THE
BEWITCHED
CONTINUUM

THE ULTIMATE LINEAR GUIDE TO THE CLASSIC TV SERIES

ADAM-MICHAEL JAMES

FOREWORD AND EDITING BY

HERBIE J PILATO

AUTHOR OF
"TWITCH UPON A STAR"

Published by Bright Horse Publishing.

Printed by CreateSpace, an Amazon.com company.

Book design by Adam-Michael James and TechnoMedia.

www.adammichaeljames.com
www.createspace.com
www.technomediapei.com

ISBN-13: 978-0692290927
ISBN-10: 0692290923

10 9 8 7 6 5 4 3 2 1

First Edition

October 2014

for
Christopher David Trentham (1953-2012),
who is still making the magic happen.

TABLE OF CONTENTS

SEASON TWO

SEASON THREE

SEASON FOUR

SEASON FIVE

SEASON SIX

SEASON SEVEN

SEASON EIGHT

WITHIN THE CONTINUUM

FOREWORD

This book is about a celebration.

A celebration of a classic television show that has meant a great deal to a great number of people.

From its inception over five decades ago to its ever-increasing popularity today, *Bewitched* has hit a chord. A chord of affection. A chord of unity. A mutual chord among all people of every heritage, culture, creed and diversity.

Some are drawn to the show's charismatic and talented cast, headed by the iconic Elizabeth Montgomery as twitch-witch Samantha Stephens; others fall under the spell of its various incantations that bespeak compelling, heartwarming and inventive stories, characters and witty dialogue; others still are drawn to its fanciful aspects, and to the wizardry of its old-school – but still very effective – special effects.

To whichever ways of wonder the show's various spirits move the viewer, *Bewitched* delivers.

In like manner, *The Bewitched Continuum* also delivers the "goods" – as it conjures up a magic of its own. With astounding perfection, author Adam-Michael James presents the facts, trivia and details of each of the show's 254 episodes, comparing one to the other with precise perception, clarity and entertaining and chronological aplomb.

With – and within – the following pages, a unique and clever take on the most beloved supernatural sitcom of all time is showcased with pizzazz and style. In the process, the heart, soul, and numerous immortal charms of *Bewitched* most joyfully live on. And that, as both Elizabeth Montgomery and Samantha Stephens might say, is "Terrific!"

Herbie J Pilato
September 17, 2014
The *Bewitched* 50th Anniversary

INTRODUCTION

When I was eight years old, I fell in love for the first time. I don't know what possessed me to sit in front of the television at five o'clock that afternoon, but on the screen, I saw a blond lady wave her hand and make a strange gesture with her nose. Suddenly, a bucket of water appeared over a man who had been bothering her, and, by the time the bucket emptied itself on him, I was hooked. Or, should I say, *Bewitched*. The supernatural sitcom that originally aired on ABC from 1964 to 1972 soon became a passion as I got to know Samantha Stephens, a beautiful witch with the ability to make magic happen by twitching her nose (Elizabeth Montgomery), her mortal husband, Darrin (first played by Dick York, then Dick Sargent), and her troublemaking mother, the formidable witch Endora (Agnes Moorehead). I was a good kid, but if I couldn't watch *Bewitched* every day at five, I admittedly had a bit of a meltdown. I'm sure my parents were more than a little exasperated.

This was 1977, when VCRs were just coming in, but too expensive for the average home. I soon discovered the simple pleasure of positioning a tape recorder next to the TV's speaker and recording the audio from as many *Bewitched* episodes as I could. I listened to them over and over again; I could recite entire scenes and knew all the sound effects. In fact, when I was ten, I actually called Screen Gems in Hollywood to ask for a tape of those effects. They said they'd send me one. I'm still waiting.

But then, you grow up. Soon there were other priorities besides my favorite television show, and I forgot about *Bewitched* for a good long while, until one day, in the mid-1990s – while channel surfing on cable, I ran across Chicago station WGN, which was airing the entire series. Faster than you could say "VHS," I loaded up tape after tape, finally able to watch at my leisure – although the network did speed up the footage a bit to make room for more commercials; it also cut out certain lines of dialogue, or sometimes entire scenes for that same purpose. I knew this since I had years of "study" under my belt. Those cassettes had served me well.

When the series slowly came out on DVD, I was thrilled. Finally, I could view episodes in their entirety, at the right speed, and in far better quality than ever before. Now that's what I call magic! But, having done my own writing by this time, including script coverage in Hollywood and opinion columns for soapcentral.com, I found myself watching with a more analytical eye, and noticing more similarities and differences within the series as a whole. For example, it seemed witches were able to negate each other's spells in some episodes, but not in others. Sometimes a witch could use her powers in another century; sometimes she lacked that ability. And why were some episodes complete reworkings of other episodes, sometimes reusing passages word-for-word?

I've come to learn that it has to be thought of in terms of historical context: TV was a whole different ball game in the '60s and '70s. Sitcoms today draft a "bible" for each season – a game plan that sets the pace for each character and what happens to them; even when individual episodes are self-contained, there's still a consistency and continuity that has become the norm. Audiences watch their shows on giant high-definition TVs, record episodes with DVRs, treat themselves to repeated viewings on DVD alongside a ton of special features, and plaster social media with posts about each boo-boo. Writers and producers *have* to micromanage their creations these days.

But, when *Bewitched* was in its original run, viewers were lucky if they saw an episode once – maybe twice if it reran over the summer. They watched on 13" or 19" screens, which were far more forgiving of flubs, particularly regarding special effects. And, since audiences weren't likely to remember details from an episode they saw a few years earlier, shows could get away with reusing actors, stories, and dialogue. They weren't concentrating as hard on continuity, simply because it wasn't necessary to.

That's what makes a closer look at Morning Glory Circle so fascinating. Remember, *Bewitched* had different writers and directors, sometimes every week. What shakes out if episodes are lined up in order and compared to each other? Do they flow together? I've wondered ever since the show's release on DVD, and I finally decided it would be fun to take on such an examination myself. After all, I do have a few decades' experience on the subject.

Of course, the question you're probably asking is: "Why now?" Simple: this year is the 50th anniversary of the premiere of *Bewitched*. What better time to delve into the magic than during the celebration of this golden milestone? And let's face it – supernatural is hot right now. Since *Bewitched* was arguably the first supernatural show on television, chances are it paved the way for the fairy tale, vampire, or fantasy series you're watching now.

So, what are you going to find here? I outline each episode with a thorough synopsis, then compare and contrast it with previous episodes – as well as with itself – in four magical sections named for beloved *Bewitched* catch phrases:

GOOD! highlights wonderful pieces of continuity and/or story aspects;

WELL? questions incongruous plot points and oversights, or special effects gone awry;

OH, MY STARS! takes Well? to the next level, calling attention to especially glaring discrepancies, often those that would change the premise of the individual episode;

SON OF A GUN! applauds excellence in any form concerning the episode in question, including its best line.

Each of the show's eight seasons starts with an introductory overview to provide a context for its collection of episodes, including changes made during hiatus that affected continuity. And, after the final episode wraps, you can venture "Within the Continuum" (a reference to the show's ethereal "atmospheric continuum") and discover fun tallies of facts and figures: How many times did Samantha twitch her nose or utter "Oh, my stars?" What did Darrin get turned into, and how many times did Larry fire him? There are also lists including witch illnesses and clients, character bios, a comparison of first and last lines – particulars that would never be noticed unless the show were looked at as a whole.

One thing you won't see in this book is behind-the-scenes information about the actors, or the production, or the show's history. There are many terrific books and fan sites out there that cover that territory, and I heartily encourage you to dive into them. What I want to do here is discuss only what is considered "canonical" – in other words, just what we see on screen. I did my best to refrain from referencing outside sources in my observations, whether paper or digital. It's just me, my laptop, and my DVDs. You have my "Witches' Honor" (another of the show's popular catch phrases) on that.

Finally, nothing written here is ever meant to be disparaging, insulting, or negative toward anyone involved in the making of *Bewitched*. That goes for writers, directors, actors, crew, special effects people – you name it. I might be analyzing and notating to the point of nit-picking, but it's always done out of love and respect for the show and its contributors. I may mention that certain things could have been done better, but I always remember that these talented folks did the very best they could with what they had available to them to put this entertaining, challenging show on the air every week.

One of my biggest hopes is that you'll not only celebrate this landmark show by exploring each of its episodes with me, but that you'll explore them for yourselves on DVD. The fashions and sentiments may sometimes seem dated by today's standards, but the fun and enjoyment, like the witches and warlocks you'll hang out with, are timeless.

Oh – that first episode I saw as an eight-year-old? "I Confess" (#135). And I have to confess: without that defining moment, this book would never have happened. I hope you enjoy reading it as much as I did writing it.

Happy 50th, *Bewitched* – and thank you for the magic!

Adam-Michael James
August 2014

SEASON ONE

(1964-1965)

Darrin Stephens discovers his wife is a witch in "I, Darrin, Take This Witch, "Samantha" (#1).

The Stephenses teach young Michael the meaning of Christmas in "A Vision of Sugar Plums" (#15).

It's "Just One Happy Family" (#10) – sort of – when Darrin tangles with his new in-laws, Maurice and Endora.

Samantha's magically inept Aunt Clara proves "There's No Witch Like An Old Witch" (#27).

SEASON ONE: OVERVIEW

On September 17, 1964, television audiences were introduced to a different kind of situation comedy: the supernatural kind. Those who tuned in that Thursday evening met a beautiful witch who revealed her magical identity to her mortal husband on their wedding night – and the rest, as they say, is history. People liked what they saw; ultimately, this new sitcom, *Bewitched*, stretched out over eight seasons, through 254 episodes, from the prim mid-'60s to the oh-so-funky early '70s.

All the core elements fans remember were established in the first weeks: witch tries to live in mortal's world while other mortals remain oblivious to her powers; mortal's world is turned upside-down by living with witch, mostly due to her family's disapproval. All the catch phrases that became staples of the show were first given voice here, too: "Oh, my stars," "Son of a gun," "Good!", and, of course, its most famous – "Well?"

Our eager young witch, Samantha, fumbled through her adjustment to mortal life while learning to cook, sew, and garden – and it should be pointed out that she was rather a quick study. We also got some tantalizing peeks into the inner workings of Samantha's family, particularly the open marriage of her parents, Endora and Maurice; also, Samantha's husband, Darrin, was thrown by the revelation that witches age at a different rate than mortals. And, for anyone who thinks that Endora did nothing but torment Darrin with witchcraft, she didn't cast a single spell on him during Season One; she changed him into a newspaper, but only to protect him from Maurice. In fact, it was Samantha who first turned Darrin into an animal: a goldfish, to get him out of the clutches of witch seductress Sarah Baker.

As with any new show, especially in this age before comedies wrote "bibles" with which to guide themselves (like their dramatic counterparts), there was definitely a sense of experimentation in these initial installments – some that worked, and some that didn't. A narrator, and characters' tendencies to break the fourth wall, disappeared after just a few weeks. Episode prologues often had nothing to do with the base story being told. Samantha offered witchy aid to an orphan, a magician, and a restaurant owner – and made strained forays into civic affairs. We even discovered she has an elf for a cousin.

Darrin also tested the waters. This successful ad man worked only ten accounts in three dozen episodes, yet managed to have thirteen fights with Samantha, not counting minor disagreements. His love for Samantha remained obvious, but he also gave a wandering eye free reign while sporting an amazingly intolerant attitude toward witches, despite being married to one – he tried to keep a friend from dating a presumed witch, and thought his own future child might be a "what."

Fortunately, while this first season sometimes perpetuated stereotypes about witches (reflecting how we mere mortals perpetuate stereotypes about races, cultures, and orientations), the show also worked to debunk them, letting us see things from a witches' perspective and turning familiar images on their ears – such as when Endora magically swept with a broom instead of riding it. Above all, the one consistent element during this premiere outing – throughout the entire series, really – was an intelligence that came through in the writing, and a presentation that immediately lifted it above its comedic contemporaries.

Many remember *Bewitched* as campy, witchy fun, thinking only of the later seasons; they're quick to remind others about the changing face of Samantha's husband and quick to forget the show was ever in black-and-white. But, whatever memories you have of the show, this genteel collection of original 36 episodes forms the basis of them. Though audiences of the 1960s easily could have rejected this sitcom that was quite unusual for its time, they instead embraced it, paving the way for Samantha, Darrin, and their eclectic circle of mortals and non-mortals to return to television screens for a second season after a memorable first.

I, DARRIN, TAKE THIS WITCH, SAMANTHA

Airdate: September 17, 1964

A narrator describes the courtship and eventual marriage of a man and woman who meet in a revolving door in New York City. On their honeymoon, the woman floats a hairbrush to herself: she's a witch! The woman is Samantha, whose mother materializes in her hotel room and learns her son-in-law is mortal. As he approaches the room, Samantha's mother sends him to the lobby by witchcraft. Satisfied that Samantha's husband, Darrin Stephens, will be driven away when Samantha tells him she's a witch, her mother disappears. Darrin is flabbergasted as his new wife substantiates her witchy confession with magic. Later, Darrin seeks counsel from his best friend, Dave, as well as his doctor and bartender; ultimately, Darrin accepts Samantha, but asks her to be a suburban housewife and refrain from using her powers.

Fashionable Sheila Sommers saunters into McMann & Tate Advertising to see Darrin, her ex-fiancé. After Darrin announces he's married, Sheila invites him and Samantha to a simple dinner gathering, but when the casually-dressed Stephenses arrive, they find that the other guests are in evening attire. Sheila seats Samantha alone at the end of the table and monopolizes Darrin's time, obliquely insulting Samantha. Miffed, Samantha fights back by magically destroying Sheila's hairstyle and gown. Darrin understands, but reminds Samantha that she broke her promise to give up witchcraft. Wanting to continue the honeymoon, Darrin excuses himself, and Samantha tackles the unkempt kitchen with a wave of her hand, telling herself she'll taper off.

GOOD!

In the prologue, there are two very effective process shots (actors positioned in front of a screen, with footage playing behind them) that make it seem Darrin and Samantha's romance is developing in the Big Apple: as they neck near a train track, and again on a ferry. A later set of process shots fluidly creates the illusion that Samantha's mother is transferring Darrin from his hotel room to the lobby.

WELL?

When Samantha's mother first appears in a flash of lightning, the open hotel window slides shut. However, when she tells Samantha, "These male witches are the worst kind," the window closes again. As for Darrin, the first time he ends up in the lobby, he asks the desk clerk for his key – but when Darrin finds himself there again, he gestures to the clerk for another. Would a hotel really keep three keys for one room?

Samantha's mother scoffs that all mortals think witches ride around on brooms, which implies witches don't. Yet, when Samantha tries to convince Darrin she's telling the truth about herself, she says she's "a real, house-haunting, broom-riding, cauldron-stirring witch." Who was wrong? As Samantha changes Darrin's drink to an Old Fashioned, and as the straw appears in the glass, someone's hand is visible at the right of the frame. Then, when Darrin exclaims, "You're a witch!" he holds the drink, but when the scene cuts back to him after Samantha magically provides him a chair, Darrin's hands are suddenly in front of him, and the drink is on the table.

As Darrin tells Sheila he's married, she comments, "If I hadn't left for Nassau when I did, it might've been me." So Darrin met and married Samantha while the traveling Sheila thought she still had a fiancé? Sheila must not mind Samantha as much as she lets on – during the cross-talk at dinner, Sheila can be heard saying, "You must bring Samantha down..." And, Samantha may deem herself an inexperienced witch, but she has no problem whipping up gale force winds by simply blowing out a candle. When Samantha waves her hand to stop the wind, the smoke from the candle wafts backwards, indicating the footage has been reversed. Plus, the light briefly catches a wire used to pull a lock of Sheila's hair in front of her face.

OH, MY STARS!

Samantha waits until her wedding night to tell Darrin she's a witch. If she was afraid Darrin would reject her, wouldn't it have been better for her to take that risk before the legal ceremony of a marriage? Skipping ahead to Darrin's reaction saves time, but not seeing Samantha's initial confession makes the scene seem incomplete. Darrin contemplates leaving Samantha over the revelation; does he think he can obtain an annulment citing the irreconcilable difference of his wife not being human?

SON OF A GUN!

"So my wife's a witch. Every married man has to make some adjustment!" – Darrin to the camera, breaking the fourth wall as he justifies his decision to make it work with Samantha.

BE IT EVER SO MORTGAGED
Airdate: September 24, 1964

EPISODE
2

The narrator extols the virtues of the typical housewife while Samantha spills beverages and burns Darrin's breakfast; Samantha relents and conjures up a decent meal for him. Later, Samantha's mother pooh-poohs her daughter's effort to live like a human and opts to observe Darrin, swearing with a "Witches' Honor" that he won't see her. Confused by Samantha's stilted affection, Darrin wants her opinion on a house he's thinking of buying. Samantha visits the property with her unimpressed mother, who magically adds landscaping to the unadorned exterior. Samantha refines it to her liking, which Gladys, a nosy neighbor, sees. Before Gladys can get her uninterested husband, Abner, to come to the window, Samantha removes the shrubbery, and the disbelieving Abner has Gladys take a spoonful of medicine.

Inside, Samantha enthusiastically furnishes the entire room by witchcraft. Gladys spies the décor through the window, but Samantha ultimately decides to buy furniture like mortals; when Gladys looks again, the sight of the empty room sends her running. Samantha asks her mother to stay and meet Darrin, but elder witch disappears, causing Darrin to assume that Gladys, who has returned to question the strange goings-on, is Samantha's mother; Gladys is stunned when Darrin kisses her cheek. Samantha later informs Darrin that their new neighbors are the Kravitzes, while Samantha's mother watches, turning to the camera and declaring that her daughter's marriage will never work.

GOOD!

The bait-and-switch of Samantha's mother making ready to leave by producing a broom, then using it to sweep away Darrin's cake crumbs, instead speaks to audience expectations about how witches travel, building on the stereotype-smashing ideas introduced in the pilot. And, unlike the reverse footage of the previous episode, in which candle smoke wafted backwards, the same technique is used here to greater effect when Samantha's mother magically puts carpet slippers on her feet.

Until recently, telephone prefixes in movies and television were listed as 555; however, the realty sign in front of the Stephenses' prospective house displays a more realistic prefix of 474.

WELL?

Samantha can't make a simple breakfast without burning something, but, later that day, she's able to bake a cake. Also, though Samantha has frosting all over her hands, she cleans it completely away with one wipe of a towel.

In the previous episode, both Samantha and her mother could "sense" Darrin entering from the other room, yet neither makes that prediction here as Darrin comes home.

Samantha promised Darrin she'd stop using her powers, but she's very liberal with them at the house: decorating its interior is one thing, but Samantha changes the entire exterior and magically opens the door in public view. Do Samantha and her mother not care about being exposed to mortals?

Abner immediately offers Gladys medicine when she reports seeing shrubbery appearing across the street, begging the question: what strange things has Gladys already seen or done that requires keeping such medicine in the house? Assuming the liquid is some sort of tranquilizer, Abner's multiple-spoon serving to Gladys surely must exceed the recommended dosage. Later, Abner takes the same medicine, which apparently isn't prescribed for him. At the end of the episode, Gladys and Abner look out the window as Darrin and Samantha stand in front of their new home; Samantha's mother is perched atop it. If the Kravitzes can see the Stephenses from across the street, they should also see someone on the Stephenses' roof – though Abner couldn't disbelieve his wife if he did.

OH, MY STARS!

Is Gladys, who runs away after the furniture she saw appears to go missing, mouthing an expletive as she turns back toward the house?

SON OF A GUN!

"Oh, they all look alike to me. Noses to the grindstone, shoulders to the wheel, feet planted firmly on the ground...no wonder they can't fly." – Samantha's mother, trying to convince her daughter that Darrin is a typical human being.

Samantha's mother reads a copy of *Harpies' Bizarre*, a tongue-in-cheek take-off on earthly glamour magazine *Harper's Bazaar*.

Samantha and her mother adding, then removing, the house's landscaping is a mammoth undertaking for the show, especially considering the scope of the crew having to physically change so much between shots outdoors, where changing light alone presents a myriad of challenges. (Only when Samantha clears the greenery do shifting shadows indicate the passage of time.) Samantha switching the front yard trees is a particularly stellar effect.

IT SHOULDN'T HAPPEN TO A DOG
Airdate: October 1, 1964

Samantha's mother arrives to find her daughter hurriedly preparing a dinner party for Darrin's client, Rex Barker. At the party, Barker tells Darrin's boss, Larry Tate, that he's interested in Samantha, who receives compliments from Larry's wife, Louise. Barker corners Samantha in the backyard gazebo; seeing Darrin coming, Samantha turns Barker into a dog. Darrin whooshes her back to the party, leaving Barker-as-dog outside; later, when Darrin checks on him, Barker darts upstairs and into bed with Samantha, who confesses the pooch is Darrin's client. Darrin is more concerned about his job than Barker's advances, so Samantha throws them both out of the bedroom.

After Samantha's mother pops in to report a cat outside, Samantha finds Barker and the feline scrapping in an alley; Samantha restores the injured client, who finds the idea of Samantha scratching him an aphrodisiac. As police officers approach, Samantha turns Barker back into a dog and is prevented from pursuing him in her nightclothes. Samantha tells Darrin the half-truth that Barker was human again, but refuses to accept Darrin's apology. The next morning, the police locate Barker-as-dog, who gets a tetanus shot, shaved fur, and a bow from a veterinarian; Darrin and Larry find the human Barker in the conference room, his appearance reflecting these changes. Barker propositions Samantha again, but this time, Darrin punches him and concedes he was wrong for not believing his wife.

GOOD!
The effect the veterinarian's grooming has on the human Barker, including a bow on his head and a tetanus shot in his rear – not to mention Barker's confused reactions to them – is priceless.

WELL?
Unlike the show's first two episodes, this installment begins without the voice of the narrator – and McMann & Tate has done some redecorating: except for the window behind Darrin's desk, and some shelving, Darrin's office looks completely different than the one seen in "I, Darrin, Take This Witch, Samantha" (#1).

Samantha has certainly caught on to cooking since she burned breakfast in the last episode: not only does she whip up a roast for more than a dozen people, but the client's girlfriend and boss' wife rave about the meal. They may not have, had they seen Samantha taking a roasting pan out of a hot oven with pot holders, then pushing it back in with her bare hands. And Barker's girlfriend, Babs, gushes to Darrin about how Samantha threw the dinner together solo, yet a maid is seen circulating the party, so Samantha obviously has help.

Darrin must be a deep sleeper, because none of the barking and meowing during Barker's literal catfight seem to disturb him. Is the exiled Darrin sleeping on the couch? If so, Samantha would have to get past him to rush outside after Barker, which would likely wake Darrin up.

Samantha is a witch. Surely when Barker-as-dog gets away, all she has to do is magically bring him back to her – but then there wouldn't be the comedy of Samantha chasing Barker and the cat through the alley. After Samantha changes Barker back, the cat sticks around as if it's waiting to resume the chase once Samantha makes him a dog again. Samantha wipes Barker's bloody face with his handkerchief, then shoves it in his mouth when the police enter the alley. Finally, is 1164 Morning Glory Circle, which is in a residential neighborhood, that close to an alley in what appears to be an urban area? And Barker-as-dog seems like a terrier of some sort, so why does Dr. Cook, the veterinarian, shave him to look like a poodle?

OH, MY STARS!

In "I, Darrin, Take This Witch, Samantha" (#1), Darrin was listed as vice president on the front door of McMann & Tate; he even had his own receptionist. In this episode, the placard on Darrin's door indicates he is only an account executive. Looks like someone demoted Darrin between the pilot and the continuation of the series. Later, Barker is a dog, but Darrin, upset about his client's transformation, barks to Samantha, "You're just a wife! He's a livelihood," which gives Darrin a rather skewed sense of priorities.

SON OF A GUN!

"Wanna bet?" – Samantha's response to her mother, who declares she won't live forever.

MOTHER MEETS WHAT'S-HIS-NAME
Airdate: October 8, 1964

EPISODE
4

The narrator returns as Samantha does over her lifeless garden with witchcraft. After Samantha has an animated witches' world versus mortal world debate with her mother, a Welcome Wagon, consisting of June Foster, Shirley Clyde, and Gladys Kravitz, throws Samantha a housewarming get-together for the purpose of snooping. To save face with the ladies, Samantha manifests dishes and silverware she doesn't yet own; meanwhile, June and Shirley's rambunctious boys race upstairs and irritate Samantha's mother, who tells them she's a witch. When the women find the kids tied up on the bed, Gladys calls Abner, not realizing that Samantha's mother has connected her daughter's out-of-service phone with magic.

Tired of her mother disparaging Darrin, Samantha says it's time they meet, so Samantha's mother offers up different versions of herself to present to her son-in-law. Later, Darrin worries that the witch may sport the expected long nose and pointy hat, which infuriates Samantha. Darrin chalks up his outburst to nervousness, then welcomes his mother-in-law, who introduces herself as Endora. After Endora chides Samantha for physically handing her an ashtray, Darrin runs afoul of Endora by calling witchcraft "nonsense." Gladys sees Endora leaving in a puff of smoke from across the street, then convinces herself she's dreaming. Samantha assures Darrin that she is committed to him regardless of Endora's approval or disapproval.

GOOD!

When seen from the perspective of witches, mortals do seem rather absurd: "I know what a bat is," Endora remarks when Samantha uses "at bat" as an expression. "Those ugly flying things that people think we're always cooking." This leads to Samantha's fun attempt to make sense out of baseball, showing how she's trying to get a handle on the intricacies of mortal life. And, in a subtle bit of continuity, Endora is still working through her issue of *Harpies' Bizarre*, the periodical she perused in "Be It Ever So Mortgaged" (#2).

WELL?

Gladys spies on the Stephenses with binoculars, and peppers Samantha with questions about Endora. Yet, Gladys somehow misses Endora appearing out of nowhere in front of the Stephens house as Samantha gardens. There's still some debate over whether witches have the ESP-like ability to sense people through doors and walls. In "I, Darrin, Take This Witch, Samantha" (#1), both Endora and Samantha knew Darrin was approaching from another room. In "Be It Ever So Mortgaged" (#2), neither witch sensed his entrance. Here, Endora picks up on the Welcome Wagon's arrival, but Samantha doesn't. And what time of year is it? This episode aired in October, yet June and Shirley's wild boys rush in during the Welcome Wagon's afternoon visit. Unless it's summer, or a weekend (and it's not the latter, because Darrin's at work), shouldn't these kids should be in school?

In a close-up, June opens Samantha's kitchen drawer all the way to find the magically produced silverware. But, when the scene cuts to a wide shot, June is still pulling the drawer open. As for Gladys, she should be cluing in that she has witches for neighbors. She's there when the tied-up boys outright admit they've seen a witch, and later, Gladys watches Endora disappear in a hail of fire. At episode's end, however, Gladys merely tells Abner she knows it's all a dream.

Ashtrays seem to be the catalyst for important moments in the show so far: in "I, Darrin, Take This Witch, Samantha" (#1), Samantha manipulated an ashtray to prove her powers to Darrin; here, it's Samantha handing one to her mother that fires up the conflict between Darrin and Endora.

OH, MY STARS!

One gets the feeling this installment was slated to be the third episode instead of "It Shouldn't Happen to a Dog" (#3). Not only is the narrator back with an intro, but the Stephenses have no dishes and no phone. If that were the case, Samantha wouldn't have been able to serve up a dinner for over a dozen people, nor call the police to check on the canined Rex Barker.

There's something to be said for building up the suspense in the show's first few episodes before finally putting Darrin and Endora in a room together. But this episode feels like two separate ones, as the first half's sole focus is on Samantha's encounter with the Welcome Wagon. The shift to Samantha inviting Endora over for dinner is too sudden; Samantha should be seen talking to Darrin about it first for the benefit of his reaction.

In "It Shouldn't Happen to a Dog" (#3), Darrin was more concerned with his client than with his wife, and here, he antagonizes Endora from the beginning of their conversation, calling witchcraft "nonsense." Naturally, Darrin wants to continue living a mortal life, and it soon becomes apparent that Darrin and Endora are to provide the show's central conflict, but he comes on a little too strong with a woman he's only just met.

SON OF A GUN!

"They play it with a ball, and a big stick called a bat. One man throws it to the man holding the bat, who tries to hit it. Then everybody chases the ball, and the man who hits it runs around in a circle on a field called a diamond before anyone else can tag him!" – Samantha, describing baseball to Endora.

Endora fashioning varying versions of herself ahead of meeting Darrin (Lavender and Old Lace, Pioneer Stock, Old World and New World) is a terrific showcase for her, plus an effective way to reveal more detail about the witch's sensibility – and abilities.

HELP, HELP, DON'T SAVE ME
Airdate: October 15, 1964

Endora thinks Darrin is philandering when she pops in and sees Samantha alone at 4:00 in the morning, but Darrin is up late working on the Caldwell Soup campaign. After Darrin labels his layouts "uninspired, pedestrian trash," Samantha invents variations, which Darrin loves until he angrily assumes Samantha created them with witchcraft. When Caldwell is unimpressed with Darrin's original concepts, Darrin debates using Samantha's improvements, but chooses not to. Samantha initially blames herself for Darrin's reaction, but, after he attributes Caldwell's disinterest – and Samantha's housekeeping skills – to her powers, Samantha makes herself invisible, packs her bags, and disappears with Endora.

The next day, Larry is upset when Darrin reveals he had another way to get the Caldwell account, but didn't use it. Larry gives Samantha's ideas to Caldwell, but when the client dismisses those as well, Darrin is ecstatic; he goes home and calls out to Samantha, apologizing and confessing he's been miserable without her. After Samantha appears, Darrin says that Caldwell not liking her ideas tells him she didn't use witchcraft. As they talk, Darrin is inspired by Samantha's casual remark and rushes off to capitalize on it. Endora suggests that Samantha has given Darrin a hint, but Samantha insists that Darrin came up with his idea on his own. Later, the Stephenses sit in a car on the beach, staring at the billboard which carries Darrin's successful new Caldwell slogan.

GOOD!

In "Mother Meets What's-His-Name" (#4), Endora alluded to having known Diogenes, a Greek philosopher. In this episode, Endora speaks of Julius Caesar, saying "he was such a nice man, too." Caesar lived from 100 B.C. to 44 B.C., and Diogenes' time was circa 412 B.C. to 323 B.C. This means that Endora is at least between 2,000 and 2,400 years old, information that adds new dimension to the witch's backstory.

The sequence of an invisible Samantha packing is quite masterful, and it gives Darrin a taste of what Samantha is capable of. Plus, it's very funny to watch Darrin talking to formerly inanimate objects, exclaiming, "Sam, you're my wife; I demand that you appear before me!"

WELL?

The narrator, whose voice-overs appeared in three of the four previous episodes, does not return to provide an introduction to this one.

Darrin substantiates his claim that Samantha used witchcraft on his layouts by telling her, "even I don't have that kind of imagination." Samantha's slogans are cute, but they're not that clever – and isn't Darrin supposed to be a brilliant ad man? After Darrin's meeting with Caldwell, Endora greets Samantha with a "Good morning, darling!" – except Caldwell has just informed Darrin that it's 2:00 in the afternoon. Perhaps Endora popped in from another time zone?

As Darrin follows Samantha's "floating" suitcases down the stairs, he grabs the railing, which wiggles considerably. Then, the invisible Samantha leaves the house, with Darrin yelling after her. If levitating luggage isn't enough to attract Gladys Kravitz's binocular-clad eye, then Darrin's full-volume pleas are. Given Gladys' suspicions in the previous episode, why is Samantha so careless as to materialize and dematerialize on the front lawn, in full view of Gladys' house? And can't Darrin hear Samantha talking to her mother outside? Finally, Endora urges Samantha, "Hold on to Mother and we'll go far, far away." But, when they fade out, it's Endora who grabs on to Samantha.

Larry comes into Darrin's office wanting to know how things went with Caldwell "yesterday." Wouldn't Larry have asked for a progress report as soon as Darrin got back from his business lunch instead of waiting a whole day to get an update?

OH, MY STARS!

Samantha might be the witch, but Darrin must have powers of his own: he darts into the bathroom fully clothed, takes a shower, and comes out wearing a robe in a mere thirty-six seconds. As Darrin dresses, Samantha scribbles all over the layouts he stayed up all night working on, yet he raises no objection.

How exactly does Darrin grinning that Samantha's ideas are no good function as an apology? He qualifies it by saying Caldwell's refusal doesn't mean Samantha lacks imagination, but, even if Samantha's slogans were magic, it doesn't necessarily mean Caldwell would automatically like them.

SON OF A GUN!

"When you're up to here in err, and you've changed into one huge lump of divine, don't say I didn't warn you." – Endora to Samantha, after Samantha lists her plans for convincing Darrin she's wrong.

When faced with using slogans he's sure are witchcraft, Darrin tells Caldwell, "If I do it once, I'll do it again. And before you know, I won't be able to do anything for myself." This is not only incredibly insightful, but it demonstrates that Darrin has a vulnerability he is very much aware of – and it explains why he is so against Samantha using her powers in any way.

LITTLE PITCHERS HAVE BIG FEARS
Airdate: October 22, 1964

EPISODE
6

Samantha discourages a high-pressure broom salesman by magically filling the room with the items. Later, Darrin's plan to play hooky with Samantha is interrupted by little Marshall Burns, who has no father and an overprotective mother. When Mrs. Burns tracks Marshall to the Stephenses', she lays into Samantha so much that Samantha almost uses witchcraft on her. Darrin feels Samantha is interfering, but softens upon discovering Marshall wants to play baseball, which Mrs. Burns deems too dangerous. At the tryouts, Gladys tells Samantha that "Marshmallow" is afraid of his own shadow, and the kids laugh at his limited ball-playing ability. To build Marshall's confidence, Samantha provides a magical assist, but Darrin fears she's given the boy a false sense of security.

That night, the Stephenses find Marshall on their patio; Darrin calls Mrs. Burns and jokingly suggests extreme ways to keep Marshall at home. Mrs. Burns threatens police action and returns the next morning for her son, who's run away to play in the big game. Trying to stall, Darrin drives slowly, while Samantha immobilizes a traffic light. At the ball field, Marshall happily reports how well he's playing, so Mrs. Burns allows him to continue. Abner dismisses Gladys' claim that Marshall improved because of Samantha, and Darrin kisses Samantha to keep her from twitching her nose on Marshall's behalf. Marshall hits a home run on his own, and his teammates carry him away. Samantha offers to "twitch up a banquet," hoping Darrin will stop her with another kiss.

GOOD!

Darrin's seen a fair amount of witchcraft so far, but his observation that Samantha can do "that" (waving fingers) and "that" (grabbing nose), "and probably a few other rituals I'm not familiar with yet" shows there's still a newness to his marriage and the way he lives because of it. Darrin kissing Samantha to keep her from twitching (the phrase he coins here to describe the nose-wiggling gesture his wife uses to perform magic) is one of the episode's best funnies.

Marshall has teammates who are African-American and Asian-American, a good bit of inclusion for a television show in the mid-'60s. And Jimmy Mathers is a little scene-stealer – Marshall has the best-written dialogue of the episode, which Mathers conveys in a way that elevates him beyond your typical child actor, outshining his adult contemporaries.

WELL?

When Darrin misses his train, he wants to honeymoon with Samantha until the next one. Shouldn't he call in to McMann & Tate and let Larry know he's going to be late? As for Samantha, she's done some brushing up on her baseball. In "Mother Meets What's-His-Name" (#4), she appeared confused trying to explain the game to Endora; here, she exhibits a much greater understanding of the sport.

Darrin and Samantha are upstairs when they hear their backyard gate open. By the time they step onto the patio, Marshall is asleep on their lawn chair. The kid knocked out that fast?

In the wide shot of Darrin realizing that the runaway Marshall is at the ballpark, Mrs. Burns stands in front of a slatted door, while Darrin stands to her left, in front of the kitchen door. But in close-up, Darrin stands in front of the slatted door himself. Darrin assures Mrs. Burns he'll drive fifteen miles an hour, which is "no faster than the law allows" – in the next shot, they're shown driving in the slow lane on a freeway. The minimum speed on such a thoroughfare is typically 45 miles an hour, so going fifteen could easily get Darrin pulled over for reckless driving. And where is this ballpark? Though Darrin takes the long way on purpose, he still drives on the freeway, then through the city to get there, indicating the field must be across town. Yet Samantha and Marshall get to the diamond without a car, and Samantha comes home from Marshall's tryouts as if they walked back.

Mrs. Burns marches onto the ball field and yells at Marshall in front of all the other kids. She's afraid strawberries will poison her child, but she doesn't seem to mind humiliating him. Of course, the story dictates that she relax her stance about Marshall playing baseball, but her switchover happens rather quickly. Is it because she senses Coach Gribben's attraction to her?

Darrin and Gladys apparently doubt each other's hearing. In full voice, Darrin tells Samantha "not so much as a twitch" with the Kravitzes sitting right behind them, and Gladys, also in full voice, tells Abner "there's something funny about her" in this same proximity. And Mrs. Burns is in earshot of all of it. Then, after Marshall hits a home run, the kids cheer and carry him away – except it's only the bottom of the seventh inning; the game isn't over yet. Finally, someone in the writing room likes their bouillabaisse: it was a Caldwell soup variety in the previous episode, and now Samantha wants to twitch some up for dinner.

OH, MY STARS!

The kids on Morning Glory Circle seem to be juvenile delinquents: in "Mother Meets What's-His-Name" (#4), the sons of June Foster and Shirley Clyde were seen running around playing in the middle of the day; here, Marshall visits Samantha's house "every morning." Is the overprotective Mrs. Burns keeping Marshall from getting an education because it's too dangerous? Maybe all the kids on the block are homeschooled. Does Marshall really sneak out every day undetected, and return before his mother knows he's missing? And, if Marshall is that sheltered, how does Gladys know who he is, let alone that he's afraid of his own shadow?

SON OF A GUN!

"Oh, bats get thrown, the ball is hard, the grass is wet, the sun is hot..." – Marshall to the Stephenses, imitating his mother and her reasons for keeping him away from baseball.

THE WITCHES ARE OUT

Airdate: October 29, 1964

Samantha's friends, Bertha and Mary, express concern for Samantha's Aunt Clara, whose waning powers land her on the freeway. With Halloween coming, the witches lament how mortals depict them as ugly old crones, while Darrin's client, Mr. Brinkman, wants exactly that image to sell his candies. After Samantha suggests recruiting Darrin to help revamp public perception, she is outraged to see Darrin drawing a stereotype witch; Darrin rips up his sketch when Samantha tells him how much it hurts to see the erroneous blacked-out teeth and warts. Brinkman rejects Darrin's sexier witch image, causing Darrin to slip that witches have feelings, too. After Darrin walks out on Brinkman and Larry, Samantha offers to magically put the other candy companies out of business, feeling that Darrin is holding the loss of his job against her.

Samantha summons Bertha, Mary, and Aunt Clara to go to Brinkman as a protest group; they create signs, but Aunt Clara, distracted by her doorknob collection, makes her sign read "Vote for Coolidge." Samantha turns Brinkman's phone into a snake when he tries to call the police; putting Brinkman in front of a French firing squad doesn't move him either, but turning him into a crone gets him to reconsider his campaign, so the witches disappear. The next day, Brinkman blankly accepts Darrin's concept, but reports that his doorknobs were stolen. Brinkman is further rattled when he sees Samantha greeting Larry in the reception area.

GOOD!

What an astute contrast, alternating the ladies' lament about mortal perception of witches with Brinkman's perpetuation of that very stereotype. Not only is there comedy in the scene, but it's strangely suspenseful. And, that Aunt Clara's protest sign is done up in shaky handwriting does a lot to subtly exemplify her declining magic.

Darrin's defense of witches in this episode shows he's come a long way even from "Mother Meets What's-His-Name" (#4), where he too easily believed that Endora might have five eyes. His argument to Brinkman that witches wouldn't want their image distorted is not just a pro-witch statement, but a commentary in support of all minority groups.

WELL?

Bertha and Mary roll their eyes when Samantha pours her tea by hand, but apparently have no issue with her manually pushing the cart before she does. Also, it's still difficult to pinpoint whether or not witches have ESP; Bertha knows someone is at Samantha's door, but can't tell it's Aunt Clara, while Samantha doesn't sense anything at all. After Samantha ushers Aunt Clara into the house, she forgets to close the door. Is it wise leaving it open for the neighborhood – and Gladys Kravitz – to see?

Mr. Brinkman makes a big show of offering his candies to Darrin – except the real-life brand name Chuckles is clearly visible on the side of the bag. Then, Bertha, Mary, and Samantha think Darrin can help change mortal perception of witches simply because he's in advertising. Darrin is one man, and one campaign is a start, but it's not going to influence billions of people. After the blow-up with Larry and Brinkman, everyone simply says Darrin lost his job, but there's no clarification as to whether Darrin quit, or if he was fired.

Samantha, Bertha, Mary, and Aunt Clara discuss their protest march at full volume downstairs in the living room; wouldn't at least one of them worry about waking Darrin? It's understandably difficult for any actor to hold still so an effect can be done, but Aunt Clara's position is all over the place as Bertha and Mary conjure up their signs. Then, the witches' visit to Brinkman is processed in soft focus, as if it were a dream. It's not, but that would explain Brinkman being terrified of the stuffed toy snake that appears in his hand. As for Aunt Clara, she can't magically pour herself a cup of tea, but she can remove 105 doorknobs from a house. What house has that many doorknobs, outside of a mansion? Brinkman's place doesn't seem like one. And does Aunt Clara always steal doorknobs for her collection?

Brinkman seeing Samantha in the office feels like a natural end to the episode (so much so, that it *was* the end in syndication), so the following tag, with Larry commenting that fathers buy Halloween candy, doesn't seem necessary. The only real benefit is seeing Samantha and Larry truly interacting for the first time, considering they didn't speak during their initial appearance together in "It Shouldn't Happen to a Dog" (#3).

OH, MY STARS!

Samantha offers to help Darrin get his job back by making every candy company but Brinkman's go out of business. Samantha would really put thousands of innocent people out of work so Darrin can keep *his* job? It's meant to be funny, but it sounds rather unethical, and it doesn't help Samantha's claim that witches are nice, ordinary people.

SON OF A GUN!

"I personally think it all begins with the children. Someone ought to rewrite those fairy tales. You know, show Hansel and Gretel for what they really are: a couple of pushy kids going around eating sweet old ladies' houses!" – Bertha to her fellow witches, trying to trace the origin of the stereotype witch.

WITCH OR WIFE

Airdate: November 5, 1964

With Darrin working late every night because Larry is overseas on business, Samantha is thrilled when Endora pops in to take her to lunch. Turning up her nose at local eateries, Endora suggests dining in Paris. After mother and daughter reminisce about past witchy escapades, Endora insists they attend a fashion show, where they bump into Larry, and his wife, Louise Tate. Samantha nervously introduces Endora, then gets sucked into making a night of it. Samantha excuses herself to pop home and call Darrin; meanwhile, Larry wants to let Darrin know he and Louise are taking care of Samantha in Paris. When Samantha returns to the table, Larry puts her on the phone with Darrin, who gets upset and drowns his sorrows at the house. Darrin later tells Samantha that Endora is right to say Samantha will tire of living like a mortal; Samantha disagrees and sullenly pops back to Paris.

Larry flies home to New York solo, and relays Louise's contention that Samantha is having a horrible time. Buoyed, Darrin books a flight; an hour later, Samantha walks into Larry's office looking for Darrin. When Larry explains that Darrin is headed for Paris, Samantha and Endora search planes for him, with Samantha peeking into windows. She finally locates Darrin, startling him before making a more subtle entrance through the lavatory. Darrin apologizes, and the couple elects to see Paris together, while Endora enjoys a drink atop the plane.

GOOD!

In this episode, the show offers a sampling of what Samantha's life was like before she met Darrin. Over their Parisian lunch, Samantha and Endora look back on a previous trip to the City of Lights, as well as their jet-set summer on the Italian Riviera. The best part? The usually critical Endora genuinely asking her daughter, "Don't you sometimes miss all this?" and Samantha's equally earnest reply, "Not really. I have other things that make up for it." It's just the right amount of backstory, seamlessly tied into the present. Another great aspect of this episode is the "worlds collide" meeting of Endora and the Tates, which weaves the canvas a little closer together.

WELL?

Darrin tells a disappointed Samantha she's going to have to amuse herself for the next few days; Samantha simply says "Bye, darling," and hangs up – which is an unusual way to end a conversation..

When Samantha pops home to call Darrin, he asks what she's been doing, and she (truthfully) tells him she's been looking at a few dresses. Shouldn't Darrin raise an eyebrow? He has the car, and there can't be that many boutiques within walking distance of 1164 Morning Glory Circle, though it is possible Samantha could have taken a taxi. More importantly, why is Samantha so indiscreet as to answer the phone after hanging up with Darrin? Does she think Darrin is calling her back? As for Larry, he dumped a mountain of work on Darrin's desk – so why does he call Darrin's house first? He knows Darrin is likely at the office, which he even mentions. It comes out that the Stephenses home number is 555-7328, but it's odd that McMann & Tate, a big-time New York advertising agency, would have a mundane, typically residential number like 555-6059. Is this Darrin's direct line? So much for non-555 prefixes, such as the 474 prefix of the real estate company of "I, Darrin, Take This Witch, Samantha" (#1).

Looking for Darrin, Samantha walks straight into Larry's office. Wouldn't she have to be announced? Plus, Larry might want to consider a new decorator, since his office is almost identical to Darrin's, save for a few pieces of furniture. Darrin's nameplate lists him as "account executive," while Larry's only sports his name – what is Larry's position in the company, anyway?

Darrin's flight is conspicuously empty, considering it's heading overseas from New York. Shouldn't its stewardess realize that Samantha did not board the plane? Does Samantha take another passenger's seat? And Samantha's "please understand how I feel" is a rather pat patch-up after the disagreement she and Darrin had.

OH, MY STARS!

Samantha's introduction to Larry happened off-camera, and they only had minor interactions in "It Shouldn't Happen to a Dog" (#3) and "The Witches Are Out" (#7). So how can Larry pick Samantha out of a crowd in Paris, with Samantha wearing a huge hat, no less? By the same token, Larry comments to Louise, "Samantha doesn't quite seem herself tonight, does she?" Odd, since Larry doesn't know Samantha well enough to make such an assessment.

Louise marvels at how Larry resisted taking her to Paris for years, while, according to Samantha's lie, Darrin and Samantha barely talked about it. Larry's response? "Well, neither did we. I can remember weeks when we didn't talk at all." Is this appropriate to say in front of someone you hardly know (Samantha), and someone else that you just met (Endora)?

SON OF A GUN!

"It's the only way to fly!" – Endora, to the audience, quoting a popular 1960s Western Airlines commercial featuring an animated bird riding on top of a plane. [The show seemed to stop breaking the fourth wall after "Be It Ever So Mortgaged" (#2), but it employs the device here once again.]

EPISODE 9

THE GIRL REPORTER
Airdate: November 12, 1964

While Darrin does paperwork, Samantha magically enlarges a needle she's been struggling to thread. The Stephenses' romantic plans are interrupted by journalism student Liza Randall, who wants to interview an advertising executive for her college paper. Darrin is flattered by Liza's obvious infatuation – until the next morning, when Liza arrives dressed to kill for her agency field trip. Samantha is visited by Liza's fiancé, athlete Marvin "Monster" Grogan, who wants to break Darrin in half. While Liza comes on strong at Darrin's office, Samantha tries to distract Monster by feeding him a huge breakfast.

As Darrin drones on about charts, Liza pours them potent drinks; Darrin soaks Liza trying to take her drink away. Darrin retreats from Liza's advances, but they fall on the couch and are caught by Larry, who calls them Mr. and Mrs. Johnson in front of a client. Back at the house, Samantha has defused the now-smitten Monster; after he and Liza leave, the Stephenses argue over how much encouragement the other provided. When Liza lies that Darrin lured her to his office, Monster confronts Darrin, ready to punch him. Samantha protects Darrin by creating an invisible shield around him, though she allows Liza, who thinks Darrin has hurt Monster, to slap Darrin in the face. Later that evening, Darrin jokes about the still-intact shield; Samantha removes it, and they make up.

GOOD!

The prologue is interesting because it's done without a single word of dialogue, nor are any necessary; it's a unique way for a sitcom to begin an episode. Plus, it's consistent that Samantha, who can't thread a needle, still hasn't got the hang of mortal life.

For someone who could have been a muscle-bound cliché, Monster is an intriguing character. His formal speech demonstrates that, while he might be a jock, he isn't a dumb jock. And, in the tag, as the Stephenses get ready for bed, it's a nice touch that Darrin is still sealed off by Samantha's magical shield – and that he has a sense of humor about it.

WELL?

Do major newspapers, even in the 1960s, print pictures of people when they move into a neighborhood? Of course, if Darrin's picture weren't in the paper, Liza would have no one to crush on, negating the whole episode. Later, the camera makes an unfortunate shift when Samantha pops out of her chair and appears next to Darrin on the couch.

The next morning, when Samantha comes back into the kitchen after answering the door, Darrin asks who it is. That's curious, since he's expecting Liza, who is 15 minutes late besides. And when Darrin escorts Liza to his car, why is it parked on the curb, when it usually spends the night in the driveway? So Samantha can watch Darrin tripping over himself opening the door for Liza? As Samantha feeds the famished Monster in the kitchen, her hairstyle is completely different than it was when he arrived on her doorstep. That's always a danger when scenes are filmed out of sequence, unless Samantha gave it a touch-up between Monster's courses.

Because Darrin takes Liza to McMann & Tate on a traditionally quiet Saturday, it seems Larry is only there with a client so he can catch Darrin with Liza and call them Mr. and Mrs. Johnson. And Samantha and Darrin have a lot of fights, even for newlyweds: nine episodes in, they've locked horns six times already. As for Monster, he tells Samantha that he and Liza are engaged; later, when he's about to clock Darrin, he refers to himself as Liza's boyfriend. Which is it?

OH, MY STARS!

Darrin defended witches to the point of losing his job in "The Witches Are Out" (#7), but here he blurts out, "What's wrong with being human? At least I'm not a..." To his credit, he saves it by calling Samantha "*bewitching* and beguiling" afterwards.

Liza offering Darrin a strange alcoholic concoction provides more problems than laughs. Darrin should be more annoyed that Liza has made a drink so early in the day – they leave his house at 9:15, and it can't even be noon by the time she plays bartender. If Darrin thinks she's offering him a soft drink, he should be able to smell the booze in his glass even before he sips it. Living in the '60s, of course Darrin keeps alcohol in his office, but where do the ice cubes come from on a Saturday morning? For all of Liza's desire to be grown-up by pouring the gin, she never drinks any, and, at home, Darrin breathes in Samantha's face, and Monster's, to prove that he and Liza only smell of alcohol. Yet, he did take a sip, which would still show up on his breath.

SON OF A GUN!

"You started it: that's one, and you started it with me: that's two." – Samantha to Darrin, after he states it takes two to make a fight.

Liza gushes over Darrin's Caldwell Soup slogan, "The only thing that will ever come between us." Darrin invented it in "Help, Help, Don't Save Me" (#5); it wasn't necessary for the show to mention the campaign, but it's excellent continuity that they do.

JUST ONE HAPPY FAMILY
Airdate: November 19, 1964

Samantha foils a TV repairman's attempt to gouge her by fixing the set with magic. Later, Endora pops into the refrigerator to warn Samantha that her father, Maurice, is coming to meet Darrin. As Samantha worries how Maurice will react to a mortal son-in-law, Darrin asks what Maurice can do about it; Samantha destroys a vase to demonstrate. Darrin stays away so Samantha can face Maurice, who declares that only a man he approves of will make her happy; Endora grudgingly helps Samantha lie about Darrin's origins and whereabouts. Samantha magically locks Darrin in a phone booth when he calls wanting to come home, while Maurice finds Darrin's mortal medicine. Maurice's silent anger shatters objects all over the room when Samantha confesses that Darrin is human.

After Endora makes the returning Darrin disappear, she sends Samantha for the evening paper; not knowing the newspaper is Darrin, Maurice grabs it, slams it against his hand, and throws it in the fireplace. Samantha restores Darrin, who stands up to his father-in-law; Maurice is impressed, but disintegrates Darrin anyway. Endora makes a case for Darrin, so Maurice strains to rematerialize him one piece of clothing at a time. The "one big happy family" then sits down to a civil dinner, where Darrin produces the rare wine that Maurice tried to conjure up earlier. Maurice wonders if Darrin might be a warlock after all, but changes his mind when the bottle isn't chilled.

GOOD!

Maurice and Endora haven't seen each other for a while, and later, Endora threatens to move in with him when he refuses to bring Darrin back. If they don't live together, and they aren't separated, then they must simply have some kind of open marriage, which is rather progressive for 1964. Could her parents' example be why Samantha wanted a traditional, mortal union?

Samantha's cover story for Darrin's mortality is quite intricate: she claims he is old stock from Massachusetts [although Darrin was established as being from Missouri in "I, Darrin, Take This Witch, Samantha" (#1)], and lies that Darrin's birth certificate is a front to fool the neighbors, adding she has pictures of Darrin "in World War I, the Spanish-American War, and the War of 1812. Before that, I have paintings." It's a clever way to reinforce that witches live for centuries.

WELL?

There is a sound effect when Samantha opens the door to Maurice, though no witchcraft is being performed in that moment. And one has to wonder if Gladys doesn't notice the limo across the street disappearing into thin air. Now, the same day Samantha obliterates a vase to give Darrin an idea of Maurice's capabilities, Larry asks Darrin, "What can he do to you? Point a finger at you and blow you up like you were made out of glass?" It's funny, but too coincidental. And when Darrin calls from the bar, Samantha excuses herself, taking her phone into the other room – a phone that has no cord. It needs one; remember, this is decades before cordless and cellular phones.

In "I, Darrin, Take This Witch, Samantha" (#1), Endora scoffed upon discovering her daughter had married a mortal, saying Samantha must have gotten the proclivity from her father. Apparently not, since Maurice's attitude toward mortals is even worse than Endora's. When Samantha references her nonexistent pictures from Darrin's supposed, multiple-decade military service, she skips the Civil War – and research indicates that the first early photographs were taken in the 1820s, which means Samantha can't have snaps of Darrin from the War of 1812.

Much is made of Larry and the bar patrons trying to help Darrin, who is locked in the phone booth by witchcraft; they even lower it to the floor. Isn't a phone booth connected to the wall with a series of thick cables? And why lower it, anyway? Darrin could just as easily be released from it upright.

Maurice catches Samantha in her lie by producing Darrin's birth certificate and medicine. How does Maurice get his hands on either? The document could be in Darrin's photo album, but Maurice would have to rifle through the medicine cabinet for the bottle. When did he have time?

Maurice slapping Darrin-as-newspaper against his thigh and hands is comical in a "that's gotta hurt" kind of way, but what makes Maurice throw it/him into the fireplace? It isn't his paper. And what is Samantha trying to accomplish when she casts her ineffective *oblivia* spell on Maurice? Either she wants to make her father disappear, or she's trying to disintegrate him, like he has Darrin.

When Maurice pops out in a plume of fire, Endora rolls her eyes, pointing out that her husband is big on exits. Yet, her own fiery exit in "Mother Meets What's-His-Name" (#4) was just as dramatic.

OH, MY STARS!

After Samantha reiterates that Maurice doesn't approve of mixed marriages, Darrin comments that Endora doesn't, either, but they "worked that out." When? Endora put Darrin on notice in "Mother Meets What's-His-Name" (#4), and they haven't had a scene together since. Would something as important as their coming to terms really happen off-screen?

Maurice, a powerful warlock, can't witch up a bottle of Chanson du Mer '53, claiming it's because there are only a few bottles left in the world, which implies his magic is limited to existing stock. Assuming Maurice really can't conjure one up from scratch, Darrin keeps a bottle of this rare vintage in the house, so Maurice should still be able to make it appear in his hand.

Darrin calls to find out when the last train leaves for Morning Glory Circle, forgetting that, at the beginning of the episode, he told Samantha the new train pulls out of Manhattan at 10:00. Would a small street in a residential neighborhood really be a train destination?

Maurice Evans flinches every time an object shatters, which rather takes away from the idea that Samantha's father is infinitely powerful. And, while the idea of disintegrating Darrin might have been funny on paper, the morbid implications of such an act veer very far away from comedy (read: Samantha is temporarily a widow).

SON OF A GUN!

"I, uh, think he'll surprise you." – Endora to Maurice, struggling to obscure the truth when asked for her opinion about Darrin.

Endora's appearances in the refrigerator and cupboard are particularly well done. And, Endora has made it quite clear that she doesn't care for Darrin, so that she goes so far as to protect him from Maurice is unexpectedly heartwarming – and a nice twist.

IT TAKES ONE TO KNOW ONE
Airdate: November 26, 1964

When Darrin needs a Miss Jasmine for his perfume account, Endora pops his photos of gorgeous models into Samantha's appliances, warning that Darrin is susceptible to other women. Janine Fleur strolls into the office and is immediately chosen Miss Jasmine; Darrin can't take his eyes off Janine, and evades Samantha's questions about her. Janine talks about quitting, so Darrin cancels Samantha's lunch date, while Endora makes sure her disheartened daughter sees Darrin in close conversation with Janine at the restaurant. But Samantha recognizes Janine as Sarah Baker, a witch seductress, and freezes all the customers. Once Sarah reveals that Endora recruited her to test Darrin's mettle, Endora recants and concurs with Samantha's demand that Sarah stay away from Darrin.

Undeterred, Janine/Sarah summons Darrin to her apartment for a late meeting. Darrin brings Larry, who falls asleep from Sarah's spiked drink. As a hexed Darrin becomes amorous, Samantha pops in and tells Sarah to let Darrin act of his own free will. When the relentless Sarah still won't fight fair, Samantha changes Darrin into an ugly fish as Sarah leans in to kiss him, then transforms her husband into a goldfish and plops him into a pitcher. Giving Sarah a final warning before restoring Darrin, Samantha makes it look like Sarah has thrown water on him to discourage his advances. Larry stays behind when Darrin leaves, but Samantha asks Sarah to also respect Larry's marriage. Later, Samantha meets Darrin for lunch and secretly defaces his Miss Jasmine billboard by magic.

GOOD!

It would have been too much of a challenge to get every single extra to hold still after Samantha freezes the restaurant patrons (as evidenced by the few that try), so the show made the very good decision to place Endora, Samantha, Sarah, and Darrin in front of footage of the suspended customers, much like when Darrin was popped from his hotel room into the lobby in "I, Darrin, Take This Witch, Samantha" (#1). It also allows more opportunities for comedy, like showing water being immobilized mid-pour. And, while it seems a little far-fetched for Endora to test Darrin so soon after protecting him from Maurice in "Just One Happy Family" (#10), her telling Sarah to stop working on Darrin shows that Samantha's happiness is really more important to her after all.

As Samantha decides Darrin should be told Janine/Sarah is a witch, Endora warns, "I wouldn't try to convince him he's susceptible to witches." Samantha swears she didn't use a single spell on Darrin, which is an excellent point for the show to explore, especially after Darrin already assumed Samantha unduly used her powers in "Help, Help, Don't Save Me" (#5).

Darrin's behavior regarding Janine/Sarah seems to indicate he has more than a business interest in her, so his "I probably had it coming" when he thinks Miss Jasmine has thrown water on him is a nice bit of responsibility-taking on his part.

WELL?

Would a young witch, raised "in the sparkle of a star," really play with something as mortally mundane as paper dolls? Samantha references them when she advises Darrin to cut out the best parts of his models' headshots and put them together "like I used to do," but it's unlikely she'd have known what paper dolls were as a child, if she was as sheltered from the mortal world as it has been implied.

Janine/Sarah is in Darrin's office seconds after Larry exits. Does Larry really not notice her in the reception area, given how much he pants over the Miss Jasmine hopefuls? At home, Samantha gets a peek at Darrin's notes on Janine/Sarah and reads them aloud next to her sleeping husband. Wouldn't that wake him up? Disgusted by Darrin's sensuous descriptions, Samantha chucks his notepad. But surely Darrin will wake up wondering why his notes are on the floor.

Samantha assumes Endora knows where Darrin and Janine/Sarah are lunching; refusing to concede Endora might be right about him, Samantha wants to take Endora to the eatery, and pops out. How does Samantha know where to go? Does Endora give her directions mid-flight? Samantha is very hurt to see Darrin dining with Janine/Sarah, but it's not like they're in a romantic clinch; they're discussing business. Then, after Samantha reveals that Darrin is her husband, Sarah plays dumb and says she'd heard Samantha had done something foolish. If that's Sarah's opinion of mortals, why does she continue pursuing Darrin (and almost Larry) once Endora tells her to back off? ("Professional pride" is not a satisfactory answer.)

When Darrin asked to know Endora's last name in "Mother Meets What's-His-Name" (#4), she said he'd never be able to pronounce it. That suggests that witches' surnames aren't relatable to the mortal world. Yet, in "Just One Happy Family" (#10), Maurice told Samantha he'd never flown into the Stephenses, and here, Miss Jasmine turns out to be Sarah Baker – these names are not unpronounceable.

After discovering the ardent Darrin and snoozing Larry, Samantha dares Sarah to let Darrin act on his own and pops out, returning the mortals to normal. How can Samantha undo the effects of Sarah's Samoan lotus leaf simply by disappearing? And how is it the same herb triggers two different reactions in Larry and Darrin? When Sarah becomes threatening, Samantha retorts that, magically, they're "pretty evenly matched." What happened to Samantha's claim in "I, Darrin, Take This Witch, Samantha" (#1) that she was inexperienced?

Samantha keeps Sarah from moving in on Larry, saying "Louise Tate happens to be a very dear friend." Samantha must have gotten close to Louise very quickly during their Paris jaunt [see "Witch or Wife" (#8)], because the only other interaction they had was in "It Shouldn't Happen to a Dog" (#3). Later, Samantha gets revenge on Sarah by vandalizing Darrin's scaled-down Miss Jasmine billboard. Does she twitch it back before anyone sees it? Perhaps the ultimate payback is the fact that Sarah is stuck continuing on as Miss Jasmine; she must be contractually obligated to do the additional television spots and photo shoots the agency has planned for her, unless she witches her way out of it.

OH, MY STARS!

After Samantha and Endora leave the restaurant, and the patrons are brought out of suspended animation, Darrin looks at his watch and opts to skip lunch, asking, "Where did all the time go?" He and the other mortals only lost two minutes and sixteen seconds – would that really necessitate going back to the office? This brings up an important question: what happens to mortals when they are frozen? Since

Darrin finds minutes missing, it can be assumed that time moves forward normally as the witches discuss him – but you'd think they could have their confrontation with mortal time stopped, and that, if Darrin was frozen, his watch would be, too.

SON OF A GUN!

"It's the spirit of conquest. It's a disease of mortal men, like chickenpox." – Endora to Samantha, who fears Darrin isn't happy with her when she sees him with Janine/Sarah.

...AND SOMETHING MAKES THREE
Airdate: December 3, 1964

Gladys sees Samantha diving into a backyard pool from across the street, but, when Gladys peeks over the fence, there's no pool. Gladys repeatedly tries to convince Abner the pool was there, while Samantha speeds herself up to make things presentable for Louise and her news: after 16 years of marriage to Larry, Louise is pregnant. Samantha accompanies Louise to the obstetrician; Larry, who is visiting an adjacent dentist, overhears Samantha talking about expecting a baby and runs straight to Darrin. After the Stephenses and Tates arrange to have dinner together, Darrin envisions a family of little witches and warlocks that fly into his office sporting hats and brooms, and wonders what he and Samantha have gotten themselves into.

At dinner, Darrin and Larry fuss over Samantha and virtually ignore Louise, who can't bring herself to tell her husband the truth. Larry kicks Louise's shin under the table to keep her from blabbing about Samantha's "pregnancy," then admits he saw the women at the doctor's office. Darrin listens as Samantha excitedly confesses that the Tates are having a baby. Larry unexpectedly embraces the prospect of fatherhood, while Darrin and Samantha agree it doesn't matter if their child is witch or mortal, as long as it's happy and healthy. Later, Samantha sees Gladys spying, so she jumps on a trampoline instead of witching up her pool; satisfied, Gladys leaves, but she blanches when she suddenly hears a splash behind her.

GOOD!

The Tates' brief appearance in "Witch or Wife" (#8) didn't reveal that much about them, particularly Louise. This episode fixes that and provides a first look at the inner workings of the Tates' marriage. As a result, Larry and Louise are more likable, plus supplied with some much-needed dimension.

That's not just Little Endora in Darrin's fantasy, that's a young Maureen McCormick, years before *The Brady Bunch* (which ran from 1969-1974 on ABC). She even pulls off a convincing witch twitch!

WELL?

In "It Takes One to Know One" (#11), Samantha classified Louise as a "very dear friend" – here, on the phone, Louise has to identify herself to Samantha by first and last name. Later, the Tates and Stephenses continue to overvalue their relatively new friendship when Larry gushes, "no two people are dearer to me than you and [Samantha]." That's a pretty big expression of affection for someone he barely knows.

When Louise calls and announces she's coming over, Samantha uses a speed-up spell to neaten the living room. In "I, Darrin, Take This Witch, Samantha" (#1), Samantha cleaned the entire kitchen with one wave of her hand, though this technique is funnier. As for Louise, she must have powers of her own: she hangs up with Samantha and arrives on her doorstep a mere 44 seconds later.

The number of Stephens children in Darrin's fantasy changes depending on the shot. Five are named (Rebecca, Samuel, Maurice, Endora, and Julius), but soon there's a sixth present with no name. By the time Samantha coaxes the children to disappear with her, there are nine of them. Is it part of Darrin's fantasy that new kids keep coming in from nowhere? Later, the doorbell rings, and Samantha thinks it's Darrin arriving with Larry. Surely Darrin wouldn't ring the doorbell to his own house.

Gladys is upset about a trampoline turning into a swimming pool, but maybe she can take comfort in the fact it's not Samantha bouncing on it, but a stunt double.

OH, MY STARS!

Gladys gets more evidence of Samantha's witchcraft when she peeks over the Stephenses' fence from the street to view what becomes a nonexistent pool. Except the Stephenses' backyard is exactly that: behind the house; it is not visible from the street. And, while Gladys' search for the pool is likely meant to counterbalance the themes of impending parenthood, it's not particularly integral to the story, and feels like it was inserted from a different episode.

Strangely, Louise jokes that Larry will hit her when he finds out she's pregnant. Not only is this not funny, but it adds an uncomfortable undercurrent to the Tates' marriage, especially after Larry said there were weeks he and Louise didn't talk in "Witch or Wife" (#8).

Darrin's fantasy about fathering little witches and warlocks is rather wonderful overall, but, in it, he withers when Samantha tells him all their children have powers, and acts as if he can't be near them. What happened to Darrin's accepting attitude of "The Witches Are Out" (#7), where he stalked out of his office over Mr. Brinkman maligning witches? To say nothing of Darrin envisioning his children in black hats and brooms; he already knows that neither are commonplace with witches from his exposure to Samantha and her parents. Back in reality, Darrin asks Samantha, "I know it'll be a boy or a girl – won't it?" For having married a witch, Darrin's misconceptions about them are unusually deep-rooted.

SON OF A GUN!

"Besides, he hates children. He says they're too young!" – Louise to Samantha, explaining why she's afraid to tell Larry she's pregnant after 16 years of marriage.

LOVE IS BLIND
Airdate: December 10, 1964

EPISODE
13

Samantha wants a reluctant Darrin to fix up her single friend, Gertrude, with someone from his office. When the unassuming Gertrude breaks a vase, Samantha secretly twitches it back together and tells her gal pal it's easily replaced. Darrin's ladykiller friend, Kermit, agrees to meet Gertrude; Kermit breaks the same vase, but Gertrude claiming it can be replaced "just like that" prompts Darrin to suspect that

Gertrude is a witch. Samantha uses magic to help Gertrude and Kermit realize common interests, while Darrin warns Kermit off Gertrude; this annoys Samantha, who tells Darrin it's impossible for a mortal to be married under a witch's spell.

Darrin tricks Kermit into meeting him at a bar to okay a layout, arranging for Kermit's ex-girlfriend, Susan, to be there. Samantha catches on and invites Gertrude; when Darrin pushes Kermit to reunite with Susan, Samantha witches Susan into dismissing her old beau. Gertrude arrives and gets a proposal from Kermit, who ignores Darrin's insistence that Gertrude is a witch. At the wedding, when the preacher asks if there are any objections, Samantha freezes the ceremony to convince Darrin that their friends' love isn't witchcraft; Darrin surmises that love can cast almost as powerful a spell. Later, he breaks the vase himself and asks Samantha to restore it, calling her over for a kiss by manually wiggling his own nose.

GOOD!

For someone so self-deprecating, Gertrude is a refreshing character, with cleverly written dialogue to boot. And, since Samantha and Darrin's wedding happened off-screen [except for a quick moment during a narrated montage in "I, Darrin, Take This Witch, Samantha" (#1)], Kermit and Gertrude's ceremony offers a chance to see what could have been, even if the Stephenses were married by a justice of the peace, and not in a church.

WELL?

Samantha and Gertrude are unusually close considering Samantha could only have known Gertrude a few months; Samantha's not even this chummy with Louise! Later, after Samantha puts the vase back together, a piece of broken glass remains in the hallway.

Kermit's office looks a lot like Darrin's, only with some artist's tables brought in and other furniture moved around. It even includes some of Darrin's layouts from "...And Something Makes Three" (#12).

Typically, when a girl excuses herself to powder her nose, she heads for the washroom. But when Gertrude returns to tell Kermit the vase he just broke can be replaced, she comes in from the kitchen. Did Gertrude make a wrong turn? And Samantha takes an awful risk restoring the vase with Kermit and Gertrude so nearby in the living room – Gertrude can certainly see the foyer from her vantage point on the couch. The third time the vase breaks, Samantha comments that Darrin doesn't like her correcting mistakes with witchcraft – yet he didn't object the second time, and that was with Kermit and Gertrude sitting a few feet away.

In the kitchen, Darrin asks Samantha if Gertrude is a witch. Samantha expresses surprise, asking, "Is that why you've been acting so funny?" She apparently forgot that he just asked her the same question in the foyer moments before. Later, Samantha is equally surprised when Darrin reports that Kermit and Gertrude have been dating every night. This can't be news; surely Gertrude is calling Samantha with updates.

Darrin's unusually gabby about witches: he tells Susan that Kermit is under a spell, then comes right out and tells Kermit that Gertrude is a witch, without stopping to think that Kermit and/or Susan might ask him how he knows. He's so busy trying to expose Gertrude that he's blind to possibility of exposing Samantha in the process.

Does Samantha simply have Susan rebuff Kermit, or does she put a truth spell on her? It's never made clear. Speaking of spells, Samantha's powers must be increasing, because now she can stop rain and move entire flocks of birds. And how come Samantha never actually confirms that Gertrude isn't a witch? She tells herself no witch would get married on a rainy day, and later, she only assures Darrin that

Gertrude's romance isn't witchcraft. Also, there are those who would suggest that Samantha using her powers in a Catholic church would be cause for lightning bolts.

OH, MY STARS!

Darrin allowed himself to be affected by the charms of Liza in "The Girl Reporter" (#9) and Janine/Sarah in "It Takes One to Know One" (#11), but here, he lustfully remembers seeing Lola and Nancy at a hospital benefit. Then, he celebrates playboy Kermit, saying "what a life that Kermit leads!" Darrin counters by admitting that a girl like Samantha doesn't come along every day, but he's on a very slippery slope: what if Endora is watching, as she swore to do in "Mother Meets What's-His-Name" (#4)?

Why is Darrin so opposed to the idea of his friend marrying a witch that he works overtime to keep Kermit away from Gertrude, and holds up business just to put Susan in Kermit's orbit? Darrin even talks about Gertrude flying off on her broom and the rain being "an omen of things to come for poor Kermit." Darrin says he has nothing personal against witches, but his words and actions say otherwise.

Are witches psychic? This has been debatable since the pilot, but the scale tips heavily in this episode. How else would Samantha know to zap the recipe of a drink Kermit created into Gertrude's head, much less know the drink exists in the first place? Then, she speeds up the migration of a flock of curlew (apparently not worried about the ecological impact of such a move) to aid in her matchmaking. Samantha might be aware Gertrude's a bird lover, but there's only one way Samantha can know Kermit is, too. And if Samantha is psychic, Darrin has a lot more to worry about than whether or not his friend is marrying a witch.

SON OF A GUN!

"All of my friends are witches, and we're just waiting for the right time to swoop down on Morning Glory Circle and claim it in the name of Beelzebub." – Samantha to Darrin, fed up with his objection to Gertrude.

SAMANTHA MEETS THE FOLKS
Airdate: December 17, 1964

EPISODE
14

A lonely Aunt Clara comes down the chimney for a visit at the same time Darrin's parents are on their way over to meet Samantha: Phyllis fusses over her adult son, while Frank is more laid back. As Samantha fields questions from Phyllis about her family, Aunt Clara surprises everyone. Darrin worries that Aunt Clara might be too much for his parents just as Aunt Clara is telling them she and Samantha are witches. Frank thinks Clara's dottiness is cute and compares her to Phyllis' sister, Madge, who thinks she's a lighthouse. Overhearing Phyllis complaining about Samantha's inability to make Darrin's favorite foods, Aunt Clara struggles to magically replace Samantha's meal with those very dishes.

After dinner, Phyllis seems upset that Samantha can cook after all, while Darrin has a gentle talk with Aunt Clara, who goes on about her doorknobs but privately packs her things. Frank scolds Phyllis for finding fault with Samantha, while Samantha's mad at Darrin for upsetting Aunt Clara. Samantha admits

Aunt Clara made the fancy dinner because she couldn't, and Phyllis confesses she felt like Darrin didn't need her anymore. After Darrin retrieves Aunt Clara, his parents connect with her, and Darrin advises Samantha to be herself, so she cleans the table by witchcraft. Darrin adds that maybe his folks aren't ready for the real Samantha yet.

GOOD!

Darrin's attitude toward witches is markedly improved here compared to the last two episodes. Meeting Aunt Clara throws him initially, but he quickly accepts her, trying not to hurt her feelings while telling her his parents won't be able to cope with witchcraft. He then lovingly tells Samantha the role of house witch has been filled, and tolerates his wife's magical tidy-up. It's nice to see Darrin back on his best behavior.

In "I, Darrin, Take This Witch, Samantha" (#1), Darrin told his new bride he had an Aunt Madge who thought she was a lighthouse. This episode builds on that revelation: we find out that Madge is Phyllis' sister. After Phyllis comes around, she speaks of bringing Madge and Aunt Clara together – now that would be an episode.

WELL?

Aunt Clara makes her entrance coming down the chimney – ironic, considering Darrin was relieved Endora didn't come down the chimney in "Mother Meets What's-His-Name" (#4). As Aunt Clara's bag and umbrella float across the foyer, the shadow of the wire manipulating them can briefly be seen on the wall. And these objects seem to have minds of their own: Aunt Clara scolds them for taking their time getting to the house, and later, Samantha reports that the umbrella told her Aunt Clara is at the bus station. Witches haven't been shown to have these kinds of interactive relationships with inanimate objects before, so it's an odd development.

If Samantha can barely make pot roast because she's "still learning," then what did she feed Kermit and Gertrude when they came over for dinner in the previous episode? What about the Tates, in "…And Something Makes Three" (#12)? The dinner party guests of "It Shouldn't Happen to a Dog" (#3)? At least Samantha's lack of culinary skill here is more consistent with her breakfast-burning debacle of "Be It Ever So Mortgaged" (#2).

Aunt Clara tells Darrin's parents she has 3,000 doorknobs in her collection, a hobby she first mentioned in "The Witches Are Out" (#7). One hundred and five of them came from her visit to Mr. Brinkman's house in that episode, but it seems his aren't the only doorknobs Aunt Clara has obtained without permission – she outright tells the elder Stephenses that "there are a lot of people having a heck of a time trying to open their doors!" Is Samantha's adorable aunt a kleptomaniac?

Aunt Clara might be eccentric, but she knows a lot more about baseball than her relatives. Apparently Bertha [from "The Witches Are Out" (#7)] helped witch the outcome of the World Series, while, in "Mother Meets What's-His-Name" (#4), neither Samantha nor Endora even knew what the World Series was. At the dinner table, Frank comments how good the food smells. Samantha laments that it's only pot roast, but when she takes the lid off the platter, it's *coq au vin*. Wouldn't a chicken dish drenched in wine smell a lot different than pot roast? For that matter, when Aunt Clara tries to conjure up the meal, she goofs and gets a live chicken that squawks loudly, which no one in the house hears.

OH, MY STARS!

In "I, Darrin, Take This Witch, Samantha" (#1), Darrin wanted to have dinner at his mother's house every Friday night; here, Darrin's parents have to fly in for a visit. If Darrin is from Missouri (also established in the pilot), is that where his parents are visiting from? Or do they live somewhere else? It's never discussed. Later, Phyllis admits she was surprised to hear Darrin got married, which means Darrin tied the knot without his parents in attendance. Darrin didn't know Samantha was a witch until their wedding night, so there was no reason for him to keep her a secret – unlike Samantha, who was rightfully afraid her disapproving parents would use their powers to dispense with Darrin [as Maurice did in "Just One Happy Family" (#10)].

Frank and Phyllis dismiss Aunt Clara's claim that she and Samantha are witches, attributing it to their new acquaintance's old age. So why then, when Frank jokingly suggests Aunt Clara is right, does Samantha confirm she is? Though the admission might sound senile in Aunt Clara's words, it's a lot more plausible coming from Samantha – yet her in-laws merely laugh it off.

SON OF A GUN!

"Oh, I don't believe in superstition." – Aunt Clara, when Samantha asks for luck making a simple dinner for her in-laws.

A VISION OF SUGAR PLUMS
Airdate: December 24, 1964

EPISODE
15

Having bought a Christmas tree, Samantha takes a shrunken version of it out of her purse and restores it to full size in the living room. Both the Stephenses and Kravitzes are bringing home children from the local orphanage for the holiday: cynical Michael picks a fight with Tommy over Tommy's belief in Santa Claus. Samantha tells Darrin it would help self-professed problem child Michael to spend time with them, but Darrin gets discouraged when Michael blows off his Santa suit as "a lot of bunk." To break through Michael's armor, Samantha admits she's a witch and offers to take him to see the real Santa Claus; the incredulous Darrin journeys with them. When Gladys sees the trio flying away on a broom, Abner pretends to believe her for Tommy's benefit, declaring he and his wife have seen reindeer.

At the North Pole, Michael meets Kris Kringle face-to-face and comes around. Darrin believes now, too, but, later, Samantha makes him think the trip was a dream. Gladys overhears Michael telling Tommy about his experience, then asks Tommy to repeat it to Abner, but Tommy plays dumb because he promised Michael he'd keep it a secret. As Darrin and Michael play, the Johnsons, who attempted to adopt Michael once before, come by and are delighted when Michael offers them a gift. They agree to be a family again, and, as Michael leaves, he and Samantha exchange winks in front of a befuddled Darrin.

GOOD!

Abner scoffs every time he thinks Gladys is seeing things, so it's a great twist for him to suddenly believe she has seen people flying through the air – and a double twist when it turns out he's just going along with it for Tommy. It's also a nice touch when Gladys finally finds a witness in Tommy, only to have him clam up out of a gentlemen's agreement with Michael.

How fun is it that even Santa Claus can't get Darrin's name right? Maybe calling him "Dennis" is Santa's way of letting Darrin know he's made this year's naughty list for ogling other women and having a less-than-tolerant attitude about witches. Or, could Mr. Claus have first heard about Darrin from Maurice or Endora?

WELL?

Orphanage administrator Mrs. Grange makes sure to introduce the Stephenses to Michael. So why does she simply let total strangers the Kravitzes approach Tommy unsupervised? Later, Darrin reports that Mrs. Grange feels Michael wouldn't appreciate spending Christmas with a family. If that's the case, why does she bother assigning Michael to a family at all?

The Stephenses put Michael up in a guest room that looks like a slightly redecorated version of their own bedroom. And, in "Help, Help, Don't Save Me" (#5), the banister on one side of the stairs was loose; now, the banister on the other side wobbles when Michael grabs it. Preparing for their North Pole trip, Samantha hands Michael his thin robe because "it's apt to be a little chilly," which is quite an understatement. Maybe Samantha's broom is heated, because her witches' outfit is even thinner, and Darrin makes the trip in his typical office suit.

As Gladys sees Michael and the Stephenses flying away, they appear to grow smaller in the sky. Yet, on Gladys' second look, the trio is in a holding pattern. Is Samantha awaiting confirmation from some witchy air traffic control? More likely, the sequence is extended so Gladys can see them more than once – so how come Abner doesn't spot them when he looks out the window himself?

At the North Pole, Samantha lovingly clears snow off Michael's head in a wide shot, but, in close-up, Michael hardly has any in his hair, and that's before Samantha attends to him. Finally, a sign indicating the North Pole may be necessary, but why is there a sign pointing the way to Santa's workshop? Who's usually up there except Santa and his elves, who already know where the workshop is? Not to mention, there are no tourists, nor any other reason for the workshop to have display tables, other than to give Michael a chance to select gifts.

Why does Samantha zap Darrin into believing that his trip to the North Pole was a dream? She'd be better off letting him retain the memory: Santa's message of acceptance would improve Darrin's tolerance toward witches. Now, if Darrin questions Santa's existence in the future, Samantha will have to explain him all over again.

OH, MY STARS!

The primary function of an orphanage is to find permanent homes for its children. Letting the kids go home with random families for Christmas seems like getting their hopes up, then dashing them. The Kravitzes and the Stephenses pick up Tommy and Michael, respectively, on December 24; that night, Christmas Eve, Samantha tells Darrin they can't bring Michael back "tomorrow" as unhappy as he was when he came. The orphans are supposed to go back Christmas Day? That's not much of a holiday. Then, Samantha laments to Darrin that "whatever disillusioned [Michael], we can't make it up to him in five minutes." He's an orphan – there's no questioning what's disillusioned him.

When Samantha proves she's a witch by changing into an ensemble similar to Endora's, Michael also wants to see Samantha's pointed hat and broom. In "I, Darrin, Take This Witch, Samantha" (#1), Endora sneered that mortals only think witches ride on brooms, and, in "The Witches Are Out" (#7), much was said against mortals' stereotypical depiction of witches. So why does Samantha present herself to Michael in the image he expects instead of gently informing the boy that witches don't look or fly that way – to say nothing of taking Michael and Darrin for a ride on a broom? Sounds like some writers want to break the stereotype of the witch, and others don't; this is a key point of the show, so it should be consistent.

Everyone knows that Santa Claus circles the globe on Christmas Eve – so why is he hanging around his workshop after bedtime on December 24? And why are the elves still busy making toys? Last-minute orders?

SON OF A GUN!

"But what difference does it make what we look like on the outside, eh? It's what we feel on the inside that counts, isn't it?" – Santa Claus to Michael, offering him – and everyone – the greatest Christmas gift of all.

IT'S MAGIC
Airdate: January 7, 1965

June Foster and Shirley Clyde [from "Mother Meets What's-His-Name" (#4)] stick Samantha with finding entertainment for a hospital benefit. A waiter suggests his magician friend, The Great Zeno, but Zeno is an alcoholic whose assistant, Roxie, leaves him for greener pastures; Samantha conjures up goldfish and a parrot to get the soused magician on the wagon. At the benefit, Samantha reluctantly agrees to assist the shaky Zeno; the audience grumbles at Zeno's lack of magical talent until Samantha gives him a boost with the real thing, which gets Zeno hired on a television show.

The night of his début, Roxie shows up ready to replace Samantha, upstaging Zeno during the live broadcast and sneering that he owes her this break. Spotting Samantha in the wings, Roxie inadvertently pulls her on stage and threatens her in front of the audience. Samantha retaliates by magically getting Roxie's hand stuck in a fishbowl, but Zeno rips off the back of Roxie's dress out of clumsiness. As Roxie moves to hit Zeno, Samantha makes her disappear, and Zeno takes command of the act. Darrin reveals that he's the one who got Zeno booked on the show, and, later, he won't come to bed until he figures out one of Zeno's illusions. Darrin accomplishes the trick, but, realizing Samantha made it happen, he gives in and joins her upstairs.

GOOD!

The haughtiness June and Shirley displayed in "Mother Meets What's-His-Name" (#4) comes to the fore again here as they maneuver Samantha into the role of entertainment chairman. Even better is Gladys' temporary change of heart: ordinarily, she looks at Samantha with near disdain, but now, she's not only friendly to Samantha, she comes to her defense as Shirley and June plan to trick her. It doesn't last – by the end of the episode, Gladys is her suspicious self again – but the brief sympathy adds some extra layers to her personality, as it does when Gladys turns the tables on the men at the kissing booth and practically flirts with Darrin.

Reverse shots for effect are easy to spot, but Samantha magically tying Zeno's tie comes off beautifully. And Samantha doesn't need to make Roxie disappear to sabotage her blatant career move – Roxie does a good job all by herself, insulting Zeno at full volume on live television, harassing the technician in the wings, and threatening Samantha on stage in front of the audience. Roxie's easy to hate, and she's supposed to be; Zeno ripping Roxie's dress is better revenge than anything Samantha could witch up.

WELL?

Samantha has fielded many questions from Gladys regarding things out of the ordinary, yet she magically steadies the waiter's tray in public, adding, with mock surprise, "It was almost like magic!" Not wise; Gladys doesn't need any more ammunition.

Samantha likes her goldfish – she gave Darrin gills in "It Takes One to Know One" (#11) to keep Janine/Sarah's lips off him; here, she zaps fish into Zeno's glass of gin to convince him he's hallucinating. Can fish swim in booze? Or are they illusions, only visible to Zeno? In either case, Zeno responds by dumping the fish down the sink, pouring his alcohol after them; would you trust rabbits and doves with this man? And, someone in the editing room cut away from two of Samantha's twitches in this scene, even clipping the sound effect that accompanies the magic gesture.

Samantha balks when she realizes she's going to have to wear Roxie's skimpy outfit. So where, in the middle of the benefit, does Samantha get the flowing skirt to go with it? She must zap it up, but it's never addressed. As for Mrs. Kravitz, she has called Samantha "Mrs. Stephens" in every appearance so far – except here, where Gladys uses her neighbor's first name. And there's a lot of hospital benefits in this town: Darrin and Samantha just mentioned seeing Gertrude at one in "Love Is Blind" (#13).

Samantha feels sorry for Zeno, and uses witchcraft to give him confidence. That must be her forté, because she did the exact same thing for young Marshall Burns in "Little Pitchers Have Big Fears" (#6). She even wears the same shawl and blouse she had on while helping Marshall at his baseball tryout.

Where does Roxie go after Samantha makes her disappear? What happens if Roxie remembers being zapped off stage and talks about it? More importantly, no live broadcast in the '60s, beaming into thousands of American homes during prime-time, would continue airing a show after the back of a woman's dress rips off, exposing her undergarments. Owing to network decency laws, somebody would pull the plug, or there would be an avalanche of viewer complaint calls, followed by a scandal. Yet Zeno is deemed a great success and booked for a 13-week engagement.

OH, MY STARS!

Samantha has learned about baseball and is getting a handle on cooking, but she doesn't know much about the workings of the mortal world yet. How else to explain her handing the drunken Zeno money without seeing what he could do first? By the same token, Samantha is pretty free about using her powers in front of mortals – she openly twitches on live television, then makes Roxie disappear in a puff of smoke. Bertha may have said it best in "The Witches Are Out" (#7): "Better take out lots of fire insurance…"

SON OF A GUN!

"You don't know much about magic." – Zeno to Samantha, as he tries to convince her he's no good without Roxie.

A IS FOR AARDVARK
Airdate: January 14, 1965

Darrin falls and sprains his ankle, then constantly pulls Samantha away from her chores to bring him various and sundry items. After Darrin sends down a paper airplane with a request for a pencil, Samantha floats one up to him. Darrin is upset until he realizes he's been running Samantha ragged, so Samantha offers to have the house fulfill Darrin's requests for him. Endora warns Samantha that, as a mortal, Darrin is too greedy to handle magic; soon Darrin says he was wrong to ask Samantha to give up witchcraft and announces that he wants to live by it from now on. Endora embraces Darrin – even remembering his name – but Samantha is decidedly unhappy, especially after Darrin "retires" from McMann & Tate.

Using reverse psychology, Samantha dons sequins and tells Darrin she can give him the memories of the exotic locales he wants to visit so they don't have to travel; when Darrin wants to sell the house, Samantha gushes about the luxuries the new one should have. Later, a package arrives containing a six-month anniversary gift Darrin bought for Samantha: a watch bearing Darrin's heartfelt inscription. Once Samantha cries that she'll go anywhere with Darrin, he decides to live like a mortal again – but, unsure he can forget his taste of power, Darrin asks Samantha to send him back to before he acquired it. She does, and this time, when the paper airplane comes down, Samantha brings Darrin the pencil manually.

GOOD!
Darrin and Samantha have gotten into a rhythm: she does something he doesn't like, he says he wants to talk to her, she asks, "When?", and he says, "Now." This same exchange took place in "Love Is Blind" (#13) and "Samantha Meets the Folks" (#14); with all the different writers on the show so far, it's nice to see some consistency taking hold.

The scene where Samantha breaks down in tears after being given Darrin's "I love you every second" watch elevates the show into serious dramatic territory. Samantha's sobs become a little maudlin, but the sequence impressively plays like a movie rather than a situation comedy.

WELL?
Darrin crawls on the floor after spraining his ankle; the scene cuts to Samantha's reaction. In the next shot, Darrin is sitting on the stairs, nursing his foot. How did Darrin get off of his stomach and onto the stairs so quickly, with a foot too painful to walk on?

The recuperating Darrin sends a paper airplane containing a request for a pencil. If Darrin needs a pencil, what did he use to scribble on the airplane? After Samantha floats a pencil to him, Darrin retorts that she used her powers just to irritate him. If she's made the purported twenty-seven trips up the stairs, surely he'd let that tiny display of witchcraft slide. Twice in this episode, he refers to those powers as "nonsense." That's partly what set Endora against him in "Mother Meets What's-His-Name" (#4), though he doesn't think magic is nonsense as he uses it to fix sandwiches and open windows, to say nothing of quitting his job and planning to live by the powers he was so quick to criticize.

It's quite intriguing that Endora feels Samantha should be exposed to mortal greed, which she helps along by siding with Darrin and encouraging the use of magic. Yet, in several episodes up to now, Endora has said that Samantha should be able to use her powers without giving a thought to whether Darrin would become greedy. Then, when Darrin and Endora do see eye-to-eye, Endora asks Samantha,

"Isn't that what you always wanted? Harmony in the family?" Samantha has, but Darrin and Endora have only locked horns in one episode, "Mother Meets What's-His-Name" (#4); the only other time they were together, in "Just One Happy Family" (#10), Endora tried to help Darrin instead, so the implication of discord seems like an overstatement.

Darrin lists foreign locales for him and Samantha to visit, including Paris – but they were just in the City of Lights a couple of months ago, in "Witch or Wife" (#8). After Darrin announces their trip around the world, Samantha packs trunks by hand. If Samantha is trying to give Darrin "too much of a good thing" regarding witchcraft, why not just twitch the trunks full and be done with it? For that matter, Darrin gets hooked on magic after Samantha has the house cooperate with him – but, after he eschews the mortal life, he never again takes advantage of the house's services.

OH, MY STARS!

Samantha's powers continue to grow exponentially. The witch who could barely move ashtrays in "I, Darrin, Take This Witch, Samantha" (#1) can now infuse an entire house with magic, plus send Darrin back to before they made their agreement. Both are intense pieces of witchcraft, but Samantha doesn't even twitch to make them happen. And this isn't the first time Samantha has played with Darrin's memory: she also made him forget their trip to the North Pole in "A Vision of Sugar Plums" (#15); at least this time, Darrin asks Samantha to do it. Seemingly, her spell negates everything that happened from the time Samantha floated the pencil to just after Darrin made the request, including his quitting McMann & Tate. Does that mean Endora has no memory of the events, either? Doubtful, since she's a witch as well. Which begs the question: does Samantha really take Darrin back in time, or does she simply restore his sprained ankle and zap him upstairs with an erased memory? Of course, then Darrin would wonder why and how he lost a few days.

SON OF A GUN!

"Don't tell me he's a convert!" – Endora to Samantha, after seeing the floating banana Darrin has summoned from the kitchen.

Darrin goes a bit overboard deciding to ditch the mortal way, but he uses some sound arguments trying to get Samantha to go along with it. "If I couldn't do it, I didn't want you to do it," he admits. "If I couldn't give something to you, I didn't want you to have it." This might be the most astute thing Darrin has ever said, even beyond acknowledging his vulnerability to witchcraft in "Help, Help, Don't Save Me" (#5). No wonder Endora remembers his name – and Darrin responds with an unprecedented "Hi, Mom."

EPISODE 18

THE CAT'S MEOW
Airdate: January 21, 1965

After Endora tells Samantha that Darrin will stray eventually simply because he's mortal, "iron tigress" Margaret Marshall of Countess Margaret's Cosmetics sashays into McMann & Tate. She likes Darrin's ideas, but wants to go over some changes at her office in Chicago. Larry warns Darrin not to let maneater Margaret know he's married, and, after Darrin is forced to cancel his seven-month anniversary celebration with Samantha, he nixes Samantha's suggestion to turn herself into a cat so she can travel with him. In Chicago, Darrin is lured onto Margaret's yacht, where he thinks a stray cat on the dock is Samantha checking up on him.

Margaret comes on strong, then excuses herself, while fidgety Darrin crawls around the room pleading his innocence to "Samantha." Margaret wants to be the Countess Margaret cover girl and returns modeling a slinky outfit; as she kisses Darrin, the cat runs out, and Darrin follows. On deck, he encounters a pelican, briefly wondering if it's also Samantha; Margaret and the crew concur they've all seen Darrin talking to animals, and Margaret realizes Darrin is married. She awards Darrin the account anyway, and tells him he should never drink champagne. Darrin brings "Samantha" home and lectures "her" for spying on him, while the real Samantha sits on the stairs. Darrin covers by presenting Samantha with the cat, and the pelican lands on the Stephenses' patio – it's Endora, who kept watch over Darrin because Samantha wouldn't.

GOOD!

Though it isn't revealed until later that the pelican Darrin talks to is Endora, it's amusing to ponder their unintentional interaction: Darrin professes his love and caresses Endora's feathers – what did Endora think of all that? She must also have a good chuckle watching Darrin talk to the cat, knowing it isn't Samantha.

WELL?

The Stephenses are shown attempting to mark their seven-month anniversary. Time sure flies, because they just celebrated their six-month anniversary in the previous episode. And Endora seems to have a hang-up about Darrin straying: she set Darrin up to do exactly that in "It Takes One to Know One" (#11), and now she spies on Darrin to make sure he *doesn't* cheat. Or, is that, to make sure he does? At the agency, Larry happily pats Darrin's upper arms in a two-shot as he revels in how much money Margaret's account will generate, yet, when the scene cuts to an over-the-shoulder shot, Larry's arms are already down.

Darrin tries to call Samantha from a pay phone on the dock, telling the operator he doesn't remember "the area code number" for his house. In this 1960s world that doesn't have the explosion of area codes today's devices require, Darrin's can only be 212, 516, or 914, presuming he lives somewhere in New York State. Do the writers have Darrin blank so they don't have to deal with a phone number on television?

Even if Darrin thinks he's in the doghouse with the cat, would he really chase "Samantha" around and talk to "her" in front of his fellow mortals? Darrin's lucky Margaret only thinks he's downed too much champagne instead of looking up the number for the nearest sanitarium; of course, Darrin's pursuit is the comedy of the whole sequence. After getting caught talking to the cat on deck, Darrin nervously claims the salt air is very refreshing. The yacht sailed out of Chicago, so the only body of water it could be on is Lake Michigan, which is a body of fresh water, not salt. Darrin also tells Margaret he's allergic to the cat one minute, but cradles it in his arms the next. Isn't he worried about getting snagged in his lie?

Margaret is sexy and confident, but what does it say about her that she's "very successful" in regard to mixing business with pleasure? Is every male Countess Margaret associate fair game?

How does Darrin get the cat home from Chicago? When he arrives, the feline is perched on his shoulder. Surely he didn't transport the kitty in cars and planes without some sort of carrier – no cat is that well-behaved.

OH, MY STARS!

When Samantha tells Endora it's her "seventh" anniversary, Endora exclaims, "You haven't been carrying on this charade for seven years!" Endora knows how long her daughter has been married; she crashed her daughter's wedding night in "I, Darrin, Take This Witch, Samantha" (#1).

Darrin tries to dissuade Samantha from joining him in Chicago by telling her, "there's an unwritten law in the advertising game: wives and business just don't mix." Mr. McMann and Larry must not know about that law, because they were the ones who wanted Samantha to host a huge dinner party for a client in "It Shouldn't Happen to a Dog" (#3), when she barely knew how to cook.

SON OF A GUN!

"Sooner or later that perfect husband of yours is going to roam. And I don't mean Italy." – Endora to Samantha, again trying to drive home the imperfection of mortals to her trusting daughter.

EPISODE 19

A NICE LITTLE DINNER PARTY
Airdate: January 28, 1965

Darrin is nervous when Endora attends a dinner Samantha is giving for his parents. Frank isn't adjusting well to retirement and mistakes Endora's friendliness for flirting, which annoys Phyllis. Frank suggests that Endora join them for a night of theatre; when Phyllis begs off, Frank declares he'll go with Endora alone. At bedtime, Darrin blames Samantha for inviting her mother and gets zapped out of bed, appearing on the couch. Phyllis tells Darrin that Frank didn't come home after his date with Endora and assumes the worst, but Frank informs Samantha he spent the night at the club because he'd forgotten his keys, with Phyllis refusing to answer the door. Frank admits that Endora makes him feel young again, and recalls proposing to Phyllis in a place called Angel Falls.

Endora assures Phyllis she's not interested in Frank, but Phyllis misunderstands and hands him over, taking a train home to her mother in Phoenix. After Frank flies to Miami for a world cruise, Samantha and Endora try to bring Darrin's parents together. Endora magically induces the pilot of Frank's plane to land in Angel Falls, while Samantha makes Phyllis pull the emergency cord on her train and disembark at the town's nonexistent depot, where the elder Stephenses meet and patch things up. Darrin is thrilled, although Samantha feels better after conjuring up the thunderstorm Frank mentioned for ambiance. When Darrin falls asleep downstairs, Samantha lovingly pops him back into bed.

GOOD!

As Darrin worries about his parents meeting Endora, Samantha reminds him that they loved Aunt Clara, who told them she and Samantha were witches in "Samantha Meets the Folks" (#14); Darrin counters that "they didn't believe she was a witch," which is a nifty bit of continuity. Darrin also comments that his parents have moved "into the city." Considering "I, Darrin, Take This Witch, Samantha" (#1) had them living close enough for Friday night dinners, and "Samantha Meets the Folks" (#14) saw them having to fly in for a visit, this is a keen story save.

After exhibiting some questionable behavior, Frank eventually owns how useless he felt after retiring, and admits that the lively Endora made him realize how drab his life had become. Comedy or drama, when any character can take responsibility for their own actions – especially after not having taken it – it's very satisfying.

WELL?

After Samantha assures Darrin that Endora will be charming, Darrin replies, "I've seen some of her charms. Bang - you're a frog!" Except that Darrin hasn't seen such behavior from Endora so far. Is there more going on off-screen?

Endora's sensational gown has a cross pattern on it; apparently there isn't any witch/church conflict. Then, while arguing with Samantha, Darrin says, "I'm beginning to understand why they used to burn witches at Salem." It's understandable that Darrin is upset about Endora's effect on his parents, but there are some lines that shouldn't be crossed.

In front of a woman he's just met, Frank disparages Phyllis, then invites Endora to go to the theatre with them in a situation where Phyllis has no choice but to agree. Later, he virtually flirts with Endora in front of Phyllis, telling his wife, "You're acting as if I've done something wrong!" Frank may be "desperate for attention" by his own account, but that doesn't do much to justify his antics.

Why are Darrin and Samantha so annoyed with Endora? Samantha asked her to be charming; she was. Endora flirted a little, but Frank took that ball and ran with it. Afterwards, Darrin tells Samantha, "I hope you're satisfied," placing no blame on his "senior delinquent" father.

Frank tells Samantha he slept at the club because his keys were in his other jacket and Phyllis wouldn't answer the door or phone. Has Frank been in town long enough to join a club? Later, Samantha tells Darrin she's gone to the beauty parlor with Phyllis and "taken care of everything," forgetting that she already recruited Endora to square things. Why doesn't Samantha call off her mother? It's only after Endora's visit that Phyllis takes off for Phoenix.

After his parents phone to say they've reunited, Darrin gushes about his father's tales of proposing to Phyllis in a thunderstorm. Samantha immediately zaps one up and says she wants everything to be perfect. Darrin must realize that his wife has been using magic to help his parents – doesn't he mind?

OH, MY STARS!

So, after 40 years of marriage, Frank and Phyllis Stephens deal with their conflicts by running thousands of miles away from each other without even having a discussion. If this is how they handle problems, what kind of an example did they set for Darrin?

Samantha and Endora using their powers to bring Phyllis and Frank together in Angel Falls is admirable, but Samantha has Phyllis pull the train's emergency cord – twice. Samantha doesn't stop to think of all the people she could injure with that stunt – and the pilots of Frank's plane will probably have to answer to Air Traffic Control and the FAA for diverting their flight. It's hard to ignore that the mother-daughter team prevents hundreds of people from reaching their own destinations just so the elder Stephenses can be reunited.

By the way, where is Angel Falls? Phyllis leaves New York for Phoenix, and Frank for Miami. There's no way the estranged couple can meet in the middle, because these destinations are on opposite ends of the country. Now, Darrin is from Missouri, and the original Angel Falls proposal happened before Darrin was born – this implies that Angel Falls is in Missouri. Yet Samantha conjures up an Angel Falls thunderstorm, and the boom can be heard on Morning Glory Circle, over 1,000 miles away. It follows that Angel Falls must be somewhere in New York State, but it means Frank and Phyllis got engaged in New York, moved to Missouri, had Darrin, and eventually moved back to New York.

Do Phyllis and Frank ever compare notes about her compulsion to stop the train and his pilot making an unscheduled detour? After both Samantha and Aunt Clara confessed they were witches in "Samantha Meets the Folks" (#14), these strange events might make Darrin's parents wonder if the confessions were true. Finally, Phyllis waits at a newly-created train depot, and Frank pulls up in a car – did Endora zap up a rent-a-car agency near her makeshift airstrip?

SON OF A GUN!

"I'll just stay calm and put the whole thing out of my mind. After all, what can happen in one evening? And now, would you like another cup of divorce?" – Phyllis to Darrin, betraying her true feelings about Frank and Endora over a pot of coffee.

Darrin and Endora's uneasy truce is wondrous to behold as they make nice in front of Phyllis and Frank. Endora calls Darrin her favorite son-in-law, and Darrin even kisses her on the cheek – not something that happens every day.

EPISODE **20**

YOUR WITCH IS SHOWING
Airdate: February 4, 1965

Endora wants Samantha to attend the wedding of Cousin Mario in Egypt, but Darrin, who's swamped with work, ruffles Endora's feathers when he says Samantha will only go somewhere with him the "old-fashioned way." At the office, Larry finds the overextended Darrin an assistant: eager young Gideon Whitsett. Their client, Woolfe, likes Gideon but ignores Darrin, who gets the hiccups. Gideon sells Woolfe on Darrin's slogan, and later covers when Darrin gets stuck in an elevator. The next day, Darrin's late after running out of gas; when he gets to the office, Woolfe is impressed by Gideon's layouts – carbon copies of work Darrin left at home. Darrin becomes convinced that Gideon is a warlock and that Endora is sabotaging him, leading to a fight with Samantha.

Endora gives Darrin a potion to combat Gideon's magic; when Darrin fumbles over his presentation, and a model home catches fire, he spritzes Endora's potion in Gideon's face, but it's only a prank meant to give Darrin confidence. As Darrin recuperates at home, Gideon stops by to pick up the Woolfe file, so Samantha magically induces Darrin into overhearing Gideon revealing his true, unscrupulous, mortal nature; once Gideon confesses using Darrin's unconscious doodling to steal his ideas, Darrin punches him. Gideon is demoted, and Darrin concedes to Samantha that his own insecurity almost did him in. After scolding Endora for the fake potion, Samantha sneezes powerfully, and Darrin's hiccups return, causing Endora to laugh from on high.

GOOD!

Building on having told Samantha he's from Missouri in "I, Darrin, Take This Witch, Samantha" (#1), Darrin relays to Woolfe that he's "Missouri U, Class of '50" – which suggests that Darrin is in his mid-to-late 30s. And Darrin's slogan is inspired, though it may not resonate with a newer generation unfamiliar with the Beatles – "He'd like to hold your hand when you're wearing your discotheque dress from Woolfe Brothers" is a play on one of the Fab Four's most famous songs (1963's *I Want to Hold Your Hand*), and was as current to audiences then as Miley Cyrus is now.

Endora has referred to Darrin by everything other than his real name from the beginning: What's-His-Name, Dennis, Whosis, Donald, You-Know-Who...she only ever got Darrin's name right in "A is for Aardvark" (#17), and that event may or may not have happened, since it was included in the time period Darrin asked Samantha to do over. Regardless, Endora's missed monikers have only ever been in conversations with Samantha – until now. Endora "forgets" Darrin's name to his face, calling him Denton, Duncan, and Derwin. If nothing else, Endora's made a choice to be more direct about it.

WELL?

Darrin and Endora nearly bonded over the use of witchcraft in "A is for Aardvark" (#17); in the previous episode, "A Nice Little Dinner Party" (#19), Endora helped reunite Darrin's parents. But here, after Darrin beats his chest about Samantha not going anywhere without him, the game changes with Endora's simple query, "You really mean to set yourself against me?" So much for peace in the family...

As soon as Gideon waltzes into Darrin's office, Darrin senses something is off. So why does it take him so long to see Gideon's true colors? Gideon pushes all the elevator buttons at the same time right in front of Darrin, but Darrin doesn't question it, even after calling Gideon on making up a false history at Yale to impress Woolfe.

When Darrin gets the hiccups during his first pitch to Woolfe, there's a sales chart on his easel. After a cutaway, the shot comes back to Darrin, but now there's a campaign slogan on the easel. Another cutaway, and the sales chart is back. Only after Larry gives Darrin a glass of water does Darrin remove the chart to expose the slogan underneath.

As Samantha and Darrin argue, she waves off his list of witchy woes by retorting, "With evidence like that, you should have been at Salem." That's the second time in two episodes – and two arguments – that the colonial locale has come up.

Darrin spends much of the episode certain that Endora has sent Gideon to sabotage him. So why, when Endora offers him "help," does he even think about accepting it? She tells him, "The only way to break a spell is with another spell," but surely Darrin would think Endora is offering him something to break her own spell. Then, Darrin chooses the moment his model home threatens to set the whole building on fire to spray the potion in Gideon's face. Why not wait until he can get Gideon alone somewhere?

Also, Darrin's getting into a habit of acting strangely in front of other mortals: in "The Cat's Meow" (#18), Darrin talked to a cat and a pelican in earshot of a client and her yacht crew, and here, Woolfe's entire board of directors witnesses Darrin's calls to Endora. Should Larry be worried? Finally, Darrin sprays a solution of baking soda, ammonia, and garlic salt into Gideon's eyes, which should burn like the blazes on contact, but Gideon just stands there.

After Gideon tips his hand, Darrin punches him and states that he doesn't think Gideon is a witch; Samantha concurs. Gideon is not out cold: why would the Stephenses talk about witches in front of any mortal, let alone Gideon? If Gideon wants revenge, all he has to do is blab to Larry or anybody else who will listen. And, Gideon's constant self-promotion supposedly made him rich by the time he hit college, yet he toils in an ad agency's copywriting department in a menial position. Why? And once Gideon's schemes are exposed, he is "back to sharpening pencils" instead of being fired for viciously trying to undermine one of Larry's top executives.

OH, MY STARS!

Darrin's sporadic intolerance regarding witches, absent the last few episodes, resurfaces when he assumes Gideon is a warlock. "Pretty soon the entire agency'll be witches. Then the building. Then the street!" Acting as if this is the most horrible thing that could happen, Darrin makes this declaration to Samantha, herself a witch. Why do the writers continue to make Darrin intolerant toward witches when he's married to one? It's amazing Samantha takes it.

SON OF A GUN!

"Wars have been won from wastepaper baskets, baby." – Gideon to Samantha, admitting that he lifted campaign ideas from Darrin's doodles.

Samantha may be getting tired of Darrin's otherworldly complaints. "This is dangerous," she tells him. "Do you know what's happening?...The way you're talking, everything bad that happens to you now is witchcraft!" Samantha setting her husband straight with a little perspective is something that needed to happen.

LING-LING
Airdate: February 11, 1965

Gladys comes by with an empty bird cage, thinking a stray Siamese cat has eaten her bird. Later, Samantha feels the exotic feline would make a perfect model for Darrin's Jewel of the East campaign. The humanized cat, Ling-Ling, wows Darrin, Larry, and nervous rookie photographer Wally Ames; Darrin decides to hold a last-minute celebration at the house, but Samantha discovers her refrigerator is empty and zaps up a feast, stunning Gladys. Welcoming Wally and the Tates, Samantha is dismayed to see Ling-Ling on the smitten photographer's arm.

Samantha tries to keep her sardine hors d'oeuvres away from Ling-Ling, and covers when the cat girl laps up her soup. Ling-Ling tells Samantha she has no feelings for Wally, but intends to be with him as long as he can give her a better life than she had as a stray. Darrin learns Ling-Ling is a cat, but can't discourage Wally, so Samantha laces Ling-Ling's drink with catnip, causing her to hiss at Wally, scratch his face, and stalk out. Gladys sets a saucer of milk out for the stray she saw at the Stephenses, but it attracts the human Ling-Ling. Before Gladys can get Abner to the window, Samantha finds Ling-Ling and changes her back; seeing only a cat, Abner hands Gladys her medicine.

GOOD!

This episode is chock full of good lines, most of them revolving around the manifestation of Ling-Ling's feline attributes (example: her turning down Wally's coffee in favor of cream). Darrin gets his moment, too – after Samantha tells him Ling-Ling is a cat, Darrin pipes up, "Why? Did she say something about Louise?"

WELL?

As Darrin talks to Samantha in the kitchen about the Jewel of the East campaign, Ling-Ling can be heard meowing off-screen. However, she doesn't show up in the kitchen until after Darrin leaves. At the agency, Wally nervously takes over for more seasoned staff photographer Rick Avery; is Avery the shutterbug Darrin pushed aside while shooting Miss Jasmine in "It Takes One to Know One" (#11)? As in that episode, all hope of finding a model is lost when the perfect one suddenly walks in, but the repeated experience never arouses suspicion in Darrin.

Darrin tells Samantha he is "leaving now," sounding like he'll be home any minute. Now, it has been said that McMann & Tate is in Manhattan, while Morning Glory Circle is out of the city, and Darrin has to take a train to get home – that implies Samantha has more time than she thinks, but the scene is engineered so Gladys sees an empty counter one minute and a smörgåsbord the next. And it's rather impolite of Gladys to help herself to an hors d'oeuvre without asking – to say nothing of leaving half of it on the serving platter. Ling-Ling does the opposite, wolfing down an entire tray of hors d'oeuvres, which is funny, but Darrin reaches down with a full platter and comes up empty in one shot; even a cat-human like Ling-Ling couldn't polish off the snacks that quickly.

Wally seems like a nice guy, but he can't have much experience with girls. He falls madly in love with Ling-Ling and wants to know if a little "nip" means more to her than he does – after knowing her less than a day. The other mortals also treat Wally and Ling-Ling like they've been dating for weeks: Larry comments how "serious" things are between them, and Darrin asks Ling-Ling what she thinks of the "lovesick shutterbug" in front of everybody, embarrassing Wally.

Darrin has a hard time believing Samantha can turn a cat into a human being, even though she made a canine of Rex Barker in "It Shouldn't Happen to a Dog" (#3). Question: does a transformee's physiology change along with their physical form? Ling-Ling handles wine like a human, although alcohol is toxic to cats, which would make her very sick, if not kill her. As for the catnip, does Samantha always keep a supply in the house? And Abner constantly shoves medicine down Gladys' throat, but what exactly does the syrup do? The implication is that it's tranquilizer, but those are typically prescribed in pill form. Maybe Gladys should try Ling-Ling's catnip.

Finally, as established in "...And Something Makes Three" (#12), Louise is pregnant. No one here mentions it, thinks to ask how Louise is progressing, or is the least bit worried when she takes a drink.

OH, MY STARS!

Wonderful as this episode is (and it's really one of the best in the series so far), it's odd that the show chose to tell two cat stories within three installments, and with the same cat. Darrin followed it around in "The Cat's Meow" (#18), then brought it home, giving it to Samantha. It hasn't been seen since; did the Stephenses just turn it loose? It would be better continuity for Ling-Ling to be the cat Darrin rescued: think of the dimension added to her speech about being tired of searching for scraps if was Darrin and Samantha who left her to fend for herself.

Gladys chats with Samantha over a fence that is either beside or behind the Stephens house. Later, Samantha peeks over a different fence to find Ling-Ling in the Kravitzes' backyard. But the Stephenses and the Kravitzes live across the street from each other, not next door – for Gladys and Samantha to see each others' patios over a fence, they'd each have to be in someone else's backyard. Are Morning Glory Circle residents all right with neighbors randomly wandering through each others' property?

SON OF A GUN!

"From now on it'll be martinis and sardines all the way!" – Ling-Ling to Samantha, telling her how it's going to be now that she's human.

Greta Chi, who plays Ling-Ling, delivers her clever, feline-tinged dialogue in a way that is fresh, believable, and a joy to watch. It truly seems Ling-Ling is a cat that's been turned into a person, even (and especially) after repeated viewings.

EYE OF THE BEHOLDER
Airdate: February 25, 1965

Endora, who feels Samantha is ignoring her witchly heritage, arranges for Darrin to find a portrait called "Maid of Salem, 1682" that looks just like Samantha. Darrin buys the artwork and becomes obsessed with it when Samantha is evasive about how old she really is; cornered, Samantha admits she will look the same as she does now when Darrin is an old man. Endora messes with Darrin, making him feel old by preventing him from lifting a heavy wheelbarrow that a little girl moves with ease. After Larry deems a marriage between a 75-year-old man and a 25-year-old woman indecent, Darrin confides in best friend Dave, his doctor, and his bartender, but gets no answers.

Darrin wanders through the neighborhood park where, thanks to Endora, a pair of chattering squirrels repeat the conversation he had with Samantha about her age. Meanwhile, Samantha finds "Maid of Salem" and is angry with Endora, who states Darrin will have to know about Samantha's age eventually. As Darrin watches an elderly couple reaffirming their love, the police spot Darrin's ticketed car at the park and call Samantha. Finding Darrin, Samantha is about to reveal her age when Darrin announces it doesn't matter. The cops catch up; having just talked to Samantha on the phone, they scold Darrin for having an affair. At home, Endora ages Darrin's picture to show Samantha what she has to look forward to, but the unworried Samantha changes it back.

GOOD!

Endora has been shown to be a powerful witch, but here it's revealed she also has a great head for detail. Her "Maid of Salem" portrait – and it's never said whether it's really of Samantha or not – even comes with dust for Darrin to blow off. And someone in the casting department had an excellent eye, because whoever posed as the older version of Darrin bears a remarkable resemblance to Dick York; remember, this is decades before CGI and Photoshop.

WELL?

It seems all is forgiven for the break-a-spell-with-another-spell prank Endora pulled on Darrin in "Your Witch Is Showing" (#20): the in-laws seem perfectly comfortable browsing an antique store with Samantha. But when Darrin brings "Maid of Salem" to the register, does Mr. Bodkin, the antique store owner, realize he's selling an item that isn't in his inventory?

Since when does Darrin do the gardening? It was Samantha who tackled that task in "Mother Meets What's-His-Name" (#4). As for little Kimmie, the girl who lifts the wheelbarrow in the backyard, she's adorable, but a stranger; Darrin knows her, but theirs is a purely off-camera acquaintance. When the newspaper delivery boy cycles by, Darrin is suddenly in the front yard, heading for the main entrance, for seemingly no other reason except to get beaned by the paper.

McMann & Tate needs sketches delivered to their Riverdale office, but if the Manhattan ad agency has this never-before-mentioned branch, it would be unnecessary for it to be in Riverdale, which is in the Bronx, only nine miles away. As for Larry, he ogles a model, then goes on to Darrin about men preferring younger women. The writers seem to have forgotten that Larry has a pregnant wife at home as of "…And Something Makes Three" (#12); these displays make him appear a scoundrel.

The show hearkens back to its first episode by mirroring Darrin's search for advice from his inattentive friend, Dave, and his disbelieving doctor, played by Lindsay Workman. That's wonderful continuity, but Workman just played the harried train conductor who dealt with Darrin's mother in "A Nice Little Dinner Party" (#19). And the bartender who rounds out this trio, portrayed by Paul Barselow, was referred to as Hal in the pilot; here, Darrin calls him Pete.

How does Endora know to have the squirrels mimic the Samantha/Darrin conversation she wasn't present for? Did she eavesdrop? And can the other park visitors see Endora laughing in the tree?

OH, MY STARS!

This must truly be the first time Darrin's thought about Samantha's age. In "I, Darrin, Take This Witch, Samantha" (#1), Darrin responded to Samantha's confession of inexperience by saying, "You're young yet!" Very young, apparently – here, when Darrin tries to guess her age, he thinks she's either 22 or 24. Samantha looks a tad more mature than that (and closer to portrayer Elizabeth Montgomery's current age of 31). Also, Darrin's surprised that Samantha doesn't look a day older than when they met, but she shouldn't; they only met a year ago. However, in "The Cat's Meow" (#18), the Stephenses celebrated their seven-month wedding anniversary; it's nearer to eight months by now, so the Stephenses must have dated for four months before getting married, which conflicts with "I, Darrin, Take This Witch, Samantha" (#1), where their courtship seemed decidedly whirlwind.

SON OF A GUN!

"Well?" – Samantha to Darrin, after he suspects that she won't look any different when he's an old man.

This episode explores a significant theme untouched so far in the series: Samantha's age. Previous episodes established that Endora is anywhere from 1,000 to 2,500 years old, so it's only natural Samantha's lifespan would exceed a mortal's as well, and that Darrin would ponder the repercussions of his wife's near-eternal youth. The exact year of Samantha's birth is purposely kept secret, leaving the audience to do a little pondering of its own.

RED LIGHT, GREEN LIGHT
Airdate: March 4, 1965

After Samantha saves Dave from being run down on a street with unrelenting traffic, the lawyer decides to campaign for a stop light. Samantha declines Endora's offer to install one by witchcraft, then attends a meeting at Dave's, where the community plans to hold a rally and invite the mayor. Darrin is recruited to come up with an ad by the next morning; as he works in the den, Endora arrives in the living room with a selection of lights, which are gone by the time the spying Gladys brings Abner over for a look. When the tired Darrin suggests Samantha just fly across the busy road, he is magically locked in the den until he finishes the ad, discouraged the next morning when Dave and Samantha want changes.

Gladys peeks in the Stephenses' window again and sees a London bobby that Endora has brought for Samantha; Abner remains dubious. At the rally, the mayor quickly deems the light unnecessary, but Endora freezes the crowd and assures Samantha that the official isn't going anywhere. Hitching a ride with the mayor after fixing his car with magic, Samantha disables its siren and horn so the bureaucrat's driver can't cut through the jammed intersection, forcing the mayor to concede the corner should indeed have a stop signal. As the Kravitzes arrive for a victory party, Gladys gulps down her medicine, no longer seeing Endora and her "guest of honor" traffic light in the room.

GOOD!

Since Dave was established as Darrin's best friend in the pilot, he's been relegated to one-note comedy relief, absently going on while Darrin revealed key information about Samantha being a witch. In this episode, the show takes the time to flesh Dave out a bit: he's a lawyer, he has some pull at City Hall, and he likes to flirt with Samantha, all of which is an improvement over Dave simply listening to Darrin in bars.

WELL?

The traffic on this all-important road evokes a silent movie, with sped-up footage that is especially glaring while Abner shuffles around at an unnatural speed at the corner. Samantha freezes traffic so Dave won't get run over, but when she restores it, Dave is still in the middle of the road, and somehow able to run back to safety, negating why Samantha stopped the cars in the first place. Later, Endora brags to Samantha that she can install a stop signal "quicker than you can say Beelzebub," a name on par with "devil" that Samantha used sarcastically in "Love Is Blind" (#13). Endora can be devilish, but certainly she wouldn't use the term in connection with herself.

In "Mother Meets What's-His-Name" (#4), Gladys was upset because the Welcome Wagon ladies volunteered her to sit down in front of a cement mixer at their freeway protest. Here, Gladys glibly suggests everyone lie down in the middle of the street for this demonstration.

Darrin works in the den while Endora brings her assortment of lights, one of which dings loudly. Wouldn't Darrin hear that from the den and wonder what's going on in his living room? Then, Darrin suddenly cops an attitude about doing the ad, which leads to a short argument about Samantha's witchcraft, followed by her magically locking him in the den until he's finished; these are all strange turns of events. When Darrin worked in the den in "Help, Help, Don't Save Me" (#5), he sketched his ideas in permanent marker. So how does Darrin produce a perfectly printed ad in there?

As Samantha wakes, the time is 7:32. A moment later, she tells Darrin it's 8:00, the deadline for the ad to make the *Morning Glory News*. But Dave and Samantha are still discussing the ad and wanting changes, despite the deadline having passed. Finally, Dave asks Darrin to add "and bring your friends" to the ad's text – however, if you take a good look at the layout, Darrin's small print already says, "be sure and bring all your friends."

When Endora first offers to help Samantha, she suggests transporting out-of-the-way signals from "little cities." She soon shows up with a bobby from Trafalgar Square; does Endora consider London a little city? Conversely, at the big neighborhood rally, no one rallies; the mayor just holds court, shoots the idea down, and answers a few questions. Afterwards, while the mayor's driver fiddles under the hood of his car, the rally attendees make their way out of the auditorium parking lot, directed by a traffic cop. If the mayor really thinks a traffic light is too expensive, why not compromise by offering the neighborhood its own policeman?

Larry comes on for a single scene to tell Darrin that trying to get a traffic light installed is pointless. This does nothing to move the story along – and neither does Abner sneaking Gladys' cookies or Darrin wolfing down Samantha's hors d'oeuvres, which the ladies have baked for a large gathering. The scenes only serve to make Abner and Darrin seem disrespectful of their wives' work, which can't be the intention.

OH, MY STARS!

Getting Samantha involved in mundane, mortal civic affairs may seem like a good idea, but the result is... mundane. Plus, Morning Glory Circle is one street in a residential neighborhood, apparently within walking distance of this contested corner where cars never stop coming; traffic from the missile plant workers aside, would this kind of two-lane road, which isn't a major highway, really be that busy? Then, mention is made of putting a traffic light *in* Morning Glory Circle, but the Circle is not the street in question, because few cars ever traverse it. Is the neighborhood itself called Morning Glory Circle? Not likely, as it's the name of a street – one that can't have its own newspaper, despite what Dave reveals.

Endora, somewhat vexed when Samantha rejects her magical help, retorts, "Sometimes I think you take after your father." The writer of this episode must not have seen "Just One Happy Family" (#10), where Samantha's father, Maurice, proved to be even more into witchcraft than Endora.

SON OF A GUN!

"Oh, Samantha, you do have an annoying way of putting a damper on my *divertissement*." – Endora to Samantha, after again being told to take a traffic light out of her daughter's living room.

Endora's prankish attempt to "help" by bringing in all manner of traffic control devices, including a London bobby, sparkles in otherwise unremarkable episode. Her impish glee as she describes the lights is contagious, particularly as she tells Samantha that jaywalking "[is] against the law, you know!"

WHICH WITCH IS WHICH?
Airdate: March 11, 1965

EPISODE
24

Endora reluctantly accompanies Samantha to "Dollar Day" at a department store, which is crawling with rabid bargain hunters. Samantha has a dress fitting but suddenly remembers another errand, so Endora offers to become Samantha to help out, confusing Gladys when "Samantha" doesn't recognize her. Endora-as-Samantha meets Bob Frazer, a writer in town on a book tour who excitedly calls his friend, Darrin, to cancel a dinner. Endora and Bob spend several days together, and, at one point, Gladys spots them in a Chinese restaurant. When Samantha returns to the department store, Bob nuzzles her ear, earning him a slap. After it dawns on her that Bob has been seeing Endora, Samantha races home and tells her mother to "stop being me."

Endora agrees to let Bob down easy; when Bob realizes he's been dating Darrin's "wife," he wants Endora-as-Samantha to profess her love for Darrin. Bob promises to keep quiet at Darrin's house that night, but, as soon as Bob gets Darrin alone, he admits he's fallen for Samantha; Darrin thinks it's a joke until Samantha privately explains how Endora doubled for her. The Stephenses are at a loss for how to make sense of things for Bob until Endora shows up as Samantha's twin. Gladys sees "Samantha" leaving with Bob and rushes over to tell Darrin, only to find the real Samantha standing at his side.

GOOD!

Endora, who has gone out of her way to get Darrin's name wrong [except for once, in "A is for Aardvark" (#17)], has to get it right here when she tells Bob that "she" is married to Darrin. Endora isn't exactly a willing participant in this correctness, but there's always sort of a secret thrill when the name "Darrin" comes out of her mouth, even when that mouth looks like Samantha's. Also, "Samantha" very grudgingly having to talk up Darrin to Bob is the highlight of the episode.

WELL?

Gladys runs into Samantha at the store and states that she'd like to meet Samantha's mother. Good thing she doesn't – Gladys would recognize Endora as the woman responsible for many of the "illusions" she's seen at the Stephens house. Endora zapping the sale sign to read "90% off" – and the resulting stampede – are funny bits, but what does she think will happen when those poor sales clerks have to face a mob of angry women at the register and explain that the merchandise isn't actually reduced that much? Endora puts more thought into transforming herself into Samantha – she even copies Samantha's heart necklace, which she's worn since "Be It Ever So Mortgaged" (#2).

Bob steps away from his book display to schmooze with "Samantha," who is having a dress fitting a few feet away. Department stores usually don't keep books and dresses together on the same floor, plus Bob and Gladys freely walk through what should be a private fitting area. On the phone, Bob and Darrin act as if they're the best of friends, so Bob should already know Darrin is married – and Bob's not the only friend Darrin calls "old buddy"; there's also Kermit, who hasn't been seen since "Love Is Blind" (#13).

Bob is surprised that "Samantha" didn't tell him she's married. She sure didn't: the script depicts Endora as single, but she is most definitely married – to Maurice, though they seem to be either separated, or in some sort of open marriage [see "Just One Happy Family" (#10)]. Regardless, Endora has made no secret of how inferior she thinks mortals are – yet she eagerly goes out with Bobby anyway.

When Bob apologizes to Endora-as-Samantha about nuzzling Samantha's ears in the department store, she gushes, "How sweet." Isn't she under strict orders to discourage the man? Plus, Endora tells Samantha she won't have to eat at the lunch date, but, when Bob wants "Samantha" to admit Darrin is the most wonderful man in the world, she thinks to herself, "Please, not while I'm eating." Finally, in the denouement, Darrin and Samantha have an animated conversation in front of Bob, during which Samantha blurts out that the whole situation is caused by magic. Why doesn't she wait until they're alone in the kitchen to bring that up? Does she think Bob won't react to such an admission? Also, when Endora shows up to save the day as Samantha's identical twin, Bob never questions the fact that, as far as he knows, both ladies are named Samantha.

OH, MY STARS!

It's common knowledge that entertainment technology wasn't as advanced in the '60s as it is now. Still, it's strange that Endora-as-Samantha's voice is markedly fuzzy and at a much lower quality than the rest of the characters. If this is a conscious choice, the muffled sound takes away from Elizabeth Montgomery's excellent characterization of Endora. Then, "Samantha" stands in front of a door labeled "Dressing Room" as she first flirts with Bob. When she tells Bob that living history was more fun, the shot is very clearly reversed, as the sign reads backwards. Was there a reason for flipping the image over?

As for Gladys, after only twenty-four episodes, it's already getting a little worn for her to always be around when Samantha or Endora perform witchcraft. Gladys sees something unusual, tries to convince Abner, and fails; the device generates much humor, but her inclusion in the Bob/"Samantha" story just doesn't seem necessary. Surely there's something else Gladys could do occasionally.

SON OF A GUN!
"I...love...Darrin...Stephens." – Endora-as-Samantha to Bob, forced to profess her love for her son-in-law.

PLEASURE O'RILEY
Airdate: March 18, 1965

As Darrin retrieves his Saturday newspaper, he notices a buxom woman moving in next door. Samantha peeks at her new neighbor through the window, while Gladys and a very pleased Abner do the same. Darrin rushes to help a fallen moving man, knocking over a box of trophies; their owner, Priscilla "Pleasure" O'Riley, reveals she won them at beauty contests. Samantha gets to know Pleasure and learns she's been engaged six times to the same man: Thor "Thunderbolt" Swenson, a jealous football player who has threatened to kill her. The Stephenses' romantic dinner is interrupted when there's a crash from Pleasure's house; Darrin discovers she has only fallen off a stepladder, but Samantha walks in to find him hovering over her.

Pleasure summons Darrin in the middle of the night, terrified because Thunderbolt has tracked her down; since Pleasure's phone hasn't been connected yet, Darrin calls the police while Samantha answers her neighbor's door. When Thunderbolt learns from Samantha that a beautiful girl (her) is next door with an attractive man (Darrin), the football player heads to the Stephens house with blood in his eye. Samantha turns Darrin into an old woman to protect him from Thunderbolt, who storms to the Kravitzes and punches Abner, landing them all on the front page of the paper. Though Pleasure gets a court order against Thunderbolt, he arrives to escort her to a modeling gig, and Samantha is amused when Thunderbolt comments that Darrin looks like his grandmother.

GOOD!
Eagle-eyed viewers will notice that Pleasure's yard sports the same real estate sign 1164 Morning Glory Circle had in "Be It Ever So Mortgaged" (#2), including its rare-for-television 474 prefix. In another full-circle moment, Samantha watches Pleasure from the window and says, "Can't let Gladys Kravitz have all the fun!" – which confirms that Samantha knows Gladys spies on her. Pleasure's presence finally gives Gladys something to do besides witnessing witchcraft, and Abner something to do besides pooh-poohing Gladys' sightings and handing her medicine.

When Thunderbolt wants to escort Pleasure to the mayor's office because he doesn't trust the official, Samantha says, "I know our mayor – there's nothing unreasonable about that!" This is a subtle, but terrific reference to Samantha's encounter with said mayor in "Red Light, Green Light" (#23).

WELL?

Houses on Morning Glory Circle must have flimsy walls, because Pleasure's tumble from her ladder can be heard from next door, and Samantha notes hearing Pleasure dropping things all day. So, the Stephenses can hear Pleasure's fall, but not her stereo, which blares at full volume? It's surprising that Samantha doesn't run to the living room to see if Aunt Clara has landed in the chimney again, because Pleasure's fall uses the exact same sound effect.

Darrin remarks that Samantha's cattiness in this episode "doesn't sound like you at all." Between Darrin's attention to Liza in "The Girl Reporter" (#9) and Janine/Sarah in "It Takes One to Know One" (#11), his observations of Lola and Nancy in "Love Is Blind" (#13), and his approval of Jewel of the East model "Ling-Ling" (#21), Samantha is probably just letting him know she doesn't appreciate his wandering eye.

Does Pleasure use a tape recorder to get Darrin to come to the window? Her summoning phrases are identical, and repeated at least three times. Later, in Pleasure's house, as Thunderbolt bangs on the door, Pleasure loudly instructs Samantha to hide her photos and trophies. If Pleasure doesn't want Thunderbolt to know she's there, why doesn't she whisper?

Thunderbolt demands to know if Samantha has seen a man next door; she replies, "Yes, indeed. A very good-looking one." Samantha knows Thunderbolt is on the warpath – instead of making a cute reference to Darrin, she should play dumb, excuse herself, and close the door as fast as possible. Of course, then there would be no reason for her to turn Darrin into an old lady, or for him to see himself in the never-before-seen mirror in the Stephenses' hallway.

What happened to the *Morning Glory News* in which Dave placed an ad in "Red Light, Green Light" (#23)? Thunderbolt and the Kravitzes end up on the front page of a different newspaper, *The Star-Dispatch*.

OH, MY STARS!

For a show about witches, this episode is decidedly unwitchy. With the exception of Samantha repairing Darrin's alarm clock and turning Darrin into a grandma to protect him, everything that happens here is completely mortal. Samantha must be pleased she's achieving such normalcy, but at times it feels like one is watching the wrong show.

As the episode begins, Samantha establishes that it's Saturday. Later that night, the frightened Pleasure asks Darrin to call the police because her phone won't be hooked up until tomorrow. Since when does the phone company connect lines on Sundays? This extends into Pleasure's court appearance; she thanks the Stephenses for helping her "last night" – which also means court was in session on a Sunday.

When Darrin calls the police to come to Pleasure's house next door, he tells them her address is 1123 Morning Glory Circle. It can't be – 1123 would be further down the street than 1164, and any house on the same side of the street as the Stephenses would also bear an even number, which 1123 is not.

Plastering Gladys' lotion-covered face on the front page of *The Star-Dispatch* as "Passion's Plaything" makes little sense. As a sports figure, Thunderbolt might command the front page, but his altercation with the Kravitzes would not be deemed that newsworthy. Plus, the sub-headline, "Pro Fullback 'Thunderbolt' Thor Swenson Arrested In Love Triangle" is not only inaccurate, but it reduces an otherwise reputable-looking newspaper to the level of a tabloid.

SON OF A GUN!

"I've only got one question for you: do you have Pleasure in this house?" – Thunderbolt to Abner, whose reply, "Not too often, but occasionally," gets him socked in the mouth.

Darrin-as-grandma comes out of nowhere, but he/she is the funniest part of the episode. The dialogue reflects a crotchety old lady, and it's clear that Dick York is having a ball playing this scene, because it translates to the screen.

DRIVING IS THE ONLY WAY TO FLY
Airdate: March 25, 1965

Darrin wants to watch baseball before teaching Samantha how to drive, causing her to magically rain the game out so the lesson can proceed. Samantha questions the accepted logic of driving to the point Darrin rushes her and withholds explanations. After following the angry Samantha into the house, Darrin tunes in his game and hears the ballpark is almost flooded, so Samantha restores the weather; the next day, Darrin restores his marriage by apologizing and arranging for Samantha to learn from Harold Harold, a proper driving instructor. But the oft-unemployed Harold is neurotic and insecure, fumbling through the house with a giant tranquilizer. As Samantha reviews what Darrin taught her about the gear selector, Harold agrees with Samantha's reasoning, and the two drive off.

Made more nervous by Harold, Samantha makes mistakes on the road and drives into an empty moving van; Harold is flustered when Samantha witches her way out of it. After Samantha clears a U-turn by removing a parked car, Harold makes her pull over, blanching when she parallel parks into a tight space by magic. Endora complicates matters by popping in and out of the backseat to toy with Harold; he runs off after she disintegrates his car. Once Samantha explains the events to Darrin, the Stephenses defend the fired Harold and convince his brother-in-law boss to give him another chance. Later, Samantha credits Harold's newfound confidence to the basket weaving class they're taking, convincing Darrin to sign up as well.

GOOD!
The effect of Endora making Harold's car reappear looks effortless. Endora and Samantha barely move, which can't have been easy: they had to hold perfectly still while someone drove the car in and got out of camera range so the scene could continue.

It's very subtle, but Harold's brother-in-law, Basil, consistently gets Samantha's name wrong over the course of the episode. Basil first refers to her as "Savannah," then "Mrs. Stephenson." Not only does it show his own ineptitude as a driving instructor, but it's kind of a nice "turnabout is fair play" moment, considering it's usually Darrin's name that gets mangled.

WELL?
Samantha tinkered with rain in "Love Is Blind" (#13) and "A Nice Little Dinner Party" (#19); here, she nearly causes a flash flood, conceivably endangering people and risking all kinds of monetary damage, simply to make Darrin teach her how to drive at that moment so she can start dinner early.

In the car, Darrin makes a show of shifting though all the gears to demonstrate what they are. Except the engine's not running, and Samantha's foot isn't on the brake; usually those conditions have to be met, or the gear shift lever remains locked. Then, Darrin becomes petulant over Samantha peppering him with questions; Samantha overreacts slightly, going from "You feel like being mean" to "You don't love me and you never did," but Darrin is unnecessarily argumentative to begin with.

Paul Lynde's fumbling, bumbling turn as Harold is fun to watch, but Harold relating his entire history growing up with four sisters and an aunt slows the story down. And Harold's neuroses are established enough by the time he arrives at the Stephens house that his sudden "Do you think we can both fit?" coffee cup joke makes him look unusually confident. Escorting Samantha out of the house, Harold clutches his bag of tranquilizer wafers in his hand, yet, once outside, the bag is gone.

As Harold tells Samantha to pull over, they're driving outdoors; when the scene cuts to a two-shot of them in the car, they are in the studio, with a backdrop photo behind them. As Endora pops in and out, the actors and camera shift in between shots, and there's a strange "light strip" that appears at the bottom of the windshield every time Endora is in the car.

At the driving school, Darrin and Samantha try to explain witchcraft to Harold. Why confirm Endora outing herself and Samantha as witches? Harold doesn't react; in fact, he never mentions it again. And Samantha's use of witchcraft in front of Harold is pretty flagrant. Avoiding the moving van is understandable, but her U-turn and "parallel parking" tricks rather rub Harold's nose in it.

Darrin tells Basil that Samantha "didn't move the car one inch" once Harold ran off. So how did Samantha get to Darrin's office? If she didn't walk, she'd have to zap herself there. Then, Basil rails that Harold "stinks" as an instructor, and Samantha counters that he's excellent. Samantha has a good heart, but Basil is closer to the mark: Harold made Samantha more nervous than she already was and had her turning the wrong way down a one-way street. In the end, Harold sheds his insecurity, and Samantha attributes it to the basket weaving class they're taking. Shouldn't his confidence come from the second chance he got with Basil?

OH, MY STARS!

Samantha notes that Darrin has been anxious for her to learn how to drive. It's true that Samantha has not been seen driving in any episode thus far, but that begs the question: how has she been getting around? She's shopped and shown up at McMann & Tate multiple times, even coming home with a Christmas tree in "A Vision of Sugar Plums" (#15). Has Samantha been using witchcraft to travel, or did the show's writers simply assume Samantha knew how to drive in previous episodes and rewrote history here to service this story?

To pull off the effect of Samantha driving up the ramp into the moving van, the car was filmed rolling slowly, with its footage sped up later. But someone went a little speed-happy in the editing room: the sequence leading up to the moving van trick gets increasingly faster, making Samantha and Harold sound like cartoon singers The Chipmunks.

SON OF A GUN!

"The engine ignites? Isn't that dangerous?" – Samantha to Darrin, wondering how safe driving actually is.

Anyone who knows how to drive presumably learned how without asking too many questions about it. So Samantha wondering why starting the car in neutral isn't labeled S or SC, declaring that D should be "F for forward," and pointing out that the designation for shifting backward should be B instead of R shines a spotlight on another mortal absurdity that's accepted as fact. And Samantha "parallel parking" Harold's car by having it slide in between two other cars is an eye-popping effect. There's no visible trickery, and the car really looks like it's gliding toward the curb – as Harold and Samantha sit inside.

EPISODE
27

Bertha [from "The Witches Are Out" (#7)] asks Samantha if Aunt Clara can stay with her until she returns from a witches' conclave in Miami. Aunt Clara refuses to be treated as a guest, so Darrin and Samantha go on to the theatre as planned; attempting to clean the house with magic, Aunt Clara smashes dishes against the ceiling and fills the house with suds. The Stephenses introduce the discouraged Aunt Clara to the Caldwells, who can't find a sitter for their son, Jimmy. Aunt Clara offers to stay with Jimmy and entertains him with little tricks; word spreads, and babysitting offers pour in. Aunt Clara continues to regale the kiddies with magic and tales of her witchy exploits, causing one mother, Agnes Bain, to lodge a formal complaint.

At the hearing, Mrs. Bain is pleased when Aunt Clara confirms she told her charges she's a witch. After the judge calls witches evil beings, Aunt Clara insists that witches only do extraordinary things and complies with the judge's request to do her own magic, getting a parakeet and a poodle instead of a rabbit. Mrs. Bain demands that Aunt Clara answer for promising to fly her children off the roof; when Aunt Clara points out she also told them she was unable to fly and did other tricks to make them happy, the judge asks if Aunt Clara can babysit his own son. Feeling better, Aunt Clara departs for Florida, but slams into the wall instead of walking through it.

GOOD!

Darrin is much more tolerant of Aunt Clara here than he was when he first met her in "Samantha Meets the Folks" (#14). He wasn't mean in that episode, but he still seemed annoyed by his aunt-in-law. Now, he hugs and kisses her, and treats her like a beloved second grandma – a nice contrast, since Darrin isn't fond of Samantha's parents. It's also an interesting twist that Aunt Clara thinks Samantha is avoiding witchcraft out of respect for her own reduced abilities, instead of realizing that Samantha has given it up because of her marriage.

Samantha certainly gets passionate out of her love for Aunt Clara: she battled Darrin and his mother over her in "Samantha Meets the Folks" (#14), and here she's ready to rumble with "whoever started this smear campaign" against Clara.

WELL?

"I offered to bring her," Bertha comments about Aunt Clara, "but she insisted on flying by herself." Bertha is rather adamant about this, because she told Samantha the exact same thing in "The Witches Are Out" (#7). That's not the only recycled bit from that episode: Bertha's walk through the wall is lifted from it, and so is Aunt Clara's, to the point Samantha wears the same blouse in this episode to match the old footage. Also, when Samantha helps her befuddled aunt out of the closet, the shadow of a boom microphone looms above them.

Aunt Clara's spell sends the dinner dishes flying up into the ceiling – a nice effect overall, except for the visible wires that facilitate it. Aunt Clara must not repair the dishes, because when she's next seen in the kitchen, only pots and pans are in the sink. Maybe Clara conjures up her ever-growing suds because she doesn't know how to use the dishwasher that's right in front of her. And apparently, Gladys Kravitz doesn't watch the Stephens house 24/7, or she'd see Aunt Clara emerging from the mountain of suds at the front door. Samantha would have to twitch them away – does Darrin not mind?

Aunt Clara's adventures in babysitting begin when she suggests staying with little Jimmy, who approaches as she stares at the Caldwell's doorknob. Only thing is, Aunt Clara can't know the boy's name, because it hasn't been mentioned at this point. Then, after Bea Caldwell and Darrin nix the idea of Aunt Clara sitting with Jimmy, Samantha approves it anyway, though that's clearly Bea's call to make. And the Stephenses should be more worried about leaving Aunt Clara alone with mortals; in "Samantha Meets the Folks" (#14), Clara immediately blabbed to Darrin's parents about being a witch, and now she announces her identity to all the neighborhood kids – and a judge. Babysitting must make Aunt Clara feel more confident; she couldn't move dishes or pour herself a glass of sherry before, but she fixes Jimmy's toy sailboat and wags a stuffed dog's tail with no problems.

Why does Aunt Clara tell Judge Winner to call her "Aunt Clara" as if everybody does? In "The Witches Are Out" (#7), Bertha and Mary simply called her "Clara." The hearing is a legal proceeding, but the judge doesn't insist on a full name, or any kind of ID – however, he's right to question Aunt Clara telling children she's a witch; if Judge Winner thinks witches are evil, some of the kids might, too.

OH, MY STARS!

Aunt Clara's speech about the wonders of youth has wonder to spare, but the accompanying music is a little syrupy, and it stops the second Aunt Clara wraps up. Later, when Aunt Clara does her tricks for the judge, he far too easily accepts what he sees. Shouldn't he and Mrs. Bain wonder how Aunt Clara is able to fit a full-sized bird cage and a poodle in her purse – and how the animals stay amazingly quiet until put on display?

SON OF A GUN!

"Oh, no, I don't want to do that." – Aunt Clara to Samantha, after it's suggested she learn the mortal way of doing things.

OPEN THE DOOR, WITCHCRAFT
Airdate: April 8, 1965

A salesman hawking garage door openers inspires Samantha to twitch her door open, which Gladys sees. Abner asks for a demonstration of the Stephenses' device, forcing Darrin to buy that instead of a new fishing rod. The garage door opener installers laugh about a job where an incorrect frequency caused a door to open and close whenever a plane flew by; the Stephenses' door has the same malfunction. Gladys peeks in after Endora zaps up a room full of fishing equipment for Darrin – naturally, there's nothing there when Gladys brings Abner over for a look. Samantha suggests returning the faulty opener, but Darrin thinks she's witching it so he can get a refund and buy his fishing equipment after all.

As the arguing Stephenses get into their car, a plane flies over, trapping them in the garage. The manual override switch is outside, so Darrin asks Samantha to twitch the door open; when a plane does it for her, Darrin believes Samantha complied, but she zaps it closed, unwilling to take responsibility for the "electronic yo-yo." Darrin comes around, and, as they kiss, another plane soars overhead, opening the door; Samantha feels this proves her innocence, since Darrin was in front of her nose. The Kravitzes overhear this, and when Darrin blathers how good women are at fixing things, Abner tells Gladys it's Darrin who's strange, not Samantha. The Stephenses' door is repaired, but, while the Kravitzes' new door is disabled, Gladys smashes into it with her car.

GOOD!

This episode feels like a natural extension of "Driving is the Only Way to Fly" (#26), where Samantha finally learned what to do behind the wheel, and she is shown here driving confidently. Plus, considering Gladys always insists Samantha is strange, it's a clever twist for Abner to label Darrin the strange one after Darrin awkwardly explains how he and Samantha got the garage door open. If the Stephenses had any remaining doubts that Gladys didn't think of them as nice, ordinary neighbors, they shouldn't now, since the Kravitzes make their judgments well within earshot.

WELL?

Maybe it was just a convention of the '60s, but it seems odd for a salesman to peddle a garage door opener in a grocery store. Also, if the store's automatic exit is out of order, how is anybody else getting out? Maybe they just walk straight through the entrance – the bag boy stands within the frame of the in door, which also has no glass in it.

This episode indicates that the Stephenses own only one car: Darrin leaves it with Samantha so that the garage door opener can be installed, opting to take a bus to work. What happened to the train Darrin rode in several earlier installments? And, if there's only one car, then why does Samantha drive it back from the grocery store the day before the installation, which is what starts the whole mess? Of course, a plane flies by just after the Magi-Door guys mention their "fluke" installation that caused a door to be opened through the aircraft bands, but there's an unusually high number of planes making their way over Morning Glory Circle compared to previous episodes, and much of this plane footage is taken from "A Nice Little Dinner Party" (#19), where Frank flew to Miami.

When Samantha tells the Magi-Door people the mechanism is being installed because of the neighbors, she says this doesn't make sense to her. Minutes later, she explains the rationale to Endora and has a perfect grasp on it. Then, Gladys drags Abner to the Stephenses' living room window to see the nonexistent fishing equipment, while Samantha blithely reads her newspaper. Can Samantha not hear the Kravitzes' voices right outside her window?

As Darrin and Samantha fight again, they are getting ready for an outing with the Tates, completely forgetting that they promised to show Abner the working garage door opener that evening, which was the whole point of buying it. After the bickering Stephenses spend many uncomfortable minutes trapped in the garage, a plane finally flies over and releases them, but Samantha zaps the door closed again, telling Darrin to choose between it and her. Would she really imprison them again just to make a point? Not to mention, this particular evening is quite dark, but the planes fly over in a daylight sky.

OH, MY STARS!

Gladys watches the Stephens house like a hawk – there's no way she would miss a truck driving up and installing a garage door opener the day *after* her neighbors said they had one. Of course, if she saw the truck, it would prove her right and negate the entire episode. As for Magi-Door, what sense does it make to install any kind of manual switch outside a garage? Even Darrin points out the switch should be inside in case people get trapped – and wouldn't being able to open the garage from the outside invite theft? That's a lot of contrivance just to trap Darrin and Samantha in the garage.

Samantha tells Darrin she watched at the window to see if the neighborhood kids were opening and closing the garage door, finally determining they must have been in school. At the rate those planes pass over, Samantha should easily connect them to the door's activity, but she doesn't. Then, she tells Darrin no was one around for miles. The Stephenses live in a residential neighborhood: inevitably, someone would be walking their dog, mowing their lawn, checking the mail, etc. And the area was so busy in "Red Light, Green Light" (#23) that a traffic signal had to be put in. So how can no one be around for miles?

SON OF A GUN!

"You mean like now?" – Samantha to Darrin, after he commands her not to use witchcraft no matter how tempted or provoked she may be.

ABNER KADABRA
Airdate: April 15, 1965

After Darrin doesn't close the front door properly, Gladys walks in to find Samantha hanging pictures by witchcraft. Her suspicions finally confirmed, Gladys thinks Samantha is from Venus. Samantha suggests that perhaps Gladys herself has caused all the strange things she's seen, but Gladys isn't convinced until she correctly guesses a number thanks to Samantha's magic. Once Gladys guesses Abner's number – a feat she only accomplishes because Abner goes along with it – Darrin comes home and sees Gladys trying to will her sprinklers on. Gladys tells Darrin that Samantha gave her the power, ecstatic when a sudden rainstorm seems to confirm it.

The next day, Samantha supposedly talks Gladys out of the idea of having powers, but Abner soon reports that Gladys embarrassed him in public by claiming to communicate with a spirit. Samantha insists that a séance is the only answer, privately telling Darrin she plans to use it to scare Mrs. Kravitz. As a gypsy-clad Gladys presides over the ritual, Abner is spooked by Samantha's displays of witchcraft. Gladys tells Abner to dry up, so Samantha changes him into a pile of dust. Samantha convinces Gladys that giving up her "powers" will bring Abner back; once restored, Abner can't understand why he's so thirsty. Later, Abner announces to the Stephenses that he's taking Gladys to the movies, but when Gladys mysteriously says she was thinking the same thing, Abner hurriedly leads her away.

GOOD!

Given the many occasions Gladys has seen witchcraft in action at the Stephenses, only to have Abner tell her she's crazy, it only makes sense that, at some point, Gladys would catch Samantha red-handed. How did that not seem inevitable until this episode? Samantha turning it around on Gladys, making her believe she has supernatural powers, is a brilliant development, as is watching Darrin and Samantha trying not to laugh as Gladys goes full-on medium. Also, Abner reminds Gladys of past fixations with yoga and karate, and confirms that she has always been a bit of an oddball, which gives Gladys a few more welcomed layers.

The show's writing is almost always intelligent and witty, but this episode is particularly snappy. The Kravitzes' extended banter is a cut above the norm, and Darrin gets in a few zingers, too. When Samantha offers to stop the rain, Darrin exclaims, "Are you kidding? Gladys will think she did it. Tomorrow she'll try for an eclipse!"

WELL?

Should Darrin be worried about the house he bought? It has loose banisters, and the front door won't close, despite Darrin pulling on it quite hard. Of course, if the door were to close properly, Gladys wouldn't see the floating pictures, and she needs to so there can be an episode.

After Gladys faints, Samantha puts a washcloth on her head – but it's dry. Later, Samantha works to convince Gladys she's manifested everything herself. Intriguing, though that doesn't explain Gladys seeing Endora's traffic lights in "Red Light, Green Light" (#23), for example, or the fishing equipment of "Open the Door, Witchcraft" (#28). Gladys comes to believe she has "the power" from guessing a single number; you'd think she'd need a few more tangible examples first. Samantha writes "19" on her pad – but after Gladys guesses the number, and the shot cuts back to the pad, the "19" is in different handwriting.

Everyone's shocked when the neighborhood is besieged by a downpour, especially Gladys, who feels she willed it to happen. Would there really be a sudden, torrential rainstorm after one thunderclap? Did no one see it was about to rain? There must have been some gray clouds in the sky; even Samantha later says the paper predicted a chance of showers, so the cloudburst shouldn't be surprising. By the way, it's been established from the beginning that Abner is retired. So why is he waiting for breakfast in a shirt and tie the next day?

At the séance, Samantha twitches up a "ghost" that smokes, which seems an unnecessary detail. And Gladys' phonograph of spooky music (which should simply be part of the score instead of being shown as source music) just happens to stop as soon as Samantha makes "Uncle Harold" disappear. As for Abner, one would think Samantha simply changed him out for dust, but when Abner reappears, he is excessively thirsty. That means Samantha literally disintegrated Abner – which makes the fact that both Samantha and Gladys handle the dust a little gruesome.

In the tag, the Kravitzes stop by to return Samantha's roasting pan – oddly, it's the same one Gladys was bringing to Samantha when she caught her witching the pictures. Gladys dropped it and didn't take it with her, so Samantha already had it back, and the Kravitzes can't be returning it.

OH, MY STARS!

Even though Gladys is quickly persuaded she possesses supernatural abilities, when Darrin spots her trying to use them to turn on the sprinklers, she tells him Samantha gave her the power. Now, maybe Gladys only means Samantha made her aware of her power, but Gladys' statement, taken at face value, changes the entire premise of the story. Also, when Samantha attempts to deter Gladys from experimenting with her "powers," Samantha is rather tipping her hand by professing to know so much about the occult. Surely, once Gladys accepts that her abilities are gone, Samantha's words will only serve to strengthen her (former) suspicions.

SON OF A GUN!

"Remember, we want peace; we're a peace-loving world. Now, we've had problems..." – Gladys to Samantha, assuming she's Venusian.

Until now, Gladys Kravitz was mostly a one-note, minor character who simply existed to witness witchcraft, then face disbelief when trying to tell anyone about it. This episode takes Gladys to the next level – she's still pure comic relief, but what a showcase for Alice Pearce. Gladys is fall-on-the-floor funny here, somehow increasingly so the more over-the-top she becomes. Abner's name may show up in the title, but it's Gladys who owns this episode.

GEORGE THE WARLOCK
Airdate: April 22, 1965

As Samantha sleeps, Darrin goes for his morning paper and gets locked out of the house, distracted by his newest neighbor, Dora "Danger" O'Riley, younger sister of "Pleasure O'Riley" (#25). Darrin accepts Danger's invitation to breakfast, then spends the day when Danger's dishwasher overflows. As the annoyed Samantha plays solitaire, Endora watches from the Queen of Spades card, then beckons Samantha's former suitor, George, to rescue Samantha from the mortal life. The next day, while Darrin takes Danger to a modeling gig, George, disguised as a raven, flies into Samantha's kitchen and rematerializes, laying on the charm. Samantha admits Darrin can be thoughtless at times, but insists she's happy with him.

George-as-raven wings his way to McMann & Tate just as they need a symbol for the Feather Touch Typewriter account. Darrin and Larry are so impressed when the bird plugs in the machine and types that Darrin brings him home in a cage to sketch him. Samantha recognizes George and changes him back; after Darrin threatens to throw George out, the warlock briefly turns Darrin into a penguin. Danger needs domestic help and George offers to provide it, but Darrin sticks his foot in his mouth about witches, angering Samantha. George tells Danger he's a warlock, but she thinks George's powers are only mortal magic tricks. Danger declares it doesn't matter what people are if they're attracted to each other, prompting the Stephenses to make up, and Endora to sigh that George has failed her.

GOOD!

This episode corrects a logistical mistake made in "Pleasure O'Riley" (#25): in that episode, Darrin told the police that the house next door is 1123 Morning Glory Circle, which isn't possible since it's on Darrin's side of the street, and his address is the even-numbered 1164. Here, the O'Rileys' address is changed to a much more plausible 1162.

Endora watches Samantha from her position on one of Samantha's solitaire cards, a quick but innovative effect. When George tells Samantha he decided to swoop down like Lochinvar, a fictitious knight who similarly rescues a damsel from a boring husband, Samantha retorts, "like Lucifer." The devilish inference is keenly appropriate, since George just pointed upwards with his index finger, pinkie, and thumb, doing the "sign of the devil" long before it was popular at heavy metal concerts. George also makes two direct references to the show: he tells Samantha he's been "put on this earth to eliminate your stale negatives and accentuate your *bewitching* positives," plus, he whistles a snippet from the *Bewitched* theme during his time as a bird.

George and Danger's meeting is where the episode gets interesting; before that, it's a revisiting of Darrin coming to the aid of a pretty girl and Samantha raising an eyebrow. Though Danger and George get together very quickly, there's an uniqueness to their budding relationship, and the best twist is that Danger isn't as clueless as she looks.

WELL?

Danger states that she's "holding down the fort" while Pleasure honeymoons. Just five episodes ago, Pleasure was so flighty that she'd been engaged sixteen times. Did she marry main contender Thunderbolt after all? For the all the throwbacks to Pleasure, the identity of her husband would be a fitting bookend.

After Darrin and Danger leave Samantha's kitchen, the scene fades out, then fades right back in as the music continues. George arrives immediately afterwards to lure Samantha back to the witchy life; he fails, flies right out as the raven, and sees Danger returning home in a taxi. Is the aforementioned fade-out meant to signify a passage of time? If not, then Danger couldn't possibly be driven to town and return in a cab in the time it takes for Samantha and George to have one conversation. Samantha tells George to "fly back home to my mama who put you up to this." Samantha always refers to Endora as "Mother" – she's never once called her "Mama."

Isn't it amazing that neither Darrin, nor Larry, nor phantom employee Porterfield, comes up with a bird symbol for Feather Touch until George flies in? And Darrin should immediately suspect witchcraft is involved: a raven flies in how many stories up and plugs in a typewriter the exact moment he's needed. Darrin concluded there was magic afoot with less provocation in "Help, Help, Don't Save Me" (#5) and "Your Witch Is Showing" (#20), yet he completely accepts George at beak value.

As Darrin and Endora get into their first full-fledged argument over her interference in his marriage, he demands, "When is this going to stop?" Darrin isn't even aware of any meddling Endora's done: he never found out Endora sicced Janine/Sarah on him in "It Takes One to Know One" (#11), or that Endora fueled his doubts about Samantha's age in "Eye of the Beholder" (#22). Endora did make an implied threat to Darrin in "Your Witch Is Showing" (#20), but she only ended up playing a prank on him, so where is Darrin getting this? Has Endora been hassling her son-in-law off-screen?

Why does Samantha make a monkey face when George heads over to Danger's house? Then, Danger reads an inaccurate, mortal-centric definition of "warlock" ("deceiver, a breaker of his word, a name for the devil") after George confesses he is one. Would her airhead sister Pleasure really keep a dictionary in her kitchen?

Darrin angrily tells George he can "always get another bird," but it's not like birds that peck on typewriters are that easy to find. Later, as Danger and George include the Stephenses in their celebration, George magically pops a champagne cork, and Samantha catches it, as she did when Maurice opened a bottle in "Just One Happy Family" (#10). Finally, George seems to fall head over heels for Danger, but he returns to his harem at the end of the episode. Does Danger get added to his collection of girls?

OH, MY STARS!

Some of Darrin's less attractive traits flare up in this episode. Danger is the latest in a long line of other women he's been intrigued by; no wonder Samantha finally gets angry. Darrin slips that he has to cope with the "copeless situation" of Samantha being a witch, then calls George "a big spook" and wants to warn Danger about him like he tried to warn Kermit about supposed witch Gertrude in "Love Is Blind" (#13). The writers ought to decide on Darrin's personality; he vacillates between loving and off-putting depending on the episode.

SON OF A GUN!

"Well, so? This is a free country, right? And anyone has the right to go to the church of their choice." – Danger to George, after he tells her he's a warlock.

EPISODE 31
THAT WAS MY WIFE
Airdate: April 29, 1965

A hair color commercial prompts Samantha to zap herself into several different wigs. Gladys peeks in the window between styles and is confused when Samantha comes to the door sporting dark hair. Samantha tells Gladys that the makeover is for a later rendezvous with Darrin at a hotel; Gladys later fails to entice Abner with her own makeovers. When Larry overhears a secretary confirming Darrin's hotel reservation, he suspects monkey business, and soon sees the brunette Samantha surprising Darrin in the lobby. Later, Samantha pops home to get Darrin's book and opens the door to Larry, lying that she's meeting Darrin at McMann & Tate. Larry heads to the hotel to warn Darrin, who goes along with Larry's infidelity assumption; Darrin can't convince his boss the brunette is Samantha, because Larry just saw her at the house.

The next day, Louise hears about Darrin's "affair" and wants to talk some sense into him at the hotel, while Samantha sends Larry there to tell Darrin an important meeting has been rescheduled – when Larry arrives, he thinks Darrin's mistress is Louise. At the office, Larry punches Darrin, so Samantha stops by in her dark wig to straighten things out. The Stephenses make sure the Tates walk in on them, Samantha turns around, and it becomes clear to everyone that Darrin was at the hotel with his own bewigged wife. Everything's forgiven, but when Larry asks how Samantha got to the hotel so fast, Darrin jokes that Samantha is a witch.

GOOD!

The Stephenses and Tates seem to be getting closer as the series progresses, and there's a palpable warmth to their foursome. And, like "Abner Kadabra" (#29), it's wonderful to see Gladys expand on her usual something's-going-on-across-the-street story and change her own look in an attempt to spice up her marriage to Abner.

WELL?

What have the Stephenses done with their TV? Except for "Just One Happy Family" (#10), it's always been at the foot of the staircase – now the stereo is there as Samantha listens to the very long Tortoise and Hare Color Preparations commercial. Samantha goes on to explain to Gladys that she's trying the dark wig because "it's easy to become bored with the same old face." Are Darrin and Samantha already tired of each other after less than a year of marriage? Then, Gladys blanches when the subject of magic comes up. In "Abner Kadabra" (#29), Gladys was convinced only she was responsible for the supernatural activity she had witnessed; here, as if that never happened, she suspects Samantha again.

It's true Darrin might not recognize Samantha right away because of her dark wig, but can he really not tell her voice? When Larry suspects Darrin of having an affair, all Darrin has to do to deny it is tell Larry about Samantha's wig – but he doesn't. Instead, he orders Samantha to appear before him with

Larry standing there, and later, when Larry can't figure out how Samantha got to the hotel so fast, Darrin pipes up that Samantha is a witch. Considering Darrin made a big case for witches in "The Witches Are Out" (#7), this "joke" could make Larry wonder if there isn't something to it. Maybe the real reason Larry thinks Darrin's a philanderer is because he saw Liza Randall on top of him in "The Girl Reporter" (#9); did Darrin ever explain the circumstances behind that potentially incriminating clinch?

Darrin wonders how Samantha didn't know Larry was at the door, saying, "I thought you were pretty good at that sort of thing." Well, she was – in "I, Darrin, Take This Witch, Samantha" (#1), she did seem to exhibit that sort of ESP, but she hasn't since.

OH, MY STARS!

Samantha tells Gladys that she and Darrin steal away to a hotel once in a while to "get to know each other all over again." Yet, at the hotel, Samantha offers to turn on the TV, and Darrin wants to finish the murder mystery he's been reading. That's romantic? Of course, if Samantha hadn't forgotten the book, she wouldn't need to pop home to get it, which brings up the next question: why does Samantha answer the door? She knows she's not supposed to be there, and even Darrin questions her logic; this plot point only happens to make Larry think Darrin is having an affair.

Darrin's had a bit of a wandering eye since the show began, but Larry's got him beat. Mr. Tate stares at a secretary, then flaunts a girlie magazine right in front of his pregnant wife. (Actually, there's no mention of Louise's condition throughout this entire episode.) And Larry's almost pleased by the idea of Darrin straying, referring to him as a "son of a gun" no less than seven times – until he thinks it's Louise that Darrin is straying with. Is Larry a "do as I say, not as I do" kind of guy?

After Gladys models her myriad of wigs, Abner only finally pays attention after his frustrated wife spikes up her hair. Abner explains that he didn't notice Gladys' makeovers because he's color blind. But Gladys has dark hair; she dons a platinum wig and a blond wig, and Abner should still be able to detect shades of light and dark, so it's an odd justification on his part.

The Stephenses worry that Larry will wonder how Samantha got to the hotel from the house so fast. Larry himself drives to the hotel "like a maniac" to warn Darrin, and gets there in 20 minutes, so what makes him think Samantha can't? This premise drives the rest of the episode, albeit on a slippery road. Samantha later compounds the mistaken identity problem by telling Larry that Darrin is at the hotel. Office emergency or not, she knows Darrin is there to convince Louise he's giving up his "other woman," so why does she glibly send Larry to the lobby?

SON OF A GUN!

"There's nothing wrong with being interested in two women. As long as they're both your wife." – Samantha to Darrin, amused over their doubles dilemma.

ILLEGAL SEPARATION
Airdate: May 6, 1965

Abner interrupts Darrin and Samantha's romantic evening with news that he and Gladys have split up. When Samantha invites the homeless Abner to stay over, he immediately requests a cup of cocoa. Though Abner's snoring keeps Darrin awake, Samantha thinks the Kravitzes will make up in no time.

Gladys rings the doorbell and sees Samantha levitating Darrin's paperwork into his briefcase, but she blows it off and hands Abner's luggage to Samantha. Darrin suggests that Samantha use witchcraft to expedite the Kravitzes' reunion, something he campaigns for even harder when he comes home to find Abner has made a nauseating Brussels sprouts dish.

After Samantha tells Darrin the Kravitzes have to come together of their own free will, Gladys breaks down and tells Samantha she's miserable without her husband; the ladies arrange for Abner to see Gladys in a provocative outfit from Samantha's window, but he draws the blinds. Annoyed when Abner keeps asking for favors, Darrin helps Samantha flesh out her idea to reunite the Kravitzes by giving them the same dream: Samantha takes them back to their college days, when the nerdy Abner proposed to the gawky Gladys. Once they wake, they dash out and meet in the middle of the street, which Samantha slows down for cinematic effect. The next night, the Kravitzes arrive with thank-yous; Gladys has a feeling that Samantha played a part in their reunion, while Abner again interrupts the Stephenses' plans for a romantic evening.

GOOD!

The show's writers take the concept "know thy neighbor" a little more seriously in this episode, revealing more of the inner workings of the Kravitzes and their marriage, plus some of Abner's own idiosyncrasies; up until now, only Gladys' have been evident. There's also the blank-filling back history that the Kravitzes met in college 30 years ago, when Gladys fell off a truck during a fraternity hayride; they took classes together, and got engaged in a malt shop.

WELL?

Samantha tells Abner the guest room is the first door to the left at the top of the stairs. Yet, in "A Vision of Sugar Plums" (#15), little Michael stayed in a room that required making a U-turn to the right. Could there be two guest rooms? Both Darrin's parents and Aunt Clara did need rooms to themselves in "Samantha Meets the Folks" (#14). Perhaps the Kravitzes are the perfect couple, after all – in this episode, they're equally impolite. Gladys looks down her nose at Samantha and basically calls her abnormal, while Abner wants his cocoa and orange juice, his clothes taken to the cleaners, and first crack at Darrin's newspaper. Add his party-crashing in the tag, and we see a whole different side to the usually-can't-be-bothered Abner Kravitz.

The Boy Scout salute has become popular: Darrin saluted to Samantha in "George the Warlock" (#30), Larry made Louise swear with the gesture in "That Was My Wife" (#31), and here, Samantha raises three fingers to Gladys.

So, the Stephenses *did* do some redecorating – their television, which was always at the foot of the stairs but replaced by the stereo in "That Was My Wife" (#31), is now at the bottom of the living room window, where the stereo used to be; it's visible as Samantha tries to get Abner to look across the street at Gladys' makeover. Now, Gladys should know that wearing a wig won't excite Abner – she tried the same thing in the last episode and failed. Plus, isn't the idea to get Abner to admit to his feelings for Gladys? Her attempts to be fetching seem calculated to elicit a seduction rather than an emotional admission.

In "A Nice Little Dinner Party" (#19), Samantha brought Darrin's parents back together from miles away without leaving her living room; now, she has to pop into Gladys and Abner's rooms separately to bespell them, and add a twitch from home to link up their dream. Samantha's idea to make the Kravitzes dream of Abner's proposal is a good one, but how can she create it in such detail? Samantha doesn't know a thing about the Kravitzes' history; does her spell allow for Abner and Gladys to fill in their own blanks? And seeing the Kravitzes in college is "keen," but it's a little hard to buy them as younger versions of themselves; wigs and university attire still can't make them look like 20-year-olds.

OH, MY STARS!

Samantha is a little too free using her witchcraft with the Kravitzes on her radar. She zaps up Abner's requested cup of cocoa (won't he wonder how she made it so fast?), then magically organizes Darrin's paperwork knowing Gladys is at the door. Later, Samantha witches Darrin's gin cards so he'll win on the first move, which Abner questions. Finally, the Kravitzes reunite because of their mutual dream, but surely they'll compare notes and wonder why they had the same one; Abner has more reason to believe Gladys now than ever before. Plus, once Gladys sees the floating briefcase, she has to know that Samantha sold her a bill of goods in "Abner Kadabra" (#29) when she said Gladys was making the magic happen herself. Darrin's even careless about Samantha's witchcraft: he calls Samantha a "devoted wife and witch" when Abner could easily be in earshot. Has Darrin changed his tune about his wife's magical "nonsense?" If not, it's hypocritical of him to push for Samantha to remove Abner as their house guest with witchcraft.

SON OF A GUN!

"Oh, Mrs. Stephens, I miss him so much, I don't know what to do. I'm an unhappy ship floating down a lonely river and this is my ninth handkerchief today!" – Gladys to Samantha, softening after seeing a picture of Abner.

A CHANGE OF FACE
Airdate: May 13, 1965

EPISODE 33

Dismayed that Samantha didn't marry a better looking man, Endora gives a sleeping Darrin different hair and a new nose. Samantha balks but adds a mustache; Gladys sees Darrin's altered appearance and runs away. Darrin's furious when he catches himself in the mirror, shaken that Samantha would toy with his looks. The next day, Darrin can't stop looking at himself, then revisits the ever-inattentive Dave, his doctor, and the bartender regarding his latest problem. After a concerned Larry calls Samantha, she realizes Darrin's ego needs boosting and transforms into "Michelle," an alluring French woman, to get the job done; Endora warns it might be mistake.

"Michelle" finds Darrin drowning his sorrows at a bar and goes on about his face, claiming to be a sculptress. Darrin doesn't rise to the bait when "Michelle" asks him to leave with her, and agrees when the bartender says his wife must be something special. Gladys watches "Michelle" drive into the Stephenses' garage, but pales when Samantha walks out. Endora feels she's right when Darrin doesn't tell Samantha about "Michelle"; later, at the office, Darrin comes on to Barbara, a substitute secretary, as Samantha walks in. Samantha is livid until Darrin explains that he knew she was "Michelle" and thought she was Barbara as well. Darrin is relieved to know Samantha cares enough to be jealous, and the Stephenses can't help but share a laugh.

GOOD!

This episode has some nice parallels to previous installments. Of course, there's the third go-round of Darrin talking to Dave, his doctor, and his bartender [as seen in "I, Darrin, Take This Witch, Samantha" (#1) and "Eye of the Beholder" (#22)] – but this time, Samantha and Endora get in on the recurring theme act: in "Be It Ever So Mortgaged" (#2), they redecorated in and around the then-future Stephens home, and here, they redecorate Darrin's face.

It's inspired that Darrin realizes "Michelle" is Samantha, but plays along. He must figure it out when the bar patron next to him gets drunk on one sip of beer; Darrin implies as much when he agrees with Joe that his wife is special. And Samantha's transformation into "Michelle" is incredibly fluid, as is the effect when "Michelle" raises her plunging neckline.

WELL?

How does Gladys not recognize Darrin? The only radically different feature on him is his nose; other than that, he looks like Darrin with a mustache and new hair. And the objects in the Stephens house continue to move around: the TV is back where it used to be, unlike the past two episodes, where it was situated under the living room window – but the mirror Darrin peers into is on the opposite side of the hallway than it was in "Pleasure O'Riley" (#25). Samantha explains that Endora got carried away giving him curly hair, a long nose, and a mustache, except Samantha added the facial hair, not Endora. Later, Darrin tells Dave that Samantha changed all of it, but, at the doctor's, he says his mother-in-law did most of it.

Dave, who finally got fleshed out in "Red Light, Green Light" (#23), reverts to type here and prattles on while Darrin tries to explain his problem. Darrin's doctor has a change of face himself: he's been played by Lindsay Workman since "I, Darrin, Take This Witch, Samantha" (#1), but Henry Hunter wears the stethoscope here. And there must be a set of triplets in New York, all serving up drinks in bars – in "I, Darrin, Take This Witch, Samantha" (#1), Paul Barselow's bartender was called Hal; in "Eye of the Beholder" (#22), it was Pete. Now, Darrin calls him Joe.

When Samantha becomes "Michelle," Endora is impressed that Samantha changes her voice. Why? Endora altered her own voice when she turned herself into Samantha in "Which Witch Is Witch?" (#24). As "Michelle" becomes Samantha again in the garage, the camera shifts downward; the garage door that's visible at the top of the frame disappears. Also, a guitar hangs on the wall – who plays? Neither Darrin nor Samantha have shown an interest in music. And, when Samantha exits the garage, why does she leave its door open after all the hoopla about getting an electronic control in "Open the Door, Witchcraft" (#28)?

Darrin works on the Feather Touch Typewriter account, as he did in "George the Warlock" (#30), which is a great piece of continuity – although these are the layouts that were dismissed once Darrin, Larry, and the mysterious Porterfield decided to use George-as-raven as their symbol. Why is Darrin working on a discarded concept? Did he have to go back to the drawing board once George became humanoid again?

OH, MY STARS!

Why would Samantha make a show of driving up Morning Glory Circle as "Michelle" in front of the Kravitzes? Surely she sees them in their front yard as she motors in. Why not change herself back as soon as she leaves Darrin at the bar? If Samantha simply forgot she was "Michelle" until she got home, she could wait to restore herself until after she's gone inside, then tell Gladys she lent the car to a visiting friend. But, if she did that, Gladys wouldn't see one woman entering the garage and another coming out.

Darrin and Samantha chuckle about him kissing Barbara, but, despite not being identified as such until years later, what Darrin does is called sexual harassment. Even in the sexist '60s, it wouldn't be unreasonable for Barbara to go to Larry or Mr. McMann to complain – and Larry already saw Liza Randall on top of Darrin in "The Girl Reporter" (#9). The Stephenses wouldn't laugh if they realized the serious trouble Darrin could find himself in.

SON OF A GUN!

"Twice. Once with a rolling pin and once with a seven-iron." – Joe the bartender to Darrin, asked if his wife ever tried to change his face.

Marilyn Hanold as "Michelle" provides a lot of *joie de vivre*. True, she's a bit of a French cliché, but she's so much fun. It really seems it's Samantha under all that bouffant and cleavage. And Dick Wilson's switch from cold sober to falling down drunk is equally effortless, and hilarious. "Pardon me, sir," he slurs as he passes the voluptuous "Michelle."

REMEMBER THE MAIN
Airdate: May 20, 1965

EPISODE 34

Eager to be more civic-minded, Samantha hosts a political meeting at the house, though Darrin doesn't relish coming home to a crowd. Ed Wright, who is running for councilman, fires Samantha up with his speech about taking opponent John C. Cavanaugh to task for having the monopoly on neighborhood infrastructure, including a questionable water main. Darrin does some ads for Wright and ultimately becomes his campaign manager. Samantha goes door-to-door, while Endora scoffs at the idea of her daughter in politics. Wright gets egged at his big rally, but Samantha twitches the next salvo back in the protester's faces, and the Wright campaign scores a victory when the governor orders an investigation into Cavanaugh's water main project.

Wright challenges Cavanaugh to a televised debate, but an expert deems the water main sound; Darrin blames Samantha for getting him involved and fears for his career. Samantha and Endora magically go through Cavanaugh's files and discover that, while the water main is legitimate, his other projects are corrupt. That night, Cavanaugh's water main bursts, causing flooding in the neighborhood; Darrin thinks Samantha ruptured it, but Endora takes responsibility, feeling her magic will reopen the governor's investigation and nail Cavanaugh, which it does. Wright is elected councilman, and later, Endora obliges Darrin when he says he'd give anything to have the fugitive Cavanaugh in the palm of his hand.

GOOD!

The scene where Endora pops in and picks apart Samantha's rationale for getting involved in politics is excellent. Not only does Endora arrive in time to interrupt Samantha's unfortunate cheer, but when Samantha explains how important politics is, Endora counters, "Only to politicians, my dear." Endora also introduces herself to Wright as Mrs. Waters, given her part in bursting the main. Leave it to Samantha's mother, who comments she hasn't seen such political mastery since the Lincoln-Douglas debates, to liven up a watered-down episode.

Ed Wright may seem like he wandered onto the *Bewitched* set from another show, but his portrayer, Edward Mallory, is certainly game. He makes Wright's jargon-filled speeches impassioned calls for change, and he takes getting egged like a trouper.

WELL?

Maybe it's only natural that Samantha wouldn't think much about how her witchcraft might impact the mortal world after living in it less than a year, but she uses her powers pretty flagrantly in it: she witches up a giant Wright banner on the house of a Cavanaugh supporter and reverses the trajectory of airborne eggs so they'll land in the faces of the men throwing them – all in public, and in broad daylight. And the ever-suspicious Gladys Kravitz, who, along with Abner, has little to do in this episode, is unusually quiet about the flying eggs. As for the vandals, they stand in plain sight and take their time reaching into their bags, glaring for dramatic effect, and not one single person in the crowd looks to see where the eggs are coming from. The second volley seems to consist of "double" eggs; is that part of the trickery necessary to make them travel backwards?

Darrin getting angry at Samantha for "dragging" him into Wright's campaign doesn't ring true. No one put a gun (or an egg, or a spell) to his head. Samantha freezing him mid-argument is a nice effect, but, when she does, her back is to him – she faces him when she reanimates him, and Darrin never stops to question what, to him, would be a sudden change in his wife's position.

Samantha and Endora make themselves invisible in Cavanaugh's office, but not their flashlights, so they're still conspicuous. Then, as they witch on the lights and materialize, the camera shifts quite a bit, taking away from the effect. Samantha handles Cavanaugh's files with her bare hands – at least Endora wears gloves. Do the witches magically erase Samantha's fingerprints later? And, for someone who claims complete ignorance about politics, Endora quickly deduces that Cavanaugh's hands are clean in regard to the water main. Mother and daughter get the goods on Cavanaugh, but that doesn't help; they can't present the incriminating info to Wright, or anyone else, without someone wondering how they obtained it. (It's called breaking and entering.)

Endora bursts the water main, potentially endangering scores of people and causing untold amounts of monetary damage, merely to help Samantha. Abner wants the Stephenses turn to radio station KXIW, except that, in New York, and most of the eastern United States, radio station call letters begin with W, not K. Even the television station that airs the debate is WXIU.

Since the water main is Wright's key issue, Cavanaugh could easily accuse him of sabotaging it in an attempt to win the election – something not addressed in the episode's watery resolution.

OH, MY STARS!

Darrin and Samantha discuss the fact that Shirley Foster can't have Wright's rally in her house. If they're referring to the woman who was part of the Welcome Wagon in "Mother Meets What's-His-Name" (#4) and the hospital benefit in "It's Magic" (#16), her name is Shirley Clyde. It's her compatriot, June, who bears the last name Foster.

As in "Red Light, Green Light" (#23), Morning Glory Circle seems to be considered an entire community, since, as indicated by this episode, it has its own water system and its own councilman. As a street type designation, "circle" is defined as a relatively small thoroughfare; to have need of representation by a councilman, the populace of a community has to number in the thousands. Morning Glory Circle, New York simply cannot exist.

Plunging Samantha into politics might be intriguing on paper, but it plays out more like a drama than a comedy, and it's strange subject matter for a show that's supposed to be about a witch married to a mortal. Even the writers seem to be aware of it: Endora tells Samantha, "I don't know what you're talking about – and neither do you."

SON OF A GUN!
"What was that incantation you were gyrating through?" – Endora to Samantha, confused to see her daughter channeling a cheerleader in support of a politician.

EAT AT MARIO'S
Airdate: May 27, 1965

Samantha and Endora enjoy a marvelous meal at an authentic Italian restaurant in which they are the only customers. The owner, Mario, explains that people want pizza, which he refuses to serve. Darrin has his hands full with the eccentric Linton Baldwin, who runs the Perfect Pizza chain, so Samantha places an ad for Mario's by witchcraft. Baldwin is upset to see his Perfect Pizza ad dwarfed by Mario's full-page spread; Darrin and Larry try to calm him with a live Perfect Pizza commercial, but Endora zaps the announcer into adding a plug for Mario's. After Baldwin fires McMann & Tate and wants to hire whoever represents Mario's, Darrin is furious with Samantha.

Endora decides to help Darrin get Baldwin's account back, kicking off her Perfect Pizza campaign by magically placing sandwich signs onto everyone that passes Baldwin on the street. Samantha alters billboards while Endora skywrites, and Baldwin loves it all. Samantha and Endora witch little kids into telling an ice cream vendor they want Perfect Pizza, even adding a talking dog to the mix. Samantha convinces Baldwin that McMann & Tate is responsible for the publicity, and, after Baldwin hires them back, Samantha tells the clueless Larry that Darrin had this planned all along. Darrin takes Samantha and Endora to the now-bustling Mario's for a celebration dinner, where Endora and Darrin almost make friends, and Mario moves the trio to the front of the line as a thank-you.

GOOD!
Listen to the wording as Endora induces the TV announcer to deliver a live commercial for Mario's – he calls the veal marsala "utterly divine." That's exactly the way Endora talks – a subtle, but accurate piece of continuity.

Having the dog run up to the ice cream cart and declare "I want Perfect Pizza, too" is corny, and an apparent take-off of *Mister Ed*, the 1961-1966 CBS show about a talking horse that was still airing during this period, but that pooch practically dares you not to smile.

There's a certain satisfaction in Larry and Darrin holding up the phone, with Baldwin on the other end, pretending they might be too busy to take back his account. It's the least Baldwin deserves for being so flaky and threatening to sue everyone in sight.

WELL?

There's no doubt that Mario is the flashpoint of the episode, but nobody can agree on how to pronounce his name. Samantha, Darrin, and Baldwin pronounce it 'mar-ē-ō, while Larry, the announcer, and Mario himself say it 'mär-ē-ō. And Endora switches back and forth between the two – interestingly, she used the latter referring to Samantha's cousin Mario in "Your Witch Is Showing" (#20). Endora trades plates with Samantha by levitating them, but there's a speed-up effect that isn't as clean as it could be, particularly when Samantha chews at hyper-speed; the sometimes visible wire is even more noticeable. Then, Endora raves about her veal marsala, which Mario calls veal scaloppine when he stops by the table.

When Darrin discovers the ad Samantha placed, she defends herself by saying, "I didn't replace a page; I only added one!" Any page she'd add would have another side, meaning she added two pages; what's on the second? And why does she zap an ad into the morning paper, knowing Darrin will see it first thing?

Samantha is understandably distraught when Darrin hangs up on her, but for her to tell Endora, "You have just won a new client, and I have just lost an old husband" is a little extreme; it's not like Darrin's going to divorce Samantha over Mario's. At the restaurant, when Samantha and Endora applaud Mario's refusal to be amalgamated into Baldwin's chain, the competitors hear the clapping behind them – but instead of craning their heads immediately, they slowly look around in front of them and don't turn all the way around until Samantha and Endora disappear. Before they do, Mario's right hand is up, with his head in one position; after they're gone, Mario's head is in another position, and both of his hands are on the chair in front of him.

Endora displays a knack for advertising, zapping up sandwich signs and slogans in the sky. Yet, in "Mother Meets What's-His-Name" (#4), when Darrin first met Endora, she barely knew what advertising was. Are Endora's sandwich signs only meant for Baldwin to see? No one in that crowd of dozens reacts to suddenly walking around wearing heavy advertisements. In the park, when the dog runs up to the ice cream cart in a wide shot, Samantha twitches her nose, but with no accompanying sound effect. Then the scene cuts to a two-shot of Samantha and Endora, and Samantha twitches again, now with the proper audio.

After Baldwin re-signs with McMann & Tate, Samantha volunteers that the sandwich signs and talking dog are part of Darrin's campaign for Perfect Pizza, and Darrin lies that he was saving it for a surprise. Is Larry really okay with Darrin mapping out and implementing an entire campaign without consulting him?

OH, MY STARS!

Mario sighs that pizza is killing his business. Given that Endora's televised plug causes Darrin to lose Baldwin's account, her decision to help her son-in-law is sweet – but all the publicity for Perfect Pizza, which far outdoes any Endora and Samantha do for Mario's, would just hurt Mario even more. Yet, Mario's clientele increases so exponentially by episode's end that reservations are required.

When Endora and Samantha realize that Baldwin must be at Mario's, they agree to pop over and check. Samantha fades out backwards, and Endora follows, saying, "That's my gal!" This footage is taken directly from the scene where Samantha and Endora decided to lunch in Paris in "Witch or Wife" (#8).

SON OF A GUN!

"Are you implying that pizza is atheistic?" – Baldwin, after Mario shrugs off Endora and Samantha's applause by saying that "somebody up there" likes him.

Linton Baldwin goes on about his humble beginnings in Modesto, California, threatens to sue everyone, compares his Perfect Pizza to the American dream, and postulates it could eliminate crime. This episode is about Mario, but Baldwin not only steals it from him, he turns around and sells it on the black market.

COUSIN EDGAR
Airdate: June 3, 1965

EPISODE
36

A mysterious feather floats by and tickles Darrin as he tries to sleep. An elf fades in, whom Samantha recognizes as her cousin, Edgar. The next morning, Samantha realizes she never sees Edgar unless she's in trouble. Edgar invisibly messes with Darrin by squirting him with shaving cream and pouring coffee on him at breakfast, which Darrin attributes to his nervousness about the Shelley Shoe account. At the office, Edgar tickles and trips Darrin to the point he thinks Endora is playing tricks on him. Endora determines that Edgar considers Samantha's mortal marriage a blot on the family name, so Samantha has Endora cook up a potion that will make Edgar sleep. Edgar accepts the spiked cocoa from Samantha, but switches cups with her.

With Samantha knocked out, Edgar ties Darrin's shoelaces together and makes him pull Shelley's chair out from under him; McMann & Tate's competitor, Froug, relishes Darrin's misfortune. The next day, Samantha explains about Edgar, who infuriates Darrin with more pranks. After Samantha insists that Darrin's welfare is important to her, Edgar disappears. While a dubious Larry lets Darrin face Shelley again, Edgar sneaks in and pulls the same tricks on the bragging Froug, even defacing Froug's layouts with insults about Shelley. Edgar then improves on Darrin's layouts by making elves a symbol for Shelley Shoes, which Shelley loves. At home, Darrin admits that he'll miss Edgar, who finally materializes in front of him and waves goodbye.

GOOD!

Endora may feel like a traitor working against Edgar on Samantha's behalf, but it's interesting to see her doing up a witches' brew the old-fashioned way. Ordinarily, Endora instantly materializes what she needs; obviously she has some experience and know-how when it comes to expected traditions, adding another layer to the formidable witch.

WELL?

This episode cuts right to the chase, showing a feather tickling Darrin's foot. Considering there's no set-up, it feels as if we're joining an episode "already in progress." Then, Samantha's ESP seems to be back, since she senses Edgar before he fades in. Edgar purposely wakes Darrin up with his feather – so why does he shush Samantha as she blurts out Edgar's name?

Samantha wants to sneak Edgar up on Darrin gradually, then invites the elf to dinner without checking with Darrin first. That's gradual? Samantha also realizes that Edgar only shows up when she's in some sort of trouble – but it's Edgar who causes all the trouble with his relentless, borderline vicious pranks on Darrin. So much for elves being gentle in addition to impish.

After Darrin's horrific afternoon fumbling and tripping thanks to Edgar, Darrin immediately suspects Endora of messing with him. Why? He and Endora nearly made friends during their last interaction in "Eat at Mario's" (#35), and Endora's hardly done anything to him, outside of a handful of attempts to break up his marriage (one he knows about, and two he doesn't).

Great care is taken to keep Charles Irving (Shelley) from getting hurt when Darrin pulls the chair out from under him, but speeding the footage up that much makes the sequence reach unintended silent movie proportions. And Darrin repeatedly yells for Endora during the Shelley meeting – Larry knows who Endora is; he spent a good deal of time with her in Paris in "Witch or Wife" (#8). Wouldn't Larry wonder why Darrin is calling out for his mother-in-law?

When Edgar goes for a second morning of shenanigans, Samantha exclaims, "Edgar, you're behaving like a child!" He is, but Samantha's assertion is a voice-over. Later, Edgar makes hilarious additions to Froug's layouts, but, when Froug shoves them back into his portfolio, they are in their original form.

The episode (and season) ends with Edgar revealing himself to Darrin and saying goodbye. Darrin laments, "I was getting used to having the little guy around the house." Darrin got used to someone who tormented him over and over?

OH, MY STARS!

How exactly can an elf be related to a witch? For Edgar to be Samantha's cousin, either Maurice or Endora would have to have a sibling that's an elf, or a sibling that had a child by one. Even then, said cousin would only be a half-elf. (Maybe that's why Edgar's so tall.) It would make more sense for Edgar to simply be a friend of the family.

If the potion meant to knock Edgar out smells so foul that both Endora and Samantha comment on it, how do they think Edgar can't detect it in his hot chocolate? Can Samantha really not smell it in her own cocoa after Edgar switches cups on her? Samantha kind of deserves to get tricked – she can't be more obvious trying to get Edgar to drink the sleepy-time concoction.

The effects of Darrin and Froug's shoelaces tying themselves are generally good, though hampered by the camera shifting as the effect is achieved. More importantly, how can Froug turn around to face Shelley with his shoes tied together? Perhaps the same way Darrin is able to walk right away after falling from the same prank.

Do elves have powers? Edgar goes around invisible, but has to pull his pranks manually – yet, he's able to magically change Froug's slogans into insults against Shelley. In "A Vision of Sugar Plums" (#15), Santa's elfin helpers displayed no such powers – surely the North Pole would crank toys out even faster if they did. Maybe Edgar truly is half-witch.

SON OF A GUN!

"I love you. And if your cousin Edgar doesn't understand that, I may have to ask you to do something horrible to him – like turn him into a human being. Now think about that for a while." – Darrin to Samantha, laying down a piece of mortal wisdom knowing Edgar is in earshot.

SEASON TWO
(1965-1966)

Samantha helps Aunt Clara change Darrin back from a chimpanzee so she can share her happy baby news in "Alias Darrin Stephens" (#37).

ABC/Photofest

In "Trick or Treat" (#43), Darrin tries to play off being turned into a werewolf for the sake of his boss, Larry Tate.

ABC/Photofest

Endora is none too pleased to see Samantha's practical-joking Uncle Arthur in "The Joker Is A Card" (#41).

ABC/Photofest

Suspicious neighbor Gladys Kravitz and her husband Abner congratulate the Stephenses on their new arrival in "My Baby, the Tycoon" (#55).

ABC Photo Archives/Disney ABC Television Group/Getty Images

SEASON TWO: OVERVIEW

Like many movie trilogies, television shows often suffer from what can be called a "sophomore slump" – somehow, their second seasons come nowhere close to capturing the magic of what got their audience's attention in the first place. The polar opposite was true for *Bewitched*, which capitalized on its own literal magic by developing ideas presented in its previous season – and forever changing the game by giving Darrin and Samantha Stephens their first child.

Yes, Samantha's pregnancy, and the ultimate arrival of baby Tabatha, drove several episodes in Season Two, as well as informed many smaller moments in a slew of other scenes. But the 1164 Morning Glory Circle that Tabatha was born into had already developed quite a bit compared to the show's beginnings. Samantha, who was glamorous but demure when introduced, became much more natural as this season progressed, making her accessible in a way she hadn't been before. Darrin, whose early caddishness and intolerance had made him almost off-putting, mellowed under the canopy of imminent fatherhood – he closed his roving eye, further opened his mind, and had less hassles with Samantha. Even Endora's impishness was sprinkled with the occasional nicety toward her son-in-law, especially as they bonded over Tabatha's birth.

The season had a much better sense of direction: episode prologues were now almost always integrated into the main story, and the show attempted to lay down ground rules about witchcraft for the first time, addressing whether or not one witch could undo another witch's spell. There were numerous disparities as this answer switched from "yes" to "no" and back again, but at least the question was raised. Our witches' spells and incantations, composed strictly of fantastical magic words during Season One, made an almost imperceptible transition to English phrases with each passing episode.

Some of the initial season's curious experiments carried over into Season Two, most notably as Samantha magically renovated a cabin, Darrin tangled with boxers, and both came to the aid of a leprechaun, who turned out to be a cousin of Darrin's. Causing much of his own distress, Darrin made an exorbitant amount of assumptions about witchcraft during this period, repeatedly assuming magic was afoot when it wasn't, which made him seem rather paranoid. And Tabatha, whose presence was heavily felt through nearly two-thirds of these 39 episodes, wound up on the backburner toward the end of the season – though she fared better than the Tates' baby, who was rarely mentioned; when he was, it was never by name.

Of course, one unfortunate aspect of Season Two couldn't be helped: the rapid decline of nosy neighbor Gladys Kravitz, whose portrayer, Alice Pearce, was dying of cancer before *Bewitched* even shot its first episode. Gladys was already becoming more shrill, but that was the writing; the ravages of Alice Pearce's illness and subsequent visible weight loss became very noticeable, particularly in "Samantha the Dressmaker" (#60) and "Baby's First Paragraph" (#62) – the latter conceivably being the last episode she lensed before passing away mid-season. The show was forced to compensate for the lack of a suspicious mortal by bringing in Gladys' sister-in-law, Harriet Kravitz, but Ms. Pearce's absence still left a sizable hole in its canvas.

Perhaps this precipitated the season's curious ending, "Prodigy" (#74), which found the Stephenses flashing back to an otherwise innocuous scenario involving Gladys and her violinist brother. "What Every Young Man Should Know" (#72), which referenced the series' pilot, would have made a more appropriate finale, but, if tacking on a Gladys-centric episode was designed as an homage to Alice Pearce, then that homage succeeded.

Less sensible were two other flashback episodes, "A Vision of Sugar Plums" (#51) and "Samantha Meets the Folks" (#56), which were merely first season shows with second season prologues added to set up the reruns. If these choice bits of filler were needed to accommodate Elizabeth Montgomery's real-life maternity leave, that's understandable, but the new scenes created major continuity flaws in both episodes; they may have gotten past audiences of the '60s, but they're glaringly obvious through even a cursory inspection today.

In the big picture, however, this season was very strong, introducing the first witch illness, the developing friendship between the Stephenses and Tates, and the début of Uncle Arthur – who, after just one appearance, seemed like he'd always been on the show. Plus, the increasing antagonism between Darrin and Endora during the season's latter episodes seemed to imply that their mortal-versus-witch conflicts were far from over.

ALIAS DARRIN STEPHENS
Airdate: September 16, 1965

Bearing gifts for Samantha and Darrin's first anniversary, Aunt Clara tries to magically resize the golf cap she brought for Darrin, but turns him into a chimpanzee instead. Aunt Clara can't remember what spell she used; without it, neither she nor Samantha can restore Darrin, who can only communicate by writing notes. Endora is installed as "chimp-sitter" when Samantha has to go out, but Larry, who thinks Darrin is home sick with laryngitis, stops by for a briefing about a client, so Darrin escapes through the window. When Gladys finds Darrin-as-chimp and brings him home, Abner calls the zoo. As the returning Samantha learns that Darrin and Endora are missing, she tells Aunt Clara that she has some very important news for Darrin – they're going to have a baby.

Samantha tracks Darrin to the zoo; she is about to let him out of the monkey cage when Aunt Clara arrives, ready to redeem herself by reversing her spell. After she accidentally changes Darrin into a seal, Samantha steps in and normalizes Darrin herself. The zookeeper is angry to find Darrin in the cage, and Darrin is even angrier until Samantha tells him they're going to be parents. Darrin melts, then wonders if their child will be witch or mortal; Samantha says only time will tell. Later, the Stephenses try their anniversary again, but Gladys stops by to ask about the chimp, blanching when she sees Darrin wearing the chimp's golf cap.

GOOD!

Although Endora's not particularly integral to this story, her amusement over Darrin's predicament, as well as her baby talk treatment of her de-evolved son-in-law, is the star of the episode. "Mother Endora will comb you," she coaxes after zapping up a playsuit for him. Later, after Darrin-as-chimp crawls out of the window, Endora beckons him to come back, admitting she was only teasing, which gives her unexpected heart.

This episode takes the premise of witchcraft to a new level by establishing a rule about how witches and warlocks use their powers. Up until now, it seemed they could undo each others' spells at random – here, it's revealed that witches need to recall the exact words of a spell, or it can't be undone by anyone. It's an effective attempt to provide structure to the show's central device, creating room for more conflict and suspense with this new rule in place.

Film buffs will notice that Aunt Clara's "abba dabba" spell is a nod to the ragtime song "Aba Daba Honeymoon," which was popularized by Debbie Reynolds and Carleton Carpenter in the 1950 movie, *Two Weeks With Love*: its primary lyric is "Abba dabba dabba dabba dabba dabba dabba, said the monkey to the chimp."

WELL?

As Darrin opens his gift from Aunt Clara in a wide shot, Samantha holds her new apron in her right hand; when the scene cuts to a two-shot, Samantha holds it in her left. On that subject, Darrin seems to be an ambidextrous chimp: he writes Samantha a note with his left paw and Endora one with his right, while, in the zoo, he's left-pawed again. Samantha gives Darrin-as-chimp the notepad a second time, even though she never took it back from him in the first place, and Darrin's handwriting is different here than it was when he left Samantha a note in "Witch or Wife" (#8).

Samantha, who railed at Darrin for allegedly hurting Aunt Clara's feelings in "Samantha Meets the Folks" (#14) and was ready to battle a troublemaking mother in Aunt Clara's defense in "There's No Witch Like An Old Witch" (#27), seems unusually upset with her aunt over Darrin's transformation. Then again, Aunt Clara probably never turned one of Samantha's beaus into a primate before.

Twice, Endora refers to Darrin as "Darwin," and later, in the zoo, when Darrin scribbles that he has nothing in common with his fellow chimps, Samantha comments, "Charles Darwin wouldn't agree with you." It's a shame these plot points aren't tied together; Endora could use it as future justification for calling her son-in-law "Darwin."

After a year in the mortal world, Samantha has certainly begun to think like one. "I don't even know where to start looking," Samantha frets to Aunt Clara when Darrin goes missing. Can't she cast some sort of locator spell? It would be better than the pat "You sure work fast!" phone call that provides her Darrin's whereabouts. The neighborhood park has been seen in "I, Darrin, Take This Witch, Samantha" (#1), "Eye of the Beholder" (#22), and "Eat At Mario's" (#35), but there's never been a zoo there before – until now.

It's lovely that Darrin gets a sense of humor about being turned into a chimp, but when Gladys makes the connection between him and the too-small golf cap on his head, the Stephenses seem to enjoy her distress a little too much.

OH, MY STARS!

Darrin has every right to be upset over getting zapped into a chimpanzee (he says nothing about being a seal), but he yells, "Sam, it's through – finished!" Is Aunt Clara's innocent mistake really enough to make Darrin threaten divorce?

Much is made of Aunt Clara needing to remember her exact words so Darrin can be turned back into a human. Yet, when she finds the spell in her book, she and Samantha each employ totally unrelated words to undo the deed. Samantha even adds and replaces words in Clara's original spell – so much for needing to remember an incantation verbatim.

SON OF A GUN!

"You mean not even you, a bloody relation?" – Aunt Clara to Samantha, as she discovers that no one can reverse her spell unless she remembers the original words.

When Endora opens the door to Larry, he reminds her, "We met in Paris." Indeed they did – in "Witch or Wife" (#8). That was nearly a year earlier; glossing over that detail after that long would be perfectly understandable, but the fact that the show doesn't makes this example of continuity that much sweeter.

In a time when season premieres didn't require slam-bang plot twists like today, this episode slyly turns the Darrin-as-chimp shenanigans into a game-changer with the revelation of Samantha's pregnancy. Darrin gently wonders if his child will inherit powers – a huge step past the squeamishness he displayed in "...And Something Makes Three" (#12). Then, Samantha puts off telling Endora, creating a cliffhanger. And Aunt Clara knows just how Endora will react to her impending grandmotherhood: "Oh, she'll be hysterical." The show took everything that was already excellent about its first season and improved on it in a single episode.

A VERY SPECIAL DELIVERY

Airdate: September 23, 1965

Darrin dotes on the pregnant Samantha, but Larry reminds him that Louise just had a baby, and suggests that an active expectant mother will have a healthier child. Meanwhile, Samantha worries how Endora will react to becoming a grandmother; Endora pops in having already heard about the pregnancy and protests, but she soon begins to look forward to the arrival. Darrin comes home and won't help Samantha make dinner, explaining his new philosophy to Endora after Samantha storms off. The next day, Darrin wakes up nauseous, with a backache and a craving for a "crazy" breakfast. At the office, Darrin gets overly emotional with Larry and argues with a client over a pickle. Darrin's doctor laughs that his symptoms point to pregnancy, but Darrin recalls his conversation with Endora and comes to the conclusion that he's about to have a baby himself.

After Samantha hears about Darrin's behavior, she realizes Endora zapped him with pregnancy symptoms; Endora refuses to remove them until Darrin has learned his lesson. Meanwhile, Darrin talks to the typically inattentive Dave – and Joe the bartender, who suggests that Darrin's "pregnancy" will make him famous. Darrin fantasizes about the media's reaction to his giving birth until Samantha finds him at the bar and assures him he's only experiencing physical sensations. With the symptoms removed, Darrin goes back to spoiling Samantha, now knowing exactly how his pregnant wife feels.

GOOD!

After the show pretty much forgot that Louise was pregnant [she made the announcement in "...And Something Makes Three" (#12)], she gets restitution as Larry reminds Darrin that Louise just had her baby. Talk about tough – she played a round of golf a day before giving birth.

As Darrin comes home from work, Endora decides to change out of her witches' outfit into something more palatable to mortals. This is before CGI, when an actor had to change clothes and place themselves in front of the camera in the exact same position to make the effect work – and this one does, beautifully.

Best friend Dave and bartender Joe (who finally has a consistent name) are once again on hand to ignore or disbelieve Darrin's problem, respectively. Even though Darrin should know better by now than to look for comfort from these guys, it's stellar continuity to include them in Darrin's pregnant pause.

WELL?

It's surprising Darrin doesn't clue in to Endora's hex on his own, considering he exhibits pregnancy symptoms immediately after discussing Samantha's condition with her. Is a lack of awareness part of Endora's spell? And Larry should be wondering about Darrin's bizarre behavior: in the past year, Darrin has defended witches and yelled for his mother-in-law – for starters. Yet when Darrin nearly jeopardizes an account over a pickle, Larry simply figures Darrin is overworked.

During Darrin's last visit to the doctor in "A Change of Face" (#33), he talked about how his features had been rearranged to the point the medic referred him to a psychiatrist. Here, Darrin apparently has all the symptoms of pregnancy, but the doctor barely reacts.

When Samantha calls to check on Darrin, the secretary answers, "Darrin Stephens' office." Darrin does not have his own secretary, despite evidence to the contrary in "I, Darrin, Take This Witch, Samantha" (#1). Plus, Miss Thatcher is stationed in the company's outer office – so wouldn't the proper greeting be, "McMann & Tate; to whom may I direct your call?" Samantha is surprised to hear Darrin's been complaining of a backache, but she shouldn't be; Darrin woke up telling her he had a backache while limping to the bathroom.

Darrin has extremely detailed fantasies: as he tells reporters about being both father and mother to his son, a WXIU news camera wheels in for a closer shot – the same camera used to televise Ed Wright's real-life debate in "Remember the Main" (#34).

When Samantha finds Darrin at the bar, she tells him, "I had a feeling you'd be here drowning your sorrows." She should – he's certainly there often enough, though her first-time appearance does add variety to Darrin's solve-problem-at-bar formula. As for Endora, she must feel very strongly about how men minimize the ordeal of pregnancy. Not only does she afflict Darrin with its symptoms to teach him a lesson, but she puts the same hex on a total stranger. Does Endora ever remove it, or does the poor man have to suffer through backaches and strange cravings indefinitely?

OH, MY STARS!

In "Alias Darrin Stephens" (#37), the show built up the suspense of how Endora would react to becoming grandmother to a mortal's baby. Instead of following through with a satisfying payoff, Endora simply appears in Samantha's kitchen already knowing about her pregnancy. Not getting to watch Endora's reaction upon learning the news is a letdown, and she's not even "hysterical," as Aunt Clara predicted she'd be. "I was hoping it was just an ugly rumor!" Endora declares. Where would she hear such a rumor? Aunt Clara was the only other person who knew besides Darrin – surely she didn't leak the info after promising Samantha she'd keep it to herself.

"If that mother of yours ever pulls a stunt like that again," Darrin tells Samantha, "I'm going to use a little magic of my own: make a few of her teeth disappear." Threatening violence isn't funny, and does Darrin really think Endora wouldn't zap him before he could curl his fist? Samantha's not even upset that Darrin wants to batter her mother; she simply replies, "And no jury would convict you."

SON OF A GUN!

"I'll have to have my pants let out!" – Darrin to Samantha, as he admits he's "pregnant."

Dick York is clearly having a ball playing this episode. Darrin's whimpering, teary-eyed conversation with Larry is topped only by his jockeying to get his hands on Mr. Martin's uneaten pickle. Then there's Darrin's fantasy, which is the perfect bookend to the one he had about having a brood of witch children in "...And Something Makes Three" (#12). And the twist of Samantha pacing in the waiting room and being told her husband just had a healthy baby boy is a clever gender-switch.

WE'RE IN FOR A BAD SPELL
Airdate: September 30, 1965

Darrin's Army buddy, Adam Newlarkin, moves to town after a sudden compulsion to leave his job in Salem, Massachusetts. Darrin thinks Samantha is responsible for the witchy pranks that befall Adam at dinner, but Aunt Clara's book reveals that Adam is under a curse from a witch sentenced by Adam's ancestor during the Salem witch hunts. Adam must kiss a dog's snout, get dunked three times, and proclaim that witches are dear while riding a horse – if he doesn't, he will be branded a common thief; Darrin's skeptical until Adam is hired at a bank. The Stephenses get Adam to kiss the dog, but when Darrin can only manage dunking Adam in a pool twice, Aunt Clara assists with the third dunk.

Samantha brings a sick Adam home from the bank, where Adam's briefcase switches itself with fellow employee Harding's. Adam balks when his friends pressure him to ride a horse while dressed like Paul Revere, but when he finds the bank's money in his briefcase, he puts stock the 17th century curse because he's from Salem. As Adam makes his ride, a police officer stops by to question him; when he returns, the cop learns the missing money is in Harding's briefcase. Adam admits he always secretly believed his grandmother's witch stories, and Darrin adds that some of his best friends are witches. Samantha revisits the book and jokes that Darrin is fated to marry a witch and live happily ever after.

GOOD!

Even though Adam is yet another "old friend" of Darrin's [like Kermit in "Love Is Blind" (#13) and Bob in "Which Witch Is Witch?" (#24), neither of whom have been seen again], his presence confirms that Darrin was indeed in the military, which was established In "Just One Happy Family" (#10). In that episode, Samantha explained to Maurice that Darrin had been a lieutenant; discovering that Darrin served in the United States Army with Adam adds to that backstory.

Darrin letting go of Adam and calling for a waiter to facilitate Adam's second dunk in the pool is right out of the slapstick comedies of old. Aunt Clara booty-bumping Adam into the water (ten years before disco) is even funnier.

There are two references to the show's title in this episode: a sped-up theme underscoring Samantha's race into the house with Adam (though no explanation is given for their faster-than-normal movements), and when Samantha warns, "Adam, you're bewitched! And you only have ten minutes to get unbewitched!" It's always a thrill to hear the name of the show woven into the script.

Adam displays a mix of humor and strength when he rightly demands to know why his friends keep putting him through the wringer. Saying he believes Zorelda's curse because simply he comes from Salem is a bit of a stretch, but having another mortal besides Darrin allowing for the possibility that witches are real proves unexpectedly gratifying.

WELL?

Samantha's ears perk up when Adam reveals he's from Salem. Why does she immediately assume Salem, Massachusetts? There's also a Salem in Oregon, and in several other states. When Aunt Clara arrives to aid Adam's cause, she comes crashing down the chimney. Shouldn't Adam have heard the noise and come running? Later, when Aunt Clara zaps her book open, a wire can be seen keeping it that way. It's revealed that a name appears in the book of spellees every time a spell is cast – if so, then Darrin must have been listed when Aunt Clara turned him into a chimpanzee in "Alias Darrin Stephens" (#37).

Adam comes down to breakfast to find a dalmatian on the patio; Darrin claims the dog belongs to a neighbor. That's convenient, but, more likely, Samantha zapped the pup up. She claims that she and Darrin kiss the "spotted dog" every morning for luck, but this is Adam's second morning at the Stephenses', and he could truthfully say he didn't see this ritual the day before. Samantha could use some schooling in thinking on her feet; she can't expect Adam to believe her claim that a musical toaster is responsible for the fanfare indicating Adam completed Part I of the antidote spell.

Adam says he got a dry suit from the inn's manager. How is it the suit just happens to fit? That suit gets wet, too, but later, at the bank, Adam's in dry clothes again. Where did he get the third suit? Speaking of clothes, Aunt Clara wears Endora's "lavender and old lace" costume from "Mother Meets What's-His-Name" (#4) for her turn as "Whistler's Mother."

Where does Adam work? His bank can't be in Manhattan, where Darrin works, because if it is, Samantha wouldn't be able to drive Adam home in five minutes (Darrin usually spends more time than that on a train), and Adam couldn't gallop past the bank from the house in less than ten. Therefore, the bank must be in whatever fictional berg includes Morning Glory Circle (it still hasn't been revealed in what town the Stephenses actually live). In any case, the business district where the bank is located looks suspiciously like the administrative buildings of a Hollywood studio lot.

OH, MY STARS!

Adam's "bewitched" state may only have made sense to "the witch Zorelda." Adam reports having had a sudden urge to leave Salem and get a job in Darrin's town. If Adam's family was cursed in Salem, why does he need to move for the curse to take effect? The endgame is for Adam to be branded a common thief, so there's not much point in his being pranked by chairs and attacked by salad, especially when those pranks are dropped once Adam gets his job. Darrin relays that Adam's ancestor – the judge who sentenced Zorelda – was witched into robbing a bank. Except Massachusetts was only one of thirteen colonies during the 1692-1693 Salem witch trials, and research indicates that there was no organized banking system until the Bank of North America was established in 1784. Finally, Adam must publicly proclaim that "witches are good, witches are dear" – yet Zorelda's revenge ruined 17th century Adam's reputation and just about took 1965 Adam down as well; so much for good and dear.

Adam gets wet at lunchtime, and Samantha comes to the bank at 4:25 to retrieve him. Catching a cold from being wet is now considered an old wives' tale; he couldn't go from perfectly healthy to sick in just four hours unless he was already coming down with something before his swim. For all that, once Adam returns to Morning Glory Circle and is told why he needs to ride the horse in costume, his cold is gone – he doesn't sneeze the rest of the episode.

SON OF A GUN!

"Samantha, I know you're going to be a mother, but would you please practice on someone else?" – Adam, after Samantha pulls rank at the bank to get the sick Newlarkin home.

MY GRANDSON, THE WARLOCK
Airdate: October 7, 1965

EPISODE **40**

The Tates call from London asking the Stephenses to take care of their baby, since their governess is sick. Gladys spies her neighbors coming home with an infant and assumes Samantha has given birth. Gladys tells a visiting Maurice about "Samantha's" baby; believing the Tates' boy is his grandson, Maurice whisks him off on "an adventure." Darrin panics, while, in London, Louise thinks she sees her baby being squired around by Maurice. As Samantha and Endora fly off in search of Maurice, the Tates call Darrin from the airport; he picks them up, but tampers with their luggage, drives slowly, and feigns car trouble to stall for time.

Meanwhile, Maurice takes baby Tate to the Warlock Club, but when Nanny Witch sees that Maurice's "grandson" can't do any magic, she declares him mortal. Back in America, as Darrin checks under his hood, Samantha pops in, and Darrin relays that Louise reported seeing the baby in London. Not finding Maurice at the Warlock Club, Samantha returns home and tries to help Darrin buy time with the frustrated Tates by witching Louise into being cavalier about her son. Finally hearing Maurice upstairs, Samantha retrieves baby Tate and sends his parents on their way, while Maurice drowns his sorrows in a giant martini. After Samantha explains about the Tates' child, Maurice's hopes about having a warlock grandson are restored – but when Gladys comes by and sees Maurice walking through the wall, she gulps down his oversized drink.

GOOD!

Louise's first time under the influence of witchcraft is spellbinding. Her "what the heck" attitude – wanting a drink and declaring, "Hit me again, honey" after she had just been frantic about the baby she thought was in London – provides great comic contrast.

There's a surprising sweetness in Maurice's attempt to bond with his "grandson," first in Samantha's bedroom, and then at the Warlock Club. His coaching the infant in front of his peers illustrates a warlock's rite of passage, even though Maurice doesn't know the boy is mortal. And Maurice's descent from beaming pride to whimpering disappointment is quite a ride.

WELL?

How does Abner know Samantha's only been pregnant three months? The Kravitzes and Stephenses don't seem close enough to be sharing this kind of sensitive information. As for Maurice, Endora mentioned his penchant for dramatic exits in "Just One Happy Family" (#10), but here, he simply pulls up in a limo like an aristocratic mortal. Not to mention, it does not look like Maurice and Gladys are talking on Morning Glory Circle. The houses behind Maurice – which are on Gladys' side of the street – are too opulent for the middle-class neighborhood, and don't resemble any other building that's been seen on the Circle so far. Finally, Samantha either has different names for Maurice, or can't stick to one: in "Just One Happy Family" (#10), she called him "Father," then graduated to "Daddy." Now she only refers to him as "Father," and no less than seven times.

Upon discovering that warlock Maurice has popped out with Larry's mortal baby, Darrin bewails, "That could mark a child for life!" That may be consistent with the Darrin of Season One, who called witchcraft "nonsense," but it feels like a step back for the more enlightened Darrin of late. Louise, on the other hand, is able to recognize a baby cradled in the arms of a stranger, in a foreign country, and in passing, at that. There's such a thing as mother's intuition, but not to this extent. Also, London and New York look very similar – the Tates' hotel and the Big Apple airport terminal are obviously filmed on the show's usual exterior street set, with the latter's entrance looking more like a bank building than an airport. By the way, how do the Tates fly back so fast? London to New York takes about 7 hours on average, yet Larry and Louise arrive just one scene after hailing a taxi at their hotel. Samantha and Endora could make the trip much faster, but they inexplicably wait until the Tates are stateside to start looking for Maurice.

Endora pops onto Darrin's car to signal him to stall the Tates, but he's already stalling them. Later, Samantha and Darrin give each other progress reports under Darrin's hood at full volume; apparently the Stephenses refrain from speaking in hushed tones with the Tates in earshot so Louise can think Darrin is talking to the motor.

A big whooshing noise tells Samantha that Maurice has arrived upstairs. It's pretty loud, but the Tates don't seem to notice. As for Maurice, when he zaps up his giant martini, there's only liquid, but when he comes downstairs, there's an equally giant olive and toothpick in the glass. Did he add them while the Tates were saying their goodbyes? Finally, Samantha smiles that once Gladys finishes the martini Maurice left her, they won't have to explain his magical exit. Maybe not, but they might have to tell Abner why the sober Gladys left his house to bring the Stephenses a baby gift and came back three sheets to the wind.

OH, MY STARS!

Throughout this episode, Larry and Louise's child is only ever referred to as "the baby." What's keeping them from giving little man Tate a name? And why is Darrin so evasive about baby Tate? If he'd just tell Gladys he's babysitting, she wouldn't think Samantha gave birth in two hours. Darrin reinforces Gladys' belief by mentioning that the baby weighs 25 pounds – but for an infant to weigh 25 pounds, it has to be at least 6-12 months old, and Larry reported that Louise "just had" her baby in "A Very Special Delivery" (#38), two episodes ago. Then, when Gladys sees Samantha is still pregnant and asks about the baby she saw, Samantha, Darrin, and Maurice just stand there silently, smiling at Gladys' confusion. It's as if they're enjoying Gladys' torment, as the Stephenses also seemed to at the end of "Alias Darrin Stephens" (#37).

SON OF A GUN!

"Oh, shut up. I'm the one who has cause to cry." – Maurice, to a very hungry, very mortal baby Tate.

THE JOKER IS A CARD
Airdate: October 14, 1965

EPISODE 41

Endora's cordial dinner with Darrin and Samantha – during which she actually gets Darrin's name right – is marred by a series of pranks. Blame goes around until Samantha realizes they are being visited by her practical-joking Uncle Arthur, whom she finds under the serving dish. All goes well until Darrin laughs at a gag Arthur pulls on Endora; she responds by giving Darrin a Beatles makeover. Uncle Arthur offers to teach Darrin simple magic so he can combat his mother-in-law; Darrin declines until unexplained mishaps at the office convince him Endora is sabotaging him.

Uncle Arthur trains Darrin to use an elaborate incantation that includes a duck call and a cowbell, but when Darrin tries it on Endora, he makes a fool of himself. Samantha hears Uncle Arthur laughing and realizes that Darrin has been tricked. Darrin and Endora unite in their anger, so Samantha recruits them for a payback scheme: Darrin casts the useless spell again, but this time, Endora turns into a parrot. Samantha cries that Darrin can't restore Endora because he doesn't know how; when a distraught Uncle Arthur admits he loves his relative and says he'll do anything to help her, Endora changes herself back and asks Arthur to give up his practical jokes. He wholeheartedly agrees, but later can't resist pranking Endora with opera glasses that leave circles around her eyes.

GOOD!

Looks like Darrin has gotten past the idea of punching Endora's teeth out [see "A Very Special Delivery" (#38)], since here they get together for dinner with Samantha and exchange pleasantries; Endora actually calls her son-in-law "Darrin," and Darrin greets her with "Hi, Mom." After Uncle Arthur plays them for fools, Darrin and Endora brainstorm revenge ideas, then team up to get back at the practical joker. Even though Darrin and Endora's distaste for each other is the main conflict of the show, it's somehow always nice to see them getting along.

Dick York and Agnes Moorehead each get a chance to shine in this episode: Darrin goes from befuddled to involved when Arthur gives him a tutorial in witchcraft (or so he thinks), and the opposite extreme, where Darrin turns the tables on his uncle-in-law with an overconfident "I've got the power now," is just as entertaining. Endora's parrot sounds quite authentic, and even though it's all in voice-over, her portrayer is clearly relishing presenting Endora from a different perspective.

WELL?

Where does the frog go once it jumps out of the dessert box? Does it spend the rest of the episode hopping around the Stephens house? Also, for some reason, when Darrin's hair changes, there's no sound effect until after the transformation – and as Darrin touches his new 'do, the wig shifts. Uncle Arthur has a finger on his tooth in a wide shot, but when the scene cuts to a two-shot, he's holding two fingers in front of him.

Feet stuck in wastebaskets? Chairs sliding out from under hapless sitters? Uncle Arthur has taken a few pages out of the playbook of Samantha's "Cousin Edgar" (#36); the show also did the pull-away chair trick with Adam in "We're In For A Bad Spell" (#39), but at least here it's done in real time, and not in silent movie speed.

Larry may not have recognized Endora's name when Darrin blurted it out before – but, since reconnecting with the lady in "Alias Darrin Stephens" (#37), Larry should find it strange that Darrin mentions Endora in conjunction with suggesting that the EZ-Open Door is jinxed. Instead, Larry's non-reaction implies he's never heard of her.

OH, MY STARS!

Uncle Arthur asks Darrin, "Endora gives you a real hard time, huh?" – and Darrin replies, "In a word, yes." Except for a few threats, a couple of minor spells, and a lot of sass, Endora really hasn't done enough to Darrin to merit these opinions. Then, while Arthur teaches Darrin his "spell," Samantha and Endora sit in the living room, where neither of them hear the distinctive noises of a duck call and cowbell coming from the nearby den. Yet Samantha does hear Uncle Arthur laughing in the den while standing at the foot of the stairs, a few feet away closer than the living room.

Arthur admits to Samantha that he tricked Darrin with his incantation; surely he realizes that Samantha will tell Darrin everything. However, when Darrin wants to try the spell again, Arthur is surprised, and acts as if Darrin doesn't know the spell is phony. After Endora changes herself into the parrot, Samantha tells Uncle Arthur that only Darrin can remove the "spell." This proprietary lock on magic is new, and different than the rule established in "Alias Darrin Stephens" (#37), where Samantha could undo Aunt Clara's spell as long she knew the original words.

SON OF A GUN!

"Your mother-in-law just turned you into Prince Valiant. That's normal living?" – Uncle Arthur to Darrin, after Endora rewards Darrin's laughter with a Beatles mop-top.

As Uncle Arthur, Paul Lynde is immediately at home, interacting with Samantha, Darrin, and Endora as if he's been on the show since the beginning. Arthur's zaniness in his own form is one thing, but his inspired appearances as the elderly mopping lady and window washer define the warlock in just a few scenes. Conversely, his panic when he thinks Endora is doomed to remain a parrot shows he has an emotional core – and brings up the tantalizing question, "How are Arthur and Endora related?"

In addition to Uncle Arthur's "spell" being in longhand, its actual words are written out all the way down the scroll. Few would notice that detail, so that the show takes the extra step to include it is magical in its own way.

When Endora plays innocent about the things she's done to Darrin, Samantha reminds her mother, "Well, if you'd like me to start at the beginning, on our wedding night you put him in the hotel lobby in his pajamas." She most certainly did, in "I, Darrin, Take This Witch, Samantha" (#1) – a wonderful piece of full-circle continuity.

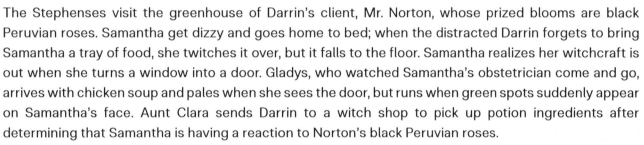

TAKE TWO ASPIRINS AND HALF A PINT OF PORPOISE MILK
Airdate: October 21, 1965
EPISODE 42

The Stephenses visit the greenhouse of Darrin's client, Mr. Norton, whose prized blooms are black Peruvian roses. Samantha get dizzy and goes home to bed; when the distracted Darrin forgets to bring Samantha a tray of food, she twitches it over, but it falls to the floor. Samantha realizes her witchcraft is out when she turns a window into a door. Gladys, who watched Samantha's obstetrician come and go, arrives with chicken soup and pales when she sees the door, but runs when green spots suddenly appear on Samantha's face. Aunt Clara sends Darrin to a witch shop to pick up potion ingredients after determining that Samantha is having a reaction to Norton's black Peruvian roses.

The shop has everything but an ostrich feather, and Darrin gets arrested trying to remove one from a woman's hat. Aunt Clara zaps up a feather instead, but when the potion doesn't work, she realizes she needs black Peruvian rose petals. Darrin goes to jail for breaking into Norton's nursery, so Aunt Clara switches places with him while he adds the petals to the potion, which does the trick. The next day, Gladys brings Abner by, but Samantha's face is spot-free, and Gladys shrieks when Aunt Clara knocks on the upstairs door from the outside. Later, Samantha zaps up some black Peruvian roses and offers a cutting to Norton as a way of making up for Darrin's infraction.

GOOD!

Isn't it interesting that Darrin *wants* Samantha to use witchcraft to determine whether she has a related illness? It's a heartwarming example of Darrin putting his wife's welfare over his desire to live a normal, mortal life. Samantha turning the window into a door can't be an easy effect to pull off, but it's quite fluid, and the Stephenses scrambling to explain it to Gladys is just as effective.

This episode, along with "We're In For A Bad Spell" (#39), goes a long way toward fleshing out the character of Aunt Clara. The bumbling witch shows she's quite knowledgeable about witch diseases and how to cure them, and her assistance further integrates her into this extended family. As for Darrin, he finally seems to be acclimating to life as a witch's husband; no longer writing off witchcraft as "nonsense," he gets arrested twice trying to cure Samantha, and there's a certain satisfaction in his having to pick through a bottle of eye of newt, given his previous attitude. Also, Aunt Clara and Darrin's jailhouse switch is arresting; their hands are in the exact same positions as they trade places.

WELL?

Both Darrin and Samantha wish Endora were around to shed some light on Samantha's illness. "When Mother wants to make herself scarce," Samantha explains, "no one can find her." Endora is almost always in earshot – if her daughter were in trouble, she'd be the first witch on the scene. For that matter, how can Samantha attempt to locate Endora or Aunt Clara if her powers are impaired?

Aunt Clara says that black Peruvian roses were used to drive witches out of Peru. If mortals had found a way to rid themselves of witches, wouldn't they implement it in other places besides one South American country? Imagine how handy those roses would have been during the Salem witch trials...

Aunt Clara sends Darrin to "a little place [where] I shop." Darrin's town has a witch supply store? Darrin learns from the clerk that modern witches wouldn't be caught dead on brooms, but, in "I, Darrin, Take This Witch, Samantha" (#1), it was established that broom riding is only a mortal misconception. And the potion requires two bat wings, although Endora denounced "those ugly flying things that people think we're always cooking" in "Mother Meets What's-His-Name" (#4).

Gladys is afraid Samantha's spots are contagious, asking Abner, "You wanna wake up with something strange?" He retorts, "I've been doing that for 20 years. Why change now?" In "Illegal Separation" (#32), the estranged Kravitzes stated they'd been married 30 years. Does Abner mean that Gladys was normal the first ten years of their union?

Aunt Clara asks the Stephenses to cross their fingers as she readies to conjure up an ostrich for the potion. Why? In "Samantha Meets the Folks" (#14), she said she doesn't believe in superstition. And if Aunt Clara can zap up the feather, why doesn't she just zap up the rest of the ingredients? Darrin exerts little effort breaking into Norton's greenhouse – a botanical building whose door has no alarm, but the rose bush does, and it only goes off after Darrin clips a flower.

After Samantha is cured, Gladys races upstairs to see the phantom door, and it's still there. Shouldn't Samantha's first act upon getting her powers back have been returning the room to normal?

OH, MY STARS!

It's enough that the sergeant at the New York State police station has a map of Los Angeles behind him, but later, when Darrin is arrested, he holds the flower as he is booked, and again in the jail cell. No one in law enforcement would let you go to your cell carrying the very item you burgled.

Despite Darrin stealing his rare bloom, Norton agrees to come to the Stephens house, and gushes at the sight of Samantha's rose-filled garden. Would he really forgive Darrin simply because his wife has a green thumb? Samantha implies that she generated her own roses from the clipping Darrin stole the night before – but Norton would never believe that, since he said it took "nine years of experimental cross-pollination" to cultivate this particular bloom. Samantha giving Norton a clipping doesn't make up for Darrin breaking into Norton's greenhouse, and, if Samantha had her own black Peruvian roses all along, that negates Darrin's excuse for stealing Norton's.

SON OF A GUN!

"Well, there's only one way to find that out. Ask a Peruvian witch who was pregnant when she got the square green spot disease. Offhand, I think the chances of finding her is not too good." – Aunt Clara, after Darrin wonders if having the disease while pregnant is serious.

TRICK OR TREAT
Airdate: October 28, 1965

Endora wants Samantha to accompany her to the Sacred Volcano for Halloween instead of entertaining Darrin's client, Rogers. Seeing Samantha upset by a box of mortal decorations Larry sent, Endora implores Darrin to let Samantha visit the Volcano, but Darrin refuses. That night, Darrin fields trick-or-treaters; outside, a trio of kids tries to prank Endora, so she turns herself into a tree to spook them. Inspired, she becomes a little girl gypsy, knocks on Darrin's door, and puts a spell on him; Darrin is amused until he starts to grow an unkempt beard. Samantha runs outside and finds Child Endora, who smugly tells Darrin he's going to be a werewolf.

When the Tates arrive with Rogers and his wife, Darrin runs upstairs to shave while Child Endora tries to remember her spell. Darrin excuses himself again when claws come in, and Larry is annoyed by his absences. The werewolf manifestations overtaking him, Darrin climbs out the window to find Endora after she disappears. Larry and Rogers spot Darrin in the backyard; Rogers, whose company makes Halloween costumes, raves over Darrin's lifelike "outfit." Darrin has Samantha lock him in a closet when he loses control, and the grown-up Endora, who never forgot her spell, returns, hoping Darrin has learned his lesson. After Samantha blasts her mother for acting like a stereotype witch, Endora apologizes and restores her son-in-law. Later, when Rogers thinks Endora's typical ensemble is also a costume, she pops a tail onto his posterior.

GOOD!

When Darrin gets frustrated by Endora's interference at his office, he flings the window open and dryly says, "Get out" – which may be his funniest offering yet. And, as in "Mother Meets What's-His-Name" (#4), Endora barely tolerates mortal kids, baits them, and then gets the better of them, in this case by turning herself into a tree in front of the shocked trick-or-treaters.

This episode follows the rule of "The Joker Is A Card" (#41): only the witch or warlock who cast a spell can undo it, indicating there's structure about witchcraft taking hold.

WELL?

Endora wants Samantha to pack her bags for their trip to the Sacred Volcano. They're going to fly there – is hand-packed luggage required? Samantha insists that Darrin isn't bigoted – yet, when Endora asks Darrin to let Samantha travel to the Volcano, he erupts, "If you think I'm going to let Sam participate in some weird rites...!"

Larry just sits there when Darrin goes ballistic over him sending Halloween decorations that upset Samantha. Mr. Tate clearly doesn't remember that Darrin also went pro-witch the previous Halloween ["The Witches Are Out" (#7)]; wouldn't it be great if Larry started to put the pieces together, forcing Darrin to throw him off the scent?

Samantha is somehow able to tell that the little girl in her front yard is Endora, simply because she wears a gypsy costume. But it's not like Endora has been seen in gypsy regalia so far. And isn't Endora supposed to be at the Volcano? Apparently werewolfing Darrin has taken precedence over her yearly pilgrimage. When Samantha first sees Darrin's "beard," she understandably exclaims, "Your face!" Ironically, in the previous episode, "Take Two Aspirins And Half A Pint of Porpoise Milk" (#42), Darrin exclaimed, "Sam, your face!" when her square green spots first appeared.

Child Endora makes a heartfelt confession to Darrin, even using his correct name, saying, "Darrin, I feel terrible; I really do. Do you really think I want my daughter married to a werewolf?" If she feels that way, why did she cast the spell in the first place, purposely forget it, and later righteously admit she transformed Darrin to teach him a lesson? And either Darrin rebuilt the backyard gazebo to its exact previous specifications, or Samantha magically restored it, because it is no worse for wear from Aunt Clara crash-landing through it in "Alias Darrin Stephens" (#37).

Rogers' wife stands right behind him when Endora zaps a tail on him – how does she not see it? Does Endora remove it before any of the mortals notice? And where is baby Tate – home with the governess the Tates had in their employ in "My Grandson, The Warlock" (#40) while his parents celebrate the child's first Halloween without him?

OH, MY STARS!

Endora demands that Samantha join her at the Sacred Volcano, telling Darrin, "We go there on Halloween." Maybe this year they do, but, in "The Witches Are Out" (#7), Samantha told Mary and Bertha that she and Endora fly to the South of France every year "'til it all blows over." Samantha's friends also stated that, in terms of improving the image of witches, Endora's "not interested in the cause at all" – here, Endora is hot to teach Darrin a lesson after thinking he sent Larry's maligning Halloween decorations.

SON OF A GUN!

"The reason our marriage is a success is because we don't give in to illogical emotion. We discuss our problems calmly and rationally, and solve them like two mature adults who realize – Darrin, how could you do this?" – Samantha to Endora, as she calls to find out why Darrin sent a box of ethnically insensitive party favors.

Two words: Maureen McCormick. Of course, she's best remembered as Marcia Brady from ABC's *The Brady Bunch* (1969-1974), but here she outdoes her turn as one of Darrin's fantasy children in "...And Something Makes Three" (#12) by truly capturing Endora's sense of impish glee; she gives the impression she's really Endora in a little girl's body, and manages to steal the episode from a werewolf.

This installment contains the strongest pro-tolerance speech heard on the show so far, as Samantha lets Endora have it for acting like a stereotype witch. "'We're not like that,' you said. 'We're nice, civilized people,' you said!" And Samantha's "You're doing it to the one person who was willing to believe we were different" argument could win a court case.

THE VERY INFORMAL DRESS

Airdate: November 4, 1965

The Stephenses are invited to a cocktail party for Mr. Barlow, who makes Mother Jenny's Jam. Samantha has nothing to wear, so the visiting Aunt Clara earns herself an invitation by zapping up a new dress for her, and a suit for Darrin. When there's nowhere to park, Aunt Clara moves a fire hydrant. While Samantha chats with Barlow, her dress sleeves disappear, forcing her to conjure up a completely different dress. Darrin and Aunt Clara offer to drive the confused Barlow to his hotel, but the fire hydrant is back, and Darrin ends up in his underclothes as a police officer tries to ticket him. The cop chases Darrin and Barlow around the car, and Aunt Clara has everyone exchanging outfits before Darrin is finally taken to jail.

Aunt Clara drives Darrin's car home by witchcraft, then peeks at the incarcerated Darrin through a crystal ball, popping him into a series of period costumes in her attempt to dress him, which unnerves his drunken cellmate. Samantha finally arrives with proper clothes and subdues the drunk by floating him into his bunk. The next day in court, the officer insists that the fully-clothed Darrin was arrested in his underwear, and calls the now-sober drunk as a witness. However, when the man relays all the witchy happenings, the judge dismisses the case. The Stephenses are relieved when Larry chooses not to handle the Mother Jenny account after hearing Barlow's strange story about Darrin.

GOOD!

Aunt Clara's moving fire hydrant moves very well, and the clothing transfers that happen as Darrin, Barlow, and the officer run around the car are seamless. Aunt Clara "driving" Darrin's car from the back seat is also a feat (though sped up a hair too much), and the effect of Samantha floating the drunk to his bunk also soars, even with the visible black wires.

Leave it to a witch to tell the truth and not resort to subterfuge like a mortal: Larry and the Stephenses keep quiet about the questionable taste of Barlow's jam, but Aunt Clara offers, "Well, I like the jar, and I think the label is very attractive. But when you open it, it's a matter of taste, isn't it? And it doesn't have any!" An ordinary enough observation, but out of Marion Lorne's mouth, it's a taste sensation.

Dick Wilson as Montague, the drunk, is the latest guest star in recent memory to steal the show from the regulars. The episode's overall plot and slapstick elements are a little silly, but Montague livens them up with his slurring, which ranges from criticism to disbelief in reaction to the magic around him. Sober, he's just as funny, recounting what he saw in his cell with pure earnestness, and even a bit of wonder. And you thought Dick Wilson just squeezed the Charmin. (He appeared as Mr. Whipple in the famous toilet paper commercials from 1964 to 1985, with a reprise in 1999.)

WELL?

When Darrin comes home and sees Aunt Clara, he grumbles to Samantha, "What's she doing here?" He was so friendly in "Alias Darrin Stephens" (#37), and surely if he were still mad at her for turning him into a chimp in that episode, she more than made up for it curing Samantha in "Take Two Aspirins And Half Pint of Porpoise Milk" (#42).

Louise is apparently at the cocktail party off-screen – if she and Larry are at McMann & Tate, where's their son? Their governess spends more time with the infant than his parents do. As Samantha listens to Barlow's droning, her Aunt Clara original has a thick border on its collar; the first sleeve disappears, and Samantha looks around in a solo shot. But when the scene cuts back to her and Barlow, the collar is missing, and it remains missing. Then Samantha replaces her green dress with a red dress – of a different style. Not that it's obvious in a black-and-white episode, but when Darrin comments on it, all Samantha offers is a weak, "Oh, well, why not," though having a different dress doesn't serve the story aside from Barlow questioning the dress' different look; Larry acts as if nothing has changed.

After the chase around Darrin's car, Barlow tells the cop that he doesn't know Darrin or Aunt Clara. Yet, in the next breath, he refers to Darrin by name and says they're not Mother Jenny's Jam people. It's amazing the police officer doesn't take Barlow in for lying to an officer. Speaking of jail, Darrin must be developing quite the rap sheet – he was arrested twice, just two episodes ago. Later that night, when Samantha pops out to bring Darrin some clothes, she is empty-handed. But as she materializes in the cell, garments are draped over her arm. Did she make a pit stop in Darrin's closet before continuing on to the jail?

Larry rejects Barlow's account, calling him a "nut" and a "king-size bore," preferring "nice, ordinary human beings" like the Stephenses. While it might be compassionate of Larry to choose Darrin over a client, a significant plot point gets dropped: Samantha, Darrin, and Larry all choke down Barlow's vegetable punch, with Samantha asking if McMann & Tate is really going to inflict the goo on "an unsuspecting public." Wouldn't that have been a better – or at least additional – reason for Larry to cut Barlow loose? Yet that aspect is never mentioned again.

OH, MY STARS!

The "blue gentleman," as Aunt Clara calls him, attempts to convince the judge that the now-dressed Darrin was arrested in his underwear, calling Montague as his witness. When the judge pooh-poohs Montague's stories about suits of armor and women appearing out of nowhere, he asks the officer if there are any other witnesses. The cop says no. Really? What about Barlow? The other people in the station when Darrin was booked? The officer that comes to Darrin and Montague's cell and listens to Montague's wild stories? Having no other witnesses makes for a simpler ending, but Barlow's presence alone upends it.

SON OF A GUN!

"Take your hands off me or put some clothes on. One or the other!" – Montague to Darrin, who tries to help the fallen drunk off the floor.

AND THEN I WROTE
Airdate: November 11, 1965

Dr. Passmore, a rest home psychiatrist, wants Darrin to publicize the facility's Civil War centennial pageant. Samantha volunteers Darrin's services, but he turns the tables by tasking Samantha with writing the script. Endora concurs with Darrin's contention that Samantha's characters are too one-dimensional, suggesting bringing them to life to inform her writing. Samantha materializes a Confederate captain who refuses to shave his beard, a Native American who won't say "ugh," and a Northern girl to serve as the captain's love interest. Gladys sees them through the window, but when she comes by under the ruse of borrowing sugar, they're gone – until Samantha goes to the kitchen. The characters tell Gladys they're out of Samantha's mind, then reappear in front of Darrin. Samantha says she can control them, but they start popping in at random with ideas for the play.

Abner sends Gladys to see Dr. Passmore, who doesn't believe she saw the characters. Later, when Darrin delivers his posters to Passmore, the fictional trio materializes before him, prompting the doc to pop his own pills. At home, Samantha's creations report that they keep appearing because they need a plot: they act out an elaborate finale for Samantha, take their bows, and vanish for good. After the pageant, Gladys arrives with congratulations, but, with Samantha considering a vaudeville act, two song-and-dance men pop in, sending Gladys screaming into the night.

GOOD!

Elizabeth Montgomery briefly stumbles over a line when Samantha tells Endora, "He thinks I should flesh them out more, " yet she recovers instantly and keeps right on going.

After forty-five episodes of Gladys reporting strange events across the street, it's about time Abner sends her to a psychiatrist: not only is it a logical next step, but it puts a fresh spin on what was becoming a somewhat worn device. Dr. Passmore tells Gladys the characters are all in her mind; when asked if she believes him, she replies, "No – yes!" Then, of course, the good doctor sees the characters himself. Too bad Gladys doesn't know about that – she could have had an ally.

WELL?

When Darrin initially balks at publicizing the Civil War commemoration, he claims his historical knowledge is "slightly less than limited," but it's not like Darrin needs to be a history buff to tell people about a play. Darrin's full plate is enough of a reason for him to say no; it's merely a set-up for Samantha to hint about her age by saying her recollection of the War Between the States is perfect.

Dr. Passmore introduces himself as the chief psychiatrist of Meadowbrook Rest Home. He would have his hands full treating his live-in residents, yet he brings Gladys in for a session. Does he see private clients on the side – at the rest home? He concludes by writing Mrs. Kravitz a prescription; what about the liquid "medicine" she's always taking – was drug interaction not a concern in 1965? And when Passmore literally gets a taste of his own medicine, he eats the pills instead of washing them down with water. Are chewable tranquilizers the next step in psychiatric treatment?

Gladys reiterates Dr. Passmore's advice to the Stephenses: "Get a hobby – join things. It's all in the mind! I'm gonna be all right!" It's very comical, but it's not like these suggestions have helped her in the past. In "Abner Kadabra" (#29), Abner decried Gladys' former obsessions with yoga and karate. As for joining things, Gladys was part of a Welcome Wagon committee in "Mother Meets What's-His-Name" (#4) and "It's Magic" (#16), and, in "Red Light, Green Light" (#23), she participated in the neighborhood effort to get a traffic light installed. Gladys must not have mentioned these events during her session, or Passmore would have offered a different suggestion.

Has Darrin not figured out by now that kissing his wife solves an awful lot of magical problems? Here, a smooch makes characters disappear – but, in "Little Pitchers Have Big Fears" (#6), Darrin necked with Samantha to keep her from giving young baseballer Marshall a twitchy assist, and it's what made Darrin realize she wasn't responsible for their "electronic yo-yo" garage door in "Open the Door, Witchcraft"

(#28). Maybe Darrin needs to Krazy Glue his lips to Samantha's if he wants to lead that normal mortal life he's always talking about.

OH, MY STARS!

Once again, can Darrin do promotion for someone who isn't a client of McMann & Tate? Darrin has moonlighted thusly before [in "Red Light, Green Light" (#23) and "Remember the Main" (#34)]; now he unofficially plugs Dr. Passmore's event. You'd think Larry would demand that Darrin devote his full attention to the agency's expansive roster of clients.

The Stephenses' really ought to invest in a nice, thick curtain for that living room window. After over a year of marriage, they know that witchcraft is a constant fixture in their house – and that Gladys spies on them. Of course, this is one of the show's shticks, but it's like Darrin and Samantha are inviting her to watch. By the way, why does Gladys wear the same dress the day after seeing Samantha's fictional characters?

SON OF A GUN!

"I'd love to go, ma'am. You're not a bad writer, but you're no Lillian Hellman." – Captain Corcoran to Samantha, wanting a resolution to her story.

Samantha interacting with her fictional characters is brilliant, in conception and execution. Informed that the South lost the Civil War, Captain Corcoran tells Samantha, "Don't dampen my spirits, ma'am – I don't know that yet." The Indian speaks in conversational English, rather than Hollywood Injun-speak, asking Darrin, "What's the matter, you don't like minority groups?" Violet gets less focus, but carries the finale of Samantha's play. And, with the three of them constantly telling Samantha what to write, it's almost a shame when she finishes her script.

JUNIOR EXECUTIVE
EPISODE 46
Airdate: November 18, 1965

As Samantha watches Darrin sleep, she remarks he must have been a cute little boy, so Endora turns him into one and makes sure he wakes up to witness his transformation. After Darrin's reaction is to call Endora "an old witch with a warped sense of humor," she makes Darrin young again in front of Larry and their client, Harding, who manufactures model ships. Darrin-as-boy has to bum a dime off a cheek-pinching matron so he can call Samantha; remembering Endora's counterspell, Samantha restores Darrin, but when Harding wants the boy to sit in on a meeting, Darrin reluctantly agrees to become his younger self to attend it.

On his way into McMann & Tate, Darrin-as-boy is accosted by two other boys who play keep-away with Darrin's model ship; when the kids scorn the toy, Young Darrin hangs out with them in a park until they reveal the boats are boring because they can't be played with. Darrin has Samantha mature him so he can tell Harding, but the client wants to hear from the boy, and becomes frustrated because Darrin and the boy are never in the room at the same time. Backed into a corner, Young Darrin "kills the kid" by acting like a brat, then puts his grown-up foot down with Harding, winning him the account. Samantha feels the park boys should be rewarded, so she zaps up kites for them, and Darrin can't help admitting he enjoyed being a kid again.

GOOD!

Darrin-as-boy gets some of the best lines of the episode, with gems like "Sam, nobody likes a smart aleck witch" and "I'll be through in a minute!" when the old woman overhears him in the phone booth talking about his mother-in-law problem. Kids saying grown-up things has always been funny, and it certainly is here.

She purposely muffles it, but Endora gets Darrin's name right as she asks Samantha to convey her apology for de-aging him.

WELL?

The show's regulars exhibit some irregular behavior here: Samantha is amused that Darrin called her mother "an old witch," Darrin initially thinks Samantha turned him into a little boy, and Endora apologizes for transforming him, even after telling Samantha in "Trick or Treat" (#43) that she would say she was sorry "once and only once."

It seems strange for the elderly lady at the phone booth to pinch Darrin-as-boy's cheek; he's ten, not five. And Larry wants Darrin to bring "the boy" in to meet Harding, saying of the client, "You know how unreasonable he can be." Darrin couldn't know that; he just met Harding a few hours before.

Darrin gets a handle on the problems with the model boat because of the two kids he runs into. These boys should be in school, not in downtown Manhattan at 9:00 in the morning on a weekday, where it's not likely there would be an adjacent park – especially one that's identical to the park near Morning Glory Circle.

Samantha looks around carefully in the park so no one will see her change Darrin back into an adult, but the boys have a clear shot of the Stephenses from their vantage point on the jungle gym, and they never say anything about it. As for the park's passers-by, they jump ahead several feet when Samantha restores her husband, and don't start walking until the kites Samantha zaps up appear. Granted, it's hard to make witchcraft effects work with a crowd of extras.

Darrin lights a cigarette after Harding demands to see the boy; though it's still in Darrin-as-boy's hand when Samantha reduces him, it's gone by the time he returns to Harding. Was something cut? Because the scene as it stands offers no point to the cigarette's presence.

With so much time to kill in Darrin's office while on call to change Darrin back and forth, Samantha must take the opportunity to give herself a makeover; her hair is completely different when she and Adult Darrin meet Larry in the outer office. And where does the offending water pistol come from? Darrin must have Samantha zap it up, since it's his idea to "kill the kid;" he sure doesn't have a problem with her using her powers now, does he?

OH, MY STARS!

Darrin's younger self has something in common with Larry Tate's infant son – neither of them have names. Young Darrin is only ever referred to as "the boy" or "sonny" – why don't the Stephenses invent a name for the wunderkind?

Samantha tells Endora that she's never seen pictures of Darrin as a little boy, but that can't be: Darrin keeps albums, as evidenced by Samantha showing honeymoon photos and a snap of Darrin in the Army to Maurice in "Just One Happy Family" (#10). Is there not a single picture of Darrin's childhood in there?

After Endora regresses Darrin the second time, Samantha reassures him she'll "try and remember how Mother did it," then changes him back. This matches the "any witch can undo another witches' spell as long as they know the words" precedent established in "Alias Darrin Stephens" (#37) – however, in both "The Joker Is A Card" (#41) and "Trick or Treat" (#43), the protocol was that a spell can only be reversed by the one who cast it. Seems the show hasn't decided which rule to stick with yet.

The big conflict at the end comes when Harding wants to see both Darrin and the boy; apparently, this isn't an option, so Darrin makes the kid a brat to discourage Harding. But Samantha could easily turn herself into the boy to satisfy Darrin's client – a feat witches are capable of, because Endora turned herself into Samantha in "Which Witch Is Witch?" (#24). Question: how did Darrin feel biting Larry and kicking Harding in the shin?

SON OF A GUN!

"Oh, Samantha, you'd better start praying for a girl." – Endora, getting a first look at Darrin-as-boy.

Billy Mumy made an impression as troublemaking orphan Michael in "A Vision of Sugar Plums" (#15), but he owns this episode with his incredibly mature portrayal of a grown ad exec stuck in a boy's body. Mumy's grown up a lot in the year since Michael's visit.

AUNT CLARA'S OLD FLAME
Airdate: November 25, 1965

Aunt Clara hides out at Samantha's because she wants to keep her one-time beau, Hedley Partridge, from discovering that her powers have dwindled; Endora, who thinks Clara needs looking after, tells Hedley where to find her. After letting himself in, Hedley opens the door to Gladys and thinks she's Samantha, so he makes flowers dance in front of the astonished woman, who runs home to look up "wizard" in the dictionary. Later, Darrin bonds with Hedley, then looks on while Clara and Hedley get reacquainted.

Aunt Clara lights Hedley's cigar magically, not realizing Samantha twitched up the flame; assuming her powers have returned, Clara wants Hedley to join her serenading lovers as nightingales, but, when she casts a spell on her own, she turns Hedley into a baby elephant and makes the bottom half of herself disappear. Darrin explains to the arriving Kravitzes that the elephant is a model for a swimsuit campaign, and, after Samantha restores Aunt Clara and Hedley, Aunt Clara tries to walk through a wall in front of the Kravitzes, which the Stephenses attribute to nearsightedness. Hedley confesses his magic was done manually; Abner confirms it by examining his rigged flowers. Hedley and Clara revel in their common ground, and later, Endora plays violin for the reunited couple amid the scent of orange blossoms. Having to leave town for his magic supply job, Hedley gives Clara a doorknob as an engagement present.

GOOD!

After Gladys tells Abner that Clara tried and failed to walk through a wall, Abner jokes, "Well, there's no point in banging your head against a brick wall." Gladys responds, "I'm starting to realize that, Abner." Wouldn't it be a great conflict if a real rift developed in the Kravitzes' marriage over her continuing sightings?

The warmth between Darrin and Hedley is an unexpected pleasure. Hedley doesn't believe Endora's stories about Darrin, and Darrin is so fascinated watching Hedley with Aunt Clara that he repeatedly has to be dragged out of the room. It's rare – and refreshing – to see Darrin liking a non-mortal off the bat.

Abner finally sees something strange in the Stephens house! He heard Samantha talking about her nose in "Open the Door, Witchcraft" (#28), but an elephant in the living room is a little harder to deny; Abner may have reason to finally start taking his wife's claims seriously. And, the Kravitzes finally meet Aunt Clara – it isn't obvious that they're strangers until they're introduced, but having them know each other now weaves the canvas a little tighter together.

WELL?

So, Aunt Clara does steal doorknobs. In "The Witches Are Out" (#7), Mr. Brinkman found himself relieved of 105 of the objects; here, Endora confirms that Aunt Clara pilfered one from Buckingham Palace. It can't be kleptomania, because Aunt Clara is aware of what she's doing – do none of the other witches have a problem with Clara stealing? She also says she can't rely on her doorknobs anymore, though they do rely on visible strings.

Are Clara and Endora sisters? Endora's annoyance with the bumbling witch is coupled with a genuine concern for her well-being; since Clara is Samantha's aunt, she has to either be Endora's sibling, or Maurice's, but the exact family connection isn't addressed.

When Aunt Clara admits her spells aren't what they used to be, Samantha replies, "That's hard to believe." Samantha already knows that what Aunt Clara says is true; surely she could agree compassionately instead of pretending this is news. On the flip side, Samantha asks Darrin to let her know when Aunt Clara needs magical assistance, and Darrin seems perfectly okay with his wife doing so much witchcraft. In a way, it's cool he's being so understanding; in another, it seems at odds with Darrin's opposition to magic. Samantha must give Hedley's lighter quite a jolt – it's still moving after it lands on the coffee table.

How does Hedley think Gladys is Samantha? If he's heard about Darrin from Endora, he's heard about Samantha, too, and should immediately realize Gladys looks nothing like her. And Gladys is doing lot of screaming lately; she shrieked over Samantha's square green spots in "Take Two Aspirins And Half Pint of Porpoise Milk" (#42), and does so here, too. It's making Gladys more caricature than character. Besides, Gladys should now be convinced there's witchcraft afoot: in "My Grandson, the Warlock" (#40), she heard Maurice say he expected Samantha's child to be a "warlock in the classic tradition;" she's too easily assuaged by explanations of rigged flowers and nearsightedness here.

Home security must have been more lax in the '60s – Gladys walks into the Stephens house uninvited, and Hedley climbs through the kitchen window to let himself in. Hedley explains to the Kravitzes that he was only able to make the flowers dance because of the wires connected to them. But Hedley merely waved at the flowers – and his hand wasn't positioned above them. Later, Hedley states that he hasn't performed real witchcraft in years. Then how did he materialize his cigar?

OH, MY STARS!

Have the Kravitzes participated in *Extreme Makeover: Home Edition*, the 2003-2012 ABC reality show? The front of their house looks nowhere close to what was shown in "Abner Kadabra" (#29).

Thinking she's levitated the lighter for Hedley, Aunt Clara blurts out, "I made a comeback!" Isn't Aunt Clara's whole rationale for taking refuge in Samantha's house the fact that she doesn't want Hedley to know her powers have waned? Celebrating a comeback is admitting something had to come back. And, once again, Samantha is able to undo a faulty spell of Aunt Clara's as long as she's privy to the original words. So the scale is tipping back toward the rule that was established in "Alias Darrin Stephens" (#37), and away from the implication that a witch can only undo their own spells, as set forth in "The Joker Is

A Card" (#41). Here's something else to consider: if the original spell is so important, why can they be uncast with completely different words?

SON OF A GUN!

"I'll just bet you did." – Samantha, as Aunt Clara recounts that she's had her moments in terms of beaus.

Endora is a witch of many moods: mischievous, vengeful, disagreeable, confident. Now she can add "sweet" to that list. Even though it initially seems she only wants Hedley to take Clara off her hands, the moment where Endora magically plays the violin for the couple is so lovely, one can almost smell her orange blossoms in the air.

EPISODE 48

A STRANGE LITTLE VISITOR
Airdate: December 2, 1965

Samantha's friends, Wally and Margaret, need to attend a witches' conclave, and ask Samantha to watch their son, Merle. As Samantha explains that Darrin is mortal, Merle's parents instruct the young warlock to pass for one. Meanwhile, Larry buys an expensive necklace for Louise's birthday; Darrin agrees to hide it, but a crook overhears and cases Darrin's house. Gladys questions Merle after she catches him practicing magic in the front yard, where Darrin unwittingly plays a game of witchcraft-assisted catch. Merle's bespelled baseball breaks the Kravitzes' window, which Merle fixes before Gladys can show it to Abner. After Merle rankles Darrin by declining Samantha's meatloaf, he works on his spells; not knowing Merle turned a hairbrush into a fire engine, Darrin tries to take the toy away, but Merle charges it with electricity, forcing Samantha to admit their guest is a warlock.

The robber returns for the necklace, but his bungling wakes Darrin. Merle comes upon Darrin tied to a chair and gets trussed up himself because he promised Samantha not to do any more witchcraft. Darrin goads the thief into taking Merle's fire engine, but Merle stops him by making the truck squirt water on him. The toy's siren alerts the police, who take the robber away; Gladys is startled when Merle laughs that a hairbrush foiled the crook. The next day, Darrin tells Merle's parents that their son behaved, and Gladys insinuates herself into the conversation, unaware that Merle and his family are disappearing behind her.

GOOD!

Sugar seems to have become Gladys' spying tool. She used it in "And Then I Wrote" (#45) to have a peek at Samantha's Civil War characters, and here she grabs her cup to check out Merle and his parents. "I came over for a snoop of – uh, a scoop of sugar!" Best of all, Samantha quickly catches on to the ruse. Merle does some convincing magic: the effects of him turning a stick into a bird and his cake changing into spinach mid-bite look effortless, plus it really does seem his baseball is hovering in mid-air. Wires can't be easy to rig outdoors; the show knocked this one out of the park.

Merle practicing witchcraft, materializing a doll and a flimsy airplane while going for a fire truck, provides a neat bit of perspective on what it's like to grow up a warlock. And his laughing at Darrin's space travel book truly is funny when you remember that, in 1965, there hadn't yet been any moon missions or space shuttles.

Samantha's been pregnant all season, but because most of the episodes have focused on other aspects of the Stephenses' lives, it's been easy to forget that they'll soon be parents. However, Merle revealing himself as a warlock gives a neat preview of what Samantha and Darrin will be like as mother and father: Darrin's gentle-but-firm approach provides stability, while Samantha outwitching Merle at the dinner table lets us know she'll be able to handle things if baby Stephens turns out to have powers.

Bumbling cat burglars aren't new in movies and television, but the neuroses Tim Herbert adds to this one offers a fresh spin. Stopping to read *Psychology of the Criminal Mind* is a master stroke – as is Darrin using reverse psychology to get Merle to magically subdue the crook with his fire truck.

WELL?

Looks like the Stephenses got rid of that pesky garage door opener that was the source of contention in "Open the Door, Witchcraft" (#28); the manual override button that was on the outside of the garage is gone, and the Stephenses always park in the driveway, anyway.

Maybe Merle's powers being underdeveloped is why wires are visible on the cake plate he floats out of the kitchen. Then, when Samantha predicts Gladys is at the door, Merle says he hasn't gotten the hang of seeing through walls. Now witches have X-ray vision?

Merle's great, but the show just did a "precocious boy" story two episodes ago with a 10-year-old Darrin in "Junior Executive" (#46). Merle's a Brocken, and Hedley spoke of Serenda Ethrington in "Aunt Clara's Old Flame" (#47), but, in "Mother Meets What's-His-Name" (#4), Endora claimed that her last name – Samantha's maiden name – is too difficult for mortals to pronounce. Will that name ever be revealed?

Samantha sends Merle outside to play in the front yard when she has a perfectly good backyard, and when she knows Gladys is snooping around. It's odd for Gladys to ask Merle if he's noticed anything strange about the Stephenses right after watching him conjure up a bird and shoot water out of his ears.

Samantha sleeps like a log: neither the robber, Darrin, nor their full-volume conversation wake her up; even the loud siren doesn't bring her around until the end of the scene. Where did the thief get all that rope? He didn't come in with it. And why does Merle come downstairs with the fire engine? As it hadn't been decided if Merle could keep it, he shouldn't have it in his possession. Was he really going to plead his case to Darrin in the middle of the night?

The officer who arrested the scantily-clad Darrin in "The Very Informal Dress" (#44) doesn't recognize him here, despite being in court with him a few weeks earlier. The cop was on the beat in Manhattan then; now he's somehow dispatched to Morning Glory Circle, which is out of the city.

OH, MY STARS!

Merle's parents recruit Samantha as sitter because they have to "attend an important conclave in London." Didn't Endora, Aunt Clara, and Bertha just attend a convention there in "Aunt Clara's Old Flame" (#47)? Was it the same conclave? And Aunt Clara went to a whole different Miami convention in "There's No Witch Like An Old Witch" (#27). Witches are certainly an organized lot.

SON OF A GUN!

"Hey, she's pretty weird – even for a mortal!" – Merle to Samantha, offering an out-of-the-mouths-of-babes reaction to meeting Mrs. Kravitz.

"I'm an engineer, Captain, not a warlock!" Well, he's exactly that in this episode – *Star Trek*'s James Doohan appears as Merle's father, a year before he boarded the *Enterprise* on the 1966-1969 NBC series. Considering it's hard to think of him playing anyone but Scotty, it's sort of a thrill to see him in a different role.

MY BOSS, THE TEDDY BEAR

Airdate: December 9, 1965

Endora wants Samantha to attend her cousin Miranda's wedding, but when Darrin says Larry won't give him the time off, Endora half-jokingly suggests turning Larry into an inanimate object. After Larry graciously agrees to clear Darrin's schedule, Endora repays the kindness by producing the sold-out teddy bear Larry wants for his son and dropping it by the office. Darrin sees the bear, which nods its head; after hearing Endora was there, Darrin thinks the toy is Larry. New client Harper and his pretty model are stunned when Darrin becomes overprotective of "Larry." Later, Louise discovers the bear and assumes Larry bought it; since she found her own bear, she returns Endora's to the toy store. Darrin and Samantha follow, but can't tell which bear is Larry, so they buy all of them.

At home, Samantha sees that one bear doesn't have a tag and realizes it's Endora's; when Endora arrives, Darrin goes off on her to the point she destroys the bear. Darrin thinks Endora has killed Larry, and he's about to tell Louise when Larry walks in, having been stuck in out-of-office meetings all day. Darrin wonders how he's going to explain his fixation with teddy bears until he realizes they'd be the perfect symbol for the Harper's Honey account. Samantha provides a magical assist by returning the departing Harper to his hotel, which Darrin excuses with a "just this once."

GOOD!

Darrin has struggled with the fallout of witchy happenings before, but when he thinks Larry is the teddy bear, he becomes comically unglued, stopping the client from holding "Larry" upside down, covering the bear's ears when Larry's ideas are criticized, and running after the model when she takes the bear into the ladies' room. Darrin's antics become just this side of overdone as the episode goes on, but they're still a honey.

What a display of contrasts: Darrin blows up at Endora like he never has before; then, after Larry turns up alive and well, Darrin tells Samantha, "Eat, drink and be merry, for tomorrow, I apologize to your mother." Too bad there's no apology scene, but there are only so many minutes in an episode; at least the intent is there.

WELL?

Cousin Miranda's wedding is the catalyst for the shenanigans in this episode. The same was true in "Your Witch Is Showing" (#20), when Endora wanted Darrin to take time off to attend Cousin Mario's wedding. Why revisit the device? And how many cousins does Samantha have, anyway? Endora thinks that by turning Larry into an inanimate object, he'll never know Darrin's been away. She doesn't really think that through: Larry would realize he'd lost two days, and Louise would be worried sick with him missing that long – to say nothing of the chaos Larry's absence would cause around the office. Another thing: won't Larry remember being a teddy bear? Darrin retained his memory when he was a chimp in "Alias Darrin Stephens" (#37).

When Darrin panics, thinking his boss is a stuffed animal, Samantha frets that she has no way of locating Endora, who is getting a wardrobe for the wedding. Yet Endora has no problem tracking Larry down to the toy shop, despite having no prior knowledge of his being there. Is Samantha just getting lazy in her witchcraft, or does Endora know a few extra tricks? Also, while Darrin turns down Endora's invitation because of his workload, Larry has no problem giving Darrin the time off. If things are that busy, Larry shouldn't be able to do without Darrin for two whole days.

No-Name Tate rides again: despite all the talk about getting a teddy bear for the child, he still has no unique means of identification. No one seems to know how old he is, either – in "A Very Special Delivery" (#38), Larry said Louise had just given birth, but now apparently her son is old enough that he's already loved a teddy bear to death and can understand his father's promise of a new one. Hopefully he's also old enough to care for himself; the Tates again run around town with no mention of anyone sitting for him.

After the extended sequence with Darrin playing mama bear to the teddy bear, Louise drops by and takes it with her to the toy store – then, the scene cuts to Darrin searching the store's shelves. Somehow, not seeing Darrin's reaction to finding out Louise took her "husband" in for a refund feels like a missed beat. Later, after "Larry" is reduced to a pile of fluff thanks to Endora, Samantha proclaims, "I can't believe Mother would do something like that!" What's not to believe? Her other parent, Maurice, similarly did away with Darrin in "Just One Happy Family" (#10) – and he didn't leave anything behind, like Endora does.

Darrin saves his hide by turning his obsession with teddy bears into a slogan for the convenient Harper's Honey account. It works so well, it can be overlooked – harder to let slide, however, is Samantha zapping Harper back to his hotel so Darrin can have a chance to talk to him; how does this even work logistically? Harper disappears from the cab, reappears in front of the hotel, and heads straight to the employee who is talking to Darrin on the phone – and Harper takes the call as if all that were perfectly normal. Harper is played by Jack Collins, who just appeared as Rogers in "Trick or Treat" (#43), six episodes ago. It's a little too soon to buy him as a different client, even in real time.

OH, MY STARS!

Not to run the "can a witch undo another witch's spell or not" question into the ground, but this episode chooses neither answer, opting for somewhere in between. Darrin expressly asks Samantha if she's sure Endora is the only one who can reverse her spell. Samantha concurs – then backtracks and says she could attempt it, adding, "not knowing the spell, there's no telling what would happen." It's like the show can't decide which spell-breaker idea is the best one; in "Aunt Clara's Old Flame" (#47), Samantha was able to undo Aunt Clara's spell, but here, she can't undo Endora's.

SON OF A GUN!

"He's the only one that doesn't have 'made in Japan' on his...here." – Samantha to Darrin, picking "Larry" out of the teddy bear crowd.

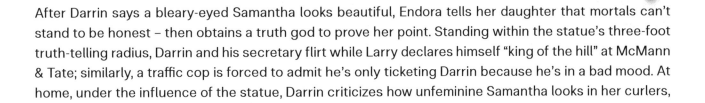

SPEAK THE TRUTH
Airdate: December 16, 1965

EPISODE 50

After Darrin says a bleary-eyed Samantha looks beautiful, Endora tells her daughter that mortals can't stand to be honest – then obtains a truth god to prove her point. Standing within the statue's three-foot truth-telling radius, Darrin and his secretary flirt while Larry declares himself "king of the hill" at McMann & Tate; similarly, a traffic cop is forced to admit he's only ticketing Darrin because he's in a bad mood. At home, under the influence of the statue, Darrin criticizes how unfeminine Samantha looks in her curlers, only to backpedal once out of range, while Endora guilts Samantha into inviting her to dinner with the Tates – and Mr. Hotchkiss, the agency's latest client.

Hotchkiss turns out to be a self-aggrandizing bore whose long-suffering wife sits in silence. When Hotchkiss invents a ridiculous slogan for his dishwasher, Larry and Darrin pretend to love it until the truth god makes them laugh at it. Endora moves the statue around to extract harsh confessions from the mortals, especially Louise and Mrs. Hotchkiss; pretty soon, Darrin, the Tates, and the Hotchkisses are battling it out. The next day, Endora takes responsibility for the statue, and Samantha uses it to make the angry Larry hand Darrin control of the account, plus admit that the Hotchkisses cleared things up without his help. After Darrin purposely has the statue reveal his adverse feelings toward Endora, she dumps a bowl of cereal on his head.

GOOD!

Samantha's Endora is showing – she thrusts the truth god at Larry so he'll admit he didn't salvage the Hotchkiss account himself, and she takes a bit of impish glee in utilizing the statue to lock down a raise for Darrin, even shaking Darrin's hand after accomplishing it. Even though it's hard to fathom Darrin going along with this, Larry has it coming after blaming him for the dinner fiasco and essentially threatening to fire him.

WELL?

There's suddenly a mirror in the Stephenses' foyer instead of the usual candelabra. It's not really integral to the story, even if the effect of Endora popping into it while Samantha peers at her own reflection is well done.

Endora procures a truth god from Hagatha, who is glad she has one in stock at her shop. How can a witch *not* have something in stock? The same question arose in "Take Two Aspirins and Half A Pint of Porpoise Milk" (#42), when the warlock clerk was "fresh out" of ostrich feathers. In both cases, why are stores necessary for witches, who can materialize objects at will? Hagatha tells Endora that the statue can be exchanged if Darrin doesn't like it, but it should be obvious from Endora "signing" Uncle Herbert's name to the card that this is not a gift.

That statue really exposes Darrin's wandering eye: he leers at Miss Thatcher under its influence, then admits these lustful thoughts to Samantha and Endora. Not that he needed a truth god to reveal his past interest in Liza, Miss Jasmine, Pleasure and Danger O'Riley...

If Larry's handling the Hotchkiss account, then the Tates should host Hotchkiss and his wife – at least then, someone would be with No-Name Tate, since the show seems to have forgotten that Louise and Larry now have a baby.

Why is Darrin driving around with the statue laying in the seat, next to its empty box? Ah, yes, because it has to be there to pull the truth out of the cop. Likewise hexed by the statue, Darrin greets Endora with a "Hi, Mom." He doesn't have the warmest feelings toward his mother-in-law, and he's being forced to tell the truth, so why the affectionate welcome? Besides, Endora told Darrin that she'd try to remember his name as long as he *didn't* call her "Mom" [see "The Joker Is A Card" (#41)].

When Hotchkiss wants Samantha to take a stab at a slogan for his dishwasher, she replies, "I'm afraid I'm not very good at that sort of thing." Yet Samantha devised slogans for Caldwell Soup that were better than Darrin's in "Help, Help, Don't Save Me" (#5), and had no trouble doing up ads for rivaling restaurants in "Eat At Mario's" (#35).

After admitting she inflicted the truth god on Darrin, Endora pops in and asks, "Where's the statue?" She has enough powers of ESP to know that Larry is coming up the walk – but she can't sense a statue that's in the same room? Speaking of powers, Darrin's bowl of cereal comes with visible wires that help Endora empty it on his head.

OH, MY STARS!

It's meant to enhance the magic, but the animated cartoon sparkle superimposed over the statue whenever a mortal comes near it detracts from the magic instead. The sound effect is enough, though it gets overused. It also seems unnecessary to have Endora zap the statue back and forth constantly, a conceptual problem that could be solved simply by extending the range of the truth god's influence. And surely one of the mortals would notice a statue disappearing and reappearing in different spots eventually.

SON OF A GUN!

"Why aren't you laughing, Ed? What happened to that sense of humor that carried you through those dark days when you were climbing that ladder?" – Frances Hotchkiss to her husband, liberated by Endora's truth god.

Next time you get pulled over by a cop, hope to get one that's forced to tell the truth under the influence of a magic statue. Listening to an officer admit he's giving you a ticket because he feels lousy and griping about taking guff from his wife and sergeant is a reminder that cops are human beings with problems of their own. Speaking of wives, Mrs. Hotchkiss is a wimpy stranger by comparison, but it's sure enjoyable when she tells her insufferable husband where to get off.

The effect of Endora floating to the ground from the backyard is so fluid that it's hard to believe Agnes Moorehead isn't actually swooping down on her own.

A VISION OF SUGAR PLUMS
Airdate: December 23, 1965

EPISODE
51

Special Note: This episode is a rerun "A Vision of Sugar Plums" (#15), with a new opening:

After Samantha shrinks a Christmas tree and puts it in her purse to make it easier to carry [as seen in "A Vision of Sugar Plums" (#15)], the scene continues with Samantha admitting she got the tree into the house by witchcraft, and Darrin forgiving her. He shows her a Christmas card from Michael, the orphan they hosted the year before; Michael thanks the Stephenses for showing him what Christmas is all about, which causes them to reminisce about the trouble they had with the boy before bringing him to the North Pole to meet Santa Claus.

In and of itself, this is a harmless Christmas episode – but, because of the new footage, and this episode's placement at this point in the series, the show's continuity is affected in the following ways:

GOOD!

It's a great touch bringing Michael back – albeit by Christmas card – because Samantha did have an especially big effect on him: the boy who thought Santa Claus was "bunk" now sends thank-yous for being taught the true meaning of Christmas. That it's revealed he's gotten over his bitterness from the previous year is a nice full circle.

WELL?

Not actually seeing Michael, however, rather lessens the impact of his presence. Granted, Michael's portrayer, Billy Mumy, just played Darrin-as-boy in "Junior Executive" (#46) a month before, so it would have been too soon for him to appear again regardless – still, a visit from Michael would be especially intriguing since he knows Samantha is a witch. Also, a brief mention of Michael's adoptive family, the Johnsons, would have added extra layers. With Bill Daily playing Roger Healey on NBC's *I Dream of Jeannie* at this point, bringing him back as Mr. Johnson would be tough, but a sentence in Michael's card about how wonderful his new parents are would have done the trick.

OH, MY STARS!

The new section featuring Michael's Christmas card is combined with the original opening from "A Vision of Sugar Plums" (#15) to play as a brand-new scene. But it doesn't work, because, when Samantha comes home, she tells Darrin "we're due at the orphanage" – then, moments later, they flash back to having met Michael at the orphanage a year ago. Unless the Stephenses are making a return trip to the orphanage, Samantha's reminder is inaccurate, to say nothing of the fact that her hair grows significantly over the course of the conversation, and that she smiles about waiting a while when Darrin says he misses having a kid in the house. That's a reference to the Stephenses' impending parenthood, but Samantha wasn't pregnant a year ago.

Who's recalling the previous year's events surrounding Michael? It can't be Darrin, because Samantha made him think his North Pole trip was a dream; Darrin wouldn't remember being there, much less having his memory erased. The flashback must be Samantha's, then – but it's not, because she wouldn't be able to recall everything experienced by Tommy and the Kravitzes. The fact that neither Samantha nor Darrin can be having the flashback negates the entire episode.

The reason Samantha is expecting this season is because Elizabeth Montgomery's real-life pregnancy was written into the show. She gave birth to her son, Robert, on October 5, 1965 – so the logical reason for this Christmas rerun was to accommodate Ms. Montgomery's maternity leave, and that's perfectly understandable. That being the case, it probably would have been better to simply run "A Vision of Sugar Plums" (#15) as is, without the continuity-destroying additions. Or, how about doing a Samantha-less episode? Example: the Stephenses get into a fight, and Endora puts an *It's A Wonderful Life* spell on Darrin to show him what life would be like without Samantha, mirroring the 1946 film. In this alternate reality, Darrin could be married to Sheila, completely miserable, and Michael could return, more disillusioned and bitter than ever, not having met Samantha. The two "A Vision of Sugar Plums" episodes are forever and always a part of the series, and *Bewitched* tried, but perhaps some better ways to cover Elizabeth Montgomery's absence could have been explored.

SON OF A GUN!

"Oh, darling, it's Christmas. No time to squabble over a little thing like making a tree." – Samantha to Darrin, after he expresses displeasure over her bringing in the festive foliage by witchcraft.

THE MAGIC CABIN
Airdate: December 30, 1965

Darrin is batting zero trying to come up with a slogan for a potato chip account; Larry attributes it to overwork and suggests Darrin take a long weekend at his mountain cabin, not realizing the retreat has fallen into rack and ruin. When rain threatens to strand the Stephenses in the hovel, Samantha zaps up a phone so Darrin can check road conditions, then refurbishes the fireplace, eventually turning the shack into a cozy hideaway. Larry is visited by Charles and Alice MacBain, who have come in response to Larry's long-forgotten ad about the cabin. While the Stephenses are out, the MacBains see Samantha's improvements and call Larry to make a down payment; he's confused because the cabin doesn't have a phone.

Samantha wants to leave the cabin refurbished for the MacBains, but Darrin wants to turn it back – until Alice admits dreaming about such a cabin and relays that Charles' doctor prescribed him fresh air. Larry arrives, forcing Samantha to remove her changes; just then, the MacBains return. Trapped, Samantha fixes it so Larry sees his crumbling cabin on one side while the MacBains see the renovated cabin on the other. Feeling guilty charging so much for his "pile of rubble," Larry deems the MacBains' down payment sufficient. Driving home through another rainstorm, the Stephenses' car runs out of gas; Samantha, who's promised Darrin no more witchcraft, compromises by filling the tank only halfway.

GOOD!
There's something neat about Samantha's "in for a penny, in for a pound" realization as she makes her first couple of magic upgrades to the cabin. Darrin resists, and Samantha replies, "You're right, sweetheart, I shouldn't be doing this way…I should just do it all at once!" If it's possible to be defiant and sweet at the same time, Samantha pulls it off.

Darrin's desperate attempts at potato chip promotion are groaners (and are supposed to be), but they do lead to Larry's comment, "This from the man who gave the world the Caldwell Soup slogan" – a great nod to "Help, Help, Don't Save Me" (#5).

WELL?
What's taking "brilliant advertising man" Darrin [as he described himself in "Junior Executive" (#46)] two weeks to come up with a slogan for potato chips? It's nice of Larry to give him some time off, but Darrin just had two days' respite in "My Boss, The Teddy Bear" (#49); guess Miranda's wedding wasn't all that restful. Maybe Larry's the one who needs rest: he says Darrin is "miserable, sleepy, grumpy – I get enough of that at home." No love for new mother Louise, eh?

Samantha pops outside to collect the goodbye kiss Darrin forgot to give her. But why would she risk appearing on the walkway, when she knows the suspicious Gladys could be watching?

For Larry to run his cabin ad for three years, he'd had to have spent far more than the $1,000 he accepts from the MacBains. About the cabin: its "country" theme plays every time the shack is on-screen – at least the "Daddy-o" reinvention underscoring Samantha's final renovation is a refreshing twist.

Where does the thunderstorm come from? The sky is clear when the Stephenses drive up; minutes later, there are lightning bolts. After the MacBains fall in love with Samantha's improvements to the cabin, Darrin tells her to remove them. How are the Stephenses supposed to explain why the MacBains see a cozy retreat one time and a hovel another?

When Larry sends Darrin to the cabin, he gives him one day off, which creates a three-day weekend – that means the Stephenses drive to the woods on a Friday. But, after the MacBains call Larry with their down payment, it's the next day, a Saturday – during which Larry dictates to Miss Thatcher as if it's a normal business day. Larry realizes there's no phone in his cabin, so he makes a whole trip up to check things out for himself; however, when he meets the MacBains, he never does ask how they made a call from there.

Splitting the cabin down the center so Larry sees the hovel and the MacBains see the coziness is pretty ambitious, but the execution has some flaws. The way the split screen is positioned, the chair and curtain are half junky, half nice. And, for as clever as this concept is, what if Larry and/or the MacBains turn around, or catch the reflection of what's behind them in the mirror? And how can Larry and the MacBains exit without seeing the split?

Darrin doesn't want to chance driving on potentially washed-out roads during the first storm because of Samantha's pregnancy, which is how they get trapped in the cabin. Yet, he has no problem making his way down the mountain during the second storm. Darrin's nice about asking Samantha not to perform witchcraft "under any circumstances," instead of making those words a command like he did in "Open the Door, Witchcraft" (#28) – yet Samantha is antagonistic when the car breaks down. They're not arguing; her attitude doesn't make sense. Nor does it when Samantha asks, "Does that little needle pointing to 'E' mean anything?" Samantha has been behind the wheel since "Driving Is the Only Way to Fly" (#26); surely she knows what a gas gauge is by now.

OH, MY STARS!

After Alice MacBain spends most of her airtime speaking for Charles, her husband finally gets a word in with, "Alice still believes in fairy tales with happy endings." Nothing wrong with that, but it explains Alice's overly syrupy personality, her claim that she saw the redecorated cabin in a dream, and the precious music that accents this admission. The MacBains are nice people, but Alice's idealistic ramblings and Charles' "They sure are, honey" responses are just too cornball to be believed.

SON OF A GUN!

"So I didn't come up with an idea. Is that any reason to send us into penal servitude?" – Darrin to Samantha, not realizing Larry is unaware of the condition of his neglected cabin.

EPISODE 53 — MAID TO ORDER
Airdate: January 6, 1966

With Samantha's due date approaching, Darrin doesn't want her doing heavy housework, but objects when she twitches the vacuum to clean by itself. Samantha reluctantly interviews a severe maid, then a flirty one, but takes a liking to nervous Naomi Hogan, who is up front about her shortcomings. With the Tates as company, Naomi curdles consommé and torches a roast. Samantha rescues the dinner with witchcraft, but lets Naomi believe she saved it herself. When Louise asks Darrin if Naomi can fill in for their absent maid and handle an important dinner party, Samantha confesses she gave Naomi "handy hints."

The Stephenses' invite themselves to the Tate affair so Samantha can monitor Naomi, but Larry turns them away. Darrin feels Larry deserves whatever Naomi serves up; Samantha doesn't, and makes excuses so she can pop outside Louise's kitchen, where Naomi is curdling and torching. Louise panics, but, when her back is turned, Samantha again makes the food edible. Darrin catches Samantha in the act, but ultimately agrees to let Samantha go on maid-sitting. With the Tate dinner a success, Samantha lets Naomi cook an awful breakfast on her own the next morning. As Naomi calculates the value of broken dishes in her head, Samantha asks Darrin if McMann & Tate can hire Naomi in their accounting department, and Samantha happily loses her help.

GOOD!

For a woman whose cooking was just as bad as Naomi's in "Be It Ever So Mortgaged" (#2), Samantha has come a long way in a year and a half. She can now make Parisian consommé, and when Naomi calls Samantha the best homemaker she's ever worked for, the expression on Samantha's face is pure delight. Maybe Samantha hires Naomi because she sees a sort of kindred spirit in her.

There's something satisfying about Darrin figuring out Samantha is helping Naomi and catching his wife red-nosed. It means Darrin has been married to Samantha long enough that he can tell when magic's afoot – and the way he softens after realizing that his beef with Larry shouldn't carry over to Louise is rather magnanimous. Darrin later washes down Naomi's terrible breakfast with a sip of water, grimacing as if the maid botched even that. If that's an improvisation on Dick York's part, it's a brilliant choice.

WELL?

It's funny that Samantha thinks Endora has shut off her vacuum cleaner instead of Darrin, since Endora did incapacitate it in "My Boss, The Teddy Bear" (#49). But why does Samantha magically send the vacuum up to clean near the ceiling, knowing Darrin is coming back with a glass of milk? She then lets the machine come crashing down after Darrin asks her to turn it off. Samantha's unusually petulant act means Darrin has to buy another vacuum, unless Samantha is planning on restoring it.

The Tates reveal that they have a maid, Esmeralda. Is this "gem" a replacement for the governess that was too ill to sit for No-Name Tate in "My Grandson, the Warlock" (#40)? Surely Esmeralda was hired after that episode, or the Stephenses wouldn't have had to drop everything to care for the child. Does Esmeralda stay with No-Name while the Tates go around as if they're not parents?

Mrs. Luftwaffe, the severe potential maid, deserves to be scared off by Samantha's magically messy kitchen. Demanding a color TV in her room – in 1966? That's like asking for a giant plasma screen today. And since when does Samantha keep the photo of Darrin that occupies the bedroom dresser on the television downstairs? She uses it to defuse her buxom interviewee, but what if the glamour girl had liked the Darrin-as-hayseed addition Samantha made to the photo instead of being turned off by it?

Louise makes such a good point: people don't have company on a maid's first night; no wonder Naomi destroys dinner. She also breaks dishes at the Tates, sweeping the shards out their kitchen door. Wouldn't Louise hear the crash and come running? And Louise isn't nearly as tolerant of Naomi's mistakes as Samantha is, but when Naomi "restores" the food (with Samantha's unseen help), Louise calls Naomi "a marvelous cook," buying the sudden changes in the disastrous dinner a little too easily. Finally, Louise hires Naomi to prepare the same meal she enjoyed at the Stephenses. Yet, after Darrin agrees to let Samantha keep helping Naomi, he's surprised that Samantha's going to zap up cherries jubilee. If Naomi's job is to recreate the dinner, shouldn't Darrin know what's for dessert?

OH, MY STARS!

Larry thinks the reason the Stephenses are trying to crash his dinner party is that Darrin wants to switch accounts with Bob Chetley; Larry tells Samantha that Darrin will be made a vice president "when the time is right, not before." However, in "I, Darrin, Take This Witch, Samantha" (#1), Darrin already was a vice president. Because this detail wasn't carried over from the pilot, it now looks like Larry demoted Darrin and plans to keep him in his current, lesser position.

SON OF A GUN!

"Maybe I'd better. In your condition, it might not be safe." – Naomi to Samantha, as they debate who's going to taste Naomi's chunky consommé.

Alice Ghostley's bumbling maid, Naomi, doesn't just have a heart of gold, she is gold. Naomi's self-deprecating asides are as hilarious as her sincerity about her failings is touching. When she chooses to quit her plum gig at the Stephenses because she knows she'll fall in love with their baby once it's born and not want to leave, it's enough to wish she'd stick around for good.

EPISODE 54 — AND THEN THERE WERE THREE
Airdate: January 13, 1966

As Darrin frantically readies to take the in-labor Samantha to the hospital, her lookalike cousin, Serena, calls with congratulations. Endora informs Darrin that Samantha has given birth to a baby girl, and the in-laws share happy tears. Endora wants to name her new granddaughter Tabatha and zaps the moniker onto the baby's bracelet. After the Stephenses discuss whether their child will have powers, Endora fills Samantha's room with flowers, annoying the strict Nurse Kelton. Later, as Serena visits Samantha, Endora tells Darrin she can turn his baby into an adult to prove she'll grow up to look like her mother. Darrin balks, but after Endora sneaks the newborn out of the nursery, Darrin meets Serena and thinks Endora aged his daughter.

Annoyed that Darrin is following her, Serena pops a pacifier into his mouth; Nurse Kelton, who has seen flowers appearing and disappearing, wonders if she's cracking up. Darrin tracks Serena to a toy store, where he nearly punches Dave for ogling his "daughter." Serena finally witches Darrin into an Indian costume, and Endora, outraged that Darrin has accused her of stealing his baby's childhood, sends him to the nursery, where Nurse Kelton tries to convince herself she isn't seeing an Indian. When Darrin finds Samantha and Serena together, Serena ties Darrin up with witchcraft and leaves, but the Stephenses convince Nurse Kelton that Darrin is simply a practical joker. Once Endora returns, Darrin offers to name his child Tabatha as a way of making up for his behavior.

GOOD!

In between visits from Endora, Serena, Darrin, and Nurse Kelton, Samantha reads a book by Dr. Spock. No, that's not a *Star Trek* reference – Dr. Spock was a highly regarded pediatrician, whose book on child rearing was outsold only by the Bible in the '60s; it makes complete sense that Samantha would study motherhood from his experienced, mortal perspective. (Besides, *Star Trek* wouldn't premiere until later in the fall.)

Though Endora shifts a little when she fills the room with flowers, the show does go to the trouble of pulling off the effect a second time when Serena also gifts Samantha with blooms. They could have shot the existing flowers in the same positions with both Endora and Serena, so that they crafted two separate sequences – with all the flowers in different places – is admirable.

Having two alternate versions of Samantha in past episodes must have inspired the creation of cousin Serena: in "Which Witch Is Witch?" (#24), Endora changed herself into a more swinging Sam, and, in "That Was My Wife" (#31), Samantha changed her own look with a dark wig. Serena appears to be an inspired hybrid of the two.

WELL?

Ever since "Be It Ever So Mortgaged" (#2), Samantha has worn a heart-shaped diamond pendant; it has to be assumed the necklace was a gift from Darrin [like the "I love you every second" watch Darrin gave Samantha in "A is for Aardvark" (#17), which has never been seen again]. So why is Samantha's necklace conspicuously absent in this installment? Does the hospital make her take it off? Or is the necklace taken out of play to prevent confusion when Elizabeth Montgomery switches back and forth between Samantha and Serena?

Darrin smokes cigarettes occasionally, but since when does he smoke pipes, much less mindlessly steal someone else's? And he's certainly taken his penchant for blabbing about witchcraft-related situations in front of mortals to a new level: he tells a stranger that he hopes that his baby will be human, and later, thinking Serena is his grown-up daughter, he pleads his case to anyone who will listen.

Twice, Darrin asks Samantha if Tabatha has powers, adding, "Can't you tell anything just by looking at her?" Samantha can't, but in "My Grandson, The Warlock" (#40), Nanny Witch was able to tell Maurice that Larry and Louise's baby was mortal without much more than a look. Speaking of Maurice, where is he during this blessed event? After all the noise he made about wanting his grandchild to be "a warlock in the classic tradition," you'd think he'd be pushing Endora out of the way to see Samantha's baby for himself. Does he lose interest once he finds out Samantha didn't have a boy?

Samantha suggests naming her child "Derek" if it's a boy (this was before ultrasounds, which, among other things, determines the gender of an unborn baby); later, Endora refers to Darrin as Derek. Is that where Samantha got the idea?

Seeing Samantha's face with dark hair shouldn't be a surprise to Darrin: in "That Was My Wife" (#31), Samantha donned a brunette wig for him in a hotel. And longtime friend Dave finally gets something to do besides give Darrin absent-minded "advice," but nearly gets a fist in his face. No wonder Dave thinks Serena's attractive – he did some heavy duty flirting with Samantha in "Red Light, Green Light" (#23); sounds like a man who knows what he wants.

How come no one ever tells Darrin he's spent the day mistaking Samantha's cousin for his daughter? Serena doesn't introduce herself, and Samantha never bothers to explain that she has a lookalike relative.

OH, MY STARS!

When Serena sees Samantha for the first time, she laughs, "Oh, my, you grew up to be a very nice looking girl," referring to their duplicate status. This would indicate that they knew each other as children – so, would the fact that they still resemble each other really be a surprise? Also, Serena is shocked to learn that Samantha married a mortal. How does she know her cousin is having a baby, but not that her cousin-in-law is human?

The Stephenses convince Nurse Kelton she's not going crazy by lying that Darrin is a practical joker. That may explain Darrin's bizarre behavior, and his random appearances dressed as an Indian, but how does that account for Endora and Serena's flowers popping in and out, or that Serena turned the nurse into a frog? Maybe Ms. Kelton is just so happy to have a reason for Darrin's antics that she happily goes into denial about everything else she saw.

SON OF A GUN!

"Sweetheart, if you don't hurry, we may ending up calling the baby 'Freeway,' because that's where it's going to be born!" – Darrin to Samantha, who is more relaxed about getting to the hospital than he is.

Darrin and Endora tolerate each other at best – at worst, they've stepped up their hostility toward each other, particularly this season. That's what makes their bonding over Tabatha's birth so wonderful; Darrin grabs his mother-in-law and hugs her, and the usually unflappable Endora bursts into tears. Whatever their differences, the salient thing they have in common is their love for Samantha, and that's never been as clear as it is in this single scene. Also, knowing that Endora has her heart set on naming the baby Tabatha, Darrin chooses it as compensation for having raged at her, even admitting his daughter "looks like a Tabatha."

Eve Arden ruled television, movies, and Broadway, especially in the '40s and '50s, so you'd think a star of that magnitude would be out of place on a humble supernatural sitcom. But, as Nurse Kelton, she fits right in, adding stability and elegance to this pivotal episode. She's strong enough to go up against Endora (her "Goodnight, Grandma" is priceless), yet bewildered enough to drive the comedy (as evidenced in her fourth-wall-breaking "Not there" when she sees Darrin as an Indian). In other words, she's just what the doctor ordered.

EPISODE 55 — MY BABY, THE TYCOON
Airdate: January 20, 1966

Darrin gets up to feed the crying Tabatha, but when the exhausted Samantha beats him to it with witchcraft, Darrin thinks his baby has powers. Later, the Kravitzes endow Tabatha with a purchase of stock, which suddenly shoots up after years of inactivity. When the accused Samantha declares that fixing the stock market by magic is unethical, Darrin briefly suspects Endora, then fingers Tabatha when the baby points to the newspaper. Darrin experiments by buying a stock Tabatha "picks out" – when that also spikes, Darrin is sure his daughter can manipulate Wall Street.

Gladys' stock broker cousin suggests that Darrin has inside information she can take advantage of; as the Kravitzes stop by, Samantha, whose hands are full, twitches Tabatha's baby doll to float upstairs, which Gladys sees. When Samantha jokes that Tabatha gave Darrin an investment tip, Gladys tears through the nursery and finds Darrin's newspaper, ready to buy the stock Tabatha points to. Afterwards, Abner advertises for a boarder, telling Darrin he lost all his money because Gladys took Tabatha's investment "advice." Darrin goes ballistic and calls Gladys' cousin, who provides logical explanations for all the jumpy market activity. Samantha is happy that Tabatha is off the hook, but when Tabatha points at the sports page, Darrin wonders if his daughter can predict horse races.

GOOD!

The effects of the bottle warmer plugging itself in and the bottle floating upstairs really look like the objects are moving of their own volition – so much so, that when wires are visible on the bottle that glides into hungry Tabatha's mouth, it can be forgiven.

In "Alias Darrin Stephens" (#37), when Darrin asked if he and Samantha had any other choice besides their child being a witch or warlock, Samantha suggested they could also have "a plain, lovable mortal baby." In this episode, Darrin accuses Tabatha of being "a full-blooded witch," so the show smartly corrects his assumption by having Samantha explain that, at best, Tabatha could only ever be a half-blooded witch. That may be stating the obvious, but it's a point that had been left unexplored ever since Darrin began contemplating having children in "...And Something Makes Three" (#12).

Darrin has mistaken mortal situations for witchcraft a lot lately; when Darrin thinks Samantha has magically manipulated the stock market, she makes it very clear that any such manipulation would be "highly unethical." This is a new detail that adds an important layer to the rules of magic – witches may have limitless power, but they have self-imposed moral boundaries in terms of what they can do.

WELL?

It only makes sense that a Hollywood show would use stock footage for the stock market – it definitely evokes the excitement of Wall Street, but the film quality of New York isn't quite on par with the rest of the episode. There also seems to be a new technique in use: when Darrin has a realization, a "ding!" sounds, as if a light bulb has gone off over his head; it's happened three times in the past two episodes. On one level, it's clever, but such a device can quickly become overkill, and viewers are smart enough to see the revelations in Darrin's expressions for themselves. Moreover, the show's sound effects are typically used to illustrate acts of witchcraft, so having one applied to Darrin for purely mortal reasons feels off somehow.

Popular trend or a case of recycling? A drawing by Shel Silverstein, a popular children's author and illustrator of the time, is shown hanging above Tabatha's crib; this exact same picture was on display in another child's room as Aunt Clara babysat in "There's No Witch Like An Old Witch" (#27).

When Darrin conducts a stock experiment to determine whether or not Tabatha is a witch, Samantha jokes, "Wait a year and ask her." Talking at that age may be advanced for a mortal baby, but in "My Grandson, the Warlock" (#40), Maurice told Gladys that Samantha was able to talk at four hours old – in six languages. Either Maurice was exaggerating, Samantha is underestimating Tabatha's magic lineage, or the writers of each episode came up with different characteristics for witch children.

Why would Samantha buy a full-sized baby doll for a newborn, complete with its own identical carrier? Of course – so Gladys will think Tabatha's flying upstairs to the nursery. Funny, but dubious – the toy is bigger than Tabatha herself. Gladys ransacks the nursery looking for the newspaper to see if Tabatha gave Darrin an investment tip – not very subtle. What is Samantha supposed to think when she comes back and finds Tabatha's toys thrown around the room? Fed up, Abner tells Tabatha that "Aunt Gladys is sick in the head and needs a thorough psychiatric examination, which Uncle Abner is now going home to arrange!" – but Gladys just lay down on the couch for Dr. Passmore in "And Then I Wrote" (#45). Maybe Abner feels the need for a second opinion. As for Samantha, how careless is it of her to twitch her dropped water bucket back into place in front of Gladys? Samantha knows her neighbor is on to her at this point – just let the water spill, and fix it later.

This episode aired in January 1966. Yet the newspaper Samantha uses to line the wastebasket – which she says is dated the day before – clearly has an ad for a "holiday sale" on its back page.

OH, MY STARS!

After Samantha's on-the-fritz witchcraft made a door out of her bedroom window in "Take Two Aspirins and Half A Pint of Porpoise Milk" (#42), the Stephenses told Gladys it was there because they were building a cantilevered nursery. Yet, when the nursery is first shown in this episode, it is of course in a more conventional place on the second floor – but Gladys never questions its location, or asks what happened to the plans for the original room.

SON OF A GUN!

"You just cured me." – Darrin to Samantha, after she warns he's going to turn into another Gladys Kravitz.

SAMANTHA MEETS THE FOLKS
EPISODE 56
Airdate: January 27, 1966

Special Note: This episode is a rerun of "Samantha Meets the Folks" (#14), with a new opening:

Tabatha receives her first letter, written by Darrin's parents, Frank and Phyllis Stephens, who are coming to visit in two weeks. Darrin recalls that their last visit was livened up by Aunt Clara; Samantha reminds him that she had no control over Clara's sudden appearance, and thinks back to how she let her lonely aunt stay while Darrin's parents were there.

As with "A Vision of Sugar Plums" (#51), adding a new sequence to a previous installment for the purpose of creating a flashback episode has the following effect on the show's overall continuity:

GOOD!

In "And Then There Were Three" (#54), Darrin seemed so busy chasing his "daughter," Serena, around that he didn't make time to inform Frank and Phyllis of their granddaughter's birth. At least it's now clear Darrin followed Endora's advice in that episode and called to let his parents know about Tabatha at some point afterwards.

WELL?

How does Samantha not realize that the food she's serving Darrin's parents is not the food she prepared? Surely she'd notice upon venturing back into the kitchen to check on her dinner that her pot roast is now *coq au vin*, and that there's a mysterious pineapple upside-down cake sitting on the counter. Yet Samantha acts as if she's seeing these dishes for the first time. Did Aunt Clara keep Samantha out of the kitchen by insisting on setting the food out herself?

OH, MY STARS!

Samantha and Darrin read a letter from his parents, which reports they're coming for another visit. This implies they live out of town, which would be consistent with the original airing of "Samantha Meets the Folks" (#14). Darrin also recalls that Frank and Phyllis met Aunt Clara the "last time they visited." Not quite – during the elder Stephenses' previous visit in "A Nice Little Dinner Party" (#19), they met Endora, and had just moved to town. So there's no need for them to write a letter announcing their arrival; all they have to do is call. Whoever wrote this tacked-on sequence didn't check with Season One's subsequent episodes.

In the new sequence, Darrin is surprised to hear how Aunt Clara came down the chimney. However, in the original airing of "Samantha Meets the Folks" (#14), Samantha explained how she found Aunt Clara in the fireplace, with Darrin asking, "She came down the chimney?" Darrin can't be surprised about an event he is already aware of.

As with "A Vision of Sugar Plums" (#51), there are inherent problems with presenting an entire episode as a flashback: a character can only remember an event he or she personally experienced. So, Darrin can't flash back to Samantha and Aunt Clara's private conversation, nor can Samantha recall Darrin meeting his parents at the airport. Say Samantha and Darrin had the flashback together – that would fill in each others' memory gaps, but they still weren't there when Aunt Clara overheard Frank and Phyllis discussing Darrin's Aunt Madge. Witchcraft could have made this device plausible somehow; the mortal way, it doesn't work.

Another question is, why was it necessary to have another flashback episode so soon after "A Vision of Sugar Plums" (#51)? Was it also done to accommodate Elizabeth Montgomery's maternity leave? Why not just run the original "Samantha Meets the Folks" (#14) as is? Adding this 36-second intro was quite a bit of trouble to go to, and it does a lot of damage to the show's continuity in a very short time.

SON OF A GUN!

"'To Miss Tabatha Stephens.' Her first letter – how about that?" – Darrin to Samantha, beaming about his infant daughter's milestone.

FASTEST GUN ON MADISON AVENUE
Airdate: February 3, 1966

EPISODE 57

Darrin, who admires how well Samantha has adjusted to the mortal life, is forced into an altercation when a drunk accosts her in a restaurant. When things turn physical, Samantha twitches Darrin's missed punch into a knockout. The next morning, the newspaper reports that the drunk Darrin clocked is Joe Kovack, a professional boxer. Abner asks for Darrin's autograph, then warns that Kovack will come after him. Kovack and his manager confront Darrin in his office, wanting to stage another fight to restore Kovack's reputation. Darrin reluctantly agrees, but after Gladys concurs with Abner's warning, Samantha, who doesn't know the rumble is rigged, finds Darrin with Kovack and again protects him with witchcraft.

While Gladys pressures Abner to get in shape, Larry sees the Darrin/Kovack article and challenges Darrin to a fight. Darrin drowns his sorrows in a bar, where a stranger recognizes him from the paper. As the stranger dares Darrin to punch him, Darrin gets up from his stool and trips, knocking the man out.

Discovering he's just KO'd reigning boxing champion Tommy Carter, Darrin is sure Samantha is there in another form and begs the bartender, whose name tag reads "Sam," to stop interfering. Samantha swears she never left the house, and Larry reveals that he settled things with Carter by arranging for him to appear at the Advertising Club's charity ball to fight the opponent of his choice: Darrin. Samantha assures him that, together, they'll be unbeatable.

GOOD!

Samantha is once again wearing the heart necklace she had on for 52 episodes [53 if you count the flashback installment "Samantha Meets the Folks" (#56)]. It's funny how the absence of the pendant made the show feel incomplete.

Darrin often imitates Samantha's twitch by grabbing his nose and wiggling it, sometimes with an accompanying "ring-a-ding-ding." So it's a nice twist here when Darrin makes the gesture only to realize how much his nose hurts from Kovack tweaking it the night before.

In "Aunt Clara's Old Flame" (#47), Gladys said she was starting to realize she was banging her head against the wall trying to convince Abner of the magical doings at the Stephenses, so she must feel an extra fillip of satisfaction finally being able to prove a claim by shoving the Darrin/Kovack newspaper headline in Abner's face. It's a subtle, but definite first for poor misunderstood Gladys.

It may or may not seem stereotypical to have an African-American boxer as the champion, but Rockne Tarkington's portrayal of Tommy Carter is a knockout. He perfectly channels Muhammad Ali, who was the real-life heavyweight champion in the '60s; this is also reflected in lines like "I'm the prettiest" and "Give it your best, put it to the test, and I'll put you to rest." Pity Tommy's rendered unconscious after such a brief appearance.

WELL?

Darrin wants to celebrate Samantha's adjustment to mortal housewifery by taking her to "the best restaurant in town." Yet his confrontations with Kovack and Carter take place in Dundee's Bar, a nice enough eatery, but hardly the "best." And why does Darrin go back there after Larry's childish display? The scene of the "crime" is the last place Darrin should frequent.

It appears the Stephenses have taken a lesson from the Tates: Gladys volunteers to babysit Tabatha when Samantha runs out to stop Darrin and Kovack from meeting again, but who watched the baby when the Stephenses went out for their aborted dinner the night before?

The sudden zooms on Darrin (when he discovers the paper) and Gladys (when she reels at Samantha's sudden wardrobe change) are meant to highlight the comedy, and they do, but it's too bad these decisions were made in the editing room; had the camera zoomed in during filming, the shots would look nice and crisp. Done in post-production, they look grainy, and lessen the impact of the moments.

In the McMann & Tate building, as Darrin receives further predictions of doom from the elevator boy regarding Kovack's potential retaliation, they ride a completely different elevator than the one in which Gideon trapped Darrin in "Your Witch Is Showing" (#20).

Darrin needs to learn to stop blurting out his assumptions about witchcraft in front of mortals. He just made a public spectacle of himself in "And Then There Were Three" (#54) – here he does it while a media darling. This particular bid for comedy is starting to wear thin, and Darrin's been around witches long enough now that if he suspects there's magic afoot, he should know to confront Samantha at home.

How many different newspapers can one neighborhood have? In "Red Light, Green Light" (#23), Darrin did up an ad for the *Morning Glory News*. In "Pleasure O' Riley" (#25), the Kravitzes were on the front page of the *Star-Dispatch*. Now, the paper in question seems to be the much bigger *New York Chronicle*, which likely has a circulation of millions. That said, why are Darrin's escapades with Kovack and Carter on its front page? Yes, on closer inspection, it's the front page of the sports section, but even then, it seems odd that these altercations would merit such media coverage, including the radio report Gladys listens to in her car.

Larry is a head honcho at McMann & Tate, but no one informs him that a professional boxer and his manager came in asking for Darrin. And by the way, is Darrin really expected to fight a heavyweight champion at a charity event? Surely Carter remembers that Darrin only fell on him and didn't even throw a punch.

OH, MY STARS!

If Kovack and his manager are arranging this fake fight with Darrin on the sly, why does the manager confront Darrin before the incident in a bar full of reporters and photographers? Any contact between them would give the ruse away, to say nothing of the manager signaling for Darrin to take a swing at Kovack in plain sight.

"Me, living next door to the man who knocked out 'Jolting Joe' Kovack!" Abner exclaims as he gets an autograph out of Darrin. Except the Kravitzes don't live next door to the Stephenses – they live across the street from them.

SON OF A GUN!

"Anything you say, mister. Only wouldn't you be just as happy if instead we got to be very good friends?" – Sam the bartender to Darrin, who thinks he's asking Samantha about promising to love, honor, and obey.

THE DANCING BEAR
Airdate: February 10, 1966

EPISODE 58

Darrin is nervous about having Endora present with his parents coming to see Tabatha for the first time, but she promises to behave, and even brings Tabatha an ordinary teddy bear. After Phyllis and Endora exchange forced pleasantries, Phyllis reveals her gift – a bear identical to Endora's. Promising Samantha she'll take care of the problem, Endora instead casts a spell to make her bear dance when Tabatha's name is mentioned. The elder Stephenses meet their granddaughter, but Phyllis spies Endora's bear, making things awkward. Once Endora's bear dances, Darrin lies that he tinkered with it – and Frank, who's still bored with retirement, wants to put the bear on the market.

With Endora on the lam and Tabatha transfixed by her dancing bear instead of sleeping, Frank heads over with Hockstedder, a toy manufacturer. Endora finally unhexes her bear, but reinstates the spell when Phyllis commands Tabatha's attention with a clown doll. Though Darrin tells Hockstedder the bear no longer works, Hockstedder wants to go into production immediately when it makes a magical comeback. To dissuade the toy titan, Samantha makes the clown dance, then laments that Tabatha will no longer be the only baby with dancing toys. Phyllis and Endora agree they don't want their granddaughter to be "one of the crowd," and the confused Hockstedder leaves. That night, Tabatha continues to cry without her toys, so Samantha slows down the rhythm of their dancing, lulling Tabatha – and Darrin – to sleep.

GOOD!

In "Samantha Meets the Folks" (#56), Darrin's parents wrote that they were coming for a visit "in two weeks." This episode indeed aired two weeks later; that the writers went to the trouble of foreshadowing their arrival two episodes ago – and followed through on it – is commendable.

Phyllis and Endora's stilted "kill 'em with kindness" banter is very effective in and of itself, but, if you recall how Endora nearly came between Phyllis and Frank in "A Nice Little Dinner Party" (#19), it adds a whole extra layer to the ladies' disdain for each other. Other carryovers from that episode include Frank continuing to be bored with retirement, flirting with Endora, and running Phyllis down – plus, he's as impulsive as ever, running to a toy manufacturer without talking to Darrin first. It's nice to see that the core personalities of Darrin's parents haven't changed.

Arthur Julian as Hockstedder is a hilarious testament to the we-can-do-it-better commercialism of the '60s. Upon seeing Tabatha, he declares, "A toy baby! Terrific! Wind it up, please." And when he's ready to mass-produce the bear, he asks for other potential product: "Anti-missile missile? Death ray gun? By any chance have you got a germ warfare kit?" Delivered in his dry, business-like tones, Hockstedder is more amusing than any dancing stuffy.

WELL?

There are a lot of recurring motifs this season: two horses, two precocious preteen boys, and now there's another teddy bear story not long after "My Boss, The Teddy Bear" (#49). Darrin was so traumatized thinking Larry had been stuffed in that episode, you'd think his seeing a teddy bear now would give him flashbacks.

The last time Endora saw Frank and Phyllis, she nearly caused them to divorce. So is it a good idea for Samantha to be so nonchalant about Endora staying for dinner as if nothing happened? As evidenced by Phyllis' chilliness and Frank's flirtation, putting them all in the same room again isn't Samantha's smoothest move.

Has Tabatha been smoking? Her cry (or overdubbed cry) is amazingly deep for a month-old baby, especially compared to her cooing whenever the toys do their dance. And the bear's choreography is a honey, but wires are visible as Frank and Phyllis discover him.

Darrin fumbles to give his parents a mortal reason for the bear's dancing, offering, "You know how I love to tinker, Pop." Since when? Darrin's never shown any interest in gadgetry. And Frank accepts Darrin's full-of-holes story a bit too easily, to say nothing of Hockstedder, who would sense a deception a mile away.

Composers often use a device they call "unempathetic film scoring," which accents a scene with a style of music that is in direct contrast to what is being presented. But in this case, it seems odd to have Samantha barring Endora from seeing Tabatha, with Endora calling that cruel, as the whimsical "teddy bear dance" cue lilts in the background.

If the elder Stephenses indeed live out of town – which negates "A Nice Little Dinner Party" (#19), where they moved into Darrin's city and had people over to their house – then how are Frank and Phyllis getting to Morning Glory Circle separately? Has Frank rented two cars? Does he hitch a ride with Hockstedder, who leaves alone? Finally, Phyllis turns the tide bringing Tabatha "a nice, friendly clown," except that "new" clown was already on Tabatha's toy shelf in "My Baby, the Tycoon" (#55).

OH, MY STARS!

Samantha attempts to derail Frank and Hockstedder by making Phyllis' clown dance, then sets Phyllis and Endora up to discourage the deal; she reasons it's a shame Tabatha won't be the only baby with dancing toys anymore once they're made public. Phyllis understandably doesn't want to go into business, and Endora doesn't want her grandchild to be ordinary, but none of this seems like a good enough reason to ditch a million-dollar deal. Hockstedder himself shoots the finale down: "If Thomas Edison had gotten mixed up with this crowd, he'd be the only man with a light bulb in his house."

Tabatha won't sleep while the toys are dancing, and she cries when they stop. Samantha's idea to slow them down as a form of lullaby is a nice thought, though not entirely sound. First, Samantha claims, "I can't stop them from dancing while they're in the crib." Why not? She's the one who made the clown dance in the first place. And Endora's bear dances only briefly after Tabatha's name is mentioned, then stops. Additionally, if Samantha can't unhex Endora's bear, how does she add to Endora's spell to slow it down? The endearing slo-mo dancing ends up being given away by the tossing of Samantha's hair, which also moves in reduced speed. Darrin is supposedly lulled to sleep by the toys, except he's already knocked out in the doorway before Samantha ever slows them down.

SON OF A GUN!

"All right, what does he do – suddenly turn into a real bear? Sing the second act from *La Traviata*?" – Darrin to Endora, questioning her gift.

DOUBLE TATE
Airdate: February 17, 1966

EPISODE 59

Inspired by Samantha's suggestion to let Darrin pick out his own birthday gift, Endora gives Darrin three wishes. Darrin unwittingly uses one to summon a busy elevator, and another to see a pretty girl in a bikini. Larry is stuck in Chicago and asks Darrin to stall his client, Mr. Turgeon; Darrin wishes he were Larry for the day and turns into his boss. Turgeon spots "Larry" and whisks him out to lunch to snag a job for his niece, Joyce; Louise slaps her supposedly out-of-town "husband" when she catches Joyce with him. Darrin-as-Larry desperately calls Samantha, but she thinks it's a prank until "Larry" declares she's a witch. Getting confirmation about the wishes from Endora, Samantha rushes to the Tates, interrupting Louise's romantic dinner for two.

Louise wants "Larry" to get rid of the lingering Samantha by dressing for bed. When Darrin-as-Larry sneaks downstairs in Larry's pajamas, Samantha discovers she can't undo Endora's spell, deducing that Darrin asking to be Larry for the day means he'll change back at midnight. As the Stephenses wait, the real Larry shows up, confusing Louise. Samantha stalls Larry when he goes to the car for his luggage; Louise demands a good-night kiss, but Darrin becomes himself again as Larry walks in on the lip-lock. To justify things to Larry, Samantha twitches Louise into sleepwalking and makes her think the night was a dream. Darrin, however, keeps quiet about how he used his bikini-clad second wish.

GOOD!

Samantha peering into "Larry's" eye to be sure he's Darrin, as if to say, "Are you in there?" is great comedy. Another nice touch is the suspense that builds as Samantha tries to keep the real Larry outside while Darrin-as-Larry is being goaded into kissing Louise good night – all as the crucial midnight deadline creeps closer. And the effect of "Larry" changing back into Darrin while kissing Louise is first-rate.

WELL?

Samantha recalling how Endora and Darrin bonded over Tabatha's birth [see "And Then There Were Three" (#54)] is poignant continuity, but adding that Endora gave Darrin a trick fountain pen as a fatherhood gift bears some scrutiny. Endora must have presented him with it after the events of that episode, because he was too busy chasing Serena and getting zapped into an Indian costume. But why would Endora give Darrin a pen that turns into a toad the very day they've made just an important connection? And why is she surprised to hear about the toad, when she cast the spell on the pen herself?

Darrin's got ladies on the brain again. His second wish zaps a voluptuous passerby into a bikini – yet he shakes off the vision. He witnesses two strange events within the course of one elevator ride, but doesn't even consider witchcraft a cause, despite usually being much quicker to suspect spells when none are cast.

Even if Turgeon is the "weirdo" Larry makes him out to be, would the client really be unreasonable about something as uncontrollable as Larry being stuck in a foggy airport, even if Turgeon's only in town for the day? More importantly, Darrin races into his office and wishes he could Larry – with the door open. Yet no one sees Darrin's transformation; not even Betty, who's just outside the door. Darrin should know something's happened as soon as he hears Larry's voice coming out of his mouth; in "Junior Executive" (#46), he questioned the "frog" in his throat before discovering he'd been turned into a kid.

The Tates' marriage isn't looking too good. Louise immediately suspects Larry and Joyce of hanky-panky [was it his girlie mags from "That Was My Wife" (#31)?]; later Louise is downright controlling, commanding "Larry" to get rid of Samantha and trying to dress him for bed. Even if it is bedtime, isn't Louise awfully hostile regarding supposed friend Samantha? Then, Larry-as-Darrin tells Samantha, "You're a witch!" and Louise replies, "Did you call me, Larry?" That's pretty loaded subtext.

No-Name Tate is apparently upstairs (and the poor little guy is still only ever referred to as "the baby"), but who sits for him when Louise walks into the restaurant alone in the middle of the day? Is Esmeralda, or the governess, on duty? And who's minding Tabatha with Samantha at the Tates 'til all hours, and the next day when she visits Darrin for lunch? Louise mentions that Samantha has "a sitter problem" – this means Tabatha is on her own.

This isn't the first time Larry thinks Darrin is fooling around with Louise. In "That Was My Wife" (#31), Larry punched Darrin after seeing him kiss a brunette Samantha. Larry should have another déjà vu as his suitcase flies open on the doorstep; in "My Grandson, the Warlock" (#40), Darrin also used this technique as a stalling tactic. But the Stephenses are getting sloppy with their attempts at resolution. In "The Dancing Bear" (#58), they gave a flimsy reason for getting Darrin and his father out of a business deal; here, Samantha fibs that Louise has been sleepwalking. And when Samantha announces that she made Louise think everything was a dream, the don't-use-witchcraft-under-any-circumstances Darrin crows, "That's using the old nose, Sam!" Good thing he doesn't know she cast a dream spell on him in "A Vision of Sugar Plums" (#15/#51) to make him forget his trip to the North Pole.

OH, MY STARS!

Having an elevator drop fourteen floors in two seconds to facilitate Darrin's first wish may make for great sitcom, but how do its occupants escape getting hurt? They fall approximately 140 feet, yet no one's even on the floor when the door opens, despite the sound of breaking glass.

In "My Boss, The Teddy Bear" (#49) and "The Dancing Bear" (#58), it seemed a decision had finally been made that one witch couldn't undo the spell of another. Here, Samantha apparently gets a spell-breaker from Endora (when? Endora popped out before they could discuss it) – and is able to at least attempt reversing Darrin's third wish.

SON OF A GUN!

"Perhaps he wanted to be his own boss." – Endora to Samantha, after being asked why Darrin has turned into Larry.

As "straight man" mortal Larry Tate, David White can only have a limited range of things to do while the magic goes on around him. But here, Mr. White gets a showcase: acting as if he's Darrin in Larry's body, White's allowed to be a little more over-the-top, and, playing Darrin-as-Larry's reluctance and confusion around Louise shows some different facets to White's skills. He's so convincing, it really seems Darrin is in there somewhere.

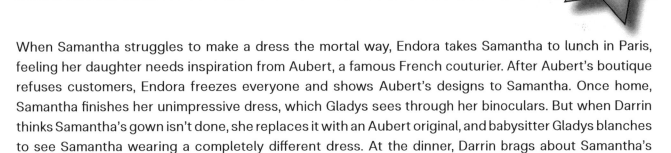

SAMANTHA THE DRESSMAKER
Airdate: February 24, 1966

EPISODE 60

When Samantha struggles to make a dress the mortal way, Endora takes Samantha to lunch in Paris, feeling her daughter needs inspiration from Aubert, a famous French couturier. After Aubert's boutique refuses customers, Endora freezes everyone and shows Aubert's designs to Samantha. Once home, Samantha finishes her unimpressive dress, which Gladys sees through her binoculars. But when Darrin thinks Samantha's gown isn't done, she replaces it with an Aubert original, and babysitter Gladys blanches to see Samantha wearing a completely different dress. At the dinner, Darrin brags about Samantha's skills to the point she gets pressured into making gowns for Glendon's wife and sister. The next day, Darrin heads to the airport to pick up a new client – Aubert.

Endora is happy when Samantha plans to twitch up Aubert's designs for the Glendon women; Gladys, who also wants a dress, returns after the fitting and briefly sees Aubert's finished gowns where there was only material before. At a top-secret cocktail party, Darrin reveals Aubert, who faints upon seeing his exclusive collection made public. Darrin fumes, relaying that Aubert thinks only Samantha looks good in his creations; Samantha visits the designer, freezing him and suggesting he create fashions for the average American woman. Aubert embraces the concept, but laments that a collection can't be produced overnight, so Samantha assures him she and Endora will handle it. Later, the Glendon women model Aubert's new line, and Gladys shocks Abner by taking a turn on the runway.

GOOD!

Dick Gautier might easily have a second career as a stunt man. Not only does he hold almost perfectly still while Aubert is frozen over his chair, but he takes a complicated spill out of it once Endora reanimates him. Then he takes his own fall down a set of stairs when Aubert goes into a dead faint over his "stolen" designs, and finishes by maintaining a mannequin-like stance as Samantha tells the frozen Frenchman how to capture the American market. Speaking of French, literally, Samantha tells Darrin that *ne regarde jamais un cheval dans la bouche* means "don't look a gift horse in the mouth." That's very close – the only word missing is "gift" (*cadeau*).

Abner, who constantly puts his wife down about her looks, culinary skills, and, of course, her sightings of witchcraft, gets a little payback at the cocktail party: when he casually asks Mr. Glendon why Samantha looks so good while Gladys looks so terrible, Glendon replies, "You must be a professional mind reader, Mr. Kravitz." And when the very bored Abner sees Gladys twirling an umbrella on Aubert's runway, his total shock is palpable – and Gladys' clumsy attempt at elegance is model perfect.

WELL?

It's good to know that Tabatha is being taken care of by Darrin's parents while Samantha sews. But, if they still live out of town, as evidenced by "A Vision of Sugar Plums" (#51) and "The Dancing Bear" (#58), then where is Tabatha – in her grandparents' hotel room? Later in the episode, Samantha lets Gladys sit for Tabatha. Is that wise, knowing what a snoop Mrs. Kravitz is? She would jump at the chance to rifle through every drawer in the Stephens house unsupervised.

Endora must love the fashionable hat she zaps onto Samantha's head in Paris – she wore the same one when she posed as Samantha in "Which Witch Is Witch?" (#24). As for Aubert's immobilized models, one of them blinks as Samantha and Endora peruse his dresses.

Samantha should know that having lunch in Paris always gets her in trouble. In "Witch or Wife" (#8), Darrin was upset that Samantha popped herself there – yet when she gets busted here, he never references the previous trip. And how does Darrin remain clueless to the fact that the very plain dress on Samantha's dummy changes pattern, design, and color once Samantha has it on? The addition of sequins alone is a tip-off.

Darrin's making a habit of volunteering Samantha for projects. In "And Then I Wrote" (#45), he stuck her with a gig writing a Civil War play, and now, he assures his client, Mr. Glendon, that Samantha will run up dresses for everyone. As for Gladys, she is getting a lot less subtle about her snooping: in "My Baby, the Tycoon" (#55), she ransacked Tabatha's nursery looking for a newspaper with supposed infant stock tips; this episode has her ripping through Samantha's bolts of material hoping to see the gowns that were there a few seconds before. For someone who's ready to kiss her sanity goodbye, Gladys recovers fast; in the very next scene, she gushes to Abner about the cocktail party she got them invited to as if nothing happened.

Darrin's developing a sense of leniency toward witchcraft, isn't he? He had no problem with Samantha putting a dream spell on Louise in "Double Tate" (#59), and he follows up now by tacitly approving of Samantha twitching up a whole line of dresses. Speaking of Tates, where is Larry in all this? The last time the agency represented a designer [in "Witch or Wife" (#8)], Larry flew to Paris to personally see a client's collection. This time, he is conspicuously absent as Darrin handles everything on his own.

OH, MY STARS!

Annoyed that Aubert's boutique won't receive customers, Endora freezes everyone and laments to Samantha, "After all that mortal money I've spent here!" Witches can zap up anything, at any time. So why would Endora need to spend money, much less frequent a store? She'd have to materialize cash to do it, so it seems like a waste of witchcraft not to zap up a dress instead. Conversely, Samantha confides to Endora that she'll "make it look like" she's sewing dresses for Gladys and the Glendon women. To wit, she engages the ladies in a fake fitting, but won't write down their measurements, which confuses them. If Samantha really wants the women to believe she's designing dresses for them, why does she skip steps instead of following the charade through to the end?

SON OF A GUN!

"Marvelous – now you're an authority on high fashion." – Samantha to baby Tabatha, who blows a raspberry after being asked for an opinion on the dress her mother made.

Haute couture has always been the territory of "half-starved fashion models," as Samantha points out. So, for Aubert to find success designing dresses for women with more typical figures is a stroke of genius on the show's part. The concept makes so much sense, it's amazing it hasn't caught on in the real-life fashion world, and it goes a long way toward smashing one more mortal stereotype.

THE HORSE'S MOUTH
Airdate: March 3, 1966

At a stop light, a horse gets out of its trailer and gallops into Samantha's backyard. Unable to understand her visitor, Samantha makes the mare human and finds out she's Dallyrand, a race horse tired of losing to her older sister. Samantha maintains Dallyrand's cover when her trainer, Spindler, comes looking for her, though sassy horse-as-human "Dolly" almost gives herself away. Darrin brings home Gus Walters, an inventor friend who needs an influx of capital; Gus is encouraged when Dolly offers him some hot race track tips. Darrin, who already suspects that Dolly is a witch, corners Samantha and finds out he's spent the evening talking to a horse.

Once the excited Gus leaves, Dolly assures Darrin she knows how to pick winners and professes a desire to finally win a race of her own. At the track, Dolly brings Gus and the Stephenses to the stables to talk to the horses: Gus wins with Dolly's first tip since she knows it's the stallion's birthday, but the inventor loses his second bet because that horse was only talking a good game. When Samantha and Dolly run into Spindler and find out Dolly's sister has been scratched, Dolly feels this is her big chance. Samantha changes her back, and the Stephenses barely convince Gus to gamble on the long shot. After a nail-biting race, Dallyrand wins, and Samantha winks at the horse Gus considers almost human.

GOOD!

Darrin starts off wanting to know if Dolly is a witch in the same negative way he did with Gertrude in "Love Is Blind" (#13). But when he figures out – on his own – that Dolly is a horse, he only mildly freaks out, then jumps in the saddle, encouraging Gus to bet on Dolly's tips and asking her how she likes life on this side of the track. That's a far cry from even "Ling-Ling" (#21), where he tried to talk co-worker Wally out of dating a cat-turned-girl; Darrin's "Oh, Sam, you did it again" seems to be a reference to that episode.

How funny is it that one of the race horses is named Favorite Martian? That's a nod to the television show of the same name that ran in prime-time on CBS during this period. And blending stock footage with the rest of an episode, which can often be uneven, is well done here, evoking the feeling that everyone is really at the races.

The friendship between Samantha and Dolly is so genuine that it's hard to let the horse return to her natural form. Samantha doesn't have a lot of friends – certainly none she can be completely herself around, like she can with Dolly.

WELL?

Dolly ditches Spindler as he sits at an intersection, which is controlled by the exact same stop/go light Endora brought in as a sample signal in "Red Light, Green Light" (#23). Doesn't it seem old-fashioned, even for 1966? Dolly runs out of her trailer in an obvious business district; in the next shot, she's on Morning Glory Circle. How does she get to a residential neighborhood so fast? And shouldn't eagle-eyed Gladys, who spotted Darrin the chimpanzee instantly in "Alias Darrin Stephens" (#37), notice a horse neighing across the street?

If there are any more horses this season, they'll be listed in the end credits. In "We're In For A Bad Spell" (#39), the bewitched Adam Newlarkin had to mount one to break a curse, and Samantha zapped one up alongside her fictional Confederate soldier "And Then She Wrote" (#45). Speaking of Adam, he was another one of Darrin's "best friends" that came and went in a single episode – the same happened with Kermit in "Love Is Blind" (#13) and Bob in "Which Witch Is Witch?" (#24). Even original friend Dave is largely only seen when Darrin's trying to drink away a witchy problem. Watch out, Gus: Darrin may be a fair-weather friend.

Dolly seems to be flirting with Gus, making a distinctive horse blow sound. Now that Dolly is human, how is she able to communicate in the language of her original form? In "Ling-Ling" (#21), the humanized cat didn't meow; conversely, when Rex Barker became a canine in "It Shouldn't Happen to a Dog" (#3), he couldn't speak like a human.

Darrin stares into a mirror and tells himself he's just talked to a horse – the same mirror that decorated the Kravitzes' foyer in "Samantha the Dressmaker" (#60). And Samantha must have liked the hat Endora zapped up for her in that episode, because here she wears it to the race track. As Dolly convinces Gus to bet on Diamond Turkey, Samantha looks toward the camera in a wide shot. But when the scene cuts to a two-shot, Samantha is looking to her right. Later, when Samantha changes Dolly back into Dallyrand, Dolly is holding a racing form. What happens to the paper? Shouldn't Dallyrand still be holding it, even if just between her teeth?

OH, MY STARS!

After Dolly becomes her equine self again to run the race, Samantha tells Gus the half-truth that Dolly had to go because of her injured sister. Tensions mount as Gus watches long-shot Dallyrand running her race, which must account for Darrin's constant slip of the tongue – instead of cheering Dallyrand on to victory, he shouts, "Come on, Dolly!" no less than three times. Dolly already dropped enough horsey hints around Gus as it was; it's a good thing he's too invested in his investment, or Darrin would have a lot of explaining to do.

SON OF A GUN!

"I tell you, the way I feel right now I'd like to sit down and have myself a good long whinny!" – Dolly to the Stephenses, upset because she's never won a race.

Patty Regan, as Dallyrand/Dolly, trots into the winner's circle in her very first scene. Her horse-centric dialogue is terrific [much like the cat chat of "Ling-Ling" (#21)], and there's something completely natural about her performance that indeed gives the earthy yet noble impression there's a horse underneath that "crazy blanket."

BABY'S FIRST PARAGRAPH
Airdate: March 10, 1966

When Samantha has trouble finding a babysitter, Endora volunteers her services, though she's never sat for Tabatha before. As Endora regales her granddaughter with pro-witch fairy tales, Gladys comes over with her "advanced" baby nephew and brags about him so much that Endora makes Tabatha "talk" to best the tyke. Naturally, Abner doesn't believe Gladys, but she rushes over to congratulate Darrin, who tries to start a conversation with his daughter. After Samantha admits Endora was babysitting, Darrin summons his mother-in-law, antagonizing her to the point she again puts words in Tabatha's mouth when Gladys brings reporters by.

The next morning, Tabatha's picture is splashed on the front page of the paper, starting an avalanche of publicity: crowds camp out in front of the house, Larry wants Tabatha to do baby food commercials, and the Stephenses field requests from Hollywood, Harvard, and the Mayo Clinic. Endora thinks the attention is wonderful, but Samantha convinces her mother that Tabatha will soon be such a public figure, she won't have time for her family. Darrin gathers the reporters to hear Endora spinning a tale about having performed in vaudeville doing baby voices; the reporters don't buy the ventriloquism claim until Endora changes Gladys' voice. Although the papers print retractions, Darrin still won't apologize to Endora, so she makes him sound like a baby as well.

GOOD!

Endora promises Samantha that she'll behave while watching Tabatha, placing her two front fingers astride her nose and swearing, "Witches' Honor," a gesture not seen since "Be It Ever So Mortgaged" (#2). It's clever of the show to pull an otherwise one-time witch sign out of mothballs. It's also revealed who's been staying with Tabatha at other times: Samantha phones an ill Sally, and goes through a list of mortal babysitters before settling on Endora.

Larry wanting Tabatha to sing a baby food jingle is perhaps the funniest part of her fifteen minutes of fame. "I like Naseley's Baby Food because it's got the taste and texture that's right!" he demonstrates, fed up enough with Darrin's resistance that he actually tries to call Tabatha himself – talk about *into* the mouths of babes. "Tabatha's" voice and dialogue also shine in this episode: "Not tonight, gentlemen," she supposedly says. "I haven't had my dinner!" The utterances sound like they're out of a cartoon, and are meant to; it's especially fun when Endora also witches Gladys and Darrin to sound like babies.

Given the Cold War atmosphere of the '60s, it's funny that the Russians come forward with their own talking ребёнок. And who's reporting this bit of news? None other than real-life Los Angeles anchor Clete Roberts.

WELL?

After a bottle floats to Tabatha, Samantha tells Endora, "For one terrible moment I thought maybe Tabatha had..." Samantha seems to be absorbing Darrin's witch phobia – yet, in "...And Something Makes Three" (#12), Samantha hoped a baby of theirs would have her twitch. And Samantha's excuse that Endora has never sat with Tabatha before doesn't wash – Gladys was allowed to babysit in "Samantha the Dressmaker" (#60), and she doesn't even have kids.

Why does Endora, who tells Samantha she's no stranger to babies, have to ask Gladys how to change a diaper? And why would Endora, who constantly derides Samantha's housewifery, bother changing a diaper the mortal way?

Reporters from the *Daily Mail* are summoned to cover the story of Tabatha talking. Yet, when Tabatha makes the front page, the paper is called the *Daily Chronicle*. With everything else going on in the world in 1966, would a talking baby headline any newspaper? The Stephenses watch a news broadcast indicating "all America" is "agog," but the station has the call letters KXIW. Only stations west of the Mississippi River can start with "K." A New York station, decidedly east of the Mississippi, would start with "W."

After his house becomes a tourist attraction, Darrin sneaks in "the back way." He couldn't: to get there, Darrin would have to park the car and go around the side of the house, both of which would be visible to the crowd. Later, Samantha freezes the throng (who can't stay still; one even blinks) so that Darrin can get out. Why do that when Gladys probably has her binoculars trained on the house more than ever? Finally, Samantha estimates there are a hundred people outside, when, in fact, there are only eleven.

Supposedly, the whole world has gone mad for Tabatha – yet, Darrin only invites the Kravitzes and the two original reporters from the *Daily Mail* over to convince them Endora is a ventriloquist. Gladys goes on about the Stephenses having supernatural powers, which the press pooh-poohs. If the reporters believe a baby can talk, wouldn't they go on alert when told that other such miracles take place in the Stephens house?

OH, MY STARS!

When Gladys realizes the red-headed woman she's talking to isn't Samantha, she exclaims, "Oh, it's you!" And Endora refers to Gladys as Mrs. Kravitz. One problem: these two have never met. Gladys should lose it the second she lays eyes on Endora; as early as "Be It Ever So Mortgaged" (#2), Gladys watched Endora perform magic from afar, and should be very uncomfortable around Endora now for that reason. After Tabatha "talks," Gladys wants to congratulate Darrin, and dashes out of a completely different house than the one she stood in front of while spying on Merle in "A Strange Little Visitor" (#48). Plus, her door is marked "204" – an impossibility considering she lives across from the Stephenses, whose house number is 1164.

SON OF A GUN!

"Well, naturally, the nice witch was concerned. I mean, who likes vandalism?" – Endora, explaining Hansel and Gretel's true impact to Tabatha.

Endora's reimagined fairy tales are absolute gold. Quoting *Snow White*'s usually evil witch as saying, "Here's a lovely apple" is hilarious enough, but the sheer delight with which Endora tells Tabatha about those "two naughty little children" Hansel and Gretel is a joy at any age. Samantha's friend Bertha must have lit a fire under someone – in "The Witches Are Out" (#7), she said mortal fairy tales should be rewritten, and now there's a whole book filled with them.

Abner has an amazing command of continuity as he reminds Gladys of her previous claims regarding her neighbors. "Once you saw people flying," he points out. [True: the Stephenses and their orphan charge Michael took off on Samantha's broom in "A Vision of Sugar Plums" (#15/#51)]. "Then you saw pictures hanging themselves on the walls!" Abner goes on. [True: Gladys did witness that in "Abner Kadabra" (#29).] Abner's complaint proves that not only does he pay attention, but the writers do as well.

THE LEPRECHAUN
Airdate: March 17, 1966

Darrin comes home and discovers he has a guest: Brian O'Brian, a leprechaun who insists they're cousins; Brian is looking for a pot of gold he hid in a fireplace that was moved to the United States from Ireland. Darrin confirms Brian's claim that the fireplace is now owned by a Mr. Robinson, a volatile businessman who refuses to advertise, so Darrin visits Robinson on behalf of McMann & Tate to nose around. After Brian drinks all of Darrin's liquor, Darrin insists that Brian make a play for his gold so he can leave; Brian climbs through Robinson's window, but goes to jail when Robinson's Great Danes subdue him.

Brian uses his one phone call to contact Samantha, and Darrin allows her to pop into Brian's cell to rescue him. Though Darrin doesn't want Samantha taking Brian back to Robinson's house, Samantha does exactly that after the leprechaun plays on her sympathies. Samantha turns Robinson's Great Danes into chihuahuas, allowing Brian to get into the fireplace, but the gold is gone; Robinson returns holding a gun in one hand and Brian's pot in the other. Samantha uses her powers to slow Robinson's advance as she pleads Brian's case – since Robinson is Irish himself, he believes Brian's a leprechaun and returns the pot to him, adding that, if Brian will be the symbol for his Irish linen, Darrin can handle the account. After Darrin forgives Samantha's defiance, Brian uses his restored magic to take his leave.

GOOD!

"Sure'n" leprechauns are expected to speak a certain way, but Brian comes with a modern twist. He laments that he lost two pots of gold: his first hiding place was "bulldozed for a real estate development," and, when his second and final pot is nowhere to be found, he exclaims, "Me security against me old age!" There's nothing like anachronistic humor, and here it works to great effect. It also comes off very well when the dogs change from Great Danes into chihuahuas – in mid-run.

Like Samantha and her friends in "The Witches Are Out" (#7), leprechauns are concerned about how they're perceived by mortals. Brian agrees to represent Robinson's line of linen if he gets "a sympathetic and understanding presentation of me image." One never thinks that a leprechaun would care whether he's stereotyped, so this is unique, especially since the witches on the show have expressed a desire to improve their own image. And, considering this episode originally aired on St. Patrick's Day, it is, as Brian would say, a "grand" time to discuss leprechauns.

WELL?

Darrin yelps that Samantha should have warned him they had company. Why would she? She already sprung Ed Wright on him in "Remember the Main" (#34), as well as young warlock Merle ["A Strange Little Visitor" (#48)] and Dolly the horse ["The Horse's Mouth" (#61)]. Darrin's correct when he says he's put up with elves ["Cousin Edgar" (#36)] and warlocks ["George the Warlock" (#30)] – but adds that he's also had to deal with poltergeists. When was that? Does he mean the fake apparition Samantha twitched up to get Gladys to stop using her "powers" in "Abner Kadabra" (#29)?

Samantha concurs that Brian's magical powers are connected to his missing pot of gold. If that's so, how did Brian get to New York from Ireland? By airplane? And with what money? It's also convenient that Samantha can't use her powers to reclaim Brian's gold because "there's a charm on it." Brian's appearance feels like an experiment out of Season One; like elves, they have very little to do with witches.

Samantha reveals that Darrin's grandmother is from Ireland's County Cork: for Darrin and Brian to be cousins, they have to have the same grandparents – but the episode stops there and doesn't make clear whether Frank's parents or Phyllis' parents can lay claim to Brian. Incredible as it sounds, either Frank or Phyllis have a sibling who had a child with a leprechaun. So far, only Darrin's Uncle Herbert ["Speak the Truth" (#50)] or his Aunt Madge [Phyllis' sister, who thinks she's a lighthouse; see "I, Darrin, Take This Witch, Samantha" (#1) and "Samantha Meets the Folks" (#14)] are contenders. And no matter how you slice it, Brian is only half-leprechaun, anyway.

Would someone as eccentric as Robinson, who doesn't want Darrin touching his imported fireplace and has two ferocious guard dogs, really leave his window unlocked for Brian to climb through? This isn't the first time Samantha's popped into prison, either: she appeared in Darrin's jail cell in "The Very Informal Dress" (#44). This time, she breaks the law by springing Brian – and Darrin allows it.

When Robinson wants to use Brian as the trademark for his linen, Samantha scolds, "Leprechauns never lend themselves to commercial enterprises!" How would she know? Are witches schooled in the ways of leprechauns? Has Samantha never seen a box of Lucky Charms? The breakfast cereal was introduced two years prior to this episode, and is perhaps one of the most famous commercial enterprises involving a leprechaun anyone's ever seen. (Maybe General Mills didn't get leprechaun approval.)

OH, MY STARS!

Darrin's right that Brian's a bungler. Samantha brings him back to Robinson's house after he's already been arrested, and he still talks at full volume. Robinson catches them and whips out a gun – but, as a witch who can do about anything, all Samantha does to stop him is move a chair and a phone. When Brian confesses he's a leprechaun, Robinson gleefully puts his gun down, hands over the pot of gold, and suddenly develops an Irish accent; this too-easy resolution strains credulity even on a show about magic. Then, Samantha, who has just flaunted her witchcraft, outs herself as Darrin's wife to the potential client. What if Robinson, who only moments before was armed and dangerous, goes public with that information? And, it's been one thing to leave open the matter of whether a witch can undo another's spell, but Brian simply rubs his pot to turn Samantha's chihuahuas back into Great Danes. Now leprechauns can reverse witch magic, too? There isn't much point in a witch casting a spell if a non-witch can cancel it out.

SON OF A GUN!

"Think of the position we're in! We have a hot leprechaun on our hands!" – Samantha to Darrin, trying to convince him to let her help Brian as he goes for the gold.

EPISODE 64

DOUBLE SPLIT
Airdate: March 24, 1966

The Kabaker account is up for grabs, and Darrin wants Samantha to be nice to Kabaker's rude daughter to help cinch the deal. Samantha tries, but Miss Kabaker is so insulting that Samantha twitches an hors d'oeuvre at her in retaliation. Darrin blows up at Samantha, and the Stephenses go to bed angry, but the next morning, Larry is caustic enough about Samantha that Darrin badmouths Louise and quits in a huff. Even though Darrin and Samantha aren't talking, he tells her about a job interview he's lined up at another agency. Louise and Samantha team up to repair their husbands' friendship; when Louise asks how, Samantha tells her she's a witch, which Louise laughs off. Samantha then zaps Darrin into reverting to childhood so he'll botch his interview.

As part of the plan, Samantha plays on the furious Darrin's pride by giving Larry credit for Darrin's success, causing him to storm out; Louise also picks a fight with Larry to drive him away. Darrin and Larry head separately to a club, where Samantha magically makes sure they end up in the same room. Realizing neither is alone in bed, Larry and Darrin flip on the lights and settle their argument. They briefly ponder living the single life, then go home to their wives, who wait for them while playing with a Ouija board. Louise winks at Samantha, and Darrin decides he's glad Samantha used her witchcraft to interfere.

GOOD!

The best part of this episode is the warm friendship between Louise and Samantha. Louise offers Samantha support as gets nowhere trying to befriend the client's snobby daughter, and later, the wives hang out, planning an elaborate reunion scheme for their husbands. Samantha even feels comfortable enough with Louise that she admits she's a witch! Louise's response? "You said it, honey, I didn't!" Samantha's "How about that" seems to imply that Louise wouldn't care if her friend was a witch – if she really believed it. (Wouldn't it be fun if Louise knew Samantha's secret and Larry didn't?) The ladies cap their evening by using a Ouija board; Samantha deems it "fascinating," which is exactly what it is seeing a *Bewitched* witch exploring another facet of the occult.

Even the smallest choices by an actor can inform a scene. As Darrin rages at Samantha post-party, she silently bends the emery board she's using to file her nails – a perfect way to express her feelings on the subject. And, in light of Darrin's unkindness, he's redeemed the next day by taking responsibility for the way he wouldn't allow Samantha to ignore Miss Kabaker.

WELL?

Asking if Samantha knows a particular plastic surgeon, Miss Kabaker says the doc does "wonderful nose work." That's almost word-for-word what Darrin's ex-girlfriend Sheila said to Samantha in "I, Darrin, Take This Witch, Samantha" (#1). Perhaps Samantha drew inspiration from Aunt Clara when she popped a canapé into Miss Kabaker's eye; Clara did that to Darrin by accident in "There's No Witch Like An Old Witch" (#27). At the risk of beating a dead horse, who's sitting with Tabatha while the Stephenses are at the Kabakers? For that matter, is someone watching No-Name Tate while the Tates are at the party, not to mention later while Larry's at the club and Louise is at Samantha's?

Did Samantha's dream spell on Louise in "Double Tate" (#59) extend to that entire evening? Louise is chummy with Samantha now, but, in that episode, Louise was so irritated by her so-called friend's presence, she even hissed "Get rid of her!" to Darrin-as-Larry.

So, Darrin comes all the way home from Manhattan on the train just to change his tie for his interview, takes another back in the dinner car (what time is this meeting?), and a third train to come home and fight with Samantha. He must take a fourth to the club, since Samantha insists on keeping the car for shopping; that confirms the Stephenses only have one car.

Isn't Samantha risking ruining Darrin's reputation in the advertising business by making him babble about "din-din" and the "choo-choo?" Ames could spread the story around – come to think of it, Darrin's probably done enough damage on his own popping off about witches during client presentations. And why is Darrin so quick to assume Samantha witched him? He's right, but usually he accuses Endora without a second thought.

After Darrin and Larry make up in the hotel room, they chat about their "newfound bachelorhood." Have they forgotten that they are both new fathers? Samantha and Louise come very close to being single mothers. At least Darrin makes up properly with Samantha, while Larry only offers a caveman-like "We're going home, Louise."

OH, MY STARS!

When watching classic movies and television, it's always a good idea to keep in mind the historical perspective in which they were filmed. But this "war of the sexes" script feels more like it came out of 1940s radio serial *The Bickersons* than *Bewitched*. This is only the Stephenses' first fight this season (as compared to their constantly butting heads last season), but Darrin yells at Samantha for "wiggling that beak" and pounds his chest that he wears the pants in the family. Then Larry approaches misogyny, calling Louise "tinted top" and a member of the "corset crowd." Larry would be happy if Samantha were crushed by a falling safe? There's comedy, and then there's cruelty.

Putting Darrin and Larry into the same room is good old slapstick shtick, but neither man hears the other walking around, Larry doesn't smell Darrin's cigarette smoke in the tiny room, and each takes it for granted that the lamp the other man turns off is going out by itself. These are sophisticated, Madison Avenue ad men – they're not this unobservant.

SON OF A GUN!

"I have a strong feeling bad words will fly/Your Daddy just came home with blood in his eye." – Samantha singing to Tabatha, after Darrin returns from his sabotaged job interview.

EPISODE **65**

DISAPPEARING SAMANTHA
Airdate: April 7, 1966

McMann & Tate is representing Osgood Rightmire and his book, *Witchcraft of the World: Fact and Fallacies*; Samantha says Rightmire is a fraud and wants to tag along to his lecture. While the Tates marvel at Rightmire's commanding presence, Samantha all but rolls her eyes at his claims. Rightmire dares any witches in the audience to target him, so Samantha twitches him into tripping, but the author counters with a nonsensical spell that makes Samantha disappear. She rematerializes right away, only to fade out more frequently once Darrin gets her home. Trying to figure out what Rightmire did, Darrin approaches him about the spell, but Rightmire claims exclusivity and begs off coming to the Stephenses' reception later that night because of Beverly, a fawning fan.

Endora bespells Beverly into arriving with Rightmire, who goes on about his witch-debunking exploits. Samantha is forced to excuse herself repeatedly as she continues to disappear, but, when Endora feels herself fading, too, mother and daughter suspect Rightmire may be a warlock. They spike a Bloody Mary with cayenne pepper and hot sauce to "test" him; after he fails, they realize he must have a talisman in his possession that's causing the disappearances. Endora spots an ornate ring on his finger and witches him into taking it off; Samantha "loses" it, zaps up a duplicate, and destroys the original, returning things to normal. Samantha can't resist one more twitch, which sends Rightmire headlong into a wall.

GOOD!

Oftentimes, the show's mortals seem oblivious to the witchcraft going on around them: a recent example is "And Then There Were Three" (#54), when Serena zapped Darrin into an Indian suit in a crowded toy store with no one the wiser. So it's a nice touch that the man sitting behind Samantha at Rightmire's lecture silently notices her disappearance, and confusedly indicates to his wife that someone was sitting there a second ago.

After Samantha's second fade-out, she summons Endora, with Darrin also calling out, "Mother!" Despite Darrin's increasing battles with his mother-in-law this season, there's respect and admiration in that one hail.

WELL?

At least now it's clear that Endora cares for Tabatha in the Stephenses' absence, since Samantha comments, "She's really awfully good about babysitting." Louise and Larry's baby isn't so lucky; he's presumably at home with governesses and/or maids while the Tates again run around without him, and he doesn't even have a name.

In "Double Split" (#64), Samantha came right out and told Louise she's a witch. Here, Samantha expresses her disapproval of Rightmire and his anti-witch sentiments, but Louise doesn't connect it to her friend's recent admission. Rightmire also makes reference to leprechauns, interesting when you consider Darrin just dealt with his mythical cousin in "The Leprechaun" (#63).

As Samantha walks toward the house from the curb, the bottom half of her briefly disappears. Now she knows how Aunt Clara felt when her own bottom faded out in "Aunt Clara's Old Flame" (#47). In plain view like that, wouldn't snoopy Gladys see, or rather not see, Samantha's missing derrière? And there doesn't seem to be much point to half of Samantha disappearing; it only happens once, as Samantha's eclipses are total the rest of the episode.

Once Endora arrives, the invisible Samantha declares, "Mama, I've got a problem." Samantha hasn't referred to Endora as "Mama" since "George the Warlock" (#30); she always calls Endora "Mother." Samantha holds her purse and wears her coat and hat when she disappears from the foyer, but when she becomes visible again, these items are gone. Samantha carries flowers during that particular invisibility stint so she can be located – when did she put her accessories down?

Samantha may be invisible, but the strings on her ice bag aren't. Also visible is sunlight, in what is supposed to be a night shot showing Rightmire and Beverly being magically summoned to Morning Glory Circle. Now, Endora arranges this through Beverly, but she doesn't know Rightmire has company, and she could just as easily give him the compulsion to come over.

If you were having company but started disappearing at random, would you sit around knowing you could pop out any second in front of everybody? Samantha does – why not stay upstairs and have Darrin tell their guests she's sick? Speaking of company, why is Beverly even there? Once she's at the Stephenses', her hilariously brainless presence doesn't move the story forward in any way; written differently, the airhead could have been integral to Samantha and Endora discovering why they're disappearing.

When Endora begins fading, without an incantation from Rightmire, she and Samantha think he may be a warlock. That's a strange conclusion – what warlock would go around debunking witchcraft? And how is it that Rightmire, fraud that he may be, never clues in to the fact he's in the presence of real witches? He knows the peppered Bloody Mary is a test for warlocks, his ring flies out of his hand, and he suddenly slams into a wall. Rightmire is a well-traveled, learned man; his car breaking down in front of the very place he's trying to avoid should be enough to make him suspect actual witchcraft.

Finally, Samantha never explains to her company how cayenne pepper got into Rightmire's drink – and how did she make sure the witch-debunker got the right one? The tray is passed around as if all the Bloody Marys are the same; Beverly, the Tates, or the visiting publisher could have ended up taking the "test" meant for Rightmire.

OH, MY STARS!

This episode builds on the idea that Rightmire's amateur incantation makes Samantha disappear, until the discovery that his ring is a talisman which possesses powers he isn't aware of. Intriguing twist, but if this ring has such adverse affects on witches, how are Samantha and Endora able to simply touch themselves with it to permanently rejoin the land of the visible? Wouldn't being so close to the ring have the opposite effect? Also, Endora electrifies the ring to get Rightmire to remove it, and Samantha zaps it out of his hand. How can their powers have any effect on it?

SON OF A GUN!

"Well, that covers me." – Darrin to Samantha, after Rightmire says witches are "the companions of dull, primitive, and ignorant people."

EPISODE 66
FOLLOW THAT WITCH (PART I)
Airdate: April 14, 1966

Abner's sister, Harriet Kravitz, is visiting while Gladys is away. Having heard Gladys' stories about Samantha, Harriet becomes a believer when she sees Samantha painting a big chair one minute and a tiny chair the next. Meanwhile, Darrin is set to lock up the Robbins Baby Food account until employee Barkley asks for an additional ten days – he's secretly having the Stephenses investigated by private eye Charlie Leach. Darrin comes up clean, so Leach turns his magnifying glass on Samantha, starting with Harriet, who lists the many strange events Gladys witnessed. Leach dismisses this until he visits Samantha under false pretenses and is chased out by witchcraft. After getting more information from Harriet, Leach spies Samantha magically repairing a dish, but when she catches him snooping around Tabatha's baby carriage, she makes it "attack" him.

Darrin grants Samantha full use of her witchcraft if Leach comes back: Leach does, so Samantha pops him onto a high-rise window ledge. Leach gets fired trying to tell Barkley about Samantha – and Charmaine, Leach's disbelieving wife, scoffs that Leach should have Samantha "witch up" the luxuries he's promised her. Inspired, Leach confronts Samantha and threatens to go public about her if she doesn't give him what he wants.

GOOD!

Darrin has spent two seasons insisting Samantha not use her witchcraft. But when Samantha worries about Leach having gotten too close to their daughter, Darrin replies, "If you see him sneaking around Tabatha or her carriage again, you have my permission to use any sort of witchcraft you like." It's heartwarming to see that his love for his baby trumps his desire for a purely mortal life.

The Gruber clan has been well represented so far, with Gladys flaunting two nephews and a cousin. Now Team Kravitz gets a turn with the introduction of Abner's suspicious sister, Harriet. Samantha's lucky Gladys is out of town; the combo of Gladys and Harriet would be a force to be reckoned with.

WELL?

There's no ESP needed for Samantha to sense Harriet will be right back – Ms. Kravitz walks out with the saucepan she came over to return. Yet Samantha shrinks her chair right away anyway after Harriet predicts she won't have enough paint for it. A bigger can would have been less conspicuous, though not as funny.

McMann & Tate advertises a lot of baby food: Larry just wanted the "talking" Tabatha to give testimonials for Naseley's in "Baby's First Paragraph" (#62). Given the Robbins company is in New York, why is there a map of Los Angeles in its office? And, when Leach first reports to Barkley, he says Darrin is "as clean as a whistle." No, he isn't – Darrin's been arrested three times this season alone [once in "The Very Informal Dress" (#44), and twice in "Take Two Aspirins And Half A Pint of Porpoise Milk" (#42)].

Samantha discovers the returning Leach in the garage when she tends to the car, which Darrin says he left "outside with the top down." But Darrin always leaves the car like that, and the Stephenses never park in the garage, which is now completely different than the one in which they were trapped in "Open the Door, Witchcraft" (#28). The retaliatory Samantha zaps Leach onto a window ledge forty stories high. What if he falls to his death? Maybe Samantha realizes that he's not that high up; he doesn't seem like he is from his vantage point. And what reason does Leach give Charmaine for being gone all night? She was already poised to leave him over not coming home to entertain her in the middle of the afternoon.

When Charmaine gives Leach the idea to extort fineries out of Samantha, he darts out of their apartment barefoot. Yet, when he arrives at Samantha's, he's wearing shoes. He takes control of the situation by declaring that Samantha is a "full-blooded, cauldron-stirring witch" – but unless Leach was in the Stephenses' honeymoon suite, he couldn't know Samantha used an expanded version of this phrase to describe herself in "I, Darrin, Take This Witch, Samantha" (#1).

OH, MY STARS!

Wary Harriet should easily put two and two together when Leach comes over claiming he's with a credit company and does nothing but ask questions about Samantha. Credit companies don't go to neighbors for information, yet Harriet is all too eager to dispense second-hand stories to a total stranger. Later, Leach peeks over Samantha's fence in time to see her rocking Tabatha's carriage by witchcraft. Whose yard is he trespassing in? It's a wonder no one calls the police on him. And why does Leach give himself away to Samantha by making a beeline for the full-sized chair, which he just saw in miniature? He's definitely not the smoothest P.I., since he blatantly rummages through the Stephenses' mail in the living room, clearly visible from Samantha's position on the patio.

SON OF A GUN!

"I didn't know if you should drink red wine or white wine with oatmeal – so I finally compromised and settled on Scotch. Breakfast is my favorite meal!" – Samantha to Leach, after his questions about bottle tops get a little too personal.

This episode provides perhaps the best continuity so far in the series. Harriet relays that Gladys saw a baby fly ["My Baby, the Tycoon" (#55)], witnessed both Samantha's square green spots and an ostrich in the living room ["Take Two Aspirins And Half A Pint of Porpoise Milk" (#42)], met a "wizard" who turned into an elephant ["Aunt Clara's Old Flame" (#47)], and caught Darrin with "a long nose and funny hair" ["A Change of Face" (#33)]. Harriet continues that Gladys saw Samantha making three dresses in ten seconds ["Samantha the Dressmaker" (#60)] and that Darrin was a chimpanzee ["Alias Darrin Stephens" (#37)]. Now, some of Harriet's information is inaccurate: Gladys never saw Aunt Clara's ostrich, which was in the Stephenses' bedroom, not the living room, and the sisters-in-law presume that Samantha turned Hedley into an elephant, which was Aunt Clara's doing. But these discrepancies can be effectively explained by the fact that Harriet's information is hearsay. And Gladys must have been watching after all as Samantha entered her house in "Disappearing Samantha" (#65), since Harriet knows Samantha's posterior faded out. Though it might have had more impact to hear Gladys describing these events herself, Harriet (and the writers) strike gold mining the show's history in this way.

Virginia Martin first appeared as Roxie in "It's Magic" (#16), but she's put to much more comedic use here as Charmaine. From her acidic volleys against her husband ("I thought I was marrying Peter Gunn; instead, I end up with Peter Rabbit") to her woebegone asides to the camera ("I wish someone would tell me what I done to deserve this"), she's memorable enough that she deserves her own show.

EPISODE 67

FOLLOW THAT WITCH (PART II)
Airdate: April 21, 1966

After a recap of "Follow That Witch (Part I)" (#66), Charlie Leach tells Samantha that he's a detective hired by Mr. Barkley of Robbins Baby Food. When being turned into a parrot does nothing to deter Leach and his threats to go public with Samantha's witchery, she agrees to grant his material requests in order to preserve Darrin's career. Leach lies to his wife, Charmaine, saying he's retained a high-profile case to justify the coming luxuries; Samantha pops in to deliver and zaps a new car into Leach's fifth-floor apartment, which he struggles to explain to his landlady. Samantha finally gives Leach the home makeover and wardrobe he wants, with the proviso that he keep his distance from now on.

Darrin's secretary, who is friends with Barkley's secretary, reports what she's heard about Robbins' investigation practices, and Darrin realizes that the man spying on Samantha must know she's a witch. Samantha confirms this and accompanies Darrin as he blasts Robbins for invading their privacy. Barkley's surveillance is news to Robbins, who fires Barkley after Samantha magically induces him into admitting he wants Robbins' job. With the Robbins account settled, Darrin approves Samantha's revenge on Leach: she systematically destroys Leach's apartment in front of Charmaine and turns the car into a toy. After Leach accosts Samantha again and gets zapped into the middle of a Mexican bullfight, he swears he'll be seeing the "witch lady" again.

GOOD!
Darrin's Part I authorization of Samantha's usually forbidden witchcraft continues in Part II, as he delightedly responds to Samantha's request to wreak havoc on Leach with a "Do your worst!" It seems Darrin may now realize that barring witchcraft "under any circumstances," as he usually postulates, is a little too black-and-white to be a sensible rule.

WELL?

This is the first time the show's done a two-part episode, so naturally there has to be a recap to remind viewers what happened the week before – this is accomplished by Samantha narrating a selection of previous scenes. But, as in the flashback/rerun episodes "A Vision of Sugar Plums" (#51) and "Samantha Meets the Folks" (#56), Samantha can't describe events she didn't witness, such as the meeting between Darrin and the Robbins people. Also, the effect of Leach being zapped onto the 40-story ledge is different (and better) than what was shown in Part I, and Leach's threat to blow the whistle on Samantha is from an alternate take.

When Samantha agrees to Leach's extortion, he promises, "I wouldn't even tell my wife." Yet, it was Charmaine's idea to blackmail Samantha in the first place, after Leach told his wife about discovering a witch in Part I. As Samantha zaps the car out of their apartment, she, Leach, and a chair shift considerably (granted, that's a hard effect to pull off). Leach tells Samantha he wants his place to look "expensive," but the result is an average, middle-class home. Does Samantha chintz in the hopes Leach won't know any better?

Samantha informs Darrin that she promised herself being a witch would never interfere with his career. She didn't mind interfering in "Double Split" (#64), when she made Darrin utter baby talk to prevent him from being hired at Ames Advertising. And why would Samantha debate terminology about witches in front of Barkley? That would only confirm the information he got from Leach. The same goes for Samantha zapping Barkley with a truth spell; Barkley himself says "someone in this room did something to me to make me say those things."

Why does Samantha go to the trouble of personally visiting Leach to take back what he demanded of her, visible or invisible? She can do that long-distance, like when she slowed down Phyllis' train in "A Nice Little Dinner Party" (#19). Samantha's powers pack quite a wallop – Leach's new coffee table snaps in two before the chandelier even hits it. Samantha also breaks down Leach's front door, but that's part of the apartment building, and nothing to do with Leach's extortion. Most importantly, why punish Charmaine? Samantha's beef is with Leach; it's not like Samantha knows Charmaine gave him the blackmail idea.

When Charmaine finds Leach in the tiny car, she cries, "The witch?" when he tries to explain Samantha shrinking it. Mrs. Leach has just been rocked like a hurricane in her apartment, and she saw multiple objects moving around by themselves – yet she doesn't even consider the possibility that Leach is telling the truth. Next question: the Leaches' apartment is a disaster area and their front door is gone. Are they really going out with things in this condition? They should be afraid their stern landlady will see the wreckage and kick them out.

Leach has spent two episodes witnessing Samantha's seemingly limitless witchcraft. So why does he arrogantly claim, "Nothing you can do can stop me?" And surely Samantha must realize from her encounter with Harriet in Part I that Gladys left a snoopy replacement, but she still zaps Leach off her doorstep when Harriet could be watching. Earlier in the episode, Samantha asks Leach, "What if I told you I didn't care if people knew I was a witch?" Maybe she means it.

OH, MY STARS!

Leach gets Samantha to do his bidding by bluffing that he'll give Barkley his report on her. Not very high stakes, are they? What can one man in a baby food company do? The reporters that Gladys blabbed to in "Baby's First Paragraph" (#62) presented a much bigger danger than that. In Part I, Leach told Samantha she was to make him "a member of the idle rich" – but, in Part II, he only requests a car, some furniture, and some clothes. Why doesn't he demand unmarked bills like most blackmailers? Finally, when Samantha takes those things back and calls Leach's bluff, he asks, "Why don't you give me what I want anyway?" Some extortionist! How about threatening to go to the papers, or the police? Leach is supposed to be a screw-up, but his actions in this second part rather blunt the suspense generated in the first, making for a weaker episode.

SON OF A GUN!

"That, Mr. Leach, would be totally redundant." – Samantha to Leach, when he worries she's going to turn him into a snake.

A BUM RAPS
Airdate: April 28, 1966

Two stylish, elderly hobos, Dilloway and Dunn, work Morning Glory Circle for handouts; Harriet catches on to Dilloway's game right away, but Samantha mistakes Dilloway for Darrin's arriving Uncle Albert. Although "Albert" gets Darrin's name wrong and thinks Tabatha is a boy, Samantha is entranced when he serenades her daughter; Dilloway reveals he was once a vaudevillian headliner. Busy with Tabatha, Samantha asks Dilloway to get the door – behind it is the real Uncle Albert. Dilloway lies that the Stephenses have moved and sends Albert on his way, then is cornered by Dunn, who wants to rob the Stephenses. Later, Harriet comes over and is confused to see that the hobo she dismissed is Uncle Albert; he filches Ms. Kravitz's watch, which Samantha sees. Harriet returns with Abner to confront Dilloway, so Samantha twitches Harriet's watch back on her arm.

Darrin asks Samantha to set out Albert's picture; when she does, she realizes Dilloway is not Albert. Having already invited "Albert" to stay, Samantha asks Darrin to humor him. After an enjoyable evening, Dilloway reluctantly helps Dunn clear out the house, but ditches his longtime friend after he realizes the Stephenses knew he wasn't Albert. Discovering the robbery, Samantha appears in her stolen television as Dunn makes his getaway, convincing him to bring the truck back to Morning Glory Circle. Dilloway comes clean, responding to the Stephenses' mercy with a promise to try and get back into entertainment, and Samantha zaps the pilfered belongings back into their proper places.

GOOD!

Nothing else is known about Harriet except that she believes Gladys' claims about Samantha [see "Follow That Witch (Part I)" (#66)] – so her interaction with her brother, Abner, satisfyingly paints a clearer picture of the Kravitz family dynamic. No wonder Abner never believes Gladys – he apparently grew up with a sister who also made unusual assertions.

This episode brings to light a problem specific to the 1960s: disenfranchised, elderly vaudeville performers who were left scratching for a living when the genre died out in the 1930s. It's hard to imagine in this day and age, but these song-and-dance performers delighted audiences for decades before talking pictures, radio, and finally television made them obsolete. Dilloway is a nice nod to their plight, and still serves as a reminder of a form of entertainment that deserves to be preserved. The episode even plays a bit like a vaudeville routine, complete with a mistaken identity plot.

Even though it's a slight cheat, having Samantha fill only part of the house with furniture is a successful effect, aided by Samantha remaining in the exact same position as the Stephenses' belongings pop back in.

WELL?

Samantha is surprisingly naïve about strangers, considering she just came through a two-part ordeal with Charlie Leach in "Follow That Witch" (#66-#67). She assumes Dilloway is Darrin's Uncle Albert, but, even after she discovers the deception, she insists on having him stick around, which is odd. But no odder than the fact that Darrin's suit just happens to fit Dilloway as if it was made for him.

When the real Uncle Albert learns that the people expecting him have moved, he slinks away, never to be heard from again. If you'd traveled all those miles to see relatives and hit such an obstacle, wouldn't you find a phone? Samantha should receive a call from Albert within minutes – and doesn't Albert have Darrin's work number? Not that the Stephenses ultimately seem very concerned with his whereabouts. By the way, how many uncles does Darrin have? Endora made her truth god look like it was from Uncle Herbert in "Speak the Truth" (#50), and now there's an Uncle Albert. Are they the same uncle? And is Albert Frank's brother or Phyllis'?

Dilloway and Dunn are referred to as hobos, bums, and tramps – all of which are homeless folks who wander around looking for work or food. Nowhere in that definition does it describe these downtrodden people as thieves, yet Dunn has no problem with the idea of stealing the Stephenses blind. If Dunn's plan is to resort to crime, he probably shouldn't declare his true intentions and identity to Dilloway in full volume on the patio when the woman he wants to hoodwink could be in earshot. Besides, if the former vaudevillians are so destitute, how can Dunn afford to rent a truck for his robbery?

Harriet brushes Dilloway off, telling him, "this is a respectable neighborhood!" Is it? This is the second robbery at the Stephenses in a few months; a thief tried to make off with an expensive necklace meant for Louise in "A Strange Little Visitor" (#48). And is Samantha's ESP back? Floating Harriet's watch out of Dilloway's pocket and calling it "one of my little funny tricks" is one thing, because Samantha witnessed its theft. But Samantha can't know Dilloway's name, and that he was part of Dilloway & Dunn, without ESP – a talent that has been nonexistent most of this season.

Even if the Stephenses are willing to give Dilloway another chance, why do they give Dunn a free pass? Samantha seems to think the act of Dilloway & Dunn has a place on television (if vaudeville was dead by the 1930s, how would networks accept it in 1966?), but the Stephenses leave them to fend for themselves, despite Darrin getting The Great Zeno on TV in "It's Magic" (#16).

Someone in the writing room is a fan of vaudeville. Samantha zapped up a couple of hoofers exploring ideas for a vaudeville-themed hospital benefit in "And Then I Wrote" (#45), and Endora claimed to be a vaudeville performer to explain a "talking" Tabatha in "Baby's First Paragraph" (#62).

OH, MY STARS!

It must be terribly difficult to deliver mail on Morning Glory Circle. In "Baby's First Paragraph" (#62), Gladys ran out of a house marked "204." Here, Harriet opens the door to Dilloway at 347. Neither number is correct; the Kravitz house is across from the Stephens house, which is 1164.

Samantha discovers that Dilloway is not Albert when she pulls the photo of Darrin's uncle out of a drawer. This can't be first time she's seen the snapshot; the way Darrin goes on about the guy, and with news that Albert is on his way, Darrin would proudly show Albert's picture to Samantha, and she'd know Dilloway isn't Albert the second she sees him. Of course, that would invalidate this entire episode.

As the Stephenses sleep, Dilloway and Dunn somehow move every piece of furniture out of their house without waking them, or their baby. All that inevitable clunking around, and it's only the sound of the robbers' truck driving away that conveniently rouses Darrin.

SON OF A GUN!

"With him, you'd have to uproot the whole tree." – Darrin to Samantha, after she's disappointed Dilloway hasn't turned over a new leaf.

DIVIDED HE FALLS
Airdate: May 5, 1966

Endora zaps Darrin into overalls and a suit of armor to mock Samantha's noble view of him, but Samantha changes him back. Later, a deadline on the Stern Chemical account interferes with the Stephenses' Florida vacation; Endora gloats, saying Darrin wouldn't have been much fun anyway. After Samantha insists that Endora can only see Darrin's work side, Endora splits him into two separate people: Fun Darrin is ready to ditch the account, while Work Darrin labors in the den. Endora convinces Samantha to tell Work Darrin they're going away together, and Fun Darrin takes Samantha to Miami.

Work Darrin bores Larry and Stern with his relentless toiling, while Fun Darrin flirts with the girls and runs Samantha ragged with his merrymaking. Fun Darrin barely remembers Tabatha and has to be twitched out of the pool because he's forgotten he can't swim. As the party continues, Fun Darrin thinks the crowd will love seeing Samantha zap up champagne, so she clears the room and summons Endora, who gets along famously with Fun Darrin. Samantha checks on Work Darrin in Manhattan, giving the stupefied Larry and Stern a chance to slip out. Work Darrin is upset, but Samantha zaps him to Miami to meet Fun Darrin – and the two don't get along. Samantha and Endora reincorporate the Darrins by having them literally run into each other, and, because Work Darrin's efforts earned a three-week vacation, Darrin decides to spend it at home with his family and his two sides.

GOOD!

It's a terrific psychological statement when it turns out Darrin's two sides don't even like each other. And, while Samantha predicts Darrin will be furious over being divided, he certainly has a sense of humor about it in the end. While Samantha is in Miami with Fun Darrin, Tabatha, who sometimes seems to lack supervision, gets to spend the week with Darrin's parents. [They *must* live in town, despite the continuity-upending assertion that they don't in "The Dancing Bear" (#58).] And the show follows through on a minor detail from "And Then There Were Three" (#54), where Darrin said he couldn't swim; he can't here, either.

WELL?

As Darrin walks away from his car, he somehow can't tell he's been changed into a hick and zapped into a suit of armor. It's not Darrin's first go-round as a knight, either; Aunt Clara accidentally put him in that same costume in "The Very Informal Dress" (#44).

The Stephenses' Floridian vacation gets canceled because Stern Chemicals has a deadline for their television commercial; this is considered an emergency. Yet, Samantha reminds Fun Darrin he has two more weeks of work in front of him, and Work Darrin grumbles that he only has only three weeks to finish the job. Where's the emergency?

In the den, Work Darrin stonily tells Samantha he can't concentrate with the "radio" (really Fun Darrin singing) blasting upstairs. But he doesn't hear Fun Darrin yelling "Fore!" in the much closer living room, much less all the full-volume conversations Samantha and Endora have there. Endora tries to keep Samantha from seeing Work Darrin in the den, "where he keeps all his books." What about all the books in the living room? Darrin hid Louise's necklace behind them in "A Strange Little Visitor" (#48). For that matter, if Darrin can't swim, why would he own a book on surfing? Maybe Samantha only acts on adrenaline to save Fun Darrin from drowning, but it's hard to believe she would witch him out of the pool in public, and in an elaborate reverse dive. This pool is supposed to be in Miami, but it's the same one Darrin pushed Adam Newlarkin into, locally, in "We're In For A Bad Spell" (#39).

How does Fun Darrin know all his fellow partiers on a first-name basis when he's only just met them? And this crowd, who's hipper than hip, probably wouldn't still be doing the Watusi, a dance that's already four years old at this point. Samantha's so desperate to keep Darrin's new friends from finding out she's a witch that she zaps them back to their rooms. Didn't she just tell Charlie Leach in "Follow That Witch (Part II)" (#67) that she didn't care if people found out? Maybe she was just bluffing, but surely some of Fun Darrin's guests would wonder why they were in his room one second and their own the next – and swap stories about it.

What happened to the heart necklace that Samantha always wears? She has it on all through the episode until she's at the pool in Miami, yet later it's around her neck again. Does she not want to lose it poolside? In the hotel, the swinging music everyone dances to blares only until Samantha makes everyone disappear, but it comes back on when Samantha leaves Fun Darrin to check on Work Darrin. And how does Samantha know where to find Work Darrin, anyway? For all she knows, he's at home or the office, but she walks into the restaurant as if she expects to find him with Larry and Stern. Not bad for a witch who didn't even know where to start looking when Darrin-as-chimp went missing in "Alias Darrin Stephens" (#37).

OH, MY STARS!

The opening segment seems to be a holdover from Season One that was tacked on to this episode, the dead giveaway being Samantha's shorter, more glamorous hair. Which episode did it get cut out of, and why resurrect it here? The only up side is that it reveals where the show got a still of Darrin dressed as a hayseed, which Samantha used to discourage her flirty domestic applicant in "Maid to Order" (#53).

SON OF A GUN!

"Well, I just hope your husband doesn't find out." – Endora to Samantha, who says she's in love with a man that loves fun and excitement.

Two Darrins are twice the showcase for Dick York: robotic Work Darrin is enough of a riot ("All right," he monotones when Larry points out Stern is making a joke), but Fun Darrin more than earns his title, whooping, "Hi, Endora! Great to see ya, baby!" He even thinks Samantha using witchcraft would be "crazy." Dick York looks like he's having a ball playing Darrin in such drastically different ways – and it wouldn't be unreasonable to assume Jim Carrey studied this episode more than once.

MAN'S BEST FRIEND
Airdate: May 12, 1966

The Stephenses look forward to marking thirty days without witchcraft, which is threatened by Rodney, a young warlock who declares he's loved Samantha since she babysat for him. After Samantha sends Rodney away, Darrin comes home with an affectionate stray dog; Samantha quickly realizes the pooch is Rodney, who knows Samantha can't use witchcraft to get rid of him. Samantha tells Rodney her marriage is based on trust and respect – to ruin both, Rodney opens the door to Harriet Kravitz, implying he's having an affair with Samantha. Rodney then answers Darrin's lost-and-found ad for the dog and witches Harriet into telling Darrin about Rodney being at the house.

During the thirty-day celebration, Darrin reveals that Harriet met Rodney, but when Samantha admits Rodney and the dog are one and the same, Darrin doesn't believe her and storms off to sleep in the den. Telling Rodney-as-dog he needs an extra blanket, Darrin sneaks outside to peek in the window, hoping Rodney will change back. Rodney doesn't until Darrin pretends to sleep; Darrin catches him and admits to Samantha that he faked his disbelief to win out over witchcraft. Harriet peeks in just as Rodney becomes a dog again. A woman arrives, responding to Darrin's ad – it's Rodney's mother, who threatens to give him a flea bath; she drags him away after he restores himself, and Samantha accidentally spoils her record by zapping up water for a choking Darrin.

GOOD!

When Darrin angrily refuses to believe Samantha's claims about Rodney, he seems to deserve Samantha turning her back on him. So how clever is it that Darrin is on to Rodney, and tricks him into revealing himself? Darrin must clue in already at the bakery, when Harriet mysteriously shows up with a craving for the éclairs she says she hates. As Darrin "rages" at Samantha for not liking the dog, his scheme is revealed in the brief moment he hesitates while pointing out, "You even said that he...fawned." Just once, Darrin hopes to defeat witchcraft without resorting to it – and does.

WELL?

How does Darrin know for sure Samantha hasn't used her powers in 29 days? She twitches without him seeing in almost every episode. And where did Darrin get a calendar with no months on it to mark her progress? There are always pictures below the clock in the kitchen; they are now absent to make room for the never-before-seen bulletin board Darrin tacks the calendar to.

When Rodney almost provokes Samantha into hitting him with a saucepan, he becomes a dog again; a second later, Darrin rushes into frame. For Darrin to get there that fast, he would have to be in the kitchen already, where he would see Rodney transform – yet, the scene plays as if Darrin is none the wiser. Rodney-as-dog does a literal flip-flop just before the fade-out, when footage of the pooch reverses for no apparent reason.

After Samantha heads to her bedroom on the heels of threatening to punch Rodney in the nose, he sits on the stairs with his hands in front of him. But when the scene cuts to a close-up, his right hand is raised conspiratorially in front of him. By the way, Rodney might be devious, but his execution is a little sloppy: he talks about "Operation Split-Up" with Harriet on the other side of the door as if he can't be heard, and again as Samantha comes down the stairs (and into earshot) with Tabatha. And either witches don't have ESP, or Rodney's could use developing, because he has to peek through the door curtain to see that Harriet's on the doorstep – carrying the same saucepan she already returned in "Follow That Witch (Part I)" (#66).

In "Divided He Falls" (#69), Samantha told Endora that Darrin keeps all his books in the den. This episode proves that's not accurate, because Samantha herself pulls a book from the living room shelf just before Rodney interrupts her celebration. And is Samantha telling Rodney that Darrin "can be very violent" to scare him, or is she remembering how her husband tangled with heavyweight boxers in "Fastest Gun on Madison Avenue" (#57)?

Darrin's scheme is sharp, but no wonder Rodney doesn't change back right away: when Darrin sneaks out the front door, he closes it normally, and the noise would tell Rodney that Darrin isn't just getting a blanket from the closet. Darrin catches Rodney, but it's amazing the warlock doesn't subdue him with witchcraft to aid his cause. As for Rodney's mother, she's a dead ringer for Mrs. Glendon from "Samantha the Dressmaker" (#60) – probably because both formidable females are played by Barbara Morrison; it seems somewhat soon for a repeat appearance.

OH, MY STARS!

Maybe the public wasn't aware of this piece of information in the '60s, but chocolate is toxic to dogs – it can make them seriously ill, or even kill them. Yet Rodney-as-dog munches on chocolate cake with ease, and no one questions the mutt's preference for the pastry. This again begs the question, do transformees retain their own physiology, or does it convert to adapt to their new form? Perhaps so – the humanized "Ling-Ling" (#21) was able to down a martini that would have made any feline very, very sick.

SON OF A GUN!

"When you want to find out something from me, just ask." – Samantha to Darrin, after he none too subtly hints about Rodney's presence.

Before Richard Dreyfuss cut his acting teeth on blockbuster feature films like *Close Encounters of the Third Kind* and *Jaws*, he cut his canine teeth as Rodney, the troublemaking warlock. Rodney's neurotic dialogue is brilliantly sophisticated, and wouldn't be out of place in 1960s theatre. Dreyfuss makes Rodney smarmy, underhanded, and charming all at the same time, plus, he holds perfectly still for Rodney's witchy changes. Considering his youth, and the fact that this is his first television role, Dreyfuss proves he can go paw-to-toe with all the veterans that surround him.

THE CATNAPPER
Airdate: May 19, 1966

Endora once again attributes Darrin's long hours to infidelity, while private eye Charlie Leach [see "Follow That Witch" (#66-#67)] returns and realizes Samantha and Endora are both witches. As Leach tells his wife, Charmaine, about the luxuries they're going to enjoy, Larry introduces Darrin to Toni Devlin, the cosmetics executive everyone thought was a man. Endora and Samantha see Darrin and Toni out at a business lunch; feeling that Toni dropping by to see Darrin at the house is going too far, the suspicious Endora turns her into a cat. Leach witnesses the transformation and spirits Toni-as-cat out of the kitchen.

Worried about the missing Toni, Darrin stalls Larry, but the Stephenses are shocked to see Leach, who wants a million dollars in exchange for the cat. Telling Leach that she can't produce that much money at once, Samantha twitches up a money tree that blooms $1,000 every 24 hours. Leach won't return Toni until he sees the tree grow the next batch, but Samantha asks him to feed Toni at a specific time; he does, and Samantha changes him into a mouse, which Toni-as-cat chases. Leach agrees to return Toni, while Samantha tracks Endora to Tibet. Endora turns Toni back, and Darrin takes the disoriented woman to their meeting. When Leach's money tree doesn't bloom, and the previous day's cash is just a pile of leaves, Charmaine rolls her eyes as Leach swears he'll visit the Stephenses again someday.

GOOD!

Despite his rampant flirting with female clients and neighbors during Season One, here Darrin sets Toni Devlin straight and tells her he *does* find her resistible. He probably shouldn't plop his hand on her shoulder five seconds after meeting her (would he do that with a male client?), but at least it's a step in the right direction.

After Endora turns Toni into a cat, Samantha twitches away Toni's purse and pearls to keep the approaching Darrin from discovering her. Later, when Toni is restored, her pearls are still gone, which is good attention to detail. Another smart moment is Darrin's quizzical look as Samantha tells Leach her powers are limited. That may have been true in "I, Darrin, Take This Witch, Samantha" (#1), but Darrin certainly knows better by now; that he's confused at first but wordlessly realizes Samantha is conning Leach speaks volumes.

WELL?

Leach figures out that Endora is a witch by watching her magical costume change. Shouldn't he make that distinction when he sees Endora popping in instead? Though Leach spends a lot of time parked in front of the Stephenses' windows, Harriet Kravitz never spots him. She does plenty of her own snooping, and Leach did have an ally in her during their last interaction [see "Follow That Witch (Part I)" (#66)]; she could help him in his latest scheme against the Stephenses, but she's somehow missing in action.

Who takes care of Tabatha while Samantha and Endora are out to lunch? And who's looking after her while Darrin's at the office and Samantha's flying around the world looking for Endora – Leach, who stops by off-screen to return the cat? In "Follow That Witch (Part II)" (#67), Leach asked Samantha if she traveled like Batman – she looks like the Caped Crusader now, all right, superimposed against grainy stock footage of foreign locales which is scored by swinger music that wouldn't be out of place on that other TV show.

Charmaine is sweet to tell Leach she doesn't need for them to be rolling in dough, but she still expresses disbelief when recapping how Barkley fired Leach over his witch stories [see "Follow That Witch" (#66-#67)]. She saw objects flying around and had a gust of wind undress her; shouldn't she at least have an open mind after what she experienced?

Why does Samantha go to the trouble of turning Leach into a mouse to coerce him into returning Toni? It does provide the catty line, "Oh, that horrible mackerel breath!" (even though Toni-as-cat never ends up eating any), but all Samantha has to do is pop in on Leach and take Toni back. The literal cat-and-mouse game is very suspenseful, considering the animals are never actually in the same frame together – however, the newspaper they run past isn't from the show's setting of New York: it's the *Silverlake Advertiser*, which is from the metropolitan Los Angeles area.

When Toni becomes human again, she doesn't wonder why she's in Darrin's lap. She just accused him of playing "the flirtatious little games between the sexes" when he put his hand on her shoulder; certainly she wouldn't give him a free pass, even in her disoriented state. Why does Toni have no memory of being a cat, while Leach remembers being turned into a mouse?

OH, MY STARS!

Charlie Leach has returned from Mexico, where Samantha left him at the end of "Follow That Witch (Part II)" (#67). How long did it take him to traverse the 2,138 miles back to New York? How did he explain his absence to the don't-you-dare-leave-me-in-this-dump Charmaine? And why does that dump look exactly the way it did before Samantha destroyed it? The show doesn't address these loose story threads, instead needle-dropping the Leaches into a new story. Granted, there's only 25 minutes of airtime, but one of them could be used to better tie the Leaches' previous appearance to their current one. Case in point: replacing the episode's prologue about Darrin and a dog snoring, which has nothing to do with what follows. And, apparently, Samantha hasn't heard of earplugs, doesn't think to silence Darrin's snoring by magic, and can hear a strange dog snoring through a closed door. Warlock Rodney just tried to be "Man's Best Friend" (#70) – surely Samantha would think that Rodney's back as a different breed.

Bringing the Leaches back from "Follow That Witch" (#66-#67) offers potentially strong continuity, but their new appearances lack the pizazz of the first go-round. Leach does hunt for bigger game, demanding a million dollars instead of home improvement like last time, but there's no point to having him discover Endora is also a witch when he never interacts with her. Endora made Toni a cat – imagine what she'd do to Leach. And the detective, who kept coming back like a horror movie villain no matter what Samantha did to him the first time, gives up too easily after just one witchy trick. Chalk it up to "sequelitis?"

SON OF A GUN!

"If that cat double-parked, wham! They'd find it!" – Darrin to Samantha, furious that the police can't find Toni-as-cat.

WHAT EVERY YOUNG MAN SHOULD KNOW
Airdate: May 26, 1966

EPISODE **72**

Darrin catches Samantha fixing a broken vase with witchcraft. As they squabble, Darrin reminds Samantha she didn't tell him she was a witch until their wedding night. When Darrin is vague as to whether he would have married Samantha if he'd known about her beforehand, Endora offers to send Samantha back in time so there will be no doubt. Samantha chooses an evening when she cooked Darrin dinner, but this time, she does it by witchcraft. Though Past Darrin flees, Present-Day Darrin demands to go back as well when he finds out his wife has been time tripping. In the alternate reality, Darrin confides to Larry about Samantha; Larry is incredulous until Samantha pops in, later interrupting Darrin's proposal with an idea to use Samantha's powers for boosting agency revenue.

In the present, Samantha fumes at Darrin's apparent complicity, and Darrin rages that he's glad he didn't meet Endora before proposing. Determined to prove himself, Darrin tells Endora to send him back again, after which Darrin throws the greedy Larry out. While making another attempt to propose to Samantha, Endora appears; Darrin is cordial, but Endora repeatedly zaps Darrin out of the room, causing him to yell that he's going to marry Samantha whether Endora likes it or not. Endora leaves, and Samantha gets an angry but sincere proposal; Samantha accepts, and all is well once everyone returns to the present.

GOOD!

To convince Darrin she's not mortal, Samantha says she's "a house-haunting, cauldron-stirring, broom-riding witch." With a slight inversion, this is the same statement Samantha made in "I, Darrin, Take This Witch, Samantha" (#1); this must just be her consistent way of confessing she's a witch, though, in that episode, Endora made it clear that witches don't ride brooms. Another satisfying touch is getting to see Samantha meet Larry – they already knew each other by the time they had their first scene together in "It Shouldn't Happen to a Dog" (#3), which always felt like the show skipped a step. Larry even finds out she's a witch; when he stutters that he's enchanted to meet Samantha, she pipes up, "How about *bewitched*, Mr. Tate?" The full-circle scene, which begins and ends with Darrin muttering, "You're a red-blooded American boy and you're in love with a witch," is ingenious.

Another connection to the pilot is Endora zapping Darrin out of his apartment and into to the hallway, which mirrors the way she zapped him out of his hotel room and into the lobby on his wedding night – the only difference is that now Darrin is aware of being relocated; Endora telling Samantha, "Don't you help him" seems to indicate she's only testing him to see how much he really wants to be with her daughter. The twist of Darrin meeting Endora right away instead of later [as in "Mother Meets What's-His-Name" (#4)], is fascinating, especially because he's much friendlier to her initially in this reality than he was in that episode.

WELL?

The fracas starts because Samantha knocks over a statuette from Uncle Albert ["A Bum Raps" (#68)]. It's just that the figurine looks exactly like the truth god Endora inflicted on Darrin in "Speak the Truth" (#50). Darrin also wants to know if Samantha uses witchcraft when he isn't home, a fair enough question considering he took it at face value that Samantha hadn't used her powers for thirty days in "Man's Best Friend" (#70).

When Darrin comes downstairs after Samantha's first time trek, she yells at him for being cowardly and walking out on her, only asking if he remembers the night she came to his apartment to cook and adding "this time you behaved very badly!" Is Darrin supposed to glean that Samantha has just taken a trip to the past from this tiny bit of information? Incidentally, why is Samantha wearing her wedding ring back in the past? She's not married to Darrin yet.

Endora casts variations of the same spell three times, always starting with "Thunder, lightning, hail, rain." Except, the first time, Endora mixes things up and says "rain, hail." Now, when everyone goes back, are they only going in their minds, or are they physically making the trip? If it's the latter, who's minding Tabatha with no one in the house? Also, are the Stephenses actually visiting an alternate reality, or can their actions inadvertently change this one? If the latter is true, they could prevent Tabatha from ever being born. Finally, Endora suggests that Darrin and Larry are to "never remember a thing" – so why does Darrin call Endora "Mom" during the tag as if he's retained some of the memory?

OH, MY STARS!

Many things about this outstanding episode hearken back to "I, Darrin, Take This Witch, Samantha" (#1), which rather brings the series full circle at this point. But, there are several inconsistencies: to begin with, Darrin lived in a house before he and Samantha were married, not an apartment. Samantha's hair was much shorter, her trademark heart necklace didn't appear until "Be It Ever So Mortgaged" (#2), and Samantha couldn't have made dinner for Darrin, because she had no idea how to cook. Darrin confides in Larry, when, in the pilot, he confided in Dave, and Larry offers to make Darrin a vice president, except he was already a vice president in the first episode. None of this takes away from the power of this installment, but even more attention to detail would have been the icing on this very tasty cake.

SON OF A GUN!

"If it were only that simple." – Samantha to Darrin, after he tells her he doesn't care if her relatives are shoplifters, moonshiners, or cattle-rustlers.

 Bewitched started with a quick montage of Darrin and Samantha's courtship, then went straight to their honeymoon, jumping to Darrin's reaction after being told off-screen that Samantha is a witch. This episode fixes that – not only do the "future" marrieds get together for a date, but Darrin proposes, and Samantha stops him so she can convince him she's a witch. Having this gap filled in, even through an alternate reality, is quite satisfying. And it only makes sense that Samantha would wonder if Darrin would have married her if she'd told him before their wedding; now she knows.

THE GIRL WITH THE GOLDEN NOSE
Airdate: June 2, 1966

EPISODE
73

As Samantha admires a mink coat in a magazine, Darrin laments that he's not getting anywhere in his career, especially after not being assigned the prestigious Waterhouse account. Once Darrin leaves for work, Louise calls Samantha with the news that Larry is giving Darrin the account anyway; when Larry mentions having seen Samantha, Darrin rejects the assignment, assuming his wife has zapped it for him. Darrin tries to repel the conservative Waterhouse with swinging slang, but it only impresses him. Darrin drowns his sorrows with Dave, who barely listens, as usual. Feeling he's been selfish in making Samantha give up luxuries she could twitch up herself, Darrin buys her the mink; later, he walks into a storm, only to be further convinced Samantha is using her powers to help him when it suddenly stops raining.

 After Darrin confidently determines that his secretary's birthplace is incorrect, a concerned Larry calls Samantha about Darrin and his "charmed life." Upset that Darrin's jumped to conclusions, Samantha zaps up a posh new décor and a butler, telling her husband they can openly live by witchcraft now that he knows she got him the Waterhouse account. Darrin balks when Samantha claims she magically arranged other accounts he knows he earned himself, and he comes to realize Samantha has stayed true to her promise not to help him succeed through spells. Samantha twitches the house back to normal, and the next day, when Darrin again walks into a storm, he gets soaked.

GOOD!

It's odd that Larry would have Darrin meet with Waterhouse after he refused the account, but Darrin's sabotage attempt is well worth the plot hole. Darrin seems to be channeling his fun side [see "Divided He Falls" (#69)] as he tries to get Waterhouse to "lay it on him," repeatedly getting his name wrong and infuriating Larry with sexed-up, modern ideas for the conservative client – all without a spell on him.

In "A Is For Aardvark" (#17), Darrin gave Samantha free reign to use her powers, then had her purge his memory of the resulting events; his current decision to secretly let Samantha pull the strings by witchcraft is a fresh take, going even deeper as Darrin realizes Samantha could have anything, "yet she chose me." He even decides that letting Samantha advance his career would be "my way of saying thanks." Darrin still shouldn't assume Samantha is magically interfering, but some of his motivations are surprisingly astute – and this time, he'll remember everything.

The Stephenses were only planning to live in style In "A Is For Aardvark" (#17) – this time, Samantha actually witches up the luxuries. The best part is watching Samantha turn the tables on her presuming husband, especially after being legitimately angry over how he'd tried and convicted her without even talking to her (great references to Salem, too). Like Samantha said in "Man's Best Friend" (#70): "When you want to find out something from me, just ask."

WELL?

Samantha moons over a mink coat in a magazine as the episode starts. A close-up reveals the fur is dark, but in the following wide shot, the coat is a much lighter shade. And Samantha must have changed her mind over the past year – in "A Is For Aardvark" (#17), she specifically told the let's-live-by-witchcraft Darrin that she didn't want a mink.

During Season One, there was an implication that Darrin was tops in his field. Here, Darrin complains about being nowhere near the top, and Larry initially withholds an account from Darrin because he's "too immature." (Immature in his mid-30s?) Now, Darrin knows Samantha is lunching with Louise, so he shouldn't think it unusual for her to talk to Larry; he also knows Samantha can perform witchcraft remotely, and doesn't need to have contact with Larry if she wants to put a spell on him, although he comes to that conclusion anyway.

It's understandable Darrin wants to succeed on his own, but his pride gets the better of him to the point he accuses Samantha of turning him into a werewolf and a chimpanzee. Has he already forgotten that it was Endora who transformed him into a werewolf [in "Trick or Treat" (#43)], and that Aunt Clara made a monkey out of him in "Alias Darrin Stephens" (#37)?

Darrin must have forgiven Dave for checking out his "daughter" in "And Then There Were Three" (#54); having Dave there as Darrin relates his latest witchy problem goes all the way back to the pilot, but his absent-minded babble is getting to be an old gag – Dave even repeats dialogue verbatim from "A Very Special Delivery" (#38). Wouldn't it be a great twist if Dave actually heard Darrin for a change?

Once again, Tabatha doesn't seem to exist. Samantha offers to drive Darrin to work with no mention of their child, and later, when Samantha zaps up servants for her *nouveau riche* house, there's a butler, an upstairs maid, a chef, and a valet, but no one to take care the baby – this after Samantha spent the whole first half of this season pregnant.

OH, MY STARS!

How many Bettys are there at McMann & Tate? Jill Foster has made three appearances as the secretary so far, the latest in "Follow That Witch (Part II)" (#67). In the next episode, "A Bum Raps" (#68), Betty had a different face in the form of Ann Prentiss; here, Betty is substantially older and played by Alice Backes. Sounds like the only criteria for getting hired as an agency secretary is that your first name has to be Betty! Darrin rocks this Betty's world, correctly predicting that her birthplace is wrong. Shouldn't he guess something innocuous instead of being willing to play games with someone's life just to prove a point?

Darrin is all too willing to believe Samantha's been fixing accounts and stopping rainstorms for him, but when he comes home to "the Taj Mahal," he suddenly doesn't want to live that way. Seeing some expensive furniture is enough to make him reconsider? Naturally, Darrin has to revert to living the mortal way, but the dots in his reversal don't quite connect.

SON OF A GUN!

"When a man can't lose, he can't win!" – Darrin to Larry, after thinking Samantha prevented his sabotage of the Waterhouse account.

PRODIGY
Airdate: June 9, 1966

EPISODE 74

Darrin briefly thinks baby Tabatha is a witch when a lamp she points to seemingly comes on by itself; setting Darrin straight and changing the subject, Samantha reminds him that Gladys has asked them over to watch her violinist brother, Louis Gruber, make his television début. The Stephenses think back to when a pregnant Samantha helped boost Louis' confidence: Abner had nothing but bad things to say about his brother-in-law, who talked a big game though he hadn't performed since his pants fell down on stage as a nine-year-old; sick of Abner's put-downs, Louis blew everyone away with his talent. Samantha arranged for Louis to perform a hospital benefit, letting Louis practice at her house.

Terrified of playing the benefit, Louis tried to break his violin, but couldn't because Samantha briefly fortified it with witchcraft. When Abner accidentally sat on the restored instrument, Louis thought he was off the hook until Samantha zapped up a Stradivarius for him. Louis was a no-show at the benefit, so Samantha witched his cab into driving backwards and delivering him to the concert hall. The self-professed "chicken fiddler" made a run for it, discovering himself on stage thanks to Samantha. Though Samantha had to get him started, Louis turned in an excellent performance on his own. In the present, the Stephenses and Kravitzes proudly watch Louis on TV, but are mortified when his pants fall down in front of an audience once again.

GOOD!

Even though this is the third flashback episode this season, it's set up much better than "A Vision of Sugar Plums" (#51) and "Samantha Meets the Folks" (#56): the quality is consistent throughout the episode, we come back to the present at the end, and what helps most of all is that, despite this being the Stephenses' recollection, these events are entirely new, so they don't feel like rehash.

Abner's quick to insult Louis, but he knows what time it is with his brother-in-law. He correctly concludes that Louis is too scared to play in public, and the resulting scene offers a fascinating look into the inner workings of the Kravitz-Gruber family that approaches straight-up drama. It's a welcome departure from watching Abner and Gladys only arguing about the witchcraft she witnesses.

Ordinarily, when Samantha tries to bolster a mortal's confidence, she magically adds to their abilities, like she did for young ball player Marshall in "Little Pitchers Have Big Fears" (#6) and prestidigitator Zeno in "It's Magic" (#16). Louis never doubts his talent – though Samantha gives him a push, he plays on his own every time.

WELL?

Gladys must be back from visiting her mother, because no mention is made of Abner's sister, Harriet, who was last seen talking to Darrin in a bakery in "Man's Best Friend" (#70). The paranoid, suspicious Gladys is remarkably subdued – she hangs out with Samantha as if she were any other neighbor. Does Gladys really not think there's anything supernatural involved in retrieving Louis or getting him to play when he stands frozen on stage?

The show's hospitals have a lot of benefits: the Stephenses recalled attending one in "Love Is Blind" (#13), and Samantha arranged to have The Great Zeno play another in "It's Magic" (#16). Samantha was the entertainment chairman in the latter, so it's conceivable she still has the connections to book Louis, though she does it without consulting him first. Later, Samantha tells Gladys that Louis has been ready for his comeback for 26 years. If Louis was nine when his pants fell down, that would make him 35 – reasonable until you recall that, in "Illegal Separation" (#32), the Kravitzes stated they had been married 30 years; unless Louis was four when his sister got married, this timeline doesn't work.

Louis is slated to play the Morning Glory Circle Auditorium. This tiny street has its own concert hall? Louis emerges from his foiled underground escape attempt in a dirty and dusty tuxedo, yet he is dragged on stage to perform for an audience without anyone trying to clean him up. And, in the wings, Darrin asks Samantha, "Is that you playing, or him?" in full volume, right next to the very woman who has spent two seasons suspecting his wife is a witch.

The episode's finale has Louis repeating history when his pants fall down on live television. Why undo his progress with such a cruel ending? More importantly, no network would continue to beam footage of a half-dressed man into millions of American homes during prime-time – they would cut to commercial before his pants hit the ground.

The flashback device here presents the same problems it did in "A Vision of Sugar Plums" (#51) and "Samantha Meets the Folks" (#56). The Stephenses are the ones recalling the events; they could never flash back to Louis' private argument with the Kravitzes, or his attempted getaway in the cab. The Stephenses and the Kravitzes could have reminisced together, which would cover everything but Louis' escape. Why do the Kravitzes come over to watch Louis' broadcast at the Stephenses, anyway? As the episode begins, Samantha tells Darrin that the Kravitzes are having *them* over.

OH, MY STARS!

There's a feeling that some episodes got moved around toward the end of this season. "What Every Young Man Should Know" (#72), which brought the series full circle by reexamining the events of the pilot, felt like a natural finale; both "The Girl With the Golden Nose" (#73) and "Prodigy" (#74) seem tacked on for no reason until you take into account that Alice Pearce, who plays Gladys, succumbed to cancer on March 3, 1966, three months before the season wrapped. This episode was evidently shot before

"And Then There Were Three" (#54) [Elizabeth Montgomery was still pregnant, and Ms. Pearce wasn't yet visibly ill]; perhaps it was moved to season's end to give Gladys a better final appearance than "Baby's First Paragraph" (#62), where she sadly looked very sick. This is not a typical "Oh, My Stars" observation, just an acknowledgment of Alice Pearce, a hilarious actress who lived by the credo "the show must go on" as long as she could – and an acknowledgment of the show, which opted to leave viewers with the best last impression of her as possible.

SON OF A GUN!

"Attaboy, Louis! Play like you eat!" – Abner, providing encouragement to his brother-in-law during the hospital benefit.

SEASON THREE

(1966-1967)

Darrin's ancestor, Darrin the Bold, must be saved from a curse in "A Most Unusual Wood Nymph" (#79).

ABC/Photofest

Endora grants Darrin's wish for a better memory in "I Remember You... Sometimes" (#97).

ABC/Photofest

Samantha is at a loss for how to deal with "My Friend Ben" (#87) when Benjamin Franklin visits the 20th century.

ABC/Photofest

"It's Wishcraft" (#103) when Samantha needs Endora's help taming Tabatha's new powers.

ABC/Photofest

SEASON THREE: OVERVIEW

The first thing viewers probably noticed when they tuned in for the third season of *Bewitched* was that Samantha, Darrin, and 1164 Morning Glory Circle were suddenly awash in what networks were touting as "living color." While it took an episode or two for the show to adjust its lighting and make-up to the new format, hues and tints were soon utilized to every advantage. The more restrained wardrobe of the first two seasons became more exotic and vibrant, particularly with its frequent inclusion of paisley, a popular pattern of the time. Endora, who had been seen in quite the variety of sophisticated ensembles before, went through the most radical reinvention, as both her clothes and hair took on a more adventurous look.

Granted, not everyone had color television sets by the fall of 1966, but there was a new vividness in the scripts that was surely evident even on black-and-white screens. The Stephenses and the Tates, who had mostly seemed like mere business acquaintances up to this point, cultivated a deepening sense of friendship. Larry, always unusually attached to his accounts but fairly mellow nonetheless, developed a tendency to brown-nose his clients – and a desire to throw his weight around at McMann & Tate, particularly with Darrin. And, a long-standing Tate mystery was solved when Larry and Louise's son was finally given a name: Jonathan. He disappeared after "Accidental Twins" (#78), but at least viewers knew what to call him.

The more genteel storylines of the black-and-white era gave way to more outlandish scenarios, including a trip back in time and historical figures visiting from the past. But it was Darrin and Endora's already strained relationship that most markedly took on a sense of theatricality. There seemed to be an unspoken, mutual agreement that allowed the in-laws to finally take the gloves off: Darrin exhibited increased hostility toward Endora, who took advantage of her supernatural superiority by putting spells on Darrin more frequently. Often, it was their differing viewpoints on how baby Tabatha should be raised that triggered these battles.

The Stephenses' daughter experienced a growth spurt, as Season Three opened on a slightly older, blond Tabatha that was quite the contrast to the brunette infant viewers had previously seen. It soon turned out that Tabatha not only inherited her looks from Samantha, but her powers; Tabatha's multiplying magic landed her parents in plenty of hot water, though there were several episodes where it seemed the witchlet had been forgotten about. And, owing to child labor laws, television children are typically played by twins; here, Erin and Diane Murphy switched off in the role of Tabatha. Eagle-eyed viewers might have been able to tell the difference between the two; while both girls were adorable, cherubic Erin seemed to have a slightly more special relationship with the camera.

Two other long-standing characters got new faces during this season as well, starting when Kasey Rogers assumed the role of Louise Tate from Irene Vernon. Louise still took a bit of a back seat to her more prevalent husband Larry, but there was something about the new Tates that made them feel more connected. More noticeably, Sandra Gould replaced the late Alice Pearce in the role of Gladys Kravitz. Sandra's Gladys certainly looked and sounded different, but it was in the scripts where the nosy neighbor underwent her greatest metamorphosis. No longer content to simply tell Abner about the strange doings across the street, Gladys became more proactive, involving city officials, and even the police, in her quest to be believed. Would Gladys have become so bold had Alice Pearce lived? We'll never know, but the Stephenses definitely had more to worry about in the sugar-borrowing snoop than ever before.

The series looked to be enjoying its success, as indicated by a seemingly higher budget. Sets were more opulent and plentiful. The Stephens house got a makeover in several areas, sporting new paintings, a new couch, and other additions and upgrades to the bedroom and foyer. There was all-new music and sound effects, and the overall feel of the show appeared to benefit from the infusion. Compare Season Three's premiere, "Nobody's Perfect" (#75), to its finale, "There's Gold in Them Thar Pills" (#107) [which introduced a "witch doctor," Dr. Bombay] – the latter is leaps and bounds ahead of the former. These 33 installments clearly demonstrated a natural evolution in the supernatural sitcom, particularly in Samantha, who started the season rather quaint but adopted a more confident and modern demeanor with every passing week.

This season does have a higher percentage of questionable episodes than the previous two, performing experiments with soapbox derbys, lunar lunacy, super cars and feisty frogs. But you'll also find some of the most sparkling episodes so far, particularly in the additions of Darrin the Bold, Benjamin Franklin, a witchcraft-controlled clown, and a little something called "wishcraft." In an era when networks still gave their shows a chance to catch on with audiences (instead of canceling them at the first sign of viewer disinterest, like today), many series came into their own during their third seasons. *Bewitched* was no exception.

NOBODY'S PERFECT
Airdate: September 15, 1966

While Tabatha is getting a glowing report from her pediatrician, Samantha sees her floating a toy across the office. Stunned to learn that Tabatha has powers, Samantha swears the happy Endora to secrecy until Darrin can be told. Left alone with Tabatha while Samantha shops, Endora gives her grandchild a few magic lessons; Darrin nearly catches them, and, after Tabatha levitates her toys, Endora taunts Darrin, barely keeping quiet about his daughter's newly-discovered witchcraft. Later, Samantha resists when the proud Darrin brings Larry and new client Robbins to the nursery; Robbins sees Tabatha as the perfect, softer image for his truck transmissions, and the men decide Tabatha's pictures should be done by child photographer Diego Fenman.

Though pleased that Tabatha twitches her nose "just like Mommy," Samantha gently beseeches her daughter to behave at the shoot, determining Darrin should learn Tabatha is a witch before she goes in front of the camera. But Samantha wakes up and finds that her husband and daughter have already left, so she zaps herself to the studio and tries to sit in on Tabatha's session, which Diego won't allow. Tabatha shocks Diego by moving his prop toys around; after Samantha peeks and magically grounds the floating playthings, Diego infuriates Darrin by calling Tabatha a "nutty baby," and Tabatha breaks a picture over Diego's head before being carried out. At home, Darrin marvels over Diego's "trick photography," and Samantha keeps Darrin from seeing Tabatha performing the same trick behind his back.

GOOD!

This episode provides some unexpected elements for the show: surprise and suspense. Tabatha magically retrieving a favorite toy becomes an impactful moment of discovery, and there's a definite tension in the air as Samantha tries to keep Darrin from finding out about his daughter's powers. The near-miss with Darrin and Endora is a moment ordinarily reserved for dramas, though Endora's repressed desire to blindside her son-in-law with the news keeps things light, as does her coaching scene, where she exhorts baby Tabatha to "Hex it for Grandmama." It's a wise decision to leave Darrin in the dark for a while rather than fill him in right away.

Samantha's speech to Tabatha about knowing what it's like to be part of the magical life is a real bonding moment for mother and daughter, with Samantha acknowledging their powers but explaining that they have to restrain them because the mortal world isn't ready for them. Samantha's joy is contagious as she realizes Tabatha shares her signature magic gesture, and Endora is equally endearing as she points out that Samantha will have to tell Tabatha "mustn't twitch."

Robert Q. Lewis as Diego Fenman perfectly exemplifies that subset of 1960s culture who went to analysts complaining of real and imagined neuroses. Diego's a little off to begin with, and Lewis hilariously takes him down the path of impending insanity as Tabatha witches the toys in Diego's studio. Tabatha getting the last laugh by bashing the "pretty pony" picture over Diego's head is not only funny, but it shows that Tabatha is much more aware of what she's doing than Samantha would like to believe.

WELL?

In response to Diego's "mistreatment" of Tabatha, Darrin refers to his daughter as "a helpless one-year-old." Tabatha has only logged eight months since her birth in "And Then There Were Three" (#54); that's not much of a difference, but, aside from Tabatha going blond since her last appearance [in the Season

Two finale "Prodigy" (#74)], she looks quite a bit older than she did in that episode. Tabatha doesn't seem to mind, because she keeps trying to untie Endora's bodice while "Grandmama" glories in her granddaughter's newfound powers. As Endora later attempts to teach Tabatha more witchcraft, she comments that Samantha "couldn't disappear past her knees until she was five." That's a charming image if you think of Samantha aging like a mortal, but "Eye of the Beholder" (#22) established that Samantha is probably around 300 years old. This begs the question, how long is a witch's childhood? Do they get to eighteen and then live hundreds of years as adults, or do they spend more time as children to correspond with their longer lifespans?

Why does Endora always change into mortal clothes when Darrin arrives? They've been family for two years now; you'd think Endora would feel comfortable wearing her usual witches' outfit in front of him. Later, when Darrin goes to bed, Samantha tells Tabatha not to use her powers, then practices her your-daughter-is-a-witch speech. Considering Samantha's secret, would she really say all this aloud when Darrin could overhear or walk back in at any second, to say nothing of sounding out the talk when she thinks Darrin is right beside her in bed? Later, after the flustered Diego exits his studio, Samantha tells her daughter "Mustn't twitch" – except Larry and Robbins aren't seen leaving, so they're still in the room to hear this.

OH, MY STARS!

As any photographer or filmmaker will tell you, lighting for color is very different than it is for black-and-white; as this is *Bewitched*'s first color episode, it's only natural the process hadn't been perfected yet. Still, it rather looks like everyone except Endora and Tabatha spent their entire summer sunning themselves on the beach. A healthy glow is one thing, but the overly bronzed faces distract from an otherwise terrific episode.

Darrin must really be in denial about Tabatha's powers. In the last episode, "Prodigy" (#74), he suspected his daughter of magically turning on a lamp; here, Tabatha floats toy blocks and several stuffed animals right in front of him, and when Endora denies having done it, Darrin demands, "Then explain how such a thing could happen!" Even when he sees Diego's pictorial evidence of Tabatha's levitation, he merely thinks it's trick photography.

It's inconceivable that Darrin would be so gung-ho about allowing Tabatha to represent Robbins and his truck transmissions. His "talking" baby was all over the news as recently as "Baby's First Paragraph" (#62); surely the public hasn't forgotten about her yet. Why risk stirring all that up again by featuring Tabatha's face in national ads? And, it's one thing for Larry to strong-arm Samantha into using Tabatha in Robbins' campaign (this *is* the man who wanted Tabatha to sing a baby food jingle), but why is Darrin so deaf to his wife's objections? Samantha's only Tabatha's mother, but the men treat her as if she doesn't have any rights at all.

SON OF A GUN!

"Well, you know what they say happens to babies who go into modeling or show business: they get their picture all over everything, they start believing their own press clippings, and they bounce from marriage to marriage!" – Samantha, nervously trying to keep Tabatha from going in front of Diego Fenman's camera.

More than her predecessors, and more even than her twin sister, Diane, little Erin Murphy is sheer delight as Tabatha. Her beaming smile is infectious, and there's a light in her that elevates her beyond merely being cute. And, because she's scarcely a toddler, her charisma is completely natural. She's a very pleasant addition to the Stephens family.

THE MOMENT OF TRUTH

Airdate: September 22, 1966

Samantha resolves to tell Darrin that Tabatha is a witch during their anniversary celebration. While Samantha is out, Aunt Clara sits for Tabatha, unaware that her great-niece has powers; when Tabatha flies things through the kitchen, Aunt Clara fears her own magic is on the fritz. Without a sitter, the Stephenses celebrate at home with the Tates, but Tabatha's floating objects cause Larry to burn a table with his cigarette and spill a bottle of champagne. Samantha tells Darrin that Aunt Clara's wobbly powers might have a delayed reaction; trying to keep the Tates from seeing items making their way upstairs, Samantha dashes to the nursery. Darrin follows just in time to witness kitchenware landing in Tabatha's crib; he is shocked when Samantha confirms their daughter is a witch.

Samantha suggests that Tabatha can be "witchcraft trained," but, with the Tates downstairs, the Stephenses realize their guests have to go. With Darrin's permission, Samantha works on convincing Larry he's had too much to drink by twitching him into flunking the sobriety tests he insists on. After Louise takes Larry home, Samantha remembers that Aunt Clara thinks she's ill and needs to be told about Tabatha. Her powers working perfectly from the relief, Aunt Clara pops out to inform the family that Tabatha is the first witch of her generation. Samantha encourages Darrin to tell Tabatha she "mustn't twitch," and Darrin lets Samantha know that he's fine with their daughter being a witch.

GOOD!

It's rather fitting that Aunt Clara should find out about Tabatha being a witch on the Stephenses' second anniversary, since she learned of Samantha's pregnancy during their first anniversary [see "Alias Darrin Stephens" (#37)]. And having Aunt Clara think her own powers are going berserk, with no idea about Tabatha's, is a nice twist.

In addition to Louise having a new face (Kasey Rogers replaces Irene Vernon in the role), there are other developments involving the Tates – their rapport is so much friendlier and intimate now, it hardly seems possible that Larry called Louise "tinted top" as recently as "Double Split" (#64). In addition, Larry and Darrin soup up their own boss/employee relationship of the past two seasons with a stronger sense of friendship. Larry shows yet another side as he unleashes his inner party animal, showing he's more than a workaholic ad man, giving David White a shot at the physical comedy that results from Larry's witchcraft-laced sobriety tests.

In the previous episode, "Nobody's Perfect" (#75), Darrin revealed intolerance again when he scoffed to Endora that he didn't want Tabatha's "normal little psyche scarred with M-A-G-I-C." Here, when Samantha worries that Darrin thinks Tabatha's powers are awful, Darrin makes up for it by assuring her, "it's been wonderful living with one beautiful witch; it'll be twice as wonderful living with two." It's simply one of the warmest moments on the show so far.

WELL?

Why do the Stephenses include the Tates in their second anniversary celebration when their first anniversary was spoiled by Aunt Clara turning Darrin into a chimpanzee ["Alias Darrin Stephens" (#37)]? You'd think Darrin and Samantha would want to be alone this time.

Aunt Clara tries to arrive more subtly by parachuting onto Samantha's doorstep. From where did Aunt Clara jump? Did she hire a plane just so she could land in front of the Stephens house? And wouldn't it be easy for Gladys, or any other passersby, to spot an old woman floating down from the sky?

The wires on Tabatha's floating objects blend better into the background with the show in color, but they're still visible when Tabatha induces the pot and spoon to come to her in the kitchen. Then, as Aunt Clara laments what she believes are her more-erratic-than-usual powers, Samantha suggests she go in for a check-up. Where? When Samantha was down with square green spots in "Take Two Aspirins and Half A Pint of Porpoise Milk" (#42), Aunt Clara had to whip up her own potion to cure her. Did this dearth of medical care prompt the witches to campaign for their own doctor? With Aunt Clara out as babysitter, Larry starts the at-home celebration by telling a joke about his golf game. In "Double Split" (#64), Larry told Darrin that golf gives him hives. Has he found a cure?

In addition to other redecoration throughout the Stephens house, their kitchen door is suddenly solid, whereas before it had slats in it. Is this part of their upgrade, or is the door this way so the Tates can't see Tabatha's floating cookware from the living room?

OH, MY STARS!

Barely having processed the news that Tabatha is a witch, Darrin asks Samantha, "How much of a witch is she?" Samantha seems to sidestep the question by replying, "She doesn't really know what she's doing." The proper answer would be for Samantha to reiterate what she told Darrin in "My Baby, the Tycoon" (#55) – that Tabatha is only a half-blooded witch. This would also answer Darrin's oblique question-within-a-question: How strong is her witchcraft? Surely being half-mortal limits Tabatha's powers somewhat, which is what Darrin really wants to know.

SON OF A GUN!

"And I'm going to tell him tonight, while we're celebrating our anniversary and he's in a good mood, just at the right time, when the lights are low, and we're in a restaurant where he can't scream, and there's a nearby exit." – Samantha to Tabatha, laying out her plan for revealing the child's powers to Darrin.

"Our Jonathan went through that phase, don't you remember?" Louise's simple, off-the-cuff question finally fills in what has been perhaps the show's biggest gap: the name of Larry and Louise's baby.

In "Nobody's Perfect" (#75), suspense was created by keeping Darrin in the dark about Tabatha's powers. That suspense continues in this episode, with yet another near-miss for Darrin in the form of the floating pot Samantha attributes to Aunt Clara. Believing his in-law is responsible is a great partial reveal – but, when Darrin camouflages the flying pot with his jacket as he runs upstairs, only to discover that his daughter is doing the magic, it infuses the moment with a kind of thrilling drama. It's as if these first episodes of the season are a two-parter.

WITCHES AND WARLOCKS ARE MY FAVORITE THINGS

Airdate: September 29, 1966

Endora wakes Samantha to tell her Tabatha's powers will be measured by testing committee the next day. Maurice labels the proceedings "women's work," but gives Samantha a silent whistle with which to contact him. Once Aunt Clara and Samantha's other aunts, Hagatha and Enchantra, arrive, they set up for Tabatha's examination; Aunt Clara tries to magically place a cape around Tabatha's shoulders, instead making it appear on Darrin at the office. Tabatha completes her tests: despite being a "product of a mixed marriage," her powers are very strong, and the child is officially certified a witch.

Endora, Hagatha, and Enchantra announce they've made decisions about Tabatha's future. When Darrin comes home and learns that Tabatha is to go away to Hagatha's school, he joins Samantha and Aunt Clara in protest. Aunt Clara and the Stephenses soon find their feet magically rooted to the floor and their voices replaced with bird chirps, so Samantha uses her whistle to summon Maurice, who zaps the testing committee to Mount Everest to goad them into changing their minds. Once they agree not to take Tabatha, Maurice ships them out, then minimizes Darrin's gratitude. At dinner, Samantha assures Darrin that Tabatha's powers are limited, though a floating fruit bowl implies otherwise. Samantha follows it to the nursery, and, when the waiting Maurice offers to send her and Darrin anywhere in the world for an evening out, Samantha says nothing can top seeing Tabatha with her grandfather.

GOOD!

Along with "Nobody's Perfect" (#75) and "The Moment of Truth" (#76), this episode seems to round out an unofficial three-parter, building on Aunt Clara popping out to tell the family about Tabatha in the latter installment. As for that family, Clara is Samantha's aunt, but it is revealed here that Hagatha and Enchantra are her aunts as well. This means these ladies are either Endora's sisters, or Maurice's. Enchantra, Endora, and Clara all have red hair, and Maurice is formal in a way that wouldn't be necessary with siblings, referring to Hagatha as "madame." Though it would have been best for the show to draw this family tree more clearly themselves, they do drop enough juicy hints to heavily suggest that Endora has three sisters in Clara, Hagatha, and Enchantra.

Maurice has loosened up quite a bit since his last appearance in "My Grandson, the Warlock" (#40): he's friendlier, he spouts Shakespeare, and he even helps Darrin by preventing Tabatha's "kidnapping" at the hands of the testing committee. Despite his "For you, nothing" response to Darrin's thanks, Maurice does offer to send Darrin and Samantha to the world destination of their choice while he babysits. Not bad for a man who disintegrated Darrin in "Just One Happy Family" (#10).

WELL?

Why is a coven necessary to test Tabatha's powers? In "My Grandson, the Warlock" (#40), Maurice thought Jonathan Tate was Samantha's baby and took him to the Warlock Club, saying Nanny Witch would "verify you've got the stuff." So where's Nanny Witch now, especially if Enchantra and Hagatha have been part of this testing committee for 308 years? Maurice takes one look at Tabatha and decides, "she's definitely got it, there's no question about that." If he's able to make that determination, why did he need Nanny Witch in the first place? And, after the way he went on about his "grandson's" education, it seems odd that Maurice would oppose a proper witches' school for Tabatha, whom he seems to have met off-screen, since he already knows her; pity to have missed their introduction.

Samantha assures Endora that Darrin will be out working during Tabatha's testing, despite it being Saturday. Aside from dressing Darrin and Larry in casual clothes, the fact that it's Saturday has no further impact on the story, which could take place on any workday. Also, the kitchen door, which always had slats but became solid in "The Moment of Truth" (#76), now has slats again.

When Samantha peeks in at Tabatha, the footage of the sleeping baby is a still frame; in a later shot, Samantha touches Tabatha's nose, and the film freezes, showing Tabatha in this very frame. Granted, it's likely difficult to get a toddler to pretend to sleep – watch how little Erin Murphy desperately tries to keep her eyes closed while "asleep" on Maurice's lap.

After Tabatha flies a blinking orb through the air, it is determined that Tabatha's powers are "very, very strong." But how strong could they be? As established in "My Baby, the Tycoon" (#55), Tabatha is half-mortal, and it's debatable that she could have full powers with that heredity. Enchantra also denotes Tabatha's "importance in the hierarchy," implying there's some sort of witches' monarchy in place – yet there's been no indication thus far that Samantha or her parents are anywhere near royalty.

It turns out witches are even more prejudiced toward mortals than mortals are toward witches. Endora and Maurice looking down their noses at Darrin is expected, but Hagatha, and especially Enchantra, take this to a whole new level, with Enchantra calling Darrin an "impudent nothing." Is this payback for mortal bigotry, or is it a case of "do as I say, not as I do" when witches call for equality, as they did in "The Witches Are Out" (#7)?

Darrin is a mortal, and Aunt Clara is a witch of wonky powers, so it seems probable that Endora and the "girls" can glue their feet and make them speak Bird. But can they really witch Samantha, whose own magic is nothing to sneeze at? Along the same lines, how is Maurice able to zap Endora, Hagatha, and Enchantra to Mount Everest against their will?

In Maurice's wide shot with the ladies, his cape is draped over his left shoulder, but, when he uses it to pop the ladies out, it is wrapped around both shoulders. At the end of the episode, when the floating fruit bowl reaches the top of the stairs, there is a shadow of a stick (or whatever other trickery was used to create the effect) cast on the wall for a brief second.

OH, MY STARS!

In "Speak the Truth" (#50), Hagatha appeared to be a friend of Endora's – she owned a witchy shop and was played by Diana Chesney. Now, Hagatha is Samantha's aunt, runs a school for young witches, and is played by Reta Shaw, who twice appeared as Samantha's friend Bertha during Season One. Hagatha even wears Bertha's dress! And where Hagatha was more genteel before, she is now decidedly anti-mortal.

Endora has always been stubborn at worst and impish at best, but here, she's unusually cruel. She says Samantha is too incompetent to raise her own child, then has no qualms about kidnapping her granddaughter over Samantha's objections. Either Endora has been written out of character, or she has a dark side that is only now surfacing for the first time.

SON OF A GUN!

"Humans emit a low-grade frequency, which upsets my instruments." – Hagatha, glad that Darrin will not be present as she runs tests on Tabatha.

ACCIDENTAL TWINS

Airdate: October 6, 1966

The Stephenses are ready for a night out with Larry and Louise, but the Tates' babysitter can't make it, so Aunt Clara is asked to sit for Jonathan as well as Tabatha. Aunt Clara entertains her charges with magic, zapping up a few unintentional toys, but a bigger misfire duplicates Jonathan. Samantha panics when she comes home to find two Jonathans; not knowing which boy is real, and because the spell requires keeping them together, Samantha talks the Tates into letting Jonathan stay overnight, as Larry is flying out on a business trip in the morning.

The next day, while Aunt Clara works on her spell, Louise arrives early to take Jonathan home. The Stephenses stall her by throwing Jonathan a birthday party on the patio so Aunt Clara can sneak his twin upstairs, but Aunt Clara opens the door to Larry, whose flight has been delayed. Samantha zaps up another party in the kitchen, and the morning becomes a mad scramble to keep Larry, Louise, and the two Jonathans apart. Samantha takes one Jonathan from Louise, but Louise finds the other with Larry. When Aunt Clara recalls making a similar duplication mistake ten years earlier, Samantha transforms her into a younger version of herself so Clara can recall the solution. Able to return the real Jonathan to the Tates, Samantha sighs when Larry tells Louise he wishes he had another just like him.

GOOD!

Samantha makes a very logical decision when she tells Darrin that hiring teenagers or little old ladies to babysit Tabatha is now out, since Tabatha hasn't learned to control her witchcraft. And, since Tabatha has spent most of her time with Samantha, and Jonathan has only appeared once [in "My Grandson, the Warlock" (#40)], it's especially nice to see Darrin and Larry as proud fathers who compete by whipping kiddie photos out of their wallets.

Darrin pulling Samantha aside and telling her they've been married long enough that he can tell when magic is afoot is a great example of how Darrin's adjusted to life with a witch. Darrin also seems to realize now that there are times to let witchcraft lead the way out of problems – he's the one who reminds Samantha about Jonathan's birthday, and hints for Samantha to zap up a party to distract Louise.

WELL?

Aunt Clara doesn't know her own strength: when she crashes into the Stephenses' door trying to walk through it, the whole house façade shakes. Then she's up to her old tricks again, literally, doing magic for children in her care as she did in "There's No Witch Like An Old Witch" (#27). The Tates' request is strange: "As long as you have Aunt Clara sitting with Tabatha, can we bring Jonathan over there?" That implies that Larry and Louise know Clara, when, in fact, they never met her until this episode. It's not unreasonable for events to happen off-screen, but the meeting of major characters shouldn't be one of them. As for Jonathan, much fuss is made over the boy having his second birthday, but, in "A Very Special Delivery" (#38), Larry reported that Louise had just given birth. Since that episode aired at the beginning of Season Two, Jonathan can only be a one-year-old.

Perhaps Aunt Clara's incantations are old-school sorcery? As the series began, every witches' spell was comprised of magic words; by "What Every Young Man Should Know" (#72), even Endora was casting spells in English. Aunt Clara seems to be the only holdout, using a dizzying array of whimsical phrases in a variety of incantations. No wonder she gets her "finchleys and bixleys" mixed up; if she'd used English, she wouldn't be as confused. Also, while amusing the tykes, Clara zaps up the same giraffe that was in Diego's photo studio in "Nobody's Perfect" (#75), plus exact replicas of Tabatha's "pretty pony," which was the catalyst for Samantha finding out about Tabatha's witchcraft in the same episode.

The Stephenses replace their kitchen door with alarming frequency. The usual slatted entrance that became solid in "The Moment of Truth" (#76) reverted to having slats in "Witches and Warlocks Are My Favorite Things" (#77), only to end up solid again in this episode. Of course, if it weren't solid, it would be harder to keep the Tates from seeing each other.

Larry's in a fog, all right – not only did he just get stuck at a foggy Chicago airport in "Double Tate" (#59), but here his flight *to* Chicago is delayed by the haze. Like father, like son: in the former episode, there were two Larrys, and now there are two Jonathans. Finally, playing Samantha's nonexistent game of hide-and-seek, Larry and Jonathan hide in the den closet – a room that was a bathroom in "Help, Help, Don't Save Me" (#5).

OH, MY STARS!

The Stephenses engage in their keep-the-Tates-apart birthday parties because Samantha insists that two Jonathans have to stay together, or Aunt Clara's reversal spell won't work. What would be the problem in letting the Tates take one of the kids home? Yes, one of them is only Aunt Clara's magic, but it's not like she needs the boys to remember the spell; all Samantha has to do once Aunt Clara comes up with it is go over to the Tates and distract them so Aunt Clara can bring Jonathan's twin in and fuse the boys. Keeping the kids together is effective for the near slapstick humor that ensues, but it isn't particularly practical.

Even if Aunt Clara made some sort of duplication mistake in the past (and the show never explains exactly what she did), having Samantha make Aunt Clara over as ten years younger doesn't make a lot of sense. Can one witch perform witchcraft on another witch? And if Aunt Clara has lived hundreds of years, a ten-year regression won't make much difference; maybe that's why she looks the same age. Regardless, the cartoon sparkles that fly from Samantha's goblet as she transforms Aunt Clara take away from the sequence.

SON OF A GUN!

"Oh, and just in case, will you keep an open mind about a larger family?" – Aunt Clara to Larry, hinting that he may not need the stork to have another child.

Two words: Jonathan Tate. After a year without a name, and only a brief mention in "The Moment of Truth" (#76), he gets almost a whole episode devoted to him. Watching Jonathan and Tabatha side by side, you can't help but wonder – wouldn't it be neat to watch them grow up together?

A MOST UNUSUAL WOOD NYMPH
Airdate: October 13, 1966

EPISODE
79

Darrin dreads a visit from long-lost family friend Gerry O'Toole, who turns out to be a pretty Irishwoman. Samantha casts a jealous eye toward Gerry, especially as her visit leans toward the indefinite. When Gerry's fear of cats and remarkable talent for weaving makes Samantha suspicious, Endora insists that

Gerry is a wood nymph. Since these sprites hate witches, Samantha goads Gerry into confessing she's there because the wood nymphs placed a curse on Darrin's 15th century ancestor, Darrin the Bold, who killed their friend, Rufus the Red; the curse also affects all of Darrin the Bold's descendants. Samantha pleads for Endora to send her back in time so she can save Rufus – and Darrin.

In 1472, womanizer Darrin the Bold relentlessly advances on Samantha until Rufus arrives seeking shelter; in the present, Gerry chases Darrin around the sofa. After arguing about payment, Rufus challenges Darrin the Bold to a duel, prompting Samantha to measure Rufus for a shroud to make him believe Darrin the Bold is murderous. Samantha likewise convinces Darrin the Bold that Rufus' opponents always die; she is thrilled when Rufus calls off the duel. Returning to 1966, Samantha foils the amorous Gerry, who doesn't believe Rufus survived until Endora materializes him in the living room. With the curse removed, the overjoyed Gerry disappears with Rufus, and Samantha briefly wonders if Darrin would look good with Darrin the Bold's mustache.

GOOD!

This is a standout episode overall, but Samantha trying to trick Darrin the Bold and Rufus out of the duel is a medieval marvel. She inventively rattles Rufus' cage by measuring him for a shroud, then chisels away at Darrin the Bold's masculinity trying to convince him Rufus is unbeatable. Undoing a curse should always be this much fun.

WELL?

In "The Leprechaun" (#63), it was established that Darrin's grandmother is from Ireland's County Cork; here, Gerry – and presumably, Darrin's great-aunt Leticia – are from Derrybrien, which is in County Galway. More importantly, Gerry tells Samantha about the curse of Killcarney County, which she reports is the manor house of Darrin the Bold. Would "county" really be part of a house's name? It must be, because there's no actual Killcarney County in Ireland – there's a Kilkenny County, and a town called Killarney, but nothing with the name Killcarney. Finally, Darrin the Bold's digs are on the ocean, but none of the aforementioned places are anywhere near the water.

Why is Samantha jealous of Gerry the second she walks through the door? Darrin isn't flirting or looking, as he's done in several episodes. Maybe Samantha senses Gerry's attraction to Darrin, which brings up a "most unusual" point: why does Gerry want Darrin at all? He's a dead ringer for the man who killed her presumed lover, Rufus the Red. Maybe it's the nymph in her.

When Gerry thinks she's heard a cat, Samantha reports that it's just the baby. Since when does Tabatha's crying or gurgling sound like meowing? And, when Samantha sends Darrin to check on Tabatha so she can confront Gerry, he walks away, goes upstairs, and closes the nursery door in only five seconds.

As Endora sends Samantha to 1472, Samantha can be heard saying, "Take care of the baby, mama!" This is only the third time Samantha has referred to Endora that way, the other two times being "George the Warlock" (#30) and "Disappearing Samantha" (#65) – strange, considering Samantha always calls Endora "Mother." In Ireland, when Samantha fits Rufus for the shroud, his weight of "13 stone 8" is a correct unit of measurement for the 15th century, but the declarations that his height is 6' 3" and his waist is 36" are not, as Imperial units weren't in use until 1824.

After Gerry leaves, Darrin is told she "got her old job back." This woman just chased Darrin around the living room but is suddenly gone without a word, and Darrin accepts it without question. Then, on the heels of her encounter with Darrin the Bold, Samantha wonders what Darrin would look like with a mustache – but Samantha already knows, as she gave Darrin that bit of facial hair in "A Change of Face" (#33).

OH, MY STARS!

It's understandable that Gerry and her fellow wood nymphs would curse Darrin the Bold for killing Rufus, but some very important details are left out. Gerry claims that the hex trickles down to all of Darrin the Bold's descendants. That includes not only whichever of Darrin's parents is in a direct line with Darrin the Bold [probably Darrin's Irish grandmother, as mentioned in "The Leprechaun" (#63)], but Tabatha. And what exactly *is* the curse? Endora says that Darrin "just might survive" it , and Samantha insists she has to "save Darrin's life" – if the curse is that deadly, why has Darrin gone his entire life without being affected by it, why are Darrin's parents alive and well, and why is Samantha not concerned about Tabatha?

In many time travel adventures (*Star Trek* and *Back to the Future*, for example), there are warnings about the dangers of polluting the timeline, but not here. Samantha displaces a conquest of Darrin the Bold's – what if the woman was supposed to be the mother of one of Darrin's ancestors? That one act could have prevented Darrin and Tabatha from being born! And what impact does Rufus' survival have? His presence could change Ireland's history, create new descendants – the list goes on. Maybe no one was thinking on such high-concept levels yet in the '60s, but, in that light, it almost seems selfish for Samantha to visit 1472 to save Darrin because she risks affecting more than her family.

SON OF A GUN!

"Oh, that's terrific! I mean, the saints be praised..." – Samantha, correcting her 1966 English in the 15th century.

Elizabeth Montgomery already flirted with an Irish accent in "The Leprechaun" (#63), but Dick York takes full advantage of his chance to put a different spin on Darrin by playing his ancestor, Darrin the Bold to the hilt. These two are having so much fun, it's absolutely infectious. That's not to leave out Michael Ansara; his Rufus is the most serious of the bunch, but he gets his moments, especially when Samantha measures the man for a shroud.

ENDORA MOVES IN FOR A SPELL
Airdate: October 20, 1966

EPISODE 80

After Samantha disapprovingly calls out to Endora because she encouraged Tabatha to levitate her teddy bear, Uncle Arthur pops in disparaging his sister. Arthur and Endora argue to the point she leaves in a huff – Darrin is happy to hear that his uncle-in-law has driven Endora away, but when the prankster warlock overstays his welcome, Darrin admits he actually prefers Endora. Wanting to monitor Uncle Arthur's influence on Tabatha, Endora zaps up a house on a nearby vacant lot. The house repeatedly appears and disappears as the siblings try to best each other; Gladys sees this activity and calls the cops, then accompanies the officers on their investigation of the supposedly nonexistent house.

Samantha blasts her mother and uncle for using her home as a battleground and demands they stop fighting, or at least fight somewhere else. Endora and Uncle Arthur decide Samantha is right and pop out; Darrin celebrates their departure until he sees that Endora's house is still on the corner. Samantha assures Darrin she can dematerialize it herself as long as Gladys and the police aren't inside. Gladys feels she finally has supporters until the house disappears, causing the cops to deny having seen it. Later, Uncle Arthur and Endora clandestinely appear in paintings, putting each other on notice because Halloween is coming up.

GOOD!

Samantha's family tree continues to grow. Uncle Arthur, who was introduced in "The Joker Is A Card" (#41), is actually Endora's younger brother, and the siblings share very little except their love for Tabatha, which causes hilarious havoc in Samantha's house.

Having no choice but to recast Gladys Kravitz after Alice Pearce succumbed to cancer the previous season, the show wisely eases Sandra Gould's Gladys onto the canvas by not putting her in a scene with Abner right away, except over the phone. It gives viewers a little time to get used to Abner having a different wife.

Not only does Samantha show an unprecedented strength in her "bluff" as she demands privacy from Endora and Uncle Arthur and tells them they're to do their fighting elsewhere, but her admission, "I'm a little torn when we get into these witches' world versus mortal world battles" provides a perspective not heard from Samantha before – and a telling one, since, in many ways, it seems she has made a complete adjustment to living a mortal life.

WELL?

In "The Joker Is A Card" (#41), Endora was annoyed by Uncle Arthur's practical jokes, but seemed tolerant enough of him. And Uncle Arthur panicked when he thought Darrin turned Endora into a parrot permanently, even exclaiming, "I love her!" There was nothing to indicate the intense feuding and jealousy seen here, unless they simply restrained themselves during their last meeting. And Endora doesn't need to make Tabatha's teddy bear dance anymore, as she did in "The Dancing Bear" (#58); here, the child does it herself, and with the same bear shown in that episode.

The Stephens and Kravitz residences got a bit of a face lift between seasons (the interior of the Kravitz house is completely different), and apparently so did Morning Glory Circle. There are never-before-seen apartment buildings behind the cops as Gladys tells them Endora's house doesn't exist, and, as for the vacant lot, it looks like it's on a whole other street. Gladys, getting more proactive in spreading the word about the magic she witnesses, tells police officers, "Actually, this is a very strange neighborhood." She's only ever had an issue with the Stephens house – isn't labeling the whole neighborhood strange a bit of an exaggeration?

Endora threatens to evaporate Uncle Arthur, who responds by saying, "I guess I'll have to paste her." Now, Maurice disintegrated Darrin in "Just One Happy Family" (#10), but Darrin is mortal. Can witches with equal power do the same to each other? Also, in "Accidental Twins" (#78), Samantha again reiterated that the witch who casts a spell is the only one who can remove it. Yet Uncle Arthur constantly makes Endora's house disappear; even Samantha can remove it, simply because her feuding relatives are "out of the way."

During Endora and Arthur's temporary truce, they reminisce about being "with" rival generals during the Civil War. They must only have been companions or confidants to Lee and Grant, because, in "Just One Happy Family" (#10), Maurice told Samantha that mortals go into the service, "not us." The siblings then settle on seeing each other only when invisible, proceeding to "divvy up" the world. Why territorialize if they're going to be invisible? Finally, Endora's house isn't the only thing appearing and disappearing: the Stephenses' kitchen door, which has gone from slatted to solid several times so far this season, is back to having slats as it always has.

OH, MY STARS!

Hearing Endora lament that she was an only child until Arthur came along is a neat bit of family history – but is it accurate? By process of elimination, "Witches And Warlocks Are My Favorite Things" (#77) implied that Clara, Hagatha, and Enchantra are all Endora's sisters. For Arthur to ruin Endora's status as an only child, he would have to have been born next – but he's quite a bit younger than the rest of the group. If Endora was indeed an only child (it's a safer bet the much older Clara had that honor), then she was so until one of her sisters came along, not Arthur, who, from this, has four sisters – just like Harold Harold, Paul Lynde's alter ego from "Driving Is the Only Way to Fly" (#26).

Darrin feels Samantha should keep a family album so Tabatha can tell her great-grandchildren about Maurice, Endora, etc. Samantha replies that, when Tabatha is old and gray, she can simply introduce her older relatives. Question: how will Tabatha age? She is half-witch, half-mortal. If she ages like a mortal, then yes, she'll be elderly in 70 years and can introduce the gang, who won't be much older. But if Tabatha ages like a witch, then it could be hundreds, even thousands of years before she's old and gray, by which time her full-witch relatives will probably be gone, because they'd all age at the same pace. With no way of knowing, Darrin is making an assumption about Tabatha's aging process, and Samantha isn't putting enough thought into it, given her own metabolism.

SON OF A GUN!

"The man has come to his senses at last. He finally appreciates the real me." – Endora, popping in after hearing Darrin say he'd choose her over Uncle Arthur any day.

A line like "Well, if it isn't my yaga-zuzzy nephew-in-law" might seem out of left field, but it's a wonderful reference to Darrin and Uncle Arthur's first encounter in "The Joker Is A Card" (#41), where "yaga-zuzzy" was part of a fake incantation Arthur taught Darrin as a practical joke. No wonder Darrin isn't happy to see his uncle-in-law.

TWITCH OR TREAT

Airdate: October 27, 1966

EPISODE
81

Building on "Endora Moves in for a Spell" (#80), the house she zapped up on the corner in that episode reappears. Samantha explains that Endora only wants to have a Halloween party there, but Darrin wants the house gone, "or else." When Samantha begs her mother to move the party, Endora dematerializes her house and decides to hold her soirée in Samantha's living room, redecorating it witches' style. Samantha insists that Uncle Arthur be invited to Endora's party and meets Darrin outside to prepare him for it; Darrin feels uncomfortable among the otherworldly guests and Uncle Arthur's practical jokes. Gladys sees a cat turn into a human being on the Stephenses' doorstep and calls on her representative, Councilman Greene, to investigate her neighbors.

As the party continues, Darrin discovers that baseball player Willie Mays is a warlock; he also gets a shock when Eva, the humanized cat who has been pursuing him all night, becomes feline again while pawing him. Uncle Arthur diverts Councilman Greene and his associate by shunting them onto the patio whenever they enter the front door. But after Arthur's wiseguy asides interrupt Endora's recitation of

'Twas the Night Before Halloween, she pops him into the party fountain and whisks her guests away. Samantha promises Darrin they can spend next Halloween with his family – and Thanksgiving with hers.

GOOD!

Darrin might be been less than thrilled to host Endora's party, but at least he gets a nicer Endora out of it. She cheerfully offers him champagne and is cordial to him the whole night – plus, he's her specially invited guest, making him the only mortal in attendance.

Gladys is getting even more aggressive in reporting her witchcraft sightings. Having already summoned the police in "Endora Moves in for a Spell" (#80), she calls them again here, as well as the fire department and the wonderfully subtle SPCA (the Society for the Prevention of Cruelty to Animals) after witnessing Eva's feline-to-human transformation.

The name Willie Mays might not mean much to modern-day audiences, but his stunt casting in *Bewitched* is notable, since he was an all-star baseball player in the '50s and '60s. The idea that witchcraft is behind his home run streak is a neat twist, and Samantha's greeting, "Say hey, Willie!" is a reference to the fact that Mays was known as the Say Hey Kid. How much fun is it to watch a ball player "pop out to the ballpark?"

WELL?

Why is Endora's house still appearing and disappearing? Samantha got rid of it in "Endora Moves in for a Spell" (#80), and, after a week, Gladys can't be the only neighbor who's noticed it. As for the witches and warlocks, they again freely undo each others' spells, add to them, and zap each other with a frequency never seen before: Endora pops Arthur out of a tree, Arthur interferes with Endora's caviar spell, and Eva's companion, Boris, finds Arthur's words in his mouth. If they have this kind of control over each other, then having supernatural powers doesn't seem like much of an advantage.

Demanding the house's removal, Darrin threatens "or else," and Samantha tells Endora that her marriage is at stake. Darrin's prepared to leave Samantha over a house? And why would Endora want a witches' Halloween party to be held in a mortal locale to begin with?

When Samantha nervously corners Darrin outside with kisses, he responds, "Swell, honey, but the neighbors." Yet, in "Man's Best Friend" (#70), he purposely kissed Samantha with the door open to give Harriet Kravitz a show. Where is Harriet, anyway? She hasn't been seen or mentioned since that episode.

Why do Boris and Eva saunter up the Stephenses' front walk instead of just popping straight in to the party? It's almost worth it for Boris' dry "Your slip is showing," regarding Eva's tail, but how can she zap it out from under her dress? If Boris had to turn Eva into a woman, then she's not a witch; if she's a familiar of some sort, then she wouldn't have powers of her own.

Councilman Green tells his associate, Morgan, that he's handled "the problems of this community year after year." No, he hasn't. In "Remember the Main" (#34), Ed Wright was elected councilman. Even if Green ultimately replaced Wright, he would only be serving his first term, which doesn't qualify as "year after year."

As Darrin dances with the amorous Eva, he tells her he's not up on the new steps. Maybe his integrated self isn't, but his Fun Side knew how to Watusi in "Divided He Falls" (#69). And this isn't the first time Darrin and Uncle Arthur have laughed together at Endora's expense: in "The Joker Is A Card" (#41), the in-laws were in stitches when Arthur zapped a stream of chocolate into Endora's eye. Also, as Arthur foils Green and Morgan, he smiles to Samantha that they make a pretty good team. How so? Samantha doesn't do anything – did a zap of hers end up on the cutting room floor?

OH, MY STARS!

Both Samantha and Endora have undergone marked opinion changes regarding Halloween compared to the last two years. Samantha tells Darrin they should "observe Halloween properly," but last year, in "Twitch or Treat" (#43), Samantha was upset by Halloween masks and avoided trick-or-treaters. Later, Samantha comments that the evening was "Mother's most unusual Halloween party," yet in "The Witches Are Out" (#7), Endora flew to the south of France to escape the holiday – and, in "Twitch or Treat" (#43), Endora wanted to take Samantha to the Sacred Volcano for the same reason. That Endora throws this party at all is out of character for her, to say nothing of having thrown enough of them that '*Twas the Night Before Halloween* is an annual rendition.

Given that this episode takes place on Halloween, there are no trick-or-treaters the whole evening. It's also Tabatha's first Halloween, but her parents spend it focused on Endora's party, and don't even mention her. Is Tabatha asleep in her crib the entire time?

The exterior of the Kravitz house looks completely different than it has the past two seasons. And, their address is now 1168 Morning Glory Circle, which can't be right. The Stephenses live at 1164, and only house numbers on their side of the street can be even; henceforth, the Kravitzes' house number has to be odd.

SON OF A GUN!

"Oh, we have our own special hookup: ghost-to-ghost." – Samantha to Darrin, explaining where the party music is coming from.

DANGEROUS DIAPER DAN

Airdate: November 3, 1966

EPISODE 82

Darrin and Endora find themselves in agreement as they lecture Samantha for listening to gossip from Louise, then from Dan, the diaper delivery man. Dan gives Samantha a promotional rattle for Tabatha, but it contains a microphone hidden by A.J. Kimberley, a competitor of McMann & Tate. When Samantha talks to Louise on the phone about Darrin's slogan for the Wright campaign, Dan takes the recording to Kimberley; Darrin and Larry are stunned that Wright has already heard their ideas. After Kimberley rubs it in, Larry gives Darrin an idea for another slogan, but Kimberley presents that as well, having heard Samantha telling Endora about it on tape. Larry becomes convinced the office is bugged and sends Darrin home handcuffed to his briefcase.

Darrin and Samantha fight when he blames her for discussing his accounts – but Kimberley needs them talking to get at Darrin's new, top-secret slogan, so Dan sends them each a present in the other's name. Comparing notes, the Stephenses conclude that Endora must have gifted them; when Endora denies it, Samantha traces her roses and discovers they're from Dan. Remembering Darrin's warning about a hidden mic, Samantha finds it in Tabatha's rattle, but not before it picks up Endora reading Darrin's all-important slogan aloud. To keep Dan from going to Kimberley, Samantha magically stops his van and gaslights him with Endora's help. Darrin gets the Wright account, and the "rattled" Dan announces he's taking time off to go to a rest home.

GOOD!

Given the triptych of season-opening episodes revolving around the discovery of Tabatha's powers, her abilities have been conspicuously absent since. So it's a great touch to include Tabatha simply levitating a plate of crackers – with Endora's encouragement – because it's a reminder that this important story point is still an issue for the Stephenses.

Samantha thwarting Dan with witchcraft is so fun and fiendish, even Endora loves it. Making his baby doll "talk" is the best bit, and Marty Ingels taking Dan into madness shows what an accomplished comic he really is. A particularly wonderful effect comes together when the lone diaper bundle flies out of the van – with no visible strings. Okay, it's a little cruel to drive a man into a rest home simply to save a slogan, and there's nothing stopping Dan from taking the tape recorder out of the disabled van and grabbing a cab to Kimberley, but this diaper man's comeuppance is anything but child's play.

WELL?

After catching Samantha dishing the dirt with Louise on the phone, Darrin tells her that he hates gossip. Maybe he needs to elaborate: in "Follow That Witch (Part II)" (#67), Darrin informed his secretary, Betty, that gossip concerning him is the only kind he's interested in. At the end of the prologue, the screen goes black mid-conversation; Samantha is still talking as the music heralds the fade-out. Perhaps something was cut for time?

Endora must like to reread her periodicals: it's spiffy continuity to show *Harpies' Bizarre*, which last appeared in "Mother Meets What's-His-Name" (#4), but it's the exact same issue. On the subject of exact sames, Kimberley's employee, Peterson, is played by Jim Bigg, who just played Morgan in the last episode, "Twitch or Treat" (#81).

Since when does Samantha talk about Darrin's slogans to anyone who will listen? Darrin and Samantha's fight comes out of nowhere, too – all Darrin does is ask Samantha to stay off the phone, which doesn't seem unreasonable considering the circumstances, but Samantha thinks Darrin is blaming her for the slogan theft, and Darrin blows up with sexist assumptions about women. And how does Dan's plan to make the Stephenses assume they've sent each other gifts patch things up? Darrin and Samantha don't resolve their issue, and once they realize they haven't sent each other presents, their fight could easily continue.

Kimberley's plot to snag the Wright account isn't quite...Wright. His entire scheme is contingent upon Wright meeting with him first before going to McMann & Tate so he can present Darrin's ideas as original. Yet it's never specified that Kimberley is first in Wright's appointment book. And so what if Wright sees the same slogan at McMann & Tate? He can't know who came up with it first, but he condemns McMann & Tate simply because of the order of his visits. If Darrin is so sure the leak is coming from his house, why not plant bad alternate decoy slogans there so his real ideas will be different and better than Kimberley's? And, while Endora is usually unfairly critical of Darrin, her contention that Darrin's slogans are "nauseating" is hard to refute: "When you fly to the moon, you'll still be writing with the Wright pen, for there's only one right way to go into space and only one right way to write" isn't one of Darrin's best.

OH, MY STARS!

Bugging Tabatha's rattle to steal advertising ideas from McMann & Tate is wonderfully diabolical, but A.J. Kimberley and his cronies would stumble on to a much bigger discovery if they didn't have selective hearing. How can Dan listen to a live feed from the hidden mic and not wonder what's going on when Endora tells Tabatha to "hex it over for Grandmama," or when Samantha instructs Tabatha, "Mustn't twitch?" Out of context, this may seem innocuous enough, but there's no mistaking the subject matter when Samantha tells Darrin that Endora is a "switchy witch," or when Endora comes right out and says she possesses "supernatural powers of the highest degree." And all of this is on tape – that's further than private eye Charlie Leach got in "Follow That Witch (Part I)" (#66)! Yet, somehow, Kimberley and the boys only hear slogans being revealed. Good thing for the Stephenses these spies aren't very observant.

SON OF A GUN!

"Oh, Mrs. Stephens, there'll be a drew niver stopping by – I mean a new driver stopping by for a while…" – Dan, after being "rattled" by Samantha.

There might be a hidden microphone, but there's nothing hidden about Larry's paranoia as the highlight of the episode. Picking through garbage, looking behind paintings, and pulling the plug on lamps is like something out of spy comedy *Get Smart* (which was running on NBC during this time) – but Larry shaking and listening to what he suspects is a bugged olive, before smashing it on the bar, lets David White play a level of comedy he rarely gets to display.

THE SHORT HAPPY CIRCUIT OF AUNT CLARA

EPISODE 83

Airdate: November 10, 1966

When the Stephenses head to the Tates to secure the MacElroy Shoes account, Aunt Clara babysits Tabatha. Shrinking a piano to take it upstairs and entertain the crying toddler, Aunt Clara is flummoxed when the instrument grows back to full size on the staircase. Aunt Clara casts a spell to make the piano light, but shorts out the lights instead. The power failure doesn't help Darrin and Larry, who are having a hard enough time drumming up MacElroy's interest in their campaign. After the Kravitzes report that the entire Eastern seaboard is blacked out, Clara summons Octavius, a warlock who dumped her for a younger witch. Ocky restores the lights, but only in the Stephens house, and only by keeping his arms up. When Larry hears the Stephenses have electricity, he rushes everyone over, since MacElroy has a plane to catch.

Aunt Clara hides Ocky in the closet as the Stephenses return with Larry and the unimpressed MacElroy. While the power company arrives to check into why hers is the only house in the neighborhood with the lights on, Samantha begins to feel Aunt Clara is responsible. Gladys sneaks in, screaming when she thinks something's in the closet; Darrin sees nothing, but Gladys faints when Ocky, who has made himself invisible except for his shoes, walks out. MacElroy loves it, thinking the "animated shoes" are part of the campaign. The next day, the newspaper attributes the blackout to a one-in-a-million accident, but Samantha's money is still on Aunt Clara.

GOOD!

Darrin shows amazing compassion for Aunt Clara in the show's prologue. "Poor old girl," he comments when he hears she was thrown over for a younger witch. "As if she didn't have enough trouble." And even if Ocky is a scoundrel, he does have his moments – his best one being his second attempt to restore the lights. Raising his arms to recast his spell, the power comes on, and Clara declares it's because of his hands. "Are they gone?" the befuddled Ocky asks.

WELL?

Why does Darrin still think Tabatha can have mortal babysitters? In "Accidental Twins" (#78), Samantha clearly stated mortals were out until Tabatha learned to control her powers. And when did the Stephenses get a piano? Watching Aunt Clara's witched instrument "losing containment" on the stairs is great, but there's never been a piano in the living room before, nor any mention of the Stephenses buying one. And isn't it kind of odd that the Tates are hosting a client dinner? Usually, that duty falls to the Stephenses.

Ocky makes a big show of wanting Aunt Clara back, claiming he "blew a year's magic" on his "little witch." Why would any witch need another witch's powers to materialize material items? Does that mean witchcraft is rationed? It hardly seems likely, given how freely the show's witches and warlocks use their powers. Ocky adds yet another wrinkle to the "can witches remove each others' spells" debate: he either partially undoes or merely adds to Aunt Clara's original spell, turning the Stephenses' lights on after she's turned them off. In "Alias Darrin Stephens" (#37) and "Accidental Twins" (#78), Aunt Clara's precise incantations were required in order to reverse them; here, she makes no effort at all to recall her original spell. And Ocky's magic must be more old school than Clara's, because even she's using English language spells now, while Ocky is still using combinations of magic words.

The Tates have some really powerful candles – just a few light their entire dining room. Later, when Samantha calls to check on Tabatha, Aunt Clara freely admits that the power is on in the house when it's out everywhere else. Why would she do that? Of course, it's a ploy by the writers to get everybody over to the Stephenses, but if Aunt Clara is so anxious to keep her goof – and Ocky's assistance – secret, all she has to say is that she also has no lights.

Gladys has been a busy girl. Between calling the police in "Endora Moves in for a Spell" (#80), adding the fire department, SPCA, and a local councilman in "Twitch or Treat" (#81), and now reporting the Stephenses to the power company, she's really burning up her phone line. Also burning up is Samantha, who is strangely hostile toward the aunt she was ready to go to battle for in "Samantha Meets the Folks" (#14) and "There's No Witch Like An Old Witch" (#27). Besides, Samantha doesn't know for sure that Aunt Clara has anything to do with the outage; is she starting to pick up on Darrin's tendency to immediately suspect witchcraft?

Larry must really want MacElroy's account, because he's stooped to using a tactic he's never used before: brown-nosing. He forces Louise and the Stephenses to stop eating, and constantly yells out for MacElroy's brandy. Maybe it all goes back to "Eat At Mario's" (#35), where Larry admitted he hated losing accounts because of the resulting sense of rejection.

Ocky's powers aren't much better than Clara's, since his shoes are amusingly visible as he steps over the unconscious Gladys on the way out the door. But what happens once Ocky gets outside? The lights stay on, which has to mean Ocky is somewhere keeping his hands up. Hopefully he's at least leaning against the house to make it easier for himself.

OH, MY STARS!

Samantha tells Darrin they have to be especially nice to Aunt Clara because she's just broken up with Ocky. Who's Ocky? Her last beau was Hedley Partridge, who came back with marriage on his mind in "Aunt Clara's Old Flame" (#47), leaving Clara a doorknob as an engagement present. Has that reunion petered out already? Either Aunt Clara got involved with Ocky on the rebound, she was two-timing Hedley, or the writers forgot she already had a fiancé.

SON OF A GUN!

"Just a little dance I learned in Scotland. It's called the Wee Kick of the Kirk." – Aunt Clara to Darrin, Larry, and MacElroy, after being caught kicking at the closet so Ocky will put his hands back up.

The power is off, but Aunt Clara is on. Not only is her dialogue snappier (especially with the reconciliatory Ocky), but the goofiness Marion Lorne brings to Aunt Clara is even more delightful than usual.

I'D RATHER TWITCH THAN FIGHT

Airdate: November 17, 1966

EPISODE
84

Darrin wants to wear his houndstooth sport coat to work, but Samantha has given it to a thrift shop, causing the Stephenses to fight. Darrin vents to Larry, who counsels Darrin based on the advice of Dr. Kramer, a psychiatrist he and Louise are seeing. After the Tates give the Stephenses conflicting definitions of what drab and colorful clothes signify, Samantha finds Darrin's dyed jacket and twitches it back to houndstooth, while Darrin buys Samantha a cheerless bathrobe. The gift-giving goes awry in the context of the Tates' advice, and the Stephenses have their worst argument yet.

Larry suggests bringing Dr. Kramer home to talk to Samantha, while Endora is horrified to hear about Dr. Kramer because psychiatrists are "anti-witch." Deciding Samantha needs the best, Endora zaps up Sigmund Freud; he listens as Samantha admits she's a witch and describes the blow-up over the coat. Freud tells Samantha that she and Darrin should only fight about important things as Darrin comes in with Dr. Kramer, who loves the houndstooth jacket. Kramer and Freud get into their own argument that nearly elevates to fisticuffs before Samantha and Endora send the doctors back where they came from. Endora scoffs as the Stephenses make up; later, Samantha dons a negligée and gifts Darrin with a stylish robe; Darrin realizes she traded in the inflammatory items by witchcraft, but decides he doesn't care.

GOOD!

The title of this episode is a paraphrase of a 1960s ad for Tareyton cigarettes, whose smokers "would rather fight than switch." And fight the Stephenses do – it's the Tates who switch. There's something almost paternal in the way Larry tries to teach Darrin about Dr. Kramer's philosophies regarding marital fighting, and Louise relaying the same information to Samantha gives Mrs. Tate some new, deeper layers. That the Tates impart nearly opposite interpretations of what clothes represent in a marriage is rather a silent indicator of the counseling not working as well as they say it is.

Psychoanalysis was almost trendy in the '60s, so it's only natural it would find its way into an episode. And, while the examinations of amphigoric, semiamphigoric and centripetal fights are interesting, it's Darrin's armchair diagnosis of Samantha that's the most revealing. "Every time you have a problem that you can't handle, or you get excited, you resort to witchcraft." Yes, she does – perhaps her conflict over giving up her powers is more deeply rooted than anyone knows. Darrin makes a psychological slip himself when Larry raves about what a wizard Dr. Kramer is, muttering, "Wizards I don't need."

As in "Dangerous Diaper Dan" (#82), the show wisely takes a moment to continue Tabatha's story while in the middle of sport jacket squabbles and dueling psychiatrists – Endora quietly zaps up a bottle for Tabatha and has her float it to herself. Getting to see the baby's magical progress is a treat, plus a nice break from the domestic discord.

WELL?

Samantha told Darrin in "Accidental Twins" (#78) that they could no longer use mortal babysitters because of Tabatha experimenting with her powers. Then why is Samantha on the phone confirming a time – with a mortal babysitter? And Darrin builds up an unusually thick head of steam in this episode – he's rude to Samantha before he even knows she gave his coat away, and storms off to "the thrift shop" in the hopes they still have it. How does he know which one to go to? Or does their area only have one such shop?

Larry admits to Darrin that he and Louise have been going to Dr. Kramer for several months. Maybe that explains why the Tates haven't been at each other's throats as much this season. Of course, Larry told Darrin in "Eat At Mario's" (#35) that he'd been in analysis for seven years – has he been seeing Dr. Kramer all along and only just recently brought Louise in on the sessions, or has he changed therapists?

It seems odd that a thrift shop would dye an out-of-style coat to increase the likelihood of selling it, considering these shops are known for having vintage duds on their racks. Later, when Darrin walks out on Samantha after the botched gift exchange, he is moving at a pretty fast clip. Yet, when Samantha pops him back inside, he is stationary. Wouldn't he still be in motion? And Samantha must be upset, otherwise she wouldn't make Darrin disappear from the front yard where the increasingly aggressive Gladys could see it, or wear the same clothes two days in a row, as indicated by the fact that Darrin spends the night at the office.

Before Endora pops in next to Tabatha's crib, a hand is visible to the left of the frame. Then, Endora backpedals on her negative assessment of psychiatrists by zapping up "the best." That's one thing, but why would Samantha blab to Dr. Freud about being a witch right after Endora said shrinks are anti-witch, and when being a witch has nothing to do with the problem at hand? Also, the rate of aging in witches again comes into question. Samantha tells Freud she realized she was a witch when she was a year old, with Endora correcting, "nine months." Doesn't this imply a mortal lifespan? Yet, in "Eye of the Beholder" (#22), it came out that Samantha could be as much as 300 years old. Do baby witches and baby mortals develop at the same pace?

OH, MY STARS!

Declining Endora's offer to take Tabatha and come home with her, Samantha decides to get Dr. Kramer's contact info from Louise, declaring, "he's the one who started the whole thing in the first place." Where is she getting that? Darrin's the one who touched off the powder keg by being so unreasonable over a lost coat. And Samantha played a hand by giving away Darrin's clothes without checking with him first; Dr. Kramer has nothing to do with this.

SON OF A GUN!

"For the first time, someone has called me in time." – Dr. Freud, thinking Tabatha is his patient.

Norman Fell is probably best known for his role as the over-the-top Mr. Roper on the 1977-1984 ABC sitcom *Three's Company*, but long before that, he turned in this subtle performance as Dr. Freud. His deadpan reactions to Samantha's admissions of witchery are just the responses you'd think Freud would have, and he makes the most sense of anyone around him, stating that the flap over the coat is "not a psychological problem." But his best moment comes when he lets his own neuroses show and allows Dr. Kramer to goad him into a fistfight. "I'll father fixation you!" he sneers. The battle of the heated head shrinkers makes the whole episode worthwhile.

OEDIPUS HEX
Airdate: November 24, 1966

EPISODE 85

Samantha is working to get new playground equipment installed in the park, and arranges to brainstorm fundraising ideas at the house with the ladies of her committee. The day of the meeting, Samantha laments Darrin's workaholic tendencies; rushing out with breakfast, Darrin is surprised to find a bowl of popcorn in the foyer – a snack Endora has hexed to induce idleness in the eater. After Darrin munches a handful, he takes the day off. As Samantha shops for her meeting, Darrin passes the bowl to the milkman and a TV repairman, who also ditch their duties. Larry storms over to find out why Darrin hasn't come in to the office and also falls victim to the popcorn. Samantha is annoyed to see her house full of devil-may-care men, but even more so when their ruckus disrupts her meeting with the stuffy committee women.

Hot-tempered client Parkinson arrives to rage at Darrin and Larry for blowing him off, but Endora's popcorn mellows him, and the cop who's followed Parkinson to give him a ticket. When the loud group raids the refrigerator because all they've had to eat is popcorn, Samantha puts the pieces together and feeds the slothful snack to the committee ladies, since the apologetic men have offered to raise their money for them. The gents exceed the committee's fundraising goal, and Samantha is happy to usher the crowd out after Endora removes her spell and restores everyone to their stressed-out selves.

GOOD!
Once the full group of lazy boys get together, their rambunctiousness becomes the best part of the episode. Rifling through the kitchen while laughing and carrying on, the actors themselves are having a blast, and there's almost a feeling they're doing some improvising in the context of the scene. Most notable is Larry, who is usually a bit of a stuffed shirt; it's fun to see him out of his element [and he doesn't even need champagne like he did in "The Moment of Truth" (#76)].

There's something sweet in the way the repentant gentlemen take over the committee's fundraiser to amass their playground equipment money for them. It's a quick sequence, in which Darrin, Larry, and this legion of character actors get a chance to shine; it's also a sort of redemption since they spend so much time annoying Samantha. As for the equipment itself, it's insightful to have Samantha suggest that Tabatha will be likely be playing on it one day.

WELL?
Samantha's worn her blue checkered dress a lot this season, but here she wears it two days in a row: she has it on when scheduling her meeting for the next day, and when that day arrives. The previous episode ["I'd Rather Twitch Than Fight" (#84)] saw her wearing the same clothes two days in a row as well –

perhaps Wardrobe isn't keeping enough tabs on Samantha's costumes. By the way, what did the wonderfully impish Mrs. Dumont do to deserve Samantha's haughty imitation of her? The lady isn't nearly as snobby as her underlings, Mrs. Wheeler and Mrs. Albright, who may have had it coming.

Endora is a witch who goes out of her way to have as little to do with mortals as possible. So how does she know so much about mortal men and their martyr-like approach toward work? Has she been researching humans since Samantha married one? As for Samantha, she should know something's wrong immediately – even though the camera pans, she's looking right at Endora as she pops the popcorn.

Why does Endora's spell need constant reinforcement? Whenever a new mortal is about to take a bite of her popcorn, she either rehexes the bowl or witches the man into reaching for the snack; maybe it saves time. But does Endora have nothing better to do than hang around and watch mortals loafing? Endora must be invisible while in the same room with the men, yet she pops out when Samantha comes home. Is Samantha able to see her?

Darrin's "Happiness House!" phone greeting is good for a giggle, but he seems to be picking up phrases from Endora. In "Dangerous Diaper Dan" (#82), she responded to Samantha's prediction of account success with "Naturally, here in Happiness House. It wouldn't dare work out any other way." The Stephenses also might want to consider replacing their TV – it already needed work in "Just One Happy Family" (#10). Finally, Darrin is having a ball playing poker with the guys, except, in "Double Split" (#64), he told Larry he hated the game.

Parkinson is either so upset at Larry and Darrin for skipping their meeting, or he doesn't know who's representing his never-mentioned product: as he barks at the receptionist, he calls the agency "*McCann & Tate*." He's ticketed by an equally forgetful cop – the same one who investigated the missing house in "Endora Moves in for a Spell" (#80). Either Paul Smith is playing a different officer, or his "Floyd" has blanked out his strange Morning Glory Circle experience already.

OH, MY STARS!

Samantha asks Darrin to mind Tabatha while she's out shopping, but he doesn't do a very good job – he's completely oblivious to his daughter's existence while passing popcorn to and playing poker with the fellas. Samantha's not much better: once she's home, she's only concerned with her meeting. Tabatha can't be able to sleep through the high-decibel racket of her daddy's playful pals, and surely she needs a bottle at some point. Good thing Tabatha knows how to zap up her own.

SON OF A GUN!

"Is it dead?" – the milkman, after Larry finds chicken in the refrigerator.

SAM'S SPOOKY CHAIR
Airdate: December 1, 1966

Samantha is intrigued by a chair in an antiques store, not knowing it "walked" to a spot where she'd be sure to see it. During a business dinner, overbearing Adelaide Cosgrove sees Samantha's chair and pressures her henpecked husband, Max, into buying it, promising Max can renew with McMann & Tate once she owns the chair. Darrin is unnerved when the chair seems to fight him; later that night, Samantha is awakened by loud noises and finds that the chair has made its way back from the Cosgroves.

The next day, the Cosgroves' uproar over the "stolen" chair threatens the renewal; Max, desperate to placate Adelaide, sees Samantha's alleged "copy" and takes the chair home. Samantha sends Darrin to the antiques store for information and also puts Endora on the case – by the time Samantha gets to the Cosgroves, Adelaide is ready to leave Max because she believes he broke the chair, which threw her to the floor. As Larry and Louise get pulled into their drama, Darrin reveals that the chair originates from turn-of-the-century Boston, and Endora learns that a smitten Clyde Farnsworth had himself transformed into the chair because Samantha rejected him. After setting Clyde straight, Samantha changes him back, and Clyde obligingly zaps up a duplicate chair for her and Darrin. The Cosgroves reunite, and Larry gets his contract signed, but Darrin is shocked when Clyde's supposedly inanimate chair kicks him.

GOOD!

The show once again gets a rare (and rather thrilling) plug in that Samantha tells Endora, "I can't give [the chair] back to the Cosgroves if it's bewitched!" That word, or derivatives of it, have only otherwise been uttered in "George the Warlock" (#30), "We're In For A Bad Spell" (#39), and "What Every Young Man Should Know" (#72). And Samantha comes a lot closer to revealing her hometown when she reports having shared a street with Clyde in Boston. It's not the first time Beantown and its environs have come up: in "Eye of the Beholder" (#22), Endora's may-or-may-not-be-fake portrait of a 1682 Samantha listed her as "Maid of Salem" (which is only 15 miles from Boston), and, in "Just One Happy Family" (#10), Samantha lied to Maurice that Darrin is "very old stock" from Massachusetts. Maybe she was just, as they say, writing what she knew.

The circus surrounding Adelaide's overreaction to what she perceives as Max's destruction of the chair is worthy of a ringmaster. Perhaps the most enjoyable part is Larry's attempt to calm the Cosgroves' conniption: Max appeals to Adelaide by calling her "love pot," prompting Larry to blurt out, "Take it from me, love pot!"

WELL?

Samantha and Darrin's battle in "I'd Rather Twitch Than Fight" (#84) started because she hated his houndstooth sport coat. So why does she wear a blouse with the same pattern to the antiques store? And Samantha sure is an easy sell: she walks into the store, sees one chair, and walks out with it in less than 90 seconds. The Stephenses never-before-seen piano in "The Short Happy Circuit of Aunt Clara" (#83) once again ceases to exist, as the chair freely runs where the instrument was last seen.

Darrin takes comfort knowing Samantha is making Tabatha's baby food by hand. Why not just pick up some Gerber's at the market? The Stephenses don't need to save money that badly, unless Samantha is just trying to go organic or take living like a mortal to a new level.

Trying to calm Larry about the Cosgrove renewal, Darrin advises him to take a pill. Darrin had to stop him from a near overdose of presumed tranquilizers in "Dangerous Diaper Dan" (#82) – would Darrin really suggest more drugs after that? Later, in the living room, when Adelaide gushes over Samantha's chair, Darrin ought to be wondering how it got there, since he just struggled to stash it in the den.

After all the hoopla over Samantha's nightwear in "I'd Rather Twitch Than Fight" (#84), Darrin must have gone back to the boutique, because Samantha is wearing the pale green robe he didn't buy her in that episode. And Samantha is right to be astonished when she finds the chair downstairs – how did it get in? Surely the Stephenses are locking their doors after having been burgled twice [in "A Strange Little

Visitor" (#48) and "A Bum Raps" (#68)]. The Cosgroves must live nearby, too, otherwise it would take a lot longer than a few hours for Clyde-as-chair to shuffle all the way to Morning Glory Circle.

When Darrin concludes that Max will re-up after receiving the chair's "copy," Samantha comments, "If he lives." But Clyde isn't fighting Max; his only beef seems to be with Darrin. Maybe Samantha inspires Clyde, because later he collapses on Adelaide, even though Clyde's *modus operandi* appears to be a desire to be near Samantha, which antagonizing the Cosgroves doesn't fit into. Then, Larry sends Louise ahead to the Cosgroves, since she's an expert on marital arguments [she should be; Dr. Kramer taught the Tates how to spat in "I'd Rather Twitch Than Fight" (#84)] – yet Larry and Louise ultimately arrive at the Cosgroves' together.

Samantha must get tired of fending off lovesick non-suitors: she just discouraged the amorous Rodney in "Man's Best Friend" (#70). As for Clyde, he was transformed in the early 1900s; Samantha says his clothes haven't changed, but he looks as mod as 1960s mod can look. And if "someone" at the antiques store loves him (in this case, a lamp), then why does he ask Samantha if there's any hope for them? Clyde spends the whole episode lovesick for Samantha, then shifts gears on a dime. It's magnanimous of him to duplicate his chair self to help Darrin, but when Samantha wanted to do it earlier, she said she needed his permission. Why? Does Clyde have some sort of copyright on his furnitured form? Finally, when Samantha brings Clyde's copy to the Cosgroves, it has collapsible legs to explain Clyde-as-chair's antics (what chair has collapsible legs?), though the inanimate object is somehow still able to kick Darrin.

OH, MY STARS!

Once again, Samantha can undo another witch's spell, but this time, doing so goes against any previous rule that's been established. As of "Alias Darrin Stephens" (#37), a witch needs to know the exact words of the original spell she cast before she can reverse it. Here, Endora simply tells Samantha that Enchantra, who transformed Clyde, used the "simple" spell, "without the ox tails." Even more baffling, Samantha commands Clyde to "become a human being again" – but Clyde isn't human, and here he has to be willing to be changed back, or the spell won't work. Maybe different rules apply to humanoid furniture?

SON OF A GUN!

"You know, we've been around the world twice. Next year we're planning to go someplace else." – Adelaide Cosgrove to her addled dinner hosts.

MY FRIEND BEN
Airdate: December 8, 1966

When Samantha struggles to fix a lamp, Aunt Clara's attempt to zap up an electrician makes Benjamin Franklin appear in the living room, which Gladys sees through the window. The stunned Samantha gently lets Franklin know he's in the 20th century and allows him to believe that modern technology transported him. Curious to see how his work with electricity has manifested, Franklin crawls around exploring wires as Darrin comes home, floored to find the inventor in his house. Larry drops by and concludes that

Franklin is Darrin's symbol for the Franklin Electronics account; Gladys is told Franklin and Clara are going to a costume party, but she is convinced the man is the real thing when Larry addresses him by name.

After Samantha decides to take Franklin on a tour to show him how his innovations have impacted the present, he wanders off by himself and attracts attention by lecturing a disrespectful teen at the library. Samantha and Aunt Clara catch up and show him a fire station; while Samantha is on a pay phone with Darrin, Franklin unwittingly starts an old fire engine, then crashes it. Franklin is arrested, and Darrin is forced to put up $1,000 in bail. Franklin's trial is set to happen in four weeks, but Aunt Clara remembers her spell and sends Franklin away, putting Darrin at risk of losing his money.

GOOD!

Samantha and Aunt Clara's search for Franklin contains a string of well done effects, such as when they pop themselves over to the library – it's an accomplishment to make it look like witches are appearing while mortals are moving. Also, Franklin's comeback to the typical, apathetic '60s teen is "right on." Franklin puts that kid in his place so thoroughly, it's hard not to cheer.

WELL?

What is it about Aunt Clara and electricity? She just caused a massive blackout in "The Short Happy Circuit of Aunt Clara" (#83), and now she's trying to zap up electricians. More importantly, Samantha has only been living the mortal life for two years out of probable hundreds – how would she even know where to start rewiring a lamp? Maybe Samantha wouldn't have been so quick to wonder at "the marvels of electricity" in "Prodigy" (#74) had she known one of its greatest proponents would soon land her in court.

Freshly zapped out of the 18th century, Benjamin Franklin is agape at the "devices" all around him, but never once does he question Samantha's wardrobe; women didn't wear pants in the mainstream until the 1930s. Another anachronism occurs when, upon seeing that his electrical experiments have borne fruit, Franklin declares, "Oh, there were those in my day who would have clapped me in the stocks for dealing with witchcraft!" Not quite – Franklin was born in 1706, and, by the time he proposed studying electricity in 1750, there hadn't been a witch trial for 57 years, the last one widely accepted as having been in 1693.

What are the odds of McMann & Tate vying for the Franklin Electronics account at the same time Aunt Clara brings its namesake into the present? Of course, coincidences make for comedy, but this one is a bit of a stretch. And why does Larry visit the Stephenses at dinnertime? Doesn't he have a wife and son at home he should be dining with?

Franklin decides to tour the city himself, and leaves Samantha a note (which will ultimately be worth a fortune if the Stephenses choose to sell it). However, unless Ben used a pencil, or the Stephenses have a quill lying around, the inventor would be perplexed by ball-point pens, which didn't exist until 1888. Ben is on foot and limited to the local area, yet Samantha and Aunt Clara seem to be running around the Manhattan set looking for him. Finally, at the library, a man needles Franklin, asking him what he's advertising. Yet, when the teenage boy gets in Franklin's face, that same needler tells the kid to "leave the old man alone."

It's standard television practice for an extra to appear in one scene, change clothes, then appear in another scene within the same episode. But the fellow who stands between Franklin and the teen gets a lot of face time, so it's glaring when he doubles as the bailiff while Franklin is arraigned.

OH, MY STARS!

As soon as Samantha meets Franklin, she tells him he's in the 20th century, gushes about how his inventions are now household words, and parades him around the city – ignoring the potential impact of giving Franklin knowledge of the future. Samantha didn't give much thought to how her activities in 1472 could reverberate into the present in "A Most Unusual Wood Nymph" (#79), either; what if Franklin goes back and applies something he learned in 1966 to an 18th century invention, or blabs to someone about his experience? Even the tiniest detail could have a mammoth effect on the timeline. As with the aforementioned episode, these musings might be out of place for a sitcom, but when you start dealing with the concept of time travel, such issues are inevitable.

Whether or not a vintage fire engine can be started by simply pressing a button is a question for qualified historians and mechanics. Regardless, a vehicle typically has to be put into gear before it can move; Ben's fire engine rolls all on its own, and its sirens go off as soon as he hits the gas pedal. Also, a plaque at the fire station says this particular engine was built in 1923, and retired in 1936. Would a fire engine that's been out of service for 30 years just...fire up like that?

SON OF A GUN!

"By your clothes and countenance, I take you to be advertising dirt, slovenliness, and a dislike for soap and water. Your demeanor proclaims your insolence and your disrespect. And by your speech, I suspect that you are advertising rudeness, vulgarity and an ignorance for the English language. Good day, sir!" – Ben Franklin, taking a 1960s teen apart.

Whatever hiccups this episode may have never takes away from the outstanding and absolutely believable performance of Fredd Wayne – it really seems Benjamin Franklin is standing in the Stephenses' living room. Contemporary audiences may not know that the accomplished actor was touring as Franklin in a one-man show at the time, which influenced this two-parter. One can only hope the real Franklin was as cool as Wayne.

EPISODE 88
SAMANTHA FOR THE DEFENSE
Airdate: December 15, 1966

Continuing on from "My Friend Ben" (#87), District Attorney Hawkins is ready to give "Benjamin Franklin" a light fine for "stealing" a fire engine instead of going to court, but Larry breezes in talking about the great publicity for the Franklin Electronics account, so Hawkins moves the trial up. Meanwhile, as bystanders and reporters gather outside the Stephens house, Aunt Clara tries to bring Franklin back, materializing Franklin Pierce instead. Gladys tells the crowd about the original spell she overheard, which jogs Aunt Clara's memory, and Franklin returns. Samantha works to influence public opinion by having Franklin speak at high schools, by changing protest signs, and by putting words in broadcasters' mouths as Franklin prepares his own defense.

In court, a librarian testifies that Franklin attempted to pay a fine on a book that was 200 years overdue, Gladys wants to testify about Samantha's witchcraft, and Darrin unwittingly helps the prosecution by confirming that a publicity stunt involving Franklin was discussed. Things look grim until Samantha remembers that the fire engine Franklin "stole" is an antique; she pops to the fire station and retrieves the plaque containing that information, then testifies that Franklin is being accused of stealing his own property, since he invented the fire department. When Hawkins threatens to charge Samantha with perjury, she twitches him silent until she can remind everyone of Benjamin Franklin's accomplishments. Franklin is found not guilty, and Aunt Clara goes out "on the town" with him after accidentally zapping herself into 18th century clothing.

GOOD!

For once, Gladys Kravitz's suspicions do some good. Seeing her neighbor blabbing to the press, Samantha smartly opens the window and lets Gladys fill in the blanks so Aunt Clara can remember how to zap Franklin back into the present. That's a brilliant twist, as is Abner finally seeing that Gladys isn't imagining things. Larry even remarks to Abner that *he's* starting to believe Franklin is the real thing.

Protest marches were oh-so-hip in the mid-to-late '60s, so having Samantha add pro-Franklin rhetoric to protest signs – with the anti-establishment kids never noticing – is especially appropriate. One of the teens has a transistor radio, on which a deejay back announces *Snarl Baby Snarl If You Love Me* – a great commentary on the changing face of music and attitudes in the '60s. The deejay: The Real Don Steele. He and his Boss Radio were all the rage in 1966, making his cameo ultra groovy.

WELL?

With everything going on in 1966 – the space race and Vietnam being two biggies – how does "every paper" consider Franklin front page news? His presence and alleged fire engine theft might qualify as human interest, but hardly a top story. People flock to the Stephenses house anyway, as they did in "Baby's First Paragraph" (#62), when Tabatha's "talking" was news. Now, Darrin himself made the front page in "Fastest Gun on Madison Avenue" (#57) – these are the kinds of things the press would build on, yet the events are never referenced.

District Attorney Hawkins is ready to let Franklin off with a fine until he believes the fire engine filching is a publicity stunt – suddenly it's a felony. Isn't taking public property the same crime regardless of its motive? And how can Hawkins ever think it's *not* a publicity stunt? He was in court when the judge used that exact term in "My Friend Ben" (#87), where Darrin agreed to put up bail. Maybe Hawkins forgot, because he also introduces himself to Darrin as if they haven't encountered each other before. As for Larry, he's obsessed with the idea that all the Franklin mania is part of a campaign for Franklin Electronics, despite Darrin not being in on the tie-in and Ben never saying one way or the other that he would lend his name to this "commercial venture."

Aunt Clara struggles to remember how she zapped up Ben the first time. Why? By this time, Aunt Clara has already recited the spell twice, the second time being hours before, as indicated by Samantha and Gladys still wearing the same clothes they had on at the end of "My Friend Ben" (#87).

Darrin sneaks "around back" to avoid the crowd, the same subterfuge he pulled in "Baby's First Paragraph" (#62). But, as in that episode, Darrin still has to be in front of the house to get to the kitchen door, where he would definitely be visible to the throngs.

The idea of Ben Franklin trying to pay a 200-year old library fine surely speaks to his integrity, but that would be quite a feat. He can't be carrying 1966 money in his pocket, and, if he had plunked down any 18th century currency, that would have attracted more attention than any fire engine. Ben is acquitted, but he still damaged a vintage fire engine, albeit unintentionally. Wouldn't he be required to pay for it?

OH, MY STARS!

The crowd around the Stephens house naturally blows off Gladys' claims about Samantha, but Franklin Pierce pops in and out in plain view of the masses. The WXIW reporter even asks about it, yet Samantha merely suggests he has something in his eye, and no more mention is made of it. Pierce's presence should have someone believing Gladys when she goes on to explain how Benjamin Franklin got there.

Hawkins' entire case rests upon whether or not Franklin stole the fire engine as a publicity stunt. He could prove his case in a minute by putting Larry, the man who contacted Franklin Electronics and spoke openly about Ben doing testimonials for them, on the stand – yet Hawkins only calls Darrin as a witness to obliquely mention that Franklin Electronics was discussed. Conversely, Franklin could have the whole case thrown out of court by questioning Aunt Clara, the only witness; she could testify that Franklin didn't even know how to start or drive a fire engine, which completely voids his motive for stealing it. Instead, Gladys, a librarian, and a high school principal do the testifying.

It's funny when Samantha twitches the D.A. into silence, but, by doing so, she's criminally obstructing justice. Gladys was shut down for talking out of turn, but not Samantha; the judge allows her to deliver a sermon from the stand that isn't even relevant to Hawkins' questions. Because a plaque names the "stolen" vehicle "Benjamin Franklin Memorial Fire Engine," Samantha says Franklin is being accused of stealing his own property, though Franklin only started the fire *department*. Besides, if Carl Benz, who invented the automobile, were to come into the present and steal a car, would he be acquitted because he'd taken his own property? No.

There's much talk around the courtroom about whether or not Ben is an impostor. But it doesn't matter – Samantha's contention that he represents Mr. Franklin and his innovations does nothing to change the case: he climbed onto that fire engine no matter what his identity is. Yet, Ben is acquitted on the basis of this speech.

The true guilty party here is Samantha. Maybe she's never had time-traveling visitors before, but she should have kept Ben in the house instead of exposing him to the outside world and making his presence a matter of public record. Talk about polluting the timeline.

SON OF A GUN!

"Oh, I'm sure they'll be all right, sweetheart. After all, they're both over 200." – Samantha to Darrin, after Ben takes Aunt Clara on a date.

Looks like Clara didn't take the womanizing Ocky back after all [see "The Short Happy Circuit of Aunt Clara" (#83)] – she's got Benjamin Franklin on her arm! They have a really sweet rapport, and Aunt Clara looks unexpectedly luminous in her 18th century garb. It's a shame Ben can't stick around – Clara's finally found a man who provides electricity.

EPISODE 89

A GAZEBO NEVER FORGETS
Airdate: December 22, 1966

Aunt Clara crashes through the gazebo that the Stephenses want to replace with a rumpus room. She accompanies Samantha and Tabatha to the park, where the girl twitches over a polka-dotted elephant belonging to another child; his mother accuses Samantha of stealing it. Later, with Darrin out of town,

Samantha negotiates a loan for the rumpus room with brusque bank president Scranton, who brightens upon learning Darrin handles his brother's soap account. Meanwhile, Aunt Clara tries to duplicate the toy elephant for Tabatha, getting a live one instead. Scranton's suspicious appraiser, Hawkins, comes by early, sees the elephant, and reports it to Scranton. Not wanting to jeopardize the soap account, Larry tells Samantha he's bringing everyone over to prove there's no elephant.

The polka-dotted pachyderm wants to be near Tabatha, so Samantha stashes them in the den. Hawkins looks for his elephant while Aunt Clara, who needs the original toy to reverse her spell, tells the woman in the park she won a contest that requires surrendering the plaything. Hawkins finds the real elephant, but Samantha leads it to another room to keep the disbelieving Larry and Scranton from seeing it. This relay continues until Larry and Scranton finally have enough and leave. When the elephant breaks through the wall, Samantha tells Hawkins that Darrin caught it on safari. Later, Samantha and Aunt Clara attempt to return the toy elephant, but Aunt Clara again zaps up the real one, sending the park woman running.

GOOD!

As with Merle's baseball in "A Strange Little Visitor" (#48), it's quite a feat when the show makes objects "float" outside. Tabatha levitating the toy elephant in the park is even more of an accomplishment, considering it's done in a wide shot, which would require the wires to run several feet high to assure the trickery stayed out of frame.

With Darrin not in an episode for the first time, the onus falls on the other mortals to believe or disbelieve the witchcraft surrounding them. Here, Larry takes up the baton along with Scranton, and their sarcastic asides as Hawkins runs around searching for the elephant more than carry the sequence.

WELL?

Aunt Clara jokes that she'd have landed dead center on the gazebo had she known Samantha wanted to tear it down. Clara made that landing in "Alias Darrin Stephens" (#37); as the gazebo has been intact since, the assumption is that the Stephenses had it repaired. Why go through all that just to tear it down a year later? At the park, after Tabatha tries to snag the toy elephant by witchcraft, Samantha rightly tells her daughter that taking someone else's property is wrong – but why doesn't Samantha return the toy to the other child's stroller first? Then the boy's mother wouldn't see Samantha with it or accuse her of swiping it; instead, Samantha just sits there with the stolen stuffed animal in her lap.

Scranton's bank must have used the same architect as McMann & Tate. Their lobbies are identical – same wood paneling, even the same conference room plaque on the door. And Samantha already knows a bank president: Mr. Abercrombie, who hired Darrin's friend Adam Newlarkin in "We're In For A Bad Spell" (#39). Wouldn't going to someone familiar for a loan be easier than broaching it with a stranger?

Steve Franken is wonderfully neurotic as bank appraiser Hawkins, but his character is almost identical to his Robbins Baby Food executive, Barkley [from "Follow That Witch" (#66-#67)], right down to his suspicions and need for character references. By the way, why another character named Hawkins so soon? That was the surname of the District Attorney from the previous episode, "Samantha for the Defense" (#88).

Aunt Clara wants to turn herself into an elephant to amuse Tabatha, but doesn't seem to know how. She did in "Aunt Clara's Old Flame" (#47), when she turned her beau, Hedley Partridge, into the mammal. Why does Samantha let this one poke its head through the front window, which faces the Kravitz house?

She knows Gladys could be spying at any moment. Finally, Samantha sounds surprised when Larry calls to say that Hawkins has been by. Why? Scranton did tell Samantha that Hawkins would be dropping in.

Samantha's logic that the men might not see the elephant on the patio is a little fuzzy. The whole point of the loan is to tear down the gazebo – the patio is the first place they'd go; Hawkins certainly does. Then, Samantha hides the animal in the den because it wants to be near Tabatha. "As long as they're both here, there won't be any problem," Samantha reasons. Does she not notice the elephant trumpeting as she says that? That would be audible from anywhere in the house, yet the elephant is inexplicably silent as the mortal men visit.

The woman in the park must have one mission in life: to sit on that bench with her kid. She's still there hours later when Aunt Clara awards her $20 for the phony contest, and doesn't recognize Clara, who was with the very woman she accused of stealing her child's toy earlier that day; it's amazing she doesn't find Clara suspicious. Honoring Samantha's request to not procure the toy elephant by witchcraft, Aunt Clara later uses magic to return it to the park woman – who is left on her own to deal with a real elephant after Samantha and Clara ditch her.

Tabatha runs out of the den, prompting the elephant to burst through the wall and make its way through the den closet before reaching the foyer. That's a lot of damage – hopefully Samantha will witch things back together before Darrin comes home. For as clever as her lie is about Darrin trapping the elephant on safari, all that does is confirm its existence to Hawkins. What's to stop him from going back to Scranton and reporting that Samantha admitted to it? Darrin's fib that Hedley-as-elephant was a model for a swimsuit campaign [see "Aunt Clara's Old Flame" (#47)] made more sense.

OH, MY STARS!

The witchcraft rule experiments continue. Ordinarily, a witch just needs to remember the right words to reverse a spell; this time, Aunt Clara must have the toy elephant from the park to zap the real one out of Samantha's living room. Is that like needing to keep the two Jonathan Tates together in "Accidental Twins" (#78)? Later, Aunt Clara suggests that Samantha pop the elephant onto the patio, and Samantha basically says she can't. So Aunt Clara having cast the original spell prevents Samantha from performing any other witchcraft in relation to it?

SON OF A GUN!

"Never mind the music!" – Samantha, to her loud and disobedient guest.

EPISODE 90

SOAPBOX DERBY
Airdate: December 29, 1966

Young Johnny Mills wants to race in the local soapbox derby, so Samantha takes him to the track, where Gladys' nephew, Leroy "Flash" Kravitz, brags he'll be the champion. Gladys sees red after Johnny beats "Flash" thanks to Samantha magically fixing a wobbly wheel on Johnny's racer. Darrin doesn't want to get involved, but softens when he hears how Johnny is hiding the racer from his mechanic father, who wants Johnny to focus on becoming a doctor. Samantha barely gets the distracted Mills to sign Johnny's racing consent form, but can't convince him to attend the derby.

The day of the race, Johnny beats all competitors except "Flash" – leaving the two to race against each other in the finals. Johnny wins, but Gladys, having watched Samantha through her binoculars, runs to the derby officials and accuses Johnny and the Stephenses of foul play. When Johnny is requested to attend an informal hearing with his parents, Johnny lies that his father is sick; Samantha goes to Mills' garage, but he is so swamped with repairs that Samantha completes a few with witchcraft to free up some time for him. Gladys insists that Johnny got "illegal help" from Samantha in the form of magic, but Johnny is able to detail the steps he took building the racer, which impresses Mills. Johnny is awarded the trophy and goes on to win the championships in Akron, earning himself a college scholarship.

GOOD!

Throughout the series, Morning Glory Circle has been said to be "out of the city," presumably somewhere in New York State. This episode finally narrows things down a bit: on the side of Johnny's racer, a placard lists his father's garage as being in Patterson, New York. Assuming the shop isn't in another town, the Stephenses and Kravitzes now have a place name to write in their return addresses. (And Patterson *is* "out of the city," some 60 miles from Manhattan. No wonder Darrin needed to take trains…)

Gladys is strangely snotty when Samantha and Johnny show up to "Flash's" practice, but she does offer an interesting bit of insight: she was never superstitious until she met Samantha! She may have a right to be – in view of Gladys' binoculars, Samantha flashes Darrin the Witches' Honor sign, which she must have picked up from her mother. Endora is the only one who's used the gesture until now, in "Be It Ever So Mortgaged" (#2) and "Baby's First Paragraph" (#62).

The effect of the tires floating onto the car in Mills' garage is masterful. Tires are heavy; it must have taken quite an effort to move them while making them look as if they're lighter than air.

WELL?

How do Samantha and Johnny know each other? Their already-in-progress connection is never established. And since when do the Stephenses drive a station wagon? They've only ever had a convertible. At the track, the shadow of the camera car can be seen as Johnny and "Flash" race.

Johnny isn't the only one with an absentee parent – where is Tabatha in all of this? The Stephenses are so busy with Johnny, they forget they have a daughter. Wouldn't it make sense to bring her to the race like other parents would? Is anybody sitting with her, or is she having to zap up bottles for herself?

Gladys has quickly reached a point where she shares her convictions about Samantha being a witch with anybody and everybody. Newspapers, reporters, courtrooms – at least this time, she limits her accusations to a handful of soapbox derby judges. But does she really think anyone is going to believe that Johnny has been helped by magic? Gladys may do well to start picking her battles. Not to mention, there was just a hearing in "Samantha for the Defense" (#88); Gladys tried to out Samantha in that episode, too.

OH, MY STARS!

Samantha comes to the aid of a young friend in need once again, in an episode identical in many ways to "Little Pitchers Have Big Fears" (#6). Samantha helps with witchcraft, Darrin objects but comes around, kid wins on his own afterwards – the main difference is, it was little Marshall under the thumb of his single mother before, and now it's a preteen being controlled by his single father. The proceedings are underscored by syrupy music that plays every time Johnny talks about his father or how he built the racer on his own. This overly sentimental story is a better fit for *Walt Disney's Wonderful World of Color* (which ran on NBC from 1961-1969) than it is for a show about mortals dealing with witchcraft.

As per formula, Johnny wins the regional race, the championship, and the scholarship, and all is right with the world. Wouldn't Johnny learn other, more important lessons if he came in second place, which is still not shabby? More distressing though, is the way Mills pushes Johnny to become a doctor. Even Darrin and Samantha go along with it; no one asks Johnny what he wants to do with his own life. It's commendable that Mills doesn't want his son to struggle like he has, but it sends a horrible message that kids should merely honor their parents' vocational wishes and shelve their own dreams. A better story would be the Stephenses encouraging Johnny to follow his own star.

SON OF A GUN!

"Well, there is, but it might shake you up a bit." – Samantha to Johnny, when he comments there must be an easier way to get his racer into Samantha's car.

SAM IN THE MOON
Airdate: January 5, 1967

Darrin watches a lunar landing on television, but Samantha would rather clean house, stating she's already been to the moon. Darrin broaches the subject with Larry, who says it would be Darrin's patriotic duty to tell the authorities if there was a faster way to win the space race. Meanwhile, Endora takes Samantha shopping in Japan, where they buy a package of warlock tea. Behind on her cleaning, Samantha zaps dust on herself to make Darrin think she's been home all day. But when Darrin sees the tea and doesn't believe Samantha had lunch with Endora locally, the annoyed Samantha yells that she's been to the moon.

Darrin wants Grand, the pharmacist, to analyze the dust and tea, suggesting it's a matter of national importance; he then has a vision in which Samantha is arrested by the military to coerce her into magically getting the U.S. to the moon before Russia. The Stephenses laugh about it until Darrin remembers giving the samples to Grand, who is coming over with Kahn, his brother-in-law from NASA. Forced to tell Darrin the tea is not ordinary, Samantha spins a tale to Grand and Kahn about Darrin having allergies and twitches up a gust of wind to blow the tea away. The Stephenses panic, but it turns out Kahn is from Nassau, not NASA. Later, Darrin asks Samantha if she's really been to the moon, and Samantha smiles that there are some things a wife shouldn't tell a husband.

GOOD!

There's a certain (and probably unintentional) time capsule quality to this episode. In 1967, the space race *was* a big deal – and 21st century youth won't know that television reception used to go berserk with interference from other electrical objects. These things seem inconceivable today, which is what makes this a cool little history lesson.

Watanabe-san is slightly stereotypical, but so much fun. Endora even gets into the spirit with her Asian-inspired hairstyle. Plus, when Samantha comes home from Japan and zaps herself into her workaday clothes, the transition is seamless.

Samantha achieves the height of mortal motherhood by taking Tabatha shopping with her. Tabatha's been home with sitters (or without) for too many episodes this season; children are usually superglued to their parents, so, even though it happens off-screen, it's nice to know Tabatha is where she should be.

WELL?

Much ado is made over the fact that it's Sunday; in the '60s, that meant stores were closed. So why is Darrin running around in his suit? Even Larry is dressed casually, in his den that looks exactly like the Stephenses'. Larry is being incredibly hostile to Darrin – okay, so he thinks Darrin is a lunar tune with all his moon talk, but that's no reason to tear his alleged friend apart.

If Samantha really needs to speed up her housecleaning, why not just accomplish it in one fell zap instead of hexing the vacuum cleaner, especially when she knows Darrin is going to be home soon? You'd think she'd stop the vacuum the second she hears Darrin calling for her, instead of casually replying, "I'll be right there" as if the machine isn't moving by itself. Finally, why does Samantha bother to zap herself with dust? It doesn't prove she's been home all day, and Darrin already accused Samantha of doing housework by witchcraft in "Help, Help, Don't Save Me" (#5). Why fulfill that prophecy?

Is Darrin's NASA vision a nightmare or a fantasy? It kicks in while his eyes are open, but ultimately, he has to be woken up from it. By the way, Samantha left Darrin a snarky note about her whereabouts before she took Tabatha shopping, so why is she sweet as pie the next time she sees him? Maybe Samantha did laundry while she was out – her shirt is clean. What happened to all the dust she zapped on it? Finally, if all the stores are closed, which is mentioned several times, how is Samantha able to go food shopping?

Tea is tea. How could even warlock tea be so chemically different that it causes a ping under analysis? It comes from a Japanese herbalist, yet Grand and Kahn make it sound like there's something alien in the package. And how thick is the Stephenses' door? They discuss their cover story with Grand and Kahn standing on the other side – the door must be made of titanium if the pharmacists can't hear them.

OH, MY STARS!

Could it be that *Bewitched* was feeling *I Dream of Jeannie* nipping at its heels and countered with an attempt to compete? This whole episode has the feel of the rival series (which ran on NBC from 1965-1970), from the quick freeze at the end of the prologue to the military uniforms that look like they're borrowed from *Jeannie*'s Tony Nelson and Roger Healey – to say nothing of all the talk about the moon, and getting there. Might as well have Jeannie blink her way into Darrin's nightmare (which, admittedly, would have been an amazing crossover).

Darrin and Samantha's fight seems to come out of nowhere. All Darrin asks is where Samantha has been, because she didn't answer the phone. Of course, Samantha feels guilty for having gone to Japan, but she overreacts to a simple question, and Darrin adds to that overreaction with his paranoia. Dr. Freud from "I'd Rather Twitch Than Fight" (#84) needs to come back and remind Samantha to fight about important things.

What on earth (or the moon) possesses Darrin to have the dust and tea analyzed? To begin with, there's not much that Grand, a neighborhood pharmacist, would be able to tell him. But what is Darrin planning to do with any information he might get? Turn Samantha in? That he'd consider choosing his country over his family is out of character, and Darrin's persistent paranoia borders on that, too.

Looking at the name "Nassau," it would appear to be pronounced "NASS-aw." As for NASA, that's generally pronounced "NASS-uh." Yet Kahn pronounces Nassau, "NASS-uh." That's coincidental enough, but not as much as Grand having a brother-in-law visiting from a place that can be confused with a space agency at the same time Darrin is obsessed with the moon.

SON OF A GUN!

"Oh, such a nice man. Lovely wife, an adorable daughter – funny name, though." – Grand, telling the "military" about the Stephenses.

Dreams or fantasies, Darrin has the best ones. In "...And Then There Were Three" (#12) and "A Very Special Delivery" (#38), they centered around future children; here, Darrin and Larry are questioned by the military, and Samantha is jailed due to Darrin's suspicions. Darrin denies knowing Samantha in a line-up, but, when Endora pops in, his "Her, I've seen" speaks volumes. Making this sequence stand out are the obscure angles, shady lighting and overall different look that allows for a lot of creativity; it's the highlight of the episode.

HOHO THE CLOWN
Airdate: January 12, 1967

Samantha is taking Tabatha to a taping of *Hoho the Clown*, for which Darrin does the advertising, so Endora invites herself along. Finding it unfair that Tabatha is ineligible for Hoho's prizes, Endora zaps Hoho into awarding them to her granddaughter on live television. Samantha attempts to diffuse the situation by giving the toys to charity, but, the next day, Hoho refuses to go on unless Tabatha is in the audience. Larry threatens to fire Darrin if Samantha doesn't bring Tabatha to the studio, where Hoho plays favorites with her and upsets Mr. Solow, the show's sponsor.

Hoho arrives at the house with a pony for Tabatha, unable to fathom his preoccupation with her. Once Samantha finally gets Endora to take the spell off Hoho, Solow cries foul because Tabatha is Darrin's daughter; Larry fires Darrin, but Solow fires Larry and Hoho. Samantha freezes the men mid-argument and devises a way out: she witches up a doll based on Tabatha and makes Hoho believe he was in on a publicity stunt designed to introduce it to the public. Solow loves it, and Darrin and Hoho get their jobs back. Later, on his show, Hoho announces that everyone who complained about his recent favoritism will receive a Tabatha doll, and Endora appears in the photo Hoho left behind so she can stick her tongue out at Darrin.

GOOD!

Endora and Tabatha are this episode's scene-stealing team. It's only natural for the impish Endora to enjoy messing with Hoho, but it's clear she's doing it all for Tabatha. Delightful little Erin Murphy nearly pulls off Hoho's clown nose (which is worked into the scene), plus she simply beams sitting next to her doppelgänger doll.

For a clown, Joey Forman gets to take Hoho through a myriad of moods: he's "on" with the kiddies, temperamental during commercial breaks, a diva in the dressing room, blindly devoted to Tabatha under Endora's spell, then completely indifferent about her once it's removed. Even Hoho's Hope Chest doesn't hold that many tricks. And Hoho must surely believe in "the show must go on," because he keeps the scene moving after accidentally letting go of one of the balloons, adding a great big "Oops."

Dick Wilson has already played his share of lovable drunks these last two-and-a-half years, but here he surprises by playing it sober. His Mr. Solow is gruff, humorless, and has no trouble putting burgeoning brown-noser Larry in his place. Who knew – he's even a good "freezer!"

WELL?

Endora must include the entire WXIU studio in her spell when she gives Tabatha the numbered badge. How else could she know some other kid doesn't already have the number 12 on his or hers? And, while the show does still switch between Erin and Diane Murphy's Tabathas during episodes, the differences are more obvious in this one. Erin's Tabatha appears with Hoho during his broadcasts, while Diane's hangs out with Samantha in the kitchen; later, when the Tabatha doll is announced on Hoho's show, Diane is placed in the chair, but Erin gets the close-up.

If Darrin is handling Solow's account, why are they meeting for the first time during Hoho's show? That would have happened long before Solow signed. When Hoho singles out Tabatha, Larry asks Darrin if he changed the program's format. Larry knows better: as ad execs, neither he nor Darrin has any control over the show's content. Then, Solow accuses Darrin and Hoho of trying to drive his toy company out of business. How would Hoho favoring Tabatha make that happen, even with viewer complaints and boycotts? Solow responds by canceling Hoho and his show, but does Solow have that kind of pull? It's a safe bet networks have more to say about the fate of their programming than one individual sponsor.

Darrin has a new habit: dressing up on weekends. In "Sam in the Moon" (#91), he wore his suit all day Sunday, and here, he spends his Saturday dressed as if he's going to the office. Also, you'd think Darrin would hang up on Gladys after the way she treated Samantha in "Soapbox Derby" (#90) instead of dishing with her about how cute Tabatha looked on *Hoho*.

Samantha doesn't think before freezing Larry, Solow, and Hoho, because she does it with the front door wide open. What about Gladys and her binoculars? Darrin's very smart to get back into position before Samantha reanimates the men, but Larry is smarter, asking why he wasn't consulted before Darrin "created" the Tabatha doll. Indeed, how can anyone market a new Solow toy without Solow's approval? Plus, given all the trouble Larry caused trying to build a publicity stunt around Benjamin Franklin in "Samantha for the Defense" (#88), surely the Stephenses would shy away from mounting their own. Incidentally, how much time has elapsed between the birth of the Tabatha doll and Hoho giving the dolls to his studio audience? It usually takes months for a new toy to go into production, but people boo Hoho as if they're seeing his very next installment.

OH, MY STARS!

Hoho's episode seems to have roots in "The Dancing Bear" (#58): Phyllis' "funny clown" is in Hoho's Hope Chest, its music cue is used as Hoho's theme song, and once again, Samantha creates a toy to solve a witchy mess. Plus, Tabatha's name was all over the papers in "Baby's First Paragraph" (#62), and her Robbins Truck Transmission ads [see "Nobody's Perfect" (#75)] must still be in magazines and billboards – so it's hard to conceive of the Stephenses generating even more publicity for her by capitalizing on her *Hoho* appearance. One last connection to "The Dancing Bear" (#58): Samantha threatening that Endora will never see Tabatha again. In both that episode and this, the stakes are pretty low, yet Samantha made no such threat in "Witches and Warlocks Are My Favorite Things" (#77) after Endora nearly kidnapped Tabatha; that's when Samantha should have banned her mother, at least for a while.

SON OF A GUN!

"A ballet, yes! A drama by Shakespeare, perhaps. But that 'ho-ho hee-hee ha-ha' business – oh, *no*." – Endora to Samantha, dismayed that Tabatha will soon be fraternizing with Hoho.

After many variations regarding the rules of witchcraft, Samantha spells it out here for Darrin: "There's a long technical explanation, but what it boils down to is that if a licensed witch puts a spell on someone, she has squatter's rights to him." There can be no more doubt that only the witch who casts a spell can reverse it. (But a "licensed witch?" Do they renew every year at a witch DMV?)

SUPER CAR
Airdate: January 19, 1967

EPISODE 93

Trying to be nicer to Darrin at Samantha's insistence, Endora zaps an experimental car he admires into the driveway. Its developers, Joe and Charlie, are stunned when the prototype goes missing from their factory. Fawning over the car, Darrin won't let Samantha drive it and forgets to thank Endora for it. Larry and current client Sheldrake come over to have a look at the car after Darrin brags about it, but Darrin discovers a placard under the hood that says the vehicle was made in Detroit. Initially thinking Endora added it for effect, Darrin blows up when Endora tells him the car is the real thing.

Joe and Charlie brainstorm how to explain the missing car to their employers, while Larry and Sheldrake view the contested auto, with Sheldrake deciding it's the perfect image for his sausage campaign. Darrin resists, but grudgingly allows Sheldrake to drive the car around the block after Larry threatens to fire him. Samantha, who has gone to the Mardi Gras to find Endora, returns with her mother, who zaps the car back where it belongs – with Sheldrake inside. Joe and Charlie make a pact to leave the country until Sheldrake and the car pop onto their platform. Larry is surprised that Sheldrake would take off with Darrin's car, but more so when the client calls from Detroit with news that the manufacturers have given him the rights to use the prototype in his campaign.

GOOD!

This episode confirms a magical point brought up in "Endora Moves in for a Spell" (#80): Samantha told Darrin she had to wait to make Endora's house disappear until Gladys and the police were clear of it, or they would disappear, too. The consequence of such a zap comes to fruition here, as Sheldrake is transported to Detroit along with the Reactor Mach II. It's always a plus when witch rules are further developed.

WELL?

Endora appearing in Darrin's portrait in "Hoho the Clown" (#92) must have been filmed in conjunction with this episode, since she is wearing the same distinctive outfit and earrings. But Samantha generalizes when she asks her mother, "Just once, can't you be nice to Darrin?" Endora was quite cordial to Darrin – and even sided with him – in "The Joker Is A Card" (#41), she cried with her son-in-law the night Tabatha was born in "And Then There Were Three" (#54), and Endora considered Darrin a welcome party guest in "Twitch or Treat" (#81); Samantha makes it sound like Endora's always nasty to him. Endora's never been one for subtlety, but with Gladys constantly lurking around, you'd think Samantha would warn her not to pop a car that stands out like a sore thumb into the driveway where anyone can see it appearing.

The garage would be safer, even if it's the most redecorated room in the house: "Open the Door, Witchcraft" (#28), "A Change of Face" (#33), and "Follow That Witch (Part I)" (#66) all featured different garages. Where is Darrin's own car during all this?

It's hard to feel sorry for Darrin in this episode, with him being so territorial about the automotive prototype and neglecting to thank Endora for it. While Darrin refuses Samantha access to the car, their wide shots are filmed outside, but their close-ups look to be filmed in-studio. As for Joe and Charlie, their prototype is displayed on a platform with a sign listing it as the Reactor Mach II. After five years of research, do these fellas really need a sign telling them what car they're working on?

The experimental vehicle comes with a hydraulic suspension system, a radar screen, and a set of problems. If Endora had zapped up a duplicate, of course it would say "Made in Detroit" – an exact copy is an exact copy. But then, Endora says her only option was to give Darrin the real thing. Why? She should be able to just zap the car out of Darrin's magazine and leave the original with Joe and Charlie. Of course, if she had, there wouldn't be any "suspension" in the story.

This episode contrasts sharply with its predecessor, "Hoho the Clown" (#92): Darrin has already forgotten Samantha's "squatter's rights" explanation that confirmed spells can only be undone by the caster, because he asks Samantha to twitch the car back where it came from. Samantha forgets, when she tells Endora that she hasn't asked her for anything important recently, that she just begged her mother to take her spell off Hoho. Larry forgets that he already threatened to fire Darrin in the previous episode. And Darrin acts surprised that Samantha is willing to travel "all the way to New Orleans" to find Endora, when she just went to Paris and Rome for that purpose a week ago.

Why does Sheldrake want Darrin's permission to use the car in his campaign? Any rights would need to be obtained from the car's manufacturer, which Endora inadvertently makes possible. Then, when Samantha pops out to look for Endora at the Mardi Gras, Larry and Sheldrake walk up to Darrin a few seconds later – there's no way they could miss Samantha disappearing. Later, as Endora works to put the Reactor Mach II back where it belongs, she and Samantha never wonder why the car is in motion (obviously either Larry or Sheldrake are driving it), and Larry never wonders why Samantha is suddenly covered in confetti and streamers. Maybe he thinks the absent Tabatha is having a party in her room.

Darrin's headache must not be too bad, because it only merits a dry washcloth. His worries are over when Sheldrake calls from the airport, but the question is, which one: Detroit or New York? The smart bet is Detroit – though, as it's now nighttime, Sheldrake could have already flown back to New York, depending on how long his negotiations were with Joe and Charlie.

OH, MY STARS!

Reusing music cues is a staple in every television show, but it can be overdone: whenever the futuristic car shows up on screen, it's accompanied by the Herb Alpert-inspired underscore composed for Charlie Leach's trip to Mexico in "Follow That Witch (Part II)" (#67); it trumpets no less than six times.

Irwin Charone's confusion at popping into the Detroit factory is the best part of his appearance, but isn't it too soon for him to play yet another character? He just appeared as the hotheaded Parkinson in "Oedipus Hex" (#85), which aired not two months earlier. Even viewers who followed the show in real time would think Parkinson had a sausage-selling twin in Sheldrake.

SON OF A GUN!

"But how do we work sausages into the space age?" – Larry to Sheldrake, not getting a satisfactory answer.

THE CORN IS AS HIGH AS A GUERNSEY'S EYE

Airdate: January 26, 1967

Depressed after Endora, Hagatha, and Enchantra tell her she's an old cow who should be put out to pasture, Aunt Clara considers turning herself into an inanimate object. Meanwhile, Larry fumes when a rival agency in the McMann & Tate building courts the Morton Milk account by putting Morton's prize-winning Guernsey cow in the lobby for National Milk Week. Samantha brings Aunt Clara to meet Darrin for lunch, then quickly pops out to pick up his watch, leaving Aunt Clara in the lobby; she talks to a plant and takes a nap in the sheltered Morton cow display. When Samantha returns and sees the cow, she thinks it's Aunt Clara, then takes it home. Louise, who has been babysitting Tabatha, finds Samantha with the cow and runs straight to Larry.

Darrin discovers the sleeping Aunt Clara in the Morton display and calls Samantha, while Larry calls Louise and is dismayed to hear about the cow in the Stephenses' living room. Larry thinks Darrin stole it to foil the rival agency, but Darrin lies that he and Samantha bought one so they can make their own dairy products. Samantha realizes her mistake and shrinks Morton's cow to purse size, enlarging it in the elevator to the shock of an amorous elevator boy. When Morton finds out Darrin is a "cow fancier," McMann & Tate is awarded the account, and the Stephenses are awarded a backyard full of cows.

GOOD!

For those unfamiliar with musical theatre, this episode's title is a paraphrase of a lyric from the classic show *Oklahoma!*: "the corn is as high as an elephant's eye." In another clever twist, this time it's Samantha jumping to conclusions and causing all the problems; usually Darrin has the monopoly on making witchcraft-related assumptions. And, magical chaos always ensues during Aunt Clara's visits, but here she's refreshingly spell-free.

Louise doesn't get a lot of opportunities for comedy with her husband getting most of the Tates' screen time, so Mrs. Tate's deadpan reaction to the cow is a nice contrast to Samantha's franticness; Kasey Rogers certainly milks her scene-stealing turn – in a good way.

Samantha's best move in this episode is shrinking the cow, then inflicting its full-size version on the randy elevator boy.

WELL?

More lamps! Samantha already got Benjamin Franklin in her living room [see "My Friend Ben" (#87)] because she chose not to fix one light fixture with witchcraft – here, she magically repairs another before Aunt Clara gets there, which is good, otherwise Samantha might be hosting Nikola Tesla this time. And so much for sisterly affection: in "Witches and Warlocks Are My Favorite Things" (#77), it was implied that Hagatha, Enchantra, and Endora are all Clara's sisters, who now tell her she's an old cow and should turn herself into something inanimate.

Larry has a cow because of the Whittle Agency's recognition of National Milk Week. This episode aired in January, but research indicates that National Milk Week is in November; at least it was when established in 1937. Even if there are two advertising agencies in one high-rise, it's a higher rise than before: in "Double Tate" (#59), the elevator indicated the building only has fifteen floors, while establishing shots as far back as "Your Witch Is Showing" (#20) revealed the skyscraper to have about twenty. Now, there's a sign saying there are as many as thirty-six, with the elevator completely different than the aforementioned episodes. It's unlikely there's a residential apartment building across the street from this Manhattan complex, but that's what's in the backdrop behind the front entrance.

That potted plant Aunt Clara changes herself into will have to be listed as a co-star if it makes any more appearances. Look closely, and you'll see it in almost every episode of *Bewitched* – several times in this episode alone, throughout the lobby of Darrin's building. And for such a big lobby, people sure miss a lot. The cop and delivery guy don't notice a cow walking away (why is it brought in for a display that isn't going to be revealed until the following week?), and nobody sees Samantha popping in and out several times, despite her not doing much to camouflage herself; strange after she specifically told the cow she'd have to be discreet.

When Samantha takes the cow back to the house, why doesn't she just zap it into the kitchen in the first place – and keep it there? She knows Louise is upstairs; even after Louise leaves, it would just be safer to keep the cow out of sight, though it would nullify Louise's reaction to seeing it.

What did the Stephenses do with all those cows after the episode? Either they found a nice farm for them to graze in (without Morton finding out, of course), or Darrin, Samantha, and Tabatha were eating hamburger for months. Maybe Samantha shrunk them all for Tabatha to play with – she's right that she should have thought of the cow-miniaturizing before, since she stuffed a scaled-down Christmas tree in her purse in "A Vision of Sugar Plums" (#15/#51).

OH, MY STARS!

Darrin rightly worries when Samantha recruits Louise to babysit, asking about Tabatha's magic. Samantha blithely says she'll just put Tabatha down for her nap first – this after her "Accidental Twins" (#78) insistence that Tabatha's constant supernatural experimentation made only witch babysitters possible. What's to stop Tabatha from waking up and floating things around the house in front of Louise? Does Samantha slip Tabatha a mickey before Louise arrives? Speaking of babysitters, who's minding Jonathan? It would make perfect sense for Louise to bring her son with her.

SON OF A GUN!

"Do you mind? This is private." – Aunt Clara to the elevator boy, who interrupts her deep discussion with a plant.

THE TRIAL AND ERROR OF AUNT CLARA

Airdate: February 2, 1967

EPISODE **95**

Endora informs Samantha that Aunt Clara, who is being put on trial for her magical missteps, wants Samantha as her defense attorney. Samantha moves the clock ahead so Darrin will miss the arriving coven; dared by Endora to pop into the den, Aunt Clara leaves her shoes behind, then makes Darrin's desk disappear during a magical refresher course. Larry needs papers from the desk, so Samantha stalls him until Aunt Clara can bring it back. Samantha barely gets Larry out of the house before Hagatha, and Enchantra, and Judge Bean arrive.

The judge feels Aunt Clara's case is open-and-shut, rejecting Samantha's call to have it thrown out "on the grounds of love." Meanwhile, Darrin discovers Larry picked up the wrong papers and heads home for the right ones. Samantha attempts to prove that Aunt Clara's powers are intact, but gives her an assist to fool the court. When Samantha gets distracted helping Darrin look for his papers – and keeping him from seeing the trial in the living room – Aunt Clara unsuccessfully tries to conjure things up on her own, causing Judge Bean to declare her earthbound. But, as Darrin heads for the living room, Aunt Clara makes a wild zap that sends everyone away. The decision is reversed; while Samantha suspects that popping the coven out was a fluke, Aunt Clara determines that her love for Samantha gave her the power she needed to redeem herself.

GOOD!

Though it isn't mentioned specifically, this episode is an extension of "The Corn Is As High As A Guernsey's Eye" (#94), in which Aunt Clara reported that Endora and the others called for her to become an inanimate object. This carries through as Endora tells Samantha how Aunt Clara can invoke "the witches' alternative" – changing herself into something useful.

Darrin's desk being gone while everything on top of it hangs in mid-air is a practically perfect effect save for a few shifting items – and Judge Bean's costume change, while cheated a bit because he bends out of frame, is very fluid. But Samantha takes the prize with her amazing zaps into and out of her witch's outfit; at this point, Elizabeth Montgomery has become a master at staying still and/or getting back into exact positions to facilitate these changes.

WELL?

Endora's appearance as a ball of light in Samantha's bedroom comes from "Witches and Warlocks Are My Favorite Things" (#77), though Endora beckoning, "Follow me" is added, and Samantha is shown running down the stairs in her same nightgown in an attempt to match the shot. The strange flash as Endora rematerializes, however, makes the transition less smooth than it could be.

No wonder Aunt Clara chooses Samantha as her defense attorney – she just watched her niece get Benjamin Franklin acquitted in "Samantha for the Defense" (#88). Does Samantha move all the clocks in the house forward, or does Darrin just take Samantha's word for it that the kitchen clock indicates he's going to be late? You'd think he'd check his watch, which was just fixed in the last episode, and there must be a clock in his car. Once Darrin leaves, Samantha opens the door to the kitchen broom closet and not only finds Aunt Clara, but the entrance to a never-before-mentioned cellar.

Endora seems to be enjoying Aunt Clara's plight; she's clearly amused when Clara makes everything disappear but her shoes. But Hagatha and Enchantra come off as hypocrites when they cry, "Poor, dear Clara," considering they're the ones who put her on trial in the first place. As discussed in "Witches and Warlocks Are My Favorite Things" (#77), these women are all more than likely Clara's sisters, so they should be helping her instead of persecuting her.

During her witchcraft tutorial, Aunt Clara zaps Darrin's desk onto the staircase, exactly where she put the Stephenses' only-here-for-this-episode piano in "The Short Happy Circuit of Aunt Clara" (#83). As for the mortals, Larry hears the second car honk in the living room, but not the first, and Darrin hears the crying of the coven all the way from the den with the door closed, but not sled dogs barking or Endora calling for a verdict. Plus, Darrin gets home awfully fast – as hinted in "Soapbox Derby" (#90), the Stephenses live in Patterson, New York; even at top speed, it would take him about an hour to drive home from Manhattan.

Samantha is right to cry witch hunt when the coven arrives having already convicted Aunt Clara, but why the fish-eye lens on Hagatha and Enchantra's cackling? Is the stereotype-perpetuating shot meant to highlight their hypocrisy? Then, Hagatha calls for Clara to be "deprived of all rights, privileges and benefits deriving from membership in the witches' community." Membership? In "What Every Young Man Should Know" (#72), Darrin asked Samantha if she was born a witch; she said yes. That suggests that any privileges are a birthright – a witch wouldn't have to become a member of a group she was born into. Moreover, Aunt Clara is a witch regardless of whether or not she has her powers.

While it's honorable of Aunt Clara to clear the "courtroom" so Darrin won't be upset by a house full of witches, she didn't have a problem when Darrin walked in and found the same group testing Tabatha in "Witches and Warlocks Are My Favorite Things" (#77). And why does Aunt Clara use the door in the tag? She already knows Judge Bean has reversed his decision. Finally, where does Clara come from if she didn't spend the night at Samantha's?

OH, MY STARS!

Hagatha and Enchantra have gotten quite the makeover since their last appearance in "Witches and Warlocks Are My Favorite Things" (#77) – Reta Shaw (Hagatha) and Estelle Winwood (Enchantra) are replaced by Nancy Andrews and Ottola Nesmith, respectively. And this is the show's third Hagatha since the character's début in "Speak the Truth" (#50). Recasts are often necessary because of actors' scheduling conflicts, and these ladies are lovely, but the lack of consistency makes it feel like Aunt Clara is being ostracized by total strangers.

Samantha tries to help Aunt Clara by levitating the judge's gavel for her. But Judge Bean shouldn't miss the assistance, because Samantha is facing him, twitching quite openly. Samantha doesn't get much of a chance to defend Aunt Clara anyway; when Samantha excuses herself to help Darrin, the trial proceeds without the defense attorney present, and, by the she time returns, Judge Bean lays down his verdict without hearing any further evidence. Aunt Clara might as well zap up a kangaroo along with her polar bear, because this is a kangaroo court.

SON OF A GUN!

"Well, I'll have a lot of company, won't I?" – Aunt Clara, as Judge Bean renders her earthbound.

THREE WISHES
Airdate: February 9, 1967

EPISODE
96

Endora pranks Darrin with a series of wrong numbers; then, after Samantha tells Endora that Darrin wishes he didn't have to go to Honolulu on business, Endora endows him with three wishes. When Larry gets to the office, he announces he has to make the trip instead; Samantha attributes it to Darrin's first wish, but Endora thinks it has more to do with Darrin now being available to entertain swimsuit model Buffy. Later, Darrin has to fly Buffy to a banquet in Boston, and Endora is sure that's Darrin's second wish in action.

Though Darrin plans to come home for dinner, he can't because a freak snowstorm grounds all the planes in Boston. Buffy is stranded as well, and the hotel is full, so Darrin gives her his room and spends the night at the airport. When a telegram arrives from Larry, Samantha calls Darrin's hotel; Buffy picks up, and Samantha believes the model's presence in Darrin's room is part of his third wish. Darrin comes home and watches as Samantha invisibly packs her things, ready to leave him – but when Darrin hears about the wishes, he uses what turns out to be his real first wish to conjure up Endora. He stops just shy of wishing Endora away forever, sending her away for a week instead. Samantha apologizes, and later, when Darrin casually wishes he could take another shower, his third wish pops him into the bath fully clothed.

GOOD!

Turnabout is fair play: after two-and-a-half years of facing constant witchcraft, Darrin gets a chance to perform a little magic himself thanks to his unwished wishes. Not only are they irrefutable proof that Darrin is innocent in regard to Buffy, but Endora and Samantha deserve to have it rubbed in their faces, though the fact that Samantha knows about Endora's spell from the get-go is a novel twist. Endora really looks terrified for a moment when Darrin almost uses his/her power to ban her from Samantha and Tabatha forever; talk about a backfire.

Samantha's sleek black witches' outfit finally gets a name – it's a "flying suit." Samantha sported it as far back as "A Vision of Sugar Plums" (#15), but only now is there a way to describe it.

WELL?

Why does Endora prank Darrin with wrong numbers? Aside from his getting fed up and yelling at Larry by mistake, it doesn't contribute to the main story, and Samantha could just as easily pick up the phone; it's surprising she doesn't. Darrin grumbles, "What are they up to?" – but he should know Samantha wouldn't have anything to do with Endora's tricks.

This isn't the first time Samantha offers to turn herself into something to accompany Darrin on a business trip: in "The Cat's Meow" (#18), she suggested becoming a cat. At least here, her potential necktie is more practical, and the Stephenses settle it right away, unlike the aforementioned episode, which Darrin spent thinking a stray cat was his wife. Can you imagine Darrin rifling through his suitcase yelling at his ties?

In the previous episode, Hagatha got a new face – now, there's yet another version of Betty, this time played by Edythe Sills. Later, Samantha tells Endora that "Darrin has to take over" when Larry goes out of town. Larry has been established as the president of the company; Darrin is a mere account executive, not a vice president, which is what Samantha's claim implies.

It's rather amazing Darrin doesn't know about the wishes until Samantha tells him. Both times when the Stephenses are on the phone, Samantha barely covers the receiver as Endora talks about the wishes she granted in full volume. Later, Darrin tells Samantha his trip to Boston is happening the next night – but when he gets there, Samantha and Endora are wearing the same clothes they had on the previous day. Darrin's probably pretty familiar with Beantown; he was just there on business in "A Gazebo Never Forgets" (#89). As for Buffy, she may be a ditz, but all she has to say when Samantha calls is that Darrin gave her his room and is cooling out at the airport. Instead, Buffy is inexplicably vague, causing Samantha to again make chaos-inducing assumptions, as she did in "The Corn Is As High As A Guernsey's Eye" (#94).

When Samantha yells that she's going home to Mother, Darrin shoots back, "Your mother's always here!" The Stephenses had the same exchange in "Dangerous Diaper Dan" (#82), albeit with slightly different wording. And you've heard of hotels being second homes, but Darrin's hotel room looks just like his own bedroom, from the layout to the color of the walls. Only the Bible sitting on the dresser gives the impression it's a hotel. Speaking of the Stephenses' bedroom, what have they done to it? The bureau and mirror that are always by the door have been replaced with a closet. And Darrin always sleeps on the right side of the bed, with Samantha on the left; now, they've switched sides.

OH, MY STARS!

If all this talk about wishes sounds familiar, it's because Endora just gave Darrin three wishes in "Double Tate" (#59), and that trio involved a model as well. The twist here is that Darrin doesn't actually make these wishes, whereas before he used them up in short order. Question: if Samantha is so sure Darrin's spending his wishes on Buffy, why not just take Tabatha and leave before Darrin gets home, instead of venting at him with magazines and coffee tables? It also seems like Samantha's planning to leave without Tabatha, since she's nowhere to be seen.

"Double Tate" (#59) isn't the only episode that "Three Wishes" (#96) borrows from. The entire sequence where Samantha makes herself invisible and "floats" her suitcases around is lifted directly from "Help, Help, Don't Save Me" (#5), down to the line where Darrin commands, "You're my wife and I demand that you appear before me!" Wouldn't it be funny if, in the middle of the sequence, the Stephenses were to stop and say, "Haven't we had this conversation before?"

SON OF A GUN!

"Aren't I in?" – swimsuit model Buffy, having trouble entering the office without her glasses.

I REMEMBER YOU...SOMETIMES
Airdate: February 16, 1967

EPISODE
97

When Darrin has trouble remembering a client's name, he buys a book to work on his memory. Endora thinks mortals would be insufferable if they possessed total recall, and sets out to prove it by casting a spell on Darrin's watch that makes him recollect the most minute details, some of which cause the Stephenses to quarrel. Pennybaker, the know-it-all client Darrin forgot, is impressed that Darrin now remembers so much about him, but quickly tires of being upstaged. Larry also becomes annoyed by Darrin's need to prove himself right, and Darrin's secretary, Betty, is upset when he reminds her of mistakes she's made with painstaking accuracy.

At dinner, Darrin and Pennybaker continue trying to one-up each other to the delight of Cynthia, Pennybaker's long-suffering wife. Samantha finally takes Darrin aside to let him know how obnoxious he's being, but he loves his sharp memory, expressing amazement over Endora saying he wouldn't be able to handle it. Samantha realizes Darrin has been hexed by Endora, who teases her by hinting the spell isn't on Darrin; she challenges her daughter to figure out the conundrum. Carefully observing Darrin with Pennybaker, Samantha makes Darrin's watch fall off, confirming Endora's spell when Cynthia picks up the timepiece, gains total recall, and shows Pennybaker how he monopolizes conversations. Samantha pockets the watch, and when Darrin guesses Endora's involvement, she forgets to give him a definite answer.

GOOD!

Like Darrin, the writers' memories are also sharp here. Darrin triggers a fight with Samantha and mentions Mrs. Dumont, who was part of the committee Samantha was on to raise funds for new playground equipment in "Oedipus Hex" (#85). Minor, but keen of the show to work the woman in. Endora also flashes Samantha the "Witches' Honor" sign, which is the fourth time overall, and the second this season.

Darrin putting down his witched watch and lapsing into *'Twas the Night Before Christmas* while reciting Lord Byron's 1815 poem, *The Destruction of Sennacherib*, is a bit worth remembering. And look who's back: Jill Foster as Betty. Edythe Sills just played the secretary in the previous episode, but, with four appearances in that role so far, Foster is the most consistent of McMann & Tate's Bettys.

Pennybaker is as annoying as he's supposed to be with his knowledge of seemingly every subject, but when Darrin pipes in – though he's just as annoying – the clash of these smarty Martys is actually something to behold. The winner: Pennybaker, by a nose, because he doesn't need a watch to rattle off his details.

WELL?

Darrin taking the train home, a typical occurrence in Seasons One and Two, makes sense now that there's an indication the Stephenses live in Patterson, New York, some 60 miles from Manhattan. Yet, many times, Darrin, Larry, and even Samantha drive back and forth from McMann & Tate. Sticking to one mode of transportation would be more consistent. Do the Tates live also in Patterson?

Does Darrin wear his watch all night, and in the shower? He must, because it comes out he has to be in constant contact with the timepiece for Endora's spell to work; if he'd taken it off at any point, he'd notice his attention to detail dwindling, as it does when he removes the watch at the office. Finally, Darrin must be "ambi-watch-trous," because he first wears it on his right wrist, then his left.

Can wives just waltz into important business meetings? Apparently, because Louise and Samantha interrupt Darrin and Larry's pitch to Pennybaker for shopping money as if it's the most natural thing in the world, and without being announced. By the way, are Jonathan and Tabatha minding each other? No sitter is mentioned, and aside from Darrin talking about improving his work performance for the benefit of his wife and child, Tabatha hasn't even been mentioned since "Hoho the Clown" (#92). Maybe she should have been shipped to Hagatha's school after all.

The cartoon sparkle of "Speak the Truth" (#50) and "Accidental Twins" (#78) is back to let viewers know that the memory function on Darrin's watch is being activated. Is that a visual cue solely for the episode, or can Darrin see his watch glittering? When Cynthia picks it up, there's a marked delay before her own total recall kicks in. Darrin's memory boost is instant; why not Cynthia's? And that's one late dinner with the Pennybakers – the kitchen clock reads 10:30 before Samantha even offers to serve, while minutes later, Darrin's watch says it's after midnight.

At the end of the episode, Samantha lies that Darrin's watch strap broke, and that she'll take it to be fixed. Shouldn't Darrin find that odd, since his watch was just repaired in "The Corn Is As High As A Guernsey's Eye" (#94)? And Samantha's not going to get very far making Darrin's breakfast on a dark burner, which should be glowing orange from the heat.

OH, MY STARS!

Endora taunts Darrin about wanting a perfect memory in the living room, while Samantha is busy in the kitchen, with the door open. Yet later, Samantha tells herself she hasn't seen Endora in two weeks. Did she really not hear her mother from the next room? Of course, if she didn't have selective hearing here, it would negate the entire episode.

Darrin's memory might be turbo-charged, but his powers of deduction, not so much. Seconds after Endora specifically asks him if he wants a perfect memory, he remembers Pennybaker, his wife, and everything about their kids, yet he credits it to his "instant memory" book. At the very least, Darrin should make the connection the two times he puts the watch down and returns to recollecting things normally. Finally, is Darrin becoming a self-satisfied know-it-all part of Endora's spell? It seems she's only given him total recall, and that his need to prove himself right is his own. But then, he brags to Samantha, "And your mother thought I couldn't handle it!" – which feels like there's more to Endora's spell than meets the eye.

SON OF A GUN!

"You mean I go on and on and on about anything – everything? Like he does?" – Pennybaker to his wife, finally seeing a mirror of himself in Darrin.

Cynthia turning things around on her husband is not only entertaining, but very satisfying. Having her blast him for telling his football story 1,560 times, then tallying up his other infractions, is a great way for her to let him know she has his number.

ART FOR SAM'S SAKE
Airdate: February 23, 1967

Endora sees pancakes magically flipped by Samantha, who is out on the patio trying to paint a still-life. Endora expects perfection from her daughter and is upset when Samantha later enters her a painting in a charity event without showing it to her first. Endora pops into the gallery and freezes its workers so she can view Samantha's artwork; feeling it amateur, she replaces it with a canvas by famed artist Henri Monchet. With the Stephenses set to attend the showing, Larry inserts art connoisseur client Cunningham into their evening. After Louise hears a news broadcast announcing that Samantha's painting has won first place, the Tates make a beeline for the showing.

Self-important Cunningham gets on the Stephenses' nerves at dinner, then decides he must have Samantha's prize-winning painting. Samantha is thrilled until she sees that the artwork isn't hers; she excuses herself to contact Endora, and triggers a bidding war in which Darrin tries to keep the painting from Cunningham. After Cunningham's $1,005 bid nets him "Samantha's" artwork, everyone gathers at the Stephenses, where Samantha learns from Endora that the painting is Monchet's, and that it will pop back at midnight. To distract Cunningham, Samantha borrows Endora's otherworldly perfume, which the fragrance manufacturer immediately wants to market. Samantha gets him to exchange its formula for the Monchet; the painting disappears as Darrin carries it away, exchanging itself with Samantha's original work that she is happy to give away to Cunningham.

GOOD!

This has little to do with story or continuity, but it's all kinds of cute the way toddler Erin Murphy tries to get away from Elizabeth Montgomery as they come in through the Stephenses front door, then succeeds to the point Montgomery has to chase Erin across the set. Of course, the scene continues as written, despite Erin's unscripted detour.

Endora's reactions at the university – and later to Cunningham's perfume – are works of art unto themselves. Endora shrugs and grimaces at the paintings and sculptures, then scrunches up her face while taking a whiff of the fragrance, topping it off with a horse blow. Endora also utters a familiar phrase: "Oh, my stars and satellites!" Did Samantha pick up her oft-spoken expression from her mother?

It very much looks like Elizabeth Montgomery signed Samantha's name to the Monchet painting. Nice touch, especially considering anyone in production could have scribbled Samantha's signature, with no one the wiser.

WELL?

Given Darrin's usual negative reaction to witchcraft, it's hard to believe Samantha would risk detection by flipping pancakes magically. Darrin could easily come downstairs early, and he wouldn't share Samantha's contention that catching the morning light for her sketch is a special occasion. Then, Endora warns Samantha that she'll be watching the painting's progress, yet somehow Samantha enters her submission without Endora seeing it first.

Endora ought to start copying objects instead of insisting on originals. In "Super Car" (#93), she zapped the real Reactor Mach II out of Detroit for Darrin when she could have just popped the car out of his magazine; here, she witches Monchet's painting out of a New York showing instead of just duplicating it. Wouldn't a well-known artist's work disappearing from a world-famous gallery be all over the news? Apparently not, but Samantha winning a local amateur art exhibit is important enough for a radio broadcast. How does Samantha not know she's a winner until she gets to the university? Wouldn't she be informed in advance, especially with the story being released to the media?

Darrin has excellent vision: he pinpoints Samantha's tiny signature on the Monchet from several feet away. But why would he mention Endora's handiwork with the Tates sitting right behind him? Samantha comments that the writing is Endora's; why didn't Endora "sign" the portrait in Samantha's "hand?"

Darrin and Cunningham are the only two patrons bidding on "Samantha's" painting. Naturally, the bidding war has to focus on them, but you'd think someone else would make even one offer. Back home, the Stephenses excuse themselves to the kitchen to appeal to Endora, but, in the next cut, only Samantha is calling for her mother. Samantha firmly tells Endora to stay until they can get the Monchet away from Cunningham, but Endora pops out as soon as she gives Samantha the warlock perfume. By offering Cunningham this supernatural scent, Samantha is opening herself up to the same problem she and Darrin dealt with in "Sam in the Moon" (#91), where the Stephenses panicked because pharmacists were analyzing her warlock tea; it carried an exotic enough ingredient that Samantha could have been exposed as a witch. What happens when Cunningham's chemists examine the contents of I Know You?

Endora assures Samantha that the Monchet painting will pop back to New York at midnight. Why the time lock on the spell? At least, in "Double Tate" (#59), the deadline made sense because Darrin had wished he were Larry "for the day," but there's no such precedent here. Finally, Cunningham decides he must have Samantha's still-life, but shouldn't this "connoisseur" notice that her signature differs from the Monchet, which is established to be in Endora's writing?

OH, MY STARS!

Larry and Darrin seem to have bought identical prefab houses. The Tates' bedroom set is the same as the Stephenses' with some different furniture in it, given away by the color of the walls and the bathroom door being in the same place. And the Tates had a very different boudoir in "Double Tate" (#59), besides.

Arthur Julian's Cunningham is snobby perfection, but he just played MacElroy, a character of similar temperament, in "The Short Happy Circuit of Aunt Clara" (#83); three months is still too soon to have an actor morph into another role.

SON OF A GUN!

"I tried some of his perfume. It burned a hole right through my robe." – Endora to Samantha, trying to make "scents" of Cunningham's fragrance.

CHARLIE HARPER, WINNER
Airdate: March 2, 1967

EPISODE 99

Darrin is visited by college chum Charlie Harper, who bests Darrin at everything. For all Charlie's success, he's surprisingly humble, but his wife, Daphne, is a relentless braggart, going on about the Harpers' material possessions. The Harpers invite the Stephenses to a weekend at their vacation house; at the resort, Charlie beats Darrin at all sports, and Daphne snarks that Charlie should give Darrin a decent job. Annoyed, Samantha collapses Daphne's hammock by magic, also witching Daphne into tossing her playing cards when she boasts about her extravagant wedding ring.

Later, Charlie offers Darrin a presidency at one of his agencies, and, when Daphne attempts to loan Samantha expensive jewelry for a formal dinner, Samantha zaps up some diamonds, then a mink coat that Daphne falls in love with. Samantha realizes her mistake when Endora pops in and lambastes her daughter for trying to improve Darrin's station by witchcraft. Although Samantha plays down the coat's value, Daphne begs Charlie to buy it for her; Darrin walks out on Samantha for giving herself something he can't afford. Samantha ultimately gifts Daphne with the mink, looking at Darrin as she explains that some things are worth much more. Once the reconciled Stephenses return home, Daphne sends the mink back, appreciative of the lesson Samantha taught her; Samantha makes the coat vanish and says she could never zap up another Darrin.

GOOD!

Darrin exhibits a wonderful pride in his wife and daughter in the company of the Harpers. He gives Samantha a smiling aside when he tells Charlie, "You're right – Tabatha is *very* special," and, at dinner, Darrin delightedly tells Daphne, who has just learned Samantha decorated the house herself, "She can do wonders with anything." There's never been any doubt Darrin loves Samantha and Tabatha, but here he displays a sense of admiration about their being witches not usually seen.

On the flip side, Samantha uses her powers to make the jealous Daphne thud those few inches to the pavement in her hammock. (The post-production zoom adds graininess to the footage, but the fluidity of seeing two angles in mid-twitch is unique.)

The Harpers don't just take the Stephenses to their vacation home, they take them into uncharted dramatic territory. When Darrin's offered a presidency and asks why Charlie doesn't want it, Harper astutely replies, "I'm much too smart to hire anybody like me." Then, in the context of Darrin's feelings about witchcraft, Samantha telling Daphne, "He likes to do things on his own" goes right to the core of

Darrin's character. But the pinnacle comes when Darrin and Samantha reach an uncomfortable impasse over the mink, which is diffused when Samantha gives it away. "Yes, you can, Daphne," Samantha says when the woman questions handing over something so valuable, "when you value something else a great deal more." All of these moments are powerful, well-acted, and wouldn't be out of place on a prime-time drama or daytime soap.

WELL?

Darrin seems to have a fair share of good buddies that show up for a visit and are never heard from again: Kermit, Bob Frazer, and Adam Newlarkin [from "Love Is Blind" (#13), "Which Witch Is Which?" (#24), and "We're In For A Bad Spell" (#39), respectively], to name a few. How about bringing one back on occasion for consistency?

The Tabatha that the Harpers admire is really a still frame, taken from "Nobody's Perfect" (#75). And the Endora that Samantha ignores in the kitchen lectures her daughter at full volume, which the Harpers are somehow unable to hear from the adjacent living room. As for Darrin, it's fantastic continuity to mention the success of the Caldwell Soup slogan he conceived in "Help, Help, Don't Save Me" (#5), but it's been almost three years – has he really not topped "The only thing that will ever come between us" since then?

What an intriguing idea, Darrin ditching McMann & Tate to run Brown & Smithers! Darrin's certainly been in advertising long enough for such a promotion, and think of the different directions the show could go in. Darrin has to stay with Larry, of course, but maybe Larry doesn't deserve that loyalty anymore, the way he's taken to firing or threatening to fire Darrin this season. Darrin's probably better off staying where he is: Charlie offers him the presidency, while Daphne tells Samantha her husband can make Darrin vice president.

This isn't the first time Samantha has zapped up finery to impress a snobby contemporary. In "Mother Meets What's-His-Name" (#4), it was china and silverware; here, she ups the ante to diamonds and furs. And the Stephenses are wrong when they say Samantha doesn't own a mink – Darrin bought her one in "The Girl with the Golden Nose" (#73).

Getting rid of the hotly contested coat, Samantha assures her husband, "I could never zap up another Darrin Stephens." Maybe she can't, but Endora can, and has, as Darrin was duplicated in "Divided He Falls" (#69).

OH, MY STARS!

Samantha proudly tells the Harpers that Darrin is McMann & Tate's "head of creative advertising." When did that happen? The only other mention of Darrin being anything other than an ordinary account executive was in "Three Wishes" (#96), when Samantha told Endora how Darrin covers when Larry goes out of town. Has Darrin been promoted? Maybe that's why Larry is so hard on him lately.

Yes, you've seen the Harpers' Oyster Bay pool before – it's where Adam Newlarkin was dunked in "We're In For A Bad Spell" (39); it was also the Miami pool where Fun Darrin partied in "Divided He Falls" (#69). By the way, in that episode, as well as "And Then There Were Three" (#54), it was established that Darrin can't swim. Here, he races Charlie across the pool. Has Darrin had lessons this season?

SON OF A GUN!

"What? Identical mink twins?" – Darrin, reacting to the level of detail in Samantha's story about the coat.

AUNT CLARA'S VICTORIA VICTORY

Airdate: March 9, 1967

EPISODE
100

Darrin's in Bridgeport on business, and Samantha relays to Aunt Clara that tyrannical new client Morgan acts like he's from the Victorian Age. Inspired to zap herself to that time, Aunt Clara instead causes Queen Victoria to preside over Samantha's living room. Former lady-in-waiting Clara tries to placate the monarch, who is critical of Samantha's manner of dress. While Samantha informs Victoria she's in the 20th century, Morgan runs roughshod over Larry and decides he needs to meet Darrin's wife. After the Queen smashes Samantha's television for displaying bikini-clad girls, Larry arrives, begging Samantha to host Morgan; he sees Victoria, whom Samantha introduces as an aunt. Looking over the newspaper, Victoria determines Providence has sent her to 1967 to settle world affairs; Aunt Clara pretends to forget her spell so she can assist her sovereign.

Morgan is intrigued by "Aunt Harriet" – he compares himself to the monarch, but is quickly reprimanded by the business side of her fan. After the frustrated Larry loses Morgan's account by telling him to shut up, Samantha first makes Morgan dream he's Queen Victoria, then a man beheaded for tyranny. Morgan returns and agrees to leave advertising to the agency, though he interrupts Larry's apology. To trick Aunt Clara into sending the Queen back, Samantha reveals herself as a witch, prompting Victoria to tell Clara she should be flogged. The angry Aunt Clara pops the monarch out, but accidentally replaces her with Prince Albert.

GOOD!

Larry's become such a "terrible tiger" himself this season, there's almost a sense of comeuppance as Morgan interrupts him, dismisses him, and puts him down. But Larry makes quite a comeback telling Morgan off. Realizing what he's done, Larry nervously babbles to Samantha, "They should put music to those words: 'Shut up!'" Larry even feels bad for asking Samantha to host Morgan in the first place. Is a new Larry in the offing?

Usually, when Aunt Clara makes some sort of goof, she spends that episode figuring out how to fix it. Not here: not only does Clara know her spell the whole time, but she pretends she's forgotten it out of her desire to improve the 20th century with Queen Victoria. If that's not a terrific twist, then the generally jovial witch getting mad when Victoria contends she should be flogged is. Samantha turns her own tables on the Queen by outing herself as a witch and becoming a Christmas tree, providing the holiday moment this season doesn't have.

WELL?

The Stephenses' television set was just repaired in "Oedipus Hex" (#85); no wonder Samantha is "not amused" to see it destroyed by the Queen, who's more than a little lucky she doesn't get electrocuted putting a fire poker through it. Later, Larry walks to the coffee table to get a look at Victoria's throne, but somehow doesn't walk through any of the glass from the television's shattered screen; some of it must be in his path on the carpet. By the time Morgan visits, the TV is intact – shouldn't Larry wonder why it's suddenly in one piece? Shouldn't Victoria?

Aunt Clara's vagueness about baseball is charming – her line, "I think it has something to do with eating hot dogs" is one of the best of the episode. But she can't be that vague – in "Samantha Meets the

Folks" (#14), Clara told Darrin's parents that she and Bertha changed the outcome of the World Series by witchcraft, which should require some knowledge of the sport. As for Queen Victoria, she sounds as if she's hearing about baseball for the first time, but she ruled from 1837 until her death in 1901, and research indicates that baseball was already dubbed America's national pastime by 1856; the first major league was formed in 1876. Victoria is aware of world events; how does she not know what baseball is?

Victoria invokes "the divine right of kings" when she assumes responsibility for overhauling the age in which she finds herself. But, when Aunt Clara is revealed to be a witch, she admonishes, "Sorcery and witchcraft are forbidden." She approves of divine intervention but condemns witchcraft? (At least that's consistent for religion.) And consider: in "The Leprechaun" (#63), Brian O'Brian declared he was the official leprechaun to Queen Victoria. That means she also believes in leprechauns...but not witches. How does she think her heavy throne got upstairs from the living room? Samantha and Aunt Clara didn't carry it up there – and one or both of them must have zapped up a globe for the Queen, unless Darrin's been hiding one in the den.

Samantha has used execution scenarios to influence unruly clients before; along with Bertha and Mary, she witched the bigoted Mr. Brinkman into seeing their side regarding their image in "The Witches Are Out" (#7). Now, Aunt Clara is considered an incompetent witch, but the proof suggests otherwise: Queen Victoria is the third historical figure she's brought out of the past this season, the first being Benjamin Franklin in "My Friend Ben" (#87), and the second, Franklin Pierce in "Samantha for the Defense" (#88). President Pierce was a "wrong number" of sorts; here, Aunt Clara likewise misfires, replacing Queen Victoria with Prince Albert. Aunt Clara points her incanting finger at Victoria, triggering a big puff of smoke, but, when it subsides, she has to raise her arm again.

OH, MY STARS!

In *Star Trek* lore, there is something called the Temporal Prime Directive, in which time travelers are not to interfere with the development of a timeline; for the same reason, visitors from the past/future are not to be given information about the time they're visiting. However, as in "My Friend Ben" (#87), Samantha is all too eager to hip Queen Victoria to the 20th century. Armed with knowledge of 1967, what's to stop the powerful monarch from using it to influence the Victorian Age in her favor? Whether or not historical figures remember skipping through time once they go back hasn't been addressed, except for Ben Franklin commenting in "Samantha for the Defense" (#88) that he wasn't aware he'd left 1967 – but that's the opposite of not remembering being there.

SON OF A GUN!

"Has neither one of you the decency to faint?" – Queen Victoria to Samantha and Aunt Clara, after seeing a girl in skimpy swimwear sashay across the TV screen.

She's regal, she's royal, she's right on! Jane Connell absolutely embodies Queen Victoria, or least our comedic, conventional image of the infamous queen. Her acidic asides rule ("Niece. You look more like a nephew"), as do her anachronisms; her panic at baseball headline "Indians massacre Chicago!" battles "Clara, your limbs are showing" for funniest line. Then there's Victoria's battle with "self-appointed" emperor Morgan, which culminates in a victory punctuated by her fan: "You will kindly (whack) show proper respect (whack) for the Crown (whack)!"

The Stephenses plan to celebrate the anniversary of their first date, but Endora is suspicious when Darrin's pretty client, Terry Warbell, gets into his car. At the office, clueless advertising manager Terry wants to go out to lunch, so Larry forces Darrin to cancel his celebration. Endora pops in as a fashion reporter and is surprised when Terry knows nothing about current trends. Meanwhile, Gladys reels when an old woman arrives claiming she's only twenty-four; upon hearing that the dowager's name is Terry Warbell, Samantha zaps herself to the Kravitzes to retrieve her. Listening to the old woman's story, Endora realizes that the Crone of Cawdor has switched bodies with Terry – if the Crone kisses Darrin, she will absorb his youth, and he will become 500 years old.

Samantha doubles as Terry's father's secretary to obtain Terry's address – meanwhile, the Crone, who has until 6:00 to make the transfer with Darrin, gets increasingly agitated when he won't respond to her advances. Samantha pops in to warn Darrin, but he won't believe her; as he readies to kiss "Terry" in retaliation for Samantha's lack of trust, the Crone becomes herself again, and the real Terry can't understand why she's in the Stephenses' living room. Gladys brings Abner over and is shocked to see the old woman is now 24-year-old Terry, whom Endora is equally suspicious of. Afterwards, Samantha and Darrin finally get to have their celebration.

GOOD!

"Terry's" confused commentaries on fashion sparkle like sequins. "I think Polly Esther is as good as the next designer," she fumbles, while being interviewed by another impostor, Endora. They have something else in common: a few risqué comments that are deceptively innocuous. When Samantha says that Darrin is just giving "Terry" a lift, Endora replies, "From what I can see, vice versa." Later, after Darrin tells "Terry" what he does for fun, she answers, "Mountain climbing? That's very good." Ponder those ponderables for a while. Finally, as the Crone switches back to her literal old self in Darrin's arms, the effect is also "very good."

WELL?

Samantha says she and Darrin are commemorating the third anniversary of their first date, then switches and says first meeting, which Darrin parrots. Unless Samantha misspoke, the implication is that Darrin and Samantha had their first date the day they met. This may be consistent with the prologue of "I, Darrin, Take This Witch, Samantha" (#1), which showed the future marrieds sitting down to dinner after repeatedly bumping into each other. If this sequence of events is correct, then they worked pretty fast.

"Terry" tells Darrin that, while her parents live in Larchmont, she's gotten a local apartment to be near McMann & Tate; this should be the first sign that "Terry" is trouble. As hinted in "Soapbox Derby" (#90), the Stephenses live in Patterson, New York, about 65 miles from Manhattan. Larchmont, also in New York, is only 25 miles from the Big Apple. This means "Terry's" closer place is actually 40 miles further away from the agency than her parents' house. When "Terry" first meets Darrin, she is matter-of-fact and confident; when next seen at McMann & Tate, she is spacey and amorous. Is this personality switch Part II of her plan? Larry also seems schizophrenic, because he's back to threatening Darrin with termination – this after telling "terrible tiger" Morgan to shut up in "Aunt Clara's Victoria Victory" (#100). Is Larry only more reasonable when Darrin isn't around?

Old Terry knocks on the Kravitzes' door, dotty and near catatonic. But when Endora questions her, she is amazingly alert and clear about what happened to her – before contradictorily adding that the only thing she can remember is her age and her name. And does this woman look 500 years old to you?

As "Terry" puts the moves on Darrin at "her" apartment, it's 5:15. The next scene shows Samantha popping in as Daddy Warbell's secretary; suddenly it's 5:55. Did it really take Samantha, a witch, 40 minutes to track down the Warbell home office? And if she can find that, she can find "Terry's" apartment without a middleman.

Darrin nervously tells "Terry" that he enjoys swimming, fishing, and mountain climbing. So he must have learned to swim sometime after Samantha saved him from drowning in "Divided He Falls" (#69) [also see "Charlie Harper, Winner" (#99)]. As for fishing, he's only ever mentioned it in "Open the Door, Witchcraft" (#28), and there's never been any indication that Darrin climbs mountains for fun, or at all.

Can Darrin really not tell something is off about "Terry?" Aside from her complete ignorance about fashion and advertising (considering she's supposed to be an advertising manager), "Terry" blurts out, "What kind of a mortal man are you, anyway?" The qualifier "mortal" should have been Darrin's tip-off. Darrin also fails to notice "Terry's" non-reaction to Samantha suddenly appearing in her apartment, instead going off on Samantha for being mistrustful and deciding to kiss "Terry" to get back at her. Darrin has no reason to disbelieve Samantha's claim about the Crone after being married to a witch this long, and, after Samantha is proven right, he doesn't even apologize.

Abner's contention has always been that Gladys sees things. Now he says that Gladys makes things up about the Stephenses. What are the Kravitzes doing in this episode, anyway? Connecting the real Terry with Samantha seems to be their only purpose.

OH, MY STARS!

With few exceptions, Samantha has worn her heart necklace since "Be It Ever So Mortgaged" (#2) [it went missing in "And Then There Were Three" (#54) and "My Baby, the Tycoon" (#55), and has played peek-a-boo since "Super Car" (#93)]. Here, in the aftermath of Darrin canceling lunch, Samantha's solid pendant changes to a heart outline – a completely different necklace. Yet in the very next scene, it's back to normal.

Heather Woodruff makes the fifth Betty to grace McMann & Tate since Season Two. And the Stephenses' bedroom set is being recycled a lot; having just doubled as Darrin's hotel room in "Three Wishes" (#96) and the Tates' bedroom in "Art for Sam's Sake" (#98), now the Kravitzes' living room takes a turn.

A simple case of amnesia? That's the best explanation Samantha can come up with for the real Terry having blanked out her entire day? Amazingly, Terry buys this. As for the Crone, she elicits more questions than answers. How does she happen to target Darrin, of all mortals? Is it a coincidence that she's picked a witch's husband? Once 6:00 comes, Darrin is safe...or is he? The Crone could just as easily come after Darrin the next day. Since absorbing mortals' youth is her thing, shouldn't Samantha and Endora stop her for good before she moves on to another mortal man? And if the Crone goes around absorbing youth, she'd always be young, never getting to 500. Does she wait 500 years between absorptions? Samantha's bedtime story come to life is such an interesting concept, but its execution is a little sleepy.

SON OF A GUN!

"Right now we have to find out where this reptile in women's clothes lives – and hope to get there in time to keep Durwood kissless!" – Endora to Samantha, actually trying to save her son-in-law.

Clearly, Agnes Moorehead relished getting to play fashion reporter Miss Krovistrod, because her enjoyment is infectious. Given Endora always gets Darrin's name wrong, it makes sense she'd call the agency "Tate-McMann." Behind her, a door is labeled McMann – so, Larry's business partner really does exist. And Endora seems to remember her encounter with Gladys in "Baby's First Paragraph" (#62): she refers to her as "Mrs. Loudmouth" before Samantha can cover the phone.

NO MORE MR. NICE GUY
Airdate: March 23, 1967

EPISODE 102

After Endora and Darrin spar over her teaching Tabatha witchcraft, Samantha informs her mother that everyone finds Darrin likable except her. Begging to differ, Endora zaps new acquaintances into nearly hating Darrin on sight. With three accounts now in jeopardy over clients' bad reactions to Darrin, Larry wants him to see Bob Farnsworth, a psychiatrist. Darrin refuses and drowns his sorrows at a bar instead, changing his mind about therapy after running afoul of a drunk.

Later, Larry calls looking for Darrin, telling Samantha about the instant dislike clients have been taking to her husband; Samantha realizes Endora's involvement and finds Darrin in session with Farnsworth. As the biased doctor implies Darrin's marriage is the cause of all his problems, Samantha zaps the shrink into admitting he's transferring his own hostility onto Darrin. Samantha tells Darrin about Endora's spell, and that his client, Baldwin, has reconsidered his stance; armed with Samantha's instruction to be extra nice to Baldwin, Darrin overdoes it and nearly alienates the man a second time, not realizing the client is no longer under Endora's influence. After Darrin blows off steam about it, Samantha assures him that she not only likes him, but loves him.

GOOD!

The clients are the stars of this episode, at least once Endora casts her spell on them. Eastwood subtly goes back-and-forth between smiling and snarling at Darrin, and it's easy to feel for Darrin when Gloria, the model, turns on him. Baldwin's vacillation is the standout, hexed or unhexed. "Sounds like you're using the hard sell," he stoically tells Darrin. "And my blankets are *soft*." Then, when Darrin offers to fetch him a club sandwich, Baldwin deadpans, "Club? Don't tempt me." Darrin thinking he's counteracting Endora's spell by brown-nosing Baldwin puts a new spin on Darrin's usual behavior, and Larry should be thrilled – Darrin's acting just like him.

The non-agency folks get a few zingers in as well. Farnsworth's over-the-top anti-marriage transference has just the right touch of neurosis, and Dick Wilson is always intoxicating playing his signature drunk.

WELL?

At breakfast, Darrin jokes that he wants to "quit my job and enjoy it all." Apparently he's forgotten he basically did that in "Oedipus Hex" (#85) after consuming Endora's sloth-inducing popcorn. Did Darrin ever find out the snack was responsible for six busy men suddenly sitting around playing poker?

Endora may just be going for theatrics when she teaches Tabatha to disappear using an ominous spell. She didn't need a spell when she attempted the same lesson in "Nobody's Perfect" (#75); she simply popped out. It also seems that Endora adds her ringing bell to her dislike hex for effect, because it doesn't change the spell, or its outcome.

Darrin knows he goes too far calling Endora a "harpy" before leaving for work, as indicated by his expression. Surely he must expect retribution – so why is he surprised when three new acquaintances in a row hate him instantly? Darrin used to be overly suspicious of witchcraft, but lately, he's going to the other extreme, not picking up on magical involvement at all. Hearing the rather square Darrin tell Larry, "I don't swing with this head-shrinking jazz" is funny (and must have been more so in 1967), if inaccurate. In "I'd Rather Twitch Than Fight" (#84), Darrin was quite open to the idea of psychiatry, and even brought Dr. Kramer home to mediate his fight with Samantha. For that matter, why is Larry recommending Farnsworth? Are the Tates not seeing Kramer anymore?

Paul Barselow's bartender must be on the run from the mob – how else to explain his constant name changes? Over the course of the series, his drink mixers have been Hal, Pete, and Joe; now he's Max. The same goes for Dick Wilson's drunks, who change identities depending on the episode. If these guys are going to make regular appearances, why not create specific characters (and names) for them? Finally, why does Wilson's Harry go off on Darrin, with Darrin thinking it's part of his "complex?" Harry isn't under Endora's spell, or at least the bell didn't appear to indicate that he is.

After Harry calls Darrin a crumb, Darrin laments to Max, "everybody treats me like that." He makes it sound like an ongoing problem, but Endora just cast the spell hours before; Darrin even tells Farnsworth that people have only disliked him since that morning. Later, Darrin is excessively nice to Baldwin, not realizing the spell is off – however, Baldwin revises his opinion of Darrin before that, which is why he wants another meeting. Has Endora's spell worn off? And, if Baldwin has mellowed about Darrin, why not Gloria and Eastwood? Finally, Larry has been established as the president of McMann & Tate – but that title is mysteriously absent from his office door.

OH, MY STARS!

The unbroken sequence of Eastwood, Gloria, and Baldwin not showing Darrin the love clocks in at eight minutes. That's a third of the episode; it starts to feel drawn out without other scenes interspersed to break it up. It begins as Eastwood sits frozen in Darrin's office, with Endora incanting, "The new acquaintance this mortal meets, he will dislike with loathing treat." Now, if the mortal Endora is referring to is Darrin, there's no problem. But as Endora says "new acquaintance," the camera is on Eastwood, as it is during "this mortal meets." This implies that Eastwood is the mortal, and Darrin is the acquaintance, which would limit Endora's spell to Eastwood, and have no affect on Gloria or Baldwin. Either the verbiage of the spell needed to be clearer, or the camera needed to stay on Darrin during that line so there wouldn't be any confusion.

SON OF A GUN!

"And it was closed." – Harry the drunk, telling Darrin about the status of Philadelphia during his trip there.

IT'S WISHCRAFT

Airdate: March 30, 1967

Tabatha has moved on to a new magical phase after solely levitating toys: wishcraft, which Darrin discovers when Tabatha pops him into her room. With Darrin's parents coming to visit, he gives Samantha permission to counter Tabatha's magic with her own. Samantha asks Endora to stay and help, but finds herself playing referee for her mother and Phyllis, who wonders if Endora has moved in. Darrin calls, angry that Endora is there; this forces Samantha to cover, as his parents are within earshot of the conversation. Catching Samantha privately scolding her son, Phyllis thinks Endora is causing trouble for Darrin, while Endora, peeved that Darrin has upset her daughter, makes it rain on him in his office.

Phyllis won't accept Samantha's claim that all is right with Darrin, who arrives under his private downpour. Endora turns it off, but, when Darrin charges in, Tabatha pops him to the nursery. Phyllis is convinced that Darrin is in the house, so Samantha has to play "keep away" with her husband and mother-in-law. Once Darrin changes out of his wet clothes, Samantha zaps him outside so he can "come home" laying on the charm; he even kisses Endora's cheek. Phyllis still believes something is wrong, so Samantha lures her to the nursery, then has Endora join her in some "tactical witchcraft" to make Phyllis think she's imagining things. Phyllis apologizes for jumping to conclusions and even exchanges niceties with Endora, but Frank sees Tabatha floating an apple, which Samantha nervously laughs off.

GOOD!

The opening sequence, in which Tabatha sits in her crib and levitates her stuffed rabbit to herself while the camera pulls back, is amazingly done in one unedited shot. That's quite a feat given there are children and special effects involved.

The Stephenses' discussion of how to handle Tabatha with Frank and Phyllis in the house has some interesting twists: Darrin gives Samantha rare permission to use witchcraft, and Samantha's contention that "it's awfully hard to break a child of what comes naturally" adds a wrinkle to Darrin's no-witchcraft rule – is it unhealthy for him to curb Tabatha's powers?

Several elements from Endora's first interaction with the elder Stephenses in "A Nice Little Dinner Party" (#19) come into play here. There's still a spark between Frank and Endora; she flirts with him more openly than before, and Frank is back to cutting Phyllis down in front of her. And, though Endora and Phyllis killed each other with kindness during their first meeting, the gloves come off now, making their genuine exchange of pleasantries at the end especially pleasant.

"Endora! Sweetheart!" Darrin's purposely overdone entrance, meant to persuade his parents everything is fine, culminates with Darrin kissing Endora's cheek – an image for the show's record books. "This has all the earmarks of a put-up job," Endora deadpans in reaction.

Heather Woodruff is catching up to Jill Foster in the Betty department: this marks her third appearance as Darrin's ever-changing secretary, and Woodruff's shocked expressions as rain pours down on Darrin in his office are enough to earn her a permanent place on the staff. She even gets her own fade-out.

WELL?

After Darrin's encounter with Tabatha's roaming rabbit, he tells Samantha that flying toys "might be hard to explain" to his parents. Oh? Darrin already explained his way out of dancing toys during their last visit in "The Dancing Bear" (#58) – and Phyllis watches the same bear floating to her granddaughter. Speaking of Tabatha, she can't make herself disappear (when Endora pops the child out of her high chair, Samantha exclaims, "You can't have started that already!"), but somehow she can zap Darrin into her nursery from different points in the house. Samantha explains, "Whenever she wishes for someone she really loves to be with her, they automatically are." Then why is Darrin the only one the girl summons?

The elder Stephenses have always flown in for visits, except for "A Nice Little Dinner Party" (#19), when they moved into a nearby house. And, in "Divided He Falls" (#69), Frank and Phyllis watched Tabatha for a week, which implied they lived within driving distance. Here, a plane is necessary again. How about deciding that Tabatha's grandparents reside in town or they don't, and sticking to it?

When Samantha tells a wet Darrin that his parents think they've had a fight, Darrin pipes up, "We have!" If so, it's one-sided: Darrin is so focused on demanding Endora leave the house, he won't understand that Samantha only wants her there to police Tabatha's wishcraft for the benefit of his parents; you'd think he'd appreciate his wife's efforts.

The dresser and mirror that were always located by the bedroom door until "Three Wishes" (#96) are again positioned in their usual place, but someone might want to have a talk with the kitchen clock: despite the chaos with Darrin's parents clearly taking place in the afternoon, the clock reads 8:30.

When Endora rings the doorbell, Samantha suggests it might be Darrin. But she just left him upstairs, and therefore knows he can't be standing on the doorstep – plus, he has a key. Then, it's Darrin who asks Samantha to pop him outside so he can make his dramatic entrance, yet he's opposed to Samantha twitching him into dry clothes. And what makes Samantha pop him onto the front walk? Zapping him into the front seat of the car would reduce the chances of Gladys seeing him appear out of nowhere.

OH, MY STARS!

All is right with the world when Samantha and Endora make so much magic happen in the nursery that Phyllis becomes convinced she's been imagining her son's "fight" with Samantha. How are flying toys supposed to accomplish this? Besides, in "Samantha Meets the Folks" (#14), both Aunt Clara and Samantha told Darrin's parents that they're witches. Frank and Phyllis laughed it off, then accepted "the old Mexican jumping bean principle" that created "The Dancing Bear" (#58) – but, between Phyllis' experience in Tabatha's room, and Frank seeing an apple floating to the child, the elder Stephenses should be starting to piece together that something supernatural is involved. Instead, Phyllis tells her husband, "Now you're imagining things!" Frank and Phyllis Stephens are intelligent people; having them stick their heads in the sand implies otherwise.

SON OF A GUN!

"Other kids leave their toys lying around. In my house, they're flying around." – Darrin to himself, after failing to catch Tabatha's self-propelled rabbit.

Tabatha is back with a vengeance: the "witchlet" who faded into the background after opening this season with a triptych of episodes runs this installment, though only in a handful of scenes. And, after having twins Erin and Diane Murphy trading off the role, the show seems to have settled on Erin, who brings the magic here without even twitching her nose.

Feeling Samantha should be living "in the sparkle of a star," Endora decides Darrin needs help and zaps Wilkerson, the representative of new client Madame Maruska, into liking everything Darrin says. Darrin is happy about how well his presentation went until Samantha mentions Endora; he correctly deduces that Endora witched Wilkerson, but assumes Larry was under her power as well. The next day, Darrin's attempt to give Larry the account is interrupted by Madame Maruska, who never makes personal appearances. Darrin thinks Maruska is Endora and throws her out, telling Larry she's a spy – but when it turns out the maven really was Maruska, Darrin is fired.

Darrin refuses Endora's offer to get his job back, instead going to see Maruska, who rejects him, Larry, and their ideas. Samantha pops into a portrait in Maruska's office and retrieves Larry's portfolio, proceeding to place Darrin's ad in the newspaper by witchcraft. While drinking in a bar, Larry and Darrin see the ad and think it was stolen until Larry investigates and discovers paperwork linking it to Darrin. Knowing Samantha is responsible, Darrin is ready to leave her until Larry comes over, thrilled that Madame Maruska wants to sign with the agency. That night, Darrin allows Samantha to twitch a blanket over Tabatha and stuns Samantha by turning off their lamp with powers of his own – really by pulling the plug from the wall.

GOOD!

Theatre buffs will know that this episode's title is a paraphrase of the 1961 Broadway musical, *How to Succeed In Business Without Really Trying*, which had just been released as a film a month before this episode aired. Now, is Endora trying to make up for the nastiness of "No More Mr. Nice Guy" (#102)? Witching Wilkerson into liking Darrin's ideas is pretty much the opposite of what she did to Darrin in that episode. Endora even feels bad for Darrin's termination, admitting, "Well, it is my fault, in a way..." Darrin has his moment of acceptance toward Endora, too, when he tells Samantha, "I'm almost used to your mother's meddling. After all, she's supposed to be a colossal pain – she's a mother-in-law."

It's the Battle of the Bettys – Jill Foster takes the lead from Heather Woodruff, putting in her fifth appearance as Betty and infusing the secretary with just the right amount of awe at Maruska's arrival.

Madame Maruska has a point: maybe Darrin *is* afraid of success. After all, he turned down a presidency at his college chum's agency in favor of remaining Larry's underling [see "Charlie Harper, Winner" (#99)]; it takes Maruska to suggest making him part of "McMann, Tate & Steffens." And Darrin assuming Maruska is Endora, then throwing her out, gives him a zaniness he rarely gets to explore.

Samantha's not the only one with a witch twitch anymore: Darrin "ring-a-dings" his own nose at bedtime, turning off a lamp with his own sound effect. Of course, he only pulls the lamp's plug, but his deadpan confidence – and Samantha's astonished reaction – light up the room.

WELL?

Out of the mouths of babes – again: as Darrin gives Tabatha a parting kiss, she cutely says, "Bye-bye," an overdub taken from "It's Wishcraft" (#103). Grandmama Endora also repeats herself – her sparkle-of-a-star speech is borrowed from "Be It Ever So Mortgaged" (#2), though shortened and slightly rewritten. After Samantha rather rudely tells Endora to blow, the resulting gale Endora whips up flies the bread box and other objects around the kitchen. Shouldn't Endora consider that Tabatha is sitting in her high chair nearby and might get hit by something?

What is Darrin's job? "I, Darrin, Take This Witch, Samantha" (#1) introduced him as McMann & Tate's vice president; afterwards, he was merely an account executive until "Charlie Harper, Winner" (#99), where Samantha bragged that Darrin was Head of Creative Advertising. Now, Larry refers to him as his assistant. Gideon, Darrin's assistant in "Your Witch Is Showing" (#20), was the low man on the agency totem pole; does Darrin have reason to be worried?

Darrin should remember that opening his high-rise window and ordering Endora to get out doesn't work. He already tried that in "Twitch or Treat" (#43); of course, this time, it's Maruska who is offered the exit. Darrin understandably wants to clean up his own mess with the cosmetics queen, but barking, "No! No!" when Samantha and Endora offer their help makes him seem overly volatile.

Samantha tries to pass off her own dress as high fashion while in Madame Maruska's artwork: she already wore it in "Charlie Harper, Winner" (#99). As Larry's portfolio floats to Samantha, it must shrink, because otherwise, it's bigger than the picture. Why does Larry leave his discarded portfolio on Maruska's office floor, anyway? Finally, Samantha has gotten much better at magically placing ads since her first go-round in "Eat at Mario's" (#35): not only does she zap Darrin's campaign on to the back page of the paper, she even creates signed authorizations in Darrin's office to go with them.

Darrin allows Samantha to magically send Tabatha a comforter, saying he's making an exception until he can afford an upstairs maid – yet he had no problem affording Naomi in "Maid to Order" (#53). Why not instead let Samantha twitch the blanket to compensate for being such a hothead about Endora's non-involvement with Madame Maruska? By the way, the credits list her as "Marushka," and that's how everyone pronounces it, but Darrin's layout (and the closed captions) spell her name without the "h."

OH, MY STARS!

As Darrin walks out on Samantha, he says he'll be at "the club," adding that he'll join one when Samantha reminds him he doesn't have a membership. Doesn't he? Darrin easily rented a room at a club after fighting with Samantha in "Double Split" (#64). Has his membership lapsed? Besides, being willing to divorce Samantha and let Tabatha grow up without a father over an account should at least earn Darrin a night on the couch, rather than getting to come home to a friendly Samantha.

SON OF A GUN!

"Stephens! Durwood – Darrin Stephens!" – Darrin, trying to correct Madame Maruska's moniker of "Steffens."

Madame "Ma-roosh-KAH" is "qvite mad": Lisa Kirk is so insanely over-the-top, yet has such a commanding, theatrical presence that it's impossible to stop smiling when she's on screen. She even seems she *could* be Endora under that fashionable Russian exterior.

BEWITCHED, BOTHERED, AND INFURIATED

Airdate: April 13, 1967

Aunt Clara pops in for a visit, zapping up a newspaper to read: the issue carries tomorrow's date and reports that Larry, who is on his second honeymoon, has broken his leg. Darrin insists that he and Samantha prevent the accident, and insinuates himself into the Tates' vacation, while the hotel manager becomes unnerved seeing Samantha turn Larry's slip on wet pavement into a backflip. The Tates' retire to their room, but when Darrin wants to monitor them from the patio, Samantha goes home. Larry carries Louise over the threshold and almost falls over a table; Darrin kicks it out of the way, and the trio lands on the couch.

Aunt Clara tells Samantha that one of Darrin's meetings has been moved up – sending Darrin to the office, Samantha nearly follows Larry into the men's steam room. Trying to make their intrusion up to the Tates with dinner, the Stephenses are shocked to learn the Tates are on their real honeymoon because Larry broke his leg during their first one ten years ago. Samantha freezes the Tates and confirms this with Aunt Clara's paper, then returns the Tates to their arrival earlier that morning; the Tates find their friends' champagne and comment it might have been fun to have Darrin and Samantha with them. The next day, Samantha prevents Darrin from tripping over Tabatha's stroller, and, wanting Samantha's flair, Aunt Clara zaps up an actual flare.

GOOD!

Larry Tate's not been as oblivious to his co-worker's behavior these last few years as he's let on. When Louise agrees that Darrin is acting a little unusual, Larry snarks, "More unusual than usual?" Among other things, Darrin has yelled for Endora and defended witches in front of his boss; it's a great inclusion that Larry has noticed.

Naturally, a stunt double does Larry's incredible backflip for David White – and a double also expertly fills in for Darrin when he falls on the couch with Larry and Louise (presumably due to Dick York's back problems, which resulted from an injury he sustained working on the 1959 film *They Came to Cordura*). But the Tates outdo any doubles, staying frozen while the Stephenses double-check Clara's newspaper.

WELL?

When Aunt Clara popped into the little room off the kitchen in "My Friend Ben" (#87), it was a broom closet. Samantha pulled her aunt through the same doorway in "The Trial and Error of Aunt Clara" (#95), but that time, it was the entrance to the cellar. Now it's a broom closet again.

Morning Glory Circle has a lot of newspapers. The latest in nearly a dozen different publications since the series began is Aunt Clara's *Morning Herald Times*, which also has a strange definition of "newsworthy" – after front-page spreads about the Kravitzes' run-in with a football player ["Pleasure O'Riley" (#25)] and Tabatha "talking" ["Baby's First Paragraph" (#62)], Larry Tate, one man from one ad agency in New York City, gets a headline by breaking his leg. In the real world, Larry would have to be the President (or Justin Bieber) to merit that kind of coverage. Also, Aunt Clara wants to use "tomorrow's" paper to bet on horse races, but Samantha said that kind of witchery was unethical in "My Baby, the Tycoon" (#55). Besides, do witches, who can zap up anything they want, need spending money? Finally, Aunt Clara tries to duplicate Samantha's traveling spell, but ends up back in the broom closet. Why is she trying to go anywhere? She's supposed to be babysitting Tabatha.

In the previous episode, "How to Fail in Business With All Kinds of Help" (#104), Darrin was ready to leave Samantha because she used her powers to place his ad in the paper. Here, he repeatedly badgers her to use witchcraft to keep Larry from breaking his leg. Samantha okays their trip, but warns Darrin that "it's dangerous fooling around with the future." That would be true if they actually ventured into tomorrow, but they are following Larry today.

Larry is unusually "lovey" to Louise in this episode, and exceptionally hostile to Darrin. Yes, Darrin is unwittingly interrupting Larry's honeymoon and making a pest out of himself, but Larry is supposed to be Darrin's friend. Both Tates see unusual things when Samantha is around – Larry even sees her appearing on the patio. In "That Was My Wife" (#31), Darrin came right out and said Samantha's a witch; in "Double Split" (#64), Samantha told Louise the same. Yet neither Larry nor Louise stop to consider that the Stephenses' contentions might be true after witnessing these phenomenons.

The Stephenses and Tates are shown moving through outdoor scenery, but other outdoor sets, especially Larry's patio, are obviously on a soundstage. The pool is outside, but it's also been in four separate locations already, the most recent of which was the Harpers' Oyster Bay house in "Charlie Harper, Winner" (#99) – just six episodes ago.

OH, MY STARS!

In "Three Wishes" (#96), Samantha told Endora that Darrin takes over for Larry when he's away – yet Darrin spends most of his Friday following Larry around, only going back to the agency for one rescheduled meeting. Who's minding the shop?

Aunt Clara asks if it's Friday, meaning tomorrow's paper must be Saturday's. But when Samantha realizes that the headline about Larry's broken leg is from "tomorrow's date, ten years ago," it causes some chronological confusion. Let's say "today" is the Friday in the week this episode aired: Friday, April 14, 1967 – "tomorrow's date, ten years ago" would be Saturday, April 15, 1957. But April 15, 1957 is a Monday, not a Saturday. For tomorrow's date to be the following day of the week, the dates have to be 11 years apart. So, either someone didn't check a perpetual calendar before writing this episode, or Larry broke his leg in 1956, not 1957.

Another time torsion happens when the Tates reveal they are attempting a do-over of the honeymoon they didn't have 10 years ago. In the 1964 episode "…And Something Makes Three" (#12), Louise found herself pregnant after 16 years of marriage, meaning the Tates married in 1948 – 19 years ago. At the end of the ordeal, Samantha sends Larry and Louise "back to this morning, when they arrived." Where – or when – are the Stephenses after this? Do they travel backwards through the day with the Tates? That seems to be the indication, because they hide on the patio in daylight. If not, the Stephenses are in the evening, but watching the Tates enjoying their morning. And where's Jonathan? Home, obviously, but the tyke is never mentioned.

SON OF A GUN!

"I'm just warming up a bottle…and when the baby wakes up from her nap, I'm going to warm a bottle for her, too!" – Aunt Clara, letting Samantha how things are going with Tabatha.

NOBODY BUT A FROG KNOWS HOW TO LIVE

Airdate: April 27, 1967

A man follows Samantha as she pushes Tabatha's stroller in the park, so she zaps him into a fountain. The man, Fergus Finglehoff, is thrilled to find out Samantha's a witch, because he's a frog. Fergus begs Samantha to make him amphibian again, but Samantha explains that only the witch who transformed him can do that. Persistent man-frog Fergus gets into the house and takes Darrin's call; an angry Darrin announces that the Tates, and current client Saunders, are coming for dinner. Samantha tells Gladys, who has seen Fergus sneaking around, that Fergus is Darrin's friend, but after Fergus croaks that he's a frog, Samantha witches him back into the fountain.

Fergus returns threatening to expose Samantha, who is forced to pop him into dry clothes as her company arrives. Before Samantha can introduce him, Gladys runs in calling Fergus a human frog. Fergus denies it, and Abner removes his hysterical wife. Samantha tries to divert Fergus' non-stop frog talk by asking about Saunders' new soup variety; Fergus goes wild when he hears it's turtle soup, so Samantha pops him into the fountain, then later discovers Fergus on the patio with Phoebe, a lady frog who's been in his pocket. Fergus explains that he bought a wish, which is a spell Samantha can undo; she humanizes Phoebe so she and Fergus can decide what form to take. Samantha grants their request to be frogs again, and Gladys runs away screaming after seeing the Stephenses talking to them.

GOOD!

Who did the backflip into the fountain? [Perhaps the same fellow who did Larry's in previous installment "Bewitched, Bothered, and Infuriated" (#105)?] That couldn't have been an easy effect to pull off, especially outside. The much more subtle effect of Samantha zapping Fergus into dry clothes is also skillful; the characters barely move.

Fergus threatening to tell Samantha's neighbors about her being a witch – starting with Gladys – makes so much sense, it's surprising this hasn't come up before. Think of the damage Fergus could do, especially with the emboldened Gladys at his side. Speaking of Gladys, as Samantha spins her tale about Fergus, Mrs. Kravitz pipes up, "Here she goes again – always an explanation." Abner adds, "I was wondering when you were gonna notice that." Abner's always one for sarcasm, but it seems he's giving his wife's claims more credence than he's letting on.

Darrin suggesting that Samantha turn Phoebe into a human being shows that he's learned a few things from being married to a witch for three years. Now, you wouldn't think there'd be a swamp for Fergus and Phoebe to inhabit in New York State, but someone did their research. There is, in fact, an area called The Great Swamp, which goes by another name: The Great Patterson Swamp. As implied in "Soapbox Derby" (#90), the Stephenses reside in Patterson, New York – so it's feasible Fergus could walk to Morning Glory Circle from the swamp. No one mentions this detail, but at least it's accurate.

WELL?

The shadow of a boom microphone follows Samantha and Fergus as they approach the Stephens house. Samantha uses a key to open her front door, but her patio door must be unlocked, because that's how Fergus gets in. Samantha apparently doesn't take better care with the doors after this intrusion, as Fergus somehow makes his way in a second time. Then, the Tates conveniently leave the front door open, allowing Gladys and Abner easy access.

The show has done a good job of sticking to the one-witch-can't-undo-another's-spell rule since elaborating on it in "Hoho the Clown" (#92), but this episode takes a slight detour around it. Samantha tells Fergus she can't change him back "unless I know where, when and why" he became a frog. That contradicts the very rule Samantha reminds him of a minute later, when she says she can't undo another witch's hex. Eventually, Fergus admits he bought a wish, and Samantha smiles, "Any witch can unhex that kind of a hex!" Now the rule has conditions? And witches, who don't need money, wouldn't go around selling spells. Along the same lines, Phoebe (who is no worse for wear after spending the day in Fergus' pocket) tells Samantha that Fergus hocked everything to pay for the old witch's wish. What frog would have underwater gear, much less an understanding of human finances?

Fergus picks up the Stephenses' phone, confirming that the number is 555-2134. However, their number has been 555-7328 since "Witch or Wife" (#8). Later, Darrin spots Fergus with Phoebe by the gazebo. Didn't the Stephenses get a loan to replace the gazebo with a rumpus room in "A Gazebo Never Forgets" (#89)? Either they changed their minds about renovating, or the polka-dotted elephant of that episode messed up the loan after all.

Why does Samantha make Fergus disappear in front of her company? Everyone sees it; surely she could put a spell on Fergus to silence him instead. Samantha also makes a boo-boo in her unusually long spell transforming Fergus and Phoebe: she incants, "With no regrets, man into toad." That might rhyme with "straight and narrow road," but frogs and toads are different species.

The Stephenses blatantly talk to frogs in front of Gladys right after her frog freak-out; they even refer to Fergus by name when Gladys just met the human version. Is this their way of getting back at Gladys for all her snooping?

OH, MY STARS!

This isn't the first time Fergus the frog has made an appearance. In "My Friend Ben" (#87), Samantha pointed to a character in Tabatha's coloring book: a frog named Fergus. Another example of recycling, which at least works as an homage of sorts, is the overdub of Alice Pearce's Gladys screaming "Abner!" as Sandra Gould's runs away.

Fergus' presence is swamped with questions. First, he says he's been trailing Samantha for hours. Has Samantha been pushing Tabatha in her stroller that long? And how did Fergus find Samantha in the first place? It's not like witches have a phone book. Then, when Samantha asks how Fergus knows she's a witch, he croaks, "Because I'm a frog!" It hasn't been revealed at this point that Fergus met a swamp witch, so his being a frog doesn't give him any obvious knowledge of witches in general. Next, how long has Fergus been human? He knows about doors, phones – and he drinks. As discussed in "Ling-Ling" (#21) and "The Horse's Mouth" (#61), can humanized animals consume human consumables? Frogs aren't usually near alcohol unless it's in a bottle in a biology lab.

Darrin gets upset immediately after hearing Fergus' voice on the phone and demands explanations from Samantha. He was mellower about Rodney's amorous presence in "Man's Best Friend" (#70), and Rodney was actually was a threat. Speaking of unexpected guests, Dan Tobin is back, this time as Saunders – but his previous incarnation, Ed Pennybaker, just appeared nine episodes earlier in "I Remember You... Sometimes" (#97). And Saunders' obsession with alcohol, which is funny at first, dries up very quickly.

SON OF A GUN!

"How do you like this bit? I'm suffering a fate worse than death, and this yo-yo wants me to fill out a questionnaire!" – Fergus to himself (and by extension, Phoebe), after Samantha requests more information about his transformation.

Frogs may not know how to live, but they know how to sass. Fergus gets the best lines here, snarking "Witches have a union?" when Samantha says she can't undo another witch's hex; he then tells Phoebe that Samantha is a "musical comedy witch" after his third trip to the fountain. When you recall that Fergus' portrayer, John Fiedler, was already famous for voicing the docile Piglet in Disney's 1966 *Winnie the Pooh and the Honey Tree* cartoon, his sardonic "big-mouth frog" is even more delightful.

THERE'S GOLD IN THEM THAR PILLS
Airdate: May 4, 1967

EPISODE
107

Endora wants to go shopping, but Samantha has to tend to a sick Darrin. As Samantha runs an errand, Endora zaps up Dr. Bombay, the family physician; Darrin is given witches' medication, which instantly cures his cold. Bombay rejects Darrin's suggestion to market the pills, but, when Larry, who's also sick, takes one and becomes healthy again, he appeals to Bombay's ego and gets the rights. Darrin and Larry leave excitedly as Samantha comes home; she is horrified to learn that Darrin has met Bombay.

Larry and Darrin pitch Dr. Bombay's Cold Bombs to the disinterested head of Hornbeck Pharmaceuticals, but the under-the-weather Hornbeck changes his tune after downing some of the medicine himself. As Larry explores how to spend the fortune he's expecting, Samantha tells Darrin about Bombay. Darrin panics, especially when his voice gets higher as a result of the pill. Darrin fakes laryngitis in a meeting with Larry, Hornbeck, and his lawyer; he tries to warn the men of the side effect via note, but they find out for themselves when their own voices pitch up. Samantha enters with Bombay's antidotal "champagne" that restores their voices but makes them sick again. Larry worries that Hornbeck is going to sue them; instead, the balding Hornbeck announces that the pills have one more side effect: hair.

GOOD!

Bernard Fox made his first appearance in "Disappearing Samantha" (#65), but his Dr. Bombay is like Osgood Rightmire on acid – in the best possible way. Bombay's egotistical declarations steal the show, and somehow it seems this family doctor has always been a part of it. Angrily popping into Bombay's witchy lab, Samantha tells him to "get up off your hassock." Got that one past Standards and Practices, didn't they? Not to be outdone, Endora's slips, "Oh, he's gone" when Darrin and Larry want to see the vanished doctor, recovering with, "Oh, I mean he's really gone. You know – way out?"

Talking in a high, squeaky voice is not the most original comedy, but the vocal afflictions of Darrin, Larry, and Hornbeck are the talk of the episode. It's humorous enough when Darrin pretends to be his secretary, but Hornbeck having the highest voice of all tops it. The best part is Hornbeck's permanently nasal lawyer, Prager, popping off, "Didn't do a thing for me" after drinking Bombay's bubbly antidote.

Only once before has the show unveiled a witch or warlock's natural habitat: George's harem, in "George the Warlock" (#30). Every other location, including The Warlock Club of "My Grandson, the Warlock" (#40), looked decidedly mortal. So what a treat to see Samantha popping into Bombay's office, which looks decidedly witchy. Turns out the "sparkle of a star" is pink (with dry ice).

WELL?

Samantha calls Max Grand's drugstore for a hot water bottle; terrific continuity, considering Max and his store appeared in "Sam in the Moon" (#91), but, after Darrin tried to have Grand analyze "moon dust" and "lunar tea," you'd think Samantha would play it safe and take her business elsewhere.

Once again, Darrin seems clueless to the witchcraft going on around him. Does he really think a pill that cures a cold instantly can be anything but magic? Not to mention, Bombay makes several non-human references that Darrin should pick up on. What is Bombay doing with pills that cure the common cold? In "Just One Happy Family" (#10), Maurice said witches have no need for medicine, at least for mortal ailments.

Endora zaps Bombay to her, then sends him back. Doesn't he have powers of his own? And, according to Samantha, Bombay is a quack simply for giving witches' medicine to a mortal, but his only misdeed is giving in to Endora's demands. As for the illness, Darrin and Larry both sound convincingly sick, but Hornbeck's sneezes are less realistic.

Larry was listening when Madame Maruska lectured Darrin in "How to Fail in Business With All Kinds of Help" (#104); the cosmetics queen told Darrin he was afraid of success, and Larry makes a similar observation here, assuming the laryngitic Darrin has stage fright on the eve of their prosperity. By the way, this isn't the first time Darrin communicates by note – he had to do the same as a chimpanzee in "Alias Darrin Stephens" (#37).

Pretending to be a secretary, the high-pitched Darrin tells Larry that "Darrin" just stepped out – but Larry never wonders who took his call. As president, he should know everyone on staff, yet it never occurs to him he's hearing an unfamiliar voice. Has he heard so many Bettys that he doesn't find this unusual? Later, as Larry asks, "And who introduced me to that kook Bombay?" it's not the word "kook" he's saying: watch his lips – it's an overdub. Finally, Larry's assertion that things have gone wrong in the three years Darrin has been with the company doesn't time out. In "I Remember You...Sometimes" (#97), Darrin recalled a birthday present Louise gave him eight years earlier, which means he's been in McMann & Tate's employ at least that long, unless he was friends with Larry first before working for him.

OH, MY STARS!

Dr. Bombay is introduced as the family physician – and twice, Endora threatens to replace him with Dr. Agrafor. This implies that witches have at least two doctors. Where were they when Samantha came down with square green spots disease in "Take Two Aspirins and Half A Pint of Porpoise Milk" (#42)? In that episode, Aunt Clara had to concoct Samantha's cure herself. She must have called a coven and lobbied for witches get their own health care – how else to explain why there's suddenly a Witches' Medical Association for Samantha to report Bombay to? And is Dr. Bombay who Aunt Clara went to for a check-up in "The Moment of Truth" (#76)?

Darrin, Larry, and Hornbeck all take a Cold Bomb, plus its antidote – yet Hornbeck is the only one who grows hair. Granted, Darrin and Larry aren't bald, but you'd think this second side effect would manifest in them somehow. The balding Prager doesn't grow hair, either, though he only took the antidote; is it only combining it with the Cold Bomb that produces results? Hornbeck doesn't know that the Cold Bombs by themselves don't grow hair, but he still wants to market the pills, even though he knows they pitch up people's voices. How unscrupulous! By the way, how long after everyone's voices are restored does this hair-raising meeting take place? All the men get sick again after taking Bombay's antidote, but, when full-headed Hornbeck returns, the trio is healthy. The episode (and season) ends with Hornbeck talking about the empire they'll build. How do Darrin and Larry get out of marketing Bombay's byproduct-laden formula?

SON OF A GUN!

"Sorry, I forgot about that." – Dr. Bombay, after Darrin reminds him he's only human.

SEASON FOUR

(1967-1968)

Tabatha causes problems while trick-or-treating for the first time in "The Safe and Sane Halloween" (#115).

Larry and Louise think Samantha has gone psychedelic in "Hippie, Hippie, Hooray" (#128).

Darrin is afflicted with a Pinocchio-like spell – only not on his nose – in "My, What Big Ears You Have" (#121).

ABC/Photofest

The Stephenses entertain extraterrestrial guests in "Samantha's Secret Saucer" (#137).

ABC/Photofest

SEASON FOUR: OVERVIEW

Society, particularly in America, was experiencing perhaps its most rapid transformation as the 1967-1968 television season progressed. Skirts got shorter, hair got longer, and new ideas about life and love were pushing against a desire to preserve the tried and true. These high-concept realities slowly made their way into a little sitcom called *Bewitched*. Hipper music and sound effects became part of the landscape and were subject to much experimentation. Conversely, even though there were new paintings in the living room foyer and the bedroom, and the patio doors boasted new curtains, the show had a more consistent look and feel throughout this season than it ever had before.

The growing hippie counterculture was wisely explored in several scripts, from repeated mentions of love-ins to dialogue peppered with new terms like "groovy" – and then there's the reintroduction of Samantha's cousin, Serena, who emerged from the cocoon of her quiet Season Two début to become the show's flower child butterfly. Not only did her "threads" reflect the mod styles that were gaining popularity, but Serena even got her own episode, "Hippie, Hippie, Hooray" (#128), in which her new brand of free love clashed sharply with the conservatism expressed by Darrin and the Tates.

Larry became more of what Serena would term "a drag," getting stuck in a pattern of regularly firing or threatening to fire supposed best friend Darrin. As for Samantha, she exhibited a new testiness, sassing mother Endora more often and even snapping at her beloved Aunt Clara – something she never would have tolerated from Darrin in the early days of their marriage.

Call it something in the writing, or a change decided upon behind the scenes, but this season found Darrin becoming quite hammy, which did not put the protagonist/antagonist in his best light. Darrin exhibited a new volatility as he fumed at Samantha with greater frequency and threatened to leave her over the slightest provocations; it felt forced, as if Dick York would have preferred to play his character differently, especially later in the season. And York, who sustained a major back injury during the filming of 1959's *They Came to Cordura*, had to be written out of four episodes because of increasing mobility issues.

Endora continued to lock horns with Darrin and began putting more spells on him – but she also got some new and different things to do, most notably in "Allergic to Ancient Macedonian Dodo Birds" (#118), which saw the formidable witch helpless without her powers, and in "Once in a Vial" (#125), where she fell under the influence of a love potion intended for Samantha. Both are showcases for Agnes Moorehead, and standout episodes into the bargain.

Tabatha really started to grow up before viewers' eyes as she went from baby babble in "Toys in Babeland" (#109) to full sentences in "Splitsville" (#140). As the young witch continued to experiment with her strengthening powers, the show leaned on Erin Murphy much more than her twin sister, Diane, even letting Erin carry a whole episode ["Playmates" (#133)]. There were other installments, however, where it seemed Tabatha didn't exist – and Jonathan Tate fared worse, only being referred to twice in these 33 episodes.

There were other continuity gaffes that stood out during this otherwise strong season. Closets moved around the Stephens house. Morning Glory Circle looked different from episode to episode, both in exterior shots and studio backdrops; the Kravitz house, long established as across the street from the Stephenses', was often nowhere to be found. Serena went through a mystifying makeover where she looked and sounded more like Samantha, and the Stephenses hired nanny Elspeth, who vanished after her one-episode appearance.

Perhaps the biggest puzzlement was season premiere "Long Live the Queen" (#108), in which Samantha was crowned ruler of her people. While it shed new light on the way witches live and conduct themselves, Samantha-as-royal seemed a strange fit for the show. The writers must have thought better of it, too, because her sovereignty was only mentioned twice more [in "Double, Double, Toil and Trouble" (#111) and "McTavish" (#130)] before being dropped without explanation. And encounters with ghosts, aliens, and a Japanese client played by a non-Asian actor made this era of the show memorable in some unintentional ways.

Still, Season Four was filled with far more shining moments than questionable ones. Darrin could only speak Italian, Samantha lost her powers, and both traveled to the 17th century with Aunt Clara for the first Thanksgiving. *Bewitched* was evolving, and, 140 episodes in, it showed no signs of slowing down.

LONG LIVE THE QUEEN

Airdate: September 7, 1967

Endora has her latest visit reported via radio broadcast, then delivers a message announcing the arrival of a witch called Ticheba. Based on Samantha's dismayed reaction, Darrin jokes that Ticheba must be Queen of the Witches, but she's exactly that – a monarch who materializes her throne to perch upon after expressing displeasure with Darrin and his house. Once Darrin leaves, Ticheba reveals that Samantha has been chosen as her successor; ignoring Samantha's concerns about Darrin, Ticheba continues redecorating the Stephenses' home. When Samantha reluctantly tells Darrin she has no choice but to accept the crown, he ultimately supports her, and all manner of witches and warlocks attend her coronation.

Deciding that royal business will only be conducted after 12 midnight, Samantha agrees to restore those that Ticheba transformed into animals or objects. Samantha fulfills her mortal duties by entertaining Darrin's prospective client, Rohrbach, but the meeting goes awry when a bird, who thinks the transformation is at 12 noon, arrives with a legion of transformees. Rohrbach runs after he opens the door to a chair and is accosted by a llama. Darrin demands that Samantha abdicate; when she confesses she must rule for a year, Darrin walks. Listening to a bar patron crying about being separated from his family for a year, Darrin comes home, much to Endora's chagrin. Darrin lovingly acknowledges Samantha's queendom as part of who she is, but, when she jokingly knights him with her scepter, she accidentally changes him into a goose.

GOOD!

After three years of not knowing where witches go when they pop out, the show wisely builds on the sight of Dr. Bombay's witchy lab in "There's Gold in Them Thar Pills" (#107) and offers a substantial glance at a supernatural meeting place that hosts Samantha's coronation. Apparently, witches like their pink (and their dry ice), because both Bombay's lab and this location sport the look, which shows consistency. It adds intrigue to finally see the world Samantha ditched for Morning Glory Circle.

Darrin running through the foyer and stopping suddenly, seeing the rocked Rohrbach from the corner of his eye, is a great bit of physical comedy – and audio comedy comes from finding out the transformed warlock has the same shrill voice he expressed himself with as a bird.

Paul Barselow's nonplussed bartender has gone through a variety of names – in this episode, he doesn't even have one – but he doles out insightful advice to Darrin, reminding him that all women have their good points. He may have singlehandedly saved the Stephenses' marriage.

WELL?

For some reason, Samantha smiles and laughs during the thunder and lightning that heralds the queen's serious arrival. (A funny in-between-scene joke, perhaps?) And Samantha may have told Darrin about Queen Victoria's visit after all [see "Aunt Clara's Victoria Victory" (#100)], because his "I forgot the question" reply to Ticheba echoes what Samantha said to the mortal monarch.

Judging by the known layout of the Stephens house, Endora is correct that the guest room and master bedroom share a wall – a wall Ticheba moves by several feet. Yet, when Samantha and Endora talk in the master bedroom, the wall is still in its usual place; it should be jutting out.

Are Samantha's feelings toward Darrin and his pro-mortal attitude different than she lets on? She tells Endora that the throne is better suited to other witches because "they don't have Darrin to contend with." Darrin's reaction to Samantha becoming queen is, "What does that make me, Prince Valiant?" In a way, yes, since Uncle Arthur equated him with the comic book hero in "The Joker Is A Card" (#41), after Endora gave Darrin a Beatles makeover. This isn't Darrin's first reference to the Taj Mahal, either: he made the same comparison when Samantha filled the living room with luxuries in "The Girl With the Golden Nose" (#73). Finally, Samantha assures Darrin she'll change everything back when Ticheba leaves, but if a witch has "squatter's rights" to a spellee, as indicated in "Hoho the Clown" (#92), then the same should hold for anything a witch manipulates by magic; ergo, only Ticheba can restore the house.

When the about-to-be-crowned Samantha makes her processional approach, ordinary yard lights are seen blinking at her right. Back in the mortal world, when Darrin is awakened by the bird, three chimes indicate the hour. But the Stephenses have never had a chiming clock in their home.

The Stephenses entertain many clients at the house, typically in the evening; daytime meetings seem to happen at McMann & Tate. So why is Rohrbach in Darrin's house before noon on a weekday? And why isn't Larry present for this meeting?

So no one, especially Gladys "Binoculars" Kravitz, sees a throng of animals and animated objects in the Stephenses' front yard? One of them is the chair seen in "Sam's Spooky Chair" (#86). And how can a lamp open a door? Do witches and warlocks still have their powers while banished to other forms?

When Samantha admits she has to be queen for a year, Darrin threatens not to come back for that long. He'd really leave Tabatha without a father for a year because of Samantha's sovereignty?

If you've just come back from being an animal or appliance, wouldn't you pop out of the Stephens house instead of leaving through the front door? And Darrin getting changed into a goose is amusing, but it's odd that Samantha wouldn't be able to control the power of the scepter, since it came with the throne.

OH, MY STARS!

Samantha becoming queen presents a kingdom of problems, starting with her claim that "certain witches are chosen at birth." This seems to go against the accepted forms of monarchy: in an elective monarchy, Samantha's installation would have to happen by vote – and, of course, in the traditional hereditary monarchy, Samantha could only have the throne passed down to her by Maurice or Endora. Is Samantha's family royalty, and it just never came up until now? In any case, Samantha being queen means that Darrin is now part of the royal family; he's up there with Princess Diana and Kate Middleton. So why is he absent from Samantha's coronation, and why do Ticheba and Endora treat him with such disrespect? Samantha's queendom also suggests that Tabatha is now a princess, and Endora the Queen Mother, but none of this is addressed. And where's Maurice? Given his love for Samantha and Tabatha, and even the pride he displayed when he thought Jonathan Tate was his descendant in "My Grandson, the Warlock" (#40), you'd think he'd be standing at Endora's side as Samantha is crowned.

Samantha's decision to take care of royal business after midnight is understandable; her choice of venue, less so. Wouldn't a witchy site be more appropriate than her own mortal house? It would keep the transformees out of Darrin's hair, and Rohrbach wouldn't pull his account – which Darrin must have a heck of a time explaining to Larry. "Well, he saw this chair, and..."

SON OF A GUN!

"You should have seen the look on Rohrbach's face when that bird flew in! And I'll bet when he saw the chair that – saw the chair?!" – Darrin to Samantha, realizing the impact the transformees are having on his horrified client.

It takes Darrin a while, but his eventual acceptance of Samantha's royal post – deeming it "part of who you are" – shows Darrin can still be the "sweetheart" Samantha always says he is.

EPISODE 109
TOYS IN BABELAND
Airdate: September 14, 1967

While sitting for Tabatha, Endora is reminded by a messenger that she is expected at a party in thrown in her honor. On the suggestion of the messenger, Endora humanizes Tabatha's toy solider to cover for her. Endora gives instructions and leaves, but the solider-as-man doesn't understand Tabatha's request for juice, so the child copies Endora's spell, eventually filling the nursery with life-sized toy people. The Stephenses are upset to see Tabatha's visitors; when Samantha can't change them back herself, she locks them in the guest room.

Meanwhile, Larry, who feels threatened by Darrin's friendship with important client Chase, sneaks over to Darrin's house after his dinner with Chase is canceled; seeing the toy people Tabatha has liberated, Larry thinks Darrin has edged him out of a costume party that includes Chase. Larry assumes Chase is setting Darrin up in his own agency and mistakes the soldier for an office employee, calling it Max. Larry takes "Max" drinking at a bar; Darrin follows and tries to explain Max's identity to his inebriated boss. While Darrin distracts Larry, Samantha uses the spell she got from Endora to turn the soldier back, and Larry swears off alcohol when he realizes he's spent the evening talking to a toy. Samantha assures Darrin she's instructed Tabatha to stop putting spells on her toys, but Tabatha still has Darrin take a long-distance call from her toy telephone.

GOOD!

Appropriately enough, this episode's title is a paraphrase of *Babes in Toyland*, the name of an operetta and two films, the most popular being the 1961 Disney version. Maybe that's why Darrin makes a reference to the famed park.

Samantha's right: Endora is "impossibly endearing" as she gets Tabatha to agree that her grandmama is "the prettiest little lady in the whole world," adding, "I believe in telling a child the absolute truth." And Tabatha, deemed a prodigy in "Witches and Warlocks Are My Favorite Things" (#77), can now humanize toys with a zap, unlock doors, and contact Pittsburgh by kiddie phone.

Larry's an entertaining drunk – or, at least, David White is entertaining taking the exec out of his usual, austere element. Hearing what he wants to hear from the nodding, silent soldier is enough cause for humor, but Larry's slurring vacillation from betrayed to confused really gives him a chance to shine.

WELL?

There's a distinct feeling that this episode was filmed during Season Three, but held back until now: almost all the music cues and sound effects are a throwback compared to the new ones presented in "Long Live the Queen" (#108) – plus Tabatha seems younger than she did during her last appearance in "Nobody But A Frog Knows How to Live" (#106), which aired nearly five months earlier.

Why is Endora lost for a replacement babysitter when she's called away? Certainly she knows her presumed sister, Clara, often cares for Tabatha in Samantha's absence. In "No More Mr. Nice Guy" (#102), Endora used a bell to cue strangers' hostility toward Darrin; here, she's ringing again, though none of the toy people ever call her using the bell she leaves behind. Endora also tells the solider, "It's a shame we can't make you talk." Witches have essentially limitless power – Endora really can't do something as simple as giving voice to a humanized toy? As for Max, he doesn't know what juice is, but he knows how to answer a phone. Tabatha cutely calls out for "juice" and "drink", but the request is a voice-over of an adult imitating a baby.

In "Hoho the Clown" (#92), Samantha made it very clear that witches can only undo their own spells – yet here, she insists she can turn the toys back herself. This discontinuity goes to the next level when Samantha arrives at the bar with a spell Endora has given her to make "Max" a toy again – but the "Hoho" rule says Endora would have to cast it, and that Endora couldn't "take care of" the other toys that Tabatha humanized.

When Samantha attempts to turn Tabatha's babysitters back into toys, her spell begins, *One-ri, or-ri, ickory ann* – which is from the series' first spell, cast in "I, Darrin, Take This Witch, Samantha" (#1). Later, Darrin stashes Tabatha's toys "until you unlearn what your dear grandmother taught you," only it isn't established at that point that Endora has anything to do with their transformations. Besides, if Tabatha can transform her toys, she can probably also unlock her toy box.

Larry's contention seems to be that Darrin's not allowed to be friends with a client, since he immediately interprets any closeness between Darrin and Chase as a plot against him. Larry needn't worry – Darrin never stays in touch with his friends. (Just ask Dave, Kermit, Bob Frazer, Adam Newlarkin, Charlie Harper...) However, Larry should be concerned about his wallet, as his modest living room of "Double Tate" (#59) is now much more opulent.

When Tabatha magically lets her dancing toy people out of the guest room, the drummer pounds the skins, but the jaunty music cue cancels out its sound. Then, as Larry eavesdrops on the "costume party," he doesn't react to Darrin screaming for everyone to go upstairs, or Samantha deciding to lock everyone away. Maybe he's too busy casting a shadow on the Morning Glory Circle studio backdrop?

Paul Barselow's bartender is back after his nameless appearance in the previous episode, "Long Live the Queen" (#108). This time, the "mixologist" is called Joe, a moniker not used since "A Very Special Delivery" (#38). Joe – and Dick Wilson's latest drunk – witness Samantha popping in to the bar (which isn't very subtle of her), yet she still risks turning "Max" back into a toy in their line of sight. And Darrin nearly tells Larry how "Max" got there – what if Larry were to remember Darrin confessing that Samantha is a witch in "That Was My Wife" (#31)?

Samantha impresses upon Darrin that Endora "apologized all over the place; she's never done that before." Actually, she has. She expressed regret for turning Darrin into a werewolf in "Trick or Treat" (#43), a little boy in "Junior Executive" (#46), and Endora even wanted to accept responsibility for messing things up with Madame Maruska in "How to Fail in Business With All Kinds of Help" (#104).

OH, MY STARS!

Darrin is in a cold sweat for fear the Chases will discover the toy people, since he's unable to cancel their dinner plans. But the Chases never show up, and they're completely dropped from the plot.

Samantha is relatively proud of Tabatha for being able to witch her toy telephone, admitting that she couldn't do it until she was five. The telephone was invented in 1876 (and the toy telephone not long after), so Samantha would have to have been born sometime after 1871 – and age like a mortal – for this claim to be true. However, this flies in the face of "Eye of the Beholder" (#22), which established that Samantha may have been around in the 1680s. Either Samantha was already an adult by the time telephones were invented, or "Eye of the Beholder" (#22) was wrong.

SON OF A GUN!

"What do I tell them when they get here – 'welcome to Disneyland'?" – Darrin to Samantha, wondering how to explain the human toys to the Chases.

EPISODE 110

BUSINESS, ITALIAN STYLE
Airdate: September 21, 1967

After Larry tells Arcarius, who represents Italian food company Chef Romani, that Darrin is fluent in the language and threatens Darrin with termination if he doesn't learn a few phrases, Darrin accepts the challenge and studies with some language records. Endora peeks in and sees Darrin struggling, so she zaps him with a spell that gives him command of Italian. The next morning, Samantha is impressed when Darrin can name objects in the tongue, but suddenly he speaks English with an Italian accent, then loses his understanding of English completely. Samantha, who can converse in Italian herself, realizes Endora is responsible, and tries to teach Darrin English out of children's books.

When Larry comes by to determine Darrin's progress, Samantha lies that Darrin can only speak Italian now because of his "total immersion" process. She sends Darrin to the office, where Romani is delighted with Darrin's fluency, but Darrin runs into trouble when Romani wants Darrin to switch over to English. Samantha drags Endora to Darrin's office, where the partially worn-off spell has him back to speaking English with an Italian accent. Slowly, Darrin's English returns, and he covers by saying he was mocking Romani and Arcarius to demonstrate how Americans are offended by dialect humor – promising it won't make its way into McMann & Tate's campaign. Later at dinner, Romani wants to hear Darrin speak Italian again, so Samantha twitches a few words into Darrin's mouth to please her guest.

GOOD!

Darrin's right that dialect humor shouldn't be funny (a great save – he's getting better at thinking on his feet), but Darrin's broken English throughout still tickles. The same goes for his "immersion" – threatening Endora in Italian puts a whole new spin on his usual routine. Samantha teaching Darrin to say simple words like "cat" is a highlight of the episode, and Elizabeth Montgomery has quite a handle on properly pronouncing Italian words; it really sounds like Samantha is fluent. (She's a witch – why wouldn't she be?)

WELL?

Romani's associate, Arcarius, must moonlight as a language instructor: Renzo Cesana, who plays Arcarius, also provides the voice for Martinelli, the record's lustful teacher. Darrin seems to have purchased lessons willy-nilly, because he acts like he doesn't know what he bought, and he shouldn't have to grab the box to determine he's listening to *Simple Phrases for the American Bachelor* in Italy, which is on the record label. That same label is visible in a close-up, even after Darrin changes records.

Endora's instant language spell doesn't quite come with no strings attached – wires are seen making it possible for Endora to hover over Darrin in the den. Her spell also gets a little preview when Darrin slips into his Italian accent before Endora freezes him. The next day, Darrin is thrilled with what he's learned, feeling "like a sponge soaking it all in." Isn't that how he felt in "I Remember You...Sometimes" (#97), when the total recall from his instant memory book turned out to be Endora's spell? You'd think that experience would make him question his sudden fluency.

First Larry threatens to fire Darrin if he doesn't learn "simple Italian." Then he says he'll be happy if Darrin can "fake a few *arrivederci Romas*." Then he threatens to fire Darrin if he doesn't *stop* speaking Italian. Since Larry has all this "fire power," why does he ask Darrin for recommendations regarding key agency positions? Darrin is only an account executive, and Larry doesn't seem interested in Darrin's opinions these days, anyway.

Darrin must be learning from Samantha's example: her *ripete* during her English lesson is overdubbed, as is Darrin's entire exchange with Romani later on. Other new dialects include Larry ringing a different doorbell than the one that's been heard the past three seasons, and Samantha's trademark twitch sound effect has been altered as well.

Samantha has a way of interrupting people's baths, doesn't she? She'd already gotten an eyeful of Dr. Bombay when she ambushed his bathroom in "There's Gold in Them Thar Pills" (#107); here, she makes Endora and her giant bathtub pop in to the living room. How can Endora think she gave Darrin an Italian "overdose?" Her spell is very specific: she arranges for Darrin to "speak like an Italian." Then Endora says the spell needs time to wear off. Odd, since it takes effect immediately, and, later, Samantha doesn't even need an incantation to recreate the same spell herself.

For a witch as sophisticated as Endora, one assumes her wardrobe is limitless. Yet here, she wears the same light green dress two days in a row. Also, Endora thinks nothing of zapping Samantha and Darrin to Italy for a "nice Italian dinner" – what happened to the authentic local eatery Endora and Samantha championed in "Eat At Mario's" (#35)? And who's watching Tabatha while everyone is in Darrin's office, then overseas? No wonder Tabatha has to make her own babysitters. [See "Toys in Babeland" (#109).]

OH, MY STARS!

As in "Toys in Babeland" (#109), Samantha tries to undo Endora's spell, continuing to forget what she told Darrin about spell exclusivity in "Hoho the Clown" (#92). Perhaps her magical concentration is going solely into remembering her languages – she says she only speaks "a little Italian," yet she knows more involved words for "art director" and "copywriter."

SON OF A GUN!

"If you counted to ten, you are a superior student. To seven, you are average. And to five, *stupido*." – Miss Petruccelli, providing encouragement on her language record.

DOUBLE, DOUBLE...TOIL AND TROUBLE
Airdate: September 28, 1967

Darrin is annoyed when Samantha's royal after-midnight meeting wakes him out of a sound sleep. Despite feeling Darrin is violating their agreement regarding the scheduling of witch business, Samantha disbands the assembly, which Endora reconvenes to announce an "evil idea" – she'll have Samantha's lookalike cousin, Serena, drive Darrin away. The next day, as Samantha leaves to volunteer at a church bazaar, Serena replaces her cousin and blasts Darrin for his interference. When a sugar-borrowing Gladys suspects the switch, Serena-as-Samantha makes her shoes disappear. Darrin seeks Larry's advice when "Samantha" wants to live a witch's life again, but Larry is rattled when Serena comes on to him.

Upping the ante, "Samantha" becomes queen and holds court, causing Darrin to walk out – but Endora feels victory is premature because Darrin hasn't taken his clothes. Darrin does return; when he protests "Samantha's" sexy hippie ensemble, she transforms herself into a bedraggled housewife. Abner comes by to return the sugar Gladys spilled, incredulous that she reported seeing Samantha at the bazaar. Darrin realizes Serena's involvement just as the real Samantha arrives; thinking his wife is Serena, he mashes her face into a pie she brought home. The outraged Samantha responds in kind with a conjured dessert, but Darrin chases her with it, resulting in Endora getting the pie in her face. Samantha sees Serena and throws a pie in retaliation, leaving the foursome covered in lemon meringue.

GOOD!

Very little is known about Serena outside of her previous – and only – appearance in "And Then There Were Three" (#54) – then, Serena was a sophisticate who didn't seem radically different from Samantha, outside of being brunette. So transforming Serena into a higher-voiced member of '60s counterculture is, as Serena would now say, "Right on." Elizabeth Montgomery's joy playing Serena-as-Samantha is infectious, especially during her amorous scene with Larry. Darrin gets his moment as well; his turnabout-is-fair-play offensive against "Serena" is another high point in this very entertaining episode. Not to mention, Serena's physical transformation to Samantha and back looks effortless.

WELL?

Darrin wakes up on the wrong side of the bed – literally – as the warlock minstrel strums outside his door; Darrin has always slept on the right, but now he dozes on the left. Can Darrin really run downstairs and interrupt royal business? That would be like Michelle Obama running into the Oval Office and telling everybody to go home.

The Stephenses may need to invest in hearing aids. Neither Samantha nor Darrin hear Endora and the masses chortling loudly in the living room once they head upstairs. Darrin can't hear Endora talking to Serena in the kitchen, despite standing a few feet away in the foyer. Then, from the same area, Darrin doesn't hear Samantha driving up, though Endora can hear the car from the kitchen. Darrin also misses an important cue from Gladys, who asks why their car isn't in the driveway; that alone should tip Darrin off to the substitution shenanigans.

Is Tabatha destined to grow up without a father? Darrin again walks out on his wife (at least he thinks it's his wife), and Endora works to get rid of Darrin for her own selfish reasons. They love Tabatha; it's inconceivable they wouldn't think of the girl's welfare.

When Endora summons Serena for her scheme, she pops into the kitchen and ducks into the laundry room – instead of popping directly into the laundry room to avoid being detected by Darrin. And when did that room get set up for laundry? It was a broom closet in "We're In For A Bad Spell" (#39), then the entrance to the cellar in "The Trial and Error of Aunt Clara" (#95). At least the doorbell is back to normal, despite being changed in "Business, Italian Style" (#110).

Seeking counsel from Larry, Darrin informs his boss/friend that he's been married to Samantha "almost four years." Actually, the Stephenses have been married just over three years. Later, when Endora freezes Larry, Serena's arm is draped around him. Endora scolds her, moves Serena's arm, and reanimates Larry – to him, Serena would have her arm on him one second, but not the next, yet he never reacts to this.

Darrin hints to Abner about the truth behind the Samantha/Serena switch, making this the second time this season he's nearly blabbed about witchcraft; he also was about to tell Larry how Endora humanized a toy solider in "Toys in Babeland" (#109).

When the real Samantha comes through the door, she sets her purse down on the cabinet in the foyer. In her next shot in the living room, she still has the purse in her hand, dropping it when Darrin grabs her for a kiss. Maybe Darrin gets confirmation about Serena's wife-swapping in the kitchen – Serena, dressed as herself, disappears with Endora just as Darrin runs in; there's no way he could miss them. And whoever levels the pie at Serena in Samantha's place aims a little too high, because Serena's brunette wig almost comes off from the impact – Elizabeth Montgomery's blond hair can be seen at Serena's hair line.

OH, MY STARS!

Serena's lucky all she gets for her machinations is a pie in the face – she's guilty of impersonating the queen. In some circles, such an act would be considered treasonous and punishable by imprisonment at the very least.

How does Darrin figure out that "Samantha" is really Serena? Darrin has only ever seen Serena once, thinking she was a grown-up version of the newborn Tabatha [see "And Then There Were Three" (#54)]. Darrin and Serena have never been formally introduced; when he clues in that there's witchcraft afoot, Serena should be the last culprit on his list. Yet, he acts as if she's pulled these stunts before.

SON OF A GUN!

"I'm sick of simmering like a watched pot. I wanna get out and boil!" – Serena-as-Samantha, explaining her thigh-high boots and mini-skirt.

The old pie-in-the-face gag – it's been a comedy staple since the early days of silent movies, and the trusty pastry prank is put to exceptional use in this episode. It isn't so much the pieing as it is the fact everyone is having such a good time. Elizabeth Montgomery visibly laughs (while trying to say "Well, how is it? Good as usual?") to the point she has to be overdubbed; one would guess the merriment is responsible for the atypical freeze frame at episode's end, because Samantha looks about ready to crack up again as the still kicks in. There's also heightened hilarity in watching lemon meringue make contact with the elegant, regal Endora – Darrin even apologizes for hitting her with it. And the show puts a new twist on the old pie standby by essentially having Elizabeth Montgomery throw a pie at herself.

When Darrin's uncomfortable with Samantha having bought an expensive coat, she offers to take it back, but Endora brands him a cheapskate. Just as Darrin is about to tell Samantha the real reason for his resistance, Endora turns him into the tightest of tightwads – he nickle-and-dimes Larry over a piece of gum and nearly reduces Betty to tears over wasting paper. But the agency's new client, Bigelow, a penny pincher himself, gets along famously with Darrin. At home, Darrin is so miserly that the annoyed Samantha realizes he must be under a spell.

The next night, Darrin has Bigelow over to dinner; Samantha tries to zap Darrin with an extravagance spell, but it "bounces" off him and hits Bigelow, who surprises his wife by suddenly being willing to spend money. Now at odds, Darrin's stinginess puts the Bigelow account at risk, but when Mrs. Bigelow loves the change in her husband, Samantha leaves the spell on him. Bigelow wants Larry and Darrin to donate to his favorite charity; just as Darrin is about to refuse, Endora returns and restores Darrin to normal, after which he agrees to the donation: $500. Darrin worries he may now not be able to afford his gift to Samantha – the coat, which he'd already bought her himself, but didn't get a chance to reveal because of Endora's spell.

GOOD!

Has Darrin remembered the events of "Charlie Harper, Winner" (#99), where Samantha zapped up a mink coat to make Darrin look good? It would appear so; when Samantha shows him the coat she bought, he says he realizes she could "zap up the most beautiful coat in the world," even adding that he finds it gratifying she bought it on sale. When it turns out the only reason he's flustered about the coat is because he already bought it for her, the moment is as warm as the coat must be.

Darrin's extreme tightfistedness is worth the cost of laughter, but the best bit is his desire to create canned leftovers. Not to be outdone, Betty (in the welcome form of Jill Foster) gets a chance for her own comic reactions to her boss' sudden thriftiness.

Mrs. Bigelow ends up dropping another clue as to the whereabouts of Morning Glory Circle when she suggests that she and her husband should also "move to the country." If the Stephenses do live in Patterson, New York, as implied in "Soapbox Derby" (#90), then talk of the expensive commute makes sense, since Patterson is over 60 miles out of Manhattan. A small, but blank-filling reference.

WELL?

Why does Samantha have the coat shipped to the house knowing that Darrin could be home upon its arrival? If she really wants to engage in "coat-and-dagger," you'd think she'd forgo delivery and bring the coat home while Darrin is at work. Also, she makes a big fuss to Endora about the tourmaline mink trim, forgetting that Darrin already gave her a full mink coat in "The Girl With the Golden Nose" (#73).

Samantha is aghast when Darrin wants to split the cost of the Bigelow business dinner with Larry – but not for the right reason. Shouldn't any McMann & Tate business dinner be paid for by the company, not its employees? Even Larry, a partner in the firm, and its president, shouldn't be expected to pay for client dinners out of his own pocket. By the way, waste-not-want-not Darrin should be thrilled with Betty for donning the same dress she wore in "How to Fail in Business With All Kinds of Help" (#104).

Samantha seems convinced lately that she can undo other witch's spells: this is the third time in five episodes she tries to remove one, though she should know from what she told Darrin in "Hoho the Clown" (#92) that this is an impossibility. She does deem the move "half foolish and half useless," but it's a move she still makes, although she tacitly changes her mind at the last minute and attempts to add to Endora's spell, rather than remove it. The fact that Samantha's new spell bounces off Darrin confirms that the witch's exclusivity clause holds. But is Samantha hoping to compensate for Darrin's frugality in trying to give him "a triple dose of extravagance?" If not, her spell would only take him to other extreme.

When Endora removes her spell and disappears, it must be earth-shaking, because not only do Samantha and Larry shift, but Samantha's chair does, too, in addition to the adjoining table and lamp. Later, in the kitchen, a miniature Endora sits in the cupboard [much like she did in "Just One Happy Family" (#10)], but, in the wide shot, it's a doll in Endora's place. That's understandable given the effect; more confusing is that Darrin changes clothes once his company leaves, but Samantha doesn't. And, while he does learn that Endora witched him, does he ever find out Samantha zapped Bigelow? For that matter, here's hoping Samantha takes the extravagance spell off Bigelow eventually, because his newfound lavishness has made him unscrupulous. What else do you call suckering Larry and Darrin into $500 donations by telling them they're down for "five?"

OH, MY STARS!

Even if Samantha can't hear Endora talking out her latest trick on Darrin from the kitchen (note to Endora: good pranksters keep their plots to themselves), surely, while the Stephenses are on the phone, Samantha can hear Endora casting her miser spell on the other end of the line. Does Endora's spell include noise-canceling? And Samantha never wonders why Darrin suddenly switches gears after being incommunicado for 18 seconds. Had the usually sharp Samantha paid more attention, she could have nipped Darrin's chintziness in the bud before it started.

SON OF A GUN!

"No. I won't cry. He'll say I'm wasting water!" – Betty, after the bespelled Darrin scolds her for inefficient use of office products.

NO ZIP IN MY ZAP
Airdate: October 12, 1967

EPISODE
113

After a celebratory Darrin leaves to sew up the Carter Brothers Industrial Products account, Tabatha pulls Samantha's breakfast tray off the dresser. Samantha tries to clean up the mess with witchcraft but can't; when Endora sees that Samantha is unable to perform magic, she summons Dr. Bombay, who determines that Samantha's powers are dammed up from lack of use. While Bombay levitates her for treatment, Darrin discovers that the Carter account has to be finalized by M.J. Nilesmunster, a girl he jilted in high school who swore she'd get back at him. When Darrin calls to stop Samantha from buying vacation tickets his bonus would afford them, Endora picks up and says Samantha is flying. Darrin sees a fly in M.J.'s hotel room and assumes it's Samantha, and, when M.J. acts as if she's meeting Darrin for the first time, he's sure Samantha has interfered.

Despite risking a power surge, Samantha has Endora put her on solid ground when an accusatory Darrin comes home drunk. Samantha insists that her lack of powers proves she didn't witch M.J., but he doesn't believe her, especially when the piano and fireplace start up on their own. After Samantha accidentally sends Darrin to a bar, he confronts M.J.; she admits she pretended not to know Darrin to clean their slate and apologizes for her teenaged behavior. Darrin asks forgiveness from Samantha, who hovers over the bed to complete Bombay's treatment.

GOOD!

W.C. Fields' "never work with children or animals" advice is not needed in this episode. Tabatha is adorably memorable despite only being seen in the prologue, and it looks like the fly really is buzzing around Darrin (albeit through manipulation), which can't have been easy to pull off. Even the abrupt edit before Darrin turns around with the fly on his nose doesn't take away from the otherwise marvelous effect.

Has Darrin-as-drunk been studying Dick Wilson's stable of inebriates? From Darrin's claim that he only had "tee martoonis" to his imitation of the fly, these moments are anything but sober. And it's amusing that Samantha knows Darrin well enough to know he'd up in a bar, with or without magic.

The "madhouse" resulting from the burst "dam" of Samantha's powers makes for an entertainingly zany scene. Fireplaces and player pianos may not be funny in and of themselves, but Samantha's uncontrollable magic – and the Stephenses' reaction to it – not only provides humor, but an intriguing look at what happens when a witch suppresses her powers.

WELL?

Darrin wakes Samantha at 6:30 because he can't wait to tell her that Carter Brothers bought his concept. Where is this industrial company, Europe? No local company would do business this early in the day. Then, Darrin leaves for the office, and Morning Glory Circle is full of pedestrians – at 6:30 in the morning.

When Darrin mentions that the Carter deal went like magic, he briefly questions if Samantha contributed any. That's the kind of suspicion he exhibited all through Seasons One and Two; he knows his wife better by now, though Samantha's "It's a fine time for my powers to get clogged up" comment after Darrin reports trouble with the account may be enough to substantiate his suspicion.

The only time a piano has ever graced the Stephenses' living room was in "The Short Happy Circuit of Aunt Clara" (#83) – until now, when Samantha needs the instrument to be there for the magical chaos that ensues later. Then, when Endora conjures up Dr. Bombay, her hands are high in a two-shot, but they're out in front of her when the scene cuts to a wide shot. And Bombay shouldn't sass Samantha – doesn't he know the Queen of the Witches has no powers? Maybe he doesn't, because Samantha's royal role has only been addressed once since "Long Live the Queen" (#108).

Endora is horrified at the thought of Samantha being earthbound, yet she lobbied to make Clara, her own sister, exactly that in "The Trial and Error of Aunt Clara" (#95). Wires show at Samantha's feet as Bombay floats her to the ceiling, where she stays until Endora brings her down. It seems Bombay should be the only one who can cancel his flotation remedy – after all, he's the doctor.

This isn't the first time Darrin and Larry make the assumption that a female client is male: in "The Catnapper" (#71), Darrin thought Toni Devlin was a man until he met her. Would Darrin really divulge his very personal back history with M.J. at full volume in two crowded elevators? Not to mention, the McMann & Tate hallway and elevator look completely different than in previous episodes.

Darrin grabs M.J.'s hotel phone to call Samantha, even though M.J. is on the line with her home office. Her phone doesn't seem to have multiple lines, since Darrin doesn't select one – by picking up the receiver, isn't he cutting into M.J.'s call?

Darrin should have a sense of déjà vu as he tries to make conversation with what he thinks is Samantha-as-fly – in "The Cat's Meow" (#18), he thought Samantha was a spying kitty. Given Darrin makes a fool of himself talking to the fly in front of Larry and M.J., you'd think she would ask Darrin about it when he returns to confront her, but she doesn't. As the former sweethearts resolve things, Darrin is cold sober. Yet, he was three sheets to the wind when he came home, and downed another drink at the bar Samantha popped him into. How did he sober up so fast?

OH, MY STARS!

Samantha sheepishly admits to Bombay that she has not been practicing her "day-to-day witchcraft," which he cites as the reason for her power clog. That's not possible – Samantha has used her powers in every episode since "Oedipus Hex" (#85), so they should be humming right along.

Darrin states that he and M.J. dated in high school. "I, Darrin, Take This Witch, Samantha" (#1) revealed that Darrin is from Missouri, a fact he confirmed when he reported attending Missouri University in "Your Witch Is Showing" (#20). Logic therefore dictates that Darrin also went to high school in Missouri, so M.J. would have had to as well. They shared classes in the same Missouri town and both ended up in New York? Granted, M.J. is traveling from an undetermined location, but the one-time lovebirds running into each other this way is a tad coincidental.

SON OF A GUN!

"If you need me, just light a match near his breath. I'll see the flames." – Endora to Samantha, commenting on Darrin's drunken state before popping out.

The various demonstrations of Samantha's power failures take magic to a new, unpredictable level of fun. The only other time Samantha had to do without her witchcraft was in "Take Two Aspirins And Half A Pint of Porpoise Milk" (#42), and her powers weren't even as erratic then.

BIRDIES, BOGIES, AND BAXTER
Airdate: October 19, 1967

EPISODE
114

Darrin has been preparing for a golf game with sporting goods client Joe Baxter, who will award his account to the agency based on whether Darrin makes a good showing. Endora feels that Darrin will be insufferable if he can once again achieve the college game he's shooting for, so Endora restores it. When Darrin brags to Larry about his improvement, Larry worries that he will try to beat expert golfer Baxter. As the big game begins, Baxter's wife, Margaret, wishes "some Sunday golfer" would best her braggart husband just once, making Samantha think.

Larry warns Darrin that his enthusiasm is annoying Baxter, who becomes even more irritated when Samantha augments Darrin's golfing with witchcraft. Although Baxter tries to unnerve Darrin, and Larry outright sabotages him, Samantha's magical additions keep Darrin on track. Baxter becomes so rattled that he misses an easy shot and loses, prompting him to hurl his golf clubs into the pool. Larry fires Darrin, and Baxter refuses to give McMann & Tate his account until Margaret pulls rank as owner of the sporting goods company, offering to set Darrin up in his own agency; Baxter realizes he's being a poor loser and relents. Later, at home, Darrin declares he's turning pro, but when Samantha admits she magically helped his game, he smiles that he already knows. After Darrin is glad Samantha taught Baxter a lesson, Samantha feels entitled to twitch on her coat.

GOOD!

From the moment Margaret Baxter mouths along to the umpteenth telling of Joe's football accomplishment [she ought to have coffee with Cynthia Pennybaker from "I Remember You…Sometimes" (#97); they could swap stories about their know-it-all hubbies], it's clear she isn't your typical client's wife. "Maggie" sasses Baxter, crosses her fingers that he'll lose (which he does, hilariously throwing his clubs into the pool), and turns the tables on his impulsive advertising decision by reminding him he's only in business because of her father's money. Margaret and Samantha have a nice rapport, too; since Samantha has no other friends besides Louise, Margaret would make a nice permanent addition to her circle.

Crafting magical effects outdoors has to be exponentially harder than doing them in a controlled studio, so the show deserves a pat on the back for the golfing goodies. Darrin's ball landing on the green, then rolling into the hole (once out of a can) is a hole-in-one for the special effects department.

When Darrin realizes that the crazy antics of the ball aren't a result of his own efforts, he sets Samantha up to believe he wants to become a professional golfer, and follows with a deadpan "Oh, really?" when Samantha confesses to fixing his game. Both plot developments are master strokes, as is Darrin *not* blowing his top. No wonder she zaps her coat on – and it's good continuity to see her wearing the one she received in "Cheap, Cheap" (#112), considering all the hassle surrounding it.

WELL?

Samantha and Endora chat at a normal volume while Darrin dozes at the kitchen table. How does he sleep through this entire pre-sunrise conversation? And how do mother and daughter know so much about golf? Samantha's lived like a mortal for three years; perhaps she's picked up an understanding of the game. But Endora, who pays little attention to anything non-witch, somehow has enough of a working knowledge of golf that she can cast a spell based on it. Samantha must be paying attention to mortal sports, because she also throws football terminology around with Margaret as if it's a second language.

Up before dawn, Darrin tells Samantha that his game with Baxter is in a couple of days. That afternoon, he and Baxter state their game is tomorrow. Which is it? And it seems Larry was being facetious when he told Darrin that golf gives him hives in "Double Split" (#64), because he isn't allergic to this fairway. Louise visiting her mother is a plausible explanation for Kasey Rogers not being in the episode, but if Louise is out of town, who's minding Jonathan while Larry's on the golf course? Did Louise take their son with her? And who's sitting with Tabatha?

Larry is never far from the Stephenses or the Baxters on the links. So how is it no one sees him plopping Darrin's ball into a can, or stomping it into a sandtrap? His footprints are clearly visible, but no one notices them – not to mention, all the mortals just accept it at face value when Darrin's ball rolls in some very bizarre directions.

That pool is getting to be almost as familiar as the McMann & Tate set. This is the swimming area's fifth different locale; it was first seen in "We're In For A Bad Spell" (#39), and most recently in "Bewitched, Bothered, and Infuriated" (#105). Is this the only pool the show has access to?

Larry tells Baxter that McMann hired Darrin, which offers a glimpse of Darrin's history at McMann & Tate, even though Larry could be lying to save face. But why doesn't Larry react when Margaret offers to establish The Darrin Stephens Agency? He worked himself into such a frenzy over the mere thought of Darrin going into business for himself in "Toys in Babeland" (#109) that he took cues from a mute, humanized toy soldier.

Samantha cutely zaps on her coat at the end of the episode with a "So sue me – it was worth it!" This isn't the first time she's uttered the sentence, though – she also did after floating Darrin's hat onto his head in "It Shouldn't Happen to a Dog" (#3).

OH, MY STARS!

This is a great episode if you're a fan of golf – but if you're not, the proceedings can get a little tedious. It's easy to get lost in the heavy amount of golf jargon, and the show spends an unprecedented 14 minutes of its 25-minute running time on the links. Plus, it's curious that securing the Baxter account is solely dependent on Darrin's skill. This is business. Baxter likes Darrin's presentation. That should be enough.

Endora thinks she'll stir up trouble by giving Darrin back his college game. Darrin fulfills her prediction by becoming cocky, but it seems out of character, and it isn't even part of the spell. Then, Samantha, who has no idea Endora already amped up Darrin's game, adds her own improvements. So what is the point of Endora casting her spell in the first place? Samantha could just witch the ball on her own; Endora's spell has no real repercussions, and no one ever finds out about it, anyway.

SON OF A GUN!

"Darrin, it's only money. And what do we need with money? Two poets like you and me?" – Larry, coaxing Darrin to let Baxter win their golf game.

THE SAFE AND SANE HALLOWEEN
Airdate: October 26, 1967

EPISODE 115

Darrin worries when Samantha reads Tabatha a mortal Halloween story; his concern turns out to be valid when Tabatha brings its gremlin, goblin, and jack-o'-lantern to life. After the creatures crawl out of Tabatha's window to follow the young witch trick-or-treating, Samantha invites them to join her. The gremlin puts a goatee on a woman and floats a man's bowl of candy to Tabatha; Samantha thinks her daughter is to blame and shoos the child's "friends" away. Samantha takes Tabatha home, where she discovers the altered book. Unable to zap the spooks back into it, Samantha goes in search of them, not realizing Gladys' nephew, Tommy, is dressed identically to the jack-o'-lantern. Mischievous Tommy switches places with it and is ultimately popped to Samantha's, while the jack-o'-lantern terrifies Gladys with its floating head.

The gremlin puts a tail on Larry, and donkey ears on Darrin; after Samantha explains the creatures' origin to Darrin, she discovers the mortal Tommy among them. The gremlin turns Tommy into a goat just as Gladys barges in looking for him; Gladys shows the goat to Larry, but he denies seeing it after Samantha changes Tommy back. Samantha convinces Tabatha to return the spooks to the book for Darrin's sake, and the vanishing jack-o'-lantern makes Larry give up alcohol. At bedtime, Darrin's afraid that Tabatha has zapped a bear out of a different book until he sees a stuffed version in her crib; little does he know, Tabatha's hidden the real bear in the closet.

GOOD!

Tabatha finally gets a Halloween! Perhaps she was too little in "Twitch or Treat" (#81), which focused solely on the adults; here, Samantha says it's her first time trick-or-treating as well, so she must have gotten over the discomfort she had with the ritual in "Trick or Treat" (#43). Samantha's right: Endora *would* have a fit, as she had in that episode, and it's mentioned that Endora hides out in the South of France on Halloween, which confirms what was originally established in "The Witches Are Out" (#7).

There's also an interesting parallel to "The Moment of Truth" (#76): Louise's contention that Larry will "celebrate anything" vibes with Mr. Tate's partying attitude in that episode, and he also swears off alcohol after his Halloween with the Stephenses, as he did before. [Louise might not want to trust that promise – Larry also briefly went on the wagon in "Toys in Babeland" (#109).]

In a subtle moment of "the show must go on," Elizabeth Montgomery spills a drink on herself as Samantha rushes to greet the Tates, but continues the scene as if nothing happened; the unscripted moment rather adds to how harried Samantha is supposed to be.

This episode contains two fascinating twists: Larry actually being able to substantiate one of Gladys' claims (though he retracts it later), and Darrin allowing Tabatha to keep a stuffed bear she zapped up because it's "a step in the right direction." Darrin choosing not to fume about the trouble Tabatha causes shows an awful lot of love for his magical daughter.

WELL?

The Kravitz-Gruber clan must be huge, because this is the fourth different nephew Gladys has hosted over the course of the series. In "Little Pitchers Have Big Fears" (#6), it was Floyd, Gladys irritated Endora with nephew Edgar in "Baby's First Paragraph" (#62), "Soapbox Derby" (#90) found Leroy "Flash" Kravitz competing for a scholarship, and here, Tommy gets pulled into the witchy doings. Why not just bring the same nephew back every time for consistency, or make it part of the joke that Gladys always has a different nephew?

When Darrin tells Samantha he can't go trick-or-treating because Larry is coming over, Samantha understandingly smiles that "business is business." Except no business is ever conducted – Larry and Louise just stop by and have a few drinks. Outside, Samantha watches Tabatha as the gremlin waves his arm to open and close a man's door and float a bowl of candy to her. So why does Samantha think Tabatha is responsible for witching her neighbors?

What stories Tommy will have for Aunt Gladys when he gets home: not only does he witness the gremlin zapping a tail on Larry and donkey ears on Darrin, he sees Samantha remove them and hears her speak openly about Tabatha's wishcraft. Maybe Tommy forgets about more than being a goat when Samantha changes him back.

It's amazing the Tates aren't cluing to the witchcraft going on around them. Aside from Larry and Louise being told Samantha is a witch [in "That Was My Wife" (#31) and "Double Split" (#64), respectively], this is the second Halloween they've come over and seen strange things [see "Trick or Treat" (#43)]. Gladys has also rushed in making strange claims both times the Tates have encountered her [in "The Short Happy Circuit of Aunt Clara" (#83) and "Nobody But A Frog Knows How to Live" (#106)]; surely two and two should equal four by now. And, it's strangely ironic that Gladys is worried about Samantha turning Tommy into a frog after all her dealings with frogs in "Nobody But A Frog Knows How to Live" (#106).

To convince Tabatha to return the creatures to the book, Samantha makes a speech about the magical life – and it's almost word-for-word what she said to her daughter in "Nobody's Perfect" (#75). Tabatha hasn't been getting the message; maybe Samantha's repeating it for emphasis?

The Stephenses are not far from their daughter's nursery, yet they don't hear all the stomping around from the creatures playing Ring Around the Rosie, nor do they hear a full-sized bear roaring. You'd think they'd come running to see if their daughter is in danger. It's also interesting that Tabatha gets both a stuffed bear and the real thing as a result of witching the second book. Does she simply not have her spell right the first time?

OH, MY STARS!

Nowadays, a lot of trick-or-treating is done before sunset, but this wasn't typically the case in the '60s. That being said, the day-for-night shots during Tabatha's candy collecting don't really put the eve in All Hallows' Eve. Also, the '60s might have been a more genteel time, but if three costumed figures you didn't recognize started following your preschooler around on Halloween, would you smile and let them trick-or-treat with her? Probably not – but Samantha does. That should be the first indicator of trouble, because Tabatha doesn't have friends. The only other kid she's been near since she was born is Jonathan Tate, and he's nowhere to be found while his parents party without him on Morning Glory Circle. Why not have Louise take the boy trick-or-treating with Samantha and Tabatha?

Tommy in the exact same costume as a jack-o'-lantern that comes from a book is enough of a stretch. But how is it possible for Tabatha's creatures to have powers? The only way that can happen is if Tabatha were to endow them with magic herself – which goes further beyond wishcraft than merely zapping them out of her storybook. And, if Samantha is unable to send Tabatha's "friends" back into it, she shouldn't be able to undo their magical mischief, either.

SON OF A GUN!

"For that, you don't need a costume." – Abner to his nephew Tommy, who says he would rather be a monster than a jack-o'-lantern.

OUT OF SYNC, OUT OF MIND
Airdate: November 2, 1967

EPISODE 116

Samantha and Darrin enjoy a leisurely lunch until Phyllis arrives in a taxi. Samantha magically speeds herself up to clean the kitchen, and Darrin listens as Phyllis announces she has walked out on Frank. Suddenly, Aunt Clara arrives in the fireplace, so the Stephenses decide to show home movies of Tabatha to keep everyone occupied. When Darrin can't get the film and its sound to match up, Aunt Clara casts a spell to fix it, which throws Samantha's voice off sync instead. Darrin tries and fails to usher his mother out of the house, so Samantha pretends to be sick while Aunt Clara fetches Dr. Bombay.

Phyllis is rattled by the doctor, who concocts a potion that cures Samantha's voice but covers her face in green stripes. The shocked Phyllis darts out the door in time to see Frank pulling up; as she tries to convince her estranged husband that Samantha has stripes, Bombay retracts his cure, which puts Samantha out of sync again. Aunt Clara remembers her spell and returns Samantha to normal just as Darrin's parents walk in. Phyllis, who thought Frank was having an affair, agrees that she's imagining things, and the couple leaves when Darrin gets stuck on a business call – but the call is just a cover, because now it's Darrin's voice that's out of sync.

GOOD!

The "home movie" with Samantha and Tabatha adds a dash of realism to the Stephenses' home life, plus presents Tabatha from a different perspective. It's also a clever twist to have Samantha grab the surgical mask out of Tabatha's toy nurse kit to camouflage her out-of-sync voice.

When Dr. Bombay readies to take Samantha's pulse, he commands her to put her leg up, then says, "Watch out" – which makes sense, if you happen to follow the trajectory of Samantha's knee. One gets the feeling Bernard Fox improvised the moment, which was kept for the episode and is quite progressive for 1967 television.

Frank Stephens strolls up the walk of 1164 Morning Glory Circle with a different face and body type – he's now in the guise of Roy Roberts. Whatever the reason Robert F. Simon didn't continue in the role, Roberts' Frank blends seamlessly into the show's framework, and even seems to bear a closer resemblance to Dick York than his predecessor.

WELL?

It's hard to believe Darrin is still asking Samantha if she's using her powers to benefit him – in this case, to zap up a lunch. He just wanted to know if Samantha manipulated his business deal in "No Zip in My Zap" (#113). She does indulge herself in a speed-up spell to clean the kitchen for his mother, and it's not the first time: she employed the same trick to tidy the living room for Louise in "...And Something Makes Three" (#12).

In "A Nice Little Dinner Party" (#19), Phyllis stated that she and Frank had been married 40 years; by now, it's been forty-three. Here, Phyllis laments Frank's lack of respect after being married 35 years. Phyllis isn't completely wrong to suspect Frank of having an affair – in the aforementioned episode, he showed a distinct interest in Endora, which surfaced again in "It's Wishcraft" (#103).

Samantha prepares to keep her magical relatives away in reaction to Phyllis' sudden arrival – but no one's worried about Tabatha, who just caused all kinds of havoc with her wishcraft in "The Safe and Sane Halloween" (#115). And Phyllis sees Aunt Clara disheveled after her slide down the chimney anyway, so why doesn't Samantha wait to neaten her aunt until she can do it privately? The touch-up zap makes Phyllis more suspicious than anything Aunt Clara could say, including when Clara sounds out spells, which Phyllis doesn't connect to the lady outing herself as a witch in "Samantha Meets the Folks" (#14).

The Stephenses know how Aunt Clara rolls – so why don't they stop her from casting her spell? They're lucky she doesn't end up summoning the Lumière Brothers, who perfected the movie projector. By the way, how is it Aunt Clara can witch Samantha with her sync spell at all? You'd think it would only affect Darrin, since he's mortal.

Aunt Clara has gone shoeless before: in "The Trial and Error of Aunt Clara" (#95), the witch disappeared without her footwear after being dared by Endora to pop out. Speaking of popping, Dr. Bombay doesn't need to be zapped up this time, unlike his first two appearances; if anything, Aunt Clara has to go to him. When Darrin is told Bombay is coming, he calls the doctor a quack. How can Darrin make that determination? He never saw Bombay treating Samantha in "No Zip in My Zap" (#113), and the only reason Dr. Bombay's Cold Bombs caused side effects in "There's Gold in Them Thar Pills" (#107) was because they weren't intended for mortals. Finally, Samantha says that Bombay is their only choice.

What happened to Dr. Agrafor, the other witch doctor Endora mentioned in "There's Gold in Them Thar Pills" (#107)?

Samantha should have a déjà vu as she stares at herself in the mirror (there's never been one in the foyer until now): her face was covered with square green spots in "Take Two Aspirins and Half A Pint of Porpoise Milk" (#42). Now it's stripes.

Where's the Kravitz house? When Frank pulls up, there's nothing but a wall of trees across the street where houses should be. And how did Darrin sneak off to the den without his parents noticing he's off sync? Frank and Phyllis walk in as soon as Aunt Clara restores Samantha's voice, so the next thing Darrin says would come out later. Did Darrin stay silent until he happened to be out of earshot of his parents? Not likely.

OH, MY STARS!

The elder Stephenses seem to live nearby, since Phyllis takes a cab to her son's house, and Frank drives there in his car. Yet, as Darrin's parents leave, Phyllis tells Samantha to write to her. So where do they live? This residential back-and-forth has been going on since their first appearance in "Samantha Meets the Folks" (#14).

If Aunt Clara and Dr. Bombay know each other to the point he mixes up a batch of Cure-All every time her spells misfire, then where was he in "Take Two Aspirins and Half A Pint of Porpoise Milk" (#42), where Aunt Clara had to cure Samantha herself? It's not like Bombay has been around for any of Aunt Clara's many goofs these last three years. Furthermore, it's peculiar that any witch's spell can be removed by a doctor's potion. Hasn't it already been established that only the witch who casts a spell can remove it? [See "Hoho the Clown" (#92).]

SON OF A GUN!

"Well, you have a choice: green stripes or out of sync. What do you want?" – Dr. Bombay to the Stephenses, after his Super Cure-All doesn't.

THAT WAS NO CHICK, THAT WAS MY WIFE

EPISODE 117

Airdate: November 9, 1967

When Larry sticks the unwilling Stephenses with a weekend business trip to Chicago for the Springer Pet Food account, Samantha installs Aunt Clara to babysit. As Springer waxes poetic about birdseed, Tabatha turns her stuffed monkey into a real one. Samantha hears about it when she calls home, so she pops in to make sure Tabatha turns it back – but Louise arrives and catches her in the living room. Samantha laughs that she stayed behind while Darrin went on to Chicago; Louise runs straight to Larry with the news. Larry scrambles to explain things to Springer, who thinks Darrin has brought a mistress to their meeting and severs ties with McMann & Tate.

The Stephenses return home, and Larry fires Darrin on the spot. Samantha and Tabatha accompany Darrin to the office to clean out his desk, where they run into Springer, who sees that Darrin's wife and "mistress" are one and the same. The Stephenses tell Springer – and Larry – that an ad exec's personal life isn't as important as the job he can do, an attitude Springer admires. Darrin goes back on the payroll, but Larry sends Louise to a psychiatrist for having seen Samantha at home. Samantha calls on Serena to pose as her twin and make sense of everything for Louise; later, "Samantha" tries to plant a kiss on Darrin, who sees through the ruse.

GOOD!

Aunt Clara is more lovable than usual in this episode, from her claim that she "zigged when [she] should have zagged," to her befuddled reaction when Tabatha's monkey crawls into her arms. And for once, it's not Clara's magic that's causing the trouble.

When "Samantha" asks for her good morning kiss, Darrin smacks her bottom and tells her not to try it again. Samantha must have told him her cousin was stopping by, but it still shows smarts that he knows the difference between them after his interaction with Serena in "Double, Double...Toil And Trouble" (#111).

WELL?

For some reason, the audio in most of this installment's wide shots sounds cavernous, as if the boom mics aren't anywhere near the actors. It wouldn't be worth mentioning if it were only one scene, but it's consistent throughout.

Darrin worries about Aunt Clara sitting for Tabatha, but, after the events of "Toys in Babeland" (#109) and "The Safe and Sane Halloween" (#115), Darrin should be far more concerned about his daughter; Tabatha does, in fact, turn a toy into a living being here, as she did in the former episode. And while it's sweet of Louise to come by and check on Tabatha, where's her own child? Jonathan might as well be raised by Tabatha's monkey for as often as his parents are seen with him.

Samantha has shoved Louise out the door before: in "The Corn Is As High As A Guernsey's Eye" (#94), it was in reaction to Louise seeing a cow in her living room. Louise is shocked to see Samantha, who's supposed to be out of town, but doesn't she wonder why Samantha is wearing her hat in the house?

The Tates have done some remodeling; their den, which was almost identical to the Stephenses' in "Sam in the Moon" (#91), now sports a much more elegant look. And Springer automatically assumes that Darrin has a mistress in tow – but suppose Samantha were sick, and Darrin simply brought a friend to pose as his wife because he knows how important family is to Springer? The client's reaction is a little extreme, but no less than Larry's – he's already fired Darrin twice this season. Finally, why doesn't Samantha tell Darrin what happened with Tabatha when he asks why she popped home? Surely he'd understand there was a crisis; leaving that out makes Samantha's check-in seem frivolous.

Either the McMann & Tate building moves around a lot, or its environs get changed frequently – the street looks completely different than it has in previous seasons; it's now more like a quaint downtown than the middle of Manhattan.

Samantha takes a big risk telling Springer that she and Darrin "created that little misunderstanding" on purpose to gauge Springer's reaction. Yet, when Darrin takes her ball and runs with it, she appears surprised as he adds that the agency doesn't have time for clients who pry into their employee's lives, which is what Samantha was leading up to. Perhaps the bigger surprise is that both Springer and Larry buy the explanation.

The split screen effect of Samantha and Serena in the kitchen is generally very good – however, if you hone in on the swinging door as Samantha enters, it looks as if it's folding in on itself. Serena should be getting tired of her relatives changing her into Samantha – Endora just effected that transformation in "Double, Double...Toil and Trouble" (#111), though Serena is a witch, and therefore can turn herself into

Samantha without assistance. Speaking of mirror images, Serena zaps up the same mirror that suddenly had a place in the Stephenses' foyer in "Out of Sync, Out of Mind" (#116).

Louise is upset at the prospect of going to see a psychiatrist – but in "I'd Rather Twitch Than Fight" (#84), it came out that both she and Larry were visiting Dr. Kramer regularly. Is Kramer the one who loses money when Serena solves Louise's doubles problem? Later, Darrin asks "Samantha" who was at the door, when he had to know Louise was on her way over. And Serena's taste for mortals must be recent – she tries to kiss Darrin here, but, in "And Then There Were Three" (#54), she thought Darrin was coming on to her, and couldn't get away fast enough.

OH, MY STARS!

When the doorbell rings, Samantha commands Aunt Clara, "Remember, I'm not here!" in full volume. Wouldn't a hushed tone be safer? Better yet, Samantha has finished her business with Aunt Clara and Tabatha – so why not just pop back to Chicago before Clara opens the door to Louise? Samantha could have prevented the whole mess, plus she should know not to risk this kind of exposure after having already created the same situation with Larry in the similarly titled "That Was My Wife" (#31).

SON OF A GUN!

"Louise? Dropped by? In the phone booth?" – Darrin, trying to understand how Samantha could have been spotted.

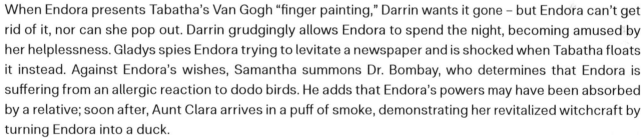

ALLERGIC TO ANCIENT MACEDONIAN DODO BIRDS
Airdate: November 16, 1967

EPISODE
118

When Endora presents Tabatha's Van Gogh "finger painting," Darrin wants it gone – but Endora can't get rid of it, nor can she pop out. Darrin grudgingly allows Endora to spend the night, becoming amused by her helplessness. Gladys spies Endora trying to levitate a newspaper and is shocked when Tabatha floats it instead. Against Endora's wishes, Samantha summons Dr. Bombay, who determines that Endora is suffering from an allergic reaction to dodo birds. He adds that Endora's powers may have been absorbed by a relative; soon after, Aunt Clara arrives in a puff of smoke, demonstrating her revitalized witchcraft by turning Endora into a duck.

While Endora purposely annoys Darrin, Aunt Clara turns Morning Glory Circle into a harbor, which Samantha restores before Gladys can show it to Abner. Endora won't leave until her magic comes back, prompting Darrin to walk out, but Samantha zaps him out of a bar so they can work together to pinpoint what's behind Endora's illness. After Samantha expresses doubt that a dodo could sap Endora's powers, Tabatha comes downstairs with the extinct animal, which she has wishcrafted out of a book. After Endora is cured with a potion Bombay brews using one of the bird's feathers, Samantha has to retrieve the once again impaired Aunt Clara from the roof, which Gladys observes. Darrin apologizes to Endora, and Samantha suggests that Darrin would rather have Endora as a witch than a mortal.

GOOD!

Usually, Darrin's suspiciousness comes off a bit grating, but, knowing Endora, his daughter *could* be at the Venice Film Festival. And Gladys is right – the floating newspaper provides proof of Tabatha's abilities. Can Gladys can use it to justify future sightings?

It turns out Endora doesn't need her powers to torment Darrin. Seeming helpless to the point that Darrin stomps off the patio, her self-satisfied smile says it all. Darrin suggests a home for senior citizens, saying, "When you're as senior a citizen as she must be, they're sure to give her the best room in the house." That's accurate – as far back as "Mother Meets What's-His-Name" (#4), Endora admitted knowing Diogenes, which makes her at least 2,000 years old. And Dr. Bombay is on hand to accurately remind everyone that Samantha lost her powers a few weeks earlier [in "No Zip in My Zap" (#113)].

Even if Darrin's episode-ending apology is a set-up for an insult, there's still a strange sincerity in it. It's just one of clever nuances sprinkled throughout this installment: Darrin looking around for birds when Bombay first mentions the allergy, Endora frowning at her thermometer, then grasping Darrin in fear of the dodo – these unspoken details add layer upon layer to this outstanding episode.

WELL?

If you're an *I Dream of Jeannie* fan, you'll notice that the sound effect accompanying Endora's attempt to blank Tabatha's Van Gogh is the same one used when Jeannie's sister blinks – Sunset Editorial created sounds for both shows. Now, "Hoho the Clown" (#92) established that a witch has "squatter's rights" to the spells she casts – yet Samantha zaps away Endora/Tabatha's portrait and gets rid of Aunt Clara's harbor.

Endora asks Samantha how she'd feel if she lost her powers, knowing full well her daughter just did in "No Zip in My Zap" (#113). Samantha forgets, too, later asking Darrin how he'd feel if she lost her powers. And Endora's hilarious helplessness is inconsistent with the Endora presented during Season One: in "Mother Meets What's-His-Name" (#4), Endora stated that just because she didn't want to cook the mortal way, it didn't mean she didn't know how. Here, she can't even pour coffee.

As Bombay listens to Endora's foot for a pulse, Samantha tells Darrin, "You should see our specialists" – except, in "Out of Sync, Out of Mind" (#116), Samantha said that Bombay was a witch's only medical choice. Later, when Bombay concludes Endora's powers could be absorbed by a relative, Endora looks at Darrin. Funny, but Bombay also stipulates the relative has to be a witch or warlock, and Endora would be the first to say Darrin doesn't fit that description. Samantha and Endora express shock at Dr. Bombay's diagnosis, but it's Samantha's voice coming out of Endora's mouth when she says, "Birds?" Finally, Endora's rib-ticking struggle with the coffee pot culminates in her grasping the pot itself, yet she doesn't get burned.

Aunt Clara's "moment of infinite glory" borrows from a few of her previous episodes. The spell she uses to conjure up her feast contains the phrase *tootles, flick* – in "Accidental Twins" (#78), she uttered *tootle fleck* trying to make a toy for Jonathan Tate. Also, Aunt Clara's wardrobe gets an upgrade along with her powers, except her hat is not new: Samantha bought it for her in "The Corn Is As High As A Guernsey's Eye" (#94). Why does Samantha think Aunt Clara "stole" Endora's powers? Was she not listening when Bombay explained that Endora's powers had gone into limbo and were subject to absorption?

Abner again wants to send Gladys to a psychiatrist. Did they give up so easily on Dr. Passmore, the head shrinker Gladys visited in "And Then She Wrote" (#45)?

Darrin is apparently in such a hurry to ditch Endora that he goes from walking off the patio to slamming the front door in two seconds flat. And what happened when Samantha zapped Darrin out of the bar with a beer in his hand? Does he ever go back and pay his bill? Tabatha hasn't learned her lesson from zapping creatures out of a book in "The Safe And Sane Halloween" (#115), because she does the same thing here with the dodo bird, which she stashes in the closet. Did the Stephenses ever find the bear Tabatha hid there in that episode? As for the bird, it's up there for two days. How is Tabatha feeding it? And does Samantha have a...mess to clean up on the closet floor?

Witch cures and feathers must go together – in "Take Two Aspirins and Half A Pint of Porpoise Milk" (#42), an ostrich feather was required for Aunt Clara's potion. It's amazing Bombay's cure works; he specifically says to stir "gently so as not to bruise," yet Endora whisks it the potion vigorously.

OH, MY STARS!

Darrin, who was seemingly over making the prejudicial remarks of the first two seasons, reverts to type here with a joke about Endora flying "past a warlock with six warts on his nose." Also, Aunt Clara turning the neighborhood into a harbor goes rather adrift. Gladys looks across the street and sees only water – where are the other houses, including 1164 Morning Glory Circle? What happens to traffic? Pedestrians? Does no one but Samantha and Gladys notice? Samantha restores the street, but only after Abner gets up and starts for the window; he should be able to see the transformation. And, when Samantha conspicuously appears on the roof to retrieve her aunt instead of quietly zapping her off it, the duo casts shadows on the "sky."

SON OF A GUN!

"It's heavy..." – Endora, after trying to lift a coffee pot the mortal way.

Samantha mentioning black Peruvian roses may seem like a trivial detail, but what continuity: the flower rendered Samantha powerless in "Take Two Aspirins and Half A Pint of Porpoise Milk" (#42).

Agnes Moorehead carries this exceptional episode in one *tour de force* moment after another. Endora's whole demeanor changes as soon as she realizes she's powerless – and from there it's an Endora that's never been seen before. Marion Lorne also gets to let loose as a powerful Aunt Clara. "No, watch it," she warns after turning Endora into a duck. [Revenge for trying to declare her earthbound in "The Trial and Error of Aunt Clara" (#95)?] But even that can't compare to the usually self-deprecating witch sashaying through the kitchen declaring, "I'm a swinger, and I like to swing." Erin Murphy does a little scene-stealing as well, merrily 'fessing up about Bobby the Bird.

SAMANTHA'S THANKSGIVING TO REMEMBER
Airdate: November 23, 1967

EPISODE
119

As Samantha prepares Thanksgiving dinner, Aunt Clara shows up in the fireplace. Darrin reluctantly listens as Aunt Clara reminisces about the first Thanksgiving, which she attended. Deciding to pop herself to Plymouth, Aunt Clara accidentally takes Samantha, Darrin, Tabatha, and the eavesdropping Gladys with her. Stuck in 1621, Samantha zaps everyone into appropriate clothes, and "translates" when John Alden invites them to dinner. All goes well except for Darrin's anachronistic speech, which alerts Phineas, a man who advocates burning witches. After warning Samantha, Darrin helps the women light a fire with matches he'd used in the fireplace back home; Phineas sees this and accuses Darrin of being a witch.

Darrin is put on trial, where he clumsily tries to explain matches to his accusers. When Phineas' words nearly condemn Darrin, Samantha steps in to defend her husband, demonstrating how easy it is to cry witch to cover human failings and making a plea for the acceptance of differences. Unconvinced, Phineas deems the match a device of witchery, so Samantha dares him to light it, providing a magical assist since it's already been lit. Darrin is freed just as Aunt Clara remembers how to zap everyone home; still in her Pilgrim clothes, Gladys runs home to show Abner, but Samantha pops her back into her own contemporary dress before she gets there. During Thanksgiving dinner, Aunt Clara suggests making plans to take Tabatha to the North Pole to meet Santa Claus.

GOOD!

Aunt Clara telling Tabatha that the first Thanksgiving was a blast is exactly that. Can't you just see a younger Clara feasting among the Pilgrims? She also has enough self-awareness to tell the Stephenses "I know what you're thinking" when she wants to try for a trip to Plymouth.

Gladys fainting at the sight of her 17th century surroundings is an understandable reaction, but it's also a clever way to render Sandra Gould motionless as co-stars more experienced with magical merrymaking facilitate Samantha's costume change. Having Tabatha stand with her back to the camera accomplishes the same thing. It's a well-done effect, as it is when Samantha puts Darrin and Aunt Clara back their in 20th century clothes.

Darrin "speaking Pilgrim" is a highlight of this very entertaining episode. "I only wisheth to explaineth about matcheth!" he blurts out to his accusers. It makes perfect sense that a 1967 man would have trouble speaking in a way a 1621 man could understand.

WELL?

Arriving in the 17th century, Samantha reports that everyone got caught in Aunt Clara's jet stream. Amusing, but Clara's spell is specific: "Take *us* back to Plymouth town." There are people living in the house they pop into; a fire is already going, and John Alden apparently stops by to see someone, though it's never specified who.

No one really eats at this first Thanksgiving feast – maybe it's because the food's not real; the turkey and fixings Phineas drops are plastic. Darrin's anachronistic speech is nothing compared to his worrying about Samantha being a witch in the 17th century within earshot of the Plymouth patriarchy. But he can easily escape his shackles if he wants to – they're plastic, too; listen as they click together.

When everyone returns to the present, there's a marked delay in Darrin's. Why? Aunt Clara says she hopes she hasn't left Darrin out of the spell, but "take us back to whence we came" doesn't leave much room for error. Also, Tabatha is not in the Plymouth courtroom, yet she comes home in the same room as Samantha; Gladys, who *is* in the courtroom, appears in the kitchen. Gladys thinks her Pilgrim clothes will convince Abner of the trip, though he could easily say she rented them from a costume shop. Would she really think her Plymouth experience was a dream? Assuming she feasted with the Pilgrims, she'd still be full – a physical sensation that disproves she was asleep.

Aunt Clara wants to take Tabatha to the North Pole, wondering how many children "get the opportunity to meet Santa Claus." Former orphan Michael could tell her: Samantha arranged just such a meeting for him in "A Vision of Sugar Plums" (#15).

OH, MY STARS!

Aunt Clara reveals that she's going to Plymouth to visit some of the girls she knew there. Clara is almost 350 years older than them at this point, a fair span of time, even in the life of a witch – would these girls recognize her? Perhaps not, because Aunt Clara speaks to no one but her fellow travelers once in Plymouth, nor is she approached by any of the settlers that supposedly know her.

Aside from declaring "Who, her?" when Phineas cries witch, Gladys has no reason to be in Plymouth. Mrs. Kravitz was ready to out Samantha to a courtroom in "Samantha for the Defense" (#88) – she'd relish the idea of airing her witchy suspicions on this particular stand, yet all she does is follow the Stephenses around, looking confused; she should have been better integrated into this special episode.

Samantha can't zap everybody home because of Aunt Clara's time travel spell, but she is able to change their clothes and twitch a lit match into firing up. This is a different rule than was established during her first trip to the past – in "A Most Unusual Wood Nymph" (#79), Endora adamantly warned Samantha she couldn't use her powers once back in time.

In the middle of this historic feast (at which Indians are only barely present), the Plymouth colonists decide to halt all festivities and put Darrin on trial for witchcraft. Not only does this seem unlikely, but it raises an important point: the potential disruption of the timeline. Surely Darrin's trial would end up in history books, to say nothing of the early appearance of the match, which isn't supposed to be invented until 1805. Samantha rightly comments that "the big witch hysteria didn't start until much later," but what if Darrin's trial fanned those flames? If someone found Gladys' measuring cup, she could end up on trial herself (the Imperial measuring system didn't exist until 1824). And wouldn't any witch paranoia exhibited by Plymouth's populace intensify after a whole group of people disappeared? Disturbing time in stories wasn't a popular concept until the 1980s, but that doesn't mean it wouldn't be a consequence assuming time travel were possible, as it is in the *Bewitched* world.

SON OF A GUN!

"How did he greet me this morn? 'Good morrow?' 'Good day?' 'Greetings to thee?' No, no, none of these – this witch just raised his hand thusly, and spake the conjure words: 'Hi, there. Everything okay?'" – Phineas, presenting his evidence against Darrin.

Samantha's defense of Darrin to the Pilgrims is a landmark moment for the show. Not only does it shed light on the possible reasons people might have cried witch in that time, but Samantha's call for tolerance is reflective of the civil rights movement taking place when this episode was filmed. And accepting each others' differences is advice that still holds today.

SOLID GOLD MOTHER-IN-LAW
Airdate: November 30, 1967

EPISODE 120

Samantha comes home to discover that the pony Endora zapped up for Tabatha is really Darrin. After the restored Darrin hits the roof, Endora considers Samantha's plea to be nicer to him and pops a photo of herself onto Darrin's desk, which he is unable to destroy no matter how hard he tries. Larry introduces prospective client Gregson, who cherishes the idea of "the perfect American home" – when he sees Endora's picture, he is amazed that Darrin thinks so highly of his mother-in-law, and asks to meet her.

Larry bullies Darrin into a dinner; all goes well until Larry's snide remarks about his own mother-in-law infuriate Louise. After the dismayed Gregson offers to set Darrin up in his own agency, Larry thinks Darrin manipulated the situation and storms out.

Darrin stays up all night devising a campaign for Gregson, planning to give Larry credit for it – but when Larry sends Darrin's office furniture to the house, Darrin angrily decides to accept Gregson's offer and shows him his layouts, unaware that Samantha has magically added Larry's name to them. The impressed Gregson signs with McMann & Tate, and Larry is so touched that Darrin attributed the ideas to him that he suggests the agency should be McMann, Tate & Stephens – someday. When Darrin comes home and sees Tabatha on another pony, he and Endora argue – and Samantha, right back where she started, covers her ears.

GOOD!

Endora (and the writers) show a lot of imagination in this installment – her winking, floating, face-making photo is inspired. Better than that, it gives Jill Foster's Betty a chance to get in on the act: asked what she thinks of a perfume called Hallucination, she sees Endora's hovering picture, and says, "I think Hallucination is a very good name for it!"

Larry's frustration with Gregson's "perfect American home" image is valid; Gregson is overly idealistic, and Larry's "perfection is something that grows" comment is surprisingly spot-on for the somewhat shallow ad exec. As for Endora, she witnesses the blow-up between Larry and Darrin and laughs, "That's what I love about mortals. They can get themselves into such hilarious messes without my even lifting a finger to cast a spell." Humorous, yes, but it's also an astute observation about the human race.

WELL?

Samantha makes Endora apologize for turning Darrin into a pony "this morning" – but reference is made to Darrin coming home before this equine effort. Since when does Darrin come from home from work in the morning? And even if you can accept the unlikely possibility that mythical creature Pegasus entertained Samantha as a child, as Endora recalls, "Eye of the Beholder" (#22) suggested that Samantha is a few hundred years old. The Pegasus of Greek mythology dates back about 2,500 years, bringing the winged horse closer to being Endora's childhood playmate instead.

The familiar McMann & Tate hallway is back to normal after it got an unprecedented makeover in "No Zip in My Zap" (#113). Endora's photographed face should be familiar to Larry, but he doesn't register the slightest hint of recognition when he sees it. And, either Samantha's familiar appliances have carried the Gregson name all this time, or she's getting to be as slick as Larry when it comes to buttering up clients, the way she laundry lists Gregson's products.

Darrin might want to reevaluate his best friend, who regularly threatens to fire him, and follows through on it. Would you include Larry in your inner circle? If anything, Darrin ought to be walking on eggshells. Gregson isn't the first client to suggest setting Darrin up in his own firm – as recently as "Birdies, Bogies, and Baxter" (#114), Mrs. Baxter put The Darrin Stephens Agency on the table. Why does Samantha work so hard to keep Darrin at McMann & Tate, when Darrin would do well to go into business for himself? (At least for a little while – until Larry learns his lesson.) Plus, it's inconceivable that Darrin wants to give Larry credit for anything under these circumstances.

Larry may run with the ball insulting Louise's mother, but Louise throws it. Given the Tates both realize how important family is to Gregson, they should know better than to pop off in front of him. Still, if they don't, Larry can't say that his mother-in-law "practically lives with" him and Louise. Is that who's taking care of Jonathan? And, after three years, Louise finally gets her chance to kick Larry under the table: in "...And Something Makes Three" (#12), Larry showed Louise the business end of his foot trying to keep her from revealing Samantha's perceived pregnancy. Larry knows what he's talking about when he says he's amazed Louise hasn't broken his leg; in "Bewitched, Bothered, and Infuriated" (#105), Larry divulged that he had suffered that very injury ten years earlier.

Larry must have been listening when Madame Maruska suggested that Darrin become part of "McMann, Tate & Steffens" in "How to Fail in Business With All Kinds of Help" (#104), since Mr. Tate dangles that carrot here. Perhaps it's fitting that Larry wants to delay the promotion: somehow, Darrin never notices that his ideas have Larry's name all over them, even though he must open his portfolio at some point before handing it to Gregson.

So Endora zaps up the exact same pony, but Samantha doesn't hear Darrin opening and closing the front door – all so she can briefly think her mother had her married to a farm animal again.

OH, MY STARS!

Darrin's empty threats to leave Samantha should have her worried. Lately, whenever he disapproves of something witchcraft-related, he's ready to bolt. Surely he's only reacting out of anger, but this is the third time this season he's been willing to ditch the three-year-old daughter who's depending on him, which isn't making him look very good, however funny his rants are supposed to be.

SON OF A GUN!

"Not every son-in-law is as cuddly as Darr-Darr and I are." – Endora to Gregson, immediately eliciting a cringe from Darrin.

MY, WHAT BIG EARS YOU HAVE
Airdate: December 7, 1967

EPISODE
121

Darrin wants to surprise Samantha with a rocking chair, but Endora assumes he's cheating after he takes a mysterious phone call regarding it. In front of Samantha, Endora casts a spell that will make Darrin's ears grow if he lies – and they do, as soon as Samantha inquires about the lady who called. Darrin asks Gladys, who senses Darrin's ears are bigger, to take delivery of the chair; Abner responds to Gladys harassing him about Darrin's gift-giving by presenting her with a table saw he bought for himself. Neighborhood gossip Hazel spots Darrin with the pretty antique dealer, but when Darrin lies that she's a client, his ears sprout.

Hazel runs to Samantha with the news, while Darrin buys a helmet. Knowing Darrin has been lying, Samantha is indifferent about Endora's spell, though she zaps up a beehive and a beekeeper hat so Darrin can cover his ears when Larry brings a client over. Afterwards, Samantha tells Darrin that Endora will normalize his ears if he can explain his lies; Darrin brings Samantha and Endora to the Kravitzes' garage to open his carton, but Abner's table saw is inside. Endora gloats until Abner explains that the hardware store took Darrin's rocker instead of his table saw. Noticing Darrin's beekeeper hat, Abner wonders if Gladys was right about Darrin's ears; Endora removes the spell so Darrin can take the covering off. Later, Samantha is horrified when Darrin's ears are huge again, but this time, they're only fake ears from a joke shop.

GOOD!

If you're going to build an episode around one of your actor's physical attributes, this is an effective way to do it. And what's not seen is funnier than what is when Darrin wears a motorcycle helmet to cover his growing appendages. Perhaps better still is the tag, where Darrin pranks Samantha with his pointy Spock ears. If nothing else, it shows that he has a sense of humor about Endora's latest trickery.

Abner has a brief moment of wondering if Gladys has been right all these years; he would never ask Darrin to take off the beekeeper hat otherwise. Wouldn't it be a cool story arc if Abner slowly started to see the Stephenses the way Gladys does? And, while Tabatha is apparently alone in the house as Endora and the Stephenses are at the Kravitzes, Samantha reporting that Tabatha fell asleep after a lullaby goes a long way toward reminding viewers that the Stephenses are still parents.

WELL?

Is Endora getting into a rut? The last time Darrin bought a surprise gift for Samantha, Endora also magically interfered [see "Cheap, Cheap" (#112)]. This is the second transformation of Darrin's ears this season: the gremlin Tabatha zapped out of her book in "The Safe and Sane Halloween" (#115) ultimately foreshadowed this episode by giving Darrin donkey ears. And then all this fuss about the rocking chair – Samantha already has one. She miniaturized it in "Follow That Witch (Part I)" (#66), which got her in trouble with Harriet Kravitz.

It must be hard to call the Stephenses: a close-up of their phone indicates they're reachable at 555-2368, yet in "Nobody But A Frog Knows How to Live" (#106), the number was 555-2134; before that, it was always 555-7328 [see "Witch or Wife" (#8)]. As for the Kravitzes, their house was yellow in both "The Safe and Sane Halloween" (#115) and "Samantha's Thanksgiving to Remember" (#119) – here, it's brown, and the house next to it is yellow. Darrin runs over and flings open the Kravitzes' garage without asking first, but he wouldn't be able to if they still had the garage door opener they installed in "Open the Door, Witchcraft" (#28), which is apparently gone now.

Only twice so far [in "Double Tate" (#59) and "Three Wishes" (#96)] has Samantha been aware of one of Endora's spells on Darrin from the get-go. But now Endora is so blatant, she hexes Darrin with Samantha standing nearby – and Samantha doesn't put up much of a fight. It's amazing she doesn't pack her bags – she was ready to leave Darrin in "Three Wishes" (#96) with much less provocation than she has here.

Darrin shrugs when Alice Swinton, the antique dealer, sees his ears and asks if he's ever done any prize fighting. His answer should be a qualified yes: in "Fastest Gun on Madison Avenue" (#57), he did inadvertently tangle with professional boxers. It can't be easy for any actor to deliver a line, have ears attached in Make-Up, get back into the exact same position, and pick up exactly where the scene left off, so it's understandable that Darrin's ear-enlarging effects aren't always the cleanest. But something goes awry during Darrin's growth spurt in the hotel; *he* does a good job of matching, but someone moves a light, because the wall behind Darrin becomes much darker, and the glare on the painting disappears.

Apparently Larry hasn't mellowed toward Darrin since the hard line he took in the previous episode, "Solid Gold Mother-in-Law" (#120). When Darrin tells Larry he's still at home, Larry barks, "I know that, idiot!" At the house, Samantha attempts to explain that Darrin can't take off the beekeeper hat because he's allergic to bees. It might be more specific to say Darrin is allergic to bee stings, which is the actual danger. Does Samantha zap the bees back to whence they came after Larry and Grayson leave, or do the Stephenses end up with a lot of honey in their kitchen?

When Abner plays that rather cruel trick on Gladys – acting like the table saw he bought for himself is a gift for her – there's never any question he's keeping it. So why does he suddenly send it back? He only seems to so the store can take the wrong carton and make Darrin look like he's lying about the rocker. These delivery folks aren't exactly efficient – certainly they would check for information on the carton before loading it, especially if there's two of them sitting there. Then, when Abner sees that Darrin's ears are a normal size, he declares he's shipping Gladys back to the psychiatrist. Back? In "Allergic to Ancient Macedonian Dodo Birds" (#118), Abner only threatened to have Gladys' head shrunk. Has Gladys gotten back into therapy since? Or was Abner talking about sending Gladys back to Dr. Passmore, who hasn't been seen since "And Then I Wrote" (#45)?

OH, MY STARS!

Who is Hazel Carter? Having this new, oh-so-mod character appear out of nowhere just to see Darrin's ears grow, report them to Samantha, and then disappear seems superfluous. Gladys already sees two phases of Darrin's ear growth – wouldn't it be better for Gladys to spot Darrin with Alice and go from there? Then, after Darrin tells Samantha about the rocker, Endora scoffs at his claim. Why? He's still under her spell; if Darrin were lying about it, his ears would grow.

SON OF A GUN!

"Well, I ran into him at the Berkeley Hotel, and we started talking, and, well, suddenly they started to sort of – bloom." – Hazel to Samantha, explaining how she literally got an earful from Darrin.

I GET YOUR NANNY, YOU GET MY GOAT
Airdate: December 14, 1967

EPISODE
122

When Endora can't babysit, Samantha installs her former nanny, Elspeth, to watch Tabatha. Darrin resists having yet another witch in his circle, but changes his mind when Elspeth protects him from an angry Endora, who feels she's being replaced. At a fancy ball, Larry wants Darrin to meet rough-and-tumble prospective client Chappell – but, before the introduction, Endora appears with Elspeth's vengeful employer, Lord Montdrako, who glues a rose in Darrin's teeth. The Stephenses pass it off with a tango; when they get home, Elspeth explains that Montdrako has no claim on her because she resigned from his employ. Larry gives Darrin another chance to present himself as a sportsman, but Montdrako arrives and transforms Darrin into a Victorian sissy just before Chappell walks in.

Darrin gives in and fires Elspeth, but she refuses to return to Montdrako, who zaps Darrin into a mirror. Samantha realizes that Elspeth has been the only company for the lonely lord, and flies to his castle to turn it into a tourist attraction, creating an English double of herself as a guide. Montdrako balks until Samantha makes a tapestry float to scare the group; he adds some "haunted" elements of his own, attracting the attention of two amorous ladies. The happy Montdrako releases Darrin, and Elspeth convinces Chappell to accept Darrin for who he is instead of who the client wants him to be. With everything back to normal, the Stephenses kiss, with Elspeth asking, "Isn't it lovely?"

GOOD!

Leaving in Tabatha's spontaneous comment about her chicken dinner makes her all the more adorable – and Elspeth's recollection of a young Samantha also falls into that category. Their rapport is so natural, you really believe Samantha grew up with this woman. And perhaps it shouldn't be, but Elspeth eyeing Darrin and declaring, "It needs a bit of fattenin'" is elitist humor that works.

This episode provides a lesson in witch etiquette. Samantha tells Darrin that witches don't fly on brooms anymore because it's "obsolete" [that witches once did might explain why mortals still think they do, as Endora pointed out in "I, Darrin, Take This Witch, Samantha" (#1)]. Then, Elspeth prevents Endora from zapping a zipper over Darrin's mouth, saying that using witchcraft on mortals "ain't sporting."

Montdrako and his tricks put Darrin into some new situations (and clothes), and Samantha's English double is another jolly addition. The split screen effect where the real Samantha disappears and her clone crosses past the split screen line is quite impressive.

WELL?

It's *Bewitched Goes Mary Poppins*, with a bit of an additional 1964 film, *My Fair Lady*, thrown in for good measure. Elspeth even floats down with an umbrella – and why not, since Hermione Baddeley played *Mary Poppins*' maid? (Too bad the wires are so visible.) Still, she's a strange inclusion; even stranger is that the Stephenses bring Elspeth in because Aunt Clara goofs up a lot. That's never stopped them from having Clara sit with Tabatha before, has it? Elspeth smiles that she's come to stay – how does she figure? Samantha has only asked her to babysit, unless she made another deal off-screen, which she wouldn't: in "Maid to Order" (#53), Samantha specifically stated she didn't want a maid.

Endora's on a windy exit kick, having already effected two in recent memory: in "How To Fail in Business With All Kinds of Help" (#104) and "Solid Gold Mother-in-Law (#120). Darrin worries that he and Samantha will be late for the Hunt Club Ball; they must be tardy after spending so much time dealing with Elspeth and Endora, but Darrin never mentions it again. When Endora and Montdrako confront Darrin and Samantha at the ball, the footage of the Stephenses is remarkably grainy. Did the editors decide a post-production zoom-in would provide more variety?

Why does big, burly Chappell want a man's man to advertise his product? The guy makes baby food. As Larry tries to add testosterone to Darrin's office, Darrin protests, "I hate stuffed fish." Does he? Darrin was upset that he had to scrap buying new fishing equipment to get a garage door opener in "Open the Door, Witchcraft" (#28), and he told "Terry Warbell" that he engaged in the sport in "The Crone of Cawdor" (#101).

Larry must be so blinded by his desire to bag Chappell's account that he doesn't wonder how Darrin changed from the old gray flannel into his "Little Lord Fauntleroy" garb in just over a minute. Darrin waits in the supply closet for his clothes to change back, but what if they hadn't? Would he have spent the night in there?

Darrin gets zapped into a mirror that hangs in a rarely seen corner of his dining room, but there wasn't always a mirror there – in "Solid Gold Mother-in-Law" (#120), a painting occupied that spot. And before Samantha learns Montdrako has made Darrin a reflection, she exclaims, "I know you're here somewhere!" Really? Darrin could be anywhere, or disintegrated [see "Just One Happy Family" (#10)].

Isn't Samantha invading Montdrako's privacy by corralling a tour group and bringing them into his home without permission? That would be quite a shock for a hermit who isn't used to company. And strangely, Tour Guide Samantha is an expert on the castle, but Montdrako is an acquaintance, and Samantha's double would only know what Samantha knows about his abode, which is very little.

Larry is aware that Darrin doesn't have a maid, but never reacts to Elspeth picking up the phone, or being there when he arrives. Elspeth tells the group that "everyone tried to act like the man Mr. Chappell wanted." How does Elspeth know what Chappell wanted? She's only just met him – unless ESP is back to being in a witch's bag of tricks.

OH, MY STARS!

If anyone shouldn't have to be reminded after three years that witches don't travel by broom, it's Darrin. So why the crack about the broom closet?

When Endora discovers that Elspeth is sitting with Tabatha, she fumes at the idea of a "stranger" taking care of her granddaughter. If Elspeth was Samantha's nanny, then Endora had to have hired her. Maurice wouldn't have, since he already considered a coven "women's work" in "Witches And Warlocks Are My Favorite Things" (#77). There is clear animosity between Elspeth and Endora, but its origin is never addressed. Maybe Maurice decided he needed the nanny more than Samantha?

SON OF A GUN!

"Him? He's not man enough to pull on stretch socks." – Endora, defining Darrin's masculinity for Montdrako.

HUMBUG NOT TO BE SPOKEN HERE
Airdate: December 21, 1967

EPISODE 123

Samantha has Darrin play Christmas tree so she can figure out where this year's will go, but he has to get to work, so she pops a tree around the living room until she finds the perfect spot. At work, crusty client Mortimer wants to discuss his instant soup campaign that evening, even though it's Christmas Eve. Larry promises the meeting won't run late, but when it does, Darrin cuts it short; Larry and Mortimer follow Darrin home, and Mortimer pulls his account when Darrin defers further business talk until December 26. Samantha wonders what Mortimer has against Christmas and pays him a visit, opting to take the disbeliever to the North Pole.

When Mortimer scorns Santa's workshop, Santa brings the curmudgeon along on his Christmas Eve sleigh ride, during which Mortimer sees his servant, Hawkins, happily sharing time with his family. After sending Mortimer home, Samantha pops in just in time for Darrin to surprise Tabatha in his Santa Claus suit. Larry also shows up dressed as St. Nick, and the men spar about Mortimer until the man himself arrives bearing gifts and apologies. When the real Santa Claus comes down the chimney, Samantha freezes the mortal adults so Santa can give Tabatha her Christmas present. Reanimated, Mortimer recognizes Tabatha's doll as the one he saw in Santa's shop, and Samantha exchanges a knowing smile with the convert.

GOOD!

It's fun to watch Darrin reluctantly moping around the living room as a tree. Even better is watching Darrin root himself into the ground by standing up to Larry and Mortimer about Christmas Eve. Darrin lets himself get pushed around by Larry enough that his turnaround is quite gratifying indeed.

Finding out that a seat belt is considered "standard equipment" in a 1967 sleigh is hilariously reflective of the time – and the weather outside might be frightful, but Darrin, Larry, and Mortimer's freeze indoors is delightful; they barely move a millimeter.

WELL?

Darrin asks Samantha if they can't just put the tree "where it was last year." Last year, the Stephenses' Christmas was off-screen, as Season Three contained no holiday episode; the pink polka-dotted elephant of "A Gazebo Never Forgets" (#89) took its place.

Larry makes a lot of fuss over Mortimer's account being worth $500,000 in billings, but you'd think he'd tell the instant soup king that his powder can wait until after New Year's; Mortimer's is a paltry sum compared to the worth of other clients, the most recent being Gregson's $10 million dollar account in "Solid Gold Mother-in-Law" (#120). Darrin laments to Mortimer that Samantha is expecting him early – 9:00 on Christmas Eve is early? And where is he expecting to buy a tree so late on this particular night? By the time the Stephenses decorate, it has to be past 10:00, yet Larry and Mortimer still invite themselves over – impolite for a regular business night, though maybe they rushed over to see the bench in the foyer, which has never been there before.

Even Mortimer's apparent role model, Ebenezer Scrooge, probably never grumbled "Humbug" in his sleep like Mortimer does. And Samantha's usual flying suit is suddenly festooned with all manner of shiny *accoutrements* – she didn't get this gussied up for her coronation in "Long Live the Queen" (#108). Does Samantha even conduct royal business anymore?

For all the timepieces Mortimer owns, his alarm clock must be state-of-the-art if he can set it for five seconds ahead – quite the trick considering it takes him eleven seconds to do it.

Remember the Big Band song that asks if you'd like to swing on a star? Here it happens literally: Samantha's broom doesn't move, but the heavenly bodies sway back and forth. At the Pole, in a wide shot, Samantha puts her hand on her waist after she magically takes back the coat she zapped up for Mortimer, but, when the scene cuts to a closer two-shot, her hand hasn't reached her hip yet.

As in "A Vision of Sugar Plums" (#15/#51), why is Santa Claus in his workshop on Christmas Eve? At least he's putting together his last shipment, but he should have been in the air hours before. He could save time by packing more of those store-bought dolls and models on his shelf that he's delivering as original creations. One elf-made toy is Suzi Bruisy, a doll who turns black-and-blue. But is she an appropriate doll for a child?

Mortimer calls for Hawkins at 10:45. Mortimer next goes to the North Pole and spends hours riding around on Santa's sleigh. Finally, he sees Hawkins spending quality time with his family. This means the Hawkinses, and their child, are celebrating in the middle of the night. On Christmas Day, Mortimer talks about his "dream" and wonders how he knows about Suzi Bruisy. But there's no indication that Samantha put a dream spell on Mortimer. You'd think he would be more moved by the fact that he flew around the world with Santa, but he never mentions it.

OH, MY STARS!

Darrin smiles that Mortimer doesn't have Samantha's "inside information" about Santa. Neither does Darrin. In "A Vision of Sugar Plums" (#15), Samantha blanked Darrin's memories of traveling to the North Pole, and, in this episode's tag, Samantha freezes Darrin to keep him from discovering she knows Santa, at least because Mortimer and Larry are there; you'd think Samantha would leave Darrin animate so he could share in the Santa experience with her and Tabatha.

Samantha is just a little too sugary about Christmas as she takes her second nonbeliever to the North Pole. Too bad Michael from "A Vision of Sugar Plums" (#15), who also visited Santa's workshop thanks to Samantha, couldn't come back to pay it forward and do a little convincing job on Mortimer.

Samantha casually comes out and tells Mortimer that she's a witch. If Mortimer can remember Suzy Bruisy, what's to stop him from remembering Samantha's confession and doing what he wants with the information? Then, Samantha carts Mortimer around on a broom – when she just told Darrin in the previous episode ["I Get Your Nanny, You Get My Goat" (#122)] that broom-riding is obsolete.

Strong headwinds or not, why is Santa Claus making deliveries on Christmas Day? And Tabatha is one of the few children who can meet the real Santa, but she never gets to interact with him – or really even notices him despite his being a few feet away – and it's Samantha who hands her the Suzy Bruisy doll. Why can't Santa give it to Tabatha himself instead of going on about Florida and suntan lotion?

What happened to Elspeth? "I Get Your Nanny, You Get My Goat" (#122) made it look like the Stephenses had decided to keep her on staff. Yet she's nowhere to be seen during all this holiday hoopla.

SON OF A GUN!

"I know he's got chronic dollar signs in front of his eyes, but you'd think he'd give them a Christmas vacation." – Darrin to Samantha, demonstrating that he really knows his friend/boss.

Samantha magically moving the Christmas tree around the living room is quite the effect, and must have taken a lot of time and effort to achieve. And there's snow in the yard, which has never been present during any winter episode, despite the show taking place in New York.

The episode's biggest gift of all? Larry declaring, "I tore myself away from Louise and little Jonathan." The boy really does still exist – and surely Larry is only in the Santa suit because he'd just played the jolly soul for his oft-missing son.

SAMANTHA'S DA VINCI DILEMMA
Airdate: December 28, 1967

EPISODE
124

After watching Samantha painting the trim on the house, Aunt Clara decides Samantha needs help and accidentally zaps up Leonardo da Vinci. Samantha thinks they should put da Vinci in Darrin's suit; Aunt Clara does so successfully, but also pops Darrin into da Vinci's period clothes. When toothpaste client Pritchfield sees Darrin, he concludes the costume is a preview for using the *Mona Lisa* in his advertising campaign. The annoyed Darrin comes home and learns that da Vinci is his house guest; Aunt Clara falls asleep listening to tales of the inventor's creations, so da Vinci wanders out of the house and into an art museum.

Samantha finds da Vinci in time to reverse the chiseling he's done on a modern sculpture he disapproves of. She brings him home, where Darrin angers him by mentioning Michelangelo. Larry arrives with Pritchfield and whips out a *Mona Lisa* likeness with an exaggerated white smile. Darrin resists the idea, so Pritchfield heads for the door, but Samantha freezes him and Larry, then shows da Vinci the alterations to his art. Horrified, da Vinci works with Samantha to create Toothpaint, which children can dab on their teeth. Back in motion, Pritchfield becomes enamored with the new product and scraps the *Mona Lisa* concept, to everyone's relief. Later, Aunt Clara has remembered how to send da Vinci back, but first she commissions him to do a new portrait: the *Mona Clara*.

GOOD!

Did da Vinci invent the special effect? Because his transition into Darrin's suit is…seamless. Leonardo's certainly one of the more animated historical figures Aunt Clara's brought out of the past – his rivalrous attacks on Michelangelo are works of art ("He painted over the cracks in an old ceiling – big deal!"), and it fits that he would take out his chisel to rework the oh-so-modern, oh-so-ironic "Man In Motion" sculpture. If only the show had revealed his *Mona Clara*.

In the previous episode, it was Darrin who knew what time it was with Larry. Here, Larry has a good handle on Darrin – when he sees his friend/employee decked out like da Vinci, he deadpans, "You're a million surprises." It shows that he's not forgetting Darrin's witchcraft-influenced actions from one episode to the next, and his inquiry, "Headed for a love-in?" is a groovy reference to the hippie culture that was making its way into the mainstream during this time.

WELL?

Aunt Clara's back in the tree, which was also her landing pad in "That Was No Chick, That Was My Wife" (#117). Her chef's hat has a mind of its own, too – in Aunt Clara's wide shot, it is puffed and pointing to the sky, but in her close-up, it's decidedly more deflated.

If you look at Leonardo's curled fist, it's holding very straight hair that's nowhere near the blades of the mixer he gets his wavy beard stuck in. And da Vinci never bats an eye at what must be, to him, people's unusual manner of dress, even though Queen Victoria, who lived centuries after him, deemed Samantha a "nephew" for wearing pants in "Aunt Clara's Victoria Victory" (#100). Why does Samantha want one of Darrin's suits for the inventor? She can't be sure her husband's clothes will even fit him. As for Darrin, he gets snagged in a unusual costume at work again, after just rocking Little Lord Fauntleroy duds in "I Get Your Nanny, You Get My Goat" (#122).

So da Vinci bores Aunt Clara by laundry-listing his innovations – thirty-two seconds later, she's asleep, he's gone, and no one hears the door. Wouldn't Samantha have been more vigilant about keeping the walking anachronism in the house after letting Benjamin Franklin slip out in "My Friend Ben" (#87)? Leonardo adapts very easily to a time period 400 years in his future – and is the museum he visits in Patterson, or New York City? It looks like a Big Apple gallery, but he can't have traversed 60 miles on foot that fast. You'd think the museum guide would come running when the artist starts hacking away at "Man in Motion"; instead, only the guard notices, and doesn't do much to stop him.

Samantha seems to be learning from her past experiences with historical figures by not blabbing about witchcraft – Leonardo simply thinks popping into the den with Samantha is "how they travel in the 20th century." But how does he know when he is? No one's mentioned the date to him.

Darrin waits a long time to tell Samantha that Larry and Pritchfield are on their way over, which is urgent enough news that you'd think it would be the first thing Darrin says when Samantha appears with da Vinci. Larry must be getting used to being frozen by now; he was just immobilized in "Humbug Not to Be Spoken Here" (#123), though he and Pritchfield execute a very good freeze. And, if Darrin's wondering where he's heard Samantha's "witchcraft got you into this mess and it can get you out" justification before, it was in "How to Fail in Business With All Kinds of Help" (#104).

Leonardo da Vinci should stare blankly at Samantha as she goes on about toothpaste, but doesn't. The toiletry did see sporadic use by the ancient Greeks and Romans, but it didn't become popular until the 19th century. It's also not likely Samantha has a chemistry set lying around for da Vinci to work with, so she must zap it up, which begs the next question: how long are Larry and Pritchfield frozen? Leonardo concocts Toothpaint from scratch, which has to take hours – yet, when the ad man and his client are reanimated, they never question where the time has gone.

OH, MY STARS!

"I can fix that," Samantha assures Darrin when he comes home in Leonardo's clothes. She shouldn't be able to – like Leonardo's journey, the wardrobe switch is Aunt Clara's spell. Darrin even asks about it, and Samantha's rule-changing rationalization that returning da Vinci to another century is "a much bigger thing" is pushing it; either a witch can change another witch's spell or she can't, and it shouldn't depend on the degree of difficulty.

Leonardo da Vinci was born in Italy in 1452. The English language was not recognized outside of Britain until the 19th century. Yet the inventor can converse with everyone around him in standard, 20th century English. Does Aunt Clara's color coded spell include a *Star Trek*-type universal translator?

As with "My Friend Ben" (#87) and "Aunt Clara's Victoria Victory" (#100), in which famous people were brought out of the past, or "A Most Unusual Wood Nymph" (#79) and "Samantha's Thanksgiving to Remember" (#119), in which Samantha and her friends traveled *to* the past, there is no consideration of Leonardo da Vinci's potential impact on the timeline. It may be easy enough to keep the museum from finding out that the original Renaissance man graced them with his presence, or the public from finding out that he invented Toothpaint, but what about when da Vinci goes back to his own time with 20th century knowledge? He could change history by coming up with a mixer or a typewriter first. This issue could be resolved by somehow mentioning that historical figures' memories of the present are purged automatically upon returning to their own time; since it isn't, it has to be assumed the visitors completely retain their experiences. Good thing Leonardo, Ben Franklin, and even Queen Victoria seem to have enough integrity to not use what they've learned in the 1960s for their own benefit.

SON OF A GUN!

"Ah, Samantha, you have arrived just in time – I have been insulted! He called me a hippie! What is a hippie?" – da Vinci, not very hip to 1967's mod lingo.

Someone's done their homework when it comes to da Vinci's inventions. The parachute, the pump, the power saw, and, more peripherally, the prefabricated house, can all be traced back to the busy innovator. Superficial research doesn't seem to establish a link between da Vinci and the revolving door he says he invented, but there's enough accuracy here to merit a *brava* or two.

ONCE IN A VIAL
Airdate: January 4, 1968

EPISODE 125

Dismayed at the sight of Samantha doing menial mortal chores, Endora recruits Samantha's old beau, Rollo, to lure her away from Darrin. Endora plays on Samantha's insecurities to manipulate her into having lunch with Rollo; he's gone when they return to the restaurant, but they run into Darrin and his no-filter client, Callahan, who declares that Endora would be perfect to advertise his perfume. Callahan arranges a business dinner with Endora, the Stephenses, and art director Bill Walters; Endora invites Rollo, and suggests he use his trademark love potion on Samantha if his own charms fail to entice her.

At dinner, Darrin and Rollo exchange uncomfortable pleasantries, and Endora chafes at Callahan's attention. When Samantha dismisses Rollo's fawning, he spikes her drink with the potion, but Endora unwittingly drinks it and falls passionately in love with Callahan. Boozehound Bill also steals a sip and becomes amorous toward his estranged wife, Harriet. As Darrin referees for the Walterses, Samantha and Rollo team up to stop Endora after she spirits Callahan away to a justice of the peace. Samantha stalls the ceremony with witchcraft, but Endora catches on and sends Samantha home, bringing those assembled to Samantha's patio after Samantha zaps Callahan from her side. Just as Endora is about to become Mrs. Callahan, the potion wears off, and Bill shifts the blame for his lovesickness on Harriet. When the dust settles, the Stephenses gently warn Endora to stop using her magic to come between them.

GOOD!

When Samantha pops home, disgusted by Endora's attempt to set her up with Rollo, she tells Endora that Aunt Hagatha's babysitting services are no longer required. This is a considerable mention, especially now that nanny Elspeth from "I Get Your Nanny, You Get My Goat" (#122) seems to be gone.

This episode features some new and intriguing duos: Darrin and Rollo's stilted banter is, as Callahan would say, "a gas" – though the way Bill and Harriet's bickering morphs into something out of a classic Pepé Le Pew cartoon (in which the Warner Brothers' skunk obliviously chased disinterested females) tops it. Finally, despite her continual rejection of him, Samantha and Rollo have an easy friendship as they join forces to keep Endora out of trouble while she's high on the "love juice." Terrific continuity, having Samantha lament, "She doesn't even remember Daddy" (not that Endora's recollection of Maurice has stopped her from dallying with bullfighters and Japanese poets), and Samantha finding herself "outwitched" by her mother turns magic into an intriguing competition.

WELL?

If Endora wants to add weight to her constant contention that Samantha should lead a witchy life, all she has to do is remind Samantha that she is a monarch. The show has virtually ignored this royal plot development since introducing it in "Long Live the Queen" (#108).

It's funny that Callahan makes perfume, yet never comments on Endora's Joie d'Anime, which Samantha detects early in the episode. Moments later, Endora conjures up Rollo, saying, "Why didn't I think of that before?" She did: in "George the Warlock" (#30), Endora also tried using an old beau to break up Samantha's marriage. Ushering Rollo in with thunder and lightning isn't very subtle; Endora's lucky Samantha doesn't come running in, wondering why there's a storm in her kitchen.

In "Business, Italian Style" (#110), Larry asked the language-afflicted Darrin to recommend an art director; Darrin's choice was Sam Kaplan. Here, the man in that position is Bill Walters.

Not since "It Takes One to Know One" (#11) have Samantha and Endora done so much popping in and out of a crowded restaurant – only then, Endora's scheme was the reverse: enlisting a witch to seduce Darrin from Samantha. Why is the Manhattan waiter the only one unnerved by all the appearing and disappearing? In Paris, Rollo's lady companion freezes, but, because a freeze frame technique is used, the other patrons temporarily immobilize along with her.

Setting her laced martini down, Samantha moves to turn on the stereo. She doesn't have to move far, since the stereo has again been switched with the television that usually occupies this space at the bottom of the stairs. After Rollo confesses that Endora put him up to using the love potion, he states that its effects last "exactly one hour." That seems odd – what happens if Rollo succeeds in seducing a lady and the potion wears off in the middle of l'amour? He'd have a lot of women walking out – or pressing charges.

When the justice of the peace says Endora will need two witnesses, he initially holds up three fingers, though he does correct himself. And Darrin inadvertently freezes with Bill and Harriet before Samantha makes her zap.

With Endora about to become a bigamist (which one would imagine wouldn't sit well with Maurice), Rollo looks at his watch and tells Samantha they have four minutes to stop her. So the first thing Rollo did when Endora imbibed his potion was look at a clock? How fortunate that Endora happens to sip at the top of the hour so a clock's chime can indicate the potion has worn off. Since when is there a chiming clock in the dining room, anyway? [Maybe that's what woke Darrin in "Double, Double...Toil and Trouble" (#111).] The Stephenses should get their money back: it's clearly 11:00, but the clock bongs twelve times.

The cold snap Morning Glory Circle had at Christmas is over; even though it's January in New York, the snow is all gone, and Samantha and Endora stand outside in thin dresses.

OH, MY STARS!

Out of all the restaurants in New York City, Darrin takes Callahan to the same one where Samantha and Endora are lunching, at the same time. That may not be witchcraft, but this episode touches off a lot of questions about the power witches have over each other, if any. Rollo's potion naturally works on mortals, but it's intended for Samantha, a witch. Is it fair, plausible, or even ethical for a witch to be able to magically manipulate a fellow witch? By the same token, Rollo worries that Endora will turn him into a frog, and Endora not only zaps Samantha home, but makes it impossible for her to pop back to the impromptu wedding. Since Rollo tells Samantha that Endora is "more powerful than both of us together," is the implication that a witch can hex another witch if her powers are stronger? Bringing it full circle, Rollo's potion leads Endora to the altar – but in "Love Is Blind" (#13), Samantha told Darrin that "no one gets married under a witch's spell." Have witches made that sort of nuptial possible since then?

SON OF A GUN!

"No. But now that you mention it, it does tickle a bit." – Endora to Rollo, who wants to know if her conscience ever pains her.

Callahan's unrestrained, unintentionally backhanded compliments are the perfect foil for the rather snobby Endora, who may finally have met her mortal match. That's what makes the turnaround so satisfying when Endora falls for the perfumer while hopped up on Rollo's potion – and what follows is an Endora as never seen before. Agnes Moorehead's girly squeals as she hugs and squeezes the man she just shot daggers at is a *tour de force* performance.

SNOB IN THE GRASS
Airdate: January 11, 1968

EPISODE
126

Larry wants Darrin to use his influence in order to land the William J. Sommers account, since Darrin nearly married Sommers' daughter, Sheila [see "I, Darrin, Take This Witch, Samantha" (#1)]. Darrin balks, but Larry arranges for them to meet with Sheila and her father for dinner; Sommers is a no-show and Larry leaves Darrin alone with Sheila, who still has a thing for him. Endora, suspicious over Darrin's recent late-night work, pops into the restaurant as a waitress and dumps a full plate in his lap. Samantha is miffed until Darrin explains how Larry and Sheila tricked him; she insists on attending a casual party that Sheila has invited them to.

After Samantha recalls how Sheila once humiliated her by "forgetting" to tell her to dress formally for a dinner party, the Stephenses arrive in full regalia, only to discover that this party is indeed casual. As before, Sheila sets Samantha at the end of the table and hogs Darrin while running Samantha into the ground. Larry and Darrin discuss business with Sommers, but Sheila moves in for the kill with Samantha, who gets fed up and sics a fly and a bee on her rival, finishing by witching a dog into destroying Sheila's outfit. Darrin feels Sheila deserved it, and, when Darrin can't find the layouts for the Webley account Sommers' was supposed to replace, Larry arrives announcing that Webley loved Darrin's ideas; Darrin casts a knowing eye at Samantha and kisses her.

GOOD!

Turns out the "I, Darrin, Take This Witch, Samantha" (#1) battle between Samantha and Sheila was only an appetizer. This time the gloves are off, and both ladies give as good as they get, although Sheila embarrasses Samantha to the point that even Larry feels bad. Samantha is more diabolical with her revenge in this go-round, especially with Gaylord, the Sommers' dog, and the effect of the loose yarn on Sheila's blouse tying itself to Gaylord's collar is particularly well done.

In "Double Split" (#64), when Samantha twitched an hors d'oeuvre into the face of a client's bratty daughter, Darrin went ballistic and spent the whole episode fighting with her. Here, Darrin shrugs off Samantha's even bigger witchy comeback by saying his ex had it coming. Darrin can be so difficult about witchcraft that it's especially touching when he demonstrates love and understanding about it.

WELL?

At least the Stephenses' television is back where it belongs after its relocation in "Once in a Vial" (#125), but their bedroom closet is by the door where the dresser should be; only in "Three Wishes" (#96) has it ever been positioned there. And the breakfast Samantha purposely ruins for Darrin is reminiscent of the burnt offerings she turned out during her first cooking attempt in "Be It Ever So Mortgaged" (#2).

Has Sheila moved? In the flashback from "I, Darrin, Take This Witch, Samantha" (#1), the front door and living room are quite different from what is seen now – not to mention, there's music playing that wasn't in the original scene. Sheila and Darrin apparently share the same taste in music; she plays the Watusi record Darrin danced to in "Divided He Falls" (#69), and the jazzy track doesn't kick in until the Stephenses see the casually-dressed gathering.

After dinner, Larry tells Sommers that Darrin has "extensive experience with your type of product." Too bad the writers don't go the extra step and reveal this product Sommers made his millions with; it would add dimension to Sheila's background. Meanwhile, Samantha tells Sheila that she and Darrin are installing new plumbing in their house. It's about time: Darrin complained about the pipes being on the fritz as far back as "Cousin Edgar" (#36).

Samantha must draw inspiration from the time Darrin accused her of turning herself into a fly in "No Zip in My Zap" (#113), because here she conjures up a real one to annoy Sheila. Its buzzing around Ms. Sommers is a challenging effect; the tiny bit of string visible in the shot is totally forgivable. Question: if Sheila has gone blond, why is she wearing a dark wig? So audiences will recognize her from "I, Darrin, Take This Witch, Samantha" (#1)? Samantha ties a thread from Sheila's blouse to Gaylord's collar and shoos Gaylord away; physics would dictate that Sheila would lurch forward and fall, rather than spin. And only Sheila's blouse is caught on Gaylord, so how do her pants fall down? Is it dawning on Sheila that strange things only happen when Darrin brings his wife over?

Does Samantha save the Webley account by witchcraft? It's only ever established that she puts Darrin's ideas in front of them, but she could have done that physically. Finally, when Larry smiles that Darrin is irascible, it's good the Stephenses don't know what it means: the word's synonyms are "irritable" and "quick-tempered." Maybe Larry's making a statement about Darrin's primary demeanor of late – to say nothing of his own.

OH, MY STARS!

Endora suspecting Darrin of cheating again? She just filled Samantha's head (and Darrin's ears) with this suspicion in "My, What Big Ears You Have" (#121). Endora stands inches away from Darrin as he loudly tells his ex, "Sheila, I'm married!" That should settle it for Endora, but she must choose not to convey Darrin's words, otherwise Samantha wouldn't be mad at him the next morning.

How exactly do events at Sheila's dinner party "blow the Sommers account?" No one sees Samantha doing anything to Sheila; for all anyone knows, the butler pulled Sheila's wig off, and what happens with Gaylord appears to be a freak accident. There's no call for Sommers to penalize Darrin, unless it's retroactive revenge for dumping his daughter for Samantha.

SON OF A GUN!

"That's right! We have to drop up at a dress-in..." – Darrin to Sheila, flustered as Samantha explains why they're in fancy clothes.

The show makes history in this episode by presenting its very first flashback to a previously-aired episode: specifically, Samantha and Sheila's introduction in "I, Darrin, Take This Witch, Samantha" (#1). Not only is it tremendous continuity, but this installment is a continuation of sorts, with Darrin telling Larry that Sheila will interpret a phone call as "a sign that my marriage is buckling." Revisiting a scene from the pilot in this context shows just how much Samantha has changed since then: no longer a shrinking violet, Samantha exudes a much stronger confidence in her dealings with the mortal world. No wonder Sheila has to step up her game.

IF THEY NEVER MET
Airdate: January 25, 1968

EPISODE 127

Endora pulls constant pranks on Darrin, including inserting a cobra into his briefcase, which gets him fired. Darrin takes it out on Samantha and agrees when she suggests he'd be happier if they never met. Suddenly Darrin disappears, and Endora reveals she's fulfilled his wish by transporting him to "the now that might have been." Samantha and Endora travel there and see a happy-go-lucky Darrin in a bigger office, still engaged to Sheila Sommers [see "I, Darrin, Take This Witch, Samantha" (#1) and "Snob in the Grass" (#126)]. Darrin and Sheila are about to be married, but he's not comfortable with his future father-in-law, Sommers, paying for everything.

Samantha and Endora observe Darrin and Sheila at Sommers' party; Darrin excuses himself, and Samantha follows him to a bar, where he chats with old friend Dave about his upcoming wedding. Hearing

Darrin question his feelings for Sheila, Samantha bumps into him, mirroring their first meeting. Darrin sees something in Samantha and rushes to break things off with Sheila; delighted, Samantha returns to this reality and has Endora rematerialize Darrin, who apologizes for his outburst. While Darrin scans the want ads for a new job, Larry stops by and congratulates him for scaring their client off with the cobra, since the man turned out to be a lawbreaker. Darrin guesses he'd be pretty miserable if he'd never met Samantha, and she smiles that they'll never know.

GOOD!

Darrin getting zapped into a kiddie car from his real one – and back – looks precise and effortless. Though it would be reasonable for the show to reuse the tiny vehicle Charlie Leach got zapped into in "Follow That Witch (Part II)" (#67), Darrin's juvenile jalopy is all new. Another fluid effect is Samantha zapping herself into her flying suit [restored from its sequined makeover in "Humbug Not to Be Spoken Here" (#123)]. And the people involved do a good job of making Samantha and Endora's pop-in next to Darrin look good – even if his cigarette smoke couldn't be trained to follow suit.

WELL?

In "The Joker Is A Card" (#41), Endora looked down her nose at brother Arthur's practical jokes. Here, she nearly outdoes him, even borrowing Edgar's shaving cream trick from "Cousin Edgar" (#36). Samantha tries to make mortal excuses for the toiletry torment, which is strange, since she already knows Endora is responsible. Endora's double door stunt is fun, but Darrin almost knocks it down when he bangs into it. Frustrated, Darrin shouts that he's going to do something desperate if Endora doesn't stop. But what can he do, outside threatening to leave Samantha again? He pulls out of the driveway onto a Morning Glory Circle that looks like it's in another city: there's no Kravitz house across the street, and the discrepant apartment building of recent episodes is replaced by a Texaco station.

This isn't the first time Endora has packed a surprise in Darrin's briefcase. In "Double Tate" (#59), it was a frog; Endora steps it up here with a defanged cobra. Naturally, Larry fires Darrin – although, the last time he fired him, in "Solid Gold Mother-in-Law" (#120), Larry swore "there won't be a next time." At the end of the episode, Samantha tells Darrin, "Larry's not going to fire you" – but he already has.

In "the now that might have been," Samantha points Sheila out to Endora. Why? Endora just saw Darrin's ex, up close and personal, in "Snob in the Grass" (#126), then reported their meeting to Samantha – if Endora really wants to cause trouble for Darrin, she should put Sheila to work. As Darrin and Sheila discuss exotic locales for honeymoons, Samantha laments that he only took her to Atlantic City for theirs, but the newlyweds' first scene [in "I, Darrin, Take This Witch, Samantha" (#1)] showed them together in a posh New York City hotel.

Samantha grimaces at the thought of Darrin wearing ruffles. Maybe that's only because it's Sheila's idea – in "Twitch or Treat" (#81), Samantha had no problem with the frills. More is revealed about Sheila's father here than was the case in "Snob in the Grass" (#126): Larry lists Sommers' worth at $28.5 million, and calls him the fourth richest man in the country. But is still isn't said how Sommers made his money; one sentence would fill in that blank.

Paul Barselow seems fated to play only bartenders on *Bewitched*; here he gets his fifth moniker since the show began. He's been Hal, Pete, Joe, Max – now he's Al. And Al's bar has a door with the exact same "private" sign that adorns Darrin's office in this different timeline. Shouldn't Darrin's name still be on his door, flaunting his upgraded title?

No one wonders where Darrin goes when he ditches Sheila's party to hang out at a bar. It seems that, in both realities, Darrin is willing to throw Sheila over for a total stranger – that works out well for the Stephenses (and the show), but, as perfectly awful as Sheila is (and you wouldn't want her any other way), it's hard not to feel bad for the socialite.

OH, MY STARS!

Darrin has a right to be angry about Endora's cobra costing him his job, and even a sitcom needs conflict, but Darrin's tirade here is excessive. Yelling "you and her against me" is unfair, since Samantha has gone up against Endora and her witchery on Darrin's behalf numerous times – and essentially agreeing that he'd be happier if they never met is crossing a line, even in anger. Moreover, Samantha, Darrin, and Endora all forget one very important thing in their game of What If: Tabatha. Endora gleefully gets rid of her father, and Samantha is so concerned about herself that she doesn't even find her child a babysitter when popping off into "the now that might have been." Samantha and Endora aren't the tiniest bit upset that Tabatha does not exist in this alternate reality, or that she won't if they let Darrin marry Sheila. Tabatha not factoring into the consequences of this story is rather shocking.

SON OF A GUN!

"I wonder what the losers get." – Samantha to Endora, as Sommers describes the oil wells, property, and lightweight airplane luggage Darrin and Sheila are to receive as honeymoon gifts.

This episode demonstrates that Darrin's anti-witchcraft stance doesn't come from nowhere – he just likes to do things for himself, as evidenced by his discomfort when Sommers throws money around on his behalf. That's definitely something to remember the next time Darrin blows a gasket over magic, because it's deeper motivation than him just being difficult or demanding.

This unofficial continuation of "Snob in the Grass" (#126) accurately pulls from the show's history: Endora rightly recalls that Darrin has been a monkey ["Alias Darrin Stephens" (#37)] and a penguin ["George the Warlock" (#30)]. The show's pilot, "I, Darrin, Take This Witch, Samantha" (#1) gets its nods, too – such as Darrin confiding in his inattentive friend Dave. Darrin calls Larry his best friend now, but seeing Dave again makes one realize how much he is missed. Best of all, the show recreates the Stephenses' first meeting by having them bump into each other at the bar door. Their initial revolving door encounter isn't referenced, and someone coming into the show at this point wouldn't realize the history, but it's a brilliant throwback for any eagle-eyed viewer – and it proves that Darrin and Samantha are destined to be together no matter what.

HIPPIE, HIPPIE, HOORAY
Airdate: February 1, 1968

EPISODE
128

Samantha barely keeps Darrin from seeing a newspaper photo of Serena, who was arrested during a love-in. Samantha zaps Serena out of jail and sends her on her way, but Larry sees the picture and assumes Samantha has gone hippie. After Larry invites himself to dinner so he can see Samantha for himself, Darrin comes home and finds Serena playing Tabatha a rock-and-roll lullaby. Darrin runs afoul of Serena, who leaves her telltale guitar out for Larry and Louise to see. When the Tates spot Serena on a news broadcast about the love-in, Darrin tries to explain that his wife and his cousin-in-law are two different people, but Larry doesn't buy it.

The next day, Serena, pretending to be a hippie Samantha, waltzes into Darrin's office and scandalizes Giddings, a conservative client. Larry still won't believe that Serena isn't Samantha, so Darrin invites the Tates to another dinner where they'll be able to see Samantha and Serena together. Samantha knows Serena won't materialize, so she switches back and forth between herself and her flower child cousin, even entertaining the Tates with some groovy guitar playing. Larry, however, catches on that Samantha and Serena are never in the room at the same time; just as the Stephenses are about to lie that Serena has taken ill, Darrin apologizes to the ether, and Serena shows up to save the day.

GOOD!

Considering hippie counterculture was at its "Haight" as 1968 began, it's very smart of the show to incorporate it, and its catch phrases, into the scripts. But it's Serena's *Rock 'n' Roll Baby to a Rock-a-Bye Beat*, and Samantha's *Iffen Song* that are really "out of sight." Elizabeth Montgomery has a ball getting her groovy on, and that translates to the catchy tunes; pity official recordings were never released.

Serena plots on the roof, where there's snow; this is certainly consistent with February in New York. Then, Darrin flips on the TV to see his Springer Pet Food commercial, which illustrates not only the endgame of the advertising process, but Darrin's campaign of "That Was No Chick, That Was My Wife" (#117).

Larry Tate not caring about an account? The greedy ad exec surprises by putting his concern for Darrin ahead of a client – and tops it off by admitting he's "one of the best truth stretchers in the business." It's not often Larry dives beneath his smooth, superficial veneer, so when he proves there's a human being behind the mustache, it's all the more gratifying.

In "Double, Double...Toil and Trouble" (#111), Serena impersonated Samantha – here, Samantha doles out the karma by stepping into Serena's go-go boots. Of course, Samantha doesn't get Serena quite right (nor is she supposed to), but her attempts to imitate her cousin, even calling Larry "Cotton Top," are "far out."

WELL?

In a close shot of Serena's newspaper article, the first two lines reflect what Samantha reads aloud. A wider shot reveals that those are the only accurate lines, but the show tried. How is the article supposed to be bad publicity for McMann & Tate? There's no direct connection to Darrin, and it's not like the identity of one account executive's wife is public information.

The Tates' kitchen is very different from the one seen in "Maid to Order" (#53); this one looks more like the Stephenses kitchen done over. At breakfast (with no Jonathan in sight), Louise tells Larry that Samantha is her "very best friend." If that's so, why hasn't she seen or talked to her in over a month?

Serena beams when it appears that Tabatha has missed her. Any interaction between them had to have been off-screen; the only other episode they shared was "And Then There Were Three" (#54), when Tabatha was hours old. And Darrin never told Serena she wasn't welcome in his house, unless that was also off-screen [punishment for messing with his head in "Double, Double...Toil and Trouble" (#111)?]. Serena retaliates by leaving her guitar at the foot of the stairs before popping out. Wouldn't Darrin and Samantha see it before the Tates' arrival? How does it end up in the living room corner? And Darrin must have grown to like poker: in "Double Split" (#64), he specifically told Larry he hated poker and bowling, yet here he deals cards like a master.

When Serena poses as Samantha in Darrin's office, her funky hat and glasses are the same she wore as "Samantha" in "Double, Double...Toil and Trouble" (#111). Similarly, Samantha wears the same pink sleeveless dress she wore in that episode, then the flowered frock she zapped Serena into in "That Was No Chick, That Was My Wife" (#117).

Larry calls Darrin his best friend here (despite having fired him four times this season alone), then recommends that "Samantha" see Louise's psychoanalyst cousin. What happened to Dr. Kramer, the shrink the Tates swore by in "I'd Rather Twitch Than Fight" (#84)? And perhaps it just seems odd by today's standards, but did average society in the 1960s really think people were crazy if they went hippie? Giddings asks if "Samantha" is out of her mind, and both Larry and Louise turn up their noses at the look and lifestyle, expressing the same viewpoint. Is this an accurate culture clash?

Samantha may be hipper than she's let on, otherwise, she couldn't grab a guitar and rock out to the *Iffen Song* – plus, it has to be assumed she's using witchcraft to play the instrument. Are Larry and Louise so not "with it" that they don't notice the guitar has no cord or amplifier, or that the song's bass line is being piped in from nowhere? Larry wonders how Samantha is changing her clothes so fast to masquerade as Serena, but, as a woman, Louise should be inquiring how Samantha is rearranging her hair and make-up so fast. Finally, Samantha laments that she can't be herself and Serena at the same time. Maybe not, but she could feasibly zap up a Serena double without any problems.

OH, MY STARS!

When Serena was introduced in "And Then There Were Three" (#54), she was a glamorous débutante. She enjoyed a mod makeover in "Double, Double...Toil and Trouble" (#111), but is it reasonable to believe the fun-loving brunette has morphed into a freaked-out blond? Her voice has even dropped from her previous, higher-pitched tones; now Serena just looks and sounds like Samantha with an attitude – an experiment that doesn't quite work.

What makes Samantha zap Serena out of jail? Serena can pop herself out if she wants to, but, by not letting Serena "cool it in the cooler," Samantha not only sets her free to wreak havoc on Darrin and the Tates, but breaks the law. Serena is now a fugitive from justice – there's nothing stopping the Tates from turning her in when they discover she isn't Samantha. If Samantha really needs to talk to Serena about the newspaper photo, which can wait, why doesn't Samantha pop her cousin back to jail afterwards – or better yet, just visit her cell?

This entire episode hinges on the fact that the Tates think Samantha and Serena are the same person – except Louise already met Serena in "That Was No Chick, That Was My Wife" (#117), after Serena helped clean up Samantha's in-two-places-at-once mess. Louise rushed right home to tell Larry about Serena, so there's no way he wouldn't know Samantha has an identical cousin, and it invalidates the entire storyline of this installment.

SON OF A GUN!

"But not too many guitars have all that psychotic paint on them." – Larry to Louise, trying and failing to be hip.

When Larry innocently suggests that Darrin speaks Giddings' language: Darrin groans, "Language? I hope he isn't Italian; I've been through that." So many of these episodes are self-contained, it gives the impression their events don't happen in tandem – this allusion to "Business, Italian Style" (#110) marvelously connects two unrelated episodes, and all it takes is one sentence.

A PRINCE OF A GUY

Airdate: February 8, 1968

When Tabatha's unsatisfied with the "happily ever after" ending of *Sleeping Beauty*, she zaps Prince Charming out of the fairy tale just as the Tates arrive to meet Darrin's cousin, Helen, and her boyfriend, Ralph. Endora tells Samantha that Tabatha can't reverse her spell, so Samantha has no choice but to modernize the prince and introduce him as "Charlie." Helen falls for him immediately, ignoring Ralph and making the intrigued Louise jealous. Ralph walks out, and Larry decides to capitalize on Charlie's charm by casting him in a commercial. Endora warns Samantha that Charlie is a product of wishcraft, which means he has no substance and can't be seen on camera. Samantha rushes to the studio, and indeed the production is halted because Charlie turns up invisible on the equipment.

At home, Helen is already talking marriage with Charlie, who doesn't want to return to his story; Endora realizes his resistance is what's preventing Tabatha from sending him back. This inspires Samantha to zap Sleeping Beauty out of the book to entice him; it works, and Charlie accompanies his true love back into the pages of fiction. Meanwhile, Ralph stops by to give the disinterested Helen a piece of his mind, but she changes hers when he says he was ready to marry her. Samantha and Endora find Helen and Ralph in an embrace, glad that Helen won't miss her other Prince Charming.

GOOD!

Because the show's veteran actors are so skilled at clothes-changing effects at this point, it's understandable when newbies' witched wardrobes don't look as smooth. But William Bassett's Charlie (likely a reference to the real-life and fictionalized "Bonnie Prince Charlie") gets zapped back and forth out of his suit in two different scenes, needing no alterations. His swaps are spot-on, and even little Erin Murphy barely moves during them.

After years of Endora botching Darrin's name, it makes perfect sense for her to mistakenly refer to Helen as "Elena." It's also intriguing that Prince Charming has no conception of Sleeping Beauty because he gets zapped out of the middle of his book, before their meeting.

WELL?

Samantha is in the right place as Endora pops in on the staircase, but the camera shifts and zooms in as Endora makes her appearance, taking away from the effect. Upstairs, Tabatha again zaps an entity out of a book, as she did in "The Safe and Sane Halloween" (#115), but it seems like a cheat to not see Samantha's reaction to discovering the prince in Tabatha's room. The sequence is joined "already in progress," following an overly long Larry/Louise/Helen/Ralph scene.

Is there more trouble in the Tates' marriage than meets the eye? Louise fawns over Charlie, and in front of Larry, at that. Is it payback for Larry ogling girlie magazines in "That Was My Wife" (#31)?

Larry wanted the "talking" Tabatha to do baby food testimonials in "Baby's First Paragraph" (#62), and Benjamin Franklin to hawk transistor radios in "My Friend Ben" (#87). Those seemed understandable, but why does Larry want a man to do a commercial for a cosmetics company? Larry remarks that Charlie is between jobs, though Samantha never conveyed that information on-screen. As for the dilemma of Charlie's invisibility, Samantha dramatically utters, "Oh, no!" three times during this section of the episode; once would be enough. Samantha follows Larry and Charlie to the TV studio by witchcraft, so she should get there long before they do. Plus, Charlie comes from a magical, fictional world – how does he know what a television camera is, let alone how to pose for it?

Helen wants to tell her mother about her marriage prospect – do these ladies come from Frank's side of the family, or Phyllis'? As for Samantha's mother, Helen has so much tunnel vision about Charlie that she fails to notice Endora wearing the same dress two days in a row. Now, Helen is apparently visiting from out of town, as evidenced by the mention of her hotel. Is Ralph visiting, too? If so, her dumping him in a strange city is rather callous. Amazingly, Ralph still wants to marry Helen – what happens the next time the wedding-obsessed woman is swayed by a pretty face? Helen seems the type to have pulled this kind of stunt before.

Endora jokes that at least Samantha didn't read Tabatha one of the *Babar* books: true, Tabatha doesn't get to materialize the titular elephant (created by Jean de Brunhoff in 1931), but she did once hide a literary bear in her closet in "The Safe and Sane Halloween" (#115). Did her parents ever find out about that? And Endora doesn't think a coffee pot is heavy anymore, as she did in "Allergic to Ancient Macedonian Dodo Birds" (#118) – she physically carries a pot, cups, and edibles on a tray without complaint.

OH, MY STARS!

With Darrin absent from this episode, of course other mortals have to take his place for balance. On paper, it makes sense to bring in Darrin's cousin, but on screen, it's baffling that she'd visit while Darrin is out of town. As Helen is a sudden, phantom relative, there's no real compulsion to invest in her, and her fickleness is unappealing; it's as if she gulped some of Rollo's love potion from "Once in a Vial" (#125).

The idea that, as a product of wishcraft, the prince has no substance, and therefore can't be seen on camera, is intriguing – but it puts Tabatha's other magical examples since "It's Wishcraft" (#103) into question. The toys Tabatha brought to life in "Toys in Babeland" (#109) were wishcraft, too, but Tabatha had to let them out of the guest room with a key; they couldn't just glide through the door like the prince does. The creatures Tabatha popped out of her Halloween story in "The Safe and Sane Halloween" (#115) also lacked transparent abilities, as did the bear in the same episode, and Tabatha's prehistoric pal from a coloring book in "Allergic to Ancient Macedonian Dodo Birds" (#118). If all wishcraft-created entities are projections, as Endora suggests, shouldn't their characteristics be consistent?

SON OF A GUN!

"The story doesn't mention where you're from, Prince Charming, but there must have been a lot of oil on the property." – Samantha, rolling her eyes at her fictional flatterer.

McTAVISH
Airdate: February 15, 1968

EPISODE
130

Aunt Clara asks for Samantha's help getting a ghost called McTavish out of a castle belonging to her former boyfriend, Ocky. With Darrin working late, Samantha flies to England, unaware that Darrin's parents are staying at the same castle. Darrin comes home early and is upset to learn that Samantha is overseas; Phyllis is upset to hear the ghost cackling, but more so when she thinks Samantha is in the hallway. Darrin stalls his mother when she calls asking about Samantha, who chats with McTavish and suggests he might like to leave his ancestral home and move to America. Samantha pops out when Phyllis spots her, only to face a drunken Darrin, who wonders if his wife prefers her witchy ways. The Stephenses make up, but McTavish scares Darrin sober when he takes up residence in their home.

Phyllis drags Frank back to New York to see Samantha at the house; warned by Darrin, Samantha talks to Ocky, who wants McTavish to return because the castle guests love him. McTavish agrees only if Ocky and Samantha install the creature comforts he's become accustomed to; Phyllis hears the conversation from the front porch, but once Ocky and McTavish leave, Samantha zaps up a TV western that mirrors her chat with them. Just as Phyllis concedes she's misinterpreted everything, Aunt Clara arrives with a gift for Samantha: a painting of McTavish that makes Phyllis faint.

GOOD!

Aunt Clara has arrived in trees, gazebos, closets – once by parachute – and, of course, the fireplace. So it's quite novel for her to walk out of the refrigerator, noting that she took the polar route. But she's not as dumb as she looks – she only pretends she can't pop out when Samantha declines to help with McTavish. As for Ocky, the show builds on his sole appearance in "The Short Happy Circuit of Aunt Clara" (#83): she didn't end up taking him back, and it turns out he's as magically inept as she is. Clara and Ocky never do interact, but that does lend credence to her considering him an ex-boyfriend.

This episode provides some additional insights into Darrin's heritage. After Ocky tells Phyllis that the woman she saw (Samantha) is the Duchess of Stephens, Frank reminds his wife that "Stephens is a fine old English name." Given that "The Leprechaun (#63) and "A Most Unusual Wood Nymph" (#79) implied that Phyllis' family is Irish, this new information can only mean Darrin is English on his father's side.

For a ghost, McTavish is very entertaining in the "horrible visage" of Ronald Long. You really believe he's been roaming that castle for 500 years, and that it's Samantha, Ocky, and the elder Stephenses who are the intruders. But it's McTavish sassing Ocky that really provides the ghostly glee. He deems the wobbling warlock puny and weak-kneed – and he's not too far off the mark.

WELL?

Samantha just got involved with castles in "I Get Your Nanny, You Get My Goat" (#122), where she helped the lonely Lord Montdrako deal with the absence of his domestic servant, Elspeth; here, Samantha helps Ocky deal with a persnickety ghost. Samantha relaying details about Ocky's castle back to Aunt Clara is a little expositional (it's to fill in the viewer, but Clara already knows this information), and it seems odd that Ocky's guests are terrified of a ghost when Montdrako's guests loved the idea of one. By the way, where is Elspeth? She hasn't been seen since the aforementioned episode.

Darrin panics as he picks up the phone and hears his mother on the other end, but there's no need for him to. He doesn't know yet that Phyllis has seen Samantha, and just because they're both in England, it doesn't mean they'll run into each other (even though they do). When Darrin wants Aunt Clara to go to Great Britain and find Samantha, she confirms what she repeatedly said in "There's No Witch Like An Old Witch" (#27): she can't fly very far. Yet she changes her mind, pops out, and makes it to the UK anyway. Then, she isn't heard from again until the end of the episode. What does she do the whole time she's in Ocky's castle?

After McTavish fails to scare Samantha by taking a swipe at her with his sword, he throws the weapon on the table, and it lands with a clunk. He is a ghost, and transparent – can an object he's taken into the afterlife be solid? He must also have spent some time in Plymouth, because he sports the same plastic shackles that detained Darrin in "Samantha's Thanksgiving to Remember" (#119). The effect of McTavish removing his head from his shoulders comes off very well...until he talks. Then his chin moves on his headless body.

Darrin is once again upset that Samantha has zapped herself to parts unknown, but you'd think he'd be used to it by now – it was Paris in "Witch or Wife" (#8), and Japan in "Sam in the Moon" (#91). His slurring pro-witch speech borrows from the former episode, particularly when he says Endora's been right all along, and that you can't expect a "proud bird" to "walk around with a smile on its beak." Darrin also appears to recall, word for word, sections of Serena's "if you had any vision" rant from "Double, Double...Toil and Trouble" (#111), and he even incorporates Endora's "sparkle of a star" lecture, first uttered in "Be It Ever So Mortgaged" (#2), even though he's never heard it.

Samantha only mentions America, not that she's from it, and it's a big country. So how does McTavish navigate his way into her living room? Does he follow her? Then, Darrin warns Samantha that she has until sundown to give up the ghost. Will he threaten to leave her again if she doesn't? Later, to dissuade Phyllis from thinking she heard Ocky begging McTavish to come back, Samantha zaps up a televised cowboy, who asks "Sam" to get his sheriff back. But Phyllis never wonders why the TV wasn't on when she first came into the house – and, if Samantha really wants to fool Phyllis, a British drama would work better than a western.

OH, MY STARS!

On one level, the show is to be commended for reminding the audience that Samantha is Queen of the Witches. On another, the mention only points up a lack of consistency, since Samantha's royal post hasn't been addressed since "Double, Double...Toil and Trouble" (#111). Has Samantha been spending all her midnights on the throne, as she vowed to do in "Long Live the Queen" (#108)? Not likely, and Aunt Clara thinking Samantha can evict McTavish, "being queen and all," is for naught; once Samantha meets the ghost, she never plays the queen card at all.

Research indicates that the United Kingdom lays claim to over 180 castles – and Samantha happens to pop into the one where Frank and Phyllis are staying. Then, Phyllis decides to fly to New York right away to make sure Samantha is home. That defies logic – if the elder Stephenses can fly back, surely Samantha can hop a flight that could get her to Morning Glory Circle ahead of them. Finally, consider: last time Phyllis saw Samantha [in "Out of Sync, Out of Mind" (#116)], her daughter-in-law had green stripes on her face, the latest in a long line of strange occurrences. Samantha told Phyllis she was a witch in "Samantha Meets the Folks" (#14) – after seeing her pop out here, shouldn't Phyllis be thinking it's true?

SON OF A GUN!

"But that's what ghosts do, lassie – scare people. What would have you have me do at my age, learn a trade?" – McTavish to Samantha, wondering how he can keep his eternity occupied if he leaves his set-up at Ocky's castle.

HOW GREEN WAS MY GRASS

Airdate: February 29, 1968

Distracted by phone calls and doorbells, Samantha saves her burning pancakes with witchcraft, infuriating Darrin. When he slams the door on the way out, the loose "9" on the house becomes a "6" – prompting delivery men to mistakenly install artificial grass on the Stephenses' lawn. Thinking Samantha has put the grass there in response to the boy who offered to reseed their lawn earlier, Darrin harangues Samantha about it so much that she makes two things disappear: the grass, and Darrin, who gets popped down to the couch. The next morning, the delivery men, who have realized their mistake, come to take the grass back; Darrin stalls them, but, because he's also insulted Endora, Samantha can't rematerialize the grass because of her mother's counteraction spell.

MacLane, the neighbor who was supposed to get the grass, comes over ready to punch Darrin, which Samantha magically prevents. The inspired Darrin suggests to Samantha that she can install the artificial grass on MacLane's lawn instead; she has trouble doing so at first, but finally succeeds. The following day, Darrin makes breakfast and burns his own pancakes as he talks to the boy about reseeding the lawn; Darrin thanks Samantha for letting them burn, not seeing her use her powers to keep him from knocking his coffee cup off the kitchen table.

GOOD!

The title of this episode is a reference to the 1941 film, *How Green Was My Valley*. And, for all Darrin's ranting in this episode, he proves not to be green when it comes to witchcraft: he rightly surmises that Samantha can zap artificial grass onto the MacLanes' lawn, since Endora's counterspell only applies to their own.

This grass menagerie gets watered by Tabatha's scene-stealing moment, in which she lobbies for "two balloons and two lollipops" on the way to the pediatrician. Samantha's "I told you to go at the doctor's!" when they return says it all when it comes to kids.

WELL?

This isn't the first time Samantha has flipped pancakes with witchcraft, nor is it the first time she's been caught. In "Art for Sam's Sake" (#98), the housewife also kept her breakfast from burning by using her nose. Endora's reaction to Samantha's hexed hotcakes in that episode was the polar opposite of Darrin's reaction here, to say the least.

Craig Hundley, the young actor who played Merle in "A Strange Little Visitor" (#48), makes his second appearance on the show, this time as a budding landscaper. Come to think of it, what happened to Merle? Has the preteen warlock had no occasion to pop in on Samantha – or Darrin, whom he made friends with? Merle would be a wonderful mentor (and sitter) for Tabatha.

The mirror is back in the Stephenses' foyer, where it was in "Out of Sync, Out of Mind" (#116); notice how it's only there when someone needs to look into it. And do Darrin and Samantha have two cars now? That's how many are in the driveway, but the Stephenses have almost always been a one-car family.

It's pitch black out when Samantha removes the artificial grass, which is the perfect cover. So why blow it by adding thunder and lightning to the spell? Is Samantha expressing her anger toward Darrin? At least Darrin looks around the street the next morning to make sure no one sees Samantha bringing the fake foliage back, but Gladys could still be watching from her window. And why, when Samantha can't rematerialize the artificial grass, does she assume someone is counteracting her spell? Her powers could be out, as they were in "Take Two Aspirins And Half A Pint of Porpoise Milk" (#42) and "No Zip in My Zap" (#113). It's ironic, too, that Endora would prevent Samantha from tending to her lawn, when she was the first to jazz it up in "Be It Ever So Mortgaged" (#2).

As Darrin looks at the delivery van parked in front of his house, the ornate buildings from "My Grandson, the Warlock" (#40) are back, but the Kravitzes' house is still missing; trees have been in its place most of the season. Then, Darrin tries to intimidate his furious neighbor by boasting that he boxed in the Navy – but "Just One Happy Family" (#10) and "We're In For A Bad Spell" (#39) established that Darrin served in the Army. If Darrin really wants to mess with MacLane, he should tell him how he knocked out professional fighters in "Fastest Gun on Madison Avenue" (#57). Darrin's right that Samantha's a great referee, because she's done it before: she magically blocks MacLane's punch the way she did jealous Monster's in "The Girl Reporter" (#9).

After her first attempt to witch MacLane's lawn, Samantha gets real grass and surmises she may be incapable of zapping up the artificial version. Since witches have nearly unlimited powers, it's unlikely Samantha can't perform such a simple spell. She specifically says, "change this lawn to verdant green," which she does. She's more specific about conjuring up "wax and sheen" the second time, so she has to be aware of her wording; there's no reason for her to think she can't produce artificial grass.

On Day 2 of the lawn saga, Darrin runs around in his suit dealing with the MacLanes' grass. It appears to be mid-morning: he should be at the office, and MacLane probably shouldn't be on his lawn with a beer. On Day 3, Darrin makes breakfast as a way of making up for "yesterday," forgetting that he actually started the whole mess two days before. Samantha saves Darrin's coffee cup before it hits the floor, but her trademark twitch sound effect is missing; she makes the gesture, but there's only the sound of her accompanying zap.

OH, MY STARS!

This episode contains perhaps the biggest continuity flaw of the entire series – the Stephenses' house number is now 192. Darrin and Samantha have always lived at 1164 Morning Glory Circle, as indicated by the plaque that has been on the house since its first appearance in "Be It Ever So Mortgaged" (#2) – however, the show goes so far as to take the plaque down to facilitate this story. If artificial grass really needs to be installed at the wrong house, why not just loosen the Stephenses' existing "6" and make the house 1194? Or have the delivery guys get the street mixed up, making them think they're at 1164 Elm Street, for example? Changing such an important detail after four seasons is about as logical as the Stephenses fighting over a lawn.

Darrin admits overreacting about the pancakes, and his either-I-can-afford-it-or-I-can't fury can be traced back to the alternate reality of "If They Never Met" (#127), where Darrin resisted Sheila Sommers' father paying for things. But there's something in Darrin's outraged reactions to pancakes and grass that actually takes him into cartoon territory. He only offers Samantha an apology so she'll bring the artificial grass back, and later, he has the cheek to tell her, "I'm a sweetheart." This is not the Darrin Stephens that viewers know and love.

SON OF A GUN!

"I see. When would be the best time?" – Samantha to Darrin, after he tells her being responsible for $2,000 worth of artificial grass is no time to start an argument.

TO TWITCH OR NOT TO TWITCH

Airdate: March 14, 1968

After catching Endora entertaining Tabatha with witchcraft – and Samantha using a speed-up spell to finish getting ready for a formal dinner party – Darrin rages that he doesn't want Samantha performing magic under any circumstances. Driving in the rain to meet new client Sharpe, Darrin gets a flat tire, but Samantha refuses to change it; the soaked Darrin has to wear Sharpe's ill-fitting tux and reacts badly to everyone's laughter. The Stephenses resume arguing at home, and, after Darrin makes some harsh allusions to Samantha's age, she takes Tabatha and "goes home to Mother."

At the office, Darrin underplays his tiff with Samantha to Larry, who wants Darrin to mend fences with Sharpe. Darrin is maneuvered into a dinner with Sharpe and expected to bring the missing Samantha; Darrin apologizes to the ether, prompting Samantha to appear. The Stephenses make up, and Darrin wants to take Samantha out privately, but, after Endora magically patches into Larry's phone call warning Darrin to show up at the Sharpes, she bets her daughter that Darrin will flake on their celebration – and Samantha has to come home with her if he does. Darrin insists they're going out alone, but Samantha influences Larry to call so she can arrange for them go to the Sharpes. On the way, when Darrin runs out of gas, Samantha secretly zaps up a filling station to help him out.

GOOD!

Samantha's "far be it for me to use witchcraft under any circumstances" comeback is exactly what Darrin deserves for barking at her about not using her powers, then sweetly asking for magical help because it suits him. And guest character Gwen Sharpe catching her own husband in a lie about his trip to Lake Athabasca, then turning it around on him, is a highlight of the episode. Sharpe's "uh-oh" expression speaks volumes.

The show hasn't hinted about Samantha's age since "Eye of the Beholder" (#22), so even though it happens over the course of an argument, it's intriguing to revisit this story point. It seemed Darrin had tacitly accepted his wife's life span, but apparently he hasn't. And Samantha shows that she is also Maurice's daughter by quoting Shakespeare the way "Daddy" did in "Witches and Warlocks Are My Favorite Things" (#77).

You know it's something when a blustery guy like Larry seems more compassionate than Darrin, but his concern for the Stephenses is on par with the softer side he displayed in "Hippie, Hippie, Hooray" (#128). Of course, his "Try using the phone" suggestion when Darrin calls out to the ether balances things out with some comedy.

It's not always apparent that the show's characters live in New York State, but the road sign next to Samantha's invented gas station provides a reminder. "Chataqua," the road the sign points to, is very much a name you'd find in that part of the country; there's a Chautauqua County in western New York. The sign misses a "u", but it still adds the local color it's supposed to.

WELL?

The Stephenses may be in an uproar again, but their closet is back to where it should be after its migration in "Snob in the Grass" (#126). Instead of getting herself ready via speed-up spell, Samantha could prevent a lot of trouble by just zapping herself into her evening clothes all at once. Why doesn't she?

Samantha and Darrin have argued in the car before: once while it was stuck in the garage in "Open the Door, Witchcraft" (#28), and most notably in "The Magic Cabin" (#52) – notable because they had almost the exact "under any circumstances" argument in the latter episode. It rained then, too, only this time, the Stephenses' interaction is far more hostile. Darrin can't justify ordering Samantha not to use her powers under any circumstances, anyway – he just asked her to twitch up a lawn in "How Green Was My Grass" (#131).

The fighting Stephenses laundry list ancient celebrities Samantha must have known: Shakespeare and Henry VIII, with Bluebeard thrown in for good measure. The implication in "Eye of the Beholder" (#22) was that Samantha was a young woman in 1682, so she may or may not have known Willie and Henry, who each lived in the 16th century. But she couldn't know Bluebeard in any age or time, since he is solely a folktale creation, first published in 1697 by Charles Perrault.

It's either rehash or great consistency: for the third time in the series, Samantha pops out, and Darrin demands that she appear before him. This exchange also occurred in "Help, Help, Don't Save Me" (#5) and "Three Wishes" (#96), although Samantha changes it up this time by dematerializing instead of surrounding Darrin with floating suitcases. In "Allergic to Ancient Macedonian Dodo Birds" (#118), Samantha reported that Endora couldn't get home without witchcraft; Samantha "goes home to Mother" here, revealing that Endora apparently lives in the clouds – clouds with very visible strings. Later, Endora tells Samantha that she'll see her on Cloud 8. Is that Endora's address?

Much tension ensues over Sharpe wanting a make-up dinner that night. Darrin could buy himself time by rescheduling instead of trying to brush off the soirée off altogether. Then, Darrin offers to take Samantha to a cozy French restaurant to celebrate their reunion when he knows he won't be able to get out of dining with the Tates and the Sharpes.

When Endora pops in to watch Larry pressuring Darrin, is she invisible to the mortals, or could they see her if they looked in her direction? And Samantha has to try three times to witch Larry into calling because Louise comes in and physically prevents him from picking up the phone. That's not the way witchcraft has been known to work; once Larry has the spell on him, his only intention should be to make that call, regardless of interruptions.

The Sharpes are shown to live in a very ritzy residence, yet the Stephenses drive there on a dirt road. A moment later, when Samantha zaps up the gas station [in "The Magic Cabin" (#52), she merely conjured up a half tank of gas], they are on a paved highway.

OH, MY STARS!

Darrin just fumed over pancakes in the previous episode, and here he loses it over speed-dressing and a flat tire. Maybe seeing Endora floating blocks with Tabatha makes for a double dose of witchcraft he doesn't need, but telling Samantha, "Why don't we use your broom?" – especially when he knows witches don't ride them – is as out of line as the rest of his resultant behavior.

Jean Blake is McMann & Tate's sixth Betty, who ushers a conciliatory Sharpe into Darrin's office. Either the agency's secretaries need to have different names, or the show needs to establish a running gag that no secretary is hired unless her name is Betty.

Samantha and Endora's bet storyline has a few chips missing. To hear them tell it, if Samantha is right that she and Darrin are going to dinner alone, Endora has to babysit; if Samantha's wrong, she and Tabatha have to come home with Endora. First off, that's an uneven bet. Then, Samantha acts as if everything is riding on Darrin confirming they're going out together – until she turns around and stacks the deck in Endora's favor by getting Larry to call so dinner at the Sharpes can happen. How does Samantha get out of the bet, anyway? Surely Endora wouldn't let such an opportunity slip through her fingers.

SON OF A GUN!

"You are one step away from making Custer's Last Stand look like a love-in.'" – Samantha, warning Darrin what will happen if he doesn't give peace a chance.

EPISODE 133

PLAYMATES
Airdate: March 21, 1968

Samantha asks Tabatha not to use any witchcraft in front of the visiting Phyllis. Mrs. Stephens is concerned that Tabatha has no friends, and feels Samantha is an overprotective mother, so she brings Tabatha to the Millhowsers for companionship. Samantha meets Gretchen Millhowser, who lets her son Michael make a mess and draw on walls in the interest of free expression. As Gretchen inundates Samantha with psychobabble, Michael and Tabatha end up playing together unsupervised; Michael grabs the sandbox shovel from Tabatha, but she floats it back to herself. Michael continues antagonizing Tabatha, and, when he wishes he were a dog so he can bite her, Tabatha turns him into the real thing.

Gretchen and Phyllis think Michael is missing and embark on a frantic search while Samantha pressures Tabatha to change him back; Tabatha can't because he's too far away. When Michael-as-dog joins the witches on the patio but the mortal women follow suit, Samantha distracts the ladies by making it sound like Michael is out front. Before Tabatha can reverse her spell, Michael-as-dog runs away, forcing Samantha to track him to a neighbor's yard and pop the animal into her arms. After Tabatha restores Michael, Gretchen thinks he's lying about having been a dog; she heeds Phyllis and Samantha's advice to try some discipline, giving her rude son a swat. Back home, Tabatha makes the stuffed bunny Phyllis brought hop down the stairs, which Samantha barely keeps Phyllis from seeing.

GOOD!

Samantha's tried to explain the problem of witchcraft in a mortal world to Tabatha before [in "Nobody's Perfect" (#75) and "The Safe and Sane Halloween" (#115)], but the twist here is that the girl is now old enough to at least try to understand what her mother is talking about. Samantha giving Tabatha a big smile, even though she's frustrated with her daughter for floating her shoes into the room, shows the loving bond between them in just one expression.

Gretchen confusing everyone with her persistent psychological excuses (suggesting that disobedient Michael is merely "sublimating anxiety" and desirous of "group identification") is a good bit of *au courant* humor, especially when Samantha turns it around on Gretchen to the point no one knows what she's talking about.

Young Teddy Quinn makes Michael the perfect brat, but he has other nuances that prove he isn't just your typical child actor. He looks both perplexed and awed when Tabatha levitates the sandbox shovel away from him, genuinely wanting to know "How do you do that?" Plus, once Michael finds himself back in his own body, his astonishment is palpable. Erin Murphy proves her mettle, too, especially during

Michael and Tabatha's battle, and both children are already expert at facilitating the show's special effects: they hardly move as Michael gets zapped in and out of Tabatha's cage, or when Tabatha turns Michael into the dog.

WELL?

Phyllis, who can be quirky, nervous, and sometimes quarrelsome, is suddenly haughty toward her daughter-in-law, with no provocation. One thing she's right about – Samantha *is* being overprotective, if only because of Tabatha's inability to control her witchcraft. Is this why Tabatha and Jonathan aren't growing up together, despite their parents being besties?

Both Samantha and Gretchen seem to have identity crises where Phyllis is concerned: Samantha calls her "Mother Stephens," a moniker she's never used before, and Gretchen refers to her as "Aunt Phyllis," though Phyllis is only a friend of her mother. Is "aunt" just an affectionate affectation? As for the kids, when Michael barks for Tabatha to get off his swing, the camera shakes; later, a wide shot shows Tabatha in a stationary position on the swing set, but when it cuts to a medium shot, the tyke is swinging away.

Tabatha can now zap with her arms and turn people into animals – yet Samantha still calls it "wishcraft." By that definition [as established in "A Prince of a Guy" (#129)], Michael-as-dog is only a projection and should be able to run through walls. Then, Samantha has Tabatha attempt to turn Michael back from a distance; had it worked, Michael would have become a boy again right in front of Gretchen and Phyllis. And Samantha's reasoning that Tabatha is too young to restore Michael unless he's right there is inconsistent with "It's Wishcraft" (#103), where Tabatha zapped Darrin off the porch all the way from her nursery a whole year earlier.

Once Michael-as-dog joins Samantha and Tabatha on the patio, mother tells daughter how she used ventriloquism to distract Phyllis and Gretchen; a moment later, Phyllis steps onto the patio, and the dog runs away. Tabatha would have had plenty of time to turn Michael back if Samantha had saved her explanation for later. Samantha must have a déjà vu as she chases Michael through the alley; she chased the similarly transformed Rex Barker though an alley in "It Shouldn't Happen to a Dog" (#3) – and now both Samantha and Tabatha have made canines out of people.

When Michael becomes a boy again, he has a full memory of having had four legs. Yet Gladys' nephew, Tommy, spent time as a goat in "The Safe and Sane Halloween" (#115) and answered with a "Huh?" when asked to talk about his experience. Samantha apparently belongs to a group that advocates the use of discipline (read: spankings), but she must not apply this to Tabatha, who only gets talked to when she uses her powers – on-screen, anyway. Maybe that's why Tabatha feels free to perform witchcraft again here.

OH, MY STARS!

Phyllis heads toward Samantha's house from a street that isn't Morning Glory Circle – this street has different buildings, and a curve that was never there before. Is the show unable to obtain the same exterior location from episode to episode?

Ever since Frank and Phyllis Stephens made their début in "Samantha Meets the Folks" (#14), their residence has been in question. In that episode, they flew in for a visit; in "A Nice Little Dinner Party" (#19), they had moved to the area – and back and forth it's gone. Now, Phyllis tells Samantha that Gretchen and her family "just moved here" as if "here" is the town Phyllis lives in, too. Isn't it time to give Frank and Phyllis a permanent home?

SON OF A GUN!

"I didn't think so. So stay close to Mommy and we'll hope for the best." – Samantha to Tabatha, who doesn't understand why she can't do witchcraft in front of Grandma Stephens.

Tabatha dominates this episode, holding her own with Michael and offering some brutal honesty about her grandmothers: "With Grandma Endora I have fun!" Tabatha has even picked up on her mother's catchphrase – "Good!" – which Samantha has been uttering since the pilot.

"Hoho the Clown" (#92) established that a witch can't undo another witch's spell; now it's revealed the rule applies to a young witch's spell as well. "I suppose I should say *you* have to change him back," Samantha tells Tabatha regarding Michael, "because it's your spell." This brilliantly takes magical consistency down to the next generation.

EPISODE 134
TABATHA'S CRANKY SPELL
Airdate: March 28, 1968

While Tabatha is willfully using her powers, Samantha is strong-armed into accepting Louise's Aunt Harriet as a babysitter so Samantha and the Tates can gang up on Baker, a client who refuses to modernize his product's packaging. Harriet brings a crystal ball to contact the spirit of her late beau and thinks he's sending signals when Tabatha flies objects around the house. Harriet excitedly phones Louise, but Samantha magically cuts the call off; when pro-paranormal Mrs. Baker hears Louise's report that Harriet summoned a ghost, the crowd follows her to the Stephenses. To discredit Harriet's claim, Samantha lulls her to sleep with witchcraft and suggests she was dreaming, but Mrs. Baker sneaks into the kitchen and sees Tabatha's hovering glass of milk. When Mrs. Baker insists that Harriet contact Baker's Uncle Willie, who designed the disputed packaging, Baker thinks it's all a scheme to manipulate him, and storms out.

Samantha brings Harriet's crystal ball to Mrs. Baker, talking her into a séance so Samantha can become Uncle Willie. But Samantha doesn't count on the real Willie's ghost showing up; he also wants Baker to keep up with the times, and recruits Samantha-as-Willie to scare Baker into changing his mind. It works, but later, when Larry makes it sound like he was the one who badgered Baker into modernizing, Samantha imitates Baker, repeating the client's orders verbatim and unnerving Larry.

GOOD!

The departed Mr. Henderson is the butt of many spectral jokes in this episode – when Harriet laments that her boozy beau "is in the spirit world now," Samantha concludes that "he was in the spirit world before he left." Getting the last word, Harriet feels cold air thanks to Tabatha's rocking horse floating out the door, and feels it can't be Henderson, because he's "in a much warmer place." Harriet tops this by going full-on mystic, confidently droning about Henderson after her "success."

Sarah Seegar, who played very unassuming characters in "A Vision of Sugar Plums" (#15/#51) and "That Was No Chick, That Was My Wife" (#117), gets a chance to shine here as believer Mrs. Baker – her overdone "Uncle Willie, come forth" says it all.

WELL?

Despite the title, Tabatha doesn't seem very cranky in this episode; her disobedience feels more gleeful than grumpy. Endora stirs the pot by suggesting Tabatha visit the witch's nursery school where Samantha learned how to fly. If this is the same school that Hagatha was said to run in "Witches and Warlocks Are My Favorite Things" (#77), Endora doesn't connect the dots. As for Samantha, her "if you can't beat 'em, join 'em" decision to take a call on Tabatha's toy telephone must be inspired by the tyke; Tabatha called Pittsburgh on one in "Toys in Babeland" (#109).

If Samantha is stuck for a sitter, and she's going to the Tates anyway, why not just bring Tabatha there to spend time with Jonathan? Larry says Harriet has been sitting for Jonathan since he was born, but that goes against "My Grandson, the Warlock" (#40), where a governess fulfilled that duty, "Maid to Order" (#53), when Jonathan enjoyed the company of Esmeralda, the Tates' now-missing maid, and most of this season, where Larry has inferred that Louise's mother is doing the sitting.

Morning Glory Circle is often a studio backdrop when seen from the Stephenses' front door, but this time shadows are cast on it, and the bottom doesn't make complete contact with the floor. Tabatha's nursery is said to be the door on the left at the top of the stairs, but previous episodes show a wall as you look out that door; if it's where Samantha says it is, the Stephenses' bedroom would be visible instead. Speaking of doors, is Harriet so entranced by the possibility of contacting Mr. Henderson that she doesn't hear the front door opening and closing as Tabatha's rocking horse makes its way through?

Samantha assumes that whatever supernatural happenings Harriet has seen are being caused by Tabatha. But Samantha should be open to the possibility of Mr. Henderson, since she just encountered a ghost in "McTavish" (#130). Then, Larry cracks that his business is dying in front of Mrs. Baker, the client's wife, which is rather bad form, not to mention an overstatement; surely McMann & Tate isn't going to go under because of one account. Besides, Baker's is only worth $500,000, and Larry wasn't nearly as concerned with the $8½ and $10 million accounts handled earlier this season. Samantha likewise exaggerates when she sighs to Endora that she and Darrin "may end up without any money in our own bank."

Endora, usually the mover and shaker of any episode she appears in, doesn't serve much purpose in this one, and it's highly unlikely that a witch of her ability doesn't know what a crystal ball is. And Willie, who at least gets metal chains instead of plastic ones like McTavish, knows Samantha is a witch simply because "in my circle, word gets around." Ghosts gossip about witches? Willie should automatically sense that Samantha is a witch just by virtue of the fact that they are both supernatural entities. When Samantha turns herself into Willie the first time, she shifts during the effect; the second time is better, but the overlay used to make Willie look transparent also makes the fence behind him look blurry, compared to the fence behind Samantha.

The secondary thrust of this episode is convincing Baker to modernize his packaging – but no one ever mentions what his product is. Does Baker make cake mix? Cough syrup? Window cleaner? Knowing what Baker peddles might explain why this upgrade is so important. Good thing Mrs. Baker faints so Samantha-as-Willie can chastise Baker privately.

Samantha shakes Larry up by imitating his word-for-word conversation with Baker – this after making him think a money bag was flying out the window. What's the point of these pranks? Is she getting back at Larry for vicariously threatening to fire Darrin? (At least Larry admitted the tactic was melodramatic.)

OH, MY STARS!

Samantha's surprised when she meets Willie, telling him, "It's not every day I meet a ghost." As previously discussed, she just tangled with one four episodes ago, in "McTavish" (#130): not only does it seem a little soon to do another ghost story, but there are several discrepancies between the two episodes. To begin with, Samantha sounds spooked when Larry tells her Harriet likes to contact the next world; this should be old hat for Samantha, unless she's play-acting for Larry's benefit. Later, Willie says he's been invisible to the Bakers for 45 years because they don't believe in him. Agnes Baker believes – and she still can't see him. While belief determining a ghost's visibility is an intriguing concept, Phyllis had no problem seeing the Scottish spirit of "McTavish" (#130). Maybe Mother Stephens' belief in the supernatural goes deeper than she's ever let on.

SON OF A GUN!

"Why not? I'm hot tonight!" – Aunt Harriet, when Mrs. Baker asks her to contact Uncle Willie.

EPISODE 135

I CONFESS
Airdate: April 4, 1968

After Samantha magically subdues an amorous drunk with a pail of water, Darrin angrily decides they should tell the world she's a witch. To show Darrin the folly of this plan, Samantha lulls him to sleep with a dream spell that demonstrates how people might react to such an admission: though dubious at first, Larry soon wants Samantha to help him control the world and fires Darrin when he won't allow it, while the Kravitzes shake in mortal terror at displays of Samantha's witchcraft. Samantha ups the ante in Darrin's dream by informing the whole world about her identity, which results in the Stephenses being besieged by crowds and telephone calls.

The United States military arrives to warn Samantha and Darrin that they're in danger because witch burning has been revived; in addition to suggesting that Samantha place everyone in protective custody, the armed forces also call on her to use her powers on their behalf. Samantha zaps Darrin and Tabatha to a desolate enclosure in the desert, which boasts a soulless trailer as their new home. Officers take Samantha and Tabatha for a briefing, leaving Darrin alone; his protestations manifest in reality, where Samantha wakes her husband from the dream. In the morning, Samantha tells Darrin she's ready to confess to the world, but Darrin backpedals, saying life is fine the way it is and causing Samantha to smile over her breakfast.

GOOD!

More than likely, the title of this episode is a reference to the 1953 Alfred Hitchcock film, *I Confess*. It's important to keep in mind that Darrin's entire dream sequence is only Samantha's interpretation of what would happen if they did, in fact, confess, and it provides some interesting glimpses into her personal insights, especially about Larry. That he becomes power mad as soon as he learns of Samantha's witchery may well stem from her observations of Larry's real-life obsessiveness over clients, and perhaps Dream Larry's claim that he's wanted to rule the world since he was a little kid is Samantha's explanation for his overbearing behavior; she knows Larry well enough that she even has him fire Darrin in the dream. Abner going circus barker while Gladys counts their take from the crowd before giving a "thrilling lecture" also says a lot about Samantha's view of the Kravitzes and what they would do with the information.

Of course, Dick Wilson can always be counted on for hilarity with his lovable, usually nameless lushes, but his going cold sober and declaring "I'm a reformed drunk" after his unexpected bath is a great twist.

WELL?

This standout episode nevertheless borrows heavily from three previous installments: "Baby's First Paragraph" (#62), in which Tabatha's "talking" caused a public craze, "What Every Young Man Should Know" (#72), where Endora showed how Darrin and Larry would react to witchcraft in an alternate reality, and "Sam in the Moon" (#91), in which Darrin's fantasy/dream had Samantha detained by the military. The elements fuse together well enough, but Larry's desire to rule the world, and his desire for "a piece of the action," comes almost verbatim out of "What Every Young Man Should Know" (#72).

Have the Stephenses' painted their bathroom? In "Out of Sync, Out of Mind" (#116), its walls were red; now they're blue. And Samantha and Darrin have switched places on the bed, probably to simplify the staging of Samantha putting her dream spell on Darrin, which is enacted with a doubled twitch.

Again, everything that happens in Darrin's dream is from Samantha's imagination: her "card-carrying, cauldron-stirring witch" admission mirrors her wedding night confession of "I, Darrin, Take This Witch, Samantha" (#1), and the Kravitzes acting as if Samantha is an alien must be Samantha's recollection of "Abner Kadabra" (#29), where Gladys caught Samantha using her powers and assumed she was from Venus. However, Samantha goes on to narrate that she and Darrin have told all their friends about her being a witch. The only friends that the Stephenses have come in for one episode and aren't seen again, except for the Tates, and Samantha leaves out Louise's reaction. Tabatha has no friends, either, as Phyllis correctly observed in "Playmates" (#133), yet Samantha laments that none of Tabatha's friends will play with her because her mother won't give them ponies.

Darrin never parks his car on the curb – unless he's going to be ambushed by a crowd; he did the same thing in "Baby's First Paragraph" (#62). In "I Get Your Nanny, You Get My Goat" (#122), Samantha adamantly told Darrin that witches don't ride "obsolete" brooms – so she wouldn't tell her dream phone caller that her broom is booked for the season. Samantha is then awed when baseball player Mickey Mantle calls to ask for her witchly help on the diamond – she should refer him to fellow big leaguer Willie Mays, who was revealed to be a warlock in "Twitch or Treat" (#81).

Samantha reminds Darrin that they've changed their phone number ten times; that's an improvement over "Baby's First Paragraph" (#62), where the Stephenses never bothered changing it, despite being media darlings. Assuming another moocher is calling, Darrin slams the receiver down on the television and leaves it there; once Agent W of the HHH gets inside the house, he's quick to close the door and curtains for privacy, but doesn't notice the phone is off the hook; someone could easily be listening in on this classified conversation.

As Samantha lists magical relatives for her military visitors, she begins to mention a cousin, cutting off a name that sounds like Edgar. This seems to be a clever reference to "Cousin Edgar" (#36), except Edgar is an elf, not a warlock. Then, Samantha and her family disappear with a grand gesture, but a shadow moves in the lower left-hand corner of the screen after they pop out.

When Darrin emerges from his nightmare, he doesn't wonder why Samantha is hovering over him with the light on. By the way, how do the Stephenses resolve this latest fight? Darrin simply wakes up and pats Samantha on the arm; the next morning, there are no apologies, nor references to their scuffle. Are they fighting so often now that they make up by default?

OH, MY STARS!

It's one thing for Darrin to be upset about the constant witchcraft that surrounds him, but his recent habit of raging over the smallest infractions seems as unreasonable as Samantha suggests it is. He's so beside himself here that he blindly suggests going public with Samantha's witchcraft, forgetting the events of "Baby's First Paragraph" (#62), where the mere implication that his newborn daughter could talk made them all paparazzi targets. If Darrin is so fed up with the magic in his life, how is telling the world about it supposed to solve his problem? It would be far wiser for him to simply lift his ban on witchcraft – especially where Tabatha is concerned, removing the forbidden fruit atmosphere from his house might make magic seem less sweet.

SON OF A GUN!

"Congratulations, sir. That's an amazing disguise!" – Larry to Samantha, after Darrin tries to tell his boss that Samantha isn't a woman.

EPISODE **136**

A MAJORITY OF TWO
Airdate: April 11, 1968

Aunt Clara, who has had another falling out with Ocky, takes refuge in Samantha's home, while a desperate Larry asks Samantha to entertain Japanese client Mishimoto in Darrin's absence. Samantha can't find a recipe for Mishimoto's favorite Japanese dish, but puts together an impressive dinner; Aunt Clara insists they sit on the floor, as per custom, and zaps herself into a kimono for ambiance. Samantha's clothes likewise change as she opens the door to Mishimoto, who is honored by the homage and finds that Clara reminds him of his departed wife. Mishimoto asks Clara out, and they spend so much time together that Larry is unable to conduct business with him.

When it seems Mishimoto is going to propose, Samantha contacts Ocky, who wants Aunt Clara back. Upon hearing that Clara has reconciled with her estranged boyfriend, Mishimoto severs ties with McMann & Tate and books a flight for Tokyo. Samantha realizes her Asian visitor has "lost face" and heads to the airport, where she tries to get him to admit he's pulling his account out of embarrassment; she magically blanks her face to get her point across. When it doesn't work, she influences a Japanese stewardess to take notice of Mishimoto and keep him in town for Larry – but it backfires, as Mishimoto proceeds to spend all his time with her. Samantha inquires into Mishimoto's favorite dish, and he laughs that the mystery recipe is broken English for "Hungarian goulash."

GOOD!

It's refreshing to have an Aunt Clara episode that doesn't revolve around her wonky powers; in fact, her skillful kimono zaps (Clara and Samantha's costume changes are first-rate effects), and effortless popping out to see Ocky shows that Aunt Clara still has a lot on the ball. She's no fool, either, chiding Ocky for running off with "that little witch," as he also did in "The Short Happy Circuit of Aunt Clara" (#83).

Samantha pops into the airport as a pair of businessmen walk by, but there's never a gap in the movement of the men as she does. Of course, if you ask anyone about this episode, they will likely cite Samantha's literally blank face – the big white blotch is admittedly not the best of effects by today's standards, but for 1968 television, it's certainly a memorable image.

Larry comments that it's only spring when Samantha calls New York City a summer festival (true; this episode aired in April), and, while the American characters call Mishimoto "KEN-su," the Japanese flight attendant pronounces it the correct way: "ken-SU."

WELL?

No one would make octogenarian Marion Lorne bash into a door more than necessary, so it's understandable that her failed wall-walking attempt from "Accidental Twins" (#78) gets recycled here. Revisiting Ocky, however, merits some questions. His only two appearances have been in "The Short Happy Circuit of Aunt Clara" (#83) and "McTavish" (#130); Clara broke up with him in the former, and had not reunited with him by the latter. This episode implies there was a reunion at some point since, or Ocky couldn't throw Clara over again, but this plot point isn't addressed.

Louise is out of town, and Larry entertains Mishimoto at Samantha's – so who's watching Jonathan? Is Harriet from "Tabatha's Cranky Spell" (#134) back on duty, with or without her crystal ball? And Larry may well be the "average American" he prided himself on being in "Business, Italian Style" (#110), otherwise he'd realize that "hong ai wong goo rash," Mishimoto's supposed favorite meal, doesn't sound Japanese; the nonsensical words actually sound closer to Chinese. Larry must not look the "Japanese" recipe up in his book, either, or he'd know the dish isn't in there before giving the book to Samantha.

If Aunt Clara is opposed to flying in a plane, then what did she parachute down from in "The Moment of Truth" (#76)? Later, Samantha tells the frustrated Larry that forgoing business for Aunt Clara is Mishimoto's prerogative. Where is she getting that? Mishimoto flew 6,700 miles from Tokyo for the express purpose of signing with McMann & Tate.

Mishimoto works fast, wanting to propose to Aunt Clara after less than a week. Samantha decides to break them up solely so Larry can do business with him, even witching Ocky into calling, much like she did with Larry in "To Twitch or Not to Twitch" (#132); pity Ocky can't put in a quick appearance to grovel in person. But why does Samantha want her favorite aunt with a three-time cheater? And why does Larry think that Mishimoto will simply take Aunt Clara's departure in stride? Larry wouldn't have been so cavalier if the infatuated Louise had run off with Prince Charming in "A Prince of a Guy" (#129).

Yamato Airways' logo is very close to the symbol for Pan Am, which was a very popular airline during this period – but where is Larry when Samantha heads to the airport? He's probably not staying behind to watch Tabatha with Aunt Clara gone, and Samantha must drive off in the car to make it look good before popping into the terminal. How is her "losing face" scheme supposed to make Mishimoto change his mind about staying? If anything, his visions would make him want to get on the plane that much faster.

It's a wonder any Mishimoto televisions get made – he spends every moment he's supposed to be setting up advertising for his company squiring women around New York. He's even got Ocky beat: Mishimoto takes up with a young flight attendant no more than an hour after coming over to propose to Aunt Clara. Finally, in "Business, Italian Style" (#110), Darrin made an impassioned speech about not finding amusement in dialect humor. Yet, this episode ends with everyone laughing about how Mishimoto's secretary called Hungarian goulash "hong ai wong goo rash."

OH, MY STARS!

What to think of British actor Richard Haydn – perhaps best known for his role as Max in the 1965 film *The Sound of Music* – playing a Japanese businessman? His performance is fine, but the casting choice is highly reflective of a Hollywood that still insisted on Caucasian performers performing roles of other ethnicities; Haydn's eyelids were even lined with silver in an attempt to make him look Japanese. *Bewitched* has otherwise been very good about populating their backgrounds with Asian children [see "Little Pitchers Have Big Fears" (#6)] and all manner of African-American residents in a time when such inclusion was not the norm, so it's kind of a letdown that Mishimoto isn't portrayed by an Asian performer – especially after Japanese actor Bob Okazaki played Tokyo warlock Watanabe in "Sam in the Moon" (#91); even this episode's stewardess, Helen Funai, is Asian.

Larry grimaces "What is this?" when he sees he's going to dine sitting on the floor, and he looks down his nose at Samantha and Aunt Clara wearing kimonos. This may be consistent with Larry being repulsed by hippies in "Hippie, Hippie, Hooray" (#128), but it's amazing Mishimoto isn't offended by Larry ostensibly putting down his culture.

Samantha encourages Aunt Clara to reunite with Ocky, telling her the heart is "seldom wrong." Clara questions this move, then traipses off to be with Ocky, forcing Samantha to dump Mishimoto on her behalf – this after accepting an expensive dress from Mishimoto the day she's expecting him to propose. It's not like the gentle witch to be so callous.

SON OF A GUN!

"Well, uh, that's very sweet of you, but I wouldn't dare go up in a plane!" – Aunt Clara to Mishimoto, after her admission that she used to fly earns her an invitation to his private jet.

EPISODE 137

SAMANTHA'S SECRET SAUCER
Airdate: April 18, 1968

Samantha has to pull Darrin away from playing with Tabatha's space toy, a remote-controlled saucer that Tabatha later flies out to the patio while her parents attend a business dinner. Babysitter Aunt Clara casts a spell to retrieve the toy and ends up with a life-sized replica that contains beings from another world. The next morning, Gladys sees the spaceship and calls the Air Force, who sends officers to investigate. Darrin lies that he's using the "model" to advertise a toy, which fools Colonel Burkett, but not ambitious young Captain Tugwell, who believes Gladys. Once everyone leaves, canine-like aliens Alpha and Orvis emerge from the ship, shocking the Stephenses.

Samantha, who feels the extraterrestrials are friendly, pops into the ship and discovers they speak "Parenthian," which mirrors English. Alpha and Orvis follow Samantha outside, where they meet Darrin and enjoy an Earth breakfast of pancakes. Gladys and Tugwell peek in the kitchen window; while Tugwell contacts his superior, Gladys attempts to make a citizens' arrest and gets blasted by Alpha's "N-gun," which infuses her with "niceness." When Burkett arrives with Tugwell, Gladys airily agrees with Darrin's assertion that Alpha and Orvis are actors dressed as aliens. Tugwell gets demoted, and Aunt Clara is able to send Alpha and Orvis back to space with the help of Tabatha, who remembers part of her spell.

GOOD!

NBC's *Star Trek* was exceedingly popular when this episode aired, and the references made within it provide some knowing laughter. Aunt Clara declares Tabatha "a better spaceman than Dr. Spock" (a published pediatrician of the time). She then tells Alpha and Orvis she'd been under the impression that spacemen had pointy ears; the Parenthians speak of their cousin Rondo, "who had the ear job." But the Parenthians do offer a little science – looking at a space map, Orvis observes, "Boy, you're really out in the boondocks, aren't ya?" In relation to the Milky Way galaxy, that's exactly where Earth is.

In "Nobody But A Frog Knows How to Live" (#106), Gladys screamed that someday, someone would believe her. That day is here: Gladys finally gets an ally in the wet-behind-the-ears Captain Tugwell. They work rather well as a team – at least until Alpha's N-gun busts them up. But Gladys, under the influence of the N, is sticky, sweet, and side-splitting, causing Darrin to wonder if an N-gun would work on Endora.

WELL?

It's cute that Darrin has more fun playing with Tabatha's remote-controlled saucer than she does – but a space toy that flies, in the late '60s? That seems a little ahead of its time. Aunt Clara has sat for Tabatha repeatedly, yet Darrin finds it necessary to ask if she has everything straight. He also tells Samantha that maybe they should stay home until Tabatha is 21, the same suggestion Samantha made in "I Get Your Nanny, You Get My Goat" (#122). And, while it's funny that Aunt Clara tries and fails to be modern by saying "O-AK," she knows better: in "The Very Informal Dress" (#44), Aunt Clara confidently declared things were "A-OK," adding she liked to keep up with the times.

Alpha wails that he and Orvis are a million miles away from Parenthia – impossible, since it's 93 million miles just to go from the Earth to the sun. Later, Alpha corrects himself when he gauges the distance to his home planet as 250 trillion miles. He might want to check their ship, though: in an overhead shot, no periscope is visible; in a straight-on shot, the periscope is up. And in close-up, the periscope simply peeks out of the ship. Similarly, in another overhead shot, the top of the spaceship is illuminated, but, when Gladys views it through the gazebo, it's not. By the way, is Danger O'Riley [from "George the Warlock" (#30)] – or whoever is living next to 1164 Morning Glory Circle these days – okay with Gladys standing in their backyard to spy on the Stephenses? After Abner pooh-poohs Gladys' latest sighting, she grabs the phone and dials the Air Force – without having to look the number up first.

In "McTavish" (#130), Phyllis stood on her son's doorstep, able to hear Ocky talking about the ghost from the living room. Gladys and the military stand in the same spot, but can't hear Samantha and Darrin in the much closer foyer concocting their publicity stunt lie. And Samantha gets from the bottom of the stairs to Darrin's side on the patio in just two seconds.

Samantha, who is about as syrupy as her pancakes in this episode, makes the risky move of popping into the aliens' ship, putting a new spin on a sci-fi cliché by promising the Parenthians she won't take them to her leader. Except she is her leader, at least in terms of witches, as of "Long Live the Queen" (#108). After Samantha pops herself into the saucer, Darrin calls, "Sam? Where are ya?" as if she didn't just say she was going to meet the aliens in their ship. Then, Darrin, who is worried about the neighbors discovering the UFO, loudly attracts attention by yelling for it to open up.

Tugwell says he'll be wearing oak leaves once he apprehends the spacemen, and pulls out a plastic-wrapped set to show Gladys. Does he really go around carrying these badges in his pocket? Gladys, on the other hand, is back to thinking her neighbors are aliens; in "Abner Kadabra" (#29), she declared Samantha a resident of Venus after witnessing her witchcraft. Finally, when Burkett gets to the backyard, and the ship is gone, he only asks Tugwell where the space people are; he doesn't bother to ask how Darrin got his giant "model" out of the backyard so quickly.

OH, MY STARS!

Samantha says it all in this episode when she utters her catchphrase, "Oh, my stars!" A show that's given audiences elves, leprechauns, and conniving crones now introduces aliens, and their plot has more holes (make that black holes) than some of sci-fi's most infamous B-movies. Alpha and Orvis speak Parenthian (really English), they have photos and maps printed on paper just like Earthlings, and they know about pancakes and syrup. Maybe there is an alien race descended from dogs – but would they give their offspring terrestrial names like Yip and Yap? And, of course, the Parenthian spaceship just happens to look exactly like Tabatha's toy. The entire cast is game, and they give it their all, but this outer space saga is just out there.

SON OF A GUN!

"I liked her better the other way." – Orvis, commenting on the sugary change the N-gun makes in Gladys.

When Darrin puts it together that only Aunt Clara can send the spaceship back, Samantha nods "you're catching on." It seems the "squatter's rights" rule set forth in "Hoho the Clown" (#92) and "Playmates" (#133) is no longer an alien concept.

EPISODE
138
THE NO-HARM CHARM
Airdate: April 25, 1968

The agency is set to become McMann, Tate & Stephens – until Darrin's campaign includes a typo listing a bank's assets at $100. Darrin is convinced witchcraft is behind it and takes to his bed, resigning himself to a magical life. Uncle Arthur arrives with his usual brand of merriment; seeing Darrin so down, he gives his nephew-in-law a pep talk – and a charm designed to protect him from all harm, including witchcraft. Darrin races to the office a new man, but, when Samantha learns that Uncle Arthur only gave Darrin the top of a lamp to restore his confidence, she barely saves her reckless husband from getting into a car accident and decides to shadow him to keep him out of danger.

With Samantha and Uncle Arthur watching, Darrin tries to convince Larry they can generate tons of publicity for the bank by exploiting the typo. Darrin visits unresponsive bank president Markham with the idea, while Samantha and Uncle Arthur pay no notice to a messenger entering Markham's office – however, the messenger is a bank robber who whips out a gun. Thinking the charm will shield him, Darrin grabs for the weapon, which impresses Markham to the point he reconsiders his association with the agency. Darrin's heroism lands him the paper, but when Samantha admits the charm is fake, Darrin realizes the impact of what he's done and faints, with Uncle Arthur popping in to catch him.

GOOD!

After four years of being Larry's invisible partner [except for a brief mention in "Birdies, Bogies, and Baxter" (#114)], McMann, the man whose name comes before Tate, is the one who ultimately decides whether or not Darrin will make partner. Now the agency chief just needs to make an appearance.

This episode boasts some masterful effects: Paul Lynde sits perfectly still as Uncle Arthur waves one clown mask on, then zaps another one off. Equally stunning is the simple addition of Samantha's jacket. And, it's obviously a stunt man making Darrin's jump off the ladder, but the match to Dick York floating to the floor is exact.

Practical joking warlock Arthur has a new trick up his sleeve: he cares about Darrin. He makes a second trip to the house just to see how Darrin is doing, and he honestly means well when he uses reverse psychology in an attempt to pull Darrin out of his slump. He even self-effacingly replies, "I deserve that" when Darrin asks if the charm explodes.

WELL?

It's funny that, lately, whenever Tabatha's on-screen, she's eating. On the subject of food, Samantha tries to cheer Darrin up with his favorite dish: beef stew. That's quite a switch from his last favorite dish: turkey soup with extra wide noodles, which Darrin gobbled up in "Pleasure O'Riley" (#25).

Is Darrin fired, or isn't he? Samantha implores the depressed Darrin to get up and go to work, but Darrin told her the night before that Larry put him on sick leave, which essentially means he's fired. Later, Larry approves Darrin's rather good idea to exploit the typo, but extends Darrin's sick leave; if Darrin's been fired, there's nothing to extend.

Uncle Arthur likes his cows – he also zapped one up in "The Joker Is A Card" (#41). Another similarity to that episode is Uncle Arthur's private encouragement of Darrin – only then, it was a prank, and now the support is genuine. However, in both "Endora Moves in for a Spell" (#80) and this episode, Arthur likens his sister Endora to "Madame Lafarge." Close – the vengeful Dickens character from *A Tale of Two Cities* is actually "Madame *De*farge."

There's never been a table with a lamp on it in front of the Stephenses bedroom window before, but Arthur needs something to shoot at that's within camera range. Telling Darrin that the charm will protect him from everything is a dangerous generalization for Arthur to make; of course, had he limited the protection to witchcraft, Samantha wouldn't have to follow Darrin around all day, and Darrin wouldn't snatch a loaded gun, which would nullify most of the episode. Darrin is ecstatic that he can no longer be "hexed, zapped, or twitched," but it isn't fair of him to imply that Samantha is also putting spells on him; she rarely has, and never with the malicious intent that Endora does.

A split screen effect makes it possible for an oncoming car to pass through Darrin's, but the demarcation line is very noticeable, as it is when Samantha and Uncle Arthur are invisible in Larry's office. For that matter, why is the uncle/niece team transparent in Larry's office (where the shadow of a boom mic tries to make a cameo in the upper left corner of the screen), but not in Omega's reception area?

There's a bank robber in Markham's office waving a loaded gun – and Darrin picks this moment to fiddle with Uncle Arthur's charm. It's meant to reinforce Darrin's possession of the charm before he lunges for the weapon, but Markham and the crook must find it pretty odd for Darrin to play catch with a trinket during a hold-up. The front page of the *Daily Chronicle* (the show's most consistent newspaper thus far) contains stories about earthquakes, taxes, and soil conservation, but they're all upstaged by an article about one foiled bank robbery. Does Darrin get this kind of coverage because he punched out a heavyweight ["Fastest Gun on Madison Avenue" (#57)] and fathered a talking newborn ["Baby's First Paragraph" (#62)]?

OH, MY STARS!

Apparently Larry revised his timeline in terms of Darrin becoming a partner: in "Solid Gold Mother-In-Law" (#120), he said the company would be McMann, Tate & Stephens "a few years from now." Maybe McMann pulled rank and offered Darrin this promotion – but how can a typo sandbag everything? There's only ever an implication that the erroneous ad was made public, and even if it were, that doesn't discount all of Darrin's other good work these past years, nor does it merit tabling the promotion and putting Darrin out of a job. When it turns out the typo isn't even Darrin's fault, Larry still suggests "forever" as the time period for postponing Darrin's advancement. The show's structure likely dictates that Darrin needs to remain Larry's underling, but Darrin's really done dirty in this episode.

Sound effects get circulated through the show all the time, especially this season, which has conducted a plethora of sonic experiments. But someone got a little zap happy in this episode, inserting the same effect into almost every magical moment and ignoring the rest of the show's library. The lesson? Anything can grate after a while.

SON OF A GUN!

"That *is* a problem. Black isn't one of your best colors." – Uncle Arthur to Samantha, who fears the "charmed" Darrin won't make it through the day in one piece.

EPISODE 139

MAN OF THE YEAR
Airdate: May 2, 1968

After Darrin is voted McMann & Tate's Advertising Man of the Year, Endora feels the accolade will make Darrin egotistical. To prove it, she casts a spell around Darrin that makes all mortals within its circle agree with everything he says. Secretaries and clients alike fawn over Darrin, who improvises uninspired slogans that people love. Agency bigwig McMann invites Darrin to his boat to congratulate him on the award, but, under Endora's spell, McMann adds that Darrin should have Larry's job. True to Endora's prediction, all the attention starts to go to Darrin's head, and he even envisions himself becoming President of the United States.

At a party thrown in Darrin's honor, Samantha watches mortals falling at his feet and begins to suspect there's magic involved, especially when Darrin continues to offer up mediocre advertising ideas. Samantha pulls Darrin out of the party when he becomes insufferable; at home, Darrin is disappointed to learn that everyone's near-worship of him is the work of Endora, who agrees to remove the spell. Samantha reminds Darrin that the best ideas are polished, and convinces him to devise better campaigns for his current clients. The next day, the clients still like his pedestrian slogans, so Darrin asks Samantha to restore Endora's spell long enough to sell them on the more effective campaigns, later realizing that his own talents and sense of worth don't need puffing up.

GOOD!

Samantha calls Endora out for expressing disgust over Darrin winning the award. "You have always claimed that Darrin was a nobody," Samantha calmly says. "Now that he's being honored by his peers, you cannot stand it." That may be the truest statement Samantha has ever uttered. Mr. McMann makes his own insightful observation when he says that Larry is "hardworking, he's not impressed by facts, he's slippery, he lies beautifully, and he's got a nice head of hair." That is Larry Tate to a T.

Endora shows how with it she is when she remarks she's going to a costume party dressed as Twiggy, the popular 1960s model who epitomized "Swinging London." And Endora adds some clever gestures to illustrate her "egdeful, eyeful, trifle, tree" spell.

WELL?

There was much *Sturm und Drang* in "The No-Harm Charm" (#138) over Darrin almost making partner, then not, after those seven zeros went missing in Omega National Bank's promotional copy. Darrin was fired, and his promotion tabled. Yet, somehow, here, he is voted Advertising Man of the Year. Were the Huckster's Club ballots cast before the Omega omission? (The name of this club sounds like an insult of some sort, but it's probably a reference to the 1947 movie *The Hucksters*, which revolved around the world of advertising.) As for Endora, even though she checks to see that Samantha is out of earshot before talking to herself about the spell she wants to put on Darrin [unlike "Cheap, Cheap" (#112)], there's no way Samantha could get that far away from her mother in six seconds.

Before Slocum is bespelled, he scoffs at having to deal with Darrin, a junior partner. "The No-Harm Charm" (#138) confirmed that Darrin is not a partner, junior or otherwise. After Slocum is bespelled, Samantha has to remind Darrin that he's already told her about the success with Slocum twice – so why does she act surprised when he tells her the slogan? It had to have come up in the first two tellings. Later, McMann says that Larry gets a cut on every account Darrin brings in. Except Darrin never brings in accounts on his own; they're always assigned to him by Larry. Buoyed by McMann's high praise, Darrin brags to Samantha that he bowled his superior over. Doing what? He did nothing but sit there, listen, and drink coffee laced with 151-proof rum.

McMann and potential client Gilbert of course can't help but be dazzled by Darrin's ideas, but it's never shown what happens when they step out of the magical circle surrounding him. Do they instantly realize that Darrin's tractor slogan doesn't track? And it may be Larry who's throwing the party, as the venue looks just like his living room, only fancier. But, if that's true, where's Louise?

Darrin talks to a political backer who wants Darrin to run for Congress, the Senate, or even President. Darrin *was* Councilman Ed Wright's campaign manager in "Remember the Main" (#34), but that's the extent of his political experience.

After Darrin realizes that everyone's ardor is a product of Endora's witchcraft, he asks Samantha, "Does that mean I'm not really one of the Advertising Men of the Year?" Strangely, she never really answers the question. She does say, "No, of course not," but goes on to elaborate how Endora cast a spell around him that makes everyone love him. Maybe Samantha should clarify by mentioning that Endora didn't cast the spell until after he won the award.

As the dust settles, Darrin tries to talk coffee client Angel into accepting his less cliché slogan for the brew, but Angel still likes the one he heard the night before. Why? When Endora's spell was in effect, all Slocum had to do to become disenchanted with Darrin's idea was to step out of the circle of influence, so Angel shouldn't still be impressed, particularly with Endora's spell off.

OH, MY STARS!

Does Endora know something about Darrin's ego no one else does? After one client loves one impromptu idea, Darrin runs home, relentlessly brags to Samantha, and fancies himself President of the United States. That level of euphoria might make sense after his successful meeting with McMann, but his rapid ascent into egomania isn't part of Endora's spell; he's even nasty to Samantha when she doesn't go along with the adulation around him. And Darrin never picks up on the spell – despite the fact that, in "How to Fail in Business With All Kinds of Help" (#104), Madame Maruska's representative, Wilkerson, got a shot of similar everything-you-say-is-gold magic, and Darrin clued in right away.

SON OF A GUN!

"'Let Herc give it a jerk.'" – Darrin's off-the-cuff slogan that blows everyone away but Samantha.

McMann's the man – after four seasons of the head honcho being only a name on a door, this corporate captain skillfully navigates the comedic waters the minute he hoists anchor. He needs no spell to make quirky asides or show that he's as slippery as he says Larry is. Best of all, McMann and Tate appear in a room together for the first time. Wouldn't it be great if McMann stuck around and put the screws to Larry once in a while, the way Larry does to Darrin?

EPISODE
140

As Samantha readies for bed, she notices Gladys sitting on the curb trying to hitch a ride. Over Darrin's objections, Samantha approaches Gladys and discovers she is leaving Abner. Samantha offers Gladys refuge in her guest room; Gladys is hesitant based on their history, but accepts the invitation. The next morning, Gladys requires wheat germ oil and annoys Darrin with her lectures about health. Darrin wants Gladys out; however, when he comes home from work, Gladys has surprised everyone with an organic vegetarian dinner. Samantha visits Abner to convince him to patch things up with Gladys, but he's more interested in his poker game and seems happy Gladys is gone.

Gladys unintentionally amuses Tabatha with her beauty treatments, while Darrin threatens to leave if Gladys doesn't. Samantha thinks it will be faster to reunite the Kravitzes with witchcraft; Darrin balks, though he eventually accepts her idea to make their butcher, Mr. Hogersdorf, fall for Gladys to make Abner jealous. After Hogersdorf makes a beeline for the Stephenses and declares his intentions to Gladys, Samantha induces Abner to come over to witness the display. Abner's indifferent, but, after some prompting from Samantha, the Kravitzes realize they still have feelings for each other and make up. Darrin is impressed when Samantha confesses Abner was only witched into stopping by, and that the reunion itself was unassisted; she adds that love is the only thing stronger than witchcraft.

GOOD!

Tabatha's either making faces at Gladys' beauty cream, or just appreciating continuity: Gladys was already slathering herself with lotions in "Pleasure O'Riley" (#25). And for all her droning about the human body being a furnace, Gladys' insistence that her curlers and creams are meant to make herself attractive to Abner is unexpectedly heartfelt. "I admit I might be fighting a losing battle," she sheepishly admits, "but at least I try." How about that – the woman who cries witch to anyone who will listen can keep it real.

WELL?

The day-for-night shots where Samantha talks to Gladys on the curb are a valiant attempt, but that's not moonlight glistening off Samantha's hair, which looks longer outside than it does indoors. Nor is it likely that so many cars would be wheeling down a residential street like Morning Glory Circle that late at night.

Gladys tells Samantha that she's always wanted to desert Abner. Why? She only claims that she's "had it" with him, but never divulges what the actual problem is – she could be leaving Abner because she's tired of him not believing her claims about Samantha, for all anyone knows. Whatever the issue, Gladys throws in the towel after 22 years of marriage – forgetting that, in "Illegal Separation" (#32), she'd already been married to Abner 30 years; by now the Kravitzes have celebrated their 33rd anniversary.

Gladys proudly asserts that she's advocated health to Abner every morning of their marriage. If she has, it was before they first appeared in the series, because she didn't start talking about getting in shape until "Fastest Gun on Madison Avenue" (#57). Later, Gladys reminds Abner that she wants any profits from their mining stock. Apparently the Kravitzes have made a new investment since "My Baby, the Tycoon" (#55), when they traded shares in Poughkeepsie Woolens for East South Dakota Petroleum based on Tabatha's "advice." However, Gladys makes no mention of the bonds Abner said she was entitled to in "Red Light, Green Light" (#23).

Darrin has a right to feel put upon over the presence of his unwanted house guest, but he slams the door on his way out, which Gladys could easily hear, grouses full-volume about the organic dinner Gladys has laid out for him, and tells Samantha that he'll leave if Gladys doesn't. There's something to be said for sucking it up and being a gracious host anyway.

Abner's got a serious crush going – he dreamt about Sophia Loren in "Samantha's Secret Saucer" (#137), and here, all his poker buddies know about his fascination with the actress. But where have these friends come from? Abner's always been portrayed as a near-hermit; is the takeaway that Gladys has kept him from having friends?

Samantha only ever mentions that Gladys has a thing for her butcher, Mr. Hogersdorf, but she never confirms that the man is single before putting her love spell on him. What if he has a wife and kid at home who won't be too pleased about the head of their household putting moves on a customer? Samantha assures Darrin that Hogersdorf will get there "as fast as he can drive" – but no one can drive from a butcher shop to Morning Glory Circle in 19 seconds. And when he leaves, there's no Kravitz house across the street – plus there's an Amoco station where an apartment building and Texaco station once stood.

OH, MY STARS!

This episode carbon-copies many elements from "Illegal Separation" (#32), where Abner took refuge in the Stephenses' home after a split from Gladys – though there's a rather keen role reversal here in that Gladys is the deserter. That said, this installment also makes an illegal separation from the show's history in several ways. Gladys Kravitz has seen all manner of supernatural events across the street for the past four years – most recently, she called Samantha an alien [see "Samantha's Secret Saucer" (#137)]. Why would she even talk to Samantha, let alone confide anything to her about Abner? Despite nervously saying that "strange things seem to happen *over there*," Gladys gleefully agrees to spend the night. That might make sense were she jumping at the chance to finally investigate Samantha up close, but she simply acts as if the Stephenses are any other neighbors – and never questions it when Hogersdorf suddenly fawns over her. As for Samantha, she makes a guest of the woman who has sicced reporters on her, tried to expose her in court, and brought the military to her door. What's to stop Gladys from searching the house from top to bottom once everyone goes to sleep? Not to mention, Endora could pop in at any time, or Tabatha could zap something up – letting Gladys into the house for any extended period is a ticking time bomb, but this story point is never explored.

SON OF A GUN!

"Mrs. Kravitz once told me she thought he looked like Henry Fonda. So, I'll make him 'Fonda' Mrs Kravitz."
– Samantha to Darrin, describing how she's going to hex Hogersdorf.

One tiny detail from "Illegal Separation" (#32) shines through to this episode: Mrs. Kravitz intends to revert to her maiden name of Gladys Gruber. Alice Pearce's Gladys mentioned her given name during that installment's Samantha-fueled dream sequence; it's impressive to see Sandra Gould's Gladys carrying the Gruber torch.

SEASON FIVE

(1968-1969)

Endora cuts Darrin down to size for rejecting "Samantha's Wedding Present" (#141).

Gladys Kravitz petitions for the removal of the Stephenses' tree in "Weep No More, My Willow" (#152).

Tabitha shows new friend Amy her own brand of magic in "I Don't Want to Be A Toad, I Want to Be A Butterfly" (#151).

ABC/Photofest

"Samantha's Power Failure" (#165) also extends to Uncle Arthur and Serena, who try to function like mortals by working in an ice cream plant.

ABC/Photofest

SEASON FIVE: OVERVIEW

Bewitched tore out of the starting gate from the top of its 1968-1969 season with a big episode about a little Darrin. But there was nothing little about the new chroma key effect used to "shrink" him, which was just the first example of the show's slicker new look. There seemed to be a bigger budget in play, as non-Stephens sets got a shot of opulence – behold Rance Butler's plantation house in "Samantha Goes South for a Spell" (#142); even the Kravitz abode saw upgrades. The real standout, however, was the string of excellent episodes that made Season Five the show's strongest offering so far in the series.

With Dick York needing to be written out more often because of his unfortunate back injury – making for eight Darrin-less episodes this season alone – the show had to find a way to compensate. Ergo, its central mortal was either somehow removed by witchcraft [as in "Darrin, Gone and Forgotten" (#143) and "Daddy Does His Thing" (#167)] or simply sent on business trips. Meanwhile, the presence of witches increased in creative workarounds that offered a fascinating look into their world – "Samantha's Good News" (#168) is the series' only episode to not feature a single mortal. Samantha, who needed to carry the show like never before, became even more "modern," bringing the appearance and sensibility of the late '60s woman to her housewifery.

Darrin's belligerence and exaggerated mannerisms reached a zenith in Season Five's early episodes, rendering him almost unsympathetic – but suddenly, starting with "Cousin Serena Strikes Again (Part I)" (#155), he began to dial it down, as if there had been a decision from on high to do so; his subsequently subdued demeanor was a welcome change by comparison. There was also more interaction between Darrin and his daughter (now Tabitha with an "i", not an "a"), who, under the natural mastery of child actress Erin Murphy, owned every episode she was in. "I Don't Want to Be A Toad, I Want to Be A Butterfly" (#151) is still a Tabitha fan favorite.

If any character found herself in Season Five, it was Serena, who developed a clear personality and style in contrast to the experimentation she underwent in Season Four. Darrin's parents finally found a home after the show had gone back and forth about whether or not they lived in town; "Tabitha's Weekend" (#163) confirmed that they resided nearby. And "Samantha's Shopping Spree" (#169) provided even more evidence that Morning Glory Circle is probably in Patterson, New York.

Perhaps the most dismaying omission of the season was the show declining to address the fate of Aunt Clara, who had been a fixture since "The Witches Are Out" (#7). Her portrayer, Marion Lorne, died between Seasons Four and Five, but Aunt Clara simply disappeared after "Samantha's Secret Saucer" (#137), never to be mentioned again. Naturally, any sitcom would be loath to sandwich the subject of death between its laughs, but the lovably bumbling Clara often wanted to change herself into something; that's just one witchy possibility that could have explained her absence. Continuing on as if she never existed seemed like a disservice to both Marion Lorne and the wonderful legacy she left behind in Aunt Clara.

Another questionable choice was the sudden recycling of dialogue from one episode to another, without a continuity-related reason for the repetition; it appeared as if the show simply latched on to certain phrases and had characters utter them at random. There was also a growing indication that one witch could hex another witch, a new "rule" that strangely put witches on the same level as mortals.

Overall, though, the season that brought audiences monkeys, mules, vanity spells and rhyming diseases took chances, crafting some of the series' most original stories to date. New music and sound effects emerged throughout, and the show added fresh layers to its already magical premise with the introduction of the authoritative Witches' Council, cosmic elements like the atmospheric continuum, and the intriguing nuts and bolts of how witchcraft actually works.

Unlike any season since the black-and-white era, there is a consistency in style and mood in these 30 episodes, giving the show its most definite identity yet; the mod fashions of the late '60s were again incorporated into that identity and helped to create a sense of time and place [especially in "Darrin, Gone and Forgotten" (#143) and "Mirror, Mirror on the Wall" (#146)]. And, at season's end, there was a revelation of a timeless nature: the Stephenses were expecting another baby. Season Five had already given birth to a whole new direction for the show, but whether Samantha would give birth to a witch or mortal would have to wait until Season Six.

SAMANTHA'S WEDDING PRESENT

Airdate: September 26, 1968

After Darrin sounds off because Endora has brought Samantha dresses through witchcraft, Endora tells him he's a small man. The next day, Darrin's clothes are too big, and Larry thinks he seems shorter. Darrin realizes Endora meant her comment literally and rushes home; Gladys gasps when she sees the four-foot Darrin running to his door. Samantha feels Endora will change Darrin back if he says he's sorry, but he refuses to out of principle. By the following morning, Darrin is only slightly taller than a coffee cup, and Gladys uses her new dog to gain entry to the Stephens house. While Samantha lies that Darrin isn't "up to" going to work, the Kravitzes' dog gets into the kitchen and chases the miniaturized Darrin into some curbside trash, which is picked up by garbage collectors.

As Samantha fearfully tells Endora that Darrin may have been eaten by the dog, O'Hara, a drunk, finds Darrin in the junkyard. Thinking Darrin is a leprechaun, O'Hara threatens to step on him unless he grants three wishes. Darrin has O'Hara take him to Samantha, while Endora amusedly searches for her tiny son-in-law. Once Darrin arrives home safe in O'Hara's pocket, Samantha grants the man's wishes – which include a Shetland pony – and Darrin learns a lesson when O'Hara remarks that it doesn't matter where a gift comes from. Endora accepts Darrin's apology and makes him full-grown again, only offering oblique regrets herself.

GOOD!

Endora starts the season in her best mood yet, even lighting up the room with her unusual but refreshing cheerfulness. Darrin bursts the bubble by being unnecessarily unpleasant with her, but at least he has a sense of humor the next morning as he jokes that he'll "baa" for Samantha if Endora goes through with her threat to turn him into a goat. Darrin's apology at the end is worth the wait; however, it's the moment that he realizes he shouldn't have questioned the source of Endora's gifts that's more satisfying.

Green screen effects are almost the norm now, but, in 1968, it was fairly new, especially for television – here, *Bewitched* employs it for the first time. Though this début effort has a few bugs in it (the footage of mini-Darrin on the kitchen table shakes for some reason, and at times the dimensions of the cup and telephone don't match), shrinking Darrin is still no small feat.

Dick Wilson has appeared as a number of lovable drunks, most without names. In Frank O'Hara, Wilson finds his best character – and performance. Not only does his soused Irishman have a heart, but he pulls off his magic wardrobe changes better than some of the show's regulars.

WELL?

This episode's opening lifts the one from "Once in a Vial" (#125), complete with Endora popping in holding a purple gift box and telling Samantha to stop sounding like a housewife. Samantha beams that Endora has gotten Darrin's name right for the first time, but she forgets that Endora already used her son-in-law's correct name as far back as "A is for Aardvark" (#17), "The Joker Is A Card" (#41), and "Junior Executive" (#46). When Darrin makes a fuss about Endora bringing Samantha a wedding gift years after the fact, she says she didn't want to waste a good spell on a bad marriage. But the dresses Endora tows through that headwind are from Paris; she only uses magic to bring them to Morning Glory Circle. Her statement implies that she zapped up the dresses herself, which wouldn't require a trip overseas.

Once Darrin realizes he's shrinking, he pushes past a secretary to declare he needs to drive home while his feet can still reach the pedals – then stops to turn around and mug for Larry and the camera. Wouldn't it be smarter of Darrin to keep going and not put a spotlight on himself?

In "The Cat's Meow" (#18), Darrin told an operator that he didn't remember what his area code was. He'll never forget now, standing next to a comparatively giant rotary dial telephone that lists the area code as 371. And there's something about the chroma key effect that makes Darrin's suit change colors. When Samantha first zaps him into it, it looks brown; other times, it's green. But when Endora restores Darrin to full size, the suit is assuredly blue.

The Kravitzes have apparently decided they'd like to have the companionship of a dog – but it only seems he's there to chase Darrin into the front yard, who hides in loosely strewn garbage. The Stephenses don't use trash bags? Samantha panics when Darrin goes missing, but surely she could cast a spell to locate him, then zap him back to the house.

When Samantha fulfills O'Hara's first wish by giving him new specs, he's evidently able to see her clearly for the first time. Does Samantha upgrade his prescription while she's at it? Then, Samantha fulfills his third wish by zapping a Shetland pony into the driveway, knowing that Gladys was just over snooping around. Why not pop the pony into the backyard? And if Darrin thinks he's heard Endora's "apology" before, he has: Endora used the "slight transgression" line after causing trouble in "Solid Gold Mother-in-Law" (#120).

OH, MY STARS!

In Season Four's opener, "Long Live the Queen" (#108), Samantha accepted the crown and upset Darrin by telling him she had to serve her people at least a year. After that, she only sat on the throne one other time [in "Double, Double...Toil and Trouble" (#111)], and her sovereignty got a final mention by Aunt Clara in "McTavish" (#130). This episode marks the passing of that royal deadline, meaning Samantha is free to abdicate the throne – however, the show goes on as if this plot point never happened; this would be the perfect time to wrap up the story by having Samantha hang up her crown, even expositionally.

The miniaturized Darrin hides in a coffee cup, which is nudged off the kitchen table by the Kravitzes' dog. Given Darrin's size, that's tantamount to falling several stories – yet he emerges from the tumble completely unscathed. He wouldn't have been so lucky if the cup had broken. The dog only gets in because the kitchen door is open, but why is it? The Kravitzes knock on the front door, and they can't have opened the kitchen door first, because Samantha is in the kitchen until they arrive. That leaves the dog opening it by himself. Finally, how does Darrin survive his trip to the junkyard? The glass mayonnaise jar in which he takes shelter is picked up by a trash collector, thrown into a garbage truck, and dumped in the dump. Any one of these impacts could do him in, to say nothing of bumping around between other trash in the truck.

Darrin is so adversarial with Endora from the get-go that it's hard not to feel he's getting what he deserves as he shrinks. He apparently retained nothing from "The Very Informal Dress" (#44), where Samantha schooled him on how to graciously accept a gift that Aunt Clara made by magic. Then, Darrin asks what Endora can do to him, when he already has four years' worth of answers to that question. And it is four years, although Darrin tells Endora that he and Samantha have been married for five.

SON OF A GUN!

"Well, what are you gonna do – knock at the door and ask to see the house midget?" – Abner to Gladys, who wants to confirm her sighting of a shrunken Darrin.

Creating overgrown duplicates of the Stephenses' foyer and kitchen to make Darrin look tiny had to be a mammoth undertaking, but the results are exemplary. Better still is the effect that shows Darrin, in a bottle, in O'Hara's inside coat pocket. The suit's label even shifts to simulate O'Hara's movement, and the show could have chosen to skip O'Hara's magic wardrobe change – but the material surrounding the bottle reflects that change. And, as Samantha holds the bottle, the foyer can be seen behind Darrin as he learns a lesson about gift-giving from O'Hara. The special effects department certainly didn't shrink from making it look as if Darrin had.

EPISODE 142 — SAMANTHA GOES SOUTH FOR A SPELL

Airdate: October 3, 1968

Serena pretends to be Samantha so she can kiss Darrin, then explains that she has turned Malcolm, a warlock who dated her without admitting he was married, into a bird. Malcolm's vengeful wife, Brunhilde, tracks him to Samantha's house, mistaking Samantha for Serena. As Serena watches, Brunhilde zaps Samantha back to 1868 New Orleans. Big Easy resident "Aunt Jenny" finds the amnesiac Samantha and takes her home to her employer, Rance Butler, who grunts at having a guest until he sees the pretty stranger in his plantation house. Meanwhile, Serena recalls Brunhilde's spell; since only a willing kiss from a mortal will restore Samantha's memory, Serena sends Darrin to the Old South to rescue her cousin.

Darrin shows Samantha's picture around and is pointed to the Butler plantation, where a lovestruck Rance asks Samantha to marry him. When Rance refuses to believe that Darrin is Samantha's husband, Darrin suggests that Samantha take off her dress to reveal a telltale mole. Rance throws Darrin out, but Darrin returns that night and climbs up a trellis to get Samantha alone. Rance catches Darrin and challenges him to a duel, during which Darrin feigns an injury to play on Samantha's sympathies. It works, and, after Samantha kisses Darrin, they disappear, leaving Rance and Aunt Jenny to wonder if they've hallucinated everything. In the present, Samantha tries to witch Darrin into thinking his 1868 experience was a dream; however, a bruise reminds him the sword fight was real, and he faints.

GOOD!

Malcolm and Brunhilde are strangers, but fun ones. Brunhilde is as appropriately wicked as her namesake suggests, but she turns to Jell-O when the sly Malcolm camouflages his affair with Serena by casting himself as the victim. Elizabeth Montgomery, given yet another chance to take Samantha out of her apron, shines as a New Orleans neophyte, and Darrin really seems to fit into the Old South – his hesitant demand for Samantha to doff her dress is one of the best parts of this time trek. But this episode would never work without the team of Isabel Sanford and Jack Cassidy: as Aunt Jenny and Rance Butler, they not only successfully evoke a time long past, but their crack timing really brings the Confederate comedy.

Astute choices in music also give this episode some real flavor. When Brunhilde arrives in a puff of smoke, there's a quick quotation from *The Ride of the Valkyries*, a signature piece in composer Richard

Wagner's *Ring Cycle* (or *Der Ring des Nibelungen*, first performed in 1876), which features, of course, Brunhilde. And Rance's workers singing *Massa's in the Cold, Cold Ground* is no accident, either: it's a Negro minstrel song written by Stephen C. Foster and published in 1852 (the second "cold" in the title was added after the Civil War). The show apparently decided to change the original word "darkies" to "people," but the tune's inclusion – especially considering the context of the workers' real feelings for Rance – hits all the right notes.

Unlike other episodes involving time travel or bringing historical figures into the present, there's nothing in this installment that would suggest any impact on the timeline. Darrin introduces himself by name, but even that has no call to ripple into the present. This aspect probably wasn't a consideration, but it's a much more effective way to approach historical hijinks.

WELL?

Why does Serena squire Malcolm-as-bird around, and why does she kiss Darrin while her supposed suitor is stashed in a closet? Darrin has no idea he's kissing Serena until Samantha walks in, yet, in "That Was No Chick, That Was My Wife" (#117), Serena pulled the same stunt, and Darrin knew it was her right away.

When Brunhilde swoops in, she immediately assumes Samantha is Serena. Now, Samantha doesn't help matters by not identifying herself right away (nor does Darrin, who continually calls his wife "Sam" instead of "Samantha" in 1868) – but does Brunhilde not recognize the former Queen of the Witches? Surely when Samantha accepted the crown, her face became familiar to all her subjects. Brunhilde also never hears Serena talking to herself, though she's only the other side of the room.

So, Darrin comes home from golf and learns that Samantha has been sent to the past – and the first thing he does is grab her photo from upstairs and pace around with it. It's not Sears Portrait Studio, either; Samantha's pic is Hollywood headshot quality. As for Serena, she insists she has to remember Brunhilde's spell word for word, but when she casts the spell, she only uses half of it, incanting "blow ye winds," while Brunhilde said "blow *the* winds." Maybe that's why Darrin arrives in 1868 some time after Samantha; if he had been sent to the same time and place, which was Serena's intention, he would encounter Samantha before or just as Aunt Jenny does, avoiding the whole thing with Rance.

Turns out it's painful for Darrin and Samantha to be pursued by others – in "Snob in the Grass" (#126), Darrin got poked with Sheila's open brooch; here, Rance's stick pin jabs into Samantha. It's a wonder Samantha's memory doesn't come back in Rance's guest room, because it looks a lot like her own bedroom, done up 19th century style. Crickets chirp as Darrin climbs up the Butler trellis, but the sky indicates there's a day-for-night sequence in progress. And, when the Stephenses return to their own time, Rance and Aunt Jenny decide they never saw the Yankee and the young lady. Won't that self-imposed denial be hard to maintain when they see the bedpost and curtains Rance slashed with his blade?

The split screen effects that allow Samantha and Serena to be seen together in this episode are generally very good, but, in the tag, there's a phantom shadow in the upper right hand corner of the screen that disappears when Serena appears. Strangely, Darrin remembers his way through the dream spell Samantha puts on him; he shouldn't, because he's never recalled being at the North Pole ["A Vision of Sugar Plums" (#15)] or living life by witchcraft ["A is for Aardvark" (#17)] thanks to Samantha's other memory erasers. But if the bruise on Darrin's posterior does jog his memory, what about the bite mark on his hand? Samantha chomped him pretty hard. And Darrin faints after his total recall, though he just passed out in "The No-Harm Charm" (#138).

OH, MY STARS!

This episode demonstrates that witches can use their powers on each other: Serena transforms Malcolm into a bird and back, while Brunhilde freezes Samantha before sending her to another century. What's the point of being a witch if another witch can bespell you at a moment's notice? Being able to zap each other rather brings witches down to the level of mortals.

When Serena recalls Brunhilde's spell, she tells Darrin it's a "beauty and the beast" curse. She figured that out from listening to a couple of couplets – yet, in previous seasons, Aunt Clara had to look spells up in books to tell what they were. Furthermore, Serena says Samantha will return to 1968 if she receives a willing kiss from a mortal. That's a good enough reason to send Darrin into the past for a rescue, but what happens if Samantha willingly kisses Rance? He's mortal – will he jump ahead a century if he plants one on Samantha?

SON OF A GUN!

"I go out to play golf, and when I come back, my wife's in *The Twilight Zone*. Links to jinx!" – Darrin to Serena, after realizing that Samantha is "gone with the wind."

During Season Four, Serena segued from groovy brunette to kooky blond, conveniently looking like Samantha to befuddle the Tates during her previous appearance in "Hippie, Hippie, Hooray" (#128). Here, Serena makes a return to her dark locks by going flower child – and what an improvement: her slightly higher tone of voice somehow gives her more of her own personality, and she even helps Darrin save Samantha from Brunhilde's time-shifting.

EPISODE **143**

SAMANTHA ON THE KEYBOARD
Airdate: October 10, 1968

The Stephenses think little Tabitha has turned on the stereo until they find her playing classical piano via Endora's witchcraft. Darrin argues with his mother-in-law, then challenges Samantha to learn how to play the mortal way as an example to their daughter. Samantha takes her first lesson with the severe Johann Sebastian Monroe; she braves his condescension and continues learning from him, displeasing Endora. When Tabitha imitates Samantha and pounds on the keys, Endora zaps her granddaughter into becoming a virtuoso again. Monroe arrives and hears the preschool "prodigy," planning to whisk her away for recordings and concert tours against the Stephenses' objections.

Samantha feels the only way to dissuade Monroe is to find him an actual prodigy, so she magically searches one out. As young Mathew Williams plays, his father Robert, a school custodian, explains to Samantha that he lets the boy practice in the school's music room since they have no piano of their own. Once Samantha is home, Monroe arrives with Maestro Ferranini, who wants to hear Tabitha play; Ferranini is disgusted when Tabitha plinks on the piano as a mortal preschooler would. Letting Monroe believe she had Tabitha fake her bad playing to scare off Ferranini, Samantha tells him about Mathew, and soon the boy is taken under Ferranini's wing. Later, Samantha impresses Darrin by playing *Born Free* without witchcraft, but Endora uses hers to have Tabitha play the fiddle instead.

GOOD!

There's something fun about watching Samantha unsuccessfully feel her way through a scale, then twitch herself into playing a Tchaikovsky concerto. But Darrin's suggestion that Endora turn herself into a four-year-old so Monroe can take her away on a concert tour tops the witchy ivory tickling, just for the images it suggests.

Jonathan Harris' Monroe is stiff and stodgy, just as you'd expect a sitcom piano teacher with delusions of grandeur to be. And the snooty instructor meets his match in the delightfully over-the-top Ferranini, who turns Monroe into a subservient wimp and throws him out of his fan club with a mouth pop that dares you not to laugh. Conversely, making child prodigy Mathew Williams African-American is a brilliant inclusion, especially in a time when the civil rights movement was heading the headlines.

WELL?

The strings of Tabitha's mini-piano aren't visible, but wires make Endora's living room levitation rather obvious. Samantha assures Darrin that Endora has only put a spell on Tabitha's fingers, but Tabitha is a witch, too: if Samantha can make herself play like a master, why does Tabitha need Endora to accomplish the same? Furthermore, how can Endora put a spell on another witch? Maybe it's because Tabitha's powers aren't fully developed, or because she's half-mortal. After Darrin drives Endora away by huffing that she's corrupting Tabitha, he says he'll buy his daughter a piano when she's old enough. What happened to the piano Aunt Clara shrunk in "The Short Happy Circuit of Aunt Clara" (#83), or the one Samantha's broken-dam powers uncontrollably played in "No Zip in My Zap" (#113)?

There's a strange audio glitch as the overdubbed Monroe takes Samantha through the *do-re-mi* scale, leaving no natural pause between his *ti* and his final *do*. Then, Endora tells Samantha that even a witch needs to practice before becoming a virtuoso – yet, Tabitha, under Endora's guidance, sits down and plays Chopin like a master, and she hasn't been practicing.

In "Tabatha's Cranky Spell" (#134), Samantha appeared shocked when would-be mystic Aunt Harriet warned against disturbing any vibrations; here, Samantha invites vibrations as a means of locating a child prodigy for Monroe. But what's the point of Samantha's second "I'm flying now and later paying" spell? It works as a joke, but does nothing to advance Samantha's mission. Once Samantha finds Mathew, his custodian father doesn't question how Samantha got in, although University High School is closed for the day, and the entrance would be locked. Finally, when Samantha returns home, she hurriedly zaps away the coat she witched up, looking worried that Darrin will react badly to it. Have things gotten to the point that Samantha thinks Darrin will blow up over a coat? It's not like "Charlie Harper, Winner" (#99), where she gave herself a mink to make Darrin look good.

When Monroe and Ferranini invade the Stephens house, Samantha nods knowingly at Darrin; as planned, Tabitha bangs on the keys, horrifying the maestro. How does Samantha know this ploy will work? Endora could easily restore Tabitha to virtuoso status knowing professionals are about to hear her granddaughter – and Tabitha could even put a spell on her own fingers. At episode's end, Endora brings Tabitha downstairs to duet on the fiddle in matching outfits, and Samantha accompanies them on the piano. Samantha just barely learned *Born Free*; how does she also know *Turkey in the Straw*?

OH, MY STARS!

Ever since her introduction in "And Then There Were Three" (#54), Samantha and Darrin's daughter has always been "Tabatha" – she even had a mobile in her nursery that spelled out her name in this way during Season Four. Now, as evidenced by the end credits (and closed captioning), Miss Stephens' name has inexplicably been changed to "Tabitha" with an "i". One can't help wondering how such a change would reflect in the Stephenses' fictional world. Is Tabitha having to learn to spell her name differently? Have the Stephenses changed her birth certificate? And how is Endora, who named her granddaughter in the first place, reacting to this alteration? It's odd that the show would change the spelling of Tabitha's name without giving a reason for it on-screen. On another point, Endora tells Monroe that Tabitha is four years old, but the girl was born in January 1966, so she isn't even three yet.

SON OF A GUN!

"Mrs. Stephens, you are playing a piano. You are not plucking a chicken!" – Johann Sebastian Monroe to Samantha, after she fumbles over her first scale.

EPISODE 144
DARRIN, GONE AND FORGOTTEN
Airdate: October 17, 1968

After Darrin makes an insulting remark about Endora, he disappears. Endora claims innocence, and Samantha wonders if Uncle Arthur is responsible, but the culprit is Carlotta, who has dispensed with Darrin so Samantha can wed her son, Juke, as per an arranged marriage agreed upon centuries before. Samantha refuses; however, when Carlotta shows Darrin perpetually running from wild animal sounds, Samantha grudgingly agrees to meet Juke. Discovering that ultimate mama's boy Juke doesn't even want to marry her, Samantha coaches him to stand up to Carlotta, imitating her for effect. Unfortunately, when it's time for Juke to face Carlotta, he caves in, so Samantha returns home.

Angry Carlotta follows, threatening to have Darrin chased by real animals if Samantha doesn't marry Juke; Samantha pretends to comply, using reverse psychology and suggesting changes she knows Carlotta will hate – particularly, zapping Juke out of his foppish clothes and into the height of '60s mod. Samantha's plan almost backfires when Juke wants to make Samantha his bride after all, but Carlotta puts her foot down and cancels the marriage, agreeing to return Darrin as soon as Juke comes home; Darrin pops in unharmed, with no memory of his disappearance. Months later, Samantha and Endora laugh as they read a letter from the newly-engaged Juke, whose fiancée is just as controlling as Carlotta.

GOOD!

Endora makes a beautifully fluid change from her wet suit into her very '60s pantsuit, and seems genuinely bothered by Darrin's disappearance – but it's her clawing with Carlotta that's the most intriguing. It's not often someone can one-up the catty Endora, but Carlotta does it with ease, and Mercedes McCambridge commands the episode as the elegantly kooky witch.

Steve Franken just put in an appearance as canine alien Orvis in "Samantha's Secret Saucer" (#137), but he was in so much make-up there that his turn here as Juke feels fresh. The consecutive effects of Samantha and Carlotta zapping Juke in and out of his groovy threads look seamless thanks to Franken's skill, and Juke's I'll-marry-Samantha-anyway roadblock is an unexpected twist.

WELL?

When Samantha gets no response from Darrin, she immediately assumes Endora has done something to him. Endora has mysteriously popped Darrin out before [in "If They Never Met" (#127)], but Samantha only ever scans the patio for him. Granted, the show doesn't have time to feature Samantha searching the house, but he could be in the bathroom, for all she knows.

Endora has somehow forgotten Samantha's arranged marriage for centuries, but Carlotta hasn't – where was she when Samantha was queen? Surely Carlotta wouldn't wait for the planet Icarus to pass between Pluto and Jupiter when her beloved Juke could become king. And Carlotta is so obsessed with her own child that she never stops to think there's another child involved – Tabitha. Endora only offers to babysit her, and Samantha doesn't mention that she has a daughter who will lose her father through this arrangement.

Carlotta warns that Darrin will be running from animal sounds forever if Samantha doesn't marry Juke. Does Carlotta's spell include a proviso that will keep Darrin from aging and dying in order to fulfill this prophecy? And what's supposed to happen if Samantha honors the arranged marriage – Darrin comes home and finds he no longer has a wife? Maybe he'd up raising Tabitha alone.

Samantha's ordinarily black flying suit has gotten another upgrade: in "Humbug Not to Be Spoken Here" (#123), sparkles were added to it; now, the bodice is a luminescent green. Juke's Little Lord Fauntleroy outfit should look familiar, too – it's the same one Darrin got zapped into in "I Get Your Nanny, You Get My Goat" (#122), only with a different shirt and tie.

Where did Carlotta get all the studio photos of Samantha to display in Juke's room? She even has the same picture Darrin showed around 1868 New Orleans in "Samantha Goes South for a Spell" (#142). It's clever for Samantha to suggest that Juke hook up with her lookalike cousin, Serena, but the photo of the young witches flies in the face of their timeline. "Eye of the Beholder" (#22) suggested that Samantha is approximately 300 years old; Carlotta and Endora having made their deal in the Middle Ages, before Samantha was born, works to substantiate this. Yet Samantha and Serena are shown as youths in what is obviously the 20th century. And Juke's room doesn't look too stable, his cloud being held up by visible black wires and all.

When Samantha returns with news that her wedding to Juke is still on, Endora laments, "What a shame." This from the woman who's spent the entire series wishing Samantha had married a warlock? Then, the emboldened Juke says that Carlotta can always phone him. Since when do witches use phones to communicate? Even the warlock drugstore clerk in "Take Two Aspirins and Half A Pint of Porpoise Milk" (#42) had barely started using a telephone to keep up with progress.

After Juke pops home, Samantha makes a dash for the kitchen to zap herself out of her flying suit, champagne glass in hand. She originally conjures up three glasses: does she remember to get rid of the other two? Then, Darrin smiles that it's been quite an evening, yet all he knows is that he and Samantha did dishes together, assuming he's been returned to the exact moment he disappeared. If not, Darrin should realize the passage of time as soon as he looks at a clock. Regardless, isn't he tired and sore from all that running?

As the episode ends, Juke becomes betrothed to a witch as domineering as his mother. If Carlotta thought Samantha giving Juke groovy upgrades was bad, how is she accepting a daughter-in-law as invested in micromanaging Juke's life as she is?

OH, MY STARS!

As Darrin laundry lists all that's good in his life, he says he'd be "ecstatically happy" if Samantha were an orphan. Samantha lets it slide by telling Darrin she may end up a widow if he makes another comment like that, but this is an unusually heartless thing to say, even for Darrin, who has grown increasingly huffy since the end of Season Two.

In the tag, Samantha states that it's been "months since Juke's emancipation." That she's wearing the same dress she wore the night of Darrin's disappearance does little to give the impression time has elapsed, but suppose it has: could this explain why, starting with "Samantha's Wedding Present" (#141), it was said the Stephenses had been married five years when they'd only been married four, and why "Samantha on the Keyboard" (#143) suggested that Tabitha is four instead of three? It appears there was a decision to age Tabitha a bit; this episode could justify that time jump, but it's a beat the show misses.

SON OF A GUN!

"What a beautiful creature you are. You don't look at all like your mother." – Carlotta to Samantha, as she plays "cat and cat" with Endora.

Is there anything Elizabeth Montgomery can't do? Here, she imitates guest star Mercedes McCambridge perfectly, her Carlotta impression being the highlight of the episode.

EPISODE 145 — IT'S SO NICE TO HAVE A SPOUSE AROUND THE HOUSE
Airdate: October 24, 1968

The Witches' Council, a supernatural authority, turns Darrin into a statue after Samantha chooses not to appear before them. When the restored Darrin refuses to let Samantha attend their meeting, Samantha recruits Serena to take her place while she satisfies the Council's demand. Tabitha recognizes Serena-as-Samantha, so Endora takes the young witch to the zoo; meanwhile, Larry suggests that the remorseful Darrin take Samantha on a second honeymoon to make up for being difficult. Serena panics when Darrin whisks her to Moonthatch Inn, the site of the Stephenses' first honeymoon; Madame Wageir, the inn's proprietress, provides the perfect romantic setting.

Samantha returns early from the Witches' Council and finds the house empty, while, at the Inn, Darrin can't understand why "Samantha" is so resistant to his overtures. As the frustrated Darrin whips out a nightie, Serena-as-Samantha makes the bed disappear. Darrin reluctantly agrees to take "Samantha" home, where the real Samantha is horrified to hear that her cousin spent the day honeymooning with Darrin. Upstairs, Tabitha tells Darrin that she saw Serena; Darrin realizes the switch and jokingly unnerves Samantha with reminders of the wild time "they" had at the Inn. After Darrin lets Samantha off the hook by asking about the meeting, the couple apologizes to each other, proposing that "Moonthatch Inn begins at home."

GOOD!

Darrin-as-statue is a nifty effect; he can't help moving once in a while, but even his eyes appear bronzed. Later, Darrin looks ready to crack up laughing as Tabitha recalls how she ended up at the zoo, making for a welcomed father-daughter moment – and Darrin making Samantha think that he and Serena shared some love in the afternoon is also a funny twist.

Serena's flower child evolution continues, and, as she stands in for her cousin, it really seems Serena is inhabiting Samantha's body. Serena zapping up a "closed for repairs" sign before adding a bed of nails to extinguish Darrin's fire is fun, and even racy for 1968 television, as is Serena-as-Samantha's comment that the combination of her, Darrin, and Mother Nature makes for "some threesome."

Intentional or not, Larry's comment that he and Louise have been married 20 years is accurate: the episode "...And Something Makes Three" (#12), which aired four years earlier, stated that the Tates had been married 16 years. Though Larry and Darrin's shouts of "whoo whoo!" might be just this side of cringeworthy, Larry's Wedded-Bliss Special does reveal the serious exec's more playful side.

When a movie or television production wants to make it look like a stationary vehicle is moving, they use something called a gimbal to simulate that movement. This gimbal gently rocks Darrin's car in front of a filmed background to create the illusion of Darrin and Serena driving down the road – an extra step that adds a nice touch of realism.

WELL?

When the Witches' Council responds to Samantha's blithe "let them do their worst" with a thunderclap, Endora replies, "I hope it's their worst." Do no witches think about how their actions will affect Tabitha? And Samantha ought to be worried about the ever-spying Gladys seeing Darrin-as-statue – instead, she tells Endora to pop out right there on the front lawn.

The again churlish Darrin should know by now that, whenever Samantha wears a pink sleeveless dress, there's going to be some cousin changing [as in "Double, Double...Toil and Trouble" (#111) and "Hippie, Hippie, Hooray" (#128)]. Failing that, "Samantha's" magic housework should be a tip-off. Besides, Darrin knew Serena was Samantha in "That Was No Chick, That Was My Wife" (#117), so why does he need Tabitha to hip him to it? As for Serena, she's tried to lock lips with Darrin more than once, most recently in "Samantha Goes South for a Spell" (#142), so why would Samantha want her cousin to stand in for her? Finally alone with Darrin, Serena freezes up instead; were here disguised kisses only pranks?

Samantha tells her cousin, "you owe me a lot of favors – here's a chance to clean the slate." That slate was already cleaned in "That Was No Chick, That Was My Wife" (#117), when Serena said presenting herself to Louise settled their account.

While Darrin changes for his golf game, he talks to a single picture of Samantha on the dresser. What happened to the double frame that usually occupies that spot? Dick Wilson is terrific as always, delivering another drunk character at the golf course bar, but he just made a notable, extended appearance as the soused Frank O'Hara in "Samantha's Wedding Present" (#141). It's a little too soon for him to appear again, and Wilson has nothing substantial to do in this episode, besides.

When Darrin comes home ready to honeymoon, Serena is flipping magazine pages by witchcraft, as Endora did in "Darrin, Gone and Forgotten" (#144) – and with the same magazine. Endora pops in to answer Serena's frantic call, but did she really leave Tabitha unattended at the zoo? And there's no way Darrin could go upstairs, change out of his golf clothes into a suit, and pack enough for a weekend trip in 24 seconds, but that's exactly what happens here.

Darrin tells "Samantha" they're staying at Moonthatch Inn, "and that's it." Does he really think this line will inspire passion in his reluctant "wife?" Darrin whistles *Here Comes the Bride*; Juke just hummed a scat version of the tune in the preceding episode, "Darrin, Gone and Forgotten" (#144). Finally, with the mistaken identity cleared up, Samantha says of the Council, "I said I wouldn't attend meetings unless they were here." Except that was an agreement she made when she accepted the crown in "Long Live the Queen" (#108), which had nothing to do with the Council. And the Stephenses shouldn't be reminiscing about their honeymoon at Moonthatch Inn, because they spent it in a posh New York City hotel [see "I, Darrin, Take This Witch, Samantha" (#1)].

OH, MY STARS!

It turns out that witches and warlocks are answerable to a Witches' Council, comprised of a "noble eight." That would make perfect sense, except it conflicts with the system of authority already established in the witch world. No ruling entity was even introduced until Queen Ticheba made herself known in "Long Live the Queen" (#108); if Ticheba was already in power, there would be no need for a Witches' Council, unless they were accountable to her. If they were, then they also would have been subject to Samantha's rule once she ascended to the throne. Perhaps Samantha instituted the Council to replace the monarchy before abdicating – but that can't be, either, because Endora says Samantha has only made two appearances before the Council since her marriage (which took place three years before becoming queen), and they wouldn't be so dismissive of the former queen's husband if Samantha had a role in the Council's creation. The Witches' Council is a great idea, but this noble eight stands in the long shadow of "Long Live the Queen" (#108).

SON OF A GUN!

"What do I do first, dust something?" – Serena to Endora, reluctantly cast as "the perfect little wife."

EPISODE 146 — MIRROR, MIRROR, ON THE WALL
Airdate: November 7, 1968

Once Endora hears Darrin is concerned about approaching middle age, she zaps him with a vanity spell that has him staring at himself in any reflective surface he can find, annoying conservative pharmaceutical client Hascomb. Despite Larry's protestations, Darrin buys himself hippie love beads and outfits himself like a '60s rock star. Listening to Darrin go on about being dashing and youthful, Samantha realizes Darrin's under a spell, but gets nowhere trying to talk him into changing for his second-chance meeting with Hascomb at a restaurant. Darrin attracts attention in his mod threads until Samantha pops him into his usual suit; Darrin examines himself in the restaurant's pond and falls in as Larry and Hascomb look on.

Undeterred, Darrin drapes himself in an expensive gold lamé jacket for a dinner party with the Hascombs. Hoping to maneuver Darrin into dressing down, Samantha zaps herself into a sequined mini-dress; the ruse almost works until he catches his reflection in her sparkles. Larry tries to turn the groovy Stephenses away, but Hascomb's "with-it" wife falls in love with their look; as Hascomb Drug's primary stockholder, she pressures her husband into letting Darrin market their new line of suntan lotion. As a result, Larry wants Darrin to continue dressing mod, but Darrin says he looks like a jackass, which Endora says can be arranged.

GOOD!

This season's implementation of chroma key effects gets even slicker as a tiny Endora fades in on the seat of Darrin's car – and the much simpler split-screen effect, where Darrin walks behind a divider in his hippie clothes but emerges in the old gray flannel, flows quite nicely.

There's an interesting, unspoken consistency in this episode: the Tates both looked down their noses at hippie counterculture in "Hippie, Hippie, Hooray" (#128), and here, Larry is obvious about his continuing derision, while Louise scrunches up her face at the Stephenses' mod makeovers. Groovy, vain Darrin, however, is delightfully over-the-top (though perhaps more fey than intended), and Dick York looks to be having a ball playing this outrageous version of his normally sedate alter ego.

William Asher – Elizabeth Montgomery's husband and the producer of the show – makes an uncredited cameo as the motorist who yells at Darrin at the traffic light. While it's not clear why Asher's car stalls as a result of Darrin being stopped at the intersection (or why he's driving a California car through New York), his road rage is spot-on; he even seems to be mouthing an obscenity if you read his lips!

WELL?

The double picture frame on the Stephenses' bedroom dresser, which was missing in "It's So Nice to Have A Spouse Around the House" (#145), returns here, but it seems Samantha isn't the only one who's gotten an upgraded studio photograph – Darrin has, too. The Stephenses' foyer also sports a giant mirror now, replacing the painting that has occupied the space since the beginning of Season Four. And Endora continues talking to herself about her plans to bespell Darrin while Samantha could be in earshot. Why doesn't she wait until she's invisible and inaudible in Darrin's car?

The time is 1968: magazines, movies, and television are full of men dressed in the epitome of mod finery. So why do the restaurant patrons nudge each other and make fun of Darrin as if they've never seen someone wearing these clothes before? Because of Darrin's age? As Darrin walks away from the mirror, he notices right away that his beads have been zapped off. But he's looking straight ahead – and it's not likely he could see the beads disappearing in his peripheral vision. Also, unless Samantha is equipped with ESP again, she can't know that Darrin is alone in that moment; she could easily effect Darrin's magical costume change in front of Larry and Hascomb.

Darrin meets Hascomb at the restaurant at 5:00. When he gets home, the kitchen clock says it's after 6:00, and Samantha is making a cake. Shouldn't she be making dinner? After all, she doesn't find out they're going to Larry's for dinner until after Darrin arrives in a fit of pique. And why is Samantha so against Darrin wearing hip clothes when she just zapped Juke into similar suits in "Darrin, Gone and Forgotten" (#144)? She must anticipate needing to shorten her sequined dress, because there's a visible demarcation on her gown that ends up being the hemline of her mini-skirt; very clean zap, though.

Herb Voland and Sara Seegar, the Springers of "That Was No Chick, That Was My Wife" (#117), appear here as the Hascombs. Another blast from the past comes when primary stockholder Mrs. Hascomb pulls rank to award Darrin an account – Mrs. Baxter did the same thing in "Birdies, Bogies, and Baxter" (#114).

When Darrin comes downstairs in his mod clothes, and Samantha briefly thinks there's another spell on him, it can't be the next morning, because Darrin reports that the agency has "a whole slew of new accounts" based on how his groovy threads influenced Hascomb. Certainly that news didn't reach this "slew" in one day – and how does the story reach any new clients at all? Did Larry put out a press release featuring a picture of Darrin dressed as a rock star?

OH, MY STARS!

It's *au courant* for the show to suggest that 80% of McMann & Tate's campaigns are designed to appeal to those under 30, but, judging by the agency's history, it's also an overstatement. In Season Four alone, Darrin devised layouts for two tractor companies and a steel company, another that invented an anti-smog device, a stuffy bank, and a retirement village; while their pet food and toothpaste slogans could certainly be aimed at a consumers of wide age range, very few of McMann & Tate's campaigns actually target the youth market. Later, Samantha tells Hascomb that his products "don't seem to get to the right people," but, up until now, Hascomb has only made pills. There's no demographic for pharmaceuticals – and if there is, it's certainly not the youth market.

Samantha's ploy to get Darrin into his more traditional clothes goes awry when he sees his reflection in her sequins. Is that all she's got? She and Darrin end up at the Tates in their glittery garments, but it's like she gave up trying to recostume him, and for no apparent reason other than he liked looking at himself in her dress.

SON OF A GUN!

"To me!" – Darrin, as he, Samantha, the Tates, and the Hascombs go around the room toasting to the new image of the Hascomb Drug Company.

EPISODE 147

SAMANTHA'S FRENCH PASTRY

Airdate: November 14, 1968

Uncle Arthur ruins Samantha's dessert when he surprises her in the oven, so he tries to conjure up a Napoléon pastry to replace it, materializing Emperor Napoléon Bonaparte instead. With the Tates on their way, Samantha convinces Napoléon to pretend he's Samantha's cousin Henri; Larry thinks "Henri" resembles Napoléon and wants to cast him in a detergent commercial, not taking no for an answer. When Napoléon goes along with it, Darrin thinks it's because he desires Louise, but the emperor relishes the idea of using fame to rebuild his army, and threatens to tell Larry that Samantha is a witch if she interferes.

Larry stops by in the morning to escort "Henri" to the studio, where Uncle Arthur pops in to tell Samantha he can't figure out how to send the emperor back. Zoom Detergent board member Bradley doesn't think "Henri" is right for the part of Napoléon, especially after his theatrical, 19th century delivery of Zoom's copy. Larry blames Darrin for the failure, and Napoléon still wants to out Samantha as a witch until Uncle Arthur returns with a guaranteed spell reverser. It doesn't work, at least not without a witchy expletive Samantha utters that sends Napoléon back to his own time. Later, Arthur invites himself to dinner with the Stephenses, but when Darrin refuses to let him join them, he disappears with their meal.

GOOD!

"Cousin Henri" proves his Napoleonic ruthlessness when he threatens to tell Larry that Samantha is a witch – and it's not often someone can hold that over Samantha's head. But the emperor's performance as Zoom Detergent's spokesman is a laugh riot – or a *Laugh-In*, since portrayer Henry Gibson was inducing yuks on that comedy show, which ran from 1968-1973 on NBC. His overdone French accent while reading Zoom's cue cards, pitching them like something out of a Victorian melodrama, proves *très, très drôle*.

Uncle Arthur's "in reverse" spell, during which he incants *un, deux, trois, quatre* backwards, truly does include those words; just invert the episode's audio to hear the normal reading for yourself.

WELL?

Uncle Arthur must enjoy popping up in food, because he was just a "stewaway" in "The No-Harm Charm" (#138), and he served himself up in a platter for his first appearance in "The Joker Is A Card" (#41). However, the mystery foyer mirror of "Mirror, Mirror on the Wall" (#146) has been replaced by its usual painting.

Uncle Arthur produces Napoléon Bonaparte trying to zap up a Napoléon dessert, but it's worth noting that the pastry isn't actually named after the historical figure, as the show obliquely implies. According to research, it's more likely the treat was called a *napolitain*, which is what the French call a resident of the Italian city of Naples. The dessert precedes Napoléon, dating back to the 17th century (Napoléon lived from 1769 to 1821) and was originally referred to as *mille-feuille*, or "a thousand leaves," due to its flaky layers. As for the Napoléon brandy "Henri" requests, Napoléon apparently did have fine cognac delivered to him, but its present-day designation isn't necessarily a reference to Napoléon himself; it's not likely the brandy carried his name in his lifetime, so he wouldn't know to call it that. One last food note: Darrin is upset when Samantha fixes Crêpe Suzette for Napoléon, forgetting she served him the same dish in "Out of Sync, Out of Mind" (#116). The thin, garnished pancake isn't guaranteed to please the emperor anyway: Crêpe Suzette didn't exist until 70 years after Napoléon died.

In "Your Witch Is Showing" (#20), Samantha worried that Darrin was starting to blame all his problems on witchcraft, querying, "Do you know what's happening?" Darrin's reply: "Napoléon was asked the same question just before Waterloo." Now Darrin can get that straight from the emperor's mouth. And why does Darrin keep demanding that Samantha pop Napoléon out? He knows many times over that she can't reverse someone else's spell; she even reminds him of this fact.

Larry has a thing for casting people in commercials without knowing whether they have any talent: he wanted Benjamin Franklin to hawk transistor radios in "My Friend Ben" (#87), and, in "A Prince of a Guy" (#129), he pressured Prince Charming to peddle cosmetics without a screen test. Shouldn't Larry be wondering why Samantha has so many relatives that resemble historical figures? He also met "Aunt Harriet" in "Aunt Clara's Victoria Victory" (#100), not realizing a monarch had given him audience.

Larry leaves the Stephens house after dinner and has everything ready for the Zoom Detergent shoot before breakfast is even finished the next morning. Then he uses his position as senior vice president of McMann & Tate to force Darrin into going along with it, but it's already been established that Larry is a full president. And what is this president, an ad executive, doing directing a commercial?

Napoléon reasons that his notoriety from the Zoom spot will enable him to rebuild his forces in France. How? As Samantha points out, nobody who claims he's Napoléon is going to be taken seriously – and he'll never be able to explain being 199 years old. When Bradley boots him from the commercial, Napoléon threatens to tell Larry that Samantha is a witch anyway, but there's no reason to blackmail her now. Is that why, when it's time to leave, he inexplicably tells the Stephenses, "I'm glad to have met you?"

When Arthur's spell reverser doesn't work, it's Samantha blurting out "bat wings and lizard tails" that sends Napoléon back. But she's just talking; she's not actually using her powers. At least this time, a historical figure doesn't leave the Stephens house with a lot of information about the future; he may be able to get a jump on the invention of television, but that's about it. However, at one point, Samantha does tell him, "I'm sure after two centuries you must be starved for affection." First, she overestimates: in 1968, Napoléon is only 147 years past his time. But this also implies that Napoléon has been told he's in the 20th century, which he hasn't, unless it was off-camera.

In the tag, Darrin yells that his roast is going to be eaten by two. So, no dinner for Tabitha?

OH, MY STARS!

Uncle Arthur's faulty spell-casting in this episode causes comedic mayhem, but it isn't consistent with the practical-joking warlock's history. He's not Aunt Clara; his powers have never acted up before, and he has no disease causing them to. Also, he is unable to send Napoléon back, but he can appear in television cameras and pop in on horses without difficulty. When Arthur changes himself into a baseball player in the studio (does the "B" on his cap stand for *Bewitched*?), the effect is hampered by the camera's drastic shift and the noticeable change in lighting; the show's so good at these transformations by now, it's a puzzlement that this one made it to air, unless the tight production schedule prevented another attempt. Finally, Uncle Arthur cheerily tells Napoléon that he and Samantha are witches. Though Napoléon was known for advocating religious tolerance, he could still have a hostile reaction to the idea of witchcraft – in "Aunt Clara's Victoria Victory" (#100), the queen was ready to have Clara flogged for being a witch, and Victoria was born 50 years after Napoléon.

It's not that Darrin doesn't have reason to dislike his supernatural in-laws, but, in this episode, he threatens Uncle Arthur with violence no less than three times. Insults are one thing, but barbarity and comedy do not go hand-in-hand.

SON OF A GUN!

"He's our dessert?" – Samantha, when Darrin asks why Napoléon Bonaparte is standing in his kitchen.

Samantha's "technical" explanation about how "kinetic vibrations" run the risk of "zonking across the atmospheric continuum" and cause unforeseen "ectoplasmic manifestations" is both humorous and fascinating – for the first time, the show gets into the nuts and bolts of exactly how witchcraft works. Of course, it's meant to explain away Uncle Arthur's unprecedented Napoléon no-no – but it far more explains why Aunt Clara's spells always brought about such bizarre results.

EPISODE 148
IS IT MAGIC OR IMAGINATION?
Airdate: November 21, 1968

Samantha has the living room in disarray when Phyllis calls to say she's coming over. Darrin objects to Samantha using a speed-up spell to neaten everything for his mother, then ducks out because he hasn't had a haircut. Phyllis pushes Samantha to enter a slogan contest for Tinkerbell Disposable Diapers, the prize being a trip to Tahiti. A month later, Samantha tries to tell Darrin she won the contest, but he's more interested his Barton Industries layouts. It turns out Tinkerbell is a subsidiary of Barton, and Larry is upset because Samantha's slogan has bested their efforts for the account. Darrin comes home jobless; the Stephenses fight when Darrin is certain that Samantha witched herself into winning the contest.

Later, Larry arrives to take Darrin back, but only because he wants Samantha to head up the agency's slogan department, so Darrin quits and walks out on his wife. Samantha installs Clarissa, a dog nanny, to watch Tabitha while she fetches the inebriated Darrin from a bar. Darrin passes out on the couch, not noticing as Samantha sneaks out with his portfolio the next morning. Larry interrupts Darrin's hangover with news that Barton has signed with the agency; Darrin figures Samantha has magically rigged Barton's computer analyzer, which evaluates slogans. Samantha's ignorance of the device leads Darrin to reveal that Samantha's own slogan tested poorly on it, which tells him it must have been imagination and not witchcraft. With "one free twitch coming," Samantha zaps Larry into giving Darrin the day off.

GOOD!

Larry's apology to Darrin may be less genuine than it seems, but it shows a degree of self-awareness not usually seen in Mr. Tate. "Everybody knows that I'm a volatile, excitable, impetuous, rash, impulsive..." Darrin fills in the blank with "blowhard," but Larry doesn't deny it. Darrin spends much of this episode personifying these attributes himself, but he's much more digestible as he fumbles through his hangover, comically asking Larry, "Did you have to ring the phone so loud?"

WELL?

When Phyllis invites herself over, Samantha lies that she's relaxing. Why? Phyllis knows Samantha is a housewife; it's not like she'd have a problem with Samantha tidying the house for her son. For Phyllis to be at the never-before-mentioned corner drugstore, she and Frank must live nearby now; they've either lived in or out of town since their introduction in "Samantha Meets the Folks" (#14). Another throwback to Season One happens when Samantha employs a speed-up spell to straighten the living room, which she did in "...And Something Makes Three" (#12), when Louise was on her way from the corner filling station. Samantha finds time to change clothes before Phyllis arrives – so what was the rush?

Phyllis laments that Darrin and Samantha never go anywhere. But the Stephenses have been to Paris ["Witch or Wife" (#8)] and Miami ["Divided He Falls" (#69)], and just last season they went to Chicago on business ["That Was No Chick, That Was My Wife" (#117)]. Then, the show skips a whole month [again lending credence to the idea that a year was added to the Stephenses' marriage; see Samantha's Wedding Present" (#141)], and Samantha makes her way to a giant, heretofore unseen mailbox on the curb. When Samantha opens her winning letter, there are plane tickets to Tahiti inside. That would never happen today, and it's doubtful it would in 1968.

Larry enrages Darrin by asking Samantha to run McMann & Tate's slogan department – since when does the agency have such a department? Darrin creates their slogans, but only as an ad executive.

Dick Wilson's latest entertaining boozer makes some fun asides about his off-screen wife, but he was just seen in "It's So Nice to Have A Spouse Around the House" (#145) as a different drunk. Then, Samantha worries about Darrin, but makes sure to change clothes again before tracking him to the bar. At least Darrin is concerned about not having paid his tab, unlike the last time Samantha zapped him off a bar stool [see "Allergic to Ancient Macedonian Dodo Birds" (#118)]. And it's reassuring that Samantha gets a sitter for Tabitha, but a dog? What if Tabitha wants some juice, as she did in "Toys in Babeland" (#109)? Clarissa can't communicate with Tabitha any more than the toy soldier from that episode could. As for this episode, how is poor Tabitha reacting to all the yelling and door slamming that's going on?

McMann & Tate is hot to get the Barton Industries account, yet Darrin has its layouts buried in the back of his den closet. Then, they're somehow in the living room for Samantha to sneak out of the house – except he'd never be allowed to bring the layouts back home after being fired. Samantha tip-toes out the front door, leaving Tabitha alone – save for her father, who's downstairs sleeping off a hangover. Is Clarissa back on duty? Larry wakes Darrin with the news that Barton loved the layouts, which is odd, because Darrin quit. There's no mention of Darrin taking his job back at any point in the tag, yet Darrin tells Samantha he'd love to stay with her "if I didn't have to go to work." Samantha obliges by magically arranging for Darrin to have the day off, but Darrin says Barton found the layouts "this morning," which means it's afternoon, and Darrin slept the morning away, so he's only getting a half day off.

OH, MY STARS!

When did Phyllis become a snob? There were rumblings of it in "Playmates" (#133), but here she gives Samantha the white glove test and has Darrin so spooked that he runs out rather than let his mother see he's gone without a haircut for a couple of weeks. At least she doesn't witness witchcraft this time.

This episode borrows heavily from "Help, Help, Don't Save Me" (#5), the first episode in which Darrin thought Samantha's ideas were witchcraft, right down to dialogue like "I'd call it imagination; I do have some, you know." Admittedly, the show takes only the kernel of that concept and puts a different twist on it, but it doesn't quite work: to begin with, why does Barton Industries need McMann & Tate if they're obtaining slogans through contests? Darrin and Larry can't not know that's how Barton operates, and surely Samantha didn't go a whole month before telling Darrin about the contest and that Phyllis put her up to it. Larry fires Darrin over Samantha entering a contest without his knowledge, and, if Barton uses a "computer analyzer" to judge slogans (which Darrin additionally calls a "consumer analyzer"), why did they declare Samantha the winner of their contest and send her airline tickets before running her slogan through their machine and deciding it's no good? Finally, Darrin ends the episode by celebrating Samantha's "lousy" slogan, as he did in "Help, Help, Don't Save Me" (#5); that conclusion already defied logic in its first go-round.

SON OF A GUN!

"Yeah – but that's dumb!" – Samantha to Darrin, after he asks if she's heard of diversification and reveals that Tinkerbell Diapers falls under the Barton umbrella.

EPISODE 149

SAMANTHA FIGHTS CITY HALL
Airdate: November 28, 1968

While Tabitha unnerves a neighborhood kid by sliding up a slide in the park, Samantha learns the park is about to be torn down to make way for a shopping center. Spurred into action after hearing the city has mysteriously forgotten to pay its nominal yearly fee on the park, Samantha organizes a protest march, and the group tries to keep a bulldozer from starting the demolition. When the driver threatens to bulldoze through the crowd, Samantha disables the machine with witchcraft, but park owner Mossler tells the women they'll be arrested if they show up again the next day. Mossler, who also owns Easy Way Rent-A-Car, strolls into McMann & Tate and laughs off the protesters.

Darrin, who has been supportive of Samantha, now tries to discourage her from continuing the fight, but gets zapped onto the couch when the marrieds have a fight of their own. In the morning, Larry sees Samantha's picture in the paper and insists Darrin stop her for the sake of preserving Mossler's account. Mossler tries to blackmail Samantha into backing down, but Darrin comes around and tells her to stand her ground, which gets him fired. When Mossler balks at Samantha reminding him that his grandfather donated the park, Samantha twitches the founder's statue to life to scold him. Mossler gives in and rededicates the park, but the statue shocks Samantha by winking at her.

GOOD!

Samantha started her married life befuddled about all things mortal, but she adjusted – perhaps a little too quickly. So it's refreshing to hear her describing the park problems to Darrin, adding, "it's so mortal, I don't understand it." Also, there's a wonderfully subtle moment with a prop: Mossler hands Samantha a flower, and, as he blackmails her, she silently crumples the bloom and tosses it aside.

Darrin is the understanding fellow of previous seasons as he helps Samantha figure out how to protest the demolition of the park, only to get blustery again when the Mossler account is threatened. So the way he comes around and stands by Samantha, even if it means getting canned (again), is particularly gratifying, and comically punctuated by his "First I'll get dressed" to Larry after he marches out in his pajamas.

Mossler receiving a dressing down from his grandfather's statue is the pinnacle of the episode. The show also used this "bronzed actor" technique when Darrin was "statuefied" in "It's So Nice to Have A Spouse Around the House" (#145); it's interesting to see what the effect looks like in motion.

WELL?

Is that Michael Millhowser from "Playmates" (#133) daring Tabitha to slide up the slide? No, but it's the same actor, Teddy Quinn, playing a new witness to Miss Stephens' witchcraft. Conversely, it's a "new" Tabitha as well, as Diane Murphy appears in place of her twin sister, Erin. Diane brings a different energy to the role, an amazing example of how much individuality there can be in identical twins.

So the neighborhood park, featured in "Eye of the Beholder" (#22), "A Gazebo Never Forgets" (#89), and "Nobody But A Frog Knows How to Live" (#106), to name a few, has been owned all along by Harlan Mossler; he happens to be advertising two of his businesses through the Manhattan-based McMann & Tate, but wants to pulverize the same park Samantha frequents in Patterson, some 60 miles away. And after all that work Samantha did to get new playground equipment installed there in "Oedipus Hex" (#85), which isn't mentioned.

Samantha asks her never-before-seen neighbor ladies how to fight City Hall, forgetting that she lobbied for a traffic signal to be installed in the neighborhood in "Red Light, Green Light" (#23); Vic Tayback appears here, as he did in that episode. It's quite a commentary on the dragged heels of governing bodies that Samantha's appointment with her councilman isn't until April 15, 1997 (and also quite an in-joke, since April 15 is Elizabeth Montgomery's birthday), but does Samantha have no pull at City Hall? She helped get Councilman Ed Wright elected in "Remember the Main" (#34). Although he was apparently replaced by Councilman Green between that episode and "Twitch or Treat" (#81), Samantha should still be able to get Wright to pull a few strings on her behalf.

If Samantha seems like a natural leader to her fellow protesters, it's because she has a little experience in this area. In "The Witches Are Out" (#7), she mobilized a supernatural protest group to convince candy maker Brinkman that stereotype witches were not the appropriate way to advertise his product. And, in "Samantha for the Defense" (#88), teen protesters ended up carrying signs benefiting Benjamin Franklin thanks to Samantha's witchcraft.

Larry fires Darrin after Samantha inadvertently jeopardizes an account; Darrin spends the night on the couch after hassling Samantha. These exact events took place one week ago, in "Is It Magic or

Imagination?" (#148), but neither Larry nor the Stephenses get the feeling they've been here before. Larry also frets that the loss of Mossler's accounts will put the agency out of business, though that's hardly likely, considering how much McMann & Tate takes in. And again, anything the Stephenses do is news: a local debate over the closure of one tiny park makes the front page, even with Vietnam and the civil rights movement going on.

After Samantha spooks Mossler into changing his stance about the park, he offers the now-unemployed Darrin all the accounts of Mossler Enterprises. For the third time in the series, Darrin has the opportunity to open his own agency – but he instead sticks with Larry, who fires him constantly.

Two other observations: the live action "statue" (played by Robert Terry) and his stationary likeness don't look very much alike, and, for all this hoopla over preserving the park for Tabitha, where is she? On the swings, where she was last seen in the prologue?

OH, MY STARS!

After the park lives happily ever after, Samantha looks over and sees the statue of Mossler's grandfather winking at her. In reaction, Samantha's jaw drops to the point Darrin has to snap her back to reality. Why is Samantha surprised? She's the one who put the spell on the statue; unless she removed it during the commercial break, the witchcraft is still active. If Samantha's merely realizing she forgot to deanimate the statue, she still has no reason to look stunned.

SON OF A GUN!

"Those mothers won't budge." – the bulldozer driver to Mossler, after Samantha and her fellow protesters dig their heels in.

EPISODE 150

SAMANTHA LOSES HER VOICE
Airdate: December 5, 1968

Samantha is besieged by two visitors: Uncle Arthur, who brings Tabitha a puppy, and Louise, who brings news she's divorcing Larry. When Arthur asks if Samantha's keeping the puppy, she says she can't speak for Darrin – so Arthur gives his niece Darrin's voice. Meanwhile, Darrin, who's been counseling Larry, suddenly sounds like Samantha. As Uncle Arthur tries to give the furious Stephenses their voices back, Larry arrives wanting to talk to Darrin, who claims laryngitis. Hearing Louise inside, Larry brands Darrin a traitor, fires him, and storms off.

Attempting to restore the Stephenses' voices, Uncle Arthur accidentally switches his with Samantha's, which they barely hide from Louise. Darrin offers Louise the sympathetic ear she wants from Samantha, but Louise feels everyone is against her and rushes upstairs. After Arthur gets everyone sounding like themselves, Darrin insults the departing warlock; when the Stephenses try to talk Louise out of also taking her leave, their voices switch again. Louise runs outside and into Larry; while they make up, Uncle Arthur returns to solidify Samantha and Darrin's voices by having them join hands. The Stephenses find their hands stuck together after Darrin sasses Arthur again, leaving the couple scrambling to explain to the Tates that they made Louise feel unwanted on purpose to bring about her reunion with Larry. Later, Arthur unsticks the Stephenses and extracts a thank-you from Darrin, handing him a bag filled with "cents of humor," which breaks and sends thousands of pennies scattering.

GOOD!

Louise Tate is usually only on hand to schmooze at business dinners, so it's nice to see Kasey Rogers getting a chance to show off her comedic talents in this episode. She's properly melodramatic as Louise sobs over a volleyball game, and flabbergasted as she hears her friends speaking in each others' voices.

This episode gives Elizabeth Montgomery, Dick York, and Paul Lynde the opportunity to act out each others' characters – vocally, anyway. Their imitations of each other are all terrific, but somehow the best is Dick York channeling Samantha as his voice comes out of his on-screen wife. Also, Darrin's affection toward Arthur at the end feels very genuine; it's heartwarming to hear him admit that his uncle-in-law is his best friend in Samantha's family. And the warmth between Samantha and Uncle Arthur, particularly in the prologue, is palpable, probably because Elizabeth Montgomery and Paul Lynde were crazy about each other in real life.

WELL?

"You know my Uncle Arthur," Samantha says as Louise barges in with her suitcases. Actually, she doesn't: neither of the Tates have ever met Arthur, at least not on screen. Louise explains that her fight with Larry started on the beach. What beach? Patterson, New York isn't anywhere near one, unless the Tates drove the hour to get to the shore.

What day of the week is this? Darrin and Larry both wear suits, which implies it's a business day – yet the men sit in a bar, then hang around Darrin's house when it looks to be afternoon outside. But it can't be a weekend, either; that would mean the Tates had their volleyball fight and dressed up afterwards. While bending Darrin's ear, Larry asks, "Have you ever seen Louise play volleyball?" Darrin has, in "Bewitched, Bothered, and Infuriated" (#105), but, since Samantha erased the Tates' memory of the Stephenses' presence, it's a fair question on Larry's part.

This isn't the first time Samantha has had a witchy problem with her voice: Aunt Clara accidentally caused a delay in Samantha's speech in "Out of Sync, Out of Mind" (#116). The big question is, how can Uncle Arthur not reverse his spell or get the Stephenses voices to "stick?" There's nothing wrong with his powers, and he can't even use kinetic vibrations zonking across the atmospheric continuum as an excuse, which is how he conjured up Napoléon Bonaparte in "Samantha's French Pastry" (#147). It's a safe bet, with Marion Lorne having passed on, that Arthur has been chosen to carry Aunt Clara's botched spell torch, but it's inconsistent with his usual abilities.

Louise asks Darrin when he started speaking for his wife; Arthur, in Samantha's voice, says "about 10 minutes ago." So Darrin sits in a bar, discovers he has Samantha's voice, races home, has his altercation with Uncle Arthur, and gets fired by Larry – all in 10 minutes? And why is Darrin so surprised to hear Louise upstairs? Surely he saw her car parked outside. When Larry arrives, Darrin feigns laryngitis; Darrin faked the same ailment in "There's Gold in Them Thar Pills" (#107), when Dr. Bombay's Cold Bombs pitched up his voice. Even if Larry doesn't wonder why Darrin's voice is out again, he should at least pay for the window he breaks once he makes nice with Darrin. What is Tabitha, who is supposedly napping the whole time, supposed to make of all this yelling, door slamming, and glass breaking?

Arthur reminds the Stephenses that there's a lonely puppy outside – a quiet one, since there's never a peep from the pup. Darrin chews Arthur out as if he knows about the puppy's existence, but this scene is Darrin's first time hearing about Tabitha's potential pet.

Louise ditching Larry over a volleyball game is funny at first, but by the time she cries that everyone is against her, she's unusually childish. Wouldn't the more mature, in-therapy Louise of "I'd Rather Twitch Than Fight" (#84) take her current version aside and remind her there's no point in an amphigoric argument?

Darrin should know not to shake hands with his uncle-in-law – this time he gets electrocuted, but in "Endora Moves in for a Spell" (#80), Arthur's hand was attached to an extra long arm. Arthur borrows another trick from that episode when he pops into one of Samantha's paintings. Strangely, when he pops out of it, the film desaturates for a moment until he appears in the chair. And since when is the fun-loving Arthur vindictive? He witches the Stephenses twice in retaliation for Darrin's insults, but that's no reason to make Samantha suffer.

Samantha recalling that Uncle Arthur taught her how to make her first pony is accurate: she first shared that with Darrin in "The Joker Is A Card" (#41). But Samantha should see Arthur's "cents of humor" joke coming – in "The No-Harm Charm" (#138), he told her it would be funny to have 5,000 pennies spill out in front of a bank teller.

OH, MY STARS!

Larry is in a rut: he has now fired Darrin three episodes in a row. The "joke" is played out, and it demeans the characters of both Stephens and Tate. Darrin ought to leave Larry in the dust, at least for a few episodes – imagine the comedy of Larry trying to conduct agency business by himself. And Darrin might earn Larry's respect if he'd stop letting Larry bully him all the time. Alas, Darrin likewise bullies Uncle Arthur, and with the threat of physical violence, as he did in "Samantha's French Pastry" (#147).

Poor Jonathan Tate – his parents are contemplating a split without even remembering he exists. Bad enough he's left all alone while his mom and dad fight; good thing they reunite, or Jonathan would have to live with having a broken family because of a volleyball game.

SON OF A GUN!

"Louise, volleyball is not grounds for divorce in this state." – Samantha, trying to convince her friend not to take Larry to a different kind of court.

EPISODE 151 — I DON'T WANT TO BE A TOAD, I WANT TO BE A BUTTERFLY
Airdate: December 12, 1968

Samantha gently instructs Tabitha not to do witchcraft in front of Phyllis, who surprises everyone by enrolling Tabitha in nursery school. Unable to get out of it, Samantha assures Darrin she will accompany their daughter to class, but Phyllis wants Samantha to go shopping, and the teacher, Mrs. Burch, won't let Samantha stick around. Left to her own devices, Tabitha magically fixes a game of musical chairs, and, when new friend Amy cries over not being cast as a butterfly in Mrs. Burch's activity, Tabitha turns Amy into a real butterfly to placate her.

Taking clothes into a fitting room as a front to fool Phyllis and a saleslady, Samantha pops in outside Tabitha's school and asks her daughter why Mrs. Burch is frantically looking for Amy. Tabitha explains what she did and that Amy-as-butterfly flew out the window, so Samantha zaps herself onto a tree in an attempt to fetch her, only to be spotted by the tree's owner. Samantha then shocks two skyscraper workers by appearing on a beam and catching Amy in a net. By the time Tabitha changes Amy back, Amy's mother is ready to press charges against a near-catatonic Mrs. Burch – and Phyllis, who has tracked Samantha to the school, wonders how she got out of the fitting room unnoticed. Later, Samantha complies with Darrin's request for a huge drink while telling him why the school is closing.

GOOD!

This extraordinary episode is not only funny, it takes chances, and it's got heart. Darrin admitting he doesn't trust Tabitha is very honest of him, and he adds real warmth when he points out that no one could trust him at Tabitha's age, either. Samantha slowly revealing the extent of the havoc Tabitha wreaked at school really works, as does Darrin simply asking for stronger and stronger drinks instead of blowing up as one might expect. And Elizabeth Montgomery really is high up in that tree as Samantha looks for Amy-as-butterfly – it's just one more way the show literally reaches new heights in this episode.

Teacher Mrs. Burch going from running "tight ship" Delightful Day Nursery School to teetering on the edge of madness succeeds as a lesson in comedy. And Phyllis may think Samantha is overprotective, but she's devil-may-care compared to Amy's mother, who greets people with "Does your child have any diseases?" Hopefully that won't stop Samantha from letting Tabitha hang out with Amy, because the girls are pure magic together. Not to mention, Amy's "Hey, that was neat!" when Tabitha changes her back says she knows Tabitha has powers, and doesn't care. What better playmate for her?

WELL?

Samantha sits Tabitha down for another lecture about witchcraft and how not everyone has powers, much like she did in "Playmates" (#133), but it doesn't do much good, because Tabitha floats a piece of cake to herself in front of Phyllis (with wires showing); it's surprising Phyllis doesn't think back to "It's Wishcraft" (#103), when Frank told her he saw an apple flying into Tabitha's hand at that same table. No wonder Phyllis brags that Tabitha's vivid imagination comes from her side of the family – she had that quality drilled into her to explain magic in "It's Wishcraft" (#103), and in "McTavish" (#130).

Someone must have given Phyllis a talking-to since "Is It Magic or Imagination?" (#148); she was a sudden snob in that episode, but here, she's back to being the down-to-earth Mrs. Stephens she's always been. However, you'd think she'd appreciate Samantha being overprotective with Tabitha; this is the woman who could barely let go of her full-grown son in "Samantha Meets the Folks" (#14).

What happened to Michael Millhowser, who was groomed to be Tabitha's friend in "Playmates" (#133)? Amy charmingly fills that position here, but isn't she a little old for nursery school? Maralee Foster, who plays the tyke, was already 7 by the time this episode was filmed.

While Samantha is stuck at the dress shop, a mannequin sports the same houndstooth coat Darrin used to keep himself warm while sleeping on the couch in "Samantha Fights City Hall" (#149). And was Mrs. Burch one of the women called upon to save the park in that episode? Her Mother Nature sign is done up in the exact same writing as said group's protest signs. Mrs. Burch must the only one on staff at Delightful Day: she answers the phone herself – it's strange that there's one in her classroom, especially when there's an empty reception desk outside. Plus, when the magic she's exposed to causes her to take a vacation, the school closes. Wouldn't a new teacher be hired to take over Mrs. Burch's class instead?

When Tabitha changes Amy back, Samantha and the butterfly are outside the classroom window. Amy and Samantha are next seen walking out the classroom door with Tabitha. There are only two ways for that to happen; Samantha and Amy climbing through the window, or Samantha popping them into the room from outside the window. Are the rest of the unsupervised kids seeing this?

With Delightful Day closed, Samantha assures Darrin he doesn't have to worry about Tabitha in nursery school anymore. Oh? What's to stop Phyllis from simply enrolling Tabitha in another school? And what semester, in any school, starts two weeks before Christmas, when this episode aired?

OH, MY STARS!

Samantha explains to Tabitha that Grandpa Stephens isn't coming over because he's in Cleveland on business. That simply can't be – Frank is retired, and has been since "A Nice Little Dinner Party" (#19), when he first mentioned struggling with his jobless state. There must have been a better way to explain Frank's absence if Roy Roberts wasn't available to fill Frank's shoes.

Art Metrano makes a terrifically cynical neighbor, scoffing at the sight of Samantha in his tree, but it's far too soon to be watching the actor again: he just guest starred as the bulldozer driver in "Samantha Fights City Hall" (#149), two episodes ago. Maybe that could have worked if Mr. Metrano appeared as the same character: "Hey, aren't you that lady who did things to my bulldozer in the park?"

SON OF A GUN!

"I'm not s'posed to fly!" – Tabitha to Mrs. Burch, when the teacher sympathizes about Samantha's daughter flying out of the nest.

How on earth does the show pull off that chair spin when Tabitha makes herself the winner of the musical chairs game? There's no platform rotating beneath it, and no wires visible anywhere.

Hiring a cute baby to sit in Tabitha's high chair was one thing, but there was no way of knowing whether the child could act. Yet Erin Murphy delivers – Tabitha commands this entire episode, whether it's during Samantha's lecture (asking "Oh, is she sick?" when Samantha explains that Phyllis doesn't fly), at the dinner table (charmingly begging, "Please cake"), in school ("Yes or no, Mrs. Burch"), or at the window with Samantha ("Is this one of those things that's called a problem?"). It's like there's a whole new range of possibilities for the show now, knowing that Tabitha can carry it when requested.

EPISODE 152
WEEP NO MORE, MY WILLOW
Airdate: December 19, 1968

The snoopy Gladys brings the Stephenses a petition demanding they remove a decaying willow tree from their front yard. In an effort to save her tree, Samantha calls Dr. Bombay, who commands the willow to weep; soon, Samantha begins bawling every time there's a breeze. Gladys, who saw Darrin giving a pretty new neighbor a ride, assumes he's having an affair and rushes to Samantha, who can't stop crying. When Gladys phones Darrin's office to give him an earful, Larry, who spied Darrin dropping his neighbor off, also suspects hanky-panky and ducks out of a business meeting to check on Samantha.

Dr. Bombay responds to Samantha's repeated summons and tries to cure her by adding laughter to his tree-healing spell – but it backfires, and Samantha cackles uncontrollably when Larry comes over to straighten things out between her and Darrin. Gladys demands that Darrin get home and make things right with Samantha; he does, and once Larry leaves, both Larry and Gladys think they saved the Stephenses' marriage. Dr. Bombay returns, admitting he "made a boo-boo" and returning Samantha to normal with a new spell. A lumberjack arrives to chop the willow tree down, but before he can take his axe to it, the dying tree becomes robust, and the confused lumberjack high-tails it out of Morning Glory Circle.

GOOD!

This episode achieves some very fluid effects, such as when Samantha changes Darrin's opaque layout into a transparent one, then back again. Its letters stay in the exact same place, as does Dr. Bombay when he changes into his tree surgeon uniform outside. The only thing that shifts is the sun, and just barely.

Samantha's incessant, purposely over-the-top weeping is a testament to Elizabeth Montgomery's talent, and the comic timing of certain moments is impeccable – like Samantha telling Gladys that "Darrin and I are a divinely happy couple," only to burst into tears. Samantha's laughter is contagious as well, but the character who caps the on-screen laugh riot is Larry, whose guffaws sound completely natural; someone must have told an off-color joke between takes to elicit this reaction. And maybe Larry really is the best friend he purports to be: despite firing Darrin in three consecutive episodes [starting with "Is It Magic or Imagination?" (#148)], the man who would do anything for an account actually ditches a client to make sure Samantha is all right.

WELL?

Samantha serves Darrin his favorite breakfast: scrambled eggs and chicken livers. However, in "George the Warlock" (#30), blueberry pancakes were his favorite. And apparently no one moves into 1162 Morning Glory Circle unless they're gorgeous: Danger O'Riley took residence there in the aforementioned episode, like her buxom sister "Pleasure O'Riley" (#25) before her. This time it's Elaine Hanson, but Darrin does behave himself with her – an improvement over the those Season One installments.

If Gladys wants to present her petition to the Stephenses, why doesn't she go to the front door? Seems she just needs a reason to peek into the house. And perhaps it's old habit on his part, but why does Darrin stash his now-transparent layout? Gladys isn't in advertising; she wouldn't know there was anything unusual about it. The Kravitzes are then shown in their kitchen, which is completely different from the one they had in "Abner Kadabra" (#29). By the way, where's the giant dog the Kravitzes supposedly adopted in "Samantha's Wedding Present" (#141)?

Ostrich races must be popular among warlocks: Samantha interrupts Dr. Bombay's participation in one to aid her tree, and Uncle Arthur just rode the favorite in "Samantha Loses Her Voice" (#150). It's nice to see outdoor footage of Samantha and Dr. Bombay on the lawn, but Samantha's intercut medium shots are done in-studio (as evidenced by the lighting), and Samantha isn't wearing her trademark heart necklace in them, though it adorns her neck in the wide shots with Bombay.

Abner goes from doing his crossword puzzle at the kitchen counter to setting up his chess board in the time it takes Darrin to say, "Mrs. Kravitz, what are you talking about?" And history literally repeats itself when Abner reads his book about the Civil War, with Gladys telling him, "the North won" – they had this same conversation in "That Was My Wife" (#31).

Samantha panics when she realizes she got "caught in the fallout" of Dr. Bombay's spell [much like getting caught in Aunt Clara's time-traveling "jet stream" in "Samantha's Thanksgiving to Remember" (#119)], but, with Gladys having just snooped around, wouldn't Samantha still have the presence of mind to close the front door after running into the house? Naturally, Gladys walks in uninvited, offering Samantha a plate of brownies. Are they soybean brownies, like she whipped up for the Stephenses in "Splitsville" (#140), or has Gladys given up vegetarianism already?

Darrin should know something's wrong when Samantha tells him she has a cold. In "Take Two Aspirins and Half A Pint of Porpoise Milk" (#42), he rightly blabbed to a client that "people like her don't get sick."

Is there a spell in place that makes Morning Glory Circle look different to everyone who drives on it? After multiple changes in Season Four, the mountains of Burbank – er, New York State – now sprawl in the background. Larry's right to tell Samantha he's an old hand when it comes to marital problems: his son Jonathan almost saw his parents split over a volleyball game in "Samantha Loses Her Voice" (#150). And, it's about an hour from Manhattan to Patterson, but Darrin does the 60-mile trip in just 45 seconds.

Before the commercial break, Samantha cackles in the left-hand living room chair – but when the tag begins, she's seated on the right. Dr. Bombay's thrashed wet suit looks to be the same one he wore in "Allergic to Ancient Macedonian Dodo Birds" (#118) – and is that producer/director William Asher providing the off-screen voice of the lumberjack's co-worker, Charlie? [Sounds like him, based on his cameo in "Mirror, Mirror on the Wall" (#146).]

OH, MY STARS!

No one ever explains why the Stephenses' willow tree is a menace to the community, but it is a menace to continuity. In four years of seeing exteriors of the Stephens house [and "How Green Was My Grass" (#131) was an episode dedicated to it], there has never been a willow tree in the front yard. It's very sweet for the show to say that Darrin planted it the day Tabitha was born, but he was far too busy in "And There Were Three" (#54) thinking his newborn had been turned into an adult to be planting trees, much less one that looks far more than three (ahem, four) years old. It's a bit like the phantom mailbox that showed up in "Is It Magic or Imagination?" (#148), which is nowhere to be seen now.

Samantha recruits Dr. Bombay because she's tried and failed to heal her tree with her own powers. This witch can stop rain and have flocks of birds fly over weeks early [see "Love Is Blind" (#13)], but she can't give magical TLC to a tree? Dr. Bombay can, though Samantha falls under the influence of his spell. This is the fourth time this season Samantha has been affected by someone else's witchcraft; being a witch herself should be enough to insulate her from outside magic.

SON OF A GUN!

"Is it another woman? Another man?" – Larry to the laughing Samantha, trying to discern who her competition is.

EPISODE 153 INSTANT COURTESY
Airdate: December 26, 1968

After Samantha comments that Endora never sees Darrin's courteous and gallant side because she's always antagonizing him, Endora zaps Darrin with a "super courtesy" spell that has secretary Betty thinking he's flirting with her and Larry becoming furious about his heightened considerateness. Up for grabs is the Adrienne Sebastian Cosmetics account; Ms. Sebastian loves Darrin's chivalry and softer approach to her product, while her brusque advertising manager, Traynor, writes Darrin off as a yes-man. As a result, Larry "courteously" gives Darrin a few years' unpaid sick leave.

Picking up on Darrin's excessive civility as he describes what happened at the office, Samantha clues in to Endora's spell and demands her mother remove it, getting only a sassy written response. In the meantime, the impressed Ms. Sebastian arrives and offers to set Darrin up in his own agency. Samantha overhears and witches Larry into coming over to apologize; Darrin, who has since been despelled, questions Larry's sincerity, and assumes he knows about Ms. Sebastian's offer. Larry doesn't; he and Darrin patch things up, but when Ms. Sebastian returns and finds Larry there, she accuses the men of faking Darrin's firing to manipulate her into giving them her account. She's about to walk when Samantha twitches her into reconsidering, and the friends/co-workers celebrate, after which Samantha giggles that Endora won't sleep for a month upon finding out she helped Darrin.

GOOD!

In this episode, it's the bodies orbiting the stars that shine brighter. Louise is a much-needed voice of reason, providing a counterpart to Larry's irrational employer/employee relationship skills – but the crass Mr. Traynor gives the installment the comedic "hard sell" it needs, not only with his blunt approach to cosmetics, but his astute observations. "Courtesy is a refuge of scoundrels and yes-men," Traynor fumes in regard to Darrin. "I've got a feeling he's both!"

WELL?

Jill Foster's Betty is back – and she's engaged. But why does Larry relish the mistaken assumption that Darrin and Betty are fooling around? As far as he knows, he just helped save the Stephenses' marriage in "Weep No More, My Willow" (#152). Also, Larry seems to have a different desk; the one he had in "Mirror, Mirror on the Wall" (#146) had a reflective surface so the vanity-spelled Darrin could stare at himself in it.

Two guest stars make return appearances here, despite having been on the show not that long ago. Herb Voland played a client the last time Endora put a spell on Darrin [in "Mirror, Mirror on the Wall" (#146)], though at least his terse Traynor is a reinvention compared to that episode's conservative Hascomb. And Sharon Vaughn, who just played comely neighbor Elaine in the preceding "Weep No More, My Willow" (#152), sits at Miss Springer's reception desk.

When Endora shoots an arrow into Samantha's kitchen wall, the attached message isn't always what Samantha reads aloud. She starts out reciting what is seen in close-up: "Tell your chivalrous husband that his courteous Mother-In-Law is regrettably unavailable." Then, the note changes to, "Guess who made me that way." But in the long shots, if you peruse the reversed message, which is visible through the paper, the calligraphy reads, "Not until I get an engraved invitation from your chivalrous husband." At least Samantha checks her wall for a hole once Endora's arrow disappears.

Even if Larry thinks Darrin's courteousness is overkill, why does he define him a "disloyal employee?" If anything, Larry should approve, since he's far more of a yes-man here than Darrin is.

Endora's pat "Disappear courtesy" spell is amusing, though it mirrors the equally short "Cancel the spell" spell-canceler she used in "Business, Italian Style" (#110), where she also asked the confused Samantha if she was expecting poetry. The timing of this spell's removal is interesting: it happens while Darrin is outside with Ms. Sebastian. If Adrienne hasn't already driven off, does she notice a change in Darrin as they talk? For that matter, does Darrin ever find out he's had a spell on him? Samantha never tells him about it, and Darrin doesn't seem to notice one way or the other.

How does Adrienne Sebastian find out Darrin's been fired? He's still on staff at McMann & Tate when Traynor escorts her out, but when Ms. Sebastian shows up on Darrin's door, she's offering him his own agency. She'd have to call the office to get Darrin's address; surely Larry would discourage her from trying to locate Darrin. Do Betty or Miss Springer fink about Darrin' termination? Later, when Larry comes over to apologize, Darrin tells him about Ms. Sebastian's offer, and Larry exclaims, "What an opportunity! For both of us!" How is Darrin getting his own agency an opportunity for Larry?

No wonder Ms. Sebastian thinks she's being swindled – Samantha zapping her into reconsidering her stance is too easy a fix. It's like the writers knew there were only so many minutes left in the episode, and picked the simplest way to wrap things up; Darrin, who has suspected Samantha of witchcraft any number of times, only says, "It's funny the way things have of working themselves out." Finally, Larry's happy that Darrin's soft sell cinches the account, but Darrin says, "You never saw it." Larry was going to let Darrin pitch a concept he didn't approve first?

OH, MY STARS!

Larry firing Darrin is getting to be like a broken record – he's done it four times this season alone. Samantha thinks Darrin has nothing to worry about, saying, "You know how he is." Have things gotten to the point that the Stephenses view Larry as a "boy who cried wolf" when it comes to his constant axings? Then, Samantha goes to work trying to reunite Larry and Darrin after Ms. Sebastian suggests starting up the Darrin Stephens Agency. These untaken job offers are just as much an overused story point, and it's bewildering that Samantha never lets Darrin advance in his career when given these opportunities, especially with Larry lowering the boom on him all the time.

SON OF A GUN!

"I want a campaign that says, 'You've got two choices: use Adrienne Sebastian products, or be ugly.'" – Mr. Traynor, describing the hard sell he expects.

Samantha's brief time on the chain gang makes for the episode's best effect. When Endora zaps her into and out of a gunny sack and chains, it looks absolutely fluid.

EPISODE 154 SAMANTHA'S SUPERMAID
Airdate: January 2, 1969

Phyllis invites herself over, insisting that Samantha needs a maid so she can socialize with women whose husbands can advance Darrin's career. Samantha tries to get out of it, but Phyllis has arranged for prospective housekeepers to come over for interviews. After the severe Mrs. Harper flunks Samantha because she has a child, the demure Amelia finds the Stephenses and their unusual schedule a "rewarding challenge." When Darrin comes home from his golf game to discover he has a maid, he tells Samantha they can't have one because of the constant magic that goes on – yet can't bring himself to fire the efficient and complimentary Amelia.

Upon hearing how Phyllis pressured Samantha into hiring a maid, Endora makes a "destructive" suggestion: destroying the living room and kitchen to discourage Amelia from staying on. At that moment, Phyllis brings stuffy socialite Leslie Otis over to meet Samantha, who lies that she and her family purposely make messes because Amelia likes to have a lot to do. Catching on to Leslie's interest in Amelia, Samantha zaps the maid into overdrive so she'll get everything cleaned up in record time. Leslie offers Amelia double her present salary, but, when Amelia wants to stay with the Stephenses, Samantha twitches her supermaid into changing her mind.

GOOD!

Tabitha simply rocks any scene she's in. Her unadulterated joy as she manually twitches the paper airplane into soaring around the patio is contagious, and Darrin makes a very good point when he reminds Samantha that there's too much magic in the house for them to have help. Endora jeering that "Durwood's mommy" wants a maid has a ring of truth to it, and her leveling the living room to expunge Amelia is fun. Although Samantha already did speed-cleaning as recently as "Is It Magic or Imagination?" (#148), watching supermaid Amelia zip around the room is worth the revisit.

WELL?

Darrin makes a paper airplane and asks Samantha if she's ever seen one before; she says no. But, in "A is for Aardvark" (#17), it was Darrin's note written on a paper airplane that set his whole let's-live-by-witchcraft declaration in motion. Darrin may not remember that due to the memory-erasing spell he had Samantha put on him, but Samantha should.

Phyllis snarks that Endora is there every time she comes over – that used to be the case, but Phyllis hasn't even seen Endora since "It's Wishcraft" (#103), despite five subsequent visits. By the way, where's Frank these days? He's been AWOL since "McTavish" (#130), with Phyllis always coming over solo. And isn't it time Darrin talks to his mother about being so presumptuous? Phyllis pushed Samantha into visiting the Millhowsers in "Playmates" (#133), into a slogan contest in "Is It Magic or Imagination?" (#148), and into putting Tabitha in preschool in "I Don't Want to Be A Toad, I Want to Be A Butterfly" (#151). Yet the Stephenses keep letting this woman walk all over them.

This episode hearkens back to "Maid to Order" (#53), where the pregnant Samantha hired lovable but inept Naomi to keep house for her. Mrs. Harper might as well be that episode's Mrs. Luftwaffe, because they are that interchangeable – plus, past and present sequences share a lot of dialogue. There *are* some reversals: "Maid to Order" (#53) saw Darrin wanting to hire a maid for his expectant wife, not thinking of the magical repercussions; here, that's all he thinks of. And Endora, who wanted Samantha to hire someone to help her through her pregnancy in "A Very Special Delivery" (#38), now expresses disdain at Samantha hiring someone to do what she can do magically.

Mrs. Harper and Amelia come over because Phyllis has fetched them from an employment agency. In the beginning of the episode, the Stephenses establish that Phyllis visits on Sundays – what employment agency sends prospective employees over on a Sunday? Then, after Mrs. Harper hires herself, Samantha tells her she has a baby. Tabitha is four; Samantha makes it sound like a newborn is sleeping upstairs.

In "Pleasure O'Riley" (#25), Darrin's favorite dish was turkey soup with extra wide noodles; by "The No-Harm Charm" (#138), it was beef stew. Here, Phyllis whips up apparent favorite shepherd's pie and asparagus with hollandaise sauce, even though Amelia has just been hired, and should be cooking the meal herself. Darrin naturally wants to get out of his golf clothes for dinner, but who wears a suit to eat in his own house?

Phyllis makes a big to-do about Samantha connecting with "the right people." So logic would dictate that Phyllis would make sure Samantha is dressed to the nines before bringing Leslie Otis over. But what does Phyllis do? She brings Leslie over unannounced.

Under the guise of getting Amelia alone, Leslie asks Samantha where she can powder her nose; Samantha says, "Into the den and to your left." Why does Samantha guide Mrs. Otis into the den closet?

That room hasn't been a bathroom since "Help, Help, Don't Save Me" (#5). And, while Samantha might think it's clever to launch Amelia into hyperspeed so Leslie will take her off her hands, she's really just setting the maid up for a world of trouble. What's supposed to happen when Leslie gets Amelia home and finds out the woman can't work that fast?

OH, MY STARS!

Phyllis was a snob in "Is It Magic or Imagination?" (#148), but not in "I Don't Want to Be A Toad, I Want to Be A Butterfly" (#151). Now she's a snob again, outdoing herself into the bargain. Since when is Phyllis Stephens interested in social climbing? Good thing she doesn't know how many times Samantha stopped Darrin from opening his own agency [see "Instant Courtesy" (#153)]. Phyllis also goes on about how "it wouldn't do" for people to think Darrin can't afford a maid, but Darrin's had two: Naomi in "Maid to Order" (#53), and Elspeth in "I Get Your Nanny, You Get My Goat" (#122). Whatever happened to Elspeth, anyway? The Stephenses presumably kept her on, but the bubbly Brit hasn't been seen since; the show misses the opportunity here to explain why.

The previous episode, "Instant Courtesy" (#153), got wrapped up in a nice, neat bow when Samantha twitched Adrienne Sebastian into considering Darrin's campaign ideas. This episode uses the same bow by having Samantha twitch Amelia into accepting Leslie's offer of employment. At this rate, Samantha will just be able to handle any conflict that comes up by witchcraft, which is the opposite of the show's basic premise.

SON OF A GUN!

"Oh, Samantha, you've been living this hum-drum life too long. Simply turn the creature into a toad and put her out back!" – Endora, when her daughter wonders how to relieve herself of Amelia.

EPISODE 155
COUSIN SERENA STRIKES AGAIN (PART I)
Airdate: January 9, 1969

After Darrin yells at Serena for waking everyone in the middle of the night with her motorcycle, Serena invites herself to a business dinner with Clio Vanita, a discriminating client Darrin is very nervous about. The Tates arrive with Italian bombshell Clio, who has a thing for Darrin and smiles while putting Samantha down. Serena promises Samantha she'll remain invisible, but, feeling Clio is trying to steal Darrin from her cousin, Serena insults Clio in Samantha's voice, then watches as Clio coos for Darrin to join her in Rome, threatening not to award McMann & Tate her account if he doesn't. While Darrin and Larry argue about it, Samantha finds Serena on the patio, having just turned Clio into a monkey.

When Darrin sees the monkey, but not Clio, Samantha lies that the client is in the den with a headache, which the departing Tates buy. Darrin offers to make a place for the monkey to sleep; after Clio jumps into the Stephenses' bed, Samantha's vehement objections tell Darrin that something is wrong. Darrin flips as Samantha sheepishly admits Serena made a monkey out of Clio, then orders Serena to turn Clio back and get out of his life forever. Stubborn Serena pops out, leaving Clio in monkey form and forcing Samantha to tie Miss Vanita up on the patio for the night.

GOOD!

This episode features two pop culture references of the time: Samantha's joke, "guess who's coming to dinner," which is the title of the landmark 1967 movie starring Spencer Tracy and Katherine Hepburn, and Samantha commenting that Serena is "Chicken Delight," a restaurant chain that was huge in the '60s. [Larry also told Darrin that Louise *wasn't* Chicken Delight in "It's So Nice to Have A Spouse Around the House" (#145).]

Four characters have shining moments in this episode: Samantha, whose imitation of Clio is uncanny [and reminiscent of her mocking Daphne Harper in "Charlie Harper, Winner" (#99)]; Serena, who makes her cousin a virtual ventriloquist's dummy; Louise, who checks on a babysitter (Jonathan Tate lives!) – and Darrin, who, even in anger, is much more subdued than he's been all season. Darrin even makes the self-aware comment, "Serena, after all these years, this is no time to start taking me seriously!" (If three years counts as "all these years," that is.)

WELL?

Perhaps Serena isn't worried about waking Samantha and Darrin at three in the morning, but what about Tabitha? There's no way the girl could sleep through the roar of her motorcycle. And aren't the Stephenses awfully conscious for having just been woken up?

Clio Vanita may be the height of fashion and glamour, but her look is so earlier this season. The sequined collar on her dress is the same material as the "heavenly creation" Samantha zapped up for herself in "Mirror, Mirror on the Wall" (#146). As for Darrin, Endora "helped" him learn Italian in "Business, Italian Style" (#110); you'd think he'd remember a few key words and phrases for Clio. If McMann & Tate did copy for Clio's magazine ad a month ago, as she says, why do they still need a slogan? Wouldn't a slogan have been included in what they submitted to the magazine?

Samantha has come a long way in the kitchen: the girl who couldn't fry eggs four years ago can now make squab, a delicacy made of baby pigeon. The show's footage of Samantha and Serena in the kitchen doesn't quite bake up as well, since it's unusually blurry compared to previous split-screen effects. As for Louise, she likes British men [Charlie, in "A Prince of A Guy" (#129)], French men [Napoléon, in "Samantha's French Pastry" (#147)], and now she oohs and aahs over Italian men. Should Larry be worried?

Darrin pooh-poohs Clio's belief in elves, but he ought to be the first to concur that they exist, thanks to "Cousin Edgar" (#36). He should also be flashing back to "Twitch or Treat" (#81), because the way Eva, the cat-turned-human, pawed him is the way Clio paws him now. And, the next time Endora thinks Darrin is cheating, all Serena has to do is tell her that she saw Darrin resisting the persistent Clio.

After Larry hears from Samantha that Clio is lying down in the den with a headache, he compliments Darrin for his "headache routine." Larry thinks Darrin *told* Clio to feign a headache so they can resume their Rome conversation later? At best, it's Clio who would make up a malady to keep working on Darrin, not the other way around. And would Larry really send Darrin overseas with the "Italian vulture" just to get her account and threaten to fire him if he doesn't go when he just stepped in to "save" the Stephenses' marriage in "Weep No More, My Willow" (#152)?

In "Hippie, Hippie, Hooray" (#128), Darrin yelled at Serena and called her a kook; after much hoopla, Darrin promised not to harass Serena again. Apparently, he's forgotten that promise, because here he flies off the handle with his cousin-in-law anyway, expecting no repercussions.

OH, MY STARS!

The Stephenses should be having some serious déjà vus, because they've uttered a lot of their dialogue before – this episode pulls much of its material from "It Shouldn't Happen to a Dog" (#3). Samantha changed Rex Barker into a canine on the gazebo; Serena turns Clio into a monkey near the gazebo. Barker-as-dog scurried upstairs and into the Stephenses' bed; Clio-as-monkey does the same. Darrin asked Samantha, "You took a live client and turned him into a dog?" – here, the pronoun and noun are different, but the question is identical. Darrin wants to let Clio sleep in the bedroom, not remembering that he offered the same accommodation to Barker – and also "George the Warlock" (#30), who was masquerading as a bird. Finally, Darrin frets that Clio has to be at a meeting the next morning, similar to "The Catnapper" (#71), where Endora having made a feline of Toni Devlin kept the client out of the boardroom. This is the first time the show has reinvented an episode so closely; it's not that they shouldn't revisit the witch-turns-client-into-animal theme, but there are other ways than straight duplication, even if they knew real-time viewers wouldn't necessarily remember seeing the same story three years earlier.

SON OF A GUN!

"Personally, I think she should see a plastic surgeon...to have her nose lowered." – Samantha to Darrin, offering her opinion of Clio Vanita.

EPISODE 156
COUSIN SERENA STRIKES AGAIN (PART II)
Airdate: January 16, 1969

Darrin has a nightmare about the events of "Cousin Serena Strikes Again (Part I)" (#155), in which Serena turned his amorous client, Clio Vanita, into a monkey. Larry comes over wanting to know if Darrin patched things up with Clio, who wanted to take Darrin to Rome; Darrin stalls and sends Larry on his way. Darrin's overjoyed when Serena returns to change Clio back – he even apologizes – but the monkey runs away before his cousin-in-law can make the transformation. As Serena babysits, the Stephenses comb the neighborhood for the missing client. Samantha ultimately tracks Clio-as-monkey to a pet store, but the owner has already sold her.

Italian organ grinder Scibetta refuses to sell Clio to Samantha, so she offers him a trip back to Italy. A police officer interrupts and demands to see Clio's animal license, deciding to quarantine the monkey when Scibetta can't produce her papers; during the confrontation, Clio gets away and runs down the street. After giving chase, Samantha zaps herself to Clio-as-monkey and takes her into the ladies' room of an office building. As the cop readies to burst in, Samantha emerges with Serena and the restored Clio. Samantha brings Clio and Scibetta to McMann & Tate, with the organ grinder illustrating a monkey-based slogan that Clio loves. At home, Serena entertains Tabitha by bringing nursery rhymes to life – but, after Darrin sasses her again, Serena entertains herself by elongating Darrin's nose.

GOOD!

Darrin's nightmare is the cleverest recap the show's two-parters have had yet; usually, Samantha narrates to bring viewers up to date. The only quibble is that Darrin wouldn't have Samantha or Serena's memories to have a nightmare about, but that was only two clips.

The parade of guest stars in this episode definitely keeps things moving: Ezekiel Lewis as the boy who provides Samantha her first clue into Clio's whereabouts has just the right combination of eagerness and comedy; Bobo Lewis as the harried mother whose house is trashed by Clio is scintillatingly sarcastic; Cliff Norton as the slightly clichéd but kooky Scibetta brings the *buono*; Richard X. Slattery's cop comically stops short of barging into the ladies' room. The pursuit of Clio down a New York street (while a little slower than may be realistic) generates a surprising amount of suspense. Plus, listen carefully: Jill Foster's Betty makes an appearance via voice-over as she announces Clio's arrival.

Serena has made several appearances so far, but it's this episode that truly sees her developing an identity of her own and breaking away from her usual storyline of switching places with Samantha. Egyptian is a natural fit for Serena (does Darrin ask her to put more clothes on because he likes what he sees? She is Samantha's double, after all), and it's novel that Serena comes back long before the typical last minute, but can't reverse her spell because her spellee is missing. The magically realized nursery rhymes are the perfect ending to this satisfying Serena sojourn.

WELL?

Clio-as-monkey chowing down on a bowl of spaghetti is about what you'd expect considering the Italian theme, but it does bring up the question of physiology. Did Clio's body chemistry change when she became a monkey, in which case spaghetti may or may not be toxic to her? Hopefully this isn't the same spaghetti the Stephenses were making while their hands were stuck together in "Samantha Loses Her Voice" (#150).

Larry comes to the house around 9:00 (according to the kitchen clock) to ask what happened between Darrin and Clio – then, after Darrin tables the subject, Larry doesn't ask about it again until 1:30. You'd think Larry would be on it as soon as Darrin walked into the office.

When Samantha makes contact with the boy who saw Clio-as-monkey, he says his friend found her "this morning," which implies it's now afternoon. But Darrin says it's only 10:15; in either case, shouldn't the little guy be in school? Samantha's coat is great, but it's the one she zapped up for herself – and got rid of – in "Samantha on the Keyboard" (#143).

The police officer makes a lot of noise about taking the monkey in because she might be a menace to public health. He ought to be even more emphatic after Clio bites him, but the subject never comes up again. Samantha gets tired of running after Clio, so she pops out to get ahead of her – almost taking a passerby with her, because the extra kept going instead of staying still for the effect.

After Serena changes Clio back, Samantha urges her to get home to Tabitha. Does that mean Tabitha is in the house alone while Serena does Samantha's bidding? Clio doesn't remember being a monkey – but young Michael remembered being a dog in "Playmates" (#133), and Amy remembered her time as a butterfly in "I Don't Want to Be A Toad, I Want to Be A Butterfly" (#151). Maybe it's only Tabitha's spells that make such recollection possible.

In "Is It Magic or Imagination?" (#148), Samantha told Phyllis she wasn't one for slogans. Yet here, her creation sells Clio on McMann & Tate. Will Larry try to hire Samantha for their nonexistent "slogan department" again? Samantha does a strange thing as she sets up her idea – she asks Darrin to tell Clio about it. Samantha knows Darrin is in the dark about what she's planned; why put him on the hot seat?

After earning himself two episodes' worth of trouble because he mouthed off to Serena, Darrin follows up his surprisingly "gracious" rebuke about Jack-be-nimble with another insult. Does he not realize there will again be retribution? Maybe he does, because he brushes his finger against his nose shortly before Serena adds to it, which might be just a tiny bit of foreshadowing on Darrin's part... or not.

OH, MY STARS!

Darrin should be proud – there are times Samantha really does think like a mortal. When Clio-as-monkey slips the noose, the Stephenses scour the neighborhood for her. Why doesn't Samantha just zap Clio back onto the patio from wherever she is? Later, after Serena makes Clio human again, Samantha shows up at Darrin's office with Scibetta and an entirely different monkey in tow. She must have twitched it up, though one wonders how she explained it to Scibetta. And if Samantha is willing to zap up a second monkey, why, when she's unsuccessful in wresting Clio from Scibetta, does she not freeze the organ grinder, conjure up a duplicate Clio for him, and pop out with the original? Of course, then you wouldn't have much of an episode.

In Part I, Larry tried to twist Darrin's arm into going to Rome with Clio, threatening to fire him and even creating a bit of a cliffhanger around it. But he never mentions it in Part II.

SON OF A GUN!

"I wanna stay and hear you scream, Daddy." – Tabitha to Darrin, when he wants to talk to Serena about zapping up Jack-be-nimble.

For as much as Part I felt like a recycled "It Shouldn't Happen to a Dog" (#3), Part II saves the two-parter by being less dependent on the Season One episode and taking on a life of its own. The Stephenses still have to find Clio, as Samantha had to find that episode's Rex Barker, but it feels fresher somehow.

EPISODE 157

ONE TOUCH OF MIDAS
Airdate: January 23, 1969

After Endora humphs at Samantha making a dress for Tabitha, a Professor MacAllister walks into McMann & Tate wanting Darrin to market a doll called "the Fuzz." The toy evokes a feeling of well-being; Betty and Darrin are ready to stock the Fuzz in a department store, but Larry isn't sold despite sharing their emotional response. Samantha and Tabitha aren't affected by the doll, but everyone else is: the store orders 200,000 the next day. Basking in his 25% cut, Darrin comes home with expensive presents for his wife and daughter, including dresses for Tabitha, so Samantha doesn't have to finish hers. Samantha thinks Endora is at it again, but Endora swears she hasn't put a spell on Darrin.

Meanwhile, Betty helps Darrin with the Fuzz franchise as bigger, more frivolous items are delivered to the house. Larry finally asks to be cut in, and Darrin shocks Samantha by deciding to buy a mansion.

Samantha is touched when Darrin gently admits he's enjoying spoiling his family as compensation for her sacrificing her witchcraft – but when he starts to go even more hog wild with purchases, Samantha gets Endora to confirm that she recruited MacAllister to plant the Fuzz. Darrin is disappointed and returns the gifts, while Larry laments losing his unmade millions after the dolls cease to generate good feelings. Later, Tabitha shows off her handmade dress as Darrin jokes that Endora must have learned to sew from Betsy Ross.

GOOD!

After Samantha tells Tabitha why she's making a dress instead of zapping one up, Tabitha's response is "silly Mommy," and Samantha remarks that Tabitha sounds just like Endora. This quick but endearing moment really speaks to the viewpoints of all three witches. Samantha's increasingly sarcastic asides as Darrin goes overboard with his newfound money – especially her comments about the Roller Derby and the his-and-hers heliports – are a tiny bit out of character for her, but a whole lot of fun.

Something's happening to Darrin: he seems to be backing away from the mugging and ranting of Seasons Three and Four, not to mention the first half of this season. He was so close to becoming a cartoon character that his restraint here is heartwarming, as is his admission that he wants the best for Samantha and Tabitha after he's denied them witchcraft for so long. Even his zinger that Endora learned sewing from Betsy Ross, which would have sounded nasty just a few episodes ago, has something tender in it. Whether it's Dick York's choice to rein Darrin in, or a directive from the powers that be, Darrin is suddenly a lot more likable.

WELL?

"My wife, the dressmaker!" Darrin beams. He shouldn't be surprised – she's designed clothes before, albeit with less successful results, in "Samantha the Dressmaker" (#60). The Stephenses also celebrate the sixth anniversary of their first date, but the time and place aren't consistent. Two years earlier, in "The Crone of Cawdor" (#101), the couple marked the third anniversary of their first date, so they should be up to five now, not six. This seems to confirm that the show *has* skipped a year, probably to explain Erin Murphy's growth; the actress is two years older than her character, which would be a marked difference in a child). "The Crone of Cawdor" (#101) also revealed that the Stephenses' first date was at La Bella Donna; here, it's Sorrento's.

After Darrin goes into partnership with MacAllister – with no contract, mind you – he asks Betty to have Hanley set up a display in his store. Betty's a secretary; she can get Hanley on the phone, but it's up to Darrin to pitch the Fuzz and propose a deal. Darrin's amazed he's in the doll business, though it's not his first time: Samantha came up with a "cute little doll" based on Tabitha to distract the hexed "Hoho the Clown" (#92). As for the Fuzz himself, he's a doll version of the gremlin that Tabitha zapped out of her book in "The Safe and Sane Halloween" (#115). Maybe he was a prototype for the costume; funny that Tabitha doesn't recognize her "friend."

In "Man of the Year" (#139), Samantha likened Darrin's advertising award to being invited to one of Truman Capote's parties; here, Darrin secures a place on the famed writer's guest list. Then, Darrin wants Betty to tell Norman Gimbel that "the New York franchise is gone." How can a franchise of any sort be developed and lost in one day – and how can the franchise be lost at all if the dolls are so successful? Besides, Norman Gimbel is a songwriter; perhaps the show meant to reference one of the unrelated Gimbel brothers of the Gimbels Department Store chain.

Darrin also tried to put 1164 Morning Glory Circle up for sale in favor of more luxurious digs in "A is for Aardvark" (#17); admittedly, he doesn't remember this, thanks to the time-reversing spell he had Samantha put on him. Samantha offers to create a sunken living room with snotty realtor Miss Dobrin at its epicenter, but is she really going to zap her in front of Betty, who's sitting on the couch?

When Darrin first tells Larry about the Fuzz, he offers to split his cut with him; Larry refuses. The next day, when the dolls start selling, Larry grimaces over his missed opportunity, but Darrin keeps things status quo. It's only after Larry offers a 10% cut of the accounts Darrin handles in exchange for a percentage of the Fuzz that Darrin brings Larry into the business. Is Darrin getting back at Larry for having been fired so many times? And, in "There's Gold in Them Thar Pills" (#107), it was Larry who spent his fortune in advance; here, Darrin spreads the wealth.

OH, MY STARS!

As soon as Darrin and Betty see the Fuzz, they are overwhelmed by a sense of well-being and compelled to form the "Fuzz factory." The doll has the same emotional effect on Larry, but he refuses the opportunity. Larry, who has admitted being a greedy person in the past, didn't need a spell to take advantage of a potential fortune in "There's Gold in Them Thar Pills" (#107); he *does* have a spell on him here, and he still says no! Why is Larry the only one not obsessed with the Fuzz?

When it seems the Fuzz is going to make Darrin rich, he goes home early. Once he overwhelms Samantha with needless extravagances, Samantha says nothing else could shock her "after all that's happened today." Yet, when Larry comes over, Darrin says he's taking care of the Fuzz business before coming into the office. That would indicate it's now the next day – except Samantha, Darrin, and Larry are all wearing the same clothes. Does that mean Darrin has taken the rest of the day off, gone shopping, done his wheeling and dealing at home, and now plans to go back to the office the same day?

Endora recruits MacAllister to plant the doll in Darrin's office so he'll ultimately end up a millionaire. Samantha must be right that Darrin also has a spell on him, because he doesn't catch on when Samantha and Tabitha don't react to the Fuzz, nor when MacAllister can produce 200,000 dolls in a couple of days. But the plot goes awry when Darrin starts buying expensive frivolities – he is fully aware that he's going overboard, which implies that the only spell in play is the feel-good quality of the dolls. So Darrin can't have a spell on him, despite Endora indirectly confirming it; Samantha even tells Darrin afterwards that he acted normally under the circumstances.

SON OF A GUN!

"I can hardly wait to see Larry's face when he finally finds out how fast the Fuzz fad flops!" – Samantha to Darrin, trying to look at the bright side of the doll debacle.

Jill Foster's increased presence as Betty is a welcomed surprise. The secretary's tenth appearance (twelfth counting two voice-overs) shows Betty stepping out from behind McMann & Tate's reception desk and taking her place as a power player on the ground floor of Darrin's Fuzz business. She's the logical choice – she's been working for Darrin since Season Two – and consistency like this gives the same feeling of well-being that the Fuzz does.

SAMANTHA THE BARD

Airdate: January 30, 1969

Samantha wakes up unable to stop talking in rhyme, so Darrin suggests summoning Endora, who thinks her daughter has come down with Venetian verbal virus. While Endora tracks down Dr. Bombay, Larry arranges for Samantha to meet the Durfees the following evening, and Samantha passes off her speech impediment as a parlor game to the invading Kravitzes. Endora returns with a potion from Dr. Bombay, but it fails to relieve Samantha's virus, forcing her to meet the Durfees uncured when their business dinner gets moved up to later that night.

As Samantha's rhymes worsen, Dr. Bombay pops in with Endora and officially diagnoses Samantha with secondary vocabularyitis. He treats it, and Samantha is able to meet the Durfees, but the rhymes come back with a vengeance in the middle of dinner, irritating the client. Samantha excuses herself and flies to Mount Everest, where Dr. Bombay is vacationing. He determines primary vocabularyitis is the culprit after all; though his sound wave injection causes an avalanche on the slopes, it cures Samantha. She returns to the restaurant explaining that she only spoke in rhyme to show Durfee, who wants to keep his decades-old dog food jingle, how outmoded that kind of advertising can be. The next day, Endora's words come out in rhyme, and when Darrin delights in his mother-in-law's malady, she turns him into a billy goat.

GOOD!

Subtle visuals do a lot to add to the proceedings in this episode. Samantha's bed head is a terrific departure from Hollywood's typical depiction of perfect-looking people. Also, the (stock footage) avalanche caused by Dr. Bombay's sound wave injection – and its ultimate reversal – is a fun demonstration of a warlock's strength.

The Kravitzes have little to do during their appearance except participate in Samantha's nonexistent parlor game, but seeing the usually expressionless Abner step out of his element, speaking in rhyme, enjoying himself, is truly sublime. And Larry earns a few points for his moment of self-awareness, telling Darrin that steamrolling him and Samantha into a dinner party is "not bad character, it's my character."

Darrin usually doesn't want Endora anywhere near him, so that he asks Samantha to call his mother-in-law because she might know what's behind the rhymes shows an unspoken respect. The in-laws pull together over their mutual concern for Samantha, creating a harmonious atmosphere – Darrin blows Endora a kiss and thanks her for fixing a shattered vase, and Endora tries to correct Bombay when he gets Darrin's name wrong. It doesn't last, of course, as Darrin can't help gloating over Endora contracting the virus [Endora confirms she really is a big baby when sick, as she was in "Allergic to Ancient Macedonian Dodo Birds" (#118)], and Tabitha's takeaway that she wants to ride her billy goat father is the perfect capper to one of the season's best offerings.

WELL?

Darrin initially thinking that Uncle Arthur has put a rhyming spell on Samantha goes back to a question that's hung over the entire season: can witches cast spells on each other? The episode provides no answer, but later, upon hearing her mother's constant rhyming, Tabitha asks if Samantha is sick; Darrin says she isn't. Why not tell Tabitha the truth? What does Darrin think he's shielding her from?

When Darrin leaves for work, he tells Samantha not to answer the phone unless it rings once, stops, then rings again. (Ah, the days before ringtones and caller ID.) But there's no break between rings when Samantha answers the call – how can she be sure it's Darrin? Then, Samantha leaves the kitchen door open for no apparent reason except to allow the Kravitzes to walk in unannounced.

Dr. Bombay's amber corpuscular evaluator reveals that Samantha's face is covered with spots, which isn't the first time; in "Take Two Aspirins and Half A Pint of Porpoise Milk" (#42), a different ailment caused square green ones.

Durfee's passion for pet food is reminiscent of Springer and his bird seed in "That Was No Chick, That Was My Wife" (#117). As it turns out, Durfee and Springer have the "same" wife: Sara Seegar, whose Mrs. Hascomb of "Mirror, Mirror on the Wall" (#146) also wanted to party. The soirée is a business dinner, so why does Mrs. Durfee keep trying to change the subject? Later, Durfee complains that Samantha "always" offers up rhymes – except Samantha speaks regularly for the bulk of the dinner.

When Samantha appears on Mount Everest next to Dr. Bombay, she is dressed in a warm fur hat and a colorfully embroidered vest; it's the same ensemble Endora wore when coming back from her first visit with Bombay. After Samantha is cured, Larry says he wasn't all that irritated by Samantha talking in rhyme – is that why he nearly threatened her when she couldn't stop her couplets? Then, Samantha jokingly rhymes to Darrin about Larry getting stuck with the check. Why toy with Darrin after the upheaval they've just been through?

When Endora starts rhyming, Samantha corrects the self-satisfied Darrin, saying her mother has primary vocabularyitis, not secondary. Wouldn't Samantha have told him about the diagnosis upgrade the night before? Samantha then zaps up the amber corpuscular evaluator to determine if Endora has the ailment's telltale spots, but it's a medical device – would Samantha have access to it? Endora's spots are pretty serious, because they're visible before Samantha gets the evaluator up to her mother's face.

It's great attention to detail that Samantha wants to have Tabitha vaccinated against the rhyming disease, but, if Endora has already caught it from Samantha, it's likely Tabitha has it, too. And Endora has had billy goats on the brain for a while – she threatened to make Darrin "get down on all four knees and apologize" in "Samantha's Wedding Present" (#141); here, she follows through on it.

OH, MY STARS!

Gladys, who's on a petition kick lately [see "Weep No More, My Willow" (#152)], comes over hoping to rally Samantha into signing so they can get a traffic light installed on their mutual corner. First off, the Kravitzes and the Stephenses live across the street from each other; they share no mutual corner. More importantly, they already lobbied for – and got – their traffic signal during "Red Light, Green Light" (#23). Has it been taken down sometime in the last four years?

SON OF A GUN!

"'Boop-doop-dee-dee?'" – Larry, making sure he's heard Samantha correctly.

Samantha and her rhymes are the star of this episode. They start off innocuously enough, but get progressively more outrageous as Samantha eventually can't stop uttering nonsense words – she even does limericks. What really makes it work is Samantha's total innocence and near helplessness while voicing her involuntary vocabulary.

SAMANTHA, THE SCULPTRESS

Airdate: February 6, 1969

EPISODE
159

Darrin gets upset when he witnesses Tabitha making clay animals with witchcraft. After a brief spell of Endora's which has Darrin eating flowers as punishment for his outburst, Samantha offers to learn sculpting the mortal way so she, in turn, can teach Tabitha. The next day, Darrin and Larry meet W.R. Campbell, the agency's first "90-proof client." As Darrin gets sloshed from his liquid lunch, Samantha attempts her first sculpture and is glad Darrin's "anesthetized" when she shows it to him. Less inhibited, Darrin more freely insults Endora, who decides to change Samantha's vague likeness of him into an exact replica that talks.

When Larry arrives, Endora tells him that Samantha may have a surprise for him later on: by the time the crocked Campbell weaves in, Endora has also zapped up a vocalizing bust of Larry. Darrin covers with the men, even after Endora has the sculptures join them in the den. The talking effigies make an increasing amount of side comments during Darrin's campaign pitch, which spooks Campbell to the point that he signs on the dotted line and swears off booze. Endora, annoyed when she learns she helped Darrin cinch the account, pops out, leaving the talking statues behind.

GOOD!

Tabitha has stolen every episode she's been in this season, and this one is no exception. Her father-daughter bond with Darrin exudes warmth, but it's her innocent demonstration of zapping up clay versions of her toys that gets the gold star. "You're a good yeller, Daddy," she smiles as Darrin has his typical reaction; Tabitha really knows her father. Endora's flower-eating spell has a sense of originality to it (plus, the particular varieties Darrin chows down on aren't poisonous) – and, after Darrin says Endora learned to read from the Dead Sea Scrolls, he's aware enough of their history to admit, "Boy, am I asking for it."

This is his Cliff Norton's third appearance in four episodes: he was Italian organ grinder Scibetta in "Cousin Serena Strikes Again (Part II)" (#156), and Professor MacAllister in "One Touch of Midas" (#157) – now he's corporate boozehound Campbell. Compare these characters and dare to say they're played by the same person; Norton is the show's father of reinvention.

The show's further experimentation with chroma key to create the talking statues works quite well, and desaturating the footage of Darrin and Larry's heads to hide the color inside their mouths is a clever workaround. Darrin's amazing composure while the sculptures interrupt his pitch is also worthy of note – it seems he's been through enough witchcraft-infused situations that he now knows how to handle them without getting ruffled.

WELL?

Darrin's favorite food – turkey soup with extra wide noodles – was consistent for nearly three years until it was suddenly changed to beef stew in "The No-Harm Charm" (#138). But Darrin's preferred meal became shepherd's pie in "Samantha's Supermaid" (#154), and now it's Irish stew. Endora's favorite food turns out to be *coq au vin*; apparently Samantha finally learned how to make it, because, in "Samantha Meets the Folks" (#14), Aunt Clara had to zap it up for her when Frank announced it was *his* favorite dish. Not to be outdone, the statues of Darrin and Larry announce that they're hungry at the end of the episode. Is that even possible? (Imagine Samantha taking a tray into the den to feed them.)

According to Samantha, Endora's "bouncing ball" note reads, "I'll be watching as he grows wide with flowers piling up inside." The ball's actual words are, "I will be watching as he grows wide as the flowers pile up inside."

Tipsy Darrin tells Samantha that Campbell is his first 90-proof client – but he forgets that alcohol-obsessed Saunders took that honor in "Nobody But A Frog Knows How to Live" (#106). Endora pops in next to the TV and talks to the statue of Darrin before adding one of Larry; presumably, the Stephenses and their dinner guests are eating in the dining room. Can no one hear Endora's voice from there? Also, Darrin, Larry, and Campbell are all good freezers, but why does Endora bother suspending them before zapping the sculptures into the den? She could easily get the statues there ahead of them without the extra zap.

It's a good thing Larry and Campbell continue to swig brandy – if they were sober, they'd never believe that Samantha made a set of the Darrin and Larry heads for each room, especially after Endora told everyone Samantha only learned to sculpt that day. Darrin's effigy essentially puts words in his mouth; Serena just did the same thing to Samantha in "Cousin Serena Strikes Again (Part I)" (#155). And Larry must be pretty confident that Darrin can sell Campbell on the campaign, because he carries a contract around in his jacket pocket the entire evening.

Once Campbell signs, Darrin gloats to Endora that he might not have gotten the account were it not for her interference. Did he think his material wasn't enough to convince Campbell on his own? Darrin's much less upset here than he was in "Instant Courtesy" (#153), when Endora also inadvertently helped Darrin get an account. And Samantha must be filling in for Betty at McMann & Tate, because that's Elizabeth Montgomery's voice announcing Campbell's arrival on the intercom.

OH, MY STARS!

So, Darrin and Larry quaff 10 or 12 martinis, then drive home – drunk. Of course, this was before the term "designated driver" made it into the lexicon (the program made its mark in 1986), but it seems very irresponsible to indicate that the ad men got behind the wheel in their inebriated state. Once home, Darrin can barely put a sentence together, but snaps out of his intoxication rather quickly – he even offers Larry a drink when the ad men were toasted an hour before. And Larry tells the Stephenses that he's glad Louise wasn't home to see him blitzed. Then who was watching Jonathan? Did the kid come downstairs and find his father passed out under the coffee table? Jokes about booze were more commonplace in the '60s, but the implications here are sobering.

SON OF A GUN!

"A bust of Durwood? He's already a bust!" – Endora, when Samantha tells her what she's sculpting.

EPISODE 160 MRS. STEPHENS, WHERE ARE YOU?
Airdate: February 13, 1969

A flirty magazine salesman puts witches down while coming on to Samantha, so she twitches herself into a hag to scare him off. Later, she helps kindly elderly neighbor Miss Parsons by zapping the lady's cat out of a tree. Serena pops in and toys with Miss Parsons, then agrees to babysit Tabitha while Samantha runs an errand. As Tabitha naps, Phyllis stops by and meets Serena. Phyllis offers her candid, but not necessarily complimentary opinions regarding Endora and Uncle Arthur – but when she calls Samantha selfish for "keeping Tabitha to herself," the angry Serena turns Phyllis into a cat. A neighborhood dog chases Phyllis-as-cat up a tree, where she is rescued by Miss Parsons.

Samantha comes home to a dancing Serena, who happily tells her cousin how she defended their family. Miss Parsons sees Samantha searching the neighborhood for Phyllis-as-cat and tells her about the stray she found. Unfortunately, the dowager's house is filled with felines, and Samantha can't tell which one is her mother-in-law. Magically ringing the doorbell to distract Miss Parsons, Samantha changes all cats but Phyllis into dogs; Miss Parsons is baffled to hear barking. With Phyllis-as-cat in her arms, Samantha returns home to find Frank, who has come for his wife. Serena grudgingly changes Phyllis back, but Mrs. Stephens is still wearing the bell Miss Parsons gave her as a cat. When the rattled Phyllis wants sherry, Serena makes a catty comment to even the score.

GOOD!

Why haven't these two been in a room together before? Serena and Phyllis [who has relinquished snobbery again since "Samantha's Supermaid" (#154)] are a fascinating duo, and their conversation not only brings out never-before-revealed details about Samantha's family, but demonstrates that the witch and the mortal have a common denominator: cattiness. Serena says that Samantha has "always had unusual taste" in people (no wonder she embraced Darrin and the mortal life), and, when Phyllis fishes for Endora's age, Serena smiles, "She admits to a thousand," while Phyllis replies, "I deserved that." Furthermore, Phyllis reiterates her opinion that Samantha is an overprotective mother [which she expressed in "Playmates" (#133) and "I Don't Want to Be A Toad, I Want to Be A Butterfly" (#151)], and Frank makes a brief return; he hasn't been seen since "McTavish" (#130).

Ruth McDevitt is a delight as the doddering, easily confused Miss Parsons – the polar opposite of her autocratic Ticheba from "Long Live the Queen" (#108). And film buffs may get a pleasing ping when Samantha's aged neighbor gives cats bells "to warn the birds" – McDevitt had a featured role in Alfred Hitchcock's 1963 film, *The Birds*. Samantha's cat/dog switch in Miss Parsons' house is all the more amazing when you consider that animals (cats especially) can't be directed to stay still for an effect. Finally, Samantha's claim that magazines *Liberty* and *Collier's* haven't been published for years is true: *Liberty*'s presses stopped in 1950 (with a brief return in the '70s), while *Collier's* disappeared from racks in 1957; interestingly, the mag made a comeback in 2012.

WELL?

When Samantha answers Darrin's telephone call, she lets the magazine salesman, who has made no secret of his interest, remain standing at the open door. Why? That's the perfect time for Samantha to get rid of the amorous pest. Of course, were she to do that, she couldn't turn herself into a crone to turn the guy off. But that's an odd development: in "The Witches Are Out" (#7), Samantha was very clear in speaking out against mortals' negative depiction of witches. So why would she embody the same stereotype now?

When Serena pops in on the front lawn, her parts of the scene are filmed in the studio, while Samantha and Miss Parsons are filmed outside. Samantha tells Miss Parsons that Serena is "a real kook" – forgetting that Darrin got in trouble for describing her cousin that way in "Hippie, Hippie, Hooray" (#128). Then, Samantha basically threatens to turn Serena into an artichoke – unlike any other season, there's an unspoken rule here that witches can do anything they want to each other. Then, Serena offers to tidy up Samantha's house – however, when Serena stood in as a mortal housewife in "It's So Nice to Have A Spouse Around the House" (#145), she didn't even know what she was supposed to do.

Phyllis blithely says she sees so little of Samantha's relatives – yet, in "Samantha's Supermaid" (#154), she inaccurately complained that Endora is there every time she visits. Now, in "Samantha Meets the Folks" (#14), Aunt Clara told Phyllis all her relatives are witches. Wouldn't Serena being able to stop an hourglass in mid-stream make Phyllis wonder if the statement was true? After giving Phyllis her feline makeover, Serena declines to give chase on the basis that Samantha wouldn't want her to leave Tabitha alone. But that's what Serena did in "Cousin Serena Strikes Again (Part II)" (#156), when she met Samantha in Manhattan to de-monkey Clio Vanita.

Samantha and Serena appearing together via split-screen looks quite good, but, in the scene where the cousins discuss Phyllis' whereabouts, the border of the split is moved to the right just enough that the flower pattern on the couch "repeats" – a phenomenon that continues all the way up to the top of the screen. As for Phyllis, it's not that she doesn't deserve what Serena dishes out, but Serena just turned a mortal into an animal five episodes ago [in "Cousin Serena Strikes Again (Part I)" (#155)].

Samantha could merely zap the missing, meowing Mrs. Stephens back like she does Miss Parsons' cat, but neglects to (because the comedy is in Samantha's search for her). But why does Samantha always call Phyllis "Mrs. Stephens?" Samantha's been married to her son nearly five years (six if you go by the show's current timeline); she ought to be on a first-name basis with her mother-in-law by now.

Serena likes her older men: as Samantha, she put the moves on Larry in "Double, Double...Toil and Trouble" (#111), and her warlock of choice was the distinguished Malcolm in "Samantha Goes South For A Spell" (#142). Here, she gives Frank the heavily-mascaraed eye! Later, when Samantha brings Phyllis-as-cat home, she's surprised to see Frank in her living room. Didn't Samantha see Frank's car in the driveway? Speaking of cars, the Stephenses have apparently gotten a new one: their usual light blue Chevrolet convertible has been traded in for a dark blue conveyance.

OH, MY STARS!

As Phyllis goes down the list of Samantha's relatives, she comments that Uncle Arthur's practical jokes can be very unexpected. They most certainly can, but Darrin's parents have never met Uncle Arthur, unless it was off-screen: Samantha's only family members to meet the elder Stephenses so far are Aunt Clara ["Samantha Meets the Folks" (#14)], Endora ["A Nice Little Dinner Party" (#19)], and now Serena.

SON OF A GUN!

"Not often, I'm sure." – Serena, when Samantha tells her that Phyllis has a husband at home.

Phyllis does correctly state that she and Frank have never met Samantha's father, Maurice – which comes up after the tantalizing revelation that Serena is a cousin on Maurice's side of the family. This means that Maurice has to have a brother or sister somewhere; Serena is the daughter of that sibling. Maybe one day this witch or warlock will make an appearance.

MARRIAGE, WITCHES' STYLE

Airdate: February 20, 1969

Inspired by Samantha's life as a mortal, a bored Serena decides to marry one. Samantha suggests finding a mate through the Human Equation, a computerized matchmaking service; Serena digs "that science fiction jazz" and can't wait to sign up. When she meets blind date Franklyn Blodgett, it's love at first sight because he knows her favorite wine, but Samantha isn't nearly as impressed. Having invited Franklyn over for dinner, Serena witches up a gourmet meal for him, but Samantha insists that her cousin cook the mortal way. What Samantha and Serena don't know is, Franklyn is a warlock.

Thinking Serena is mortal, Franklyn follows his father's advice and fakes clumsiness to endear himself to her, suffering through her inedible food. The date only brings them closer, and Serena hopes for a proposal when Franklyn hints he wants to discuss something important. Samantha thinks it's time Serena tell Franklyn she's a witch; after discovering each other's magical identities, Serena and Franklyn laugh about how they were looking for the same thing. However, when Franklyn criticizes Serena's flamboyant style of magic, the honeymoon is over. Serena tries another electronic dating service, but Ted, the new prospect, turns out to be a warlock prankster that zaps a crown onto the owner's head, and Samantha and Serena exchange knowing glances.

GOOD!

The insights Samantha passes on to Serena about living the mortal life not only hearken back to the pilot, "I, Darrin, Take This Witch, Samantha" (#1), but they show how much Samantha has learned the past five years. Claiming herself to be "an authority on the subject" – and she would be by now – Samantha tells Serena that "mortals are uncomfortable with perfection," which Darrin has proven himself to be. The episode also offers a flip-side perspective when Samantha comments to Serena that "the hard part" will be telling Franklyn she's a witch, which Samantha advises she do before Franklyn proposes. Sounds like Samantha has learned from waiting until her wedding night to inform Darrin of her supernatural lineage.

With Darrin out of episodes again, it falls to the show's other cast members to fill in for him, which is why Serena is back after having just appeared in the previous installment, "Mrs. Stephens, Where Are You?" (#160). But how she and Franklyn fill in – it's almost like watching a spinoff as they try to pass themselves off as mortals. Their seductive effect on each other is palpable (the highlight: Serena rolling her eyes during their kiss), and, by the time they discover they're both witches, they seem like such a good couple that it's almost a shame they implode – except that their argument over how to use magic (with Franklyn comparing Serena to a "demented windmill" and Serena retorting that Franklyn is a "road company Cary Grant") is such a fun implosion.

WELL?

Serena magically cuts herself a piece of Samantha's cake, but dark strings are visible on the knife, and the sped-up footage unfortunately makes the effect look like an effect. By the way, is Serena older than Samantha? Her calling Samantha "little cousin" begs that question, though there's no clear answer.

Serena can't wait to boogie on down to the Human Equation; what doesn't add up is that Samantha says Tabitha is napping. With the cousins out mate-hunting for Serena, who's watching the witchlet? Speaking of boogieing, Serena gets her groove on after the second commercial break, but it's Elizabeth

Montgomery's double (who fills in when Samantha and Serena appear together without split-screen) that's doing the dancing. Similarly, Serena doesn't look like herself at the end of the episode, when the cousins sit on a couch facing the camera. It's unusual for the show to let Samantha/Serena's double be so visible.

When Serena fills out her form, she jokes that her name isn't a problem – but does she have a last name? Despite Franklyn and Ted having surnames like Blodgett and Perkins, respectively, Endora said her family name would be too difficult for mortals to pronounce in "Mother Meets What's-His-Name" (#4). Later, Serena fires off a "like Grandma always said" quote. Samantha and Serena do share a grandmother because they're cousins; the ancestor in question would have to be Maurice's mother. Wouldn't it be fascinating to learn the identity of a witch who could produce a son as outlandish as Maurice? And, at least Franklyn's father makes it known that the Warlock Club still exists; it hasn't been mentioned since Maurice took Jonathan Tate there in "My Grandson, the Warlock" (#40).

Serena has to be blinded by her attraction to Franklyn, because she never questions how the "mortal" could produce a bottle of the extremely rare Château Lafite Rothschild 1923, which just happens to be her favorite vintage.

The gourmet feast Serena pops in for Franklyn is obviously her own spell, yet Samantha zaps it away in one fell twitch. Are witches back to being able to undo each other's spells? However, Serena's first attempt at cooking mortal style isn't any better than Samantha's was in "Be It Ever So Mortgaged" (#2); pity Serena isn't seen stumbling through her preparations as well. Incidentally, is Franklyn at any time aware that he's wooing Serena in her cousin's house?

When Serena tells Franklyn the truth, she pops in and out, asking, "Get it?" Suppose Franklyn really were mortal: would he really be able to glean that Serena is a witch just from her appearing and disappearing? Serena doesn't even use the word "witch" until after her second example; in "I, Darrin, Take This Witch, Samantha" (#1), Samantha said she was a witch right away and had to do a litany of magic before Darrin finally caught on. Franklyn's comment that Serena's style of popping out would be gauche in his circle is amusing, but Serena has never waved her arms around to disappear until this episode. Finally, why does Samantha pick that moment to come downstairs? Yes, so she can get showered with champagne – but, if your cousin was on an important date in your living room, wouldn't you wait until it was over to make yourself known?

There's a strange discoloration in the split screen as Samantha and Serena sit on Mr. Lovelace's couch, as if the set was lit just a bit brighter when Samantha did her scene. Then, when Ted zaps the crown on Lovelace's head, the matchmaker isn't in the least bit rattled by the fact that an object has suddenly appeared out of nowhere, only attributing this to Ted's "irrepressible sense of humor." Does Lovelace know that Ted is a warlock? And/or is Lovelace a warlock himself?

OH, MY STARS!

As Samantha tries to steer Serena away from dating mortals, she says, "You know what's available among the warlocks." Indeed she would, given there are only so many of them – so why doesn't Serena recognize Franklyn the moment they meet? More importantly, it seems Franklyn is mortal until he's suddenly being chauffeured by an invisible driver in witchy surroundings at the top of a scene. There's no payoff in that; there must have been a better, more suspenseful way of revealing Franklyn's identity.

SON OF A GUN!

"And a man pops out of the machine?" – Serena, as Samantha explains the factors of the Human Equation.

GOING APE

Airdate: February 27, 1969

After Samantha hurries Tabitha home from the park by zapping roller skates onto her feet, Bonzo, a chimpanzee, follows them. The primate tries to communicate with Samantha, but when she can't make sense of his grunts and gestures, she turns him into a human being. Bonzo doesn't care about the little boy he ran away from, relishing the idea of finally being a man. Meanwhile, Ms. Tucker and Mr. Flynn of Brawn Cologne stun Larry with their mediocre campaign idea; Darrin is flying back from Canada, so Ms. Tucker insists on seeing him as soon as he gets home. Before Samantha can change Bonzo back, Larry arrives with Ms. Tucker, who decides the humanized Bonzo is the perfect image for her cologne.

As "Harry Simian," Bonzo has trouble warming up to his modeling gig, but ultimately, he does so well that Larry and Ms. Tucker arrange a press conference for him. "Harry" has had enough of the human world and wants to return to his little boy; Samantha bets that Bonzo can be fired if he acts like himself. At the press conference, "Harry" pinches Ms. Tucker, pulls off her wig, and swings around the photo studio on a rope. Samantha tells Larry that "Harry's" actions are tied into Darrin's "original" concept for Brawn Cologne, which Ms. Tucker accepts – as long as she doesn't have to see "Harry" again. Later, at the park, Samantha sees Bonzo and tells his boy to take good care of him.

GOOD!

Lou Antonio doesn't monkey around when it comes to playing a primate. He engenders sympathy as he insists he's a chimpanzee and not a monkey, and his growing disillusionment is palpable as the workaholic humans around him show him he was better off before Samantha transformed him. Her comment, "I thought humans were complicated" not only speaks volumes about *Homo sapiens*, but of her five years' exposure to the race. Bonzo biting into wax fruit further points up how ridiculous the mortal world can be, and the episode's centerpiece, where "Harry" gets himself fired by wreaking havoc, is a fun chimpanzee/human culture clash. But watch Bonzo's subtler moments, where Antonio scratches himself or carries himself like a chimp would; they're equally effective, as are the back-and-forth changes between Bonzo and "Harry."

WELL?

In "Mrs. Stephens, Where Are You?" (#160), the Stephenses sported a new(er) blue car with the license plate 90-63C5. However, as Samantha wheels Tabitha home from the park, that plate is on a yellow car parked at the curb. Also, it seems Tabitha's parents have bought a swing set for her, because it was never in the backyard until now – of course, neither was there a human version of a monkey that needed something to climb around on.

If Samantha's comfortable talking to Bonzo-as-human, it's because she's turned animals into people before: in "Ling-Ling" (#21), it was a cat, and, in "The Horse's Mouth" (#61), a humanized thoroughbred gave out hot racing tips. If Darrin weren't in Canada, he and Bonzo could compare notes, since they've each spent time in both human and chimp form [see "Alias Darrin Stephens" (#37)]. Bonzo's lucky – in that episode, Gladys called the pound on Darrin-as-chimp; now, she's nowhere to be found. By the way, what's in Bonzo's back pocket? Either chimps have credit cards, or Lou Antonio forgot to take his wallet out of his jeans before lensing.

If Larry asking, "Models?" sounds familiar, it's because he posed the exact same question, the exact same way, in "Cousin Serena Strikes Again (Part II)" (#156). Later, when Larry tries to introduce Endora to his clients as "Mrs....", Endora hesitates and simply reiterates her first name. This seems consistent with "Mother Meets What's-His-Name" (#4), where Endora told Darrin that her (and presumably Samantha's) last name is too difficult for mortals to pronounce. Yet, as recently as "Marriage, Witches' Style" (#161), warlocks Franklyn and Ted both had mortal-sounding last names. Did the magic men make them up so they could pass themselves off as human?

Endora tells the mortals that "Harry" is "Darwin's cousin," but Larry never raises an eyebrow at Samantha's mother getting his employee's name wrong. It's also hard to believe that Larry is threatening to fire Darrin through Samantha again; he did that in "Tabatha's Cranky Spell" (#134), too, only then he admitted he was being melodramatic. This time he's serious.

Does Samantha zap up that giant alarm clock for Bonzo/"Harry"? Speaking of zapping, when she makes Bonzo human the second time, she uses the same spell she initially cast, which includes the line, "a monkey you are, a monkey you'll be." Only thing is, the first time, Samantha didn't know Bonzo is a chimp – now she does. So why continue referring to him as a monkey, even in a spell? At the shoot, both Bonzo and the photographer wear light blue, short-sleeved shirts; "Harry" wore his when meeting everyone the day before. Samantha couldn't find him fresh clothes?

Before Larry prevents his return to primate status, Bonzo happily grasps Samantha's arm, shakes it wildly, and declares, "You're a queen among witches." Well, she's not now, but she was: did news of Samantha's coronation in "Long Live the Queen" (#108) somehow make it to the chimp world? Bonzo's photos turns out so well that Larry books him for a press conference – why is he required to model for more pictures when he gets there? It's not much of a press conference, anyway, not with representatives from only two magazines in attendance.

OH, MY STARS!

Monkey see, monkey do? Okay, Bonzo's a chimp, but Serena just de-evolved Clio Vanita in "Cousin Serena Strikes Again" (#155/#156). At least Bonzo discovering Samantha is a witch is handled better than "Nobody But A Frog Knows How to Live" (#106), where "human frog" Fergus figured it out just by following Samantha around; Bonzo does see Samantha using her powers. That said, how does a chimp know what a witch is, much less anything about magic? Moreover, how can he look sexy on command? "Harry" is smart, and he may have enough of a primal urge that he can pinch Ms. Tucker (and, by extension, kiss her), but it's hard to imagine he knows so much about the human world. Do chimps read chimp encyclopedias when people aren't looking?

SON OF A GUN!

"That's life! Think of the poor fella who invented 6-Up." – Samantha to Bonzo, after he says he missed being human by one rung on the evolutionary ladder.

TABITHA'S WEEKEND

Airdate: March 6, 1969

EPISODE 163

When Phyllis learns that Endora has spent time alone with Tabitha, she wants the same privilege, but Samantha makes excuses, so Frank comes by to pressure Samantha on Phyllis' behalf. Afraid Tabitha won't be able to contain her witchcraft in front of her mortal grandparents, Samantha tags along, much to Phyllis' chagrin. Phyllis tells Tabitha she can do anything she wants during her weekend, then shows her granddaughter a talking mynah bird. Frustrated that the bird only mimics a few phrases (including "Frank, I have a sick headache"), Tabitha witches it into having a real conversation, which Phyllis overhears; Samantha makes Tabitha restore the bird before Frank can hear for himself.

Endora pops in for a visit, and Phyllis wants her to take Samantha home; Tabitha watches as the grown-ups fight about what's best for her, then disappears. Frank and Phyllis think Tabitha is playing hide-and-seek, but Samantha thinks Endora has removed Tabitha by witchcraft until Endora reminds Samantha that a young witch can turn herself into an object instead of running away. As the elder Stephenses catch Samantha and Endora talking to household articles, Samantha sees one of Phyllis' raisin cookies moving. Samantha grabs Tabitha-as-cookie and demands she change herself back; Frank and Phyllis decide to go on a cruise after they witness the transformation. At home, Endora sends the punished Tabitha a dessert, but when Samantha objects, Endora pops out in a huff.

GOOD!

Once again, Tabitha rules an episode – good thing Phyllis doesn't know she prefers her witch grandmother, and has as far back as "Playmates" (#133), when she declared, "With Grandma 'Dora I have fun!" A mynah bird may be a poor substitute for a dodo bird, but the tiny talker almost steals the show from its human co-stars, even if its dubbed-in voice belongs to Phyllis' portrayer, Mabel Albertson. The fact that it's picked up Phyllis' "sick headache" phrase is a strong piece of continuity [Phyllis' first complaint was in "Samantha Meets the Folks" (#14)], and the bird's hilarious insights into its own life via Tabitha is a feather in this episode's cap. Not to be outdone, the grown-ups' squabbling over Tabitha provides terrific comedy – and throughout, Tabitha wears the dress Samantha made for her in "One Touch of Midas" (#157).

Endora sparkles in this episode, too. She cracks Samantha up by suggesting she could lose Phyllis in a game of *chemin de fer* (that Samantha laughs says a lot about her feelings toward her pushy mother-in-law) – and later, when Tabitha wants Endora to have one of Phyllis' raisin cookies, Endora asks if they're from an Alice B. Toklas recipe. The show got away with that one – they couldn't very well say Endora was asking for marijuana-laced treats...

WELL?

Tabitha spends a lot of time at the zoo with Endora – they made a trip in "It's So Nice to Have A Spouse Around the House" (#145), and here, Endora offers another outing, after having just taken her granddaughter the week before. Speaking of animals, Endora and Uncle Arthur like their horses – Endora sits astride one in the same place Arthur did in "Samantha's French Pastry" (#147), though her horse faces the other way. It's curious that Endora's desire to show her granddaughter "all the fascinating relatives on our side of the family" includes Arthur: the siblings used Samantha's house as a battleground in "Endora Moves in for a Spell" (#80) and were ready to divvy up the world so they wouldn't have to see each other. Maybe they've made up since then?

After the normally docile Frank twists Samantha's arm into letting Tabitha come over, Endora asks Samantha when she can be ready to leave for Barcelona – except she just said they were going to "swinging London."

Patterson must have a lot of tract housing. Frank and Phyllis' foyer is exactly the same as Miss Parsons' ["Mrs. Stephens, Where Are You? (#160)], and their kitchen is a duplicate of the Kravitzes ["Weep No More, My Willow" (#152)]. Back at Samantha's house, Tabitha's room has consistently been "first door to the left at the top of the stairs" [as Samantha indicated in "Tabatha's Cranky Spell" (#134)], but here, Tabitha's room is on the right, and presumably where the master bedroom should be; the master bedroom seems to have taken the place of what was once the guest room.

Frank is so excited about his new booze-vending invention that he forgets he already told Samantha about it in "The Dancing Bear" (#58). And Phyllis was never seen drinking sherry until Serena offered her some in "Mrs. Stephens, Where Are You? (#160); here she asks for a tall glass.

When Phyllis carries Tabitha out of the kitchen, the child holds a cookie in her left hand, but, a second later on the patio, Tabitha's got it in her right hand. As for Samantha's childhood, this installment conflicts with her aging as described earlier in the series. Endora says that Samantha enjoyed a champagne and caviar snack in Tivoli Gardens as a four-year-old; the Disneyland prototype opened in 1843, but "Eye of the Beholder" (#22) suggested Samantha was already an adult by 1682.

As Samantha holds Tabitha-as-cookie, she seems to be casting a spell to change her daughter back. Isn't Tabitha supposed to be changing herself back? If so, the spell sound effect isn't necessary; Samantha's not performing witchcraft. In either case, how does Endora speed it along by jumping Samantha's count of three?

Endora has visited with Darrin's parents any number of times, but she's never gone on about her witchy activities in front of them before. In "Samantha, the Sculptress" (#159), Endora also freely discoursed about magic in front of Larry; she seems to be on a kick that way.

OH, MY STARS!

This first-rate episode revolves around Frank and Phyllis' claim that they have never spent a weekend alone with their granddaughter. But they did – in "Divided He Falls" (#69), newborn Tabitha was in her grandparents' care for a week – and even up to three weeks – while Samantha and Darrin frolicked in Miami. True, Samantha has kept Tabitha away from them since her powers emerged in Season Three, but for Phyllis to say she's never had Tabitha over for the night is a definite overstatement.

Endora's delight over taking Tabitha to see unicorns and dodo birds at an apparent witch zoo is fun, but, according to "Allergic to Ancient Macedonian Dodo Birds" (#118), Endora is exactly that – allergic. She can't be near one without losing her powers! Perhaps when Dr. Bombay restored them in that episode, he also cured the allergy, but this was never specified.

When Samantha denies Tabitha her grandmother's floating pudding (undoing someone else's spell again?), Endora storms off, calling her daughter an "insensitive, selfish, mortal-marrying child." All this over a dessert?

SON OF A GUN!

"Oh! Beginner's luck." – Endora, when Phyllis tells Frank and Samantha that she has an idea.

There's no more doubt – Frank and Phyllis Stephens live nearby. Although Darrin's parents don't live in the same house they occupied in "A Nice Little Dinner Party" (#19), the show seems to have finally decided whether or not they reside in town, after going back and forth about it for five seasons.

The Stephenses entertain J. Earle Rockeford, a rich socialite whose account McMann & Tate is courting. Rockeford invites Darrin to join Burning Oak, his exclusive country club – but when the uncomfortable Darrin defers, Rockeford takes his wife and leaves. At Larry's insistence, Darrin plays golf with Rockeford at Burning Oak, prompting Endora to predict that Darrin will soon be "outsnobbing the snobs." To hasten her prediction, Endora casts a spell which makes Darrin snooty; he even looks down his nose at Burning Oak's golf course, but Rockeford seems to like the change.

Meanwhile, Samantha lunches with the wives of Burning Oak, most of whom dismiss her. Samantha is furious, but Darrin is ready to move to a more luxurious house near the club and wants a fancier dinner than Samantha offers. Samantha realizes Darrin is under a snob spell and asks babysitter Aunt Hagatha to dig up dirt on Rockeford and the others while she dines with Darrin at Burning Oak. As Darrin haughtily declares that too many undesirables are in membership, the crowd freezes; Endora has brought the witchy background check Samantha requested and agrees to despell Darrin. Samantha goes on to skewer the snobs with choice bits from their sketchy ancestries, even outing herself as a witch. The history lesson gets the club's screening process abolished, Darrin admits he enjoyed Samantha's equalizing, and Endora skywrites to apologize for her spell.

GOOD!

Although it's unspoken that Samantha gave up luxuries that would make the ladies of Burning Oak look like trailer trash, her time in the mortal world has grounded her so much that she easily trounces the stuck-up luncheon ladies, assailing one with the revelation that her "couturier" is Sears and Roebuck. The country club's elitism goes much further than anything reflected in the dialogue: the show wisely cast African-American caddies and servants to show just how far Burning Oak goes to literally whitewash its surroundings. But perhaps the best part of Samantha's disastrous lunch is when Hortense Rockeford smiles at Samantha's department store comeback. In that one moment, Hortense shows she's really not like her husband or friends at all.

Endora arrives to save the day, having just picketed a "new movie about witches." That movie is none other than *Rosemary's Baby*, which came out nine months earlier (not exactly new) and equates witchcraft with Satanism. *Bewitched* witches certainly would be concerned about such a representation, and it makes Samantha's "if the shoe fits" comment regarding Endora's latest spell on Darrin that much more amusing.

WELL?

Endora really sees Samantha as a slave these days, zapping a ball and chain onto her daughter's ankle – in "Instant Courtesy" (#153), it was chains and a sack dress. Later, when Mrs. Rockeford asks Samantha how long she's been without help, Samantha says, "Quite some time now," but the correct answer is, since Amelia moved on to greener pastures in "Samantha's Supermaid" (#154).

The Stephenses don't belong to a club now, but in "A Change of Face" (#33), "Double Split" (#64), and "Birdies, Bogies, and Baxter" (#114), allusions were made to Darrin carrying a membership card. And what product or service of Rockeford's is so important that Larry's brown-nosing reaches new heights? It never comes up.

Mrs. Rockeford's comment that a club should be exclusive – and Samantha's flip retort about how little breeding there is in the world – echoes the snotty sentiments of Sheila Sommers' in "Snob in the Grass" (#126). Sheila was also the first to mention plastic surgeon Dr. Hafter to Samantha [see "I, Darrin, Take This Witch, Samantha" (#1)]; prissy Miss Kabaker did the same in "Double Split" (#64). Here, Cynthia suggests "Dr. Haf*ner*."

Darrin snarks that Larry has spent "too many years on the public links." Isn't that where Darrin has been golfing? Darrin wants to live in a ritzier neighborhood again as a result of Endora's spell, but he just suggested relocation under the influence of a different spell in "One Touch of Midas" (#157).

Darrin's favorite food has changed three times in the past year, most recently in "Samantha, the Sculptress" (#159); now, a new preferred dish takes top honors: corned beef and cabbage.

Doreen McLean makes the fourth actress to play Aunt Hagatha since she was introduced in "Speak the Truth" (#50); the shopkeeper and witches' school administrator has more recently only been an off-screen babysitter. As Samantha tasks Hagatha with snooping into the snobs, she suggests getting Aunt Bertha to stay with Tabitha. Who's Aunt Bertha? Samantha had a friend named Bertha in "The Witches Are Out" (#7), but she didn't seem to be related to Samantha one way or the other. How about getting Aunt Enchantra, who hasn't been mentioned since "The Trial and Error of Aunt Clara" (#95)? Speaking of whom, Clara's portrayer, Marion Lorne, died between Season Four and Season Five, and the lovable witch has been missing in action since her last appearance in "Samantha's Secret Saucer" (#137). Witches live thousands of years, but presumably not forever – Samantha could say that she wishes her favorite aunt were still around to babysit. Or maybe Clara finally turned herself into something. One tiny mention would fill in a very huge blank; as it stands, it's like Aunt Clara never existed.

The Burning Oak set makes a huge deal out of checking people's backgrounds. Have they checked Darrin's? Surely the fact that he's been arrested three times [twice in "Take Two Aspirins and Half A Pint of Porpoise Milk" (#42) and once in "The Very Informal Dress" (#44)] would have the snobs keeping their distance from him. Samantha relaying the results of her own witchy background check is magical, but shouldn't she be worried about Darrin getting kicked off the Rockeford account as a result? She would be if Larry was there, but for some reason he is absent from the festivities.

Finally, this isn't the first time Endora's taken a stab at skywriting: she did it once to save one of Darrin's accounts in "Eat At Mario's" (#35).

OH, MY STARS!

Samantha declaring that it's "sock-it-to-you time" is a paraphrase of one of the signature lines of comedy show *Laugh-In* (which ran on NBC from 1968-1973), but there's nothing funny about Darrin threatening to sock Endora, no matter what she does to him.

What possesses Samantha to out herself as a witch in front of her Burning Oak dinner companions and all the other members standing by? Yes, in the world of *Bewitched*, witches are the greatest minority, but exposing her identity so blatantly, even to make a very good point, is essentially realizing the cautionary dream Samantha put on Darrin in "I Confess" (#135), which was meant to talk him *out* of telling the world she's a witch. What's to stop Rockeford or any of the others from going public with this information? Does Samantha really think Rockeford won't tell Larry about it? The scene is powerful, but "I'm a witch" comes with exponential repercussions.

Endora apologizes by skywriting "I promise never to bother What's-His-Name again" one hundred times. Aside from the fact that the entire city can see her cloudy capitals, Endora uses a broom to literally get this message across. She said in the very first episode that witches don't ride brooms – why would she get on one now?

SON OF A GUN!

"I think we all know that there's no such thing as a purebred American – unless it's the Indian. And an American Indian could never get in here!" – Samantha, showing the condescending country clubbers the fallacy of their screening process.

The fire Samantha "lit under Burning Oak" is one of the most satisfying moments of the series. Not only does it point out that all Americans can trace their origins elsewhere, but it is also an understated call for equality.

SAMANTHA'S POWER FAILURE
Airdate: March 20, 1969

EPISODE
165

Endora wakes Samantha with news that the Witches' Council is fed up with her marriage to Darrin. When Samantha refuses to dissolve it, the Council strips her of her powers. Endora urges Samantha to change her mind for the sake of her birthright, while Uncle Arthur and Serena arrive to support their powerless relative. After Endora exchanges barbs with them, the Council gets wind of their standing behind Samantha and removes their witchcraft as well. Samantha's uncle and cousin assure her they can function like mortals, offering to get jobs to prove their point.

Serena and Arthur are confident after getting hired at an ice cream plant, though Serena has to discourage the attentions of Buck, their amorous manager. The now-mortals are assigned to a conveyor belt where they are to dip frozen bananas in chocolate. All goes well until the belt speeds up, and Arthur and Serena make a mess trying to compensate; the job ends when they get into a chocolate fight with Buck. Later, Samantha agrees to face the Witches' Council, pointing out that they're guilty of the same injustices that mortals inflicted during the Salem witch trials. When Uncle Arthur catches Tabitha using her powers, he attempts a tablecloth trick "without" witchcraft, leading the group to realize the Council has restored their magic.

GOOD!

The Witches' Council was unheard of until "It's Nice to Have A Spouse Around the House" (#145), and all they did then was turn Darrin into a statue when Samantha refused to meet with them. Here, their power and influence proves to be far greater than that, stripping three (and a half) witches of their witchcraft. It would appear that the witch world has been given some formidable structure.

There was no real animosity between Endora and Arthur during his first appearance in "The Joker Is A Card" (#41), but it ramped up when they were revealed to be siblings in "Endora Moves in for a Spell" (#80) – they still have the same sardonic crackle, despite not having shared the screen since the latter episode. Also, Arthur quickly develops a hilariously adversarial relationship with mortal manager Buck, whose attempted seduction of Serena would be considered sexual harassment today; it's worth it for Serena's reactions, which are colder than any ice cream they're pushing.

WELL?

Reusing effects can work very well (and can always save a show money), but Endora's "bouncing ball" from "Witches and Warlocks Are My Favorite Things" (#77) was already reused in "The Trial and Error of Aunt Clara" (#95). Having Samantha wear the same nightgown is a nice effort, but her hair being inches longer once she meets Endora downstairs makes it obvious the scenes were filmed at very different times. Samantha also has an incongruous recollection of her wedding: in the pilot, Darrin was only seen slipping a ring on Samantha's finger during a narrated montage, so there could have been thunder from the Witches' Council – but there probably weren't wedding bells, since the Stephenses appeared to be married at a justice of the peace, and not in a church. By the way, how do Darrin and Tabitha sleep through the Councils' present, discourteous display of thunder?

Uncle Arthur tells Samantha that he and Serena have come to support her stand against the Witches' Council – yet he acts surprised when he first sees Serena. Also, in "Samantha, the Bard" (#158), the rhyme-afflicted Samantha recited the familiar lyrics, "the foot bone's connected to the leg bone," etc., which come from the spiritual, *Dem Bones*, written by James Weldon Johnson (1871-1938); here, Uncle Arthur sings passages from the song as a dancing skeleton.

Endora responds to Arthur and Serena's sass by zapping their lips shut with a button and a zipper, respectively; this is before their powers are taken away. How can Endora zap them at all? Again, witches seem to have an unprecedented power over one another. Once without witchcraft, Serena thanks Endora for the "groovy threads" as if she's seeing the dress for the first time, but Serena already wore it in "Double, Double...Toil and Trouble" (#111). Then, Endora melodramatically swears they've all seen the last of her, and Uncle Arthur replies, "Well, hurry up. We'd like to be alone." This is virtually the same exchange the siblings had in "Endora Moves in for a Spell" (#80).

Minutes after losing their powers, Serena and Uncle Arthur tell Samantha they'll get jobs. Why? It's not like the Stephenses can't afford to put them up for a while – shouldn't they wait on employment until their reduction to mortal status appears to be permanent? Privately, Serena berates Uncle Arthur for telling Samantha, "We're behind you 100%," but those were Serena's words, not Arthur's. Plus, Arthur struggles to light a match, though Serena's ex-beau, Franklyn, had just that struggle in "Marriage, Witches' Style" (#161). Finally, Arthur wants to fulfill Darrin's "expectation" of a hot foot, despite telling Darrin in "Samantha Loses Her Voice" (#150) that he stopped pulling that trick 400 years ago.

The Stephenses always had a light blue car, until "Mrs. Stephens, Where Are You?" (#160), which put a dark blue car in their driveway. Now Samantha's car is green. Speaking of colors, while confronting the Witches' Council, the witchy background behind Samantha and Endora is red, white, and gray in a wide shot; in Endora's medium shot, it's pink and purple.

At home, Samantha doesn't want Uncle Arthur attempting a second tablecloth trick, since his first broke all but her best dishes, which have been in Darrin's family for generations. Have these heirloom dishes come along since "Cousin Serena Strikes Again (Part I)" (#155), where Samantha reminded Darrin that they only had one set of china?

Endora's attitude in this episode is strange. She expresses no surprise when the Witches' Council strips her daughter's powers, meaning she knows this is their plan all along – it's almost as if she's in on it. Later, when everyone's witchcraft is restored, Endora grumpily pops out. Endora ought to be happy that her daughter has retained the birthright she worried would be lost; are the sour grapes because Samantha got to retain her marriage as well?

OH, MY STARS!

Endora says the Witches' Council has "finally had it" with Samantha's mortal marriage. So why have they waited five years to act on it? Then, Uncle Arthur grumbles that he voted for the Council, which hasn't reversed a decision in 3,000 years, but a monarchy and a democracy can't exist at the same time – in "Long Live the Queen" (#108), Ticheba was sovereign until passing the crown to Samantha; if the Council is a Parliament of sorts, and under rule of the queen, there'd be nothing to vote for. Has the monarchy been abolished since Samantha abdicated?

Additionally, if the Council has been around for millennia, why did Endora and her sisters need to call a coven in "The Trial and Error of Aunt Clara" (#95) to have the aging witch declared earthbound, since the Council now renders Samantha so without the benefit of a trial? And why punish Tabitha? She's committed no crime. Not to mention, Samantha's fellow witches always forget that dissolving the Stephenses' marriage would deprive Tabitha of her father. Just once, it would be great to see Tabitha stand up and tell her parents' detractors to leave her daddy alone.

SON OF A GUN!

"It's something you need when you can't twitch." – Samantha, when Tabitha asks what luck is.

Uncle Arthur and Serena are a genius comic pairing; it's amazing they've never been on screen together until now. As helpless "mortals," their power failures rule the episode, particularly their *I Love Lucy*-inspired chocolate free-for-all (the original sequence aired on CBS in 1952). There's a feeling that Elizabeth Montgomery and Paul Lynde are improvising their dialogue – and, once Ron Masak's "chocolate covered manager" enters the fray, the trio looks to be having so much fun, they can't stop laughing.

Samantha's appeal to the Witches' Council is spot-on. Of course, she's had practice making do-the-right-thing speeches [see "Samantha for the Defense" (#88) and "Samantha's Thanksgiving to Remember" (#119)], but turning the Council's prejudices around on them by invoking the Salem witch trials is brilliant, and Samantha's call for freedom for those who "choose to be different" goes far beyond any television show.

SAMANTHA TWITCHES FOR UNICEF

Airdate: March 27, 1969

EPISODE 166

Samantha gets suckered into shadowing E.J. Haskell, who has flaked on a $10,000 donation he pledged to the United Nation's Children's Fund. When Samantha's attempt to discuss the donation with Haskell gets a door slammed in her face, Samantha makes sure her face is visible to him everywhere: she takes the place of Haskell's chauffeur and secretary, and even projects her image onto a moose head. Haskell decides to see a psychiatrist – Samantha eavesdrops on the session, then induces the doctor to leave so she can take his place, mustache and all. Endora pops in, spooking Haskell; she tells Samantha to look to his fiancée, Lila, for answers.

Cabaret performer Lila is indifferent to Samantha and refuses to ask wealthy Haskell for anything before their wedding – privately, she hides another man in her dressing room. Endora catches on and spikes Lila's restaurant soup with "truth salts," which force her to admit she's only marrying Haskell for his money. Haskell sends Lila on her way, then blanches when he sees Samantha, determining that she represents his conscience. He agrees to the UNICEF donation, but, when Endora appears, he thinks she's there about his doubts and anxieties. Later, the committee leader who tasked Samantha with following Haskell reports that he came through on his own, but asked if she'd ever seen a blond conscience.

GOOD!

Samantha's chairs going from unpainted to painted and back again are flawless effects. There's also some terrific continuity when Mrs. Wehmeyer recalls that Samantha saved the neighborhood park [see "Samantha Fights City Hall" (#149)]. And, though Endora initially thinks that hungry children are a petty problem, she comes on board to help Samantha with Haskell, culminating in the builder thinking Endora represents his doubts and anxieties. ("I don't know why," Endora wonders, "but I have the distinct feeling that I've been insulted.")

Three particular guest stars keep this donation appropriation cooking. Sharon Vaughn is the perfect baffled bimbo who gets her just desserts during the soup course. Herb Voland, who has made several appearances on the show so far, finally gets a chance to play a character with a wider comedic range than his usual group of grumpy clients (without frequent "wife" Sara Seegar, who appears here as Mrs. Wehmeyer without crossing his orbit). Finally, Bernie Kopell's stereotypical shrink doesn't shrink from making every heavily-accented word out of his mouth as funny as possible.

WELL?

Samantha lets herself get pressured a lot: Phyllis pushed her into hiring help in "Samantha's Supermaid" (#154), Frank twisted her arm into bringing her daughter over for "Tabitha's Weekend" (#163), and now Mrs. Wehmeyer railroads Samantha into hunting Haskell. Is Endora the only person she can stand up to? Speaking of whom, with Darrin out of town (nice touch mentioning he's asleep upstairs during the tag; it keeps him in the Darrin-less episode), Endora wants to take Samantha and fly off on a cloud. Surely she doesn't intend to leave Tabitha home alone during their flight?

This community center where the ladies are slated to congregate must be in a small neighborhood, because Haskell's driver later takes him through the same area the committee women were parked. Both locales are on a Hollywood street near the studio.

Has Betty quit McMann & Tate to work for E.J. Haskell? Jean Blake, who played the constantly changing secretary in "To Twitch or Not to Twitch" (#132), shows up here as Haskell's receptionist, Miss Blake, who wears Samantha's outfit from the previous episode, "Samantha's Power Failure" (#165). And it's not the first time Samantha has magically replaced a secretary: she also temped in "The Crone of Cawdor" (#101), trying to track a seductress who wanted to kiss the youth out of Darrin. For that matter, Haskell's office is identical to the one bank president Markham occupied in "The No-Harm Charm" (#138).

Dr. Chomsky – an apparently Russian psychiatrist with a German accent – listens as Haskell talks about his fiancée, whom Endora terms a "vixen." Except Haskell doesn't provide any information that would cause Endora to come to this conclusion. Later, at the restaurant, Endora distracts a waiter while Samantha sprinkles truth salts in a bowl of soup on his tray. How can Samantha know that the bowl she's selected is meant for Lila? That soup could get served to Haskell, or even to someone at another table. Do witches have ESP again? And, if Endora considers truth salts "tools of my trade," then why didn't she use the honesty-inducing seasoning in "Speak the Truth" (#50) instead of procuring a truth god from Hagatha?

Lila has to be pretty high on her soupy serum, because she doesn't notice Samantha sitting at a table behind Haskell; Samantha was just in her dressing room, wearing the same easy-to-spot red, yellow, and black plaid coat. When Haskell finally gives in and agrees to the donation, Samantha produces a blank check for him to sign. It is funny that he insists he can't give a check to his conscience, but where did Samantha get it? Did she zap it out of his checkbook? She'd have to, because any old check wouldn't have his account information on it. Endora's presence causes Haskell to dash out of the restaurant – hopefully he paid his bill first. And, Samantha and Endora already have their own table, so why do they take over Haskell's when he leaves?

The next day, Mrs. Wehmeyer rushes over to tell Samantha she needn't waste time following Haskell. Yet she told Samantha "yesterday" to case Haskell for 48 hours. Does she think Samantha hasn't started yet?

Despite the episode's title, Samantha zaps and pops for UNICEF, but never actually twitches. And, when Samantha tells Endora to paint the clouds with sunshine, she's referencing the 1929 song (and 1951 movie) *Painting the Clouds with Sunshine*.

OH, MY STARS!

Once Samantha and Endora hear about Lila, they target her in an effort to get Haskell to pony up. But how does ruining Haskell's engagement secure the UNICEF money? Yes, Lila originally talked him out of his pledge, but getting rid of her doesn't necessarily mean he's going to make good on it. Haskell only does because he realizes he won't get rid of Samantha otherwise; Samantha and Endora don't need Lila to complete their mission.

SON OF A GUN!

"Oh, well, that's good. Because it's easier to be general than specific. That is, usually, but not always, although sometimes it's harder to be general." – Samantha to Haskell, struggling to understand what he's talking about when he mistakes her for an interior decorator.

Samantha has gone out of her way to live a mortal life these last five years. So, while one slammed door might seem an extreme catalyst to provoke Samantha into behaving like a witch again, her clever zaps on the errant donator are a whole lot of fun. Of course, Samantha could save herself the trouble of hassling Haskell by magically persuading him to write a check, but then she couldn't do her fall-on-the-floor imitation of Dr. Chomsky.

DADDY DOES HIS THING
Airdate: April 3, 1969

EPISODE
167

Samantha has a surprise for Darrin on his birthday, but they're interrupted by the arrival of Maurice, who presents Darrin with a lighter he can use to perform witchcraft. When Darrin gently refuses it, Maurice becomes furious and turns Darrin into a mule. Gladys sees Darrin-as-mule from across the street, then comes over the next morning and witnesses him downing a human breakfast. Samantha recruits Endora to help her find Maurice; while they argue with him in a Paris café, Gladys calls the animal shelter, and Darrin is taken away.

Samantha pops over to the shelter and retrieves Darrin, confounding the attendants. Maurice attempts to change Darrin back, but when he has trouble doing so, he zaps up a chess board, suggesting their "mutual concentration" will aid in the process; Gladys enters mid-game and can't wait to tell chess enthusiast Abner. Finally, Maurice re-enacts Darrin's transformation in the living room painting, running the images backward to bring Darrin back from "his recent hee-haw." When Abner stops by, not believing Gladys' story about a chess-playing mule, Maurice turns himself into one to engage Abner in a game.

GOOD!

Based on their past interactions [especially in "Just One Happy Family" (#10)], the last thing you'd expect Darrin and Maurice to be is cordial with one another. Yet Maurice acknowledges Darrin's birthday, and Darrin doesn't make a fuss over Maurice having tunneled through the wall. The niceties don't last – nor should they – but they're a refreshing change of pace. And Tabitha's reaction to the spiteful witchcraft being leveled at her father is finally taken into consideration: Samantha's relieved Tabitha's not having a trauma over her daddy being turned into a mule.

In "Weep No More, My Willow" (#152), Abner played chess with himself. That's a minor plot point, so it's sharp attention to detail that Abner's pastime is brought back here. He not only plays against his invisible opponent, he's challenged by Maurice-as-mule. The episode ends there, but picturing Abner going through with the game is quite the image.

WELL?

It's nice to see a character celebrating a birthday, even on the wrong day. In "Double Tate" (#59), Endora was the in-law who gifted Darrin, but then he blew his candles out in February; here, it's April. Samantha giving Darrin a watch is reminiscent of Darrin presenting Samantha with his "I love you every second" timepiece of "A is for Aardvark" (#17) – whatever happened to that present?

The Stephenses know something witchy is about to happen based on the sudden blast of *La Marseillaise*, the French national anthem. But their heads snap in the direction of the wall before Maurice's tunnel even appears. At least Maurice doesn't pull up to the curb for the neighbors to see this time, as he did in "My Grandson, the Warlock" (#40), but his giant martini glass comes from that episode, and he got his "Spanish gin, Italian vermouth and a Greek olive" recipe from Endora, who ordered a martini that way in "Mother Meets What's-His-Name" (#4). The observation that Maurice wouldn't be in anything but magnificent health comes from "Just One Happy Family" (#10), and Maurice grouses that Samantha has "picked a lemon in the garden of love," which is what Endora said about Samantha's choice in "How to Fail in Business With All Kinds of Help" (#104).

Be careful what you wish for: in "Mirror, Mirror on the Wall" (#146), Darrin said his '60s mod clothes made him feel like a jackass, and now he is one. As for Samantha, she apparently didn't learn from "A Gazebo Never Forgets" (#89), where she let Aunt Clara's pink polka-dotted elephant peek out the front window; here, she ushers Darrin-as-mule to that same window, even though she just talked about how thick the grass is in the *backyard*. It's late at night, too – what is Gladys doing peeking across the street at exactly that moment?

The next day at breakfast, Gladys comes to see the mule, gleefully reporting she spent the night trying to convince Abner of its existence. The only way Gladys could know about the mule is if she spied on the Stephenses, an act her statement confirms for them. Then, strangely, Gladys' excitement changes to disapproval as she insists Samantha can't keep a mule as a pet – that's as abrupt as the fact that the Stephenses' kitchen door now faces a wall, though it's always faced the street. As for that breakfast, the scrambled eggs and chicken livers deemed to be Darrin's favorite in "Weep No More, My Willow" (#152) have changed to eggs Benedict, and Abner complains that all he ever gets is lumpy oatmeal, when, in "Splitsville" (#140), Gladys' organic offerings were more exotic; she also served Abner pancakes and bacon as far back as "Abner Kadabra" (#29).

When Samantha and Endora pop in to the café in Paris, the patrons continue as if people appear out of nowhere all the time. At least Maurice's lady friends, Yvette and Angelique, register shock when Maurice vanishes; apparently it's all right for Maurice to flirt with mortals, despite not wanting Samantha married to one.

This is the second time Gladys has reported Darrin to an animal shelter, although in "Alias Darrin Stephens" (#37), Darrin was a chimpanzee. Tabitha seems to take her father's removal in stride – shouldn't she be more upset? Later, Gladys can hear Darrin-as-mule's braying from all the way across the street, and tells Samantha she knocked, when she clearly didn't.

The day is saved when Maurice reverses "footage" of the previous night's events (from an omniscient perspective, and with multiple camera angles) – but he got the idea from Uncle Arthur, who sent Napoléon Bonaparte back to his own time by performing a spell in reverse in "Samantha's French Pastry" (#147).

What inspires Maurice to turn himself into a mule for Abner's benefit? It almost seems he's trying to protect Gladys by substantiating the presence of the animal for her. Then, Maurice-as-mule tells Samantha he can't resist a game of chess, but why can Maurice talk in his "asinine condition," while Darrin could only bray? At any rate, the next time Gladys speaks of strange events at the Stephenses', maybe Abner will take her seriously – he can't very well deny seeing a chess-playing mule for himself.

OH, MY STARS!

At the beginning of the episode, Samantha tells Darrin she has a birthday surprise for them both, but it's interrupted by Maurice, and the Stephenses never revisit the subject once things return to normal. And Darrin is nice enough in turning down Maurice's magic lighter, but he had to know what his father-in-law's reaction would be. He'd have been smarter to accept the gift, then simply not use it; of course, then there wouldn't be an episode.

It's inconceivable that Samantha and Endora, who love Tabitha fiercely, would leave her in the care of Darrin-as-mule, even for a minute. Endora jokes that Darrin can "bray for help," but that would be useless if there were an actual emergency. Finally, Maurice claims that "mutual concentration on a common problem" will help him change Darrin back, but Maurice is a powerful warlock, and there's nothing wrong with his powers; one zap is all it should take to make Darrin human again.

SON OF A GUN!

"I listen to you all the time, except when you talk – there I draw the line." – Abner to Gladys, not wanting to hear they have a jackass for a neighbor.

Maurice is back! Samantha's father hasn't made an appearance in 90 episodes [see "Witches and Warlocks Are My Favorite Things" (#77)], and this is only his fourth visit overall – but the way he commands this installment, it's as if he were around a lot more often. True, Maurice's antics sometimes borrow from past episodes (at least he's consistent?), but his surrounding himself with French *femmes* and reporting that "Dr. Bombay forbids me to discuss family problems at the aperitif hour; it gives me heartburn" shows new facets to the warlock's personality.

SAMANTHA'S GOOD NEWS

Airdate: April 10, 1969

Maurice pops in, having picked up on Samantha's radiance via the atmospheric continuum. After Samantha shrugs off the observation, Maurice reveals that he has taken on a private secretary: the beautiful Abigail Beecham. Sensing a connection between her father and Abigail, Samantha summons Endora, who is immediately jealous. Although Abigail proves her witchy secretarial skills, Endora changes her into an old crone. After restoring her, Maurice argues with Endora while Samantha gets to know Abigail better. Maurice and Abigail share a kiss in front of Endora, who threatens to file for an ectoplasmic interlocutory, then pops out.

Maurice seems unconcerned with Endora's fury; later, Endora approves Samantha's suggestion to make Maurice jealous with John Van Millwood, a Shakespearean competitor. Maurice chafes at Endora's choice of companion, and soon he and John attempt to one-up each other delivering sonnets. Abigail tires of the fighting, and leaves with the amorous John – but, after Endora and Maurice make up, they concur that there's something unusual about Samantha, coming to the conclusion that Samantha is going to have another baby. Samantha confirms her good news and shares it with Tabitha, who wants to know if her new sibling will be a witch or a warlock, ultimately deciding she'd rather have a pony.

GOOD!

Even though the atmospheric continuum was never mentioned until "Samantha's French Pastry" (#147), the show develops the idea here by having Maurice pick up on Samantha's aura via the ethereal field. Perhaps the continuum has roots in "George the Warlock" (#30): the titular troublemaker similarly felt the "vibrations" of Samantha's unhappiness.

As Endora and Samantha discuss Maurice's fascination with Abigail, Endora asks, "Am I on Durwood's side of the bed or yours?" Not only is this a great way to keep Darrin in yet another Darrin-less episode, but Endora's potential disdain is a subtle addition to her already blatant feelings about her son-in-law.

Even after only five appearances, Maurice's personality is established enough that it becomes immediately obvious he's met his match in John Van Millwood, who calls his co-star "Morris" (actually the proper British way of pronouncing "Maurice") and snarks that audiences can't understand a word Maurice says. As Maurice has a way of lording over everyone, it's fun to see him get a little comeuppance.

WELL?

Fulfilling Tabitha's request for a present, Maurice zaps a huge swing set into the backyard. What happened to the one Bonzo/"Harry" climbed around on in "Going Ape" (#162)?

Endora and Maurice's open marriage seems to be a bit complicated. Endora, who barely batted an eye when Maurice cavorted with Yvette and Angelique in "Daddy Does His Thing" (#167), is immediately jealous of Abigail. Likewise, Maurice has not been shown to object to Endora keeping company with Japanese poets, Spanish bullfighters, and numerous princes, yet his hackles are up as soon as John pops in on Endora's arm. Could it be time for Samantha's parents to reevaluate the boundaries of their relationship?

Endora may be right when she says any witch can type a Shakespearean soliloquy: Abigail types invisibly, while Endora made a typewriter clack independently in "And Then I Wrote" (#45), though she wasn't particularly accurate. Chatting with Abigail, Samantha wants to know if the secretary is interested in marrying Maurice. How can Samantha ask that? Her father already *is* married.

Upstairs, Samantha suggests trying "the old jealousy approach" on Maurice. She's certainly had success with this technique: she used it to reunite the Kravitzes in "Splitsville" (#140). It turns out that popular '60s actor Steve McQueen is Dr. Bombay's nephew; Serena also mentioned him when she rode her motorcycle through the living room in "Cousin Serena Strikes Again (Part I)" (#155).

Who knew: William Shakespeare, who lived from 1564 to 1616, considered John Van Millwood the best of the warlocks in his original production of *Romeo and Juliet*. So Willie not only knew about warlocks, but didn't mind hanging out with them.

As Maurice and Endora reason out why Samantha looks so radiant, he asks, "How old is Tabitha?" If he doesn't know, then maybe he needs to visit more often. Thankfully, Endora and Maurice have a surprisingly positive reaction to the prospect of a grandchild, which wasn't necessarily the case in "A Very Special Delivery" (#38) and "My Grandson, the Warlock" (#40), respectively. Samantha grabs the phone, saying she wants Darrin to be the first to know, after her parents. Now, it would seem that her pregnancy news was the birthday surprise that Maurice interrupted in "Daddy Does His Thing" (#167), though the show doesn't make this connection directly. If that's the case, why didn't Samantha tell Darrin he's going to be a father again as soon as the mule business was over with, instead of waiting until her parents forced the issue?

OH, MY STARS!

Somewhere along the line, the floor plan of 1164 Morning Glory Circle has changed. Initially, the Stephenses' bedroom was the first right at the top of the stairs, and beyond that was the guest room. Here, it's as if Tabitha's room replaced the master bedroom, and the master bedroom replaced the guest room: Samantha exits Tabitha's room and continues to the audience's right, where the second floor dead ends at the master bedroom.

Maurice says he last saw Endora "two or three months ago...maybe eighteen." This is meant to highlight their separate-ways marriage, but they were just together one episode ago, in "Daddy Does His Thing" (#167). They're also so busy reminiscing that they don't realize Attila the Hun can't be the "young witch" Endora had drafted into the army – Attila, who lived in the 5th century, was a man.

SON OF A GUN!

"I beg your pardon!" – Abigail Beecham, when John Van Millwood asks if she's a thespian (an innuendo that's quite progressive for television in 1969).

This is a history-making episode – unlike the 168 before it, there's not a mortal in sight. Given the show's premise – a witch living in a mortal world – an all-witch episode shouldn't work, but it does, and it's a fascinating way to cover Dick York's absence.

This installment builds on a concept that dates all the way back to "Just One Happy Family" (#10): Endora and Maurice don't live together, as confirmed here when Maurice tells Abigail about his "informal marriage." Maybe before the sexual revolution, this couldn't be explored, but now it can. The dynamic between Maurice and Endora, and how they function as a couple, is brought to the fore for the first time; if they've had these spats for "centuries", as Maurice points out, just imagine Samantha as a girl witch listening to them go at it. All this begs one tantalizing question: if Samantha's parents have such an unconventional union themselves, how can they object to hers?

Darrin doesn't need to feel bad anymore – Endora just has a thing about making sure she mispronounces the name of anyone she doesn't like. She called Darrin's cousin Helen "Elena" in "A Prince of a Guy" (#129), and Abigail gets her last name mangled here as much as Darrin's first name typically does.

Darrin did say in "Just One Happy Family" (#10) that he's partial to large families – Samantha is pregnant again, an unexpected, game-changing development. The news allows Elizabeth Montgomery's real-life pregnancy to be written into the show, and Tabitha's reaction is priceless. "Boy or girl," Samantha wonders. "Witch or warlock? Which?" That's one solid cliffhanger.

EPISODE 169
SAMANTHA'S SHOPPING SPREE
Airdate: April 17, 1969

Samantha is readying to take Tabitha shopping when Cousin Henry, a practical joker like Uncle Arthur, invites himself along. Endora accompanies them, then watches as the bored Henry toys with neophyte salesman Joseph Hinkley, Jr. – Henry magically rips a sports jacket, then replaces Hinkley with Jack Snow, a football player. Desperate to impress his father, Hinkley tries to push a sale on Henry, so the warlock responds by turning him into a mannequin. Samantha demands that Henry change Hinkley back, but Henry stubbornly pops out instead.

Attracting attention by talking to Hinkley-as-mannequin – who can talk back – Samantha ducks into a men's fitting room to check on Endora's search for Henry, not seeing department store workers Fred and Harry removing all the dummies for a new display. While Endora argues with Henry on the moon, Hinkley-as-mannequin's outbursts have Harry and Frank thinking the other is speaking, sparking an argument of their own. Samantha approaches them under the ruse of buying the dummy; when it doesn't work, Samantha zaps Hinkley home with her, nearly bringing the coworkers to fisticuffs over the missing mannequin. With her elders unable to restore Hinkley, Tabitha reports seeing Henry cast his spell; Endora uses it to make Hinkley human again, and Samantha brings him back to the store believing he helped her make multiple purchases, which surprises Hinkley's father.

GOOD!

The gold in this episode is in the subtleties. When Henry first messes with young Hinkley, Endora silently contemplates chucking an ashtray at the mischievous warlock (reflecting a time when smoking was allowed – and encouraged – in stores). Then, when Hinkley-as-mannequin "talks" and gets Samantha into a sticky wicket with the clerk, she quietly bops the dummy with her purse as the scene fades out. As for Hinkley going from chummy to dummy, he hovers over Henry, with the camera following Samantha's cross to Endora; Henry announces he's ready to go, and Samantha crosses back to Hinkley, who's now a mannequin – rather incredible when you realize it was all done in one shot.

Cameos can be hit-or-miss, especially with sports figures who may shine at their game but not on camera. So the show scores a touchdown in getting Jack Snow of the then-Los Angeles Rams to become the butt of Henry's joke. Snow is properly befuddled by his sudden 1,600-mile relocation from Dallas, and exudes a natural charisma on screen. The team of Dave Madden and Herb Ellis also wins big – the duo played automotive experts Joe and Charlie in "Super Car" (#93), but return here as frenemies Fred and Harry. Their horn-locking is topped only by the risqué moment they sneak in: Harry asks Fred if he really thinks Samantha wants the dummy for making suits; shaking his head, Fred replies, "Takes all kinds, Harry."

WELL?

Endora and Uncle Arthur share some common ground after all: the warlock is off picketing the 1968 witches-as-demons film *Rosemary's Baby*, as his sister did in "The Battle of Burning Oak" (#164) – despite the film probably being out of theatres at this point, having been released ten months earlier. Henry's live jack-in-the-box calls Samantha a "nudge," a Yiddish term Maurice used to describe his daughter in "Daddy Does His Thing" (#167). As for Samantha, it appears she's already given up on making dresses for Tabitha, buying one instead of taking needle to thread again like she did in "One Touch of Midas" (#157) – where hexed toy "the Fuzz" was on sale at Hanley's Department Store; here, it's Hinkley's. And, while Henry claims that Arthur steals his jokes, Henry does the plagiarizing by insulting Endora with Arthur's "when I think of you as a blood relative, I long for a transfusion" line from "Samantha's Power Failure" (#165).

The "technical" explanation of how Uncle Arthur zapped up Napoléon Bonaparte instead of a Napoléon dessert – words with multiple meanings causing kinetic vibrations to zonk across the atmospheric continuum; see "Samantha's French Pastry" (#147) – must be how Henry gets Jack Snow, an L.A. Ram, when his plan is to turn Hinkley into a ram. Either that, or Henry's powers are on the blink. As for Hinkley-as-dummy, he yells out "Don't touch me!" when Harry goes to undress him, so obviously Hinkley can still feel. It's a wonder, then, that Hinkley says nothing when Harry picks him up from underneath his legs and carries him out of the Men's Department.

In "Sam in the Moon" (#91), Darrin suspected that his wife could make a lunar landing; this episode confirms that witches can, since Endora and Henry are on the satellite while the Apollo astronauts are still working to get there. Nice set, but is that blue glob above it supposed to be Earth? Later, when Tabitha tells her grandmother how to change Hinkley back, Endora identifies the move as "the transcendental triple." It looks to be a pretty general zap, so how can it do something as specific as turn a man into a mannequin and back?

The store clerk decides on a checkup when he catches Samantha popping out with the mannequin – yet when Samantha and Hinkley return, the clerk doesn't react. Samantha saves Hinkley's hide by twitching up packages to evoke the titular shopping spree, but does she also zap up receipts and adjust Hinkley's inventory to reflect the shifting of merchandise? The boxes Hinkley, Jr. drops are empty, judging from the sound they make – and, with Hinkley so hot to impress his father, why does he throw the last package on the floor in front of him?

OH, MY STARS!

Cousin Henry's presence brings up many questions that are never answered. For Henry to be a cousin to Samantha, he has to be the child of her aunt or uncle; Endora narrows things down by referring to Henry as her nephew, making him the son of one of Endora's siblings. Aunt Clara? Not likely. Aunt Enchantra or

Aunt Hagatha? Possibly. But the information given here implies that Uncle Arthur is Henry's father. They share a resemblance, Henry says he taught Arthur everything he knows about practical jokes, and, when Endora first sees Henry, she calls him "the clown prince of the cosmos" and wonders where "King Arthur" is. There's also a feeling that this was meant to be an Uncle Arthur episode; perhaps Paul Lynde was unavailable, so the prank-pulling warlock got a son. This is an acceptable development, but it would be nice if the show drew its family tree a little clearer.

When Henry makes Hinkley a dummy, Samantha asks, "Mother, can you release him?" Samantha, of all people, should know better – she's the one who said whoever casts a spell on someone has "squatter's rights" to that person back in "Hoho the Clown" (#92). It's intriguing that Tabitha demonstrates Henry's transcendental triple, but Endora shouldn't be able to use it to restore Hinkley.

SON OF A GUN!

"I keep telling his mother, that kid is a dummy." – Hinkley, Sr., not realizing Hinkley, Jr. is exactly that.

Steve Franken has made several memorable appearances on the show so far, but he seems to have found his niche in Cousin Henry. He's zany, creative, and even temperamental – what a kick it would be to see him in a scene with Uncle Arthur.

It's official: The Stephenses live in Patterson, New York! This was implied in "Soapbox Derby" (#90), but only on the side of a racer; here, Samantha confirms it when she tells Jack Snow what city he's in. After five seasons, it's good to finally know where the series is actually set.

EPISODE 170

SAMANTHA AND DARRIN IN MEXICO CITY
Airdate: April 24, 1969

The Stephenses look forward to traveling to Mexico for the Bueno soft drink account, but Larry pulls rank and makes the trip with Darrin's ideas instead. While Darrin sulks, Samantha secretly pops south of the border to zap Larry into insulting the client's country so he'll have no choice but to bring Darrin in. After Larry lies that Darrin is fluent in Spanish, Darrin scrambles to learn the language; in his stressed state, he offends Endora, who casts a spell to make Darrin's fear of speaking Spanish disappear. However, en route to Mexico, it's Darrin who disappears whenever utters the language. Samantha flies home to implore Endora to remove the spell, and a stewardess gets rattled watching Darrin and Samantha pop in and out of the plane.

Forced to limit his vocabulary to English, Darrin continually refers to Bueno as "the product," then suggests changing the name to Zap to appeal to American consumers. Samantha twitches Bueno's reluctant president into considering the idea, but Larry is angry that Darrin didn't speak Spanish after he talked Darrin up. Endora reverses her spell, only now it has Darrin disappearing when he speaks English. Since Darrin has to deliver a speech to Bueno's executives in both languages, Samantha fixes it so everyone except Larry hears Darrin bilingually, even though he's only speaking Spanish. Darrin is a hit, and, after Samantha coaxes Darrin into apologizing to Endora, his use of English is restored.

GOOD!

There's a certain knowingness in Larry telling Señor Aragon that Darrin is "quite a linguist." Is Larry recalling how Darrin "mastered" Italian in "Business, Italian Style" (#110)? Larry doesn't appear to be volunteering Darrin out of hand, as in that episode; he seems to legitimately believe that Darrin can achieve fluency quickly based on past experience.

WELL?

Larry's "*presidente* to *presidente*" rationale for going to Mexico City makes a certain amount of sense. But then Larry should have established that from the beginning instead of popping it on Darrin at the end of the meeting. And what's so big about Bueno that Larry feels he has to run Darrin down once in Mexico City?

History has proven that Larry doesn't have the best attitude about different cultures: he had an aversion to flower children in "Hippie, Hippie, Hooray" (#128), and displayed ignorance about Japanese tradition in "A Majority of Two" (#136). So, when Samantha zaps Larry into making disparaging remarks about Mexico and its people, is she putting words in his mouth, or inducing him to tell his truth? It's not clear; if it's the latter, she does it without Endora's truth salts, which she needed to pull confessions out of cabaret performer Lila in "Samantha Twitches for UNICEF" (#166). Why didn't Samantha just zap Lila like she zaps Larry here?

Darrin calling Endora "the old lady of the sea" comes out of nowhere – which makes it all the more unusual that Endora's spell doesn't seem like a prank; she looks genuinely surprised when she learns her zap is making Darrin pop out. Speaking of which, when he first disappears on the plane, how does Samantha know Darrin is actually there, albeit invisible? The last time he vanished like that, the matchmaking Carlotta had removed him completely to make room for her son [see "Darrin, Gone and Forgotten" (#144)]. There's also a similarity to "Disappearing Samantha" (#65), when Osgood Rightmire's "incantation" made Samantha invisible; now Darrin knows how it feels.

Darrin gets out of speaking Spanish by suggesting that Bueno change its name to Zap for the American market. Foreign products are domesticated all the time – it's surprising McMann & Tate doesn't think of this before anyone goes to Mexico. Once there, Larry is upset that Darrin avoided Spanish, grunting, "Why do you think I brought you down here?" Darrin replies, "Probably because you blew the first meeting." Larry is often rude and condescending, but usually it's Darrin who blows meetings under the influence of witchcraft. Then, Samantha lies that Darrin isn't calling Bueno by name because he's superstitious about saying the name of a product before landing an account; Larry should be crying foul, since such "superstition" has never been an issue before. When Larry wants to know why Samantha suggested calling the drink Zap, she begins, "Larry, I hate to tell you this…" What is she going to do, admit to Larry that witchcraft is preventing Darrin from speaking Spanish?

After Endora reverses her spell, Samantha takes a big risk fibbing to Larry that Darrin wants to be immersed in the Spanish language – because it's the same excuse she used in "Business, Italian Style" (#110), when Darrin could no longer understand English. Reminded of her spell, Endora says she forgot about Darrin – which runs counter to her previous insistence that she would only remove the spell after Darrin learned his lesson. Finally, what is the likelihood that a Mexico City hotel, whose signage is probably all in Spanish, would label a room "Suite B?"

OH, MY STARS!

Given how many times Larry has run roughshod over Darrin these past three seasons, there's a sense of justice as Samantha messes with Larry at the Mexico City restaurant. But has she thought her retaliation through? Señor Garcia could easily fire McMann & Tate over Larry's discriminatory remarks, and nearly does, until Samantha twitches him into giving the agency a second chance – but none of this guarantees that Larry will send for Darrin. Nevertheless, Larry makes that call, which means Samantha does all this just so she and Darrin can go to Mexico. Darrin has many times unjustly accused Samantha of magically interfering with accounts – so why does she do it here? Later, Samantha zaps Garcia a second time so he'll consider changing Bueno to Zap, and gleefully makes sure that Larry can only hear Darrin's speech in Spanish. Perhaps Darrin has been gone too much lately; Samantha is actually acting more like Endora in this episode.

On the flight to Mexico, Darrin can barely fumble his way through the simplest of Spanish phrases. Yet, when he is locked into disappearing if he speaks English, he can carry on a complete Spanish conversation with Garcia, plus make a speech in the tongue without writing it down – and all just a few hours later. It's as if Darrin has an additional spell on him; there's no way he could pick up Spanish that fast without one.

Samantha's witch twitch is the show's most famous and endearing sound effect – but its overuse in her multiple translation spells proves that there is something called too much of a good thing: Samantha twitches no less than nine times during Darrin's speech. Why doesn't Samantha just zap him once? And the Spanish-speaking group should be able to tell from Darrin's lips that he's speaking Spanish with English coming out of his mouth.

This is the last episode of the season, but there's something anticlimactic about it, because a cliffhanger of sorts was created with "Samantha's Good News" (#168), in which Samantha revealed her pregnancy and questioned whether her new child would be witch, warlock, or mortal. With Dick York having missed so many episodes because of his back injury, it rather feels this installment was tacked on so the season could end with a Darrin episode. The show seemed to do this in Season Two as well, placing "Prodigy" (#74) after natural finale "What Every Young Man Should Know" (#72) to give the deceased Alice Pearce a proper send-off. Whatever the good intentions, the episode shuffling doesn't feel right in Season Five, either.

SON OF A GUN!

"Jadies and lentlemen, we are now approaching Cexico Mity." – daunted stewardess Liza, after seeing Darrin pop in and out one too many times.

SEASON SIX

(1969-1970)

Expectant father Darrin (now played by Dick Sargent) asks Dr. Bombay what's behind "Samantha's Curious Cravings" (#174).

"Tabitha's Very Own Samantha" (#189) plays with the young witch, who is jealous of her new baby brother.

When "Daddy Comes for a Visit" (#180), Maurice gives Darrin his own powers, which Darrin tries to keep Larry from discovering at the office.

courtesy The Everett Collection

Uncle Arthur's witchcraft-related illness turns out not to be as bad as the cure in "Super Arthur" (#190).

ABC/Photofest

SEASON SIX: OVERVIEW

When viewers of *Bewitched* tuned in for its sixth season premiere on September 18, 1969, they undoubtedly weren't prepared for a revamped theme – or a new Darrin. Aside from the magic, the switch from Dick York to Dick Sargent is easily what people remember most about the show. While the debate rages to this day over which Darrin was better, one fact cannot be disputed: Dick Sargent owned the role from the moment he uttered his first line, "Sam, how many times have I told you never to talk during somebody's backswing?" Despite a new look and approach, this Darrin blended seamlessly into the show, interacting with the mortals and witches around him as if he'd always been there. Additionally, the often huffy Darrin was markedly calmer, at least for a while. If Dick York was the Darrin Stephens for the '60s, then Dick Sargent was going to be a Darrin Stephens for the '70s.

Another new face on Morning Glory Circle was the nervous but well-meaning witch Esmeralda, whom the Stephenses took on as domestic help. While Esmeralda had the same penchant for causing witchy disasters as Samantha's Aunt Clara – whose absence continued to go unexplained – the way the "yoo-hoo maid" sneezed up fictional authors (Mother Goose) and familiar Christmas characters (Santa Claus) was truly her own.

Naturally, the show built on "Samantha's Good News" (#168), the Season Five near-finale in which viewers discovered the Stephenses were expecting their second child. Again incorporating Elizabeth Montgomery's real-life pregnancy into storylines, the show started with Tabitha's difficulty in accepting a soon-to-come sibling ["Samantha and the Beanstalk" (#171)] and culminated in the beautiful moments of "And Something Makes Four" (#175), which brought Adam Stephens into the world. Adam didn't generate as many episodes focusing on him as his sister did as a newborn, but his presence was still felt as Tabitha struggled to deal with her feelings of rivalry [see "Samantha's Lost Weekend" (#186) and "Tabitha's Very Own Samantha" (#189)], even if Adam rather faded into the background in the season's latter half.

With Darrin-less episodes no longer necessary, Samantha's relatives, particularly Uncle Arthur and Serena, were not called upon as often. However, Serena came to be credited as "Pandora Spocks" – a paraphrase of "Pandora's Box" crafted to imply that Serena and her cousin were played by two different ladies. Another lady, Louise, appeared only three times this season, but she made an impression regardless by ditching her brunette 'do in favor of fiery red hair. Speaking of firing, the show wisely backed Larry off from his tendency to terminate Darrin at the drop of a hat, which had dominated Seasons Four and Five. And finally, the "thoroughly modern Samantha" retained that quality throughout these 30 episodes: she refrained from using witchcraft more than ever before, but replaced her powers with the power of backtalk, as both Darrin and Endora discovered that Samantha had developed a slightly sharper tongue.

Perhaps to make the transition between Darrins as seamless as possible, 1164 Morning Glory Circle remained mostly the same, save for a few cosmetic changes. Outside, the sounds of birds and crickets joined the backyard's new furniture and backdrops, while on the road, viewers were treated to scenes of characters driving on real streets instead of against process shots in the studio. New effects, both special and sound, were sprinkled into the footage, with duplicate Endoras and Arthurs, and Esmeralda's continual fade-outs. As for the dialogue, it got a bit saucy at times, as if to mirror the ongoing sexual revolution; it also contained more slang and pop culture references, which made their way into witches' spells. Non-mortals made frequent visits to other planets as the show expanded on Season Five's cosmic concepts – and on Earth, the show finally presented irrefutable proof of the Stephenses' hometown: Westport, Connecticut.

As for McMann & Tate, it didn't feel like the agency was in Manhattan anymore, with Darrin and Larry quickly arriving at Morning Glory Circle despite a 50-mile distance. Props seemed to know when and where they were needed, as the bar moved around and mirrors were suddenly available to peer or pop into with increasing frequency. Most notably, scenarios from earlier seasons began showing up as reinvented new episodes; perhaps having a new Darrin gave the show tacit permission to revisit storylines, which it did at least six times during this season.

However, the show still had a strong sense of originality, sending Tabitha into a fairy tale, having Serena hang out with rock stars, and even trapping everyone in the Stephens house via a magical vapor lock – this was just for starters. Despite an occasional pull from the past, there was a consistent, contemporary feel to Season Six, and it felt as if there were a new energy just from having a new Darrin in the house. Despite having moved out of the Top 20 in the Nielsen ratings for the first time, *Bewitched* was ready for the '70s – and a seventh season.

With the Stephenses' new baby coming, Tabitha gets upset when she thinks her parents prefer boys. Deciding to replace herself with a boy, Tabitha zaps Jack out of her *Jack and the Beanstalk* book, then pops into the story. Samantha finds Jack in Tabitha's room and realizes that her daughter has run away through witchcraft just as Phyllis comes to visit. While Phyllis befriends Jack, Samantha pops into the book and climbs the beanstalk to look for her runaway child. At the top, Samantha meets the wife of the fairy tale giant, who warns Samantha that her husband eats trespassers.

Tabitha witches the castle guard to sleep, then introduces herself to the giant – when he becomes annoyed by her constant questions, Tabitha threatens to "make a no-no" at him. Back in the real world, Jack confuses Phyllis with details from his impoverished storybook experience. By the time Samantha reaches the castle, the hen's golden eggs aren't golden, the giant's harp plays rock music, and the giant is miniaturized. Samantha makes Tabitha restore everything and takes her home, and Jack's sudden disappearance has Phyllis questioning her sanity. Tabitha comes to understand that she is loved, and Darrin says two out of three isn't bad when he expresses love for Samantha and Tabitha, but not Endora.

GOOD!

It's nice to see the Stephenses have pulled Tabitha's crib out of storage in anticipation of their new arrival. Samantha even touches up the pony she first painted on it in "Fastest Gun on Madison Avenue" (#57).

Even though Jack, Tabitha, and Samantha are really crawling on a beanstalk mural painted on the floor, their climbs still look convincing: Darrin's hand is seen next to the book, and some of the leaves move as Tabitha brushes past them. Also, the chroma key effect the show started using in Season Five is back, deftly changing the sizes of Tabitha and the giant.

Tabitha again proves she can carry an episode, and not only is she growing, but her powers are, too – now she can pop out and shrink giants. And Erin Murphy holds her own next to powerhouse Ronald Long (assuming they didn't film their scenes separately due to the chroma key). Tabitha's battle of wits with the giant is the crowning moment of the episode, and its gems are Tabitha's changes to the castle, particularly the harp that rocks out.

The giant's other battle – with his wife – comes in a close second as she takes advantage of her domineering husband's temporarily shrunken state to vent with verve. Bobo Lewis' sarcastic wench doesn't seem like she should fit into this fairy tale world, but it's the contrast that makes her appearance work so well. And, of course, Johnny Whittaker's eager but clueless Jack ties the whole episode together.

WELL?

Endora magically honoring Darrin's request to knock should sound familiar to him – she also rapped an invisible door in "Mirror, Mirror on the Wall" (#146). Then, Endora refers to Darrin's golf equipment as a "ball and bat." Endora knows what golf clubs are – she built a whole spell around them to improve Darrin's game in "Birdies, Bogies, and Baxter" (#114). And, while Darrin threatened both Uncle Arthur and Endora with physical violence throughout Season Five, Darrin's softer approach here at least creates the illusion it's funny when he tells Endora what he wants to do with his golf club.

Tabitha has run away before, though in that instance, she stayed in the room as a raisin cookie [see

"Tabitha's Weekend" (#163)]. But it sure is noisy at the top of a beanstalk: in wide shots of Samantha and the giant's wife, there's a low roar, perhaps a dry ice or fog machine, or some other studio equipment whirring in the background. Interestingly, the giant shrinking and growing is reminiscent of last season's premiere, "Samantha's Wedding Present" (#141), in which Darrin was cut down to size and restored – the show even uses the same trumpet blare effect as the giant grows. Samantha may want to rethink chuckling at the giant's wife's vow to squash her husband under her heel, since it wasn't that long ago she also had a shrunken spouse.

Phyllis is amazed to think that Jack had a cow "in this neighborhood" – of course, she wasn't around in "The Corn Is As High As A Guernsey's Eye" (#94), when the Stephenses had a cow in that very room. Then, Jack happily wolfs down some milk and cookies – can storybook children eat real world food?

Upstairs, Darrin yells at Endora in Tabitha's room with the door open, making it easy for Phyllis to hear the in-laws arguing about Samantha, the beanstalk, and Endora's refusal to climb it in her Lili Arlege original. And Darrin knows from Lili Arlege: he bought Tabitha a playsuit by the fictitious designer in "One Touch of Midas" (#157). Endora assures Darrin that a witch can zap herself into and out of stories at whim, because, as a child, she did the same with the works of Shakespeare. That must tickle Maurice no end, but, in "Mother Meets What's-His-Name" (#4), Endora said she knew Diogenes, indicating she's about 2,500 years old; as Shakespeare lived from 1564 to 1616, Endora would have been an adult witch long before popping into his plays.

Showing Samantha that the castle's hen no longer lays golden eggs, the giant's wife says Tabitha wanted an omelet for breakfast. Has everything that's happened up to this point taken place in the early morning? Finally, after Jack vanishes, Phyllis wants the address of a qualified psychiatrist – apparently the world cruise she dragged Frank on after seeing Tabitha's magic in "Tabitha's Weekend" (#163) did nothing to shore up her nerves.

OH, MY STARS!

Getting a glimpse of Jack's fictional world is fascinating, but it conflicts with "A Prince of a Guy" (#129), where Prince Charming was plucked from the middle of his book and didn't know Sleeping Beauty was waiting for him near its end. Here, the giant and his wife both know Jack will eventually show up, as if they're privy to the entire story. Not only that, but the giant is aware that other children exist besides storybook children, and everyone's heard of witches, even though witches aren't a part of Jack's story. As for the mortal world, Jack has no clue what golf is, but the giant's wife has heard of The Rolling Stones. None of this takes away from the fun of the episode, but it seems that either the rules for fairy tale characters aren't consistent – or there are no rules.

SON OF A GUN!

"I am so a boy!" – Jack, confirming he's the gender the Stephenses supposedly prefer after he misunderstands Samantha.

There's no way to address this episode without mentioning the fact that Darrin suddenly has a new face after five seasons. Dick York and Dick Sargent are two different-looking, different-acting actors with their own takes on Samantha's mortal husband, but Dick Sargent makes a seamless transition into Morning Glory Circle. This Darrin's interactions with Tabitha, Endora, and Phyllis are completely natural, and there's no mistaking his love for Samantha, particularly in the final moments of the installment. It's regrettable that Dick York's continuing back problems forced him to step out of Darrin Stephens' shoes, but at least a capable actor is here to fill them.

SAMANTHA'S YOO-HOO MAID
Airdate: September 25, 1969

With Samantha's due date approaching, Endora, who feels her daughter should have a maid, introduces Esmeralda, an insecure witch with erratic powers. Darrin is hesitant to take on someone who fades out when she gets nervous, but he agrees to give Esmeralda a try. When Darrin wants to work at home, Endora zaps Larry into insisting Darrin report to the office so Darrin won't see Esmeralda's witchcraft acting up. Esmeralda sneezes, making the living room furniture float to the ceiling. Meanwhile, car manufacturer Hampton shows up at McMann & Tate unexpectedly; Darrin left home without his layouts, so Larry cheerfully forces Darrin into bringing Hampton over to see them.

As Esmeralda reads Tabitha a fairy tale on the patio, she sneezes up a unicorn. Just then, the businessmen arrive; Samantha takes Darrin aside to explain what's happening, and, while Larry turns his back to make a drink, Hampton momentarily floats up in his chair thanks to Esmeralda. The Stephenses try to keep Larry and Hampton away from the patio, then scramble to explain when Tabitha opens the door and reveals the unicorn; Darrin sells Hampton on the idea that the animal is the new symbol for his economy car. Later, Samantha arranges for Esmeralda to be an on-call "yoo-hoo" maid instead of a live-in maid – but even then, Esmeralda sneezes an elephant into Tabitha's room.

GOOD!

What's happening to Darrin? The man who once lost it over magically flipped pancakes [see "How Green Was My Grass" (#131)] continues exhibiting the more rational behavior he adopted in the latter half of Season Five, actually listening when Endora wants to explain why Esmeralda is acceptable as a maid. Darrin's also getting increasingly better at thinking on his feet regarding accounts, as he did while working around talking statues in "Samantha the Sculptress" (#159) – and he even chuckles as Esmeralda's elephant trumpets upstairs. Either the powers that be decided Darrin was becoming too much of a cartoon and ramped him down a bit, or they realized that Darrin should be used to witchcraft enough by now that it wouldn't make him angry all the time. The result is a much more pleasant Darrin.

WELL?

When Endora drops the ketchup bottle, it splatters in a wide swath on the floor. But when the bottle repairs itself, the shards are fewer and bigger, and the spilt ketchup is concentrated in a much tighter area. Then, as Endora pops in to hold the suspended bottle, there's a moving shadow in the left side of the frame before she appears. And, after many seasons of not exhibiting ESP, Endora predicts Esmeralda's arrival, as she would have in the show's early episodes.

Alice Ghostley makes an appearance here as new maid Esmeralda. The Tates also had a maid called Esmeralda in "Maid to Order" (#53), who went out of town on a family emergency and was replaced by Naomi, who was played by...Alice Ghostley.

Darrin decides to work at home, telling Larry he'll come into the office around noon. What's the point of that? It takes almost an hour to make the trip, so Darrin can't get much work done, anyway. Just how early is it?

Perched on her couch several feet in the air, and staring at the tree Esmeralda sneezed up, Samantha jokes she'll have to pay the gardener extra to rake up the living room. The Stephenses have a gardener?

As recently as "Daddy Does His Thing" (#167), Samantha told Darrin-as-mule to be glad he procrastinated mowing the lawn.

At the office, Larry cordially introduces Darrin to Hampton – but, in their previous scene, Larry berated Darrin for loafing during the nonexistent, spell-induced "crisis" created by Endora. Did Larry ever tell Darrin what the "crisis" was, or apologize for overreacting? Then, Darrin has egg on his face as he tells Hampton he left his layouts at home. Darrin specifically tried to work on the Hampton account in the den – was he so flustered by Larry's barking that he forgot to take them with him?

Perhaps Endora was inspired by all the mule-related chess playing in "Daddy Does His Thing" (#167), because now she challenges herself to a game. On the patio, Esmeralda reads *Sleeping Beauty* to Tabitha – a story the young witch knows well, since she zapped Prince Charming out of it in "A Prince of a Guy" (#129). You'd think Tabitha would be bored with fairy tales by now, having just lived one in the preceding episode, "Samantha and the Beanstalk" (#171).

When the unicorn first appears on the patio, it whinnies with fervor. But somehow, neither Samantha nor Endora hear it, despite sitting on the couch a few feet away. The unicorn also stays amazingly quiet the entire time Larry and Hampton are at the house – until Tabitha opens the patio door. Tabitha continually calls the creature a "funny pony," but she knows what a unicorn is: Endora brought her one in "If They Never Met" (#127), and the witchlet happily recalled seeing one at a witch zoo in "Tabitha's Weekend" (#163). Samantha describes "making" the unicorn to Hampton: "You find yourself a white pony, add a lot of glitter, and some *papier-mâché* and presto!" Of course, that's exactly how the show did it.

The Stephenses have moved their liquor to the counter that joins the living room and kitchen. Of course, if they hadn't, Larry's back wouldn't be turned when Hampton floats off the ground. Finally, it's a little odd that Samantha tells Tabitha unicorns weren't on Noah's Ark, then responds to Esmeralda's sneeze with "Bless us." Witches don't usually make Biblical references – though Noah's apparent exclusion of unicorns is an intriguing enough reason why they don't frolic through the real world.

OH, MY STARS!

When Samantha was pregnant with Tabitha In "A Very Special Delivery" (#38), Endora wanted Samantha to get "someone to help with the heavy work." Yet, when Samantha finally hired Naomi in "Maid to Order" (#53), Endora was nowhere to be seen. Then, Endora was violently opposed when Phyllis pressured Samantha into hiring help in "Samantha's Supermaid" (#154) – here, Endora is not only back to suggesting that Samantha take on a maid, but she foists one on her in a pushier way than Phyllis did. What's the takeaway here – a maid is only okay if it's Endora's idea?

Esmeralda's magical bumbling is immediately reminiscent of another witch with wonky powers – Aunt Clara, who hasn't been seen since "Samantha's Secret Saucer" (#137). Now, Marion Lorne unfortunately passed away not long after that episode lensed, but wouldn't this be a wonderful opportunity to explain Clara's absence? Perhaps the show didn't want to venture out of sitcom territory by revealing that Clara died (witches live thousands of years, but not forever) – but they could say she's on a long trip, scouring the globe for doorknobs. Or Clara could have suggested that Endora bring Esmeralda in to take over for her. Instead, Aunt Clara just fades away like Esmeralda's trees and animals – only without an explanation.

SON OF A GUN!

"Why should today be different than any other day?" – Endora to Darrin, after he suspects she's anxious to get rid of him.

Making Esmeralda invisible for a while before letting viewers see her is quite possibly the best new character reveal on the show thus far. Portrayer Alice Ghostley already shone like a diamond as inept mortal maid Naomi in "Maid to Order" (#53), so it's no surprise the show thought enough of her to bring her back as inept witch maid Esmeralda. Like Dick Sargent in the previous episode, it rather feels like Esmeralda has been on the show longer than one episode, plus, her connection to Samantha – and Tabitha, specifically – is instant.

SAMANTHA'S CAESAR SALAD
Airdate: October 2, 1969

Her hands full with Tabitha, Samantha calls on Esmeralda to make a Caesar salad, but the yoo-hoo maid produces Julius Caesar instead. Darrin is none too pleased to find the emperor in his kitchen, especially with Larry on his way over to talk business. After Samantha explains to Caesar that he came into the present by witchcraft, Larry arrives; Esmeralda tries to pop Caesar into 20th century clothes and misfires by putting Darrin in Caesar's toga. Later, while Larry tells Darrin how he plans to conquer Evelyn Charday and her Top Tiger cologne account, Samantha shows the original conquerer his place in history books. Upset over being defined a dictator, Caesar wants the texts rewritten, so Esmeralda opens the door and points him toward City Hall.

At the mayor's office, the emperor finds his way into a hippie protest group; Samantha intervenes just as the belligerent Caesar is about to be subdued by a police officer. That evening, the Stephenses stash Caesar in the den while they entertain Larry and Charday. After Esmeralda's spells fail to send Caesar back to his time, Samantha realizes that Caesar's obsession with changing history books is keeping him in the present, so she zaps up Cleopatra to entice him just as Larry and Charday walk in. Darrin invents a slogan for Top Tiger based on great romances of history, and, the next day, Esmeralda's attempt to prepare a hearts of palm salad pops a palm tree into the living room.

GOOD!

It's Caesar's reactions to the 20th century that conquer this episode. He calls Darrin's suit "binding," then displays pride, anger – and, of course, humor – as he reads about himself. As for Darrin's off-the-cuff slogan, "Top Tiger Cologne: the reason why Cleopatra let Julius seize her," it's so bad, it's good.

In the previous installment, "Samantha's Yoo-Hoo Maid" (#172), Larry looked stunned as he watched Esmeralda fading in and out. This episode silently picks up that story thread as Larry is left alone in the kitchen with Esmeralda; he seems to recognize her, and gets that funny look on his face all over again.

Herb Ellis' very serious cop is a nondescript role in and of itself, but compare it to Ellis' last appearance as the goofy Harry in "Samantha's Shopping Spree" (#169), and it becomes quite the reinvention.

WELL?

There's a sudden jump cut when Tabitha claps her hands and spills her milk. Was trickery necessary to make it appear that Erin Murphy had knocked over her moo juice? Something similar happens when Esmeralda fades into her clothes in front of Samantha, but that probably has more to do with the chroma key effect; the show had only 1969 technology to work with, but Esmeralda being invisible except for her clothes doesn't look as good as desired, especially with her yellow dress appearing white.

Of course, there are legal reasons behind it, but it's unintentionally funny that the brand names on Samantha's salad fixin's are covered over with tape. And no wonder Caesar has never heard of Caesar salad: the dish seems to have been invented by restaurateur Caesar Cardini in the 1920s, some two millennia after Caesar roamed Rome.

Darrin should know he'll end up wearing Caesar's clothes – in "Samantha's da Vinci Dilemma" (#124), Aunt Clara popped Darrin into that historical figure's garb. Larry and Caesar are in the Stephens house at the same time, but amazingly, they don't see each other; that's fortunate for the emperor, because given Larry's history of casting Samantha's visitors in commercials [see "Samantha's French Pastry" (#147)], Larry probably would have Julius hawking salad dressing.

After Caesar is zapped back into his own clothes, the scene continues with a zoom-in. Perhaps the only usable take was a wide shot, and the show opted for variety by moving in closer in post-production, but that stretch looks particularly grainy compared to the rest of the episode. When Caesar wants to have his "dictator" label stricken from the history books, Samantha says, "You can't fight City Hall" – but that's exactly what she did for the neighborhood park in (what else) "Samantha Fights City Hall" (#149). "All you have to do," Esmeralda tells the departing imperator, "is go right through this door." And what? He doesn't know what a taxi is – and even if he did, there wouldn't be many trolling Morning Glory Circle for fares.

Like Prince Charming in "A Prince of a Guy" (#129), all attempts to send Caesar back fail because he doesn't want to leave. Interesting: Uncle Arthur's return spell for Napoléon in "Samantha's French Pastry" (#147) also didn't work, yet Bonaparte couldn't wait to leave. Samantha zaps Cleopatra out of the past – without a spell, mind you – to remind the emperor what he's missing. He read about her in Samantha's history book; was the lady pharaoh never on his mind after that? At least Prince Charming had the excuse of not being aware of Sleeping Beauty's existence.

The Stephenses' den seems unusually big, with bookshelves lining the left wall. Either the den has never been shown from that perspective, or it was enlarged to make room for Cleopatra and her servants. At least the bar is back in its usual place, after it moved in "Samantha's Yoo-Hoo Maid" (#172).

Esmeralda's on a roll: during her introduction in the previous installment, she sneezed up a tree, saying she hadn't gotten one in a long time. Here, she materializes a palm, making for two trees in two episodes.

OH, MY STARS!

When Esmeralda was introduced in "Samantha's Yoo-Hoo Maid" (#172), it was established that her powers are mostly gone, and involuntary at best. Here, she casts no less than five spells very purposefully. Unable to remember her original spell, Esmeralda wants to travel back to 103 B.C. – but how does going to the year before Caesar was born help zap him out of 1969 A.D.? If Esmeralda's powers are so faint, she certainly couldn't pull off a spell that big, and when she finally does cast it, it has nothing to do with going back in time.

When Napoléon Bonaparte visited in "Samantha's French Pastry" (#147), the 19th century Frenchman could understand English, though the ruler certainly could have learned the language. Caesar and Cleopatra can also understand English, but this shouldn't be possible: Caesar spoke Greek, Cleopatra spoke Egyptian, and modern English didn't come into being until 1,500 years after their deaths. Then, Samantha cheerfully shows Caesar his future via historical accounts – including the time and place of his assassination, and his killers. Armed with this information, surely Caesar's first order of business upon his return would be to make sure the Ides of March turn out differently; Samantha's loose tongue could change the face of the modern world, all because Caesar doesn't die when he's supposed to. Too high-concept for a comedy, perhaps, unless witches' return-to-your-own-time spells come with memory erasers, which is never made clear.

SON OF A GUN!

"Is nothing sacred?" – Caesar, finding his relationship with Cleopatra splashed across Samantha's history book.

SAMANTHA'S CURIOUS CRAVINGS
EPISODE 174
Airdate: October 9, 1969

While Darrin networks with neighbors in case he's not home when Samantha goes into labor, Samantha craves chocolate cake, which suddenly appears. Samantha shrugs it off until food inconveniently pops in during a visit to Dr. Anton, her obstetrician. Later, at home, Larry wants the Stephenses to attend a business-related cocktail party, but Samantha is unable to keep him from seeing a skewer of shish kebab that came out of nowhere. After being cured by Dr. Bombay, Samantha gets a craving for a corned beef sandwich and disappears. Now going to the food, Samantha calls Darrin from a deli, so he begs off the party by hinting to Larry that Samantha is in labor.

Once home, Samantha suddenly announces that the baby really is coming – en route to the hospital, Darrin gets pulled over for speeding, but Samantha gets hungry again and disappears before Darrin can explain the emergency to the cop. At the hospital, Darrin receives a call from Samantha, who is enjoying a hot dog at a baseball stadium. After Samantha returns for admission to the hospital, Dr. Bombay pops in and runs afoul of Dr. Anton, then zaps the mortal doctor into another patient's room for a chance to give Samantha a proper cure. Later, Dr. Anton reveals that Samantha only had a false alarm – but Larry, who was to be awarded an account in celebration of her baby, wonders if he can borrow an infant from the nursery to pass off to his client.

GOOD!

Food is the star of this episode, as it pops in all over the place, especially the chop suey accompanied by an appropriately Chinese sound effect. Darrin's panic when he thinks Samantha's in labor is both funny and realistic, but Endora's knowing amusement makes the moment heartwarming. And Dr. Bombay is the zaniest he's been so far in the series, dispensing one-liners faster than any medicine he's ever prescribed. The witch doctor also evokes "And Then There Were Three" (#54) by zapping Dr. Anton into another room to give a male patient pregnancy progress, the way that episode's Nurse Kelton witnessed witchcraft in her own hospital.

Darrin makes a very good point when he asks why Dr. Bombay doesn't leave someone on call when he's unavailable, and shows he's been paying attention where Larry is concerned: telling Samantha how Larry took the news of their absence, Darrin smiles, "With his usual good grace." Larry *would* only accept going into labor as an excuse for not being at a business function – and only Larry is outrageous enough to suggest borrowing a baby to please a client, which is actually excellent continuity.

The show has a new capability this season: characters are seen driving on the road instead of sitting behind the wheel in a studio, which adds a touch of realism as Darrin rushes Samantha to the hospital. And, at the stadium, there's a graffiti heart next to the pay phone that reads, "B.A. & E.M." That can only stand for "Bill Asher and Elizabeth Montgomery" – a unique way of incorporating their real-life relationship into reel life.

WELL?

Darrin instructs Samantha to call Mr. Lutkins, their next door neighbor, should she go into labor while home alone. Mr. Lutkins must live in the house to the left (if you're facing the street), because only a gaggle of pretty ladies have ever occupied the house to the right, most recently Elaine Hanson in "Weep No More, My Willow" (#152). At Dr. Anton's office, Samantha goes to great lengths to deal with the candied apple and chop suey that pop into her hand. But what does she do with the honeydew melon – leave it as a tip?

Endora has become unusually open about divulging witchy details in front of Larry. It started in "Samantha the Sculptress" (#159), when she told him she had to be in Paris in 20 minutes; here, she confesses that she craved hummingbird wings while carrying Samantha – quite different from the discreet sophisticate Larry met in "Witch or Wife" (#8).

Dr. Bombay is delayed because he's scaling the Matterhorn. Mountain climbing must be his new hobby, because he just planted the same flag on Mount Everest in "Samantha the Bard" (#158). As they wait for him, Samantha assures Darrin that she'll do her best not to think about food at the cocktail party – that would be a feat, considering all the eatables likely to be served there.

In "Samantha's Yoo-Hoo Maid" (#172), Samantha referenced a never-before-mentioned gardener. Darrin confirms they've hired one, saying theirs could do a better job of doctoring than Bombay, who boasts that he never "bombs out." The medic has rather an inflated view of himself – is there a cure he's administered that *hasn't* backfired, at least initially? After he leaves, Samantha says that Bombay takes pulses through the left foot because he "likes to be showy." That's not the explanation he offered in "Samantha the Bard" (#158), when he pointed out that the appendage was "centrally located."

Perhaps Samantha peeked when Serena zapped a pay phone into placing a call in "Marriage, Witches' Style" (#161), because she employs the same trick to call Darrin from the deli. On the way to the hospital, the Stephenses whip past houses – though in the next shot, they're passing industrial buildings. Is quiet little Morning Glory Circle that close to a business district?

Samantha's come a long way since "Mother Meets What's-His-Name" (#4), where she could barely explain baseball to Endora; she now excitedly tells Darrin about the home run hit by Los Angeles Dodger Willie Davis. And, incidentally, Larry should let client Paxton go – who awards an account based on the birth of an employee's child, albeit drunkenly, giving that priority over whether or not the campaign is any good?

OH, MY STARS!

Endora insists to Darrin that Dr. Bombay is their most "prominent witch doctor." That seems right, as he's the only physician seen curing anyone; there was a Dr. Agrafor mentioned in "There's Gold in Them Thar Pills" (#107), but he's been absent since. Later, Samantha tells Darrin that Dr. Bombay is "the only witch doctor we have." So, which one is it: prominent or only? Then, when Samantha's cravings send her to food, she, Darrin, and Endora all lament that Dr. Bombay reversed his spell. What spell? Samantha has an illness – there's no spell to be reversed.

SON OF A GUN!

"I don't see how that would hurt – at least you'd know your child would be able to cut the mustard." – Dr. Bombay to Darrin, who fears that his baby will be born at a hot dog stand.

Dr. Anton only received off-screen mentions in "Alias Darrin Stephens" (#37) and "Take Two Aspirins and Half A Pint of Porpoise Milk" (#42), episodes that aired four years prior – so that the show puts a face to the doctor after all this time is incredible attention to detail.

EPISODE 175

AND SOMETHING MAKES FOUR
Airdate: October 16, 1969

The Stephenses' new baby is on its way, and Darrin is so flustered that he drives off without Samantha. At the hospital, Maurice pops in for the blessed event; though Maurice and Darrin are uncomfortable being in the waiting room together, they are overjoyed when they learn Samantha has had a boy. After zapping cigars into everyone's mouths, Maurice is dismayed that his grandson isn't front and center in the nursery, so he casts a spell that makes anyone who sees the infant fall in love with him. Meanwhile, the Stephenses revel in the fact that they have a son.

As a crowd gathers around the nursery, Larry falls under Maurice's spell and wants to cast baby Stephens in a baby food commercial; Darrin smells a rat, as does Samantha when she relays how the hospital is commissioning a mural of their son. Maurice pops in and admits to his spell, but he pops right back out after Darrin antagonizes him. Endora, arriving with congratulations, can't get anywhere with Maurice and frets over Larry exploiting the baby; Samantha theorizes that the Witches' Council will boot Maurice out of the Warlock Shakespearean Society for his act, which convinces him to remove his spell. At home, Samantha and Darrin are introducing Tabitha to her baby brother when a rattle appears; after the adults wonder if a newborn can exhibit powers, Tabitha admits the rattle is her "being born" present.

GOOD!

Considering that Endora was on hand when Tabitha was born in "And Then There Were Three" (#54), it's very fitting that this time Maurice is here for the birth of a grandchild. When Darrin is told he has a son, the rare warmth between him and Maurice is palpable. There's also warmth to spare as Maurice and Endora recall the night Samantha was born, disagreeing about the interplanetary details like Maurice Chevalier and Hermione Gingold singing I Remember It Well in the 1958 film Gigi; even Darrin can't help but smile at their reminiscence.

It would be enough for Maurice's spell to make onlookers fall in love with "Stephens, Boy", but turning them dopey, dreamy, and near catatonic gives the joke an extra jolt of humor. Larry even wants to trade his own son for Darrin's, worth it all by itself to hear he remembers having a child – Jonathan Tate lives! And it's a novel twist when the seemingly random Mrs. Paikowski turns out to be the daughter of the client Larry hopes to impress.

In the tag, the show wisely brings the baby home to meet Tabitha. "He's very nice," the witchlet says of her new brother. "How long is he going to stay here?" Witch or mortal, sibling rivalry is alive and well.

There's genuine suspense created when the baby seemingly gives himself a rattle, and it's exceeded only by Tabitha's endearing confession that she witched up the toy as a "being born" present. That she already loves her sibling is a great way to wrap up this game-changing episode.

WELL?

It may not have been feasible to do proper night photography for television back in the '60s, but the day-for-night technique used as Darrin backs out of the driveway without the in-labor Samantha takes away from the moment, simply because being able to discern sunlight is so distracting. If anything's dark, it's the Stephenses' car, which is navy blue again like it was in "Mrs. Stephens, Where Are You?" (#160); in "Samantha's Caesar Salad" (#173), it was green.

Though there's generally little call to discuss the show's music, much of this episode's underscore comes from Season Three. What's unexpected is that the 1966 cues don't work in a 1969 episode; styles changed so fast back then that this music, recorded only three years earlier, feels out of place. The baby also gets Tabitha's hand-me-downs in the form of her past and present themes – with all the new music composed for this season, couldn't the boy have been given a theme of his own?

In "Samantha's Curious Cravings" (#174), Dr. Anton predicted that Samantha's baby would be born in the middle of the night, and the waiting room clock indeed indicates it's 4:49 in the morning. So where *is* Anton? There are only nurses present, and not even Nurse Kelton, who was on duty when Tabitha was born; granted, that was at the Perkins Hospital, and this is Memorial. It also seems the giant's wife from "Samantha and the Beanstalk" (#171) has a real-life counterpart: Bobo Lewis is such a unique presence that it's too soon to feature her as Nurse Horgan only four episodes later. Can Nurse Horgan really not hear bassinets moving around behind her as Maurice repositions his grandson? Naturally, he'd want the boy front and center, but it's amazing Maurice doesn't whisk him off to the Warlock Club to have his powers verified. He mistakenly did that with Jonathan Tate in "My Grandson, the Warlock" (#40); surely he'd do the same for his actual grandson.

Larry doesn't need a spell on him to cast a Stephens infant in a commercial – in "Baby's First Paragraph" (#62), he wanted the supposedly talking Tabitha to peddle baby food. Here, Samantha and Darrin vehemently object to letting their son do commercials, though they didn't mind letting Tabitha take a turn at it: not only did Darrin himself push to make Tabitha the symbol for truck transmissions in "Nobody's Perfect" (#75), but Samantha zapped up a doll and called it "Tabatha" (her daughter's then-spelling) so it could help save an witched performer's reputation in "Hoho the Clown" (#92). Amazingly, Endora is upset by the idea of mortals exploiting her new grandson – but she was okay with the buzz generated from making Tabitha "talk" in "Baby's First Paragraph" (#62), and never raised an objection in "Samantha on the Keyboard" (#143), when Tabitha nearly became a touring piano virtuoso thanks to Endora's witchcraft.

Samantha gets Maurice to remove his spell by pointing out that the Witches' Council would be furious upon finding out how he is publicizing her witch-mortal marriage. Finding out? Shouldn't the Council already know? In both "It's So Nice to Have A Spouse Around the House" (#145) and "Samantha's Power Failure" (#165), they reacted instantaneously to statements and actions.

Before discovering Tabitha is responsible for the floating rattle, Samantha asks Endora if a warlock can "start that young," forgetting that, in "My Grandson, the Warlock" (#40), Maurice told her a baby warlock is born with certain powers, though they need to be developed.

OH, MY STARS!

The spell Maurice surrounds the baby with includes the line "whatever mortal sees your face will fall straightway in love with you." Whatever mortal. That means all mortals. Yet this spell has no effect whatsoever on Darrin. Does Maurice's incantation include an exemption because Darrin is the baby's father? And, for a guy who's supposed to think his child is "the greatest thing that ever happened," as Samantha says, all Darrin can muster when Larry goes on about the tyke is, "he's kinda cute."

SON OF A GUN!

"You dialed the wrong number." – Darrin to Samantha, after her calls for Maurice produce Endora.

The scene between new parents Samantha and Darrin transports the show from sitcom to heartwarming drama, helped along by the theme-quoting underscore that plays as the camera pans from roses to glowing mother. The Stephenses' original "I'm a mother!/And I'm a father!" sequence in "And Then There Were Three" (#54) was also wonderful, but this is a much stronger scene – one that somehow does a lot to cement Dick Sargent in his role as Darrin, plus this Darrin's love for, and connection to, Samantha.

EPISODE 176
NAMING SAMANTHA'S NEW BABY
Airdate: October 23, 1969

The Stephenses' newest addition receives visits from both sets of grandparents – all goes reasonably well until Maurice finds out the baby is named after Frank. The elder Stephenses are flabbergasted when objects suddenly start shattering around the room; Samantha tries to calm her father, but he wants to discuss the matter without Darrin's parents, and zaps Phyllis into insisting upon leaving immediately. Maurice then sends Endora on her way and tells Darrin that "Frank" is an unsuitable name for a warlock. Darrin infuriates Maurice by sticking to his guns and soon finds himself zapped into a mirror.

Having been despelled by Maurice, Phyllis returns with Frank and is surprised to see the mirrored "portrait" of Darrin. Samantha fibs that Maurice invented a device which projects an image into a mirror, intriguing Frank. As the grandfathers discuss Maurice's supposed innovation, Frank confides that being named after his own grandfather left him dubbed "Little Frank" by his family. After the elder Stephenses leave, Maurice zaps Darrin out of the mirror, happy that the baby can now be called "Maurice" – but Samantha thinks her son will be nicknamed "Maury," and proposes the name "Adam" instead; Darrin pretends not to like the new moniker so Maurice will accept it. Later, Frank comes by wanting to show Darrin's "picture" to a photography professional, and is disappointed to learn it "fades."

GOOD!

It's exposition, but accurate exposition, when Darrin comments that Samantha has only been home from the hospital for a week; she did indeed come home in "And Something Makes Four" (#175). And, five years and a recast later, the spark that first ignited between Frank and Endora in "A Nice Little Dinner Party" (#19) is still there – and Phyllis knows it. Other great unspoken moments come when Endora reacts to the "tremor" excuse Darrin uses to explain Maurice's temper tantrum, and later, as Endora silently realizes that Phyllis has been zapped by Maurice, her expression is pure glee.

Samantha laughs that Frank should go with number two "because they try harder" – that's a reference to the long-running slogan used by car rental company Avis; it was their trademark up until 2012.

WELL?

In "Samantha and the Beanstalk" (#171), the Stephenses went over a list of potential boys' names: James, Scott, and Timothy, in particular. Neither parent mentioned Adam, a name Samantha now says she's very fond of. Later, Frank and Phyllis declare they've waited all week to meet the baby. In "And Something Makes Four" (#175), Phyllis was said to be coming by the hospital. Was Adam not introduced to his mortal grandmother that day?

Samantha explains to the befuddled Phyllis that the ritualistic "spells" her parents cast is a family custom. So why wasn't this done for Tabitha when she was born? Frank has bought a block of stock for his ultimately temporary namesake – interesting when you consider the Kravitzes bought shares for Tabitha in the episode after her arrival [see "My Baby, the Tycoon" (#55)]. In another parallel, Darrin shows his parents a tree he planted the day their grandson came into the world; Darrin apparently also did this for Tabitha, as revealed in "Weep No More, My Willow" (#152). Whatever happened to Tabitha's dying tree once it was rejuvenated? It's not been in the front yard since.

Maurice expresses his anger through shattered objects, just as he did when first learning about Darrin's mortality in "Just One Happy Family" (#10). And, as Frank drives, he and Phyllis wheel down a real road, though no New York street would sport California palm trees.

When Samantha sighs she almost hoped for twins so she wouldn't have to hassle over namesakes, Maurice says that can be arranged. Good thing Darrin stops him – Aunt Clara already gave Jonathan Tate the double treatment in "Accidental Twins" (#78). As Maurice goes on about his grandson bearing an appropriate warlock name, Darrin snarks, "Maybe we'll be lucky this time and the baby will turn out to be 100% mortal." If Tabitha had heard that, she'd have run further away than raisin cookies and beanstalks. So much for the kinder, gentler Darrin: he blows his top with Maurice, as in days of yore.

The usual painting in the foyer is replaced by the same mirror that occupied the space in "Mirror, Mirror on the Wall" (#146), of course so Darrin can be zapped into it, which the elder Stephenses see. Funny they notice that, but not that Darrin's "image" wasn't in the mirror when they were there the first time, nor when they left. Frank surprises Maurice by admitting that being a namesake has its drawbacks; Maurice concurs. So why does Maurice still want the baby named after him? As he empathized about Frank having been called "Little Frank" all his life, wouldn't Maurice worry that the kid will likewise be called "Little Maurice?"

Phyllis asks Samantha what Maurice "does," which means one of two things: either she forgot that Serena already told her Maurice "basks" in "Mrs. Stephens, Where Are You?" (#160), or Phyllis wasn't satisfied with Serena's answer and decided to tap another source. As for Frank, he has a lot of friends in high places – in "The Dancing Bear" (#58), he summoned a toy manufacturer to investigate Darrin's Mexican jumping bean powered stuffed animal; here, he knows "the head of the number one photo outfit in the country."

OH, MY STARS!

It is apparently news to Maurice that his grandchild is to be named "Frank," but it shouldn't be. In "Just One Happy Family" (#10), Maurice didn't *want* Samantha's first-born boy named after him, which relieved Darrin because he had already promised that honor to his father. More incongruous is Samantha smiling, "You've met my father" when the elder Stephenses see Maurice; in "Mrs. Stephens, Where Are You?"

(#160), Phyllis specifically said she and Frank hadn't met Maurice, so their encounter here is their first, and should be treated as such.

Maurice must know Lord Montdrako from "I Get Your Nanny, You Get My Goat" (#122), who also zapped Darrin into a mirror – and it's as cold inside this mirror as it was inside the first. It's too distinguishable a gag to repeat less than two years later.

Maybe the reason Samantha is so fond of the name Adam is because of Darrin's old Army buddy, Adam Newlarkin, who believed in witches [see "We're In For A Bad Spell" (#39)]. Too bad Adam is another friend of Darrin's who never returned; had he visited once in a while, it would have made perfect sense for the Stephenses to name their son after him.

SON OF A GUN!

"An appellation you have to share with the lowly hot dog." – Maurice, after finding out "Frank" is not short for "Franklin."

It's the gathering of the grandfathers: Maurice interacts with Frank for the first time, and he even seems to have a certain affection for his mortal counterpart during their meeting of the minds, which leads to the twist of Frank expressing dismay over being named after his own grandfather. This progenitorial pairing is a rare combination that puts a fresh spin on the show's usual proceedings.

EPISODE 177 — TO TRICK-OR-TREAT OR NOT TO TRICK-OR-TREAT
Airdate: October 30, 1969

When Endora catches Samantha making Halloween costumes for Tabitha and the neighborhood children on behalf of UNICEF, she is outraged that Samantha would perpetuate mortal stereotypes about witches, and blames Darrin for Samantha's involvement. Darrin asserts his right to take Tabitha trick-or-treating, but when he likens Endora to one of the crone masks, he develops warts and blacked-out teeth the next day. On the way home, he is pulled over by a cop and forced to explain his witchy appearance. Darrin apologizes to Endora, saying he should have known better than to project a witch in the image he now personifies; shocked, Endora changes him back, but she makes him a hag again when he continues to protect his right to celebrate Halloween as he chooses.

Samantha backs out of trick-or-treating for UNICEF so Endora will restore Darrin, but Larry is upset because the wife of his client, Bartenbach, heads the chapter Samantha abandoned. Darrin argues with Endora and gets zapped into "costume" again; he joins Tabitha and the other children collecting candy and money for UNICEF, yielding a record-breaking donation because of his witch outfit. When Bartenbach wants to use the image for his personal care products, Samantha suggests supplanting the crone with the Good Witch of the North from *The Wizard of Oz*. Satisfied, Endora restores Darrin, who sells Bartenbach on the idea with the help of Samantha-as-Glinda.

GOOD!

A little kid like Tabitha *would* ask if she'd get more candy trick-or-treating as an ugly old witch – and Samantha's right to concur. Their discussion about witches not looking like mortals' interpretation of them borrows heavily from "The Witches Are Out" (#7), but, in the context of a mother witch sharing these ideas with her daughter, it's a wonderful exchange. And Samantha is still working with the United Nations' Children's Fund, as she did in "Samantha Twitches for UNICEF" (#166).

Darrin and Endora have been at each other's throats for five years, so to hear Endora say that he has finally pushed her too far is quite a statement, one as potentially chilling as Samantha's poufed tresses, caused by her mother's gale-force departure, are comical. Darrin's continually smooth changes back and forth into his crone costume are masterful, and he even gets something right that Uncle Arthur always got wrong: he refers to Endora as Madame Defarge. [Arthur likened his sister to *A Tale of Two Cities* villain "Madame *Le*farge" as far back as "Endora Moves in for a Spell" (#80).]

WELL?

Samantha slips a little when she tells Tabitha about witch equality. "They're just the same as everyone else," Samantha observes. Isn't she a they? After Endora zaps a real crown on Tabitha's head, she pops in, prompting Tabitha to immediately remove the crown and hand it to her mother. Tabitha just asked if she could wear it with her costume – is she that obedient regarding the house rule against witchcraft, or did she just anticipate the scene a bit?

There's never been a mirror in Darrin's office until now – of course, he couldn't look at his slowly transforming face if it wasn't there, unless he went to the washroom. At least the phantom mirror that appeared in the Stephenses' foyer in "Naming Samantha's New Baby" (#176) has once again been replaced by the usual painting. And Jean Blake is back as Betty – but, considering she last appeared as Miss Blake in "Samantha Twitches for UNICEF" (#166), it looks like Betty has quit working for E.J. Haskell and taken back her original job.

Darrin's gradual morph from mortal to misshapen is evocative of other episodes, specifically "Twitch or Treat" (#43), where he became a werewolf one step at a time, and "Samantha's Wedding Present" (#141), where he wasn't immediately aware he was shrinking. Darrin already has three arrests on his record [see "Take Two Aspirins and Half A Pint of Porpoise Milk" (#42) and "The Very Informal Dress" (#44)], and now he has two speeding tickets: here, and from "Samantha's Curious Cravings" (#174). But the cop who flags Darrin can't quite make up his mind: in one breath, he seems to at least tolerate "long-hairs," and in the next, he obliquely implies Darrin is gay based on his appearance. Rather progressive for 1969 television in either case.

Samantha has who knows how many people counting on her to make Halloween costumes for UNICEF – can she really just drop out on October 31 without repercussions? Larry couldn't have any other reaction, since he was equally annoyed that Samantha jeopardized his accounts in "Is It Magic or Imagination?" (#148) and "Samantha Fights City Hall" (#149), and UNICEF's Mrs. Bartenbach just happens to be the wife of the client McMann & Tate is courting

The crickets are chirping, but it's Halloween day-for-night as Tabitha and the gang trick-or-treat. And Darrin is on the front page of the paper yet again – though the copy that Samantha reads does match what's on the page. Speaking of accuracy, Endora's arrow hits its mark – with a little help from the black wire that is unfortunately visible in the closer shot.

Samantha adds a sparkly hat to her usual flying suit to become the Good Witch of the North; strangely, Bartenbach loves the idea of telling people that using his products will make them look like Glinda. Equally strange is Darrin's comment that the stereotype witch image is all right for kids; if you're trying to teach tolerance, aren't kids the first place to start, so that eventually tolerance won't have to be taught at all?

OH, MY STARS!

There's something off about the timeline of this episode. As it starts, Darrin insists that he's celebrating Halloween with Tabitha "tomorrow night," which indicates the current date is October 30. The next day, Darrin gets his witchy makeover on what should be on October 31 – but it isn't, because nobody's trick-or-treating. Darrin brings his original Bartenbach presentation to the office the following morning, runs afoul of Larry, lectures Samantha, and gets turned back into a hag – *then* everyone goes trick-or-treating, except it's now November 1. Finally, the Stephenses contend with the day after Halloween, which, by this example, is November 2. Either someone in the writing room made a mistake charting out this sequence of events, or Darrin misspoke when he said Halloween was "tomorrow night."

This episode borrows concepts and virtually word-for-word dialogue from "The Witches Are Out" (#7), the show's first Halloween installment. Tabitha thinks they should tell everyone they're witches because "then they'll find out what wonderful, nice people we are" – that's what Samantha's long-missing friend Mary said five years earlier. In the aforementioned episode, candy maker Brinkman was turned into a crone; here, it's Darrin. Brinkman also wanted to use an ugly witch to sell his product, like Bartenbach does now. And Larry should be having déjà vu after déjà vu listening to Darrin talk about how witches have feelings, too. All these ideas are well-integrated into the current story, but that's not enough of a reason to avoid crafting something original.

There are sharp contrasts to "The Witches Are Out" (#7) as well. That episode established that Endora flies to the south of France on Halloween to escape the ugly masks, something she also did in "The Safe and Sane Halloween" (#115); here, Endora hangs around. Samantha pointed out in the former installment that Endora thought "we should try and forget" mortals' depiction of witches, but now Endora takes the opposite stance, championing the very cause she always dismissed. And Darrin, who five years ago suggested that Brinkman go with Glinda to sell candies, has to ask, "Who?" when Samantha proposes alluding to the more aesthetically pleasing witch.

By the way, where is baby Adam in all this? He just got a name in the last episode, but is seemingly alone while his family is out trick-or-treating.

SON OF A GUN!

"I don't suppose you get lucky very often." – the traffic cop to Crone Darrin, who comments this isn't his lucky day.

"This time, I am fully aware that I am responsible for your irascible behavior." Darrin is cognizant of being the one person who knows what witches really look like, and it's unprecedented to see him make amends to his mother-in-law for going against that. Also, his turnaround in reminding Endora that his family is going trick-or-treating regardless of her opinion shows he's got a lot of backbone. [He must have looked up the meaning of "irascible" since not knowing its definition in "Snob in the Grass" (#126).]

EPISODE 178

A BUNNY FOR TABITHA
Airdate: November 6, 1969

It's Tabitha's birthday, and Uncle Arthur pops in to give her a "wish box." Tabitha wishes for a bunny rabbit, and Uncle Arthur decides to entertain at Tabitha's party with a "witchcraft show" – meanwhile, the agency's client, A.J. Sylvester, is blue because his girlfriend left him, so Larry brings him to the party to cheer him up. After performing some traditional magic tricks, Uncle Arthur casts a spell involving Tabitha's rabbit and accidentally humanizes it. Arthur can't change it back, so Samantha passes buxom "Bunny" off as his assistant; Sylvester takes an instant liking to Bunny, which unsettles Darrin. With everyone distracted, Sylvester and Bunny leave. Samantha and Uncle Arthur track them to a bar, invisibly observing Sylvester's ex-girlfriend telling him she's still available. Uncle Arthur wants to crash a Tasmanian party, but pops out after Samantha lectures him; Samantha then approaches the rabbit/human couple to invite them to a vegetarian dinner, knowing it will entice Bunny.

At the table, Sylvester and Bunny announce their engagement, which Darrin unsuccessfully tries to discourage. Samantha has better luck getting Bunny to admit she'd like hundreds of children – and when Bunny finds out that Sylvester shoots rabbits at his lodge, she slaps him and leaves. The next day, Sylvester has made up with his girlfriend, and Uncle Arthur, having gotten his powers recharged by Dr. Bombay, returns to change Bunny back – however, his spell referencing the opposite sex puts six Bunnys in the backyard.

GOOD!

It's nice to see "Samantha's Shopping Spree" (#169) wasn't wasted; here, Tabitha wears the dress bought during that Hinkley's run. The show also follows through on an unintentional boo-boo Paul Lynde makes – Uncle Arthur bops a tree branch behind him as he zaps up Tabitha's wish box, causing the branch to shake; the crew makes sure the branch is still shaking as the wish box appears, creating a fluid effect.

This episode could never work without Carol Wayne as bubbly bimbo Bunny. But Bunny's not as dumb as she looks: she's on a mission to procreate, and Wayne is aware of it. If *Larry* can tell Darrin, "Will you stop with the layouts?", then Bunny is having an effect. The comedy in this episode benefits from clever writing and the gameness of the performers: trying to get Bunny to tip her foot, Samantha tells Sylvester, "I hope you like large families," ultimately leading Bunny to smack her new beau because he calls rabbits pests – and the often uptight Darrin gets a kick out of the whole exchange, deadpanning that Bunny is "hopping mad." There's also something strikingly astute about Bunny adding that rabbits are "nicer than people."

WELL?

Darrin blows up his balloon with two hands. By the time Uncle Arthur appears in it, Darrin uses only his left hand; then, in the wide shot, the balloon is in Darrin's right. In the balloon, Arthur tells Darrin that purple isn't his best color – interesting, considering Arthur said the same thing to Samantha about black in "The No-Harm Charm" (#138).

Speaking of colors, Samantha should know that wearing this yellow dress will herald merriment from her uncle; the last time she had it on, Arthur altered her speech in "Samantha Loses Her Voice" (#150) – an episode in which the practical-joking warlock said he stopped giving hot foots 400 years ago. Sounds like he's revived the trick, as it gets him in trouble with a Tasmanian count. One other parallel: Arthur pops Darrin's balloons to service his pun, "Napoléon Balloon-Apart." Is this not a sore subject considering he had the real emperor standing in that very spot in "Samantha's French Pastry" (#147)?

Tabitha is told that whatever she uses the wish box for, she'll find inside. Samantha then fondly remembers using one to wish up a pin-striped unicorn. How could an animal that big fit in the box? Samantha recalls getting her wish box on her sixth birthday. This again brings up the question of witches and their aging process: "Eye of the Beholder" (#22) hinted that Samantha's been around since at least

1682, and Samantha reminded Darrin that she doesn't need beauty aids to keep her young in "Samantha's Caesar Salad" (#173). A witch's longer life span would indicate they have more early years, too, but Samantha referencing her sixth birthday implies that a witch's childhood is only as long as a mortal's.

A room full of kids helps Tabitha celebrate her birthday...in the middle of a business day. Why aren't these kids in school? And Larry must be especially anxious about Sylvester's account – he spirits his client the 60 miles from his office in Manhattan to Darrin's house in Patterson in 48 seconds.

Why do Samantha and Arthur pop in and out of the bar when they can just appear as miniatures on Sylvester and Bunny's booth? Yes, so Dick Wilson's latest drunk can witness it. How does no one else in the bar see this? The spot where Samantha materializes is in Sylvester's direct line of sight. As for his ex, Anita, she's awfully friendly and flirty toward a man she just dumped. And can Bunny's rabbit metabolism handle a martini? Usually bunnies are only given alcohol in labs.

After Sylvester announces his lightning-fast engagement to Bunny, Samantha asks her to help clear the table, saying she's going to have to get used to it; Bunny responds, "You're so right." Up until a few hours ago, Bunny was a bunny. How can she know about mortal things like clearing tables? And Darrin must sense something familiar as he tries to convince Sylvester not to marry Bunny – he made a similar plea to his long-gone friend Wally in "Ling-Ling" (#21), who was interested in a humanized cat.

In the tag, Samantha smiles that Sylvester and Anita could never have reconciled without Bunny. What did Bunny do to bring about their reunion besides breathily introduce herself to Anita? Notice where Uncle Arthur is pointing when he says Dr. Bombay gave him "a recharge right in my..." Did Paul Lynde sneak one by the censors? Finally, Bunny starts out as Tabitha's birthday present. Assuming Uncle Arthur manages to merge the six human Bunnys back into one cute critter, is Tabitha allowed to keep her? Or does Bunny join the kitty Darrin brought for Samantha in "The Cat's Meow" (#18) as another discarded pet?

OH, MY STARS!

Like father, like daughter! Darrin's birthday changed months between "Double Tate" (#59) and "Daddy Does His Thing" (#167), and now it's Tabitha's turn: Tabitha was born on screen in the January episode, "And Then There Were Three" (#54), but this birthday happens in November. And Tabitha's party begs three important questions: who are these kids [Tabitha had no friends as of "Playmates" (#133); has Samantha remedied this?], where is Adam (the infant wouldn't be locked away in the nursery), and where is Jonathan Tate? Darrin and Larry are supposedly best friends, but their kids aren't growing up together; the only episode Tabitha and Jonathan ever shared scenes in was "Accidental Twins" (#78).

SON OF A GUN!

"Sweetheart, it really isn't his fault – I mean, you know how fast rabbits multiply." – Samantha to Darrin, after Uncle Arthur makes sextuplets out of Bunny.

After Darrin bans Endora from his home, she tells Samantha she'll change him into a mouse at midnight unless he reconsiders. Samantha visits an apothecary, who suggests a three-part prevention spell: Darrin must touch a buffalo between the eyes, drink a potion underwater, and "fly over water by day in the dark." At the office, Larry institutes security for the Illinois Meatpackers account, while Samantha and Tabitha arrive to take Darrin to the zoo, hoping to get him near a buffalo. But Darrin's co-worker, Ralph Jackman, is a member of a Buffalo lodge, which satisfies the spell's first condition. To fulfill the second, Samantha convinces Larry to let Darrin go home sick, ultimately holding a glass of water over Darrin's head as he imbibes the necessary potion.

Samantha lies that she has to pick Serena up at the airport, maneuvering Darrin onto a helicopter; pulling a ski hat over his head completes the spell. The Stephenses are surprised to find Larry in the terminal, accusing Darrin of stealing the now-missing layouts. Darrin realizes he has switched briefcases with Ralph, who borrowed Darrin's keys and took the layouts from Larry's locked cabinet. At midnight, the contrite Ralph visits Darrin as Endora's spell calls for the mortal under the roof to become a mouse; Samantha panics when she sees a rodent, but the transformee is Ralph, whom Samantha deems "a funny looking buffalo."

GOOD!

It's a novelty for Samantha to know about one of Endora's spells ahead of time – the conditions of Samantha's "anti-spell" are daunting, but the creative ways Samantha satisfies them by playing on their wording also satisfies.

There's nice attention to detail in this episode. Darrin remarks "it's an hour's drive to the airport," which is accurate considering Patterson is 60 miles out of New York City. Then, after Samantha talks Darrin into the helicopter ride, she says, "I'll tell Esmeralda we're leaving" – so that's who's been taking care of Adam when it seemed the Stephenses left their newborn alone. Samantha lies that Serena is into doing things the mortal way, but it's not that far-fetched: Samantha's cousin eschewed witchcraft trying to hook a human husband in "Marriage, Witches' Style" (#161), then was forced to do manual labor in "Samantha's Power Failure" (#165). And, at the airport, though Larry suspects Darrin of stealing the Illinois Meatpackers layouts, he doesn't want it to be true, which humanizes the often one-dimensional ad man.

WELL?

Endora zips Darrin's lip literally, a tactic she used to silence Serena in "Samantha's Power Failure" (#165). It's not the first time Samantha has gotten soaked in that blue dress, either: here, it's because of Endora's kitchen downpour; in "Marriage, Witches' Style" (#161), it was Serena's champagne that did the dousing.

This episode introduces Postlethwaite, an apothecary who offers potions and other magical solutions. Has he always been around? In "Take Two Aspirins and Half A Pint of Porpoise Milk" (#42), Aunt Clara sent Darrin to a similar shop located in the mortal world. And has Dr. Bombay been getting his ingredients from Postlethwaite all this time?

Larry has taken work-related security measures before: in "Dangerous Diaper Dan" (#82), he handcuffed a briefcase to Darrin's wrist when a rival agency was after their campaign ideas. The current layouts are missing, but so is the phantom mirror that showed up in Darrin's office in "To Trick-or-Treat or Not to Trick-or-Treat" (#177).

Ralph is a bundle of coincidences: he just happens to be a member of the Loyal Order of the Buffaloes the minute Samantha needs one, he's at the airport just in time to run into the Stephenses and switch briefcases, and he shows up on Darrin's door just when Endora's spell needs to bounce onto another mortal. And he completely misses the paint Samantha smudges on his head, despite wiping the exact spot with a handkerchief.

It's one thing for Darrin to grudgingly take the medicine Samantha offers, but surely he'd at least question what the elixir is for. The bottle has no label, and Darrin should catch on that there's magic involved, especially after he hears the indicator bell a second time.

Samantha gets Darrin aboard a helicopter, saying she needs to be at the airport to meet Serena in 20 minutes. It could take some or all of that time just driving to the heliport, and that's assuming there's a helicopter ready for take off as soon as the Stephenses get there.

What does Ralph stand to gain by stealing the layouts? He's on his way to Chicago, so he can't be taking them to competitor Frazer & Kolton; they're also in New York. Is he taking them to the Illinois Meatpackers' home office in hopes of opening his own agency? His motivation is never made clear. Then, finding Darrin with the stolen layouts, Larry tells him he's under arrest. Neither Larry nor the security guard have the power to make arrests; if Larry means a citizen's arrest, he should specify.

There's a new clock in the dining room to indicate that it's midnight, but it chimes fourteen times instead of twelve. After Endora casts her mouse spell, Samantha is actually surprised that Endora wants to go into the kitchen to make sure it worked. And Darrin just hangs out by the cellar/closet/laundry room door, when Endora could easily walk in and see him standing there.

At least Ralph can evade the police during his 1-2 week stint as a mouse – surely Larry's called the law. But Ralph must have friends and/or family who will be worried about him being missing that long, which no one considers.

OH, MY STARS!

Much of the material in this episode is lifted from "We're In For A Bad Spell" (#39), where Darrin's Army buddy, Adam Newlarkin, was forced into a similar triptych of rituals to avoid being branded a common thief. Instead of buffaloes, underwater potions, and dark flying, Adam had to kiss a spotted dog, get dunked three times, and champion witches on horseback – also without being aware he was enacting a spell. Here, Ralph's unbelievably identical briefcase containing the stolen layouts is switched with Darrin's, the way Adam's was switched with a bank employee trying to make off with a cache of cash. And, in both episodes, the satisfaction of a spell component is announced with an audible signal. This episode is still entertaining as a stand-alone, but this is the second near-remake so far this season [the first being "To Trick-or-Treat or Not to Trick-or-Treat" (#177)]. *Bewitched* is a show with oodles of originality; why copy episodes?

The final component of Samantha's anti-spell is that Darrin must fly over water by day, in the dark. All goes well until the Stephenses are in the helicopter, presumably on the way to one of New York City's major airports from Patterson. The thing is, there are no bodies of water, or at least nothing the size of what's shown, between these cities.

SON OF A GUN!

"Now, all I have to do is put the potion in there, and get him to stick his head under the water." – Samantha, contemplating using a nozzle to complete the second part of the spell.

It's hard to believe: the grizzled apothecary of this episode and last episode's sophisticated client A.J. Sylvester are played the same actor. Bernie Kopell proves he is a master of reinvention, giving even the shape-shifting Cliff Norton a run for his money.

Hearing about Endora's imminent mouse spell, Darrin finally asks a question that looms every time she uses her witchcraft on him: "I know your mother doesn't care about me," he tells Samantha, "but how about you and the kids?" Indeed – Tabitha must feel awful knowing her beloved grandmama hates her even more beloved daddy so much. It's brilliant that the show finally addresses this very large elephant – make that mouse – in the room.

DADDY COMES FOR A VISIT
Airdate: November 20, 1969

EPISODE
180

In honor of his first grandson, Maurice gifts Darrin with a watch that can be used to perform witchcraft. Darrin refuses to accept it, so Maurice turns him into a dog. Samantha gets her father to reverse the transformation by quoting Shakespeare, and Darrin is hard pressed to deny Maurice's contention that he should try the magical life, since Samantha has lived like a mortal for five years. Darrin agrees to use the watch for a day; once Maurice shows him how to pop into the office with it, Larry is confused because he just talked to Darrin at home. After invisibly sitting in on Darrin's not entirely successful presentation to Bliss Pharmaceuticals, Maurice suggests Darrin attend the Bliss board meeting the same way and takes him to lunch in Hong Kong. When Darrin won't use the watch to advance himself, Maurice hypnotizes him into changing his mind.

Eavesdropping on the Bliss executives, Darrin hears that they're going with a rival's old-fashioned approach rather than McMann & Tate's modern one. Darrin pops back to the office and persuades Larry to change their campaign based on his "inside information." High on the power, Darrin comes home and tells Samantha they're going to live by witchcraft, which has Samantha very, very worried.

GOOD!

Maurice tells Samantha that he's entered Adam for membership in the Warlock Club. This is consistent, considering Maurice took Jonathan Tate to the magical lodge by mistake in "My Grandson, the Warlock" (#40). It's also insightful of Maurice to observe that Darrin's refusal to allow witchcraft stems from feeling inferior in comparison to it. Samantha has lived the mortal life for five years without complaint; Maurice is fair-minded to suggest that Darrin use the watch.

Bliss, Jr.'s definitely/maybe pendulum swinging during his meeting with McMann & Tate is rather karmic payback for Larry, who purposely makes on-a-dime changes to brown-nose his clients. Larry does essentially threaten to fire Darrin by confirming that he's staked his job on his inside information, but he hasn't made that threat since "Going Ape" (#162), nor has Larry actually fired Darrin since "Instant Courtesy" (#153). It's a much more effective plot device when it's used sporadically like this.

WELL?

Samantha notes that her baby is ten weeks old; considering he was born in "And Something Makes Four" (#175), the tyke can only be five weeks old. Then, Maurice gets very specific about the fancy witches' breakfast he wants – yet he was perfectly happy eating a mortal lunch in "Samantha's Good News" (#168).

Samantha apparently took note when Maurice recited Shakespeare's "the quality of mercy is not strained" from *The Merchant of Venice* in "Daddy Does His Thing" (#167), because she wisely baits her father with the quote to get him to un-dog Darrin; in turn, Darrin thanks Maurice "from the bottom of my jowls," much as he did "from the bottom of my withers" in the aforementioned mule-morphing episode. And, while Maurice reminds Darrin that Samantha has acquiesced to the mortal life for "five long years," this correct chronology actually conflicts with "Samantha's Wedding Present" (#141), which stated that the Stephenses celebrated their fifth anniversary a year ago. Perhaps Maurice's observation is meant to calibrate the show's timeline?

Darrin now has an idea how Aunt Clara felt as he pops out without his shoes; she unintentionally went shoeless in both "The Trial and Error of Aunt Clara" (#95) and "Out of Sync, Out of Mind" (#116). Darrin's technical, purposely confusing mind-over-matter explanation of his sudden presence is fun, but it still doesn't tell Larry how he dialed the Stephens house and got Darrin's office instead.

Maurice whisks Darrin to Hong Kong to discuss the watch over lunch. When they arrive, it's daytime, but there's a thirteen-hour time difference between New York and Hong Kong; if Maurice and Darrin were to leave Manhattan at noon, they'd be at the restaurant at one o'clock the next morning. Then, Maurice threatens to strand Darrin in China for refusing to be dishonest in his business dealings – how did Samantha end up with so much integrity? Finally, Maurice's "sparkle of a star" speech is captivating, but Darrin already knows it – he cited part of it when he was upset with Samantha for ghost chasing in "McTavish" (#130); Endora also used it as an anti-mortal argument in "Be It Ever So Mortgaged" (#2) and "How to Fail in Business With All Kinds of Help" (#104). Is this just a big saying in Samantha's family?

No wonder Bliss Pharmaceuticals likes the old-fashioned approach: their board room was Omega National Bank's office in "The No-Harm Charm" (#138), as well as E.J. Haskell's in "Samantha Twitches for UNICEF" (#166). Darrin reminds Bliss, Jr. that their sales have dropped 23% in five years owing to their antiquated advertising techniques. So what does Bliss do? Stick with the exact same mail order approach that's put them in the red. Then, they give McMann & Tate another crack at their account – after the entire board already voted to give it to Gilbey.

Ready to embrace a life of witchcraft, Darrin tells Samantha that he married her for who she is, and that, if he loves her enough, he has to accept that. Those are noble words, but they're also word-for-word what he told her when she became a monarch in "Long Live the Queen" (#108). Darrin also thinks that minks might be extinct by the time he can afford to buy Samantha this type of coat, not knowing that Endora made the same mink/extinct observation in "The Girl With the Golden Nose" (#73), and forgetting that he already bought Samantha a mink in that same episode. She also received a separate coat with mink trim from him in "Cheap, Cheap" (#112).

OH, MY STARS!

Maybe Darrin doesn't remember the events of "A is for Aardvark" (#17) because of the memory-erasing spell he had Samantha put on him. And maybe real-time viewers weren't likely to recall an episode that aired five years earlier. But someone in the writing room remembered, because said episode is where

Darrin was first seduced by magic. This installment borrows that concept, and several lines, including Maurice's claim that Darrin has "opened the forbidden can of peas." Another blast from the past is that Maurice just offered Darrin a witchcraft-charged gift in "Daddy Does His Thing" (#167), and turned Darrin into an animal for refusing it. A final parallel is the repeated use of the watch-activating spell, *zolda, prancan, kopec, lum*; in "The Witches Are Out" (#7), this incantation was only used to pour tea. So how can it enable the watch to do everything Darrin commands it to?

When Darrin refuses to use the watch to win the Bliss account, Maurice seems to lull his son-in-law with a type of hypnosis; he doesn't use an incantation, but he does zap Darrin out of the stupor. Setting up for a cliffhanger, Darrin exclaims that he knew Samantha would be thrilled with his decision to embrace witchcraft. Now, Darrin must be under a spell, because he's been with Samantha long enough to know she'd be anything but thrilled. But it's hard to tell whether Maurice hexed Darrin or not, and either option drastically changes the stakes: Darrin choosing magic of his own free will would have much more serious implications.

J. Edward McKinley and John Fiedler are two terrific character actors, but their appearance as father and son rather defies logic. Not only did McKinley just play auto maker Hampton in "Samantha's Yoo-Hoo Maid" (#172), but McKinley was born in 1917; Fiedler, in 1925. Even a show about witchcraft can't make actors with only an eight-year age difference look like senior and junior.

SON OF A GUN!
"'Shanghaied you to Hong Kong'? That pun is worthy of Uncle Arthur." – Maurice to Darrin, knowing a thing or two about his brother-in-law.

DARRIN THE WARLOCK
Airdate: November 27, 1969

EPISODE 181

Following the events of "Daddy Comes for a Visit" (#180), Samantha is sure Darrin will give up using Maurice's magic watch and revert to living like a mortal. After Maurice refreshes Samantha's memory of previous events by projecting an image onto the refrigerator, Darrin decides to zap up a French feast for breakfast. Popping into the office, Darrin experiments by floating a book to himself, but Larry catches him; Darrin explains it away, then is offered a hefty bonus for the "inside info" he scored regarding Bliss Pharmaceuticals. Samantha insists to Darrin that she wouldn't stay if she didn't enjoy being a housewife, but sadly honors Darrin's wish to keep living by witchcraft.

When Larry can't make sense of Darrin's magical comings and goings, Darrin demonstrates his "mind over matter" technique by correctly guessing what Betty had for breakfast. Larry excitedly predicts great wealth and power, but Samantha's words echo in Darrin's head, causing him to rethink the magical life. Darrin returns the watch to Maurice, but, during a dinner for Bliss and his son, Maurice zaps the timepiece over to Darrin to tempt him. Darrin holds to the modern concept he devised before eavesdropping on the Blisses, jeopardizing the account and his job. Maurice leaves in a thunder-and-lightning huff, and, the next day, Larry announces that Bliss awarded the account to McMann & Tate based on Darrin's integrity.

GOOD!

Early on, the series' witches (Endora especially) made frequent and astute comments about humans and their habits, but not so much in recent years – so it's refreshing for Maurice to subtly mention that work is "the all-consuming possessor of mortals." For Darrin's part, it's fascinating that he tells Samantha, "I've made you live like a mortal for so long that you're beginning to act like one": Samantha's certainly not the naïve witch she was five years ago.

For once, the Stephenses don't take one of Larry's firings lying down. Samantha announces to Darrin that "an ex-friend of yours is here" – then, when Larry requests Darrin's signature on the Bliss contract as if nothing happened, Darrin scoffs, "Me? Oh, you fired me." The Stephenses know by now that Larry will probably put Darrin back on the payroll – but at least they make him sweat it out a bit first.

WELL?

Samantha is unusually chipper at the top of the episode, considering she's had all night to brood about Darrin embracing witchcraft. And though Maurice "tuning in the refrigerator" is one of the more unique ways the show has recapped the first part of a two-part episode, he already cast a similar reminder projection into a painting in "Daddy Does His Thing" (#167). By the way, how is Maurice able to display events he didn't personally witness, such as Darrin's private "today Bliss Pharmaceutical, tomorrow the world" moment? Does the magic watch have a secret recording device?

Darrin tests his powers by making a book float to him; he also levitated a book in "A is for Aardvark" (#17), which he doesn't remember thanks to Samantha blanking his memory. It hardly seems possible that Larry considers mind over matter "bunk," since he told Darrin to tap into exactly that to conquer a "toothache" in "To Trick-or-Treat or Not to Trick-or-Treat" (#177). And, *zolda, prancan, kopec, lum* has to be uttered or thought about to access the watch's magic – yet Darrin is able to say "Book, return" and "Take me to Samantha" aloud, apparently thinking out the spell simultaneously. That shows more versatility than walking and chewing gum at the same time.

After telling Samantha their doing without is over – a sentiment he already expressed in previous installment "Daddy Comes for a Visit" (#180) – Darrin inquires into Maurice's whereabouts, wanting to tell him "the good news." Why didn't Darrin tell him the night before, after he told Samantha? Or at breakfast, when it was just the two of them at the table? Samantha is surprised to hear that Darrin used the watch to obtain "inside info," even though Maurice just told her about it during the refrigerated recap. And Samantha's "you may have given up but I haven't" speech is still powerful, but it's what she told Darrin almost verbatim after he "repealed Prohibition" in "The No-Harm Charm" (#138).

Apparently Larry threatens to fire everyone on his staff over nothing; Betty almost gets axed for not jotting down what she ate for breakfast. Larry must be so blinded by greed that he can't see Darrin popping into his office, despite making it to the doorway by the time Darrin appears. But Darrin obviously comes to feel very strongly about giving up the watch – he takes a 60-mile cab ride, which can't be cheap.

In "Samantha's Good News" (#168), Maurice's rival, John Van Millwood, boasted that William Shakespeare deemed his performance the best of the warlocks. Here, Maurice indicates that "Will" *is* a warlock. Later, when Maurice returns, neither Bliss Sr. nor Jr. see him pop in, despite facing his direction while talking to Larry.

Historically, Larry is often the definition of two-faced to please a client, but, in this episode, he outdoes himself like never before. Can the Blisses not see through this brown-nosing? Not that they'd know he already used his "doesn't feed the bulldog" line in "My, What Big Ears You Have" (#121). Darrin also revisits what he told Endora in "How to Fail in Business With All Kinds of Help" (#104) by noting that Maurice threw the Bliss account into his lap, so he's throwing it out.

Maurice needs a new way to express anger: he just shattered objects five episodes ago, in "Naming Samantha's New Baby" (#176). Plus, he should check with Endora before underscoring a pop-out with thunder and lightning; Endora departed just that way in "To Trick-or-Treat or Not to Trick-or-Treat" (#177).

OH, MY STARS!

As a way of reminding viewers what happened in "Part I," Maurice recalls how easily Darrin accepted his "magic gift." Easy? Maurice had to turn Darrin into a dog first, and later had to hypnotize his son-in-law before he'd even consider using the watch to get ahead. And the question remains: did Maurice put a spell on Darrin? He must have – but surely Darrin couldn't break it just by deciding he's had enough of the watch's magic. As for Samantha, if there's a spell in play, she should sense it; the last time Darrin wanted gourmet delicacies was in "The Battle of Burning Oak" (#164), where Samantha quickly sussed out Endora's snob spell. Is Samantha so much in denial this time that she really thinks Darrin is just indulging Maurice's whim?

Secretary Betty finds her seventh incarnation here in Irenee Byatt [whatever happened to Jill Foster's Betty? She went into the Stephenses' kitchen for a cup of coffee in "One Touch of Midas" (#157) and never came out], replacing Jean Blake's Betty of "Samantha's Secret Spell" (#179). What makes the recast significantly glaring is that Byatt's Betty is quite a bit older than Blake's. Betty should also feel like she's done this before: in "The Girl With the Golden Nose" (#73), Darrin thought Samantha was magically fixing things for him, and bet Betty that she wasn't actually born in Minneapolis, resulting in the discovery that she was born in Saint Paul. At least Darrin doesn't rock Betty's world this time.

"You remember Larry Tate," Samantha says to her father. Once again, important characters are said to have met off-screen – to audiences, Maurice and Larry have never set eyes on each other until now. Samantha also had Larry pegged in "I Confess" (#135), programming his predicted reaction to witchcraft into Darrin's dream: Larry aspired to juggling the stock market and seizing control of the national economy, owing to the fact he's wanted to rule the world ever since he was a little kid. Here, Larry shares the exact same ambitions with Darrin, only this time, everyone's awake. It's a wonder Darrin doesn't have a déjà vu hearing Larry quote from his dream.

SON OF A GUN!

"French toast is...well, it isn't French, and it isn't toast, and that gives you an idea of what you're going to be up against in this world." – Samantha to Adam, serving up a life lesson with breakfast.

SAMANTHA'S DOUBLE MOTHER TROUBLE
Airdate: December 4, 1969

EPISODE 182

Tabitha asks for nursery rhymes to be read aloud, but Adam gets hungry, so Samantha calls for Esmeralda to take over. Unable to control a sneeze, Esmeralda materializes Mother Goose just as Phyllis arrives seeking refuge after a fight with Frank; Samantha is forced to introduce Mother Goose as an aunt. Frank comes by to square things with Phyllis, who is upset that her husband obliquely disapproved of her modern, groovy outfit. Mother Goose thinks everyone she meets is a character from her rhymes; Frank is impressed with the "old-fashioned lady" and engages her in conversation. Darrin comes home from his golf game, unhappy to find his house in an uproar.

When Darrin can't pull his father away from Mother Goose, Samantha makes sure Phyllis sees them together, twitching Frank into making quaint overtures toward the fictional author. Samantha's ploy to inspire jealousy in Phyllis is about to work when Esmeralda sneezes again, turning Mother Goose into an actual goose. Frank and Phyllis witness the transformation and make up on the basis that they're going over the hill together. Samantha thinks Darrin should thank Esmeralda for reuniting his parents, so Darrin silences his wife with a kiss.

GOOD!

Through Esmeralda, the show further explores the inner workings of witchcraft as she reasons out how she conjured up Mother Goose: "the involuntary act [of sneezing] generates abnormal powers which materialize the thought nearest my cerebellum." This neatly ties in to the "zonk across the atmospheric continuum" explanation Samantha offered when Uncle Arthur zapped up Napoléon in "Samantha's French Pastry" (#147).

It seems perfectly natural for Mother Goose to perceive everyone around her as figures from her rhymes – Darrin being labeled "Georgie Porgie" is probably the best example. And, for once, Samantha tattling to an anachronistic visitor about the 20th century presents no danger to the timeline, since Mother Goose is a fictional character that can't influence history.

Phyllis as "the woman of tomorrow" is an intriguing reinvention of the typically bourgeois matron – but her behavior is rooted in the past. "I have left Frank forever," she announces melodramatically. "Again?" Samantha replies, and rightly so – Phyllis also ditched her husband in "A Nice Little Dinner Party" (#19) and "Out of Sync, Out of Mind" (#116). The sick headaches Mrs. Stephens has had over the course of the series are too numerous to list [they've plagued her since "Samantha Meets the Folks" (#14)], but her theatrical addition, "Why should I bore you with the details of my throbbing pain" rather three-dimensionalizes the malady. Phyllis never drank sherry until "Mrs. Stephens, Where Are You?" (#160), but she also chugged it in "Tabitha's Weekend" (#163), so it's great continuity that she pours it for herself here and takes the whole bottle upstairs with her. And the relatively new Esmeralda quickly figures Phyllis out, wryly commenting to Samantha, "We know *she's* not going to fade."

WELL?

Samantha's tongue sharpens in this episode, at least in talking to herself: when Darrin plays golf instead of staying home to help out, Samantha snarks, "I hope you get a caddy that snickers." As he is about to discover Mother Goose in the house, she says, "Just what I needed – Little Boy Blue to come blow his cool." And, in response to Darrin wanting to try "the direct mortal approach" on his father, Samantha rolls her eyes, smiling, "Gee. I wish I'd thought of that." Has Samantha built up some unspoken resentment against her hubby?

Both here and in "Is It Magic or Imagination?" (#148), Phyllis heralded her arrival by calling from a corner drugstore. It must be fairly new; Darrin used to have to go "into the village" to buy the most rudimentary items, and Samantha needed a hot water bottle delivered in "There's Gold in Them Thar Pills" (#107). In any case, it's odd there's a drugstore on a residential street like Morning Glory Circle.

Phyllis, who pushed for Samantha to hire help in "Samantha's Supermaid" (#154), now compliments "that fabulous Esmeralda." But how does Phyllis know about her? Esmeralda only first arrived in "Samantha's Yoo-Hoo Maid" (#172), and she's never met Phyllis – on-screen anyway.

Nursery rhymes attributed to Mother Goose date back to the 1600s; the first book to make mention of "her" (whether or not she was real is disputed) was published in 1695. The book this Mother Goose is sneezed out of must be a more modern publication, otherwise she wouldn't know about iceboxes, which only came into use in the mid-1800s. Curiously, Tabitha wants Mother Goose to recite *Hey Diddle Diddle*, though Samantha just did – and the girl never got an answer from her mother as to why the dish ran away with the spoon; Tabitha has the opportunity to get it straight from the source, but never does.

As Phyllis sits on the couch, the footage is its usual good quality, but when the scene cuts to Samantha and Mother Goose, it's very grainy; obviously, the duo was filmed at a wider angle, and a decision was later made to magnify them.

Frank knows Phyllis is at the house, because she left a note in his money clip. Wouldn't her car also be in the driveway, unless she took a taxi? Likewise, Darrin has to be told his parents are there, despite the fact that his parents' car(s) is/are parked in front of his house.

In the den, with the door open, Samantha tells Darrin how Mother Goose arrived. With the elder Stephenses roaming around, is this wise? Then, Samantha and Darrin, who rants as of olde, blame each other's family for the current fracas – except Esmeralda isn't family.

Esmeralda feels it's her fault Frank is flirting with Mother Goose. But how can Esmeralda know that? She went upstairs to fix up the guest room for Phyllis before Frank ever arrived. In early seasons, the guest room was the last door on the right. Over time, the master bedroom took over that space, and the former master bedroom is either Tabitha's room or Adam's nursery; it must be the nursery, because Samantha peeks down to the patio from a never-before-seen window after "tending to Adam's appetite." So where is this giant guest room where Phyllis nurses her sick headache, which also looks down on the backyard?

Phyllis removes her funkalicious wig in order to lie down. Isn't part of her gripe that she wants to be a modern woman? She no longer looks like one with her own hair, and it's not like she can't snooze in the wig, which she leaves behind when she takes off with Frank. What are Darrin and Samantha supposed to do with it?

OH, MY STARS!

The main comedy of the show comes from keeping its mortals in the dark regarding any witchcraft they witness. But Frank and Phyllis Stephens should have clued in by now. Frank blanches while seeing a goose and floating glasses; this after seeing strange things in "It's Wishcraft" (#103) and "Tabitha's Weekend" (#163). Phyllis claims here that she's *starting* to see things, when she made a production out of seeing things in "It's Wishcraft" (#103) – and she's certainly noticed unusual events since then. Besides, Aunt Clara told her in-laws that she and Samantha are witches in "Samantha Meets the Folks" (#14), which Samantha jokingly "confirmed" – so why would Samantha provide Phyllis with a reminder by saying that her family is "wacky as witches?" Frank and Phyllis having short memories may be a part of the self-contained nature of each episode, but when you take the series as a whole, Mr. and Mrs. Stephens seem either clueless or in denial for not acknowledging what's right in front of them.

SON OF A GUN!

"Oh, my goose – it's Mother Stars!" – Samantha, inverting her trademark phrase at the sight of the nursery rhyme "author."

As this book is generally meant to discuss continuity, there's not much call to explore what goes on behind the scenes unless it has to do with a special effect or noteworthy performance. But it's worth pointing out that David White, who plays lovable, bootlicking Larry, directs this episode – and skillfully.

EPISODE 183
YOU'RE SO AGREEABLE
Airdate: December 11, 1969

At Samantha's insistence, Darrin tries to be pleasant to Endora, who refuses to reciprocate. After Samantha complains that everyone but Endora finds Darrin agreeable, Endora zaps him into a state of excessive agreeability; he signs an absurd petition of Gladys', then concurs with everything conservative client Shotwell says, despite contradicting himself. Shotwell writes Darrin off as a yes-man and storms out the door, causing Larry to give Darrin extended time off without pay. Realizing he's been fired, Darrin considers an opening at a rival agency, so Samantha uses her powers to plant Darrin's name everywhere she can with that company's bigwig.

Darrin is hired at the new firm, but, between agreeing to a significantly lower salary and joining Gladys' ridiculous committee, Samantha realizes Endora's been at it again. Endora removes her spell with the incantation *lleps eht esrever*, after which Darrin becomes unusually ill-tempered. Just as Samantha figures out Endora meant "reverse the spell," Larry comes over to apologize and take Darrin back. But when Darrin practically throws Larry out, Samantha freezes the men and insists Endora return things to normal. Darrin and Larry celebrate their reunion, and later, the Stephenses are heading out for their own celebration when Gladys comes over to retrieve Darrin, who promised to address her committee. Darrin doesn't remember agreeing to it, but Samantha persuades him to make a speech anyway to keep Gladys happy.

GOOD!
Given that the show's mortals are kept blissfully unaware of the witchcraft going on around them, it's a terrific inclusion when Larry notes that Darrin sometimes goes overboard with clients, and tells Shotwell that Darrin has a peculiar sense of humor – it means Larry's been paying attention the last five years. And Endora's "disagreeable" spell might be mean, but it finally gives Darrin a chance to express some unfiltered feelings about Larry firing him yet again. Samantha seems to be on this wavelength as well – usually, she twitches her nose to keep Darrin and Larry in business, but here, she quietly advises her husband, "Maybe it's time you made a change," even going so far as to magically help him get hired elsewhere. The continuing theme of Larry's firings benefits from these novel twists.

WELL?
After Darrin huffily chastises Samantha for floating a plate to herself, she asks him to come back in and act as if it never happened – and he does. Isn't he too annoyed to just forget like that? And the effect of Samantha putting the broken plate back together is nearly perfect, except for her hair giving away the reversed footage.

Darrin relishes the fact that it's been 3 days, 8 hours, and 45 minutes since Endora's last appearance, but it's really been four weeks – Endora hasn't been seen since she tried to turn Darrin into a mouse in "Samantha's Secret Spell" (#179). How can Endora ethereally "hear" Darrin's request for advance notice, but not Samantha coaching him to be agreeable seconds later?

Darrin volunteers to "duck out the back way" to avoid Gladys, which is futile considering that door is in plain view of her house – and Samantha tells Gladys that Darrin has left already, when his car is still in the driveway. Darrin takes the petition from Gladys and signs it – then it's back in Gladys' hand, but Darrin is never seen giving it back to her.

Champion brown-noser Larry now knows what he sounds like, listening to Darrin agree with anything a client says; too bad Larry doesn't have a moment of clarity seeing himself in Darrin. Larry advises Darrin not to compromise his principles, which is odd, considering he just fired Darrin for sticking to his principles in "Darrin the Warlock" (#181).

In "Follow That Witch (Part II)" (#67), Samantha told Darrin that she promised herself being a witch wouldn't interfere in his career. Maybe, to her, there's a difference between being a witch and using witchcraft, because she definitely interferes here. When she pops in outside Washburn's office, she reaches for the door, but is stopped by the exiting mortals. What does she think she's going to do once she gets inside?

Her Washburn mission accomplished, Samantha pops back into the kitchen, although that's where Darrin was when she left. Does she have some sort of witch GPS that tells her to appear in the kitchen to avoid being seen by Darrin and Gladys in the living room? Later, when Endora utters *lleps eht esrever*, Samantha asks, "What kind of an incantation is that?" It shouldn't sound unfamiliar: all witches, including Samantha, cast spells using whimsical words of this type instead of English throughout Seasons One and Two.

Though the disagreeable Darrin is engulfed in his newspaper, he should still be able to see Samantha's giant cursive letters in his peripheral vision. Failing that, he should hear her finger snaps and bark that she isn't making the drink he demanded. As the bespelled Darrin battles the unusually sheepish Larry, Samantha zaps at them in a flamboyant gesture, both to freeze and unfreeze them. Shouldn't Larry, especially, wonder why Samantha is snapping her fingers in their faces?

Samantha finally breaks down Endora's beef with Darrin: "She just doesn't care for mortals." Darrin replies, "Well, I'm going to be one as long as I live" – a strange statement for him to make, considering only weeks ago, he was, for all intents and purposes, a non-mortal [see "Daddy Comes for a Visit" (#180) and "Darrin the Warlock" (#181)]. It's also incongruous that Darrin doesn't remember the agreements he made while under Endora's spell; generally, he always has total recall of his witchcraft-influenced movements.

OH, MY STARS!

When Samantha asks Darrin why he signed Gladys' petition, he says, "Just to be agreeable, I guess." Then, after Larry fires him, Darrin tells Samantha that Shotwell hates people who disagree with him. Samantha just told Endora that everyone finds Darrin agreeable – shouldn't the repeated instances of the word clue Samantha in to Endora's spell long before it does? And how does *lleps eht esrever* make Darrin cantankerous? Reversing the spell should restore him to normal, not take him to the other extreme.

J. Edward McKinley might have shaved his mustache since "Daddy Comes for a Visit" (#180) and "Darrin the Warlock" (#181), but that doesn't distract from the fact that he just appeared as a different character two weeks ago. In those episodes, McMann & Tate also handled a pharmaceutical company run by a conservative client who used an ineffective, old-fashioned ad campaign. Why the duplicate story point so soon?

Samantha magically gets Darrin hired by Washburn, who has never heard of Darrin, yet somehow knows his home phone number. (Darrin must be listed in the white pages.) But later, when Larry comes to apologize, Darrin never throws his new job in his ex-boss' face, so there's not much point to Darrin accepting another position. And Darrin is expected to report to Washburn the next day; how does he get out of it when he chooses to return to McMann & Tate? The show never resolves it; Darrin taking a new job nearly puts a new, refreshing spin on Larry's hire/fire game, but it's scuppered when the Washburn angle gets dropped.

SON OF A GUN!

"They don't sound like they have room for anyone else." – Samantha, discussing Darrin's prospects at Stone, Fraser, Moreheim, Cooper, Cooper & Washburn.

EPISODE 184
SANTA COMES TO VISIT AND STAYS AND STAYS
Airdate: December 18, 1969

After enjoying a moment of Adam's first Christmas, and gently lecturing Tabitha about telling her mortal friend they know Santa Claus, Samantha calls for Esmeralda to help out over the holidays. Esmeralda proceeds to sneeze up a goat and "Christmas seals," but the Stephenses are floored when Esmeralda accidentally brings Santa to their kitchen. Because St. Nick got there through Esmeralda's witchcraft, he is essentially stuck until her spell wears off. Gladys comes by to remind the Stephenses of a neighborhood decorating contest and sees Santa, thinking it's Darrin in costume. Larry also visits, upset because Louise bought herself a mink stole.

With Santa's time getting short, Samantha convinces Darrin to escort Larry out, after which she zaps up Santa's elves to help her jolly friend. Curious about Santa's legendarily mammoth output, Darrin peeks at Kris Kringle and the elves working at super speed; Gladys also sees but can't convince Abner of the Christmas miracle. By December 24, Santa is still grounded at the Stephenses, so Samantha summons his sleigh to the front yard. Abner thinks it's a bid to win the decorating contest, shocked Gladys watches the fast-forward elves loading the sleigh, and Larry, who suddenly sees the Stephenses' "display" in the sky, briefly believes it could be Santa, admitting he's just disappointed because he wanted to buy Louise the mink stole himself. On Christmas Day, Samantha defers scolding Tabitha for turning her disbelieving friend into a mushroom.

GOOD!

The opening sequence, where Samantha squires baby Adam around the tree, is beautifully shot, and done in a much more cinematic way than is usual for a sitcom. As for Tabitha, she knows what she's talking about when she tells Sidney her family knows Santa Claus: in "Humbug Not to Be Spoken Here" (#123), she saw Santa and her mother in discussion, and was asked to keep a gift from him a secret. And

Samantha's "everyone is entitled to believe in what they want" speech goes beyond just Santa Claus, especially when she adds, "If they don't want to believe, that's all right, too."

Darrin meeting Santa officially undoes the events of "A Vision of Sugar Plums" (#15), where Darrin "forgot" his first Kris Kringle confab thanks to Samantha's spell. It was always a shame that Darrin wasn't allowed to retain that memory; now Darrin knows for sure that Santa is real.

WELL?

Esmeralda's powers are increasing: now when she goofs, her sneezes are accompanied by thunder and earthquakes, which hasn't been the case since she was introduced in "Samantha's Yoo-Hoo Maid" (#172). Not to mention, Esmeralda always fades out when she gets nervous; here she pops out.

Calming the off-screen Louise about the mink stole via telephone, Samantha advises, "Maybe you should have consulted him before you bought it." But Samantha didn't, when she snuck home a coat with mink trim in "Cheap, Cheap" (#112). Then, as far as Darrin knows, he is meeting St. Nick for the first time, as Samantha's magic blocked him from remembering their previous encounter in "A Vision of Sugar Plums" (#15). So why does Samantha never officially introduce them? And, since Santa is twiddling his thumbs waiting to be popped back to the Pole, why not let Tabitha spend time with him? She didn't get a chance to interact with him the last time he visited, either. [See "Humbug Not to Be Spoken Here" (#123).]

Later, Santa grouses that his elves won't know how to proceed without him. They've done how many hundreds of Christmases, and they still need him there to supervise? If Santa is that worried, he should just call the Pole; surely his workshop has a phone line.

Larry decries "the crass commercialism that has invaded the Christmas holiday" – ironic, since "crass commercialism" is his middle name. Larry can't hear Santa's booming voice emanating from the kitchen, but Darrin can hear the elves. As for Gladys, she decides to hang around the Stephenses' front window at 3:03 in the morning, then rushes back to her bedroom to tell Abner about Santa and his elves – a room that is a duplicate of the Stephenses' guest bedroom from "Samantha's Double Mother Trouble" (#182).

Now an insider, Darrin wants to know how the North Pole practitioners turn out so many toys so quickly, which begs the question: do they always wait until the last minute to go into production? Santa and the elves were still making toys on Christmas Eve in the previous two holiday installments as well.

Samantha's spell cautions Santa's reindeer to duck the antennas, but Rudolph and the gang ought to be flying over them – and Gladys frowns that the Stephenses won't decorate for Christmas, but where are the Kravitzes' decorations? They have a few outside, yet there's nary an ornament or a piece of tinsel inside. And amazingly, Abner doesn't see the sleigh appear, despite not bending down for his paper until after it materializes.

Tabitha watches Santa's sleigh from her upstairs room, meaning it faces the street. That was the case in "The Safe and Sane Halloween" (#115), when her kiddie book creatures climbed out the same window – but it means "Tabitha's Weekend" (#163) was wrong: that episode showed Tabitha's as the first room to the right, which, according to "Samantha's Double Mother Trouble" (#182), faces the backyard. Then, Larry excuses himself to pick up Louise's mink stole, a present she already bought for herself, which is the catalyst for the Tates' entire conflict in this episode.

While Santa "stays and stays," Esmeralda's spell could still wear off at any moment. So what happens if Santa pops back to the North Pole while flying the sleigh? And does absolutely everything that happens to the Stephenses end up on the front page of the paper? Julius Caesar's cab driver just made headlines in "Samantha's Caesar Salad" (#173); in "To Trick-or-Treat or Not to Trick-or-Treat" (#177), it was Darrin-as-witch – now it's Santa's sleigh. Finally, where does Esmeralda disappear to? The last time she's seen is when Samantha zaps up the elves, but the maid was asked to stay on through the holidays.

OH, MY STARS!

Samantha tells Darrin that Esmeralda's spells don't usually last as if he's hearing this for the first time. The audience may need reminding, but he doesn't – he's known about Esmeralda's magic since he first met her in "Samantha's Yoo-Hoo Maid" (#172). More importantly, there's a recurring pattern with Esmeralda's spells: her animals all spend only a short time materialized, but "Samantha's Caesar Salad" (#173), "Samantha's Double Mother Trouble" (#182), and this episode seem to indicate that humanoids stick around.

When Darrin asks why Samantha popped Santa's sleigh on the front lawn, she smiles, "Because there wasn't room out back." Aunt Clara landed a UFO out there in "Samantha's Secret Saucer" (#137) that was certainly bigger than Santa's ride, especially because the famous sleigh only sports four reindeer. Then, Samantha cues the elves to load the sleigh, telling them, "there's no one out there now." If Gladys can see them from her window, so can anyone else – why doesn't Samantha just zap everything onto the sleigh? Gladys freaking out over the sped-up helpers isn't that necessary a beat.

A final reflection: why aren't the Stephenses ever visited by relatives at Christmas? This is the third holiday episode [not counting the recut "A Vision of Sugar Plums" (#51)], and neither Samantha's nor Darrin's parents are anywhere to be seen. You'd think there'd be a big family gathering, especially now that there are two children involved.

SON OF A GUN!

"Well, maybe instead of toys, you could leave each child a gift certificate." – Esmeralda, offering Santa a way to deal with his lack of Pole position.

EPISODE
185

SAMANTHA'S BETTER HALVES
Airdate: January 1, 1970

The Stephenses prepare for a Caribbean vacation, although Larry covertly tries to get Darrin to make a trip to Chicago for him instead. When Darrin tells Samantha he can't be in two places at once, Samantha thinks back to the last time he said that: months earlier, Darrin didn't want to leave a pregnant Samantha to fly to Tokyo on business. Hearing Darrin's indecision, Endora divided him – Business Darrin went to Japan while Doting Darrin stayed home and hovered over Samantha. After Samantha caught on, Endora convinced her to keep Darrin split for a while. Business Darrin annoyed his client, Tanaka, while Doting Darrin annoyed Samantha with his constant attention.

Samantha implored Endora to put a reintegrated Darrin in Tokyo, but when Endora tried to, Doting Darrin ended up overseas while a furious Business Darrin came home. Endora's second attempt fused Darrin, who wound up in both his business suit and golf clothes. The flashback ends with Samantha trying to explain, since Darrin couldn't remember being divided. In the present, the Stephenses turn their attention toward their imminent vacation; as predicted, Larry returns with a sudden back injury, but

Samantha, knowing he's still scheming to trick Darrin into going to Chicago, zaps up a vampire bat to frighten Larry into bolting upright. Their vacation saved, the Stephenses run upstairs to finish packing.

GOOD!

The double Darrins inspire doubly nice effects in this episode. Darrin dividing via split screen is quite effective, but Darrin getting popped into his half-and-half wardrobe looks even better. The Doting Darrin/ Business Darrin switch is the perfect peak to their story, with Doting Darrin humorously scrambling to explain his presence to Tanaka.

WELL?

Samantha can't wait to ditch "diapers, dinners, and demand feedings." She's tired of caring for Adam after only 2½ months? Then, as Samantha remembers having two husbands, she tells Darrin, "You were so anxious for me to get to the hospital to have that baby." Not "my baby" or "our baby?" Louise doesn't fare much better – she's "used to being alone," and Jonathan is, too: Samantha suggests that Larry take Louise to Chicago without ever mentioning their son. Why give the Tates a child if he's never on the canvas? And no wonder Larry thinks he can manipulate Darrin into going to Chicago – he did exactly that in "That Was No Chick, That Was My Wife" (#117).

Business Darrin takes a 12-hour, 6,700-mile flight just so he can make a presentation to Tanaka that shouldn't take more than a half an hour. And he's still going on about it at dinner; wouldn't he run out of material on the plane? Maybe the reason Tanaka is staring at his stewardess is because she's wearing the same colorful uniform as the flight attendants of "Samantha and Darrin in Mexico City" (#170); at least Larry doesn't try to make Darrin learn Japanese for this trip.

On Day 2, Doting Darrin feeds Samantha an inedible breakfast – yet he makes Samantha a lunch on Day 1 she has no complaint with. When Samantha commands Endora to fuse Darrin in Japan, the camera drops suddenly, as if they're in an elevator, and, when Doting Darrin replaces Business Darrin in Tanaka's house, the camera shifts significantly between pops.

Tanaka is right that Larry shouldn't make Darrin go to Tokyo when Samantha's about to have a baby. So why was Tanaka in New York? His wife is expecting any day, too. It's not clear whether Mrs. Tanaka can understand English; regardless, you'd think Tanaka would speak Japanese to his wife when they're alone together.

Darrin has used his "double/triple/tell me the story after I pass out" bit on Samantha before, after learning of Tabitha's nursery school naughtiness in "I Don't Want to Be A Toad, I Want to Be A Butterfly" (#151). And he uses Uncle Arthur's long-incorrect nickname of "Madame LeFarge" for Endora, despite accurately referencing the Dickens character, "Madame *De*Farge," in "To Trick-or-Treat or Not to Trick-or-Treat" (#177).

If the Stephenses didn't know before that Larry was trying to con them (and it's insightful that they do), they would figure it out from the way he hobbles in with a "back injury." If your back gave out, would you stop at someone's house en route to the hospital? Wouldn't you call an ambulance instead of driving yourself? Even the ailing Louise could get Larry to the hospital in an emergency. Fortunately, Samantha sees through the ruse and conjures up a bat, though its materialization happens off-screen, and it makes its flight with visible strings. Once Larry gets over his initial shock, won't he wonder how a bat got into his friends' house?

OH, MY STARS!

Darrin comments that he and Samantha haven't had a real vacation in five years – actually, it's been three-and-a-half since they frolicked in Miami, in "Divided He Falls" (#69). Ironically, that's where most of the source material for this episode comes from. The build-up is different, but there are several chunks of dialogue that are exactly the same, and the fact that Samantha has seen her husband divided before should have her suspecting Endora right away. "Haven't we been through all this?" Doting Darrin paradoxically asks. It's also a shame the two Darrins don't interact, which was the highlight of "Divided He Falls" (#69).

Darrin's business trip to Japan is a better flashback/recut than the show's previous attempts, specifically, "A Vision of Sugar Plums" (#15/#51), "Samantha Meets the Folks" (#14/#56), and "Prodigy" (#74). Pre-flashback, however, Darrin says it would be easier to forget his name than what happened in Japan – yet, *in* the flashback, Darrin doesn't remember his double duty. This means, in the present, he shouldn't be able to recall the trip, because he has no memory of the events. As for Samantha, it's not possible for her to think back to Darrin's private experiences on the plane, or in Tokyo.

Tanaka leisurely leers at a stewardess on the long New York-Tokyo flight, then tells stodgy Business Darrin, "You really should learn how to play a little!" Obviously, Tanaka does – with other women, while he has a very pregnant wife at home.

There are several wonderful books out there about the behind-the-scenes aspects of *Bewitched*; the focus here is primarily the show's fictional aspects. That said, there are times when real-life events have to be discussed, because of the way they affect continuity. According to Herbie J Pilato in *Bewitched Forever*, this episode was the first that Dick Sargent lensed after taking over the role of Darrin from Dick York. However, it "contained dialogue that both he and Elizabeth [Montgomery] thought was inappropriate," particularly Samantha's line, "I only want one Darrin." Obviously, it would have been too soon for Samantha to utter such a sentiment after the high-profile recast – so, the original sequences were shelved until audiences became more familiar with the new Darrin and then incorporated into this episode, creating the Stephenses' "flashback."

SON OF A GUN!

"Quiet!" – Samantha shutting Business Darrin up on the condition he won't remember her doing it.

This episode rights a wrong committed in "A Majority of Two" (#136), where the show cast the decidedly non-Asian Richard Hadyn in the role of Japanese businessman Kensu Mishimoto. That's how Hollywood rolled during much of its golden era, but it was sad to see the misrepresentation still happening on television in the late '60s. Thankfully, this episode fills the screen with Asian actors, namely Richard Loo as Tanaka, Frances Fong as his wife, and Debbie Wong as the stewardess. The giggling Mrs. Tanaka is still a bit of a stereotype, and casting Chinese-Americans Loo and Fong as Japanese characters rather gives off a "they all look the same" vibe, but the trio's appearance is a step in the right direction.

EPISODE
186
SAMANTHA'S LOST WEEKEND
Airdate: January 8, 1970

Rebelling against her new baby brother, Tabitha refuses to eat, so the worried Esmeralda puts a spell on her milk that's meant to get the child to clean her plate. But Tabitha has been punished, and when

Samantha sees Esmeralda taking the glass to Tabitha's room, she grabs it and drinks the milk herself. Esmeralda can't alleviate Samantha's uncontrollable urge to eat, so she goes to the frisky apothecary and asks him to whip up a cure. Abner comes by to get Samantha to sign a petition, but Samantha is so busy eating that she barely acknowledges him. Thinking she has voracious ravenousitis, Samantha puts in a call to Dr. Bombay, then takes Darrin to the grocery store, where she eats items out of strangers' carts. Later, Bombay gives Samantha a cure that puts an end to her excessive hunger.

The next day, Samantha falls asleep at random, confusing Abner, who has returned with his petition. The apothecary finally finishes Esmeralda's potion, but will only give it to her in exchange for a kiss. Complying, Esmeralda then pops in at the Stephenses and tells them about the spell on Tabitha's milk; it turns out Samantha's narcolepsy is a side effect of Dr. Bombay's unnecessary cure. Bombay voids it, and, before the hungry Samantha can eat again, Esmeralda makes her drink the potion, returning Samantha to normal.

GOOD!

Samantha eating everything in sight – including Adam's baby food – definitely satisfies a viewer's hunger for comedy. The best moments are Samantha taking a bite out of the hippie's lettuce, and Darrin pretending not to know his wife as the grocery store manager chides her for eating food without paying for it. Less obvious are Samantha's sudden, unscheduled naps, which steal the show from Samantha's gorging.

Dr. Bombay scoffs when Darrin offers up Samantha's left elbow to aid in removing the voracious ravenousitis cure, but at least Darrin tries – and he's never done that before.

WELL?

Samantha tells Esmeralda that Darrin is going out to hit some golf balls, "or at least to swing at them." What's up with the put-down? Samantha knows from "Birdies, Bogies, and Baxter" (#114) that her husband can play a decent game of golf. Her snideness continues when she paraphrases his book, *How to Line Up Your Fourth Putt*; Darrin calling it *How to Improve Your Swing* is wrong, too, because the title is actually *Secrets of the Perfect Golf Swing*.

Twice, in wide shots, Tabitha clutches her fork in her right hand just above the table. But, in her medium shots, her hands are down and the fork is next to her plate. Esmeralda could save herself a lot of trouble by just popping into Tabitha's room with the hexed milk instead of walking there the mortal way. And, maybe Esmeralda doesn't want Samantha to get mad at her for interfering, but why doesn't the maid tell Samantha what the milk is for as soon as she grabs the glass? As for Esmeralda's apron, it can't be easy to create an effect of it walking independently, but it faces forward after Esmeralda invisibly sneaks out of the kitchen, then it's suddenly in profile as Esmeralda reappears in it.

If the apothecary's potions can cure witches, why do they need Dr. Bombay? Conversely, if witches have Dr. Bombay, why do they need the apothecary? Pharmacists don't come up with cures, they dole out medicine prescribed by doctors; you'd think the Bombay/apothecary association would work the same way. And the next question is, how can a potion by either practitioner undo a witch's spell? Dr. Bombay whipped up some Super Cure-All to help Aunt Clara restore Samantha's voice in "Out of Sync, Out of Mind" (#116), but it would seem that only a witch's counterspell can undo an original spell. Even so, why doesn't Esmeralda just get some Cure-All from Bombay?

The Kravitzes are into petitions lately: Gladys just circulated one for upholstered bus benches in "You're So Agreeable" (#183). It's nice to see Abner, but there's a feeling that his scenes with the hungry/ sleeping Samantha were originally intended for Gladys; it seems out of character for Abner to willingly take part in Gladys' civic improvements. The last time Abner was over [in "Daddy Does His Thing" (#167)], he saw a chess-playing mule; this time he sees Samantha narcoleptic after eating to distraction. Abner ought to realize Gladys is right about her by now.

Samantha, having eaten everyone's dinner, now feels a grocery run is in order. Why? Was that the only food the Stephenses had left in the house? At least there are actual products in the market (in previous episodes, brand names were covered with tape; there are too many to camouflage here), but what store stocks a display of cherry tomatoes next to a shelf that carries ketchup and booze side-by-side? Later, the refrigerator is packed full, but the Stephenses are only seen bringing one bag of groceries into the house. Were the rest of them in the car?

Dr. Bombay may not "believe in a lot of mumbo-jumbo," but he does believe in reusing cures: he treats Samantha with the same tuning fork he used in "Samantha the Bard" (#158), although this time the sound waves don't break things. After everyone thinks Samantha's nonexistent voracious ravenousitis is cured, she claims she's stuffed. She's been wolfing down incompatible types of food all day – shouldn't she also be sick? And, in a rare show of appreciation, Darrin says he'll use Dr. Bombay if he ever becomes a warlock, forgetting that he basically was one thanks to Maurice's magic watch in "Daddy Comes for a Visit" (#180) and "Darrin the Warlock" (#181).

Once all is back to normal, Samantha jokingly pretends to fall asleep, needlessly worrying Darrin. Isn't that rather a cruel jest?

OH, MY STARS!

This episode again implies that witches can put spells on each other, a rule that hasn't been established one way or the other. As the show finally decided after three seasons that a witch can't undo another witch's spell, a similar decision as to whether one witch can bespell another would help clarify things.

If Esmeralda's tiny eating spell makes a grown witch like Samantha a "foodaholic," what would it have done to witchlet Tabitha? Speaking of whom, the show spends so much time focusing on Samantha's "ailment" that it forgets to resolve the original problem: Tabitha's hunger strike. Samantha assured Tabitha that she was loved after she ran away in "Samantha and the Beanstalk" (#171); wouldn't similar parenting be appropriate now so the child doesn't starve herself? And, as wonderful as this episode is overall, it's a bit odd for Samantha to have another eating problem so soon – she just had an unnamed affliction that caused whatever food she desired to appear in "Samantha's Curious Cravings" (#174).

SON OF A GUN!

"Oh, Dr. Bombay, now, listen quick before I fall asleep. Esmeralda has a potion that will remove her spell – now, if you can remove your cure, her cure can cure me!" – Samantha, explaining things between snoozes.

EPISODE **187**

THE PHRASE IS FAMILIAR
Airdate: January 15, 1970

Endora and the Stephenses agree that Tabitha needs a more formal education than Samantha's home schooling, so Endora summons warlock teacher Professor Phipps. Darrin allows him to tutor Tabitha as long as he doesn't use witchcraft; Phipps agrees, then criticizes the use of clichés in Darrin's ad campaign.

When Samantha comments that Darrin's success is dependent on coming up with clever slogans, Endora zaps him into speaking in nothing but clichés. After Darrin overwhelms Larry with a laundry list of sayings, he dashes home and discovers that Phipps has brought the Artful Dodger out of *Oliver Twist* as a teaching aid for Tabitha. Endora removes her spell, though she replaces it with a new one, under which Darrin acts out his clichés.

Larry introduces Darrin as the Slogan King to new client Summers, but when Darrin physicalizes maxims by involuntarily crossing his eyes and throwing himself to the floor, he ends up literally bowing out of the meeting. Undeterred, Larry brings Summers to Darrin's house, climbing through the window when the Stephenses won't answer the door. Darrin agreeing to "play ball" with Summers puts the men in baseball uniforms, so Samantha freezes everyone and makes Endora normalize Darrin. Samantha has Darrin help her move the frozen Larry and Summers so they can pretend they were talking about Summers' campaign the whole time. Afterwards, the Artful Dodger, who earlier tried to filch Samantha's ring and Darrin's watch, absconds with Summers' cufflinks as Phipps leads him away.

GOOD!

Sometimes, it's all in the details: Endora's love for baby Adam is tangible, and Darrin and Summers getting zapped into baseball uniforms in front of Larry comes off flawlessly – as does their getting changed back while frozen. David White and Cliff Norton, as Larry and Summers, do a masterful job of remaining motionless – and physically moving deanimated mortals is a new concept for the show. Finally, on the Stephenses porch: snow. The flakes are most appropriate for New York State in January; it's an environmental touch the show doesn't have to add, but does.

It's possible – even probable – that viewers watching Season Six for the first time were waiting to see if Dick Sargent would pass the test of being Darrin Stephens after the recast; maybe the show was, too. After this episode, there can be no doubt that Dick Sargent has come into his own as Darrin, and he proves it with a brand of physical comedy Darrin hasn't been able to explore until now; Dick York's pratfalls were unfortunately limited by his back injury. York will always be the Darrin of the '60s – it's just that now there's also a Darrin for the '70s.

WELL?

The Stephenses are getting rather lenient about their daughter's witchcraft – they don't even scold Tabitha when she makes apples disappear during her home schooling with Samantha. Darrin's mellowing, too; in "Witches and Warlocks Are My Favorite Things" (#77), he vehemently insisted that Tabitha would attend mortal schools only, but here, he lets warlock Phipps tutor her without much of a fight. Endora's getting to be like Phyllis: she sees what she defines as a problem, then solves it without consulting Samantha first; in "Samantha's Yoo-Hoo Maid" (#172), it was bringing Esmeralda in as a domestic, now it's an instant teacher for Tabitha.

Why is Darrin carrying around his ad for Kitty Kakes, which has already been sold to that client? Endora inquires into Darrin's "so-called phrases" as if she's learning about them for the first time, but, in "Dangerous Diaper Dan" (#82), she was quite vocal about Darrin's "nauseating slogan." And, after Darrin suffers his first bout of clichés, he questions his speech. He's under a spell: in "Mirror, Mirror on the Wall" (#146), Darrin certainly didn't stop to wonder why he was behaving like a narcissist.

Even warlocks read abridged versions of books: Phipps' passage from *Oliver Twist* is very different from Charles Dickens' original 1838 description of the Dodger. Samantha interrupts Tabitha's lesson by walking into the den without knocking first – it's her house, but you'd think Phipps would be more than irked. When Samantha is upset to see the Dodger, Phipps says he hasn't taught Tabitha witchcraft – but hasn't he, by example? And Samantha knows from pickpockets: in "A Bum Raps" (#68), Darrin's "Uncle Albert" lifted a watch from Harriet Kravitz. Whatever happened to Abner's sister, anyway?

Larry strolls into Darrin's office with a list of Multiple Industries' products, asking if Darrin can have a slogan ready by noon as if he's dropping off his dry cleaning. Darrin's already mapped something out for the conglomerate's farm machinery division, which is amazing considering he only just that moment found out what their products are.

Endora is at least learning to talk to herself about bespelling Darrin out of earshot of Samantha, but she does it in earshot of Darrin, who somehow doesn't hear her on the roof as he treads the front walk.

Darrin's watch must be fast: the strings on it are visible before his latest cliché makes it float off his wrist. Larry walks in on Darrin's frantic phone call to Samantha – does he not wonder why his friend/ employee needs Endora found fast?

Is McMann & Tate in Manhattan anymore? Larry follows Darrin the previously established 60 miles to Patterson like he's going next door. And Larry has a fascination with the Stephenses' front window – in "Samantha Loses Her Voice" (#150), he broke it; now he climbs through it. As for the Stephenses, can't they tell sooner that Larry is coming through? They just stand there, allowing Larry to catch them in the hall. After the baseball uniform fiasco, Samantha could make things much easier on herself by just zapping the incapacitated Larry and Summers onto the couch, but that doesn't generate the comedy of their frozen forms being moved manually.

Phipps escorts the Artful Dodger into the foyer after Tabitha's lesson and announces their departure, though the perfunctory professor would be more likely to zap him back into the book before ever leaving the den. Where do Phipps and Dodger go after walking out the door? Phipps still has to pop out, and Gladys – or anyone else looking out the window – could see them vanish.

OH, MY STARS!

Darrin, having just uttered "an encyclopedia of clichés," goes in the opposite direction and tells Summers, "I won't have anything to do with a campaign based on slogans." Isn't that what the advertising business is all about? Aren't slogans what Darrin has offered every single client since the show began? If Darrin means he isn't going to rely solely on clichés to craft a slogan, then that's what he should say; this small semantic error changes an entire vocation – not to mention one of the key premises of the entire series.

It probably works on paper to have everyone laugh off the baseball uniforms, but it feels like far too easy an ending. If it were only Summers, say, who had seen himself dressed as a ballplayer, he could feasibly convince himself he was only imagining it. But Larry can corroborate his story – would these men really just pretend they haven't seen anything? And how come Larry never wonders why something strange happens every time he comes over?

SON OF A GUN!

"You're sure he won't break?" – Darrin to Samantha, proving that he's green when it comes to moving frozen mortals.

Samantha comes home from shopping and discovers that Endora has filled the house with Louis XIV furniture. Mother and daughter have a zap-off, but Phyllis comes by, sees the décor changing back and forth, and faints. After Phyllis comes to the conclusion she's losing her mind, Samantha tells Darrin she has no choice but to finally reveal to her mother-in-law that she's a witch. Darrin reluctantly agrees, and Phyllis watches as Samantha gently performs witchcraft to back up her claim. Phyllis is surprisingly open to the idea of having a witch for a daughter-in-law, but blurts Samantha's identity to Frank after the Stephenses asked her not to. Cornered, Samantha tries to fix a broken vase for Frank, but nothing happens, and Frank escorts Phyllis out, questioning his wife's sanity.

Endora explains that the Witches' Council has restricted Samantha's powers to prevent her from needlessly exposing herself. Meanwhile, Frank takes Phyllis to a psychiatrist who finds her problem amusing; he secretly tells Frank his wife is seriously ill. Sensing the shrink's deception, Phyllis runs away; Samantha guesses she has committed herself to a rest home and finds her via locator spell. Unable to do any more magic in front of Phyllis, Samantha magically induces her new friend, Mrs. Quigley, into swallowing one of Phyllis' tranquilizers, then makes her see impossibilities everywhere. The doctor determines that Phyllis has been taking hallucinogenics, and she is relieved to learn that the pills caused her strange sightings.

GOOD!

It's not easy to do a scene, freeze in position, then get back into the same position after the crew has completely redecorated the room you were standing in – which makes Samantha and Endora changing the living room back and forth an incredible series of effects. Elizabeth Montgomery and Agnes Moorehead do some inevitable shifting (more so Ms. Moorehead), but it barely takes away from the result, especially considering what it must have taken to pull this off.

Phyllis reaches a zenith of zaniness by suggesting that Frank can remarry and give Darrin a baby brother, not to be outdone by Bernie Kopell's madcap Teutonic shrink, Dr. Rhinehouse. And Roy Roberts gets a chance to show Frank's comedic side like never before; usually Frank is only there to react to Phyllis. Frank even pulls the elder Stephenses' entire storyline together by remarking that Phyllis has "complained of aches and pains for years" – she's come down with sick headaches ever since her introduction in "Samantha Meets the Folks" (#14).

As Mrs. Quigley, Nydia Westman sneaks up on her scene with her repeated "What are you in for?" inquiries, then lets loose with her shocked reactions to Samantha's "hallucinations" and side-splitting pro-drug proclivities. To put it in a way she would understand, Mrs. Quigley is a trip.

WELL?

Samantha's hands are full, and she gets distracted by Endora's redecorating, but she could prevent a whole episode of trouble by just closing the front door. Leaving it open caused a similar scenario with Gladys back in "Abner Kadabra" (#29). But the real issue is, can Samantha just zap away Endora's furniture? It's Endora's spell; if "Hoho the Clown" (#92) is correct, and a witch has "squatter's rights" to her own magic, Samantha shouldn't be able to restore her living room.

How is it Phyllis only now thinks she's losing her mind? Both she and Frank thought they were "going over the hill" as recently as "Samantha's Double Mother Trouble" (#182), and Phyllis has seen a multitude of unusual incidents for over five years. Deciding Phyllis has to be told she's a witch, Samantha notes that a wise man said, "honesty is the best policy" – that man is Sir Edwin Sandys, who first uttered the phrase in 1599.

When Samantha first admits to witchcraft, Phyllis doesn't believe her. Why? Phyllis has known her daughter-in-law isn't mortal since "Samantha Meets the Folks" (#14): Aunt Clara's claim of witchery has had to be in the back of Phyllis' mind all along. Even if she forgot about it, Samantha just provided a refresher by saying her whole family is "wacky as witches" in "Samantha's Double Mother Trouble" (#182). And what about Frank? Having also heard Clara's confession, and himself having seen strange things since "It's Wishcraft" (#103), he should be more apt to believe the confirmation than not.

Phyllis has tranquilizers in her purse, and her visit to Dr. Rhinehouse doesn't seem to be her first. Did Phyllis make good on her vow to see a psychiatrist after encountering Jack in "Samantha and the Beanstalk" (#171)? Dr. Rhinehouse asks, "What seems to be the trouble?" Phyllis goes on about how she's lost her mind, then contends, "I still think my daughter-in-law's a witch" – except the subject of witches hasn't come up. Dr. Rhinehouse's office is identical to the one in which Samantha had a consultation with her obstetrician, Dr. Anton, in "Samantha's Curious Cravings" (#174). And it may be good that Samantha never sees Dr. Rhinehouse; she might find he's a dead ringer for Dr. Chomsky from "Samantha Twitches for UNICEF" (#166) – after all, both docs are played by Bernie Kopell.

If Samantha can cast locator spells, why has she waited until now to implement one? There are dozens of times Samantha could have saved herself from running around looking for missing people and animals over the years. Here, Samantha finds Phyllis with Mrs. Quigley, who calls the adult Samantha a "teenager" – Mrs. Quigley must know the apothecary, because that's what he called Esmeralda in "Samantha's Lost Weekend" (#186).

OH, MY STARS!

"Samantha's Power Failure" (#165) demonstrated that the Witches' Council can remove a witch's power at will. And it makes sense that they'd exercise this option to keep a witch from "frivolously flaunting" herself to mortals. So where have they been the last five-and-a-half years? There are too many instances of witch-outing to mention here, but Endora herself started the ball rolling in "Mother Meets What's-His-Name" (#4); Aunt Clara continually spilled the beans in the early seasons [two examples are "Samantha Meets the Folks" (#14) and "There's No Witch Like An Old Witch" (#27)]; Uncle Arthur tattled to Napoléon Bonaparte in "Samantha's French Pastry" (#147) – and Samantha made two Christmas confessions [see "A Vision of Sugar Plums" (#15) and "Humbug Not to Be Spoken Here" (#123)], plus informed an entire country club of her witchhood in "The Battle of Burning Oak" (#164). For that matter, why did the Council allow Samantha to tell Darrin about herself in "I, Darrin, Take This Witch, Samantha" (#1)? Granted, the Witches' Council has only been part of the canvas since "It's So Nice to Have A Spouse Around the House" (#145); have they retroactively gotten tired of the loose lips in the witches' community and decided to do something about it?

SON OF A GUN!

"I'll take a gross!" – Mrs. Quigley, putting in her order for Phyllis' "hallucinogenic" pills.

Although the show is developing a pattern this season of borrowing too heavily from previous episodes, the events surrounding Samantha revealing herself to Phyllis brings the whole series full circle by mirroring her initial confession of "I, Darrin, Take This Witch, Samantha" (#1). As with Darrin, Samantha tells Phyllis she's a "cauldron-stirring, card-carrying witch" (notice she left out "broom-riding" – smart continuity considering she has repeatedly said witches don't ride brooms), and she proves her powers by levitating an ashtray, like she did for Phyllis' son; Darrin takes the reveal in stride, even smiling and nodding. The show continues reaching back to the first episode by mentioning Darrin's Aunt Madge, who thought she was a lighthouse (given the past tense, it has to be assumed Phyllis' sister has since passed away) – and Samantha's imitation of Madge, who hasn't been mentioned since the recut "Samantha Meets the Folks" (#56), is deliciously bizarre. Based on Phyllis' own family, she *would* be okay with Samantha being a witch – maybe that appreciation of the unusual is what attracted Darrin to Samantha in the first place.

Apparently, "Durwood doesn't count" when the Witches' Council blocks Samantha's powers in front of mortals. Have they inadvertently shown Darrin some tolerance because he's known about Samantha and her brethren for so long?

TABITHA'S VERY OWN SAMANTHA
Airdate: January 29, 1970

EPISODE 189

Upset at having to share her mother's attention with Adam, Tabitha wishes up her "very own very special Mommy" that is oblivious to everyone but her. After the real Samantha nearly catches them together, Tabitha suggests they pop out to an amusement park, where they run into Gladys and her nephew. Gladys becomes concerned when "Samantha" denies knowledge of the baby, so she calls Darrin, who, in turn, calls Samantha and lectures her for taking Tabitha on a fun trip after misbehaving. Confused, Samantha finds Tabitha's room empty and thinks Serena is entertaining her – but the carnival's Ferris wheel worker is more confused when Tabitha and Fake Samantha disappear from the attraction just as Real Samantha approaches asking about them.

Gladys and Darrin unknowingly encounter both Samanthas at the house, unable to account for the discrepancies in "her" behavior. The real Samantha gets rid of Gladys by explaining about Serena, and news of his cousin-in-law's probable presence has Darrin wanting to cancel a client dinner. With Larry and the Nickersons in the living room, and Samantha tending to Adam, Tabitha comes downstairs with "Samantha," who overdoes it gushing about "her" daughter. Samantha finally confronts them and extracts a confession from Tabitha, assuring her she has enough love for both her children. Tabitha returns Fake Samantha to the ether, and Real Samantha later tells Darrin he's lucky Serena wasn't around to hear the things he said about her.

GOOD!

Like Endora before her [she discussed her resentment toward Arthur for spoiling her only child status in "Endora Moves in for a Spell" (#80)], Tabitha's issues with having a baby brother are right on the money. What kid wouldn't ask why the maid can't do all the baby chores? It rather puts witches and mortals on the same level.

There have been two Samanthas on screen before, but the split-screen effects in this episode are among the best in the series. When Real Samantha enters Tabitha's room, Fake Samantha ducks into the closet, and it really seems there are two of them. "Samantha" and Tabitha popping on and off the Ferris wheel is perfectly matched, too, the ride continuing to move fluidly both times.

It's a blink-and-you-miss-it moment, but when Nickerson tells Darrin he has a very special little lady in Samantha, Darrin knowingly smiles, "I know." His expression exudes such warmth; with one look and two words, he acknowledges he's married to a witch and loves her madly.

WELL?

As Tabitha enters the kitchen with a Band-Aid on her chin, Samantha indicates that the injury came from Tabitha trying to fly. This brings up an interesting question: what's the difference between popping and flying? Tabitha easily popped herself into a book in "Samantha and the Beanstalk" (#171), but she's apparently too young to fly; is popping simply the act of disappearing from one place and appearing in another, or does a witch disappear, literally fly to their destination, and then appear in it? Regardless, you'd think Samantha would be more wary about eating Tabitha's ice cream cone – the last time she gulped down her daughter's dairy products, she became a "foodaholic" thanks to Esmeralda. [See "Samantha's Lost Weekend" (#186).]

When Real Samantha interrupts Tabitha's game with Fake Samantha, she asks her daughter, who has been shouting giddily, to play a little quieter. Considering Tabitha has given herself playmates before, shouldn't Samantha be wondering if Tabitha is alone up there? Fake Samantha's hair is perfectly coiffed at home, but much looser at the play park; when she comes home, her hair is sprayed again, but Real Samantha sports the looser hair while looking for Tabitha.

Seymour is fifth in a long line of Kravitz nephews: Floyd, Edgar, "Flash" and Tommy. Why not pick one and let him come around once in a while so viewers can get to know him and watch him grow up?

Gladys isn't the least bit alarmed when Samantha asks about Aunt Hagatha, which is curious, because Gladys is positive Samantha and her family have powers of some sort, and "Hagatha" isn't exactly a mortal-sounding name. As for Real Samantha, it's not like her to flagrantly disappear in front of a mortal, no matter how much of a hurry she's in. When she pops out, a purple-clad play park extra jumps ahead several feet – and there are palm trees behind the Ferris wheel, which are not common in New York State. At home, Gladys doesn't see Samantha appearing out of nowhere in the foyer, despite facing that direction while on the phone.

When Tabitha wants real food for her tea party, "Samantha" pops down to the kitchen to do up a tray. But this Samantha could zap up a feast for Tabitha without leaving her chair – and Tabitha could just twitch up goodies herself. Of course, then Darrin wouldn't run into "Samantha" in the kitchen. How is it the double ignores Gladys, but is immediately friendly toward Darrin, who makes the hour drive home from McMann & Tate in just a few minutes?

After the Nickersons arrive, Tabitha tells Fake Samantha, "You have to dress just like Mommy." Tabitha wouldn't make that request without intending to take her downstairs, but her motivation for doing so is never made clear. Now, the Nickersons are over to dinner, and Tabitha is not invited. (Come to think of it, she never dines with her parents' company.) Has the girl been fed? Maybe not, because Darrin sends Tabitha to bed – at 6:00 – and, if the one deviled egg Fake Samantha gives her makes her that full, Real Samantha would have noticed Tabitha's distress at the table. Why is Tabitha only nauseous now? The way she stuffed herself, she'd have been ready to hurl before coming back from the park.

Gladys, who ordinarily looks upon the Stephenses with disdain and shrinks from going over to their house, suddenly tries to be a good neighbor. Is this a new tack, becoming friendly with the Stephenses so she can snoop from the inside?

OH, MY STARS!

Larry asks, "Who?" when the secretary tells Darrin that Gladys Kravitz is calling. Larry knows very well who Gladys is – he sat in a courtroom with the Kravitzes in "Samantha for the Defense" (#88) and watched a hysterical Gladys making a fool of herself in "Nobody But a Frog Knows How to Live" (#106) and "The Safe and Sane Halloween" (#115), the latter of which saw him agreeing with her about seeing a goat in the kitchen. There's no way Gladys wouldn't have made a lasting impression on Larry – unless he's purposely choosing to "forget" about her.

Aunt Hagatha is becoming the Betty of the witch world. While the face-changing secretary has had seven incarnations so far, Kay Eliot becomes Hagatha #5 in this installment. Perhaps the show felt they could get by casting different actresses because Hagatha appears so infrequently, but her constant reinventions make it feel like a stranger is being asked to babysit. [When you think about it, it's a little amazing that Samantha lets Hagatha anywhere near her daughter: this is the woman who wanted to forcibly remove Tabitha for her now-forgotten school in "Witches and Warlocks Are My Favorite Things" (#77).]

SON OF A GUN!

"I consider Tabitha an adult." – Fake Samantha, after offering Tabitha a tray of "goodies" Darrin says are for the grown-ups.

SUPER ARTHUR
Airdate: February 5, 1970

EPISODE **190**

Darrin puts in weekend work on the Top Pop account, but is interrupted by Uncle Arthur, who appears in mirrors, then accidentally shatters them popping out. Arthur refuses to call Dr. Bombay until he gets doused by the bucket of water he's magically rigged for Darrin. Bombay diagnoses Arthur with Bombay's Syndrome, an allergy to horse feathers – Arthur is furious when Bombay tries an experimental cure on him, but afterwards, he is able to zap a palm tree into the living room, which the visiting Larry sees. Too distracted to work, Darrin storms out to play golf when Arthur starts turning into things – including a colt and an Indian – as a result of his cure's side effect.

To keep Uncle Arthur's mind off himself, Samantha teaches him how to drive; the lesson is disastrous, and, when Arthur insists he'd rather fly, he turns into Superman and lifts off. Morning Glory Circle comes to a standstill as neighbors are mystified by the soaring Arthur, and soon police arrive to investigate. Larry, who catches Darrin playing golf and drags him home to work on Top Pop, also wonders why Arthur is flying; Darrin creates a Top Pop slogan around the Superman image, and Samantha lies that Arthur is using a jet pack. Bombay returns and gives a proper cure to Arthur, who promises Darrin he'll vacate the premises, then zaps all the furniture out of the room.

GOOD!

Uncle Arthur getting drenched by the bucket of water he intends for Darrin isn't what makes that sequence funny. It becomes that when you consider all of Arthur's tricks over the years; his soaking takes on a karmic quality that is actually quite satisfying. Paul Lynde is also rather adept at making the show's magic happen – when Arthur zaps himself out of his wet clothes, the effect is fluid.

Dr. Bombay and Uncle Arthur: a match made in the cosmos. They've never had occasion to share scenes before, but their back-and-forth between friendly and adversarial is most complex, and most entertaining. "I know I have to put up with his malpractice," Arthur remarks, "but about those jokes." What was that about karma?

Even though Darrin's slogan, "Try Top Pop: it's groovy, man; it's tasty, man; it's super, man" is set up as a groaner, it's actually pretty clever. Speaking of groovy, the Blue Meanies that Samantha says are plaguing Darrin is a reference to the colorful antagonists of the Beatles' 1968 animated film, *Yellow Submarine*.

WELL?

The Stephenses have never had a mirror in the den, or at the top of the stairs, and there's usually only a painting in the foyer – unless a mirror is required for the plot. Paul Lynde casts shadows as Arthur inhabits the den and foyer mirrors, and his hand comes into frame as Arthur zaps himself out of the den mirror.

There are two loose cannon warlocks in the living room, and the doorbell rings. What do you do? If you're Darrin, you open the door and let Larry in; you'd think he would just step outside with his boss instead. The den's not far away from the living room – can't Larry hear Arthur shouting at Dr. Bombay? And does Samantha zap the den mirror back together so Larry won't step into the room and wonder why it's broken?

Arthur inadvertently steals a joke from Esmeralda when he pops a palm tree into the living room the way she unintentionally did in "Samantha's Caesar Salad" (#173). Look carefully: there's a ring on the carpet before the tree appears in the same spot. After Larry leaves, Darrin swears to do the same; he hasn't made an "either he goes or I do" threat since Season Four, but it isn't endearing now, either.

The show has said from the beginning that witches don't ride brooms – so why does Arthur joke about him and Samantha riding a broomstick built for two? Samantha suggests that Uncle Arthur brush up on his driving in case he's grounded – but forgets that he was already made earthbound on her behalf in "Samantha's Power Failure" (#165).

This isn't the first time Samantha has had to make cars pass through each other to prevent an accident because of her uncle – she did the same to protect the supposedly untouchable Darrin in "The No-Harm Charm" (#138). This pass-through effect starts out better than the first, but gets spoiled by a dark line that throws a spotlight on the split screen.

Obviously, copyright prevents the show from using Superman's logo, but Uncle Arthur's costume rather makes him look like he's wearing a red diaper. As for Samantha's reference to *The Flying Nun*, the 1967-1970 Sally Field series was running concurrently on ABC, the same network that broadcast *Bewitched*. And Betty #7, otherwise known as Irenee Byatt, gets soaked in an uncredited, unrelated role.

Gladys Kravitz would be the first neighbor to run out of her house at the sight of Superman – yet she's conspicuously absent, and so is her house, as Morning Glory Circle returns to the unfamiliar layout first seen in "My Grandson, the Warlock" (#40). There are other discrepancies on the Circle: Samantha and the police seem to be filmed on a cloudy day, or even in the studio, while Larry and Darrin stand in a sunny outdoor spot.

Dr. Bombay boasts that he's been practicing witch medicine for hundreds of years. So where was he in "Take Two Aspirins and Half A Pint of Porpoise Milk" (#42), when Samantha came down with her first witch disease? As Bombay leaves, he laughs that he buys his pills at the drugstore. Does that mean these meds come from the apothecary, like Esmeralda's did in "Samantha's Lost Weekend" (#186)? Again, if witches have the apothecary, they don't need Bombay, and vice versa.

OH, MY STARS!

In "Tabitha's Very Own Samantha" (#189), Larry forgot who Gladys Kravitz was. Here, he doesn't remember Dr. Bombay, despite trying to make a mint off his Cold Bombs in "There's Gold in Them Thar Pills" (#107). Samantha forgets something in this episode, too – her kids. Who's watching them while she's teaching Arthur to drive and Darrin's out at the golf course?

SON OF A GUN!

"I read palms." – Uncle Arthur to Larry, explaining his palm tree's presence in the living room.

So what if it's not actually Paul Lynde flying around the backlot – the effect still soars. At one point, wires can be seen on Arthur's stunt double, but they'd have to be mighty sturdy to lower a grown man so smoothly. Super Arthur gets way up there – how did the show pull that off? Not to be outdone, Arthur magically clears the entire downstairs level of furniture. It truly looks like Darrin, Samantha, and Arthur are standing there as the furniture disappears, since they all get back into exactly the same position; remember, this is long before the effect could be done with CGI.

Series continuity is respected, ignored, flirted with, or forgotten about depending on the episode. In this one, continuity is revered as the show references "Driving Is the Only Way to Fly" (#26) and puts a whole new spin on its events. In that installment, Harold Harold, played by a pre-Arthur Paul Lynde, taught Samantha how to drive. Here, the show flips it by casting Samantha as the instructor, and it turns out that uncle and niece share similar thoughts about the "logic" of mortal driving. As a novice driver five years before, Samantha felt starting a car should be indicated with S or SC. Today, Arthur thinks "G for go" will move the car, and he looks for a B to hit the brakes. Best of all, when Samantha discusses the gear shift selector, she says, "I always thought it should be 'F for forward'" – she did indeed think that in "Driving Is the Only Way to Fly" (#26). This kind of consistency may be the norm for current shows, but it wasn't when *Bewitched* was on the air – so it's golden when it happens.

WHAT MAKES DARRIN RUN
Airdate: February 12, 1970

EPISODE
191

Feeling Darrin has no drive, Endora zaps him with ambition so powerful that he immediately bucks for a raise and works to undermine Larry with Braddock, a new client. Armed with personal information, Darrin impresses the sporting goods manufacturer and locks up the account. High on his success, Darrin tells Samantha they should have Larry's partner, McMann, over for dinner, and reveals a plan to take over the agency. Samantha confronts Endora, who keeps her spell on Darrin in favor of making him a multimillionaire.

Darrin won't listen when Samantha tells him he's been hexed, so she makes sure the Tates show up while McMann is over. Darrin fills McMann's ear with backhanded compliments about Larry; by the time the Tates arrive, McMann is ready to put Darrin in Larry's job. Samantha capitalizes on McMann's fondness for booze and twitches him into downing enough that he can't talk straight. But when McMann moves to demote Larry anyway, Samantha freezes everyone and gets Endora to despell Darrin, then privately tells him he'll have to get himself out of his own mess. Darrin butters Larry up for McMann's benefit, confusing the honcho; McMann comes to the conclusion that Darrin and Larry are a team that shouldn't be broken up. Later, as the Stephenses ready for a trip Darrin earned as a bonus, they inform a happy Endora that they've bought a yacht – a model boat that Samantha is perfectly happy with.

GOOD!

This episode has some interesting subtleties. Endora admits to herself that Samantha is a woman in love; given her ill feelings toward Darrin, that's quite a thing for her to acknowledge. And Larry proves he's been paying attention to Darrin's eccentricities over the years (of course not knowing it's all been a reaction to witchcraft): when Darrin tells Larry he'll be at the Braddock lunch with bells on, Larry sighs, "Just come as you are," which sounds like a man who remembers that Darrin has presented in a myriad of costumes, from Little Lord Fauntleroy ["I Get Your Nanny, You Get My Goat" (#122)] to Roman chic ["Samantha's Caesar Salad" (#173)]. Later, to McMann, Larry advises, "Now you see what I go through with this young genius. Don't try to make any sense out of what he says; just look at the results." This shows that Larry has even learned to embrace Darrin's unusual behavior. And Louise Tate, who has been AWOL since "Cousin Serena Strikes Again (Part I)" (#155), is back, reinventing herself as a groovy redhead and kicking up her usually staid wardrobe a funkalicious notch.

Drunken, slurring characters have been a comedy staple for years, but McMann's inebriated inaccuracies are intoxicating: he calls Darrin "Stephensy" and can't get the name of his own agency right – first it's "McMann & Tates," then "McTate & Mann." And though the little-seen character is now played by film actor Leon Ames instead of Roland Winters, who originated the CEO in "Man of the Year" (#139), McMann is consistent: he like his booze now as much as he did then. He even gets a first name – Howard – and a wife.

WELL?

Endora scoffs that Darrin "hasn't an ounce of ambition." Now, she has a point: Darrin's had several chances to open his own agency, all of which he's turned down; perhaps Madame Maruska from "How to Fail in Business With All Kinds of Help" (#104) was right that Darrin's afraid of success. Or maybe Endora's spell pulls the truth out of Darrin when he tells Braddock he stays at McMann & Tate because of Larry. That said, Endora is contradicting herself: as far back as "Help, Help, Don't Save Me" (#5), she put down ambition as "foolishly mortal."

If Darrin wasn't under Endora's ambition spell, you'd swear he'd taken backstabbing lessons from former assistant Gideon Whitsett; in "Your Witch Is Showing" (#20), the unscrupulous newbie also used personal information to cozy up to a client. And, when Darrin bribes the maitre d' to pull Larry away with a fake phone call, Darrin's right hand is up in a wide shot, but down in the subsequent two-shot.

The schmoozing Darrin tells Braddock that Larry's not a credit grabber. Darrin *must* be under a spell – he was very upset when Larry took credit for his work on the Bueno account in "Samantha and Darrin in Mexico City" (#170), and, in "Tabitha's Very Own Samantha" (#189), Larry told a client he was pleased with "the way Stephens worked up my ideas."

As Darrin takes "all the oxygen out of the room" telling Samantha about his takeover plans, he starts with an unusual overdub that doesn't match what's coming out of his mouth. Darrin shrewdly chooses McMann as his target since he's president of the agency – but it's long been established that Larry is president. Certainly McMann is a senior partner, and CEO; it's a wonder this is only his second appearance in the entire series.

Samantha realizes that Darrin is under Endora's spell as he schemes to have the McManns over the following night. Just before the dinner, Samantha tries to tell Darrin what Endora did. Surely she wouldn't wait an entire day to reveal this important information. Samantha expressly tells Darrin to invite the Tates, but has to witch them into coming over – did Darrin purposely ignore Samantha's wishes in his quest to commandeer McMann & Tate, or did something get left out of the script? Samantha thinks zapping Larry into calling McMann is the answer, but all Larry can do is call his partner and maybe find out he's dining at Darrin's; that doesn't necessarily mean Larry is going to show up. How is the Tates' presence supposed to stop Darrin, anyway? It's not one of Samantha's better-thought-out saves.

In the 1967 episode "I Remember You...Sometimes" (#97), Darrin recollecting a birthday gift led to the implication he'd been at McMann & Tate at least 8 years, which makes his hire date 1959 – 11 years ago. In "There's Gold in Them Thar Pills" (#107), which also aired three years earlier, Larry stipulated that Darrin had only been on staff 3 years; now six. Either way, Darrin can't know Larry was "a ball of fire" fifteen years ago, not unless he heard it through the grapevine.

Continuing with chronology, Darrin casts Larry as a member of the old guard. A year ago, in "Samantha's French Pastry" (#147), Larry said he was 47, so now he's 48. In "Your Witch Is Showing" (#20), Darrin said he graduated the University of Missouri in 1950; assuming he studied the usual four years, Darrin would have been 22 when he got his diploma, making him 42 now. That means Larry is only six years older than Darrin – if Larry's ready to be put out to pasture, Darrin's not far behind.

McMann gets drunker each time he gulps booze at Samantha's magical urging. Doesn't it usually take time for alcohol to get into the system? Maybe the instant drunkenness is part of Samantha's spell – or, her powers could be on the blink, as Louise blinks when she's supposed to be frozen.

OH, MY STARS!

When Endora first responds to Samantha's accusation of witchcraft, she says she's been on Venus, and that she "planted a broom up there." Yet it was Endora who stated in the very first episode that witches don't ride brooms – why would she revert to a stereotype she herself decried? Besides, in "And Something Makes Four" (#175), Endora and Maurice debated over whether he had flown to her beside from Venus the night Samantha was born. That was at least three centuries ago, so Venus hardly needs claiming.

Something is off in the resolve of this episode. After Endora removes her ambition spell, Samantha leaves Darrin to founder on his own, saying he would have realized he was hexed if he had listened to her earlier. Usually, when Darrin is under a spell, he thinks he's behaving normally: case in point, "You're So Agreeable" (#183), where he didn't even remember his actions. Yet Samantha thinks telling Darrin about the ambition spell is going to help, then punishes him for something he couldn't control. McMann's not blameless – he's ready to sack Larry, and he's not even under a spell. Finally, McMann listens to Darrin talking Larry up minutes after he ran him down, correctly pointing out that Darrin is contradicting himself. Doesn't late arrival Larry wonder what Darrin is contradicting himself about? And there's nothing to stop Mrs. McMann from going to Louise with how Darrin was about to throw Larry to the wolves before the Tates got there, so McMann declaring his underlings a team he doesn't want to break up is not the happy ending it appears to be.

SON OF A GUN!

"Well, I guess that's what's it at – uh, where it is..." – McMann, flunking out of Hip 101.

SERENA STOPS THE SHOW
Airdate: February 19, 1970

As entertainment chairman for the Cosmos Cotillion, Serena is on the hunt for singers just as Darrin comes home announcing that his client, Breeze Shampoo, is sponsoring a TV special starring hot recording artists Boyce and Hart. After grooving on their record, Serena wants them to headline her dance and witches her way in to see them – however, their manager, Chick Cashman, writes Serena off as a song plugger and throws her out. Appealing to Darrin to intervene, Serena performs her song, *I'll Blow You A Kiss in the Wind*; when Darrin doesn't like it, Serena casts a spell that turns fans off from Boyce and Hart and has venues canceling their gigs.

After Breeze Shampoo pulls out of the Boyce and Hart TV special, Larry, who opposed the deal, declares he was right when trade papers call the group over. Serena revisits Cashman, who, in light of declining record sales, agrees to let Boyce and Hart perform at the Cotillion. Since Serena has ignored her calls, Samantha pops over to the Cosmos Club to talk her cousin into reviving the singers' careers; Serena complies after their rendition of her song results in thunderous applause. Boyce and Hart reappear in Cashman's office and learn they've received a flood of offers, and Samantha predicts that Breeze Shampoo will return to the agency in no time.

GOOD!

Serena plays Boyce and Hart's groovy record in mid-air – which is a groovy effect. The crazed fan sequence is also well done; it's rather realistic for a sitcom, and definitely creates a feel of time and place: in this case, 1970.

Serena's hallmark is her spontaneous, emotion-driven witchery – so it's amazingly courteous of her to go to Darrin for help with enough self-awareness to ask, "Would you rather I handle this in my own way?" And, while it may not be the first time Elizabeth Montgomery has sung on the show, it's Serena's – remember, it was only Samantha-as-Serena who sang *The Iffen Song* in "Hippie, Hippie, Hooray" (#128). Serena's rendition of *I'll Blow You A Kiss in the Wind* (actually *I'm Gonna Blow You A Kiss in the Wind*, written by Boyce and Hart) is, as she herself would say, " right on."

Rock stars aren't always the first to make fun of themselves, so it's nice to see that Boyce and Hart can plant their tongues firmly in their cheeks. Confused by all the "black marks," the pair is asked if they can read music. In unison, the rockers point to each other and reply, "I do – he doesn't." Their take on "Serena's" song had to have been the epitome of hot in 1970, and it's a perfect representation of that time when seen though today's lens.

WELL?

When Samantha and Serena exit the kitchen to meet Darrin and Larry in the dining room, Elizabeth Montgomery's double is doing her best to hide her face. Serena has had a thing for Larry since meeting him in "Double, Double...Toil and Trouble" (#111), though she was pretending to be Samantha at the time; ironically, it was Samantha-as-Serena who first called Larry "Cotton Top" in "Hippie, Hippie, Hooray" (#128) – Serena must have decided she liked the nickname. As for Larry, how does he even recognize Serena? He's only ever met her in that latter episode, when she was blond. His attitude about the counterculture carries over from that episode as he voices his opposition to "putting those hippies on television" – so much for the youthful approach McMann was told Larry had in "What Makes Darrin Run" (#191). Darrin must still have a little of the previous episode's ambition spell clinging to him – why else would he go over Larry's head to seal the deal with Breeze Shampoo?

Tommy Boyce pulls a piece of the shirt the screaming girls tore off him out of his robe pocket to show Serena. Why is it there? Is he keeping it as a souvenir? Then, as Serena dickers with Cashman, she tells the manager, "in my circle, money isn't important." Maybe it isn't now, but in "Take Two Aspirins and Half A Pint of Porpoise Milk" (#42), Darrin had to fork out cash to buy medicinal ingredients at a witches' shop, and, in "Samantha the Dressmaker" (#60), Endora lamented "all the mortal money" she spent at a Paris couturier. After Cashman boots Serena, she appears in the Stephenses' TV with a "sigalert" – for non-Californians, that's a report relaying the latest traffic tie-ups, which her puns refer to. But she's wrong when she exclaims, "They were rude to me!" Only Cashman was rude; Boyce and Hart were ready to take Serena to bed.

Serena's always been grandiose, but she could save time by either putting a spell on Cashman to allow Boyce and Hart to perform, or zapping up doubles of the boys to sing at the Cotillion. Sandbagging the rockers' careers seems about as unethical as Samantha said magically fixing the stock market was in "My Baby, the Tycoon" (#55).

Despite Serena's instant failure spell, Breeze Shampoo waits several days to cancel Boyce and Hart's special, and no one notices the slump until Larry brings the trade paper in. Darrin also shows a remarkable lack of business savvy; no one seals a deal with a verbal contract in the advertising business.

Serena threatens revenge after her first encounter with the singers and their manager – yet, she strolls right in a few days later to refresh her offer. Cashman would have ordered extra security for Serena, who is wearing Samantha's contested mink-trimmed coat from "Cheap, Cheap" (#112).

The footage of the crowd at the Cosmos Club is actually taken from Samantha's coronation in "Long Live the Queen" (#108); apparently Ticheba's dogs are waiting for Boyce and Hart to perform. Now, the guys don't read music, but they're not playing instruments, either – don't they wonder how their backtrack is being piped in? The "guys and gals in the cosmos" must really love Serena's song, because they clap nearly a minute for a performance that lasted about as long. However, it's not likely Serena will be asked back as entertainment chairman: she brought in one act to sing part of one song for an entire dance. Finally, when Boyce and Hart return to Cashman's office, their manager comments that they haven't left yet, and Bobby Hart says, "That's what you think." His answer implies that he remembers the Cotillion, except Serena's spell specified, "Forget where you were and what you did."

OH, MY STARS!

There are several continuity flaws in this episode with regard to time. After Serena sings her song, Samantha offers her a midnight snack. A moment later, when Serena pops back to Boyce and Hart's venue to assure their failure, it's still daytime, and not long after her first visit, because the same fans are camped out there. When Serena meets Boyce and Hart, she says her Cotillion is "a week from Saturday night" – she casts her spell soon after. The next scene shows Larry reporting that the duo hasn't sold a record in three days, the same amount of time Samantha has been trying to reach Serena; it's the night of the dance at this point, because Samantha pops there in the same clothes she wears during Larry's visit. But it can't be Saturday, because Larry brandishes "today's issue of *Weekly Variety*," which doesn't publish on weekends (nor would a weekly publication put out daily editions), and it can't have only been three days since Serena cast her spell, because the dance was still over a week away when she did. The only way this works is if Boyce and Hart stopped selling records over four days into Serena's spell, but that doesn't gibe with the fans turning off from their idols instantly.

SON OF A GUN!

"Aw." – Boyce and Hart, when they realize Serena's "trip" only involves a magic carpet.

JUST A KID AGAIN
EPISODE 193
Airdate: February 26, 1970

Samantha and Tabitha visit Hanley's Department Store, where salesman Irving Bates is more interested in playing with toys than selling them. When Irving wishes he were a boy again, Tabitha turns him into a nine-year-old. Junior Irving runs afoul of his boss – then a cop intervenes as Irving unsuccessfully tries to drive his car. Tracking down the Stephenses, Irving-as-boy presents himself to Samantha and explains how Tabitha "shrunk" him. After Samantha reveals that she and Tabitha are witches, Irving realizes he's stood up his girlfriend, Ruthie; he has Samantha call to make his excuses, but Ruthie hangs up. When Darrin comes home, Samantha tries to get young Irving to pretend he's Tabitha's friend; privately, Irving tells Tabitha to forget about changing him back.

Darrin is dismayed to learn that his daughter has turned a 32-year-old man into a boy, and when Tabitha's attempt to restore Irving doesn't work, Samantha calls Dr. Bombay, who concludes that Irving and Tabitha want Irving to stay a child. Samantha realizes that Ruthie is the only way to change Irving's mind – she takes Irving to see Ruthie and twitches Ruthie's boss into amorously chasing her around the room. After Irving-as-boy comes to Ruthie's rescue, she gratefully lavishes attention on him. Sold, Irving gently tells Tabitha that he wants be an adult again, so she grants his request.

GOOD!

Ron Masak doesn't spend as much time on screen as his junior counterpart, but his arrested development as disillusioned grown-up Irving is a treat for the kid in all of us, balanced by the salesman's natural rapport with Tabitha. As for Master Irving Bates, his transformations from 32 to 9 – and back again – are crackerjack effects, and Richard Powell's grown-up declarations are hilarious coming through his out-of-the-mouths-of-babes filter. Young Irving's deadpan deliveries, especially during *The Story of Irving and Tabitha*, look like child's play; he's got as much lip with Darrin as he does heart with Tabitha when he tells her why she needs to change him back. Child actors of Powell's caliber don't come along every day.

WELL?

Maybe the grocery store manager from "Samantha's Lost Weekend" (#186) got fired after Samantha consumed his profits, because he shows up here as Irving's boss – or, at least, it's the same actor, Jonathan Hole, making an appearance as a different character only seven episodes later. Irving tells Samantha and Tabitha that the hippie doll they settled on costs $9.95 – yet, the amount at the register is

$7.50 for every customer. And Samantha should easily hear Irving yelling, "Hey! Little girl!" from the nearby gift wrap kiosk; the store doesn't even have Muzak to drown out his cry.

For all Tabitha's excitement about the idea of keeping the shrunken Irving around as an older brother, the Stephenses never mention that she already has a baby brother in Adam, whom she was still jealous of in "Tabitha's Very Own Samantha" (#189). Shouldn't Samantha be worried about retaliation from the Witches' Council when she tells Irving she's a witch? She just got her powers popped in "Samantha's Secret Is Discovered" (#188) for making the same admission to mother-in-law Phyllis.

When Irving tries to light his pipe, Samantha stops him, saying, "Little boys do not play with matches." Where is she getting that? She knows Irving is a 32-year-old in a kid's body. Irving doesn't think things through when he moves to call the cops on Samantha and Tabitha; they could have an APB out on him for kicking a cop in the shin earlier that day.

Darrin clunking his golf clubs around when he comes through the front door is the only way he could miss hearing Samantha magically shattering the cookie jar in the kitchen to coerce Irving into behaving. And Tabitha has a swing set again – there was one parked in the backyard in "Going Ape" (#162), but nothing since, except for the temporary one Maurice zapped up in "Samantha's Good News" (#168). If anyone should be sympathetic to Irving's plight, it's Darrin: he himself was turned into a ten-year-old in "Junior Executive" (#46), so he ought to be comparing notes with the toy salesman, not giving him a hard time.

Samantha tells Darrin that Dr. Bombay is the best witch doctor they have, which implies there's more than one. Yet, in "Samantha's Curious Cravings" (#174), Samantha said Bombay was the only one. And his solution is to cast a spell to make Irving an adult again – but Samantha could do that. Neither adult should think they can undo Tabitha's spell, anyway; she has squatter's rights to Irving, as stipulated in "Hoho the Clown" (#92).

What to do when an unwanted guest won't cooperate? Tempt him into going back where he came from. Samantha got rid of Prince Charming in "A Prince of a Guy" (#129) by zapping up Sleeping Beauty for him; Samantha also had Cleopatra's curves do the talking to send Julius Caesar home to Rome in "Samantha's Caesar Salad" (#173). It works here as well, as young Irving gets to see up close and personal two very good reasons to go back to his life as an adult. Speaking of Ruthie, she never wonders how this strange boy knows her name, and her boss, Drucker, falls under Samantha's love spell, but it's a wonder he can see her – there are no glasses in his glasses. And would you use a travel agency that's got brochures for an event that happened three years ago? Drucker's has them, in the form of rack cards for Montréal's Expo 67.

After Tabitha restores Irving to full size, he asks Samantha to send him to Ruthie; in turn, Samantha asks Darrin if he minds. That's a silly question – she just took Irving-as-boy to Ruthie without getting Darrin's permission. Irving's glad to return to life as a grown-up, but maybe he shouldn't be; hours earlier, he was certain he'd been fired from a job he wasn't happy in, and his girlfriend said she'd been stood up for the last time. That's not much of a life to go back to.

OH, MY STARS!

When did Morning Glory Circle move? For the first two seasons, it was only said the Stephenses lived in New York State. In "Soapbox Derby" (#90), there was a hint that narrowed the town down to Patterson, a detail that seemed to be confirmed by Samantha in "Samantha's Shopping Spree" (#169). Maybe only the store was in Patterson, because Irving tracks Samantha and Tabitha to a town called Westport! Ironically, hobo Horace Dilloway, posing as Darrin's Uncle Albert, told the real Albert that the Stephenses had moved to Westport in "A Bum Raps" (#68) – if they live in Westport now, Horace couldn't say they moved there, so Irving's revelation is a history rewrite all the way around. Assuming this relocation is what the writers have decided on, which Westport are they referring to? There's one in New York, but it's 273 miles from Manhattan – Darrin wouldn't commute that far. There's another Westport that's only 51 miles from NYC, but it's in Connecticut – and cars on the show have always had New York license plates. It's good to finally have a definite setting for the show; it's just a shame it conflicts with series history.

SON OF A GUN!

"Well, I won't hold that against you. I'm a liberal." – Irving, finding out that Samantha and Tabitha are witches.

Doesn't it just crackle with possibilities that Irving knows Samantha's secret? All the mortals that should have figured it out by now – Larry, Frank, Phyllis, etc. – are kept in the dark for the sake of comedy, so it's fascinating that Irving has been brought into the magical loop. True, he can't tell anyone – note Darrin's knowing smile when Irving mentions this – but Irving's witchy knowledge sounds like a good reason to have him stop by once in a while. Besides, he's great with Tabitha, and they're forever bonded because of their experience.

EPISODE 194

THE GENERATION ZAP
Airdate: March 5, 1970

Darrin is assigned to mentor Dusty Harrison, a college girl who's interested in advertising. Suspicious Endora promises Samantha she'll butt out, but gets Serena to zap the stoic Dusty with a love spell. Darrin senses that Dusty is attracted to him, so he sends her on a long errand; at home, Darrin tells Samantha about Dusty, who shows up on the doorstep dressed to kill. Samantha is amused by Dusty's fawning, but, the next day, when Darrin tells Dusty he's finding her another mentor, the bespelled girl runs out of his office in a flood of tears. Dusty's father thinks Darrin has been toying with his daughter's affections, which puts Harrison's account with the agency in jeopardy.

Samantha deduces that Serena is involved and pops out to look for her – but Serena pops in and replaces her, suggesting to Darrin that they have Harrison over to straighten things out. While Darrin explains to Harrison that Dusty's crush is one-sided, "Samantha" makes faces behind Darrin's back. After Dusty barges in pledging her devotion to Darrin, Serena-as-Samantha leads Harrison to the patio to make advances. Samantha returns and sees Dusty chasing Darrin, then catches her double with Harrison. Once Serena removes her spell, Dusty is horrified, and Harrison wants to punch Darrin, which Samantha prevents – though she does let Dusty slap her husband. Later, Darrin hears that Harrison has been busted for embezzlement and decides to tell Larry that he sabotaged the account on purpose.

GOOD!

Endora hasn't tried to break up Samantha's marriage for a couple of years – not since "Once in a Vial" (#125), where her scheme backfired to the point a love potion had her violently in love with Bo Callahan – ironically, also played by Arch Johnson, who appears as Harrison here. Endora was making too many attempts there for a while; after the long break, this new scheme feels fresh. Fresher still is Serena, who bats her eyelashes as the witched Dusty falls hard for Darrin.

There is something about Elizabeth Montgomery's performance in this episode that really creates the impression Serena is inhabiting Samantha's body, particularly when the "identical" cousins argue on the patio. The way Serena's voice and mannerisms express through "Samantha" is genius.

WELL?

The fancy mirror that took the place of the painting in the foyer in "Mirror, Mirror on the Wall" (#146) and "Naming Samantha's New Baby" (#176) is back, though the den mirror that was only ever seen in "Super Arthur" (#190) is gone. As for the Stephenses, Samantha is just upstairs, but doesn't hear Serena's loud cackling in the living room, and later, Darrin can't hear Serena and Endora from the den, despite just having heard Samantha saying she's going out.

Endora doesn't need to zap Serena into appearing – Serena can pop in herself; besides, the last time Endora conjured Serena up to wreak havoc [in "Double, Double...Toil and Trouble" (#111)], she at least picked the more clandestine laundry room. Now, as Serena is Samantha's cousin on Maurice's side of the family [as established in "Mrs. Stephens, Where Are You?" (#160)], Endora would certainly be Serena's aunt, at least by marriage. So why has Serena never referred to Endora as an aunt until now?

Serena and Endora may be manipulating Dusty's heart strings, but there's no hiding the strings holding the witches up in Darrin's office. Then, they double zap Dusty (Serena placing the spell and Endora unfreezing the mortals); in their two-shot, they are both pointing at Dusty and Darrin, but in the wide shot, only Endora is pointing.

How old does Darrin think Dusty is? He offers her root beer and ginger ale like she's a teenager, despite knowing she's a college student. Once again, the bar is on the kitchen counter for no apparent reason, as it was in "Samantha's Yoo-Hoo Maid" (#172), and, although Darrin asks Samantha to fix everyone a snack, she just makes a snarky comment and joins Dusty on the couch, ignoring the request. Dusty should be a lot colder toward Samantha – she's in love with Darrin through a spell and would be more apt to view Samantha as a threat, yet she's perfectly cordial to her perceived rival.

Serena's note is delivered by the "butterfly" that Tabitha turned preschool friend Amy into in "I Don't Want to Be A Toad, I Want to Be A Butterfly" (#151). After Samantha disappears, Endora pops in and tells Serena, "She's getting to be almost as dumb as he is," which seems out of character knowing how much Endora loves her daughter. But Darrin doesn't help this cause – when Samantha pops into the dining room, Darrin doesn't see it, despite facing that direction while talking to Dusty.

Darrin tells Dusty it's "not true" he doesn't know about unrequited love. His known romantic interests, outside of Samantha, are Sheila Sommers [see "I, Darrin, Take This Witch, Samantha" (#1)] and Mary Jane Nilesmunster ["No Zip in My Zap" (#113)], both of whom he dumped. So who did Darrin long for?

When the news report reveals Harrison's shifty activity (which doesn't include the shift the frozen Harrison makes when Serena-as-Samantha pops out next to him), Darrin shushes Samantha, but he does it before the anchor ever mentions Harrison's name. And Darrin's had a little experience telling Larry he purposely sabotaged the account of a criminal client – that's what he did in "If They Never Met" (#127), when he assured Larry there was a good reason for Endora's cobra being in his briefcase.

OH, MY STARS!

Perhaps Braddock, the sports manufacturer Darrin schmoozed in "What Makes Darrin Run" (#191), has a twin brother in Harrison, because they're both played by noted character actor Arch Johnson. Gruff

Harrison is different from the more affable Braddock, but a three-episode gap is too soon to bring back such a recognizable actor. (By the way, he and Melodie Johnson, who plays Dusty, are not related.)

This time, the show copies content from "The Girl Reporter" (#9), in which young Liza Randall crushed on Darrin while writing an article for her college newspaper. There *are* marked differences: unlike Liza, Dusty requires a spell to fall in love with Darrin and doesn't have a jealous boyfriend, while Samantha thinks the whole thing is funny, and Darrin doesn't respond to Dusty's flirting; neither was the case with Liza. There's even an interesting, inadvertent comparing of 1964 and 1970 – Liza was a "typical American school kid with freckles, short socks, and sneakers," while Dusty is "your average know-it-all college girl; a little on the plain side, studious, dedicated, wearing a mini-skirt and a great big smile." That said, much of the dialogue (including "Give me a quarter and I'll go to the movies" and "I've had enough of this whole silly farce") is lifted directly from the original episode. Since the Stephenses have already experienced these events, continuity would dictate that they realize it; they don't. If the show really felt it necessary to double up on a story, it would be only natural for ad man Darrin to mentor a second student – why not recall what happened with Liza, then move on to this different but similar scenario using completely new dialogue?

SON OF A GUN!

"I'm just dying to have you look at my coffee pots." – Dusty to Darrin, breathily reporting that she's completed his errand.

EPISODE 195 OKAY, WHO'S THE WISE WITCH?
Airdate: March 12, 1970

Darrin needs to get to a presentation for a housing development, but none of the doors or windows will open. When Darrin's hammer and Samantha's witchcraft can't provide a way out, Samantha summons Endora, thinking she's responsible. Swearing her innocence with a Witch's Honor and agreeing to track down next likely suspect Uncle Arthur, Endora discovers that she can't pop out. Larry calls, wanting to know where Darrin is, so Samantha lies that he's sick; later, Darrin's attempt to escape through the chimney fails. Samantha yoo-hoos for Esmeralda, but the maid hasn't cast any backfiring spells and is disappointed to be stuck in the house because she finally has a date.

Samantha drives Larry away by telling him the house is under quarantine, then calls for Dr. Bombay, hoping he can solve the riddle of their entrapment. Using his atmospheric oscillator, Bombay confirms the house is sealed off by a "vapor lock" thanks to undistributed metaphysical particles left behind by Samantha's non-use of witchcraft. Bombay can only cast his curing spell outside, so Samantha transfers him to a "photograph" and slides him under the door. It works, setting everyone free; to help Darrin explain his delay to Larry, Samantha adds an extendable roof to Darrin's model house, and Endora shrinks the playground equipment she zapped up for Tabitha, creating an indoor/outdoor play yard for rainy days. The client loves it, and Samantha later distributes metaphysical particles by sending Esmeralda to Jupiter for her date.

GOOD!

This episode has a high percentage of great lines, especially in its second half. As Samantha theorizes that the house is sick, Darrin declares he has "a contagious disease that's about to change me into a raving maniac" – Endora rolls her eyes and claims, "The change will be imperceptible." Dr. Bombay gets strange readings on his atmospheric oscillator, causing Endora to opine, "Maybe you're holding it too close to Durwood." Not to be outdone, Darrin listens as Bombay says, "I'm in favor of relieving the suspense with a little humor," then replies, "So am I. Why don't you try some?" The show's dialogue is always well-written, but these snappy and clever exchanges are outstanding.

Perhaps it's the relief of not being stuck in the house anymore, but Darrin and Endora show an unprecedented appreciation for each other in the moments following the removal of the vapor lock. "Endora, I never thought I'd say this," Darrin says after his mother-in-law miniaturizes Tabitha's playground equipment per Samantha's instruction, "but you've been a big help!" Tickled, Endora gushes to Samantha, "What would your husband do without us?" This unexpected warmth is the perfect capper to an already stellar episode.

WELL?

Darrin tries to get out the window with a hammer, but chucks it in frustration and accidentally breaks a cookie jar – the same jar Samantha shattered and reassembled to show Irving Bates the extent of her power in "Just A Kid Again" (#193).

Endora surmises that an entrapment spell would be cast by someone who wants to make trouble for Samantha's marriage. How is sealing the Stephenses in their house supposed to cause a rift between them? Endora makes up for this hinky hypothesis by incorporating the 1967 Fifth Dimension hit, *Up, Up, and Away*, into her ultimately ineffectual departure spell – but when she realizes Darrin is part of the family she's stuck with, Endora sighs, "You can't have everything." Ironic, because when she split Darrin in "Samantha's Better Halves" (#185), she bragged, "Who says you can't have everything?"

There's no real purpose to the Stephenses moving the model house from the foyer bench to the living room coffee table – are they just trying to occupy their time since they're stuck inside? Esmeralda is thrilled to have a date with Ramon Verona after 75 years of hoping; she reminds Endora that Ramon is a salad chef. Do witches really need food preparation employees when they can zap up their own salads? Maybe Esmeralda can learn something from Ramon; she did have trouble making salad in "Samantha's Caesar Salad" (#173).

Larry's worried about not having access to the model house, but he can't be too worried, or he'd climb through the window, as he did in "The Phrase Is Familiar" (#187). Luckily he doesn't, or Samantha would have to explain why it's "locked."

Different swing sets were stationed in the backyard in "Going Ape" (#162) and "Just A Kid Again" (#193), but Tabitha didn't get to keep either of them – even now, she only gets to play on Endora's for 24 seconds before being dragged away in anticipation of Dr. Bombay's arrival. Why can't Tabitha stay? She's old enough now that she doesn't need to be shielded from witchy doings. Bombay determines that the vapor lock is caused by Samantha's witchcraft being "sharply curtailed" – maybe Darrin's right to reply, "Who said so?" because she truly uses her powers more episodes than not.

Why does Bombay need Samantha to turn him into a photograph when he's perfectly capable of transforming himself? Once outside, Bombay casts his curing spell and places his hands on the door, only to stumble into the house and crash into the swing set once the door is opened. It's not likely he'd have that much momentum from the door opening; he'd probably just fall on the floor in front of him.

Trying to get to Jupiter to meet Ramon Verona, Esmeralda pops in for help, saying she's landed on Venus and Pluto in her attempts. When Esmeralda was introduced in "Samantha's Yoo-Hoo Maid" (#172), Endora said the domestic had lost most of her powers – yet now Esmeralda is able to fly around to different planets. Samantha concurs that "Jupiter's a toughie" – in "Sam in the Moon" (#91), Darrin lost it over the idea of his wife being able to make a lunar visit, which she neither confirmed nor denied; here, he gets evidence that she's flown even further than that, but doesn't react. Maybe after almost six years of being married to a witch, he's decided these things are no longer worth the fuss.

After Samantha zaps Esmeralda to Jupiter, she puts forth that she should use her powers once a day to avoid another vapor lock. Darrin resists. Wouldn't it be better to let her do some subtle zapping if it means not getting stuck in the house again? After all, if the takeaway is that repressing yourself is detrimental to your overall well-being, isn't it negating the message for Darrin to expect Samantha to continue her repression?

OH, MY STARS!

When Darrin realizes he's stuck in the house, he has 38 minutes to get to his meeting – except it's an hour's drive from Westport to Manhattan, so he's already late. Later, Larry drives two hours to get from McMann & Tate to Morning Glory Circle and back, making him over an hour and a half late for the same presentation. But somehow, after the house is released from the vapor lock, Darrin is able to meet with the housing development folks and impress them with Samantha's indoor/outdoor play yard idea. Did Larry end up postponing the meeting, as he suggested he might? And could busy executives really reschedule it for the same day?

SON OF A GUN!

"Durwood, sit down and relax. The centuries will pass quickly.'" – Endora, as everyone realizes they are trapped in the house.

This episode, whose title derives from a phrase Samantha first uttered in "Marriage, Witches' Style" (#161), can be summed up in just one line from Endora: "What an original spell!" This is one of the most unique tales the series has spun so far – there's even a mystery as to what's sealing off the house; usually the magical culprit is evident right away, though it often takes Samantha a while to figure things out. The show goes even further, hinting that Samantha is doing herself more harm than good by suppressing her natural magic, which builds on an idea first presented in "No Zip in My Zap" (#113), where "neglect of her metaphysics" had clogged up Samantha's powers; it's perfectly sensible that undistributed metaphysical particles would continue to cause her problems. And, considering how many remakes there have been this season, it's wonderful to see that the show can still conjure up something completely new and innovative.

EPISODE 196

A CHANCE ON LOVE
Airdate: March 19, 1970

Overbooked Samantha has forgotten that she's committed herself to selling raffle tickets for charity – so when Serena pops in, Samantha persuades her cousin to take her place. As Samantha, Serena hits it off with sexy George Dinsdale; they want to expand their lunch date into a dinner date, but Dinsdale has a business obligation. Meanwhile, the Stephenses attend an agency dinner where Samantha runs into – George Dinsdale. Samantha is horrified when Dinsdale nuzzles her, but she soon realizes it was Serena he met. Samantha tries to explain, but Dinsdale laughs off the double duty as romantic intrigue. On their next date, Serena reiterates to Dinsdale that she and Samantha are two different people, but he still thinks "Samantha" is just playing games.

Undeterred, Dinsdale kicks Darrin off his account and goes to the house to assure "Samantha" that Darrin won't be a problem. The disbelieving Dinsdale parrots Samantha when she brings up Serena, and becomes one after he grabs Samantha for a kiss. Darrin arrives with Larry, amazed when the parrot squawks that he's Dinsdale; by the time Larry leaves, Darrin knows the bird isn't a bird, and Samantha tells him that the only way to set Dinsdale straight is to get her and Serena in the same room. Samantha restores Dinsdale, who is apologetic when he sees the cousins together – though later, he returns to the Stephenses in a daze after Serena took his "fly me to the moon" crooning literally.

GOOD!

The show's special effects team seems to have gotten the kinks out of their split screening, because none of those pesky lines divide Samantha and Serena as in previous installments. It's also astute of Samantha to know she can manipulate Serena into covering for her by suggesting that Darrin will have a fit if he finds out about their switch. No wonder Serena swoons over George Dinsdale; Jack Cassidy brings a sex appeal never before seen on the show. Plus, the restaurant which hosts their dates – and the way those scenes are shot – has a very sophisticated look compared to the rest of the episode.

The other characters surrounding the Serena/Dinsdale/Samantha triangle offer up some geometry of their own. Red-headed Louise barely says a word but still manages to be memorable in her funky, furry ensemble that's a far cry from her couture of yesteryear. [What would the Louise of "I'd Rather Twitch Than Fight" (#84) have to say about the psychological ramifications of her future self's choice in clothing?] Larry owns his client paranoia when he suggests Dinsdale dropped Darrin over the way he makes martinis; Darrin says he isn't making sense, and Larry replies, "I know, but I'm desperate." Darrin even demonstrates that he's been paying attention to witchcraft the last six years, as he knows right away that Samantha's parrot is a person and puts it to the test.

WELL?

In the opening sequence, Serena magically piles Samantha's groceries into the cupboard, but its door starts to close during the effect. After her arrival, Serena jokes that Samantha is choosing to "tote that barge and lift that bale" – the lyric is from *Ol' Man River*, a song featured in the 1927 Broadway musical *Showboat*, and it's exactly what Darrin said Samantha was lucky she didn't have to do in "To Twitch or Not to Twitch" (#132). Additionally, Serena's comment that Samantha "needn't develop biceps" doing housework repeats Endora's sentiment from "Be It Ever So Mortgaged" (#2) word for word.

Samantha tells Serena that selling raffle tickets is so easy, "Even you could do it." Maybe Samantha is remembering Serena's disastrous turn as a powerless frozen banana maker in "Samantha's Power Failure" (#165). Serena adding a "smidgen" to the hemline of her mini-dress is a flawless effect, but when Serena gets to the hotel as "Samantha," the smidgen is removed; either Serena changed it back, or someone in Wardrobe made a boo-boo. Question: in asking Serena to double for her, why does Samantha let her cousin keep the dollar sign "tattoo" stenciled near right eye? Admittedly, Serena's sported similar marks appropriate to the situation since "Marriage, Witches' Style" (#161), but, if Samantha wants to be represented accurately, you'd think she'd insist on Serena making herself an exact duplicate.

As Dinsdale first appears, he tells Larry that they need to "close up the generation gap." The guy makes soup – what kind of generation gap could there be? Later, at the party, Darrin doesn't see Dinsdale having a long, intense conversation with his wife, but Larry, Louise, or the many others in attendance could report this sighting to Darrin; apparently, they don't.

Answering Samantha's late-night summons, Serena's sultry response is, "Boy, do you have rotten timing." Serena must not be as interested in Dinsdale as she lets on if she's already entertaining another gentleman. Serena assures her cousin that her flirtation with Dinsdale is perfectly innocent – yet, a moment earlier, Serena admitted, "innocence is not my bag." Samantha shouldn't be surprised that Serena is into Dinsdale: after all, her cousin was on the hunt for a mortal in "Marriage, Witches' Style" (#161).

Maybe "broom" has become a witch euphemism – it's been clear since the pilot that witches don't actually ride them, but the word's being used a lot lately, so maybe the obsolete method of travel has just worked its way into the lexicon, since Serena tells Samantha not to "bust her broom."

Dinsdale doesn't recognize "Samantha" as a brunette, just as Darrin and Larry didn't recognize a non-blond Samantha in "That Was My Wife" (#31). But he should be able to tell that Serena sounds very different from Samantha – does he think she's just putting on a voice to aid in her pretense? At home, Samantha turns the client into a parrot to fend off his advances; she effected the same change in blackmailing detective Charlie Leach back in "Follow That Witch (Part II)" (#67). After Samantha makes the transformation, her hair is much looser than it was when Dinsdale was kissing on her.

Musical theatre veteran Jack Cassidy gets a brief chance to display his considerable vocal talent as Dinsdale describes how singing *Fly Me to the Moon* (a standard written in 1954) earned him a trip to the real place. Serena once again copies from Endora, who told Samantha how she fulfilled a beau's request to make that same journey in "Witch or Wife" (#8). Samantha makes light of Dinsdale's lunar launch by saying he did it cheaper than NASA, but, given how hung up Darrin was on "the NASA men" in "Sam in the Moon" (#91), she might want to reexamine her choice of words. Did Darrin's tacit acceptance upon learning she'd been to Jupiter in "Okay, Who's the Wise Witch?" (#195) make her feel like she could broach the subject again?

OH, MY STARS!

Why would Samantha want Serena to impersonate her after she caused so much trouble hitting on embezzler Harrison in her form in "The Generation Zap" (#194)? If Samantha really wants Serena to do her a solid, she should say it's the least her cousin can to do make up for that incident. Or, if Samantha really needs to be in two places at once, she could simply split herself, like Endora did to play chess in "Samantha's Yoo-Hoo Maid" (#172).

After the originality of "Okay, Who's The Wise Witch?" (#195), the show pulls this episode's central plot from "Which Witch Is Which?" (#24), where Endora attended a dress fitting in Samantha's stead and came back with a boyfriend. Samantha even asks Serena to lower her hemline a smidgen, whereas before, Endora-as-Samantha wanted to lower her neckline "two smidgens." It's not as blatant a redo as other episodes this season, but it also doesn't have the crackle of the original, despite fine performances all around.

SON OF A GUN!

"Well, turn him off!" – Samantha to Serena, who confesses she turns Dinsdale on.

IF THE SHOE PINCHES
Airdate: March 26, 1970

While Darrin struggles with a slogan for Barbour Peaches, Tabitha entertains imaginary friends in her new playhouse – until Tim O'Shanter, a real leprechaun, approaches her for food. Darrin doesn't believe Tabitha's feeding a leprechaun and thinks his daughter is guilty of zapping a pointy nose and donkey ears on him, but Samantha catches Tim and demands to know why he's there. Tim says he needs a witch to restore his magic; Samantha does, but it turns out that Endora, who rendered Tim powerless in the first place, has sicced the leprechaun on Darrin. Later, Tim leaves Darrin a pair of shoes, which makes him lazy. With the Barbour deadline approaching, Larry comes by to check on Darrin's progress and threatens to fire him over his new devil-may-care attitude.

When Tim won't remove Darrin's shoes, Samantha cooks up a leprechaun-controlling potion, explaining to Tabitha that witchcraft is all right in emergencies. After Tim eats chicken soup laced with the potion, he complies with Samantha's command to get rid of the shoes – then slips that Endora is behind his presence. Samantha sends him away, and Endora grudgingly restores Tim's powers so he can leave. Larry returns for the Barbour slogan; Samantha has Endora zap one into Darrin's head, but it's bad enough that Endora has to add a zap to make Larry love it.

GOOD!

Tabitha doesn't have much to do in this episode, but she steals it anyway. Proving she knows nosy neighbor Gladys Kravitz quite well, Tabitha pretends to give "her" a requested cup of sugar; Gladys has been asking for those since Samantha was pregnant with Tabitha in "And Then I Wrote" (#45). Tabitha then goes up against the leprechaun, countering Tim's refusal to nosh nonexistent food with, "You eat what's in front of you or you don't eat at all!" Tabitha's turn for the serious is also wonderful, as she soberly reminds Samantha, "I thought we had a rule: no witchcraft!" And Samantha teaching Tabitha that there are times rules have to be broken simply rules.

Both times Endora and Tim are on the roof, there are very realistic-looking clouds behind them, and the backdrop changes depending on the time of day, as do the bird sound effects that become twilight crickets. And Darrin's observation that Endora has "run out of ideas to torment me" brings the whole series full circle in a subtle way.

WELL?

Samantha insists that Tabitha is "behaving like any normal six-year-old." In real time, Tabitha is four; she was born on-screen in 1966 ["And Then There Were Three" (#54)]. But Maurice pointed out that the Stephenses had been married "five long years" as of this season's "Daddy Comes for a Visit" (#180) – so suggesting that Tabitha is six rather puts another slant on why Darrin hurriedly dumped Sheila Sommers to marry Samantha in the pilot. [Of course, Samantha didn't announce her pregnancy until a year after her wedding, in "Alias Darrin Stephens" (#37).]

Endora tells Tim to stop stalling, but in voice-over, since the words don't match what's coming out of her mouth. Samantha's hair doesn't match, either; it bounces loosely when she opens the door to Larry, then it's sprayed down in a close-up, and it finishes by getting even looser after she drags Tim in to answer for Darrin's reconstructive surgery. Darrin's ears have been tampered with before: Tabitha's goblin friend zapped him with similar (but not identical) donkey ears in "The Safe and Sane Halloween" (#115), and Endora made Darrin's own ears grow in "My, What Big Ears You Have" (#121). As for Darrin's nose, Serena made an addition to that in "Cousin Serena Strikes Again" (Part II)" (#156). Hopefully Tabitha got the proper apology her parents promised; they should know better than to think their daughter is responsible for Darrin's makeover.

Maybe leprechauns can't fly without wires: they're visible when Samantha lifts Tim off the living room carpet, and when Endora floats him to the roof. Does no one on Morning Glory Circle see a witch and an even more conspicuous leprechaun on top of the Stephens house?

Endora makes Darrin lazy through Tim's trademark shoes, but her slothful popcorn did it first in "Oedipus Hex" (#85). With Darrin under Tim's power, Samantha searches for a potion to control the leprechaun. Samantha had Endora concoct a similar brew in "Cousin Edgar" (#36) to incapacitate an elf – but Samantha forgets how that scheme backfired when Edgar switched drugged hot chocolate on her. For Tim to be doing Endora's bidding, maybe he's already under the influence of a potion. Tim can't be all bad, though – he pretends to hear "a baby's cry," which is more acknowledgment than Adam gets from his own family members the entire episode.

At the table, Tim and Samantha play switch-the-soup, but both do so without making any noise with the dishes at all. If Samantha sees Tim putting the spiked soup in front of her, why doesn't she just zap the bowls into the right places instead of floating them? And where's Tabitha? The child almost never shares a meal with her parents.

After Tim slips that he's working for Endora, Samantha makes him disappear. She implies she's sending him back to "the old sod," but he pops in next to Endora on the roof. Did Endora intercept him? As Tim happily reacts to the news he can leave, he holds his hat behind him in a wide shot, but, in the ensuing two-shot, the hat is in front of him.

Samantha has Endora zap a slogan into Darrin's head – a bit of an easy story wrap-up – but then, she wonders if her mother can put a spell on "the entire peach-buying public." This from the woman who told Darrin it would be unethical for a witch to influence the stock market in "My Baby, the Tycoon" (#55); it seems this would apply to the supermarket, too.

OH, MY STARS!

There's an inherent connection between this episode and "The Leprechaun" (#63), but the show doesn't take the opportunity to make it. Samantha was much friendlier to Darrin's magical cousin, Brian O'Brian, than she is to Tim; in an interesting reversal, Samantha wants Tim gone while Darrin is rather mellow towards him, and that's before he puts on Tim's shoes. Darrin and Phyllis' Irish heritage, established in "A Most Unusual Wood Nymph" (#79), is never mentioned. And the leprechaun community can't be that big – do Tim and Brian know each other?

Brian required his pot of gold before he could perform magic; Tim's magic is wrapped up in a legendary *shillelagh*. Samantha restores Tim's powers, but Endora still has to make him fly to the roof. Do Samantha's powers actually have an effect on Tim, or is Endora's original magic-depleting spell blocking it? Also, Tim indicates that Endora has only sapped his power to travel, but he'd still need his magic *shillelagh* to pull his pranks, which is in Endora's custody the whole time – yet Tim can put a nose and ears on Darrin, and later remove his shoes.

Samantha cooks up a potion to gain control over Tim; a sound effect signifies it's working. Then Samantha yells for Tim to take his sloth-inducing shoes off Darrin – and Tim resists. It's only after Samantha threatens him with a count of three that he complies with her demand, but the potion should make Tim obedient to Samantha right away, forcing him to tell her who sent him without stalling. It's like the potion isn't even part of the plot once Samantha feeds it to him.

Lastly, Endora seems to be starving Tim while he does his "job." What job is this, exactly? To get Darrin fired? It's never really clear why Endora brings Tim in. Endora says later that sending the disruptive leprechaun was part of a test to see "where the breaking point is in this mortal marriage" (sponsored by the Witches' Council, no less), but even then, Tim's worst antics could only be inconveniences; they'd hardly bring the Stephenses to a breaking point.

SON OF A GUN!
"I wish you and Daddy would find something to do while I'm entertaining." – Tabitha, to her parents, undoubtedly mimicking what she's been told over the years.

MONA SAMMY
Airdate: April 2, 1970

EPISODE 198

Endora invites herself to dinner with the Tates and brings a gift – a da Vinci painting that looks like Samantha. Though the artist's muse was Samantha's great-aunt, Cornelia, Darrin stashes the portrait, which Endora prominently displays so the Tates will notice. When Louise won't stop talking about it, Endora lies that Darrin painted it, and Larry pulls rank to pressure him into doing a portrait of his wife. Once the Tates leave, the Stephenses go off on Endora, who threatens never to return. Darrin and Samantha explore a myriad of solutions – including telling Larry she's a witch – but they settle on Samantha zapping Darrin with the ability to paint Louise's picture.

The next day, Darrin can barely set up an easel; after Samantha witches him, he paints like a madman. While Samantha and Larry play cards, Endora magically forces Darrin to alter Louise's beautiful portrait; by the time Larry peeks, it's a grotesque representation. Larry shields Louise from it, so she follows the Stephenses home and demands a look. Samantha is able to restore the painting, and Louise is upset that Larry found her likeness ugly. Samantha calms Louise, who decides she also wants a portrait of Larry; explaining that Darrin is actually allergic to paint, Samantha twitches him into sneezing and jerking uncontrollably. Afterwards, when Darrin is still unnerved by Cornelia's lookalike portrait, Samantha assures him that their different aging processes don't matter.

GOOD!
Darrin makes some unprecedented observations where Endora is concerned in this episode. First, he says her lobster thermidor is "brilliant" – though he's trying to distract Louise from the painting, the compliment sounds genuine, as does Endora's thank-you. Then, speaking to Samantha after he defaces his painting, Darrin remarks, "I thought your mother couldn't change one of your spells," substantiating the rule set forth in "Hoho the Clown" (#92). Samantha points out that Endora merely added to her spell, a new aspect of witchcraft that opens up a slew of intriguing possibilities.

Ordinarily, the show's mortals simply accept the Stephenses' explanations for any magical goings-on. Larry lets it slide when Samantha suggests he only perceived Louise's portrait as ugly because he lost at cards, but his "I'd like to believe that" shows that he's not necessarily buying the fancy footwork this time. And Dick Sargent gets another chance to deliver his special brand of physical comedy with Darrin's witchcraft-induced sneezing and nervous tic.

WELL?

Apparently, the long-forgotten Aunt Clara isn't the only member of Samantha's family to sit for Leonardo da Vinci [see "Samantha's da Vinci Dilemma" (#124)] – Great Aunt Cornelia had the same honor. In Clara's episode, Leonardo was a serious artist focused only on his work, but here, Endora describes him as a "sweet, dirty old man." Plus, it turns out Serena isn't Samantha's only lookalike relative. As for Larry, does mention of the *Mona Lisa* give him flashbacks to when he wanted to sully the masterpiece to sell toothpaste?

To dodge Darrin's questions about whether his wife is the subject of the painting, Samantha exclaims, "Oops, there's the doorbell," and it rings. Is Samantha back to having ESP-like powers, which she hasn't exhibited since "I, Darrin, Take This Witch, Samantha" (#1)? Then, Darrin doesn't want the Tates seeing da Vinci's painting, yet he stashes it near the staircase in plain view, and more obviously leaves a noticeable blank space on the wall.

Louise doesn't need to ask who painted "Samantha's" portrait; the signature is visible from her vantage point. Endora changes the signature, but it's not the first time she's messed with paintings – she similarly credited an Henri Monchet still-life to Samantha in "Art for Sam's Sake" (#98). And Larry should be suspicious of the Stephenses and their sudden talents by now – in "Samantha the Sculptress" (#159), he was told she turned out two sets of masterful busts after having only sculpted for the first time that day.

After Darrin compares her to the Marquis de Sade, Endora spouts, "he was just a classmate." She's being facetious, one would imagine, because the sadistic Frenchman lived from 1740 to 1814, and Endora would have completed any education long before that.

To avoid doing Louise's painting, Darrin suggests telling the Tates that Samantha is a witch. But the Tates already know: in "That Was My Wife" (#31), Darrin made that confession to Larry, and Samantha revealed herself to Louise in "Double Split" (#64). Does Samantha object now because she's worried the Witches' Council will pull the plug on her powers again, like they did when Phyllis was told about her magic in "Samantha's Secret Is Discovered" (#188)? Maybe it would be good for Larry or Louise to be in the loop, with one helping to hide the truth from the other; it would put a fresh spin on the show at this point.

Samantha offers Darrin a tranquilizer, but since when does he take them? Did Phyllis leave some behind in "Samantha's Secret Is Discovered" (#188)? Supposed proficient painter Darrin being unable to set up an easel is comical, but wouldn't Samantha zap the talent into him before arriving at the Tates? And, once again, little Jonathan Tate is presumably in his room somewhere, because neither Tate mentions their son; the boy was last acknowledged by Darrin in "And Then There Were Four" (#175).

Darrin (or, rather, his stunt artist) sketches and paints Louise's portrait in a matter of hours, which should have the Tates on alert. Darrin doesn't need much time to destroy it, either: even under Endora's spell, he couldn't change the picture that drastically in 33 seconds. By the way, if Samantha can "subtract Mother's little addition" (which makes sense, because the spells are on Darrin, and not the painting itself), why doesn't she do that while still at the Tates and save herself Larry's diatribe?

After almost six years, Larry finally has proper justification for firing Darrin – defending his wife's honor. But after the painting is restored, and Louise wants another one, Larry reminds Darrin that he's his boss – except Darrin hasn't been rehired. Larry must wonder why Darrin always picks hobbies he's allergic to: in "My, What Big Ears You Have" (#121), it was beekeeping; of course, Darrin was only in its signature getup to conceal his enlarged appendages. And Larry's Brownie isn't a tasty dessert – in this case, it's a 1930s Kodak camera; amusing when you recall Kodak was the show's sponsor for years.

OH, MY STARS!

Darrin's foggy about the details of his first date with Samantha, but he's not the only one: in "The Crone of Cawdor" (#101), the Stephenses said they shared their first meal at La Bella Donna; in "One Touch of Midas" (#157), it was Sorrento's. Here, Samantha reminds Darrin that they wanted to eat at The Lobster but ended up at the automat (a sort of self-serve, coin-operated holdover from the '30s and '40s).

There are also some marked inconsistencies in regard to witches' aging processes, and the time periods in which they age. Samantha reminds Darrin that Endora is ageless – but, in "It Shouldn't Happen to a Dog" (#3), Endora said she wouldn't live forever. Samantha then divulges that "the family" was in Italy when da Vinci took a shine to them. "Eye of the Beholder" (#22) established that Samantha was likely the subject of a "Maid of Salem" drawing done in 1682; Leonardo da Vinci died in 1519. Samantha would have to be much older than that episode implied to be included in the "us" da Vinci liked. And if everyone was so tight with Leonardo, he should have recognized Samantha when he visited in "Samantha's da Vinci Dilemma" (#124), or at least thought she was Cornelia – unless he was zapped from a time before he met "the family."

Samantha agrees that she could have been painted by Toulouse Lautrec (1864-1901) or Renoir (1841-1919), which is the first time she's ever given Darrin concrete information about her age – but her subsequent conversation with him is virtually verbatim from "Eye of the Beholder" (#22), with some updated lingo, as they wonder what people will say when Darrin gets old while Samantha stays young.

Darrin suggesting that he kill himself as a way out of painting Louise, even as a joke, is simply inconceivable. The man's got two children – orphaning them shouldn't even cross his mind.

SON OF A GUN!

"Out of pot roast?" – Endora, when Louise says that any good cook can make lobster thermidor.

Louise Tate is back, and groovier than ever – not only does she continue her visual evolution, she also gets an active part in a story for the first time since "Samantha Loses Her Voice" (#150). Though Louise weeps here like she did in that episode, she proves to be a much stronger character this time, and even a bit of a force to be reckoned with. As an added bonus, her interaction with Endora is satisfying, especially when you consider these ladies haven't had any major screen time together since "Witch or Wife" (#8).

TURN ON THE OLD CHARM
Airdate: April 9, 1970

EPISODE 199

When Endora expands her trademark unpleasantness to playing pranks on Darrin, Samantha remembers that Maurice has a magic amulet that can make her mother friendly. Under its influence, Endora calls her son-in-law "Darrin" and apologizes for her behavior – but, after Darrin leaves for work, Endora thinks her graciousness is a sign of illness. At the office, Darrin upsets greeting card maker Augustus Sunshine by giving an honest appraisal of the client's old-fashioned couplets. Samantha worries when Dr. Bombay deems the suspicious Endora healthy; Darrin, who has left the amulet upstairs, is confronted by Endora and turned into a dog. Samantha tucking the amulet under Darrin's paw gets him changed back, but she feels they're playing with fire.

The next day, Larry wants to bring Sunshine over, so Samantha calls Esmeralda to babysit while she and Darrin shop in preparation. Esmeralda sees the amulet and swipes it – hoping it will work on reluctant beau Ramon Verona, she leaves the Stephenses defenseless as Endora pops in, furious that they used Maurice's magic on her. As revenge, Endora zaps them into fighting in front of Larry and Sunshine, further jeopardizing Sunshine's account. After Esmeralda brings the amulet back and indirectly gets Endora to remove the hostility spell, Samantha magically induces Larry and Sunshine into returning, explaining that she and Darrin were demonstrating how Sunshine might modernize his rhymes with funny insults. Sunshine's first attempt references outer space, but Samantha wishes "people wouldn't knock outer space if they haven't been there."

GOOD!

"Ramon Verona" could just have been a random name dropped during "Okay, Who's the Wise Witch?" (#195), but the show brings him back off-screen and ties Esmeralda's unrequited love for him to the amulet, causing the Stephenses big problems when she takes the charm for herself. And, after twice reusing Endora's ball of light footage from "Witches and Warlocks Are My Favorite Things" (#77) [in "The Trial and Error of Aunt Clara" (#95) and "Samantha's Power Failure" (#165)], the show takes the time to craft a new light bubble for Endora's private arrival. No need to excuse Samantha's French, either: *L'enfer n'a aucun furie comme une sorcière microbé* does translate to "Hell hath no fury like a bugged witch," as she says.

The Stephenses' bickering while under the influence of Endora's spell is mean, nasty – and highly entertaining. Elizabeth Montgomery and Dick Sargent rarely get to take their characters out of their cordial confines; their enjoyment translates to the screen.

WELL?

Does Endora's shaving cream gag bring back any memories for Darrin? The last time he was covered in the toiletry, it was thanks to Samantha's "Cousin Edgar" (#36).

It's interesting that there's a magic amulet in play after Dr. Bombay asked, "Anything else? Potions? Magic amulets? Flu shots?" in "Okay, Who's the Wise Witch?" (#195). When Samantha produces Maurice's charm, she tells Darrin it's been around for centuries. Yet it contains a peace symbol, which didn't exist until Gerald Holtom designed it in 1958; it wasn't used to signify harmony until 1960. At least Darrin has some practice keeping such a talisman with him "at all times" – he was given the same instruction by Uncle Arthur in "The No-Harm Charm" (#138), only this charm is real; no wonder Darrin is so giddy when he tells Samantha, "It works!"

Darrin knows he's courting disaster by using this amulet on Endora. So, when she appears in the kitchen, and he realizes he doesn't have it, the last thing he should do is conspicuously fish around in his pocket for it. This absence of protection causes Endora to turn Darrin into a dog – exactly as Maurice did in "Daddy Comes to Visit" (#180). But, amulet or no amulet, Endora, a witch who proclaimed a coffee pot heavy in "Allergic to Ancient Macedonian Dodo Birds" (#118), would never make Darrin a sandwich by hand.

When Larry brings Sunshine over, the Stephenses act as if his wanting to "hang on to the account with a little socializing" is new and novel – despite the fact that's what they've been doing for six years. What's novel is Endora's fury toward her beloved daughter; Samantha should realize right away that Darrin doesn't have the amulet on him. "You bet your sweet broomstick," Endora says in regard to knowing about the charm – strange when you consider she wouldn't likely reference brooms, after being the first to insist witches don't ride them. Maybe she picked the phrase up from Darrin, who uttered it in "Your Witch Is Showing" (#20) and "How to Fail in Business With All Kinds of Help" (#104).

After Samantha and Darrin drive Larry and Sunshine away with their hostility, Esmeralda returns with the amulet, and Samantha prominently displays it while making Endora do her bidding. Why the flaunt? So that if Endora comes back, she'll know doing so will force her to be nice? Good thing Tabitha doesn't venture downstairs while her parents are taking pot-shots at each other, though at least this time Darrin's under a spell; he meant every similar fightin' word he said in "Double Split" (#64).

On the road, Larry and Sunshine are hit with the compulsion to turn around and head back to the Stephens house, thanks to Samantha's spell. In "Naming Samantha's New Baby" (#176), Maurice compelled Darrin's parents to do the same. In both instances, palm trees line streets that aren't supposed to be in California.

Maurice ultimately replaces the amulet with a tie "that doesn't do anything," noteworthy since his last two gifts to Darrin [in "Daddy Does His Thing" (#167) and "Daddy Comes for a Visit" (#180)] were programmed with witchcraft. It's actually a magnanimous gesture on Maurice's part, because it's his amulet to begin with – which makes Samantha telling Darrin not to bother sending a thank-you note because Maurice has no address all the more puzzling. Darrin knows that all he has to do is shout his gratitude to the ether and Maurice will hear; you'd think peacemaker Samantha would encourage it.

In conclusion, Endora finally makes good on her threat to move in with Maurice, which she vowed to do in "Just One Happy Family" (#10) – and Darrin now knows for sure that Samantha has been to outer space, which she only implied in "Sam in the Moon" (#91) and "Okay, Who's the Wise Witch?" (#195). Amazingly, Darrin doesn't seem spaced out by it.

OH, MY STARS!

Samantha has apparently known about Maurice's amulet all along. So why has she waited six years to tell Darrin about it? He could have used the protection long before now; did she see the amulet as a last resort? And, if "Daddy used it throughout the centuries," why didn't Maurice control his wife with it in "Witches and Warlocks Are My Favorite Things" (#77), when Endora was ready to kidnap their granddaughter, or in "Samantha's Good News" (#168), in which a jealous Endora wanted an ectoplasmic interlocutory (read: divorce)?

The question of whether witches can undo each others' spells was resolved long ago, but, ever since the beginning of Season Five, there's been another question mark hanging over the show: can witches gain power over one another? Though this has never been specifically addressed, the amulet makes Endora nice against her will, and Samantha falls under Endora's hostility spell. What exclusivity – or even safety – can there be for a witch if another witch can bespell her? Witches might as well be mortals if that's the case.

SON OF A GUN!

"'Married life is never humdrum when you're stuck with such a dum-dum.' Samantha Stephens, number 86." – Samantha's greeting card idea, as influenced by Endora's hostility spell.

Endora usually vacillates between impish and nasty, with little variance. So when Agnes Moorehead is given a chance to show another side to the formidable witch [as in "Allergic to Ancient Macedonian Dodo Birds" (#118) and "Once in a Vial" (#125)], it's sheer gold. Endora's "disgustingly sweet behavior towards Durwood" has added dimension knowing how she really feels about her son-in-law, and even Esmeralda gets showered with compliments.

MAKE LOVE, NOT HATE
Airdate: April 16, 1970

Esmeralda is depressed because Ramon Verona [see "Turn On the Old Charm" (#199)] has thrown her over for another witch. Samantha calls Dr. Bombay for a remedy, even hoping he'll take an interest in the maid; instead, he sets Esmeralda up on a blind date with his ne'er-do-well friend, Norton. When Norton doesn't groove on Esmeralda, Bombay mixes up a love potion for them. Darrin calls with news that he and Samantha have to entertain client Meiklejohn and his wife as Bombay finishes his potion, which is meant to trigger an attraction to the first person the "imbibee" sees; when the nervous Esmeralda fades out, Norton falls head over heels for Samantha.

Darrin comes home to find his wife fleeing a warlock; after Samantha explains, Larry arrives early with the Meiklejohns, who have had a fight. Unbeknownst to everyone, Bombay's potion has spilled into Samantha's clam dip, so when Esmeralda takes a bite, she falls in love with Darrin. Meiklejohn and his wife continue squabbling until he ingests the potion and becomes smitten with his sparring partner; Mrs. Meiklejohn tastes the dip and begins flirting with Larry. Samantha chastises Bombay, who puts a reverse spell on the potion; she then keeps Meiklejohn from the antidote so he'll continue lavishing attention on his wife. Darrin is upset when his client is lovey-dovey days later, but the potion only lasts 24 hours – Samantha suggests Meiklejohn needed a push, then pushes Darrin into her arms by witchcraft.

GOOD!

Unfortunately for Esmeralda, Ramon Verona has moved on, but it's brilliant to close his off-screen chapter that started in "Okay, Who's the Wise Witch?" (#195). Another terrific, silent piece of continuity is Tabitha's playhouse, which has been ensconced in the backyard since "If The Shoe Pinches" (#197). And Darrin, who once flipped over magically flipped pancakes [see "How Green Was My Grass" (#131)], shows how much he's mellowed by telling Samantha she can "take a few shortcuts" with their short-notice dinner if she wants to; the warmth in that moment far overshadows any compromising of the show's central conflict (Darrin's opposition to witchcraft).

Dr. Bombay, who has only ever dispensed witch remedies, wise cracks, and bad jokes, is given a chance to do something different in this episode as he tries to help Esmeralda get over Ramon. Instead of just curing a patient and popping out, Bombay lingers a while, and not just in doctor mode – the warlock actually has friends: Cliff Norton's acidic, rude Norton is great by himself, but when love takes over via the potion, both Nortons shine. Who knew a man imitating a pigeon could be so funny?

Samantha briefly tries to encourage a love match between Bombay and Esmeralda – which isn't as far-fetched as it sounds; though Bombay balks, and the episode doesn't revisit it again, merely planting the seed of the idea is most intriguing. As for real relationships, Meiklejohn becoming besotted with his estranged wife provides Charles Lane a different character to play than his usual curmudgeons. And, the camera zooming in on each love object as the potion kicks in is really quite effective.

WELL?

Maybe the audience needs an expositional reminder of who Ramon Verona is, but Darrin doesn't; he was on hand as Esmeralda first told Samantha and Endora about him in "Okay, Who's The Wise Witch?" (#195). Speaking of that episode, Esmeralda reported then that Ramon was the salad chef at the Interplanetary Playboy Club. Now he's livening up lettuce at the Warlock Club. Is Ramon a freelance salad chef? And how does Samantha know so much about the hat check girl at any club? It's not like she ever goes out painting the cosmos red.

Dr. Bombay rightfully notes that he's not Dear Abby when Samantha hopes he can give Esmeralda something to cure her depression. What's he supposed to prescribe her, some kind of witchy Valium? Bombay then brags that he cured Norton of "the incurable square green spots disease." Mentioning the ailment from "Take Two Aspirins and Half A Pint of Porpoise Milk" (#42) is a snazzy bit of continuity, but, in that episode, it was Aunt Clara who provided the cure.

If Bombay really needs a love potion, why not get some from Rollo? Samantha's old beau carried a supply in "Once in a Vial" (#125), which this episode borrows from; while not a straight-up remake by any means, Bombay's potion also causes devotees to chase their targets, as Rollo's did. However, Rollo's potion only lasted an hour, and Bombay's lasts twenty-four.

Samantha hopes Oscar of the Waldorf will entertain the Meikeljohns: she is referring to Oscar Tschirky, a maitre d' who became famous during his 1893-1943 tenure at the Waldorf-Astoria Hotel in Manhattan. Samantha's not wrong to suggest that Larry put her on the payroll for cooking up so many client dinners over the years – maybe she remembers Larry being ready to do just that in exchange for her dreaming up slogans in "Is It Magic or Imagination?" (#148).

Dr. Bombay makes very sure to clarify that his potion can only induce interest in members of the opposite sex. That's 1970s television for you; perhaps it's progressive that the show even hints there's another possibility.

Now, the Stephenses know that Bombay has brewed a love potion, and that it's affecting Norton; how do they miss the change in the suddenly emboldened Esmeralda? Her near-worship of Darrin should tell them that she ingested the potion somewhere in the kitchen – and, by process of elimination, that the potion is probably in the dip. Instead, they merrily take the bowl to the Meikeljohns, whom Samantha regales with the tale of Abner recently taking Gladys to her first baseball game. It's nice to know the Kravitzes are still around [they haven't appeared since "Tabitha's Very Own Samantha" (#189), but one of the first times Samantha saw Gladys was at a baseball game, back in "Little Pitchers Have Big Fears" (#6).

When everyone goes "amok," Bombay insists he doesn't know how the potion got into Samantha's dip. Norton and Esmeralda hear this, but don't react to the news of being drugged. Does their bespellment by the potion render them incapable of processing such information? Mrs. Meiklejohn returns to normal after one bite of the antidote-laden dip, but it takes effect before she even swallows it. Doesn't it have to get into her system? Finally, Samantha magnetizes Darrin to her and laughs, "So sue me; it was worth it!" She's used that justification for similar bonding moments: in "It Shouldn't Happen to a Dog" (#3) and "Birdies, Bogies, and Baxter" (#114), specifically.

OH, MY STARS!

So, a brown liquid spills into Samantha's creamy, off-white clam dip – it even puddles on the surface – and Samantha doesn't notice. It's not like the potion is going to soak into the dip; it'll stay on top until Samantha is ready to serve it. Perhaps Samantha overlooks Dr. Bombay's empty flask pointing toward the bowl when she cleans up the kitchen with witchcraft – but even if Samantha doesn't lay eyes on the dip again, Esmeralda should see something very undiplike floating in Samantha's bowl and tell her about it posthaste. Instead, Esmeralda simply samples it for herself. Of course, had either witch seen the potion in the dip, there wouldn't be a free-for-all in the living room.

SON OF A GUN!

"I wonder if that's what they mean by 'life, liberty, and the happiness of pursuit.'" – Esmeralda, inverting the Declaration of Independence quote as she watches Samantha running from Norton.

All the witchcraft-induced fawning sequences in this episode are wonderful, but it's Sara Seegar's Mrs. Meiklejohn who steals the show. Her giddy, girlish attention to Larry is like something out of the old Warner Brothers' *Bugs Bunny* cartoons, and Larry's nauseated reactions offer the perfect counter.

SEASON SEVEN

(1970-1971)

Larry and the Stephenses tour Massachusetts in "Samantha's Bad Day in Salem" (#207).

ABC Photo Archives/Disney ABC Television Group/Getty Images

Dr. Bombay studies the results of Darrin's hexometer scan in "Samantha's Magic Potion" (#212).

ABC/Photofest

Endora's latest attempt to show Samantha what the future holds being married to a mortal turns Darrin into "Samantha's Old Man" (#210).

Serena goes back in time to pay a visit to Darrin's ancestor in "The Return of Darrin the Bold" (#217).

SEASON SEVEN: OVERVIEW

Whatever *Bewitched* intended for its 1970-1971 season, surely those plans were scuppered by an unforeseen event during its summer hiatus: a fire at Sunset Gower studios that destroyed the Stephenses' kitchen set (visit bewitchvic.tripod.com/reviews for details). Needing to rebuild, the show sent Samantha and company to Salem, Massachusetts for a witches' convention. Inevitably, episodes were shot out of order so the eight-part Salem saga could kick off at 1164 Morning Glory Circle – which, in addition to sporting a different kitchen, underwent extensive renovations to bring the house into the '70s. And it didn't stop there: Tabitha got a new room, and the backyard gazebo was removed; even the Kravitz house enjoyed an extreme makeover, and the updated décor likewise made its way into McMann & Tate, where Darrin and Larry suddenly worked out of different offices. The changes looked great, but, aside from Endora making one general observation about the house, these revamps were never acknowledged, which rather made for an elephant in the room the entire season.

The Salem sojourn made up over a quarter of the season's 28 episodes, with back-to-back two-parters that interspersed the show's characters with establishing shots of Massachusetts landmarks – then featured Larry, the Stephenses, and Serena in actual maritime locations. New music and sound effects fashioned just for the trip added to this fresh, on-the-road feel.

But the call of home always beckons, and it was pretty much business as usual once the Stephenses returned from Salem. It's borderline trivial to note that the heart necklace Samantha had worn for six seasons was gone [last seen in "A Chance on Love" (#196)], with no explanation of why the trinket was significant in the first place; less trivial was Samantha seemingly starting to find Endora's pranks on Darrin funny, such as when a pig's head sat on his shoulders in "This Little Piggie" (#220). And Esmeralda, brought on in Season Six to much sneeze-worthy fanfare, appeared in only a trio of this season's episodes. In fact, "Samantha's Magic Mirror" (#226) found Esmeralda engaged, which suggested that her days as the Stephenses' yoo-hoo maid were over.

The characters who exhibited figurative and literal growth during Season Seven were Tabitha and Adam. Yes, Erin Murphy was quickly becoming a young lady, but her on-screen, infant brother was aged slightly and recast with toddler twins David and Greg Lawrence. Tabitha settled into an endearing role as Adam's big sister, and confirmed she could still carry an episode – "Sisters At Heart" (#213), the season's Christmas offering, put her at the forefront of a tale that tackled racism and equality with regard to her African-American friend, Lisa. Tabitha even traded in the manual twitch she'd utilized since Season Three for full-fledged zaps and a new finger-crossing gesture that was all her own.

There was, however, a growing sense that the magical well was threatening to run dry. More scenes and scenarios were borrowed from previous seasons, especially the early ones, even if some of the reinventions demonstrated a good amount of ingenuity [particularly "Out of the Mouths of Babes" (#224)]. The sudden mirrors that conveniently advanced plots in Season Six increased in number, as did what one might call "convenient slogans." Darrin's accounts had timed out with witchy happenings before, but it was becoming more of a stretch – a furry doll getting zapped to full size just as Darrin needed a slogan for hair tonic, for example.

Not only did Morning Glory Circle look different depending on the episode, but so did McMann & Tate's trusty secretary, Betty, who changed faces four times this season alone. Beyond the focus on Salem and the proliferation of remakes, the show did test out some new ideas – though not all of them worked. Serena and Samantha were linked by a spell of Endora's, Darrin spent time in an ape suit and monkeyed around with gangsters, and the Stephenses were visited by the tooth fairy (who was never referred to as such) in a peculiar two-parter that felt like separate episodes instead of a single, cohesive one.

Yet, Season Seven does boast some of the most imaginative episodes in the entire series. Darrin got aged, Endora got duplicated, and Arthur got lucky – so did Serena, with Darrin the Bold from "A Most Unusual Wood Nymph" (#79), of all people. Samantha's psychological state affected her witchcraft in two very intriguing installments, and the show finally answered the invisible question of whether or not witches could hex each other (they could, as long as they caught their subjects off guard). And somehow, the most satisfying moment of the entire season was the quiet 45-second appearance of Larry and Louise's son, Jonathan Tate, after a five-year absence – which corrected *Bewitched*'s biggest oversight. A show that still had this much magic in it surely had a few more tricks up its sleeve for its legions of fans.

TO GO OR NOT TO GO, THAT IS THE QUESTION

Airdate: September 24, 1970

Darrin's suspicion that Endora has an ulterior motive for being friendly turns out to be justified when she brings a directive from the High Priestess Hepzibah: Samantha must attend the upcoming Witches' Convocation in Salem, Massachusetts. Samantha declines, but, after an argument between Darrin and Endora gets him turned into a toad, she reconsiders. The restored Darrin confuses Larry by suddenly asking for time off when, the day before, he demanded involvement in a prestigious account. Samantha informs Endora that Darrin will be traveling to Salem with her; the news instantly reaches the Witches' Council, who announces that Hepzibah is coming for a visit.

The High Priestess arrives in a flurry of witchy fanfare, angry that Darrin wants to attend the convention; though the Stephenses try to tell her Darrin is only interested in seeing Salem, Hepzibah sends them to their room, invisible. She summons Endora, and they discuss the fact that Endora's interference through the years has all been an attempt to break up Samantha's marriage under Hepzibah's direction; Endora admits that Darrin abides the harsh treatment because he loves Samantha. Hepzibah is further intrigued when Darrin stands up to her, so she decides to stay the week to observe the Stephenses' marriage – and determine whether or not it should be dissolved.

GOOD!

Endora sings, which is not something the formidable witch usually does; she warbles here to great comic effect, overdoing her high notes for viewers' amusement. And Darrin being changed back from a toad while he's still on a lily pad in the bathtub – and getting soaked while fully-clothed – is not only funny, but something that had to have been done in one take. Now, in "Tabitha's Very Own Samantha" (#189), Darrin asked what Samantha would do if one of her relatives turned him into a frog; she replied she'd become one, too. She doesn't do that here, but she does expand on the idea by suggesting that she and the children can join him in amphibian form if he'd prefer. Finally, the living room was just magically cleared of furniture in "Super Arthur" (#190), but, as in that episode, this laborious effect is pulled off with aplomb.

WELL?

When Samantha summons her singing mother to the living room, there's a shadow moving in the lower right corner of the screen just before Endora pops in. Endora compliments Samantha's decorating choices, saying, "It's all you" – yet, in "Samantha's Secret Spell" (#188), Endora said the Salvation Army wouldn't even send a truck for Samantha's furnishings. And Tabitha's playhouse, which had been on the patio since "If the Shoe Pinches" (#197), seems to be gone.

In "Witches and Warlocks Are My Favorite Things" (#77), Endora said she didn't ordinarily get involved in committee work; here, she not only organizes the Witches' Convention, but accepts an appointment as Lord High Chairman. Samantha's note says the Convention starts when the planet Icarus passes between Jupiter and Pluto, but it just did in "Darrin, Gone and Forgotten" (#144) – and, in actuality, Icarus is an asteroid, which instead crosses the orbits of Mercury, Venus, Earth, and Mars.

Darrin reminds Endora that she's turned him into a horse, a mule, and a monkey. It was indeed Endora's zap that made Darrin a pony in "Solid Gold Mother-in-Law" (#120), but Maurice made him a mule [in "Daddy Does His Thing" (#167)], and Darrin was a monkey via Aunt Clara's goof-up in "Alias Darrin Stephens" (#37). At least Endora realizes a long-held dream when she turns Darrin into a toad: she already wanted to make that transformation in "Help, Help, Don't Save Me" (#5).

Larry is right to deem Darrin's request for a vacation outrageous, considering Darrin just demanded the Gotham Industries account. Why doesn't Darrin simply tell Larry that he needs to leave town on a family emergency? Instead, Darrin declares he hasn't had a vacation in four years, when he and Samantha just cavorted in the Caribbean after "Samantha's Better Halves" (#185), and enjoyed Darrin's vacation bonus after "What Makes Darrin Run" (#191). Endora says that Samantha and Darrin will benefit from separate vacations, but the Witches' Convention is hardly a vacation for Samantha, and Darrin doesn't even need one.

Why is Hepzibah, who must have more important things to do than assure the attendance of one individual witch, getting herself involved? The Witches' Council already sends a note ahead of the High Priestess, so shouldn't she just let them deal with Samantha?

When Samantha compares Hepzibah to Julius Caesar, neither she nor Darrin remember that they hosted the Roman emperor in "Samantha's Caesar Salad" (#173). Samantha ought to compare the High Priestess to Ticheba instead; having been through the former monarch's royal treatment in "Long Live the Queen" (#108), Darrin would instantly know what he's in for. Incidentally, the wonderful Jane Connell played a different sovereign, albeit a mortal one, in "Aunt Clara's Victoria Victory" (#100).

What exactly is the problem with Darrin coming to Salem? When Hepzibah hears that Darrin isn't coming near the convention itself, that should be the end of it. For that matter, most witchy events, like Samantha's coronation in "Long Live the Queen" (#108) and the Cosmos Cotillion in "Serena Stops the Show" (#192), are held in cosmic locales that mortals can't even access – so it's not necessary for any witches to travel to Salem in the first place.

Darrin has made his impassioned speech about giving up the right to express himself in his own house before, after Endora shrunk him in "Samantha's Wedding Present" (#141). Samantha tells Darrin they'll go out to dinner, but surely she realizes that Hepzibah, who has fashioned herself an observer, would insist on accompanying the Stephenses to any restaurant. Finally, Darrin is perturbed to see that his home has undergone some regal refurbishing, but it's not the first time: Endora affected a similar extreme makeover in "Samantha's Secret Is Discovered" (#188), Ticheba added luxuries in "Long Live the Queen" (#108), and even Samantha had a go at it to teach Darrin a lesson in "The Girl With the Golden Nose" (#73).

OH, MY STARS!

Probably the most notable element of this season premiere is the very different décor of the Stephens house. Their master bedroom is now blue instead of green, their living room has all-new furniture and carpet, and their kitchen has been completely remodeled and enlarged – it even sports a never-before-seen staircase. And Larry has a new office! However, this was a true case of necessity being the mother of invention. According to Scott Viets on Vic's *Bewitched* Page (bewitchvic.tripod.com/reviews), a fire at Sunset Gower Studios between Seasons Six and Seven gutted the original kitchen set, so the Stephenses were sent to Salem to give the show time to rebuild. From that, it's fair to assume the rest of the set was given a similar facelift while they were at it, bringing the house into the '70s. While it certainly couldn't be helped that this real-life event impacted the show, its handling creates a substantial gap in continuity: the only reference made to the renovations is Endora's throwaway line about the living room. Had Samantha added that she and Darrin decided to do some home alterations, it would have eliminated the subconscious question mark generated by the new furnishings.

Hepzibah is forbidding and fun, but her presence royally conflicts with the rest of the series. In "Long Live the Queen" (#108), Ticheba sat on the throne until she passed the crown to Samantha, who was expected to reign a year. With Hepzibah ruling now, one assumes she took power when Samantha abdicated. But then, Hepzibah reminds Endora, "You promised us this marriage would not last" – which implies that Hepzibah has been on the throne from the beginning. That can't be if Samantha was queen just three years ago. Perhaps, if a High Priestess outranks a queen in the hierarchy, each could be in power at the same time, but usually the reverse is true – and that would have had Hepzibah serving under Samantha. The dubious experiment of "Long Live the Queen" (#108) continues to have repercussions, and much of Hepzibah's introductory material comes from that episode as well.

Hepzibah decides to study the Stephenses because theirs is "the first and only mixed marriage of witch to commoner." Actually, it's not: in "Just One Happy Family" (#10), Samantha told Darrin that Maurice "doesn't approve of mixed marriages," and Endora reminded her husband that they "happen in the best of families." Samantha corroborated this, albeit in the alternate reality of "What Every Young Man Should Know" (#72), by pointing out to Darrin that "not many of our people have fallen in love with human beings before." The Stephenses having an exclusive witch/mortal marriage makes for a better plot, but it's a history rewrite that flies in the face of what the show established in its beginnings.

SON OF A GUN!

"At three furlongs, I'm unbeatable." – Darrin, as Hepzibah sizes him up.

The discovery that Endora's torment of Darrin has been by Hepzibah's command all along adds the extraordinary layer that the tricks and spells haven't just been random or for fun. And, when Hepzibah is amazed that mere mortal Darrin has repeatedly subjected himself to these witchcraft-related ordeals, Endora simply replies, "He loves my daughter." This is not something it ever appeared Endora would admit; it's as if six years of the show's history is wrapped up in that one wonderful revelation.

SALEM, HERE WE COME

EPISODE 202

Airdate: October 1, 1970

Following the events of "To Go or Not to Go, That Is the Question" (#201), Darrin resents having to attend a formal dinner in his magically renovated house. After Darrin expresses displeasure at his individuality-removing designation as "mortal" and rejects witch delicacies at the table, Hepzibah issues demerits: if Darrin receives ten, he will be "dissolved." The Stephenses are forced to explain Hepzibah and her redecoration when Larry shows up unannounced; he samples the non-human cuisine, shocked when Tabitha tells him it's pickled eye of newt. The next day, Hepzibah is fascinated by the idea of mortal work and pressures Samantha into taking her to Darrin's office.

Hepzibah barges into McMann & Tate as Larry and Darrin are meeting with their client, Hitchcock; the gruff executive is about to rebuke Hepzibah for her presence, until Samantha twitches him into becoming smitten instead. Swept off her feet by Hitchcock, Hepzibah returns seeing mortals in a new light – but Darrin antagonizes her, causing her to exhaust Darrin's demerits and announce that the Stephenses' marriage will be dissolved at midnight. Samantha assures Darrin she can talk Hepzibah into mortalizing her, but Darrin won't let her give up her identity; he goes to Hepzibah to apologize and finds the priestess with Hitchcock. Again influenced by Hitchcock's charms, Hepzibah relents, allowing the Stephenses to remain married, and to travel to Salem together.

GOOD!

Tabitha-as-princess can hardly be the same little girl who had imaginary friends during her last appearance in "If the Shoe Pinches" (#197) – there's a certain poise to Erin Murphy now; she's growing up fast. The only thing funnier than the idea of baby Adam making "a no-no" on Hepzibah is Darrin deadpanning, "Darn. I wish I'd thought of that."

Given the climate of continuing desegregation in the early '70s, it's a cool correlation for Hepzibah to serve "ethnic food" like kidney of iguana (*bourguignonne* in neat-feet oil), especially since it's not typical to think of witches as an ethnic group. This cuisine is consistent with the delicacies Uncle Arthur listed in "Twitch or Treat" (#81): sea urchins with *bordelaise* sauce, for example – and interestingly, his salad of oak leaves and Spanish moss was drizzled with "neat's-*foot* oil." Larry diving in to Hepzibah's feast is played for comedy, but it also gives the impression that witchy delights might be palatable to mortals after all.

Most viewers of the time knew him as the sinister Joker in *Batman* (which ran on ABC from 1966-1968), but here, Cesar Romero delivers a one-two "biff/wham" as ordinary human Ernest Hitchcock. The sharp contrast between his brusque businessman and his "lovesick adolescent" is terrific, particularly the latter persona. Plus, Hepzibah changing the house back from "Buckingham Palace" is an astronomical effect.

WELL?

Samantha looks lovely in her pink-and-white gown, but you'd think she'd present to royalty in something *au courant*: she donned this particular frock as far back in "Charlie Harper, Winner" (#99). And Darrin complains that Hepzibah must live in the Taj Mahal, forgetting he said exactly that about Queen Ticheba in "Long Live the Queen" (#108).

"Postlethwaite" must be a popular warlock name: in "Samantha's Secret Spell" (#179), it was also established as the first name of the apothecary. Darrin needn't take Hepzibah's demerits too seriously; the wires holding them up are distinctly visible whenever they appear.

Larry ought to recall that Samantha had another aunt who thought she was a queen in "Aunt Clara's Victoria Victory" (#100), especially since the two "relatives" look and sound alike (Jane Connell plays both monarchs). Larry also reports he's "meeting Louise at the club for dinner" – but where's Jonathan? Do the Tates ever spend time with their son?

Plates are placed in front of Darrin and Tabitha in the scene's opening wide shot, but, in close-ups, Hepzibah, Samantha, and Tabitha all have empty dishes in front of them. After Larry leaves, Samantha motions for Darrin to do something, but it's never clear what, because the scene immediately transitions to the next morning.

At the office, both Darrin and Larry are amazingly patient as they handle Hepzibah – especially Larry, who's only humoring Samantha's crazy aunt as far as he knows. But when Hitchcock readies to insult Hepzibah, only to stop himself with a romantic overture, the High Priestess inexplicably misses that Hitch has been witched, despite Samantha clearly twitching in Hepzibah's line of sight.

Once home, Darrin paces around, asking Samantha, "How could you do it?" They've obviously been home for a while; wouldn't they have had this discussion long before this moment?

Again faced with Hepzibah's demerits, Darrin is shown to have four against him, but when the markers were last on-screen, Darrin had only accumulated three. Soon, Hepzibah decrees that the Stephenses' marriage will be dissolved at midnight; Samantha tells Darrin this involves dissolving him. But what about the repercussions this would have in the mortal world? Is Hepzibah planning to zap all public records of Darrin and his marriage out of existence as well? Will all mortals Darrin has come into contact with – specifically his parents and the Tates – have their memories purged of him, or will they think Darrin is missing or dead?

In "To Go or Not to Go, That Is the Question" (#201), much was made of Darrin taking on the prestigious Gotham Industries account – is Hitchcock connected with that company? Gotham is never mentioned, yet it doesn't seem likely Larry would hand Darrin a whole new account with Gotham still on the table.

The scene after Hepzibah rescinds her marriage-dissolving decision, the Stephenses are in different clothes. Did Hepzibah really stick around a whole extra day once she rendered her final judgment?

Darrin's mother gives the Stephenses a lot of vases – in "Samantha's Secret Is Discovered" (#188), Samantha shattered and reassembled one Phyllis had gifted them with to demonstrate her powers; here, Hepzibah destroys another of Phyllis' presents as a show of superiority. Samantha assures Larry the vase is easily replaced; then, when he sees it intact moments later, she blurts out, "I told you it was easily replaced!" This is the same exchange Samantha had with her long-missing friend Gertrude in "Love Is Blind" (#13).

OH, MY STARS!

1164 Morning Glory Circle isn't the only location that's gotten an upgrade: Larry already had a new office in "To Go or Not to Go, That Is the Question" (#201), and now Darrin's in a larger suite with a different layout. Like the previous episode, there is no reason given for these reinvented rooms. Did Larry see Darrin's home renovations and convince McMann the agency needed them, too?

Darrin's later behavior with Hepzibah is unfathomable – he risks his marriage, and even his existence, just so he can pop off at the priestess. A story needs conflict, but the stakes are far too high here for Darrin to be so reckless. Looking for a loophole, Samantha suggests talking Hepzibah into "drumming me out of the witch world," which she claims has never been done before. Has Samantha so quickly forgotten that her magic was eliminated by the Witches' Council in "Samantha's Power Failure" (#165) *and* "Samantha's Secret Spell" (#188)?

Threatening to dissolve Darrin is tantamount to a death threat. Maurice was bad enough disintegrating Darrin in "Just One Happy Family" (#10), but Darrin didn't have children then. No one considers what Darrin's termination would do to Tabitha and Adam – Hepzibah issues her dissolvement ultimatum *right in front of Tabitha*, who goes on eating her pickled eye of newt as if it were any other day. And Samantha just sits there, not lowering the boom in defense of her kids. Maybe the sitcom wanted to avoid the dramatic implications of this storyline, but they're simply unavoidable.

SON OF A GUN!

"So, you're a world traveler. Perhaps you've used my airline: the regal bird with the silver beak?" – Hitchcock to Hepzibah, paraphrasing "the proud bird with the golden tail," the popular Continental Airlines slogan of the day.

With two-part episodes, the show has historically either done a recap, or given one or both of the Stephenses a flashback or dream to remind viewers what took place the previous week. Here, the episode simply picks up where the last one left off, ingeniously refreshing memories by having Darrin complain about Hepzibah. And, the show offers unprecedented continuity by having Hepzibah's trumpeteer announce "ex-queen Samantha." Considering Samantha's foray into sovereignty was dropped immediately after her coronation in "Long Live the Queen" (#108), the mention is amazing, even if the continuity problems regarding the witches' monarchy addressed in "To Go or Not to Go, That Is the Question" (#201) still exist. Is Hepzibah's admitted soft spot for Samantha because they're both royalty?

THE SALEM SAGA
Airdate: October 8, 1970

Samantha and Darrin bid farewell to Tabitha and Adam as they board a plane to Boston; Endora appears on the wing, then pops into the cabin and zaps a passenger off the flight for not giving his seat up to her. In Salem, Samantha and Endora school Darrin on what was really behind its infamous witch hunts – and Potter, a drunk, sees Endora changing a sign's ugly witch to a pretty young witch. Later, the Stephenses tour the House of the Seven Gables, where an antique bedwarmer comes alive and hassles Samantha. The tour guide, Miss Ferndale, castigates the Stephenses for handling the bedwarmer; when it goes missing, she reports their license plate number to the police.

En route to the hotel, Samantha and Darrin argue over the bedwarmer and are shocked to find it in the back seat of the car. Samantha reasons that someone has been trapped inside the antique since the time of the witch hunts; Endora concurs, and suggests looking for answers at the Witches' Convention. While Darrin fights with the animated bedwarmer, the police arrive at the hotel, not taking Potter's reports of witches seriously. The Stephenses continue debating what to do until the cops come knocking; after Samantha unsuccessfully tries to zap the bedwarmer away, she and Darrin hide it in the closet and get ready to face the music.

GOOD!

Maybe it's something in their half-witch metabolism, but first Tabitha experienced an unusual growth spurt between Seasons Two and Three, and now Adam, who was young enough to make a "no-no" on the High Priestess Hepzibah in previous installment "Salem, Here We Come" (#202) is a curly-headed toddler on Endora's lap. But it's all worth it to see Tabitha has gotten over her sibling rivalry from Season Six. "Hear that, Adam?" Tabitha lovingly warns. "You better mind me!"

Endora and Samantha on the wing of the plane is one of the most memorable images of this episode – second only to its self-propelled bedwarmer, which gives Samantha a lot of comedy to play with: she feigns insanity to explain talking to the antique when she gets caught by a tour guide, then makes a show of bringing the item to the hotel for the drunken Potter. There's also great attention to detail in "Salem" – the Stephenses' rental car has Massachusetts plates, and its registration reads "1970."

Between the bedwarmer seeming alive and Dick Sargent's physical comedy, Darrin's battle with the antique is as epic as it is funny. Best of all, this episode finally solves a mystery that has been hanging in the air since "Eye of the Beholder" (#22) – Samantha's age. She's always been vague about the number, but here, Samantha admits she was a child during the Salem witch hunts of the 1690s. The aforementioned episode allegedly showed Samantha as a young woman in a "Maid of Salem" drawing dated 1682, but it was never established that the picture was actually Samantha, so this new information is perfectly acceptable, and fills in a lot of blanks.

WELL?

Samantha tells Tabitha that the next Witches' Convention is being held "in about 100 years." Then what were the Miami conclave ["There's No Witch Like An Old Witch" (#27)] and the two London conclaves ["Aunt Clara's Old Flame" (#47) and "A Strange Little Visitor" (#48)] that all took place five years ago?

Does McMann & Tate's Betty have a twin? Irenee Byatt, Betty's last incarnation from "Darrin the Warlock" (#181), sits behind the Stephenses on the flight. For a woman who becomes so frazzled by the sight of Samantha and Endora on the wing, she's unusually calm after gulping down her pill. What's in that bottle? And Endora zapping Samantha onto the wing against her will is another example of one witch having power over another, which has never been officially established as a rule.

In "Three Wishes" (#96), Darrin told Samantha that they ought to go to Boston sometime. Here, they finally do, but "Sam's Spooky Chair" (#86) revealed that Samantha's family lived in Boston at the turn of the 20th century; Endora scoffs that she and Samantha have seen Salem, but neither witch makes mention of their former hometown.

It was probably impossible for the crew to drag their camera rig all the way to Salem, but, as a result, the show is back to the process shot driving that was jettisoned in favor of location driving in Season Six. And the "Salem" park Potter staggers in front of is identical to the usual Westport (then Patterson) park that Samantha saved in "Samantha Fights City Hall" (#149).

It makes sense that Endora would alter Salem's witch signs, given her fury over the misrepresentation of witches in "To Trick-or-Treat or Not to Trick-or-Treat" (#177). But, in "I, Darrin, Take This Witch, Samantha" (#1), Endora also stated that mortals only think witches ride brooms – so why does she keep a broom in the sign's logo at all? Darrin shouldn't require an explanation about witch stereotypes – he fought against them in both "The Witches Are Out" (#7) and "To Trick-or-Treat or Not to Trick-or-Treat" (#177) – and he also doesn't need to be told that only mortals were persecuted during the witch trials, since he himself was accused in "Samantha's Thanksgiving to Remember" (#119). Incidentally, this mortals-only contention goes against "The Girl With the Golden Nose" (#73), in which Endora stated that Samantha's Aunt Agnes was burned at the stake in Salem.

Miss Ferndale's guided tour jumps in and out of voice-over as the Stephenses fuss with the bedwarmer, though it's not immediately obvious. Samantha, on the other hand, sees the bedwarmer coming at her, but instead of darting into the next room to get ahead of it, she simply stands there and lets it block the doorway. Does no one – not Miss Ferndale nor anyone in the tour group – see the Stephenses trying to get the bedwarmer out of their way? It's a smart bedwarmer, too: it somehow knows which car Samantha arrived in, when it couldn't have seen Samantha pull up to the House.

Driving back to the hotel, Darrin is strangely furious at Samantha for the bedwarmer's antics. He's not wrong when he says "it wouldn't be the first time" she's hidden something from him – but, when he thinks Samantha is hitting him in the head, he threatens, "Sam, you do that one more time and I swear..." Promising battery doesn't sound like Darrin at even his angriest! So much for the peace that has reigned supreme between the marrieds since "Samantha Fights City Hall" (#149), a long stretch considering the Stephenses used to scrap like junkyard dogs. [Their witchcraft-fueled bickering in "Turn on the Old Charm" (#199) doesn't count.]

Scuffling with the bedwarmer should remind Darrin of doing the same with Clyde Farnsworth, a piece of fighting furniture from "Sam's Spooky Chair" (#86). Darrin asks Samantha to zap the bedwarmer back where it belongs, when she already told him she couldn't because it's a transformed warlock. As for Miss Ferndale, in a world full of rapists, murderers, and genocidal world leaders, she calls people who steal museum pieces "the lowest form of criminals." And the Salem police stand right outside the

Stephenses' hotel room, but never hear Darrin yelling about getting an ax, nor do they become insistent when their suspects take forever to answer the door.

OH, MY STARS!

The Stephenses' flight to Boston has a few inconsistencies on its radar. Endora shifts considerably when Samantha pops in and out next to her on the wing. There are clouds chroma-keyed under the wing, but not above it, and the "sky" is clearly a blue screen, which would pass if it didn't ruffle under the power of the fans and bunch up to the right of the frame. Inside the plane, nobody reacts to Endora popping in out of nowhere, and not a single crew member approaches this woman who didn't take off with them; even in a pre-9/11 world, Endora would be viewed as a security risk. Then, Samantha, Darrin, and Endora proceed to argue about making a passenger disappear in full volume, while standing up in their seats, at that. Not to mention, Endora and the Stephenses don't deplane from the same American Airlines jet that touches down; the stock footage of the landing has a different logo on its tail.

SON OF A GUN!

"You witches have the dumbest rules – and at the dumbest times." – Darrin, after Samantha explains she can't make the bedwarmer disappear because it doesn't want to go.

Miss Ferndale's presentation about the House of the Seven Gables is only meant to be background noise as Samantha struggles with the bedwarmer, so it isn't necessary that she's accurate. But the show goes the extra mile here, getting the history of the site exactly right: Miss Ferndale states that the House of the Seven Gables was built in 1668 by John Turner, and that it was purchased in 1908 by Caroline O. Emmerton for the purpose of turning it into a museum, providing for quite a history lesson.

SAMANTHA'S HOT BEDWARMER
Airdate: October 15, 1970

EPISODE 204

Continuing on from "The Salem Saga" (#203), the Stephenses almost convince the Salem police that the House of the Seven Gables' bedwarmer isn't in their possession – until it floats out of the closet. After Darrin tells the cops Samantha is blameless, he is arrested and taken to jail. Samantha flies to the Witches' Convention and has to blackmail Endora into letting her address the attendees about the bedwarmer, and the warlock who inhabits it. When no one comes forward with information, Endora sends out a summons on Samantha's behalf. As Samantha waits, she pops into Darrin's cell, shocking Potter, the drunk who witnessed witchcraft earlier that day.

Back at the Convention, Serena admits transforming the warlock; hoping to clear Darrin, Samantha has Endora zap Serena to Old Salem so she can remember her spell. In the past, Serena cats around on wimpy warlock Newton; when her mortal lover arrives, she lies that Newton is suspected of witchcraft and offers to turn him into something inanimate – the bedwarmer. Armed with Serena's spell, Samantha magically sneaks past the police station's desk sergeant to change Newton back. With the evidence "missing," Samantha twitches the arresting officers into talking about the bedwarmer's unusual behavior, prompting the judge to dismiss Darrin's case. After Newton and the House of the Seven Gables' Miss Ferndale hit it off, Samantha jokes that the tour guide now has another bedwarmer.

GOOD!

Having defeated Darrin in "The Salem Saga" (#203), Newton-as-bedwarmer's new challengers are the cops. Richard X. Slattery and Ron Masak, specifically, get a chance at some physical comedy as they battle the mischievous antique. Their experiences nicely come full circle when Samantha zaps them into telling the truth about what Newton put them through; Ron Masak's officer adds to it by revealing that Newton tried to bite him after Darrin's arrest.

The show does a great job matching the "ferny dell" where witches were first seen congregating in "Long Live the Queen" (#108). That episode's footage was reused in "Serena Stops the Show" (#192), so it's commendable that the crew recreates this area for these proceedings. And most of Serena and Samantha's appearances in the dell are done with a double instead of split-screen, but it works well, especially when Samantha puts her hand on Serena's shoulder.

WELL?

When Miss Ferndale and the cops storm the Stephenses' hotel room, the bedwarmer opens the closet door to reveal himself. Given that he floats and attacks mortals, it may be that the warlock interned within can still perform witchcraft, but the writers never address this. And for some inexplicable reason, Samantha talks to the bedwarmer in front of the cops, and gets it to hop over to them. It's not like her to flaunt witchery like that – she was even punished for outing herself in "Samantha's Secret Is Discovered" (#188). As for Darrin, he's racking up quite a rap sheet – this is his fourth arrest, following "Take Two Aspirins and Half A Pint of Porpoise Milk" (#42) and "The Very Informal Dress" (#44).

It was Endora who suggested taking the problem of the bedwarmer to the convention attendees in "The Salem Saga" (#203) – now, she resists when Samantha comes to her for that help. And where's Hepzibah? She coerced Samantha into attending the convention; you'd think the High Priestess would be there herself.

Darrin is likely having a déjà vu – he shares the slammer with one of Dick Wilson's drunks, and Samantha appears in the cell, both of which happened in "The Very Informal Dress" (#44). The men are trying to sleep, but the establishing shot of the police station indicates it's the middle of the day.

In Old Salem, Serena is surprisingly compassionate as she frees the Widow Patterson from her stocks, though it's odd she'd show off her powers in an atmosphere where mortals are paranoid about witches. Now, when Serena first appeared in "And Then There Were Three" (#54), she was a mellow socialite. So how was she a wild child 300 years earlier? Newton worries he'll be accused as a witch, but he won't be – in "The Salem Saga" (#203), both Endora and Samantha confirmed that no actual witches were tried. After Newton is transformed, Serena vanishes from Captain Nichols' arms, essentially taking her 17th century counterpart, whom she is inhabiting, with her.

How does Samantha know where the cops are keeping Newton-as-bedwarmer? Assuming she located him by witchcraft, she ought to just pop straight into the room instead of sedating the desk sergeant. Incidentally, Newton would never think Samantha is Serena: he saw her returning to the hotel with Darrin and was privy to all their conversations; likewise, he shouldn't need Darrin to tell him that Samantha is spoken for. And the Stephenses risk all kinds of trouble by spouting off about stealing evidence a few feet away from a judge and three cops.

The judge dismisses Darrin's case based on the arresting officers' tales of the animated, now missing, bedwarmer. Yet Miss Ferndale, her associate, and Potter all saw the Stephenses with the bedwarmer – Potter even saw them taking it into the hotel; the cops' magical recollections do nothing to change these facts. Finally, none of Salem's residents are willing to entertain the idea that witches might be real – though Darrin's Army buddy, Salem native Adam Newlarkin ["We're In For A Bad Spell" (#39)], certainly was a believer. Where has Adam been the last five years, anyway?

OH, MY STARS!

The show's last two-parter ["To Go or Not to Go, That Is the Question" (#201) and "Salem, Here We Come" (#202)] was connected by a very effective pick-up-where-we-left-off scene that made that transition beautifully. This episode continues from "The Salem Saga" (#203) with Potter briefly recapping events for the crowd amassed in front of the hotel – but follows by backing up into "Part I" with a partially rewritten, incongruous, and expositional scene that has Darrin dropping his suggestion for Samantha to disappear. Simply starting with Darrin opening the door to the cops would be a much smoother segue; such a technique worked for the previous pair of episodes.

In "Marriage, Witches' Style" (#161), Serena threatened to tell Darrin that Samantha cavorted with Sir Walter Raleigh if she didn't help her find a mortal to date. Here, Samantha blackmails Endora with the same information, only Maurice is to receive the news. He wouldn't care; he and Endora have an open marriage. But then, Samantha indicates she was a little girl when she witnessed Endora and Sir Walter in a clinch. Raleigh lived from 1544 to 1618. In "The Salem Saga" (#203), Samantha said she was a child during the Salem witch trials, which mostly took place in the 1690s. So, unless Samantha's childhood spanned 70 years or more, she couldn't have caught Endora with the English writer.

Oddly, Samantha forgets her own statement from "Hoho the Clown" (#92): only the witch who cast a spell can undo it. All goes well having Serena journey into the past to remember how she transformed Newton, but once she returns to 1970, Samantha wants to restore him herself; she should have Serena change Newton back, since that's the only way it can happen. And why is Endora needed to send out a message to the atmospheric continuum and transport Serena to Old Salem? Samantha's powers are strong enough to put out her own ethereal feelers, and, if Aunt Clara could zap herself to 1621 Plymouth unassisted [see "Samantha's Thanksgiving to Remember" (#119)], then Serena can fly to the same century by herself, too.

Serena appears next to her younger self, freezes her, and inhabits her body. Erring on the side of originality and assuming this is an ability that just hasn't been demonstrated before, why does Serena not even attempt to behave like her 17th century counterpart? It is humorous, hearing an Olde World woman saying things like "groovy," but you'd think Serena would invisibly fade in and watch her 1690s self turn Newton into a bedwarmer. The incantation Serena uses on Newton can't be right, because it's delivered in 20th century English – nor should it work when Samantha incants "snickery snack" instead of Serena's original "snickety snack." And consider: in "The Salem Saga" (#203), Samantha said she was a child during this period – Serena should be a child, too, instead of the full-grown witch that she is, which invalidates this entire part of the story.

SON OF A GUN!

"By keeping my ears open and my lid shut." – Newton, explaining to Samantha how he got "so hip" as a bedwarmer.

DARRIN ON A PEDESTAL

Airdate: October 22, 1970

In Salem, Massachusetts, Samantha gets called away to an emergency witches' meeting, so Serena offers to sightsee with Darrin instead. The cousins-in-law travel to Gloucester, where Serena gets the hots for the town's Fisherman's Memorial statue and zaps it to life. After Darrin demands that Serena replace the monument, she does – with Darrin. Serena takes the Fisherman to a romantic getaway spot, while Samantha arrives in Gloucester, only to find Darrin-as-statue in place of the memorial. Larry, in town on business, brings umbrella manufacturer Barrows to meet Darrin; Samantha scrambles to explain Darrin's absence and distract Larry, who thinks the statue looks like his associate.

Forced into a lunch with Larry and Barrows, Samantha excuses herself and searches for Serena – meanwhile, Serena shows up at the restaurant with the Fisherman, annoying Barrows. When Samantha returns, she confronts her cousin and gets her to humanize Darrin again, concurrently sending the Fisherman back where he belongs. Darrin meets Barrows, but the client is ready to walk until Samantha convinces him to listen to an improvised slogan which ties Barrows Umbrellas to the Fisherman's Memorial. Barrows loves it, and later, the Stephenses visit the statue so Darrin can work on a layout. Serena returns, but when Darrin balks at thanking her for his concept, she whips up a gale and ruins the umbrella Darrin has positioned on the monument.

GOOD!

The humanized Fisherman's Memorial is no ordinary statue. He has a bad back from 50 years of hunching over a wheel, and it's a brilliant touch that he's terrified of water, considering he "stands for all the able-bodied seamen that drowned." And, while lots of witchy hijinks have inspired Darrin's slogans over the years, making the Fisherman a "masculine symbol" for Barrows Umbrellas is one of the show's better tie-ins.

When Samantha and Serena are at the Gloucester House bar with Potter [the drunk from "The Salem Saga" (#203)], the cousins chat via split screen in front of a process shot (basically, a video backdrop), and the dual effect works quite nicely. But that's nothing compared to the scenes of Larry/Samantha/Barrows and Darrin/Samantha/Serena in front of the statue: all the dialogue from these sequences is dubbed in. Most likely, the maritime wind and other ambient noise from the ocean, boats, and traffic were picked up by the microphones, so overdubs were necessary – but you'd never know the trick had been employed were it not for the one moment of double tracking when Darrin tells Serena, "I'll thank you to blow out of here." All the actors do a masterful job of matching their dialogue (sort of reverse lip-syncing) later on in the studio.

WELL?

Darrin feels guilty for dumping the Barrows Umbrella account on Larry; Samantha rightly reminds him they're on vacation. Is Darrin the only ad executive at McMann & Tate? And what happened to the prestigious Gotham Industries account Darrin lobbied for and postponed in "To Go or Not to Go, That Is the Question" (#201) – or Salem-goer Ernest Hitchcock, to whom Larry offered his assistance in "Salem, Here We Come" (#202)? These clients are nowhere to be seen as Larry and Darrin concentrate solely on Barrows.

Samantha gets called to an emergency meeting of the Witches' Council, which can't be right, because Samantha is not on the Council. And Endora's demonstration of past, present, and future incantations is hardly that urgent; it sounds like typical convention fare.

It doesn't seem like Serena would need to go sightseeing in Salem and its environs – in "Samantha's Hot Bedwarmer" (#204), it came out that Serena was a Salem resident in the 17th century. Does she just want to see how her town has grown? Street level, Darrin is shocked when Serena zaps up a car for them, saying he expected a broom – this despite Samantha telling him as far back as "I Get Your Nanny, You Get My Goat" (#122) that witches consider broom-riding obsolete.

From a moving car, hundreds of feet away, Serena decides the Fisherman's Memorial statue is hot stuff. After she animates him, he states that "it's been 50 years since I've kissed a lassie." He's a statue – what lassie could have kissed? Darrin barks that "there's going to be trouble" if Serena doesn't restore the memorial, but that's laughable, considering the mortal is no match for any witch. Once Darrin is "statuefied," Serena's comment that cars are made for "transportation and air polluting" is as astute as it is funny, but her Fisherman has just spent half a century immobilized next to a busy road; he shouldn't have to ask what a car is.

The haven that Serena has "whipped up" comes complete with a spying, tattling groundskeeper who doesn't much seem like a witchy creation. As for the mortals, Larry knows where to find Darrin because the hotel desk clerk has Darrin's itinerary. When you're on vacation, do you tell the hotel staff where you're going? Probably not; it's just a device so everyone can get together in Gloucester.

It's too bad the show has to rely on a freeze-frame to present Darrin as a statue, especially since that wasn't necessary when Darrin was bronzed in "It's So Nice to Have A Spouse Around the House" (#145). Larry drives Samantha and Barrows to the Gloucester House; most viewers probably don't know that the restaurant is only half a mile from the memorial; they could walk it in 10 minutes. Of course, doing so wouldn't offer a chance to hear that spiffy "Salem theme" again as everyone gets out of the car – which, on its third listening, starts to lose its spiffiness.

Samantha trails Serena with a locator spell, building on "Samantha's Secret Is Discovered" (#188), where she first cast that type of incantation. Granted, Samantha tires of the groundskeeper's tangent, but she's there for information – why does she pop out before he finishes?

Dick Wilson's latest drunkard – Potter from "The Salem Saga" (#203) – identified the Stephenses to the police regarding that episode's missing bedwarmer. So why doesn't he recognize Samantha now? Even toasted, Potter should find her face familiar.

Does Gloucester have only one restaurant? Serena and the Fisherman inexplicably end up there the same time as Larry and Barrows – and, even odder, seat themselves at their table. Samantha and Serena leave Larry and Barrows, getting all the way into the bar in three seconds, but people seem to move fast in Gloucester: an extra appears outside the window and starts walking as the Fisherman disappears.

Outdoor shoots can be tricky, so it's forgivable when a boat lurches forward as Serena pops in, and when Darrin and Serena are bathed in sunlight while Samantha's sky is cloudy in her pick-up shots. But that doesn't change the dialogue: Samantha tells Darrin that "even the men who go down to the sea in ships" is a great idea – except she's the one who came up with the slogan.

OH, MY STARS!

When she first pops into the Stephenses' hotel room, Serena giddily apologizes for being a few days late for the convention – but she was at the convention on its first night, helping Samantha to change the warlock Newton back from a House of the Seven Gables antique in "Samantha's Hot Bedwarmer" (#204). Was something shot out of order, or did the writers just forget this detail?

SON OF A GUN!

"Chicken of the sea – that's me." – the Fisherman, comparing himself with the famous brand of tuna.

PAUL REVERE RIDES AGAIN
Airdate: October 29, 1970

EPISODE 206

In Salem, Esmeralda pops in with an update on the kids and takes Samantha's pile of packages back with her, including an "antique" Paul Revere teapot Larry wants to use to lure Sir Leslie Bancroft of British Imperial Textile Mills. When the vacationing Stephenses resist Larry's push for Darrin to meet with Bancroft, Larry demands his teapot back; since the package is now in Westport, Darrin agrees to see the Englishman while Samantha retrieves the teapot from Esmeralda. Samantha can't pop home because Louise is visiting Tabitha and Adam, so Esmeralda tries to zap the teapot to Samantha and puts Paul Revere in her hotel room instead. When Revere overhears Sir Leslie talking about "invading the American market" with his product, he thinks it's time to warn his countrymen – which he is able to do when Esmeralda accidentally materializes his horse.

Bancroft walks when Darrin tries to explain Revere's presence with the slogan, "The British are coming," while Samantha chases the horse-riding historical figure in a taxi. Though Salem's tourists think Revere is part of the town's attractions, the police don't, and he is taken to jail. Visiting his cell, Samantha listens as Revere concedes his ride wasn't necessary in the 20th century; she then takes him to Boston to show him a statue commemorating his impact on history. Esmeralda returns Paul to his own time, and Sir Leslie signs with McMann & Tate after seeing the full-page ad that Samantha placed by witchcraft.

GOOD!

Considering Tabitha and Adam's whereabouts are often ignored while the adults get most of the air time, it's great attention to detail for Darrin to ask Esmeralda who's sitting with his kids in her absence (in this case, it's Aunt Hagatha). The young Stephenses are even visited by Louise – who could well have brought Jonathan with her. And, when Samantha wants to pop home, Darrin shows he's learned from past witchy troubles and warns her to make sure Louise isn't there first; Louise showed up when Samantha popped home from Chicago in "That Was No Chick, That Was My Wife" (#117).

It's encouraging to see the Stephenses at least try to put their foot down with Larry about their vacation, and it's only right that Larry utters "Who?" at the mention of Esmeralda, since the maid and the ad man have never been formally introduced, despite sharing the screen three times in Season Six.

The Salem photo backdrop outside the Stephenses' hotel room, and the zoom out from it, combine to make a very nice shot. Also well-done is Paul Revere's ride through "Salem" – the crane shots, tilted angles, and quick edits make for quite a suspenseful sequence; tourists certainly would think it's put on for show. Finally, the "statue" that sits astride his horse is a bronzed actor who stays perfectly still both as the camera zooms in on him, and in reverse shots with Paul and Samantha below.

WELL?

Apparently, the maitre d' from the Gloucester House [see "Darrin on a Pedestal" (#205)] has a second job as a Salem bellhop, since Jud Strunk plays both parts in these back-to-back episodes. And either the Hawthorne Hotel has the same taste as the Stephenses, or they sold some old furnishings to the inn, because the painting hanging behind Darrin during his call to Larry is the same one that hung in the Stephenses' living room for years.

Esmeralda leaves her shoes behind when she pops out, just like Aunt Clara used to – and even Darrin, who went shoeless trying to master his "powers" in "Daddy Comes for a Visit" (#180). But who knew: witches have a video chat system that is decades ahead of Skype and FaceTime! It's got a few bugs though, as both the operator and Samantha are seen at one angle, then much closer up in subsequent shots. Question: if Samantha is so anxious to regain the teapot but can't pop home, why doesn't she just twitch it back to the hotel instead of depending on Esmeralda to magically deliver it? (Answer: because then Esmeralda wouldn't zap up Paul Revere.)

When Esmeralda complains that her throat is hoarse, it triggers witchcraft that pops Revere's horse to him. But it's only a play on words; Esmeralda isn't actively trying to cast a spell in that moment.

Since when is Darrin into history? He told Samantha that his knowledge of the Civil War was "slightly less than limited" in "And Then She Wrote" (#45), and he always has to be told who his visiting historical figures are. Besides, any history buff would correct Samantha when she says Paul's rock group is the Sons of Liberty – that's the name of the actual organization Paul Revere belonged to; Samantha means Paul Revere and the Raiders, who racked up hits in the late '60s and early '70s.

How does Paul get his horse down to street level from the Stephenses' hotel room – in the elevator? And the Stephenses have seen a man in Paul Revere garb on horseback before: it was part of a curse-breaker that Darrin's friend, Adam Newlarkin, had to complete in "We're In For A Bad Spell" (#39). Interestingly, according to research, Paul Revere never actually shouted, "The British are coming." Historical accounts reveal him as saying, "The Regulars are coming out" – which, admittedly, isn't nearly as dramatic.

Samantha jumps into a taxi to chase Revere and his horse through Salem. Why? The Stephenses have a rental car, and she could just zap the escaping Paul off his horse. Two officers from "Samantha's Hot Bedwarmer" (#204) return here, but neither recognize Samantha, even though they just went through a court case with her. And surely the desk sergeant – most likely a Massachusetts resident – wouldn't have to be told about the Sons of Liberty; he's probably heard about them all his life.

The "Boston" park Samantha brings Revere to looks nothing like the actual Boston Mall where Revere's statue stands; it's really the show's usual neighborhood park, with the mountains of Burbank in the background. It's understandable that passersby shift when Larry's teapot pops into Samantha's hands, but how can Paul claim the pot as his own? Larry bought an obvious copy, and no speech about how Revere didn't get to put his mark on it because he had to make his ride changes that fact.

Darrin has a much bigger problem than getting the teapot back to Larry – Samantha and Paul generate some serious electricity just before Esmeralda sends the militia man back. Samantha even grins, "He wasn't bad, was he?" when Bancroft compliments Paul's "performance." Would Samantha be so intrigued if she knew Revere was flirting with her despite being married his entire adult life?

OH, MY STARS!

Samantha never learns when it comes to discussing current events with visiting historical figures. She's announced the 20th century five times before: to Benjamin Franklin, Queen Victoria, Leonardo da Vinci,

Napoléon Bonaparte, and Julius Caesar. How can she be sure she's not changing history by telling Revere about planes, submarines, and moon landings? Worse, Samantha cheerily tells Paul Revere, who was born just 45 years after the Salem witch hysteria, that she's a witch – there's nothing stopping him from revealing Samantha's identity to his arresting officers, and Samantha's lucky the Witches' Council doesn't lower the boom on her for being such a chatterbox.

After Esmeralda sends Revere to Salem, she's next seen in the kitchen, casting a spell to put the militia man back where he belongs – the thing is, Esmeralda doesn't know she's materialized him at this point. The only possible connection is when Samantha picks her mirror back up for a second call to the operator – but the call isn't shown, so either there's a deleted scene, or a gap in the writing. Later, Samantha saves the day by zapping Darrin's "the British are coming" ads into Salem's newspapers – except she wasn't present when Darrin devised the slogan because she ran out to chase after Paul, and Darrin never gets a chance to tell her about his concept. As for Larry, he's with Darrin the whole time, so he knows Darrin can't have placed the ad – yet he never wonders how it got in the paper.

Finally, by zapping Paul Revere out of his cell, Samantha is breaking the law. This isn't her first time magically busting someone out of the joint, either; she likewise obstructed justice by liberating Brian O'Brian in "The Leprechaun" (#63). Once the cops get over their shock, do they initiate a citywide manhunt for the errant horse rider? And are witches exempt from mortal laws?

SON OF A GUN!

"It's an authentic original reproduction." – Larry, on whether his teapot was actually made by Paul Revere.

EPISODE 207 SAMANTHA'S BAD DAY IN SALEM
Airdate: November 5, 1970

At the ongoing Witches' Convention in Salem, Samantha runs into Waldo, a childhood friend who never got over his crush on her. After the dismissive Samantha leaves, Waldo zaps up a duplicate that swoons over him; goaded by his critical mother, Waldo decides to take action. The next day, Samantha tends to "family business" while Larry tries to badger the sightseeing Darrin into working. Larry changes his tune after seeing "Samantha" with Waldo and confuses Darrin by suddenly insisting he spend more time with his wife. Larry gives Samantha the cold shoulder at lunch and nearly chokes when Waldo approaches the table; privately, Waldo tells Samantha he just wanted to meet Darrin, while Larry nervously tells Darrin about seeing Samantha and Waldo together.

As Samantha excuses herself, but misses Darrin in the lobby, Waldo reinstalls her double and implores her to steal away with him; Darrin overhears and demands answers, so Waldo turns him into a crow. Seeing Darrin-as-bird packing his suitcase with his beak, Samantha suspects Endora and confronts her at the convention, where the attendees applaud Darrin's predicament. Waldo changes Darrin back, and, at the hotel, Samantha can't believe Larry and Darrin think she's fooling around. She summons Waldo, who sheepishly reveals the double; Larry sees it and throws a punch at Waldo, getting himself turned into a crow. Samantha asks Waldo to zap up a blond "Serena," which convinces the restored Larry that Samantha has been true to Darrin.

GOOD!

Not only is installing a "resident witch" in Salem to make sure ignorant mortals never fire up another witch hunt a good idea, it connects this episode with "To Go or Not to Go, That Is the Question" (#201), where Endora first brought up the appointment. And, when Samantha's fellow supernaturals delight at Darrin being a bird, she cries, "You call yourselves decent witches – bullies, that's what you are!" She's not actually wrong: Endora and most of her brethren have been bullying Darrin for years; it's interesting that Samantha finally calls them on it.

Waldo changes Darrin into a crow in a restaurant full of people – nobody moves, rendering the effect flawless. Watching the feathery Darrin "pack" is also very entertaining – but it's Larry's ornithological transformation that's the highlight; his crow even has white "hair."

Fake Serena outshines her imaginary, automaton cousin for sheer grooviness. She is only Waldo's interpretation of Serena; she goes from smiling to severe, and it's always fascinating to watch Serena's voice issuing forth from Samantha's likeness. Not to be outdone, Anne Seymour as Waldo's caustic mother defines her son in a far too brief 30-second appearance. "Let me count the ways," Mama sneers as Waldo tells "Samantha" how-do-I-love-thee: "One, like some kind of nut; two, like a case of arrested development…"

WELL?

Witches have zapped up food and drink ever since Bertha and Mary magically poured themselves tea in "The Witches Are Out" (#7). So doesn't it seem odd that the convention attendees serve themselves mortal style at the refreshment table? Waldo isn't very original zapping up a worshiping Samantha clone; Tabitha did it first in "Tabitha's Very Own Samantha" (#189). More to the point, Waldo might want to consider an upgrade – his artificial paramour wears Samantha's wedding ring, which can't be very romantic for him.

Darrin reminds Larry that he's on vacation because he's "pizzazzed out." No, Darrin was forced into a vacation in "To Go or Not to Go, That Is the Question" (#201) because of Samantha having to attend the Witches' Convention. And, as discussed in the exploration of that episode, this is not the first vacation Darrin has had in four years, as he insists to Larry.

After Darrin is changed into a crow, how does he get up to his room? The doors and windows are closed, and it's not like Darrin can use a key in that state. Does he squawk at the bellhop to let him in? And Samantha immediately suspects Endora of having a hand in the bird – true, her mother is usually guilty, but this time, Samantha knows Waldo is on the scene, and she should be more open to him being the culprit.

Darrin is ready to leave Samantha over Waldo; maybe this his retaliation for the times Samantha falsely accused him of philandering in "Three Wishes" (#96) and "Snob in the Grass" (#126). Later, Samantha threatens to zap Waldo into another century. What if he doesn't want to go? After all, Newton-as-bedwarmer wouldn't budge when Samantha tried to relocate him in "The Salem Saga" (#203).

So much for Larry being the competent boxer he said he was in "Fastest Gun on Madison Avenue" (#57) – he misses Waldo by a mile. And isn't it dangerous for everyone to discuss witchcraft in front of Larry-as-crow? Darrin retains his memories of being a bird; it's a little too convenient that Larry doesn't.

Larry is surprised to see Serena as a blond, but he shouldn't be – he met her with that hair color in "Hippie, Hippie, Hooray" (#128). By the way, since "Serena" is Waldo's creation, how does she know to call Larry "Cotton Top," which is her personal nickname for him? Larry asks if the "cousins" have been to a costume ball, but you'd think he'd recognize the green-and-black flying suits as Samantha's

Glinda costume from "To Trick-or-Treat or Not to Trick-or-Treat" (#177). And, if Fake Serena fades out at the slightest touch, as she does when Larry puts his arm around her, Waldo's "relationship" with Fake Samantha must be rather chaste!

OH, MY STARS!

Darrin's expositional history lesson about Salem doesn't quite work. Considering he and Larry are actually seen in the real Salem, showing them against process shots during the early part of the tour is a disappointing contrast. Were there budgetary and/or logistical restraints involved? Darrin offers up a chronicle of colonist Roger Conant, which would be fine if he hadn't just chatted with Sir Leslie about him in "Paul Revere Rides Again" (#206). Then, Darrin caps his sightseeing trip by going back to the House of the Seven Gables – why would he show his face there after he was accused of stealing their bedwarmer in "The Salem Saga" (#203)?

Endora says that the High Priestess Hepzibah installed the first resident witch of Salem in 1692. That's a very enlightened thing for her to do, but if Hepzibah was already in power in 1692, why were Ticheba and Samantha queens in 1967? [See "Long Live the Queen" (#108) and "To Go or Not to Go, That Is the Question" (#201).] Then, it is revealed that this pink, smoky gathering place for witches is considered hallowed ground – so, when Darrin materializes there, why doesn't Hepzibah? She was the one who didn't want Darrin anywhere near it when the season began.

SON OF A GUN!

"If she's the chairman, it should be called the Ways to Be Mean committee." – Darrin, on Endora pulling rank to put Samantha on the witches' Ways and Means committee.

Larry starts off as his usual demanding self in this episode, trying to pull Darrin away from his vacation – but, as soon as he sees "Samantha" with Waldo, he does a one-eighty into some very nervous, very funny territory. He babbles to Darrin, snarks at Samantha, and gives David White a chance to play a style of comedy that proves Larry Tate doesn't just care about accounts.

SAMANTHA'S OLD SALEM TRIP
EPISODE 208
Airdate: November 12, 1970

The Stephenses return early from Salem because the Witches' Council doesn't want Samantha seen in public with Darrin. While Samantha checks on the kids, Esmeralda intercepts a Council message demanding that Samantha return to Salem immediately – so she zaps Samantha there herself. Soon Endora pops in, wondering where Samantha is; in analyzing Esmeralda's spell, Endora determines that Samantha has been sent to 17th century Salem with no memory or powers. Endora elects Darrin to rescue Samantha with a magic coin that will restore her, but, because of Darrin's 20th century approach, he gets himself clapped in the stocks for lewd conduct.

The next day, Samantha uses Darrin's anachronistic ball point pen, which gets them both accused of witchcraft. Darrin turns their trial to his advantage by announcing he can prove Samantha's witchery with the coin; the judge permits the demonstration, which gives Samantha total recall. Samantha uses her powers to prove that the colonial persecutors have only ever tried their fellow mortals, and calls the group out on their senseless hysteria before taking Darrin home. Back in 1970, Samantha sets the Witches' Council straight, closing the Salem chapter, and Esmeralda's attempt to make a Spanish omelet results in plain eggs and the maid in a flamenco dress.

GOOD!

Adam's lucky to have a big sister who can use her powers to interpret his infantile ramblings, which also demonstrates her growing warmth toward him. Tabitha also shows a nice bit of consistency when she asks if Samantha brought her anything from Salem; she requested a Salem souvenir as her parents left in "The Salem Saga" (#203).

Darrin smartly realizing that the honey from the jail cell will stick the magic coin to Samantha's head (a condition of her memory restoration) creates an opportunity for Samantha to out herself as a witch and teach her mortal accusers a lesson or two about their witch hysteria. Darrin doesn't even seem to mind Samantha using her powers to scare them straight, commenting, "What a ham" when she turns herself into a floating bucket of water.

The detail on the tavern's 17th century menu is very realistic, at least based on a modern-day understanding of that period. But Esmeralda is on the menu in 1970: her flamenco foible at the end of the episode even has Darrin amused.

WELL?

The makeover of 1164 Morning Glory Circle continues: Tabitha has a new room, but it looks just like her parents' bedroom; it seems to be situated in the same place, too, judging by the location of the door and hallway. Trying to keep a hold on the squirming Adam, Esmeralda tells Tabitha her parents will be back "next week, which won't be soon enough for me." That's an unusually sarcastic thing for the placid Esmeralda to say, especially in front of Tabitha.

In "Salem, Here We Come" (#202), Hepzibah was asked if she had ever flown "the regal bird with the silver beak." Here, Darrin frowns upon flying home via "the proud witch with the golden nose." Once again, Samantha flying into a flock of geese raises the question, when witches fly, do they actually levitate from Point A to Point B? Because they're generally seen just vanishing from one place and materializing in another.

Samantha was pressured into attending the Witches' Convention in "To Go or Not to Go, That Is the Question" (#201). So why didn't Esmeralda have to go? And you'd think the Witches' Council would send their message arrow to Tabitha's room, where Samantha actually is, instead of to the living room with Esmeralda. How does Darrin simply continue up the stairs after the arrow makes a loud thwack a few feet behind him, causing Esmeralda to noisily drop a pair of suitcases? And the Council's demand for Samantha to return to Salem makes little sense: if their "hallowed ground" is in a witchy locale [see "Samantha's Bad Day in Salem" (#207)], Samantha could just stay home and pop over to wherever she needs to go, as she does at episode's end.

This Old Salem jaunt has origins in more than one previous episode: Darrin asking if he'll be a perfect stranger to his wife, and Endora's response, "A stranger, yes, but hardly perfect" comes from his exchange with Serena in "Samantha Goes South for a Spell" (#142), and Endora tells Darrin to "throw in a lot of thees and thous," which is what Larry wanted Benjamin Franklin to utter in "My Friend Ben" (#87). Now, Samantha coached Darrin in Pilgrim-speak in "Samantha's Thanksgiving to Remember" (#119), so he should know how to conduct himself in the 17th century – instead, he makes no attempt to blend in, calling Samantha "Sam," as he did in "Samantha Goes South for a Spell" (#142). He even snarks, "Sorry, wrong century" when asking a shocked colonist for a pencil. To be fair to Darrin, the Salemite should know what a pencil is: they came into use in the 1560s, and research suggests that American colonists imported pencils from Europe.

After Darrin is clapped in the stocks, Samantha still has his coin and pen the next day. Why didn't she thrust his items back at him the moment he ran afoul of her? Later, when Darrin misses trying to wing the coin into Samantha's cell, his jailers allow him to pick it up. No prison guard, in any century, would let a suspect keep any kind of money – they'd confiscate it.

The judge tells Samantha and Darrin they'll be hanged if they don't confess – if they do confess, they'll be hanged for being witches. Darrin heard this same threat 70 years earlier in "Samantha's Thanksgiving to Remember" (#119). As for the honey-covered coin, it has been thrown, picked up, and carried around in Darrin's pocket. How can it still be sticky?

Samantha electrifies her captor; maybe she got the idea from watching Uncle Arthur shock Darrin in "Samantha Loses Her Voice" (#150). And of course, not much could be done to prevent the fire and smoke in the wastebasket from shifting considerably as Samantha became and unbecame the bucket of water. The Witches' Council sapped Samantha powers for "frivolously flaunting" herself as a witch in "Samantha's Secret Is Discovered" (#188); her flaunting is even more frivolous here, but maybe she makes such a good point during this pivotal time in witch history that the "noble eight" is willing to look the other way.

When Samantha returns from confronting the Witches' Council, she is pleased to announce she doesn't have to go back to Salem. In "Salem, Here We Come" (#202), Samantha told Darrin that once they returned, she would remove the spell that made his client, Hitchcock, fall in love with Hepzibah. Does she?

OH, MY STARS!

Why is the Witches' Council having issues about Darrin appearing in public with Samantha now? Did they not get the memo in "Salem, Here We Come" (#202) that the High Priestess Hepzibah gave Darrin permission to travel there with Samantha?

Endora's decision to send Darrin to the 17th century to rescue Samantha doesn't quite track. The great and powerful Witches' Council is supposed to be near-omnipotent – so how are they not aware that Esmeralda miscast a spell, and why don't they just zap Samantha back to the present themselves? For that matter, Esmeralda uncharacteristically remembers her original spell [she didn't in "Samantha's Caesar Salad" (#173)], so why can't she simply undo it herself? Another wonky element of this time trek is Samantha's loss of memory and powers. Endora determines this witchy condition based on the retelling of Esmeralda's very basic spell. Yet, Endora sent Serena to the same time period in "Samantha's Hot Bedwarmer" (#204), and Serena didn't lose *her* powers – is it that Serena gave her consent to time travel, and Samantha didn't? Also, Esmeralda's powers aren't the greatest to begin with; sending Samantha back in time is far beyond her capabilities. Finally, it's strange that Samantha automatically speaks in 1690s vernacular upon arrival, while Darrin uses 1970s lingo making the same trip.

The show's witches and mortals continue to run the risk of altering history. It's enough that Samantha introduces a ball point pen into Old Salem 200 years early (it was invented in 1888), but Samantha and Darrin's influence causes the judge to declare "an end to these and future trials." Even if one judge had the power to do that, it's unlikely this is the exact time and place the Salem witch trials are supposed to stop. Imagine the butterfly effect of just one person surviving who isn't supposed to – the changes could easily ripple into the present. As is always the case with these historically-based episodes, the show is first and foremost a comedy, but, through the lens of how time travel stories are executed today, it's hard not to notice the Stephenses' impact on the timeline.

SON OF A GUN!

"Take this coin, and do what I tell you." – Darrin to an amnesiac Samantha, forgetting that the world's oldest profession was already around in the 1690s.

SAMANTHA'S PET WARLOCK
Airdate: November 19, 1970

After Samantha's old beau, Ashley Flynn, fails to recapture her interest, he decides to see what the all fuss is about Darrin. Ashley visits McMann & Tate and invisibly catches Larry and Darrin digging themselves into a hole with dog food manufacturer Gibbons; Larry claims Darrin owns an unusual breed. Gibbons wants to see the nonexistent pet, so Larry and Darrin make a beeline for the pound, where Ashley becomes the dog they're looking for. Darrin brings Ashley-as-dog home, but Samantha sees the "canine" turning Adam's baby food into a steak and realizes Ashley has shape-shifted. Samantha forces him to humanize, then introduces him to Darrin, who tells Larry the dog ran away. Larry demands the dog be found for Gibbons, so Samantha turns Ashley back into man's best friend.

While Darrin is out stocking up on Gibbons' products, Gladys stops by to see the Stephenses' new "dog," commenting how ugly it is; Ashley gets revenge by trotting over to the Kravitzes and turning himself into different breeds to spook Gladys. Once Larry brings Gibbons over, Ashley-as-dog locks himself in a closet, then shrinks from Darrin to create the impression he mistreats animals. Catching on, Samantha feeds a Gibbons Dog Burger to Ashley, who turns it into a steak; the Stephenses use the transformation to suggest a steak-like dog treat for Gibbons' line. Rewarding Ashley-as-dog for playing nice, Samantha changes him back, after which he pops out for fun and games with Endora.

GOOD!

It's no wonder that dog fanatic Gibbons thinks that everyone has one – he seems like just that kind of guy, as much as Larry seems like someone who would have a nervous white poodle, as Gibbons guesses. Also, watching Darrin and Larry contradicting each other, with their description of Darrin's "dog" getting more and more outrageous, it's understandable why Ashley laughs.

Can a warlock perform witchcraft as an animal? It's never been seen until now, which means it's not impossible – and that's what makes Ashley-as-dog the star of this episode. From zapping baby food to tormenting Gladys, the magical mutt brings something new and exciting to the show. It's ingenious that, in the confines of Ashley's "sheepdog beagle," he can only change himself into those two specific breeds. Best of all, the canine "performer" is somehow able to hold still to accomplish his food-changing effects.

It turns out that Gladys still takes her medicine – Abner hasn't foisted it on her since the earlier seasons, but, considering Gladys first took a spoonful in "Be It Ever So Mortgaged" (#2), it's particularly awesome continuity. And Darrin confirms that he and Samantha live in Westport; the show changed locales in "Just A Kid Again" (#193).

WELL?

Darrin reports reading four books in one night. How? *Lassie Come-Home*, originally a magazine story written by Eric Knight in 1938 and expanded into a novel in 1940, is already more than an evening's curl-up at 256 pages. As for Samantha, her little black book must have been filled to capacity before the mortal life, because Ashley is yet another torch-carrying warlock left in her wake, this after Waldo was just in that role two episodes ago in "Samantha's Bad Day in Salem" (#207). Is Samantha having multiple déjà vus listening to Ashley's seduction attempt? "George the Warlock" (#30) wanted to rescue Samantha from her "domestic cage," and Rodney, the warlock Samantha once babysat (who also became a dog), described their interaction as "love/hate" and professed a preference for complex relationships in "Man's Best Friend" (#70), as Ashley does now.

Larry takes an awful chance with Gibbons, claiming Darrin's dog is a sheepdog/beagle mix. Larry's not a dog expert, but Gibbons is; Larry could easily have come up a hybrid that doesn't exist. Then, the champion brown-noser atypically tells his client, "When you've seen one mutt, you've seen them all." Someone as smooth as Larry Tate would never stick his foot in his mouth like that.

Darrin accepts Ashley-as-dog far too readily. Larry creates an impossible-sounding pup they just happen to find at the pound – and Darrin's six years of experience doesn't tell him that witchcraft is involved?

Ashley isn't a very sneaky warlock-as-dog; he tips his paw right away, changing Adam's mush into a steak. Now, this has been a question as far back as "Ling-Ling" (#21): do metabolisms change when humanoids turn into animals, and vice versa? Because if Ashley's system doesn't convert to canine, then he's a warlock eating a raw steak.

The Stephens house continues to be full of non-stop magic – but, for some reason, Gladys decides the possibility of a new dog is a good reason to snoop instead. Whatever happened to the behemoth the Kravitzes adopted in "Samantha's Wedding Present" (#141)? And the Kravitzes must believe in keeping up with the Joneses: following the Stephenses' lead, Abner and Gladys' house has gotten a makeover as well – it's now white instead of yellow, the living room walls are blue instead of green, and the spacious brick kitchen they sported in "Weep No More, My Willow" (#152) is now tiny, with an ordinary linoleum floor.

Morning Glory Circle morphs yet again, this time inserting a house on the end of the street where there's usually a curve and a gas station. When Samantha runs across the street to retrieve Ashley, who's watching Adam? Esmeralda is at the movies with Tabitha, and Darrin is out buying Gibbons Dog Burgers – meaning Samantha leaves her toddler all alone in the house.

When Ashley-as-dog acts up, Darrin reminds him, "You gave me your word!" When did that happen? Ashley was sassing Darrin right up to the time Samantha put the warlock on all fours again, so Ashley didn't promise anything one way or another. Then, to explain Ashley turning the dog burger into a steak, the Stephenses tell Larry and Gibbons that the hand is quicker than the eye. Reasonable, except neither Samantha nor Darrin's hands get anywhere near the plate. When the mortals leave, Endora returns, and Samantha says of Ashley, "If it hadn't been for him, Darrin never would have gotten the account." What kind of show of confidence is that?

OH, MY STARS!

Does Ashley have a twin that just came back from being a bedwarmer? Noam Pitlik is swarthy and shifty as Ashley, but identifiable enough in his distinct style that it's just too soon to see him again after just he played warlock Newton in "Samantha's Hot Bedwarmer" (#204). Ashley being a dog for half the episode lessens the effect, but perhaps the show should have waited longer to tell Ashley's story, or at least hired another actor to play Ashley while casting Pitlik later in the season.

SON OF A GUN!

"Then why does everybody call you Durwood?" – Ashley, as Darrin insists on the correct use of his name.

Since Season Five, and even before that, a question hanging over the show has been, "Can a witch perform magic on another witch?" It didn't seem logical that they should be able to, yet instances abounded. So it's most intriguing when Samantha pops Ashley into a pooch, and Darrin asks, "How come you can do that to a warlock?" That alone means the writers are asking themselves this same question. Samantha's reply? "I caught him by surprise!" Finally, it's explained how witches can zap each other. Granted, it rather implies that witches have to constantly live with their guard up to prevent others from putting spells on them, but it's a plausible enough explanation, and it adds a whole new layer to the inner workings of witchcraft that didn't exist before.

SAMANTHA'S OLD MAN
Airdate: December 3, 1970

EPISODE 210

To remind Samantha that Darrin will grow old long before she does, Endora turns him into a senior citizen. Darrin can't stop looking at himself, so Samantha takes him to a drive-in movie to distract him. Samantha bumps into the Tates; they're suspicious since Samantha begged off a game of bridge by saying Darrin is sick. Larry and Louise stop by Samantha's car and meet the aged Darrin, whom Samantha introduces as Darrin's grandfather, Grover. Inspired, the Tates excuse themselves and return with Louise's grandmotherly Aunt Millicent. Hip Millicent grooves on "Grover," so the Tates set the old-timers up on a date.

The next day, Darrin worries that he'll miss a meeting with Booker of Beau Geste cologne; since Darrin hasn't met Booker, Samantha encourages Darrin to attend the meeting in his elderly form. All goes well until Larry shows up and scolds "Grover" for impersonating Darrin, but "Grover" blows Larry and Booker away with his salesmanship. Later, Darrin is forced to keep his date with Millicent because the Tates bring her by the house, so Samantha turns herself into an old woman and barges in as "Grover's" supposedly dead wife. After she reams him out for philandering, the Tates take Millicent home. Endora is upset to see her daughter as a blue-hair and agrees to change Darrin back; Samantha assures Darrin that she can alter her appearance in coming years, which will allow them to grow old together.

GOOD!

In both "Eye of the Beholder" (#22) and "Mona Sammy" (#198), Darrin wondered how people would react to a perpetually young Samantha hanging around him as an old man. Now he knows – and if the teenagers in the next car flashing him a "Right on!" are any indication, Darrin can probably lay that six-year fear to rest.

Ruth McDevitt has been a witchy monarch ["Long Live the Queen" (#108)] and a dotty cat lady ["Mrs. Stephens, Where Are You?" (#160)], but her Millicent, in all her groovy glory, is an anachronistic delight. Not to be outdone, Samantha as "Grover's" wife, in the form of Hope Summers (from the 1960-1968 series, *The Andy Griffith Show*) is one of the many highlights of this outstanding episode. Samantha's voice might be emanating from "Carolyn," which is how the credits list her (the dubbing is amazing), but Summers' expressions are priceless.

It's solid continuity for Endora to pass on an invitation from Samantha's old beau Rollo; his love potion was the catalyst for "Once in a Vial" (#125), though he hasn't been seen or mentioned again until now.

WELL?

This isn't the first time Endora appears in the refrigerator [she did it to warn Samantha about Maurice in "Just One Happy Family" (#10)], nor is it the début of her Knave of Hearts costume, which she wore in "Samantha's Secret Spell" (#179). Endora wants to take Samantha to the Cosmos Cotillion – but, when Serena was its entertainment chairman in "Serena Stops the Show" (#192), she said the dance only took place once a year. It hasn't been a year yet, and the last Cotillion wasn't a costume ball.

Darrin gazes at himself in a multitude of reflective surfaces, including the latest convenient mirror to replace the painting in the foyer [there hasn't been a mirror there since "The Generation Zap" (#194)]. But should Darrin be this furious with Endora? He understood Samantha changing him into a grandmother to protect him from a jealous football player in "Pleasure O'Riley" (#25), after all.

Larry is unusually intrigued by the idea of Samantha cheating on Darrin, considering he was just a nervous wreck thinking he saw Samantha with another man in "Samantha's Bad Day in Salem" (#207). And Larry's argument for pushing his theatre tickets on "Grover" isn't his strongest – Darrin lies that he's seen the musical in question, and Larry says that's impossible, because it's opening night. Does Larry mean the world premiere? A show simply having an opening night doesn't mean it's never played anywhere else.

Why does Larry describe Darrin to Booker as "young Stephens?" As explored in the analysis of "What Makes Darrin Run" (#191), Darrin and Larry are probably only six years apart. Samantha knows that Larry generally joins Darrin for meetings with clients, yet she suggests that Darrin meet Booker as "Grover" – sure enough, Larry shows up at the restaurant. Then, Samantha inexplicably calls and interrupts Darrin's meeting; of course, she needs to, so Darrin-as-Grover can step away from the table, with Larry's arrival creating conflict.

"Grover" feels it necessary to tell Larry that Darrin woke up with an infected throat, but Larry already knows Darrin is "sick" – that was Samantha's reason for canceling bridge with him and Louise the night before. Darrin slips, though, telling Booker, "What *I* have in mind is a saturation campaign for television." This makes the slogan sound like "Grover's" idea, when "Grover" just said Darrin filled him in on the concept. After impressing Booker, Darrin laughs that Larry offered to make "Grover" Darrin's supervisor. That's amazingly generous for Larry, but isn't Larry already Darrin's supervisor?

Louise smiles that Millicent doesn't care what she and "Grover" do, "as long as they're together." What together? They haven't known each other 24 hours; Louise makes it sound like "Grover" and Millicent are a couple. Samantha's change into the first older version of herself is superb; if only that camera hadn't moved. It's curious, though, why Samantha chooses to become two different elderly ladies: she begins by completely altering her outward appearance to be "Grover's" wife, then creates another version for Darrin that is simply herself, only older. Hope Summers is a joy to watch as she socks it to "Grover," but it's rather a shame that Elizabeth Montgomery gets put into all that wonderful movie-quality make-up and doesn't end up doing both scenes in that guise.

OH, MY STARS!

When Darrin tells Samantha that Larry has just joined Booker at the table, he says, "I'm thinking of cutting my wrists." That's not as terrible as when Darrin suggested killing himself in "Mona Sammy" (#198), but the father of two shouldn't be telling this joke. Explaining his older appearance, "Grover" tells Larry that

Darrin misunderstood: his wife died, not him. So, when "Grover's" better half shows up very much alive, it looks like he lied about his wife being dead. Yet everyone's more upset about his catting around than they are about what appears to be a cold-hearted lie.

Booker informs Larry that the Darrin Stephens he just met is 70 years old. This gibes with Endora's math, since she wants Samantha to see what Darrin will look like in three decades, and Darrin is in his early 40s. This even works when Samantha, as "Grover's" wife, says they've been married 53 years; "Grover" could have gotten married at seventeen. It's just that "Grover" can't be only 70: Darrin's father and "grandfather" would each have had to have kids at the age of fifteen to total the thirty years. Assuming Darrin's "progenitors" were of legal age instead, "Grover" is at least 76, if not 80 or more.

One substantially missed beat: not showing Tabitha's reaction to her aged father.

SON OF A GUN!

"What about 30 years from now, when whatever dubious charms he has wrinkle up?" – Endora to Samantha, questioning her daughter's future attraction to Darrin in a line that's pretty racy for television in 1970.

Dick Sargent turns in what may be his finest performance yet as old-timer "Grover." His curmudgeonly asides are a caution ("Passable, for a talkie," he deadpans, describing the drive-in movie to Larry), but it's his Grover-as-businessman scene where he really shines. Clearly relishing the opportunity to play a different character within his character, Sargent makes "Grover's" sales pitch as mesmerizing as the twinkle in his eye when he delivers it. "I am young, in here," Darrin-as-Grover remarks, pointing to his heart, "and in here, where it counts," he finishes, tapping at his temple – a powerful lesson, capped only by "Grover" turning things around on Larry and calling *him* a "son of a gun."

Darrin has worried about how people will react to the increasing gap between his age and Samantha's before, but here, he also ponders what his own life will be like as an old man. Obliging, Samantha offers him a "preview" by turning herself into an old woman and informing him that she can arrange it so they appear to age at the same rate. Not only does this sequence have a lot of heart – and stunning old-age make-up – but Samantha's demonstration finally provides an answer to the question Darrin's been asking since Season One. It's also a sneak peek into the lives of the Stephenses decades down the line, and creates a good explanation for why they appear to be aging together, since their portrayers are.

THE CORSICAN COUSINS
Airdate: December 10, 1970

EPISODE
211

Hoping to remind Samantha of the witchy life she's given up, Endora casts a spell that makes her experience Serena's emotional and physical sensations. Meanwhile, McMann & Tate works to land the Bigelow Industries account, which requires the Stephenses to join the country club of J.J. Langley; when Larry stops by to tell Darrin and Samantha that ladies from its screening committee are coming over, Samantha bursts out laughing because Serena is being tickled by a beau. Samantha rushes to the grocery store to satisfy Serena's craving for ring-tailed pheasant, then dances in the aisle as Serena hits the floor with her date – who pops out before his wife can see him. Serena becomes furious, and soon Samantha is channeling her cousin's hatred of men.

The committee ladies arrive early, and Larry is befuddled by the antagonism Samantha levels at him and Darrin. Before long, Samantha is crying Serena's tears – and Endora, feeling Serena's negative emotions are ruining her spell, zaps up a potent drink to brighten Serena's spirits. Serena becomes intoxicated immediately; Samantha "drunkenly" reminds Mrs. Langley about the rumor that her husband gained control of Bigelow Industries through a hostile takeover. The committee ladies storm out, and, later, Larry returns confirming the rumor, happy that the agency is no longer associated with Langley. Samantha pretends she sabotaged the account on purpose, and, when Larry wants to know how Samantha knew about Langley, Darrin smiles that his wife is a witch.

GOOD!

Serena's party girl behavior expressing through Samantha is, of course, the centerpiece of this episode, but perhaps the most outrageous moment is Samantha dancing in the grocery store, looking very confused while having Serena's good time. Then there are "Samantha's" entertaining emotions, ranging from hostile to teary-eyed, ending at falling down "drunk" – but Serena's original feelings and inebriation are the most tickling. Asked why she's crying over a warlock running out on her, Serena sobs, "Because! Now I don't have anything to do this afternoon." It's quite a showcase for Elizabeth Montgomery.

WELL?

In "Samantha's Old Man" (#210), Darrin "broke 80" in his golf game; here he reports letting their client win by shooting a 68. That's great, but what if you don't follow golf? Sometimes the show assumes every viewer knows how to play, as it did in "Birdies, Bogies, and Baxter" (#114), the last time McMann & Tate won an account by golfing instead of delivering a good advertising strategy. The Stephenses also had to join a country club in "The Battle of Burning Oak" (#164); this time Darrin applies for membership without running it by Samantha first, and he's not even under that episode's snob spell.

Endora reminds Samantha that Serena is "quicksilver" and lives "in the sparkle of a star." That must be a witches' motto, because Endora first uttered it in "Be It Ever So Mortgaged" (#2), and Maurice used its phrases to hypnotize Darrin in "Daddy Comes for a Visit" (#180). It does seem unusual that Endora is able to connect her daughter and niece by witchcraft; maybe she caught them by surprise, which was the criteria Samantha needed to turn fellow supernatural Ashley into a dog in "Samantha's Pet Warlock" (#209). The even bigger surprise is, there's a never-before-seen door at the top of the stairs.

Larry – who is wearing the golf cardigan Darrin first sported in "Birdies, Bogies, and Baxter" (#114) – may be wondering where he's heard Samantha compulsively laughing before. Answer: "Weep No More, My Willow" (#152). But Larry should be more worried about Louise – he comes home from a game of golf to find her sleeping, and when he leaves Darrin's to wake her up, Samantha wants lunch. Why is Louise knocked out in the middle of the day? Is Jonathan having to fend for himself? Speaking of knocked out, the Stephenses' foyer ceiling seems to be missing during Larry's visit.

The hungry Samantha serves up some lobster salad, only to develop Serena's taste for ring-tailed pheasant. Darrin recalls that, the last time Samantha hankered for the delicacy, they learned Adam was on his way. Not quite: in "Samantha's Good News" (#168), the traveling Darrin was told by telephone that Samantha was expecting, and only because her parents guessed her condition first; ring-tailed pheasant had nothing to do with it.

The Stephenses might want to stay out of that supermarket. The last time they were there, in "Samantha's Lost Weekend" (#186), Samantha was also under the influence of witchcraft; at least this trip, she doesn't eat food from the baskets of her fellow shoppers. For all that, Samantha and Darrin come home with no groceries, leaving them with nothing to serve Mrs. Langley and Mrs. Hunter. So how is Samantha able to make canapés, and when does she prepare them? Aside from rustling up liquid refreshment in the kitchen with Darrin, Samantha is never out of her visitors' sights.

Darrin thinks Samantha's severe mood shifts stem from a spell of Endora's. But Endora doesn't typically cast spells on her daughter, the exception being "Turn on the Old Charm" (#199), in which Endora put a hostility spell on both the Stephenses. When Darrin asks if witches have psychiatrists, Samantha replies, "They don't." Isn't she a they?

Larry worries about losing Langley's account when "we don't even have it yet." Yes, they do: Darrin came home confirming that the agency had gotten the account after he let Langley win their golf game. Samantha must feel pretty strongly about Darrin moving on from McMann & Tate, because, after the Langley debacle, she tells him, "Maybe it's time for a change," as she did after Larry canned him in "You're So Agreeable" (#183). But Darrin never gets canned here: the only thing Larry says as he tailgates the ladies out the door is, "Darrin's just an employee – I'm the president of McMann & Tate!" For once, Larry doesn't actually fire Darrin, nor does he threaten to; are the Stephenses so used to Larry's terminations by now that they're just reading between the lines?

Out of nowhere, Darrin tells Larry that he's married to a witch – this after pooh-poohing doing exactly that to explain Waldo's duplicate Samantha in "Samantha's Bad Day in Salem" (#207). Larry laughs it off – but Darrin already made this confession in "That Was My Wife" (#31), and Larry's certainly seen enough strange things that this would make sense to him. Darrin's lucky the Witches' Council doesn't step in; they sure did when Samantha revealed herself to his parents in "Samantha's Secret Is Discovered" (#188).

OH, MY STARS!

Endora complains that Samantha is a live-in maid, a cook, and a babysitter. Of course she is: she's caring for her own kids – Endora's supposedly precious grandchildren. "She doesn't worry about diapers!" Endora says of Serena. Is Endora suggesting that Samantha ditch Tabitha and Adam in favor of partying and romancing? Endora's *Corsican Brothers* spell (inspired by the 1844 novella by Alexandre Dumas) is an interesting concept, but how is giving Samantha her cousin's emotions and physical experiences supposed to remind her of what she's given up? Dancing around the room and vicarious drunkenness don't seem like much of an enticement.

This episode's boy-are-we-glad-we-avoided-that-crooked-client finale [also used in "If They Never Met" (#127) and "The Generation Zap" (#194)] creates a lot of corporate confusion. Early on, Samantha asks Darrin why Langley is running Bigelow's company; Darrin replies there's a rumor that Langley bought up Bigelow's stock in a hostile takeover – Samantha alludes to this in her tipsy tattling to Mrs. Langley. By episode's end, Larry's relieved they're no longer associated with Langley, because he just heard about the swindle on the radio and claims it will be "front page stuff." But how could any client's shady business dealings within his own company hurt the agency one way or another? And Darrin knows about the rumor from the beginning, so presumably, Larry does, too – yet he continues buttering up the Langleys as if he doesn't. Maybe something was cut from the script, because the show doesn't usually go from Point A to Point C without going through Point B.

SON OF A GUN!

"That is not true. We have one member from Brooklyn." – Mrs. Langley, denying Samantha's claim that the country club is against foreign-born members.

SAMANTHA'S MAGIC POTION
Airdate: December 17, 1970

When Darrin strikes out with clients, he begins to wonder if witchcraft isn't involved. Endora swears innocence, but Darrin still meets resistance trying to pitch a campaign to the president of Harmon Savings and Loan, who hates it before Darrin has a chance to explain it. Larry feels Darrin is projecting a lack of confidence and sends him home to rest; after Endora maintains she has nothing to do with Darrin's problem, Samantha has Dr. Bombay check Darrin over with a hexometer, which detects the presence of witchcraft. When the scan doesn't achieve concrete results, Darrin throws in the towel and decides it's time to live by magic.

Samantha twitches up a potion and tells Darrin he should continue working, as her powers can bring him unparalleled success. Darrin drinks the potion, which initially turns him purple, then charges into the office, insisting to Larry that he present the same campaign to Harmon. The bank president is again dismissive, but Darrin takes control of the situation and demands to be heard; once Harmon sees where Darrin is going with his concept, he loves it. Darrin comes home victorious, though unsure about continuing to get ahead magically; Samantha admits she faked her potion to bolster his confidence, and Darrin realizes that he used witchcraft as an excuse for his completely mortal slump.

GOOD!

It's an interesting twist that Larry, who usually only likes Darrin's ideas if a client does, admits he still approves of Darrin's "insect" concept after Harmon shoots it down. Larry's observation that Darrin is projecting a lack of confidence is also remarkably astute for a man who would just as soon fire his supposed best friend – here, Larry simply suggests that Darrin take time off to rest, though he can't resist threatening to fire him twice: once in good humor, and once in bad. For Larry, that's progress.

Unknowingly spurred by Samantha's confidence booster, Darrin assumes command with Harmon, and it's very satisfying; he should be like this more often. Perhaps if he were, Samantha's prediction of "Stephens & Tate," an interesting glimpse into one possible future, would be likelier to come true.

Endora has been at the root of Darrin's problems for about five years (she rarely cast spells on him in the black-and-white seasons), so it's refreshing that she is absolutely innocent here. Dr. Bombay's brief appearance livens things up, especially when he becomes a kind of Liberace (older viewers will well remember the accomplished pianist with a flair for sequins). Also, Bombay changing back into his football uniform and popping the hexometer out are very fluid zaps. There's even a nifty bit of quasi-continuity with the hexometer: looking at the results of Darrin's scan, Dr. Bombay reports that witchcraft exhaust is clean while mortal exhaust is dirty; this is on par with Aunt Hagatha's declaration in "Witches and Warlocks Are My Favorite Things" (#77), where she said mortals emit a low-grade frequency.

WELL?

Darrin comes down the new stairs in the kitchen, which is part of the Stephenses' implied remodeling that was introduced in "To Go or Not to Go, That Is the Question" (#201); later, Samantha climbs them. Where do they lead? There's no connection to the second level that's visible to the audience; this suggests that there's more upstairs than previously shown. Once Endora arrives, she honors Samantha's request to knock by rapping at the air with the appropriate sound effect – Endora performed this same trick in "Mirror, Mirror on the Wall" (#146) and "Samantha and the Beanstalk" (#171).

After bombing out with Harmon three times, Darrin worries about his fourth attempt. Even a boss that doesn't engage in hair-trigger firings like Larry would be loath to let Darrin continue with this client; aren't there other executives at McMann & Tate who could take a whack at Harmon? Maybe it's just accounts for banking institutions that Darrin has problems with – in "The No-Harm Charm" (#138), Darrin thought witchcraft removed seven zeros from his copy describing the assets of Omega National Bank. When Larry half-jokingly asks if Darrin's slump is attributable to black magic, Darrin responds, "Would you believe me if I said yes?" That's innocuous enough until you remember Darrin just told Larry that Samantha is a witch in "The Corsican Cousins" (#211). Wouldn't Darrin's statement confirm this?

Endora ethereally comments "I've not only lost a daughter, I've gained a bullhorn." She also made this aside to Samantha in "It's So Nice to Have A Spouse Around the House" (#145). Samantha references Dr. Bombay's hexometer in her hailing spell and tells Darrin that using it won't hurt. If she knows so much about this witchcraft-detecting machine, why has it taken Samantha seven years to suggest utilizing it? Perhaps Bombay only just invented it, but still, Samantha, who isn't a doctor, shouldn't know so much about it.

Samantha is shocked to find that Darrin is still in bed, saying he'll be late for the office; Darrin replies he's not going. Either Darrin has forgotten that Larry just gave him a few days off to rest, or he's keeping this news from his wife. Samantha lingers while making up *pinchley, finchley, potsy, rex* off the top of her head; perhaps she is recalling that Aunt Clara used *pinchley finchley* as part of her spell to fuse the two Jonathan Tates in "Accidental Twins" (#78). Samantha must also draw inspiration from the memory-restoring ritual of "Samantha's Old Salem Trip" (#208), where she had to bow three times while incanting; here, Darrin has to turn three times after incanting. Finally, Samantha completes her deception by turning Darrin purple, a trick she picked up from Uncle Arthur, who similarly tinted Darrin in "A Bunny for Tabitha" (#178).

Harmon is probably one of those blustery people who respects it when someone stands up to him. Darrin taming him is wonderful, but Harmon's switch is a bit too easy, considering how violently opposed he was to Darrin's concept moments before. Later, Samantha tells Darrin, "Just because the client is difficult to convince doesn't mean the idea will fail – you said that yourself." Darrin recalls uttering these words, but it must have been off-camera, because he has never used that maxim toward advertising in an episode, which is too bad; had he done so, it would have given Samantha's reminder a lot more impact.

OH, MY STARS!

This installment, while fine as a self-contained episode, is a mishmash of no less than five previous episodes, borrowing dialogue from them all. Darrin's contention that he can't stand people feeling sorry for him, and Samantha's response, "Especially when you're doing such a good job of it yourself," comes from "Witch or Wife" (#8). Darrin anticipates being able to do things with Samantha's magic they couldn't otherwise for 20 years, as he did in "A is for Aardvark" (#17), but he had Samantha purge his memory of the events of that episode, which Darrin's current "back up time" request mirrors – and Samantha must recollect Darrin telling her back then that not knowing where your next meal is coming from helps you work up an appetite, because she repeats it back to him now. Samantha also paraphrases the let's-tell-the-world-I'm-a-witch dream she gave Darrin in "I Confess" (#135), where Dream Larry said he could control the world with "my brains and your voodoo"; here, Samantha predicts success using "your know-how and my witchcraft." Much of the current episode originates in "The No-Harm Charm" (#138), including Darrin's entire "I give up" speech, in which he declares he's "tired of bucking all this witchcraft," and Samantha tries to improve on that episode's confidence-building scheme, replacing Uncle Arthur's placebo magic charm with color-changing orange juice – this hearkens back to "Samantha's Secret Spell" (#179), in which Samantha tried to prevent Darrin from being turned into a mouse by tricking him into drinking a potion. All of these elements are wonderful in and of themselves, but mixing them together to form this premise cooks up a stew that can't help but feel like leftovers when the series is taken as a whole.

SON OF A GUN!

"Bugs? Again? What's he got, a fetish?" – Harmon to Larry, rejecting Darrin's campaign for the smaller investor a second time.

SISTERS AT HEART
Airdate: December 24, 1970

Lisa, the daughter of Darrin's coworker, Keith Wilson, is spending the night; Tabitha and Lisa are fixated on the idea of being sisters, especially after another girl says they can't be because they're different colors. Meanwhile, Darrin's client, Brockway, investigates Darrin's home life and is stunned when Lisa answers the door claiming to be Tabitha's sister. After Brockway pulls his account because Darrin isn't "stable," Lisa spills paint on herself, so Tabitha cleans her up with witchcraft. Desperately wanting to be Lisa's sister, Tabitha accidentally gives her friend white polka dots, also covering herself in brown ones. Samantha tries removing them, but Tabitha unconsciously blocks the attempt.

To show Brockway how stable Darrin is, Larry has the office Christmas party at the house; Brockway sees Keith's wife, Dorothy, and tells her how much he admires her courage in being with Darrin. After Samantha explains to Tabitha that her strong friendship with Lisa makes them sisters regardless of color, Tabitha is able to remove their polka dots. Brockway wants Darrin back on his account upon learning Samantha is his wife, not Dorothy, but Larry surprises himself by telling Brockway to find another agency. To teach Brockway a lesson, Samantha makes him see Larry, Darrin, and herself as African-American; Brockway returns the next day to apologize to the Wilsons and admit that he's guilty of racism. Samantha invites Brockway to Christmas dinner, saying he can start to change by accepting the white and dark meat of their "integrated" turkey.

GOOD!

Adam is getting to be as cherubic as Tabitha was at his age. Better yet, there's a definite affection forming between the Stephens siblings that is a joy to see. Samantha being "outnumbered" by Tabitha and Lisa is a fun contrast, with the kids enjoying their witchy predicament more than Samantha would prefer. Plus, there's just something about Lisa's wonder and amazement at being surrounded by magic for the first time. "This is better than Disneyland!" she exclaims.

Keith and Dorothy Wilson seem like they've been on the show the whole time. Their interaction is very natural, and Larry's warmth toward Keith gives the ordinarily grouchy ad man extra dimension. The writers (including William Asher, the show's producer/director who doesn't usually pen scripts) really know Larry: after Keith secures the Fenmore account, Tate wants to hear "every exquisite economic detail" – it's just like Larry to think the victory means a white Christmas. Keith's response? "Uh, watch that!" This episode seamlessly blends comedy with matters of equality, such as when Samantha posits that the Wilsons would accept her and Tabitha being witches because "they understand about minority groups."

Brockway, for all his sugar-coated intolerance, brings out some of the best moments of the episode. Young Lisa becomes the mature little lady while talking to him at the door, and Brockway gifting Adam with a panda because he "wasn't quite sure whose side of the family he takes after" is still funnier than it is offensive. Of course, Brockway's racist revelation in the tag, where he reaches out to the Wilsons, is as satisfying as it's intended to be, and then some. The perfect finishing touch: snow on the ground, which is rarely seen during these Connecticut winters.

WELL?

Phyllis should be pleased – after haranguing Samantha about Tabitha not having friends as far back as "Playmates" (#133), the girl has finally made one. Her connection to Lisa is tangible right away, but, had Lisa first appeared a few episodes back, their fast friendship wouldn't seem so fast. And no wonder Tabitha can recite Samantha's "don't fly" instruction; she's been getting that lecture since "I Don't Want to Be A Toad, I Want to Be A Butterfly" (#151).

Parley Baer is solid as Brockway, but it's a little soon to see him again, unless Brockway has a twin brother who's a desk sergeant in Salem [see "Paul Revere Rides Again" (#206)]. The Stephenses are lucky Brockway isn't as serious about digging into their home life as baby food employee Barkley was in "Follow That Witch" (#66-#67) – Barkley hired private detective Charlie Leach, who stumbled upon Samantha's magical identity.

Tabitha and Lisa change colors faster than your average screensaver, but the black-as-white girl facing Tabitha in the wide shot doesn't seem to be Lisa. One can't help but ponder what on-set happening made a double necessary, seeing that Venetta Rogers already has her white make-up on. Tabitha, trying to determine how to be Lisa's sister, goes from "I know a way!" to not knowing how she turned them polka-dotted. If Tabitha's intention wasn't to unify her and Lisa with spots, what did she have in mind? The polka dots seem more a product of Esmeralda's sneezing or Uncle Arthur's powers going flooey; there's nothing wrong with Tabitha's witchcraft, so how does she end up making the boo-boo?

The Stephenses are usually very upset when Tabitha uses her powers, but they uncharacteristically take it in stride here. Not only that, but neither Darrin nor Samantha seem particularly concerned that Tabitha tattled to Lisa about being a witch; they simply continue on as if Lisa has always known their biggest secret. Irving Bates found out in "Just A Kid Again" (#193), where Tabitha also couldn't reverse a spell because of a psychological desire not to, causing Samantha to seek Dr. Bombay's advice, as she does here. Samantha should know from that episode that no other witch can undo Tabitha's spell, which means no "cure" from Bombay would work, either.

Think of the dozens, maybe even hundreds, of lunches, snacks, and dinners Samantha has prepared for clients on behalf of McMann & Tate – *now* Larry hires a caterer. During the party, Samantha only signals for Darrin to wait after she makes Brockway see through black-colored glasses. Does she ever tell her husband what she did?

Watching the Stephenses and Wilsons gather around the Christmas tree with all the kiddies is genuinely heartwarming, but it points up the fact that, usually, only the residents of 1164 Morning Glory Circle are in attendance at Christmas. As discussed in "Santa Comes to Visit and Stays and Stays" (#184), Endora and Maurice ought to pop in for some festive fun with their grandchildren, and the same goes for Darrin's parents.

OH, MY STARS!

Darrin begins the episode very pleased to meet Lisa. However, Tabitha and Lisa obviously know each other quite well for Lisa to be spending the night – so how is Darrin only seeing Lisa for the first time? Lisa is Keith's daughter, and Keith works with Darrin; isn't it likely Darrin and Keith realized they had daughters in common and introduced them to each other? That's a meeting Darrin would have been present for.

Samantha explains that Tabitha and Lisa's spots are not created by witchcraft, but "wishcraft." That's a nice throwback to "It's Wishcraft" (#103), where Samantha first revealed that type of magic, but Tabitha's powers have grown far beyond that since. And, if there's a whole book devoted to counteracting wishcraft, why hasn't Samantha gotten her hands on it before? It would have come in very handy when Tabitha turned Michael Millhowser into a dog ["Playmates" (#133)] and Amy Catherine Taylor into a butterfly ["I Don't Want to Be A Toad, I Want to Be A Butterfly" (#151)]. Where are these kids, anyway?

SON OF A GUN!

"Witches don't ride brooms, and they don't wear pointy hats, and have warts on their nose." – Tabitha, breaking down yet another stereotype for Lisa.

This story may be by 1970's tenth grade English class at Los Angeles' Thomas Jefferson High School, but it has more heart, originality, and impact than many a regular episode of *Bewitched*. While its message of equality is clear, the installment has the solid feel of the show, creating a perfect blend that makes this one of the best – if not *the* best – episodes of the series. Samantha has made lots of speeches in seven years, but her "all men are brothers" lesson is her most memorable, and it's just as applicable now as it was in 1970.

"Excuse me," Larry says after Brockway expresses relief that Darrin is married to a white woman. "I just want to make sure it's me talking." It's not like Larry has never dismissed clients before [he did so in "The Very Informal Dress" (#44) and "Aunt Clara's Victoria Victory" (#100)], but he's never done it on principle until now. And Parley Baer's doubling to create the effect of Brockway looking at an African-American version of himself in this episode's forgivable convenient mirror is spectacular: Samantha's "black Christmas" is all due to Darrin, who actually encourages her to twitch her nose because he's full of "holiday cheer."

Tabitha has retired her childlike manual twitch in favor of zapping like mommy – and the effects of Tabitha and Lisa's skin colors going back and forth are extraordinary when you consider the amount of time and make-up involved, and the fact that Erin Murphy and Venetta Rogers had to assume the exact same positions to make the transformations work. Finally, it's very novel that Lisa now knows Samantha and Tabitha are witches. Though most characters who stumble upon this secret don't return, Lisa and her parents would make a welcome permanent addition to this series.

THE MOTHER-IN-LAW OF THE YEAR

EPISODE 214

Airdate: January 14, 1971

With Bobbins Candies experiencing sluggish sales, Endora suggests a campaign giving mothers-in-law chocolates on their own special day. Darrin dismisses the concept, but Endora zaps him into mentioning it to Bobbins, who loves it. Darrin works to dissuade the client, insisting they can't institute an official

Mothers-in-Law Day; later, Bobbins proposes crowning a Mother-in-Law of the Year on his live television show instead. Endora zaps Bobbins with a love spell so he will select her for the honor, then leaves on Bobbins' arm. The next day, Darrin unsuccessfully tries to talk Larry and Bobbins out of having Endora appear on the show.

The morning of the broadcast, Endora has other plans and leaves Darrin in the lurch – so Samantha turns herself into her mother to do Bobbins' commercial. Just as Samantha-as-Endora is about to go live, Endora pulls Samantha backstage; furious at being imitated, Endora turns herself into Samantha. "Endora" returns and reads her cue cards as written, but "Samantha" pops in during the broadcast with sarcastic asides, forcing the real Samantha to improvise to get the spot back on track. Endora ups the ante by becoming herself in front of the audience; Samantha likewise normalizes and ends the commercial on a positive note. Bobbins is thrown, but when he ultimately likes the unique way his candies are presented, the Stephenses breathe a sigh of relief.

GOOD!

There's an almost unprecedented earnestness in the way Endora makes her Mothers-in-Law Day suggestion. She really means it, and she's not being sneaky or deceptive about it any way – unlike later, when she moves in on Bobbins to get herself cast as Mother-in-Law of the Year. "Mercy!" she exclaims, trying to pass herself off as the old-fashioned woman. She's rather a good match for Bobbins, who is quietly demanding on his own – it's not often a client runs roughshod over Larry. "I've seen the commercial; that's the only part that interests me," Bobbins declares after Darrin's "surprise element." Isn't that just what a sponsor would say?

After six-and-a-half seasons, Larry reveals that he doesn't live far from Darrin. His frequent visits have always hinted that he's nearby; there's just never been confirmation until now.

WELL?

The Stephenses can't seem to decide whether their schooner painting should stay in the foyer – it's back, replacing the latest convenient mirror of "Sisters At Heart" (#213). Now, Endora should already know there's no such thing as Mothers-in-Law Day; Samantha made this clear to her in "Snob in the Grass" (#126). And listen: *The Sweetheart Parade*'s closing theme is the same "Salem underscore" used repeatedly in "Darrin on a Pedestal" (#205) as the cast frolicked through Gloucester, Massachusetts. Ironically, that episode's client, Barrows, wanted everyone in the world to own his umbrellas, while here, Bobbins wants people to buy his candy whether they like it or not.

Endora rather squanders her witchcraft making Darrin the mouthpiece for her Mothers-in-Law Day idea: she casts a whole spell when she could just zap words into his mouth, as Samantha did to Larry in "Samantha and Darrin in Mexico City" (#170), for example. When Darrin comes home angry that Endora made him tell Bobbins about the idea, Samantha asks, "Why are you so upset?" and suggests that Endora is just trying to help him; she even deems Darrin irrational. That's a very different reaction for Samantha – is she easing off regarding her mother's interference in Darrin's life?

Endora hits Bobbins with a love spell without bothering to ascertain his marital status first; what if Bobbins has a wife waiting at home while he's out on the town with Endora? Apparently, Endora runs around telling everyone Darrin's name is "Durwood" – Bobbins wants to refer to Darrin thusly, just like Samantha's ex, Ashley, did in "Samantha's Pet Warlock" (#209). But Larry must have been listening when Darrin used hay fever as an excuse for Samantha's bizarre behavior in "The Corsican Cousins" (#211), because he cites the same reason for Darrin's resistance to Endora appearing in the commercial.

Contrary to everything currently known about thunder, it's revealed here that Endora's ski date, Peabody, is responsible for "inventing" the weather phenomenon. Does that even make sense? So far, no witch or warlock has been said to be more than 3,000 years old – maybe 4,000. Did nothing accompany lightning in all the storms before that? As for Samantha, this is the first time she's become Endora, but Endora's had a little practice playing Samantha, since she took her daughter's place at a dress fitting in "Which Witch is Which?" (#24).

Samantha and Endora appearing on Bobbins' live television commercial may seem odd to younger viewers, but live daytime programming was still the norm in 1971; in fact, soap operas didn't switch to tape until 1975. Samantha's change back into herself packs a punch, because the Bobbins Candy box moves slightly as she ceases being her mother. For Darrin's part, he explains the Samantha/Endora switch by claiming he got the technique out of an electronics manual. Shouldn't Larry be crying foul? Darrin used the same excuse for being in the office seconds after Larry talked to him at the house in "Daddy Comes for a Visit" (#180).

Once Bobbins is happy with his unusual commercial, Samantha hears Peabody's thunder, deduces Endora is with him, and utters a "Thanks, Mom!" to the ether. Thanks for what? For flaking out on the commercial, pitching a fit at Samantha's attempt to save it, and trying to sabotage her in front of millions of viewers?

OH, MY STARS!

Endora's motivations are very confusing in this episode. She invents Mothers-in-Law Day, zaps it into Darrin's head, and zaps Bobbins into casting her as Mother-in-Law of the Year – only to ditch it all to go skiing with Peabody. Samantha reports that Endora promised to do the commercial, but when Endora pops in, she asks, "What television show?" as if this is the first time she's hearing about it. What's the point of her machinations if she doesn't end up on the show? And, if she's so interested in Bobbins, why does she throw him over for Peabody? Endora doesn't even bother taking the love spell off Bobbins. Of course, it's all meant to bring Endora and Samantha to a place where they play each other on live television, but Endora always has a method to her magical madness, which makes her behavior here unusually inconsistent.

SON OF A GUN!

"You're also a couple of other things which I won't mention!" – Samantha-as-Endora, adding to Endora's self-proclaimed status of "inimitable."

"How about a little kissy-poo?" Those words to Darrin, coming out of Endora's mouth but in Samantha's voice, is just one of the many hysterical moments that comes from Samantha and Endora's mother/daughter switcheroo. It also features two Endoras arguing with each other – as well as "Samantha" telling the director, "I wanted to be with my mommy" via Elizabeth Montgomery's pitch-perfect channeling of Agnes Moorehead. And Samantha and Endora doing battle on live television while playing each other is inspired: "If you honor your mother-in-law this one day," Samantha-as-Endora starts to say, "you can forget about her for the rest of the year," Endora-as-Samantha finishes.

MARY, THE GOOD FAIRY

Airdate: January 21, 1971

Tabitha, who is losing a tooth, argues with Gladys' nephew, Sidney, over whether the Tooth Fairy exists. That night, the real fairy retrieves Tabitha's tooth from under her pillow and runs into Darrin. Samantha is delighted to see the fairy, whom she as introduces Mary; chilled from visiting children in the middle of the night, Mary has searched out a witch's house for a quick rest. Darrin offers Mary some brandy to warm her up, but the fairy quickly gets drunk and refuses to go back out; feeling responsible for Mary's condition, Samantha agrees to switch places with her and finish that night's tooth-gathering duties, even though becoming the fairy cancels out her powers.

The next morning, Mary tells Samantha she's going to have to be the good fairy from now on – as the Stephenses bicker over what to do, Gladys brings Sidney by, curious from having seen Samantha flying the night before. With Darrin distracted by the Kravitzes, Mary sneaks out; afraid Mary will reveal who and what she and Samantha are, Darrin searches the neighborhood for the missing pixie while Tabitha shows the sardonic Sidney that there really is a Tooth Fairy – her mother.

GOOD!

Young Sidney's inclusion in this episode is a terrific piece of continuity: he was the off-screen friend Tabitha turned into a mushroom because he didn't believe in St. Nick in "Santa Comes to Visit and Stays and Stays" (#184). This time, Tabitha wants to ditch him as a playmate because he won't acknowledge the Tooth Fairy, which gives the boy consistency. Sidney also gets a backstory: it's revealed he's a Kravitz, and through and through at that. "Your father gets excited a lot, doesn't he?" Sidney deadpans, apparently around enough to make some accurate observations. And, when Tabitha exposes Samantha as the Good Fairy, Sidney snarks, "Boy, your whole family's freaked out." He must get his stoic sense of comedy from Uncle Abner, who tells Darrin, "If Sidney bugs you, don't hesitate to get rid of him. I don't care how you get rid of him, just don't send him back to us!"

WELL?

This episode looks to have been filmed before "Sisters At Heart" (#213), because Tabitha has more teeth here than she did before. And Gladys has a lot of nephews: Sidney is the sixth since the series started. It's a wonder the show doesn't just pick one and let him come back occasionally. It also goes against lore that everyone refers to Mary as the Good Fairy. Mary has arrived to collect Tabitha's tooth; she is very obviously the Tooth Fairy, but the show never uses the term. Why the generalization?

Tabitha's room has moved yet again. In "Tabitha's Very Own Samantha" (#189), it was on the left at the top of the stairs, but here, it resumes its place adjoining her parents' bedroom on the right [see "Tabitha's Weekend" (#163)]. Mary tells Samantha – who is remarkably awake considering she was nearly comatose a moment before – that she picked a witch's house so she could rest up. But most witches don't live in houses: for example, Carlotta and her son Juke lived among the clouds in "Darrin, Gone and Forgotten" (#144), and Endora always tells Samantha she should be living "in the sparkle of a star" like the rest of her brethren. Mary tiptoes out of Tabitha's room, and is only seen because Darrin decides to go to the kitchen. What was Mary going to do, crash at a witch's house without permission?

Samantha is a fast worker: it only takes her 35 seconds to make a roast beef sandwich for Mary, and she also finds time to fix her hair while saying goodnight to Adam, because she comes back downstairs with much neater tresses.

Whether it's Mary or Samantha doing the fairy flying, wires very visibly do the job instead of wings. What makes Samantha pick the front step as the place to test them out? She'd still be conspicuous from the backyard, but not as much as she is facing Morning Glory Circle. And ultimately, Samantha descends through the roof, so why not ascend the same way? Naturally, Gladys sees her, and Gladys should remember that she's witnessed Samantha flying before – on a broom, in "A Vision of Sugar Plums" (#15).

Tabitha is only surprised to see that her mother is now the Good Fairy. Wouldn't this revelation be more upsetting to a child? Then, in the foyer, Samantha and Darrin lock horns about Mary dumping the Good Fairy job on her. The living room is definitely within earshot; why argue in front of Mary like that? Samantha insists to Darrin there's nothing she can do – why not call Endora? Mary's a mere fairy, and not even that without her wand and wings – Endora could easily intimidate Mary with witchcraft; even Tabitha could turn Mary into something on Mommy's behalf. Instead, Samantha hides while Darrin introduces Mary to the Kravitzes as Samantha's aunt. Not the most original explanation: the Stephenses just passed off the High Priestess Hepzibah as an aunt in "Salem, Here We Come" (#202), and Mother Goose before that in "Samantha's Double Mother Trouble" (#182). And those are just two examples.

There's something thrilling about Darrin admitting he's finally gotten used to being married to a witch; it rather brings the show full circle. But why does Darrin make this statement at full volume when Sidney is on the nearby patio with Tabitha? The kids play on the Stephenses' latest phantom playground equipment, the last of which Tabitha had in "Just A Kid Again" (#193). For her part, Tabitha goes against her mother's direct orders, not only telling Sidney that Samantha is the Good Fairy, but showing him. What's to stop Sidney from running to Aunt Gladys and corroborating her story about seeing Samantha airborne? Samantha lies that she's thinking of dressing as the fairy for Halloween. No wonder Sidney sees through it: this episode aired in January.

OH, MY STARS!

Samantha could save herself a lot of trouble by just remembering she's a witch. All she has to do is zap herself into fairy garb, give herself a wand, and do her own flying to complete Mary's route for the night. Instead, she trades places with Mary when she doesn't have to. Of course, if Mary and Samantha don't switch, there's no episode, but consider this: Samantha knows that if she assumes the form of the Good Fairy, she will no longer be a witch. It's hard to believe she's willing to sacrifice her powers for a drunken fairy. Why not just pop the coins under the remaining children's pillows and retain her identity? Another question is, where do Samantha's powers go when she and Mary trade places? Mary doesn't absorb them – are they in the wand? At the end, Sidney sasses Samantha, saying she's too old to go out for Halloween, and the scene freezes as it appears Samantha is about to hit the boy with her wand – in front of Tabitha. If that's supposed to be a funny finale...it isn't.

SON OF A GUN!

"Gee whiz. Everything good that happens here is a secret." – Tabitha, irritated that she can't tell Sidney about her mother being the Good Fairy.

Consummate comedienne Imogene Coca, who made a name for herself on NBC's *Your Show of Shows* from 1950 to 1954, takes the role of the Good Fairy, which might have been too oddball a character for other actresses, and gives her a subversive side by turning her into an old-school, almost vaudevillian drunk. "Oh, my goodness gracious!" Mary exclaims as she's supposed to signal Darrin to stop pouring brandy. "I forgot to say when." Coca also makes Mary's drunken "White Swan" rendition intoxicating.

THE GOOD FAIRY STRIKES AGAIN
Airdate: January 28, 1971

EPISODE
216

Following the events of "Mary, the Good Fairy" (#215), the Stephenses panic over the missing sprite, who is drinking at the Kravitzes'. Gladys is shocked when her visitor reports giving Samantha her Good Fairy job – as Gladys runs to Abner with the news, the marinated Mary staggers out and gets picked up by the cops. Darrin goes to the police station to retrieve the errant fairy; meanwhile, his client, Ferber, arrives a day early to hear the agency's ideas on selling his weight-loss suit, the Reducealator. Since Darrin is supposedly working at home, Larry brings Ferber to the house to check on his progress.

Samantha hides in the den to avoid being seen in her fairy costume, but that's where Larry wants to discuss the campaign – Darrin stalls until Samantha invites everyone in, covering her wings by wearing Ferber's Reducealator. After Samantha breaks off the button that controls its heat, Larry and Ferber help her out of the suit and are stunned to see her wings; the Stephenses invent a slogan that uses the Good Fairy as a symbol for the Reducealator. Satisfied, Ferber and Larry leave, but the now-sober Mary is unhappy that Samantha's wings are drooping. After Samantha "accidentally" spills a Bloody Mary on her delicate dress and is willing to collect teeth anyway, an incensed Mary demands that Samantha make her the Good Fairy again, which is exactly what Samantha had planned.

GOOD!
Larry rarely holds firm with a client instead of brown-nosing – but here, when Ferber demands details on his Reducealator campaign, Larry reminds the man he's a day early and is perfectly willing to wait until tomorrow to connect with Darrin about his ideas. Could it be that, after sending bigot Brockway on his way in "Sisters At Heart" (#213) and being bulldozed by Bobbins in "The Mother-in-Law of the Year" (#214), Larry's relaxed his attitude about his accounts?

Part II of the Good Fairy's visit doesn't quite have the same energy as the first. In fact, it feels like a different episode most of the time – except when the show goes back to the core of what made Part I work: the conflict between Samantha and Mary. Samantha employing reverse psychology on Mary to get her to take her job back is clever, especially when she says she's "ashamed" she didn't get to the last two children on Mary's list and pours a tomato-based, hard-to-clean drink on herself. Samantha knows just how to yank Mary's chain, and Darrin smiling as he catches on is another great touch. When Mary and Samantha finally do restore themselves, the effect is superlative.

WELL?
Gladys hasn't tried to inflict her chicken soup on anyone since "Take Two Aspirins and Half A Pint of Porpoise Milk" (#42), but doing so here indicates that her vegetarianism of "Splitsville" (#140) was just a phase. That can happen, but why did the Kravitzes undo their living room makeover so quickly? Their

walls are green again, as they'd been since the series went to color in Season Three; the walls were light blue in "Samantha's Pet Warlock" (#209). Was this episode filmed prior to that one?

Larry is amazingly understanding when he tells Ferber that Darrin wants to devise his ideas at home, but strangely, Ferber calls it insubordination. Granted, Darrin probably should be at the office – he'd certainly be free of Mary's distractions there – but you'd think Ferber would be happy his campaign is at least being worked on. Of course, Darrin's not working on it, since he's at the Westport police station, which looks just like the Salem precinct where he was detained in "Samantha's Hot Bedwarmer" (#204). And Paul Smith, who plays the more aggressive of Mary's arresting officers, again compares himself to "Charlie Prince Charming," as he did while balking at the idea of 9-year-old Irving Bates being 32 in "Just A Kid Again" (#193).

When it appears Larry and Ferber have arrived, Samantha suggests not opening the door, but it's hard to fake not being home with a car parked in the driveway. Gladys, on the other hand, simply lets herself in when the Stephenses don't answer the doorbell. Once Larry and Ferber finally show, Samantha ducks into the den to hide, but where does Larry like to go to discuss accounts with clients? The den. Samantha would be better off stashing herself upstairs in her bedroom – or Tabitha's room, or even Adam's nursery, since the kids are nowhere to be seen in this installment.

Darrin states that Larry knows he doesn't like to show unfinished work. True: Darrin first made this point to Larry in "Samantha's Yoo-Hoo Maid" (#172). But, trying to get Darrin off the hook, Samantha throws the Reducealator on over her fairy costume – in ten seconds. Then she turns up the heat, literally, by inadvertently pulling the Reducealator control knob off its panel. She can't just stick it back on?

The Stephenses coming up with questionable slogans has become part of the comedy of this show. But Samantha really ought to let Darrin finish before interjecting with "Fly now, Reducealator." Even her "whittle while you work" is catchier. Amazingly, Ferber likes the slogan, and praises Darrin's "all-out effort." Darrin replies, "You'd be surprised how much of that Sam is responsible for." If he's blaming Samantha for all the slogan scrambling he's had to do, surely he knows this fairy fuss is Mary's fault, and other supernatural happenings are typically brought about by in-laws or illnesses, not Samantha.

How absorbent is that spun milkweed dress of Mary's? When Samantha purposely douses it with a Bloody Mary, the stain is dark and orange, but, in wider shots, it's much less pronounced. Finally, when Mary becomes the Good Fairy again, she asks Samantha to zap her to the nearest wheat field so she can use the spears to clean her sullied dress. Samantha obliges, but how would she know where to find a wheat field in Westport – is there a wheat-locator layered into her zap? Maybe Samantha is just declining to twitch Mary's dress clean as a touch of revenge for the uproar she caused.

OH, MY STARS!

How to successfully bridge a two-part episode: have Part II pick up where Part I left off, and layer in a few connective threads to remind viewers where they are in the story [as in "Salem, Here We Come" (#202)]. How not to: backtrack to before the end of Part I, throw out the original finale, and completely rewrite that part of the episode while using a handful of exact lines from the previous installment. Sidney, who saw Samantha in Mary's costume at the end of Part I, is neither present nor accounted for here. Mary talks to Samantha in the kitchen, except she's already supposed to be gone. Samantha discusses Mary's disappearance with Darrin in the den, despite discussing it in the foyer before, and it was Tabitha who told Darrin that Mary was gone, not Samantha, as happens here. Darrin went out to look for Mary in the previous episode, but does so now again as if his original search never happened. Then, Samantha calls Darrin back in, announcing a phone call from Larry, who had nothing to do with Part I. The show must have had a good reason for succeeding "Mary, the Good Fairy" (#215) in this way, but, if so, it's not evident as Mary continues her adventures with the Stephenses.

SON OF A GUN!

"In broad daylight? Some nearsighted duck hunter's apt to shoot me out of the sky!" – Samantha, when Darrin suggests she use her "dumb" wings to escape Larry and Ferber's visit.

THE RETURN OF DARRIN THE BOLD

Airdate: February 4, 1971

EPISODE **217**

Endora continues to feel Samantha should live according to their witchly heritage, so she visits the Old Man of the Mountain for a way to turn Darrin into a warlock. She is given an potion that is to be administered to Darrin's 14th century ancestor, Darrin the Bold [see "A Most Unusual Wood Nymph" (#79)], which will change his "cosmic chromosomes." Endora sends Serena back in time to get the job done; suddenly, both Darrins are able to pop in food and drink on demand. Summoned by Samantha for answers, Endora claims that Darrin has been absorbing witchcraft through osmosis, and is thereby exhibiting powers of his own after years of exposure.

Upset over being able to perform magic, Darrin unintentionally pops himself to a bar; while Samantha calls around looking for him, Serena appears, unusually dismayed when Samantha suggests Darrin might leave her. After Serena slips about having met Darrin the Bold, Samantha realizes that Endora's osmosis explanation is a cover for her latest scheme, so Samantha travels to the 14th century herself to "cure" Darrin's ancestor. Meanwhile, Darrin comes home and is accosted by Ferguson, a neighbor who is angry about a bush Darrin dematerialized; Ferguson rears back to punch Darrin when Samantha pops in and magically blocks his fist. Samantha explains to Darrin that his powers were a trick, but laughingly opts to wait until he's at the office to go into details about it.

GOOD!

Because the natural movement of smoke is unpredictable, edits involving it are usually detectable by the unfortunate jumps in special effects. That's not the case here: when Endora casts her spell to send Serena to the past, the smoke wafts by, and suddenly Endora is by herself. The real smoldering, however, happens due to the unexpected chemistry between Darrin the Bold and Serena. Their playful, racy banter gives them a certain rooting value as a couple, and Serena is actually left with a new appreciation of present-day Darrin. Elizabeth Montgomery (ahem; Pandora Spocks) and Dick Sargent look like they're having a blast playing the scene, which definitely translates to the screen.

WELL?

Endora and Serena get together to cause havoc for Darrin again, as they did in "The Generation Zap" (#194), an episode where the aunt/niece duo was also suspended by visible wires – and fashion plate Serena uncharacteristically wears the same outfit here that she did in that episode. Serena sniffs, "I never did dig what Sammy dug about that dodo." Funny alliteration, but Serena conversely stated in "Samantha's Power Failure" (#165) that her cousin and Darrin were a set.

Endora's idea to turn Darrin into a warlock is not her most original: Maurice just did that in "Daddy Comes for a Visit" (#180). Where was Endora when Darrin *wanted* to live by witchcraft in "Samantha's Magic Potion" (#212)? At "the top of the world," Endora tells Serena the air is too thin for levitation. It didn't seem to be when Maurice zapped Endora and her sisters to Mount Everest in "Witches and Warlocks Are My Favorite Things" (#77), or when Samantha met Dr. Bombay on the same peak in "Samantha the Bard" (#158) – to say nothing of Endora flying to the moon in "Samantha's Shopping Spree" (#169), where there is no air.

In "A Most Unusual Wood Nymph" (#79), Endora warned Samantha she wouldn't have powers in Darrin the Bold's time – yet Serena does. There's no way of knowing if Serena arrives before or after Samantha's original visit, but there are some marked differences in Darrin the Bold's world: in "A Most Unusual Wood Nymph" (#79), he had brown hair and a mustache; here, he sports red hair and a beard. The castle exterior is different, and the main room, while a close match, contrasts a bit with the room shown the first time. Plus, this Darrin the Bold has Gawain for a servant – before (or after), Muldoon held that position.

When Samantha determines that Darrin is under a wish spell, he wishes for her to call Endora, but instead of being compelled to do it right away, she makes a joke. As Endora spins her lie about Darrin absorbing witchcraft, she says, "Your father told me this might occur!" That's risky: all Samantha has to do is go to Maurice for confirmation. Then, Darrin grouses that he can't live by zapping things up – apparently not remembering that he relished doing exactly that in "Darrin the Warlock" (#181), and was ready to again as recently as "Samantha's Magic Potion" (#212). [Darrin also got a kick out of using witchcraft in "A is for Aardvark" (#17), but Samantha's memory-erasing spell is still in place.]

Distressed, Darrin wants to cool out in a bar to think. He always used to, right from "I, Darrin, Take This Witch, Samantha" (#1); it's amazing he hasn't since "Is It Magic or Imagination?" (#148).

Samantha burns up the phone line trying to find Darrin, when she could just cast a locator spell, like she did in "Samantha's Secret is Discovered" (#188) and "Darrin on a Pedestal" (#205). Now, Serena may not be the smartest witch in the world, but she's never been dumb – she shows up at Samantha's after her encounter with Darrin the Bold, though that's the last place she should be. When Samantha worries that Darrin will go away, Serena says, "Oh, Sammy, that's terrible!" Yes, it is – Darrin shouldn't even start to consider leaving Tabitha and Adam simply because he can't cope with zapping things up.

If Serena needs Endora to send her to the 14th century, then how does Samantha get there? And would a man living in the 1300s utter such a 20th century phrase as "blonds have more fun?" Aside from the fact that he'd be speaking Gaelic, not English, but that's another story.

The Stephenses have new neighbors in the Fergusons; the last person to occupy 1162 Morning Glory Circle was Elaine Hanson, in "Weep No More, My Willow" (#152). Richard X. Slattery's neighbor characters always get mad about gardening: Ferguson loses it over a bush, but in "How Green Was My Grass" (#131), Slattery's man McLane fumed about Darrin receiving his artificial lawn by mistake. Like McLane, Ferguson gets his punch magically blocked as well, though Slattery's trying to hit a different Darrin.

OH, MY STARS!

Endora's scheme actually has a lot of merit until she zaps Serena back to the 14th century to work on Darrin the Bold: when Darrin's ancestor was introduced in "A Most Unusual Wood Nymph" (#79), he was living in 1472 – the *15th* century. Altering Darrin the Bold's cosmic chromosomes is clever, but won't all other relatives on the Irish side of Darrin's family, including Brian O'Brian ["The Leprechaun" (#63)] and Darrin's mother, Phyllis, also suddenly inherit witchcraft? And what if, on the basis of discovering his magic powers, Darrin the Bold decides to bear children with a different woman than he would have had he remained mortal? Darrin won't be born, and Tabitha and Adam won't be, either. Endora probably doesn't think of that; it's just one of the many things that can result from messing with time.

Where does Samantha get her potion to return Darrin the Bold to normal? She merely shows up with it in the 14th century – does she visit the Old Man of the Mountain first? Not to mention, Samantha doesn't have to pluck Darrin the Bold's beard or make him inhale this potion's vapors like Serena had to; Samantha just dumps it on his head, and she doesn't even stick around to make sure the treatment works. That's either a great display of faith, or a decided lack of quality control on her part.

SON OF A GUN!

"So what? The impossible just takes a little longer." – Endora, when Serena says turning Darrin into a warlock isn't possible.

Dick Sargent amazes again, this time as the lecherous Darrin the Bold – it really seems Darrin and his ancestor are two different people. It's brilliant for the show to link back to an episode that aired five years earlier – Endora would know about Darrin the Bold, since she helped Samantha save him in In "A Most Unusual Wood Nymph" (#79). And, the idea that Darrin might actually become a warlock after years of being exposed to witchcraft, even if it's only Endora's lie, is most intriguing, largely because it would be such a sensible twist.

THE HOUSE THAT UNCLE ARTHUR BUILT

Airdate: February 11, 1971

EPISODE
218

Uncle Arthur arrives and plays a few pranks on Darrin before telling Samantha he's going to be married. But his fiancée, Aretha, is a snob who hates practical jokes – which Arthur can't resist pulling on Samantha in private. Aretha's uptight attitude quickly has Arthur zapping her into a clown suit to lighten her up, but Aretha condemns his sense of humor and leaves, breaking Arthur's heart. At the office, humorless furniture mogul Rockfield shuts down McMann & Tate's campaign ideas, but agrees to hear more at dinner. However, Arthur, thinking he can win Aretha back by getting rid of his practical jokes, casts a spell that plants them in Samantha's house.

After Samantha finds a dancing skeleton in the closet, and Darrin is doused by a bucket of water, the Stephenses hunker down for their dinner with Larry and the Rockfields: the evening becomes a disaster between glasses being glued to the table, a boxing glove that punches Larry, and a barrel of monkeys that unnerves Mr. Rockfield. Uncle Arthur pops in with Aretha on his arm, but his amusement at the monkeys drives her away for good. Shrugging it off, Arthur assimilates his practical jokes, leaving the Stephenses to work his pranks into a slogan for Rockfield. Later, popping in to say goodbye, Uncle Arthur literally boxes Darrin's ears.

GOOD!

Uncle Arthur is the flashpoint of several fluid effects in this episode. He puts giant boxing gloves on Darrin, then shrouds and unshrouds him in a suit of armor, while all the actors reclaim the exact same positions. Arthur also makes his squirting flower vase disappear in Samantha's one hand as she's wiping her brow with the other, with no obvious edit. And his monkeys pop out of the living room while Larry is talking – in mid-sentence. Arthur has always flown solo, so his falling in love is unique, and so is his distributing practical jokes through the Stephens house as if they're actual physical entities. The show still has a lot of original ideas seven years in – including Uncle Arthur's giant ear (even if it's not the most realistic), and the gift boxes that get zapped onto Darrin's ears after he threatens to box Arthur's.

Rockfield is the third client since "The Mother-in-Law of the Year" (#214) to run roughshod over Larry, whose brown-nosing backfires when Rockfield sees his furniture in Larry's office and declares, "I don't fall for that kind of bait, Tate." Is the show consciously doling out some karma to the ultimate yes-man?

WELL?

Miniature Arthur is awash in a halo of blue as he stands on the couch – but then, blue screening was still a relatively new technology in 1971. Arthur also seems taller in the wide shot than he does when Samantha first pulls away the pillow to reveal him. The "new" Arthur extends beyond his tux and cape: he has always referred to Darrin by his actual name [aside from one instance of "Dum-Dum" in "Samantha Loses Her Voice" (#150)]; here, Arthur calls his nephew-in-law "Digby" three times. Not new is Arthur's "in a war of wit, you're unarmed" joke – he already used it in "A Bunny for Tabitha" (#178), though that time, it was a "battle of wits."

Arthur claims to have reformed for Aretha, but if he's gone with the witch long enough to get engaged, surely he'd have cured himself of the jokes she hates before ever arriving at Samantha's. Instead, he pranks Darrin as soon as he sees him, and deems Aretha's hand "finger-lickin' good" (the Kentucky Fried Chicken slogan that lasted until 2011), a strange way for him to compliment her knowing she isn't receptive to humor. Samantha's right – Aretha is a phony: Aretha copies Ticheba's "Where is the main house" question from "Long Live the Queen" (#108), as well as the haughty way cabaret singer Lila talked about "undesirables" in India in "Samantha Twitches for UNICEF" (#166).

Samantha must give herself a zap walking out of the kitchen, because her hair is dry despite Uncle Arthur's vase dampening it moments before. It's understandable that Arthur would pull Samantha aside for a prank, but how does he lose control in front of Aretha so quickly? He swears he'll never let it happen, but he does – 50 seconds later.

Betty, McMann & Tate's trusty, face-changing secretary, hasn't been seen since "Darrin the Warlock" (#181) – but she's back, in a different size, shape, and age than her predecessor; unfortunately, this Betty is uncredited, so her portrayer remains a mystery. Darrin must be inspired by the success of "The Mother-in-Law of the Year" (#214), because here he suggests that Rockfield cast a Secretary of the Year in his furniture ads.

Uncle Arthur has made himself a clown before – twice, in "The No-Harm Charm" (#138) – but this clown sings. Some of his discarded jokes will be familiar to eagle-eyed viewers: Arthur *was* the dancing skeleton in "Samantha's Power Failure" (#165), and he finally makes good on the bucket of water he unsuccessfully tried to dump on Darrin in "Super Arthur" (#190). Isn't Darrin's anger just a little extreme – and misdirected? He somehow thinks Samantha is responsible for drenching him, which he knows she would never do. By the way, with Arthur's practical jokes strewn throughout the house, are Tabitha and Adam getting pranked, too?

"There's nothing I can do," Samantha insists to Darrin. That's getting to be her stock answer: she offered the same non-solution when Tabitha covered herself and her friend Lisa with spots in "Sisters At Heart" (#213), and when "Mary, the Good Fairy" (#215) forced Samantha into assuming her tooth-collecting job.

The Rockfields can't hear the groovy music coming from the kitchen when Samantha opens the door to the dancing skeleton (would she really do this with company over?), and Darrin doesn't recall that his shoes were glued to the carpet another time as well, by Endora in "Trick or Treat" (#43). Darrin citing furniture polish as the reason his guests' glasses are stuck to the table is reasonable, yet no one really questions how a boxing glove shows up out of nowhere to punch Larry – a glove that ought to be floating instead of popping in on a stand. At least Larry gets a wet washcloth here; all the other washcloths administered over the years have been dry.

The only thing that stands between Arthur and Aretha is his practical jokes – yet he brings her to the very house where he distributed them. Given how nonplussed he is when Aretha dumps him the second time, deep down he must be hoping that popping into Samantha's will push Aretha away. And Darrin's ears are always getting messed with: Endora made them grow in "My, What Big Ears You Have" (#121), while "The Safe and Sane Halloween" (#115) and "If the Shoe Pinches" (#197) found Darrin with donkey ears. Here, Uncle Arthur wraps the trick up by replacing Darrin's ears with gift boxes.

OH, MY STARS!

This "fun house" story proceeds nicely until Samantha utters a line that seems to throw things off. While all manner of chaos is happening around Larry and the Rockfields in the living room, Samantha reports to Darrin that Uncle Arthur has "made up with Aretha and given us back his practical jokes." Back? Arthur hasn't reclaimed his jokes at this point in the story. Samantha's statement comes out of nowhere; perhaps a scene was deleted, or a change was made in the script that didn't ripple into later scenes.

SON OF A GUN!

"You're right – she's a phony. Stacked, but a phony." – Uncle Arthur to Samantha, admitting his true regret over losing Aretha.

SAMANTHA AND THE TROLL

Airdate: February 18, 1971

EPISODE 219

Startled by Samantha, Tabitha breaks the cup of milk she's floating to the sink for Adam; Samantha tries to twitch the cup back together and discovers that her powers aren't working. Serena pops in and insists Samantha go for a check-up, which will require her to be out late. Overhearing Darrin telling Larry that Samantha won't be able to make a client dinner, Serena changes herself into her cousin to make a liar out of him. Later, with Darrin at the office, Serena brings several of Tabitha's toys to life so they can play hide-and-seek with her; engrossed in the game, no one notices that the humanized Fuzz is still hidden in the closet downstairs.

With Serena filling in for Samantha, Darrin asks his cousin-in-law to prepare a simple mortal dinner, and to be nice to his client, Berkley, who is having trouble selling his hair tonic to a generation of long-hairs. Under the guise of "sensitivity awareness," Serena-as-Samantha comes on to Berkley so much that Mrs. Berkley wants to leave. Darrin gets "Samantha" into the kitchen, but only after she demands a kiss from any man in the room; Samantha pops home early and takes over for the annoyed Serena, who pops out in a huff. Samantha successfully manages to do damage control with the Berkleys – but suddenly, Fuzz runs out of the closet, forcing Darrin to tie the shaggy doll into a slogan for Berkley's hair tonic, which saves the day.

GOOD!

For an only child who had so much trouble adjusting to a sibling, Tabitha has become quite the big sister to Adam. Portrayer Erin Murphy shows a palpable warmth toward the tyke as Tabitha gives him a witchy assist with his milk. Tabitha and Serena's game of hide-and-seek is fun, and their rag doll participant is Diane Murphy, Erin's twin sister, who also played Tabitha in Seasons Three and Four. Diane hasn't made an appearance since "Samantha Fights City Hall" (#149); this is an ingenious way to bring her back.

It's strangely intriguing to watch Darrin and Serena function as husband and wife, with him asking her to make dinner for the Berkleys. Of course, the scene's peak is Serena changing herself into Samantha to obtain a kiss from Darrin; it's always a thrill to hear Serena's voice coming out of Samantha.

WELL?

When Tabitha floats Adam's cup around the kitchen, it happens by visible strings, which is understandable – less so is Samantha feeling it necessary to magically clean up Tabitha's mess before Darrin sees it. What's the fuss? All Samantha has to do is say she dropped the cup. She can't repair it, but she does manage to put the broken glass in the sink without making any noise.

Ever since Dr. Bombay first made his presence known in "There's Gold in Them Thar Pills" (#107), it's been customary for witches to summon him at the first sign of illness. So Serena doesn't need to send Samantha away for her "10,000-spell overhaul"; she just needs to be on hand to cause havoc all day. Serena pops Samantha out with a spell that starts *weebus worbus tootle flick*; these are the same words Aunt Clara used to zap up a feast in "Allergic to Ancient Macedonian Dodo Birds" (#118) – ironically, in that episode, Samantha told the powerless Endora she had a "pooped popper," while here, Serena learns that Samantha has a "pooped twitch."

Season Seven offers up its third convenient mirror [after "Samantha's Old Man" (#210) and "Sisters At Heart" (#213)] to allow Serena to tell one joke – and Samantha should know she's going to be imitated, since she was the last time she wore that blue blouse in "The Generation Zap" (#194).

Larry wants to have the Berkley dinner at Darrin's, since Louise is visiting her mother. Hopefully Jonathan is with her, or the child will be home unattended. Later, at the office, Larry suggests a slogan for Berkley's Hair Tonic – novel, since normally Darrin has to come up with all the ideas.
Tabitha also played hide-and-seek with her mother's double in "Tabitha's Very Own Samantha" (#189), and she doesn't need Auntie Serena to turn her toys into people – she had that mastered by "Toys in Babeland" (#109), an episode where she made a real phone call on a toy telephone, as Serena does here. But how does Fuzz open and close the door to the closet he hides in, when he doesn't have hands?

At dinner, Larry wonders why "Samantha" is acting strangely, but, considering Samantha just exhibited bizarre behavior in "The Corsican Cousins" (#211), you'd think he'd be getting concerned. Serena-as-Samantha's claim that everyone should love each other hearkens back to the hippie creed she embraced in "Hippie, Hippie, Hooray" (#128), but why, when Berkley and his wife finally connect, does he suddenly share his wife's desire to go home? Mrs. B. only wanted to leave because "Samantha" was grooving on her husband; Berkley is there to hear McMann & Tate's new slogan. And Samantha has to be told about Serena flirting with Berkley – so how can she start talking about the sensitivity awareness she wasn't present for?

Do the Stephenses realize Fuzz is a live version of Tabitha's doll? Because they don't seem at all alarmed that there's a creature suddenly running around their house. Samantha renaming Fuzz "Harry" is reminiscent of "Going Ape" (#162), where Endora gave former chimpanzee Bonzo the same moniker. And Larry should be noticing that, every time he comes over, strange things happen that lead to slogans: he just got punched by a phantom boxing glove and watched monkeys hopping about in preceding episode "The House That Uncle Arthur Built" (#218).

OH, MY STARS!

Serena suggesting that "Super Boob" is "too cheap to hire a maid" might ordinarily be a funny statement, but someone has forgotten that the Stephenses already have a maid – Esmeralda. Surely Serena has heard about her – and where is Esmeralda these days, anyway? She hasn't been seen since "Samantha's Old Salem Trip" (#208).

It's a Hollywood fact of life that all productions have budgets – especially television shows, which often have to find creative ways of staying within those limits. Naturally, this show reuses a lot of props (especially that big plastic plant), and perhaps first-run viewers weren't likely to remember the exact events of Seasons Four and Five – but Fuzz's presence creates a fair share of problems. To begin with, Fuzz was the goblin that Tabitha zapped out of her storybook in "The Safe and Sane Halloween" (#115). Her current doll, the miniature version of Fuzz, should ring bells for Larry and Darrin – they were on the brink of making millions off the same doll, also called The Fuzz, in "One Touch of Midas" (#157); is the doll Serena humanizes the one Darrin gave Tabitha in that episode? Bringing back both sizes of Fuzz is a shrewd way of utilizing an old prop and costume, respectively, but, in terms of continuity, it's unfathomable that no one – not Tabitha, her parents, or Larry – remember seeing the very conspicuous Fuzz before.

SON OF A GUN!

"I think it's Martha." – Berkley, regarding his jealous wife when Darrin tries to tell Serena-as-Samantha that something's burning.

THIS LITTLE PIGGIE
Airdate: February 25, 1971

EPISODE 220

After Darrin has trouble deciding between ties, then campaigns, Endora zaps him into constantly changing his mind, leading Gladys to think he's being sarcastic. Gladys reports Darrin's confused state to Samantha; meanwhile, at the office, Darrin concurs with Larry's approval of his hip tie, then goes out to buy another one. Samantha pops over to McMann & Tate to investigate Darrin's indecisive behavior, but Larry pulls Darrin away to make a pitch for Colonel Brigham's Spare Ribs. When Darrin can't determine which of his concepts he likes better, Brigham decides against both, prompting Larry to send Darrin home to work on a new idea.

Unable to choose a route to the house, Darrin spends hours driving around; Samantha demands that Endora undo her spell, pointing out that Darrin sticks to his decisions. Endora takes this to mean that Darrin is pigheaded, and makes Darrin look the part before zapping him up to the roof. Before Samantha can retrieve him, Larry and Brigham drive up, confused to see Darrin standing on top of his house in a pig's head; Samantha says Darrin is modeling a revolving sign for Brigham's restaurants and improvises a satisfactory jingle to go with it. Samantha gets Endora to remove the head, but when Endora thinks she should be thanked for inspiring Brigham's campaign, Samantha says she'll get hers – later.

GOOD!

Endora turning things around on Samantha by implying that Darrin's decisiveness signifies pigheadedness is a very witty comeback – and Samantha does open that door. There's a neat sense of full circle for the series when Samantha assures Larry and Brigham, "You'd be surprised how many ideas have been born in this house." And, as for that "E-I-E-I-O" jingle of Samantha's, it's supposed to be cringeworthy, but it's also so bad, it's good.

WELL?

After Endora criticizes Darrin's indecisiveness, Samantha asks her mother to leave her fangs at home on her next visit. Where is home? In "Allergic to Ancient Macedonian Dodo Birds" (#118), Samantha told Darrin one couldn't "get there from here" without witchcraft; in "To Twitch or Not to Twitch" (#132), Samantha took Tabitha "home to Mother," which seemed like a cloud that Endora later referred to as "Cloud 8." It might be nice to see Endora's place after all these years.

It's different for Endora to stop Darrin's moving car before casting a spell, but his brake lights stay on as she incants, and they only go out when she unfreezes him. And Gladys has a fixation with trash – in "Samantha's Lost Weekend" (#186), she sent Abner out with a petition to change trash day; here she wants to have the neighborhood's garbage cans painted. At least her visit reveals that the usual painting is back in the foyer, replacing the convenient mirror of "Samantha and the Troll" (#219).

Larry tells Darrin, "Your trouble is, you worry too much!" That's ironic considering Larry has nearly worried himself into ulcers over the agency's accounts. He's also amazingly mellow in this episode: for one thing, he likes Darrin's oh-so-contemporary tie – quite a contrast, as he's hated everything cool and modern since "Hippie, Hippie, Hooray" (#128). Larry even thinks the idea of losing a client over a tie is ridiculous – this after he thought Darrin ruined an account over a martini in "A Chance on Love" (#196).

When Samantha hears that Darrin went out to buy a tie, she asks, "What was wrong with the one you were wearing?" That would indicate that Darrin's not wearing his original tie anymore, but he is. Larry hustles Darrin out of his office a moment later, so Samantha pops home - won't Betty wonder why Mrs. Stephens went in, but never came out?

Much is made over Colonel Brigham not being from the South, just because he deals in spareribs. But his geography ultimately has no impact on the plot one way or the other. Then, after Brigham gets frustrated by Darrin not standing behind either of his campaigns, Larry takes Darrin aside and says, "You'd better come up with something to replace the idea you just shot down." Except that Darrin actually shot down two ideas by virtue of flip-flopping on the first.

Samantha should know that demanding a spell be undone on the count of three, then extending that count to five, doesn't do any good – that was her condition when the lovesick Arthur filled every room with practical jokes in "The House That Uncle Arthur Built" (#218), and he certainly didn't show. When Endora does arrive, Samantha tells her not to deny putting a spell on Darrin. "Who's denying?" Endora admits. Yet, her earlier note contained a comical, but definite, denial. And either Endora's spells really are getting nastier, or the Stephenses are unclear about how to rate them: Samantha says zapping a pig's head onto Darrin is the lowest thing Endora has ever done – but, in "Samantha's Old Man" (#210), Darrin proclaimed Endora's aging spell her most atrocious. Samantha tries not to laugh when the pig's head appears on her husband; she also bit her lip when Tim the leprechaun gave Darrin donkey ears in "If the Shoe Pinches" (#197). After all this time, is Samantha starting to find Darrin's predicaments funny?

After Samantha makes Endora return Darrin's head to normal in the kitchen, Larry joins them to talk about how well things went with Brigham, whom they leave by himself in the living room. This was before he could whip out a smartphone to check messages; what is he supposed to be doing out there all alone?

OH, MY STARS!

This episode contains two very conspicuous recasts, at least when compared to other episodes. First, there was a much younger, uncredited Betty in "The House That Uncle Arthur Built" (#218) – here, a more mature version sits at Betty's desk, played by Ann Doran, making her Betty #9. Is this proliferation of Bettys an in-joke at this point? If not, it might be better to give McMann & Tate secretaries different names, or just have Larry admit that the agency doesn't hire secretaries unless they're named Betty, which would actually be funny. Also, Aunt Hagatha hasn't been around since "Tabitha's Very Own Samantha" (#189), so the show can get away with giving her another new face – but Ysabel MacCloskey just played the very mortal Mrs. Rockfield two episodes earlier in "The House That Uncle Arthur Built" (#218). It's difficult to believe that even that viewers seeing the show in real time wouldn't have noticed these changes.

SON OF A GUN!

"Darrin, will you get your – !" – Larry, stopping himself before finishing a colorful demand in front of Samantha (a progressive inclusion for a TV sitcom in 1971).

MIXED DOUBLES
Airdate: March 4, 1971

EPISODE 221

Worried after Louise lends her a book about boredom in marriage, Samantha tosses and turns – and wakes up in Larry's bedroom. When he thinks she's Louise, Samantha pops over to the house, where Louise and Darrin perceive Louise as Samantha. Endora answers Samantha's call for help and suggests that a metaphysical molecular disturbance is in place, affecting the mortals Samantha comes into contact with. As Louise, Samantha sends Larry and Jonathan into their day before Endora brings Dr. Bombay to the Tate house. He confirms Endora's diagnosis and gives Samantha a cure – however, upon investigation, Louise still sees herself as Samantha.

While waiting for Bombay to return, Samantha visits Darrin at the office and twitches her nose to convince him she's not Louise. Not wishing to end the evening in their swapped spouse state, Darrin and "Louise" concoct a surprise party for Larry at the house; when it gets late, Larry makes noise about going home to bed. Samantha does her best to stall – until finally, Dr. Bombay arrives with his new potion, which also fails to work. Samantha recalls having a dream about her concern for Louise the previous night, so Bombay adds dream inversion to his diagnosis and is able to administer a treatment that restores Samantha and Louise to their proper identities.

GOOD!

Even though Larry is Darrin's boss, it's nice to see him dealing with something else besides clients once in a while. It's a treat to see Louise in a new situation as well, standing in the Stephenses' bedroom and coming down the stairs as if she lived there, all the while expressing confusion because nothing is familiar. Samantha's magic wardrobe changes are always masterful (like the one she performs in the Tates' bedroom), but Larry's freeze in that scene is equally impressive.

Samantha's had spots and stripes. She's talked in rhyme. And she's had her powers conk out under the influence of more than one witchy illness. So what a neat twist that Samantha is only a carrier of metaphysical molecular disturbance (MMD), and that the ailment only affects mortals. There's a wonderful originality to this episode, and Samantha's final diagnosis of dream inversion is a smart touch, because it's particularly believable.

WELL?

Samantha has known Louise for seven years. So why does Samantha refer to her by last name as if Darrin doesn't know who his boss' wife is? When Samantha appears in the Tates' bedroom, the editors zoom in on the footage in post-production for dramatic effect, but it looks rather grainy compared to the next, crystal clear shot. The Tates – who still sleep in separate beds in 1971 – have another new bedroom; the previous versions of "That Was My Wife" (#31), "Double Tate" (#59), and "Art for Sam's Sake" (#98) hint that Louise likes to redecorate a lot.

Darrin and Louise could easily see Samantha popping out as they exit the bedroom; why doesn't Samantha just make herself invisible? Samantha and Endora discuss the whole matter in front of Tabitha's door; you'd think Tabitha would hear them and dart out to ask Mommy and Grandmama what's wrong. How does Endora know so much about MMD? As Dr. Bombay points out, she is a "laywitch" – does Endora read witch's medical journals in her spare time?

Is Samantha wearing her own clothes, or Louise's? Louise seems to be in Samantha's, even saying her robe is tight, but Samantha fits into Louise's wardrobe just fine. Like their bedroom, the Tates' kitchen, first seen in "Maid to Order" (#53), is radically different here; its homey look doesn't quite match the opulence of the rest of the house.

Jonathan Tate not only makes a sudden and welcome appearance, but he seems to sense that something isn't right with his "mother." MMD is said to affect all mortals: Jonathan should think Samantha is Louise without question. Does Bombay mean all grown-up mortals? No wonder Louise is reading *Marital Unrest* – when his "wife" gives him a non-committal peck on the cheek, Larry deadpans, "That's the kind of passion I'm accustomed to."

Why would Samantha think Larry is taking Jonathan to the office? Because Samantha has always kept Tabitha out school, except for "I Don't Want to Be A Toad, I Want to Be A Butterfly" (#151)? Once Dr. Bombay treats Samantha's MMD with his specially-coated harmonica, Samantha returns to the house to see if it worked. That seems a futile zap – if order were restored, Samantha and Louise would simply switch places, like they did at the start. The bigger mystery is why Bombay is suddenly making moves on

Endora. He's never shown the slightest interest in her since they first appeared together in "There's Gold in Them Thar Pills" (#107).

Darrin should clue in that "Louise" is his wife the second Samantha mentions MMD. Where would Louise come up with something like that? To prove herself, Samantha twitches up some ringing bells (and some unfortunately visible wires that hold them up). Does Darrin perceive this as Louise twitching her nose? Samantha then asks Darrin not to be furious, just annoyed. He shouldn't be either: Samantha just told him the MMD isn't her fault. Not wanting the Tates to find out about their predicament, Samantha invents a surprise party for Larry – but the odds of the Tates discovering that Samantha is Louise because of MMD are astronomical; it would be stranger to them that "Louise" is wearing Samantha's wedding ring.

Larry reminds "Louise" that she hates martinis, then whispers to Darrin that she gets mean after imbibing them. Yet Louise downed the same drink in "…And Something Makes Three" (#12) and remained perfectly docile. And it seems that no matter what form Jonathan's mother takes, the kid ends up alone – who's sitting with him while the Stephenses avoid unintentional wife-swapping?

Samantha's MMD/dream inversion must also affect the molecules in the living room, because Darrin, Louise, and Larry somehow don't hear Dr. Bombay and Endora talking to Samantha in the adjacent kitchen. And Bombay apparently likes old movies: his "every little breeze seems to whisper Louise" is from the Maurice Chevalier song *Louise*, performed in the 1929 film *Innocents of Paris*.

OH, MY STARS!

Endora tells Samantha she should give Larry a chance because he might make a better husband for her. That's funny, but is Endora forgetting that Tabitha, Adam, and Jonathan are involved? Also, at some point during the day, Louise must feed Tabitha and Adam – MMD only affects mortals, and Tabitha is half witch, so she should know right away that Louise isn't her mommy. (Similarly, this would be quite the acid test for Adam – whether he's inherited powers is unknown, but, if he can tell Louise isn't Samantha, that would be the answer.)

Does Betty also generate a metaphysical molecular disturbance that makes her look different every time? Natalie Core becomes the third Betty in just four episodes; this after Ann Doran just played her in previous installment "This Little Piggie" (#220). And perhaps it's just from looking at life through a 21st century lens, but it seems unnecessary for the Stephenses to avoid getting into bed with different partners. Of course the comedy comes from preventing it, but all Darrin and Samantha have to do is lie down next to Louise and Larry, respectively, put off any marital duties, and go to sleep. Maybe the implication was still too much for network standards in 1971.

SON OF A GUN!

"Sam, in our marriage, boredom will never be a problem." – Darrin to Samantha at bedtime, ironically not knowing he's going to wake up next to Louise.

Jonathan Tate lives! He's hasn't been on screen since "Accidental Twins" (#78), and in those five years, his parents have largely acted as if their son doesn't exist – that's what makes his brief appearance here a thing of beauty. "Jon" doesn't look much like Larry or Louise, but it's revealed here that he's in school, and that he gets driven there by Larry. As the Tates and Stephenses should have had their kids growing up together all along, this could be the beginning of resolving the biggest inconsistency of the entire series.

DARRIN GOES APE
Airdate: March 11, 1971

Serena brings Darrin a magical portable television as a peace offering, but becomes furious when Darrin won't accept the gift. With Samantha and the kids out shopping, Serena returns in Samantha's form to get Darrin to change his mind; when he insults Serena instead, she turns him into a gorilla. Gladys spots the primate in the Stephenses' living room and tries to show Abner just as Serena makes Darrin human again; Darrin won't apologize, so Serena returns him to simian status. Gladys calls the disbelieving cops, who, in turn, call Johnson's Jungle Isle; the Johnson brothers' female gorilla, Tillie, needs a mate, so they collect Darrin for their sanctuary.

When Darrin turns up missing, and Gladys excitedly tells her about the gorilla, Samantha realizes that Serena has been monkeying around. Samantha pops over to Johnson's Jungle Isle and brings Darrin-as-gorilla home – but Gladys hears him, and soon the Johnson brothers and the cops are searching the house for the animal. Samantha twitches Darrin from room to room to throw everyone off, then pops him on the roof, where Gladys sees him. As Gladys, the cops, and the Johnson brothers close in, Samantha threatens Serena into normalizing Darrin, who lies that the gorilla ran down the street. Serena confuses the officers by zapping Darrin off the roof, and later, Samantha jokes with Darrin about his supposed connection to Tillie.

GOOD!

It's not every day Serena owns up to being "a little stubborn," but she does – albeit behind the mask of Samantha – and that's just one of several small but mighty details that permeate this episode. Darrin, who has raised Cane over much smaller matters than being turned into a gorilla, simply tells Samantha, "It's all part of the adjustment a man has to make when he marries a witch." Ysabel MacCloskey's presence as Aunt Hagatha was strange in "This Little Piggie" (#220) because she had just played Mrs. Rockfield two episodes before that, but Hagatha's return in MacCloskey's form is most welcome here. And, assuming the writers knew about this, "Johnson brothers" is 1920s slang for criminals, which the Jungle Isle proprietors may well be, given their reaction to the police.

WELL?

Icarus is a busy planet. Actually, it's an asteroid, and Serena indicates that the celestial body has passed between Venus and Jupiter; in "To Go or Not to Go, That is the Question" (#201), it was about to pass between Jupiter and Pluto. In either case, Icarus only crosses the orbits of Mercury, Venus, Earth, and Mars. And Earth's weather may be controlled by witches after all, because Darrin watches a forecast by "*the* weatherman" on his new TV, while "The Mother-in-Law of the Year" (#214) reported that a certain Mr. Peabody invented thunder.

The opening of this episode borrows heavily from "Samantha's Wedding Present" (#141): Serena suggests that if Samantha has to be "saddled with a mortal," Darrin is "as good as any" (Endora said the same thing in that Season Five opener); Darrin infers that a witch's gift is made of "bats' wings and eels' eyes" (he had the order reversed the first time), and Serena-as-Samantha tells Darrin that "people give gifts the way they know how" (which Samantha taught Darrin after his rejecting Endora's goodwill got him miniaturized). The Stephenses should be wondering where they've heard all this before.

Once Darrin becomes a gorilla, his flailing breaks a vase in the living room – the same one Hepzibah magically shattered in "Salem, Here We Come" (#202). Interesting, when you consider there's usually no vase on display in that spot. And Abner should be more open to the idea of there being a gorilla across the street – he played chess with a mule there in "Daddy Does His Thing" (#167).

Serena can't seem to levitate without wires these days; maybe they're just harder to camouflage against lighter backgrounds. As for Gladys, she's spelled her last name for potential witnesses before, only here it's for cops; in "Baby's First Paragraph" (#62), it was for reporters. Incidentally, Paul Smith frequently plays cops on the show; if he's the same officer every time, isn't he wondering why he always gets called to tiny Morning Glory Circle? He responded to complaints of a flying man in "Super Arthur" (#190) and picked up a drunken Tooth Fairy ["The Good Fairy Strikes Again" (#216)] before arriving on the scene this time to deal with a gorilla.

Either wildlife sanctuary proprietor Alex Johnson moonlights as a janitor, or he's got a twin, since Allen Jenkins plays Johnson and the gent who cleaned the McMann & Tate building in "This Little Piggie" (#220). And usually, when there are incongruous beasties in the Stephens house, Gladys calls animal shelters herself [see "Alias Darrin Stephens" (#37) and "Daddy Does His Thing" (#167)]; here she needs the cops to do it.

Maybe these officers are rookies: they secure the entire Stephens house in 13 seconds, then tell Gladys there's no sign of a struggle, despite the broken vase in the living room that indicates otherwise. Darrin had no time to sweep up the glass, and Serena certainly didn't reconstruct the vase, so Samantha and Tabitha should see it as soon as they get home from shopping, but don't.

The Witches' Council, introduced in "It's So Nice to Have A Spouse Around the House" (#145), now boasts a "Royal" in its title – but they can't be royal, because they weren't a ruling body when Samantha was on the throne ["Long Live the Queen" (#108)].

The Maharajah of Janipur (whether the show is referring to the Janipur in India or Bangladesh isn't clear) seems to be the guy everyone hangs out with: Samantha interrupts Aunt Hagatha's visit with him, but Endora kept him busy in "This Little Piggie" (#220). Too bad the Stephenses don't remember that Darrin could write when he was a chimpanzee ["Alias Darrin Stephens" (#37)] – not only could he have communicated again, but, he could have kept working on his Cushman Cosmetics layouts. Paul Smith's officer enters the Stephenses' kitchen and finds the Johnson brothers there – the "jungle people" are essentially breaking and entering, yet all the cop does is ask if they've seen the gorilla.

In "This Little Piggie" (#220), Endora zapped the literally pigheaded Darrin onto the roof to humiliate him. Is that where Samantha gets the idea to pop Darrin-as-gorilla up there herself? It's not any less conspicuous a choice than Endora's. Do Tabitha and Adam ever find out their father has de-evolved? Hard to say, but viewers find out Serena is from Babylon, not "the cabbage patch," as she hinted to Mrs. Parsons in "Mrs. Stephens, Where Are You?" (#160) – an episode that also saw Serena accosting mortals in the front yard, as she does with the cops here.

OH, MY STARS!

No one would expect the show to use a real gorilla, like they were able to use a real chimpanzee during Darrin's turn for the primate in "Alias Darrin Stephens" (#37), but, because the "big ape" is so obviously an actor in a gorilla suit, it lessens the impact of Darrin having been transformed – and it adds an element of camp the show probably wasn't going for.

The Stephenses' neighborhood gets monkeyed around with in this episode, too. Morning Glory Circle has never looked so different – there's no Kravitz house across the street (where is Gladys running to every time?), the road follows a different path, and there are apartment and industrial buildings to the right instead of the usual filling station, making the area look less residential than it really is. Inside the Stephens house, there's yet another convenient mirror in the foyer so Darrin-as-gorilla can look at himself – why not just put a mirror in that spot and keep it there? But the oddest feature is the sudden wall that now exists in the kitchen, just past its door. Looking in from the outside, a clock and a spice rack hang there – but from the inside, no wall occupies that space. Even when there's a close-up of what the cops and Johnson brothers see through the door, it's a direct line into the kitchen. So why is the wall there?

SON OF A GUN!

"Gladys, if you had any compassion for your fellow neighbor, you'd move!" – Abner, when Gladys feels he doesn't care if the Stephenses have been eaten by a gorilla.

MONEY HAPPY RETURNS
EPISODE 223
Airdate: March 18, 1971

After Endora criticizes Darrin for being unable to buy his children a pool, he finds an envelope stuffed with cash in the back of a taxi. Darrin assumes Endora zapped it up, but she swears her innocence with a Witch's Honor. Meanwhile, a mysterious man recalls the taxi in search of the envelope; the driver remembers giving it to Darrin, so the man follows him home from the office. Darrin shows Samantha $100,000, refusing to believe Endora isn't responsible and scoffing when Samantha suggests the money might belong to a gambler or criminal. When Darrin implies that Samantha zapped up the cash herself, she becomes furious and pops out, dematerializing the envelope.

The mystery man, Kosko, arrives and pulls a gun on Darrin when he says the money isn't there. Darrin calls Louise looking for Samantha, but Louise won't put her on the phone; hearing from Louise that Darrin sounds frantic, Samantha returns home and meets Kosko, whose associate, Braun, isn't far behind. Larry interrupts, thinking Darrin is accepting a bribe; rewarding Darrin's "loyalty" with a raise, Larry unwittingly leaves Kosko and Braun to hold the Stephenses at gunpoint. Samantha turns their weapons into toys and twitches up sirens, which attracts actual cops. Kosko and Braun are arrested after Samantha brings the money back and reports their suspicious activities. Darrin apologizes to Samantha and admits the truth to Larry, who cancels the raise.

GOOD!

In an episode with suspense, intrigue, and criminals, Louise ends up bringing the big guns. It only makes sense that Samantha would seek refuge with her friend, and Louise's witticisms are not to be missed. "Let him cook 'til he's well done!" Mrs. Tate suggests in a show of girl power against Darrin. "It's always life or death," she adds, not knowing Darrin may be facing exactly that. It's really one of Louise's finer moments, as is Samantha turning Kosko and Braun's very real guns into child's toys and psyching the men out with sirens. [Did Samantha recall young warlock Merle similarly subduing a prowler with a toy fire engine in "A Strange Little Visitor" (#48)?]

So, McMann & Tate really is in the International Building. It was in "The Corn Is As High As A Guernsey's Eye" (#94) and "That Was No Chick, That Was My Wife" (#117); the high-rise sports different plaques and a different door now, but the name still is the same.

WELL?

The Stephenses live in Westport, Connecticut. This episode aired in March. Isn't it a little chilly for Tabitha and Adam to splash around in a pool? And Darrin has gotten drenched a lot this season: in "To Go or Not to Go, That Is the Question" (#201), it was in the bathtub as he came back from being a frog, and, in "The House That Uncle Arthur Built" (#218), the practical-joking warlock's bucket of water got him; here, the dousing happens in Endora's instant pool. Notice how Samantha starts to giggle at Darrin's soaked self; she also sniggered at the sight of Darrin's pig head in "This Little Piggie" (#220). Maybe Samantha's realizing the irony of her statement that the family needs to wait on a pool until they can afford one; she had no problem twitching up a pool for herself in "...And Something Makes Three" (#12).

Darrin speaks of the Cushman Restaurant account, despite just having worked on the Cushman Cosmetics account a week earlier ["Darrin Goes Ape" (#222)]. When Darrin realizes how much money is in the envelope, he leans over so he can drop the phone on top of the cash within camera range. Later, a valet brings Darrin his car, and Larry has one, too – so why did they take a cab to their meetings? As for Kosko, his racket must rake it in, because he springs for a 51-mile cab ride from Manhattan to Westport.

Endora tells Darrin that if he doesn't watch out, she'll make him "get on all four knees and apologize" as a billy goat. She made the same threat in "Samantha's Wedding Present" (#141), and carried it out in "Samantha the Bard" (#158). Then, a smiling Samantha posits that a bookie or gangster could have lost the hundred grand. Samantha finds the possibility of criminal activity amusing?

"I don't blow up at Darrin often," Samantha tells Louise, "but this time he really asked for it." True on both counts: except for one quick skirmish in "The Salem Saga" (#203), the Stephenses haven't fought since "Samantha Fights City Hall" (#149), and Darrin kicks it old school, thinking his wife has used her powers to help him advance – he made similar accusations all through Seasons One and Two. In response, Samantha loses her cool a little too quickly; it's interesting that she calls Darrin pigheaded, a trait she denied he possessed in "This Little Piggie" (#220). At least Darrin doesn't get paranoid when Samantha growls she might go to the moon, as he did in "Sam in the Moon" (#91).

Once again, the painting is back in the foyer, replacing the convenient mirror of "Darrin Goes Ape" (#222). But when Kosko arrives for the money, it's a little bit like "How Green Was My Grass" (#131): Darrin accused Samantha of zapping up an artificial lawn, she got mad and dematerialized it, and the real owner showed up looking for it. Darrin desperately calls Louise, saying he knows Samantha isn't there yet – but how does he know his wife will end up there at all? She's a witch; her potential destinations are endless. Darrin also fields several of Louise's questions about his family. Why does Louise ask about Phyllis? They've never met.

Larry must see Braun entering the Stephens residence, yet he rings the doorbell only 21 seconds later and says he didn't know Darrin had guests. But Larry's come a long way, baby: he brings Darrin a campaign that incorporates Women's Lib, the polar opposite of the man that called Louise a member of the "corset crowd" in "Double Split" (#64). Larry reacting to Kosko and Braun's nonexistent bribe rather slows down the story, especially since Kosko has a gun. Why does Kosko pull it on Darrin, only to hide it when Samantha comes home? Then, when he and Braun both aim guns at the Stephenses, it's played as if this threat is brand-new.

Gordon Jump's character must bartend at night to pay for the police academy, because the drink purveyor of "The Return of Darrin the Bold" (#217) is now one of Westport's finest. He's gotta be a rookie – what seasoned cop approaches a potentially volatile situation alone, with his partner sitting in the car? The officer triumphantly drags Kosko and Braun away solo, but they could easily overtake him.

When Samantha finally produces the much-ballyhooed money, it's in a wide shot where she twitches it up behind her back. Or rather, there's a twitch sound effect, but Samantha doesn't actually twitch her nose. Finally, Darrin bemoans the fact that Larry reneged on his 15% raise and six-week vacation – except, when Larry made the offer, it was a 15% raise and a $2,500 bonus, which Samantha reiterates.

OH, MY STARS!

He's a janitor. He's a Johnson brother. And now, he's a cabbie. Accomplished character actor Allen Jenkins is wonderful, but he has played three different characters in just four episodes. Some of the show's guest stars, like Cliff Norton and Bernie Kopell, have the ability to reinvent themselves to the point you wouldn't know they were the same actor even if they played back-to-back scenes, but Jenkins is so distinctive that it's jarring to see him in appearances so close together. What precipitates such casting decisions?

"The kids are fine," Darrin assures Louise during their phone call. No, they're not – they're upstairs while a criminal has a gun pointed at their daddy. By the time Samantha and Braun enter the picture, there are two guns in play, and the Stephenses don't seem the least bit concerned; they don't even try to talk the gunmen down for their kids' sake. Of course, this is a sitcom, not a crime procedural, and everyone knows Samantha can handle Kosko and Braun with witchcraft. However, it's still odd that the safety of Tabitha and Adam, who appear early in the episode, is never a factor; the Stephenses don't even tell the arresting officer that these men were waving guns around with their kids in the house.

SON OF A GUN!

"You work for that fruitcake?" – Kosko to Darrin, offering a perspective on Larry only fresh eyes can provide.

OUT OF THE MOUTHS OF BABES
EPISODE 224
Airdate: March 25, 1971

Darrin has to shelve his weekend golf game when Larry announces that Sean Flanagan of Mother Flanagan's Irish Stew is coming to town early. Darrin tries to work, but Endora arrives and wants to take Tabitha to the Unicorn Handicap; finding Darrin's refusal childish, Endora turns him into a 12-year-old. Larry returns, forcing Samantha to introduce the "preteen" as Darrin's nephew, Marvin. When Larry won't leave, "Marvin" goes to the park with Tabitha and plays basketball with Herbie, who wants him to help challenge a tough neighborhood team. Samantha serves Herbie some Mother Flanagan stew, but when the boy deems it awful, Darrin thanks Endora for youthening him, because it's made him realize the agency shouldn't advertise the product.

Larry tastes the stew and hates it as well, but he won't give up the account; as Flanagan arrives, Samantha suggests to Darrin that "Marvin" tell the truth about the stew. Larry nervously disputes "Marvin's" opinion, but Flanagan thinks back to his own childhood and remembers that he never cared for his mother's recipe, either. With Flanagan's stock threatening to go to waste, Samantha convinces him to market it as dog food. Later, Darrin and Larry have a date to play golf, but Herbie stops by needing "Marvin" for his basketball game, so Samantha turns Darrin into a boy one more time to reward Herbie for his honesty.

GOOD!

By itself, Samantha making it rain on Larry must seem a little cruel. But when you add Larry sticking Darrin with the Mother Flanagan account to all his other manipulations over the years, the soaking has a strangely satisfying karmic quality. And Darrin, who's usually annoyed by Samantha's magical displays, actually laughs at the result.

There's a wonderful moment of bonding between Darrin-as-boy and Tabitha as they go to the park to play. Darrin isn't usually seen hanging out with the young witch for one reason or another, so there's a warmth to their father-daughter time, even with father closer to daughter's age. Then, there's Herbie – his dry, almost wise-beyond-his-years delivery is exceeded only by the "player incentive" he tries to bribe "Marvin" with. Herbie truly earns his reward for telling the Stephenses about the unpalatable stew.

Darrin rarely offers regrets to Endora – two instances that come to mind are a shrunken Darrin saying, "I'm sorry" in "Samantha's Wedding Present" (#141), and his under-duress pig squeal apology in "This Little Piggie" (#220) – but here, Darrin breaks records by telling Endora that he's sorry, contrite, and grateful.

At the table, Larry comes across as a little boy himself as Samantha feeds him; there's almost a nurturing quality about the scene. Larry thinking he's "compassionate" for not telling Flanagan how bad his mother's recipe is comes as a step above his usual brown-nosing, and, while Darrin's "integrity with humor" campaign could use polishing, it's actually not a bad idea; more than one product has found success by copping to its less appealing traits.

Of course, "Marvin" saves the day, and it's not the first time Darrin has used his boyish appearance to get to the truth about a product: the main premise of this episode comes from "Junior Executive" (#46). But everything's presented in such a new way that it doesn't feel like a "rerun," and the unexpected twist is that "Marvin's" confession gets Flanagan to recall how "lousy" his mother's stew is. Darrin doesn't even have to scramble for a slogan this time; Flanagan himself puts the finishing touch on Samantha's doggie stew idea.

WELL?

In "Birdies, Bogies, and Baxter" (#114), Darrin revealed that he's been golfing since college. So why now does he need a book to tell him how to swing a club?

When Endora changes her daddy into a contemporary, Tabitha giggles. Is that just kiddie cuteness, or does Tabitha have a darker streak somewhere? Endora is a witch who probably doesn't like to repeat herself; Darrin should remind her she's doing exactly that, giving him an unplanned second childhood as she did in "Junior Executive" (#46). In that episode, and when Irving Bates went through similar de-aging thanks to Tabitha ["Just A Kid Again" (#193)], the "boys" spoke in the unchanged voices of the young actors playing them. Here, Darrin is 12, but retains an adult voice that he has to alter so he can sound like a convincing "Marvin." The humor is successful, but, because it can be hard for one actor to match another actor's speech for a voice-over, "Marvin's" voice sounds stilted at times, especially during his big speech about standing up to Endora, which was lifted word-for-word from "Samantha's Wedding Present" (#141); Samantha's "You're hardly in a position to debate the issue" response comes from that episode as well.

Larry somehow never notices that "Marvin" and his supposed uncle are dressed identically, right down to a pair of conspicuous striped pants – and Mr. Tate is also not the slightest bit upset to hear that Darrin's gone on a multiple-hour errand to a nursery when he's supposed to be at home working on the Mother Flanagan account. Twice, Larry believes Darrin isn't home, yet Darrin's car must still be in the driveway, and the same goes for Darrin-as-boy, who asks Samantha if the coast is clear when the presence or absence of Larry's car would answer that question.

The Stephenses' kitchen door has almost always faced Morning Glory Circle. But when "Marvin" and Tabitha come home, there are only trees where there should be a street. Samantha serves Herbie and "Marvin" generous portions from the one can of stew Larry brought – don't Tabitha and Adam get any? And it's ironic that Darrin considers this Irish stew "blech," because it's his favorite food, according to "Samantha the Sculptress" (#159).

Though it's a little convenient for Samantha to magically extract a confession from Flanagan regarding how much profit he makes per can, her suggestion that the not-fit-for-human-consumption stew be used to feed dogs is quite resourceful. Question: has Darrin ever told Larry that Ashley the dog from "Samantha's Pet Warlock" (#209) is no longer part of the household? It's a wonder Larry doesn't ask to test the rechristened doggy stew on the pooch. Finally, Larry is understandably irritated when Darrin stands him up to play basketball, but he derisively asks, "At his age?" as if the sport has an age limit.

OH, MY STARS!

Since when *does* Darrin play basketball? Naturally, not everything is known about him, even after seven seasons, but the only other sport besides golf he's ever shown an interest in is fishing ["Open the Door, Witchcraft" (#28)]. He once mentioned swimming and mountain climbing ["The Crone of Cawdor" (#101)], but Darrin didn't even learn to swim until after "Divided He Falls" (#69), where Samantha had to magically save him from drowning. He seemed comfortable throwing a baseball around with young warlock Merle in "A Strange Little Visitor" (#48), and "What Makes Darrin Run" (#191) revealed that Darrin ran track in college, so maybe it's possible he shot hoops there, too – it's just that, if he was good enough at basketball that he was an all-star forward at Missouri State, surely this would have come up before now.

SON OF A GUN!

"I'm beginning to feel like a yo-yo." – Darrin to Samantha, after repeatedly going from boy to man.

SAMANTHA'S PSYCHIC PSLIP
Airdate: April 1, 1971

Darrin is about to give Samantha an expensive bracelet to celebrate 30 days without witchcraft when he catches her magically cleaning the kitchen in preparation for Phyllis' arrival. He shrugs it off, but Samantha feels guilty: she hiccups, and bicycles appear all over the room. Darrin takes his inquisitive mother upstairs to see the kids while Samantha summons Dr. Bombay, who declares it unnatural for Samantha to suppress her witchcraft; after suggesting that her guilt manifested the bikes, he cures her. Samantha and Phyllis go shopping, but Darrin worries when another of Samantha's hiccups makes a mirror disappear from the foyer.

A cheery Larry comes over to see Darrin, but he quickly becomes unnerved when babysitter Serena appears out of nowhere, followed by Dr. Bombay. Meanwhile, Samantha and Phyllis are confronted by a store detective after Samantha hiccups and dematerializes a high-priced necklace. Dr. Bombay wonders if eliminating Samantha's guilt is eliminating gilt instead, and uses his latest invention to locate Samantha, who stands accused of stealing the necklace. Bombay administers the right cure to Samantha, the necklace pops back into place, and Larry is flustered when the foyer mirror reappears in front of him. Later, Darrin sasses the exiting Serena, so she turns him into a baby goat.

GOOD!

To magically tidy her kitchen, Samantha does a little twirl as Darrin walks in, but her turn is fluidly edited, and Darrin doesn't move; it's quite the excellent effect. The five-part effect when Dr. Bombay gets rid of Samantha's bikes, with doctor and patient looking around the room, must have been time-consuming to shoot, but it appears effortless.

Larry gets another shot at a non-client storyline when he bonds with Bombay over martinis [he has indeed had "the pleasure" of meeting the doc, in "There's Gold in Them Thar Pills" (#107)], and his later "I've been looking all over for you and I couldn't find you everywhere" freak-out to Darrin shows a hilarious new side to the usually collected ad man. Not to be outdone, it's a rare day when Darrin and Dr. Bombay exchange civil words, so watching them work together to help Samantha is a rather gratifying development. Finally, Irwin Charone is back, this time in the form of the store detective; he hasn't made an appearance since "Samantha's da Vinci Dilemma" (#124), so his presence feels new and fresh.

WELL?

Three cents a can on waxed beans, three mentions on the show. In "Witch or Wife" (#8), Darrin felt that kind of savings couldn't be exciting for a witch new to the mortal life, and Samantha bought 60 cans in "Fastest Gun on Madison Avenue" (#57), which Darrin said should last 14 or 15 years. It's only been five; this time Darrin thinks they're covered 15-16 years.

No wonder Darrin's mellow about Samantha's kitchen magic – at least she straightens things for Phyllis' benefit all at once, unlike "Out of Sync, Out of Mind" (#116), where she sped herself up into a lean, mean, cleaning machine. And Darrin's tried to reward Samantha for 30 non-witchcraft days before, in "Man's Best Friend" (#70). However, Samantha just used her powers repeatedly in "Out of the Mouths of Babes" (#224); to first-time viewers, that was only a week.

Samantha gives Darrin a choice: Dr. Bombay, or Phyllis institutionalized, perhaps remembering that her mother-in-law went to the funny farm after seeing witchcraft in "Samantha's Secret Is Discovered" (#188). Ironically, Phyllis asks Adam where his teddy bear is; she spent a whole episode involved with that particular stuffed animal in "The Dancing Bear" (#58).

Bombay sported sequins and a candelabra *à la* Liberace the last time he tickled his computer's ivories in "Samantha's Magic Potion" (#212) – that identical machine was a hexometer that detected witchcraft. Has Bombay modified it into something new? His tuning fork also finds new life as a "prank-quilizer," though it had different uses in "Samantha the Bard" (#158) and "Samantha's Lost Weekend" (#186). And there's yet another convenient mirror in the foyer – the last one appearing in "Darrin Goes Ape" (#222); at least this one is better integrated into the story.

Serena has been designated babysitter in Samantha's absence – the kids will be glad to see her, but where's Esmeralda? No one yoo-hoos for her, and the wonky witch has been AWOL since "Samantha's Old

Salem Trip" (#208). For that matter, why is a sitter necessary when Darrin is home? Maybe it's because Darrin says he's heading to Larry's; oddly, Larry shows up on Darrin's door instead.

Dr. Bombay must take magic lessons from Maurice. The witch doctor "tunes in the refrigerator" for a recap the way Samantha's father did in "Darrin the Warlock" (#181), and even reverses the footage, a technique Maurice used to de-mule Darrin in "Daddy Does His Thing" (#167). Bombay then proudly shows off his "which witch went which way" invention, but it's just showmanship; there's no reason Bombay can't cast a locator spell to find Samantha instead.

Phyllis asks if Tabitha can spend a Saturday and Sunday with her; Samantha, who fought it tooth and nail in "Tabitha's Weekend" (#163), agrees readily here. Perhaps Samantha feels more relaxed about the idea since Lisa spent the night in "Sisters At Heart" (#213)?

Questioning the spinning arrow of Dr. Bombay's invention, Larry is told the machine is a "witch hunter." How much more confirmation does Larry need? In both "The Witches Are Out" (#7) and "To Trick-or-Treat or Not to Trick-or-Treat" (#177), Darrin made a case against portraying witches as old crones in ads. Then, Darrin came right out and told Larry that Samantha is a witch in "That Was My Wife" (#31) and "The Corsican Cousins" (#211). The premise of the show is that mortals either don't believe such claims or simply ignore them, but Larry's smart enough to realize that the word "witch" always coming up must mean something.

At the department store, which is strangely devoid of music (and other customers), there's a camera shift that happens as Samantha's hiccup makes the necklace disappear – but the bigger offenders are the maps of Los Angeles that hang in the detective's offices when his store is on the opposite coast in Connecticut. Also, Samantha twitching the detective into checking the status of the necklace is cute, but it's another one of her easy fixes.

Chess with real kings must be the latest witch fad: Serena is into the game now, but, in "Super Arthur" (#190), Dr. Bombay participated in the life-size game. And goats are on everyone's minds – Serena turns Darrin into one, though Endora just threatened to in "Money Happy Returns" (#223) [and actually did in "Samantha the Bard" (#158)]. "What if the children heard you talk like that?" Samantha scolds as Darrin bleats. She needn't worry; last time Darrin was a goat, Tabitha wanted to ride him.

OH, MY STARS!

Without the benefit of subtitles – which viewers of the series' first run, and initial syndication run, didn't have access to – there's a risk of confusing the words "guilt" and "gilt." The pun is intentional so that ornate things will vanish once Dr. Bombay calls for Samantha to "eliminate all of guilt" – but, because "gilt" (which means "covered thinly with gold leaf or gold paint") is not one of the English language's more common words, it's easy to interpret Bombay as saying, "anything that's *guilt* will disappear," as in anything that resembles the expensive bracelet which triggers Samantha's initial psychological reaction. The result is ultimately the same; it's just that the soundalike words make things a tad unclear.

SON OF A GUN!

"Careful there, fellow! Don't you signal before you turn?'" – Dr. Bombay, after Larry nearly runs into him.

Darrin has finally learned to pick his battles when it comes to witchcraft – instead of blowing a gasket over Samantha cleaning the kitchen with magic, he simply says, "That was an emergency. It doesn't count." This is a lot of growth from the man who sparked a battle royal over twitched pancakes in "How Green Was My Grass" (#131).

The show makes an excellent point about repression in this episode, as Dr. Bombay discusses the reason for bicycles appearing. Reminding Samantha that, as a witch, stifling her powers causes inner conflicts and guilt is a clear message – to her and to viewers – that it's important to be oneself even when pressured not to. Exploring this "cycle-logical" aspect gives the episode a layer of substance that sitcoms of this period don't typically have.

SAMANTHA'S MAGIC MIRROR

Airdate: April 8, 1971

EPISODE
226

Esmeralda is blue because her old boyfriend, Ferdy, is coming to visit, and she doesn't want him to see that her powers have waned. After Larry stops by fresh from an argument with Louise and sees an elephant Esmeralda sneezed up, Samantha gives Esmeralda a mortal makeover to boost her confidence. When Darrin's forced compliments fail to improve Esmeralda's outlook, Samantha zaps the mirrors so Esmeralda will see a younger, prettier version of herself. The newly-empowered Esmeralda comes on to Larry, which drives him out of the house, though Esmeralda is still nervous about Ferdy's impending arrival.

Because only Esmeralda can see her beautified self, she's confused when Ferdy doesn't notice her new look. Ferdy easily conjures things for himself, so, after Esmeralda botches his drink, Samantha agrees to do her magic for her. Unbeknownst to Esmeralda, Ferdy's witchcraft is being performed by his nephew, who hides outside until a police car scares him off. Samantha steps away when Darrin calls to report that Larry is heading back; unattended, Esmeralda and Ferdy zap up consecutive disasters and realize they're both keeping the same secret about their powers. Ferdy and Esmeralda get engaged, and Larry walks in as they fade out; Samantha suggests that what Larry saw can be attributed to his dismissive attitude toward Louise. Larry calls to invite his wife along on his business trip, but he only triggers another fight.

GOOD!

Though Esmeralda has been absent since "Samantha's Old Salem Trip" (#208), the mousy maid comes roaring back in a *tour de force* that Alice Ghostley must have had a ball playing. Buoyed by the sight of Esmeralda 2.0 in Samantha's mirrors, the real Esmeralda finds her confidence, and then some: she sashays down the stairs, flirts with Darrin, and propositions Larry – which rattles the ordinarily unshakable ad exec.

As for Samantha's mirrors, to quote Esmeralda, "I just can't get over the effect!" Nancy Priddy doubling as Esmeralda via split-screen looks amazing; true, sometimes things don't match when Esmeralda and her younger reflection turn away from or toward the mirror (it can't be easy to sync up when you can't see behind you), but the overall illusion works very well.

Actor Tom Bosley became famous for ABC's *Happy Days* starting in 1974 (the series ran until 1984), but, three years before Howard Cunningham, Bosley brought the delightfully kooky Ferdy to *Bewitched*. Ferdy and Esmeralda are entertaining enough while they're trying to impress each other, but it's when they do witchcraft unassisted that the fun really begins: Ferdy reverting Samantha's pearls to oysters and Esmeralda getting a literal Scotch on the rocks instead of the drink are their best bungles. And, though his name is never revealed, Ferdy's nephew – who, appropriately, looks like he walked off the set of ABC's 1970-1974 series, *The Partridge Family* – is groovier than groovy, and he even offers a glimpse of what it must be like to be a hip, young warlock. His only flaw is that he pops out too soon.

Though this installment focuses on Esmeralda and Ferdy, Larry gets his moment, too, as he argues with Louise during the episode's tag. It's clear from their phone conversation who wears the pants in the Tate family; maybe that's why Larry's always on a power trip at the office – to compensate.

WELL?

This episode borrows its central premise from "Aunt Clara's Old Flame" (#47), in which Clara didn't want *her* old boyfriend, Hedley Partridge, to find out her powers were kaput. The main difference is, Aunt Clara didn't know Samantha was doing her magic for her, and here, Esmeralda does, as she makes the request of Samantha herself. The pair of waning witches have something else in common besides former paramours: Esmeralda sneezes up an elephant here, while Aunt Clara turned Hedley into one in the aforementioned episode.

Lately, whenever Darrin's sketching a layout, he's in the den; he never goes to the office anymore. As for the foyer, a whole different mirror replaces the one that hung there in "Samantha's Psychic Pslip" (#225). Once Esmeralda arrives, she sneezes up a palm tree – her second since "Samantha's Caesar Salad" (#173) – then Darrin tells her she needs to do something about her cold. Esmeralda hasn't sneezed since "Santa Comes to Visit and Stays and Stays" (#184), where she also materialized trained seals; maybe the audience needs to be reminded that her actualizing ahchoos are involuntary, but Darrin knows she doesn't have a cold – he found out during Esmeralda's introduction in "Samantha's Yoo-Hoo Maid" (#172) that his housekeeper's sniffling is nothing to sneeze at.

It's understandable that Esmeralda wants to settle down in a home of her own, but she doesn't live with the Stephenses, and she hasn't sat for the children in almost 20 episodes – where is she living now? Perhaps it's just the way of witches to want to become a potted plant when powers start fading: Aunt Clara considered the same solution in "The Corn Is As High As A Guernsey's Eye" (#94).

Samantha prides herself on giving Esmeralda a mortal makeover, but where does the hairpiece come from? Esmeralda's own hair isn't long enough to curl like that, and Samantha probably doesn't have a drawer full of wigs at her disposal, so she must have zapped it; so much for the 100% mortal approach. As for Esmeralda, she gets out of Samantha's bathrobe and into her pink dress in 25 seconds flat.

Larry and Louise fight because she wants him to spend time with her before he heads off on a business trip. What about Jonathan? Have the Tates already forgotten the boy who made a brief comeback in "Mixed Doubles" (#221)? And when Darrin suggests going bowling, Larry says he hasn't played since hurting his back. Does this mean Larry really does have an old football injury, as he claimed in "Samantha's Better Halves" (#185)?

Samantha assures Darrin that, if things work out with Ferdy, Esmeralda won't be at the house so often. But Esmeralda is supposed to be the Stephenses' maid, and she's only paid three visits this season. Later, Samantha remembers Ferdy, and interacts with him as if they've met, yet that can't be: Esmeralda says it's been 400 years since she last went out with Ferdy – in "The Salem Saga" (#203), Samantha said she was a child during the Salem witch trials of the 1690s, 120 years after Ferdy would have been around. Even if Samantha were old enough to remember him, she wouldn't know him, since she only just met Esmeralda two years ago, in "Samantha's Yoo-Hoo Maid" (#172).

When Larry comes over, he's wearing a suit. When he comes back from hitting golf balls, he's wearing a suit. Does he always go to the driving range dressed for a business meeting? Speaking of appearances, Esmeralda and Ferdy fade out with Samantha's reflection-changing spell still in play, presumably only affecting mirrors in Samantha's house. Won't Esmeralda be upset when she peers into a mirror somewhere else and finds out Samantha has deceived her?

OH, MY STARS!

"You know Esmeralda," Darrin says to Larry after his hot-to-trot help slinks into the foyer. Technically, Larry doesn't: despite having been in the same room with her three times [in "Samantha's Yoo-Hoo Maid" (#172), "Samantha's Caesar Salad" (#173), and "Make Love, Not Hate" (#200)], Larry and Esmeralda have never officially been introduced. And, while it's sweet that Esmeralda and Ferdy come together over their erratic powers, shouldn't they get to know each other again before any engagement? People can change a lot in four years, let alone four centuries.

As Ferdy's nephew hides under the Stephenses' living room window, the backdrop indicates there's nothing but trees behind him – not even Morning Glory Circle. However, in the reverse shots with the cops, the tiny street is more developed than ever, with a whole new house at the end, and an industrial-looking building near a giant, three-story apartment house. As if that weren't enough, when Darrin drives up to stop Larry, Morning Glory Circle is restored to its usual exterior, with the telltale gas station replacing the completely different infrastructure seen earlier in the episode.

SON OF A GUN!

"What's going to happen when she asks the mirror who's the fairest one of all, and the mirror tells her?" – Darrin to Samantha, who has instructed Esmeralda not to look at herself until her makeover is complete.

LAUGH, CLOWN, LAUGH
Airdate: April 15, 1971

EPISODE 227

Endora strides through the living room on a camel, but when Darrin doesn't find it funny, she insists he has no sense of humor. To lighten Darrin up, Endora zaps him into involuntarily telling obnoxious jokes to secretary Betty, then grumpy Jameson of Mount Rocky Mutual Insurance. Larry sends Darrin home early; although Endora removes her spell per Samantha's demand, she turns around and casts another that makes Darrin laugh at serious things. Darrin doesn't make it out of the driveway before he realizes he's been bespelled again, as he can't stop chuckling at bad news about Gladys' sister.

Samantha calls in sick for Darrin, but Larry decides to bring Jameson and his wife by the house anyway. Before they get there, Gladys arrives to tell Samantha about Darrin's strange behavior; Samantha covers when Darrin, who's hiding behind the door, chortles at the mention of a car accident. Gladys promises to keep what she's heard to herself, but runs straight to the nearest neighbor. When Darrin can't stop laughing at the sourpuss Jamesons, Samantha explains away his levity by telling jokes – soon Larry and Mrs. Jameson offer up their own, and Jameson notices that laughing has alleviated his bursitis. Together, the Stephenses invent a campaign for Mount Rocky that puts a humorous spin on the otherwise serious insurance industry, making everyone happy.

GOOD!

Throughout Seasons Three, Four, and Five, Larry fired Darrin over the most minor infractions, usually due to behavior caused by Endora's spells. Here, after Darrin subjects a client to a series of tacky jokes that two years ago would have earned him another pink slip, all Larry does is send him home early. Calling Samantha later, Larry merely says that he and Darrin "had a little misunderstanding." The change in Larry makes him much more three-dimensional. Then, Larry tells the Jamesons that Darrin is "erratic, but talented," demonstrating he's taken note of Darrin's conduct the past seven seasons. Finally, while telling his joke, Larry recalls a former boss who would give his employees a raise, then fire them so they'd be losing a better job – could this be where Larry got his ideas about employer/employee relations?

Things rather come full circle for Gladys Kravitz as she comes to the Stephenses' door. Samantha, knowing her neighbor too well, asks where Gladys' cup is – an apt question, since Gladys has been using sugar as an excuse to snoop since "And Then I Wrote" (#45).

McMann & Tate's Betty has an eleventh incarnation in the form of Marcia Wallace, but her wonderfully neurotic version of the secretary is the best since Jill Foster's Betty disappeared in "One Touch of Midas" (#157).

In an interesting, unrelated connection between episodes, the title "Laugh, Clown, Laugh" comes from the song that Arthur-as-clown sang in "The House That Uncle Arthur Built" (#218) – which he picked up from the 1928 Lon Chaney movie of the same name.

WELL?

Endora can't seem to make up her mind. Atop her camel, she says Darrin's sense of humor needs replacing, but later, she says Darrin has no sense of humor at all. Samantha scolds her mother's opinion of Darrin, asking, "Does a turkey laugh at an ax?" That's a strange joke, and puts a darker spin on Endora's motivations than the show likely intended.

Endora casts her first spell on Darrin, unfreezes him, then disappears. Shouldn't she disappear first? Darrin could easily see her out of the corner of his eye in those couple of seconds of awareness. And having a chime go off every time Darrin's about to tell an off-color joke makes sense as an indicator for the audience, but it's already clear Darrin is bespelled, not to mention the sound effect gets a little old after a while.

Hearing that Endora's been at it again, Samantha smiles, "Oh, dear. Did she do something mean?" The query makes Samantha sound like she's not taking Darrin seriously. Endora returns, saying she was just trying to give Darrin a sense of humor – but, if that's so, why did she cast a spell that specifies hair-curling jokes?

Gladys tells Darrin she has a sister in St. Louis who needs an operation. Could this sibling be the mother of one, some, or all of the six Kravitz nephews that have shown up over the years, the latest being Sidney in "Mary, the Good Fairy" (#215)?

The Stephenses have apparently decided to put the sailboat painting back in the foyer after hanging mirrors in that spot the last two episodes. On the phone, when Samantha lies that Darrin can't come back to work because he isn't feeling well, Larry actually yells at her, which he's never done before – Samantha would be within her rights to hang up on him. Perhaps Larry is truly that upset over Jameson, because he tells the departing client they can stop at Darrin's on the way to the airport. The only way Westport, Connecticut is on the way to the airport from New York City is if the Jamesons are flying out of New Haven or Hartford.

Endora's second spell has Darrin giggling at serious things: "the graver the note, the more it will tickle." So, when Darrin hurts himself dashing up the stairs, he should be roaring with laughter. Conversely, as the jokes with the Jamesons flow, Darrin guffaws at them all – isn't he only supposed to be amused by somber situations? Samantha laughs about an uncle of hers that's always complaining. She must be making this up, because she only has one uncle who's ever been mentioned – Arthur – and when he's around, she and Darrin do the complaining.

Samantha is right that laughter is the best medicine; health can certainly be affected by mental states and attitudes. But, after all the merriment, Jameson exclaims that his bursitis is gone. After a few jokes? Bursitis is an inflammation; whether through medication or an improved frame of mind, the relief wouldn't be that instant, or at least that total. Samantha celebrates by announcing, "Laugh and the world laughs with you," causing everyone in the room to split their sides. Why? Samantha's making a declaration, not a joke. Finally, at the end of the episode, Darrin chuckles over a gag gift Jameson has sent, but there's no mention of whether Endora has removed her only-laugh-at-serious-things spell yet or not.

OH, MY STARS!

When did Mrs. Rockfield from "The House That Uncle Arthur Built" (#218) become Mrs. Jameson? For that matter, when did Aunt Hagatha marry a mortal? These questions simply mean that Ysabel MacCloskey has been cast in yet another role this season, despite being established as Aunt Hagatha in "This Little Piggie" (#220) and "Darrin Goes Ape" (#222). Switching MacCloskey's roles from mortal to witch and back again is particularly jarring – she makes a terrific Hagatha, so why not keep her in that role and find an equally capable character actress for the one-off role of Jameson's wife, instead of recycling MacCloskey in such a strange way?

SON OF A GUN!

"Sam, if you love me – don't talk to me!" – Darrin, desperate to avoid hearing anything serious that could make him laugh.

SAMANTHA AND THE ANTIQUE DOLL
Airdate: April 22, 1971

EPISODE
228

Phyllis visits with gifts for the kids – including a doll for Tabitha that belonged to Phyllis' grandmother. Adam wants to play with it, but Tabitha floats it out of his hands. Trying to explain what Phyllis saw, Samantha implies that Phyllis moved the doll herself by sheer force of will; Phyllis tests her "powers" when she recalls that her grandmother was said to have supernatural abilities. Phyllis immediately tries to demonstrate her paranormal gifts for Frank, but returns to Samantha's when the attempt doesn't work. Phyllis feels a familiar is necessary to act as a conduit for her powers; when Tabitha again levitates the doll, Phyllis believes the toy is that conduit.

After Phyllis calls the disbelieving Frank an old goat, Samantha is inspired to try "hyper-hallucinogenic revelation": she'll scare Phyllis straight by turning Frank into a goat. However, when the time comes, Phyllis refers to Frank as a stubborn mule instead, so Samantha switches mammals. As Phyllis can't change Frank back, Samantha suggests a séance in which Phyllis can contact her grandmother for help; voiced by Samantha, "Grandma" advises Phyllis that only the power of love can restore her husband. Phyllis speaks to Frank-as-mule from the heart, Samantha makes him human again, and Phyllis swears off her powers for good. Later, after Darrin observes how nice it is not having Endora around, she turns him into a goose from afar, so Samantha likewise transforms herself to keep him company.

GOOD!

This episode's references to Phyllis' supposedly supernatural Irish grandmother may seem random, but they actually do tie in to Darrin's heredity as established in past seasons. In "The Leprechaun" (#63), it was revealed that Darrin's own grandmother was from Ireland's County Cork – and Frank said in "McTavish" (#130) that Stephens is "a fine old English name," so, process of elimination suggests that it's Phyllis' side of the family that's Irish. Phyllis having "the power" is delightfully over-the-top (thanks to Mabel Albertson's unrestricted performance) – and if Phyllis can have a sister who thought she was a lighthouse [see "I, Darrin, Take This Witch, Samantha" (#1) and "Samantha Meets the Folks" (#14)], then why not a grandmother who claimed to have unusual powers?

After Samantha makes Frank a mule, Phyllis acts as if she's going to abandon her power, only to turn around and state she'll have to discipline her thoughts, which is quite a twist. This leads to the séance, featuring Elizabeth Montgomery's fun interpretation of Phyllis' Irish "grandmother." Darrin cleverly adds to Samantha's plan by advising his mother to tell Frank how much she loves him; it's a satisfying moment.

Robert F. Simon is back, after not having made an appearance as Frank since "It's Wishcraft" (#103). [Roy Roberts took over the role in "Out of Sync, Out of Mind" (#116).] Interestingly, Dick Sargent's chemistry with Simon's Frank is even more natural, plus they bear a closer father-son resemblance, much as Dick York's Darrin did with Roy Roberts' Frank. And, in a subtle bit of continuity, Frank wants Phyllis to see Dr. Rhinehouse, the psychiatrist she had a session with over a year ago in "Samantha's Secret Is Discovered" (#188).

This season ends with the discovery that Tabitha has a new way of expressing her powers – instead of her old manual twitch, or even just plain zapping like she did in "Sisters At Heart" (#213) and "Samantha and the Troll" (#219), Tabitha now crosses fingers from opposite hands and bends them in unison. It's an unspoken way of saying that the witchlet of yesteryear is quickly growing into a young lady witch.

WELL?

When Samantha says Phyllis shouldn't bring gifts every time she visits, Phyllis retorts, "Well, if I were here as often as your mother, you'd probably be right." It's true that Endora always seemed to be on hand when Phyllis was over, but Phyllis hasn't even seen Tabitha's other grandmother since "Samantha's Secret Is Discovered" (#188). Phyllis also gripes to Samantha that Darrin is too thin, despite telling him he looked "simply wonderful" in "Samantha's Psychic Pslip" (#225). Phyllis follows by offering to give Samantha recipes for Darrin's favorite foods, as she did when encountering Samantha for the first time in "Samantha Meets the Folks" (#14). Phyllis waited seven years to try this tactic again?

Tabitha is right to be concerned that Adam might damage the doll – in "Sisters At Heart" (#213), she told her mother that Adam was always breaking her toys. Samantha directs Tabitha to let the whining Adam play with her doll anyway – but what possesses Tabitha to be so brazen as to make the doll float in front of Phyllis? Tabitha is talented enough now that she could just zap it out of Adam's hands and into her own; Phyllis need never have seen it. Of course, then you wouldn't have an episode.

Frank, who is known for calmly blowing off his wife's visions and claims, is unusually hostile toward Phyllis in this installment. Phyllis tries to float an hourglass to Frank, ironic considering how rattled she was by Serena's giant, backwards-running model in "Mrs. Stephens, Where Are You?" (#160). But the elder Stephenses' house is different from both their previously established abodes [see "A Nice Little Dinner Party" (#19) and "Tabitha's Weekend" (#163)].

When Phyllis can't manipulate objects in her house, she races to Samantha's for answers. But, by the time she gets there, she already knows why her powers only work in her son's house. Does she read about it while Frank's driving? Samantha plays dumb at the mention of familiars; obviously, she knows about them, but she and her fellow witches never seem to require them for their sorcery.

Samantha employs "hyper-hallucinogenic revelation" to make Phyllis believe she's turned Frank into a mule. But how is it a hallucination if Frank is actually an animal? Darrin's parents come full circle, in a way, when Phyllis calls Frank an old goat – that's what he called himself for flirting with Endora in "A Nice Little Dinner Party" (#19). And now father and son have even more in common: Darrin was also a mule, courtesy of Maurice, in "Daddy Does His Thing" (#167).

Trying to change Frank back, Phyllis raises her arms and intones, "Undo the spell." What spell? Despite her talk of familiars, the feats she "does" are more indicative of telekinesis than witchcraft. Then, as Phyllis' "grandmother," Samantha tries to scare Phyllis with talk of a family curse. Is she thinking of the real curse placed on Darrin's family in "A Most Unusual Wood Nymph" (#79)?

Endora borrows the two lightning bolt arrows with which the Witches' Council sent messages in "Samantha's Old Salem Trip" (#208) to herald changing Darrin into a goose. At least Samantha finally follows through on her pledge to turn herself into an identical animal; in both "Tabitha's Very Own Samantha" (#189), and "To Go or Not to Go, That is the Question" (#201), Samantha said she would change herself into a frog if Darrin ended up in an amphibious state. Maybe Samantha's transformation is her way of making up for accidentally turning Darrin into a goose herself in "Long Live the Queen" (#108).

OH, MY STARS!

There have been at least eight episodes this season whose premises stem from previous installments. This one joins their ranks, as the ideas of "Abner Kadabra" (#29) – where Gladys caught Samantha using magic only to be told she herself had powers – are reworked. Samantha should be having a déjà vu as she convinces Phyllis of her "abilities" the way she did Gladys; she then scares her mother-in-law by making her believe she's turned Frank into a mule; Samantha turned Abner into a pile of dust for the same reason. Samantha even encourages both women to hold séances to get everything back to normal – good thing Gladys and Phyllis don't know each other, or they could compare notes. Phyllis' adventures do make for a highly entertaining episode, but, it's lamentable that the show again relies on the past to give viewers a present.

The last time Phyllis was over, in "Samantha's Secret Is Discovered" (#188), she was told that Samantha is a witch [as she was in "Samantha Meets the Folks" (#14)], though Samantha led her to believe that hallucinogenics were responsible for the revelation. Seeing Tabitha's doll floating across the room now, Phyllis should immediately recall the confessions of witchery and realize that they're true. But she doesn't even mention it, despite the fact that she was perfectly fine with the idea of having a witch for a daughter-in-law.

SON OF A GUN!

"Samantha, if you'll forgive me, this is one subject you know nothing about." – Phyllis, as Samantha tries to persuade her mother-in-law that supernatural powers come and go.

SEASON EIGHT

(1971-1972)

Esmeralda struggles to restore a famous Italian landmark in "Samantha's Not So Leaning Tower of Pisa" (#232).

ABC/Photofest

"Tabitha's First Day in School" (#248) turns out to be a battle between a class bully and her witchcraft.

ABC/Photofest

Grandpa Maurice gives little Adam a tutorial in witchcraft to answer the question, "Adam, Warlock or Washout?" (#242).

ABC/Photofest

When "Samantha's Witchcraft Blows a Fuse" (#253), the Stephenses work to remove her telltale red stripes.

ABC/Photofest

SEASON EIGHT: OVERVIEW

This final season of *Bewitched* is somewhat notorious, both for producing the highest number of remakes it had ever lensed, and the fact that the series ended on a regular episode, without any kind of wrap-up. Make no mistake: a Season Nine was in the works (see *Bewitched Forever* by Herbie J Pilato), but ABC canceled the show after Season Eight had wrapped. Networks are much more willing to give long-running programs the chance to craft proper finales today, but that wasn't the way in the '70s. And so, the most popular and acclaimed supernatural sitcom on the air disappeared, not with a grand Maurice-style puff of smoke, but a quiet Esmeralda fade-out.

These concluding 26 episodes came with pluses and minuses, but started by sending the Stephenses to different ports of call in Europe, much like Season Seven began with a trip to Salem. The only difference was that the show's actors stayed in the studio this time, rather than embark on a new location shoot. Samantha's encounter with Henry VIII was a remake that came across as epic, while an original episode of Serena tangling with the Loch Ness Monster was a bit out to sea. Conversely, a Parisian rework of "Just One Happy Family" (#10) didn't live up to the original, while Samantha's battle with an English ghost was mesmerizing. After spending seven "European" installments on this fence, the Stephenses and Tates returned home with the scale tipping in neither direction.

Young Tabitha and Adam provided some of the freshest moments of the season – not only was Tabitha blossoming, but she carried episodes that saw her becoming a TV star and a champion skater. Plus, she was finally allowed to go to school, where she ran afoul of a bully, then flirted with genius thanks to "grandmama". Not to be outdone, Adam literally found his voice and got a whole episode to himself to determine whether or not he had powers – at once a remake *and* a continuation of Tabitha's Season Three certification.

Darrin became the most accepting of witchcraft he'd ever been, even allowing his wife to zap up The Darrin Stephens Agency as a way of getting back at Larry. Darrin's progressive viewpoint was temporarily stymied by the oddly placed "A Good Turn Never Goes Unpunished" (#252), a Season One reboot that reinstalled his paranoia about magic; thankfully, it didn't stick. Samantha, on the other hand, went through quite the evolution: her hair got longer and straighter, her clothes got hipper, and her attitude got bigger. One gets the impression that Elizabeth Montgomery had a desire to make her character stronger, but, in this season, Samantha giggled at Darrin's Endora-related predicaments, growled at him, and gave him the evil eye – she even threatened to zap him. If this was a bid to incorporate the growing Women's Liberation movement, it succeeded, but Samantha's new aggressiveness seemed out of character for the good-natured witch viewers had seen for seven years.

There was a little more of Louise, a lot more of Maurice, and even more Bettys, bringing the number of actresses playing the secretary to fourteen. It also seemed like the show couldn't quite decide what to do with Esmeralda: ignoring her Season Seven engagement to Ferdy, the ever-bumbling witch became more friend than maid, going her own way after a successful magic show only to be back in service to the Stephenses without clarification. Even more curious, Uncle Arthur, Darrin's parents, and the Kravitzes all vanished from the screen for no perceptible reason; only Abner and Gladys got a cursory off-camera mention. Like Aunt Clara before them, this seemed a disservice to both the show's quintet of legacy characters, and the actors who portrayed them.

The gulf between the world of 1964, when *Bewitched* premiered, and the world of 1972, when it ended, was probably on par with the Grand Canyon – but the sights, sounds, and sensibilities of the forward-thinking early '70s colored the show in a way it hadn't been since the middle of its run. Viewers heard up-to-date new music and sound effects, as well as dialogue that sometimes bordered on bawdy ("He can do *everything* right," Samantha informed Endora. "I oughta know!"). Themes of self-empowerment were explored as Samantha's continual suppression of her natural abilities resulted in illness; she even told Darrin that preventing Adam from practicing witchcraft could be detrimental to the boy. These concepts also played on a larger stage as the arrival of George Washington heralded examinations of rights, freedoms, prejudices, and patriotism.

Despite the plentiful amount of reworked episodes, the show still laid claim to a lot of imagination – a hippie warlock made Larry do his bidding, while Serena made Larry back up a few decades. Samantha faced literal ups and downs thanks to an illness that defied gravity, while Maurice faced his first bout of powerlessness. Certainly there was enough supernatural gas in the tank for another season, but *Bewitched* faced stiff competition in its new time slot (from a little newcomer called *All in the Family*), and ultimately, the decision was made to end the series – leaving behind 254 reasons why a show about a witch who married a mortal still enjoys unprecedented popularity in reruns, and on DVD, a half century after its début.

HOW NOT TO LOSE YOUR HEAD TO KING HENRY VIII (PART I)
Airdate: September 15, 1971

Vacationing in England, the Stephenses tour the Tower of London, where a figure in a portrait begs Samantha to release him from it – the figure is Herbie, a warlock who has been imprisoned there since the time of Henry VIII. Samantha zaps Herbie out of the painting, incurring the wrath of his captor, Malvina. After Samantha reluctantly returns Herbie to the portrait, Malvina sends her to Henry VIII's court as punishment. With Samantha missing, Darrin contacts Endora, who learns from Herbie that Samantha is marooned in 1542 with no memory, and no powers. As Samantha can only be restored by a kiss from a man in the present day, Endora delivers Darrin to the 16th century, giving him a talisman he can use to summon her if he runs into trouble.

Wandering amnesiac Samantha meets and joins a band of minstrels set to entertain King Henry VIII. Impressed by Samantha's singing, Henry offers to keep her on as a palace performer, but later threatens to throw her in the dungeon if she tries to leave with the minstrels. Despite having executed his fifth wife that morning, Henry decides Samantha should be his next bride, making her a lady-in-waiting, while Darrin makes his way into the palace.

GOOD!

Adam may or may not be a warlock, but at least now he can verbally communicate with older sister Tabitha. The stronger family connection, however, happens when Darrin and Endora work together to find out what happened to Samantha, then plan her rescue. The mortal-witch adversaries continue to bicker, of course, but the mutual love for Samantha that ties them together is most palpable here.

This episode beautifully evokes the English Renaissance period, from the instrumentals that entertain the king to the minstrel's brief performance of *The Hunt Is Up*, a ballad written by William Gray during the reign of Henry VIII. This installment also offers a *Bewitched* first: Samantha singing. Elizabeth Montgomery provided vocals for Serena in "Serena Stops the Show" (#192), and Samantha-as-Serena in "Hippie, Hippie, Hooray" (#128), but Samantha herself has never broken into song until now – her rendition of *Early One Morning*, said to date back to the 16th century, is lovely. And it all takes place at Hampton Court, where Henry VIII actually ruled.

Cliffhangers are usually the territory of dramas and soap operas, but Darrin making a beeline for the palace as Samantha struggles to fight off Henry VIII creates a healthy bit of suspense for the supernatural sitcom – though the comedy of Samantha telling the king, "Your wife expectancy isn't too great" keeps things balanced.

WELL?

In England, Darrin says Larry "knows, but he doesn't care" that the Stephenses are on vacation, which he also reported in "Samantha's Bad Day in Salem" (#207) – and his hotel phone only gives off one ring at a time, whereas UK phones emit a two-ring signal. Endora calls on a toy telephone, like Samantha and Serena before her [in "Tabatha's Cranky Spell" (#134) and "Samantha and the Troll" (#219), respectively]; Tabitha first instituted the practice in "Toys in Babeland" (#109).

Endora wanted to give Tabitha and Adam a pool in "Money Happy Returns" (#223), and finally does so here. When Darrin objects, Endora advises him, "Don't get your giblets in an uproar," which is what her brother, Arthur, said after his failing powers shattered a mirror in "Super Arthur" (#190).

It's exciting to come back from commercial zooming into the Tower of London, but the cars aren't moving; it's a still photo. And poor Samantha can't travel anywhere without being accosted: in "The Salem Saga" (#203), Newton-as-bedwarmer confronted her at the House of the Seven Gables – now it's Herbie's turn. Herbie comments that Samantha is the first witch to take the tour in 400 years. Considering the Tower was still being used as a prison in 1571, any tours then were conducted in an entirely different way.

This installment could well be the best time travel story in the series, but it borrows from similar sagas. Darrin asks how he's supposed to kiss a perfect stranger, forgetting he already did so successfully in "Samantha Goes South for a Spell" (#142) – an episode in which Samantha was also punished by a vengeful witch. In "Samantha's Old Salem Trip" (#208), Endora furnished Darrin with 1690s duds without having to zap clothes out of a painting, and Samantha draws as much attention to her "minimal covering" here than she did in that episode. In both instances, Samantha arrived in the past with neither magic nor memory.

Endora hasn't browsed *Harpies' Bizarre* since "Dangerous Diaper Dan" (#82), but, either the magic mag folded after one issue, or Endora rereads old ones, because it's the same copy from five years earlier. Darrin calls to tell Endora about Malvina's curse, but how did he find out about it? Herbie couldn't have told him, because he is frozen in the portrait as Endora gets further information from him. For that matter, how does Herbie know Samantha has been zapped to 1542? Was that the year he was banished to the painting?

At the castle, Samantha picks up an instrument and declares, "It's called a lute." It's called exposition: the minstrels already know what a lute is. How is Samantha able to learn *Early One Morning* in just a few hours?

Endora first attempts sending Darrin to the past by incanting, "Backward, turn backward, oh, time in thy flight." This is the same line she used to send the Stephenses to an alternate reality in "What Every Young Man Should Know" (#72). When she brings Darrin back to the present, she gives him a talisman, "in case you get into trouble again." Darrin didn't need a talisman to get Endora to zap him out of Henry I's 11th century court – all Darrin had to do was call out; nor was he in trouble. Darrin's in the ballpark when he says Endora "missed the target by 500 years" – they're aiming for 1542, and Henry I reigned from 1100-1135. However, despite being in one of London's biggest tourist attractions, Darrin and Endora discuss Samantha's plight and facilitate two trips into history without a single visitor or group wandering by.

When Darrin finally arrives in the right year, it startles the friar, who didn't bat an eye when it was Samantha that suddenly appeared. Shouldn't Darrin wonder why telephone wires are hanging above the path leading to the palace in both the 11th and 16th centuries?

Was Henry VIII's appearance inevitable? Fighting about Samantha's age in "To Twitch or Not to Twitch" (#132), Samantha yanked Darrin's chain by claiming she knew the king, Esmeralda revealed she was once his lady-in-waiting as she interviewed in "Samantha's Yoo-Hoo Maid" (#172), and Serena alleged she cooked for the sovereign in "Samantha and the Troll" (#219).

OH, MY STARS!

The longest-standing rule on this show, officially established in "Hoho the Clown" (#92), is that one witch cannot undo the spell of another. That rule does get broken on occasion, but this episode is the biggest violator, as Samantha casually zaps Herbie out of a painting without even an incantation; there is no way Samantha should be able to break Malvina's curse. Another questionable bit of witchcraft is Endora accidentally sending Darrin to 11th century England instead of Henry VIII's time. Endora has been shown to be one of the most powerful witches in the cosmos – she can't possibly be "seven Henrys off," especially when her spell specifies sending Darrin "back to the time of Henry VIII." Endora is not Esmeralda or Aunt Clara; unless she's sick with a witch disease, her aim should be perfect the first time.

Though the show very correctly depicts Henry VIII's fifth wife, Catherine Howard, as being beheaded in 1542, it's interesting that the king most remembered for disposing of his brides only did so with two of them: this one, and Anne Boleyn, who, ironically, was charged with witchcraft. His marriages to Catherine of Aragon and Anne of Cleves both ended in divorce, Jane Seymour died due to postnatal complications, and his sixth and final wife, Catherine Parr, remained married to Henry until his death. Malvina must be too furious to care about disrupting the timeline: she purposely sends Samantha to this exact moment to meet Henry VIII, which could result in Samantha taking Catherine Parr's place in the history books – and who knows how Catherine not being queen could change history? It's true that television shows weren't thinking on this level when *Bewitched* aired, but time travel stories do rather beg questions like these.

SON OF A GUN!

"'I know not'? What a strange name – you must be Irish." – King Henry VIII, misinterpreting Samantha's identity crisis.

Two new characters charge this episode with electricity, the first being the properly evil Malvina, played to delicious over-the-top perfection by Arlene Martel. She makes such an impression in less than a minute that Malvina would make a welcome addition to the show's roster of recurring characters. And Ronald Long is perfect as Henry VIII, arguably giving the definitive performance of the oft-portrayed monarch. Not only does his theatrical experience in England infuse the king with the regal quality he demands, Long even makes Henry VIII funny.

EPISODE 230

HOW NOT TO LOSE YOUR HEAD TO KING HENRY VIII (PART II)
Airdate: September 22, 1971

After a narrator recaps the events of "How Not to Lose Your Head to King Henry VIII (Part I)" (#229), Darrin hears Samantha singing and discovers that the king plans to make her his sixth wife. Masquerading as a pastry boy, Darrin witnesses Henry presenting Samantha with the royal jewels; when the king steps out of the room, Darrin tries and fails to jog Samantha's memory. Henry catches Darrin with Samantha and wants him executed, but Samantha's compassion persuades Henry to imprison Darrin in the dungeon instead. Darrin summons Endora with the talisman she gave him, but she can't perform witchcraft in the past; instead, she hypnotizes the dungeon guard and breaks Darrin out of his cell.

Crashing the king's masked ball, Endora tempts Samantha with memories of her mother and steers her toward the disguised Darrin – but when Samantha sees him, she balks, and when Henry sees him, he decrees that Darrin will be beheaded. Endora stalls by playing on the king's reputation as a wrestler, forcing Darrin into a match to get a reaction out of Samantha; it works, and the defeated Darrin gets his kiss as a dying wish, which restores Samantha's memory. After Darrin, Samantha, and Endora disappear, Henry VIII is convinced he is having a royal dream, while in the present, Endora frees Herbie from Malvina's painting and takes him home, causing Samantha to relabel the artwork "The Missing Horseman."

GOOD!

Darrin's overblown Brit is as funny as his "I never dreamed I'd welcome your interference" admission while calling Endora is poignant. For as much as they can't stand each other, the witch/mortal team works well together – and Endora using her "native ingenuity" to manipulate the guard, lull him to sleep, and give him the post-hypnotic suggestion of feeling rotten shows a clever side to the witch who is used to zapping up results.

The music for Henry VIII's masked ball is beautiful, and very of the period. However, Endora rules the room far more than the king when she forces herself to campaign for Darrin: she chokes trying to tell her amnesiac daughter that Darrin is handsome and charming, and, when Samantha shrugs that Henry is merely short for his weight, Endora pipes up, "You mean he'd be thin if he were ten or eleven feet tall?" There *is* a feeling that Endora would find it fun to watch Darrin get crushed in a wrestling match, but that's quickly overtaken by an earnestness as Endora implores Darrin to trust that she knows what she's doing.

It doesn't surface often, but there's a real affection emanating from Endora when she tells the Stephenses, "Hang on, kids – here we go!" as they disappear. And, looking at the episode through a sci-fi lens, it seems that the only impact Samantha and the gang had on the timeline was the king's chamberlain suggesting their presence was a royal dream.

WELL?

Apparently, the minstrels that were evicted in "How Not to Lose Your Head to King Henry VIII (Part I)" (#229) had time to teach Samantha two songs, because here she does a lovely lute/flute duet. The only question is, who's on flute? It's just Samantha and the king in the room. She starts again from the beginning as Darrin nears her window below, but maybe Henry just enjoys previewing new material: Samantha's song, *Of All the Birds That Ever I See*, was written by Thomas Ravenscroft in 1607 – some 65 years after the events of this episode.

In "Paul Revere Rides Again" (#206), Darrin was revealed to be a history buff, yet he walks into the court of Henry VIII and has to ask who Catherine is when told Samantha will replace her. And British architecture must not vary that much – the inside of Hampton Court looks just like the inside of the Tower of London, where the Stephenses start and end this journey.

Once Darrin finds Samantha, he asks, "You really don't recognize me, do you?" Strange, considering he's dealt with Samantha in amnesiac states before – in "Samantha Goes South for a Spell" (#142) and "Samantha's Old Salem Trip" (#208). At least he makes a better attempt to connect with his wife here than in those two episodes; instead of just calling her "Sam" like usual, he gives her a quick précis of their life together. Is Samantha carrying a subconscious awareness of her true identity? She must be, or she'd have a much more negative reaction to being told she's a witch; remember, Henry VIII had his second wife, Anne Boleyn, executed on charges of witchcraft.

The king finds Darrin with his intended and comes at him with a dagger, but Henry seems like the kind of guy who have Darrin killed, rather than do the dirty work himself. As Darrin is dragged away, Samantha wonders, "Why did he call me 'Sam?'"; she posed the same question when Darrin tried to rescue her from Rance Butler in "Samantha Goes South for a Spell" (#142). Given Samantha's 16th century frame of mind, perhaps her name truly is unfamiliar, as there were no recorded instances of "Samantha" until the 18th century.

When Darrin wails that Samantha won't have anything to do with him, Endora replies, "Oh, if that had only happened when you first met!" Granted, she's never warmed up to Darrin, but she loves Tabitha and Adam – if Samantha had initially rejected Darrin, the kids would never have been born. Samantha, however, seems to know how to perform an English court dance, though it's doubtful anyone would have had time to teach her the steps.

First a strange man (Darrin) tries to plant his lips on Samantha, then a strange woman (Endora) wants Samantha to smooch what she must perceive as a second strange man (also Darrin). Is Samantha not wondering why there's so much interest in her kissing habits? Then, Endora shrewdly talks King Henry into wrestling Darrin, hoping to trigger an emotional response from Samantha, but it's not much of a match: Henry just puts Darrin into a headlock and gives him a big bear hug. Her plan working, Endora tells Samantha, "I wouldn't want his death on my conscience!" Wouldn't Samantha find that odd, considering Endora started the wrestling match in the first place? Then, outraged when it seems Darrin has been killed, Samantha cries, "You simply have no feelings, you big klutz!" The humor is in the anachronism, but Henry isn't clumsy.

The whole reason Malvina sent Samantha to 1542 was because she freed Herbie from his canvassed curse. Yet, at episode's end, Endora does the exact same thing – and no one seems worried that Malvina will return.

OH, MY STARS!

Endora only being able to pop herself to and disappear from the 16th century might add an extra element of drama to Samantha's rescue attempt, but only once before, in "A Most Unusual Wood Nymph" (#79), was it implied that a witch traveling back in time could not access her witchcraft. Behold the series' other time travel episodes: Samantha zapped everyone into Pilgrim duds in "Samantha's Thanksgiving to Remember" (#119) and disrupted a witch trial with magic in "Samantha's Old Salem Trip" (#208). Serena froze her 17th century self in "Samantha's Hot Bedwarmer" (#204), then Darrin's ancestor in "The Return of Darrin the Bold" (#217). Plus, the whole family just spent Christmas in the 14th century in "Sisters At Heart" (#213). Now suddenly Endora can't use her powers in the past because "I wasn't even born yet." That statement goes against the show's very beginnings – in "Mother Meets What's-His-Name" (#4), Endora admitted knowing Diogenes, who lived 300 years before Christ, and many episodes afterward indicated that Endora is anywhere from 1,000 to 3,000 years old; here, Endora isn't even 400. There's dramatic license, and then there's ignoring rules established over seven seasons.

SON OF A GUN!

"Well, they're not born yet – but they will be if you'll just cooperate a little!" – Darrin, trying to convince Samantha to kiss him for the sake of their children.

In "The Good Fairy Strikes Again" (#216), the show segued into the second part of a two-parter by completely changing the ending of the previous episode. That mistake is corrected here with a proper recap, narrated by someone with an omniscient perspective instead of Samantha, who has only ever been privy to certain events [example: "Follow That Witch" (#66-#67)]. There are a few different angles and takes compared to Part I, but this is the best introduction to a Part II seen so far in the series.

SAMANTHA AND THE LOCH NESS MONSTER

Airdate: September 29, 1971

Samantha sends Tabitha and Adam a magic video "postcard" from Inverness, Scotland, where the Stephenses are visiting Darrin's cousin, Robbie. Despite insisting that he's seen the fabled Loch Ness Monster, Robbie faints when the creature pops out of the water. Samantha recognizes the beast and talks it down, later becoming concerned when the severe Baron von Fuchs arrives with a plan to kill it for $3 million in reward money. Samantha finally tells Darrin that the Loch Ness Monster is really a warlock named Bruce, transformed by Serena. Agreeing to Samantha's plea to take the creature out of harm's way, Serena visits the bottom of the loch and restores Bruce – but he exacts revenge on her by turning her into a mermaid.

After the Stephenses get Serena-as-mermaid back to their hotel, Samantha zaps the obstinate Bruce out of a party at the Warlock Club. Bruce wants Serena to remain a mermaid for 40 years, since he was a monster that long; Robbie rushes in, thrilled that the monster sighting means more tourism for Inverness, and Samantha plays on Bruce's ego by casting Serena-as-mermaid as the town's new attraction. Bruce admits he's a better monster than a warlock, so he normalizes Serena in exchange for being sent back to the lake. As the Stephenses ready to leave Scotland, a worse for wear Baron emerges from the water, having been bested by Bruce-as-monster, who needs a case of antacid after eating the Baron's submarine.

GOOD!

Samantha twitching up live footage of Loch Ness for Tabitha and Adam to see on their chalkboard is a fun bit of witchcraft, plus it subtly drives home the point that witches really can do anything. It's also not surprising that Samantha can speak the Baron's native German fluently – after all, she demonstrated a total command of Italian in both "Business, Italian Style" (#110) and "Cousin Serena Strikes Again (Part I)" (#155).

After Bruce-as-monster first surfaces, the camera zooms in on Robbie. Darrin remains standing as Robbie faints. Then, the camera pans as Samantha checks on Robbie – but when it pans back, Darrin has fainted as well. And this is all done in one shot. More slick camera work comes via the cinematic crane/ zoom combination that reveals the Baron von Fuchs and his mini-sub. As for the Baron himself, Bernie Kopell's latest memorable character is stern, stereotypical – and exactly what *Herr Doktor* ordered. Who knows if the epithets the disheveled von Fuchs spouts at the monster are actually German or not – Kopell nearly dares you not to laugh at him, and he's a highlight of the episode.

Serena's underwater adventures may not rival today's television standards (fans blowing on her with the footage slowed down to approximate sunken slinking, with an aquarium for a lake floor), but the show does try. In fact, the on-the-water shots are not only different for the show, they're incredibly ambitious – true, the boat and camera move considerably when Serena pops out, but that can't be helped. And making Serena look as if she's swimming like a mermaid couldn't have been easy to pull off. Two other nice touches: the aquatic rendition of Serena's groovy theme, and her flawless dry-off in Bruce's pad. Darrin's even impressed with Serena's potential skill set as a mermaid.

WELL?

Robbie is introduced as Darrin's cousin. "The Leprechaun" (#63) and "Samantha and the Antique Doll" (#228) both established that Darrin is Irish on his mother's side; "McTavish" (#130) established that Darrin is English on his father's. So where does this Scottish cousin come from? Granted, England and Scotland are both part of the United Kingdom, but this is the first mention of any Scottish lineage.

Insurance company Boyd's of London has offered a $3 million reward for the monster. Cute: the real company is Lloyd's of London; perhaps the show wasn't allowed to use their actual name. Darrin later concurs that it's shocking to learn the Loch Ness Monster is really a warlock. Why? In seven years, Darrin has dealt with leprechauns, elves, ghosts, enchanted bedwarmers – Bruce's identity should roll right off his back. As Samantha explains Bruce to Darrin, there's a post-production zoom that's meant to break up the shot, but the effect is unintentionally grainy. And Serena certainly likes to change suitors into things: married Malcolm was a bird in "Samantha Goes South for a Spell" (#142), and, in "Samantha's Hot Bedwarmer" (#204), she let Newton languish as an antique for three centuries.

Since split-screen is impossible to use when people are on the water, a double is used so Samantha and Serena can be in the boat at the same time. However, the double's face is visible, and Samantha's voice-over is just a little stilted, likely from trying to match the double's dialogue.

Serena changes Bruce back from being a monster, only to get zapped with a mermaid tail for her effort. Were Bruce and Serena both caught off guard, which Samantha said was the criteria for witches transforming each other in "Samantha's Pet Warlock" (#209)? Now, transformations are one thing – but Bruce turning Serena into a mermaid takes away her witchcraft. Is this on par with Samantha's powers being canceled out by substituting for "Mary, the Good Fairy" (#215)?

Darrin rightly has Serena cover her tail when Robbie is about to enter, but why does he insist on the camouflage before, when Samantha zaps everybody to the room, as if someone's going to see Serena in her fishy altogether? Later, as Samantha tracks Bruce, her spell indicates that the Warlock Club is located "36.6 degrees north by northwest on the cosmic continuum." Isn't the Warlock Club in London, as indicated in "My Grandson, the Warlock" (#40) and "Daddy Comes for a Visit" (#180)? Is the cosmic continuum the same as the atmospheric continuum first mentioned in "Samantha's French Pastry" (#147)?

Bruce threatens to report Samantha to the Witches' Council for "the illegal use of teleportation spells." The real crime is that Samantha has never used them before! If she can simply twitch Bruce into appearing in front of her, why hasn't she done so the many times her family members bespelled Darrin and made themselves scarce?

The vindictive Bruce wants Serena to remain a mermaid for 40 years, because he was a monster that long. He's relatively accurate: though the Loch Ness Monster was referenced as far back as the 6th century, he didn't enter popular culture until 1933. That being the case, if Bruce has been underwater for four decades, he can't know about television satellite system Telstar, since it wasn't launched until the early 1960s. Finally, Serena brainstorms ways to entertain Inverness as a mermaid, saying she can fool around with the fishermen. Why not – she already made merry with the Fisherman's Memorial in "Darrin on a Pedestal" (#205).

OH, MY STARS!

After Serena finds herself with a tail in place of legs, Samantha asks her to remember Bruce's spell, insisting, "Maybe I can reverse it." Samantha knows a witch can only reverse her own spell – with few exceptions, that's been the rule since "Hoho the Clown" (#92). So her logic becomes even more confounding when remembering that, earlier in this same episode, Samantha said only Serena could restore Bruce.

Television shows have never been allotted the larger budgets granted to feature films, so it's understandable that there are limitations in creating this episode's aquatic *accoutrements* – it's just too bad there wasn't a way to put something a little more realistic on the screen. The allegedly foreboding Loch Ness Monster looks like he wandered in from a kiddie show, and he's not much taller than Serena to boot. Serena's mermaid tail looks better, but it's not very scaly, and it's hard to take green cloth with black lines criss-crossing it seriously. It was a valiant attempt; it's just that these pivotal props are memorable in a way the show didn't intend.

SON OF A GUN!

"Yes, but only on a can of tuna." – Darrin, when Serena asks if he's ever seen a mermaid before.

SAMANTHA'S NOT SO LEANING TOWER OF PISA
Airdate: October 6, 1971

EPISODE 232

With the Stephenses now in Italy, a distraught Esmeralda pops in, asking to be relieved of her babysitting duties because she accidentally turned Tabitha's friend into a dinosaur. Pained upon seeing the Tower of Pisa from the Stephenses' rented villa, Esmeralda admits she made it lean 800 years ago while dating its builder, Bonanno Pisano. Larry, hoping to bottle up the Count Bracini Olive Oil account, brings the count by the villa; after Bracini takes a shine to Esmeralda and invites her to sightsee with the group, she feels so empowered that she's motivated to fix the Tower, sending the city of Pisa into a frenzy over their straightened landmark.

Samantha reminds Esmeralda that the Tower is a world-famous tourist attraction, and begs her to remember how she originally made it lean. When Esmeralda draws a blank, Samantha takes her to the 12th century to reunite with Bonanno. Trying to whip up a lunch involving lean roast beef, Esmeralda tilts the Tower again, to Bonanno's horror; in the present, Count Bracini arrives to break his date with Esmeralda because of the Tower emergency, only to find it in all its leaning glory. Later, he reports that the global attention to the Tower will double the city's tourism and summons everyone to a party, while Larry remains annoyed that, one way or another, discussing business with Bracini seems impossible.

GOOD!

The show does a very good job of making it look like the Stephenses are actually in Italy – Samantha and Darrin's rented villa is stunning, the outdoor sets and populace feel authentic, and it's a nice touch that Darrin, as an ad man, wants to check out Italian television commercials. The panicking *Pisanis* demonstrating how a town might react to the "miracle" of a straightened tower also give viewers an idea of the potential mass impact of witchcraft, an aspect that hasn't been explored before.

WELL?

At least witches' video chat "technology" is consistent: in "Paul Revere Rides Again" (#206), Samantha was shown in a close angle, then in medium as she spoke to Esmeralda; here, Esmeralda starts in a medium shot that widens so Tabitha can fit into the frame. It's also ironic that Esmeralda tries to reconnect her "call" with a spell that ends, "in the land once ruled by Caesar," considering she caused the famed emperor to visit in "Samantha's Caesar Salad" (#173).

Esmeralda's fades require Alice Ghostley to put blue screen material over whatever part of her needs to be invisible and get back into position, with the show removing any blue in post-production. Esmeralda's first fade-out starts well, but when she fades back in, her fully-realized upper body comes in at a completely different angle. Her second lack of cohesion, in front of Larry and Bracini, looks better; however, as she solidifies, her legs and feet shift considerably to the right. Curious – in "Samantha's Yoo-Hoo Maid" (#172) , Endora said Esmeralda fades when she gets tense. Esmeralda is happy when Bracini wants to take her sightseeing. So why does she fade?

Esmeralda admits that making the Tower of Pisa lean ended her engagement to its builder, Bonanno Pisano. So Esmeralda agreed to marry a mortal 800 years before Samantha wed Darrin, and met no resistance from the Witches' Council? Bonanno has to know Esmeralda and Samantha are witches; he doesn't react when they do witchcraft in front of him, and he even asks Esmeralda for a "Tower Special" – this is rather progressive for a man who lived in a time when suspected witches often met with execution.

When this episode was written, the Tower was, in fact, attributed to Bonanno Pisano; he was a sculptor in the 1170s, so the timeline is right. However, studies now suggest that perhaps another builder, Diotisalvi, actually constructed the Tower; no one knows for sure. At any rate, only the ground floor and second floor had been built by 1178 – once the structure began to lean, work on it was abandoned until 1272. So Esmeralda couldn't have climbed to the top of the Tower, where she says she's been, unless she came back after its completion in 1372 – and that's not likely, since Esmeralda also admits she hasn't been in Pisa since making the Tower lean.

Larry asks what Esmeralda is doing there – surprising, considering the two still have never been formally introduced after two seasons. After Bracini capitalizes on squiring Esmeralda around Pisa by asking her to dinner, Samantha remarks that the yoo-hoo maid has scored two dates. When was the first? Esmeralda and Bracini did lunch in the company of Larry and the Stephenses; not much of a date.

Samantha is unusually hostile toward Esmeralda, but maybe it's warranted: Esmeralda straightens the Leaning Tower of Pisa, in broad daylight, *with people inside.* Why not wait until late at night when no one would be in danger? Samantha offers to send Esmeralda to the 12th century to make the Tower lean again, but Esmeralda asks, "What if I got stuck back in time?" She wouldn't – Samantha could just zap her back to the present.

In 12th century Italy, Bonanno Pisano has a conversation with Samantha and Esmeralda – in English. Does Samantha's time travel spell come with an instant translator? Esmeralda says she was a girl when she dated Bonanno, yet he doesn't notice that she is considerably older when she arrives to bring him lunch. And where is the Esmeralda of the 1100s? The 1971 Esmeralda could just watch *her* cast the original spell. And how does Esmeralda botch Bonanno's building by commanding, "one Tower, and make it lean" 800 years before the lingo of 20th century diners? Finally, it seems Bonanno invented the telephone 700 years early: one can be heard ringing on-set as he first approaches Samantha.

In "Business, Italian Style" (#110), Endora wanted Darrin to learn the language, telling Samantha, "If you ever do make a trip to Europe, Dum-Dum wouldn't be a source of embarrassment." Darrin finally takes the trip, but is baffled when Bracini freely converses with him in Italian, apparently remembering nothing from his language records. And Larry still seems to discriminate against other cultures: in "A Majority of Two" (#136), he turned up his nose at Aunt Clara's sit-on-the-floor Japanese dinner, he didn't seem very open to his Latino clients in "Samantha and Darrin in Mexico City" (#170), and here, he complains, "I don't understand these Europeans" when Bracini puts sightseeing before business, commenting that, "In

Italian, everything sounds like an emergency." After his wonderful acceptance of the African-American Wilsons in "Sisters At Heart" (#213), Larry's attitude is kind of a letdown.

OH, MY STARS!

Darrin lets Samantha know that Larry is coming over with a client. But where did Larry come from? In "How Not to Lose Your Head to King Henry VIII (Part I)" (#229), it was established that the Stephenses had come to Europe for a vacation – now Larry is in Italy, stopping by with a client. He even tells Bracini, "Darrin brought his wife along" as if this were a business trip and Samantha just happened to be there. Of course, Larry would insinuate himself into the Stephenses' vacation, but there's no connective thread to justify his sudden presence.

When last seen in "Samantha's Magic Mirror" (#226), Esmeralda became engaged to her former boyfriend, Ferdy. This episode ignores that event, portraying Esmeralda as the most insecure she's ever been – she'd really be this despondent over a broken vase and a dinosaur? And what happened to Ferdy? Esmeralda simply accepts Bracini's overtures as if her fiancé never existed. Though real-time viewers had a summer between "Samantha's Magic Mirror" (#226) and this episode, it still would have been better to include a line about things not working out with Ferdy so Esmeralda would be free to move forward.

SON OF A GUN!

"No, with her it's *buffa, buffa, buffa* all day long." – Samantha, when Bracini continues mistaking Esmeralda's truth-telling for joke-telling.

BEWITCHED, BOTHERED, AND BALDONI
Airdate: October 13, 1971

EPISODE
233

Convinced that Darrin will be tempted by the beautiful women of Rome, Endora decides to prove it by bringing the city's famous Venus statue to life. Darrin is instantly beguiled by "Vanessa"; he misses a business meeting and then suggests to Samantha that they take "Vanessa" home to be their maid. When Larry becomes smitten with "Vanessa" as well, Samantha begins to suspect her mother's involvement, especially when their newly-hired help saunters in wearing only an apron. Later, McMann & Tate's client, Baldoni, brings his wife to spend the weekend at the Stephenses' rented villa in Pisa [see "Samantha's Not So Leaning Tower of Pisa" (#232)]; Mrs. Baldoni is annoyed when her husband also succumbs to "Vanessa's" charms.

Baldoni, who is on the board of trustees of a museum, soon receives a call that the statue of Venus has been stolen. Samantha clues in to "Vanessa's" identity, but can't get Endora to appear, so she returns to Rome and makes the classic Adonis statue sentient to counteract "Vanessa." Mrs. Baldoni is captivated by "Alberto," but Samantha manages to get the living statues out to the patio, where Endora agrees to send them back. Just as mother and daughter get ready to zap them, Venus and Adonis hold hands and are remarbled that way. Endora laughs it off as "one more miracle in the enchanted city of Rome," and Samantha teases Darrin over his attraction to "Vanessa."

GOOD!

As statues, "Vanessa" and "Alberto" do their best not to move; it's hard to stay perfectly still, but the effect is not spoiled by their slight, occasional motion. And Venus gets away with some pretty racy shows of skin for 1971 television – it's all tasteful, even when she exposes her entire hip and leg when first humanized, and again as "Vanessa" backs out of the Stephenses' boudoir wearing only an apron. Perhaps the statues' best bit happens when Venus and Adonis quietly clasp hands just as Endora and Samantha restore them. It's always enjoyable to view familiar images in bizarre situations, by way of absurdist humor.

"Vanessa" and "Alberto's" magnetic lips are the highlight of their time as humans, but an actual human steals the spotlight from them both: Mrs. Baldoni. Her jealous asides as her husband drools over "Vanessa" (Baldoni reads "Vanessa's" palm, causing the missus to bark, "In a minute you'll be reading the back of my hand!") provide comic contrast to Dona Baldoni later going gaga for Adonis.

WELL?

Rome shouldn't look too foreign to the Stephenses – the museum they visit there looks exactly like the museum they visited in London. [See "How Not to Lose Your Head to King Henry VIII" (#229-#230).] The effect of Endora appearing as a doll in the museum's case looks great, but, when the shot moves in closer, Endora gets zoomed up as well, which throws off her dimensional perspective. Darrin wonders why Endora can't go to the market for spaghetti instead of traveling to Rome for it – after seven years, he really has to ask? Then, Endora assures the Stephenses that Esmeralda is home babysitting, but the yoo-hoo maid was last seen on Count Bracini's arm in "Samantha's Not So Leaning Tower of Pisa" (#232). Are they still seeing each other?

Darrin has a business meeting in Rome, and tells Samantha he'll see her in Pisa. It's a four-hour drive between these cities – how are the Stephenses' traveling? Let's assume they drive to Rome together, and that Samantha is to drive back by herself, with Darrin hitching a ride with Larry and Baldoni. Except he can't, because he ditches his boss and client to sightsee with "Vanessa," and she certainly doesn't drive. Is everybody taking planes between Rome and Pisa?

After Darrin flakes on his meeting, he tells Larry things can be made up to the Baldonis when they spend the weekend, as if this is the first time Larry is hearing about the visit; surely he already knows the Baldonis' itinerary. As for Samantha, she reminds Darrin that they don't need "Vanessa," since "the villa comes with four in-help." The helpful quartet is indeed shown – so why does Samantha, who is on vacation in a foreign country, have to do her own grocery shopping?

Darrin says that Samantha could use "Vanessa's" help around the house. But Samantha doesn't remind Darrin that they already have a maid: Esmeralda. Then, in "The Generation Zap" (#194), Darrin glossed over details about the nubile Dusty Harrison, so Samantha clarified with, "You didn't say it was a he, so I figured it had to be a she"; Samantha comes to the same conclusion about Darrin's "European cousin." Now, up until a few hours before, "Vanessa" spent centuries as a statue. So how does she know how to make drinks, or what a working visa is? She doesn't even know to put an apron on over her uniform.

What was under the red sheet Endora zapped up to keep Venus from being missed? Obviously, someone pulled the sheet away and discovered that Venus was gone; why didn't Endora just zap up a duplicate statue? As Samantha realizes "Vanessa" is the "crime of the century," Venus seems to nod as the camera zooms in on her – it's odd she would she give herself away. And, while the show opted to break up a long, static wide shot by zooming in during post-production, as they often do, the effect is again grainy, making the Stephenses' private conversation about "Vanessa" not look as good as the rest of the episode.

That night, the huge, cavernous museum is silent except for the guard's footsteps – a guard that somehow can't hear Samantha casting her spell and talking to Adonis, despite barely being out of earshot. Back at the villa, Ernesto Baldoni wants "Vanessa" to be "the House of Baldoni's goodwill ambassador." What exactly does the House of Baldoni do that necessitates such a position? His service or product is never mentioned. Also, no one notices that Samantha goes upstairs to nurse her "headache," but comes back through the front door with Adonis – who leaves the museum with a smooth chest and arrives at the villa with a hairy one. As for Samantha's own hair, it alternates between flatter and fuller depending on the scene, despite events happening in tandem, just as it did in "Samantha's Not So Leaning Tower of Pisa" (#232).

Surely it's only Endora's impish nature that makes her send the hand-holding statues back to the museum in that state? Hopefully she restores them to their proper, separate forms before anyone discovers them. Afterwards, Darrin tells Samantha it was "touch and go" with Venus, and Samantha replies, "Touch what and go where?" This is same exchange they had over college cutie Liza Randall in "The Girl Reporter" (#9).

OH, MY STARS!

Endora's clear intent in siccing Venus on Darrin is to get him to stray from Samantha and prove her point about mortal fidelity. Forget for a moment that Endora has put Darrin through this very test dozens of times already; at this point she ought to take the hint that Darrin hasn't cheated and isn't likely to. The issue is this time is, does Darrin have a spell on him, or not? As soon as he sees "Vanessa," the sound effect that usually indicates a spell is in play is heard, and Darrin's cavalier attitude about business also lends itself to that conclusion. Yet, Larry, who is also smitten initially, doesn't end up as enamored of Venus as Darrin, and Darrin later seems aware that the sultry statue is having an effect on him. So, is Darrin acting from his own free will when he wants to take "Vanessa" back to America with him, or are he, Larry, and Baldoni under Endora's influence?

SON OF A GUN!

"Let me guess: you were kidnapped, and you escaped. Anything less I won't accept." – Larry to Darrin, rightfully perturbed over Darrin missing the Baldoni meeting.

PARIS, WITCHES' STYLE
Airdate: October 20, 1971

EPISODE 234

In Paris, Samantha again sends Tabitha and Adam witchy video "postcards" of the sights [see "Samantha and the Loch Ness Monster" (#231)]. Soon, Endora pops in, warning that Maurice is angry because Samantha didn't stop off to visit while in London [see "How Not to Lose Your Head to King Henry VIII" (#229-#230)]. Hoping to appease her husband, Endora zaps up a phony Darrin, who is so subordinate that Maurice feels he's broken his spirit. As Maurice gives "Darrin" a pep talk in another room, the real Darrin comes back from a meeting with Europa Tours, but fails to go along with the doppelgänger scheme; Darrin argues with Maurice and finds himself zapped to the top of the Eiffel Tower.

On the ground, Darrin returns to the hotel and tells Maurice off – Endora turns Darrin into a statue to save him from Maurice's retaliation, but Maurice identifies Darrin-as-statue and shatters him. When Samantha demands that Maurice restore her husband, he has trouble doing so until Endora decides to move back in with him. After Darrin rematerializes, Monsieur Sagan, the president of Europa Tours, arrives, threatening to pull his account unless Darrin can explain the newspaper photo of him atop the Eiffel Tower. Maurice crafts a slogan based on the picture, and Sagan is happy until he witnesses Maurice zapping everyone into dinner clothes.

GOOD!

Samantha's Parisian "postcards" are not only fun to watch, they're a beautiful continuation of "Samantha and the Loch Ness Monster" (#231), where Samantha provided her children similar insights into her Scotland trip. Samantha's getting nervy, too, simply twitching up the "postcards" in front of Darrin; maybe, after seven years, they've come to an agreement that witchcraft that doesn't affect outcomes is okay. Maurice uses his witchcraft to finally give himself a spotlight, after spouting Shakespeare sonnets since "Witches and Warlocks Are My Favorite Things" (#77), and Endora uses her own powers to protect Darrin. There's something heartwarming about her actions, just as her "Dummy Darwin" puts a new spin on her son-in-law.

This episode corrects a major continuity flaw from "How Not to Lose Your Head to King Henry VIII (Part II)" (#230), in which it was stated Endora hadn't been born by 1542. As Endora was said to be over 2,000 years old as far back as "Mother Meets What's-His-Name" (#4), her telling Tabitha and Adam that she was present when the Louvre Museum lay its cornerstone is more true to her history – the Paris landmark was originally built as a fortress in 1190.

The "Picasso" that Endora zaps up for Maurice is a great touch – in 1971, famous painter Pablo Picasso was still around. He was 80 at the time (he lived until 1973), and at the height of a prolific period, creating daring works just like the kind Maurice is presented with here. Other notable details are Maurice zapping himself and his family into fancy dining duds – it's a very well-done effect – and, *Le Figaro* is an actual French newspaper that's been in print since 1826. Its front page, featuring a mortal worker with a crane, addresses the silent question, "Just how did Darrin get down from the Eiffel Tower?"

WELL?

Neither Darrin nor Samantha mention it, but they've been to Paris together before, in "Witch or Wife" (#8). Samantha notes in her video "postcard" that Paris' Louvre Museum is almost 900 years old, but, as it was built in the 12th century, it isn't quite 800 years old when Samantha drives by.

Maurice pops into 1164 Morning Glory Circle and is angry to discover his daughter has been in Europe without visiting him. Witches are often privy to information via the atmospheric continuum, so why would Maurice have to go to Samantha's house to find out she isn't there? For that matter, it's odd that Samantha and Darrin didn't drop in on Maurice when they were in London [see "How Not to Lose Your Head to King Henry VIII" (#229-#230)] – did their forced trip to the 16th century throw off their itinerary? Samantha hopes to make Maurice understand that their presence in Europe is "part work and part vacation," except it was all vacation until Larry inexplicably showed up in "Samantha's Not So Leaning Tower of Pisa" (#232).

Maurice's dramatic entrance via black smoke works, at least until he wafts into the hotel room; not as effective is the voice-over of "Dummy Darwin," who says, "Actually, we should have called you while in London" right after telling Samantha, "We should have at least called him in London." Besides, call Maurice where? It's not like he has a phone.

With the fake Darrin in the other room, Samantha tells the real Darrin, "You've got to help me get rid of you." A reasonable request, except Endora just agreed to pop Darrin's double out. She gives him the hiccups, prompting Maurice to fetch him a glass of water; when Maurice sees the real Darrin, Samantha says her husband is having a drink to combat a headache. Shouldn't mother and daughter have gotten their story straight before telling Maurice anything? And since when does Maurice engage in manual labor to obtain liquids?

Maurice zaps Darrin onto the Eiffel Tower, which is funny as long as you don't think about it too much – Darrin could have fallen to his death. Returning to the hotel, Darrin angrily recalls that Maurice has turned him into a monkey [that was Aunt Clara, in "Alias Darrin Stephens" (#37)], and a raven [that was Waldo, in "Samantha's Bad Day in Salem" (#207)]. Plus, if Darrin ever existed as "a pair of old galoshes," it was off-screen. The only animal Darrin sort of gets right is a donkey: Darrin was a mule in "Daddy Does His Thing" (#167), and a mule is the offspring of a male donkey and a female horse.

Endora turns Darrin into a statue while Maurice is looking into a mirror with his back turned. Can't he see what Endora is doing in its reflection? Maurice comically picks up a pineapple, thinking its Darrin, but otherwise, he finds Darrin-as-statue a bit too quickly.

Pressed by Samantha to apologize for shattering Darrin-as-statue, Maurice shrugs that he was goaded into "a slight transgression." He must have picked that up from Endora, who offered the half-hearted regret in "Solid Gold Mother-in-Law" (#120) and "Samantha's Wedding Present" (#141).

Darrin's headline, *Un marchant Americain escaled la Tour Eiffel*, is so close: it generally translates to "An American Businessman Climbs the Eiffel Tower," but *marchand* means "businessman," and the show probably meant *escalade* instead of *escaled*, which is closer to English than French. Maurice helps Darrin by coming up with a slogan for Europa Tours, but the warlock knows nothing about advertising outside of his brief exposure to it in "Daddy Comes for a Visit" (#180). By the by: in "Samantha and the Loch Ness Monster" (#231), Darrin's cousin, Robbie, mentioned a Europa Travel. Is Europa Tours the same company?

OH, MY STARS!

This episode is, for all intents and purposes, a Parisian version of "Just One Happy Family" (#10). That Maurice "wouldn't have it any other way" in regard to his perfect health comes from that episode [and "Daddy Does His Thing" (#167)], as do his shattered objects [see also "Naming Samantha's New Baby" (#176)]. Then there's his attempt to intimidate Endora, where she again responds, "Perhaps you frighten Samantha, but you certainly don't frighten me." And Endora threatens to move back in with Maurice, which she actually did do at the end of "Turn on the Old Charm" (#199).

In "Just One Happy Family" (#10), Maurice was furious to learn that Samantha had married a mortal. While his subsequent disintegration of his son-in-law was still tantamount to killing him – which is a little much for a sitcom – Maurice had a far more legitimate reason for his upset then. Here, Maurice is ready to pulverize Darrin because he didn't bring Samantha to visit while in London! Another reason Maurice's second destruction of Darrin doesn't work is because now, there are children involved – and no one ever mentions Tabitha and Adam, or how Darrin's disappearance will affect them. As a result, Maurice comes off as selfish, and just this side of evil, which can't be the intention.

SON OF A GUN!

"Don't worry, it's a dummy Darwin. Not too different from the real thing." – Endora to Samantha, as she zaps up a brown-nosing double for the purpose of placating Maurice.

There's an interesting moment between Maurice and Darrin's double – despite having just bullied his "son-in-law," Maurice takes his subservience to mean he's "broken the poor chap's spirit." He even goes so far as to tell Darrin, "It's all very well to appreciate your betters, but you mustn't tear yourself down in the process." It's very brief, and of course Maurice doesn't realize he isn't talking to the real Darrin, but, for one moment, Maurice shows his mortal son-in-law some unprecedented affection.

EPISODE 235

THE GHOST WHO MADE A SPECTRE OF HIMSELF

Airdate: October 27, 1971

The Tates join the Stephenses on their return trip to London, and Larry arranges for the foursome to spend the weekend at an English castle. Its duke explains that the grounds are haunted by Harry, the ghost of a womanizer. As a witch, Samantha asks the noisy poltergeist to quiet down so the guests can sleep, but the amorous Harry soon inhabits Darrin's body to be near her. Louise overhears Samantha and Harry-as-Darrin in heated conversation, assumes they're having a fight, and has Samantha spend the night in her room while Larry bunks with "Darrin."

The next morning, "Darrin" is annoyed by the duke's cavalier attitude toward the ghost; hoping to patch things up for the Stephenses, Louise tries talking to "Darrin" and is shocked when he comes on to her. Samantha realizes that the only way to get Harry out of Darrin's body is by summoning the ghost of the Duchess of Windermere, whose jealous husband killed Harry. After Harry eagerly moves on with the Duchess, a confused Darrin wonders why Louise wants Larry to punch him. Samantha quickly points out that Larry added too much work to their vacation, and that Darrin was just demonstrating what could happen if the stress continued; Larry accepts the explanation, and peace reigns over the Stephenses' final day in Europe.

GOOD!

Louise Tate appears infrequently enough that, when she becomes a major player in a story instead of just Larry's wife, it's a joy to behold. Her spunkier attitude of the last couple of seasons is intact: she tells Samantha to make Darrin apologize [after advising her to let Darrin stew in "Money Happy Returns" (#223)], and she shares an unexpected chemistry with "Darrin." [Good thing she doesn't remember kissing the real Darrin, after he changed back from being Larry's clone in "Double Tate" (#59).]

Larry's not much for self-awareness – he hasn't often talked about what makes him tick since admitting that losing accounts makes him feel rejected [see "Eat At Mario's (#35)]. So it's rather amazing when he owns his behavior by admitting that Louise can handle "Darrin's" ugly mood because "she's been handling mine for years." Think about it: given what a bear Larry has been to Darrin, imagine what Louise has had to put up with. Conversely, Louise coming to the conclusion that her traveling companions think someone has to be crazy to find her attractive is as humorous as Samantha's long-winded backpedaling

– and it's a great nod to the foursome's history when Samantha reminds them that business is "how we all got together in the first place."

Bewitched has covered all manner of supernatural situations in 235 episodes, but ghost inhabitation is a new one. Harry's voice coming out of Darrin – especially in front of the duke – is a highlight, and it's a neat twist when Harry reminds Samantha that hurting him will also hurt Darrin. There's even a brief look into the life of a ghost: the spirit of "Uncle Willie" Baker sported chains in "Tabatha's Cranky Spell" (#134), too, but here it's revealed that the accessory is only a mortal expectation, much like brooms are for witches.

WELL?

In "To Go or Not to Go, That is the Question" (#201), Larry resisted Darrin's choice of Salem as a vacation spot, exclaiming, "When I've just offered you London, Rome, Paris?" Now Darrin's been to all three. But, this European jaunt was not, as Samantha says, "a vacation with a little business on the side." In "How Not to Lose Your Head to King Henry VIII (Part I)" (#229), Samantha sighed at the thought of Larry calling, saying, "He knows we're on vacation" – work was never a factor. It's also curious that *now* the Stephenses come to London, after all the fuss about not having visited Maurice there in "Paris, Witches' Style" (#234). Maybe they saved money on airfares by flying in and out of the same city, but, looking at a map, their London-Inverness-Pisa-Rome-Paris-London route is a bit of a mess. However, the Stephenses were able to get the exact same hotel room for their second stay in London.

During his last vacation in "Darrin on a Pedestal" (#205), Darrin felt guilty for dumping the Barrows account in Larry's lap; now he feels guilty for dumping the Regal Silverware account in Larry's lap. Then, Larry shows up on the door – where has he been? Larry conducted business with Darrin in "Bewitched, Bothered, and Baldoni" (#233), but not "Paris, Witches' Style" (#234) – did he fly back to New York from Italy only to make another trip overseas? Larry ushers Louise in just as the Stephenses are scheduled to leave for the States; not very good planning. And who's with Jonathan? Interestingly, the last time the Tates were in London – in "My Grandson, the Warlock" (#40) – Louise unwittingly saw Maurice squiring baby Jonathan around the British capital.

Europe is a land of many cultures, influences, and architectural styles – so how come Whitsett Castle looks exactly the same as the museums of the Tower of London ["How Not to Lose Your Head to King Henry VIII" (#229-#230)] and Rome ["Bewitched, Bothered, and Baldoni" (#233)]? And Samantha just can't travel without being harassed: in "The Salem Saga" (#203), it was by an enchanted bedwarmer, Herbie-in-a-painting got Samantha into trouble in "How Not to Lose Your Head to King Henry VIII" (#229-#230), and now, it's Harry's turn.

Darrin pooh-poohs the idea of a ghost, but he should be way past being a nonbeliever, since a spirit moved into his living room in "McTavish" (#130). As for Harry, he doesn't know Samantha's a witch until she shows him – but, in "Tabatha's Cranky Spell" (#134), the ghost of Uncle Willie was aware of Samantha's identity right away. Harry tries to touch Samantha, but she passes through him with a usual fade-out sound effect, implying that she's using her powers to avoid him. Harry's a ghost. Samantha is corporeal. He'd pass through her regardless.

In "McTavish" (#130), Samantha commented, "If there's one thing I can't stand, it's a pushy ghost" – no wonder she's annoyed when Harry invades Darrin's body. But when he tries to grab her, she needlessly makes herself invisible and exits through the door when she could just pop out. Of course, Harry-as-Darrin has to follow her and involve the Tates, who wonder why "Darrin" refers to himself as a ghost, yet never question Samantha saying she can have the castle fall on him. And Larry may not remember that he and Darrin shared a bed once before, when they walked out on their wives in "Double Split" (#64).

Larry assures Samantha that Louise has a lot of experience handling marital tiffs. She should – the Tates went to a psychiatrist that taught them how to argue constructively in "I'd Rather Twitch Than Fight" (#84). When Louise wants Larry to punch Darrin for making a pass at her, he hesitates – however, he had no problem clocking Darrin for supposedly moving in on Louise in "That Was My Wife" (#31).

Both Harry and the Duchess of Windermere are depicted in castle portraits, looking to have lived in the 1800s. So how is it their "paintings" look like photographs? The Duchess wants Harry to get rid of "those silly chains," so he merely zaps them away. Question: how can ghosts of mortals possess powers they didn't have while living?

In "Tabatha's Cranky Spell" (#134), Uncle Willie said his descendants couldn't see his ghostly form because they didn't believe. Darrin must believe after all; not only can he detect Harry and the Duchess, he can see through them. Finally, Larry wants to look up a psychiatrist for Darrin, but it's not the first time: Larry sent Darrin in for some "head-shrinking jazz" in "No More Mr. Nice Guy" (#102).

OH, MY STARS!

The relationship between witches and ghosts is, of course, open to debate, as they're typically only considered real in movies and television. But Samantha having power over her spectral counterparts raises some interesting questions. First, Samantha threatens to zap Harry out of existence – can she even do that? Also, Harry exists as the ghost of a mortal, but does Samantha having to pop the Lady Windermere out of her painting mean she's only Samantha's creation? If not, where has she been since becoming a spirit? And Lady Windermere ought to recognize Harry right away instead of being confused – she was only having an affair with the man, which caused his death.

SON OF A GUN!

"I'm sorry, I forgot. You're in charge of that." – Larry to Louise, after she tells him not to pry.

EPISODE 236

TV OR NOT TV
Airdate: November 3, 1971

With their parents back from Europe, Tabitha and Adam enjoy an episode of *Steamboat Bill* – until Tabitha takes exception to the kiddie show's Punch and Judy puppets, who influence Adam to hit her arm. Tabitha exasperates her mother and father by popping in to the live show to lecture Punch and Judy, but the show's sponsor, McMann & Tate client Silverton, loves the addition and wants the "TV mystery girl" to perform with the puppets every day. When Larry and Silverton come to the house to discuss finding her, Darrin gets caught in his lie about her identity because Silverton recognizes Tabitha; he offers the excited girl a starring role on his show, much to the Stephenses' dismay.

But stardom loses its luster for Tabitha before she's even through rehearsals, so Samantha stealthily suggests that she purposely go up on her lines to discourage the show's director. Meanwhile, Samantha magically makes sure that Silverton's wife brings their actress daughter, Robin, to the studio. As Silverton becomes annoyed by Tabitha's apparent unprofessionalism, his wife and daughter arrive, and Samantha twitches him into casting Robin instead. That night, Tabitha is glad to hear that Robin got Punch to ease up on Judy, feeling that "there's too much hitting on TV."

GOOD!

The witchlet who started out only being able to levitate her "pretty pony" in "Nobody's Perfect" (#75) can now simply pop herself from one place to another like any adult witch – and Tabitha can even talk to her brother and mother through the television. Plus, it's hard to argue with Tabitha's logic: even by 1971, there was a lot of violence on TV; Adam following Punch's example and whacking Tabitha is an potent example of what millions of children are susceptible to learning from the medium.

While Samantha is asking her kids what they want for lunch, Steamboat Bill quickly cuts to a commercial for its sponsor, Silverton Toys, which is a clever and realistic touch. And surprise – Larry actually agrees with Darrin's desire to recast Tabitha, at least after Silverton denounces nepotism; that's what makes the twist of the client wanting to keep Tabitha on the show anyway because he places profit over nepotism all the more effective.

Tabitha's time on set is rather a slice of show biz life, portraying what cast and crew have to do to put a show together. The hair, make-up, and script people all stress about their particular departments, and a dress gets thrown over Tabitha's face while the director goes over line changes. He can even be seen lecturing Tabitha in the background as Samantha is magically convincing Silverton to use Robin.

WELL?

Samantha seems amused when Adam is enthralled by Punch hitting Judy. Shouldn't she back Tabitha up by telling her brother that domestic violence is not okay? The director of Steamboat Bill must have migrated from the set of The Sweetheart Parade [see "The Mother-in-Law of the Year" (#214)]: both show biz men are played by Robert Q. Lewis. This director wants to tell his analyst about Tabitha popping in – ironic, considering Lewis' photographer from "Nobody's Perfect" (#75) wanted to tell his analyst about Tabitha floating toys around his studio. Steamboat Bill is a live show, yet the on-set music seems to be piped in from nowhere, and there's no studio audience. As for the puppeteers, they can tell that Tabitha has zapped away Punch's slapper, despite being behind a curtain.

Tabitha wants to know why her mother does "stuff" sometimes; Samantha replies that she only uses witchcraft in emergencies. The video postcards of "Samantha and the Loch Ness Monster" (#231) and "Paris, Witches' Style" (#234) were emergencies? Samantha uses her powers in non-calamitous situations all the time – no wonder Tabitha thinks it's allowed. Tabitha also asks what a catastrophe is; maybe she was too young to remember Samantha using that word to describe her transformation of Amy in "I Don't Want to Be A Toad, I Want to Be A Butterfly" (#151).

Darrin lies that he had an usher pick a girl out of the audience to appear with Punch and Judy. It's doubtful Larry would believe Darrin took such a chance – what if the kid couldn't act? Plus, an ad man's only responsibility to a show is to come up with good commercials, not add content. At home, Darrin unfairly notes that Samantha "let" Tabitha pop into the studio; why would he accuse Samantha of complicity? He's right that Tabitha's lack of discipline regarding her powers could cause problems for her when she's older, but he and Samantha "let" their daughter get away with a great deal.

The Stephenses must have had a new doorbell put in while they were away in Europe, because the chimes sound different than they have for most of the run of the series. Silverton has a string installed in his suit so he can emulate a talking doll, but he stole the bit from Uncle Arthur, who used it first in "Samantha Loses Her Voice" (#150). And perhaps the Silvertons are a non-traditional family: John Gallaudet (Silverton) was 68 when this episode taped, while his "daughter," Kathleen Richards, was only twelve. Conversely, isn't Robin a little old to still be saying "Mommy?"

The giant's harp from "Samantha and the Beanstalk" (#171) seems to have a new place on the set of *Steamboat Bill*. Samantha tells Tabitha that "taking a break" means getting ready for the next scene – but how does Samantha know so much about show biz? This isn't information your typical suburban housewife has access to. And even if Tabitha weren't purposely forgetting her lines, she can hardly be blamed for not knowing them: the clock reads 11:30, and Tabitha only just got her script a couple of hours before, with tons of line changes since.

When Samantha tries to steer Silverton toward casting Robin, he shrugs that Robin isn't there. That's not insurmountable; all he has to do is call her. She's not in school, anyway – shouldn't she be? Only Tabitha seems to be exempt from public education. After Silverton casts Robin, Samantha tells his wife that she's taking Tabitha to the zoo, the museum, and the movies – all the activities she heard the woman planning for Robin while invisible. Why would Samantha taunt Mrs. Silverton like that? Hopefully, someone will sit with Adam while Samantha and Tabitha are out at all these places – come to think of it, who's with him while everyone's at the studio?

At the end of the episode, Tabitha says she could get Punch to stop hitting Judy completely if she were on the show – an odd thing for her to say, since she couldn't wait to get off it.

OH, MY STARS!

Samantha and Darrin are determined to keep Tabitha from *Steamboat Bill*, but they never really say why; if Tabitha legitimately wants to do the show, it seems strange that her parents would discourage it. Are they worried the girl will use witchcraft on live television? If so, that concern should be in the dialogue. Besides, Tabitha ought to be a sensation – she's already a proven commodity, having appeared on "Hoho the Clown" (#92), after which she had a toy modeled after her. How many kids still have Tabatha dolls in their rooms? You'd think Larry would be capitalizing on that.

The Stephenses get maneuvered into allowing Tabitha to appear on television, and all Samantha has to do to fix the situation is twitch Silverton's wife into bringing their daughter – who just happens to be an actress – down to the studio, then zap Silverton into replacing Tabitha with her. If Samantha always relied on solutions like that, episodes would only be five minutes long.

SON OF A GUN!

"Not only have I not laughed, chuckled, or smiled, but I'm actually in pain." – Darrin to Larry, sitting through an episode of *Steamboat Bill* for the benefit of the sponsor.

EPISODE 237

A PLAGUE ON MAURICE AND SAMANTHA
Airdate: November 10, 1971

Samantha has lost her powers, apparently permanently, because of her long-term exposure to mortals. Endora helps Samantha keep this news from a visiting Maurice by obliging his desire to see Samantha turn herself into a unicorn – but Darrin comes home wondering how Samantha made the transformation.

Learning the truth, the furious Maurice moves to turn Darrin into a lizard, only to discover he is now without witchcraft as well. Dr. Bombay pops in and tells Samantha she only has perimeridictamitis, an ordinary witch disease that Maurice contracted from welcoming Samantha with a kiss. Though Endora has trouble adjusting to her husband's powerlessness, Maurice views living like a mortal as a challenge and forces his way into accompanying Darrin to McMann & Tate.

While Samantha's attempt to procure Bombay's antitoxin gets her chased by the amorous apothecary, Maurice takes a shine to Betty, then takes a stab at coming up with a slogan for Benson's Chili Con Carne. Benson shoots down Darrin's ideas, but loves Maurice's more aristocratic concept. Samantha, having arrived with the antitoxin, covers when Maurice says he didn't need a spell to create his slogan. At home, Maurice kisses his sometime wife, but only so he can infect her and strip away her powers; however, he makes sure to share the cure with her before they vanish together.

GOOD!

As the episode starts with Samantha's power loss already in progress – a unique alternative to the usual formula of discovering her lack of witchcraft in the prologue – Endora rightly asks how Samantha could get in touch with Bombay without magic (answer: Esmeralda). Endora also exudes a surprising amount of compassion, telling her daughter she "might even learn to live with the disgrace" of her powerlessness; this is not a typical Endora reaction, especially where Darrin is involved.

When Darrin remains human after Maurice fails to turn him into a lizard, Endora cautiously taps Darrin's arm to make sure for herself. But the usually detached witch falls apart trying to brave her way through Maurice's reduction to mortal status, which gives her new comic dimension. Samantha's parents are always good for good-natured bickering, though this time, Maurice and Endora also offer a rare glimpse into the early relationship they must have had, with Maurice laying on the charm and Endora playing coy. Of course, he's only romantic to prank her into contracting perimeridictamitis, but saving half the antitoxin for her shows clear affection, and her cleaning "cooties" off the container shows she hasn't lost her sense of humor.

Over the years, episodes have shown Samantha, Endora, Serena, and even Uncle Arthur losing their powers, but never before has the formidable Maurice had to go without magic. Surprisingly, he embraces it, shaving with a razor and taking an interest in the way "the other half lives" – a terrific turnaround, considering Darrin tried the witchy life at Maurice's behest in "Daddy Comes for a Visit" (#180). Seeing Maurice in his trademark formal attire, the confused Larry asks him if he's going to a wedding, but it's Maurice's pitch for Benson's Chili Con Carne that shows him at his temporarily mortal best. Adding that he's "an authority on human foibles" is rather a nice throwback to the observations he used to make about mortals during the black-and-white seasons.

WELL?

As the episode opens, Dr. Bombay has already been there to examine Samantha and diagnose her with a permanent loss of powers. So why does Samantha pick that moment to try her witchcraft? Yes, the audience needs to learn something's wrong, but the experiment implies that Samantha is in denial about her ailment. She then tells Endora that Bombay's hexometer found nothing wrong with her – except the hexometer, introduced in "Samantha's Magic Potion" (#212), was designed to detect the presence of witchcraft, not make diagnoses. Facing a life without magic, Samantha determines, "Maybe I can adjust." Isn't that what she's spent the last seven years doing?

Samantha and Endora worry for Darrin's "continued existence" if Maurice finds out Samantha is powerless because of him. Considering Maurice just obliterated Darrin for failing to bring Samantha for a visit in "Paris, Witches' Style" (#234), that's a legitimate concern. Excusing his ailing driver, Maurice says, "Alas, poor Yorick; he isn't well." Those not familiar with Shakespeare may not know that Maurice is quoting *Hamlet*, which explains his "Danish prince" costume.

When Tabitha developed powers, she got a whole episode devoted to it ["Nobody's Perfect" (#75)]; this after the second half of Season Two included many is-she-or-isn't-she moments. Here, Maurice asks how Adam is coming along with his witchcraft, and Samantha replies, "Fine." That is the very first mention of Adam having powers, and quite the revelation to throw into a casual conversation. Maurice is perturbed to hear that Tabitha hasn't flown yet. Then what do you call Tabitha popping into a live broadcast in "TV or Not TV" (#236)? Are flying and popping two different skills? The metabolism of witches again comes into question as Maurice recalls Samantha being three when she first flew. If Esmeralda was a "girl" at 100 [see "Samantha's Not So Leaning Tower of Pisa" (#231)], then Samantha would still have been an infant at three.

Samantha and Endora just put one over on Maurice with a Darrin double in "Paris, Witches' Style" (#234); Maurice is unusually gullible, falling for their trickery again, when Endora turns Samantha into a polka-dotted unicorn in Maurice's line of sight. After she gets snagged, Samantha is told by Endora that "circumventing the truth is not the way around your father," despite the fact Endora just helped fake Maurice into thinking Samantha could still do witchcraft.

Learning that Samantha's power loss is related to long-term exposure to mortals, Maurice confesses that he wanted to turn Darrin into a "leaping lizard" when they first met. If so, it's an impulse he hid; during that first meeting in "Just One Happy Family" (#10), he simply disintegrated Darrin.

Bombay tells Samantha's parents that they must avoid direct contact with her, "and, above all, no one must kiss her." Granted, Endora doesn't kiss Samantha, but she certainly has direct contact with her daughter; why does she still have her powers? What about Tabitha, and, presumably, Adam?

Endora spends the night at the Stephenses without issue – amazing, given how hard Darrin fought her stay in "Allergic to Ancient Macedonian Dodo Birds" (#118), an episode where Endora herself was powerless. At breakfast, Maurice marvels at trying Samantha's very mortal meal of ham and eggs, but he's had ham before: he considered his ham-and-cheese sandwich a "gourmet lunch, mortal style" in "Samantha's Good News" (#168).

Maurice likes his secretaries – he practically goaded Endora into an "ectoplasmic interlocutory" over "amanuensis" Abigail Beecham in "Samantha's Good News" (#168), and here, he grooves on Betty. It appears Maurice has found a new calling, too: his chili slogan here is preceded by a slogan for Europa Tours in "Paris, Witches' Style" (#234). Darrin opens that door by telling Maurice to let him know if he thinks of a campaign idea for Benson. Is Larry okay with this strategy?

The apothecary examines Samantha to make sure Bombay's diagnosis of perimeridictamitis is correct – that would be like going to your pharmacist for a second opinion, and Samantha herself says that Bombay is the only one who treats witches. However, in "There's Gold in Them Thar Pills" (#107), Endora threatened to ditch Bombay for a Dr. Agrafor – is the aged apothecary Postlethwaite Agrafor? Apparently Esmeralda didn't warn Samantha he's a literal skirt-chaser after also being pursued by him in "Samantha's Lost Weekend" (#186).

Maurice invades Darrin's meeting, raving about Benson's chili. Where and how did he taste it? It's 1971; there's no microwave in the lunch room. Finally, when Darrin makes a sarcastic aside to Maurice in the tag, the warlock exclaims, "Darby!" But that's not what his lips are saying.

OH, MY STARS!

When Larry encounters Maurice, Darrin tells his friend/boss, "You know my father-in-law." Actually, Larry doesn't: despite unknowingly seeing Maurice on the streets of London [carrying his baby, in "My Grandson, the Warlock" (#40)], and standing with him in a hospital hallway admiring newborn Adam ["And Something Makes Four" (#175)], Larry has never been introduced to Maurice. As for Betty, maybe they're cheaper by the dozen: redhead Marcia Wallace ["Laugh, Clown, Laugh" (#227)] steps aside to make pretty blond Susan Hathaway the agency's Betty #12. One more, not so minor note: Bombay says perimeridictamitis is communicable through kisses or direct contact with an infected witch or warlock. So who did Samantha catch it from? Esmeralda?

SON OF A GUN!

"He seems to think that it's a manifestation of molecular mortal linkage, caused by a formation of polymers and certain hydrogen elements in a biological unity of two or more dominant species." – Samantha, telling Endora what Dr. Bombay attributes to the loss of her powers.

HANSEL AND GRETEL IN SAMANTHALAND
Airdate: November 17, 1971

EPISODE
238

As Tabitha reads *Hansel and Gretel* to Adam, she feels sorry for the starving siblings and zaps them out of their book so she can feed them. Samantha follows a leg of lamb that's floated out of the oven and discovers Hansel and Gretel, but no Tabitha, who has popped into the fairy tale to ask her new friends' father if they can spend the night. Concerned that Tabitha might encounter the evil witch of the story, Samantha follows her daughter into the book, leaving Darrin to explain Hansel and Gretel to the visiting Tates. Samantha finds the wicked witch's gingerbread house; the witch denies having seen Tabitha, but actually has her locked in a cage to take Hansel's place as a pie.

Learning from Darrin that Hansel and Gretel are co-stars in a play of Tabitha's, the Tates let the kids "go home," so Darrin searches the neighborhood for them. Meanwhile, Samantha talks to the woodcutter's wife and realizes she's been had by the wicked witch; she storms back to the gingerbread house and turns the witch into a fairy godmother until she agrees to let Tabitha go. Back in the real world, the cops pick Hansel and Gretel up for stealing ice cream, so Samantha zaps the kids out of their custody; later, at dinner, Samantha gets railroaded into actually putting on Tabitha's "play" when Louise insists on helping.

GOOD!

Samantha's right: Tabitha is old enough to read to Adam, and their big sister/little brother relationship gets warmer every time they appear. Tabitha also continues her pro-witch crusade of "Sisters At Heart" (#213) by letting Hansel and Gretel know that the witches of her world aren't mean, ugly, or old hags – and, although she's zapped herself into books before [see "Samantha and the Beanstalk" (#171)], she does so here with a never-before-seen confidence. Cautioned by Hansel that she doesn't know his father, Tabitha responds, "He doesn't know me."

Objects "float" on the show because there are strings or wires attached, manipulated from above the set with the ceiling removed. Here, the pan containing the leg of lamb floats over to the kitchen stairwell, then ducks *under* its ceiling and up the stairs; ordinarily, wires from above would make that effect impossible. To quote Hansel, "That's some trick!"

Of course, it's not a storybook without Bobo Lewis in it. Even though she also functioned as the giant's wife in "Samantha and the Beanstalk" (#171), her smart aleck comments again add spice; she even thinks her woodcutter husband is fooling around with Samantha, making her sardonic sassiness that much edgier.

WELL?

In "Be It Ever So Mortgaged" (#2), Samantha began wearing a diamond-studded heart necklace that was seen in almost every episode until "A Chance on Love" (#196), after which it disappeared. She wore no necklace all through Season Seven, or into this season – but now, a letter "S" has taken the place of the heart. Changing out jewelry is no big deal, but for Samantha to have worn her heart pendant for six seasons, there must have been some significance to it. Unfortunately, that significance was never mentioned; most likely, it was a present from Darrin shortly after their marriage, but having Samantha wear a new necklace and say why she took off the old one would have been a great nod to history.

Maybe Tabitha really is as undisciplined as Darrin made her out to be in "TV or Not TV" (#236): though she means well, she zaps Hansel and Gretel out of the book despite having been lectured about using witchcraft two episodes before. Perhaps her parents will consider Tabitha redeemed when they hear how she told Hansel and Gretel that she and Adam have been taught to share, a lesson Samantha passed on to them in "Samantha and the Antique Doll" (#228). Question: Samantha zaps herself to the same spot in the book that Tabitha does. So why is the picture zoomed out when Samantha gets there?

The fairy tale's gingerbread house is not big, and the witch can hear Samantha from inside. Wouldn't it stand to reason that the imprisoned Tabitha can, too? Why doesn't she yell for help? For that matter, the witch tells Samantha that she's "sick and tired of you snooping around" as if Samantha has made a pest of herself, despite the fact that she just arrived. The humor is that the witch's hearing is supposed to be bad, but Samantha's isn't much better – she leaves, and a few seconds later, the witch cackles with glee. With Tabitha missing, you'd think Samantha would rush right back.

Once again, the Tates come over without a word regarding Jonathan's whereabouts. And maybe Hansel and Gretel deserved their fate in the book, because they're very disobedient; no sooner than Darrin tells them to stay upstairs do they venture into the living room to meet Larry and Louise.

After realizing his fictional guests have left, Darrin yammers to the Tates that they just live down the street, though it's a long block. It's not the downtown core; it's just Morning Glory Circle. Besides, Darrin only has himself to blame: as Larry points out, Darrin repeatedly told the kids to go home, essentially tossing them into the street. That won't help when Samantha gets back and Tabitha can't zap Hansel and Gretel back into the book because they're gone.

When Samantha turns the wicked witch into a fairy godmother, her frilly outfit comes with the same wand Samantha inherited from "Mary, the Good Fairy" (#215). Then, back home, a shadow moves over Tabitha's bed before mother and daughter pop in. As for Hansel and Gretel, it's a wonder they ever got by in the forest: turned loose on the streets of Westport, the starving kids steal two gallons of ice cream instead of any actual food. Finally, Darrin's roped Samantha into getting involved with a play before, in "And Then I Wrote" (#45). Will Tabitha have to zap Hansel and Gretel back for a command performance, considering Louise is sold on staging the siblings?

OH, MY STARS!

When it comes to fairy tales, and interacting within them, anything goes, but the show seems to have some differing ideas from one episode to another. Samantha worriedly zaps herself into Hansel and Gretel's story to find Tabitha before the wicked witch does – sounds reasonable, except, in "Samantha and the Beanstalk" (#171), Endora dispassionately assured Darrin, "any child that can zap herself into a fairy tale can zap herself right out of it." Yet Tabitha just sits in the witch's cage waiting to become a pie. Once Miss Stephens finally threatens to use her powers, the witch laughs that "storybook witches are stronger than real little girl witches." That doesn't even make sense – in the aforementioned episode, Tabitha was able to subdue the storybook giant with one manual twitch.

Back in "A Prince of a Guy" (#129), Prince Charming had no idea that Sleeping Beauty was waiting for him, because Tabitha zapped him out of the middle of his book. Here, Hansel and Gretel know about the witch, the witch is expecting them, and the woodcutter's wife grouses about being talked into the story, when she shouldn't be aware there's anything but the story. The same goes for the witch, who laments that millions of little children will be disappointed by the presence of a fairy godmother. Was "A Prince of a Guy" (#129) wrong?

SON OF A GUN!

"You don't belong here. This is a restricted story – not that I'm prejudiced, or anything." – the wicked witch, protesting Samantha's presence in her fairy tale.

Already famous for giving the world Witchiepoo in NBC's 1969 kids' show *H.R. Pufnstuf* (which gained fame through repeated syndication in the '70s), Billie Hayes brings her unique brand of humorous villainy to *Bewitched*'s group of witches. In a nod to the fact that the witch in the real-life *Hansel and Gretel* story has vision problems, Hayes makes great use of impaired hearing, serving up marvelous modern asides in trying to get rid of Samantha. The best example: when Samantha asks who the witch's supper will be, and the witch smirks, "I don't give out recipes."

THE WARLOCK IN THE GRAY FLANNEL SUIT
Airdate: December 1, 1971

EPISODE
239

When Darrin can't take time off from work so Samantha can attend her cousin Panda's wedding, Endora coerces Alonzo, a hippie warlock, into infiltrating McMann & Tate to put Darrin out of a job. Alonzo casts a spell on Larry to make him go along with everything he says and presents some far-out ideas for the conservative Montecello Carpets account. Darrin catches on that there's witchcraft afoot, but Larry is so impressed by Alonzo that he curtly tells Darrin he should open his own agency. Darrin walks, and when Samantha can't get a hold of Endora, the Stephenses decide it's time to start Darrin Stephens Advertising.

Samantha transforms an empty office across the hall from McMann & Tate, filling it with furniture just as Larry heads in to have a look; Larry thinks Darrin has been planning to defect all along and drags Montecello Carpets client Cushman away to meet Alonzo. Samantha invisibly observes Cushman rejecting Alonzo's radical approach, and makes her witchy presence known when Alonzo gets ready to zap Cushman. Alonzo takes his spell off Larry and leaves, while Cushman visits Darrin's new office and green-lights his concepts. Larry comes crawling back, so Samantha tries to twitch him into making Darrin a partner, but Larry still manages to postpone the idea of McMann, Tate & Stephens.

GOOD!

This episode's title seems to paraphrase *The Man in the Gray Flannel Suit*, a 1955 book which became a 1956 movie, both of which are set in, of all places, Westport, Connecticut. (Did the show change its locale from Patterson, New York based on this movie about ad men?)

Interestingly, all the major players of this episode exhibit unexpected moments of compassion and understanding. Endora is sincere as she tells Darrin how important it is that Samantha attend Cousin Panda's wedding; Darrin responds by saying he wants Samantha to attend, but he's backlogged because they got just came home from Europe. [The Stephenses' Salem trip was forgotten as soon as they got home, so it's great continuity to mention that this vacation just wrapped in "The Ghost Who Made A Spectre of Himself" (#235).] As for Larry, the normally grouchy ad exec is under Alonzo's spell and still has the insight to tell Darrin, "I realize that you feel your position at McMann & Tate is being threatened by a talented newcomer." Even after Darrin opens his own agency, Larry wants to be friends, which is more than Darrin got the many times Larry fired him.

"Which one of you is McMann?" Alonzo's simple question reminds viewers that even Larry has a boss, one that hasn't been seen since "What Makes Darrin Run" (#191). And, for the first time, it's Larry who's under a spell, and getting some magically-induced karma in the process: the man who's looked down his nose at hippies since "Hippie, Hippie, Hooray" (#128) now tells Darrin, "It's not my fault if you don't dig the universal vibrations." Larry's near-worship of Alonzo is balanced out perfectly when later, with the spell off, he nearly bursts into tears realizing the absurdity of Alonzo's ideas.

WELL?

The Stephenses should remember that, whenever one of Samantha's many cousins has a wedding, Endora will make sure Samantha can attend. In "My Boss, the Teddy Bear" (#49), Endora asked Larry if Darrin could have time off. And, in "Your Witch Is Showing" (#20), Darrin thought Endora had sent Gideon Whitsett to "un-job" him, as she does with Alonzo here. Darrin even tells Endora, "You bet your sweet broomstick," which is what he said to Samantha regarding Gideon.

On the Stephenses' roof, Endora materializes Alonzo amid thunder and lightning. Not very subtle – any neighbor could see them up there, and surely Samantha would hear the rumbling and raise an eyebrow. Now, Endora's never had an issue with Serena being part of the hippie culture – so why does she think Alonzo looks disreputable?

A brunette Samantha Scott steps in as Betty #13, replacing the blond Betty of "A Plague on Maurice and Samantha" (#237) – but at least it's consistent when Darrin says that Larry's eyes light up at the mention of money; Larry replies, "Of course! I'm a greedy person," as he did in "How to Fail in Business With All Kinds of Help" (#104). Darrin should know right away a spell is being cast when Alonzo suddenly waves his arms for no perceptible reason, and Darrin's strangely averse to having someone else brainstorm slogans, considering he just had Maurice do the exact same thing in "A Plague on Maurice and Samantha" (#237).

After Samantha finds out Alonzo is working with Endora, she can't get her mother to appear. Why not just zap Endora to her? She produced Serena's friend Bruce in "Samantha and the Loch Ness Monster" (#231), and Endora just popped Alonzo in against his will earlier in the episode. Speaking of popping, no one reacts when Samantha suddenly appears in a crowded bar; she tells Darrin that Alonzo's magic only covers getting Larry to like his ideas, but she can't know that, and neither can Darrin, because he was frozen when Alonzo cast his spell.

When Cushman meets Samantha, he compliments Darrin on his choice of wives, causing her to pipe up, "I chose him." Interesting, but the events of "I, Darrin, Take This Witch, Samantha" (#1), suggest otherwise. Later, when Samantha makes herself "invisible" and kisses a befuddled Darrin [as she did in "Follow That Witch (Part II)" (#67)], Alonzo can "sense" and "feel" her in the room, but not see her, which is curious, since they're both witches. Alonzo doesn't know the other witch is Samantha – it could be Endora checking up on him – yet he inexplicably takes his spell off Larry anyway.

After Samantha counters Larry's disparaging comments about Darrin with complimentary ones [a tactic she also used in "Samantha and Darrin in Mexico City" (#170)], Cushman "flows over" to Darrin's new office and tells him they have a deal. Deals involve contracts. Darrin Stephens Advertising has no employees, nor the legal status to conduct business, not unless Samantha popped paperwork in with Darrin's new furniture.

As Larry stops by on his way home, Darrin tells him, "This isn't on your way home," and, when told Larry is making a gesture, Darrin replies, "I'm making one, too: goodbye." Darrin said both these things in "You're So Agreeable" (#183). Finally, under Samantha's twitch, Larry proposes making the agency McMann, Tate & Stephens, then backtracks and says one day "that's how it's going to read." Larry sidestepped promoting Darrin the same way, without witchcraft, in "Solid Gold Mother-in-Law" (#120).

OH, MY STARS!

Sophisticated witch Endora and groovy dude Alonzo obviously travel in different circles. So how do they know each other? And how would any warlock know as much about copywriting and advertising as Alonzo does? Plus, it's established that Samantha and Alonzo know each other, but Samantha doesn't react upon hearing that "some freak named Alonzo" is in Darrin's office. Shouldn't she recognize the name instantly and realize what Darrin is up against?

Samantha's pretty blatant with her witchcraft here, zapping Larry into giving Darrin a promotion, which Darrin would have railed against not that long ago – yet Larry still avoids making Darrin a partner. Samantha shrugs that "where Larry is concerned, even witchcraft has its limits." No mortal on this show has ever been able to will himself past the influence of witchcraft – and Samantha just forced Larry to say what she wanted in his previous scene. So how can he not do her bidding here?

SON OF A GUN!

"Mr. Tate! I think you dig my philosophy!" – Alonzo, when Larry grooves on slogans like "flurpity flurp."

Once again, Bernie Kopell is a reinvented revelation. It's hard to believe this bespectacled hippie was just a German creature hunter in "Samantha and the Loch Ness Monster" (#231) and the grizzled apothecary of "A Plague on Maurice and Samantha" (#237). Not to mention, warlock Alonzo has an interesting grasp on the logic of mortal advertising.

Darrin was told the agency should be McMann, Tate & Stephens as far back as "How to Fail in Business With All Kinds of Help" (#104), and he's squandered several chances to open his own agency since. For Samantha's part, she usually intervenes so Darrin will stay in Larry's employ; this time, when Darrin threatens to go into business for himself, Samantha replies, "Why don't you?" There's a certain satisfaction in seeing what could be as Samantha creates Darrin Stephens Advertising – and the anti-witchcraft Darrin "bends the rules" to let her create it. Larry deserves the comeuppance, and the next step would be letting Darrin run his own agency for a few episodes to really teach Larry a lesson.

THE EIGHT-YEAR ITCH WITCH
Airdate: December 8, 1971

Concerned when Darrin's briefcase is filled with pictures of pretty models, Endora summons Ophelia, a feline familiar she turns into a gorgeous woman to tempt Darrin. McMann & Tate has trouble finding a "cat girl" to appear at Tom Cat Tractors' sales convention until Ophelia slinks in, wowing Darrin, Larry, and Tom Cat's representative, Mr. Burkeholder. Ophelia aces her photo shoot, but when she hears Darrin won't be in attendance at the convention, she magically induces Larry and Burkeholder into insisting he fly to Albany with them. Darrin opts not to stay overnight and plans a romantic late dinner for Samantha, even making a request for babysitter Endora not to go away.

Ophelia is a hit in Albany, but as Darrin gets ready to leave, she calls using a disguised voice and lies that the airport is fogged in. When Ophelia stops by Darrin's hotel room for a drink, Darrin nervously asks Larry to join them; annoyed, Ophelia zaps Larry into taking a nap, but Samantha has figured out Endora's scheme and confronts her catty competition, daring her to do her worst – without witchcraft. As Samantha predicts, Darrin doesn't take Ophelia's bait and leaves for the airport, after which Samantha steps in again to keep Ophelia from working her wiles on Larry. When Darrin gets home, he finds Endora has apologized to him with a message written across the sky.

GOOD!

This episode provides an interesting insight into Larry's legendary browbeating: Samantha suggests that his ultimatums are "merely a cry for help." It adds dimension to dig into Larry's motivation in this way, and Samantha's comment is consistent with "Eat At Mario's" (#35), where Larry himself admitted he didn't like losing accounts because it makes him feel rejected.

"Brace yourself for a famous first from Darrin to you," Samantha prepares Endora, "*don't* go away." Considering the heavy animosity between the in-laws over the years, this moment is unexpected – and even touching.

If Julie Newmar looks "familiar," she should: she infuses Ophelia with the special brand of feline fatale she was famous for during her 1966-1967 run as Catwoman on ABC's *Batman*. She truly comes across as a cat personified, especially during her photo shoot – and, even though her Mohawk Airlines "representative" is purposely overdubbed (is that Bobo Lewis' voice?), Ophelia's mannerisms and facial expressions make the scene.

WELL?

This episode is fun as a standalone, but it's also a fusion of three previous installments. In "It Takes One to Know One" (#11), Endora recruited a seductress to work on Darrin, Samantha found headshots of models in her kitchen appliances, Larry magically fell asleep in the company of a gorgeous woman, and, like the Sarah Baker of that episode, Ophelia turns her attentions to Larry when her seduction of Darrin fails. In "Ling-Ling" (#21), Samantha transformed a feline to help Darrin with his Jewel of the East campaign; now Endora transforms Ophelia for the convenient Tom Cat Tractor account. Ophelia also shares Ling-Ling's preference for cream in favor of coffee, though she adds a reason: "I'm on a diet." And, in "Three Wishes" (#96), Darrin was forced to attend a convention alongside a woman Endora thought Darrin was fooling around with, complete with bad weather and a hotel room. It all still works, though you'd think everyone would feel as if they've lived it all before.

In "Solid Gold Mother-in-Law" (#120), Darrin questioned why Endora felt his marriage license was her deed to his house; this time he only asks the question in regard to his briefcase. Then, Endora asks if Samantha knows about the famed seven-year itch, apparently forgetting she claimed Darrin was getting that itch five years early in "The Catnapper" (#71), which also involved a kitty. Samantha retorts that she's been married eight years, despite the fact that the beginning of this season marked her seventh anniversary – and Sam's getting saucy: in "The Warlock in the Gray Flannel Suit" (#239), she said, "Darrin's a fast worker. I oughta know"; here, she declares, "He can do everything right. I oughta know."

Didn't Endora just try to tempt Darrin with another woman in "Bewitched, Bothered, and Baldoni" (#233)? Her incantation that begins *one-ri or-ri ickory ann* must be an all-purpose spell: Samantha used it trying to make Endora disappear in "I, Darrin, Take This Witch, Samantha" (#1), and again trying to restore Tabitha's humanized dolls in "Toys in Babeland" (#109). And clouds do get bigger, but somehow Endora also gets bigger once Ophelia-as-cat pops into her arms. Are the cloud's very visible wires part of its silver lining?

Tom Cat Tractors has likely been planning their sales convention for months – and McMann & Tate waits until the day of the event to cast their Cat Girl? Ophelia saves the day, but there would be paperwork and identification involved in hiring her to represent a client; even Darrin wants her references checked.

Endora hears Darrin saying he has to go to Albany, and that there's a woman involved. So how does she miss Darrin instructing Samantha to have her mother *not* go away? The rare nicety ought to induce Endora to fly straight to Ophelia and call her off.

"Stuck" in Albany, Darrin wants to rent a car and drive back, which Samantha says will take three hours (close: two-and-a-half). But he'd have to go to a rental agency first, so it would be well past 2:00 in the morning before he pulled into Westport – a little late for a candlelight supper, outside of a 24-hour diner. Darrin's original promise to be home by midnight was overly ambitious, anyway: his hour-long flight is scheduled for 11:00; as there's no airport in Westport, he'd have to fly into New York and drive home from there – so it would be at least 1:00 no matter how he got home.

Ophelia zaps up a room service waiter in the guise of Roger Lajoie, who just played the neighbor Darrin approached while looking for "Hansel and Gretel in Samanthaland" (#238). Endora tries to prove Darrin is lying about Albany's fog by claiming the city's weather is "fair and warmer, and clear" – yet this episode aired in December, and Albany would be hovering around the freezing mark.

Endora promises to stop bothering Darrin via skywriting, using the same message from "The Battle of Burning Oak" (#164); only now it's nighttime, the sky is dark blue instead of gray, and there's no broom involved. Plus, this time, "anyone who's looking" can see the writing, whereas the Stephenses weren't concerned about that before.

OH, MY STARS!

Either the Stephenses had a lot of first dates, or someone's not clear on exactly when it was. Previous first-date anniversaries took place in March ["The Crone of Cawdor" (#101)], January ["One Touch of Midas" (#157)], and April ["Mona Sammy" (#198)] – now the Stephenses mark it in December. Such anniversaries would be more meaningful if they happened the same time every year instead of getting tossed about the calendar.

Ophelia is a familiar, but *Bewitched* witches don't use them; only mortal Phyllis ever required one when she thought she had powers in "Samantha and the Antique Doll" (#228). Ophelia reminds Samantha that she can only follow orders, but she's not Endora's familiar, so whose is she? And how does Samantha know her? None of this is ever addressed.

The next question is, are familiars different from ordinary felines? The humanized Ophelia drinks alcohol and understands her convention duties, which seems beyond a cat's typical experience [not to mention, booze is toxic to a cat; see "Ling-Ling" (#21)]. Finally, it isn't clear whether familiars have powers of their own, but, assuming they do, can Samantha simply undo their magic? And Ophelia tugs at her ear, just like *Sabrina, the Teenage Witch* of comic book, cartoon, and television fame; Sabrina first appeared in print in 1962, followed by an animated series on CBS from 1971-1974, and a 1996-2003 live action series on ABC. Interestingly, Sabrina's world also contains a Witches' Council. Who got what from whom?

SON OF A GUN!

"If you don't know, it's too late to teach you." – Endora to Samantha, who asks just what act Darrin has been caught in with Ophelia.

THREE MEN AND A WITCH ON A HORSE
EPISODE 241
Airdate: December 15, 1971

After the Kravitzes win big at the horse races, Endora feels Darrin isn't brave enough to take such chances, so she zaps him with a gambling spell and installs a talking rocking horse in Tabitha's room to give him insider tips. Darrin is so distracted listening to his races during a business meeting that he irritates Larry and cautious client Spengler – but when Darrin wins a hefty chunk of change and cites an "unbeatable source," Larry and Spengler decide to place their own bets. Samantha insists that Darrin winning this way is against witch ethics; Endora responds by zapping the rocking horse into steering Darrin wrong so he'll lose the money.

Fearing the repercussions of Larry and Spengler also taking a dive, Samantha pops down to the track and turns Darrin's horse, Count of Valor, into a human being. Though the Count is sure he'll be retired once he throws the race, the stableman predicts the horse will have a more permanent fate. Larry and Spengler worry when Count of Valor trails, so Darrin lets them out of their bet – but the Count rallies, and Darrin is again a winner. With Endora's spell removed, the Stephenses' give their winnings to charity, while Larry returns to collect his and Spengler's cut for the good of the account – and himself.

GOOD!

This episode's title is most likely a reference to *Three Men on a Horse*, a 1935 Broadway play by George Abbott and John Cecil Holm that centers on man who can pick surefire race winners – it was made into a movie in 1936, and Endora mentions the title in a line of dialogue. It's also possible/probable that Darrin's story is equally inspired by *The Rocking Horse Winner*, in which a boy can predict outcomes by riding a hobby horse; D.H. Lawrence published the book in 1928, which was followed by a British film in 1949.

Endora's "watch out" warning, after which she generates an earthquake in the den, is a different method of heralding her arrival than she's used before. Other new elements include Endora dragging Darrin's car backwards into the driveway through witchcraft, and Samantha asking Tabitha to summon her troublemaking grandmama, since she knows Endora won't answer if she does the calling herself.

It's hard to argue with Endora in this episode: Darrin *does* stay on a treadmill. For some reason, the writers never have Larry promote Darrin, who seems destined to remain an ordinary account executive despite years of successful campaigns – Darrin even had a chance to start his own agency in "The Warlock in the Gray Flannel Suit" (#239), and he still returned to McMann & Tate. In her prejudice, Endora usually underestimates Darrin, but here, she is bang-on.

Hoke Howell is a source of horselaughs during his quick appearance as the humanized Count of Valor, who puts a unique spin on race horses by purposely plotting to be put out to pasture. And Scatman Crothers, the film veteran who was just breaking into television at this time, puts his special stamp on the Aqueduct stableman. Another nice touch is that the Aqueduct Race Track really is in New York City.

Having gotten some insight into why Larry coddles clients in "The Eight-Year Itch Witch" (#240), Larry himself adds to it here by surmising that "with a client, you can't always be rational." That certainly helps to explain Larry's often irrational business behavior.

WELL?

Samantha reports that Abner has bought Gladys a diamond ring with his horse race winnings. He's learning; he gifted her with a table saw in "My, What Big Ears You Have" (#121). Darrin backs a dark green car out of the driveway, as opposed to the light blue one that's shuttled him around of late. The car sports a New York license plate; given the show suddenly put Morning Glory Circle in Westport as of "Just A Kid Again" (#193), the car should have Connecticut plates. And so much for Endora's promises: she just told the whole neighborhood via skywriting that she wouldn't "bug What's-His-Name" anymore [see "The Eight-Year Itch Witch" (#240)], but she's right back at it again one episode later.

Darrin has asked Tabitha to pick horse race winners out of the newspaper before – though in "My Baby, the Tycoon" (#55), she was a newborn who could only randomly point. Later, a shadow appears over the upper left corner of Tabitha's door as Darrin leans down to talk to the hobby horse. Darrin questions why the talking toy wants him to get on his back, but he should be doing whatever the horse says without question, as he's under Endora's gambling spell. Then, finding Darrin in Tabitha's room, Samantha says she thought he left. Didn't she hear the front door as he came back in?

Larry tells client Spengler that all creative people "have a screw loose," an analysis he picked up from another client, H.B. Summers, in "The Phrase Is Familiar" (#187). And Endora delights in saying that Darrin's willingness to bet on races with advance information is proof of his lack of character – but he's only doing so because of her spell, so where's the lack of character?

Samantha's learned a lot about horse races since her last trip to the track in "The Horse's Mouth" (#61) – she spouts all manner of racing jargon as if it were second nature. After her frustrating conversation with the bespelled Darrin, Samantha slams the den door, but neither Larry nor Spengler react to it. Wouldn't the display of anger make one or both of them uneasy? Undeterred, Darrin reveals it's Saturday when he says the horse races are broadcast on TV. If it's the weekend, why are Darrin, Larry, and Spengler running around in suits and having business meetings? Darrin lets Samantha know they're going back downtown – he must mean downtown Westport, or else it's three men in a car driving almost an hour each way between Westport and Manhattan.

With the ad men and their client set to lose their investments thanks to Endora's misinformation, she reminds Samantha that they can't tamper with the future. That didn't seem to be an issue when, working with what they thought was tomorrow's newspaper, the Stephenses tried to keep Larry from breaking his leg in "Bewitched, Bothered, and Infuriated" (#105) – an episode in which Aunt Clara purposely looked for the next day's racing results so she could place a winning bet. But Samantha does have experience turning horses into people: she made a lady of Dallyrand back in "The Horse's Mouth" (#61), who came up from behind like Count of Valor does here, though at least "Dolly" was only trying to beat her sister, not a trip to the glue factory.

Samantha tries to calm Darrin at episode's end by reminding him that he won a lot of money thanks to Endora's spell. Didn't she just get through telling Endora he wasn't entitled to his winnings? When Larry comes around for his and Spengler's percentage, Samantha advocates giving it to them, but they're not entitled to the money, either – though it would be tough to tell them why. Larry thanks Samantha, telling her, "it's people like you that make me proud to be an American." He also displayed this kind of "patriotism" in "Samantha's Bad Day in Salem" (#207), after Samantha encouraged Darrin to ditch sightseeing in favor of helping Larry with an account.

OH, MY STARS!

This episode starts with Samantha telling Darrin about the money the Kravitzes won at the track. Where are Abner and Gladys these days? They have been witness to all manner of witchy events since "Be It Ever So Mortgaged" (#2), but they haven't appeared together since "Darrin Goes Ape" (#222), and Gladys last stopped by solo in Laugh, Clown, Laugh" (#227). The Kravitzes have always been an important part of the canvas, so it's odd they'd suddenly be missing from the proceedings without some sort of explanation; at least they get this off-screen mention.

SON OF A GUN!

"For your information, Durwood won $890. You tell me the last time that dimwit made that kind of money!" – Endora to Samantha, not knowing much about mortal economics, even for 1971.

Rules are made to be broken, but, on a television show, when rules are followed, it's a kind of glue that holds everything together. Samantha rails at Endora, asserting that predicting anything with magic "is strictly against witch ethics" – this aligns with "My Baby, the Tycoon" (#55), where Samantha told a suspicious Darrin that no witch would influence the stock market because they consider it unethical. It's commendable that all-powerful witches have a boundary like this in place – and even more so that the show chose this moment to reinforce it.

EPISODE
242
ADAM, WARLOCK OR WASHOUT?
Airdate: December 29, 1971

As her family enjoys a weekend breakfast, Samantha is asked to join Endora in the refrigerator for an emergency discussion about Adam, whose powers are slated to be tested that day. Samantha has trouble getting Darrin out of the house until Maurice arrives, anxious to put Adam through his paces. Maurice gives Adam some private coaching and is dismayed when his grandson can't perform the most elementary witchcraft, so he infuses the child with a portion of his own powers. During the test, Endora, Samantha, and the ladies of the testing committee are shocked when Adam floats around the room, an ability he is too young to exhibit.

Darrin gets zapped out of his golf game by Adam and is none too thrilled when Endora and the committee deem the boy a prodigy who should be taken away for decades of training. When the committee replaces Darrin's protests with dog barks, Samantha summons Maurice, who admits he gave his grandson an assist; upon hearing that Adam has no powers, the committee wants to dissolve Samantha's marriage. But Samantha, with Darrin's permission, encourages Adam to try levitating an object on his own, and everyone is thrilled when he does it. Satisfied, Maurice, Endora, and the committee take their leave, but the empowered Adam pops Samantha into the kitchen, earning him his first witchcraft-related talking-to about restraint.

GOOD!

Maurice is the driving force of this episode, and not just because he gives Adam powers. There's something heartwarming in the way he coaches the lad [it even parallels his tutoring Jonathan Tate in "My Grandson, the Warlock" (#40)], especially as Maurice only saw Adam as an infant during Season Six. Maurice's caustic interaction with his open-marriage wife is as satisfying as ever, and Tabitha even gets in on the fun in a rare scene with her grandpapa: when Maurice says his voice has a unique quality, Tabitha pipes up, "And it's so loud, too!" – a great way of referring to Maurice's booming theatricality.

Most of the ritualistic aspects of the show's witches were dropped as the show got into its second and third season, so it's intriguing that Samantha, Endora, Enchantra and Grimalda silently greet each other by touching their flattened hands together. Regarding Adam, Samantha explains to Darrin that witchcraft is a talent, and one whose suppression can be harmful; this has been cited as the cause of more than one of Samantha's witch diseases, and here she offers her best explanation on the subject to date; perhaps if she had put it in these terms when she first married Darrin, he wouldn't have been so difficult about the slightest use of witchcraft. The highlight of Samantha's wonderful mother-son test, however, is Darrin gently letting Adam know it's okay to try and float the shell himself – and Adam is able to, which is a game changer all around.

WELL?

This episode is less of a remake than a continuation of a concept explored in "Witches and Warlocks Are My Favorite Things" (#77): the testing of witch children. However, there's still plenty to compare and contrast: the Witches' Council is involved in Adam's test, but they weren't in Tabitha's, as the "noble eight" wasn't mentioned until "It's So Nice to Have A Spouse Around the House" (#145). Maurice called Tabitha's test "women's work," though he's on hand for Adam's – and, as with Tabitha, the committee wants to remove Adam for special training, but they never say where; at least Hagatha had a school when Tabitha was tested. Maurice again steps in on Samantha's behalf, though you'd think he'd be the first to support Adam's witchly education. And Darrin would remember Tabitha's testing, so Adam's shouldn't come as a surprise; he ought to be glad for the novelty of having his voice replaced with barking, since last time, it was bird chirps.

Samantha and Endora discuss Adam's upcoming testing in the refrigerator, with the door closed. Why is there light? Samantha is reminded that, so far, "Adam hasn't shown the least talent for witchcraft." Then was Samantha feeding Maurice a line when she told him Adam was doing "fine" with his witchcraft in "A Plague on Maurice and Samantha" (#237)?

Tabitha has had a new room since "Samantha's Old Salem Trip" (#208); here, it seems Adam has inherited her old one, except now it's blue instead of pink, and tile replaces the carpet. Question: why was Tabitha booted out of the room she had from birth to the end of Season Six? Maurice wants Adam to float the toy puppy across the room, but does the boy even understand what he's being asked to do? He's a toddler who has never exhibited witchcraft, and he's been shielded from it all his young life. Maurice does take news of Adam's apparent humanity extremely well, considering he slid into a martini-fueled depression when mistaken descendant Jonathan turned out to be mortal in "My Grandson, the Warlock" (#40). And Maurice's help must include wires, since they are visible both times Adam flies.

When Maurice flirts with Enchantra and Grimalda, Endora snarks that he's a hit with the "geriatric set." What does that make Endora? It's been peripherally suggested that Enchantra is Endora's sister [see "Witches and Warlocks Are My Favorite Things" (#77)]. In the refrigerator, Endora says that Adam has never performed witchcraft – yet she's surprised he can't levitate a ball. And why can't he? Did Maurice only give him the power to fly?

Some committee – they adjourn after Adam does a single trick. Wouldn't they want more comprehensive tests after seeing him float around the room? Endora watches her grandson "fly" with disbelief, looking at Maurice as if she knows he's up to something – then insists to Darrin that Adam needs special training. How does Endora go from smelling a rat to believing Adam is a prodigy?

Darrin storms out of the den and shoves his golf club at Samantha, who looks like she's going to hit him with it – that's quite a change from the Samantha that only lived to please Darrin in Season One (or, at least, a demonstration of how much things changed between 1964 and the early '70s).

Adam is overdubbed in all his scenes; something in the recording of young David Lawrence must have precipitated going back for fixer-uppers. Now, Maurice goes to a lot of trouble to make Adam look good to the committee – so why does he immediately confess that Adam is working off his power and has none of his own? It also makes little sense that the news of Adam's humanity would result in the committee deciding to dissolve the Stephenses' marriage. What is that supposed to fix? It won't give Adam powers, Tabitha's already an accomplished witch, and depriving both children of a parent is cruel in any case.

Adam goes a little crazy using his newfound powers: he zaps up a glass of milk, then pops Samantha into the kitchen. Maybe Adam *is* a prodigy: Tabitha was only able to levitate objects for two years, until she first transported Darrin in "It's Wishcraft" (#103). How can Adam, who's never zapped anything before this afternoon, relocate a full-grown witch? Was Samantha taken by surprise, which is how she implied one witch could have control over another in "Samantha's Pet Warlock" (#209)?

OH, MY STARS!

Television budgets have limits, and shows are also limited in terms of time, but that lightning bolt Maurice hits Adam with looks like something out of a 1950s B-movie. The sound effect indicating Adam's got the power would have worked just as well by itself.

In "Witches and Warlocks Are My Favorite Things" (#77), the testing committee was comprised of Endora, Aunt Clara, Hagatha, and Enchantra. Aunt Clara has been gone since the end of Season Four (the show never has explained her absence, and misses another opportunity to here); at least Endora provides some consistency. But Hagatha (and her school) are missing in action, while Enchantra, who hasn't been seen since "The Trial and Error of Aunt Clara" (#95), is portrayed here by Diana Chesney – the actress who played *Hagatha* in her first appearance ["Speak the Truth" (#50)]. And Grimalda is properly witchy, but there have been any number of other supernaturals introduced over the years whose reappearance would be great for continuity, instead of bringing in a stranger, and without indicating how she ties in to the canvas.

SON OF A GUN!

"Thank you, Endora, your charm is ageless. So sad about the rest of you." – Maurice, after his wife scoffs at his being escorted into the room by sexy slave girls.

SAMANTHA'S MAGIC SITTER
Airdate: January 5, 1972

EPISODE
243

The downhearted Esmeralda pops in as the Stephenses head out for a business dinner; upon hearing that Aunt Hagatha is already babysitting, Esmeralda becomes even more despondent. But when Darrin's client, Norton, can't find a sitter for his son, Esmeralda volunteers her services. Esmeralda defuses the mischievous Ralph with demonstrations of witchcraft, but her spells conjure up unintended results, such as a plush mountain lion turning into a real one. When Larry, the Stephenses, and the Nortons return, Samantha sees the lion prowling through the house and zaps it outside, changing it back into a toy before the Nortons see it. Esmeralda feels awful, but Samantha considers the subject closed.

The next day, the angry Mrs. Norton shows Samantha her son's black eye, administered by schoolmates who made fun of him for believing in witches. Norton pulls his account, but Samantha decides to explain Esmeralda's witchcraft by having her perform in a magic show; the Nortons refuse to come until Samantha performs a little magic of her own. Esmeralda predictably botches her simple mortal tricks, and the Nortons are convinced Esmeralda is a magician after her convincing "illusion" of turning Norton into a monkey. The experience leaves Esmeralda feeling confident again, although, when she pops out, she ends up in the refrigerator.

GOOD!

The kiddies have fun in this episode, but the grown-ups are great as grumps. When Larry suggests that the Stephens children are no different from other kids, Darrin retorts, "Wanna bet?" Samantha shuts Darrin down when he complains about Esmeralda's babysitting technique; has she just gotten tired of his grousing after seven years? Of course, the topper is Mrs. Norton, who, receiving an invitation from Samantha, smirks, "I'm going to tell you exactly what you can do with your party." That's tame by today's standards, but in 1972, it must have pushed an envelope or two.

A few rays of sunshine do poke through the cast's cantankerous clouds, however. Darrin's "I'll pretend I didn't hear that" gives Samantha tacit permission to magically induce the Nortons into attending Tabitha's "party," which is almost sweet – Darrin's even amused when Esmeralda shows up in his refrigerator. And Larry, who tries to blow Samantha off when she calls with her invitation, actually shows a soft spot when he hears the party is for Tabitha, admitting, "That's a hard one to turn down."

The magic show is, of course, the highlight of this episode, as Esmeralda adds her signature no-nos to ordinary tricks; turning Norton into a primate is the best of her monkeyshines.

WELL?

This episode is another of this season's witches' brews, combining elements from two previous outings. First, in "There's No Witch Like An Old Witch" (#27), babysitting breathed new life into a depressed Aunt

Clara, who also got in trouble for telling her charges she was a witch; Esmeralda surely got the idea to have a water pistol backfire in a naughty boy's face from her. Other Aunt Clara-isms, though not from that episode, include Esmeralda coming down the chimney, getting magically cleaned up by Samantha, and her subsequent compliment, "You're so talented." As for the magic show, Uncle Arthur blazed that trail in "A Bunny for Tabitha" (#178), where a different boy punched a different girl in the stomach, with the same "Where should I punch her?" response. Samantha should be more upset that it's her daughter getting socked this time, and Larry should be wondering where he's seen all this before. Finally, Esmeralda also uses Uncle Arthur's "bats in the belfry, pigs in a poke" spell, substituting "bunny" for "monkey."

Darrin admits that he hates business dinners – this after hundreds of them – stating that "wine, dine, and sign" is part of Larry's selling concept. Does this mean real-life advertising agencies don't actually use this method, and that it's just a conceit for the show? And it's always good to see Esmeralda, but why is she depressed again? She just had her confidence boosted by the amorous Count Bracini in "Samantha's Not So Leaning Tower of Pisa" (#231); has that romance fizzled already?

Norton tells his worried wife that their son, Ralph, is "sensitive" because of the way she fusses over him. That's old code-speak for "gay"; it's confounding that a show known for its tolerance lessons would throw in such a stereotype, which doesn't even advance the plot. Norton could be a retired cop, since Richard X. Slattery just played one five episodes prior [in "Hansel and Gretel in Samanthaland" (#238)], and Ralph's portrayer, Ricky Powell, was Tabitha's frenemy Sidney in "Mary, the Good Fairy" (#215).

Ralph gets a good soaking from Esmeralda's booby-trapped water pistol, yet, by the time Esmeralda's bear disappears less than two minutes later, his hair and pajamas are dry again. And how do both Ralph and Esmeralda miss a live mountain lion being in the room?

Samantha zaps at the advancing lion in the Nortons' line of sight. Why not remove it with a subtle twitch instead? Outside, Darrin very correctly comments that Samantha can't undo Esmeralda's spell; Samantha replies that she can circumvent Esmeralda's witchcraft by creating a stuffed version of an existing animal. Interesting, but then why didn't Samantha do that when Aunt Clara turned a plush, polka-dotted elephant into the real thing in "A Gazebo Never Forgets" (#89)? And how can Samantha zap up a toy lion that looks exactly like the one Ralph already has when she's never seen the original? Not to mention, the Norton family is going to wonder how it got outside from Ralph's room.

It seems very bad business for Norton to pull his account with McMann & Tate because of an employee's babysitter. Maybe there's more magic involved in Samantha's party than she's admitting to, because she gets a whole crowd of people there, despite not inviting anyone until the day of the event. As Esmeralda performs, Tabitha is surrounded by strange kids – where's her best friend, Lisa? [See "Sisters At Heart" (#213).] And, for all Larry's affection regarding Tabitha, why is his son Jonathan not in attendance? He hasn't been seen or mentioned since "Mixed Doubles" (#221). At least Adam is there.

Larry looks shocked in a wide shot after Esmeralda zaps up a goose, but, in his close-up, he's smiling and applauding. And it turns out that Norton-as-monkey can talk, though when Darrin was a monkey in "Alias Darrin Stephens" (#37), he could only communicate by writing notes. Incidentally, the kids must feel cheated – they went to a magic show, and the magician only performed four tricks.

First Norton tells Larry that Ralph is talking about witches and spells. Then Larry witnesses Norton turning into a monkey. Larry has twice been told Samantha is a witch [see "That Was My Wife" (#31) and "The Corsican Cousins" (#211)], and Darrin has consistently jumped to the defense of witches ["The Witches Are Out" (#7) and "To Trick-or-Treat or Not to Trick-or-Treat" (#177)] – does Larry need Endora to write it in the sky for him? He doesn't even react when Samantha talks about Hagatha, which is clearly not a mortal name.

In the previous installment, "Adam, Warlock or Washout?" (#242), Endora and Samantha conversed in the refrigerator. Here, Esmeralda accidentally pops into it; perhaps the show needed to reuse the set. Darrin asks Esmeralda if the light really goes out when the door closes – her answer should be no, since the light stayed on while Samantha and Endora talked.

OH, MY STARS!

Esmeralda's backstory loses cohesion in this episode. Larry and the Nortons refer to Esmeralda as Samantha's aunt, but Samantha didn't even meet her until "Samantha's Yoo-Hoo Maid" (#172). Esmeralda was brought on as domestic help – yet, when she appears, Darrin asks why she's there, and Samantha says she thought of Esmeralda right away when needing a sitter, but installed Aunt Hagatha instead. Isn't caring for Tabitha and Adam part of Esmeralda's job? Then, Esmeralda has a farewell party, when no one has announced that her services are no longer required; Samantha even contradicts Esmeralda's farewell by telling her to come back soon. Esmeralda's place on the canvas was unmistakable when she started, so it's peculiar the show is being so vague about it now.

SON OF A GUN!

"Now, you stop that! I'll tell you when to applaud!" – Esmeralda to the kids, who love her magic mistakes.

SAMANTHA IS EARTHBOUND
Airdate: January 15, 1972

EPISODE **244**

Sluggish Samantha can barely move, and when Darrin helps her to the couch, it collapses. Samantha summons Dr. Bombay, who determines she weighs over 500 pounds because of a condition called gravititis inflammitis. Bombay gives Samantha a cure, but, instead of normalizing her gravitational pull, it makes her float to the ceiling. Dr. Bombay pops off to procure an antidote while Samantha is forced to honor a commitment volunteering at charity bazaar, where she is expected to model in a fashion show. Darrin raises eyebrows wrapping his arms around Samantha to keep her on the ground, but when he steps away, Samantha has to sell the bolt of material she's using to weigh herself down; only a tree keeps her from floating away.

Darrin makes a scene trying to pull Samantha back to earth, annoying his client, Prescott, whose wife is running the charity event. The Prescott Shoes account is at risk until Samantha grabs a heavy urn to accessorize the Egyptian dress she's modeling; Darrin uses the image as a springboard for his new slogan, "With Prescott Shoes, you don't walk, you float." The Stephenses sneak home, but curious Prescott follows and arrives just in time to see Samantha hovering. Dr. Bombay, who has returned with his antidote, zaps up a ladder to fool Prescott; the client accepts that Samantha was able to float thanks to wires just as Bombay floats off the ground himself.

GOOD!

Gravititis inflammitis: a unique witch disease. It's impressive to see such an original story amid this season's revisited ones. And usually, Dr. Bombay's gone by the time his cures backfire – here, he's still around as Samantha's heaviness turns to lightness. Best of all, the show builds on the idea of witchcraft suppression being bad for witches; in "Adam, Warlock or Washout?" (#242), Samantha told Darrin that keeping their son from expressing his powers could cause him harm, and her own guilt feelings over using witchcraft made her sick in "Samantha's Psychic Pslip" (#225).

There are a couple of spiffy, blink-and-you-miss-them details in this episode: Mrs. Prescott can see into the Stephenses' living room because the curtains that usually flank the door are at the cleaners. It's never been obvious that those curtains existed until now: clever plot device. And, at the bazaar, as Darrin reaches over for a bolt of material to weigh Samantha down, she quietly, and without sound effect, starts to float until the bolt gingerly lands her in the chair.

WELL?

Everyone made a big show of Esmeralda saying farewell at the end of the preceding episode, "Samantha's Magic Sitter" (#243). So why are Tabitha and Adam at the park with her? At breakfast, Darrin tells Samantha she has "finally achieved the ultimate in housewifery" by volunteering at Mrs. Prescott's bazaar. Finally? Samantha volunteered for a hospital benefit as far back as "It's Magic" (#16). Then, Darrin mentions the necessity of "getting next to the client's wife." Phyllis advocated that in "Is It Magic or Imagination?" (#148), but Darrin never has, except under Endora's ambition spell of "What Makes Darrin Run" (#191). Besides, does Darrin think Samantha has been making client dinners for eight years for the fun of it?

Dr. Bombay pops in carrying his medical bag, but, in the next wide shot, the bag is suddenly on the coffee table. And the carpet covering the part of the floor that ultimately collapses slides as Bombay steps onto it. As for his *weebus warbus tootle flick* incantation, Aunt Clara uttered its intro to magically cater a party in "Allergic to Ancient Macedonian Dodo Birds" (#118), and Serena used the same to send Samantha for a 10,000-spell overhaul in "Samantha and the Troll" (#219).

Bombay zaps up a scale, telling Darrin it needs a penny to help pay for a witches' pension plan. That's cute, but in "Serena Stops the Show" (#192), Serena told Boyce and Hart's manager that money wasn't important in her circle. The scale indicates that Samantha weighs over 500 pounds (515, to be exact) – so how could Darrin possibly pick her up and carry her to the couch from the kitchen?

Samantha decides she wants a second opinion, but who is she going to get it from? In "A Plague on Maurice and Samantha" (#237), she confirmed that Bombay is "the only one who treats witches." If she's referring to "Dr. Calm Pewter," Bombay's electronic diagnosis machine, he didn't even use one until "Samantha's Magic Potion" (#212), and that was only developed to detect the presence of witchcraft. Amazingly, Bombay has the exact potion for gravititis inflammitis in his tiny little bag, but, when it doesn't work, he says he'll have the apothecary whip something up. Isn't the apothecary, as an equivalent to a mortal pharmacist, simply there to prepare Bombay's prescriptions?

How about that – Darrin doesn't have the slightest sniffle until he needs to keep Samantha on the ground; having the cold from the beginning would be a less manufactured plot development. Dozens of people witness Samantha's public floating, yet the Stephenses don't seem concerned, and the bazaar patrons go right back to browsing tables as if nothing happened. Then, Samantha tells Darrin to take a cab home to check on Bombay's progress. That's hardly necessary; Bombay can easily pop into the bazaar himself with any updates.

Samantha panics when Mrs. Brock wants to buy the material she's using to weigh herself down, but surely she could just hold on to the chair she's sitting in to stay grounded. Furthermore, her offer to take the bolt to Mrs. Brock's car isn't going to help; there may be nothing in the parking lot to stop Samantha from floating straight up into the sky after Mrs. Brock takes her purchase home.

When Darrin returns, Samantha gets his attention with a loud whisper, as if no one can see her tree-sitting. Darrin very pointlessly asks his wife, "How'd you get up there?" (even Samantha responds with, "You *are* kidding"), then climbs the tree and sits on the branch next to her. After the Prescotts leave in disdain, Darrin shimmies down the tree and pulls Samantha's leg to bring her back to earth. Why didn't he do that in the first place?

Darrin laments the idea of losing a $200,000 account, but considering the agency has handled accounts worth $2 million [in "Samantha the Bard" (#158)] and even $10 million [in "Toys in Babeland" (#109)], Prescott Shoes is chicken feed. And Darrin handles this account solo, without Larry, which rarely happens. Darrin manages to get Samantha into the makeshift backstage area so she can change into her Egyptian costume – aren't there other women back there who would be freaking out at the sight of a man? Once Samantha is on the runway, no one uses the nearby record player to cue up the Egyptian music she floats around to.

It feels like a wink-wink-nod-nod when the Stephenses tell Prescott that Samantha hovers because of invisible wires, since that's how the show pulls off the trick. Alas, they're not always invisible when Samantha hovers around the house – and, as Darrin helps her down the ladder, Dr. Bombay is already hooked up to wires that pull him off the ground later in the scene.

OH, MY STARS!

As the Stephenses fumble to explain Samantha's "invisible wires," Dr. Bombay suddenly rises into the air, presumably having contracted gravititis inflammitis himself. This might be amusing, but it's not possible: Bombay established that Samantha's ailment is the direct result of sublimating her magical instincts, which does not apply to the doctor. There is no indication that this disease is contagious, and even if Bombay were susceptible, catching it would make him crash through the floor – Samantha only started floating after he dispensed the initial cure.

SON OF A GUN!

"I can't help it. I really dig this chick!" – Darrin, explaining to Mrs. Prescott why he has a vise grip on his wife.

SERENA'S RICHCRAFT
Airdate: January 22, 1972

EPISODE
245

Serena surprises the Stephenses at the door, having taken a cab to the house – the Contessa Piranha has rendered Serena powerless in retaliation for romancing her fiancé. Serena becomes intrigued by Darrin's wealthy client, Harrison Woolcutt, who picks Darrin up in his helicopter. Deciding that money is a decent substitute for magic, Serena flirts with Harrison, over Darrin's objections. Harrison takes Serena out on his yacht and finds it endearing when Serena can pinpoint little-known details about famous paintings, but can't light a match, which generates more than a few sparks between them.

As Harrison is ignoring business with McMann & Tate in favor of seeing Serena, Samantha takes her place at their next lunch date so "Serena" can break things off. But Harrison, who won't take no for an answer, brings Larry and Darrin to the house to talk some sense into his wayward lady friend. Samantha summons the Contessa Piranha on Serena's behalf, and, when Piranha shows an interest in Harrison, Samantha twitches him into throwing Serena over for her. Avenged, Piranha restores Serena's powers, but Darrin is annoyed when Harrison again postpones business, not returning until days later and reporting that Piranha took him to the moon.

GOOD!

Serena's sultrier than ever, probably because the mores of 1970s television were changing. As she and Harrison discuss the chronology of Woolcutt Towers, she coos, "I'm not too young for any hotel." She also replies to his leading question about whether she travels with her husband by oozing, "Never with my husband." [True: Serena cavorted with married men in both "Samantha Goes South for a Spell" (#142) and "The Corsican Cousins" (#211).] Then, on the yacht, when Harrison tells Serena the chemistry between them is good, Serena ups the ante with, "And the biology isn't bad, either."

This episode adds some nice touches. Serena calls Larry "Cotton Top," which she hasn't since "Serena Stops the Show" (#192); then, when Samantha masquerades as Serena in the restaurant, Elizabeth Montgomery does a wonderful balancing act letting Samantha's mannerisms show through her free-wheeling "cousin." And, the yacht's chandelier sways, really evoking the feeling of being on the water.

Ellen Weston's Contessa Piranha is regal, a force to be reckoned with, and a great big flirt. The show even provides a royal bit of continuity by making Piranha the niece of the High Priestess Hepzibah. [See "To Go or Not to Go, That is the Question" (#201) and "Salem, Here We Come" (#202).] Piranha's so entertaining, she's one character it would be fun to go swimming with again.

WELL?

This episode has Season Eight music cues and sound effects, but there's a distinct feeling it was filmed for Season Seven and shelved until now. The giveaway? Samantha's sweatshirts and scarves, a look she sported toward the end of the previous season, and her hair, which recently has been flatter, straighter, and longer than the more bouffant style seen here. At any rate, in "Samantha's Secret Spell" (#179), Samantha told Darrin that Serena didn't know anything about cabs; now Serena manages to take one after getting zapped onto the freeway by the Contessa. And, in a case of literally seeing double, the Stephenses open their home to Elizabeth Montgomery's stand-in, whose face is visible in the doorway.

This is the second time this season Serena's been stripped of her powers, though at least now it's not because she's a mermaid [see "Samantha and the Loch Ness Monster" (#231)]. Samantha compassionately tells Darrin that Serena will need "mortal basic training," forgetting that Serena was already schooled in that subject in "Samantha's Power Failure" (#165).

Outside, Darrin's light blue car is back, reclaiming its place from the dark green one Endora "towed" in "Three Men and a Witch on a Horse" (#241). Inside, Samantha invites her powerless cousin to stay – moments after Darrin told her, "anywhere but here." And since when does Darrin plagiarize slogans? In "Paris, Witches' Style" (#234)], Maurice created "Europa Tours towers above them all," which Darrin repackages here as "Woolcutt Towers: above the rest." Larry then asks Harrison if he'd like a drink before they start discussing the campaign – which they already have, because Darrin just pitched his concept.

Serena excitedly introduces herself to Harrison as Samantha's younger cousin. This runs contrary to the fact that Serena has been calling Samantha "little cousin" since "Marriage, Witches' Style" (#161). And Darrin ought to hold his tongue when he's hosting a house full of mortals: Serena walks in as Darrin decries his house becoming "a home for delinquent witches," but it could easily have been Larry.

Has Serena always known so much about art? She's never shown the slightest interest in painters before. And surely even a witch knows how to take a napkin out of its holder; Serena's not that helpless. She apparently dallied with Vincent Van Gogh, too, so why was the idea of dating a mortal so novel in "Marriage, Witches' Style" (#161)?

Darrin's definitely getting more permissive about witchcraft – in "Samantha's Magic Sitter" (#243), he purposely turned a blind eye to magically solving the problem of Esmeralda and the Nortons; here, when Samantha suggests taking Serena's place to deflect Harrison, Darrin declares, "I love it." One hole in her scheme: who's taking care of Tabitha and Adam while Samantha's with Harrison? Darrin's at work, and Serena is in a state of suspended animation upstairs.

In a bit of a role reversal, Larry encourages Harrison's pursuit of Serena, while Darrin is upset about the pursuit getting in the way of business. In "A Majority of Two" (#136), Larry was frustrated by client Mishimoto's courting of Aunt Clara, and more recently, he was annoyed that Count Bracini was wooing Esmeralda ["Samantha's Not So Leaning Tower of Pisa" (#231)].

Harrison points out that Serena can't dial a telephone, but she must be faking, because she very expertly used a pay phone in "Marriage, Witches' Style" (#161). Harrison also marvels that Serena "doesn't care about my loot," apparently missing the fact that hoping he owns the originals of priceless artwork and inquiring into his status as one of the world's ten richest men indicates otherwise.

The Contessa Piranha appears as a witch of great power and stature. So why is she doing her nails by hand as if she were a teenage mortal girl? As for Serena, Samantha apparently freezes her mid-laugh; but it's never mentioned what she found so funny. Serena replies to Samantha's question as soon as she's unfrozen, so the implication is that Serena could hear her – odd, considering that mortals in the deep freeze hear nothing and lose time while in that state. By the way, Larry and Harrison are mortals: wouldn't they find a name like Piranha strange?

Piranha doesn't know who hit Harrison with a love spell, despite Samantha twitching him in her line of sight; she also doesn't seem to care that his affections are brought about by magic. Question: when Harrison comes back from his lunar lovefest, does he still have Samantha's spell on him, and, if not, when did she remove it?

OH, MY STARS!

This episode is not necessarily a remake of two other episodes, but it does liberally cut-and-paste from both. In "Marriage, Witches' Style" (#161), Serena's favorite wine was Château Lafite Rothschild, 1923 – here, she sips its 1945 vintage. Serena also misconstrues a matchbook's "close cover before striking" instruction, which Franklyn, her supposedly mortal date in that episode, also had trouble with; Uncle Arthur later made the same mistake of pounding on matches in "Samantha's Power Failure" (#165). Then there's "A Chance on Love" (#196): Bernie Kuby appears then and now as a waiter with a customer who becomes confused by his date disappearing, and the Contessa Piranha pimps Serena's style by wanting Harrison to take her on an evening of "dancing, merrymaking, et cetera," a line Serena used on then-date George Dinsdale. Finally, Dinsdale and Harrison, played by accomplished singers Jack Cassidy and Peter Lawford, respectively, both croon a line from '50s standard *Fly Me to the Moon*, then speak of how they were spirited away to the satellite. You'd think the Stephenses would look at each other and wonder why so many of Serena's beaus like this song.

SON OF A GUN!

"I mean, there's not much difference between witchcraft and richcraft – except maybe you fly a little slower." – Serena, telling Samantha why diamonds are also a witch's best friend.

EPISODE **246**

SAMANTHA ON THIN ICE
Airdate: January 29, 1972

Tabitha is excited to receive an invitation to an ice skating party until Samantha reminds her that she doesn't know how to skate. After Darrin and Endora bicker over whether Tabitha should learn by witchcraft, Darrin challenges Samantha to take mortal lessons alongside Tabitha to set an example. Samantha accepts, and, while she's fending off advances from the instructor, Endora turns the struggling Tabitha into a wunderkind skater. Samantha rushes Tabitha home, but they are followed by the egomaniacal Billy "Blades" Bookoltzer, a former Olympic skater who wants Tabitha to train for the Games. Cornered by Blades' obsessiveness, the Stephenses have no choice but to take Tabitha to the rink the next day for a private audition.

With Endora's spell removed, Samantha assures Darrin that Tabitha will easily discourage Blades; however, Endora pops into the rink and reinstates her granddaughter's superior ability for the instructor. Samantha begs Endora not to let Tabitha become a public figure with no time for her family, so Endora acquiesces; when Blades arrives, Tabitha again stumbles like an amateur. Peeved when the Olympian calls Tabitha a klutz, Endora makes Blades and the instructor fall all over themselves, then knocks Darrin off his feet for insulting her, which makes Samantha laugh.

GOOD!

It's actually quite novel that Darrin stays with Adam while Samantha and Tabitha are out at the skating rink. The Stephens boys don't seem to spend much father-son time together; that they do here helps deepen that relationship. And, as Endora realizes her interference is about to make Tabitha a media darling, she exudes a palpable warmth in removing her spell that's not always evident with the formidable witch.

Billy "Blades" Bookoltzer, under the command of portrayer Alan Oppenheimer, is severe and melodramatic – and just wouldn't work any other way. He steals the episode as he badgers the Stephenses into letting Tabitha skate for the sake of God and country. Billy's blazer even carries the emblem for the 1960 Olympic Games in Squaw Valley, California – where the nameless instructor, real-life Olympic skater Bob Paul, won a gold medal for Canada.

WELL?

Is Endora letting Darrin know her offer still stands? She suggests making him "a carrot growing in a field of rabbits," which she also proposed in "Samantha the Sculptress" (#159). When Tabitha announces the ice skating party, the Stephenses' only concern is that she can't skate – they must be past not wanting her around mortal children for fear she'd use magic in front of them [see "Playmates" (#133)]. Then, Endora reminisces that Samantha qualified for the Cosmic Icecapades at three – but witches don't age like mortals, not if Esmeralda was a girl at 100 [see "Samantha's Not So Leaning Tower of Pisa" (#231)].

Samantha meets Darrin's challenge to learn skating the mortal way by saying, "If I can't, I will be more careful in the future about accepting challenges"; this was how she reacted to piano lessons in "Samantha on the Keyboard" (#143).

The term "sexual harassment" was relatively new in the 1970s, but it certainly applies here: Samantha tells the instructor she's married, and he still hits on her. She could have him fired faster than she could twitch herself into a crone, which she does here without moving her nose; there's only the sound effect. Endora's spell packs a punch, too – when the fallen Tabitha stands up and skates away, she's considerably taller. Of course, Erin Murphy is doubled by a professional skater, as Elizabeth Montgomery is; freeze "Samantha" while she's spinning, and her double's face can be seen.

As Tabitha magically glides over the ice, Samantha calls for her daughter to "stop that" – rather hypocritical, considering Samantha did the exact same thing just moments before. Samantha also wants Tabitha to cease "in spite of your grandmama," but she can't know for sure Endora is involved; maybe Tabitha watched Samantha-as-crone on the ice and decided it was okay for her, too. At home, Tabitha tells Darrin, "we both kept our promises," meaning they skated mortally, but it's not like her to tell bald-faced lies. Similarly, Samantha holds up two fingers as if she's going to zap Darrin when he laughs at her bruised bum – and she's never threatened her husband with witchcraft before.

Both Blades and the instructor gush over Tabitha's abilities, yet show no interest in Samantha's apparently expert skating – which Darrin somehow never finds out about. Blades pushing for Tabitha to compete in the Olympics times out well, as this episode aired just five days before the start of the 1972 Winter Games. But Blades should specify that he wants to groom Tabitha for the 1976 event; surely he's not talking about Tabitha going for the gold in less than a week. Besides, this is all a mirror of Johann Sebastian Monroe viewing Tabitha as a potential concert pianist in "Samantha on the Keyboard" (#143).

Samantha might have missed spotting Endora in the rink the first day, when it was jammed with people, but the second day, with the arena empty, the Stephenses should be able to see and hear Endora talking to herself. Endora swears her spell isn't on Tabitha, and Samantha deduces that it's on Tabitha's feet – another parallel to "Samantha on the Keyboard" (#143), in which Endora witched Tabitha's fingers. How can Endora cast spells on Tabitha at all? Is Tabitha simply susceptible to zapping because she's only half-witch?

In "Baby's First Paragraph" (#62), Endora caused a media sensation by making it appear that then-newborn Tabitha could talk, and Samantha warned that Tabitha would end up belonging to her public; Samantha makes the same argument here. Tabitha may be destined for celebrity, though: not only is her "talking" still in newspaper archives, she was the poster girl for Robbins Transmissions ["Nobody's Perfect" (#75)], and she's flirted with television stardom twice – in "Hoho the Clown" (#92), where a doll was named after her that's probably still in millions of homes, and, more recently, she was a champion for non-violence in "TV or Not TV" (#236).

Endora's counterspell includes the phrase, "you'll find you don't know how to skate." Given how wordings in spells often have literal results, does this mean Tabitha just won't know how in the present, or is the lack of knowledge permanent? Then, Endora is quizzical when Blades calls Tabitha a klutz, but she's heard the word before: that's how Samantha described the reigning monarch of "How Not to Lose Your Head to Henry VIII (Part II)" (#230). Finally, Samantha bursts out laughing when Endora makes Darrin fall on the ice, capping an episode in which she has shown an unusual amount of attitude.

OH, MY STARS!

Admittedly, the skating instructor has some retribution coming for making disparaging comments about witches – but what an affront to continuity! Samantha once turned herself into a crone to spook an amorous magazine salesman [in "Mrs. Stephens, Where Are You?" (#160)], but at least that was in the privacy of her own home; here, she parades the stereotype witch image in front of a skating rink full of mortals. Endora merely smiles that Tabitha's mama is a show-off – yet, in "To Trick-or-Treat or Not to Trick-or-Treat" (#177), she was "incensed" by the idea of Samantha "depicting your own kind as toothless old hags" – she even replaced crone witches on tourist signs with beautiful witches in "The Salem Saga" (#203). So how can Endora be okay with this misrepresentation? And what about the Witches' Council, who would sooner zap Samantha off the ice than let her malign her brethren in such a way? After Samantha becomes herself again, she continues to flaunt her skating abilities and publicly reveals that she has two different faces. It's just not like Samantha to make a magical spectacle of herself, and she already had her powers taken away for displaying them to mortals in "Samantha's Secret Is Discovered" (#188). This one-minute sequence shockingly reinforces the stereotype the show has spent nearly eight years trying to smash.

SON OF A GUN!

"I learned my important lesson someplace else." – Samantha, telling Darrin that Tabitha got the message upstairs while hers was delivered downstairs.

EPISODE 247

SERENA'S YOUTH PILL
Airdate: February 5, 1972

Serena is babysitting the kids when Larry stops by; Serena flirts with him, but when he refers to himself as a "senior citizen," she offers him Vitamin V, which she promises will make him feel younger. Louise is shocked to see her husband come home sporting the red hair he had in his youth; Larry credits his new look to the vitamin, and tells the Stephenses he wants to market it. Samantha worries that Serena might have given him a youth pill, and, the next day, Serena confirms it, while Louise rushes over reporting that Larry romanced her 'til all hours of the morning and searched the dial for a television show that's long since been off the air.

Indeed, when Darrin gets to the office, Larry is reliving their first meeting from 1961. By the time Samantha arrives, Larry has reverted to a college kid who only remembers the '50s; the Stephenses bring the chronologically-challenged Larry to the house, where he turns into a boy who doesn't know what television is. Samantha has to get Child Larry past Louise to take him upstairs, where Serena has an antidote that makes Larry the proper age again. At dinner, Darrin shows Larry an agreement from "1961" that he signed under the influence of the pill: it states Darrin is to become a vice president after two years with McMann & Tate. Larry, however, claims that the statute of limitations has run out, and Darrin is kept in his usual position.

GOOD!

Larry and Serena have never been left alone together before [his time with Serena-as-Samantha in "Double, Double...Toil and Trouble" (#111) doesn't count], so their interesting chemistry is an unexpected surprise. Larry really does seem to come alive as he cautions Serena not to turn him into "the red devil of yesteryear" – considering his freewheeling attitude toward women over the years, young Lawrence Tate must have been a heartbreaker. Darrin's "1961" meeting with Larry offers a glimpse of their pre-show lives, and if Larry hasn't evolved, Darrin has – he actually apologizes to Serena, which is not something he does every day.

Louise mentions that she and Larry have been married over 20 years. She's right: in "...And Something Makes Three" (#12), the Tates had already been married 16 years, so, by now, they've celebrated their 23rd, or even 24th anniversary. Louise's meltdown over Larry's revitalization is a lot of fun, and she proves that she knows her husband when she observes, "Larry, when you get those dollar signs in your eyes, no amount of warning will help."

When the Stephenses walk Collegiate Larry to their doorstep, he lags behind out of frame – suddenly his voice changes, Samantha and Darrin turn around, and the camera pulls back to show Child Larry; this is all done in one shot. Another masterful effect happens when Samantha reverse tailors Child Larry's overgrown clothes: little Ted Foulkes is placed into the exact same position after his change, and he doesn't move a muscle.

WELL?

Serena babysits because both Samantha and Darrin are out, meaning there is no car in their driveway – yet Larry rings the bell as if somebody's home. He inexplicably goes around back and finds Serena, who wonders if he knows how his baby blue eyes "kind of turn me on." He should – she made the same confession in "Serena Stops the Show" (#192). Likewise, she asks him, "Did I ever tell you that I'm simply wild about gray hair?" Answer: yes, but as Samantha, in "Double, Double...Toil and Trouble" (#111).

Season Seven was full of mirrors that conveniently appeared in the foyer when someone needed to appraise themselves. There have been none this season, until now, as a mirror replaces the Stephenses' painting for the first time since "Samantha's Magic Mirror" (#226). After taking his Vitamin V, Larry borrows Adam's unfortunate B-movie lightning bolt from "Adam, Warlock or Washout?" (#242) to indicate that the pill is working. Then, Larry pulls up to his house – really the Nortons' house from "Samantha's Magic Sitter" (#243) – and walks in the front door, which was on the other side of his living room throughout Seasons Five, Six, and Seven.

Serena seems to have gotten the only existing issue of *Harpies' Bizarre* from Endora, who read it in "Be It Ever So Mortgaged" (#2), "Mother Meets What's-His-Name" (#4), and "How Not to Lose Your Head to King Henry VIII (Part I)" (#229). Elizabeth Montgomery's stand-in "plays" Samantha when Serena's face is visible, but listen carefully: that's not Samantha's voice calling out for her cousin when the Stephenses return home, nor is it Samantha telling Child Larry, "I hope so."

Are the curtains that flank the Stephenses' front door at the cleaners again? They were gone in "Samantha Is Earthbound" (#244), then back in their usual place after that; here, Larry peeks through windows that are curtainless. Maybe Larry and Darrin don't get déjà vu from their "piece of the action" exchange because they've never had it in the real world: the co-workers spoke the same words during Endora's alternate reality of "What Every Young Man Should Know" (#72), and the dream Samantha fed Darrin in "I Confess" (#135). The next morning, after Darrin blames Samantha for Serena's antics, his subsequent kiss is met with an uncharacteristic growl – strangely, her hostility from "Samantha on Thin Ice" (#246) continues.

The Tates had to have left Jonathan alone in the middle of the night to go traipsing off to Lover's Lane. And Jonathan must have noticed his father's different appearance; for that matter, since Jonathan was born in 1965, did Larry even recognize him? Jonathan's experience is never addressed, but the Tates dance until 2:00 in the morning – and the wee small ones are a little late for Larry to flip the dials for *The Jack Paar Show* (which ran from 1957-1962 on NBC); even by 1972, he'd only find a test pattern. The next day, Larry utters nautical terms and tells Darrin he was in the Navy, although, in "Oedipus Hex" (#85), Larry said he served in the Army. Does anyone else at McMann & Tate react to Larry's red hair, or question his '60s references?

It requires a little suspension of disbelief to buy that Larry just happens to be reliving the day Darrin started working for him, which he claims is October 15, 1961. However, in "I Remember You...Sometimes" (#97), Darrin stated that he'd given Louise a birthday present eight years earlier, which meant Darrin was probably at McMann & Tate by 1959. Ten episodes later, in "There's Gold in Them Thar Pills" (#107), Larry commented that Darrin had been with McMann & Tate three years, placing their meeting in 1964. Regardless of the date of their first encounter, Larry tells Darrin he'll become a first vice president if he stays with the company two years. That makes sense, when you consider that the show's pilot, "I, Darrin, Take This Witch, Samantha" (#1), which aired in 1964, showed Darrin listed as a vice president – but he hasn't held the position since, so what happened to Larry's actual 1961 offer?

Busy ad exec Larry must have a calendar in his office somewhere; does he not once refer to it and see that it's 1972? He might be living in the past, but Samantha is, too, because she wears the same knit dress two days in a row. Soon, Collegiate Larry is in Mr. Tate's office; do any of his associates wonder why? Perhaps not – Louise, who is sitting for Tabitha and Adam with no Jonathan in sight, never wonders why Serena is suddenly upstairs, or how she got past her.

Back to normal, Larry concedes that Samantha tried to warn him about Vitamin V's potential side effects. The last time he took a mysterious drug in the Stephens house was in "There's Gold in Them Thar Pills" (#107), after which he emitted a high, screechy voice thanks to "Dr. Bombay's Cold Bombs." That's not something a person forgets; surely he would have thought twice about even suggesting Vitamin V be marketed after that debacle.

OH, MY STARS!

What exactly is Vitamin V? Samantha describes it as "sort of a youth pill," but witches live hundreds, even thousands of years, owing to their natural metabolisms; they wouldn't need a pill to stay young. And by the way, why does Larry never promote Darrin? He gets out of his underling's sudden Machiavellian attempt to get ahead by saying the statute of limitations has run out on the paper he signed – but, according to this episode, Darrin has busted his tail for Larry and the agency for over 10 years, only to be kept in the same job all that time. Darrin deserves to advance – wouldn't it provide new story opportunities for everyone if he got a chance to move up in the world?

SON OF A GUN!

"It's radio with pictures." – Samantha, trying to explain television to Child Larry.

Larry doesn't often get an episode devoted to him, but David White hits the ground running with this chance to show another side to his straight man ad man. And both Collegiate and Child Larrys bring proper befuddlement to the proceedings.

After the Board of Education demands that Tabitha be enrolled in school, Samantha grudgingly registers her daughter. Tabitha immediately runs afoul of class bully Charlton Rollnick, who plants a frog in Tabitha's desk; Samantha, who's been hovering outside the door, sees Charlton pulling Tabitha's hair and shocks him through witchcraft. The teacher, Mrs. Peabody, gives the troublemaking boy detention – afterwards, a menacing Charlton corners Tabitha in the hall, so she changes him into a frog. Mrs. Peabody assumes Charlton-as-frog is part of the class terrarium and makes Tabitha return him; with the teacher's back turned, Tabitha grabs her amphibious tormentor and runs home.

Tabitha sneaks out to the patio to change Charlton back, but can't undo her spell; Samantha realizes that her daughter must have brought the wrong frog home and pops into the locked classroom to switch them, spooking the school janitor. Before Tabitha can restore Charlton, his intense mother comes by to pick him up. While Samantha keeps Mrs. Rollnick busy, Tabitha rushes her magic, causing the rehumanized Charlton to croak at his mother like a frog. Once Tabitha successfully normalizes the boy, Samantha suggests a psychological connection between "bullfrog" and "bully." Mrs. Rollnick agrees to ease up on Charlton, who wants flies with his hot fudge sundae, and Tabitha lobbies for the same "love and understanding" that Charlton is now receiving.

GOOD!

Charlton's as intimidating as a televised bully should be, but Tabitha immediately shows she can handle him, defending her "dumb name" – and without witchcraft. Of course, Tabitha turning Charlton into a frog is the fun of this episode, but their rapport once she changes him back is interesting; there's almost a feeling these two could end up friends. Not to be outdone, Samantha charging Tabitha's braids with electricity to stop Charlton from pulling them is a neat show of mother-daughter solidarity.

Under the comedic command of Nita Talbot, Charlton's mother is domineering, volatile, and bewildered all at the same time; she even brings an certain earthiness to the show. Samantha's bullfrog/bully correlation is right on the money, and Tabitha is amusingly shrewd as she turns Samantha's parenting advice around on her.

WELL?

The front door curtains are back, and the sailboat painting once again takes its proper place from the latest convenient mirror of "Serena's Youth Pill" (#247). The Stephenses wonder if "school is ready for Tabitha," given her past displays of witchcraft, but that seems unfair; Tabitha behaved herself beautifully in front of mortals in both "Samantha's Magic Sitter" (#243) and "Samantha on Thin Ice" (#246). The acidic Mrs. Hickman deserves to get a devil tail zapped on her *derrière*, but it's far too soon for Jeanne Arnold to play another dragon lady; she was the equally acidic Mrs. Norton in "Samantha's Magic Sitter" (#243).

Samantha anxiously tells Mrs. Peabody that this is Tabitha's first school experience. Not quite: Tabitha did attend preschool (for a day) in "I Don't Want to Be A Toad, I Want to Be A Butterfly" (#151). Samantha constantly walking in and interrupting class does merit Mrs. Peabody deeming her overprotective [a label Phyllis applied as far back as "Playmates" (#133)] – it's just that Samantha's been mellow about Tabitha for some time now, even allowing her to be around mortal kids without incident. So why is Samantha a nervous Nellie again here?

It's a weekday, because Tabitha is in class – so why is Darrin home at 2:45 in the afternoon? Hopefully he took the day off to stay with Adam, otherwise the boy was alone while Samantha and Tabitha were at school. Darrin mockingly chides himself for asking "How do you know?" when Samantha predicts that Tabitha is about to walk through the door, but Samantha having advance information isn't the norm: she's only ever exhibited psychic powers in "I, Darrin, Take This Witch, Samantha" (#1) and "Mona Sammy" (#198). Maybe the terrarium frog has ESP instead; it remains completely quiet in Tabitha's pocket and only starts croaking so Samantha can hear him.

It's understandable that Samantha would want to give her daughter other options besides magic, but she tells Tabitha that punching Charlton in the nose would have been "more ladylike" than turning him into a frog. Violence as an alternative to witchcraft? Even Tabitha knew better.

Tabitha got home 15 minutes after class let out, and it's about five minutes after that when Samantha pops over to the school to retrieve Charlton-as-frog. Wouldn't Mrs. Peabody still be there grading papers or preparing the next day's lesson instead being gone only 20 minutes after dismissing her students? And it's not necessary for Samantha to stick around and hide Charlton-as-frog from the entering custodian; she could pop out before he even looks up from the doorknob.

To retrieve her disobedient son from the Stephenses, Mrs. Rollnick removes her curlers, changes clothes, fixes her hair, and is on the doorstep far sooner than her 10-minute estimate. When Charlton's mama asks where her boy is, Samantha tells her he's on the patio with Tabitha. Why would she do that when he's out there as a frog? Naturally, Mrs. Rollnick makes a beeline for the patio; Samantha would have been safer stashing Charlton up in Tabitha's room, as the woman would be less likely to charge upstairs in a stranger's house. Then, Mrs. Rollnick says nothing when it turns out her missing son isn't on the patio after all.

Samantha must have retained the child psychology she learned from Gretchen Millhowser in "Playmates" (#133) to suggest to Mrs. Rollnick that Charlton is suffering from "ego identification." Asked how he changed into a frog, Charlton points to Tabitha and says "She made me one!" The mother-daughter witches are very lucky Mrs. Rollnick doesn't pursue that further.

OH, MY STARS!

Samantha is developing more and more of an edge as this season progresses. She gleefully flaunts her witchcraft by disappearing in front of the custodian – something Serena or Endora would do – and she's surprisingly hostile when Darrin wants to know what's going on with Charlton and Tabitha. It's almost as if Elizabeth Montgomery got tired of playing Samantha as Ms. Nice Guy and needed a change; characters do evolve, but, if this is a purposeful evolution, some mention of it in the dialogue would be helpful.

This is an outstanding episode overall, but then, so was "I Don't Want to Be A Toad, I Want to Be A Butterfly" (#151), which this story liberally borrows from. The wonderful Maudie Prickett played that episode's Mrs. Burch, but she's back as Mrs. Peabody, and her latest teacher observes that "no child is essentially different from any other child," just as her old one did. As for Tabitha, she chipperly told Mrs. Burch, "I'm not s'posed ta fly!" in the aforementioned episode; here, Tabitha assures Samantha she knows she's not supposed to. Yet Samantha told Maurice that Tabitha *hadn't* flown yet in "A Plague on Maurice and Samantha" (#237).

SON OF A GUN!

"When Charlton's mother comes, all I have to do is explain to her that her son, the frog, is safe in a terrarium at school. Meanwhile, she can take this one home as a receipt!" – Samantha, not sharing Tabitha's contention that realizing they have the wrong frog has solved "the whole problem."

Tabitha's been around the house so much that it's easy to forget she's not getting a formal education; it seems unspoken that the Stephenses have kept their daughter out of the mortal school system since her disastrous attempt at nursery school in "I Don't Want to Be A Toad, I Want to Be A Butterfly" (#151). But Samantha is right when she informs the caustic Mrs. Hickman that she's been tutoring Tabitha at home – she was first seen doing so in "The Phrase Is Familiar" (#187), an episode which briefly had Tabitha under the tutelage of warlock Professor Phipps. However, as Mrs. Hickman points out, public education was still compulsory during this period (home schooling was not as popular then), so the idea to finally build on this story thread and send Tabitha to school earns an A+.

GEORGE WASHINGTON ZAPPED HERE (PART I)
Airdate: February 19, 1972

EPISODE
249

When Tabitha isn't allowed to take Darrin's rare George Washington collection to school for show-and-tell, Esmeralda tries to zap the items out of a history book, but gets the real president instead. The Stephenses are upset, yet intrigued by the presence of the father of the United States; Washington is shocked to learn that he has traveled to the 20th century through witchcraft. Samantha updates Washington on how the country has progressed in 200 years, while Esmeralda struggles to remember the spell that materialized him. As Samantha checks on her progress, Washington decides to go for a walk and strolls into the park, to the amazement of those who witness him.

As Samantha searches the neighborhood for Washington, the president engages people about the state of the union – but, when a cop accuses him of holding a rally without a permit, Washington pulls his sword, which gets the historical figure arrested. Washington is released in Samantha's custody, and Darrin has his trial reduced to a hearing – yet Esmeralda remembers her spell and sends Washington back to the 18th century, noticing that his shoes didn't travel with him. In her attempt to return them, Esmeralda makes Washington reappear – this time with his wife, Martha Washington, at his side.

GOOD!

A lesson in continuity: Tabitha's still in school. She was seemingly pulled from public education after one day of nursery school [see "I Don't Want to Be A Toad, I Want to Be A Butterfly" (#151)], so it's gratifying that she not only continues as a pupil following "Tabitha's First Day In School" (#248), but that her show-and-tell dilemma is what leads to George Washington's visit. And, once the Stephenses think Washington is gone, Darrin admits he'll always cherish the experience, which is quite a lot of progress for a guy who couldn't abide magically flipped pancakes in "How Green Was My Grass" (#131).

President Washington grumbling that his birthday is on the 22nd of February, not the 21st, is not only a terrific bit of absurdist humor, but a great commentary on the absurdity of holidays. The show also deserves extra credit for having Darrin mention that "next Monday is George Washington's birthday," as this episode aired on February 19, 1972; indeed, the following Monday was the 21st.

The neighbor Samantha approaches is none other than Dick Wilson, who, amazingly, does *not* appear as a drunk. The only other time he's played sober on the show was in "Hoho the Clown" (#92); his inebriates are legendary, but it's good that the actor is given a chance to break away from the bottle.

WELL?

What do George Washington and Benjamin Franklin have in common? They both lived in the 18th century, they became friends and confidants after their first meeting in 1775 – and they've both visited Morning Glory Circle. Perhaps Ben told George about his flashforward [see "My Friend Ben" (#87)], because Washington also calls Darrin "an enlightened gentleman of the 20th century" and follows in Franklin's footsteps by getting arrested, released on bail, and put on trial. Once again, Samantha wants a trial moved up "due to the advanced age" of the accused, who blabs his true age like Franklin did, and both men disappear before their court dates. Last, but not least, it was Aunt Clara who materialized Franklin, while Esmeralda witches Washington. Do the Stephenses not feel they've been through all this before?

So Darrin Stephens, who never showed an interest in history until "Paul Revere Rides Again" (#206), now keeps a collection of 200-year-old George Washington relics that belong in a museum. And yoo-hoo maid Esmeralda is back, despite having a farewell party in "Samantha's Magic Sitter" (#243) as if she'd hung up her apron. As for Tabitha, no wonder she's interested in George Washington – she learned all about him while almost starring on *Steamboat Bill* in "TV or Not TV" (#236). Incidentally, Tabitha is an expert at zapping things out of books ["Hansel and Gretel in Samanthaland" (#238), most recently], so why does she need Esmeralda to obtain Washington's literary buckle and button?

In "Aunt Clara's Victoria Victory" (#100), Samantha was deemed Clara's nephew after the 19th century monarch saw her in pants; Washington makes no such observation about Samantha's shirt and slacks here, even though he was president decades before Victoria was born. And why does Washington think to ask what century he's in? It's not like he'd have any frame of reference about the future.

After Darrin unbelievably tells Larry via telephone that he's running late because he's paying homage to Washington, Larry's huffy response on the other end is him saying, "It's brilliant; a machine that bears the name of the father of our country." Is the mere mention of Washington enough to give him another crass marketing idea?

Darrin must have inherited the giant U.S. map that hung in McMann & Tate's reception area in "The Warlock in the Gray Flannel Suit" (#239), because it now adorns the Stephenses' den. As Darrin leaves, he tells Samantha not to let the president out of her sight – and the first thing she does is run to the kitchen to check on Esmeralda, where the witches make tea in the 20 seconds it takes for Washington to stroll out the door. By the time Samantha gets to the front porch, the president is nowhere to be seen. How far could he go in less than a minute? Samantha's used locator spells before – if little Adam could zap Darrin off a golf course in "Adam, Warlock or Washout?" (#242), certainly Samantha can twitch Washington back to the house.

1162 Morning Glory Circle has always had a high turnaround: Dick Wilson's lawn-mowing neighbor now replaces grumpy gardener Ferguson from "The Return of Darrin the Bold" (#217). In the park, Washington thinks being called a hippie is an insult, as did Leonardo da Vinci in "Samantha's da Vinci Dilemma" (#124). Also mirroring that episode, Samantha asks, "What'd the dodo do?" when the cop labels Washington as such; a museum guard had the same opinion of Leonardo.

Westport seems to have gotten a new police station since Darrin retrieved the drunken Mary in "The Good Fairy Strikes Again" (#216); maybe Samantha is retrieving Washington from a different precinct, but why is there a map of New York City hanging in this Connecticut division? Darrin later shares that he pulled some strings to get Washington's hearing moved up to the next day. He's an advertising executive; what possible influence could he have with the courts?

Esmeralda tries sending Washington back by reciting her original spell backwards, but it's her not being able to remember the spell that's causing the problem – and all she has to do is ask Tabitha, who witnessed her casting it. Washington's shoes get left behind; Tabitha wanted a Washington relic for show-and-tell, so why doesn't Esmeralda, whose hair is suddenly wavy for this scene, just keep the footwear? Instead, Esmeralda tries to zap the shoes back, horrified when she materializes both Washingtons. Curious: Esmeralda is only seen incanting *Size eleven, shoes of leather/George needs you for the winter weather*, after which she tells the Stephenses she got Martha by rhyming "life" with "wife." Neither word has anything to do with transporting shoes.

OH, MY STARS!

Yet again, Samantha tells visiting historical figures about the future. As mentioned in previous analyses of similar episodes, pollution of the timeline was not a widely-explored fictional concept in the '60s and '70s, but think of the damage Samantha could inflict on the present just by showing Washington a map of America's 50 states. And, unlike all other instances of anachronistic visitors, this episode confirms they go back to their own time with 20th century knowledge, because Martha Washington believes what George has told her about his trip. The Stephenses could wake up to a whole different United States because Samantha's loose lips caused Washington to change history.

SON OF A GUN!

"Then why is President Lincoln's name on a five dollar bill, while the father of his country is only on a one dollar bill?" – President Washington to the Stephenses, after discovering he's second billing when it comes to bills.

Will Geer is simply the living embodiment of George Washington – or at least, how he's perceived two centuries after his presidency. George is at once gentle, spirited, determined, and confused – plus, his presence offers the show a unique opportunity to discuss world affairs, most particularly the then-current Vietnam War and the apathy of many American citizens, without being preachy. The episode also tackles prejudice in perhaps the most comprehensive way it ever has: after Samantha reveals herself as a witch, Washington asks, "Even in the 20th century, people are not prepared to accept you?" Not only is that a clear statement about the plight of gays, African-Americans, etc., but it neatly dovetails the fictional realm of witches with the real world.

GEORGE WASHINGTON ZAPPED HERE (PART II)
Airdate: February 26, 1972

EPISODE
250

After a narrator recaps the events of "George Washington Zapped Here (Part I)" (#249), the Stephenses are stunned to see that Martha Washington has taken up residence alongside her husband. While Samantha shows her kitchen's modern miracles to an unimpressed Martha, the president draws Darrin into a deep discussion concerning his legal troubles as a result of being charged with disturbing the peace and assaulting an officer. The next day, Larry swings by and meets the Washingtons, convinced that "Honest George" would be the perfect symbol for Whirlaway Washing Machines. The first president of the United States quickly clashes with Whirlaway president Jamieson and socks it to the executives over the appliance's misleading claims of superiority.

At the hearing, Washington's arresting officer presents his case to the judge, while Samantha acts as the president's attorney. The hearing's participants discuss Washington's sword, free speech, and the rights given by the Constitution, but when the subject comes around to whether Washington is the real deal, Samantha states that he serves a reminder of the principles on which America was founded, and insists that Washington had the freedom to engage in peaceful assembly. The president is exonerated, and Esmeralda sends the Washingtons back – but the judge makes a frantic visit to the Stephenses when Washington's signature on a release form seems authentic, which Samantha neither confirms nor denies.

GOOD!

Having recovered from some of the less effective connective threads between two-part episodes [see "The Good Fairy Strikes Again" (#216)], the show does a traditional recap here, bringing back the announcer from "How Not to Lose Your Head to King Henry VIII (Part II)" (#230). There are different angles of the cop pulling his gun on Washington, and of Washington's shoes, but the refresher is accurate, and the announcer gets some of the best jokes as he describes Esmeralda and the situation she caused.

Washington's private conversation with Darrin briefly moves the show into straight dramatic territory – and, since Darrin doesn't usually spend much time interacting with the historical figures that visit his house, there's something satisfying about their extended dialogue. Darrin also comes up with an original explanation for Samantha's "relatives": "Washington" is a touched history professor, and his wife dresses alike to humor him, a nice change from time travelers usually being "aunts" or "cousins."

Introducing Martha to the kitchen conveniences today's society takes for granted, Samantha sighs, "Nowadays, snowy white comes in a box" as Martha describes laundering her linens by hand. When Martha loses sleep because of "the big birds," Samantha refers to the "species" as *Turbo jetus*. And, in a moment of perhaps unintentional continuity, Samantha says the neighborhood is on a flight pattern, which explains why planes constantly soared overhead in "Open the Door, Witchcraft" (#28).

Tapped to lend his name to Whirlaway's appliance, Washington asks, "Does this Abraham Lincoln have a washing machine named after him?" This is a great connection to Part I, where Washington felt slighted over Lincoln being on a $5 bill. And, Samantha's best point during the hearing is that George could easily think he's Benedict Arnold or John Wilkes Booth instead.

WELL?

Part II, like Part I, borrows heavily from "My Friend Ben" (#87) and "Samantha for the Defense" (#88), the two-parter which brought Benjamin Franklin to Morning Glory Circle. As with Franklin, Washington is amazed that Larry wants him to participate in a "commercial venture," Darrin offers to forfeit $2,000 bail for Washington [he stood to lose $1,000 over Franklin], Samantha again tells a judge that it doesn't matter whether the accused is the historical figure he claims to be, and both Franklin and Washington wrap up with "although I shall continue to be _____, for I can be no other, I shall no longer be that untimely gentleman in your gracious presence."

Why does Samantha get on Esmeralda about remembering the spell to send the Washingtons back when the maid just cast it a few minutes before? Martha believes George's "fanciful tale," but later, she has to be told about the hearing. Did Washington not get to that part before Esmeralda zapped them into the present?

George and Martha Washington are sitting at your table. The doorbell rings. What do you do? If you're Samantha, you casually answer the door as if nothing's out of the ordinary. At least Larry has a fuzzy memory, because he doesn't recall already telling Darrin, "My seat belt's broken and I want you to hold me in the car," as he did in "Samantha and the Troll" (#219). Larry acts as if this is the first time he's seen strange people in period costume at Darrin's house, and he never notices that Samantha's "aunts" from "Aunt Clara's Victoria Victory" (#100) and "Salem, Here We Come" (#202) are dead ringers for Martha; all three first ladies were played by Jane Connell. But Larry was listening in "Aunt Clara's Victoria Victory" (#100) when then-client Morgan said of the queen, "If you have to go out of your mind, go out in a big way"; this is his comment about Washington now.

Larry sees dollar signs as he envisions "a machine that bears the name of the father of our country" – that's what Darrin heard during his phone call with Larry in Part I. Then, Samantha, who kept Washington from going public about his plight in Part I because she was afraid witches would be exposed, talks about the hearing in front of the otherwise unaware Larry. She also hypocritically tells Darrin not to let Washington out of his sight, when there's only a hearing because she let the president out of *her* sight in Part I.

Jack Collins, who appeared as McMann & Tate client Prescott in "Samantha is Earthbound" (#244), is back already as another client, Jamieson. Now, Larry only gets the idea to have Washington pitch when he comes to pick Darrin up for the meeting. So when did Larry write the copy – in the car?

For a housewife, Samantha knows an awful lot about ceremonial swords. Then, she insists to the judge that the crowd's chatting started Washington chatting, but she wasn't even in the park when the president spouted off, so her testimony is hearsay, and thereby inadmissible. If Washington really wants to plead his case, he should bring in some of the park people as witnesses. He does fib that "providence" brought him to 1972 [Queen Victoria really believed this was responsible for her trip in "Aunt Clara's Victoria Victory" (#100)], then leans over to tell Samantha he answered without lying. Wouldn't the judge demand to know what the accused is whispering about?

As Esmeralda incants her spell backwards to send the Washingtons home, Darrin asks, "What is she doing?" though he already heard her attempt this method in Part I. Question: Esmeralda used an entirely different spell when she brought Washington back with his wife. So how is it her original spell-reversal works on both of them?

OH, MY STARS!

As discussed in Part I, Samantha often violates what the *Star Trek* universe calls "the temporal prime directive," which advocates withholding information to avoid altering the future. It wasn't clear that historical visitors remembered their experiences until now; Samantha's got a lot of faith in the Washingtons, because she shows Martha all her modern kitchen appliances. It's a cute scene, but Washington has proved to be a blabbermouth, telling Martha about his trip and then yapping about his arrest in front of Larry and Jamieson after Samantha asked him to keep that quiet. What's to stop Martha from telling her friends about 20th century innovations and hastening the inventions of the dishwasher and washing machine, neither of which showed up until the 1850s? Plus, Washington's 1972 signature is now a matter of public record, like Samantha's pro-Franklin campaign of "Samantha for the Defense" (#88). The show has never chosen to address the implications of time travel, but that doesn't mean these implications aren't there.

It's too bad that Martha Washington doesn't get more to do: Part I's cliffhanger focused on her arrival, but all she does in Part II is comment about appliances. It feels as if she should have been a more integral part of this two-parter's conclusion. Maybe she babysat Tabitha and Adam while her husband was in front of the judge?

SON OF A GUN!

"Oh, no. It's more popular than ever." – Samantha, when Martha is glad the bed hasn't gone out of fashion.

Larry's certainly wanted historical figures to do commercials before (not knowing they were historical figures), but he gets more than he bargained for when President Washington tries out as spokesman for Whirlaway Washing Machines. Will Geer's stilted phrasing is excellent, but Washington wows when he questions Whirlaway's superiority claim and vehemently rejects taking part in "falsehoods." And the best part is, Darrin loves it.

SCHOOL DAYS, SCHOOL DAZE
EPISODE 251
Airdate: March 4, 1972

Tabitha will skip from first grade to second if she passes a test given by her teacher, Mrs. Peabody [see "Tabitha's First Day In School" (#248)]. Perturbed that her granddaughter is getting a mortal education, Endora zaps the nervous Tabitha with a spell that instills her with knowledge on all subjects. Tabitha astounds Mrs. Peabody by correctly completing her test in 30 seconds and doing long division in her head, so the teacher has Mr. Roland, the school's principal, meet Tabitha, who then exhibits mastery in science, art and literature. Knowing Endora has been at it again, Samantha brings Tabitha home, but Mrs. Peabody follows and witnesses Tabitha performing witchcraft while playing with Adam in the backyard.

After Adam outs Tabitha as a witch, Samantha catches Mrs. Peabody with her kids and is forced to confirm her magical identity, displaying her powers as proof. Roland won't believe Mrs. Peabody, so they make a surprise visit; Darrin is stunned to hear Samantha telling the educators she's a witch until she zaps up a trunk full of magic tricks. Camouflaging her witchcraft within normal mortal illusions, Samantha passes the family off as magicians called The Witches, which satisfies Roland, but not Mrs. Peabody, who still believes Samantha is a witch. Endora, who has removed her genius spell from Tabitha, apologizes by leaving behind a blackboard with "Endora promises not to interfere" written 500 times.

GOOD!

Mrs. Peabody flirts with becoming a regular character as Maudie Prickett's teacher from "Tabitha's First Day In School" (#248) comes roaring out of the terrarium, quickly graduating from explaining Tabitha's "genius" to the principal to discovering that Samantha and her brood are witches. The ingenious twist is, it's Adam who tells her; considering he's been a minor player so far, his involvement in a development this big is major. Mrs. Peabody imitates Tabitha's more recent finger-cross zap [introduced in "Samantha and the Antique Doll" (#228)], then Samantha's signature twitch before getting zapped into a tree, and her continuing belief that Samantha is a witch at episode's end leaves the delicious hint that the Stephenses may not have seen the last of her.

Accuracy goes to the top of the class in regard to Tabitha's complicated math solutions – 267.583 *ad infinitum* and 1,013, respectively, are correct answers. Tabitha's other advanced abilities, where she discourses on Einstein, da Vinci, and Shakespeare, have a humorous "out of the mouths of babes" quality to them, but her most developed talent is her easy rapport with little brother Adam. For a girl who wanted a pony instead of a little brother in "Samantha's Good News" (#168), Tabitha clearly has embraced being a big sister. And, in another subtle indicator of her growth, she calls out, "Coming, Mother!" when she has always referred to Samantha as "Mommy."

Extra credit points: Charles Lane, who has only played clients since his first appearance in "Speak the Truth" (#50), finally breaks out of that mold by stepping into the shoes of Principal Roland. There's even a portrait of George Washington in his office, which may or may not be a nod to the fact that the show just spent two episodes with the president ["George Washington Zapped Here" (#249-#250)].

WELL?

Endora's a witch who always seems know what's going on at the Stephenses. Tabitha has been in school three weeks. So how is Endora only hearing about it now? There's something strangely sour in the way she imitates Tabitha's half-hearted "Hi, Grandmama" – Endora's always friendlier to her granddaughter than that. To help the nervous girl on her test, Endora freezes her and puts a genius spell on her. Has Tabitha been caught off guard, as was said to be the criteria for one witch to hex another in "Samantha's Pet Warlock" (#209)? And Endora just gave Tabitha an extraordinary ability in "Samantha on Thin Ice" (#246); she should remember that she took her skating spell off Tabitha to keep her from becoming a public figure, which this new spell has as much potential to do.

If Mrs. Peabody thought Samantha was overprotective in "Tabitha's First Day In School" (#248), Samantha proves her right by asking to sit in as Tabitha takes her test. After Tabitha gets 100% in record time, Samantha insists to Mrs. Peabody that her daughter is "a perfectly normal child" – yet, in the aforementioned episode, Samantha introduced Tabitha as "a very unusual child." Mrs. Peabody's a bit of a prodigy herself: she checks all 30 of Tabitha's answers in only five seconds, and remarks that Tabitha's especially proficient in math; how can the teacher determine that if Tabitha answered all questions on all subjects correctly?

Mrs. Peabody has had Tabitha as a student for three weeks. Instead of deeming her a genius from one test, shouldn't the teacher be wondering why Tabitha has never exhibited this kind of excellence before now? Tabitha comments that Principal Roland has a Salaino *Mona Lisa* hanging on his wall, not a da Vinci, never mentioning that there would only ever be a print in an elementary school. Then, Samantha drags her knowledgeable daughter out – isn't she still supposed to go to class?

When Mrs. Peabody comes over about her article on Tabitha, Samantha says, "When you barge in here uninvited, you do a thing more courageous than you think." Perhaps Samantha picked up menacing tips from "gangster" Kosko in "Money Happy Returns" (#223), who told Darrin, "When you use an ill-considered tone to me, you do something more courageous than you realize." Samantha ushers her children off the patio after catching Mrs. Peabody with them, but who is Tabitha nodding at as she makes her exit?

When Mrs. Peabody gets zapped into a tree, she thinks Samantha is a alien. So did Gladys Kravitz, in "Abner Kadabra" (#29) and "Samantha's Secret Saucer" (#137). Why isn't the Witches' Council intervening? They stripped Samantha of her powers for "frivolously flaunting herself as a witch" in "Samantha's Secret Is Discovered" (#188), and she's far more frivolous here than she was with Darrin's mother. Later, Samantha tells Darrin that Endora's spell on Tabitha included "algebra, advanced trigonometry, physics" and "the complete works of Shakespeare." Yet Samantha can't know *what* her mother's spell included, because she wasn't in the room when her mother cast it, and Tabitha didn't do algebra or trigonometry while at school.

Samantha laughs that zapping up a drink is helpful if you're passing through a "dry state." Darrin originally pondered that convenience in "I, Darrin, Take This Witch, Samantha" (#1), only then, Mississippi was the last state to have laws against the sale of alcohol; they were repealed in 1966, so the joke is outdated now. It's clever that Samantha tries to fake Roland and Mrs. Peabody into believing the Stephenses are magicians, but she has to be remembering "Baby's First Paragraph" (#62), where Endora solved the problem of Tabitha's "talking" by pretending she was a ventriloquist; she even kept Esmeralda's magic triangle from "Samantha's Magic Sitter" (#243). Then, the teacher rightly asks how a trunk full of magic tricks explain her ending up in a tree; Darrin merely jokes that Samantha shouldn't do "that tree bit." With a non-answer like that, no wonder Mrs. Peabody still thinks Samantha is a witch.

What happens when Tabitha no longer exhibits genius in school? Are Roland and Mrs. Peabody supposed to believe she's simply holding back these "abilities?" Mrs. Peabody takes a year's sabbatical, but so did Maudie Prickett's last teacher, Mrs. Burch, who went on leave after encountering Tabitha in "I Don't Want to Be A Toad, I Want to Be A Butterfly" (#151). Finally, Darrin questions whether Endora really "wrote" 500 promises on the blackboard: when the flip side reads, "Ditto," Samantha laughs that at least there are 250 statements, but there's really only eighty-two. And at times, Endora spells "interfere" as "interffere" and "interffre."

OH, MY STARS!

Much is made of Tabitha skipping to the second grade – yet, she has been said to be seven years old. Since boys and girls have to be five before they can enter kindergarten, Tabitha should already be in second grade. And it's March, which is awfully late in the school year; why not just have her jump to third grade when school starts back up in September?

SON OF A GUN!

"You've just answered your own question." – Endora to Darrin, when he asks what's wrong with Tabitha attending a mortal school, like he did.

EPISODE 252
A GOOD TURN NEVER GOES UNPUNISHED
Airdate: March 11, 1972

Darrin labors over the Benson Sleep-Ezy Mattress account, but finds his advertising concepts uninspired. Samantha makes some effective improvements, but Darrin thinks she twitched them up to assure a bonus trip to Bermuda that Larry has offered. Samantha furiously denies it, but, after Darrin fails to impress Benson with his original ideas, he still believes there's witchcraft in play. Deciding she might as well act like the guilty witch she's accused of being, Samantha makes herself invisible, then zaps Darrin out of bed, continuing to remain out of sight over breakfast, where Tabitha has to mediate between her squabbling parents.

Endora wants Samantha and the kids to come away with her, but Samantha reconsiders her hard line against Darrin. Meanwhile, Larry finds the additions Samantha made to Darrin's layouts and wants to use them, but Darrin refuses; Benson walks in while they're fighting over them. Larry puts Samantha's concepts in front of Benson, but when the client doesn't like those either, Darrin is thrilled and rushes out. Samantha, who has joined Endora on Cloud 9, hears Darrin's apology and pops home, where the Stephenses make up. Samantha ultimately inspires a new idea, which Darrin sells to Benson – but, because Darrin has gotten so little sleep recently, he knocks out during his celebration with Samantha.

GOOD!

"If I'm going to be stuck with the name, I might as well enjoy the game." Samantha's fiercer approach toward Darrin [which began developing in "Samantha on Thin Ice" (#246)] is used to improved effect here, as she makes herself invisible after Darrin accuses her of magically adding to his layouts; it's hard to argue he has it coming. Samantha's been invisible before, but it's never looked as good as when she's reading in bed, her legs tenting the blanket. Then, when Samantha zaps Darrin out of bed, his side of the blanket floats down, adding realism to the supernatural effect.

Just like mortal kids, Tabitha referees her parents' fight by being a "Mommy, Daddy said/Daddy, Mommy said" liaison – she even lends Samantha an ear after Darrin leaves, and, when Tabitha wants to know who won the fight, she is told her mother and father are both losing. Meanwhile, Darrin and Larry get into their first physical scuffle over a layout, adding a new layer to their somewhat adversarial relationship. When Benson catches them, Larry says they're mulling over ideas; Benson cracks, "It looks more like you were mauling them."

WELL?

When Darrin reports that he might earn a trip to Bermuda as a bonus, Endora jokes that the closest Samantha will get to Bermuda is an onion, a comment she already made in "How to Fail in Business With All Kinds of Help" (#104). Plus, it's not accurate anymore, since the Stephenses' presumably went on another Bermuda vacation Darrin earned in "No Zip in My Zap" (#113). As for the home turf, the U.S. map that conveniently hung in the den in "George Washington Zapped Here (Part I)" (#249) is now gone.

Larry tells Benson that the agency is on the 32nd floor. This seems consistent with "The Corn Is As High As A Guernsey's Eye" (#94), which indicated that McMann & Tate's building has 36 floors. However, Season One establishing shots showed the building as having only about 20 stories, and, in "Double Tate" (#59), the elevator's highest number was fifteen. Now, Darrin knows his ideas are subpar when he leaves the house; Larry must recognize that, too. Why, then, does Larry allow Darrin to pitch them, and why does he assure Benson they're the best?

As in "To Twitch or Not to Twitch" (#132), Darrin makes disparaging remarks about Samantha's age, only here, instead of Henry VIII and Bluebeard, the Stephenses cross swords over Samantha having "known" Socrates and Plato. That worked before, when Darrin could only guess at Samantha's age, but "The Salem Saga" (#203) made it clear that Samantha was a child during the late 17th century; Plato and Socrates lived around 400 B.C. Samantha has, in fact, zapped Darrin onto the couch before [in "A Nice Little Dinner Party" (#19), "How Green Was My Grass" (#131) and "Samantha Fights City Hall" (#149)], except this is the first time it's Dick Sargent's Darrin being transferred.

Samantha serving and eating breakfast while invisible is new, and an innovative idea, but perhaps a little more difficult to execute than it was to conceive. There's a jump cut edit after invisi-Samantha brings Tabitha her cereal; then, she picks up her plate and glass from the table and walks to the ironing board, but the objects appear to float when they should move at normal speed. And, though the show certainly tries, the chroma key used to facilitate Samantha's fork-waving and toast-eating is exposed by blue borders and a glass that becomes partially invisible as the iron spouts off its steam. When Samantha pops back in, her orange juice appears with her, but the glass wasn't invisible; before she materializes, the glass should look as if it's suspended in mid-air.

Darrin believes Samantha's ideas are witchcraft and outright refuses to use them – so why does he bring them to the office in the first place, much less leave them on his desk overnight for Larry to find? Larry and Darrin also venture into new territory: they argue in front of a client. With Benson looking on, Darrin snarks that he's Larry's "property" – they're lucky Benson doesn't walk right out. Then, Larry shows the client Samantha's ideas, which are only Darrin's original layouts with Samantha's scribble all over them – talk about an unprofessional presentation.

Would an ethereal place like Cloud 9 really provide mortal lawn chairs for its witchy guests? Maybe they're now serving the Witches' Joy Juice that Endora created in "The Corsican Cousins" (#211), because the drinks she and Samantha sip are also served in giant glasses with swan decorations. As Samantha calls the drink heavenly, a squeaking door can be heard from somewhere backstage; she then praises the smog-free air, as Endora did at Cloud 8 in "To Twitch or Not to Twitch" (#132).

It's interesting to finally hear what witches hear when someone calls out to the atmospheric continuum, but Darrin's apology being audible to everyone at Cloud 9 seems a bit invasive. Finally, Endora shifts considerably when Samantha pops out, capping an episode that contains several unusually below-par effects.

After Darrin rushes off to develop the idea Samantha inspires, she tells Endora that it's her place to "inspire her husband with occasional witchly wifecraft." Is she saying she really did zap this new concept into Darrin's head, after not using magic to craft her original ideas? Finally, during the Stephenses' celebration, a plane can be heard flying overhead when Darrin spills his champagne.

OH, MY STARS!

This installment lifts entire sequences and dialogue from "Help, Help, Don't Save Me" (#5), with a little bit of "Is It Magic or Imagination?" (#148) thrown in – and the latter episode was already a remake of the former. For sheer continuity, the Stephenses should feel like they've lived all this before: Darrin thinks nothing of it when Samantha draws on his layouts like she did eight years prior, Endora utters her "up to here in err/one huge lump of divine" phrase from the original episode, and Larry repeats his "don't you want to the sun to rise in the morning/don't you want me to live 'til tomorrow" speech. After the Stephenses make up, Samantha again inspires a slogan (at least the old Caldwell Soup slogan *was* inspired; Benson's, not so much); Darrin deciding Samantha is innocent of using witchcraft simply because the client didn't like her ideas was a weak resolution the first time, and it doesn't get stronger here.

But the real reason this episode doesn't work is because, by now, Darrin has evolved too much as a character. In "Help, Help, Don't Save Me" (#5), he was still getting used to being married to a witch, so it was natural for him to suspect his bride of magical help. But after nearly eight years, Darrin has adopted a more tolerant attitude regarding magic, not to mention gotten to know Samantha and what she is and isn't capable of – and *now* he thinks she's using witchcraft? Throwing Darrin back into that mindset is a glaring step backwards. He concedes that he should have known Samantha wouldn't lie to him; she replies, "That's right, you should've." There's never been a truer line of dialogue in the history of *Bewitched*.

SON OF A GUN!

"A toast: to Benson Sleep-Ezy Mattresses. When you're exhausted, a bed of nails is just as good." – Samantha, inventing her own slogan after Darrin snoozes through their celebration.

SAMANTHA'S WITCHCRAFT BLOWS A FUSE

Airdate: March 18, 1972

EPISODE 253

Darrin and Aunt Hagatha become concerned when Samantha seemingly gets drunk off one sip of an exotic cocktail from Mr. Fong's Chinese restaurant, a client of Darrin's. The intoxication passes, but vertical red stripes appear on Samantha's face. After Darrin relays that Samantha's drink contained a Himalayan cinnamon stick, Dr. Bombay concludes she's having an allergic reaction: they have eight hours to administer a cure, or Samantha will have the stripes for a year. Hagatha zaps Samantha to the apothecary for the potion; he chases her around before providing it, but the cure doesn't work, and soon horizontal stripes join Samantha's vertical ones.

Bombay returns to inform everyone he left out an ingredient: the tail feather of a dodo bird. Samantha has Hagatha zap the extinct animal out of one of Tabitha's books; it scurries to the roof, where it attracts the attention of the cops. Darrin pursues the bird and falls from the roof making a grab for the feather, which fails to activate the potion; meanwhile, Dr. Bombay returns, having remembered that the Himalayan cinnamon stick is the potion's most important component. After Hagatha and the Stephenses gang up on him, Dr. Bombay vanishes. Darrin steals the rare cinnamon from Mr. Fong and gets arrested; this final ingredient does the trick, and Samantha's stripes disappear, but it happens in front of the officers who come by asking about the dodo bird.

GOOD!

There's something so welcoming and calm about Mr. Fong that it's only natural to wish he'd stick around a little longer. And his portrayer, Benson Fong, had a chain of real-life restaurants called Ah Fong, which Darrin represents here. Samantha calls Fong's drink "bewitching" – it's always a bit of a thrill to hear the show's title, or a derivative of it: this is only the seventh time it has found its way into the scripts [it was referenced in "The Girl Reporter" (#9), twice in "George the Warlock" (#30), "We're In For A Bad Spell" (#39), "What Every Young Man Should Know" (#72), and "Sam's Spooky Chair" (#86)].

It may seem that Dr. Bombay has always had a bevy of nurses, but there's only ever been an appearance by one, in "Samantha's Lost Weekend" (#186) – until now. Suzanne Little's sultry Nurse Often is just the kind of receptionist Bombay would be expected to have, and her oozing, "I'm very receptive" is as funny as it is frisky. It's also a subtle touch when Samantha tells Bombay, "Lately I haven't been any further than a PTA meeting," which testifies that Tabitha is still in school.

A grown actor chasing another grown actor in an animal costume shouldn't be amusing, but Darrin's battle with the bird sings. Not only does it give him a rare chance for more advanced physical comedy, but he proves how far he's willing to go for Samantha as he scales his own roof. The police sergeant who shrugs at his officers' non-report about the bird is Herb Vigran, who was equally exasperated in "Darrin Goes Ape" (#222); it's a nice piece of continuity that the sergeant is still manning this desk.

WELL?

Mr. Fong tells the Stephenses that his Heavenly Himalayan ingredients are secret except for the cinnamon stick. Wouldn't such a rare spice sooner be kept secret than whatever else is in the drink? Less rare, however, is latest convenient mirror that replaces the Stephenses' painting in the foyer so Samantha can view her stripes; the last such mirror was seen in "Serena's Youth Pill" (#247).

Aunt Hagatha hasn't been around since Ysabel McCloskey played her in "Darrin Goes Ape" (#222); here, Hagatha's played by Reta Shaw, who once appeared as the character in "Witches And Warlocks Are My Favorite Things" (#77). Curiously, Shaw wears the same costume as her other character, Bertha, who fell off the canvas after "There's No Witch Like An Old Witch" (#27). Hagatha and Darrin are unusually hostile toward one another considering they barely know each other – and when Samantha drunkenly stumbles into the house, Hagatha exclaims, "witches aren't subject to such mortal frailties!" Then why was Serena crocked in "The Corsican Cousins" (#211)? Serena also read the one and only copy of *Harpies' Bizarre* that exists in "Serena's Youth Pill" (#247); Hagatha reads it here, though Endora perused it as far back as "Be It Ever So Mortgaged" (#2).

There must only be so many ways to call Dr. Bombay – Hagatha's "from Tripoli to Timbuktu" spell is how Samantha summoned him in "Weep No More, My Willow" (#152). Bombay also passes off his hexometer [from "Samantha's Magic Potion" (#212)] as a new and different invention every time; now, the souped-up synthesizer is an "ultra-vascular self-denominating powered trichroscope." Samantha is told she can get her potion "from your apothecary," as if there's more than one, and his reputation must be pretty widespread if even Hagatha knows he's a "dirty old druggist." That said, Samantha goes to him in earnest and is still surprised when he chases her, even though he just did in "A Plague on Maurice and Samantha" (#237).

Bright Red Stripes disease must be pretty common, because the apothecary ignores Bombay's prescription, hands Samantha a bottle, and lets her take it home. Later, Samantha wants Hagatha to talk to the Witches' Council about replacing "that quack" Dr. Bombay; if he's only rarely right, as the apothecary commented in "A Plague on Maurice and Samantha" (#237), then why hasn't Bombay already been replaced?

Darrin mentions that he'll "never be able to talk about" a dodo bird being in his living room. That's what he said about Kris Kringle in "Santa Comes to Visit and Stays and Stays" (#184). Now, dodo birds don't fly – so how does this one get up to the Stephenses' roof? And whatever the cops drive up on, it's not Morning Glory Circle, which was probably too hard to recreate accurately in the studio.

How does Darrin come out from hiding in the front yard bushes, run around back, and return with a ladder in less than ten seconds? His roof is also far smaller than it should be for a house that size. After Darrin falls, but credits the dodo with indirectly saving his life, Hagatha grouses, "I knew there was something I didn't like about that bird." So Hagatha would rather the father of her great-niece and great-nephew split his head open?

Darrin goes out to steal a cinnamon stick in a jacket that's torn and soiled from his dalliance with the dodo – yet neither his arresting officer nor the desk sergeant have anything to say about this shifty look. As for the beat cops, it's amazing they come back just to ask the Stephenses about a giant bird – even more amazing is that Darrin leaves the front door open so the cops can see his striped wife.

Armed with the cinnamon stick, Samantha whips her potion into a frenzy, despite Bombay's instruction to mix slowly to avoid bruising it. A full minute and 43 seconds goes by (not including the commercial break) before her stripes disappear – which, of course, happens in front of the cops. These officers think the Stephenses will know what's hopping around on their roof, and they never ask why

Darrin's all roughed up. Finally, after Aunt Hagatha confirms that Dr. Bombay didn't mention the cinnamon, she goes missing the rest of the episode.

OH, MY STARS!

Like Dr. Bombay's potion, there are many ingredients in this installment, starting with "Take Two Aspirins and Half A Pint of Porpoise Milk" (#42); that episode's square green spots become bright red stripes, both diseases last a year, and Himalayan cinnamon is known to drive witches out of the Himalayas, just as black roses were known to drive witches out of Peru. As before, Darrin is arrested for stealing a rare ingredient needed to cure Samantha, though now it's a throwaway scene with Mr. Fong saying nothing at the police station; Darrin's account isn't even in jeopardy this time. And, like "Take Two Aspirins..." (#42), Darrin would never be allowed to keep an item that he stole. There are also borrowed elements from "Out of Sync, Out of Mind" (#116), which put green stripes on Samantha's face as a result of Dr. Bombay's "cure," which conflicted with Aunt Clara's original voice-displacement spell. And then, the titular feathered friend from "Allergic to Ancient Macedonian Dodo Birds" (#118) puts in an appearance, but the guess would be it's because the show needed to reuse the costume. Not only is a tail feather again needed for a potion, as in "Take Two Aspirins..." (#42), but it's zapped out of Tabitha's book, as in "Allergic..." (#118), where Endora had the "pooped popper" Samantha has now. In and of itself, this is an enjoyable episode, but it requires ignoring a triptych of previous episodes.

SON OF A GUN!

"My husband wanted to see what I look like in stripes.'" – Samantha, when the police ask about her criss-crossed face.

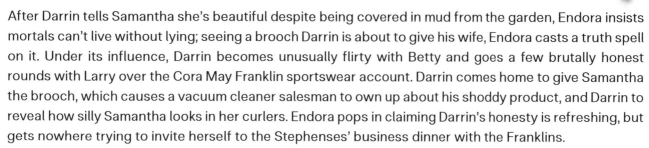

THE TRUTH, NOTHING BUT THE TRUTH, SO HELP ME, SAM
Airdate: March 25, 1972

EPISODE 254

After Darrin tells Samantha she's beautiful despite being covered in mud from the garden, Endora insists mortals can't live without lying; seeing a brooch Darrin is about to give his wife, Endora casts a truth spell on it. Under its influence, Darrin becomes unusually flirty with Betty and goes a few brutally honest rounds with Larry over the Cora May Franklin sportswear account. Darrin comes home to give Samantha the brooch, which causes a vacuum cleaner salesman to own up about his shoddy product, and Darrin to reveal how silly Samantha looks in her curlers. Endora pops in claiming Darrin's honesty is refreshing, but gets nowhere trying to invite herself to the Stephenses' business dinner with the Franklins.

Darrin and Larry endure the self-aggrandizing Cora May and her wimpy husband, Walter, but when Samantha walks in wearing her truth-telling brooch, the ad men laugh hysterically at Cora May's preposterous slogan idea. Endora fades in to watch the evening's descent: the long-suffering Walter bursts Cora May's egotistical bubble, Darrin and Larry differ on how to handle her account, and the quartet of mortals get into a loud argument as Samantha sighs. The next day, Samantha, now aware of Endora's spell, uses the brooch to make the annoyed Larry concede that he needs Darrin at the office. Then, also in its power, Darrin admits how much he loves Samantha; despite not being affected by the brooch, Samantha lovingly reciprocates Darrin's feelings.

GOOD!

Emily Banks, McMann & Tate's fourteenth Betty, has a naturalness about her that is very appealing, and the show even divulges a bit of Betty's back history: in "Instant Courtesy" (#153), she told Darrin she was engaged; it appears she still is, and has been for eight years. And Bernie Kuby, who usually only plays waiters, is a persistent vacuum cleaner salesman who unwittingly asks a witch, "Do you believe in magic?" before being forced to tell his potential customers "what a dog" his Mindmaster vacuum is.

For perhaps the first time, the foyer mirror isn't convenient – it's just still there from "Samantha's Witchcraft Blows A Fuse" (#253), and not suddenly included to advance a plot. Maybe it should have been there all along?

While this episode is virtually an exact remake of "Speak the Truth" (#50), it improves on the original in several ways. It was overkill to watch Endora zapping the truth god around the room the first time, so making the unicorn brooch mobile by tacking it to Samantha works much better. Endora stayed for dinner before; now Darrin won't allow it, leaving her to invisibly watch the proceedings instead; her joy as the chaos goes on in front of her is strangely infectious. Walter's liberation mirrors Frances Hotchkiss' from "Speak the Truth" (#50) almost word-for-word; they're both good scenes, but it's interesting to compare the change in social attitudes between 1965 [when the first episode aired] and 1972: Frances was a mousy wife, but here the roles reverse as Cora May lords over Walter, which puts some color in the old black-and-white episode.

WELL?

Darrin asks for Endora to provide a little warning before popping in, "like the flu," a comparison he also made in "Instant Courtesy" (#153) by complaining, "All of a sudden she's here, like the flu."

Endora may have had good reason to doubt Darrin's fidelity when he first married Samantha, but she's tested him repeatedly – she should know by now he isn't going to stray, yet she is certain his gift for Samantha is meant to make up for cheating. Endora herself told the High Priestess Hepzibah, "He loves my daughter" in "To Go or Not to Go, That is the Question" (#201)! Is she still under Hepzibah's directive to break up Samantha's marriage? Maybe that's why she interferes again, despite promising to stop in "School Days, School Daze" (#251).

Why is Betty so taken aback by the fact that the brooch Darrin bought for Samantha is a unicorn? Surely even by 1972, unicorns were ingrained enough in popular culture that Darrin shouldn't have to clarify that the animal is his wife's "mythical" favorite. In the close-up of the unicorn, Darrin's hand moves, even though he's been frozen by Endora, and Betty's notepad is in her right hand while apologizing for flirting with Darrin, though it's in her left by the next shot. Regardless, Betty's sudden befuddlement should be Darrin's first indicator that there's witchcraft in effect, yet he misses the clue.

Larry's truth-telling reveals that he hates working with women; given his provincial attitudes over the years, that's not surprising, though he had no problem working with Mary Jane Nilesmunster ["No Zip in My Zap" (#113)] or Evelyn Charday ["Samantha's Caesar Salad" (#173)], to name a couple, unless he was covering his disdain then, too.

Samantha tries to assuage Cora May after Darrin and Larry guffaw at her "dressy-wessy" slogan, saying "they always do this with a new account." Apparently Samantha didn't get the memo that the agency has had this account for a year. Being a witch, Samantha should be able to see, or at least sense, that Endora has invisibly invited herself to the party; Alonzo picked up on Samantha's invisibility in "The Warlock in the Gray Flannel Suit" (#239). Additionally, if you know that your mother always sends messages in balloons that pop, wouldn't you step away when the next one floats down? Samantha doesn't, though this episode and "Three Men and a Witch on a Horse" (#241) are only the most recent examples of Endora's frequent balloon-popping.

Larry tries to calm the Franklins by saying that "this type of constructive argument is very healthy for a marriage." He should know, thanks to all the how-to-argue training he got from Dr. Kramer in "I'd Rather Twitch Than Fight" (#84). Interestingly, every mortal in the room gets zapped by the truth spell except for Cora May, who has no trouble telling it like it is without assistance. As for Samantha, she walks into the living room, and conversation proceeds normally until she stands next to Darrin; plus, every time she gets near someone, they spout off. How does Samantha not realize that she is the catalyst for all the caustic confessions?

Though there's usually a final scene in which Endora removes her spell, gets read the riot act, and either apologizes or makes excuses for herself, she is conspicuously absent during the episode's tag, leaving Samantha to tell Darrin that her mother admitted to witching the unicorn. Another curiosity: why does Endora leave the spell on the pin? Of course, if she took it off, Larry couldn't acknowledge that he needs Darrin, and it wouldn't be revealed that Darrin is honest about his love for Samantha with or without a spell.

OH, MY STARS!

As previously discussed, this episode is a remake of "Speak the Truth" (#50), but it may contain the highest percentage of cut-and-paste scenes in the entire series. In that episode, Endora obtained a truth god to inflict on Darrin and his fellow mortals. Here, it's a unicorn pin, but that's where the differences end: Endora accuses Samantha of lapping up the syrup of white lies (before, it was treacle) after mimicking their entire original conversation. Darrin and Betty's "dress" scene is nearly word-for-word, as is Larry's distaste for his current account; the names are interchangeable. The same goes for Darrin's feelings about Samantha's curlers, Cora May's absurd "Confucius say" slogan, and Darrin and Larry's reaction to it. While the chaotic climax is not as verbatim, it's still essentially the same scene, as it is when Larry comes over to berate Darrin, only to get witched into admitting how much he relies on him. One element missing from this remake is Louise, who provided much fire in "Speak the Truth" (#50); she would have been a welcome addition here. This season has demonstrated enough originality that the show shouldn't have to go to the well to remake three episodes in a row.

SON OF A GUN!

"That's like asking Niagara to fall up." – Darrin, after Samantha tells Endora to stop being suspicious.

When this episode ended, viewers didn't know it would be the last in the series – and apparently, neither did the cast and crew of *Bewitched*. According to Herbie J Pilato in *Bewitched Forever*, a ninth season was planned, but, with lower ratings and competition from CBS' wildly successful *All in the Family*, perhaps the show sensed it might not be back: Samantha giggles to Larry that she can't wait to tell Endora the Franklins made up because her mother "just loves happy endings," the Stephenses profess their love for each other in a way that feels like a happy ending of its own, and, just before the final fade, Darrin kisses Samantha on the nose as if to acknowledge her unique expression of witchcraft. Surely, all that would have been innocuous had there been a Season Nine, but at least the show provided an inadvertent wrap-up of sorts, whether they intended to or not.

SERIES FINALE

If you've made it this far, chances are you've traversed eight seasons of analysis regarding the Stephenses and their inner circle of witches and mortals. Naturally, it's human nature (and perhaps also non-human nature) to sooner point out what's wrong with something, rather than what's right, and surely I've spent a lot of time focusing on the continuity flaws on Morning Glory Circle. That's why I'd like to insert a gentle reminder: whatever glitches are part of *Bewitched* aren't necessarily a commentary on the show – this is true of any series, really. *Bewitched* had many different writers, and many different directors. Episodes were filmed out of order, and were generally intended to be self-contained. Those responsible for getting the show on the air every week were inevitably faced with budgetary limitations and time constraints, to say nothing of pressures from the network. Likely there were last-minute changes in scripts – and, one would assume, deleted scenes and/or dialogue. All these factors played a part in series continuity. But it's also important to keep this in mind: the show has been off the air for over 40 years; it's not like anything can be done to change it now!

Is delving into the imperfections of *Bewitched*, as well as its good points, suggesting that people shouldn't watch the show? As Endora once said, "Hex, no!" One of the series' most salient qualities is how intelligently it was written – and that was so from the pilot all the way through to the final episode. Speaking of which, as mentioned in Season Eight, it's doubtful the cast and crew knew that "The Truth, Nothing But the Truth, So Help Me, Sam" (#254) would forever and always mark the end of the series. Neither they, nor audiences of the time, were allowed proper closure – but maybe we can have it now. Based on what I know of the show's direction, not to mention my own preferences and opinions, I've dreamed up what you could call a "fanfic" finale, just for fun.

Let's say it's the week after "The Truth, Nothing But the Truth, So Help Me, Sam" (#254) was broadcast. Perhaps, in this alternate universe, there was still a two-part *Bewitched* episode yet to air, and maybe it went something like this:

I, SAMANTHA, TAKE THIS MORTAL, DARRIN (PART I)
Airdate: April 1, 1972

EPISODE 255

Larry is congratulating Darrin for his stellar work on the Montgomery Industries account when McMann enters, declaring it's time to make the agency's signs read McMann, Tate, and Stephens. An overjoyed Samantha plans a party to celebrate the promotion: on the guest list are the McManns, the Tates (including their son, Jonathan), and co-worker Keith Wilson, along with his wife, Dorothy, and their daughter, Lisa [see "Sisters At Heart" (#213)]. Frank and Phyllis Stephens have been invited as well, and, when Gladys comes by to borrow sugar, Samantha includes the Kravitzes. Though the McManns are forced to beg off the party, the other guests toast to Darrin's success. However, Tabitha's former teacher, Mrs. Peabody, who still believes Samantha is a witch [see "School Days, School Daze" (#251)], snoops outside the window.

Darrin and Larry wax nostalgic about previous campaign victories, with accompanying flashbacks. The guests mingle: Frank and Phyllis meet the Kravitzes, then Louise. Tabitha and Adam play with Jonathan and Lisa, but, when the older kids tease Adam, he goes running to Samantha – and the mortal guests are shocked when the inconsolable toddler suddenly turns Jonathan into a baby zebra. Mrs. Peabody watches from outside, and, when the Stephenses can't explain their way out of the magic, Samantha reluctantly tells everyone that she and her children are witches. Before anyone can react, there is a flash of lighting – and every mortal, including Mrs. Peabody, disappears – leaving only Samantha, Tabitha, and Adam in the room.

Let's also say that this cliffhanger resolved not only itself, but the entire series, the following Saturday evening:

EPISODE
256
I, SAMANTHA, TAKE THIS MORTAL, DARRIN (PART II)
Airdate: April 8, 1972

Endora reports that the High Priestess Hepzibah ["To Go or Not to Go, That Is the Question" (#201)] has demanded to see Samantha. Along with the Witches' Council, Hepzibah announces that Samantha must leave the mortal world, showing, through flashbacks, why mortals cannot have knowledge of witches – following a brief hearing, Darrin's memories of Samantha will be purged. Samantha calls Michael Johnson ["A Vision of Sugar Plums" (#15)] and Irving Bates ["Just A Kid Again" (#193)], who know she's a witch, to testify on her behalf. Additionally, Lisa affirms Tabitha's positive influence on her, and Darrin is allowed to speak of his eight-year exposure to witches. The Council is unmoved until Tabitha pipes up that if Lisa accepted witches, maybe the other mortals will, too, so Hepzibah zaps everyone back to the Stephens house, where Adam restores Jonathan, and Samantha's confession is met with silence.

However, slowly but surely, everyone admits they've always known about Samantha – Phyllis and Frank, Lisa's parents, and the Tates back up their assertions with flashbacks. Mrs. Peabody barges in, wanting Samantha taken away – but Gladys surprisingly defends her longtime neighbor and tells the teacher to knock it off. Hoping to engender further acceptance, Samantha summons Endora, Maurice, Serena, Uncle Arthur, Esmeralda, and Dr. Bombay to the party. As all combinations of witches and mortals interact in harmony, Hepzibah clandestinely tells Samantha that she and the Council have decided there is hope for witch-mortal relations after all, while Endora and Darrin admit to a mutual respect for each other. Moved by all the support, the Stephenses marvel at how far they've all come.

Of course, that's just one possible finale – you may love it, you may hate it. You may also have your own ending in mind. But consider this: has *Bewitched* ever really ended? Maybe it has in terms of first-run episodes, but even before those were done, installments from earlier seasons were being rerun in syndication. And the entire series has been in syndication ever since; it's never been off the air. Fans watch it on local stations, cable stations – plus, every episode is now available on DVD, and through on-line services. There are many beloved television shows which disappear into the ether after their original runs – *Bewitched* is simply not one of them.

As they say in Hollywood, that's a wrap. I hope you've enjoyed this exploration of *Bewitched* – I had a lot of fun discovering the show all over again through writing this for you. But if DVDs and Blu-rays can have special features, so can we: on the following pages, you will be permitted "Within the Continuum," a special section that includes tallies of clients, witch illnesses, family trees, first and last lines, and more. Stay a while – I promise you'll be spellbound.

A final thought: the magic of *Bewitched* lingers on because hundreds of thousands, if not millions of people – from multiple generations and from all over the world – still adore the Stephenses. We each have our own reasons for that adoration, but those reasons all boil down to one thing: *Bewitched* is special. It was in the '60s and '70s. It is now. And it will be in some future where it's seen via hologram. Every episode is like an old friend that's always there for us – and each one is part of a show that has always served to remind us of the magic that exists within us all.

WITHIN THE
CONTINUUM

BY THE NUMBERS

Two hundred and fifty-four episodes of props, nicknames, catch phrases and story points can generate more facts and figures than a McMann & Tate sales report. Like taking your taxes to an accountant, all of *Bewitched*'s infamous elements are now tallied in this section for you. How many times does Larry fire Darrin? How many sick headaches does Phyllis have? Sometimes classic moments don't occur as often as memory suggests, sometimes they happen more often – here's how it all adds up.

THE STEPHENSES

number of times Samantha is rendered powerless: 9

number of episodes in which Samantha twitches her nose: 139
>   [141 counting off-screen or invisible twitching]

number of episodes in which Samantha doesn't use her powers: 29

number of times Samantha turns an animal into a human being: 4

number of spells Samantha casts on Darrin: 5

number of episodes in which Samantha wears her heart necklace: 162

number of episodes in which Samantha wears her "S" necklace: 8

number of fights Darrin and Samantha have: 28
>   [29 counting one Darrin picks as a ruse in "Man's Best Friend" (#70)]
>   [30 counting a witchcraft-induced "fight" in "Turn on the Old Charm" (#199)]

number of episodes with no Darrin: 14

number of times Darrin goes on trial for witchcraft: 2

number of times Darrin travels back in time: 4
>   [5 counting the alternate reality of "What Every Young Man Should Know" (#72)]

number of times Darrin is fired by Larry: 15
>   [16 counting the dream of "I Confess" (#135)]

number of times Larry threatens Darrin with termination: 24

number of times Darrin quits McMann & Tate: 3
>   [4 counting the alternate reality of "What Every Young Man Should Know" (#72)]

number of times Darrin is offered his own agency or considers opening one: 5

ENDORA

number of times Endora is rendered powerless: 2

number of spells Endora casts –
      that change Darrin's behavior: 19
      that change Darrin's physical form: 16
      that are cast around Darrin: 3

number of times Endora impersonates Samantha: 2
number of times Endora is impersonated by Samantha: 1

number of times Darrin refers to Endora as "Mom": 5

number of times Endora refers to Darrin as –
      Durwood: 133
      Darwin: 33
      What's-His-Name: 22
      Dum-Dum: 17
      Dumbo: 13
      Donald: 10
      Darwood: 7
      Durweed: 7
      Dobbin: 5
      Duncan: 5
      Derek: 4
      Dagwood: 3 (once in a dream)
      David: 3
      Dennis: 3
      Dexter: 3
      Darius: 2
      Dogwood: 2
      Whatchamacallit: 2

      Darrin: 12

MAURICE

number of times Maurice disintegrates Darrin: 2

number of animals Maurice turns Darrin into: 2

number of times Maurice refers to Darrin as –

        Dolphin: 13

        Dustin: 6

        Dustbin: 5

        Darryl: 2

        Dobbin: 2

        Darrin: 4

SERENA

number of times Serena is rendered powerless: 3

number of times Serena impersonates Samantha: 8 (twice at Samantha's request)

number of times Serena is impersonated by Samantha: 2

number of times Serena calls Larry "Cotton Top": 3

        [4 counting Serena's double in "Samantha's Bad Day in Salem" (#207)]

number of times Serena refers to Darrin as –

        Ding-Dong: 9

        Dumbo: 7

        Dum-Dum: 4

        Durwood: 3

        Poopsie: 3

        Superboob: 2

        Tall, Dark, and Nothing: 2

        Darrin: 4

ARTHUR

number of cows Arthur zaps up: 2

number of times Arthur turns himself into a clown: 3

number of times Arthur refers to Darrin as –

        Digby: 3

        Dum-Dum: 1

        Darrin: 15

OTHER MORTALS

number of Gladys' nephews: 6

number of Phyllis' sick headaches: 7
> [8 counting the recut "Samantha Meets the Folks" (#56)]

number of historical characters that visit the Stephenses: 11

number of Bettys: 14

number of mortals who have been told Samantha is a witch: 22
> [27 counting historical figures]
> [32 counting those that overheard in "The Battle of Burning Oak" (#164)]

OTHER WITCHES

number of times Esmeralda sneezes up a no-no: 12

number of times Aunt Clara comes down the chimney: 6

number of Aunt Hagathas: 6

number of fictional characters Tabitha zaps out of books: 8

MAGIC MISCELLANY

number of mirrors that conveniently show up to advance the plot: 24

number of times the show's title is referenced: 6
> [7 counting a raven whistling the theme in "George the Warlock" (#30)]

number of times Samantha asks, "Well?": 86

number of times Samantha asserts, "Good!": 41
> [42 counting the recut "A Vision of Sugar Plums" (#51)]

number of times Tabitha utters, "Good!": 1

number of times Samantha exclaims, "Oh, my stars!": 54
> "My stars!": 2
> "Well, my stars!": 1
> "Oh, my goose – it's Mother Stars!": 1
> "Oh, my stars and satellites" (by Endora): 1

number of times Larry refers to Darrin as a "son of a gun": 39
> [40 counting the recap from "Darrin the Warlock" (#181)]

number of times the Stephenses refer Larry a "son of a gun": 5

number of others Larry calls a "son of a gun": 2

number of others who utter "son of a gun" besides Larry and the Stephenses: 1

number of times Darrin manually imitates Samantha's twitch (with or without a "ring-a-ding-ding"): 44

number of times "Witch's Honor" is sworn: 29

SQUARE GREEN SPOTS AND SICK HEADACHES

Witch or mortal, health is important. But no matter which side of the cosmos one calls home, it's inevitable to sometimes feel under the weather – the symptoms just manifest a little differently. Find out how with this list of what character came down with what ailment during eight seasons of *Bewitched*. Whether case of the sniffles or power-plugging illness, a little ibuprofen or sound wave injection will make it all better.

THE MORTALS

DARRIN

MALADY	EPISODE
sprained ankle	"A is for Aardvark" (#17)
black eye	"That Was My Wife" (#31)
common cold	"There's Gold in Them Thar Pills" (#107)
common cold	"Samantha Is Earthbound" (#244)

LARRY

MALADY	EPISODE
broken leg (past)	"Bewitched, Bothered, and Infuriated" (#105)
common cold	"There's Gold in Them Thar Pills" (#107)
back injury (past)	"Samantha's Magic Mirror" (#226)

LOUISE

MALADY	EPISODE
"upper respiratory something"	"Samantha's Better Halves" (#185)

PHYLLIS

MALADY	EPISODE
sick headache	"Samantha Meets the Folks" (#14/#56)
	"The Dancing Bear" (#58)
	"It's Wishcraft" (#103)
	"Tabitha's Weekend" (#163)
	"Samantha and the Beanstalk" (#171)
	"Samantha's Double Mother Trouble" (#182)

ABNER

MALADY	EPISODE
required bridgework	"Pleasure O'Riley" (#25)

THE WITCHES

SAMANTHA

MALADY	EPISODE
square green spots disease	"Take Two Aspirins and Half A Pint of Porpoise Milk" (#42)
clogged powers due to metaphysical neglect	"No Zip in My Zap" (#113)
primary vocabularyitis	"Samantha the Bard" (#158)
unspecified ailment	"Samantha's Curious Cravings" (#174)
a vapor lock caused by undistributed metaphysical particles	"Okay, Who's the Wise Witch" (#195)
unspecified ailment	"Samantha and the Troll" (#219)
metaphysical molecular disturbance/ dream inversion	"Mixed Doubles" (#221)
subconscious manifestation of objects resulting from guilt feelings	"Samantha's Psychic Pslip" (#225)
perimeridictamitis	"A Plague on Maurice and Samantha" (#237)
gravititis inflammitis	"Samantha Is Earthbound" (#244)
bright red stripes disease	"Samantha's Witchcraft Blows A Fuse" (#253)

ENDORA

MALADY	EPISODE
allergic reaction to dodo birds	"Allergic to Ancient Macedonian Dodo Birds" (#118)
primary vocabularyitis	"Samantha the Bard" (#158)
perimeridictamitis	"A Plague on Maurice and Samantha" (#237)

MAURICE

MALADY	EPISODE
perimeridictamitis	"A Plague on Maurice and Samantha" (#237)

ARTHUR

MALADY	EPISODE
unspecified ailment	"A Bunny for Tabitha" (#178)
Bombay's syndrome (an allergic reaction to horse feathers)	"Super Arthur" (#190)

DR. BOMBAY

MALADY	EPISODE
gravititis inflammitis	"Samantha Is Earthbound" (#244)

McMANN & TATE'S DATABASE

This hotshot Manhattan advertising agency was cranking out campaigns decades before *Mad Men*. Now, take a peek through Darrin and Larry's Rolodex with this comprehensive list of every client that's ever set foot in their office. It's information Betty would have at her desk – if she wasn't constantly changing faces, that is.

CLIENT	COMPANY	EPISODE	BILLINGS
Mr. Angel	Angel Coffee	"Man of the Year" (#139)	-
Mr. Arcarius	Chef Romani	"Business, Italian Style" (#110)	$500,000
Monsieur Aubert	Aubert of Paris	"Samantha the Dressmaker" (#60)	-
Mr. Austen	-	"The Girl Reporter" (#9)	-
Edgar Baker	-	"Tabatha's Cranky Spell" (#134)	$500,000
Ernesto Baldoni	House of Baldoni	"Bewitched, Bothered, and Baldoni" (#233)	-
Horace Baldwin	Baldwin Blankets	"No More Mr. Nice Guy" (#102)	-
Linton Baldwin	Perfect Pizza	"Eat At Mario's" (#35)	-
Sir Leslie Bancroft	British Imperial Textile Mills	"Paul Revere Rides Again" (#206)	-
Rex Barker	Barker Baby Food	"It Shouldn't Happen to a Dog" (#3)	$500,000
Charles Barlow	Mother Jenny's Jam	"The Very Informal Dress" (#44)	-
Mr. Barrows	Barrows Umbrellas	"Darrin on a Pedestal" (#205)	-
Harold Bartenbach	Bartenbach Beauty Products	"To Trick-or-Treat or Not to Trick-or-Treat" (#177)	-
Mr. Barton	Barton Industries	"Is It Magic or Imagination?" (#148)	-
Joe Baxter	Baxter Sporting Goods	"Birdies, Bogies, and Baxter" (#114)	$1 million
Mr. Benson	Benson's Chili Con Carne	"A Plague on Maurice and Samantha" (#237)	-
Mr. Benson	Benson Sleep-Ezy Mattresses	"A Good Turn Never Goes Unpunished" (#252)	-
Mr. Berkley	Berkley Baby Foods	"And Something Makes Four" (#175)	-
Roland Berkley	Berkley Hair Tonic	"Samantha and the Troll" (#219)	$500,000
Mr. Bigelow	Bigelow Tires	"Cheap, Cheap" (#112)	-
Silas Bliss, Sr.	Bliss Pharmaceutical	"Daddy Comes for a Visit" (#180)/ "Darrin the Warlock" (#181)	-
Mr. Blumberg	Abigail Adams Cosmetics	"A Prince of a Guy" (#129)	-
Bernard Bobbins	Bobbins Candies	"The Mother-in-Law of the Year" (#214)	-
Jennings Booker	Beau Geste Cologne	"Samantha's Old Man" (#210)	-
Count Bracini	Count Bracini Olive Oil	"Samantha's Not So Leaning Tower of Pisa" (#232)	-
Bob Braddock	Braddock Sporting Goods	"What Makes Darrin Run" (#191)	-
Mr. Bradley	Zoom Detergent	"Samantha's French Pastry" (#147)	-

CLIENT	COMPANY	EPISODE	BILLINGS
Mr. Brigham	Colonel Brigham's Succulent Spare Ribs	"This Little Piggie" (#220)	-
Mr. Brinkman	Brinkman's Candies/ Witches' Brew Candy	"The Witches Are Out" (#7)	-
Mr. Brockway	-	"Sisters At Heart" (#213)	-
Mr. Burkeholder	Tom Cat Tractors, Inc.	"The Eight-Year Itch Witch" (#240)	-
Mr. Caldwell	Caldwell Soup	"Help, Help, Don't Save Me" (#5)	-
Bo Callahan	Autumn Flame Perfume	"Once in a Vial" (#125)	-
Waldon R. Campbell	W.R. Campbell Sporting Goods	"Samantha, the Sculptress" (#159)	$2 million
Roy Chappell	Chappell Baby Foods	"I Get Your Nanny, You Get My Goat" (#122)	-
Evelyn Charday	Top Tiger Cologne	"Samantha's Caesar Salad" (#173)	-
Bob Chase	-	"Toys in Babeland" (#109)	$10 million
Max Cosgrove	-	"Sam's Spooky Chair" (#86)	-
Mr. Cunningham	Cunningham Perfume	"Art for Sam's Sake" (#98)	-
Mr. Cushman	Montecello Carpets	"The Warlock in the Gray Flannel Suit" (#239)	-
Toni Devlin	United Cosmetics	"The Catnapper" (#71)	-
George Dinsdale	Dinsdale Soups	"A Chance on Love" (#196)	-
Oscar Durfee	Durfee Dog Food	"Samantha the Bard" (#158)	$2 million
Mr. Ferber	The Reducealator	"Mary, the Good Fairy" (#215)/ "The Good Fairy Strikes Again" (#216)	-
Sean Flanagan	Mother Flanagan's Irish Stew	"Out of the Mouths of Babes" (#224)	$250,000
Mr. Fong	Ah Fong's	"Samantha's Witchcraft Blows A Fuse" (#253)	-
Mr. Foster	EZ-Open Door	"The Joker Is A Card" (#41)	-
Bernie Franklin	Franklin Electronics	"My Friend Ben" (#87)/ "Samantha for the Defense" (#88)	-
Cora May Franklin	Cora May Sportswear	"The Truth, Nothing But the Truth, So Help Me, Sam" (#254)	-
Raul Garcia	Bueno	"Samantha and Darrin in Mexico City" (#170)	-
Charlie Gibbons	Gibbons Dog Food	"Samantha's Pet Warlock" (#209)	-
Mr. Giddings	Giddings Tractor	"Hippie, Hippie, Hooray" (#128)	-
Charles Gilbert	Hercules Tractor	"Man of the Year" (#139)	-
J.T. Glendon	-	"Samantha the Dressmaker" (#60)	-
Mr. Grayson	-	"My, What Big Ears You Have" (#121)	-
Mr. Gregson	Gregson Home Appliances	"Solid Gold Mother-in-Law" (#120)	$10 million
Mr. Hampton	Hampton Motors	"Samantha's Yoo-Hoo Maid" (#172)	-
Jim Hanley	Hanley's Department Store	"One Touch of Midas" (#157)	-
Mr. Harding	-	"Junior Executive" (#46)	-

CLIENT	COMPANY	EPISODE	BILLINGS
Mr. Harmon	Harmon Savings & Loan	"Samantha's Magic Potion" (#212)	-
Mr. Harper	Harper's Honey	"My Boss, The Teddy Bear" (#49)	-
John J. Harrison	Harrison Industries	"The Generation Zap" (#194)	-
Whitney Hascomb	Hascomb Drug Company	"Mirror, Mirror on the Wall" (#146)	$500,000
Mr. Henderson	-	"One Touch of Midas" (#157)	$2 million
Ernest Hitchcock	-	"Salem, Here We Come" (#202)	-
Mr. Hornbeck	Hornbeck Pharmaceuticals	"There's Gold in Them Thar Pills" (#107)	-
Ed Hotchkiss	Hotchkiss Appliances	"Speak the Truth" (#50)	-
Harold Jameson	Mount Rocky Mutual Insurance	"Laugh, Clown, Laugh" (#227)	-
Hector Jamieson	Whirlaway Washing Machines	"George Washington Zapped Here (Part II)" (#250)	-
Mr. Kabaker	-	"Double Split" (#64)	-
J.J. Langley	Bigelow Industries	"The Corsican Cousins" (#211)	-
Mr. MacElroy	MacElroy Shoes	"The Short Happy Circuit of Aunt Clara" (#83)	$1 million
R.H. Markham	Omega National Bank and Trust	"The No-Harm Charm" (#138)	-
Margaret Marshall	Countess Margaret's Cosmetics	"The Cat's Meow" (#18)	$1 million
Mr. Martin	Stanwyck Soap	"A Very Special Delivery" (#38)	$500,000
Mr. Martin	-	"A Bum Raps" (#68)	-
Madame Maruska	Madame Maruska Lipstick	"How to Fail in Business With All Kinds of Help" (#104)	$1 million
George Meiklejohn	-	"Make Love, Not Hate" (#200)	-
Kensu Mishimoto	Mishimoto Electronics	"A Majority of Two" (#136)	-
Mr. Morgan	Morgan Mattresses	"Aunt Clara's Victoria Victory" (#100)	$1 million
Jesse Mortimer	Mortimer's Instant Soups	"Humbug Not to Be Spoken Here" (#123)	$500,000
C.L. Morton	Morton Milk	"The Corn Is As High As A Guernsey's Eye" (#94)	-
Harlan Mossler	Mossler Enterprises	"Samantha Fights City Hall" (#149)	-
Mr. Nickerson	-	"Tabitha's Very Own Samantha" (#189)	-
M.J. Nilesmunster	Carter Brothers Industrial Products	"No Zip in My Zap" (#113)	-
Elliott Norton	-	"Samantha's Magic Sitter" (#243)	-
Mr. Norton	-	"Take Two Aspirins And Half A Pint of Porpoise Milk" (#42)	-
Randolph Parkinson, Jr.	-	"Oedipus Hex" (#85)	-
Mr. Paxton	-	"Samantha's Curious Cravings" (#174)	$2 million
Ed Pennybaker	-	"I Remember You...Sometimes" (#97)	-
Mr. Pickering	Jewel of the East	"Ling-Ling" (#21)	-

CLIENT	COMPANY	EPISODE	BILLINGS
Wilbur Prescott	Prescott Shoes	"Samantha Is Earthbound" (#244)	-
J.P. Pritchfield	Mintbrite Toothpaste	"Samantha's da Vinci Dilemma" (#124)	-
Osgood Rightmire	-	"Disappearing Samantha" (#65)	-
Mark Robbins	Robbins Transmissions	"Nobody Perfect" (#75)	-
Mr. Robbins	Robbins Baby Food	"Follow That Witch" (#66-#67)	-
James Robinson	Westchester Consolidated Mills	"The Leprechaun" (#63)	-
J. Earle Rockfield	-	"The Battle of Burning Oak" (#164)	-
Lionel Rockfield	Rockfield Furnishings	"The House That Uncle Arthur Built" (#218)	-
Jack Rogers	-	"Trick or Treat" (#43)	-
Mr. Rohrbach	Rohrbach Steel	"Long Live the Queen" (#108)	$8.5 million
Monsieur Sagan	Europa Tours	"Paris, Witches' Style" (#234)	-
Mr. Saunders	Saunders Soup	"Nobody But A Frog Knows How to Live" (#106)	-
Tom Scranton	Super Soapy Soap	"A Gazebo Never Forgets" (#89)	$1 million
Adrienne Sebastian	Adrienne Sebastian Cosmetics	"Instant Courtesy" (#153)	several million
Dwight Sharpe	-	"To Twitch or Not to Twitch" (#132)	$500,000
Mr. Sheldrake	Sheldrake Sausages	"Super Car" (#93)	-
Mr. Shelley	Shelley Shoes	"Cousin Edgar" (#36)	-
Mr. Shotwell	Shotwell Pharmaceuticals	"You're So Agreeable" (#183)	-
Lester Silverton	Silverton Toy Company	"TV or Not TV" (#236)	-
H.J. Simpson	-	"Maid to Order" (#53)	-
O.J. Slocum	-	"Man of the Year" (#139)	-
Mr. Solow	Solow Toy Company	"Hoho the Clown" (#92)	-
William J. Sommers	-	"Snob in the Grass" (#126)	-
Mr. Spengler	-	"Three Men and A Witch on a Horse" (#241)	-
Alvin Springer	Springer Pet Food	"That Was No Chick, That Was My Wife" (#117)	-
Sanford Stern	Stern Chemicals	"Divided He Falls" (#69)	-
Mr. Stewart	-	"Weep No More, My Willow" (#152)	-
H.B. Summers	Multiple Industries	"The Phrase Is Familiar" (#187)	-
Augustus Sunshine	Happy Heart Greeting Card Company	"Turn on the Old Charm" (#199)	-
Alvin Sylvester	-	"A Bunny for Tabitha" (#178)	-
Mr. Tanaka	Tanaka Enterprises	"Samantha's Better Halves" (#185)	-
Evelyn Tucker	Brawn Cologne	"Going Ape" (#162)	$800,000
Randolph Turgeon	-	"Double Tate" (#59)	-

CLIENT	COMPANY	EPISODE	BILLINGS
Clio Vanita	Vino Vanita	"Cousin Serena Strikes Again" (#155-#156)	$500,000
Jay Warbell	Warbell Dress Company	"The Crone of Cawdor" (#101)	-
J.P. Waterhouse	Waterhouse & Company	"The Girl With the Golden Nose" (#73)	-
Leroy Wendall	Prune Valley Retirement Village	"If They Never Met" (#127)	-
Harrison Woolcott	Woolcott Towers	"Serena's Richcraft" (#245)	-
Harrison Woolfe	Woolfe Brothers' Department Store	"Your Witch Is Showing" (#20)	-
Mr. Wright	Wright Pens	"Dangerous Diaper Dan" (#82)	-
-	Barbour Peaches	"If the Shoe Pinches" (#197)	-
-	Breeze Shampoo	"Serena Stops the Show" (#192)	-
-	Cushman Cosmetics	"Darrin Goes Ape" (#222)	-
-	Cushman Restaurants	"Money Happy Returns" (#223)	-
-	Feather Touch Typewriters	"George the Warlock" (#30)	$2 million
-	Ganzer Garage Doors	"The Trial and Error of Aunt Clara" (#95)	-
-	Gotham Industries	"To Go or Not to Go, That is the Question (#201)	-
-	Hilgreen Coffee	"The Generation Zap" (#194)	-
-	Illinois Meatpackers	"Samantha's Secret Spell" (#179)	-
-	Jasmine Perfume	"It Takes One to Know One" (#11)	-
-	Kingsley's Potato Chips	"The Magic Cabin" (#52)	-
-	Naseley's Baby Food	"Baby's First Paragraph" (#62)	-
-	Regal Silverware	"The Ghost Who Made A Spectre of Himself" (#235)	-
-	Sleggershammer's Dairy	"Red Light, Green Light" (#23)	-
-	Top Pop	"Super Arthur" (#190)	-
-	Tropical Bathing Suits	"Three Wishes" (#96)	-
-	Webley Foods	"Snob in the Grass" (#126)	-

HAVEN'T I SEEN YOU SOMEWHERE BEFORE?

In the days before VCRs and DVDs elevated casual television viewers into eagle-eyed experts, shows had a habit of casting the same character actors over and over in different roles, and *Bewitched* was no exception. For better or worse, part of its enduring legacy is that many of the same faces show up with different names – and now you can keep track with this all-inclusive collection of guest stars. Every actor who played multiple characters is here – but only multiple characters: Jill Foster, for example, appeared 10 times as single character Betty, so she's not on this list. And, if an actor repeated a character, even if through a two-parter or a recut episode, that distinction comes after their name. Enjoy dissecting this directory of delightful déjà vus.

2

Edward Andrews	Lauren Gilbert	Stuart Nisbet
Jeanne Arnold	Julie Gregg	Henry Oliver
Baynes Barron	Beryl Hammond	Barbara Perry
Larry Barton	Jonathan Harris	Arthur Peterson
Billy Beck	Tim Herbert	Noam Pitlik
Henry Beckman	Lew Horn	Ricky Powell
Jim Begg	Craig Hundley	Mala Powers
Danny Bonaduce	Kendrick Huxham	Nancy Priddy
Peter Brocco	Hollis Irving	Teddy Quinn
Nellie Burt	Gordon Jump	Ron Randell
Jeff Burton	William Kendis	Jay Robinson
Jack Cassidy	Roger Lajoie	Joe Ross
Diana Chesney	Mary Lansing	Charlie Ruggles
Jonathan Daly	Art Lewis	Cosmo Sardo
Myra De Groot	Robert P. Lieb	Maida Severn
Molly Dodd	Dave Madden	Anne Seymour
Ann Doran	Monty Margetts	Edythe Sills
Allen Emerson	Maureen McCormick	Jeanne Sorel
Hal England	Oliver McGowan	Jud Strunk
Herbie Faye	Joseph Mell	Robert Terry
Jack Fletcher	John Mitchum	Frank Wilcox
John Gallaudet	Elmer Modlin	
Henry Gibson	Byron Morrow	

3

Arthur Adams
Alice Backes (2 as June Foster)
Dick Balduzzi
Gordon De Vol
Kay Elliot
John J. Fox
Alex Gerry
Jonathan Hole
Joan Hotchkis (2 as Miss Ferndale)
David Huddleston
George Ives

Robert Q. Lewis
Laurie Main (2 as British Tour Guide)
Judy March
Ruth McDevitt
Billy Mumy (2 as orphan Michael)
Burt Mustin
Pat Priest
Kevin Tate (2 as orphan Tommy)
Vic Tayback
Dan Tobin
William Tregoe

4

Martin Ashe
Irenee Byatt
Dort Clark
Sidney Clute
Jack Griffin
Harry Holcombe
Allen Jenkins
Bobo Lewis
Karl Lukas

Ysabel MacCloskey (2 as Aunt Hagatha)
Virginia Martin (3 as Charmaine Leach)
Barbara Morrison
Joseph Perry
Jerry Rush
Reta Shaw (2 as Bertha, 2 as Aunt Hagatha)
Paul Sorensen
Sharon Vaughn
Herb Vigran

5

Irwin Charone
Herb Ellis
Henry Hunter
Arch Johnson
Arthur Julian
Nancy Kovack (3 as Sheila Sommers, 2 as Clio Vanita)
Larry D. Mann
Ron Masak (2 as Officer Clancy)
Art Metrano
Maudie Prickett (2 as Mrs. Peabody)

6

Jane Connell (2 as Hepzibah, 2 as Martha Washington)
John Fiedler (2 as Silas Bliss, Jr.)
Ronald Long (2 as Henry VIII)
Cliff Norton
Herb Voland

7
Jean Blake (5 as Betty)
Steve Franken (2 as Mr. Barkley)
Bernie Kuby
Lindsay Workman

8
Jack Collins
Charles Lane

9
Parley Baer (2 as Salem Desk Sergeant)
Paul Barselow
Bernie Kopell (4 as the Apothecary)
Richard X. Slattery (2 as Salem Police Officer)
Paul Smith

10
J. Edward McKinley (2 as Silas Bliss, Sr.)

11
Sara Seegar (2 as Mrs. Grange)

18
Dick Wilson (3 as John Paul Potter III)

WHICH WITCH IS WHICH?

Everyone knows who Adam and Tabitha's parents are, and that Larry works for McMann & Tate. But how many cousins does Samantha have? And what is Darrin's educational background? Eight seasons of casual mentions add up to a lot of family trees, résumés and entries in little black books – peruse these short character profiles that cover biographical details of all the show's major witches and mortals, based on airdates and other clues culled from the episodes themselves: how it all comes together is fascinating.

ABNER

OCCUPATION
retired

MARRIAGES
Gladys Gruber (1935)

RELATIVES
Harriet Kravitz (sister)

ADAM

DATE OF BIRTH
October 16, 1969

RELATIVES
Darrin Stephens (father)
Samantha Stephens (mother)
Tabitha Stephens (sister)
Frank Stephens (grandfather)
Phyllis Stephens (grandmother)
Maurice (grandfather)
Endora (grandmother)
Frank (great-great-grandfather)
Albert (great-uncle)
Arthur (great-uncle)
Herbert (great-uncle)
Max (great-uncle)
Agnes (great-aunt, deceased,
   by stake during Salem witch trials)
Bertha (great-aunt)
Clara (great-aunt)
Enchantra (great-aunt)
Hagatha (great-aunt)
Madge (great-aunt)
Cornelia (great-great-aunt)
Emma (great-great-aunt)
Letitia (great-great-aunt)
Lorenzo (great-great-great-uncle)
Brian O'Brian (first cousin once removed)
Edgar (first cousin once removed)
Helen (first cousin once removed)
Henry (first cousin once removed)
Mario (first cousin once removed)
Miranda (first cousin once removed)
Panda (first cousin once removed)
Robbie (first cousin once removed)
Serena (first cousin once removed)

ARTHUR

OCCUPATION
former ice cream plant worker

RELATIVES
Clara (sister)
Endora (sister)
Enchantra (sister)
Hagatha (sister)
Samantha (niece)
Adam Stephens (great-nephew)
Tabitha Stephens (great-niece)

CHILDREN
Henry (presumed son)

RELATIONSHIPS
Aretha

CLARA

RELATIVES
Arthur (brother)
Endora (sister)
Enchantra (sister)
Hagatha (sister)
Samantha (niece)
Adam Stephens (great-nephew)
Tabitha Stephens (great-niece)

RELATIONSHIPS
Hedley Partridge (broken engagement)
Octavius/"Ocky" (dated)
Benjamin Franklin (dated)
Kensu Mishimoto (dated)

CRIMINAL RECORD
stole 105 doorknobs from Mr. Brinkman
stole doorknob from Buckingham Palace

DARRIN

DATE OF BIRTH
February (or April) 1928

OCCUPATION
advertising executive at McMann & Tate
    started in 1959 (or 1961, or 1964)
Advertising Man of the Year, 1968

EDUCATION
University of Missouri, Class of 1950
graduated cum laude
student body president

MILITARY EXPERIENCE
United States Army, lieutenant

OTHER PLACES OF RESIDENCE
New York City
Missouri

MARRIAGES
Samantha Stephens (1964)

RELATIVES
Frank Stephens (father)
Phyllis Stephens (mother)
Frank (great-grandfather)
Albert (uncle)
Herbert (uncle)
Max (uncle)
Madge (aunt)
Emma (great-aunt)
Letitia (great-aunt)
Brian O'Brian (cousin)
Helen (cousin)
Robbie (cousin)

CHILDREN
Tabitha Stephens (daughter)
Adam Stephens (son)

RELATIONSHIPS
Mary Jane Nilesmunster
(broken engagement)

Sheila Sommers (broken engagement)

CRIMINAL RECORD
arrested for attempting to steal a feather
from a woman's hat

arrested for stealing a black Peruvian rose

arrested for resisting arrest and indecent
exposure

arrested for stealing a bedwarmer

arrested for stealing a Himalayan cinnamon
stick

2 speeding tickets

ENDORA

DATE OF BIRTH
circa 300-400BC

MARRIAGES
Maurice (open marriage)

RELATIVES
Arthur (brother)
Clara (sister)
Enchantra (sister)
Hagatha (sister)
Henry (nephew)
Serena (niece)
Adam Stephens (grandson)
Tabitha Stephens (granddaughter)

CHILDREN
Samantha (daughter)

RELATIONSHIPS
Bo Callahan (broken engagement)
Bernard Bobbins (flirtation)
Frank Stephens (flirtation)

ESMERALDA

DATE OF BIRTH
the 11th century

OCCUPATION
housekeeper/babysitter
former lady-in-waiting to Henry VIII

RELATIONSHIPS
Bonanno Pisano (broken engagement, 1100s)
Ferdy (broken engagement, 1500s)
Ramon Verona (dated)
Count Bracini (dated)

FRANK

OCCUPATION
retired

OTHER PLACES OF RESIDENCE
Missouri

MARRIAGES
Phyllis Stephens (1925)

RELATIVES
Frank (grandfather)
Adam Stephens (grandson)
Tabitha Stephens (granddaughter)

CHILDREN
Darrin Stephens (son)

RELATIONSHIPS
Endora (flirtation)

GLADYS

BIRTH NAME
Gladys Gruber

OCCUPATION
housewife

MARRIAGES
Abner Kravitz (1935)

RELATIVES
Louis Gruber (brother)
Edna Gruber (sister)
name unknown (sister)
Julius (cousin)
Edgar (nephew)
Floyd (nephew)
Leroy (nephew)
Seymour (nephew)
Sidney (nephew)
Tommy (nephew)

LARRY

DATE OF BIRTH
1920 (or 1921)

OCCUPATION
senior vice president/partner at
McMann & Tate

MILITARY EXPERIENCE
United States Navy

MARRIAGES
Louise Tate (1948)

RELATIVES
name unknown (mother)
name unknown (sister)

CHILDREN
Jonathan Tate (son)

LOUISE

DATE OF BIRTH
December, year unknown

OCCUPATION
housewife

MARRIAGES
Larry Tate (1948)

RELATIVES
name unknown (mother)
name unknown (brother)
Harriet (aunt)
Millicent (aunt)

CHILDREN
Jonathan Tate (son)

MAURICE

OTHER PLACES OF RESIDENCE
London

MARRIAGES
Endora (open marriage)

RELATIVES
Serena (niece)
Adam Stephens (grandson)
Tabitha Stephens (granddaughter)

CHILDREN
Samantha (daughter)

RELATIONSHIPS
Abigail Beecham

PHYLLIS

OTHER PLACES OF RESIDENCE
Missouri

MARRIAGES
Frank Stephens (1925)

RELATIVES
name unknown (mother)
name unknown (grandmother)
Madge (sister)
Adam Stephens (grandson)
Tabitha Stephens (granddaughter)

CHILDREN
Darrin Stephens (son)

SAMANTHA

DATE OF BIRTH
June 6, mid-to-late 1600s

OCCUPATION
housewife
former queen of the witches

EDUCATION
Hagatha's school

OTHER PLACES OF RESIDENCE
Boston, Massachusetts

MARRIAGES
Darrin Stephens (1964)

RELATIVES
Maurice (father)
Endora (mother)
Arthur (uncle)
Agnes (aunt, deceased,
   by stake during Salem witch trials)
Bertha (aunt)
Clara (aunt)
Enchantra (aunt)
Hagatha (aunt)
Cornelia (great-aunt)
Lorenzo (great-great-uncle)
Edgar (cousin)
Henry (cousin)
Mario (cousin)
Miranda (cousin)
Panda (cousin)
Serena (cousin)

CHILDREN
Adam Stephens (son)
Tabitha Stephens (daughter)

RELATIONSHIPS
Ashley Flynn
Clyde Farnsworth (dated)
George
Henry VIII (broken engagement,
   while amnesiac)
Rance Butler (while amnesiac)
Rollo

SERENA

PLACE OF BIRTH
Babylon

OCCUPATION
former ice cream plant worker

EDUCATION
Witches' University

OTHER PLACES OF RESIDENCE
Salem, Massachusetts

RELATIVES
Maurice (uncle)
Endora (aunt)
Samantha (cousin)
Tabitha Stephens (first cousin once removed)
Adam Stephens (first cousin once removed)

RELATIONSHIPS
Bruce
Captain Nichols
Clyde
Darrin the Bold
Franklyn Blodgett
George Dinsdale
Harrison Woolcott
Malcolm
Newton
Otto
Vincent Van Gogh
the Gloucester Fisherman's Memorial

CRIMINAL RECORD
arrested for causing a riot at a love-in

TABITHA

DATE OF BIRTH
January 13, 1966

EDUCATION
Delightful Day Nursery School
Towner's Elementary

RELATIVES
Darrin Stephens (father)
Samantha Stephens (mother)
Adam Stephens (brother)
Frank Stephens (grandfather)
Phyllis Stephens (grandmother)
Maurice (grandfather)
Endora (grandmother)
Frank (great-great-grandfather)
Albert (great-uncle)
Arthur (great-uncle)
Herbert (great-uncle)
Max (great-uncle)
Agnes (great-aunt, deceased,
    by stake during Salem witch trials)
Bertha (great-aunt)
Clara (great-aunt)
Enchantra (great-aunt)
Hagatha (great-aunt)
Madge (great-aunt)
Cornelia (great-great-aunt)
Emma (great-great-aunt)
Letitia (great-great-aunt)
Lorenzo (great-great-great-uncle)
Brian O'Brian (first cousin once removed)
Edgar (first cousin once removed)
Helen (first cousin once removed)
Henry (first cousin once removed)
Mario (first cousin once removed)
Miranda (first cousin once removed)
Panda (first cousin once removed)
Robbie (first cousin once removed)
Serena (first cousin once removed)

TRANSFORMATIONS

1164 Morning Glory Circle became a veritable zoo over the course of eight years – and that's just based on how many animals Darrin was turned into. But Larry Tate once found himself imprisoned in feathers – and so did Endora. This section will tell you who spent what episode in what form, and who caused the reinvention. The focus here is only on animals and objects, not a mortal or witch becoming another type of humanoid, but there's plenty here in regard to the surprising shape-shifting of these characters.

THE MORTALS

DARRIN

OBJECT/ANIMAL	BY WHOM	EPISODE
newspaper	Endora	"Just One Happy Family" (#10)
big mouth bass/goldfish	Samantha	"It Takes One to Know One" (#11)
penguin	George	"George the Warlock" (#30)
chimpanzee/seal	Aunt Clara	"Alias Darrin Stephens" (#37)
werewolf	Endora	"Trick or Treat" (#43)
goose	Samantha	"Long Live the Queen" (#108)
pony	Endora	"Solid Gold Mother-in-Law" (#120)
statue	The Witches' Council	"It's So Nice to Have A Spouse Around the House" (#145)
billy goat	Endora	"Samantha the Bard" (#158)
mule	Maurice	"Daddy Does His Thing" (#167)
dog	Maurice	"Daddy Comes for a Visit" (#180)
dog	Endora	"Turn on the Old Charm" (#199)
toad	Endora	"To Go or Not to Go, That is the Question" (#201)
statue	Serena	"Darrin on a Pedestal" (#205)
crow	Waldo	"Samantha's Bad Day in Salem" (#207)
gorilla	Serena	"Darrin Goes Ape" (#222)
baby goat	Serena	"Samantha's Psychic Pslip" (#225)
goose	Endora	"Samantha and the Antique Doll" (#228)
statue	Endora	"Paris, Witches' Style" (#234)

LARRY

OBJECT/ANIMAL	BY WHOM	EPISODE
crow	Waldo	"Samantha's Bad Day in Salem" (#207)

ABNER

OBJECT/ANIMAL	BY WHOM	EPISODE
pile of dust	Samantha	"Abner Kadabra" (#29)

FRANK

OBJECT/ANIMAL	BY WHOM	EPISODE
mule	Samantha	"Samantha and the Antique Doll" (#228)

PHYLLIS

OBJECT/ANIMAL	BY WHOM	EPISODE
cat	Serena	"Mrs. Stephens, Where Are You?" (#160)

MISCELLANEOUS MORTALS

TRANSFORMEE	OBJECT/ANIMAL	BY WHOM	EPISODE
Rex Barker	dog	Samantha	"It Shouldn't Happen to a Dog" (#3)
Toni Devlin	cat	Endora	"The Catnapper" (#71)
George Dinsdale	parrot	Samantha	"A Chance on Love" (#196)
Joseph Hinkley, Jr.	mannequin	Henry	"Samantha's Shopping Spree" (#169)
Ralph Jackman	mouse	Endora	"Samantha's Secret Spell" (#179)
Nurse Kelton	frog	Serena	"And Something Makes Three" (#54)
Sidney Kravitz	mushroom	Tabitha	"Santa Comes to Visit and Stays and Stays" (#184)
Tommy Kravitz	goat	a goblin	"The Safe and Sane Halloween" (#115)
Charlie Leach	parrot/ mouse	Samantha	"Follow That Witch (Part II)" (#67)/ "The Catnapper" (#71)
Michael Millhowser	dog	Tabitha	"Playmates" (#133)
Elliott Norton	monkey	Esmeralda	"Samantha's Magic Sitter" (#243)
Charlton Rollnick	frog	Tabitha	"Tabitha's First Day In School" (#248)
Amy Catherine Taylor	butterfly	Tabitha	"I Don't Want to Be A Toad, I Want to Be A Butterfly" (#151)
Clio Vanita	monkey	Serena	"Cousin Serena Strikes Again" (#155-#156)

THE WITCHES

SAMANTHA

OBJECT/ANIMAL	BY WHOM	EPISODE
Christmas tree	herself	"Aunt Clara's Victoria Victory" (#100)
bucket of water	herself	"Samantha's Old Salem Trip" (#208)
goose	herself	"Samantha and the Antique Doll" (#228)
polka-dotted unicorn	Endora	"A Plague on Maurice and Samantha" (#237)

ENDORA

OBJECT/ANIMAL	BY WHOM	EPISODE
pelican	herself	"The Cat's Meow" (#18)
parrot	herself	"The Joker Is A Card" (#41)
duck	Aunt Clara	"Allergic to Ancient Macedonian Dodo Birds" (#118)

MAURICE

OBJECT/ANIMAL	BY WHOM	EPISODE
mule	himself	"Daddy Does His Thing" (#167)

TABITHA

OBJECT/ANIMAL	BY WHOM	EPISODE
raisin cookie	herself	"Tabitha's Weekend" (#163)

SERENA

OBJECT/ANIMAL	BY WHOM	EPISODE
mermaid	Bruce	"Samantha and the Loch Ness Monster" (#231)

ARTHUR

OBJECT/ANIMAL	BY WHOM	EPISODE
skeleton	himself	"Samantha's Power Failure" (#165)
colt	himself	"Super Arthur" (#190)

CLARA

OBJECT/ANIMAL	BY WHOM	EPISODE
plant	herself	"The Corn Is As High As A Guernsey's Eye" (#94)

MISCELLANEOUS WITCHES

TRANSFORMEE	OBJECT/ANIMAL	BY WHOM	EPISODE
Ashley	dog	himself/ Samantha	"Samantha's Pet Warlock" (#209)
Dr. Bombay	photograph	Samantha	"Okay, Who's the Wise Witch?" (#195)
Bruce	Loch Ness Monster	Serena	"Samantha and the Loch Ness Monster" (#231)
Clyde	chair	Enchantra	"Sam's Spooky Chair" (#86)
George	raven	himself	"George the Warlock" (#30)
Hedley	elephant	Aunt Clara	"Aunt Clara's Old Flame" (#47)
Malcolm	bird	Serena	"Samantha Goes South for a Spell" (#142)
Newton	bedwarmer	Serena	"The Salem Saga" (#203)/ "Samantha's Hot Bedwarmer" (#204)
Rodney	dog	himself	"Man's Best Friend" (#70)

TOP 10 BEST AND WORST EPISODES

Every episode of *Bewitched* is a jewel, but, while some shine bright, some shine even brighter. Naturally, everyone has their preferences, and any list of favorites (and not-so-favorites) is going to be subjective depending on those preferences. Whether agreeing or disagreeing with the rankings this list has to offer, the explanations as to why its selected episodes settled into these particular positions provide compelling arguments.

THE WORST

10 "BIRDIES, BOGIES, AND BAXTER" (#114)

With holes in the plot as well as on the golf course, Endora's attempt to magically improve Darrin's game spends two-thirds of an episode on the links and utters so much golf jargon, it's easy for the average viewer to get lost. At least it's a nice way to get everyone out of the studio.

9 "OPEN THE DOOR, WITCHCRAFT" (#28)

A garage door opener set to the frequency of planes flying over Morning Glory Circle has Darrin thinking Samantha is responsible, and Samantha magically trapping him in the garage to prove a point. Even with Gladys keeping up the with the Jones', the proceedings are still a bit mechanical.

8 "RED LIGHT, GREEN LIGHT" (#23)

The Stephenses join forces with the Kravitzes to get a needed traffic signal installed on a street that suddenly has its own newspaper and plunges Samantha into community service. Thankfully, there's Endora's "*divertissements*" to keep things from going into gridlock.

7 "THE MAGIC CABIN" (#52)

A very pregnant Samantha can't be blamed for twitching Larry's rustic hovel into something hospitable, but when the too-good-to-be-true MacBains come knocking, one supply the retreat no longer needs is sugar. Ambitious for the effect of a half-and-half cabin.

6 "SAMANTHA'S SECRET SAUCER" (#137)

Floppy-eared aliens descend upon the Stephens house after Aunt Clara unsuccessfully tries to retrieve Tabitha's toy UFO – then Gladys brings *I Dream of Jeannie* military men to have a peek at the canine come-latelies. Notable as Aunt Clara's final appearance before portrayer Marion Lorne passed away.

5 "LITTLE PITCHERS HAVE BIG FEARS" (#6)

Samantha goes *Leave It to Beaver* with the next best thing: the Beav's real-life little brother, Jimmy Mathers. While he's a scene-stealer, all the ballpark brouhaha makes Samantha, who's admittedly still adjusting to the mortal life, look like she wandered onto the wrong set.

4 "HOW GREEN WAS MY GRASS" (#131)

Containing the biggest continuity flaw of the series (the Stephenses now live at 192 Morning Glory Circle), Darrin and Samantha tussle over grass real and artificial. Chaos ensues when people come looking for the lawn after Samantha zaps it away. It's Darrin at his blustery best.

3 "REMEMBER THE MAIN" (#34)

The phrase "politics make strange bedfellows" has never been truer. Ad man Darrin becomes a campaign manager. Witch Samantha becomes a cheerleader. And Endora joins the fun by magically bursting a contested water main. What's a little civic improvement between witches?

2 "SUPER CAR" (#93)

Endora gifts Darrin with a prototype automobile that drives everybody crazy, as does a music cue that trumpets every time the vehicle appears. A client wanting to use the futuristic car to sell sausages (!) leaves the comic team of Dave Madden and Herb Ellis as the high point of a tale that runs out of gas.

1 "SOAPBOX DERBY" (#90)

Samantha helps squeaky-clean Johnny Mills win a kiddie car race despite an absentee father and Gladys making public accusations of witchcraft. Distinctive only for revealing that the Stephenses probably live in Patterson, New York, and for Samantha's first display of the Witches' Honor sign.

THE BEST

10 "SAMANTHA'S POWER FAILURE" (#165)

It's one thing for Samantha to lose her powers, but here, the newly-minted Witches' Council also strips Serena, Uncle Arthur, and even Tabitha of their magic. This results in the ingenious pairing of Serena and Arthur, who have never shared a scene, and their chocolatey attempt to adjust to the mortal world.

9 "TAKE TWO ASPIRINS AND HALF A PINT OF PORPOISE MILK" (#42)

This first witch illness episode not only demonstrates just how easily magic can go awry, but takes Aunt Clara out of her doddering witch role by casting her as a healer and mother figure. Pages of sparkling dialogue add up to an episode in which laughter truly is the best medicine.

8 "I CONFESS" (#135)

What would happen if the world found out Samantha's a witch? This episode takes a question that hung in the air for four seasons and answers it in a fun dream sequence that also serves as a commentary on the absurdities of mortal life, particularly how humans react to anything new and different.

7 "ALLERGIC TO ANCIENT MACEDONIAN DODO BIRDS" (#118)

Felled by an ornithological sensitivity, the formidable Endora is at her magicless, helpless best – and, on the flip side, there's a rare glimpse of what Aunt Clara would be like if she were running on full power. A true *tour de force* for Agnes Moorehead and Marion Lorne.

6 "I DON'T WANT TO BE TOAD, I WANT TO BE A BUTTERFLY" (#151)

Tabitha's the student, but the young witchlet schools every adult contemporary in an installment that shows off little Erin Murphy's completely natural abilities. Miss Stephens charms as she innocently sasses her preschool teacher and gives her new friend wings; gold stars all the way.

5 "SAMANTHA'S GOOD NEWS" (#168)

The show's only non-mortal episode cleverly deviates from its usual mortal-reacts-to-witchcraft formula by taking advantage of Darrin's absence and delving into the entertaining repercussions of Endora's open marriage to Maurice. There's even a cliffhanger: Samantha's pregnant!

4 "OKAY, WHO'S THE WISE WITCH?" (#195)

Six years in, Samantha's neglect of her powers causes a metaphysical "vapor lock" that traps her, Darrin, Endora, Esmeralda, and Dr. Bombay in the house. Set up as a mystery, but ending as pure comedy, this venture into new territory is one of the series' most original episodes.

3 "MIXED DOUBLES" (#221)

Samantha wakes up to a world in which mortals think she's Louise Tate. This inventive case of mistaken identity offers a unique look at Larry and Louise, a brilliant new ailment (metaphysical molecular disturbance), and an appearance by Jonathan, the Tates' rarely-mentioned son.

2 "SAMANTHA'S OLD MAN" (#210)

The Emmy-nominated old age makeup deserves all its accolades, but it's Dick Sargent's geriatric *joie de vivre* that steals the show – and Samantha finally reveals how she'll bridge the gap between Darrin's eventual aging and her own protracted youth. This episode's got seniority in the best possible way.

1 "SISTERS AT HEART" (#213)

This quiet call for acceptance and equality has Tabitha wanting to be sisters with African-American friend Lisa so badly that she mistakenly covers them with different pigments of polka dots. And Samantha schools a bigot in literal living color, a reflection of the series' entire mission statement.

FIRSTS AND LASTS

The mere mention of *Bewitched* always conjures up certain words and images. Surely the Witches' Council was always around, and the Stephenses always lived in Westport? This collection of auspicious beginnings and happy endings chronicles exactly when a reference first appeared, as well as when it stopped being a reference. Also included are the first and last lines of every major character, which are fascinating to view side-by-side.

CATCH PHRASES

PHRASE	FIRST REFERENCE	LAST REFERENCE
"Well?"	"Eye of the Beholder" (#22)	"The Truth, Nothing But the Truth, So Help Me, Sam" (#254)
"Good!"	"I, Darrin, Take This Witch, Samantha" (#1)	"A Good Turn Never Goes Unpunished" (#252)
"Oh, my stars!"	"The Witches Are Out" (#7)	"Samantha's Witchcraft Blows A Fuse" (#253)
"Son of a gun!"	"It Shouldn't Happen to a Dog" (#3) [by Rex Barker; not by Larry until "...And Something Makes Three" (#12)]	"A Good Turn Never Goes Unpunished" (#252)
"Witch's Honor!"	"Be It Ever So Mortgaged" (#2)	"The Eight-Year Itch Witch" (#240)
twitch	"Little Pitchers Have Big Fears" (#6)	"Samantha and the Troll" (#219)
pop	"That Was My Wife" (#31)	"Samantha's Witchcraft Blows A Fuse" (#253)
zap	"Samantha Meets the Folks" (#14)	"Samantha's Witchcraft Blows A Fuse" (#253)

PEOPLE, PLACES, AND THINGS

PARTICULAR	FIRST REFERENCE	LAST REFERENCE
Samantha twitching her nose	"I, Darrin, Take This Witch, Samantha" (#1)	"School Days, School Daze" (#251)
Darrin's manual twitch	"Help, Help, Don't Save Me" (#5)	"Mary, the Good Fairy" (#215)
Endora's spells on Darrin	"Eye of the Beholder" (#22)	"Three Men and a Witch on a Horse" (#241)
The Witches' Council	"It's So Nice to Have A Spouse Around the House" (#145)	"Samantha's Witchcraft Blows A Fuse" (#253)
Westport, Connecticut	"Just A Kid Again" (#193)	"Money Happy Returns" (#223)

PARTICULAR	FIRST REFERENCE	LAST REFERENCE
Larry threatening to fire Darrin	"That Was My Wife" (#31)	"The Truth, Nothing But the Truth, So Help Me, Sam" (#254)
Larry firing Darrin	"Hoho the Clown" (#92)	"Mona Sammy" (#198)
basing slogans on witchcraft-related events	"Eat At Mario's" (#35)	"Samantha Is Earthbound" (#244)
Samantha's heart necklace	"Be It Ever So Mortgaged" (#2)	"A Chance on Love" (#196)

LINES

SAMANTHA

FIRST LINE	"Mother! What are you doing here?"	"I, Darrin, Take This Witch, Samantha" (#1)
LAST LINE	"Well, it doesn't work on me. But I love you. And that is the truth, the whole truth, and...et cetera."	"The Truth, Nothing But the Truth, So Help Me, Sam" (#254)

DARRIN

FIRST LINE	"Must be the champagne."	"I, Darrin, Take This Witch, Samantha" (#1)
LAST LINE	"Honey, you're beautiful, sweet, clever, adorable, and I love you madly. It works."	"The Truth, Nothing But the Truth, So Help Me, Sam" (#254)

ENDORA

FIRST LINE	"What am *I* doing here? What are *you* doing here?"	"I, Darrin, Take This Witch, Samantha" (#1)
LAST LINE	"You're right, Durweed. I don't have to be angry to be difficult. But it helps."	"The Truth, Nothing But the Truth, So Help Me, Sam" (#254)

GLADYS

FIRST LINE	"There are two of them, Abner – both women. One older...maybe a sister. Maybe a mother. Come take a look, Abner!	"Be It Ever So Mortgaged" (#2)
LAST LINE	"Oh, Mrs. Fremont!"	"Laugh, Clown, Laugh" (#227)

ABNER

FIRST LINE	"Leave me alone. I'm retired."	"Be It Ever So Mortgaged" (#2)
LAST LINE	"Gladys, if you had compassion for your fellow neighbor, you'd move!"	"Darrin Goes Ape" (#222)

LARRY

FIRST LINE	"Well, how'd we make out?"	"It Shouldn't Happen to a Dog" (#3)
LAST LINE	"Well, I'll see you later at the office, Darrin."	"The Truth, Nothing But the Truth, So Help Me, Sam" (#254)

LOUISE

FIRST LINE	"Ah, no thank you. Oh, that was a marvelous dinner, Samantha."	"It Shouldn't Happen to a Dog" (#3)
LAST LINE	"Oh, Larry, you're your old self again."	"Serena's Youth Pill" (#247)

CLARA

FIRST LINE	"Oh, I got the spell all wrong, I got all mixed in the spell, and I landed in the middle of the freeway."	"The Witches Are Out" (#7)
LAST LINE	"Oh, thank you, Darrin. Thank you, Darrin. Oh, darling!"	"Samantha's Secret Saucer" (#137)

MAURICE

FIRST LINE	"Samantha! Of course it is. You've got to be my daughter – you're positively gorgeous."	"Just One Happy Family" (#10)
LAST LINE	"Scene stealer!"	"Adam, Warlock or Washout?" (#242)

PHYLLIS

FIRST LINE	"I can't wait to see him. Oh, I hope she hasn't let him lose weight."	"Samantha Meets the Folks" (#14)
LAST LINE	"Oh, Frank!"	"Samantha and the Antique Doll" (#228)

FRANK

FIRST LINE	"Oh, he's probably in the last stages of malnutrition."	"Samantha Meets the Folks" (#14)
LAST LINE	"Phyllis!"	"Samantha and the Antique Doll" (#228)

ARTHUR

FIRST LINE	"Forgive me for not rising, but I'm up to my neck in work."	"The Joker Is A Card" (#41)
LAST LINE	"Now there's an idea!"	"The House That Uncle Arthur Built" (#218)

SERENA

FIRST LINE	"Samantha? This is Serena. Your cousin, Serena."	"And Then There Were Three" (#54)
LAST LINE	"Bye-bye."	"Serena's Youth Pill" (#247)

TABITHA

FIRST LINE	"Bye-bye, Daddy."	"Nobody's Perfect" (#75) [first appearance: "And Then There Were Three" (#54)]
LAST LINE	"Cheers."	"A Good Turn Never Goes Unpunished" (#252)

DR. BOMBAY

FIRST LINE	"For your information, I was about to enter my bath."	"There's Gold in Them Thar Pills" (#107)
LAST LINE	"In that case, it's obvious I didn't mention it. And having done so, I shall leave."	"Samantha's Witchcraft Blows A Fuse" (#253)

ESMERALDA

FIRST LINE	"Hello, Endora. I hope I'm not too early."	"Samantha's Yoo-Hoo Maid" (#172)
LAST LINE	"Oh. In that case..."	"George Washington Zapped Here (Part II)" (#250)

ADAM

FIRST LINE	"Hello, Mommy."	"How Not to Lose Your Head to King Henry VIII (Part I)" (#229) [first appearance: "And Something Makes Four" (#175)]
LAST LINE	"That she's a witch."	"School Days, School Daze" (#251)

ACKNOWLEDGMENTS

There would be no such thing as *The Bewitched Continuum* were it not for the magic provided by the following people:

Herbie J Pilato, consultant, editor, and contributor – thank you for helping to shape this book into what it is, and for all your support and encouragement. And, of course, thank you to Melissa McComas for helping to connect us;

Amanda Mecke, Paul Levine, Jeff Serena, and Mark Clark (of *Star Trek FAQ*), thank you for your expertise;

Polly Haas of MPTV, Andrea Gordon of The Canadian Press (for the Everett Collection), and especially Todd Ifft and Derek Davidson of Photofest – thank you for the help and assistance in making it possible for me to have so many wonderful *Bewitched* images in this book;

Scott Viets and Vic's *Bewitched* Page for making show information available back in the '90s, and for letting me refer to it today; also, gratitude to springfieldspringfield.co.uk for making episode transcripts available so I didn't always have to search through DVDs to double-check dialogue;

Charles Tolbert for performing miracles;

Blair Sweeney and Roberta McLean of TechnoMedia for perfecting my crude book cover concept and for being experts "in design";

Bonnie Winings, Laurel Lambert, and Susan Szotyori of SWPR Group for helping to send the message out to the atmospheric continuum;

Phil Farrand for his enterprising example, which introduced me to continuity;

Leo Marchildon for making *Bewitched* available to me in a way I'd only dreamt of as a child;

An extra special thank you to Chris Wilson for last-minute saves;

And, to my friend and former boss Maggie Field, thank you for believing in this book from the beginning – without you, this would still only be an idea rolling around in my head.

ABOUT THE AUTHOR

Photography by Erin Brown

An expert at continuity, Adam-Michael James has a long history in the entertainment industry. He spent two years writing script coverage for film production companies such as Centropolis Entertainment, Carsey-Werner-Mandabach, and Beacon Pictures. He also has three years' experience writing continuity scripts for radio. His exposure to the television industry through his work as an agency assistant and background actor give him a unique and qualified standpoint from which to write *The Bewitched Continuum*. James' literary output includes the book and lyrics for the musical drama *The Nine Lives of L.M. Montgomery*, *Extra Extra!: Memoirs from a Piece of Human Furniture*, a humorous how-to book on being a Hollywood extra, and the novel *Undo the Deed*, a time travel story with a child abuse theme that was influenced by *Bewitched*. Since 2009, James has been a columnist for soapcentral.com, where his commentaries on the continuity and structure of the soap opera *The Bold and the Beautiful* reach an estimated 250,000 readers. He also appears frequently on soapcentral.com's corresponding Internet radio show, *Soap Central Live*. For more information about Adam-Michael James, please visit adammichaeljames.com.

ABOUT HERBIE J PILATO

Photography by Dan Holm

Herbie J Pilato is the foremost authority on *Bewitched*, having interviewed stars Elizabeth Montgomery, Dick York, Dick Sargent, David White, series creator Sol Saks, producer/director William Asher (former husband to Montgomery), and more. Pilato's original *Bewitched Book* was the first to document the show, and was later revised as *Bewitched Forever*. He served as a consultant and/or producer on Nick at Nite's initial broadcast of *Bewitched*, *Bewitched: The E! True Hollywood Story*, Montgomery profiles on A&E's *Biography* and MSNBC's *Headliners & Legends*, the *Bewitched* DVD release, and Nora Ephron's *Bewitched* movie. His new books include the best-selling and critically-acclaimed *Twitch Upon A Star: The Bewitched Life and Career of Elizabeth Montgomery*, *The Essential Elizabeth Montgomery: A Guide To Her Magical Performances*, and *Glamour, Gidgets and the Girl Next Door: Television's Iconic Women From the 50s, 60s and 70s*, among others. Prolific beyond *Bewitched*, Pilato has worked on TV shows for TLC, Syfy, Bravo, Warner Brothers, NBCUniversal, and Sony; founded Television, Ink. and The Classic TV Preservation Society; serves as Contributing Editor to Larry Brody's prestigious www.TVWriter.com, and has many TV shows and movies in development. He lives in Burbank, California, which he describes as a cross between Hollywood and Mayberry.

MAR   2016

Made in the USA
Middletown, DE
05 March 2016